Y0-BCG-916

21st Century
ECONOMICS
A Reference Handbook

21st Century ECONOMICS
A Reference Handbook

Volume *2*

Edited by
Rhona C. Free
Eastern Connecticut State University

⑤SAGE | reference

Los Angeles | London | New Delhi
Singapore | Washington DC

Copyright © 2010 by SAGE Publications, Inc.

All rights reserved. No part of this book may be reproduced or utilized in any form or by any means, electronic or mechanical, including photocopying, recording, or by any information storage and retrieval system, without permission in writing from the publisher.

For information:

SAGE Publications, Inc.
2455 Teller Road
Thousand Oaks, California 91320
E-mail: order@sagepub.com

SAGE Publications Ltd.
1 Oliver's Yard
55 City Road
London EC1Y 1SP
United Kingdom

SAGE Publications India Pvt. Ltd.
B 1/I 1 Mohan Cooperative Industrial Area
Mathura Road, New Delhi 110 044
India

SAGE Publications Asia-Pacific Pte. Ltd.
33 Pekin Street #02-01
Far East Square
Singapore 048763

Printed in Mexico

Library of Congress Cataloging-in-Publication Data

21st century economics: a reference handbook / editor, Rhona C. Free.
       v. ; cm.
Includes bibliographical references and index.
ISBN 978-1-4129-6142-4 (cloth)
   1. Economics—Handbooks, manuals, etc. I. Free, Rhona C. II. Title: Twenty-first century economics.
HB171.A19 2010
330—dc22   2010001776

This book is printed on acid-free paper.

11   12   13   14   10   9   8   7   6   5   4   3   2

Publisher:	Rolf A. Janke
Acquisitions Editor:	Jim Brace-Thompson
Developmental Editor:	Sanford Robinson
Reference Systems Manager:	Leticia Gutierrez
Reference Systems Coordinator:	Laura Notton
Production Editor:	Kate Schroeder
Copy Editors:	Gillian Dickens, Matthew Sullivan, Karen Wolf
Typesetter:	C&M Digitals (P) Ltd.
Proofreaders:	Kristin Bergstad, Sally Jaskold
Indexer:	Joan Shapiro
Cover Designer:	Candice Harman
Marketing Manager:	Amberlyn McKay

Contents

Volume One

Preface		**xi**
About the Editor		**xv**
About the Contributors		**xvii**

PART I. SCOPE AND METHODOLOGY OF ECONOMICS

1. History of Economic Thought — 3
   Paola Tubaro, University of Greenwich; Centre Maurice Halbwachs

2. Economic History — 13
   Sue Headlee, American University

3. Economic Methodology — 23
   Timothy A. Wunder, University of Texas at Arlington

4. Twentieth-Century Economic Methodology — 33
   Peter J. Boettke, George Mason University

5. Econometrics — 45
   Peter Kennedy, Simon Fraser University

6. Marxian and Institutional Industrial Relations in the United States — 55
   Michael Hillard, University of Southern Maine

PART II. MICROECONOMICS

7. Supply, Demand, and Equilibrium — 69
   Kevin C. Klein, Illinois College

8. Consumer Behavior — 79
   Frederick G. Tiffany, Wittenberg University

9. Demand Elasticities — 89
   Ann Harper Fender, Gettysburg College

10. Costs of Production: Short Run and Long Run — 101
    Laurence Miners, Fairfield University

11. Profit Maximization — 111
    Michael E. Bradley, University of Maryland, Baltimore County

12. Imperfectly Competitive Product Markets — 125
    Elizabeth J. Jensen, Hamilton College

13. Predatory Pricing and Strategic Entry Barriers 135
    Bradley P. Kamp, University of South Florida

14. Labor Markets 141
    Kathryn Nantz, Fairfield University

15. Wage Determination 153
    Kenneth A. Couch, University of Connecticut
    Nicholas A. Jolly, Central Michigan University

16. Role of Labor Unions in Labor Markets 163
    Paul F. Clark and Julie Sadler, Penn State University

17. Game Theory 173
    Indrajit Ray, University of Birmingham

18. Economics of Strategy 185
    Quan Wen, Vanderbilt University

19. Transaction Cost Economics 193
    Christopher Ross Bell, University of North Carolina at Asheville

20. Asset Pricing Models 203
    Peter Nyberg, Helsinki School of Economics

21. Portfolio Theory and Investment Management 215
    Thomas W. Harvey, Ashland University

PART III. PUBLIC ECONOMICS

22. Externalities and Property Rights 227
    Mahadev Ganapati Bhat, Florida International University

23. Public Choice 237
    Peter T. Calcagno, College of Charleston

24. Taxes Versus Standards: Policies for the Reduction of Gasoline Consumption 247
    Sarah E. West, Macalester College

25. Public Finance 255
    Neil Canaday, Wesleyan University

26. Regulatory Economics 265
    Christopher S. Decker, University of Nebraska at Omaha

27. Cost-Benefit Analysis 275
    Mikael Svensson, Örebro University, Sweden

PART IV. MACROECONOMICS

28. Economic Measurement and Forecasting 287
    Mehdi Mostaghimi, Southern Connecticut State University

29. Measuring and Evaluating Macroeconomic Performance 297
    David Hudgins, University of Oklahoma

30. Macroeconomic Models 307
    Christopher J. Niggle, University of Redlands

31. Aggregate Expenditures Model and Equilibrium Output 319
    Michael R. Montgomery, University of Maine

32. Aggregate Demand and Aggregate Supply 333
    Ken McCormick, University of Northern Iowa

33. IS-LM Model 341
    Fadhel Kaboub, Denison University

34. Economic Instability and Macroeconomic Policy 349
    John Vahaly, University of Louisville

35. Fiscal Policy 357
   Rosemary Thomas Cunningham, Agnes Scott College

36. Government Budgets, Debt, and Deficits 369
   Benjamin Russo, University of North Carolina at Charlotte

37. Monetary Policy and Inflation Targeting 381
   Pavel S. Kapinos, Carleton College
   David Wiczer, University of Minnesota

38. Debates in Macroeconomic Policy 391
   John Vahaly, University of Louisville

39. New Classical Economics 399
   Brian Snowdon, Durham University

PART V. INTERNATIONAL ECONOMICS

40. International Trade, Comparative and Absolute Advantage, and Trade Restrictions 411
   Lindsay Oldenski, Georgetown University

41. Balance of Trade and Payments 419
   Lawrence D. Gwinn, Wittenberg University

42. Exchange Rates 431
   Carlos Vargas-Silva, Sam Houston State University

43. Comparative Economic Systems 441
   Satyananda J. Gabriel, Mount Holyoke College

44. World Development in Historical Perspective 451
   Douglas O. Walker, Regent University

45. International Finance 467
   Steven L. Husted, University of Pittsburgh

46. The European Economic and Monetary Union 477
   Leila Simona Talani, King's College London

47. East Asian Economies 485
   Kiril Tochkov, Texas Christian University

48. Globalization and Inequality 493
   Rachel McCulloch, Brandeis University

49. The Economics of Fair Trade 503
   John D. Messier, University of Maine at Farmington

Volume Two

PART VI. ECONOMIC ANALYSES OF ISSUES AND MARKETS

50. Economics of Education   515
    Ping Ching Winnie Chan, Statistics Canada

51. Economics and Justice   525
    George F. DeMartino, University of Denver

52. Sports Economics   533
    Aju Fenn, Colorado College

53. Earnings of Professional Athletes   543
    Lee H. Igel and Robert A. Boland, New York University

54. Economics of Gender   553
    Lena Nekby, Stockholm University
    Peter Skogman Thoursie, Institute for Labour Market
      Policy Evaluation (IFAU), Uppsala

55. Economics and Race   563
    Sean E. Mulholland, Stonehill College

56. Economic Analysis of the Family   577
    Steven Horwitz, St. Lawrence University

57. Economics of Aging   585
    Agneta Kruse, Lund University

58. Agricultural Economics   597
    Patricia A. Duffy, Auburn University

59. Real Estate Economics   607
    Erick Eschker, Humboldt State University

60. Economics of Wildlife Protection   617
    Rebecca P. Judge, St. Olaf College

61. Environmental Economics   631
    Jennifer L. Brown, Eastern Connecticut State University

62. Economics of Energy Markets   637
    Stephen H. Karlson, Northern Illinois University

63. Political Economy of Oil   645
    Yahya M. Madra, Gettysburg College

64. Transportation Economics   655
    Anthony M. Rufolo, Portland State University

65. Urban Economics   665
    James D. Burnell, College of Wooster

66. Economics of Gambling   677
    Douglas M. Walker, College of Charleston

67. Economics of HIV and AIDS   687
    Roy Love, Health Economics Consultant

68. Economics of Migration   697
    Anita Alves Pena and Steven J. Shulman, Colorado State University

69. Health Economics   707
    Shirley Johnson-Lans, Vassar College

70. Economics of Health Insurance   717
    Amy M. Wolaver, Bucknell University

71. Economics of Information   729
    Viktar Fedaseyeu, Boston College

72. Forensic Economics   739
    Lawrence M. Spizman, State University of New York at Oswego

73. Economics of Crime   747
    Isaac Ehrlich, State University of New York at Buffalo

74. Economics of Property Law   757
    Richard D. Coe, New College of Florida

75. Queer Economics: Sexual Orientation and Economic Outcomes   767
    Richard R. Cornwall, Middlebury College

76. Economics and Religion   777
    Carmel U. Chiswick, University of Illinois at Chicago

77. Economics and Corporate Social Responsibility   785
    Markus Kitzmueller, University of Michigan

78. Political Economy of Violence   797
    Shawn Humphrey, University of Mary Washington

79. The Economics of Civil War   807
    Marta Reynal-Querol, Pompeu Fabra University

80. Economic Aspects of Cultural Heritage   819
    Leah Greden Mathews, University of North Carolina at Asheville

81. Media Economics   827
    Gillian Doyle, Centre for Cultural Policy Research, University of Glasgow

82. Microfinance   837
    Shannon Mudd, Ursinus College

83. Latin America's Trade Performance in the New Millennium   847
    Maritza Sotomayor, Utah Valley University

PART VII. EMERGING AREAS IN ECONOMICS

84. Behavioral Economics   861
    Nathan Berg, University of Texas–Dallas

85. Experimental Economics   873
    Seda Ertaç, Koç University
    Sandra Maximiano, Purdue University

86. Complexity and Economics   883
    Troy L. Tassier, Fordham University

87. Ethics and Economics   891
    Victor V. Claar, Henderson State University

88. Feminist Economics   901
    Gillian Hewitson, University of Sydney

89. Neuroeconomics   913
    Dante Monique Pirouz, University of Western Ontario

90. Evolutionary Economics   921
    Clifford S. Poirot Jr., Shawnee State University

91. Matching Markets   931
    Thomas Gall, University of Bonn

92. Beyond Make-or-Buy: Advances in Transaction Cost Economics   941
    Lyda S. Bigelow, University of Utah

Index   **951**

PART VI

ECONOMIC ANALYSES OF ISSUES AND MARKETS

50

ECONOMICS OF EDUCATION

PING CHING WINNIE CHAN

Statistics Canada

Economics is a study of making choices to allocate scarce resources—what to produce, how to produce, and for whom to produce. With education being one of the top social priorities to compete for scarce resources, economic analysis on returns of education, the optimal allocation of education resources, and evaluation of education policies has become increasingly important. In addition to the theoretical development and empirical applications of human capital theory, different areas of economics have also applied to education issues, such as the use of the economics of production to study the relation between education inputs and outputs.

Since the release of the 1983 National Commission on Excellence in Education report *A Nation at Risk*, the U.S. government has initiated different education reforms to improve failing student performance. In recent years, rich data sets (often longitudinal) have become available from different education policy experiments—for example, voucher programs in Milwaukee and accountability policies in different states. Research that takes advantage of these policy experiments has shed some light in the current education debate by providing empirical evidence of the impact of different policies and suggestions for policy design.

In this chapter, the human capital theory and an alternative screening hypothesis are first introduced to provide some theoretical background in the area. Next, the impact of various education inputs on student performance is discussed to apply the production theory on education and to highlight some of the empirical challenges in evaluating the impact of key factors in education. Then, theoretical and empirical evidence on school choice and accountability policies in the elementary and secondary school markets is described to highlight the policy relevance of the field.

Theory

Human Capital Theory

Education is often regarded as one of the main determinants in one's labor market success. The primary model used to measure the returns to education in the field is the human capital theory. Drawing an analogy to the investment theory of firms, each worker is paid up to his or her marginal productivity—the increment of output to a firm when an additional unit of labor input is employed. Human capital theory postulates that education is made as human capital investment to improve one's productivity and earnings.

The essence underlying human capital theory can be traced back to Adam Smith's classic theory of equalizing differentials, in which the wages paid to workers should compensate for various job characteristics. The modern human capital theory, building on the seminal work of Theodore Schultz (1963), Gary Becker (1964), and Jacob Mincer (1974), has drawn attention to conceptualizing the benefits of education and to modeling education as a form of investment in human capital.

As a first step to calculating the rate of returns to education, Schultz (1963) categorized a list of education benefits, including the private benefits in terms of wages and the social benefits that are accrued to the economy as a whole (e.g., research and development to sustain economic growth and better citizenship). In calculating the costs of education, in addition to the direct costs of tuition, transportation, books, and supplies, the indirect costs of forgone earnings—the opportunity costs incurred while acquiring the human capital during schooling—should also be included.

Introduced by Becker (1964), one way to determine the optimal level of education is to compare the internal rate of return (i) earned by acquiring that level of education and the market rate of interest (r) in financing to acquire that level of education. The internal rate of returns to education corresponds to the implicit rate of return earned by an individual acquiring that amount of education, and the market rate of interest represents the opportunity cost of financing the investment required to obtain the amount of education. Because of diminishing returns, the present value of marginal benefits of education generally declines with years of education. The present value of marginal costs (direct cost and the opportunity cost of forgone earnings), on the other hand, generally increases with years of education. The combined actions of marginal benefits and marginal costs of education result in a falling internal rate of return when education attainment rises. As a simple illustration, assuming a constant cost of borrowing in the capital market, Figure 50.1 shows that one will continue to invest in education as long as the internal rate of return (i) exceeds the market rate of interest (r) and that the optimal equilibrium education (E^*) level has been attained when $i = r$.

Estimating the Rate of Returns to Education

To empirically estimate the rate of returns to education, cross-sectional data on earnings of different individuals at a point in time can be compared, and the differences in earnings can be attributed to differences in the levels of education after accounting for other observable differences. Mincer (1974) developed a framework to estimate the rate of returns to education in the form of the human capital earnings function as follows:

$$\log y_i = a + rS + bX + cX^2 + e, \qquad (1)$$

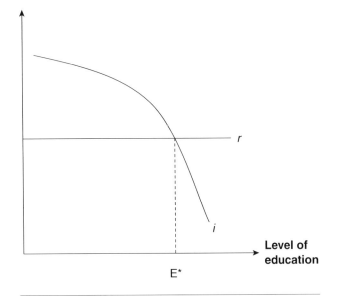

Figure 50.1   Optimal Education Level Determination

NOTE: i is the rate of return; r is the market interest rate; E^* is the optimal level of education.

where y are the earnings of individual i. S represents the years of education acquired, X represents individual's potential experience that is usually approximated by $X = \text{age} - S - 6$, and e is the stochastic term.

The Mincer (1974) model is widely used to estimate returns of schooling, and the estimate r can be interpreted as the rate of returns to education when assuming that each additional year of education has the same effect on earnings and the years of schooling are measured accurately. Using the U.S. Census data, James Heckman, Lance Lochner, and Petra Todd (2006) showed that the data from recent U.S. labor markets do not support the assumptions required for interpreting the coefficient on schooling as the rate of returns to education; the review calls into question using the Mincer (1974) equation to estimate rates of returns to education. To better fit the data in modern labor markets, many studies have extensions and modifications of the original Mincer equation—for example, allowing wage premiums when one completes elementary school in Grade 8, high school in Grade 12, and college after 16 years of completed education (the sheepskin effect), as well as incorporating other interaction terms or nonlinearities into the earnings equation.

A growing literature has also attempted to measure the causal effect of schooling by addressing the concern of ability bias in standard earnings equations. By assuming that, because of their same genetic makeup, identical twins' innate ability would be the same, Orley Ashenfelter and Cecilia Rouse (1998) estimated the rate of returns to education on a large sample of identical twins from the Princeton Twins Survey. Their results confirm that there is ability bias in the standard estimation, and once the innate ability is controlled for, the estimate of the returns to education is lowered.

Screening

The human capital theory emphasizes the role of education in enhancing one's productivity. An alternative model based on the work of Kenneth Arrow (1973) and Michael Spence (1973) argued that education plays a role as a signal of workers' productivity when productivity is unknown before hiring because of imperfect information. The assumption is that if the individuals with higher ability have lower costs of acquiring education, they are more likely to acquire a higher level of schooling. In such a case, the level of education one possesses can act as a signal to employers of one's productivity, and individuals will choose an education level to signal their productivity to potential employers.

It is empirically difficult to distinguish between the human capital theory and the screening hypothesis because high-ability individuals will choose to acquire more education under either theory. In an attempt to contrast the two models, Kevin Lang and David Kropp (1986) examined U.S. enrollment data and compulsory attendance laws from

1910 to 1970. Under the human capital theory, the effect of an increase in minimum school-leaving age should be apparent only among individuals that have optimal years of education lower than the minimum school-leaving age. Under the signaling model, the increase in minimum school-leaving age will also affect individuals that are not directly affected under the policy in the human capital theory. The reason is that a rise of the minimum school-leaving age from t to $t + 1$ would decrease the average ability level of individuals with $t + 1$ years of education. To signal higher ability, the high-ability individuals will choose to stay in school for $t + 2$ years. Therefore, the human capital theory and the signaling theory would yield different implications for the changes in compulsory attendance laws. Lang and Kropp's analysis showed that enrollment rates did increase beyond those directly affected by the rise in minimum school-leaving age

Thus far, empirical evidence in the area is still limited, and the results have not been conclusive in determining the role of the two theories in education investment decisions. On one hand, the pure signaling model cannot explain the investment decision in professional education programs such as medical science or law because it is only through the professional programs that one can accumulate the knowledge and skills necessary for those occupations; on the other hand, it is impossible to discount the value of signaling completely from the empirical data. Given the important role of education in our society, both theories contribute in explaining the motivation of education investment decisions, and the current literature suggests that the importance of each theory might differ by the level and program in which an individual enrolls.

Education Production Function

In the production theory, a production function typically indicates the numerical function by which levels of inputs are translated into a level of output. Similarly, an education production function is usually a function mapping quantities of measured inputs in schooling (e.g., school resources, student ability, and family characteristics) to some measure of school output, like students' test scores or graduation rates. A general education production function can be written as follows:

$$T_{it} = f(S_{it}, A_i, F_{it}, P_{it}), \qquad (2)$$

where T_{it} is the measured school output, such as test scores of student i at time t. For the inputs in the production function, S measures resources received by students at schools that are affected by school expenditure, teacher quality, class size, as well as curriculum planning and other school policies. A denotes the innate ability of a student, F measures the family background characteristics that are related to student education attainment, and P measures peer effects from classmates and close peers.

Many empirical studies have attempted to measure the impact of school resources on performance because school inputs can be more directly affected by policies targeted to improving student performance. One of the earliest studies in the area is the landmark 1966 *Equality of Educational Opportunity* report led by James S. Coleman. Aiming to document the different quality of education received by different populations in the United States in response to the 1964 Civil Rights Act, the author collected detailed information on schools, teachers, and students. One of the most controversial conclusions from the report is that measurable characteristics of schools and teachers played a smaller role in explaining the variation of student performance compared to family characteristics. Though the Coleman report's interpretation has been criticized from the regression framework (e.g., in Eric Hanushek and John Kain, 1972), the report remains a benchmark study in assessing education outcomes.

In a widely-cited paper, Hanushek (1986) surveyed the literature on the impact of school inputs and concludes that there is no evidence that real classroom resources (including teacher–pupil ratio, teacher education, and teacher experience) and financial aggregates (including teacher salary and expenditure per pupil) has a systematic impact in raising student performance. Reviewing research with new data and new methodologies in a follow-up, Hanushek (2006) maintained that the conclusion about the general inefficiency of resource usage in public schools is still warranted; further, he suggested that more research is needed in the area to understand when and where resources are most productively used.

Class Size

A popular policy proposal is to reduce class size to improve student performance. With smaller class sizes, students can have more personal interactions with teachers during class time. However, as pointed out by Caroline Hoxby (2000), measuring the impact of class size has been difficult because the greater part of class size variation documented in administrative data "is the result of choice made by parents, schooling providers, or courts and legislatures" (p. 1240). The observed variations in class sizes, therefore, are correlated with some unobservable factors that might be correlated with student performance.

To ascertain the effect of class size reduction, the Tennessee Department of Education conducted a 4-year longitudinal class size study, the Student Teacher Achievement Ratio (STAR). The cohort of students who entered kindergarten in the 1985 to 1986 school year participated in the experiment through third grade. A total of 11,600 children were involved in the experiment over all 4 years. The students were randomly assigned into one of three interventions: small class (13 to 17 students per teacher), regular class (22 to 25 students per teacher), and regular-with-aide class (22 to 25 students per teacher with a full-time teacher's aide). Classroom teachers were also randomly assigned to the classes they would teach. The class size cutoffs were designed following the study conducted by Gene Glass and Mary Smith (1979). They summarized the findings on the performance impact of class size from 77 studies comparing student performance in different class sizes and concluded that the greatest gains in achievement occurred among students who were taught in classes of 15 students or fewer.

The STAR project provides an opportunity to study the causal effect of class size given that the students are assigned to different class size randomly to avoid the endogeneity problem of the class size variable. Alan Krueger (1999) controlled for observable student characteristics and family background and found that relative to the standard deviation of the average percentile score, students in smaller classes performed better than those in the regular classes (both with and without an extra teaching aide). The effect sizes are 0.20 in kindergarten, 0.28 in first grade, 0.22 in second grade, and 0.19 in third grade, which suggest that the main benefit of small class size tended to concentrate by the end of the first year. In light of this finding, Krueger suggested that small class size "may confer a one-time, 'school socialization effect' which permanently raises the level of student achievement without greatly affecting the trajectory" (p. 529).

Using an alternative measurement approach, Hoxby (2000) exploited the natural variation in population size from a long panel of enrollment data in Connecticut school districts. Similar to Project STAR, the class size variation that resulted from cohort size variation is exogenous in the estimation because class sizes are not driven by choices of parents or the school authority. However, using this natural population variation in class size, the analysis found no significant impact of class size on student performance.

Family Factors

In addition to school resources, innate ability is an important contributor in student performance that is often unobservable in data analysis. To further complicate the analysis, family background, especially parental education, is often correlated with unobserved student ability. While reviewing the literature on school resources and student outcomes, David Card and Krueger (1996) pointed out that the presence of omitted variables might bias the relation between school resources and student outcomes because children from better family backgrounds are likely to attend schools with more resources.

Having some family controls in the empirical analysis is important to control for the influence family factors might have on student outcomes. Nonetheless, there has been limited evidence identifying the impact of family factors on student performance separately. Take family income as an

example: Most studies can show only a suggestive correlation between student outcomes and family income but not of a causal relationship between family income and student outcome (Mayer, 1997). Family income is likely to suffer from the problem of endogeneity under such a reduced-form regression model because children growing up in poor families are likely to face other adverse challenges that would continue to affect their development even if family income were to increase. To address the issue of endogeneity, different papers have attempted to isolate the exogenous variation of income using different research designs. Gordon Dahl and Lance Lochner (2008) exploited the income shocks generated by the large, nonlinear changes in the Earned Income Tax Credit (EITC) in the past two decades. Their analysis found a positive impact of income on student mathematics and reading scores, and the effects were stronger for children of younger ages. Exploiting the policy variation in child benefit income among Canadian provinces, Kevin Milligan and Mark Stabile (2009) also showed that child benefit programs in Canada had significant positive effects on different measures of child outcomes. More research in the area is still needed to understand the impact of family factors and to prescribe relevant policy recommendations.

Peer Effects

A distinct feature of the education production function is that there is a public good component in student performance. Classroom teaching simultaneously provides benefits to more than one student at the same time, and the learning experience of one student is being affected by the average quality of his or her classmates (peer effects). Edward Lazear (2001) explicitly modeled the negative externalities created from the disruptive behavior of one student on all other classmates and provided the theoretical intuition to reconcile the mixed results documented in the class size reduction analysis. In particular, the model implied that class size effects are more pronounced in smaller classes for students with special needs or from disadvantaged populations.

Empirical evidence in identifying peer effects, however, has been rather limited. Charles Manski (1993) pointed out that analyses from standard approaches that regress students' outcomes on peer outcomes cannot properly isolate peer effects from the selection effect, in which it is difficult to separate a group's influence on an individual's outcome from the individual's influence on the group—the reflection problem. To put it simply, the reflection problem occurs when the performance of Student A is influenced by the presence of Student B, and vice versa. Another challenge in identifying peer effects empirically is that peers are rarely assigned randomly. Parents are likely to select neighborhoods through residential location to associate with good peers in good neighborhoods with good schools. A positive correlation between peer and individual might reflect this unobserved self-selection instead of any direct impact of peers on student performance.

The effect of increased sorting from increased school choice initiatives is often discussed in the choice policy debate. When more choice is given to parents, students remaining in the public school will suffer if the better students choose to leave the public school and switch to the alternative and thereby lower the peer quality remaining in the public school. The impact of sorting based on outcomes is discussed in the school choice section.

Education Policy

To improve the efficiency and effectiveness of public schools, a variety of reform strategies have been proposed on the policy front. These include restructuring the school organization and decision-making process, improving accountability, and providing more choice among schools as reflected in policies such as open enrollment programs that increase choice in the public school system or private school vouchers and tuition tax credits between public and private schools. In this section, the policy implications and empirical evidence on school choice and accountability measures are discussed to highlight the policy relevance of economic analysis in education.

School Choice

The promotion of choice among schools through the use of financing mechanisms such as vouchers and tuition tax credits has a long history. Milton Friedman's original essay on the government's role in education, published in *Capitalism and Freedom* (1962, chap. 6), is often regarded as the source that reinvigorated the modern voucher movement. In the essay, Friedman advocated the use of government support for parents who chose to send their children to private schools by paying them the equivalent of the estimated cost of a public school education. One of the key advantages of such an arrangement, he argued, would be to permit competition to develop and stimulate improvement of all schools.

The concepts of choice and competition are closely related and tend to be used interchangeably in this area of research. Yet, as defined in Patrick Bayer and Robert McMillan (2005), there is a clear distinction between the two, with choice relating to the availability of schooling alternatives for households and competition measuring the degree of market power enjoyed by a school. Typically, one would expect a positive correlation between the two, with an increase in choice being associated with an increase in competition. According to the standard argument, increased competition will force public schools to improve efficiency in order to retain enrollment. Yet in principle, increased choice need not always improve school performance, as illustrated in a model developed by McMillan (2005). His model showed that rent-seeking public schools could offset the losses from reduced enrollment by cutting costly effort.

Using public money in the form of vouchers or tax credits to support private schools is perhaps one of the most contentious debates in education policy today. School choice advocates claim that increasing school choice could introduce more competition to the public system to improve overall school quality and increase the access to alternative schools for low-income students, minority students, or both, who would otherwise be constrained to stay in the public system. Opponents argue that it is inappropriate to divert funds from the already cash-strapped public system because it would have a detrimental impact on school quality. According to the opponents' view, voucher or tax credit policy is likely to benefit only affluent families who could afford the additional cost of attending private schools given that the vouchers and tax credits are unlikely to cover the total cost of attending private schools.

Despite the controversy of school choice debate, there are now a number of U.S. states implementing various forms of school choice programs: Arizona, Florida, Illinois, Iowa, Minnesota, Pennsylvania, and Puerto Rico have adopted some forms of tax credit, deductions, or both; Colorado, the District of Columbia, Florida, Ohio, and Wisconsin have publicly funded school voucher programs in place; and Maine, Vermont, and New York have voucher programs funded by private organizations.

Empirical studies that examine the effect of private schools as well as different choice programs are discussed to highlight the important role of economic analysis in evaluating policy programs and the challenge in identifying the school choice impact.

The Effects of Private Schools

One strand of the choice literature has focused on public versus private provision, to see whether student outcomes differ across sectors, controlling for student type. In practice, students self-select into public or private schools, and this nonrandom selection might bias the performance effect in a comparison of outcomes between public and private schools since private school students may be unobservably better.

In an early study, Coleman, Thomas Hoffer, and Sally Kilgore (1982) used data from the High School and Beyond Survey of 1980 and showed that Catholic schools were more effective than public schools. Jeffrey Grogger and Derek Neal (2000) used the National Educational Longitudinal Survey of 1988, which allowed analysis of secondary school outcomes conditional on detailed measures of student characteristics and achievement at the end of elementary school. They found achievement gains in terms of high school graduation rates and college attendance from Catholic schooling, and the effects were much larger among urban minorities. Given the difficulty in controlling for selection bias in the measurement approach, only suggestive evidence on positive private school effects can be drawn from these studies.

Small-Scale Randomized Voucher: The Milwaukee Experiment

Wisconsin was the first U.S. state to implement a school voucher program, the Milwaukee Parental Choice Program, to low-income students to attend nonreligious private schools in 1990. Only students whose family income was at or below 1.75 times the national poverty line were eligible to apply for the vouchers. The number of successful applicants was restricted to 1% of the Milwaukee public school enrollment in the beginning of the program and was later raised to 1.5% in 1994 and 15% in 1997. One thing worth noting in the Milwaukee program is that only nonreligious private schools are allowed to participate in the program.

Using the normal curve equivalent reading and math scores from the Iowa Test of Basic Skills (ITBS), which was administered to the Choice students every year and in Grades 2, 5, and 7 for students in the Milwaukee public schools, Rouse (1998) compared the test scores of Choice students with those of unsuccessful applicants and other public school students. The sample consisted of African American and Hispanic students who first applied in the years 1990 to 1993 for the program, and a matching cohort was drawn from the public student data with valid test scores for comparison. Rouse's results showed that the voucher program generated gains in math scores, and students selected for the voucher program scored approximately two extra percentage points per year in math when compared with unsuccessful applicants and the sample of other public school students. In contrast, there was no significant difference in reading scores.

Tuition Tax Credit: Ontario, Canada

In 2001, the provincial government of Ontario, the most populous province in Canada, passed the Equity in Education Tax Credit Act (Bill 45), which led to an exogenous increase in choice between public and private schools. The tax credit applied to the first $7,000 of eligible annual net private school tuition fees paid per student. Although 10% of eligible tuition fees could be claimed for the tax year 2002, a 50% credit rate was scheduled to be phased in over a 5-year period, resulting in a maximum tax credit of $3,500 when the program was fully implemented in 2007, which was a comparable amount to that offered in the Milwaukee experiment (about $3,200 in 1994 to 1995). The tax credit was large in scope because about 80% of private schools participated in the program, irrespective of their religious orientation. In 2003, the credit was switched off unexpectedly because of a change in the provincial political party in power.

Taking advantage of this unique opportunity to study a large-scale increased choice experiment in North America,

Ping Ching Winnie Chan (2009) examined the Grade 3 standardized test (an annual assessment administered by the Education Quality and Accountability Office in Ontario) of Ontario public schools before and after the introduction of the tax credit policy. The empirical evidence indicates that the impact of competition was positive and significant in 2002 to 2003 (the year the tax credit was in full effect). The average proportion of students attaining the provincial standard was found to be about two percentage points higher in districts with greater private school presence—districts where competition from private schools would be higher because of the tax credit. The Ontario experience provides evidence that increasing private school choice could help public schools to improve their performance.

Choice Within the Public System

In addition to an increase in school choice from private schools, there are other forms of choice within the public system—for example, open enrollment policies, magnet schools, and charter schools. Students in North America typically attend a neighborhood public school assigned within the school attendance boundary, and the application to out-of-boundary schools varies from jurisdiction to jurisdiction. Open enrollment policies allow a student to transfer to another school either within or outside his or her school attendance area. This form of choice is indeed the most prominent form of choice available to students in the public system. Magnet schools are schools operated under the public system, but they exist outside of the zoned boundaries and offer academic or other programs that are different from the regular public schools to attract enrollment. Charter schools, on the other hand, are not subjected to the administrative policies within the public system even though they are also publicly funded. The charter documents the school's special purpose and its rules of operation and will be evaluated by the declared objectives in the charter. In the United States, there are about 200 charter schools, mostly situated in Minnesota and California, and in Canada, Alberta is the only province with charter schools. The magnet schools and the charter schools aim to provide more diversity within the public system to meet the needs of students.

Open Enrollment Policy: Chicago Public Schools

In Chicago, students have more flexibility in their high school selection and may apply to schools other than their neighborhood schools when space is available through the Chicago Public Schools (CPS) open enrollment policy. The take-up rate of the policy among Chicago students is quite high, and more than half of the students in CPS opt out of their neighborhood schools.

Using detailed student-level panel data from CPS, Julie Cullen, Brian Jacob, and Steven Levitt (2005) compared the outcomes of those who did versus those who did not exercise choice under the open enrollment program. Students opting out of their assigned high schools (i.e., those exercising choice) were found to be more likely to graduate compared to those who remained in their assigned schools. An important insight in their study, though, is the presence of potential selection bias in the sample of students who take advantage of the choice program. If the more motivated students are more likely to opt out of local schools and to fare better academically than students with lower motivation, then opting out may be correlated with higher completion rate. This calls into question whether to interpret the higher education outcomes as an effect from the school choice program itself or from the selection bias in motivation or other unobservable characteristics among the students who opted out.

As mentioned, one of the important issues in the school choice literature relates to the performance impact from increased student sorting. Although competition varies, the mix of students between public schools and alternative schools would also vary. Thus, in a more competitive environment, the average ability of students in public schools may be systematically different from students in public schools operating in a less competitive environment. When school choice increases, productivity responses from schools and sorting effects due to changes in the mix of students are likely to operate together. It is an empirical challenge to separate the effects of sorting from productivity responses, and more research in the area is still required in this direction.

Accountability

Much of the earlier debate in U.S. educational policy for raising performance concentrates on providing more resources to the system, such as increasing educational expenditures, reducing pupil–teacher ratios, or supporting special programs to target students with different needs. As performance responses to these policy initiatives have shown to be less than encouraging (see Hanushek, 1986), federal policy since the 1990s has moved to emphasize performance standards and assessments. Since the passage of the No Child Left Behind Act (NCLB) in 2001, all states are required to follow standards and requirements laid down by the Department of Education to assess the annual performance of their schools. The policy has been controversial, and debates have focused on its effectiveness in improving student performance as well as other unintended outcomes— for example, grade inflation, teaching-to-the-test, or gaming the system, which might result when the system responds to specific objective measures. Working with the CPS, Jacob and Levitt (2004) presented an investigation of the prevalence of cheating by school personnel in the annual ITBS. The sample included all students in Grades 3 to 7 for the years from 1993 to 2000. By identifying "unusually large increases followed by small gains or even declines in test scores the next year and unexpected patterns in students' answers" (p. 72) as indicators of cheating and a retesting

experiment in 2002, the authors concluded that cheating on standardized tests occurs in about 4% to 5% of elementary school classrooms. The frequency of cheating was also found to increase following the introduction of high-stakes testing, especially in the low-performing classrooms. The investigation showed that cheating is not likely to be a serious problem in high-stakes testing but confirmed that unintended behavioral responses would be induced under a different incentive structure. This creates a challenge for policy makers to design incentive structures that could minimize the disruptive behavior. In this section, an overview of the NCLB legislation and empirical evidence on student performance impact from stronger accountability measures in Florida and Chicago are discussed.

The No Child Left Behind Legislation

Immediately after President George W. Bush took office in 2001, he proposed the legislation of NCLB, aiming to improve the performance of U.S. elementary and secondary schools. The act requires all states to test public school students in Grades 3 through 8 annually and in Grades 10 to 12 at least once, subject to parameters set by the U.S. Department of Education. The states set their own proficiency standards, known as *adequate yearly progress* (AYP), as well as a schedule of target levels for the percentage of proficient students at the school level. Such performance-based assessment reinforces the accountability movements that were adopted in many states prior to NCLB (by 2000, 39 states had some sort of accountability system at the school level). If a school persistently fails to meet performance expectations, it will face increasing sanctions that include providing eligible students with the option of moving to a better public school or the opportunity to receive free tutoring, which the act refers to as *supplemental educational services.* States and school districts also have more flexibility in the use of federal education funds to allocate resources for their particular needs, such as hiring new teachers or improving teacher training.

Florida's A+ Plan for Education

Florida's A+ Plan for Education, initiated in 1999, implemented annual curriculum-based testing of all students in Grades 3 through 10. The Stanford-9 Achievement Test (SAT-9) was instituted as the Florida Comprehensive Assessment Test (FCAT) in 2000. All public and charter schools receive annual grades from A to F based on aggregate test performance, and rewards are given to high-performing schools, while sanctions as well as additional assistance are given to low-performing schools. The most controversial component of the plan is the opportunity scholarships, which are offered to students attending schools that received an F grade for 2 years during a 4-year period. In 2006, the Florida Supreme Court issued a ruling declaring the private school option of the Opportunity Scholarship Program unconstitutional, and students are no longer offered the opportunity to transfer to a private school; however, the option to attend a higher-performing public school remains in effect.

Prior to the A+ Plan, in 1996 Florida had begun rating schools based on their aggregate test performance (based on a nationally norm-referenced test such as the ITBS or SAT-8) on students in Grades 3 through 10 in reading and mathematics. Based on student performance, schools were stratified into four categories on the Critically Low Performing Schools List, and schools receiving the lowest classification were likely to receive a stigma effect because of the grading.

David Figlio and Rouse (2006) examined the Florida student-level data from a subset of school districts from 1995 to 2000 to assess the effects of both the voucher threat and the grade stigma on public school performance. The analysis showed positive effects on student outcomes in mathematics in low-performing schools, but the primary improvements were concentrated in the high-stakes grades (prior to 2001 to 2002, students in Grades 4, 8, and 10 were tested in reading and writing, and students in Grades 5, 8, and 10 were tested in math). Their results also found that schools concentrated more effort on low-performing students in the sample.

Chicago Public Schools

In 1996, Chicago Public Schools (CPS) introduced a school accountability system in which elementary schools were put on probation if the proficiency counts (i.e., the number of students who achieved a given level of proficiency) in reading on the ITBS were lower than the national norm. Schools on probation were required to implement improvement plans and would face sanctions and public reports if their students' scores did not improve.

After the introduction of NCLB in 2002, CPS designated the use of proficiency counts based on the Illinois Standards Achievement Test (ISAT), which had been introduced by the Illinois State Board of Education in 1998 to 1999 as the statewide assessment, as the key measure of school performance. Subject to the requirement of the act, the ISAT test in 2002 changed from a relatively low-stakes state assessment to a high-stakes exam under the national assessment.

Derek Neal and Diane Schanzenbach (in press) examined data from CPS to assess the impact of the introduction of these two separate accountability systems. The analysis compared students who took a specific high-stake exam under a new accountability system with students who took the same exam under low stakes in the year before the accountability system was implemented. The results show that students in the middle of the distribution scored significantly higher than expected. In contrast, students in the bottom of the distribution did not score higher following the introduction of accountability, and only mixed results could be found among the most advantaged students.

Both the Florida and the Chicago results show performance effects on public school performance after the introduction of stronger accountability measures. However, given that the effects are not uniformly distributed across students with different abilities and are often concentrated in students of high-stakes grades, both studies raise concerns about resource allocation when responding to such accountability measures and call for more research on policy design that can minimize disrupted incentives.

Conclusion and Future Directions

The economics of education is a growing and exciting field in economic research. As reviewed in this chapter, the empirical analysis in the field has already provided many insightful ideas for current education issues that are relevant to public policy. The new research in the area has started to adopt a more structural approach to understand the impact of education reform policies that have often induced responses from different players—for example, using general equilibrium analysis to model the linkage between housing decisions and school consumption to measure the potential benefits on school quality with school choice policy (see Bayer, Fernando, & McMillan, 2007; Nechyba, 2000). These new papers use innovative measurement design and more detailed microlevel data and can complement the findings from reduced-form analysis in the literature as well as identify the channels through which the policy effect is being brought about.

References and Further Readings

Arrow, K. (1973). Higher education as a filter. *Journal of Public Economics, 2*(3), 193–216.

Ashenfelter, O., & Rouse, C. (1998). Income, schooling, and ability: Evidence from a new sample of identical twins. *Quarterly Journal of Economics, 113*(1), 253–284.

Bayer, P., & Fernando, F., & McMillan, R. (2007). A unified framework for measuring preferences for schools and neighborhoods. *Journal of Political Economy, 115,* 588–638.

Bayer, P., & McMillan, R. (2005). *Choice and competition in local education markets* (Working Paper No. 11802). Cambridge, MA: National Bureau of Economic Research.

Becker, G. (1964). *Human capital.* New York: Columbia University Press.

Belfield, C. (2000). *Economic principles for education.* Cheltenham, UK: Edward Elgar.

Benjamin, D., Gunderson, M., Limieux, T., & Riddell, C. (2007). *Labour market economics: Theory, evidence, and policy in Canada* (6th ed.). Toronto, Ontario, Canada: McGraw-Hill Ryerson.

Card, D., & Krueger, A. (1996). School resources and student outcomes: An overview of the literature and new evidence from North and South Carolina. *Journal of Economic Perspective, 10*(4), 31–50.

Chan, P. (2009). *School choice, competition, and public school performance.* Unpublished doctoral dissertation, University of Toronto, Ontario, Canada.

Checchi, D. (2006). *The economics of education.* Cambridge, MA: Cambridge University Press.

Cohn, E., & Geske, G. (1990). *The economics of education* (3rd ed.). Oxford, UK: Pergamon.

Coleman, J. (1966). *Equality of educational opportunity.* Washington, DC: Government Printing Office.

Coleman, J., Hoffer, T., & Kilgore, S. (1982). *High school achievement: Public, Catholic and private schools compared.* New York: Basic Books.

Cullen, J., Jacob, B., & Levitt, S. (2005). The impact of school choice on student outcomes: An analysis of the Chicago Public Schools. *Journal of Public Economics, 89,* 729–760.

Dahl, G., & Lochner, L. (2008). *The impact of family income on child achievement: Evidence from the earned income tax* (Working Paper No. 14599). Cambridge, MA: National Bureau of Economic Research.

Figlio, D., & Rouse, C. (2006). Do accountability and voucher threats improve low-performing schools? *Journal of Public Economics, 90,* 239–255.

Friedman, M. (1962). *Capitalism and freedom.* Chicago: University of Chicago Press.

Glass, G., & Smith, M. (1979). Meta-analysis of research on class size and achievement. *Educational Evaluation and Policy Analysis, 1*(1), 2–16.

Grogger, J., & Neal, D. (2000). Further evidence on the effects of Catholic secondary schooling. *Brookings-Wharton Papers on Urban Affairs, 1,* 151–193.

Hanushek, E. (1986). The economics of schooling. *Journal of Economic Literature, 24,* 1141–1177.

Hanushek, E. (2006). School resources. In E. Hanushek & F. Welch (Eds.), *Handbook of the economics of education* (Vol. 2, pp. 865–908). New York: Elsevier North-Holland.

Hanushek, E., & Kain, J. (1972). On the value of "equality of educational opportunity" as a guide to public policy. In F. Mosteller & D. P. Moynihan (Eds.), *On equality of educational opportunity* (pp. 116–145). New York: Random House.

Hanushek, E., & Welch, F. (Eds.). (2006). *Handbook of the economics of education* (Vols. 1 & 2). New York: Elsevier North-Holland.

Heckman, J., Lochner, L., & Todd, P. (2006). Earnings functions, rates of return and treatment effects: The Mincer equation and beyond. In E. Hanushek & F. Welch (Eds.), *Handbook of the economics of education* (Vol. 1, pp. 307–458). New York: Elsevier North-Holland.

Hoxby, C. (2000). The effect of class size on student achievement: New evidence from population variation. *Quarterly Journal of Economics, 115*(4), 1239–1285.

Krueger, A. (1999). Experimental estimates of education production functions. *Quarterly Journal of Economics, 114*(2), 497–532.

Jacob, B., & Levitt, S. (2004, winter). To catch a cheat. *Education Next, 4*(1), 69–75.

Lang, K., & Kropp, D. (1986). Human capital versus sorting: The effects of compulsory attendance laws. *Quarterly Journal of Economics, 101*(2), 609–624.

Lazear, E. (2001). Educational production. *Quarterly Journal of Economics, 116*(3), 777–803.

Levin, H. (1989). Mapping the economics of education: An introductory essay. *Educational Researcher, 18*(4), 13–16, 73.

Manski, C. (1993). Identification of endogenous social effects: The reflection problem. *Review of Economic Studies, 60,* 531–542.

Mayer, S. (1997). *What money can't buy: Family income and children's life chances.* Cambridge, MA: Harvard University Press.

McMillan, R. (2005). Competition, incentives, and public school production. *Journal of Public Economics, 89,* 1131–1154.

Milligan, K., & Stabile, M. (2009). *Do child benefits affect the wellbeing of children? Evidence from Canadian child benefit expansions* (Working Paper No. 12). Vancouver, British Columbia, Canada: Canadian Labour Market and Skills Researcher Network.

Mincer, J. (1974). *Schooling, experience, and earnings.* New York: Columbia University Press.

Neal, D., & Schanzenbach, D. (in press). Left behind by design: Proficiency counts and test-based accountability. *Review of Economics and Statistics.*

Nechyba, T. (2000). Mobility, targeting, and private school vouchers. *American Economic Review, 90*(1), 130–146.

Rouse, C. (1998). Private school vouchers and student achievement: An evaluation of the Milwaukee Parental Choice Program. *Quarterly Journal of Economics, 113*(2), 553–602.

Schultz, T. (1963). *The economic value of education.* New York: Columbia University Press.

Spence, M. (1973). Job market signaling. *Quarterly Journal of Economics, 87*(3), 355–374.

51

ECONOMICS AND JUSTICE

GEORGE F. DEMARTINO

University of Denver

Exploration of the connections between economics and justice is complicated by the fact that both economics and justice are variously defined and deeply contested. Economics can be thought of as the study of the determinants of wealth creation, which was the view taken by many classical economists; the study of choice and allocation under conditions of scarcity, which is the view of contemporary neoclassical theory; the study of the production, appropriation, and distribution of the social surplus, which informs Marxian theory; the study of the manner in which communities provision for themselves, which is the view of many institutionalists; and in other ways. Justice is likewise a controversial concept. Here, too, one finds that distinct approaches yield diverse accounts of what is just and unjust. Justice can be defined in terms of fairness, respect for inviolable rights, or equality. Making matters more interesting, each of these definitions can be (and is) also theorized in diverse ways. For instance, egalitarians (those who define justice in terms of equal distribution) often disagree among themselves about whether a just distribution is one that assures equality of income, wealth, opportunities, rights, or something else entirely. Finally, many economists tend to avoid discussion of ethical matters, including justice, which they define as lying outside their field of expertise. As a consequence, notions of justice are implicit rather than explicit in much of economics.

This diversity implies that it is a mistake to think that there is any one right way to conceptualize economics, justice, or the connections between them. It is both intellectually honest and far more rewarding to embrace the conceptual diversity that one encounters in this context and then to explore the ways in which distinct approaches to

economics engage distinct notions of justice. This allows for an informed investigation of conceptions of economics and justice. One stands to learn much about the controversies among economists over policy and the assessment of economic outcomes by attending to the justice conceptions that inform their judgments. In a reciprocal manner, one can better evaluate contending justice claims by attending to their economic implications. After all, an approach to justice that seems entirely plausible in the abstract may generate concern if one finds that its economic policy implications are damaging or even repugnant in fundamental ways.

This chapter proceeds in just this way. It begins with and gives most attention to neoclassical economic theory—the orthodox approach to economics that has predominated in the profession for many decades. One encounters a deep ambivalence among neoclassical economists about the place of moral judgments in economics—including but not limited to judgments concerning justice. This suggests that there is no one neoclassical conception of justice. This chapter instead investigates the theoretical strategies that have emerged within the tradition to manage this ambivalence. Despite the reluctance of neoclassical economists to engage matters of morality, a conception of justice has emerged within important strands of neoclassical thought. It is associated with what are called *negative* liberties, rights, and freedoms. This is an approach that focuses on the individual's freedom from illegitimate constraints on his or her decision making. This approach informs the work of Nobel Laureate Milton Friedman and other economists. A particularly clear statement of this approach appears in the work of libertarian philosopher Robert Nozick (1974), and the chapter examines his central arguments and their implications for economic justice.

Then the chapter turns to one heterodox approach to political economy, Marxian theory, and explores alternative notions of justice that inform this approach. Marxian theory is exemplary of many other heterodox approaches that embrace positive rights and freedoms. These reach far beyond the requirements associated with negative rights. This chapter explores two relevant aspects of Marxian theory: (1) its notion of exploitation and (2) its conception of a just distribution of burdens and rewards. These are derived from its normative grounding in an egalitarian notion of justice.

It bears emphasis that the controversy in economics over justice is not just of academic interest. The debate is deeply consequential. To demonstrate this, this chapter investigates what each approach implies about the legitimacy of the market as an institution for distributing income, wealth, and opportunity. This is one of the most important of all policy debates in economics and politics. One sees that what a school of economic thought has to say about this question depends directly on the conception of justice to which it is committed.

Neoclassical Economics

There is a profound difficulty within neoclassical theory in speaking about justice. This difficulty stems from the conception of economics as value-free science that informs neoclassical thought. Advocates of neoclassical theory tend to view economics as an objective science, the goal of which is to theorize the functioning of economic processes and outcomes as they are, undistorted by normative judgments. Just as physics seeks to describe the physical world as it is, not as the physicist would like it to be, so must the economic scientist describe the operation of the social world independent of normative biases. Neoclassical economics holds to a rigid distinction between positive economics—the objective explanation of economic phenomena—and normative economics—the evaluation of economic outcomes and the formulation of policy prescription. In this dichotomy, positive economics is by far preeminent. Considerations of justice reside in the domain of normative economics and are taken to be far less scientific than the considerations that inform positive economics. As a consequence, most neoclassical literature is altogether silent on justice concerns.

Neoclassical theory incorporates the effort to remain value free in the specification of the assumptions with which it begins its work. Human actors are presumed to be rational, where rationality is defined in particular ways. For neoclassical theory, rationality implies self-interested, egoistic behavior. Rational actors seek their own welfare. Moreover, they always desire more of the things they like. Rationality also implies that they know best what is good for them. This requires an assumption that each agent has a preference ordering that maps his or her full set of likes,

dislikes, values, commitments, tolerances, intolerances, fears, and passions. When confronted with a choice between two commodities or courses of action, rational agents simply consult their preference ordering and make those choices that benefit them most, all things considered. By *benefits most* is meant maximizing their personal happiness or utility, or more prosaically, simply choosing those options that best satisfy their preferences.

The assumption of rationality yields an important implication. In this framework, there is no basis for the economist or the economic theory to judge the choices that economic actors make. Because they are rational, they know best, full stop. It is of critical importance that this theoretical strategy spares the economist from having to make the value judgments that assessing actors' preferences would require. Hence, the assumption of rationality allows economics to undertake its investigation of economic matters in an apparently objective way.

Rational agents have virtually limitless desires, but they populate a world of finitude. This is because all output requires inputs from nature, but nature's bounty is finite. At any one moment, only so much can be produced. Hence, economic actors confront a world of scarcity. This leads to the central economic problem in neoclassical thought: choice and allocation under conditions of scarcity. How can the scarce resources that society has available to it be best allocated across the diverse purposes to which they can be put? Should more energy go into auto production or into mass transportation? Which choice will leave society best off, where best off is theorized in terms of maximizing people's satisfaction of desires, according to their own respective preference orderings?

It would seem that the neoclassical emphasis on scarcity and allocation of resources would immediately call forth questions of economics of justice, because in a world of scarcity there is not enough to go around. There would seem to be a need here for normative criteria to assess the justness of any particular distribution of total social output. For reasons already discussed, however, this is not the case. Neoclassical theory's commitment to objective science requires that it attempt to answer questions surrounding allocation of scarce resources and distribution of final output while minimizing value judgments. Shunning value judgments has led the profession to emphasize efficiency as its chief evaluative criterion rather than alternative, value-laden criteria like justice. In this approach, an economic outcome is taken to be inefficient if at least one person could be made better off given existing resources and technologies without making at least one other person worse off. For example, if one person prefers apples to bananas but has in his or her possession only bananas, while another person has the opposite preference but possesses only apples, the situation is inefficient because both could be made better off simply by exchanging with each other. In contrast, an efficient (or Pareto optimal) outcome is one in which no one can be made better off without making at least one other person worse off. If one assumes that these two people do trade bananas and apples, the situation that results after the trade is made is efficient.

Notice that the assessment of efficiency does not seem to require of the economist any value judgments. The economist does not ask or care why one person prefers apples and another bananas. The economist does not ask how many apples or bananas each possesses prior to or after the exchange takes place. That is taken to be none of the economist's business. And so it appears that judgments pertaining to efficiency are largely value free.

Neoclassical Economics, Distribution, and Justice

What does this approach suggest about distribution of income and wealth? Efficiency considerations imply that income should be distributed in whatever way best ensures the enhancement of social welfare. That distribution is best that permits the maximum satisfaction of preferences, given existing resources and technologies. This distribution can be summed up as follows: In the first instance, to each according to his her contribution.

Most neoclassical economists emphasize the efficiency benefits of rewarding each agent according to his or her contribution (rather than the intrinsic rightness of such arrangements). The efficiency argument is simple and is understood by its advocates to entail little in the way of value judgments. The argument is this: An economic system that rewards agents for their contributions will give them an incentive to contribute more—perhaps by investing in training (and so enhancing their human capital) or by acquiring other productive assets like land or capital. The assumption of rationality implies that individuals do this for themselves, in pursuit of increasing income, but the unintended consequence of their doing so is increasing total social output owing to their increasing productivity. Hence, the argument for rewarding agents according to their contributions is, for most economists, a simple matter of wise economic management. Economies that reward contribution will grow prosperous, and that will allow for greater satisfaction of people's desires.

But what about distributive justice as opposed to efficiency? A central theme in neoclassical thought is that this is largely a noneconomic question, because it entails value judgments of the sort that neoclassical theory does not permit. For example, imagine that a professor distributes $100 among all his or her students, equally. Is this arrangement efficient? The answer is yes, because once the distribution is made, no one can be made better off without making another worse off (the only way for one student to get more is for another to get less). But what if, instead, a professor gives all $100 to just one student? Is this distribution efficient? The answer is again yes because the only way to make any one of the unfortunate students who received nothing better off is to take some amount of money away from the lucky student who possesses the $100. Both situations are equal in an efficiency sense. This implies that efficiency has nothing to do with equity, fairness, or justice. And because neoclassical thought emphasizes efficiency over other evaluative criteria, one is led to the conclusion that there is little more to be said about them.

Free Choice, Negative Freedom, and Justice

There is more to the story, however. Neoclassical theory's attachment to rationality entails a strong commitment to individual free choice, which in turn implies a certain sense of justice that some (though by no means all) leading neoclassical economists embrace. Because the agents know best what is in their best interest, that economic system is best that allows them the freedom to choose from among the opportunities they face. There are constraints in this choosing, of course. As discussed, choices are constrained by scarcity. In a world of scarcity, each and every action taken entails an opportunity cost in terms of what must be forgone to pursue it. The material that goes into a bicycle tire is unavailable for producing an automobile tire. In a market economy, scarcity is imposed on each agent via his or her budget constraint. Individuals can purchase whatever they choose, provided they do not exceed the resources they have available to them (through income or borrowing).

This sense of economic freedom is often described as *negative freedom* and is associated with negative rights or liberties (Berlin, 1958). Negative freedom entails the right to choose from among the opportunities one confronts, given one's circumstances (such as one's budget), without coercion by others (and especially by government). In this account, a poor person and a rich person may be equally free, provided that each can choose without interference from among the opportunities each confronts. Naturally, the rich person will have a greater set of opportunities than the poor person. But if both can choose freely from among the options available to them, each is equally free in the sense of the enjoyment of negative rights.

This manner of thinking then leads to a particular conception of justice. A distribution is taken to be just, provided that it arises from the exercise of free choice defined as negative freedom. Agents are to be free to make the best deals available to them within the constraints set by their budgets. Whatever aggregate distribution of social wealth arises from each agent acting in this manner is on this account just, because it arises from the equal enjoyment of negative freedom of all agents, no matter how rich or poor they might be. In this account, an unjust distribution would be one that arose from the violation of some people's (negative) rights. For instance, a distribution that arises from theft, extortion, or physical coercion (such as through the threat of force) would be unjust because it violates persons' negative rights.

This conception of justice emerges in the work of some important neoclassical economists who engage matters of justice. Friedman (1962; Friedman & Friedman, 1990) is particularly notable in this regard. In work such as *Capitalism and Freedom* and *Free to Choose,* he advocates forcefully for negative rights in the form of freedom of choice as restricted only by one's budget constraint. For Friedman, the enjoyment of such rights is vital to economic prosperity, for the reasons already discussed—and even to justice. He argues strenuously against physical coercion in economic affairs, especially by the state, as inherently unjust. He equates freedom with the absence of such coercion.

The equation of justice with the outcome of free choice derives from the work of political theorists like John Locke (1690) and is developed more fully in contemporary libertarian work. Locke argues that people have an inherent right to own that which they create—both directly through their own labors, and indirectly through the capital they employ to hire the labor of others. Locke reaches this important normative conclusion on the basis of a simple intuitive argument. First, Locke contends that "every Man has a *Property* in his own *Person.* This no Body has any Right to but himself" (MacPherson, 1962, p. 200). This is a natural right that cannot be legitimately abridged by society or government. Second, people have a right to attempt to survive, and this can be accomplished only by their appropriating for themselves elements of nature. One achieves this by mixing labor with nature, thereby transforming it into necessary goods. Hence, though nature is provided to humankind in common, the act of individual labor provides the normative foundation for individual appropriation. Each person acquires the exclusive right to possess and consume that which his or her own labor has created. In Locke's words, "The *Labour* of his Body, and the *Work* of his Hands, we may say, are properly his" (MacPherson, p. 200).

Locke extends this right of property to include that output produced by the labor of others whom one has hired. He reaches this conclusion by emphasizing that the right of property in one's own person and labor must entail the right to alienate it to others through voluntary exchange. In this respect, one's labor is no different from other property.

The modern libertarian view of distribution, such as that advocated by prominent libertarian theorist Nozick, is consistent with these Lockean propositions. In this view, any distribution of a society's output is just, provided that it arises only from legitimate processes. In Nozick's (1974) words, "The complete principle of distributive justice would say simply that a distribution is just if it arises from another (just) distribution by legitimate means" (p. 151). Presuming a just prior distribution—that is, one that did not arise via the infringement of people's rights—the outcome of a series of voluntary exchanges between free individuals must also be deemed just, regardless of the patterns of distribution that arise as a consequence. If those who make the greatest contribution are able to secure through voluntary exchange a greater reward, then the consequent

inequality is entirely just. Indeed, from this perspective, government initiatives to redistribute income in pursuit of greater equality are unjust. In Nozick's view, because such initiatives essentially force some to work, uncompensated, for others, redistributive measures are even tantamount to slavery.

Just one matter remains. Tying reward to contribution (or voluntary exchange) speaks to distribution in the first instance. But what of those who do not contribute or who have nothing to exchange? Many in society produce nothing at all, either during portions of their lives (when they are infants, elderly, or infirm), or during their entire lives (if they are in some way incapacitated in ways that prevent so-called productive work). Few would argue for their complete exclusion from a share of total output: Beneficence toward the deserving poor is widely accepted among advocates of most theoretical perspectives.

This begs the question: What degree of provisioning should society make for the unproductive? Here, neoclassical theory provides little guidance because this question is seen to lie squarely in the domain of value judgments. Instrumental (efficiency) arguments still apply, of course: In cases where the unproductive can be made productive, the argument can be made that a sufficient distribution should be made to induce this rehabilitation. In this case, value neutrality might be (apparently) preserved via the recommendation of the use of cost-benefit analysis as the appropriate scientific means for making this judgment. But this then would be seen as the nonnormative matter of determining just what distribution to the unproductive will generate an efficient outcome. Beyond this, neoclassical theory has little to say.

Egalitarianism and Heterodox Economics

Many alternative approaches to economics and political economy differ from neoclassical theory in their initial assumptions, substantive propositions, analytical methods, and especially in their normative judgments. Not least, approaches as diverse as Marxian, institutionalist, socioeconomic, and feminist theory tend toward the embrace of egalitarian normative commitments, as do many contributions to political theory (see Anderson, 1990; Lutz, 1999; Tool, 1979; Walzer, 1973, 1983). These are commitments that emphasize equality among society's members. As Amartya Sen (1992) has argued at length, however, most normative frameworks emphasize the equality of something that is taken to be fundamental. Distinct frameworks differ primarily in what it is that each seeks to equalize across society's members. And so it should not be surprising that distinct heterodox approaches tend to define what it is that is to be equalized differently. Indeed, even within each of these traditions, we find normative controversy including, but not limited to, what makes for a just outcome.

The Marxian approach is representative of the many diverse schools of thought that embrace some form of egalitarianism, and so this chapter investigates it in some detail here. Like other heterodox approaches, the Marxian tradition reaches beyond negative freedom (associated with negative rights) to embrace positive freedom (tied as it is to positive rights). Positive freedom (sometimes called *substantive freedom*) concerns not just the absence of constraints on a person's actions. Instead, according to Sen (1992) it speaks to the full range of beings and doings that a person can actually achieve or enjoy, given his or her income, wealth, race, gender, level of schooling, and all other factors that bear on what a person can be or do. This account recognizes that two individuals with equal negative freedom (in the sense of freedom from coercion) may enjoy very different levels of positive freedom. The relatively poor person who is entirely free to choose may face a very bleak opportunity set as compared with that of a rich person. Egalitarian frameworks that privilege positive as opposed to negative freedom are inclined to find ethically deficient a social arrangement that fails to address this inequality. They seek reform that expands the opportunity set of the disadvantaged in order to equalize the life chances (and not just the negative rights) of society's members.

John Rawls (1971) has been particularly influential in shifting the attention of political theorists and others to positive conceptions of freedom. In *A Theory of Justice*, Rawls advances an approach to justice as fairness. He investigates what kind of social arrangements concerning distribution (and other things) would arise voluntarily from a process of rational deliberation among society's members. He asks us to join him in a thought experiment in which we suppose a committee of deliberators who will decide on the best institutional arrangements for the society that they will inhabit. Critically, he requires that one envisions this committee as doing its work behind a veil of ignorance—that is, they must design the rules under which they and all other members of society will live, without knowing as they deliberate into which group in society they themselves will be placed. This ensures that they will consider the fairness of the arrangements they propose from the perspective of all the groups that make up society. Rawls argues that the outcome of this thought experiment would be just, because it would potentially be deemed fair by all of society's members.

What principles would such a committee of deliberators agree on to govern distribution in their society? Rawls (1971) argues that the committee would settle on two fundamental principles. The first requires the equal distribution of primary goods to all of society's members. Primary goods are the "basic rights, liberties and opportunities, and the . . . all-purpose means such as income and wealth," but also the "bases of self-respect." These goods, Rawls continues, "are things citizens need as free and equal persons" (pp. 180–181). Justice as fairness requires that these goods be equally provided to all of society's members so that each has equal substantive ability (positive freedom) to pursue his or her life plans.

Rawls's (1971) second principle, the difference principle, modifies the first. It allows for the case in which the equal distribution of primary goods may harm all of society's members. Justice as fairness permits inequality in the distribution of primary goods, provided that the worst off benefit most thereby. This test for inequality is quite demanding: It requires evidence that unequal distributions help most those who will receive least. Absent such evidence, Rawls argues that inequality in primary goods is illegitimate.

Rawls's work has been deeply influential. In economics, Sen has taken up and extended Rawls's work in ways that relate to economic conceptions of justice (see also Nussbaum, 1992). Sen argues that while Rawls is right to emphasize equality of positive freedom, he errs by focusing on the means to achieve freedom rather than on the actual freedom that people enjoy. This is because individuals differ in their abilities to convert primary goods into achievements. This implies that two people with equal bundles of primary goods may nevertheless face distinct levels of substantive freedom. For instance, a disabled person may need greater income and support than others to achieve the same level of beings and doings (such as mobility or occupational success). Were all individuals identical, this problem would not arise. But because interpersonal differences are so dramatic, the goal of promoting equality in substantive freedom requires that we focus on substantive equality directly, rather than on the means to achieve it. And this implies that we may need to distribute primary goods and other means to achieve unequally if we are to achieve the most important kind of equality: equality in the positive freedoms that people enjoy.

Positive Freedom and Marxian Economics

Look at how this emphasis on positive freedom bears on normative judgments within the Marxian framework. This framework begins with a simple, intuitively plausible assumption: To exist over time, all societies must produce a surplus. That is, those who perform the labor necessary for provisioning (producing food, clothing, health care, shelter, etc.) must produce not just enough to sustain themselves, but to sustain others. This is because at any particular moment, some in society will be unable to produce for themselves. This is true of infants, young children, the elderly, the infirm, and the otherwise disabled. If the productive workers produced only enough to sustain themselves, society would be unable to reproduce itself over time.

The Marxian framework concerns itself principally with the diverse ways that societies organize the production, appropriation, and distribution of the surplus (Resnick & Wolff, 1987). Who is assigned to produce the social surplus, and what means are used to ensure that they are induced to perform this social necessity? Who is entitled to appropriate the surplus so produced? That is, who receives it, and by what juridical, political, cultural, or other means are they ensured that the surplus flows to them? Finally, what norms, rules, laws, or conventions dictate the distribution of the social surplus across society's members, including those who participate in and those who are excluded from the practices of producing and appropriating the social surplus?

Unlike neoclassical theory, many heterodox approaches explicitly engage normative questions and even base their theoretical frameworks on normative judgments (DeMartino, 2000). This is certainly true of the Marxian approach. Vital questions arise immediately in this approach about the rightness of the arrangements that societies adopt to manage the production, appropriation, and distribution of the social surplus. First, one finds in the Marxian tradition a normative indictment of what is called *exploitation*. This term is used to describe any social arrangement in which those who produce the surplus are excluded from its appropriation. This happens whenever others in society enjoy the right of appropriation at the expense of the producers. For instance, in slave societies, the surplus is produced by slaves but appropriated by the slave owners. This, for Marxists, represents a particularly clear example of exploitation. On this ground (among others), slavery is deemed unjust. And so would be any other social arrangement that shared the feature of exploitation.

The Marxian tradition has much to say not just about who should appropriate the surplus, but also about how that surplus should ultimately be distributed (DeMartino, 2003; Geras, 1985, 1992; Lukes, 1987). In this approach, a distribution of the social surplus is just when it is based on need. This conception is consistent with Sen's framework, as already discussed. Those who require more, perhaps because of physical disabilities (permanent or temporary), age, geography, or other challenges, are entitled to greater shares of the social surplus. In contrast, distributive justice requires that those who require the least because of good fortune or other factors are to receive less (Marx, 1938).

Distribution according to need relates directly to the positive freedom that underlies the Marxian approach. Allocating more to those with the greatest need ensures that they enjoy increasing substantive freedom to live valued lives. It expands their opportunity sets by increasing the beings and doings that are available to them. Distributing more to those who are most impoverished in terms of their freedoms and who face the greatest challenges thereby contributes toward the equalization of positive freedom across society's members. It generates what its advocates see as genuine equality. This is equality in positive freedom—in what people can actually achieve—rather than in what this approach's proponents view as the hollow freedom associated with neoclassical theory's emphasis on negative freedom.

The equality that underpins Marxian and other heterodox approaches is much more demanding than is the equality to which neoclassical theory is committed. The latter requires only the removal of certain kinds of constraints—especially those imposed by the state, given its monopoly over the legitimate use of violence to enforce its dictates.

For those who value positive freedom, the removal of these constraints may not be at all sufficient to the achievement of genuine equality. Indeed, the value placed on negative rights might often interfere with the realization of equality of positive freedom. This would be the case, for instance, when the exercise of rights by those who are best off interferes with and reduces the opportunity sets of those who are less advantaged. Hence, we find a tension between these two kinds of freedoms and especially between demands for equality of the one as opposed to the equality of the other.

Applications and Policy Implications

Normative judgments matter deeply—not only at the level of abstract debate, but also in the design and evaluation of institutions, policies, and outcomes. Indeed, the positions economists take on the most important public policy questions are tied directly to the normative frameworks (including their judgments about justice) that underlie their approaches to economics. To see this, consider the question of whether the economic outcomes associated with the market economy are just. Here one finds a sharp controversy between those who embrace negative and those who embrace positive accounts of freedom.

In Friedman's (1962) account, distribution of total social wealth under the free market results from free exchange in the marketplace. Free exchange here entails only that there is no coercion. In the absence of such coercion, agents are taken to be entirely free to pursue their own interests as they see fit. This ensures that they will enter into only those agreements (or undertake those market exchanges) that improve their personal welfare. It is not for the economist to evaluate a person's judgments in this regard. When someone consummates an exchange, economists must presume that that person has made the best bargain available to him or her.

This conception of market interactions and outcomes implies that agents will receive rewards in the marketplace that are commensurate with their contributions to social welfare. Those who have produced the goods that society deems most useful or desirable will secure a higher price when they sell these goods than will other agents who are selling less desirable goods. Moreover, those with the greatest skills and with savings that they are willing to invest will make the greatest contributions to total output, which in turn serves as the means to enhance social welfare. In a free market, these agents will be able to bargain for rewards that reflect these greater contributions. In contrast, those with few skills or other endowments will receive low rewards that are commensurate with their lower contributions to total output. This is as it should be: Justice prevails when agents secure the share of total income they are due owing to what they contribute and the choices they make, unconstrained by illegitimate infringements on their rights or the rights of others.

From this perspective, the free market is viewed as the optimal form of economic arrangement. Not only is it apt to promote economic efficiency owing to the incentives it provides each actor to make greater contributions, but it also is just in the sense that it ensures equal negative rights to all actors. Unlike other economic arrangements that are based on dictates from the state that necessarily compromise negative freedom, the marketplace operates on a logic of freedom that allows each agent to pursue his or her self-interest unimpeded by illegitimate interference. So it is that Friedman can equate capitalism with freedom.

Those who embrace positive, as opposed to negative, freedom reach a radically different conclusion about free market processes and outcomes. The Marxian tradition argues that the negative rights associated with the marketplace both obscure and deepen substantive inequality. In a capitalist economy, those who produce the social surplus, the wage laborers, are exploited by the firms that hire them because the legal right to claim the surplus produced by laborers is monopolized by the firm. The surplus is extracted from workers unfairly, despite the illusion of fairness given by the fact that under capitalism workers are free to work or not as they see fit (Bowles & Gintis, 1990; Resnick & Wolff, 1987; Roemer, 1988). In this sense, the apparently free workers under capitalism are no different from slaves because both are deprived of the right to appropriate their own surplus. Hence, Marx can call employment under capitalism wage slavery.

From the Marxian perspective, there are other reasons to deem the free market unjust. The market economy does not ensure that those with the greatest need will secure the greatest allocations of the social surplus. Instead, those who are worst off in terms of their needs will often be least able to bargain for a fair price for what they have to sell. This is particularly the case for workers. Because under capitalism the means of production are monopolized by capitalists, workers cannot sustain themselves independently in the ways that they could were they to have in their possession the means of production. They are therefore compelled to sell their labor power in a market that is stacked in favor of the capitalists. Hence, free exchange leads to systematic unfairness owing to the asymmetry in bargaining power between capital and labor.

This concern about the inherent injustice of the labor market is shared by other heterodox traditions, such as radical institutionalism (see Dugger, 1989; Dugger & Sherman, 1994). For instance, institutionalist economist John Commons (1924) argues that workers must secure a wage regularly in order to survive: Because what they have to sell is perishable, they are forced to take what they can get (Ramstad, 1987). In contrast, the firms to which they must sell their labor power often can wait. This asymmetry in the ability to wait leads to an asymmetry in bargaining power, which in turn ensures that wages will be depressed below the fair level that would exist were workers and firms to confront each other as equals. For Commons, the outcome of such asymmetric bargaining is on its face unjust. In his view, reasonable value in exchange is realized only when both parties enjoy equal ability to wait.

Future Directions

Much works remains to be done on the connections between economics and justice. At present, neoclassical theory is undergoing substantial change owing to new avenues of research. For instance, developments in behavioral and experimental economics are demonstrating the severe limitations of the rationality assumption. Research indicates that individuals are often driven in their decision making by notions of fairness, justice, the welfare of others (not just family members but even strangers), and other ethical concerns. This implies new avenues for research on several fronts, as Sen (1987) has argued. What conceptions of justice do individuals hold when they make decisions? How do these conceptions affect their behavior? How are these conceptions (and behavior) affected by the social milieus in which individuals act? And what kinds of institutional arrangements might be desirable in promoting the conceptions of justice that individuals value? Although the answers to these questions will require substantial research, it is increasingly apparent that the simplistic account of rationality that has informed neoclassical economics for many decades is unlikely to survive much longer in economics. This may encourage neoclassical economists to revisit their historical antipathy toward normative judgments in their work.

Heterodox economic research can and likely will be extended to encompass a greater focus on normative matters and the kinds of institutions and policy strategies that are consistent with the conceptions of economic justice that heterodox approaches value. Greater attention must be paid to the relationship between positive and negative economic rights, for instance. A second question concerns the kinds of policy measures that might generate equality of positive freedoms in ways that are widely taken to be ethically defensible—even perhaps by those who would do worse under such arrangements. And what challenges are posed to the equalization of positive freedom by the dramatic increases in international economic integration over the past several decades? What kinds of policy initiatives are now necessary at the multilateral level to promote global equality? These are difficult questions, to be sure, but providing compelling answers to them is vital to the success of heterodox research and political projects.

Conclusion

This chapter has established that distinct approaches to economics value distinct notions of rights and freedom, which in turn generate distinct notions of justice, and these differences bear heavily on their respective assessments of economic policies and outcomes. Neoclassical thought entails a strong aversion toward value judgments, and this leaves it with little to say about economic justice. That said, there is implicit in the tradition a commitment to negative rights and negative freedom. Those who embrace this conception of freedom (such as economist Friedman and philosopher Nozick) are led to view any economic outcome as just, provided it arose through just means, where just means is defined as voluntary exchange, free of coercion. In this conception, then, free market outcomes are just because they arise from the exercise of people's rights. Even grossly unequal distributions of income are beyond reproach, provided they arose from processes (such as free exchange) that violated no one's rights.

In contrast, many heterodox traditions explicitly engage moral judgments, and many of these adopt a positive conception of rights and freedom. These approaches place emphasis on what a person can actually be or do, and many also view a just outcome as one that entails equality in positive freedom.

The case of bargaining between capital and labor examined in this chapter is just one example of what Marxists and other heterodox economists view as a general ethical problem in free market economies. Those who enjoy greatest substantive freedom are in positions to extend their own freedoms at the expense of those with least substantive freedom, because the enjoyment of substantive freedom facilitates greater bargaining power in market exchanges. Those with the greatest income, wealth, connections, and so forth will gain at the expense of those who lack these resources. This leads to the conclusion that the equality of negative rights that the free market enshrines may often deepen inequality in the positive freedoms that people enjoy.

References and Further Readings

Anderson, E. (1990). The ethical limitations of the market. *Economics and Philosophy, 6*(2), 179–205.

Berlin, I. (1958). *Two concepts of liberty.* Oxford, UK: Oxford University Press.

Bowles, G., & Gintis, H. (1990). Contested exchange: New microfoundations of the political economy of capitalism. *Politics and Society, 18*(2), 165–222.

Burczak, T. (2001). Ellerman's labor theory of property and the injustice of capitalist exploitation. *Review of Social Economy, 59*(2), 161–183.

Commons, J. R. (1924). *Legal foundations of capitalism.* New York: Macmillan.

DeMartino, G. (2000). *Global economy, global justice: Theoretical objections and policy alternatives to neoliberalism.* London: Routledge.

DeMartino, G. (2003). Realizing class justice. *Rethinking Marxism, 15*(1), 1–31.

Dugger, W. (1989). Radical institutionalism: Basic concepts. In W. Dugger (Ed.), *Radical institutionalism* (pp. 1–20). New York: Greenwood Press.

Dugger, W., & Sherman, H. J. (1994). Comparison of Marxism and institutionalism. *Journal of Economic Issues, 28*(1), 101–127.

Ellerman, D. (1992). *Property and contract in economics.* Cambridge, MA: Blackwell.

Friedman, M. (1953). The methodology of positive economics. In M. Friedman (Ed.), *Essays in positive economics* (pp. 3–43). Chicago: University of Chicago Press.

Friedman, M. (1962). *Capitalism and freedom.* Chicago: University of Chicago Press.

Friedman, M., & Friedman, R. (1990). *Free to choose: A personal statement.* San Diego, CA: Harcourt Brace Jovanovich.

Geras, N. (1985, March/April). The controversy about Marx and justice. *New Left Review, 150,* 47–85.

Geras, N. (1992, September/October). Bringing Marx to justice: An addendum and rejoinder. *New Left Review, 195,* 37–69.

Locke, J. (1690). *Two treatises of government* (2nd ed., P. Laslett, Ed.). Cambridge, MA: Cambridge University Press.

Lukes, S. (1987). *Marxism and morality.* Oxford, UK: Oxford University Press.

Lutz, M. A. (1999). *Economics for the common good: Two centuries of economic thought in the humanistic tradition.* London: Routledge.

MacPherson, C. B. (1962). *The political theory of possessive individualism.* Oxford, UK: Oxford University Press.

Marx, K. (1938). *Critique of the Gotha Program.* New York: International Publishers.

Nozick, R. (1974). *Anarchy, state and utopia.* New York: Basic Books.

Nussbaum, M. (1992). Human functioning and social justice: In defense of Aristotelian essentialism. *Political Theory, 20*(2), 202–246.

Ramstad, Y. (1987). Free trade versus fair trade: Import barriers as a problem of reasonable value. *Journal of Economic Issues, 21*(1), 5–32.

Rawls, J. (1971). *A theory of justice.* Cambridge, MA: Harvard University Press.

Resnick, S., & Wolff, R. D. (1987). *Economics—Marxian versus neoclassical.* Baltimore: Johns Hopkins University Press.

Roemer, J. E. (1988). *Free to lose.* Cambridge, MA: Harvard University Press.

Sen, A. K. (1987). *On ethics and economics.* London: Blackwell.

Sen, A. K. (1992). *Inequality reexamined.* Cambridge, MA: Harvard University Press.

Tool, M. R. (1979). *The discretionary economy.* Boulder, CO: Westview Press.

Walzer, M. (1973). In defense of equality. *Dissent, 20*(4), 399–408.

Walzer, M. (1983). *Spheres of justice.* New York: Basic Books.

52

SPORTS ECONOMICS

AJU FENN

Colorado College

Sports economics is arguably the most popular under-graduate elective in the collegiate economics curriculum today. Of the top 50 liberal arts colleges surveyed, 61% of the respondents offered an elective in sports economics. Details of the survey are available upon request. The rankings are based on the *U.S. News & World Report* rankings ("Liberal Arts Rankings," 2009). Of the top 50 economics departments at research universities surveyed, 43% of the respondents offered a course in sports economics (Dusansky & Vernon, 1998). The *Journal of Sports Economics* has added special issues to keep up with the flow of scholarship, and more than one textbook has emerged on the subject. What is sports economics? Why might a topic such as sports stimulate pedagogical and scholarly interest among academics and students who usually pursue more serious subdisciplines, such as econometrics and mathematical economics?

Sports economics is the study of the allocation of scarce resources among competing desires in the context of sports. Although this definition is not very different from the definition of economics itself, it does reveal how the subdiscipline of sports economics was born. It also reveals the breadth of the field. Anything that carries the title of sports, from professional football to a lumberjack competition on ESPN, has the potential to stimulate a paper in this subdiscipline. Established economic scholars from other disciplines brought their standard tool kits to bear on professional and amateur sports data sets. At first, they studied baseball extensively because it was a sport that they had played and followed. Many of these scholars were tenured at prestigious research universities but undertook these projects because the sports industry was fun to study. At first, there were no textbooks for sports economics classes, and syllabi looked suspiciously like a list of applied microeconomics topics. Labor economists studied everything from wage discrimination to managerial efficiency. Industrial organization scholars promptly investigated the concept of market power on the field in wins and off the field in dollars, and environmental economists used contingent valuation methodology to determine the value of a sports team to a city or region. This chapter discusses the various strands of the literature in detail.

There are also other factors that contributed to the emergence of sports economics. Department chairs discovered that offering an elective in sports economics with a principles prerequisite was a good way to boost departmental enrollments. Other faculty members discovered that students who would normally run screaming at the mention of regression would sit patiently through the explanation of a multiple regression model that explained the determinants of competitive balance in the National Football League (NFL). With the advent of the Internet, sports data sets became readily available. Other students wanted to conduct applied econometric research in the context of sports with the aid of user-friendly econometrics software packages. At the Western Economics meetings (the formal partner for meetings of the North American Association of Sports Economists), the 8:00 a.m. sports economics sessions seemed to be drawing a crowd. Once in a while, participants would catch the guilty look of a macroeconomist who was having a little too much fun at that particular session. Economists are onto something here. Economics has not looked this appealing since the IS-LM model.

The rest of this chapter proceeds as follows. The various strands of the sports economics literature are discussed in each of the subsequent sections, as they apply to sports economics theory; the later sections discuss applied work, policy implications, and directions for future research. The major strands of the literature include the theory of the firm, the theory of the consumer, economic impact studies, discrimination in sports, and collegiate sports. In each instance, the chapter strives to point out the classic readings and some more current work in the area. A brief section covers some of the many sports economists who have been instrumental in the birth and progression of the discipline. The chapter concludes with some discussion about the future directions of the field. First, the chapter turns to a loose classification of topics in sports economics.

A Loose Classification of Topics in Sports Economics

Any classification of sports economics along traditional *Journal of Economic Literature* lines will be challenged by the differences between professional sports, amateur sports, and recreational sports. To be clear, professional sports are those where the contestants are paid for participation, amateur athletes are not directly paid for their participation by the contest organizers, and recreational sports are those undertaken for pure consumption value of participation and perhaps for the health benefits from exercise. Rather than attempt to construct an airtight classification that will be rendered obsolete by the evolving nature of the discipline, this chapter attempts to classify the literature based on the underlying big ideas in economics, such as the theory of the firm, the theory of the consumer, public policy regarding funding of stadiums, competitive balance, and discrimination in sports. In sports economics, as in economics, new branches often emerge from the cross-pollination of these big ideas. Any discussion of the classification of the literature on sports economics should begin with the original paper that brought economic ideas to bear on the sports industry. It is to that paper that this chapter now turns.

Origins of Sports Economics

Sports economists agree that the original work in the field was Simon Rottenberg's paper on the labor market for baseball players (Rottenberg, 1956). In this paper, Rottenberg describes the existing rules of the baseball industry and their implications for competition. He discusses concepts such as the reserve clause, territorial rights, the drafting of minor league players into the majors, competitive balance, and market size. He also introduces the notion of a production function as it applies to sports, where the number of games (weighted by revenue) put on by a team is a function of its players and all other inputs, such as competing players, managers of both teams, transportation, and the ballpark, are considered a second factor of production. Rottenberg discusses the reserve clause—which allows the team to renew a player's contract at a wage set by the team, at not less than 75% of the current year's salary. He dismisses the argument that the reserve clause is desired to protect small-market teams (teams with smaller fan bases and lower revenues) from higher-paying large-market teams. Rottenberg cites the domination in the count of the number of pennants won by the Yankees and the St. Louis Browns as evidence of unequal player talent distribution. He also discusses territorial rights—the exclusive right to be the only Major League Baseball (MLB) team in a region—and the notion of competitive balance. Competitive balance refers to the ability of teams to have a roughly equal chance of winning a game. This topic is related to the uncertainty of output hypothesis, which maintains that there is greater fan interest when the outcome of who will win the event is fairly uncertain. Rottenberg discusses player drafts, territorial rights, and the reserve clause, which are all factors that impact the distribution of player talent and consequently impact the competitive balance in a league. Rottenberg then closes with his free market prescription for exciting and close baseball games. Many of the ideas raised by Rottenberg have grown into branches of sports economics today. For example, competitive balance has been an area of study in all of the major professional sports in the United States. Allen Sanderson and John Siegfried (2006) provide a 50th-anniversary perspective on Rottenberg's original work and the strength of his conclusions after 50 years of industry developments.

The Theory of the Sports Firm

The key distinction between sports teams and rival firms in traditional economics models is as follows: Although sports teams seek to compete on the playing fields, they need their competitors to survive financially in order to put on a game or a match. This key point serves as the springboard for many of the departures from standard microeconomic models of the firm when applied to sports teams and leagues. Sports economics models of firms are based on three big ideas: (1) profit maximization behavior of sports teams and leagues, (2) market power of sports teams as both sellers of a unique product and almost exclusive employers of a highly skilled set of professional athletes, and (3) firms' decision-making process about hiring players and coaches. This chapter turns to each of these big ideas regarding the sports firm in as much detail as a single chapter will allow.

Profit Maximizing Behavior

Several of the economic models treat a single team as the firm. Alternatively, some models deal with the league as a cartel or social planner, and each individual team is considered to be a member of this group. There is a healthy literature on modeling both firms and leagues in the context of competitive balance. Papers in this area cover the measurement of competitive balance and the optimal policies to promote competitive balance in a league. Those studies are discussed in the section on competitive balance.

A simple model of static profit maximization of a sports firm is contained in the leading undergraduate textbook on sports economics. Michael Leeds and Peter von Allmen (2008) define profits as the difference between revenues and costs. Team revenues are broken down into gate revenues, broadcast revenues, and licensing and other stadium-related revenues, such as concessions and naming rights. Costs are usually dominated by players' salaries in the major leagues. Other costs include items such as travel, marketing, and administrative costs, including league costs.

There are more dynamic and complex models available as well. Most of these models deal with profit maximization in the context of multiple teams and the optimal policy for promoting competitive balance in a league. For example, Mohamed El-Hodiri and James Quirk (1971) develop a model of profit maximization for a sports team over time. They conclude that profit maximization of a given team and the promotion of competitive balance across a league are incompatible. Donald Alexander and William Kern (2004) explore some of the more dynamic elements that impact the franchise value of a team, such as team relocation, the presence of a new facility, market size, and regional identity.

In the traditional theory of the firm, the firm chooses its output level to maximize profits by taking market price to be either given in a competitive setting or subject to the constraint of the market demand curve if the firm is a monopolist. There is little debate over what exactly constitutes a unit of output. If a firm is making and selling jeans, for example, output is measured in terms of the number of pairs of jeans that are produced and sold. Another firm theory concept is the choice of product quality that a firm must consider. In sports economics, one has to consider the notion of output carefully. Is it just the number of games played by a team, or is it the winning percentage of the team that matters for profits? Is it merely winning or closeness of the outcome that boosts revenues? Thus, in sports, the concepts of quantity and quality are inextricably linked. In most other markets, one can segment the market by quality levels and then examine the output decision of the firm at a given choice of quality level. In sports, the number of games is not a team choice variable. It is set by the league. The quality of a team that a franchise chooses to field, however, is a choice variable. So it all comes down to two questions. Does winning matter (and at what cost)? What about the owner's utility maximization problem?

Andrew Zimbalist (2003) provides an overview of the profit maximization debate. He concludes that owners' objectives vary among leagues and that further research is needed. Alternative hypotheses of ownership do not preclude profit maximization but also include the owners' utility as part of the objective function. Such utility may come from being seen as a mover and shaker in the big city, like Jerry Jones, the owner of the Dallas Cowboys, or simply one who gets to call the shots, like Al Davis, the owner of the Oakland Raiders. D. G. Ferguson, Kenneth Stewart, J. C. Jones, and Andre Le Dressay (1991) examine the premise of profit maximization and find support for profit-maximizing behavior. Ferguson et al. assume that profit maximization is synonymous with revenue maximization.

The main challenge in doing empirical work in this area is to come up with good data on the cost side of the equation. Team revenues based on attendance and average ticket prices can be easily calculated. Broadcast revenues and revenue-sharing agreements are made public as well. Player salaries are usually available, but bonuses, travel costs, and other general and administrative costs may not be as easily available for teams. How much does it cost a team to put on a single game? The lack of precise data on this subject can make profit maximization a tough hypothesis to test. However, for the interested reader, a simple win maximization model that should be accessible to advanced undergraduates is discussed in Stefan Kesenne (2006).

Sometimes, static profit maximization may not be validated by the data because of a combination of the owners' desires to win and their goals to increase the long-term value of the franchise. Often, owners will try to break even each year while investing the profits back into player talent, coaching staff, or facilities. In the minor leagues such as AAA baseball, arena football, or lacrosse, the audience goes for the experience, and the weather may make a bigger impact on the attendance than the earned run average of the starting pitcher.

Market Power in Sports

Another characteristic of sports teams is that they usually possess some degree of market power in both the product and input markets. A team is usually the only seller of a particular professional sports product in the output market (monopoly) and often the only employer of professional athletes in that sport in that particular city (monopsony). Recent empirical evidence by Stacey Brook and Aju Fenn (2008) seems to suggest that NFL teams do possess market power over their consumers. When college football athletes look at professional football as a career, there are a limited number of leagues or employers. Such an employment scenario with a single employer meets the classic definition of monopsony.

Lawrence Kahn (2000) provides an overview of the studies that discuss monopsony and other labor market issues in sports. Harmon Gallant and Paul Staudohar (2003) examine how antitrust law in the United States has influenced the evolution of professional sports leagues. Stephen Ross (2003) considers 10 important antitrust decisions where courts have ruled against sports leagues and examines whether these decisions were in the best interest of the public from an economist's point of view. In general, economists argue that a monopolist will charge a higher than competitive price and will appropriate a portion of the consumer's surplus. Should the government then disband all operating professional leagues? What could possibly justify a legal monopoly in sports? Kahn (2003) argues that expansion to too many teams would lower player quality and that the optimum structure lies somewhere between a monopoly and a competitive solution. What complicates the issue further is that for every sold-out stadium in the NFL, there are additional fans at home that get to watch the game on television. This issue returns when this chapter explores the consumer side of sports economics.

Sports firms are supposed to hold power over their employees—and the players as well, because professional sports employment opportunities are somewhat limited. One of the oldest ideas in this area is the so-called invariance principle, which is an application of the Coase Theorem to sports leagues. Professional athletes have a unique set of skills and are in a position to generate an economic rent as a result. The invariance principle in sports economics states that regardless of whether the player or the owner controls the rights to the player, the mobility of players between teams should be the same. In the case of free agency, players reap the benefits by playing for the highest bidder. In the case of the team owning the rights to the player, the team may sell the player to the highest bidder. The origins of this idea are attributed to Simon Rottenberg (Sanderson & Siegfried, 2006). John Vrooman (2009) finds that if owners are win maximizing in nature, then they will erode their own monopsony power and compete aggressively for player talent. He states that the fact that most professional payrolls are about 60% of the revenue generated is evidence of the erosion of monopsony power by team owners. This is a budding area of policy in sports economics, but practical measurement of monopoly and monopsony power may be challenging because the details of cost and salary data are often private. This chapter turns next to the choices facing the sports team regarding talent evaluation and coaching.

Input Decisions of the Firm: Which Players and Coaches to Hire?

Because sports teams spend vast amounts of money on player payroll, it stands to reason that most aspects of the labor market are well documented. It is not the number of units of labor (players) or human capital (coaches and players) that is important. In most leagues, these numbers are set by league rules. What matters here is how league owners and unions agree to split total revenue among owners and players and the ability of the team to evaluate the talent of players and coaches.

Rodney Fort (2006) has excellent coverage of the history of player pay, the value of sports talent, and labor relations in professional sports. The traditional explanation is that players are paid their marginal revenue products. In sports, this is often defined as the product of their marginal contributions to each win multiplied by the revenue earned for the franchise by that win. There is some disagreement among scholars about whether players' marginal revenue products are equal across teams. Stefan Szymanski and Kesenne (2004) argue that the marginal revenue of a win will be larger for a large-market team than for a small-market team.

So do players get paid their marginal revenue products of wins? What does the research say? In most leagues, such as the NFL, the league is a monopsony buyer of player talent, and there are some limits to compensation, such as a salary caps or disincentives such as a luxury tax. In a given league and within the limits of the salary cap, each team competes for the best players, thereby bidding up the wage for a player. In addition, players are often organized into unions so that overall negotiations between players unions and the team owners represent a bilateral monopoly (where a single buyer of talent, the team, faces a single seller of talent, the players union). In a bilateral monopoly, the equilibrium often comes down to the bargaining power of the two sides. If owners prevail in these negotiations, then through the use of salary caps or other restraints on compensation, players' wages are restricted to levels below their marginal revenue products. On the other hand, if players unions prevail in negotiations, then the aggregate share of total revenue that goes to the players becomes larger. Given these nuances, in sports it makes sense to review the evidence whether players are actually paid the marginal revenue product of wins.

Scully (1974) is among one of the first to study the issue of pay and performance in MLB. He finds that in the 1970s, baseball players were exploited by teams under the reserve clause, which prohibited players from seeking competitive employment with other teams. He finds that baseball players' average salaries over the length of their careers were only about 11% of their gross and 20% of their net marginal revenue products. Since then, many papers have been written about the determinants of wages and the impact of the type of contract (length, time in the contract, etc.) on performance. Alternatively, a more recent study by Vrooman (2009) finds that in most North American professional major leagues, players share about 60% of the revenues earned. Vrooman reports that all leagues except MLB have imposed salary caps just below 60% of league revenue. In short, with the advent of free agency, the balance of power between players and owners has evolved, and player salaries have risen.

What, then, are the determinants of an individual player's salary? Factors such as the performance of a player on and off the field, race, the revenue of the team, the type of arbitration scheme, the contributions of teammates, and league salary caps influence the salary that a player receives (Barilla, 2002; Berri & Krautmann, 2006; Brown

& Jepsen, 2009; Idson & Kahane, 2000). Kahn (2000) argues that the presence of rival leagues leads to higher salaries for players in baseball. Whenever competing leagues merge, the result is stronger monopsony power of owners over players and a decline in players' salaries. In most major league sports in North America, players are drafted by a team, which gives the team exclusive rights to negotiate with that player. Within a given league, it is presumably the ability of a player to contribute to wins and boost attendance that determines his or her level of salary.

Todd Idson and Leo Kahane (2000) examine the team effects on player compensation in the National Hockey League (NHL). They find that players' wages depend on their individual contributions and the impact of their teammates' play on their productivity. Idson and Kahane (2004) have gone on to study the themes of discrimination, market power, and compensation in their subsequent papers on the National Basketball Association and the NHL. They have also investigated the impact of characteristics of workers, such as language skills, on the pay and performance of coworkers (Simmons, Kahane, & Longley, 2009). There is also a large literature on the determinants of coaches' salaries and the retention of coaches. The interested reader is directed to the books mentioned for further reading at the end of this chapter.

The ability to spot talent is important in leagues where teams are constrained by league rules in the amount of money that they can spend on payroll. Player talent evaluation is often touted as the reason why small-market baseball teams such as the Oakland As and the Minnesota Twins can compete with large-market teams such as the Dodgers. The Patriot's three Super Bowl wins under coach Bill Belichick in the age of the salary cap is often attributed to the ability of the organization to spot talent. Contrary to the popular misconception that coach Belichick was a film major, it turns out that he actually majored in economics. What characteristics make certain players successful in the big leagues? Both front office general managers and sports economists alike would love to know the answer to this question. David Berri (2008) has devoted considerable effort to measuring productivity on the basketball court and examines how success in college may or may not translate into success in the professional leagues. J. C. Bradbury (2007) is to baseball sabernomics (the analysis of baseball using economic principles and econometric tools) what Berri is to productivity in the NBA. This is a budding area of research.

In summarizing the theory of the firm, one has to return to the question of whether sports firms maximize profits. The preponderance of evidence indicates that the majority of professional major league sports franchises seek to operate in the black in the short run while maintaining the goal of increasing the value of the franchise. There is also a certain utility associated with owning a major league team. However, to most owners, this utility is more than a hobby because they strive to make their franchises financially viable and competitive on the playing field at the same time. This chapter turns next to the individuals that are responsible for the growth of sports into big business: the fanatic or the supporter, as they are known in Europe.

The Theory of the Sports Consumer

Readers may find this area easier to follow because most are consumers, if not sports consumers, and are thus familiar with the reasons and the ways in which consumers enjoy sports. Consumers attend sporting contests in person, watch them on television, or participate in sports. This chapter sets the participation aspects aside for now because the vast majority of consumers are not professional athletes. In each of these markets, fans that attend games or television audiences, the consumers, may be further divided into groups based on their intensity of preferences. Some fans are die-hard fans and live and die with the fortunes of their teams. Other casual fans, while interested, do not suffer these same highs and lows. Finally, there are those that happen to attend a sporting event or watch a game on television because it is just another entertainment option that they happened to choose. Some or all of these fans may choose to buy sports apparel either to proclaim their loyalty to their teams or as a fashion statement. All of these consumers have one thing in common. They are all maximizing their own utility functions.

Attendance at Sporting Events

Fans may choose to attend games or matches because they believe that the experience will enhance their utility, subject to their budget and time constraints. Do fans have more fun watching their teams win, lose, or win in close games? Which outcome yields the most fan attendance?

Sports economists claim that winning is a very important determinant of attendance (Davis, 2009; Welki & Zlatoper, 1994). Most fans prefer a close contest, with their teams winning in the end. There has been much work done on the uncertainty of outcome hypothesis (Knowles, Sherony, & Haupert, 1992). The age of the sporting facility also matters. Brand new stadiums and arenas tend to draw more fans. John Leadley and Zenon Zygmont (2006) find that increased attendance due to a new stadium lasts for about 5 years. The prevailing wisdom about superstar players is that they promote attendance through winning at home and sell out games on the road because everyone wants to see them play (Berri, Schmidt, & Brook, 2004). The demand for sporting events in North America is considered to be unresponsive to changes in ticket price (Coates & Humphreys, 2007). Are sports fans addicts? According to traditional studies on rational addiction, the past and expected future consumption of a good should be significant determinants of current consumption of that good. In other words, if a fan has attended the games for a given team in the past and plans on attending games in the future, that will impact the fan's decision to attend games in the present. Fans are like addicts in that watching games provides excitement. Fans experience exhilaration when their teams score and feel down when their teams fall dramatically behind. Die-hard fans follow the fortunes of their teams throughout the off-season and miss the Sunday ritual of watching their favorite NFL teams. During the season, they plan on watching their teams every Sunday. It is in this sense that fans are likened to addicts (Becker & Murphy, 1998). Sports economists have begun to consider this question as well. Young Lee and Trenton Smith (2008) find evidence that Americans are rationally addicted to baseball while Koreans are not. The literature in this area is fairly thin because it is a recent development in the field.

Sports on Television

Most major league sports are broadcast on television in North America. The NFL has a blackout rule to prevent a reduction in ticket sales. If a game is not sold out 72 hours before kickoff, then it is blacked out in the local television viewing area. It tends to be the case that winning teams seldom have to worry about this rule, and about 90% of the games are sold out. In Europe, however, televising a game sometimes depresses attendance (Allan & Roy, 2008). The NFL currently has contracts with the major television networks to broadcast games through 2011. The value of these contracts is about $20.4 billion. This aspect of television viewing tends to be in the category of a public good. If enough people attend a game, a viewer can sit at home and watch the game without paying for a ticket. In some senses, this makes U.S. local television broadcasts nonrival and nonexcludable. The category of pay-per-view (PPV) is a little different. If one wants to watch an NFL team that is not being carried on the local television stations, one may have to purchase a special package from a cable or satellite television provider. Similarly, one may also purchase the opportunity to view certain other sporting events, such as boxing matches or soccer matches, which are available only on PPV. Either way, it is big business, and teams are able to extend their audiences beyond the confines of their stadia. There is a large literature on the economics of broadcasting and how certain systems impact consumer welfare. The consensus view among sports economists is that leagues that tend to share national television revenue equally, like the NFL, have greater competitive balance and consequently a greater demand for their product. On the other hand, leagues that have revenue imbalances, like MLB, where large-market teams like Los Angeles and New York have larger broadcast revenues, have less competitive balance and consequently a lower demand for their product. However, there is not much published academic research on the determinants of television ratings for sports events in North America. One reason for this may be that the data are proprietary information, and researchers may have to purchase data sets from a media research organization. This may be a potential area of expansion for the academic literature.

Sports Merchandise and Memorabilia

Consumers purchase sports jerseys, baseball hats, and other assorted items. Other consumers are collectors and purchase items such as baseball cards and other autographed memorabilia. There is a literature on baseball cards and the impact of a player's performance and race on sales. However, the impact of championships or star players on sports apparel has yet to be investigated.

When one brings sports firms and consumers together, one often gets into the arena of public policy. It is to this subject that this chapter next turns its attention.

Sports and Public Policy

Even those who do not care about sports will probably have a few thoughts on the subject when asked whether they think their taxpayer dollars should be used to fund a new stadium for their local professional team. In the 1950s, most professional sports teams played in privately owned stadiums or arenas. Most professional football teams were the tenants of professional baseball teams and played football games around the baseball schedule. All professional hockey teams played in private arenas. Many professional basketball teams played in college arenas and played their games around the collegiate schedule. In the 1990s, U.S. cities spent $5,298 million on 57 new venues in the four major professional sports. The public's share averaged $218 million for each of these venues. This is approximately 66% of the cost (Depken, 2006). This section considers some of the economic arguments presented for and against public funding for stadiums. Sanderson (2000) provides an excellent overview of this debate.

Proponents of public funding argue their cases on the basis of indirect and direct benefits of the team to the area. Indirect benefits—or benefits not accruing to the team—include the multiplier effect of job creation in the area due to team- and stadium-related activities. Teams often claim that the new stadium will be an engine of economic growth and revitalization for an area. Games draw crowds, and those crowds need to eat, drink, and shop. The direct benefits of a new stadium are those that accrue directly to the team and their fans. Teams contend that with the revenue from a new stadium, they can afford better players and contend for a championship. They claim that a new stadium enhances civic pride from living in a major league city. Last but not least, a new stadium would keep the team in town, and fans that attend games would retain their entertainment values, as would the fans that watch the televised games at home.

Critics of public funding for stadiums argue that the multiplier effect is overstated because of the so-called substitution effect. The substitution effect occurs when fans substitute attendance at sports events for other entertainment options like a movie at their local mall. Thus, the economic impact in the stadium area comes at the cost of spending at other entertainment venues. Critics claim that the benefits to consumers are not large enough to justify the subsidies given to sports teams. The consumer surplus generated from attending games is not large enough to justify the expenditures required to construct new stadiums (Alexander, Kern, & Neill, 2000). Critics also claim that stadium moves not only increase revenues through higher prices and attendance but also lower costs through favorable rental agreements. Most rental agreements provide attendance-based rents. This shifts the risk to the landlord, which in this case is the taxpayer. Robert Baade, Robert Baumann, and Victor Matheson (2008) find that megaevents such as the Super Bowl have no statistically significant impact on taxable sales. Yet in the end, city after city builds stadium after stadium for professional sports teams. Why is this so? Fenn and John Crooker (2009) examine the willingness of Minnesotans to pay for a new Vikings stadium given the credible threat of team relocation. They find that on average, households are willing to pay approximately $530 toward a new Vikings stadium. These results were obtained from a representative urban and rural sample of 1,400 households in Minnesota. There are two plausible explanations for the stadium building boom. Either the civic pride aspects have been undervalued or stadium advocates have been politically more successful at outmaneuvering their critics. Past studies fail to find any statistically significant relationship of the impact of a stadium on the income in the standard metropolitan statistical area (Baade & Dye, 1988). Similarly, Brad Humphreys (1999) analyzes data from every U.S. city that had a professional football, basketball, or baseball franchise over the period from 1969 to 1994. He finds that, contrary to the claims of proponents of sport facility subsidies, the presence of a professional sports team or facility has no effect on the growth rate of local real income per capita, and it reduces the level of local real income per capita by a small but statistically significant amount. The problem with all the studies done on valuing civic pride is that they are surveys with no binding commitment on the part of the respondents to actually spend the money. There is room for a study that uses the experimental economics approach by giving participants a sum of money and a credible scenario of a relocation to see how much money they actually donate. Jesse Ventura, governor of Minnesota from 1999 to 2003, asked people to turn their tax rebates in to support funding a new stadium. The electorate greeted him with the usual response of bewildered amusement.

Having discussed the sports firm, the sports consumer, and how professional sports impacts public policy, this chapter turns to issues of competitive balance, discrimination, and collegiate sports.

Competitive Balance in Sports

Competitive balance refers to a situation where teams have a more or less equal chance of winning a game. This does not necessarily mean that all teams in the league must be of the same talent level. The NFL, in fact, takes past success into account while making the schedule for the next year. They pit stronger teams against stronger opponents, and weaker teams get easier opponents. Why should one care about competitive balance? U.S. sports economists argue that competitive contests are what drive attendance. European sports economists are not as concerned with competitive balance. In the English Premier League, for example, teams at the top vie for championships, while teams at the bottom strive to avoid relegation. The supporters are regionally loyal to their teams. They would love to win, but winning is not all that matters. The competitive balance literature bifurcates into two major strands. The first branch deals with constructing indices to measure and observe competitive balance. The second deals with policy prescriptions to promote competitive balance.

Sanderson and Siegfried (2003) present a useful review of the different measures of competitive balance. Measures range from simple measures of dispersion, such as standard deviations of winning percentages around league means, team means over time or at a point in time, modifications of Gini indices, and the deviations of the Herfindahl-Hirschman Index. There is also a considerable literature on the use of these measures in North American major league sports.

The second branch of this literature deals with both the measurement and policy prescription for a more competitive league via practices such as revenue sharing and the reverse order draft. For example, Andrew Larsen, Fenn, and Erin Spenner (2006) find that the NFL did indeed become more competitive as a league after the institution of the salary cap and free agency in 1993. There are also theoretical models that examine how competitive balance in a league may be improved. Crooker and Fenn (2007) examine the state of competitive balance in MLB and provide a league transfer payment mechanism for improving parity and, consequently, league profits.

Discrimination in Sports

Given that one can observe a player's performance and compensation with some degree of clarity, sports economists have used the data to test for racial and gender discrimination in sports, both in the professional and collegiate arenas. Sports economics textbooks such as

Leeds and von Allmen (2008) classify discrimination into employer discrimination, employee discrimination, consumer discrimination, gender discrimination, and positional discrimination. The interested reader is referred to their book for an extensive discussion of the theory and applied work on discrimination in sports economics. In general, most studies regress wages against performance statistics and race and gender variables to examine the role of race and gender. Other studies cover the values of baseball trading cards and the race of the player involved. The big idea in this area is that discrimination did exist in the past, both in terms of salaries and consumer preferences. For example, Mark Kanazawa and Jonas Funk (2001) find that predominantly white cities enjoy watching white players play for their hometown NBA team. However, both employer and consumer discrimination has been decreasing in recent years. Title IX and its influence on gender balance in collegiate sports is another big idea that dominates the literature on discrimination and college sports.

Collegiate Sports

The big elephant in the room is the unpaid professional: the college athlete. Collegiate athletic directors claim that college athletes for big-time programs bring in revenues that are redistributed to other programs in the athletic department and sometimes even to the rest of the school. The financial details of National Collegiate Athletic Association (NCAA) Division I programs are available in a report from the NCAA (2008).

Title IX and its impact on collegiate athletics have dominated the literature recently. Sports economists have also become fascinated with the question of a national playoff in NCAA football. Zimbalist (2001b) has an excellent book on the subject of college sports that covers the relevant issues. This topic is a chapter unto itself and goes well beyond the scope of an overview of sports economics.

Conclusion

The world of sports economics is constantly evolving. Some topics, such as the Olympics, bowling, golf, NASCAR, professional bass fishing, and distance running have not been covered in this chapter because of space limitations There is, however, a literature on each of these sports. Among the issues that present excellent opportunities for new research are the connections between gambling and sports. In particular, are there aspects to watching sports that are addictive? Another area of interest is the connection between sports and the joint consumption or depreciation of an individual's health stock: Some fans may choose to drink beer while watching sports, and others may be motivated to participate in adult recreational sports leagues after watching an exciting contest. The economics

of youth sports and adult recreational sports has been largely unexplored; this will also be an area of interest in the years to come. Older topics that pertain to the impact of institutions and rules on sports, such as free agency and drug testing, will be examined time and again as the institutions and rules evolve. The economic impact of a sports team on a region will remain a constant topic of research as long as teams seek public funding. Studies and statistics on unlocking the keys to winning will also be around for quite some time. If a sport is televised and people watch it, sooner or later a sports economist will analyze it. Be prepared for the first study on competitive balance in the World's Strongest Man competition; it could happen.

Author's Note: This chapter is dedicated to the memory of Larry Hadley.

References and Further Readings

Alexander, D. L., & Kern, W. (2004). The economic determinants of professional sports franchise values. *Journal of Sports Economics, 5*(1), 51–66.

Alexander, D. L., Kern, W., & Neill, J. (2000). Valuing the consumption benefits from professional sports franchises. *Journal of Urban Economics, 48*(2), 321–337.

Allan, G., & Roy, G. (2008). Does television crowd out spectators? New evidence from the Scottish Premier League. *Journal of Sports Economics, 9*(6), 592–605.

Andreff, W., & Szymanski, S. (Eds.). (2006). *Handbook on the economics of sport.* Northampton, MA: Edward Elgar.

Baade, R. A., Baumann, R., & Matheson, V. A. (2008). Selling the game: Estimating the economic impact of professional sports through taxable sales. *Southern Economic Journal, 74*(3), 794–810.

Baade, R., & Dye, R. (1988). An analysis of the economic rationale for public subsidization of sports stadiums. *Annals of Regional Science, 22*(2), 37–47.

Barilla, A. G. (2002). *An analysis of wage differences in Major League Baseball, 1985–95.* Unpublished doctoral dissertation, Kansas State University.

Becker, G., & Murphy, K. (1998). A theory of rational addiction. In K. Lancaster (Ed.), *Consumer theory* (Vol. 100, pp. 581–606). Northampton, MA: Edward Elgar.

Berri, D. J. (2008). A simple measure of worker productivity in the National Basketball Association. In B. Humphreys & D. Howard (Eds.), *The business of sport* (pp. 1–40). Westport, CT: Praeger.

Berri, D. J., & Krautmann, A. C. (2006). Shirking on the court: Testing for the incentive effects of guaranteed pay. *Economic Inquiry, 44*(3), 536–546.

Berri, D. J., Schmidt, M., & Brook, S. (2004). Stars at the gate: The impact of star power on NBA gate revenues. *Journal of Sports Economics, 5*(1), 33–50.

Bradbury, J. C. (2007). *The baseball economist: The real game exposed.* New York: Dutton.

Brandes, L., Franck, E., & Nuesch, S. (2008). Local heroes and superstars: An empirical analysis of star attraction in German soccer. *Journal of Sports Economics, 9*(3), 266–286.

Brook, S. L., & Fenn, A. J. (2008). Market power in the National Football League. *International Journal of Sport Finance, 3*(4), 239–244.

Brown, K. H., & Jepsen, L. K. (2009). The impact of team revenues on MLB salaries. *Journal of Sports Economics, 10*(2), 192–203.

Coates, D., & Humphreys, B. R. (2007). Ticket prices, concessions and attendance at professional sporting events. *International Journal of Sport Finance, 2*(3), 161–170.

Crooker, J. R., & Fenn, A. J. (2007). Sports leagues and parity: When league parity generates fan enthusiasm. *Journal of Sports Economics, 8*(2), 139–164.

Davis, M. C. (2009). Analyzing the relationship between team success and MLB attendance with GARCH effects. *Journal of Sports Economics, 10*(1), 44–58.

Depken, C. A. (2006). The impact of new stadiums on professional baseball team finances. *Public Finance and Management, 6*(3), 436–474.

Dusansky, R., & Vernon, C. J. (1998). Rankings of U.S. economics departments. *Journal of Economic Perspectives, 12*(1), 157–170.

El-Hodiri, M., & Quirk, J. (1971). An economic model of a professional sports league. *Journal of Political Economy, 79*(6), 1302–1319.

Fenn, A. J., & Crooker, J. R. (2009). Estimating local welfare generated by an NFL team under credible threat of relocation. *Southern Economic Journal, 76*(1), 198–223.

Ferguson, D. G., Stewart, K. G., Jones, J. C., & Le Dressay, A. (1991). The pricing of sports events: Do teams maximize profit. *Journal of Industrial Economics, 39*(3), 297–310.

Fort, R. (2006). *Sports economics.* Upper Saddle River, NJ: Prentice Hall.

Gallant, H., & Staudohar, P. D. (2003). Antitrust law and public policy alternatives for professional sports leagues. *Labor Law Journal, 54*(3), 166–179.

Gerrard, B. (2007). *Economics of association football.* Northampton, MA: Edward Elgar.

Humphreys, B. (1999). The growth effects of sport franchises, stadia and arenas. *Journal of Policy Analysis and Management, 18*(4), 601–624.

Humphreys, B. (2002). Alternative measures of competitive balance in sports leagues. *Journal of Sports Economics, 3*(2), 133–148.

Idson, T., & Kahane, L. (2000). Team effects on compensation: An application to salary determination in the National Hockey League. *Economic Inquiry, 39*(2), 345–357.

Idson, T., & Kahane, L. (2004). Teammate effects on pay in professional sports. *Applied Economic Letters, 11*(12), 731–733.

Kahn, L. M. (2000). The sports business as a labor market laboratory. *Journal of Economic Perspectives, 14*(3), 75–94.

Kahn, L. M. (2003). *Sports league expansion and economic efficiency: Monopoly can enhance consumer welfare* (CESifo Working Paper No. 1101). Munich, Germany: CESifo Group Munich.

Kanazawa, M. T., & Funk, J. P. (2001). Racial discrimination in professional basketball: Evidence from Nielsen ratings. *Economic Inquiry, 39*(4), 599–608.

Kesenne, S. (2006). The win maximization model reconsidered: Flexible talent supply and efficiency wages. *Journal of Sports Economics, 7*(4), 416–427.

Knowles, G., Sherony, K., & Haupert, M. (1992). The demand for Major League Baseball: A test of the uncertainty of outcome hypothesis. *American Economist, 36*(2), 72–80.

Larsen, A., Fenn, A. J., & Spenner, E. L. (2006). The impact of free agency and the salary cap on competitive balance in the National Football League. *Journal of Sports Economics, 7*(4), 374–390.

Leadley, J. C., & Zygmont, Z. X. (2006). When is the honeymoon over? National Hockey League attendance, 1970–2003. *Canadian Public Policy, 32*(2), 213–232.

Lee, Y. H., & Smith, T. G. (2008). Why are Americans addicted to baseball? An empirical analysis of fandom in Korea and the United States. *Contemporary Economic Policy, 26*(1), 32–48.

Leeds, M., & von Allmen, P. (2008). *The economics of sports* (3rd ed.). Boston: Addison-Wesley.

Liberal arts rankings. (2009). *U.S. News & World Report.* Available at http://colleges.usnews.rankingsandreviews.com/college/liberal-arts-search

NCAA Publications. (2008). *2004–2006 NCAA revenues and expenses of Division I intercollegiate athletics programs report.* Available at http://www.ncaapublications.com/ProductsDetailView.aspx?sku=RE2008

Rosentraub, M. S., & Swindell, D. (2002). Negotiating games: Cities, sports and the winner's curse. *Journal of Sport Management, 16*(1), 18–35.

Ross, S. F. (2003). Antitrust, professional sports, and the public interest. *Journal of Sports Economics, 4*(4), 318–331.

Rottenberg, S. (1956). The baseball players' labor market. *Journal of Political Economy, 64*, 242.

Sanderson, A. R. (2000). In defense of new sports stadiums, ballparks and arenas. *Marquette Sports Law Journal, 10*(2), 173–192.

Sanderson, A. R., & Siegfried, J. J. (2003). Thinking about competitive balance. *Journal of Sports Economics, 4*(4), 255–279.

Sanderson, A. R., & Siegfried, J. J. (2006). Simon Rottenberg and baseball, then and now: A fiftieth anniversary retrospective. *Journal of Political Economy, 114*(3), 594–605.

Scully, G. (1974). Pay and performance in major league baseball. *American Economic Review, 64*, 915–930.

Shmanske, S. (2004). *Golfonomics.* River Edge, NJ: World Scientific.

Simmons, R., Kahane, L., & Longley, N. (2009). *The effects of coworker heterogeneity on firm-level output: Assessing the impacts of cultural and language diversity in the National Hockey League* (Working Paper No. 005934). Lancaster, UK: Lancaster University Management School, Economics Department.

Szymanski, S., & Kesenne, S. (2004). Competitive balance and gate revenue sharing in team sports. *Journal of Industrial Economics, 52*(1), 165–177.

Vrooman, J. (2009). Theory of the perfect game: Competitive balance in monopoly sports leagues. *Review of Industrial Organization, 34*(1), 5–44.

Welki, A. M., & Zlatoper, T. J. (1994). U.S. professional football: The demand for game-day attendance in 1991. *Managerial and Decision Economics, 15*(5), 489–495.

Zimbalist, A. (Ed.). (2001a). *The economics of sport.* Northampton, MA: Edward Elgar.

Zimbalist, A. (2001b). *Unpaid professionals: Commercialism and conflict in big-time college sports.* Princeton, NJ: Princeton University Press.

Zimbalist, A. (2003). Sport as business. *Oxford Review of Economic Policy, 19*(4), 503–511.

53

EARNINGS OF PROFESSIONAL ATHLETES

LEE H. IGEL AND ROBERT A. BOLAND

New York University

One of the greatest challenges facing professional sports has been the rapid increase in earning power of professional athletes during the past quarter century. This challenge is likely to dominate the sports business landscape in the coming decades, especially as salaries and endorsements that have reached averages in the millions of dollars encounter an increasingly turbulent, complex, and transnational economy. But now, more than ever before, the income potential of professional athletes has significant implications for the relationship among sports, business, and society.

As professional sports became more organized during the twentieth century, professional athletes in all developed countries were increasingly paid several times the average worker's salary. But even the relatively high-paying jobs that persisted through the first 70 or so years of the century did not parallel the rise, magnitude, and capacity of the professional athlete's earning power during the latter part of the century, especially in the professional baseball, football, basketball, and hockey leagues in the United States. The rise of the professional athlete paralleled that of the blue-collar worker, albeit with much better pay. That is, both professional athletes and blue-collar workers carved out a livelihood based on a cash wage with few fringe benefits until unionization increased their capacities to earn higher salaries and gain benefits. This increased both their social standing and their political power. But just as dramatically as the status of the blue-collar worker has fallen during the past 30-plus years, the status of professional athletes has experienced growth.

The Evolution of Athletes' Salaries

To fully perceive the economics of modern athletes' earning power, it is helpful to bear in mind the rapid transformations that have occurred as sports shifted from pastime to business. There is perhaps no better starting point for such explanation than in the evolution of athletes' salaries, which have traditionally served as the greatest portion of their incomes.

Talk of athletes' salaries has often been considered in the context of team sports. Yet whether athletes play team or individual sports, professional athletes by definition receive pay for their performance in athletic competition. One of the early forms of paying individuals for athletic performance was established with the emergence of prizefighting in the late nineteenth and early twentieth centuries. In particular, the influx of European émigrés to the United States during this period of time, combined with the emancipation of slaves in the post–Civil War era, resulted in the ascension of social minorities through participation in sport. While white Irish Americans were the first to gain mass popularity—and to be paid accordingly—as prizefighters, Jack Johnson, a black man, had become heavyweight champion by the end of the first decade of the twentieth century. Johnson's ability to come out on the winning side of fight after fight elevated him to the status of pop culture icon, which brought with it all the benefits and trappings of such a position.

However, much of the standard for today's salary structures across the sports landscape has its modern roots in the advent of professional baseball in the United States. During the late nineteenth century and for more than half of the twentieth century, baseball was the most popular professional team sport, and Babe Ruth was baseball's—and, arguably, the country's—most popular and dominant figure. Ruth, who played for the New York Yankees, was among a few stars whose presence on a team had such an impact on the press and at the turnstiles that he had the power to command an exceptionally high salary. And as one well-known anecdote relates, when reporters asked Ruth, whose contract at one point was valued at $80,000 per year, why he should be paid more than President Herbert Hoover, Ruth reportedly replied, "Why not? I had a better year than he did."

Nevertheless, the contracts of such stars were outliers. The average salary for a professional baseball player at the time was approximately $7,000, and although this figure was upward of five times that of the average working family, the disparity within the sport tells of how little impact stars had on the salary demands of other players on their teams. It also hints at the extent to which most players were bound to the whims of ownership.

As in almost any organization, payroll allocation has historically been one of the primary influences on sports franchises' decisions when negotiating player contracts. In fact, the infamous Black Sox scandal, in which eight members of the 1919 Chicago White Sox conspired with gamblers to intentionally lose that year's World Series, is generally considered to be the players' reaction to having felt underpaid by team owner Charles Comiskey. Yet the players' earnings were constrained not only by the actions of a penny-pinching owner. They were also severely limited by the existence of the reserve clause.

The Reserve Clause and Free Agency

The reserve clause was one of the longest standing provisions in player contracts of both the major and minor leagues. It bound a player to a single team, even if he signed contracts on an annual basis. The term of reserve, therefore, effectively restricted a player from changing teams unless ownership granted his unconditional release from the team.

From the late 1800s until the 1960s, when the amateur draft was instituted, the only conceivable license that players had over their careers was the freedom to negotiate as an amateur with any team willing to sign them to a professional contract. Once the contract was signed, it was at the team's discretion to trade, sell, reassign, or release the player. The only alternative leverage that players held at contract time was to hold out—that is, refuse to play unless their preferred conditions were met.

One of the earliest serious studies on the reserve clause and its implications was conducted by Simon Rottenberg

in a 1956 article, "The Baseball Players' Labor Market." Rottenberg concluded that the reserve clause inevitably transferred wealth from the players to the owners. He also determined that the best players tended to play for teams in the largest markets because these teams were in the optimal position to exploit the players' talent for the benefit of attracting fans to the ballpark.

But only a couple of years prior to the publication of Rottenberg's (1956) study, the Major League Baseball Players Association (MLBPA) had been established. As it functioned early on, the MLBPA was largely unassuming, to the point of being ineffectual until 1966 when the players hired Marvin Miller, a former negotiator for American steel workers, as the head of their union. The appointment of Miller would forever change the standards of player compensation—first in baseball and then across all professional sports.

On behalf of the players, Miller began to press for increases in such contract provisions as the minimum salary and pension contributions by owners. In so doing, he was progressively beginning to disrupt the basic assumptions of player contracts and, by extension, the relationship between ownership and players. Not long thereafter, things reached a tipping point when Miller challenged the legitimacy of the reserve clause.

In 1970, Curt Flood was a star player for the St. Louis Cardinals who had been traded to the Philadelphia Phillies. Flood, however, did not want to move from St. Louis and informed the Cardinals, Phillies, and the baseball commissioner's office of his intention to stay put and play out the remainder of his contract in St. Louis. Commissioner Bowie Kuhn ruled that such action was not within Flood's rights as a player and ordered him to play for Philadelphia or not play at all. Flood chose the latter and sued Major League Baseball (MLB) for violation of U.S. antitrust laws.

The case of *Flood v. Kuhn* (1972) eventually reached the U.S. Supreme Court, which ultimately sided with MLB. The Supreme Court cited, if somewhat dubiously, MLB's decades-old exemption from antitrust law. But losing in court did little to deter Miller and the players he represented. They instead took the owners head-on in a series of labor negotiations.

By 1972, a labor impasse boiled over when team owners refused to bargain with the players union on salary and pension issues. Now that they were firmly organized and unified by Miller, the players responded with the first leaguewide strike in American professional sports history. Only after nearly 100 games were lost to the strike did the owners finally concede to the players' demands. (The players found the labor stoppage so successful a tactic that they used it again in 1981, 1985, and 1994; the owners took a similar tack in 1976 and 1989, when they locked out the players during other labor disputes.)

As the players gained increasingly equal leverage in negotiations with owners during the 1970s, they pushed for a growing number of concessions. Of these, none was perhaps as influential to the earning power of professional athletes as the advent of free agency.

In 1974, Jim "Catfish" Hunter, a pitcher for the Oakland Athletics, became the first player to qualify for free agency. Hunter and team owner Charles Finley negotiated a contract that included a clause that required Finley to make a payment into an annuity for Hunter on a certain date. When Finley missed the date and subsequently attempted to pay Hunter directly rather than honor the clause, Hunter and Miller filed a complaint charging that the contract was null and void because Finley had broken the terms of the contract.

The case was sent to an arbitrator, who sided with Hunter. The voided contract made Hunter a free agent, which created a bidding war for his services. When Hunter signed a contract, he did so with the New York Yankees for a guaranteed salary that was precedent setting in both size and duration: $750,000 per year for 5 years. Even the immediate implications of the deal were far reaching: Hunter not only became the highest paid player in baseball history, but he also was one of the first players to receive anything more than a 1-year contract—and a guaranteed one at that. More important, the deal effectively established free agency across all of baseball.

As free agency took shape in the mid-1970s, the concept of the reserve clause was undergoing its final days of existence. In 1975, pitchers Andy Messersmith and Dave McNally played under the terms of the reserve clause. But when it came time for them to sign their contracts, they, with Miller's encouragement, argued that the reserve clause could not be applied if no contract was signed. Their case went before arbitrator Peter Seitz, who struck down the reserve clause and thereby resolved that the players could become free agents and sell their services to the highest bidder.

With the constraints of the reserve clause compromised and the rise of free agency, it was but a matter of time before these transformations would recast the expectation for player contract lengths and values and reconstitute the leitmotiv of the individual over the team.

On the Implications of Free Agency

The players' gaining the right to freely offer their services to any team (on expiration of contract) had an astonishing impact on salaries. In 1975, the minimum salary in MLB was $16,000, and the average salary was $44,676; by 1980, the salaries had jumped to $30,000 and $143,756, respectively; within 10 years of the start of free agency, the salaries had risen to $60,000 and $371,571, respectively; and by the 20th anniversary, they had risen to $109,000 and $1,110,766, respectively. And while minimum and average salaries continued to rise year after year,

nothing did more to demonstrate the extent of free agency than the 10-year, $252 million contract that Alex Rodriguez signed with the Texas Rangers in 2000.

The team's bid, which exceeded the next highest offer by approximately $100 million, personifies the theory that free agency is an auction market for athletes. According to work popularized by Richard Thaler (1992), this particular type of auction is a common value auction, in which the item being auctioned is more or less of equal value to all bidders, though bidders do not know the market value of the item when placing their bids. To place a bid, however, each bidder must have independently and expertly estimated the value of the item prior to bidding. When the auction is complete, the winner of the auction almost always is the one who provided the highest estimate. But as Thaler propounded, the winner of the auction ends up the loser because either the winning bid usually exceeds the true value of the item and the enterprise therefore loses money, or the true value of the item is less than the independently and expertly furnished estimate.

Despite most bidders' awareness of the "winner's curse," it fundamentally occurs because the thought processes of those doing the bidding—that is, ownerships—is irrational. The epitome of this reality is that the Rodriguez contract was eclipsed in 2007 when Rodriguez himself, who had by then been traded to the New York Yankees in 2004, signed a contract extension worth $275 million over 10 years. Most remarkable about the deal is not the numbers associated with it but that Yankees home games had been reaching sellout capacity and that every team Rodriguez played for had an improved win-loss record after he was no longer with them.

As such, the "winner's curse" is, in this context, of enormous benefit to the players. Because free agent salaries in professional sports are set from the top down, Hall of Fame–caliber players inevitably command the highest salaries. But because the free agent market persists on a scarcity of talent available in a given year, even second-level talent can expect to be compensated at a disproportionately higher amount, relative to their actual value of performance.

Although professional baseball was the forerunner of almost every significant policy for the movement of players between teams, the labor market for all athletes in every professional league is, fundamentally, a result of bargaining between owners and players. Over time, both owners and players have tended to agree that free agency is a means through which to provide the greatest perceived individual economic benefit. For owners, the costs associated with procuring and developing young talent has become so high as to insist that their best protection is through policy that requires a newly professional player be bound to his original team for a short period of time; in MLB, for instance, the period is 6 years. When this period of time lapses, the player qualifies for free agency and, under the rules of restricted free agency, can negotiate a new contract with any team, including his original one.

The conditions under which an athlete qualifies for restricted free agency vary among the major professional sports leagues. But the rules generally hold that although the athlete has freedom to negotiate with any team and agree on terms of a contract, the athlete's current team has an opportunity to match the terms of the deal before a contract is signed with the new team. Quite often, league rules specify that when a restricted free agent signs a deal with a new team, that team must compensate the athlete's prior team with an equitable number and level of picks in future drafts of amateur players. This framework is different from that of unrestricted free agency, under which the athlete has either been released outright from the team, not been offered a renewal upon expiration of contract, or not been selected in the amateur draft. Unrestricted free agents are, therefore, permitted to entertain and decide for themselves about contract offers from any team, an opportunity that can be especially lucrative for those who are the top performers in a league.

Yet even within the span of time between the beginning of a professional career and becoming eligible for free agency, and though it is in ways reminiscent of the reserve clause, the athlete is not entirely constrained by the whims of the owner. During this period, contracts are typically structured to provide players with annual salary increases, while annual minimum salary increases and salary cut percentages are mandated by the league, and as a result of the collective bargaining agreements between owners and players unions, players have the right to have their contract grievances with the owners ruled on by an independent arbitrator in the first couple or few years of the original deal. Given that these mechanisms essentially compare one player to other players in the league and their salaries and that the market value for players has increased over time, athletes stand to earn better than an "honest day's pay." In fact, they possess an increasing opportunity to create generational wealth for themselves and their families.

Since athletes have become more and more successful at increasing their salaries, a good many teams have in turn had to repeatedly relinquish key players. At the same time, in an attempt to remain competitive in both the game and the business, managements have discovered combinations of human intuition and statistical measurement that predict player performance. One result has been that a variety of teams in a number of leagues have begun to develop cost-containment strategies specific to their rosters.

Although Branch Rickey pioneered such systems during his years as an executive with the St. Louis Cardinals in the 1930s, perhaps the most popular of modern-day philosophies is that detailed in the book *Moneyball: The Art of Winning an Unfair Game* by Michael Lewis (2003). Lewis's treatment is an examination of Billy Beane, who as general manager of the Oakland Athletics MLB franchise, has used sabermetrics—mathematical examination of baseball-specific statistics—to make decisions about which amateur players to draft and which free agents to sign according to a notoriously low budget by league standards. With this system, which has the capacity to illuminate traits of the game that may not be immediately apparent, the team is theoretically able to obtain large numbers of undervalued, serviceable players at all positions. It is, in practice, a cost-containment strategy that helped Oakland compete with high-spending teams and qualify for the playoffs regularly in the 1990s and throughout the first decade of the 21st century, despite having the second lowest payroll in baseball.

By now, several other roster cost-containment theories have also been applied with success throughout professional sports. One of these involves the notion of free agency avoidance, in which teams essentially resist pursuit of high-priced free agents, including their own, and instead purposefully plan to replace those players with other talent already in the organization. Another theory involves teams extending substantial longer-term contracts, with submarket signing bonuses, to young players before they are eligible for free agency. This theory inherently provides an element of security to both the team and the player; they both effectively bet against the uncertainty of free agency.

The successful management of such human resources and salary allocation theories is evidenced in sports that operate both with and without salary caps. For example, in the National Football League (NFL), which does limit the amount of money a team can spend on total player salaries, teams such as the New England Patriots, Pittsburgh Steelers, and Philadelphia Eagles have implemented cost-containment theories and consistently appeared in the playoffs during the late 1990s and early 2000s. As a further example, Bill Belichick, head coach of the Patriots, and his staff have managed roster concerns by actively seeking players at positions less influenced by free agency and shying away from overvaluing and overpaying players at quarterback, wide receiver, and cornerback positions. Still, despite the relative success of these methods of controlling player costs, no team is immune from the reality of the rising costs of player contracts.

Although numerous factors contribute to the values of player contracts, the dollar amounts and conditions basically settle on that most fundamental of economics concepts: supply and demand. As referred to earlier, there is a limited supply of individuals who are able even in the first place to perform at the professional level. When a team plans to acquire an individual who is among the best performers in the sport, the decision makers in the organization must prepare to deal with the realities of smaller supply and higher demand.

According to application of economic theory, the supply curve's inelasticity in this relationship means the value of contracts will be determined by the demand curve. The increase of the demand curve expresses the rise in the individual player's value and, to be specific, the value of the individual player's contract. But this simple relationship tells only part of how and why player contracts are valued as they are today. What is further said to explain current thinking about player contracts dates to the early days of modern economic theory: the neoclassicists' creation of marginal utility theory circa 1870.

Within marginal utility theory, which has taken to being called *microeconomics* since the establishment of Keynes's economic synthesis, there is the marginal revenue productivity (MRP) theory of labor and wages. Marginal revenue is the return obtained from the last unit sold and is a function of change in total revenue divided by change in quantity. As applied to labor and wages in general, it holds that workers are paid according to the value of their marginal revenues to the enterprise. In the context of player contracts, this means salary is based on and differentiated by performance, productivity, and output. More simply, players are paid based on whatever is considered to be their contributions to the enterprise.

Assuming that ownership is willing to pay a productive player for adding to the financial earnings of the franchise, what exactly is contained in the player's contribution? The answer has generally been to reduce MRP to the number of tickets sold to fans as a result of a player being a member of the team. But this is conceivably too simple an explanation. Given the amount of revenue streams flowing into the sports leagues and the business as a whole, it is increasingly difficult to ascertain a valid and reliable MRP for the professional athlete. This is in large part why those who have devoted a considerable amount of recent scholarship to understanding sports economics—certainly Andrew Zimbalist of Smith College and *The Wages of Wins* authors David Berri, Martin Schmidt, and Stacey Brook—have stated that salary structures are questionable and misguided and that there is by now a need to modify the way salaries are determined. At the heart of their arguments is the relationship among player salary, performance statistics, and which statistic matters most in determining player pay.

There is no doubt that the terms, considerations, and values of player contracts have experienced explosive growth since the advent of free agency. They have, in turn, brought significant change to sports and the sports business. Prior to free agency, professional athletes had generally been subject to the benevolent interests of owners; the typical athlete's acts of defiance amounted to some combination holding out for higher salary, overcoming the influence owners held over members of the press, and the occasional (though ultimately prohibited) acts of collusion in which owners tacitly agreed not to bid on each other's free agents. Today, professional athletes are arguably no longer exploited, inasmuch as athletes and owners have an increasingly balanced amount of control over the rules and courses of making money from sports. This is perhaps as much a result of successful labor negotiations as of rising exposure across the various means of communication—radio, television, newspapers, magazines, and the World Wide Web—that reach and influence the sports fan and the public at large.

The Evolution of Athletes' Endorsements

In addition to the labor triumphs achieved by professional athletes in the last quarter of the twentieth century, there has been no greater or more powerful transformation than that of professional athletes basing their salary demands on the revenue streams afforded by television broadcasts. When television sets penetrated the media market and became an increasingly mainstream household item beginning in the 1950s, teams and leagues found a fresh medium by which to transmit their product to audiences, especially those that were outside the range of a particular radio signal. The broadcast of professional sports events was a natural fit for programming executives, who rapidly signed teams and leagues to lucrative contracts. But although these deals almost immediately increased the income and value of teams and leagues, only a very small minority foresaw the unintended consequence they would have on the incomes of professional athletes.

The Impact of Television and Media on the Earnings of Professional Athletes

Because the boom in media rights deals made plenty of news, the public reporting of deals meant team revenue figures were no longer shrouded in secrecy, as they had been previously. So while owners celebrated having parlayed successful television broadcasts and distribution contracts, players and their representatives rejoiced in having a definitive figure to target in contract negotiations. That is, owners, who with closed financial books had been able to effectively cry poverty, could no longer do so with any sense of veracity.

In the United States, the NFL has thus far proven to be the most successful sports entity when it comes to consistently maximizing media revenue. But this success has come at the cost of a labor battle that spanned nearly two decades and spilled over into legal disputes to be tried in courts of law. However, one method to achieve labor peace emerged in 1992, when the NFL owners offered to open their financial books and give players a large share of the list of defined revenue streams.

The list was dominated by the league's multibillion-dollar media deal, and the owners offered the players a 63% share (later as much as 65%) in exchange for the players' agreement to cap their salaries at the 63% level. This salary cap, which was similar to the agreement reached a decade earlier within the National Basketball Association (NBA), guaranteed players the lion's share of revenue from the league's media deals and gave the owners cost certainty over their team rosters.

Yet despite the ostensible advantage a salary cap grants to both sides, salary caps have not proven to be as effective in providing cost certainty in all sports. After the NFL and its players association negotiated a collective bargaining agreement in 2006, the prospect of even a slight change in calculation has given rise to speculation that salary caps may not be as effective a tool of cost control as ownership has believed them to be until now. The potential sticking point is that salary caps are tied to overall revenue and contain minimum salary guarantees, and there are a host of other exceptions that have been—and could be even more so going forward—exploited by either ownership or player interests.

But while salary cap controversies and related contract negotiations persist on one hand, on the other hand, for athletes in most major professional sports, both with and without salary caps, compensation is tied to the overall media-earning capacity of their particular teams and leagues. In capped sports, the figures are, by definition, generally fixed; in uncapped sports, the figures are more variable, though ultimately based on media earnings. And in any case, because they have largely signed over their media income to players, owners have turned to new ways of maximizing facility-based revenue streams, a direct result of which is the boom in stadium construction, naming rights, and sponsorship deals during the past 20-plus years.

Owners are, however, not alone in gaining revenue streams through sponsorship and related deals. Since the earliest days of modern professional sports, all manner of corporations and organizations have intended to reach existing and potential customers by aligning themselves with athletes. Professional athletes tend to be able to draw people to an event, which provides the opportunity for organizations to do such things as promote their products and services or motivate and entertain customers and employees. In exchange for making an appearance and performing some relative function, whether in person or through some electronic medium, the athlete typically receives some form of compensation. Player contracts are by and large the primary embodiment of this because athletes possess the status to make their teams and sports more marketable.

Yet over time, especially as the reach of sports and media has grown across the globe, endorsement income has also become an important part of the athlete's overall earnings potential. It is indeed extreme, the case of professional golfer Tiger Woods, who, until derailed by self-destructive behavior that led to personal scandal, was estimated to earn upwards of $100 million per year in endorsement income. But to whatever extent Woods's actions hurt his own earning power and may in the long term impact athletes' endorsements, well-known and recognizable athletes—both current and retired professionals—can earn many millions of dollars annually for endorsing both sport-specific equipment and apparel and consumer products; this is typically in addition to receiving quantities of these items for free.

An athlete's ability to act as a successful endorser is, on the surface, a function of likeability and recognition. But below the surface, the athlete-as-endorser is a tool that is used in an attempt to persuade other individuals to do something in the interest of whatever product, service, or organization is being promoted.

Robert Cialdini of Arizona State University has researched and developed accepted theories about how and why people tend to be influenced by others. Within his framework are the realities that people tend to behave as they see others behaving (so-called social proofs), are likely to outright obey the requests of authority figures, and are easily persuaded by other people they are fond of, especially if they find those individuals somehow attractive. One dominant theme of the literature on the subject is that people are willing to be swayed because it allows them to identify with successful others, which is a means by which to enhance one's self-esteem. That is, when a person joins a renowned group and draws attention to membership in it, that person is likely to feel more satisfied with himself or herself.

Although the theories propounded by Cialdini (1993) are settled in a greater social context, they originate in his and his colleagues' having verified that following a sports team victory, fans are more likely to brandish their team's logo and share the recognition by saying, "We won"; following defeat, the same fans declare, "They lost." These dual concepts—basking in reflected glory and cutting off reflected failure, respectively—help explain the traditional allure of popular and well-behaved athletes as endorsers and the rejection of athletes whose personalities are disagreeable or whose behavior runs afoul of the law or social norms.

Although the basic reasons for using professional athletes to make promotional statements remains the same as anytime before, the advancement of such a strategy and tactic looks very much different today than it did in 1960, when Mark McCormack, founder of International Management Group, began to craft the image of professional golfer Arnold Palmer into one suitable for all manner of endorsements. Palmer was not, of course, the first professional athlete to take on the role of product pitchman. But with McCormack acting as his agent, Palmer is considered to have become the first professional athlete to seriously market, promote, and license himself and his likeness—and to have built a corporate enterprise from it.

The effectiveness of Palmer as a spokesman is a result of advertisers' having chosen to align him with products and services that he either used personally or had confidence in promoting to the public. But the underlying strength of the endorsement strategy rested on and concentrated on something more profound: Palmer as an upstanding human being rather than as a championship golfer. By focusing more on the former than on the latter,

Palmer's value as an endorser was guarded against any likelihood of poor performance on the golf course.

Countless professional athletes across virtually every professional sport have in the interim used the basic tenets of Palmer and McCormack's strategy to convert image into income. And it may well be argued that NASCAR and the teams and drivers within it have individually and collectively built themselves up on much the same premise. What is undeniable, however, is that professional sports have grown to compete variously as part of or side by side with the entertainment industry, and athletes are by now equivalent to entertainers in terms of status, function, and compensation. For high-performing athletes, especially those who have a particular marketability, there are often opportunities to earn more money from endorsing products and services than from playing their sports.

Global Considerations and Future Directions

In today's global economy, business concerns and information flows are no longer local, regional, or multinational, even if they are organized as such. Business and the flow of information are transnational, which means factors including marketing, pricing, and management do not know national boundaries. But if this analysis is United States–centric, it is only because professional sports in the United States have provided the basic model for the composition, image, and interests of today's professional athletes the world over.

Professional sports teams in the United States, beginning with baseball, have increasingly set about finding players from outside the country. This has been a response, first, to the desire to expand the pool of available talent and, more recently, to increasingly high salaries being paid to players who might not pan out. It is ever more also due to the fantastic attempts by individuals and organizations within the sports business to tap new markets by attracting foreign fans who are conceivably interested in consuming anything that might be related to a favorite professional athlete playing abroad.

With the possible exception of premier football (soccer) players and Formula One race car drivers, both of whom benefit from relative free agency and concomitant auction markets for their services, professional athletes who compete in U.S. leagues are by and large paid a higher salary than their counterparts around the world. This is in great measure due to the victories of their organized labor unions over management. Yet it is fast becoming an old reality.

Although leagues abroad follow the United States in many ways, they tend to have different issues with player movement because they permit the largely unencumbered free flow of players between leagues. In the United States, the existence of one high-professional league per sport

means there are a finite number of available roster spots on a team and, by extension, in the league. This phenomenon, combined with the prospects of media exposure, explains, for example, the unprecedented contracts extended to Alex Rodriguez, the first of which doubled the previous record for a sports contract, which was a 6-year, $126 million agreement signed in 1997 between forward Kevin Garnett and the NBA's Minnesota Timberwolves.

The years since the advent of free agency have been a great period of time for the earnings of professional athletes, most of whom have increasingly benefited by attracting owners and sponsors that are willing to compete against one another for the athletes' talents and services. Their status has become more profitable and their access to financially rewarding opportunities has risen steeply. And the farther up the talent and status scale a player has gone, the better the pay. But this much is also true for athletes who compete in individual sports.

Both in and across the team and individual sports labor markets, there is, as in any labor market, inequality of income distribution. The enormous amount of information pertaining to the salaries of professional athletes has permitted reliable Gini coefficients—measurements of inequality in income distributions—to be computed, and the results demonstrate that plenty of inequalities exist. Generally speaking, even in consideration of capped sports, individual versus team sports, and the economic policies specific to each, there is a significant discrepancy between 90% of earners and those in the top 10%, who anyway lag well behind the top 1% (to say little of those in the top 0.1%). Yet given salary increases over time, and despite the few instances of stagnation or decrease, most professional athletes can be assured of receiving better than a living wage.

Consider, for example, that the average salary for an MLB player is at present more than $3 million; when Donald Fehr became executive director of the MLBPA in late 1985, the average player's salary was a little more than $300,000 (approximately $600,000 in 2008 money). The billions of dollars committed to salaries in today's domestic and foreign sports leagues and associations tell nothing of the days when a good many athletes supplemented their incomes by taking jobs during the off-season, which was the impetus for the creation of preseason training camps. Players now typically train year-round and may even receive additional compensation for doing so.

Even so, there is a line of argument that asserts athletes are being exploited because they are being paid wages lower than the MRP, the revenue that is generated. There is, in addition, subtext about the existence of prevailing structures of race and gender discrimination. Although there is not by any means a final word on the matter, it is becoming clear that the argument over whether professional athletes are any longer paid lower wages because they are of ethnic and racial minorities appears to be obsolescent: Alex Rodriguez is Latino; Tiger Woods is of

African American and Asian descent; and NBA players, who are the highest paid of all league athletes in the United States, are a majority black. To be clear, disparities in salary due to racial, ethnic, and even language biases is an existent though decreasing issue in the context of player salaries. However, the same cannot be said for gender. Although female participation in sports has risen dramatically since the latter part of the twentieth century and women's professional leagues have been created in reflection of that change, female athletes are not as well compensated as their male counterparts. One overarching reason for this is because, whatever social stereotypes predominate, professional women's sports have yet to achieve the levels of viewership and, by extension, revenue that men's sports generate.

To be sure, as private investors and public institutions in many parts of the developed world have for the past two decades-plus invested in sports teams and leagues, demand for top players has become increasingly competitive. The U.S.-based leagues have not yet ceased to be the market leaders, but they are beginning to experience realities of the open market that have existed for quite some time almost everywhere else. Most notably, several players in the NBA and the NHL have decidedly gone to play—and be paid handsomely—in elite European leagues. And the implications of acquiring the best talent available has become so fierce that teams in more than a few sports are willing to pay posting and transfer fees across teams and leagues simply for the right to negotiate with a player. Yet no one can say with any certainty whether any of this experience is likely to ring true in years come.

Conclusion and the Challenges Ahead

Throughout history, professional sports have generally not let outside factors, such as the economy, control business. Executives and personalities have taken charge of external forces, especially during periods of downturn, and acted to endow their assets with various capacities to gain wealth. Having been more proactive than reactive, they have tended to not let economic factors affect business performance any more than those factors set limits on how they conducted their business.

Easy access to credit and other economic factors that existed during the first three quarters of the twentieth century allowed professional sports entities to think and behave as they traditionally had. But significant economic and social transformations in more recent years have led to upheaval of much of what everyone knew to be true. One question that is beginning to be asked is, "Do companies that pay athletes to endorse products and services really benefit from the relationship?"

The existing research is mixed regarding whether athlete endorsements are any longer a defensible corporate decision from a marketing, advertising, or branding standpoint. Now more than ever before, in an era of increased media exposure and player scandal, the company risks gaining negative public attention over the athlete who engages in behavior that is not consistent with the corporate image. But even more profound is that such endorsement deals will be so overused as to be ineffectual, should they continue to proliferate at the rate they have in the past. The problem is, primarily, that companies may well be left with little to distinguish their investments—even if they employ the most renowned athletes and those whose images and values unquestionably connect with the corporate brand. The prospect of this actually happening cannot be dismissed, because collapse eventually emerges in any market in which participants overpay for products or services that do not hold the possibility of producing a fair return on their investments.

Although this and other observations and conclusions outlined in this analysis are based on a wealth of data and literature, there is, altogether, little evidence that today's facts are being interpreted by anything but yesterday's theories. Thus, there is a need to examine and think through the basic assumptions of the sports business and, specific to this discussion, how athletes are compensated for their services.

The first challenge of this effort is to cast a new and functional economic theory for the sports business in general and for player contracts in particular. The formulas for how professional athletes should be compensated for their performance and contributions are often complicated and rather unscientific. But if the proud achievement of billions of dollars being exchanged throughout the sports business is any indication, they have served the interests of both athlete and owner quite well for quite some time. Now given the fits and seizures of the shift to a transnational and knowledge-based economy, the question is, "How much longer can traditional principles and policies be sustained?"

The highest levels of professional sports effectively function as monopolies. As with the majority of monopolistic enterprises, the activity and innovation that begot prosperity was so successful for so long that they find it reasonably difficult to abandon those practices and habits. Thus, if leagues and owners continue to increase the price of admission to games and access to content in order to turn a consistent profit while keeping up with increasing player costs, are they destroying the mutual trust they have with fans? Are the player contracts themselves corrosive because the wages and benefits paid out through them are increasingly so disparate from those of the average fan? Will these circumstances generate waves of contempt that turn athletes who are paid millions of dollars from heroes into villains? If the answers are yes, can players then expect to be paid as much tomorrow as they are today?

Such questions prompt the second challenge, which is to deal with the justification for the terms of player contracts. A long-standing argument has been that professional athletes have a limited window during which to cash in on their skills. This may well be so; a good case for this could certainly be made for any period prior to free agency. Yet some athletes go so far as to announce that such contracts are necessary if they are to "feed the family." What they mean to say is that the contracts are necessary to feed the family according to a certain standard. This too may be fine, because there is sound argument in paying high-performing individuals according to whatever is deemed an appropriate market value. But in light of today's salaries, benefits, retirement policies, and the access to opportunities afforded to even the least competent professional athletes, the question is whether the rationale matches the reality. When it no longer does (and it may already not), customers—be they fans who attend games or owners who woo players to their teams—reject what is being marketed to them. As a consequence, the entire system lurches toward instability.

A third, but related, challenge is to produce a better and more honest definition of what in the sports business is meant by *short term* and *long term* and what is needed to balance the expectations of both—regardless of whether player contracts are guaranteed. Although much of the subject is beyond this analysis, it nevertheless signals here the need for conscious development of programs that educate and assist professional athletes, whatever their level of financial success and length of professional career, in every aspect of transition to life after their playing days are over. A spectrum of professional athletes, from the extremely well known to those who appeared in the ranks momentarily, have found themselves impoverished by wrestling with the frustrations of trying to find post-career outlets that in even a small way replicate the sense of competition, camaraderie, and notoriety associated with being a professional athlete.

These are not, of course, the only challenges facing the incomes and earnings of professional athletes at the outset of the twenty-first century. But in considering the rapid and impressive changes to athletes' salary and endorsement prospects, these challenges are certainly high among the list of priorities going forward.

References and Further Readings

Berri, D., Schmidt, M., & Brook, S. (2006). *The wages of wins: Taking measure of the many myths in modern sport.* Stanford, CA: Stanford University Press.

Cialdini, R. (1993). *Influence: The psychology of persuasion.* New York: Quill William Morrow.

Coakley, J., & Dunning, E. (2002). *Handbook of sports studies.* Thousand Oaks, CA: Sage.

Drucker, P. (1993). *Post-capitalist society.* New York: HarperCollins.

Helyar, J. (1994). *Lords of the realm: The real history of baseball.* New York: Villard Books.

Lewis, M. (2003). *Moneyball: The art of winning an unfair game.* New York: W. W. Norton.

MacCambridge, M. (2004). *America's game: The epic story of how pro football captured a nation.* New York: Random House.

Miller, M. (1991). *A whole different ball game: The sport and business of baseball.* New York: Birch Lane.

Palmer, A., & Dodson, J. (1991). *A golfer's life.* New York: Random House.

Rosner, S., & Shropshire, K. L. (2004). *The business of sports.* Sudbury, MA: Jones & Bartlett.

Rottenberg, S. (1956). The baseball players' labor market. *Journal of Political Economy, 64*(3), 242–260.

Thaler, R. H. (1992). *The winner's curse.* Princeton, NJ: Princeton University Press.

Zimbalist, A. (1992). *Baseball and billions.* New York: Basic Books.

54

ECONOMICS OF GENDER

LENA NEKBY

Stockholm University

PETER SKOGMAN THOURSIE

Institute for Labour Market Policy Evaluation (IFAU), Uppsala

This chapter on the economics of gender discusses the role of gender in the labor market from an economic perspective. Focus on the labor market is motivated by the fact that labor earnings are arguably the most important component of an individual's income and a major determinant of living standards. Earnings are also correlated with employment opportunities, occupation, promotion, and job mobility, all of which, for reasons that are discussed in greater detail below, are influenced by gender. Although there are other arenas where gender is of economic importance (e.g., gender differences in the division of child care and domestic labor, access to day care, and health), these topics are not covered in this chapter. Interested readers should instead turn to the chapters on the economics of the family and feminist economics. This chapter focuses on the theoretical foundation for gender differences in the labor market as well as the empirical evidence on gender discrimination and gender differences in preferences.

The chapter begins with an overview of country differences in gender wage and employment gaps. This section discusses how gender differences in employment rates and differences in wage dispersion may relate to the gender wage gap. This is followed by a theoretical overview of gender differences in the labor market covering both supply-side differences in human capital acquisition—the role of gender-specific preferences—and demand-side discrimination. The next section discusses the empirical problem of identifying discrimination in the labor market. The

chapter rounds off with two sections covering, in turn, the empirical evidence on discrimination and gender differences in preferences.

Gender Differences in the Labor Market: Overview

Studying differences in labor earnings is of fundamental importance for anyone interested in understanding poverty, social stratification, and the economic incentives facing workers. Labor earnings are the most important component of an employed individual's income and a major determinant of living standards. This chapter therefore begins with a comparison of gender labor market gaps in a selected number of industrialized countries. First, an overall picture of gender wage gaps and differences between countries is provided, followed by a description of the trends in these gaps during the last 20 years. Country differences in gender wage gaps are related to differences in female employment rates as well as varying wage distributions across countries. Possible explanations for the wage gaps observed, such as productivity differences, occupational gender segregation, preferences, and discrimination are discussed in subsequent sections.

Table 54.1 reports the gender wage gap, the female employment rate, and the fraction of female employees who work part-time for a selected number of countries during the period from 1989 through 2006. The gender wage gap is defined as 1 minus the ratio of the annual averages of female and male mean hourly wage rates, which can then be interpreted as how much less, as a percentage, women earn per hour relative to men. For example, a gender wage gap of 23% in the United States in 2006 means that the female wage rate is 23% smaller than the male wage rate. In other words, for every $100 that men earn per hour, women earn 23% less—that is, $77. As shown in Table 54.1, gender differences in pay prevail in all countries, even though the size of the gaps varies considerably across countries. In 2006, the female hourly wage rate in France was 11% smaller than the male hourly wage rate. Thus, wages of employed women in France are closer to men's wages than in the case of the United States. When one looks at the period from 1994 through 1998, where information on the gender wage gap for the full set of countries is available, one sees that the gender wage gap is 36% in Japan, 10% in France, and 24% in the United States. Table 54.1 also shows that there seems to be a tendency toward decreasing gender wage gaps over time in most countries since the late 1980s.

An interesting question to ask is why gender differences in labor market outcomes vary across countries. For example, why do women earn less relative to men in a country such as the United States compared with France or Sweden? One reason could be that women have acquired different skill levels across countries and that women in France and Sweden are more qualified than women in United States. Because skills are rewarded through higher pay in the labor market, this is one potential reason for observed country differences in pay. According to Francine Blau and Lawrence Kahn (2000), however, there seems to be little reason to believe that women in the United States are less qualified relative to men than women in other countries. An alternative explanation is that there are country differences in economic returns to skills and therefore differences in economic incentives. Countries with high rewards to skills have wage structures that encourage skill acquisition among workers. This suggests that the wage structure in a country plays an important role in determining the gender wage gap, given that there are gender differences in skills and qualifications. Consider, for example, two countries where women have lower levels of labor market experience than men, but the gender difference in experience is the same in the two countries. If the return to experience is higher in one country, this country will have a larger gender wage gap, all else equal.

Moreover, centralized wage-setting institutions tend to reduce wage dispersion across firms and industries and raise the relative pay of low-wage workers (regardless of gender), which in turn may reduce the gender wage gap. Because most European countries have more centralized wage setting compared with the United States, the degree of centralization of wage setting may be an important explanatory factor behind country differences in the gender wage gap. Empirical evidence suggests that the overall wage structure is of major importance in explaining gender wage gaps, where the higher level of wage inequality in the United States compared with other countries tends to increase U.S. gender differentials relative to those in other countries (see, e.g., Blau & Kahn, 1996a, 1996b).

These explanations of the gender wage gap are based on the assumption that women on average are less qualified than men. It is therefore interesting to see how the gender wage gap has evolved over time as female labor force participation has increased in most countries since the 1970s. Human capital skills, such as level of education and labor market experience, have also increased for females relative to males during this period. Because a stronger attachment to the labor force would increase other labor market skills as well, this suggests that gender wage gaps should shrink over time. According to Table 54.1, the female employment rate has increased slightly in most countries, together with a decrease in the gender wage gap. Thus, it appears that women to some extent have caught up with men by accruing more skills. It should be stressed, however, that even if women to a large extent have caught up with men in terms of level of education, they systematically chose different types of educations. For example, men to a larger extent than women chose technical educations. If technical educations and the occupations associated with these educations yield higher returns in the labor market than other types of educations, this would improve men's labor earnings relative to those of women.

Furthermore, because women have lower employment rates than men, women might be a more selected group in the labor market than men with, on average, higher tastes and skills for work compared to the population of women. Such selection into employment makes it difficult to study trends in gender wage gaps because the group of female workers from one time period to another might not be comparable when female employment rates change over time. This also makes across-country comparisons of gender wage gaps difficult because female employment rates are very different across countries, implying that the selection of females who participate in the labor market in one country is potentially very different from the corresponding selection in another country.

Difficulties in comparing trends in gender wage gaps across countries are supported by the striking international variation in female employment rates. It is apparent in Table 54.1, for example, that France had the lowest gender wage gap in 2006 (11%) but also one of the lowest female employment rates. Only 59% of women were employed in France at that time, compared with 66% of women in the United States. One hypothesis, therefore, is that selection into employment is not random and might affect the size of gender wage gaps. In particular, if employed women have relatively high-wage characteristics, low female employment rates are consistent with lower gender wage gaps because women with low-wage characteristics are not included in the observed wage distribution. This may explain the negative correlation between gender wage and employment gaps that are observed in Table 54.1.

The pattern of countries with high gender wage gaps tending to have high female employment rates might also

Table 54.1 Gender Wage Gaps, Female Employment Rates, and Female Part-Time Work Rates Among the Employed (Percentages)

	1989–1990	1994–1998	2006
Austria			
Gender wage gap	33	31	—
Female employment rate	—	59	64
Female part-time work rate	—	30	40
France			
Gender wage gap	15	10	11
Female employment rate	52	53	59
Female part-time work rate	25	32	30
Italy			
Gender wage gap	20	17	—
Female employment rate	—	37	46
Female part-time work rate	—	14	26
Japan			
Gender wage gap	41	36	—
Female employment rate	57	57	59
Female part-time work rate	—	—	—
Sweden			
Gender wage gap	21	16	16
Female employment rate	73	68	71
Female part-time work rate	—	34	40
United Kingdom			
Gender wage gap	32	25	21
Female employment rate	61	64	66
Female part-time work rate	44	44	42
Unites States			
Gender wage gap	29	24	23
Female employment rate	64	67	66
Female part-time work rate	—	—	—

NOTES: Female part-time work rates are the fraction of employed women who work part-time. Female employment rates and female part-time work rates are from Eurostat (2009). Gender wage gaps are based on hourly wage rates. Gender wage gaps for the periods from 1989 through 1990 and 1994 through 1998 are taken from Blau and Kahn (2000), and the gender wage gaps in 2006 are from Eurostat. The gender wage gap for the United States in 2006 is based on annual earnings for full-time workers (Institute for Women's Policy Research, 2009).

be reinforced by differences in the extent to which women work part-time. In France, the fraction of employed females working part-time in 2006 was 30%. The corresponding figure for Sweden, which had a larger gender wage gap as well as a higher female employment rate in 2006, was 40%. Working part-time implies that a smaller amount of work experience is accumulated over time in comparison to full-time workers. It might also be the case that working part-time is associated with lower chances for promotion and wage raises. Taken together, there are, therefore, a number of explanations as to why a higher female employment rate, together with high female part-time rates, might be associated with a higher gender wage gap within a country.

Different patterns of employment selection across countries may in turn stem from a number of factors. First, there may be country differences in the gender role of household work, social norms, or both, affecting labor force participation. Second, labor demand mechanisms, including social attitudes toward female employment and those attitudes' potential effects on employer choices, may be at work, affecting both the employment rate as well as the level of wage offers by gender. Claudia Olivetti and Barbara Petrongolo (2008) suggest that the international variation in gender employment gaps can indeed shed light on across-country differences in gender wage gaps. This study suggests that sample selection into employment explains nearly one half of the observed negative correlation between gender wage and employment gaps. They also show that while the raw wage gap is much higher in Anglo-Saxon countries than in southern Europe, the reason is probably not to be found in more equal pay treatment for women in the latter group of countries but rather in different selection processes into employment. Female participation rates in southern European countries are low and concentrated among high-wage women. Correcting for lower participation rates in southern European countries widens the wage gap to levels similar to those of other European countries and the United States.

Theoretical Explanations for Gender Differences in the Labor Market

Gender differences in labor market outcomes stem from supply-side differences in productivity, labor supply, or preferences or to demand-side differences in opportunity—that is, gender discrimination in employment, wage-setting, or promotion of equally qualified individuals (see Altonji & Blank, 2003, for an overview). Supply-side differences in productivity and labor supply between men and women are often analyzed within the human capital framework (Mincer & Polachek, 1974). The human capital model postulates that individuals invest in education and training and are rewarded for these investments in the labor market, either via enhanced employability, higher wages, or both (Mincer, 1958; Mincer & Polachek, 1974). Within this framework, gender differences in labor market outcomes are attributable to gender differences in human capital investment.

A number of explanations have been forwarded as to why women historically have invested less in education, skills, and other qualifications valued in the labor market. A partial explanation can be found in traditional gender norms concerning child care and housework within families. If women expect to spend more time out of the labor market, they consequently have less time in the labor market to reap the benefits of their human capital investments. As such, women will invest less in market-oriented human capital and, in addition, will direct their investments toward educations and skills with lower depreciation rates due to time out of the labor market (Polachek, 1975). Notice that gender differences in the types of academic training being invested in, due to differential depreciation, also help to explain patterns of occupational segregation by gender. Shorter duration in the labor market as well as more frequent interruptions for child rearing also influence employers' willingness to finance on-the-job training for female employees as well as promotion possibilities, reinforcing, over time, gender differences in productivity. Note that there is a literature that questions the degree to which human capital models can explain occupational segregation by gender (Beller, 1982; England, 1982).

Not only are there social norms concerning women's division of labor between home and market production but there are also norms concerning what constitutes typically female or male pursuits in the labor market (Akerlof & Kranton, 2000). In other words, preferences for certain types of occupations or educations may be due to social norms or preconditioning regarding what is considered appropriate for women and the costs of deviating from these norms (Akerlof & Kranton, 2000; Gundersson, 1989; Polachek, 1984). Differences in type of academic training can also be the result of historical differences in remuneration and access to jobs by gender. If women historically have had lower access to (due to norms or discrimination) or lower payoffs from certain occupations, then investments in education and training for these occupations will also be lower. This implies that historical discrimination in the labor market can lead to subsequent differences in human capital investment and that gender differences in the labor market can become a self-fulfilling prophecy (Darity & Mason, 1998). Claudia Goldin (2006) argues that lower remuneration in typically female occupations has an historical basis in the segregation of jobs as women increasingly entered the labor market in the early 1900s. As white-collar positions opened up for women, policies were instituted at the firm level, creating sex-segregated positions. Jobs were increasingly classified as either female or male, where the majority of female jobs were dead-end, providing little room for advancement to higher positions or earnings growth.

Over time, shifts in the norms concerning female participation in the labor market, greater and more continuous time in the labor market, as well as more equitable distribution of housework and child care will increase incentives for women to invest in human capital accumulation and for firms to invest in female employees. Indeed, the salience of gender differences in human capital investment as an explanation for gender differences in labor market gaps has decreased over time as women increasingly have closed the gender gap in education, at least with regard to level of education. However, hard-to-break differences in remuneration attributable to occupational segregation remain due to either cultural devaluation of female jobs or dual labor market and crowding theories, where exclusion from male jobs leads to crowding in female jobs and consequently lower wages as well as lower returns to education (Bergmann, 1974; Doeringer & Piore, 1971). Occupational segregation by gender is therefore both a cause and a consequence of gender differences in pay. Occupational segregation can lead to gender differences in human capital investment and productivity, but it is also a partial explanation for gender wage and income differentials in a society characterized by occupational gender segregation and lower remuneration for female jobs.

On the demand side, two forms of discrimination are commonly discussed within the economics framework: taste-based discrimination and statistical discrimination. Taste-based discrimination arises because of a disutility among employers (customers or coworkers) for interacting with female workers or because of a preference for male workers (Becker, 1971). If tastes for discrimination are large and the demand for preferred male workers is lower than the supply, a wage differential arises between male and female workers, the implication of which is a competitive advantage for firms that hire equally productive women. This suggests that wage gaps will disappear in the long run as nondiscriminating employers enter the market. Frictions to free entry, imperfect information, collective bargaining, search costs, and other infringements to perfect market competition may, however, lead to sustainable wage gaps due to taste-based discrimination over time. There are a number of empirical studies examining the degree to which competition decreases gender discrimination; see, for example, Orley Ashenfelter and Timothy Hannan (1986); Sandra Black and Elizabeth Brainard (2004); Black and Philip Strahan (2001); Judith Hellerstein, David Neumark, and Kenneth Troske (2002); Xin Meng (2004); and the references therein.

Statistical discrimination arises because of the inability to acquire, or costs of acquiring, perfect information about job candidates. Instead, employers use readily available group statistics to assess candidates (Arrow, 1973; Phelps, 1972). This implies that if women on average have lower relevant labor market experience for a given position, are expected to leave the labor market for child rearing, or both, to a larger extent than male candidates, employers will be less inclined to interview and hire female candidates. Notice that statistical discrimination is individual discrimination based on actual group statistics. The individual in question may deviate from mean group characteristics, but employers are unable to assess this information, or the costs of doing so are high. Statistical discrimination is also based on the assumption that unbiased group statistics are readily available. This may not be the case, and agents may act on the presumption that their beliefs are statistically correct but actually base decisions on biased information because of erroneous perceptions of group productivity. In the sociological literature, this is termed *error discrimination* (England, 1992).

The Empirical Problem of Identifying Gender Discrimination in the Labor Market

The most common method of estimating gender differences in labor market outcomes is through wage, earnings, or employment regressions using register or survey data. Typically, variations of the following basic model are estimated:

$$y_i = \alpha + \beta_1 female_i + X_i \beta_2 + \varepsilon_i$$

where y_i is a labor market outcome (employment, wages, income) of individual i, *female* is a binary (dummy) variable equal to 1 if female and 0 otherwise, and X is a vector of other control variables, typically both demographic and human capital indicators that may influence the outcome variable and systematically differ between men and women. Finally, ε is the random error component measuring the impact of unobserved characteristics in the equation that also influence the outcome variable. In estimation of this type of equation, the coefficient for *female* indicates to what degree labor market outcomes differ between men and women with similar characteristics (the observable characteristics included in the vector X). It does not, however, tell us whether these gender differences are due to discrimination— that is, to unequal treatment of equally qualified individuals. The reason is that it is impossible for researchers to control for all possible supply-side differences in productivity by gender. For a causal interpretation of the effect of gender on a given outcome, the correlation between the *female* dummy variable and the random error component must be equal to 0. This is called the *zero conditional mean assumption,* stating that there should be no systematic differences in unobserved factors between men and women that influence the outcome of interest. If there is such a factor—for example, if women have systematically lower on-the-job training than men and this is unobserved in an income equation—then the measure for gender differences in income will be biased if differences in labor market training are not accounted for in estimation. This implies that observed gender differences in labor market outcomes may be due to supply-side differences in productivity by gender, uncontrolled for in estimation (unobserved characteristics) or discrimination.

Note that there is a large literature concerning the decomposition of gender wage gaps into an explained and unexplained component, the so-called Oaxaca-Blinder method, where the unexplained component measures wage differentials that remain after controlling for all observable characteristics in estimation (Blinder, 1973; Oaxaca & Ransom, 1999). (For extensions of this method, see also Juhn, Murphy, & Pierce, 1991.)

Recently, attention has turned to estimating gender differences in the labor market using experimental methods. The reason is that a well-executed controlled experiment can unequivocally identify a causal effect of gender on an outcome of interest. Experiments are based on random assignment of a given population into a treatment group and a control group. Random assignment guarantees that both observable and unobservable individual characteristics are, on average, similar in treatment and control groups. This implies that any differences in outcomes due to treatment are attributable to gender alone. Studies based on experimental methods are often characterized by high internal validity but low external validity. High internal validity implies that experiments are credibly able to identify a causal effect of gender on outcomes of interest. Low external validity implies that results often cannot be generalized to the population at large. This is due to the fact that experiments are often performed on limited subsamples of the population only. Experimental methods have been used to study the presence of gender differences in preferences as well as employer discrimination. The next two sections provide an overview of the recent empirical evidence within these two strands of research on gender and the labor market.

Evidence of Gender Discrimination

Two commonly used methods to study gender discrimination in the labor market are so-called audit and correspondence testing studies (Darity & Mason, 1998; Pager, 2007; Riach & Rich, 2002). Audit studies use actual test persons to apply for jobs and participate in job interviews, while correspondence testing studies send written applications (CVs) to actual job openings and measure differences in callbacks to interviews. Audit studies have the advantage of testing discrimination in the entire application process, from initial contact with employers to actual job offers. On the other hand, audit studies are unable to credibly control that test persons are similar in all characteristics of relevance to employers (Heckman, 1998; Heckman & Siegelman, 1993). Although test persons are trained to behave and dress in a similar manner, their use introduces uncertainty into the experiment. Female test persons may, for example, internalize expected discrimination and subconsciously behave differently than male test persons. These issues are avoided in correspondence testing studies, where interpersonal contact between test subjects and employers is avoided via the use of written applications only. Many studies also suggest that the majority of employer discrimination occurs at this stage—that is, in callbacks to interviews from formal applications (Riach & Rich, 2002). As such, the correspondence testing methodology is equivalent to a randomized controlled experiment where gender is signaled by, for example, the names assigned to CVs.

The first field experiment to study gender discrimination in hiring was carried out by Peter Riach and Judith Rich (1987) in Victoria, Australia, using the correspondence testing methodology. This study finds that women encountered discrimination 40% more often than men. In a more recent work, Neumark (1996) studies the prevalence of gender discrimination in restaurant hiring in Philadelphia (United States) using both audit and correspondence testing methods. Female and male pairs were matched and trained to apply for waitress and waiter jobs in low-, medium-, and high-price restaurants after providing written CVs to restaurant managers. This experiment design therefore metes out possible differences in test person behavior by testing employer responses to both written applications and job interviews. Results showed that high-priced restaurants were significantly more likely to interview men than women (gender difference in callbacks to interviews) and significantly more likely to offer men jobs after interviews. Gender differences in hiring were not significant in low- and medium-priced restaurants. As wages and tip earnings are significantly higher in high-priced restaurants relative to low- and medium-priced restaurants, hiring discrimination in high-priced restaurants provides a partial explanation for within-occupation gender wage differentials in the restaurant sector.

Other correspondence tests of gender discrimination in hiring attempt to explicitly link hiring discrimination to statistical discrimination, either via experiments set up to test the effect of employer expectations concerning forthcoming childbirth among young female applicants (Duguet & Petit, 2006) or by signaling unobserved stereotypical personality traits associated with gender (Weichselbaumer, 2004). Emmanuel Duguet and Pascale Petit (2006) find that for qualified job positions, younger childless women have lower callbacks to interviews than men. This difference vanishes for older women, regardless of whether they have children. Doris Weichselbaumer (2004) tests whether women experience less hiring discrimination in traditionally male jobs if they signal stereotypical male personality traits (ambition, assertiveness, competitiveness, dominant individualism), which are normally not observed on written CVs but are nonetheless assumed to be important for the hiring decision. Three applications were sent to each job opening: two female and one male, where the male applicant and one of the female applicants signaled typically male personality traits while the other female applicant signaled traditionally female personality traits. Results showed that women were treated equally, regardless of variation in personality traits. Unfavorable

treatment for women applying to masculine occupations was not mitigated for women signaling masculine traits, and preferential treatment for women in feminine occupations was not threatened by masculine traits among female job candidates.

More recent field experiments attempt to link occupational segregation and hiring discrimination. Riach and Rich (2006) use the correspondence testing methodology to test for sexual discrimination in hiring in England, explicitly testing occupations that can be categorized as typically female, male, or mixed. Men were found to be discriminated against in the female occupation (secretary), and women in the male occupation (engineer). However, and somewhat unprecedented in the research literature to date, significant discrimination against men was found within mixed occupations (trainee chartered accountant and computer analyst programmer). Mangus Carlsson and Dan-Olof Rooth (2008) test 13 occupations in Sweden with varying gender composition and find no hiring discrimination against women in male-dominated occupations and a slight preference for women in female-dominated occupations as well as mixed occupations. This study therefore suggests that present hiring discrimination is not likely to explain substantial occupational segregation by gender.

Another innovative field study uses the introduction of blind auditions to analyze potential hiring discrimination against female musicians within symphony orchestras (Goldin & Rouse, 2000). In the 1970s and 1980s, many major U.S. orchestras changed their audition policies and adopted so-called blind auditions—that is, auditions behind a screen preventing the identification of applicants' gender. Interestingly, many auditions took the added precaution of muffling the sound of footsteps, which may otherwise have betrayed the gender of candidates, either by rolling out a carpet to the stage or by asking candidates to remove their shoes. Results from this study indicate that the adoption of a screen increased by 50% the probability that a female musician advanced beyond preliminary rounds and by several-fold the likelihood that a female musician would win in the final round.

A recent study on discrimination in hiring attributable to the gender composition of evaluation committees ties together the two strands of research discussed in this chapter—namely, gender differences in preferences and discrimination. Manuel Bagues and Berta Esteve-Volart (2008) use unique evidence provided by the public examination of candidates applying for positions within the Spanish Judiciary. Candidates are randomly assigned to evaluation committees with varying gender composition. Results from this study indicate that female candidates are less likely to be hired and male candidates more likely to be hired when randomly allocated to a committee with a larger share of female evaluators. A careful analysis of the data suggests that the quality of male candidates is overestimated in committees with female majorities. If women systematically overestimate the quality of male candidates, this could partially explain female reluctance to compete, as well as relatively poor performance in competitive environments, as noted in several studies that are discussed in the next section on gender differences in preferences.

The studies discussed in this section have spawned a large research interest in testing the presence of gender discrimination in different countries, labor markets, and populations. The consensus in this literature is that gender continues to be a salient factor in hiring within many labor markets and that more research is necessary to understand the extent to which discrimination explains labor market gaps today as well as the extent to which discrimination influences the preferences and human capital acquisition of coming generations.

Evidence on Gender Differences in Preferences

There is a vast literature aimed at explaining gender differences in preferences. Gender differences in preferences are interesting in and of themselves but also have potential importance in explaining gender labor market gaps. Men and women might have different preferences with respect to risk taking and competition, as well as different reactions to competition. For a survey of the research literature on gender differences in preferences, see Rachel Croson and Uri Gneezy (2009). Different degrees of risk taking among individuals can translate into different choices concerning jobs and occupations, according to the individuals' risk exposure to unemployment, work injuries, and so forth. If workers are compensated for such risks through higher earnings, one explanation for observed gender wage gaps would be gender differences in risk taking. If women are less likely to compete, it not only reduces the number of women who enter competitive environments—for example, in terms of competition for jobs or wage bargaining—but it also decreases the chances for women of succeeding in these competitions.

The general finding from studies on gender differences in risk-taking behavior, most of which are based on laboratory experiments, is that men are more prone to risk taking than women. There are several explanations as to why men are more risk-prone than women. A number of studies, for example, find men to be more overconfident than women. Muriel Niederle and Lise Vesterlund (2007) test this using a controlled laboratory experiment where pairs of two women and two men perform a task, namely adding up sets of five 2-digit numbers for 5 minutes. Participants were first asked to perform the task with piece-rate compensation and thereafter in a tournament setting. After having experienced both compensation schemes, participants were asked to choose one of the two payment schemes in the final round (either piece rate or tournament). Although there were no gender differences in performance in either compensation scheme, Niederle and Vesterlund find that 73% of men prefer the tournament scheme compared with only 35% of women. To elicit participants' beliefs on their relative tournament performance, at the end of the experiment, participants were asked to guess how their performances ranked relative to those of other participants. While 75% of men thought they were best in their group, only 43% of women held this belief. Participants who were more confident about their relative tournament performance were also more likely to enter a tournament.

Although numerous studies such as this have found men to be more overconfident than women on average, this difference may not hold for all tasks or for selected participants. One example of this is provided by Lena Nekby, Peter Skogman Thoursie, and Lars Vahtrik (2007), who use a large running race to study the behavior of women who choose to compete in a male-dominated setting and the consequences of this behavior on performance. Participants were given the opportunity to self-select into start groups based on individual assessments of running times. Overconfident behavior was measured as self-selection into start groups with lower time intervals than final results in the same race (or in the previous year's race) would motivate. Only runners who participated in the same race on the same course during the previous year were sampled so that results would not be contaminated by potentially lower knowledge of individual capabilities among women. Results show that there are environments (male dominated) in which the selection of women who participate are more likely to be confident and competitive and that, within this group, performance improves equally for both genders.

This result is important because gender differences in labor outcomes may be underestimated in selective environments, such as among executives. Earlier studies on the gender wage gap, for example, have found a glass ceiling for women in the upper part of the income-wage distribution (see, e.g., Albrecht, Björklund, & Vroman, 2003). One interpretation of a glass ceiling is that women have greater difficulties than men in obtaining higher positions for observationally equivalent qualifications due to unobservable differences in competitiveness. If there are women in male settings who are as competitive as men, women who compete for higher positions may be evaluated on average female behavior and statistically discriminated against and prevented from reaching higher positions. Another example of this is found among professional investors. Although men are more risk taking than women on average, there are no differences in risk propensities among professional investors, as indicated by their investment behaviors (see, e.g., Atkinson, Baird, & Frye, 2003). Thus, while fewer women are selected into positions such as investors and executives, those who do choose to enter these professions have similar risk preferences to the men in these positions.

In terms of gender differences in competitive behavior, men seem to choose competitive environments to a larger extent than women. In contrast to Niederle and Vesterlund (2007), there is also some evidence that men perform better than women in competitive environments. For example, in a study by Gneezy, Niederle, and Aldo Rustichini (2003), men and women were asked to solve mazes on a computer for 15 minutes. Participants were paid either according to a piece rate (a dollar amount per maze solved) or according to a winner-take-all tournament. Under the piece-rate scheme, no significant differences in performance between men and women were found. When participants were paid on a competitive basis, however, the performance of men significantly increased, relative to the performance of women. However, similar to this result concerning selective participation, there is evidence that women who choose to compete perform as well as men in these settings (see, e.g., Datta Gupta, Poulsen, & Villeval, 2005).

In a field study, Gneezy and Rustichini (2004) study children's running performance in a regular school physical education class. Children were asked to run twice over a short track while the teacher measured their speed. First, the children ran alone. Thereafter, the children were paired according to running times. This led to pairs of runners with different gender compositions. When the children ran alone, no gender differences in performance were noted. However, when the children ran in pairs—that is, in competition, running times for boys improved by 0.163 seconds on average, while the performance for girls decreased by 0.015 seconds relative to the when they ran alone. Boys were apparently spurred by competition to a larger extent than girls. One objection to these types of studies is the degree to which the produced results can be generalized to actual labor market settings. A similar concern is the extent to which results are task or location specific.

One area where competition has a potentially strong impact on labor market outcomes is in situations concerning bargaining. Deborah Small, Michele Gelfand, Linda Babcock, and Hilary Gettmen (2007) study bargaining using a laboratory setting where participants were told in advance that they would be paid between $3 and $10 for participation at the end of the experiment. After the participants finished their assigned tasks, the experimenter thanked them for their participation and asked, "Here is three dollars. Is three dollars OK?" Only 2.5% of female participants but 23% of male participants requested more money. In another study, Jenny Säve-Söderberg (2007) uses data from two surveys of recent law graduates on their transitions from school to work. Results in this study indicate that in wage negotiations, women consistently submitted lower wage bids than men. It was also found that women received lower wage offers, even when women and men submitted the same wage bid. Negotiating for wages was, however, found to lead to higher wage offers than not submitting any wage bid at all.

The discussion thus far has pointed out that there seems to be evidence of gender differences in preferences, but no discussion on the possible reasons why there might

be differences in preferences. Explanations for observed gender differences in preferences include possible genetic differences (see Colarelli, Spranger, & Hechanova, 2006). In contrast, Gneezy, Kenneth Leonard, and John List (2009) use an experimental approach to explore whether there are gender differences in selecting into competitive environments across cultures by examining a patriarchal society (the Maasai in Tanzania) and a matrilineal society (the Khasi in India). Similar to the evidence presented for Western societies, Maasai men opt to compete at twice the rate as Maasai women. The opposite result is found among the Khasi, where women choose the competitive environment considerably more often than men. These results suggest that existing societal structures are linked to observed gender differences in competitiveness. Croson and Gneezy (2009) summarize this literature and conclude that there is support for both genetic and cultural explanations for gender differences in competition. The interesting question for further research is what weight to attach to each of these factors in explaining gender labor market gaps.

Taken together, results from studies on gender differences in preferences suggest that men on average are more inclined to take risks than women and that men also prefer competitive environments to a larger extent. These findings potentially explain a portion of observed gender differences in the labor market because risk taking and competitive behavior are likely to be associated with pecuniary awards. To what degree observed gender differences in preferences are genetic or socially determined is an open question for further research.

Conclusion

This chapter has discussed the role of gender in the labor market from an economic perspective. Theoretically, there are potential supply-side differences by gender in skill acquisition and preferences that can explain why women earn less on average than men. On the other hand, there are also potential gender differences in opportunity—that is, discrimination prior to entering the labor market, affecting skill acquisition and working norms, as well as direct discrimination in the labor market, affecting employment and earning. Employers may, for example, expect women, to a larger extent than men, to have longer and more frequent absences from the labor market. Women as a group may then be perceived as a greater risk by employers then men, leading to lower wages and promotion possibilities and also to lower incentives to invest in human capital for future generations.

Evidence from studies on gender discrimination suggests that unequal treatment of equally qualified men and women continues to be important in the labor market. Experimental studies on discrimination tend, however, to be carried out on limited subsamples of the labor market, implying that it is difficult to make any general conclusions about the extent to which discrimination can explain gender gaps in the labor market.

Studies on gender differences in preferences, in turn, suggest that men on average are more inclined to take risks than women and that men also prefer competitive environments to a larger degree than women. These findings potentially explain a proportion of gender differences in the labor market because risk taking and competitive behavior are likely to be positively awarded by employers.

The consensus in the research literature on gender and economics is that both preferences and discrimination matter for labor market outcomes, outcomes that are of crucial importance for lifetime income, living standards, and intergenerational transmissions of income and opportunity, implying that attention must be paid to minimizing the impact these two overriding factors have in creating gender labor market gaps. There are also social changes in force that with time are likely to alter the underlying mechanisms behind these gender differences; among them, changing norms concerning the within-family allocation of labor between household and market, access to day care, and legislation promoting equal opportunity. The question remains to what degree social changes alone will eliminate differential opportunities by gender and to what degree more active measures are necessary to enforce equal opportunity.

References and Further Readings

Akerlof, G. A., & Kranton, R. E. (2000). Economics and identity. *Quarterly Journal of Economics, 115*(3), 715–753.

Albrect, J., Björklund, A., & Vroman, S. (2003). Is there a glass ceiling in Sweden? *Journal of Labor Economics, 21*(1), 145–177.

Altonji, J. G., & Blank, R. (2003). Race and gender in the labor market. In O. C. Ashenfelter & D. Card (Eds.), *Handbook of labor economics* (Vol. 3C, pp. 3143–3260). New York: Elsevier North-Holland.

Arrow, K. (1973). The theory of discrimination. In O. A. Ashenfelter & A. Rees (Eds.), *Discrimination in labor markets* (pp. 3–33). Princeton, NJ: Princeton University Press.

Ashenfelter, O. A., & Hannan, T. (1986). Sex discrimination and product market competition: The case of the banking industry. *Quarterly Journal of Economics, 101*(1), 149–174.

Atkinson, S. M., Baird, S. B., & Frye, M. B. (2003). Do female fund managers manage differently? *Journal of Financial Research, 26,* 1–18.

Bagues, M. F., & Esteve-Volart, B. (2008). *Can gender parity break the glass ceiling? Evidence from a repeated randomized experiment* (FEDEA Working Paper No. 2007-15). Madrid, Spain: FEDEA.

Becker, G. (1971). *The economics of discrimination* (2nd ed.). Chicago: University of Chicago Press.

Becker, G. (1993). *Human capital: A theoretical and empirical analysis, with special reference to education* (3rd ed.). Chicago: University of Chicago Press.

Beller, A. H. (1982). Occupational segregation by sex: Determinants and changes. *Journal of Human Resources, 17*(3), 371–392.

Bergmann, B. (1974). Occupational segregation, wages and profits when employers discriminate by race or sex. *Eastern Economic Journal, 1*(1–2), 103–110.

Black, S. E., & Brainard, E. (2004). Importing equality? The impact of globalization on gender discrimination. *Industrial and Labor Relations Review, 57*(4), 540–559.

Black, S. E., & Strahan, P. E. (2001). The division of spoils: Rent sharing and discrimination in a regulated industry. *American Economic Review, 91*(4), 814–831.

Blau, F. D., Brinton, M. C., & Grusky, D. B. (Eds.). (2006). *The declining significance of gender.* New York: Russell Sage.

Blau, F. D., & Kahn, L. M. (1996a). International differences in male wage inequality: Institutions versus market forces. *Journal of Political Economy, 104*(4), 791–837.

Blau, F. D., & Kahn, L. M. (1996b). Wage structure and gender earnings differentials: An international comparison. *Economica, 63,* S29–S62.

Blau, F. D., & Kahn, L. M. (2000). Gender differences in pay. *Journal of Economic Perspectives, 14*(4), 75–99.

Blinder, A. S. (1973). Wage discrimination: Reduced form and structural estimates. *Journal of Human Resources, 8,* 436–455.

Carlsson, M., & Rooth, D.-O. (2008). *An experimental study of sex segregation in the Swedish labour market: Is discrimination the explanation* (IZA Discussion Paper No. 3811). Bonn, Germany: Institute for the Study of Labor.

Colarelli, S. M., Spranger, J. L., & Hechanova, M. R. (2006). Women, power, and sex composition in small groups: An evolutionary perspective. *Journal of Organizational Behavior, 27,* 163–184.

Croson, R., & Gneezy, U. (2009). Gender differences in preferences. *Journal of Economic Literature, 47*(2), 448–474.

Darity, W. A., & Mason, P. L. (1998). Evidence on discrimination in employment: Codes of color, codes of gender. *Journal of Economic Perspectives, 12*(2), 63–90.

Datta Gupta, N., Poulsen, A., & Villeval, M.-C. (2005). *Male and female competitive behavior: Experimental evidence* (IZA Discussion Paper No. 1833). Bonn, Germany: Institute for the Study of Labor.

Dimand, R. W., Forget, E. L., & Nyland, C. (2004). Retrospectives: Gender in classical economics. *Journal of Economic Perspectives, 18*(1), 229–240.

Doeringer, P., & Piore, M. J. (1971). *Internal labor markets and manpower adjustment.* New York: D. C. Heath.

Duguet, E., & Petit, P. (2006). Hiring discrimination in the French financial sector: An econometric analysis on field experiment data. *Annals of Economy and Statistics, 78,* 79–102.

England, P. (1982). The failure of human capital theory to explain occupational sex segregation. *Journal of Human Resources, 17*(3), 358–370.

England, P. (1992). *Comparable worth: Theories and evidence.* New York: Aldine de Gruyter.

Eurostat. (2009). The European Union labour force survey. Available at http://epp.eurostat.ec.europa.eu/portal/page/portal/labour_market/earnings/main_tables

Gneezy, U., Leonard, K. L., & List, J. A. (2009). Gender differences in competition: Evidence from a matrilineal and a patriarchal society. *Econometrica, 77*(3), 1637–1664.

Gneezy, U., Niederle, M., & Rustichini, A. (2003, August). Performance in competitive environments: Gender differences. *Quarterly Journal of Economics,* 1049–1074.

Gneezy, U., & Rustichini, A. (2004, May). Gender and competition at a young age. *American Economic Review Paper and Proceedings,* 377–381.

Goldin, C. (2006). The rising (and then declining) significance of gender. In F. D. Blau, M. C. Brinton, & D. B. Grusky (Eds.), *The declining significance of gender?* New York: Russell Sage.

Goldin, C., & Rouse, C. (2000). Orchestrating impartiality: The impact of "blind" auditions on female musicians. *American Economic Review, 90*(4), 715–741.

Gundersson, M. (1989). Male-female wage differentials and policy responses. *Journal of Economic Literature, 27*(1), 46–72.

Heckman, J. (1998). Detecting discrimination. *Journal of Economic Perspectives, 12,* 101–116.

Heckman, J., & Siegelman, P. (1993). The Urban Institute audit studies: Their methods and findings. In M. Fix & R. J. Struyk (Eds.), *Clear and convincing evidence: Measurement of discrimination in America* (pp. 187–258). Washington, DC: Urban Institute Press.

Hellerstein, J., Neumark, D., & Troske, K. R. (2002). Market forces and sex discrimination. *Journal of Human Resources, 37*(2), 353–380.

Institute for Women's Policy Research. (2009). *The gender wage gap: 2008.* Available at http://www.iwpr.org/pdf/C350.pdf

Juhn, C., Murphy, K. M., & Pierce, B. (1991). Accounting for the slowdown in black-white wage convergence. In M. Kosters (Ed.), *Workers and their wages: Changing patterns in the United States* (pp. 107–143). Washington, DC: AEI Press.

Meng, X. (2004). Gender earning gap: The role of firm specific effects. *Labour Economics, 11*(5), 555–573.

Mincer, J. (1958). Investment in human capital and personal income distribution. *Journal of Political Economy, 66*(4), 281–302.

Mincer, J., & Polachek, S. (1974). Family investments in human capital: Earnings of women. *Journal of Political Economy, 82*(2), S76–S108.

Nekby, L., Skogman Thoursie, P., & Vahtrik, L. (2007). Gender and self-selection into a competitive environment: Are women more overconfident than men? *Economics Letters, 100,* 405–407.

Neumark, D. M. (1996). Sex discrimination in restaurant hiring: An audit study. *Quarterly Journal of Economics, 111*(3), 915–941.

Niederle, M., & Vesterlund, L. (2007). Do women shy away from competition? Do men compete too much? *Quarterly Journal of Economics, 122*(3), 1067–1101.

Oaxaca, R. L., & Ransom, M. L. (1999). Identification in detailed wage decompositions. *Review of Economics and Statistics, 81,* 154–157.

Olivetti, C., & Petrongolo, B. (2008). Unequal pay or unequal employment? A cross-country analysis of gender gaps. *Journal of Labor Economics, 26*(4), 621–654.

Pager, D. (2007). The use of field experiments for studies of employment discrimination: Contributions, critiques and directions for the future. *ANNALS of the American Academy of Political and Social Science, 609,* 104.

Phelps, E. S. (1972). The statistical theory of racism and sexism. *American Economic Review, 62,* 659–661.

Polacheck, S. W. (1975). Discontinuous labor force participation and its effect on women's market earnings. In C. B. Lloyd (Ed.), *Sex, discrimination, and the division of labor* (pp. 90–124). New York: Columbia University Press.

Polachek, S. W. (1984). Women in the economy: Perspectives on gender inequality. In U.S. Civil Rights Commission (Ed.), *Comparable worth: Issue for the 80s* (Vol. 1, pp. 34–53). Washington, DC: Government Printing Office.

Reskin, B. F., & Bielby, D. D. (2005). A sociological perspective on gender and career outcomes. *Journal of Economic Perspectives, 19*(1), 71–86.

Riach, P. A., & Rich, J. (1987). Testing for sexual discrimination in the labour market. *Australian Economic Papers, 26,* 165–178.

Riach, P. A., & Rich, J. (2002). Field experiments of discrimination in the market place. *Economic Journal, 112,* F480–F518.

Riach, P. A., & Rich, J. (2006). An experimental investigation of sexual discrimination in hiring in the English labor market. *B.E. Journal of Economic Analysis & Policy, 6*(2), Article 1. Available at http://www.bepress.com/bejeap/advances/vol6/iss2/art1

Säve-Söderbergh, J. (2007). *Are women asking for low wages? An empirical analysis of individual wage bargaining and ability signalling* (Working Paper No. 7/2007). Stockholm: Swedish Institute for Social Research.

Small, D., Gelfand, M., Babcock, L., & Gettman, H. (2007). Who goes to the bargaining table? *Journal of Personality and Social Psychology, 93,* 600–613.

Weiselbaumer, D. (2004, Spring). Is it sex or personality? The impact of sex-stereotypes on discrimination in applicant selection. *Eastern Economic Journal, 30,* 159–186.

55

Economics and Race

Sean E. Mulholland

Stonehill College

Race is a construction of society. These small, observable differences, often in pigmentation and physical characteristics, have, throughout time, played a role in defining and reinforcing other less easily observed differences. This is true both across groups and within groups. However, even using the term *groups* may be misleading. This spectrum of observable differences has two important consequences. First, unique individuals that may have little else in common are grouped as similar by others. Second, by being treated as a member of said group, one's own identity of self is altered. This chapter first looks at socioeconomic measures for those defined as members of certain racial groups. Traditional measures such as earnings, education, and segregation present the reader with foundational knowledge of racial differences across time and space. Second, the chapter discusses theories and empirical research that seek to explain these differences across and within these various racial groups, as well as policies seeking to reduce the disparate results.

To analyze the nexus between race and economics, a definition of race is required. Yet defining race as distinct, mutually exclusive categories is misleading at best. Physical characteristics, such as skin color, nose width, and hair texture, are often used to define race. Unfortunately, as any introductory anthropology text will tell you, human characteristics are on a continuous gradient, not in unique categories. Thus, much of the historical data presented and many of the academic works cited use basic categories such as black, white, and Asian in the analysis. New data and innovative researchers have begun to look within these groups, such as Asians with varying types of eyelids and the darkness of skin tone of blacks and African Americans, to gain a better grasp of the importance these subtle differences play within each traditional race category.

Attempting to group individuals into various categories in order to compare across and within groups often requires the use of averages or medians. No one is the average member of a group, and only one in millions is the median of that group. Thus, the average or median of the group one identifies with in no way reflects one's individual outcome.

One of the difficulties associated with empirical analysis is that correlation does not imply causation. Even though one group may have lower earnings or higher unemployment, this does not necessarily mean that it is due to current or past discrimination. For instance, as demonstrated in this chapter, African Americans have lower annual earnings than Asian Americans. Although one possible explanation may be current discrimination, another plausible hypothesis is that Asian Americans have more years of schooling, more years of experience, or another aspect that may affect the group's productivity and, therefore, earnings.

Characteristics, such as educational attainment, that affect a person's earnings may have been subject to past policies. The history of the United States includes a vast number of examples where minority groups have been at a disadvantage compared to settlers who were predominantly white, of northern European origins, and Protestant in faith. Any person who did not match this description had a significantly lower standing in early American society. Blacks were enslaved and perceived as objects, not as human beings; Chinese and Japanese immigrants were abused and denied citizenship, even into the second and third generations; Catholics were often treated with suspicion; and Jews were persecuted. Even the whites of southern or eastern European descent did not enjoy the same privileges and opportunities as the whites of, say, English or German origins. So while it may be the case that discrimination is not present in the current labor market, legacy effects, or past discrimination and social policies, may affect current economic outcomes. Thus, when analyzing differences in outcomes, researchers attempt to include as many current and past characteristics in their analyses as possible.

This chapter first lays out some current and historical statistics on earnings, education, geographic distribution, marital status, and occupational choices of African Americans and whites. It then discusses recent developments in the economic literature on how economists have attempted to explain these differences between African Americans and whites. Next, the chapter focuses on Asian Americans and research seeking to explain their economic welfare. Then this chapter discusses the effects of the Civil Rights Act of 1964 and affirmative action. Because the chapter is about race, it focuses on differences between African Americans, Asians, and whites. Ethnic differences, such as the differences between Cuban and Dominican, or Korean and Chinese, though important because of their unique histories and experiences, are discussed only when the emphasis is on differences within race categories.

Data on African Americans

Figure 55.1 shows the median earnings of full-time, year-round male workers by race in the United States from 1955 to 2007 as reported by the Current Population Survey of the U.S. Census.

These data, reported in real 2007 dollars, show that full-time, year-round white workers received higher earnings than African American workers. In 1955, the median earnings for full-time white male workers were $29,618, while African American workers earned about 61% of whites' amount: $18,033. Over time, however, full-time African American workers have witnessed a decline in earnings disparity. By 1980, African American males earned about 70% of male white workers' earnings. By 2007, the ratio of African American male to white male worker was about 0.78. Although this chapter focuses on differences within the United States, it is important to stress that race also matters in most other countries. For example, African Canadian men earn 18% less than Canadian whites, and nonwhite immigrants in Britain earn less than similarly skilled white immigrants (Howland & Sakellariou, 1993; Stewart, 1983).

Figure 55.2 tells a slightly different story for full-time, year-round female African American and white workers.

In 1955, the median earnings for full-time white female workers were $19,339, while for African Americans, the year's earnings were about 51% of whites' amount: $9,933. Over time, however, full-time African American female workers have witnessed a greater decline in earnings disparity than their male counterparts. By 1980, African American females earned about 93% of female white workers' earnings. By 2007, the ratio of African American female to white female worker had fallen to about 0.86.

These differences are often attributed to racial discrimination. However, at least a portion of this difference may occur even if market participants are not prejudiced. One possible nonprejudicial difference may result from differences in education. Figure 55.3 shows the average years of schooling for African American and white workers in the United States from 1880 to 2000 (Turner, Tamura, & Mulholland, 2008).

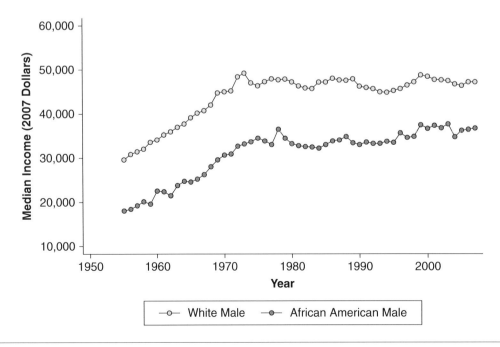

Figure 55.1 Median Income: African American and White Male Workers, Full-Time, Year-Round, 1955–2007

SOURCE: U.S. Census Bureau (2008b).

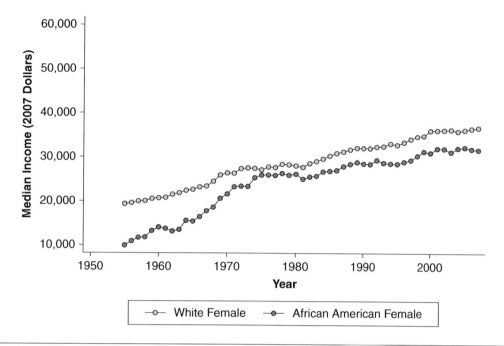

Figure 55.2 Median Income: African American and White Female Workers, Full-Time, Year-Round, 1955–2007
SOURCE: U.S. Census Bureau (2008b).

Again, one sees a similar pattern: Whites averaged just over 4 years of schooling in 1880, while African Americans averaged just over one half of a year of schooling. Even with educational disenfranchisement among African Americans in the South, African Americans witnessed an increase in years of schooling. By 1950, the average years of schooling completed by an African American worker were just over 6.5 years. White workers in 1950 had 9.5 years of schooling. In 2000, African American workers possessed just over 12 years of schooling, while whites had completed just over 13 years of schooling. Thus, some of the differences in earnings may be explained by differences in educational attainment.

Furthermore, geography can play a role, especially if local labor markets differ. Table 55.1 shows the geographic distribution of whites and African Americans across the various regions of the United States. African Americans are located primarily in the South, while whites are more concentrated in the Northeast and West. John Bound and Richard Freeman (1992) emphasize that labor is largely

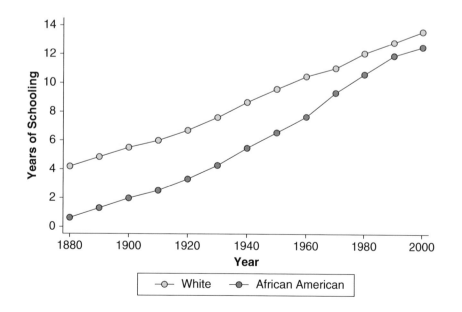

Figure 55.3 Average Years of Schooling: African American and White Workers, 1880–2000
SOURCE: Turner, Tamura, and Mulholland (2008).

Table 55.1 Geographic Distribution by Race: African Americans and Whites

	Percentage of Total Group Population	
	African American	White
Region		
Northeast	18.00	19.54
Midwest	18.78	25.22
South	53.62	34.25
West	9.60	20.98

SOURCE: U.S. Census Bureau (2000).

NOTE: Percentages may not add to 100 due to rounding.

Table 55.2 Marital Status by Race: African Americans and Whites

	Percentage of Total Group Population	
	African American	White
Married, spouse present	31.8	53.9
Married, spouse absent	1.7	1.2
Widowed	6.2	6.1
Divorced	11.0	9.8
Separated	4.4	1.8
Never married	45.0	27.2

SOURCE: U.S. Census Bureau (2008a).

NOTE: Percentages may not add to 100 due to rounding.

immobile in the short run, and these differences in regional location will also shape labor market outcomes, such as earnings. Because African Americans are more highly concentrated in the South, where wages and earnings are lower, a portion of the white–black earnings gap may be due to geographic location.

Another factor that affects the incentives and constraints of individuals is their family arrangements. Table 55.2 shows the marital status of African Americans and whites. Whites are much more likely to be married, with their spouse present, than African Americans. In addition, African Americans are much less likely to have ever married. Empirically, studies show anywhere from 0 to a 50% wage premium for married men. Theoretically, this marriage premium could arise from various sources. First, marriage can make men more productive by allowing them to specialize in nonhousehold production. Second, it could be that employers discriminate in favor of married men, and third, it could be that married men possess some unobservable characteristic that makes them more productive. Attempting to eliminate much of the unobservable characteristics, both Harry Krashinsky (2004) and Kate Antonovics and Robert Town (2004) use twin data to study the impact of marriage on wages. Although Krashinsky finds a 6% marriage premium for within-twin estimates, Antonovics and Town find a 27% married wage premium. Because African Americans are less likely to be married, they are either unable to specialize in nonhousehold production or less likely to possess the unobservable characteristic that makes them more productive.

The industry in which one chooses to work may also affect labor market outcomes. Table 55.3 shows the distribution of employment by industry and race. African Americans are more likely to work in industries that face more regulation: transportation and utilities, education and health, public administration, and the armed forces. African Americans are also more likely to work in information and leisure and hospitality. When one compares industrial distribution, the difficulty often arises as to whether occupation is a choice or a constraint. If one believes that firms in certain industries discriminate against certain types of employees, the data above may reflect more of a constraint and less of a decision by those employed.

Given that these differences may be choices not affected by race, economists must search for ways to isolate how and where discrimination is possible and, more important, how to disentangle its effects from these and other possible explanations.

Theories of Discrimination

Employer-Based Discrimination

In 1955, Gary S. Becker wrote his Nobel Prize–winning doctoral dissertation on the economics of discrimination. His work advances the theory that discrimination, contrary to the Marxist view, is costly to the individual who discriminates. He hypothesizes that because employer-based discrimination is costly, in the sense that employers must forgo profits in order to pay for their tastes for discrimination, increased competition will lower profits and thus the ability of discriminating firms' to practice discrimination. According to Becker (1957),

> If an individual has a "taste for discrimination," he must act as if he were willing to pay something, either directly or in the form of a reduced income, to be associated with some persons instead of others. When actual discrimination occurs, he must, in fact, either pay or forfeit income for this privilege. This simple way of looking at the matter gets at the essence of prejudice and discrimination. (p. 14)

Table 55.3 Industrial Employment Distribution by Race: African Americans and Whites

	Percentage of Total Group Population	
	African American	*White*
Agriculture, forestry, fishing, and hunting	0.29	1.68
Mining	0.28	0.57
Construction	4.25	8.60
Manufacturing	9.88	11.09
Wholesale and retail trade	12.48	14.60
Transportation and utilities	7.78	5.02
Information	2.75	2.30
Financial activities	6.11	7.06
Professional and business services	9.61	10.92
Educational and health services	26.27	20.38
Leisure and hospitality	9.48	8.70
Other services	4.45	4.69
Public administration	6.31	4.38
Armed forces	0.04	0.01

SOURCE: U.S. Census Bureau (2008a).

NOTE: Percentages may not add to 100 due to rounding.

Therefore, the market structure in the output market affects the ability of individual firms to discriminate. By refusing to hire individuals based on characteristics that have nothing to do with productivity and thereby reducing the pool of possible employees, discriminating firms will, in the long run, face higher labor costs. Increased competition in the output market will force these firms to find lower cost production methods. Increased competition will squeeze higher cost firms, including discriminating firms, out of the market. According to Becker's theory, only nondiscriminating firms will continue to operate. The result also suggests an important implication for wage equality across races. In the long run, each employee will be paid his or her marginal product multiplied by the price of the output she or he is producing. Or stated another way, workers will be paid a wage that reflects exactly the value they add to the firm. Without any racial or other type of discrimination, wage gaps between equally skilled and productive whites and non-whites should no longer exist.

This does not mean that average wage inequality across races will disappear or even decline. Kenneth Arrow (1972, 1973) and Edmund Phelps (1972) stress that a skills gap and imperfect information can explain racial wage differentials. African American workers have on average fewer years of schooling; thus, their wages may be lower. One way to test Becker's (1957) model is to analyze firms that have experienced an increase in competition through an exogenous change in regulation. In the 1970s, the banking system experienced such a regulatory change.

Before the 1970s, banks were unable to operate across state lines. Banking regulations up to this point required banks to operate as independent entities within each state border. Although Bank of America could have branches in any state, each state operation had to operate independently. Customers who wanted to change the address of their accounts were required to open new accounts if they moved across state lines. These restrictions limited banking competition to within the state borders; banks in one state were not in competition with banks in another.

Innovations, such as the automated teller machine, that make distance banking easier weaken the desire and ability of banks to fight regulatory changes that eliminated these state controls. Most states deregulated geographic restrictions on banking between the mid-1970s and 1994, when the federal Riegle-Neal Act effectively eliminated these restrictions. Granting banks the ability to compete across state borders increased the level of competition in the banking industry.

Becker's theory predicts that such an increase in competition will lead to the elimination or, at least, the reduction of a wage gap that exists due to racial discrimination. To test the validity of that prediction, Ross Levine, Alexey Levkov, and Yona Rubinstein (2008) collected data on earnings of black and white non-Hispanic male workers aged between 18 and 65 from 1977 to 2007. They also compared the actual ratio of interracial marriages in each state from the 1970 census to the same ratio based on hypothetical random pairing of partners to assess the level of racial bias. Their research showed that in the states with high levels of racial prejudice, the increase in market competition significantly reduced the wage gap between African American and white workers. In the states with lower-than-average bias, where the actual and hypothetical interracial marriage ratios were very similar, the reduction was almost unnoticeable. Their results suggest that Becker's theory holds empirically only when the initial degree of racial bias in the economy is high. If the degree of racial bias is already low, less of the wage differential is due to racial discrimination, and thus, increases in competition will have little effect on racially based wage differentials.

The banking industry is not the only example of increased competition in the output market due to regulatory changes. Looking at the racial wage gap in the for-hire trucking industry, Nancy Rose (1987) finds that increased competition due to deregulation reduced the racial wage gap in the trucking industry. Expanding on this work, James Peoples and Lisa Saunders (1993) find evidence that deregulation reduced the wage gap for both union and nonunion drivers. Peoples and Rhoda Robinson (1996) extend this line of research to the telecommunications industry by showing that the earning disparity between black and white males decreased with the divestiture of AT&T and the resulting increase in competition. John Heywood (1998) examines the effects of deregulation in airlines, trucking, rail, and telecommunications on racial earnings. His results suggest that all industries, except airlines, witnessed a decline in the racial earnings gap.

Becker (1957) writes that, in the long run, discriminating businesses, operating in a competitive market, will become less profitable than the nondiscriminating ones, lose market share, and eventually fail. In response, discriminating firm owners could simply sell their firms, offer their labor for a salary, and earn higher returns. However, rational people seek to maximize their utility, not their monetary earnings alone. Though monetary income has a large effect on utility, prejudiced employers would rather suffer pecuniary losses than employ minority workers. Kerwin Charles and Jonathan Guryan (2007) claim that, because of such preferences, those formerly prejudiced employers would remain prejudiced as employees and work only at firms whose owners were equally prejudiced. In an economy with a significant number of such white, racially biased workers, there might still be some prejudiced firms at which these biased employees will work. If at least one such firm operated, wage gaps could continue to exist.

In the same study, Charles and Guryan (2007) also find that there is a close relationship between the level of prejudice and the magnitude of the wage gap. They construct a prejudice measure by using six questions asked in the General Social Survey (GSS) from 1972 to 2004. These questions included respondents' "feelings about interracial marriage, their sense of whether racially restrictive housing covenants were appropriate, their views about children being racially segregated in schools, and their view on whether the government should be obligated to help blacks." They find the racial wage gap to be larger in communities with higher levels of prejudice. Charles and Guryan conclude that the most prejudiced region in the United States is the Southeast, while New England and the West Coast are the least.

Customer-Based Discrimination

Though Becker's model predicts that increased competition will eliminate employment discrimination in the long run, this is not true for customer discrimination. Customer discrimination exists when customers have and are willing to pay for their discriminatory preferences. If customers wish to avoid contact with a certain group of people, customers will repeatedly pay more to avoid contact with individuals from that group. Lawrence Kahn and Derek Shearer (1988) investigate racial differences in the 1985 to 1986 salaries of individual basketball players and the attendance effects of replacing one black player with a white player. Holding constant various factors, such as productivity, market, and player draft position, they find that black players earn 20% less than white players. In addition, they show that "replacing one black player with an identical white player raises home attendance by 8,000 to 13,000 fans per season" (p. 40).

Even without direct contact, customer discrimination may be present. Clark Nardinelli and Curtis Simon (1990) address this possibility by analyzing the value as listed in the 1989 issue of *Beckett Baseball Card Price Guide* of Topps baseball cards issued in 1970. Because the two important measures of card value, player's lifetime performance and the number of cards issued, are easy to measure, they are able to construct a model to determine the effect of race on card value. They find a card value gap of 10% among hitters of comparable ability and a 13% gap in card value among pitchers. Torben Anderson and Sumner La Croix (1991) look at baseball cards from 1977, when the number of cards issued did not vary by player, and find results that support those found by Nardinelli and Simon.

Keith Ihlanfeldt and Madelyn Young's (1994) work on fast-food restaurants in Atlanta show that a 10-percentage-point increase in white customers reduces African American wages by about 1%. Ihlanfeldt and David Sjoquist (1991) use the racial composition of residents in subcounty areas as proxies for customer composition and find that the racial composition of an employment area affects the type of job held by black workers. Using data from four metropolitan areas, Holzer and Ihlanfeldt (1998) show that racial composition of the customers affects whom employers hire. They find that the magnitude of these effects vary by "occupational category and the degree of direct contact with customers on the job" (p. 862). Holzer and Ihlanfeldt suggest that these differences may be increasing in importance as the distribution of jobs shift from those with little customer contact, such as manufacturing, to those with greater customer contact, such as retail.

Neighborhood Effects

Customer discrimination may also account for the failure of inner-city blacks to migrate to the suburbs (Kain, 1968). Transportation difficulties or information limitations may also result in spatial mismatches (Holzer, Ihlanfeldt, & Sjoquist, 1994). Unfortunately, discrimination in the credit market may reduce the ability of blacks to move households or businesses. Faith Ando (1988) finds blacks are less likely to be approved for loans even after accounting for various factors that influence approval rates. David Blanchflower, Phillip Levine, and David Zimmerman (2003) find that "black-owned firms, in particular, are substantially more likely to be denied credit than other groups and are charged higher interest rates for those loans that are approved than are other firms that are otherwise comparable" (p. 930). Furthermore, a study of the Boston mortgage market during the early 1990s reveals substantial racial differences in the likelihood that a mortgage application would be rejected, even after controlling exhaustively for differences in credit history and various other factors (Munnell, Tootell, Browne, & McEneaney, 1996).

The lack of migratory ability leads to another possible reason for differences in earnings discussed in a vast literature on peer group effects or social interaction and neighborhood effects (Borjas, 1995; Case & Katz, 1991; Glaeser, Sacerdote, & Scheinkman, 1996). Building on this work and the work of Kain (1968), David Cutler and Edward Glaeser (1997) find African Americans in segregated communities are worse off than those in nonsegregated communities. Cutler and Glaeser show that a one-standard-deviation reduction in segregation would eliminate one third of the education and earnings gap between whites and blacks.

Statistical Discrimination

Statistical discrimination, first described by Arrow (1972, 1973) and Phelps (1972) and further developed theoretically by Joseph Altonji and Charles Pierret (2001), occurs when an individual's estimated productivity is based on the group to which he or she is categorized and not by his or her individual characteristics. William Wilson (1996) reveals that both black and white employers are reluctant to hire young, black urban males. In addition, "statistical discrimination can be quite damaging to both the efficiency of market allocations and to equity. This is due to the very real possibility that the empirically valid statistical generalizations lying at the heart of such discrimination can be self-fulfilling prophecies" (Loury, 1998, p. 123; see also Coate & Loury, 1993; Lundberg & Startz, 1983).

Recent Research on African American Discrimination

These categorizations can be based on a large range of factors. Racial stereotypes that are the bases of prejudices are often identified with one or more physical characteristics. But as suggested theoretically by Kevin Lang (1986), speech patterns and nonverbal communication may also be a source of discrimination. A recent study of speech patterns carried out by Jeffrey Grogger (2008) collected the phone recordings from interviews for the National Longitudinal Survey of Youth and removed all the information that could reveal each interviewee's gender, race, and age. He then asked people to identify the speaker of each recording as either black or white. Comparing the reported earnings of the black interviewees identified as sounding black to those black interviewees identified as sounding white, he finds that blacks who sound black earn 10% less than blacks who do not. In comparison, whites who sound black earn 6% lower salaries than whites who do not.

Not only does it appear that African American–sounding speech may be associated with wage differentials, but a person's name may also play a role. Marianne Bertrand and Sendhil Mullainathan (2003) test whether having a typically white-sounding name is more advantageous for job applicants than having a black-sounding name. Using the frequency of names given to African American and white newborns in the state of Massachusetts between 1974 and 1979, they sent four resumes to each job posting in *The Boston Globe* and the *Chicago Tribune*. Each group of four resumes, which included detailed information, had two of high quality and two of low quality. One high-quality and one low-quality resume were always given distinctly African American names, while the other two would always get white-sounding names.

Resumes with white-sounding names had a callback rate of 10%, while black-sounding names had a rate of only 6.7%. The results suggest that an applicant with a white-sounding name can, on average, expect an invitation for a job interview for every 10 resumes submitted, while an applicant with an African American–sounding name will only receive 1 for every 15. This result suggests that employer-based discrimination plays a role in the interview process.

However, statistical discrimination and neighborhood effects may also be present. Bertrand and Mullainathan's (2003) experiment also looks at the effect a person's address has on whether an applicant receives an invitation for an interview. Consistent with neighborhood effects, applicants whose neighborhood residence was whiter, with higher earnings and levels of education, realized a greater callback rate than those whose address represented the lower earning, less educated, predominately African American neighborhoods. However, living in a whiter, higher earning, more educated area neighborhood does not help the applicants with distinctively black names very much.

Moreover, employers seemed to be more willing to acknowledge the difference between high- and low-quality white applicants than differences between high- and low-quality African American applicants. High-quality white applicants received invitations for interviews from about 11% of their applications, while low-quality white applicants received invitations from only 8.8%. In contrast, high-quality blacks experienced a callback rate of just less than 7%, while low-quality blacks received callbacks on 6.4%.

Speculating that distinctively African American–sounding names convey information about socioeconomic background, Roland Fryer and Steven Levitt (2004) seek to determine consequences and causes of black-sounding names. Using California birth certificates, they collected data on the first names given to black and white non-Hispanic newborns between 1961 and 2000. Using these data, they created the black name index (BNI) to measure the distinctiveness of a given name by dividing the fraction of black children given that name over the fraction of both black and white children receiving the exact name. Babies born in predominantly black hospitals, over time, were more likely to receive distinctively black names than those born in predominantly white hospitals. Blacks living in segregated neighborhoods were more likely to give their children distinctively black names than those living in integrated communities. Moreover, a woman's first name can indicate to her potential employer the circumstances she grew up in and her current situation, both of which can imply her labor productivity. Fryer and Levitt also found that a woman with a BNI of 100 (a name that no whites have) is 20.9% more likely to have been born to a teenage mother and 31.3% more likely to have been born out of wedlock than a similar black woman with a BNI of around 50. Once a potential employer realizes that a resume has been submitted by an individual with a distinctively black name, he or she has a reason to believe the applicant has poor credentials without reading it in detail. This could explain why black applicants receive so few callbacks, regardless of their qualifications. If this is employer-based discrimination, instead of statistical discrimination, then the employers simply reject the applicant because of their taste for discrimination.

Focus on African Americans versus white, however, may miss a subtle yet important difference in how various shades of discrimination are expressed. Preferences for those with lighter pigmentation have been cited by historians who show that both whites and lighter skinned blacks often found ways to maintain distinct social networks (Gatewood, 2000). These culturally defined restrictions have serious consequences. Robert Margo (1992) finds that light-complected slaves were more likely to receive skill training. Shawn Cole (2005) reports that 40% of freed slaves were mulattoes, and less than 6% of slave sales in late eighteenth- and early nineteenth-century Louisiana involved mulatto slaves.

Looking at Los Angeles neighborhoods in the 1900s, James Johnson, Elisa Bienenstock, and Jennifer Stoloff (1995) discover that the combination of black racial identity and a dark skin tone reduces an individual's odds of working by 52%, after controlling for education and including quality, age, and criminal record. A lighter complexion is also associated with higher incomes and life chances than a darker complexion in blacks in the United States (Keith & Herring, 1991; Ransford, 1970). Andrew Goldsmith, Darrick Hamilton, and William Darity Jr. (2006) find that blacks with lighter-colored skin earn higher wages than black workers whose skin color is identified as medium and dark. The wage gap between medium-skinned blacks and whites is 16%; the wage gap between dark-skinned blacks and whites is 17%. In comparison, the gap between light-skinned blacks and whites is only 7.6%.

Data on Asian Americans

Repeating the data exercise performed with African Americans but substituting data on Asian Americans reveals a different story. Even though it has been fewer than 70 years since some of their ancestors were held in internment camps, Asian Americans seem to be faring better than the population at large.

These data, reported in real 2007 dollars, show that full-time, year-round white and Asian American male workers have, at least for the last 20 years, similar earnings.

In 1988, the median earnings for full-time white male workers was $47,598, while for Asian Americans, the yearly earnings were about 99% of whites' earnings: $47,287. Over time, however, full-time Asian American male workers have witnessed slightly higher earnings growth than white male workers. By 2007, Asian American males earned about 108% of what white male workers earned.

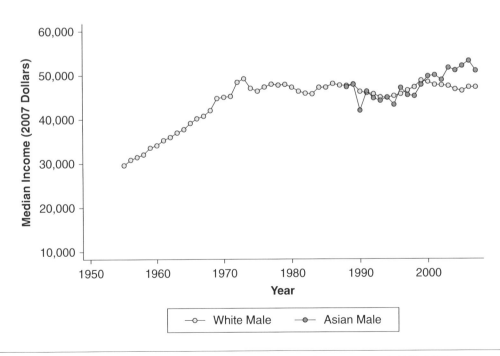

Figure 55.4 Median Income: Asian American and White Male Workers, Full-Time, Year-Round, 1955–2007

SOURCE: U.S. Census Bureau (2008b).

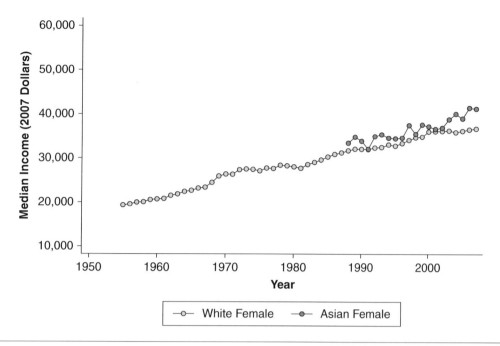

Figure 55.5   Median Income: Asian American and White Female Workers, Full-Time, Year-Round, 1955–2007

SOURCE: U.S. Census Bureau (2008b).

Figure 55.5 shows a similar story for full-time, year-round female Asian American workers relative to their white female counterparts.

In 1988, the median income for full-time white female workers was $31,701, while Asian American women earned about $33,426. By 2000, Asian American females earned about 104% of what white female workers earned. By 2007, the ratio of Asian American female earnings to white female worker earnings was about 1.12.

Presenting the difference in education will help to suggest why both Asian American females and males now earn more than their respective white colleagues. Figure 55.6 shows the average years of schooling for Asian American and white workers in the United States from 1940 to 2000 (Ruggles et al., 2008)

In the 1940s, whites had just over 7 years of schooling, while Asian Americans had just fewer than 6.9 years of schooling. By 1980, Asian Americans had on average

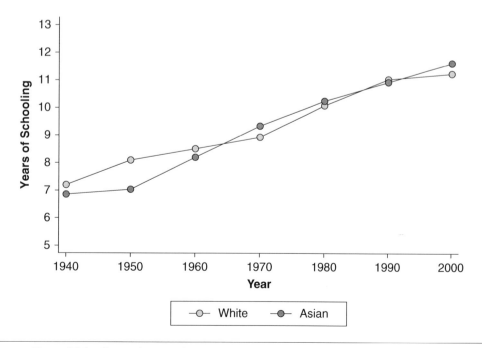

Figure 55.6   Average Years of Schooling: Asian American and White Workers, 1940–2000

SOURCE: Data from Ruggles et al. (2008).

obtained more years of schooling than whites. The ratio of the average years of schooling for Asian Americans relative to whites was 1.04. From 1980 to 2000, this ratio varied little.

Geography can also play a role, especially if local labor markets differ. Table 55.4 shows the geographic distribution of whites and Asian Americans across the various regions of the United States. Asian Americans are primarily located in the west and northeast, much like their fellow white citizens, where wages and earnings are higher.

Another factor that affects the incentives and constraints of individuals is their family arrangement. Table 55.5 shows the marriage status of Asian Americans and whites. As presented above, empirically, studies show anywhere from 0 to a 50% wage premium for married men. Because Asian Americans are more likely to be married and less likely to be divorced than white Americans, Asian Americans can more easily specialize in nonhousehold production, or they are more likely to possess the unobservable characteristic that makes them more productive. Asian Americans are also less likely to be divorced than whites.

Industry of choice may also affect labor market outcomes. Table 55.6 shows the distribution of employment by industry and race. Although Asian Americans are more likely than whites to work in some industries that face greater regulation, such as education and health, they are also more likely to work in industries that face much less regulation: manufacturing, information, financial, professional and business services, leisure and hospitality, and other services. As mentioned above, the difficulty often arises as to whether occupation is a choice or a constraint. If one believes that firms in certain industries discriminate against certain types of employees, the data above may reflect a constraint and not a decision by those employed.

Research on Asian American Discrimination

The data presented in Table 55.6 suggest that Asian Americans have attained higher levels of earnings, education, and family stability than the overall population, the other minorities, or both. A study conducted by Barry Chiswick in 1983 seems to reinforce the idea that Asian Americans have achieved higher socioeconomic welfare. Using data from the 1970 census of population, which identifies Asian Americans by their origins—Chinese, Japanese, and Filipino—Chiswick compares U.S.–born Asian male workers' earnings and employment to a control sample of U.S.–born whites. Chiswick finds that Asian American men had higher levels of earnings, employment, and education in 1969 than white men. In aggregate, the Asian Americans earned about $10,000, while white men earned only $9,900; Asian Americans had completed more schooling (12.6 vs. 11.9 years), and worked more hours (48.7 vs. 48.3 weeks). However, only 77% of Asian American men were married and living with their wives, compared to a rate of 86% for white men.

Within the Asian American group, the Chinese Americans and Japanese Americans performed better in all categories than the whites; however, the Filipino Americans fared worse. In 1969, Chinese Americans earned $10,400, had completed 13.1 years of schooling, and worked 47.6 weeks; the Japanese Americans earned $10,300, had been in school for 12.7 years, and worked 49.4 weeks. The Filipino Americans earned only $7,000, had completed 11.3 years of schooling, and worked 46.8 weeks. After controlling for human capital, demographics, and geographic area variables, the weekly earnings for those of Chinese, Japanese, and Filipino origins were lower than those of the whites by 2%, 4%, and 16%, respectively. But because both Chinese Americans and Japanese

Table 55.4 Geographic Distribution by Race: Asian Americans and Whites

	Percentage of Total Group Population	
	Asian American	*White*
Region		
Northeast	15.03	19.54
Midwest	11.80	25.22
South	20.82	34.25
West	52.35	20.98

SOURCE: U.S. Census Bureau (2000).

NOTE: Percentages may not add to 100 due to rounding.

Table 55.5 Marital Status by Race: Asian Americans and Whites

	Percentage of Total Group Population	
	Asian American	*White*
Married, spouse present	58.3	53.9
Married, spouse absent	2.6	1.2
Widowed	4.5	6.1
Divorced	4.3	9.8
Separated	1.4	1.8
Never married	28.9	27.2

SOURCE: U.S. Census Bureau (2008a).

NOTE: Percentages may not add to 100 due to rounding.

Americans worked more weeks than the whites, their annual earnings were higher. On the other hand, the Filipino Americans had both significantly lower weekly earnings and more workable hours. Chiswick (1983) concludes that those of Chinese and Japanese origin, despite being minorities, are as successful in the labor market as whites and therefore do not suffer any discrimination.

Pramod Junakar, Satya Paul, and Wahida Yasmeen (2004) claim that the results obtained by Chiswick (1983) might not be very accurate because "estimates of discrimination based on studies of earnings are likely to be underestimates as they usually ignore the probability of finding employment in the first place" (p. 6). However, the year analyzed by Chiswick, 1969, was a year of full employment, with the unemployment rate of only 2.1%—the lowest in the post–World War II period. Therefore, the probability of being without a job was very small, regardless of race or ethnicity.

Even though Chiswick (1983) finds no evidence of discrimination against the Chinese and Japanese born in the

Table 55.6 Industrial Employment Distribution by Race: Asian Americans and Whites

	Percentage of Total Group Population	
	Asian American	*White*
Agriculture, forestry, fishing, and hunting	0.38	1.68
Mining	0.07	0.57
Construction	2.89	8.60
Manufacturing	13.44	11.09
Wholesale and retail trade	12.28	14.60
Transportation and utilities	3.92	5.02
Information	2.33	2.30
Financial activities	7.52	7.06
Professional and business services	13.97	10.92
Educational and health services	21.48	20.38
Leisure and hospitality	12.08	8.70
Other services	6.20	4.69
Public administration	3.45	4.38
Armed forces	0.00	0.01

SOURCE: U.S. Census Bureau (2008a).

NOTE: Percentages may not add to 100 due to rounding.

United States and some researchers have subsequently concluded similarly, others have found that Asian Americans still earn less than similarly educated whites. One explanation for this discrepancy is the heterogeneity within Asian Americans. Although Chinese Americans and Japanese Americans tend to do well with respect to education and earnings, other nationalities, such as the Filipino Americans and southeastern Asians do not fare as well. The combination of these Asian subgroups into one large category creates the gap between the Asian Americans in general and whites in data from the 1970s.

Another possible weakness of Chiswick's (1983) study is the exclusion of foreign-born Asian Americans. A study conducted by Zhen Zeng and Yu Xie (2004) looks at place of birth and education to explain why there is no consensus on whether the Asian Americans have lower or higher earnings than whites and, if they do, why this gap in earnings exists between similarly educated Asian Americans and whites. Using 1990 census data supplemented with data from the National Survey of College Graduates, they divide Asian American male workers into three distinct groups: U.S.–born Asian Americans (UBA), U.S.–educated Asian immigrants (UEAI), and foreign-educated Asian immigrants (FEAI). FEAI are compared to the UEAI to assess the effects of the place of education on earnings, UEAI to UBA for the effects of nativity, and UBA to U.S.–born whites (UBW) for the effects of race.

Zeng and Xie (2004) show that UEAIs have 2 more years of schooling and 37% higher earnings than FEAI. In addition, one third of UEAIs work in professional occupations, while only 13% of FEAIs do. Although Asian Americans have higher earnings overall than whites, they earn less at each level of education, which means they have to obtain more education in order to have parity in earnings. UEAIs earn more than FEAIs but still less than UBAs. That said, it seems as though earnings differ both by nativity and by place of education. The results from the two models show that UBWs have the highest earnings, followed UBAs (5% less than UBW), UEAIs (5% less than UBA), and FEAIs (16% less than UEAI). However, only the difference between UEAI and FEAI is statistically significant. Although the effects of race and nativity are very small and negligible, where Asian Americans are educated has a substantial effect on their earnings. The results show that much of the discrimination of Asian Americans is directed against the immigrants, especially those who have completed their education prior to arriving in the United States. This suggests that Chiswick's (1983) decision to only include U.S.–born Asian Americans may be driving his results.

Chiswick's (1983) results might also be biased because he includes wages, salaries, and earnings from self-employment. Using data from the 1992 Characteristics of Business Owners (CBO) survey, Alicia Robb and Robert Fairlie (2007) show that Asian American–owned firms are 20.6% more likely to have profits of $10,000 or more,

27.2% more likely to have employees, and have 60% higher sales than white-owned businesses. Asian American–owned firms also have higher survival rates: an 18% probability of closure versus 23% for white-owned firms. By including self-employed Asian Americans, who on average are much more successful than the typical owner, Chiswick's results might be upwardly biased. Moreover, people who are self-employed usually do not face the kind of discrimination from their employers that wage and salary earners face; thus, including business owners in an attempt to measure employer discrimination may reduce the likelihood of findings even if customer and statistical discrimination is present.

Because the growth of the Asian population in the United States is a recent phenomenon, there are relatively few studies that analyze the labor market outcome experienced by Asian Americans. The few studies available seem to disagree as to whether Asians in the United States are subject to discrimination in the labor market. The problems that scholars have to confront are lack of adequate data and the heterogeneity of the Asian group in terms of their ethnicity, nativity, and education.

Policy

Two policies most often cited as having the greatest impact on racial discrimination are the Civil Rights Act of 1964 and affirmative action. Before the enactment of the Civil Rights Act of 1964, employment and contractual actions based on race were legal. The act established the Equal Employment Opportunity Commission (EEOC) and prohibits employment discrimination by large employers (more than 15 employees), whether or not they have government contracts. The resulting reduction in the black–white wage gap was large and abrupt (Card & Krueger, 1992; Donohue & Heckman, 1991).

Though the Civil Rights Act of 1964 sought to prohibit current discrimination, affirmative action was developed to overcome persistent disparate outcomes. The result was a system of preferences for minority college applicants, minority job applicants, and minority-owned businesses. Affirmative action has generated much debate on both constitutional and equity grounds. Although space here does not allow for a thorough discussion of the challenges to current court decisions or a thorough presentation of research looking at the redistributive and efficiency effects of affirmative action, a few noted theoretical and empirical studies are presented.

Finis Welch (1976) develops a theoretical model with taste-based discrimination and a quota-based system to show that affirmative action may cause unskilled workers to be assigned to skilled positions and vice versa. Lundberg and Startz (1983) develop a model to show that affirmative action can increase efficiency in human capital investment but lower efficiency in the labor market, resulting in an ambiguous net effect. Coate and Loury (1993)

find that affirmative action can, theoretically, have negative effects on those it seeks to help. They show that if "identifiable groups are equally endowed ex ante, affirmative action can bring about a situation in which employers (correctly) perceive the groups to be unequally productive, ex post" (p. 1220).

Empirically, Jonathan Leonard (1984a) finds no negative productivity effects on federal contractors after affirmative action implementation. Leonard (1984b) finds that the share of employment accounted for by minorities rose at contractor establishments covered by affirmative action between 1974 and 1980, while those accounted for by white males declined. Using microlevel data, Holzer and David Neumark (2000b) discover that employers using affirmative action in job searches recruit "more extensively and screen more intensively" and "are more likely to ignore stigmatizing personal characteristics and histories when they hire" (p. 269). These affirmative action hires, however, come at the expense of white males, who see a 10% to a 15% decline in employment at these establishments.

In a meta-analysis of sorts, Stephan Thernstrom and Abigail Thernstrom (1997) report that black enrollments as a percentage of all enrollments in schools, excluding historically black colleges and universities, rose from 1.8% in 1960 to 9.0% in 1994. William Bowen and Derek Bok (1998) report that from 1960 to 1995 the percentage of blacks aged 25 to 29 who had graduated from college rose from 5.4% to 15.4%. Looking at data for selective institutions, Frederick Vars and Bowen (1998) and Bowen and Bok (1998) find some evidence that test scores are worse predictors for blacks. Thus, because African Americans with similar standardized test scores to whites' perform better in college and are more likely to graduate than their white classmates, affirmative action may have simply reduced the bias present in the college application process.

Although the program may place slightly less qualified individuals into positions and possibly lead to negative fit or stigma effects, it may also create positive externalities. Minorities benefiting from affirmative action may generate social benefits, such as working in underserved areas, which do not generate private pecuniary benefits. Overall, Holzer and Neumark (2000a) conclude, "Affirmative action offers significant redistribution toward women and minorities, with relatively small efficiency consequences" (p. 559).

Conclusion

Race continues to play a role in whether and how employees are hired and compensated, the level of education one receives, and where and how one lives. As has been shown, many of these effects can be measured in various manners. Competitive markets can, theoretically in the long run, reduce employer-based discrimination and eliminate earnings and wage differences based on characteristics that have no effect on labor productivity. However, customer and statistical discrimination can persist. Unfortunately, discrepancies in employment opportunities, wages, neighborhood effects, and loan approval can simply occur because of one's name, accent, address, or physical characteristics. Even with equal opportunity legislation and (or despite) affirmative action, African Americans appear to experience a greater difference in earnings relative to whites and Asian Americans.

References and Further Readings

Altonji, J. G., & Pierret, C. R. (2001). Employer learning and statistical discrimination. *Quarterly Journal of Economics, 116*(1), 313–350.

Anderson, T., & La Croix, S. J. (1991). Customer racial discrimination in Major League Baseball. *Economic Inquiry, 29,* 665–677.

Ando, F. (1988). Capital issues and the minority-owned business. *Review of Black Political Economy, 16*(4), 77–109.

Antonovics, K., & Town, R. (2004). Are all the good men married? Uncovering the sources of the marital wage premium. *American Economic Review, 94*(2), 317–321.

Arrow, K. (1972). Some mathematical models of race in the labor market. In A. H. Pascal (Ed.), *Racial discrimination in economic life* (pp. 187–204). Lexington, MA: Lexington Books.

Arrow, K. (1973). The theory of discrimination. In O. A. Ashenfelter & A. Rees (Eds.), *Discrimination in labor markets* (pp. 3–33). Princeton, NJ: Princeton University Press.

Becker, G. S. (1957). *The economics of discrimination.* Chicago: University of Chicago Press.

Bertrand, M., & Mullainathan, S. (2003, January). *Are Emily and Greg more employable than Lakisha and Jamal? A field experiment on labor market discrimination* (Poverty Action Lab Paper No. 3). Cambridge: MIT.

Blanchflower, D. G., Levine, P. B., & Zimmerman, D. J. (2003). Discrimination in the small business credit market. *Review of Economics and Statistics, 85*(4), 930–943.

Borjas, G. (1995). Ethnicity, neighborhoods, and human capital externalities. *American Economic Review, 85*(3), 365–390.

Bound, J., & Freeman, R. (1992). What went wrong? The erosion of the relative earnings and employment among young black men in the 1980s. *Quarterly Journal of Economics, 107,* 201–232.

Bowen, W. G., & Bok, D. (1998). *The shape of the river.* Princeton, NJ: Princeton University Press.

Card, D., & Krueger, A. B. (1992). School quality and black-white relative earnings: A direct assessment. *Quarterly Journal of Economics, 107*(1), 151–200.

Case, A. C., & Katz, L. F. (1991). *The company you keep: The effects of family and neighborhood on disadvantaged youths* (NBER Working Paper No. 3705). Cambridge, MA: National Bureau of Economic Research.

Charles, K. K., & Guryan, J. (2007). *Prejudice and the economics of discrimination* (NBER Working Paper No. W13661). Cambridge, MA: National Bureau of Economic Research.

Chiswick, B. R. (1983). An analysis of the earnings and employment of Asian-American men. *Journal of Labor Economics, 1*(2), 197–214.

Coate, S., & Loury, G. C. (1993). Will affirmative-action policies eliminate negative stereotypes? *American Economic Review, 83*(5), 1220–1240.

Cole, S. (2005). Capitalism and freedom: Manumissions and the slave market in Louisiana, 1725–1820. *Journal of Economic History, 65*(4), 1008–1027.

Cutler, D., & Glaeser, E. (1997). Are ghettos good or bad? *Quarterly Journal of Economics, 112*(3), 827–872.

Donohue, J. J., III, & Heckman, J. (1991). Continuous versus episodic change: The impact of civil rights policy on the economic status of blacks. *Journal of Economic Literature, 29*(4), 1603–1643.

Fryer, R., & Levitt, S. (2004). The causes and consequences of distinctively black names. *Quarterly Journal of Economics, 119* (3), 676–805.

Gatewood, W. B. (2000). *Aristocrats of color: The black elite, 1880–1920.* Fayetteville: University of Arkansas Press.

Glaeser, E. L., Sacerdote, B., & Scheinkman, J. A. (1996). Crime and social interactions. *Quarterly Journal of Economics, 111*(2), 507–548.

Goldsmith, A., Hamilton, D., & Darity, W., Jr. (2006). From dark to light: Skin color and wages among African Americans. *Journal of Human Resources, 42*(4), 701–738.

Grogger, J. (2008, July). *Speech patterns and racial wage inequality* (Harris School Working Paper No. 08.13). Chicago: University of Chicago.

Heywood, J. S. (1998). Regulated industries and measures of earnings discrimination. In J. Peoples (Ed.), *Regulatory reform and labor markets* (pp. 287–324). Boston: Kluwer Academic.

Holzer, H. J., & Ihlanfeldt, K. (1998). Customer discrimination and the employment outcomes of minorities. *Quarterly Journal of Economics, 113*(3), 833–865.

Holzer, H. J., Ihlanfeldt, K. R., & Sjoquist, D. L. (1994, May). Work, search, and travel among white and black youth. *Journal of Urban Economics,* 320–345.

Holzer, H. J., & Neumark, D. (2000a). Assessing affirmative action. *Journal of Economic Literature, 38,* 483.

Holzer, H. J., & Neumark, D. (2000b). What does affirmative action do? *Industrial Labor Relations Review, 53*(2), 240–271.

Howland, J., & Sakellariou, C. (1993). Wage discrimination, occupational segregation and visible minorities in Canada. *Applied Economics, 25*(11), 1413–1422.

Ihlanfeldt, K. R., & Sjoquist, D. L. (1991). The role of space in determining the occupations of black and white workers. *Regional Science and Urban Economics, 21*(2), 295–315.

Ihlanfeldt, K. R., & Young, M. V. (1994). Intrametropolitan variation in wage rates: The case of Atlanta fast-food restaurant workers *Review of Economics and Statistics, 76*(3), 425–433.

Johnson, J. H., Jr., Bienenstock, E. J., & Stoloff, J. A. (1995). An empirical test of the cultural capital hypothesis. *Review of Black Political Economy, 23*(4), 1–27.

Junakar, P. N., Paul, S. & Yasmeen, W. (2004, June). *Are Asian migrants discriminated against in the labour market? A case study of Australia* (IZA Discussion Paper No. 1167). Bonn, Germany: Institute for the Study of Labor.

Kahn, L., & Shearer, D. (1988). Racial differences in professional basketball players' compensation. *Journal of Labor Economics, 6*(1), 40–61.

Kain, J. D. (1968). Housing segregation, Negro employment, and metropolitan decentralization. *Quarterly Journal of Economics, 82,* 175–197.

Keith, V., & Herring, C. (1991). Skin tone and stratification in the black community. *American Journal of Sociology, 97,* 760–778.

Krashinsky, H. A. (2004). Do marital status and computer usage really change the wage structure? *Journal of Human Resources, 29*(3), 774–791.

Lang, K. (1986). A language theory of discrimination. *Quarterly Journal of Economics, 101*(2), 363–382.

Leonard, J. (1984a). Anti-discrimination or reverse discrimination? The impact of changing demographics, Title VII, and affirmative action on productivity. *Journal of Human Resources,19*(2), 145–174.

Leonard, J. (1984b). Impact of affirmative action on employment. *Journal of Labor Economics, 2*(4), 439–463.

Levine, R., Levkov, A., & Rubinstein, Y. (2008). *Racial discrimination and competition* (NBER Working Paper No. 14273). Cambridge, MA: National Bureau of Economic Research.

Loury, G. C. (1998). Discrimination in the post–civil rights era: Beyond market interactions. *Journal of Economic Perspectives, 12*(2), 117–126.

Lundberg, S., & Startz, R. (1983). Private discrimination and social intervention in competitive labor markets. *American Economic Review, 73*(3), 340–347.

Margo, R. A. (1992). Civilian occupations of ex-slaves in the Union army, 1862–1865. In R. W. Fogel & S. L. Engerman (Eds.), *Without consent or contract: Markets and production: Technical papers, Vol. 1* (pp. 170–185). New York: W. W. Norton.

Munnell, A. H., Tootell, G. M., Browne, L. E., & McEneaney, J. (1996). Mortgage lending in Boston. *American Economic Review, 86*(1), 25–53.

Nardinelli, C., & Simon, C. (1990). Customer racial discrimination in the market for memorabilia: The case of baseball. *Quarterly Journal of Economics, 110,* 575–595.

Peoples, J., & Robinson, R. (1996). Market structure and racial and gender discrimination: Evidence from the telecommunications industry. *American Journal of Economics and Sociology, 55,* 309–326.

Peoples, J., & Saunders, L. (1993). Trucking deregulation and the black/white wage gap. *Industrial and Labor Relations Review, 47,* 23–35.

Phelps, E. S. (1972). The statistical theory of racism and sexism. *American Economic Review, 62,* 659–661.

Ransford, E. (1970). Skin color, life chances, and anti-white attitudes. *Social Problems, 18,* 164–178.

Robb, A., & Fairlie, R. (2007, January). *Determinants of business success: An examination of Asian-owned businesses in the United States* (IZA Discussion Paper No. 2566). Bonn, Germany: Institute for the Study of Labor.

Rose, N. L. (1987). Labor rent sharing and regulation: Evidence from the trucking industry. *Journal of Political Economy, 95,* 1146–1178.

Ruggles, S., Sobek, M., Alexander, T., Fitch, C. A., Goeken, R., Hall, P. K., et al. (2008). *Integrated public use microdata series: Version 4.0* [Machine-readable database]. Minneapolis: Minnesota Population Center. Retrieved October 20, 2008, from http://usa.ipums.org/usa

Stewart, M. B. (1983). Racial discrimination and occupational attainment in Britain. *Economic Journal, 93*(371), 521–541.

Thernstrom, S., & Thernstrom, A. (1997). *America in black and white: One nation, indivisible.* New York: Simon & Schuster.

Turner, C. S., Tamura, R., & Mulholland, S. E. (2008). *Productivity differences: The importance of intra-state black-white schooling differences across the United States, 1840–2000* (MPRA Paper No. 7718). Munich: University Library of Munich, Germany.

U.S. Census Bureau. (2000). *Census 2000.* Available at http://www.census.gov/main/www/cen2000.html

U.S. Census Bureau. (2008a). *Current population survey, annual social and economic supplement.* Available at http://www.census.gov/cps

U.S. Census Bureau. (2008b). *Historical income tables: People* (table P-36). Available at http://www.census.gov/hhes/www/income/histinc/incpertoc.html

Vars, F. E., & Bowen, W. G. (1998). Scholastic aptitude, test scores, race, and academic performance in selective colleges and universities. In C. Jencks & M. Phillips (Eds.), *The black-white test score gap* (pp. 457–479). Washington, DC: Brookings Institution.

Welch, F. (1976). Employment quotas for minorities. *Journal of Political Economy, 84*(4, Pt. 2), S105–S139.

Wilson, W. J. (1996). *When work disappears: The world of the new urban poor.* New York: Knopf.

Zeng, Z., & Xie, Y. (2004). Asian-Americans' earnings disadvantage reexamined: The role of place of education. *American Journal of Sociology, 109*(5), 1075–1108.

56

ECONOMIC ANALYSIS OF THE FAMILY

STEVEN HORWITZ

St. Lawrence University

One of the notable characteristics of economics over the end of the twentieth and start of the twenty-first century is the extension of economic analysis to subject matter that was not traditionally thought of as economic. Books like *Freakonomics* (Levitt & Dubner, 2005) demonstrate these new applications of economics, and these books' popular success indicates that there is a demand for the use of economics to shed light on a variety of social issues. The origins of this extension of economics to the noneconomic in this fashion are often associated with work at the University of Chicago, in particular the work of 1992 Nobel Laureate Gary Becker. Much of Becker's (1960, 1973, 1974) seminal work in economics was devoted to showing how "the economic way of thinking" could enhance our understanding of a wide variety of social phenomena. One of the first social institutions Becker explored in this fashion was the human family.

In the almost 50 years since that first contribution, the economics of the family has exploded as an area of economic research. A whole variety of family-related phenomena, from how people choose marriage partners to how families make decisions about market versus household production to how household production is divided to how many children couples have to why and how frequently they get divorced to large-scale issues about the evolution of the form and function of the family, have all been subject to economic analysis. This literature has grown substantially in the last few decades, and this entry should be seen as an overture to the much richer work cited in the references.

Theory

The economics of the family has explored almost every aspect of what might be termed the *life cycle* of the family: the time from marriage to divorce or death. In each case, the general strategy is similar in that it makes use of the economic way of thinking to analyze the choices that men and women make about the formation, continuation, and dissolution of families. At its most basic, the economic way of thinking proceeds as follows:

1. Identify the relevant decision makers and attempt to assess the costs and benefits they face in making the decisions in question, recognizing that both costs and benefits may have a large subjective component to them.
2. Note that the relevant costs and benefits are on the margin and that costs may be opportunity costs rather than explicit ones.
3. See whether the empirical data are consistent with predictions that emerge from the specification of the marginal costs and marginal benefits.

With respect to the family, this means that the economist is trying to understand decisions from marriage to childbirth to divorce as being the outcome of marginal benefit versus marginal cost comparisons by the people involved. When economists first started analyzing family issues this way, many objected that it was an attempt to reduce the romance and mystery of marriage and family down to cold calculations, especially financial ones. A further look at how the economics of the family proceeds shows that these concerns are largely misplaced.

The economics of the family simply argues that like all other human decisions, considerations of costs and benefits matter for decisions about the family, and the relevant costs and benefits need not be construed as narrowly financial or pecuniary. It is the focus on the margin and the comparison of costs and benefits that makes it an economic analysis, not any specification of what those costs and benefits might be.

The simple example of choosing to get married illustrates many of these points. First, how do spouses decide that each is the one? Conventionally, one might tell stories of love at first sight, or stars in their eyes, or a sign of some sort. All of those might be part of the decision, but at the very least, the lovers must consider whether someone "better" is out there. After all, rarely do we find perfection in a partner. Why stop looking now and choose this person to marry? From an economic standpoint, we might raise a number of considerations.

The love that spouses have for one another is a significant benefit from deciding to get married. They do get to spend the rest of their lives with one another. There are more material benefits to marriage, or more precisely to household formation. For the purposes of this chapter, we will assume that marriage and household formation happen together, even though in reality the latter sometimes comes first, which is in itself a question in the economics of the family: What are the costs and benefits of living together versus marriage? If the couple marries and moves in together, the spouses benefit from economies of scale (lower average costs of production). For example, if each one has a vacuum cleaner and a washer and dryer, they no longer need two of each. It is also cheaper, per person, to cook for two people, not to mention saving one set of utility payments.

On the cost side, prospective spouses have to consider the down sides of sharing space and resources. One of those costs is *imperfect preference satisfaction.* When decisions are made jointly, one or both partners frequently do not get exactly what they would like, especially as compared to each making the decision alone. The joint decision about what car to buy is often a good example here, because neither party gets exactly what he or she wants, as the number of people driving minivans they would not have bought on their own suggests. Compromise is a cost of marriage. Marriage is also a long-term legal commitment that is not cheap to end. Finally, there is the opportunity cost question: Could one have done better? Analysts of the economics of marriage have constructed search cost models that attempt to show at what point it no longer makes sense to keep looking for someone better, much like the way in which drivers at some point decide they do not think there will be a cheaper gas station up the street and just take the one at the next corner.

Economics can also be used to analyze changes in the frequency of marriage overall. For example, economists know that marriage rates have fallen over the twentieth century, and they know that people have been getting married later and later in life over the last 50 years. One way of looking at both phenomena is to ask whether the net benefits of marriage have fallen, especially for younger people, in recent decades. Historically, when women's economic opportunities were fewer and less well paying, the benefits to them from marriage were greater. Being able to share the much higher income of a husband was the key to economic survival for many women, certainly so if they wished to be able to support any children they might have.

Even for men, the benefits of marriage have fallen in modern times. To see why, one needs to examine the concept of household production. One way of conceiving the household that marriage creates is that it has a series of outputs it produces, and the members of that household are the human capital of the production process that leads to that output. The outputs of household production include everything from children and child rearing to cooking and cleaning to managing the household finances. Assuming the household is not completely self-sufficient, it will also require resources from outside the household (what is often termed *market production*) to be combined with household labor to produce those outputs. As with any other production process, household production involves a division of labor, in this case between the spouses.

Over time, the costs and benefits of marriage have changed. In particular, as women have become more equal participants in the labor market and as less labor has been required for household production, thanks to increased technology and more widely available and reasonably priced market substitutes, the benefits related to the household division of labor have fallen substantially. Women no longer need access to men's market incomes, and men no longer need someone to manage the household. Because of microwaves, automatic clothes washers and dryers, the much lower cost of dining out or using a dry cleaners, and the widespread use of child care providers, households produce fewer goods and services themselves and require less labor in the process. These changes in the costs and benefits of marriage have in turn led to different choices by men and women. These changes can help explain why one sees later and fewer marriages.

One of the important contributions to the economics of marriage is the idea of *assortative mating.* If one assumes that individuals are net benefit maximizers and that the marriage market has enough participants (both male and female), theory predicts that we will get assortative mating, which means that people will tend to marry those who bring similar levels of benefits to marriage as they do. Economists use the terms *high* and *low benefits* to refer to the human capital of the potential marital partners. High-benefits partners are those who bring high earnings potential, higher education (implying, perhaps, more interesting and desirable consumption preferences), and good health. In general, a high-benefit partner will do better marrying another high-benefit partner than a low-benefit one, unless there is a very unequal distribution of the total benefits of the marriage. Given the competitiveness of the marriage market, that outcome is unlikely. And because high-benefit people are so likely to marry each other, there are few high-benefit people left for low-benefit people to marry; hence, they tend to marry other low-benefit people, resulting in the pattern predicted by assortative mating.

Economic theory can also say something about the decision to have children and how many. Prior to economics examining this question, there were few rigorous examinations of how fertility decisions got made. Once again, the logic of costs and benefits and the margin are central to the analysis. Children clearly provide their parents with benefits, both psychological (or emotional) and economic. Having a child can be a great source of joy to parents. Children also have value as economic assets, particularly as a source of support for parents in their old age. Children can also provide labor for market or household production. All of these benefits must be weighed against the costs. Obviously, children must be fed, clothed, and educated, each of which requires explicit monetary costs from the parents. Children also demand much of the parents' time, reducing the time they have for market production, other forms of household production, or leisure. Having children is a loss of freedom for the parents, because their choices now must take into account the effects on the child. Finally, there are economies of scale in child production. The average cost of raising a child declines with each successive child, because the marginal costs of additional children are declining. It clearly does not require twice as much labor to raise two children as it does one, and things like clothes and toys can often be passed down to the younger child.

Even choices about raising children can be understood using economics. If parents wish to discourage problematic behavior in children, thinking in terms of incentives, costs, and benefits can be very effective. Take the case of children who forget to bring their lunches to school. The parents can simply bring the children's lunches whenever this happens. Soon, the children will recognize that they can impose the costs of their own mistakes on the parents with the parents' cooperation, which dramatically reduces children's incentive to remember to bring their lunches. The parents, in this case, would like to find a way not to bear the costs of the children's decision. Specifically, one might wish to strive for situations where the parents are indifferent to the children's decision to remember or forget their lunches. The simplest way to do that is to refuse to bring the lunches. If the children remember them, great. If the children forget, the parents bear no cost; the children will survive a day without lunch and will learn that remembering is their responsibility and that they will pay the costs of not remembering. In essence, the parents have used responsibility as a proxy for the role played by property rights in economic analyses. By delineating what is whose, property rights set up spheres of responsibility, and parental assignments of responsibility do as well. As long as parents are willing to stick to those assignments, they can prevent children from imposing costs on them and creating the inefficiencies that go with those costs (Wittman, 2005).

One of the most famous economic explanations of parent–child relationships is Gary Becker's (1991) Rotten Kid Theorem. He argues that if parents are altruistic and wish to help their children, those children will act in ways that maximize family income. Put differently, we might expect that a child whose parents want to help him or her would choose to shirk obligations to the whole family and attempt to live off the parents' generosity. Becker's analysis suggests that this expectation is wrong. The child's degree of selfishness turns out not to matter, because even the most self-interested child will still take into account the effect of his or her actions on the rest of the family, effectively internalizing all possible externalities. As Becker points out, this theorem can be applied beyond the parent–child relationship to a variety of interactions within the family. He also notes that this does not mean that families will be without conflict. All the theorem predicts is that all have an interest in maximizing total family income. How that income is distributed among beneficiaries can still be the source of much conflict.

The economics of divorce is in many ways the mirror image of the economics of marriage. When the benefits to marriage fall, ceteris paribus, the opportunity cost of divorce falls and one sees more divorces; when the benefits to marriage rise, one should see fewer divorces. If couples gain less from the specialization that the household division of labor involves, then the incentive to stay married in the face of any sort of dissatisfaction with the marriage—especially of a psychological or emotional nature—is that much less. The legal environment matters a great deal here as well, because there are significant transaction costs to a divorce (much more so than a marriage). If the law makes divorce costly and difficult, one should see fewer divorces, even if couples are unhappy. To the extent the law reduces the transaction costs associated with divorce, divorce rates will rise, all else equal. As some have noted, these legal rules are not completely external to the economics of marriage. If the economic benefits to marriage were falling, one would expect that the margin of unhappiness that would produce a possible divorce would be lower as well (i.e., people will put up with less unhappiness if they are not getting other benefits from the marriage). In turn, this would produce a greater demand for divorces, which might well pressure political and legal institutions to reduce the transaction costs of divorce. A complete economics of the family has to account for the possible endogeneity of the institutional framework within which individuals decide.

Applications and Empirical Evidence

Understanding some of the basic theory behind the economics of the family can help economists make sense of a great deal of history and current economic and demographic data. The evolution of the Western family over the last several hundred years illustrates a number of the core economic principles discussed in the prior section. The transition from agriculture to industry is particularly instructive.

Several features of the family in the era of agriculture are worth noting. First, marriage was predominantly based on economic considerations rather than emotional ones. Marriage was necessary for survival, so finding a good mate was much more akin to finding a good work partner than anything else. Love, as we understand it today, was much more the province of the very, very few who did not have to worry about day-to-day survival. Second, the household was run by the husband. In this world, there was no real distinction between market and household production, because even crops that were sold on the market were produced by the household. Although women still disproportionately labored at what one today would call household production, they, along with children, were also expected to help with the crops or the cattle. And all of this was under the direction and supervision of the man. Third, children were viewed as economic assets. They were needed to contribute to production. This explains why families in the past (and families in agricultural areas today) tended to be larger. With falling marginal costs of children and potentially rising marginal benefits for the first several children, having a family of five, six, or seven made much more economic sense.

Industrialization changed the costs and benefits facing a number of family-related decisions and thereby changed the way families look and function. The crucial change was that the development of factories meant the physical separation of market and household production as men went out to work to earn an income, eventually leaving women at home in charge there. This heightened the division of labor within the family, which reached its peak in the late-nineteenth-century concept of men's and women's separate spheres. By ending the economic partnership component of marriage, industrialization was also a catalyst for the development and spread of love-based marriages. Finally, industrialization led to higher wages, which eventually allowed children and women to get out of the factories and into the homes, once their incomes were not necessary for survival and comfort. One result of this development was that children progressively lost their roles as economic assets and acquired new costs, because they could now devote time to education rather than production. This shift in the relative costs of children led to the (still ongoing) reduction in the size of the family and the related development of increasingly reliable birth control technology. Many of the features we associate with the modern Western family are products of the transition from agriculture to industrialization and the way in which it altered the costs and benefits facing parents. Economic theory is extremely useful in elucidating the process by which that evolution occurred.

As noted briefly earlier, one of the notable demographic trends of the last 40 or 50 years has been the decline in the marriage rate and the rise in the median age of first marriage. Between 1950 and 2000, the percentage of women aged 20 to 24 who were never married jumped from 32.3% to 72.8%, with the male numbers being 59.0% and 83.7%. For those aged 25 to 29, one sees a tripling of the percentage of women never married (38.9% in 2000) and a more than doubling of the male percentage (51.7% in 2000). The rates for those aged 30 to 34 also more than doubled in that 50-year period. The median age of first marriage for men rose from 23.0 to 26.9 and for women from 20.3 to 25.1 over roughly the same 50-year period. The overall marriage rate fell from 10.7% to 8.2%, and consistent with what theory would predict, birthrates over that period fell by 50% (Jacobsen, 2007).

Economic theory offers several possible explanations for the changes in the marriage rate, all of which emerge from the basic insight that marginal benefits and costs matter when people make marriage decisions. Women's greater productivity in the market has reduced the differences in comparative advantages between men and women, thereby reducing the benefits from the elements of specialization and exchange that characterize marriage. As men's and women's human capital look increasingly similar, the benefits of marriage fall while the costs remain roughly the same. This tendency may be somewhat offset by elements of assortative mating in that as men's and women's human capital converge, their tastes and the opportunity cost of their time converges as well, which might lead to more complementary consumption preferences, which would in turn increase the benefits of marriage. As marriage has evolved from narrowly economic to more about emotional and psychological factors, concerns about complementarities in production have gradually been replaced by concerns about complementarities in consumption. Signals about what one reads, watches, listens to, or eats are becoming far more relevant to the marital decision than what one does for a living or one's preferences about household or market production.

Men's incomes relative to women have fallen, and this is another potential factor. Men may delay marriage until they have levels of income that are, in their minds, sufficient in comparison to that of potential mates, perhaps because they wish to ensure a certain level of power in the household. A smaller income gap between men and women would mean it might take more time for men to get to that threshold, thereby leading to later first dates of marriage by men.

Two longer run social changes are of relevance here as well. Aside from the decline in the direct benefits of marriage, family formation may offer fewer benefits than in the past because more and more of the social functions that were once met by the family are now met outside of it. Other social institutions have, over time, taken on more of the economic, educational, religious, and social functions of the family, leaving the family with the core developmental and socialization functions (though market substitutes such as paid child care exist here too). These changes mean that families are less important to achieving important social goals, reducing the benefits of marriage. At the same time, substitutes for marriage are less costly than they used to be since social disapproval of nonmarital cohabitation has almost disappeared, allowing couples (including same-sex ones) to get many of the remaining benefits of household formation and family outside legal marriage.

Countertrends for each of these explanations have also been identified in the literature, because respecification of the relevant costs and benefits can produce different predictions. For example, the reduction in the social functions of the family might make marriage more attractive to women who wish to pursue a career, do not want to engage in much household production, and would prefer having a committed companion to share valuable leisure time. As with other areas in economics, the economics of the family continues to explore which costs and benefits seem to be the most powerful in explaining observed outcomes.

The decline in birthrates also reflects powerful economic factors. The shift from agriculture to industry and the corresponding shift of children from being net producers to being net consumers are clearly borne out in the data. At the same time, the development of more reliable contraception, most likely an endogenous response to children becoming increasingly a net cost to parents, and changes in women's expectations about their own participation in market production have contributed to the fall in birthrates. In addition, reductions in infant and child mortality have made it possible for parents to have a given number of children survive to adulthood with fewer pregnancies and births. The decline in the birthrate may reflect not just a desire for fewer children but an increase in the efficiency of the cycle from pregnancy to adulthood. In addition, children were for many years a source of support for adults in their old age. With higher levels of wealth, parents are more able to save for their own old age, particularly through organized retirement plans, both public and private. This also reduces the benefits of having children.

Models of child production decisions often treat the decision as one about child-based consumption. That is, parents wish to produce a certain combination of the number of children they have and the investment in each of those children that delivers a multiplied total of child-based consumption. The investment can take the form of either parental time or market-acquired goods and services. In these models, the growth in parental wages over the last several decades has both income and substitution effects on child-based consumption. Rising income will lead parents to want more of it. However, rising wages imply rising opportunity costs of having children, which will reduce the amount of child-based consumption being sought because parents substitute less-time-intensive forms of consumption than those involving children. However, the increase in wages can also lead to families substituting market goods and services for their own time in the production of child-based consumption (e.g., hiring a nanny, providing children more toys to keep them entertained after school, or even sending older children to a boarding

school). It might also be cheaper as wages rise to increase parents' child-based consumption by investing more resources in a small number of children rather than having more children, even given the economies of scale in child production.

The empirical evidence on the size of some of these effects varies. Empirical studies in the United States and Europe indicate that a 10% increase in women's wages will produce anywhere from an 8% to a 17% decline in births, depending on the wealth of the region being studied, while a 10% increase in men's wages would increase births by anywhere from 10% to 13% (Winegarden, 1984). The negative elasticity associated with women's wages reflects the substitution effects of women's time, while the positive elasticity of men's wages reflects the pure income effect that a higher male wage has for his wife. Even with correlation data such as these, causality remains controversial: Do women have fewer children because they are working more, or are they working more because they are having fewer children? Economists do not have a very good understanding of how long-run changes in the economy affect social choices, and standard econometric studies can show only correlation, not causation.

An additional application of the basic economic theory of the family regards the division of labor within the household. The standard model argues that the spouse with the lowest opportunity cost of his or her time as measured by their market wage should specialize in household production, while the other should specialize in market production. The model assumed that differences in wages between men and women were large enough that they mattered for such purposes. The model would also predict that as male–female wage differentials disappeared, one should see a more even distribution of work in the household. As women's wages rise, one should see men taking on a more equal share of household production.

Empirically, we have seen convergence in the time men and women spend on household production, but not to the same degree as the convergence in wages. That is, women still do a disproportionate (to the opportunity cost of their time) amount of the household production. Recent empirical work shows that men and women with roughly the same human capital and the same demographic features (e.g., age and marital status) working in the same job will earn close to the same wage. However, married men and women still do significantly different, though less so than in the past, amounts of housework. In 1965, the average for married men with a child aged 5 or over was 5.3 hours of housework per week, while women averaged 30.3 hours. By 2004, the men in that group averaged 9.5 hours per week, while the women fell to 16.9 hours. In relative terms, women went from doing almost six times the housework to almost twice as much. There is no question that the economic model can explain a good deal of this, but the disparity by gender remains, with women putting in 7.4 more hours per week, despite the fact that the wage differential is nowhere the 2:1 ratio.

It is also worth noting that the total amount of time spent on housework fell from 35.6 hours per week to 26.4 hours (all data as reported in Jacobsen, 2007, p. 111). That overall reduction is due to a combination of better household technology and cheaper market substitutes, as well as lower standards of cleanliness.

Even if one takes away the children at home, the men do only 0.7 hours more per week, and the women do 1 hour less, leaving a differential of 5.7 hours. The explanation for the difference cannot be the presence of children alone. A complete explanation for the remaining difference will likely focus on factors giving the male more bargaining power in the discussion over the division of housework, perhaps deriving from the higher cost of exiting the relationship for women, particularly when there are children involved. Economists have used a variety of bargaining models to explore both marital choice and the division of household labor (e.g., Lundberg & Pollack, 1993).

The economics of divorce provides yet another application of the basic model. Divorce rates in the United States are notably higher today than 40 years ago, despite a slow downward trend since about 1980. After a long-run slow increase since the early twentieth century, interrupted by a spike at the end of World War II and a leveling off for the 20 years afterward, the divorce rate more than doubled in the period between the mid-1960s and the early 1980s. Two of the most straightforward explanations of the long-run increase are the increased ability of women to survive economically outside of a marriage, discussed earlier, and the reduction in the birthrate. Both of these reduce the marginal cost of divorce. The first does so by reducing the financial burden on women and the second by reducing the number of marriages with any children, or with minor children, at a given time. Married couples with minor children are more likely to try to stick it out in a bad marriage, so anything that reduces the number of such children lowers the cost of divorce, inducing more divorce.

The large jump from the mid-1960s until the early 1980s and the relatively high plateau maintained since then require additional explanations. The mid-1960s date is not accidental, because it reflects the beginning of the loosening of divorce law across the country. In particular, the advent of no-fault divorce is often credited as a key factor in the rising divorce rate of that period. This change in divorce law allowed couples to divorce without having to prove adultery, abuse, or abandonment by the spouse. They could simply decide they did not wish to be married anymore. In most states, by the late 1970s, the unilateral desire by one partner to leave the marriage was sufficient to get a divorce. The controversy in the literature is the degree to which no-fault was a cause or consequence of a rising desire for divorce. Certainly, by lowering the cost of divorce, no-fault made divorce more likely, but others argue that it was a shift in the demand for divorce that led to the changes in the law. In fact, the divorce rate does seem to start its climb before no-fault had really spread to most states, lending credence to the idea that it was the intensification of the longer-run factors noted previously that pushed states to liberalize their divorce laws. Once liberalized, however, the lowered cost induced a movement along the demand-for-divorce curve, causing another jump.

A second explanation for that increase and sustained plateau is that there are expectation-matching and signaling problems as men and women adjust to new norms (Allen, 1998). Couples who married under the mutual assumption of a more strict division of labor by gender may well have found themselves 15 years later in a world where the wife was working, leading to tensions in the marriage because the reality did not match their expectations. The jump in divorces that quickly followed the advent of no-fault suggests that there were latent divorces waiting to happen, and these might have been one type. The signaling problems reflect the uncertainty that has come with changing social norms and gender roles. By the 1970s, couples were less likely to expect a strict division of labor, but men in particular may have had a difficult time in determining whether a prospective spouse was likely to want a career or to stay home. Rather than a flat-out wrong expectation, the signals about what expectation to have became increasingly noisier, making it more likely that mistakes would be made. Even for women, determining whether a potential husband would be accepting of their deciding later on to take up a career became more difficult in the new environment. This would likely generate more bad matches that would reveal themselves down the road, which is consistent with the ongoing high divorce rate.

This signaling theory should also predict a decline in the divorce rate, at least on the margin, as social norms become more predictable. Recent divorce data suggest this might be happening. The divorce rate has been very slowly falling, and when it is looked at from a cohort perspective, we find that divorce rates among those married just a few years have fallen more notably. A decade ago, couples married just 5 to 10 years were more likely to get divorced than couples today married that long. An explanation for this is that couples are making better matches today because they are facing less-noisy signals in the marriage market. Men and women have more similar life goals and are more tolerant of the need to bend their own goals to those of spouses. Even as the marriage rate continues to fall, the most recent evidence suggests that those marriages that are happening are more likely to stay together than in years past (U.S. Census Bureau, 2007).

Policy Implications

The economics of the family can inform an analysis of various policy proposals. In this section, three such issues are examined using the approaches outlined in previous sections.

One of the more fascinating questions worth exploring is how policy choices can affect women's labor force participation decisions. As an example, consider the way in which the U.S. tax system treats secondary earners. The typical economic model of the family assumes that labor force decisions are made sequentially—that is, the higher-earning spouse is assumed to work in the market, and given that person's decision, the family decides whether the lower-earning spouse should also work in the market and how much. More often than not, the secondary earner is the woman. Tax policy enters into the picture because married couples are almost always better off filing jointly than using the IRS's *married, filing separately* category, even given the discussion to follow. Filing jointly means that the secondary earner's first dollar of income is taxed at the marginal rate applicable to the primary earner's last dollar. So rather than paying lower rates on portions of the secondary earner's income, the couple filing jointly sees a much larger portion of all secondary income taxed. When that effect is combined with the law's refusal to treat child-care payments as an expense of employment, the incentives for the secondary earner in a family with small children are such that the disposable income from the secondary earner's work is actually quite low. Some analysts (McCaffery, 1999) have suggested that if married couples could file truly separately (as distinct from married, filing separately, under current law), with each one's income being taxed separately, this problem would be substantially lessened.

Analyzing the policy of no-fault divorce is another area in which the economics of the family can contribute. Historically, a spouse had to show abuse, abandonment, or adultery in order to get a divorce. For couples who were just unhappy, this often meant having to lie to have the grounds necessary for divorce, and it placed one spouse in the position of being at fault for the divorce. From an economic perspective, this process involved rather high transaction costs for unhappy couples. In the late 1960s and early 1970s, more states moved to so-called no-fault divorce, by which one or the other spouse could terminate the marriage for whatever reason he or she desired. This policy is probably more accurately called *unilateral* divorce, because the divorce does not require the consent of both parties. One advantage of so-called fault-based divorce is that couples who were unhappy at the very least had to cooperate in a lie to get a divorce. The need to cooperate in a lie meant that the divorce could take place only if both parties were willing to take affirmative steps to give up on the marriage. This may well have made for fewer adversarial divorces and greater ease in dividing up assets because both parties thought they would be better off separated. Today, the decision is unilateral in most states and therefore does not require any cooperation of this sort.

The problem with no-fault is that unilateral divorce puts the weaker party, usually the woman, at the mercy of the stronger. Imagine the wife who has given up her own career to help her husband's, to raise children, or both. If he decides he wants a divorce, she has very little leverage to prevent him or to negotiate reasonable terms (Cohen, 1987). Prior to no-fault, she could at least

hold out on cooperating to convince a judge that there were sufficient grounds. Or if one imagines a divorce regime where mutual consent replaces unilateral desire or abuse, abandonment, or adultery as the grounds for divorce, the financially weaker party gains significant bargaining power.

This can perhaps best be seen by using the Coase Theorem, one implication of which is that if transaction costs are sufficiently low, any situation involving external costs can be renegotiated to make the harmed party whole. What a mutual consent divorce regime would do is force couples into a negotiation process that would ensure that the weaker party is able to make a credible claim to compensation for the breaking of the marital contract. This effect of such a policy is a clear benefit. However, this shift would come with costs as well. One of the advantages of unilateral divorce is that it makes it very easy for a harmed party to exit the marriage. Imagine a situation where a wife was deeply unhappy but not abused, nor was there any adultery. Under unilateral no-fault, she could file for divorce and get out. If she were in fact being abused, she would not need to demonstrate to a judge that abuse was present. By raising the costs of divorce, going to a regime of mutual consent does make it harder for the victimized spouse to lose out economically, but it also makes it harder to get out of a bad marriage in the first place. An economic analysis of the family can help policy makers think through the trade-off here and try to find a set of policies that would make it easier for victimized spouses to exit bad marriages but to do so in ways that do not leave them substantially worse off.

The economic approach to child production also sheds light on policies designed to reduce birthrates in parts of the world where the population is thought to be growing too quickly. In the past, policy makers often focused on improving education and access to birth control—for example, by distributing condoms in third world countries. The assumptions were that population was, in fact, too high and that parents wanted smaller families but simply did not know how to make that happen or lacked the resources to do so. The economic approach suggests that all of these assumptions may be faulty. It may well be the case that parents in the third world are having the number of children they actually desire to have, given the circumstances in which they find themselves. The marginal benefits of additional children often do outweigh the costs in poorer societies for reasons this chapter has already touched on. At the very least, the economic approach to child production leads analysts to ask a different set of questions about this situation. Many have noted that freely distributed condoms often do not get used for their intended purpose and end up being used for other things. The economics of the family can explain that by asking whether the reason for large families in these societies is not ignorance or lack of resources but a reasonably rational calculation of the benefits and costs of child production. That population growth rates in the developed world are different might just reflect a difference in those costs and benefits, rather than education or access to resources per se.

These are but a few examples of how economic analyses of the family can inform policy discussions. Too often, family decision making is understood as standing outside the province of rationality and the kind of marginal benefit and marginal cost thinking of economics. Ignoring the economic approach to the family can lead to bad policy decisions if families are, in fact, making decisions along the lines that economics suggests.

Future Directions

The social institution of the family has changed enormously over the last 50 years, which is roughly the same length of time it has been a serious object of study for economists. There is little doubt that the change will continue in the years to come. Economists will likely be kept very busy trying to understand the continued evolution of gender relationships and the household division of labor, particularly as communications technology appears to be making it increasingly possible to work from home. Analyzing child production and raising decisions in a world where genetic choice might be possible and where the cost of raising kids continues to climb will provide another set of challenges. The same can be said of the developing world as globalization brings economic pressures on family forms and gender roles there. Finally, as same-sex marriage remains on the policy agenda, and as more same-sex couples create households and raise children, economists may find interesting research questions there because such households face the same decisions as opposite-sex ones have over the years.

Conclusion

Exploring the social institution of the family through the eyes of economics not only demonstrates the variety of phenomena that can be examined using the economic way of thinking, it also provides a different and valuable perspective on how families function and the choices that individuals make within them. Economics brings into relief the constraints under which family members choose and the various marginal benefits and marginal costs that might inform their decision making. Seeing the family in this light can help us make sense of some of the major demographic changes of the last few generations as well as inform policy makers as to the likely consequences, both intended and unintended, of various family policy proposals. Like all other social institutions, the family exists to reduce transaction costs and to solve human coordination problems. Economics helps us identify exactly how families do so and thereby informs our attempts to improve them.

References and Further Readings

Allen, D. W. (1998). No-fault divorce in Canada: Its cause and effect. *Journal of Economic Behavior and Organizations, 37,* 129–149.

Becker, G. S. (1960). An economic analysis of fertility. In Universities-National Bureau (Ed.), *Demographic and economic change in developed countries* (pp. 209–231). Princeton, NJ: Princeton University Press.

Becker, G. S. (1973). A theory of marriage: Part 1. *Journal of Political Economy, 81,* 813–846.

Becker, G. S. (1974). A theory of marriage: Part 2. *Journal of Political Economy, 82,* S11–S26.

Becker, G. S. (1991). *A treatise on the family* (Enl. ed.). Cambridge, MA: Harvard University Press.

Becker, G. S., & Lewis, H. G. (1973). On the interaction between the quantity and quality of children. *Journal of Political Economy, 81,* S279–S288.

Cohen, L. (1987). Marriage, divorce, and quasi rents: Or, "I gave him the best years of my life." *Journal of Legal Studies, 16,* 267–303.

Coontz, S. (2005). *Marriage, a history: From obedience to intimacy or how love conquered marriage.* New York: Viking.

Grossbard-Shechtman, S. (1993). *On the economics of marriage: A theory of marriage, labor and divorce.* Boulder, CO: Westview Press.

Hadfield, G. (1999). A coordination model of the sexual division of labor. *Journal of Economic Behavior and Organization, 40,* 125–153.

Jacobsen, J. P. (2007). *The economics of gender* (3rd ed.). Malden, MA: Blackwell.

Levitt, S. D., & Dubner, S. J. (2005). *Freakonomics.* New York: HarperCollins.

Lundberg, S., & Pollack, R. (1993). Separate spheres bargaining and the marriage market. *Journal of Political Economy, 101,* 988–1010.

McCaffery, E. J. (1999). *Taxing women.* Chicago: University of Chicago Press.

Parkman, A. (2000). *Good intentions gone awry.* Lanham, MD: Rowman & Littlefield.

Posner, R. A. (1992). *Sex and reason.* Cambridge, MA: Harvard University Press.

Robinson, J. P., & Godbey, G. (1997). *Time for life: The surprising ways Americans use their time.* University Park: Pennsylvania State University Press.

Rosenzweig, M. R., & Schultz, T. P. (1985). The demand for and supply of births: Fertility and its life cycle consequences. *American Economic Review, 75,* 992–1015.

Rosenzweig, M. R., & Stark, O. (Eds.). (1997). *Handbook of population and family economics.* Amsterdam: Elsevier.

Shorter, E. (1975). *The making of the modern family.* New York: Basic Books.

U.S. Census Bureau. (2007). *Survey of income and program participation (SIPP), 2004 panel, wave 2 topical module.* Retrieved February 2, 2009, from http://www.census.gov/population/socdemo/marital-hist/2004/Table2.2004.xls

Winegarden, C. R. (1984). Women's fertility, market work, and marital status: A test of the new household economics with international data. *Economica, 51,* 447–456.

Wittman, D. (2005). The internal organization of the family: Economic analysis and psychological advice. *Kyklos, 58,* 121–144.

57

Economics of Aging

Agneta Kruse

Lund University

Population aging is a worldwide phenomenon. The demographic transition from a state with high fertility and mortality rates to a state with low fertility, low mortality, and increased longevity has changed the well-known population pyramid into what looks more like a rectangle or a skyscraper. This means fewer children and more old-aged people in relation to those of working age. Aging started in the industrialized world and has thus gone farther in these countries than in developing countries, where it started later. The transition is far from complete in the industrialized world, and aging is forecast to go on during the entire period of prognosis, up to the year 2050.

Population aging has caused anxieties about the economic effects of aging: the possibilities of supporting an increasing number of older persons with a shrinking workforce. This chapter focuses on the economics of aging in the industrialized world. The next section describes the demographic changes and aging, their history and prognoses of future development. The following section uses a life cycle approach to give a theoretical foundation for analyzing the economic aspects of aging, from both the individual's and society's points of view. Later sections analyze the effect of aging on production and consumption patterns. As old age pensions constitute such a large part of life cycle redistribution, special attention is given to pensions and the eventual strain caused by aging. The conclusions from these sections are that demographic changes will cause substantial economic pressure, ceteris paribus. The final section discusses possible remedies and concludes the chapter.

Aging Populations

Historically, aging started with a drop in fertility rates, which had already started to decline in many industrialized countries in the nineteenth century. In 1950, the total fertility rate was 3.45 in the United States (meaning that on average each woman was expected to give birth to 3.45 children), 2.66 in Europe, and 2.75 in Japan; it had fallen to 2.04 in the United States, 1.41 in Germany, and 1.29 in Japan by 2000. A fertility rate below 2.1 is below reproduction rate; the population will eventually shrink if immigration does not compensate for the low fertility. There is a rather large dispersion in fertility rates between countries within Europe, with Italy and Germany having the very low fertility rates of 1.29 and 1.35, respectively, while Sweden has a fertility rate of 1.67 and the United Kingdom 1.70 (United Nations, 2007).

It takes some 20 years before a birth cohort enters the labor market. Thus, low fertility rates will give rise to successively smaller cohorts entering the labor force.

In the next phase, population aging was driven by a drop in mortality and increases in longevity. Between 1950 and 2000, life expectancy at birth increased by 8.5 years in the United States, 11.2 years in Germany, 13.9 years in Italy, and 18 years in Japan, and population prognoses forecast that life expectancy will increase by at least 5 years by 2050 (United Nations, 2007).

A way of measuring aging is by dependency ratios, where the child dependency ratio is the number of children in relation to the number of people of working age, and the old age dependency ratio is the number of people aged 65 or older in relation to those of working age. The development of these ratios is shown in Table 57.1.

Table 57.1 Dependency Ratios

Region	Child Dependency Ratio[a]					Old Age Dependency Ratio[b]				
	1950	1975	2000	2025	2050	1950	1975	2000	2025	2050
Europe	40	37	26	23	25	13	18	22	32	48
Sweden	35	32	29	28	28	15	24	27	36	41
Germany	35	34	23	21	24	14	23	24	39	54
Italy	40	38	21	20	25	13	19	27	39	60
United Kingdom	33	37	29	27	27	16	22	24	32	40
United States	42	39	33	30	28	13	16	19	28	34
Canada	47	40	28	24	27	12	13	18	33	44
South America	69	71	49	34	28	6	8	9	16	29
Australia and New Zealand	42	44	32	28	27	13	14	18	31	41
Africa	76	86	78	61	43	6	6	6	7	11
Asia	61	71	48	34	28	7	7	9	15	27
Japan	59	36	21	19	22	8	12	25	50	74

SOURCE: United Nations (2007).

NOTES: Number of children or older persons per 100 working-age people from 1950 to 2000 and prognosis up to 2050, medium variant. (a) Ratio of population between 0 and 14 years of age to population between 15 and 64. (b) Ratio of population 65 and older to population between 15 and 64.

As can be seen in the table, aging started in most regions and countries with a drop in fertility; the child dependency ratio fell. In the next phase, population aging gave rise to increases in the old age dependency ratio. The table shows that aging has been going on for a long time and is forecasted to continue.

Table 57.1 shows the UN population forecasts with the medium variant. It should be emphasized that demographic forecasts are highly uncertain. For example, fertility rates have shown great variability in the past; the forecasts assume a constant fertility rate. Also, so far, the drop in mortality has constantly been underestimated in population forecasts, as have the increases in longevity. Even with great uncertainties in the forecasts, there is no doubt that the population is rapidly aging.

Aging brings forward changes in consumption and production patterns.

Life Cycle Approach

No human being can support himself or herself by his or her own labor during a whole lifetime. Infancy is an obvious

example, as is old age. Figure 57.1 sketches some important economic events in an individual's life: entrance into and exit from the labor market plus the length of retirement period. Individuals need to consume in periods when they do not have any income. To survive, individuals have to cooperate. The main institutions for cooperation are the family, the market, and the state, which exist side by side, and their importance differs in different countries as well as historically in the same country. The way of mixing the institutions and organizing them has effects on the pressure caused by aging, as is evident later on in this chapter; for a comprehensive analysis, see Lars Söderström (2008).

E is the time of entry into adulthood and the labor market. Childhood extends up to the point E. The period from E to EX represents working years; EX is the exit from the labor market into retirement. D is the time of death; the period between EX and D is the number of years as a retiree. During the working years, the individual earns an income, assumed to increase with age. Assume that the individual wants to maximize lifetime utility, subject to the budget constraint determined by lifetime income. The planning problem is then to transfer income from working years to nonworking years and to smooth consumption possibilities.

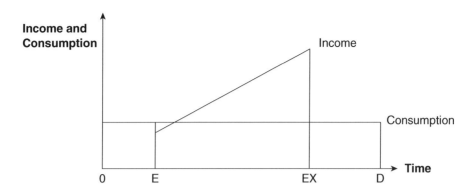

Figure 57.1   Life Cycle Income and Consumption Planning Problem

The assumptions in Figure 57.1 are that income is increasing with age and that an even consumption stream over the years maximizes utility. Of course, other patterns are possible; they are discussed in the analysis of aging and the welfare state.

Figure 57.1 may also be used as an illustration of a society at a specific time. The number of children is then the number between origo and E, the number of people of working age is between E and EX, and the number of retirees is between EX and D. The income of those in working years is used for the support of all coliving individuals.

The figure highlights the planning problem faced by the individual and society—that is, how to organize transfers over years and between generations in an efficient and utility-maximizing way. The figure is drawn as if there were total certainty in life, the income stream is certain, the possibility of working until the age of EX is certain, and the time of death is certain, to mention but a few uncertainties that one meets in real life. Apart from childhood and old age, the risk of periods of work incapacity during working age, due to sickness or unemployment, for example, are examples of individuals' inability to always support themselves. The purpose of the institution for cooperation—be it the family, the market, or the state—is then not only to even out consumption possibilities over the life cycle, but also to function as an insurer against income losses, the risk of high consumption needs, like health care and old age care, as well as poverty.

The life cycle illustration gives an intuitive insight into the problems that an aging population might cause. The following sections analyze it further.

Production and Labor Supply

So far we have shown a purely demographic view. However, more important from an economic point of view is the labor force in relation to the number of people being supported. At any given time, the number of people being supported is determined by the demarcation line between childhood and adulthood, between working ages and retirement, and finally between retirement and death. The UN figures used in Table 57.1 with the delimitation of age groups 0 to 14, 15 to 64, and 65 and older do not describe the economic-support reality in the industrialized world. In Western societies, there has been a trend of postponing entrance into the labor market. The expansion of higher education means that an increasing portion of each cohort studies at high school and university and delays entrance into the labor market. Besides, retirement age has shown a declining trend for several decades, even if it seems to have turned upward the in last decade. Economic growth is a common explanatory factor for both trends. Early retirement occurs both because pension systems have subsidized early retirement (see Gruber & Wise, 1999, for international comparisons) and because leisure is a normal good with positive income elasticity.

Furthermore, what is economically important is labor supply. Table 57.2 shows total labor force participation rates and the participation rates in different age groups.

Table 57.2   Labor Force Participation Rates in Different Age Groups, 2007

	Ages 15 to 24	*Ages 25 to 54*	*Ages 55 to 64*	*Ages 15 to 64*
Germany	51.3	87.1	58.0	75.6
Italy	30.9	77.6	34.6	62.5
Sweden	57.1	90.0	73.0	80.6
United Kingdom	65.3	84.5	59.3	73.6
European Union 15	48.8	84.6	48.8	72.5
United States	59.4	83.0	63.8	75.3
Japan	44.9	83.3	68.4	73.6

SOURCE: Organisation for Economic Co-operation and Development (OECD, 2008).

If the labor force is defined as people between 15 and 64 years of age, the participation rate is around three quarters in the countries shown in the table, far less in Italy, and somewhat higher in Sweden. Labor supply changes over the life cycle, with a rather low supply in young and old ages. The ages between 25 and 54 may be seen as the most productive years with high participation rates. The differences between age groups mean that the age structure and changes in it will influence a country's production capacity.

Using labor force participation figures for calculating what might be called an effective old age dependency ratio gives quite different and higher ratios than the ones shown in Table 57.1; see Table 57.3.

The use of the labor force instead of the number of persons increases the old age dependency ratio by 6 percentage points (for the United States) at the least and 18 percentage points (for Italy) at most—that is, quite substantial increases. Moreover, the use of population figures to forecast the old age dependency ratio in 2050 gives substantial increases in the ratio, as seen in Table 57.1. The effective old age dependency ratio exceeds these significantly; by the middle of this century, there will be one retiree per working person in Japan and almost one retiree per working person in Italy. However, even these figures are underestimates if we are interested in actual work performed; unemployed people are included in the labor force, as are people on sick leave, holiday, and parental leave. In addition, participation rates only partly capture the labor supply; they do not tell how many hours per week or how many weeks per year a person works, or how many years constitute a working life. All these aspects matter, and the chapter comes back to this when discussing pension systems.

These future prospects have given rise to numerous alarm reports, but these are often built on static calculations. It is worth emphasizing that economies are flexible and that there are adaptation possibilities. Prices will change, giving incentives to adapt to new circumstances. As an example, there is empirical evidence from cross-section and time-series data that a slower growth in labor force induces a more rapid productivity growth (Cutler, Poterba, Sheiner, & Summers, 1990) Furthermore, institutions matter; the way of organizing life cycle redistribution and support of older persons will most certain change.

The last 50 to 60 years have seen important changes in the labor market and in different groups' participation in the labor market. One trend is the increase in market work by women. There has also been a very marked downward trend in the participation rates by older men. Lately, this trend seems to be taking a turn upward. Gary Burtless (2008) shows that there is a trend of postponing retirement in industrialized countries; the age at retirement is increasing. Gabriella Sjögren Lindquist and Eskil Wadensjö (in press) discuss factors behind the decision to exit the labor market. They divide these into individual factors, such as health, family situation, and social and occupational pension schemes, influencing the supply side, and institutional factors, such as wage system and mandatory retirement age, influencing the demand for older workers. They conclude that the closing down of roads to early exit and the reformed pension system has delayed retirement in Sweden.

Table 57.3 Old Age Dependency Ratios, 2005 and 2050

	2005		2050	
	65 and Older / (Number of Persons)	*65 and Older / (Labor Force)*	*65 and Older / (Number of Persons)*	*65 and Older / (Labor Force)[a]*
Germany	0.28	0.37	0.54	0.71
Italy	0.30	0.48	0.60	0.97
Sweden	0.26	0.33	0.41	0.50
United Kingdom	0.24	0.33	0.40	0.55
United States	0.18	0.24	0.34	0.45
Japan	0.30	0.40	0.74	1.0

SOURCE: Author's calculations using figures from United Nations (2007) and OECD (2008).

NOTES: Age range for *number of persons* and *labor force* is 15 to 64. (a) Calculations are made with the assumption that labor force participation rates are the same in 2050 as those reported in Table 57.2.

Aging and Capital

Aging may also influence savings and capital accumulation. Albert Ando and Franco Modigliani's (1963) hypothesis of consumption and saving over the life cycle assumes borrowing during childhood, positive saving during working ages, especially during the later phase of working ages, say between 50 years of age to 64, and dissaving during retirement. There is empirical evidence to support the theory—among others, Solveig Erlandsen and Ragnar Nymoen's (2008) empirical study of private consumption and capital accumulation using Norwegian data strongly supports the theory—even if some contrasting evidence also exists.

The population forecasts show that the number of people in working ages will decrease, which means that capital per worker will increase, other things being equal. If the capital–labor ratio was optimal at the outset, there will be too much capital; savings can be reduced and consumption increased. This is a conclusion drawn by, for example, Cutler et al. (1990). However, with fewer workers to support an increasing number of older persons, an increase in productivity caused by more capital per worker should be a welcome effect. The effect of aging on savings and capital is further analyzed in the discussion of pension reforms.

Production and Consumption Patterns

Cutler et al. (1990) use what they call a support ratio to highlight changes in production capacity and changes in consumption patterns as the population ages. The support ratio is defined as

$$\alpha = LF\ /\ CON, \qquad (1)$$

where LF is the effective labor force and CON is the effective number of consumers.

Cutler et al. (1990) start by assuming that LF and CON simply are defined as the number in different age groups—that is, an analysis very similar to the analysis discussed earlier called *pure* demography.

As pointed out in the introduction, aging started with a decline in fertility, which means that the support burden of children lessens. There is a time span before the old age dependency ratio increases; thus, there is a period in which the support burden is lessened. However, in the next phase of the demographic transition, the number of older persons increases, and so does the old age dependency ratio. The per capita consumption demands (needs) from older persons surpass by far that of children. A changing age structure, with fewer children and more older persons, does not have a neutral effect on the support burden. Cutler et al. (1990) therefore qualify the support ratio, taking different consumption patterns in different age groups into account as well as age-specific labor force participation rates.

The support ratio will decline in the decades to come. One of their conclusions is that the support ratio is more sensitive to changing consumption patterns than to changes in the labor force participation rates (see also Erlandsen & Nymoen, 2008).

Aging and the Welfare State

In many countries, a large part of life cycle redistribution takes the form of publicly provided or subsidized consumption and transfers. Division of public expenditure in accordance with the problems the welfare state aims to remedy gives essentially three categories: (1) life cycle redistribution, (2) risk insurance, and (3) what may be called redistribution in accord with our ethical preferences—that is, support of the genuinely weak. A comparison of expenditures in five countries, Britain, Hungary, Italy, Poland, and Sweden, in the middle of the 1990s shows that life cycle redistribution constituted by far the largest part. It ranged from 60% in Britain to more than 80% in Poland. The aid to the weak was the smallest part, below 10% in all the countries except in Britain, where it counted for just above one fifth (Kruse, 1997).

Of course, the importance of life cycle redistribution in the welfare state makes it sensitive to aging. During childhood, the individual is a net receiver of public expenditure; during working ages, a net contributor; and during old age, again a net receiver. During childhood, the main items are education, publicly provided or subsidized child care, and child allowances, to mention a few. During old age, the most important expenditure areas are public pensions, health care, and old age care. With a welfare state model, these expenditures are financed mostly by taxes, which give high tax wedges and are detrimental to employment.

There is widespread concern that population aging will put the welfare state under strain and force a retrenchment. With aging, the tax base decreases if the decline in the number of workers is not compensated for by productivity increases. At the same time, aging increases the demand for pensions, health care, and old age care. Prognoses of these important expenditure areas until the year 2050 are reported, for example, in EU Economic Policy Committee (EU, 2003). Table 57.4 shows these prognoses for a selection of European countries. Per capita expenditure is assumed to be constant; combining per capita expenditure with demographic changes, one gets the following expenditures.

Take health care as an example. The consumption of health care increases strongly with age. Björn Lindgren and Carl Hampus Lyttkens (in press) present figures showing the per capita cost for persons aged 80 and older to be around four times the cost for persons aged 30 to 50 years. This figure stems from a simulation model for Sweden. EU (2003) shows an even more marked increase with age. Note that taking this into consideration would change the consumption pattern in the stylized life cycle picture in

Table 57.4   Public Expenditures on Public Pensions, Health Care, and Old Age Care as a Percentage of GDP in 2000 and Projections of Change From 2000 to 2050

	Pensions		Health and Old Age Care	
	2000	*Change From 2000 to 2050*	*2000*	*Change From 2000 to 2050*
Belgium	10.0	3.3	6.1	2.1
Denmark	10.5	2.9	8.0	2.7
Finland	11.3	4.7	6.2	2.8
France	12.1	3.8	6.9	1.7
Germany	11.8	5.0	5.7[a]	1.4
Italy	13.8	0.3	5.5	1.9
Sweden	9.0	1.7	8.8	3.0
United Kingdom	5.5	−1.1	6.3	1.8

SOURCE: EU (2003).

NOTE: (a) Applies to health care only.

Figure 57.1. In all the countries in Table 57.4, the number of people in the age group 80 and older will increase rapidly. From 2000 to 2030, the 80 and older share in the population will increase from 4.0% to 9.0% in Italy, from 3.7% to 7.5% in France, and from 3.5% to 7.2% in Germany (United Nations, 2007).

To what extent the increased number of elderly people will actually lead to increases in the health care costs is, however, a matter of dispute. Friedrich Breyer and Stefan Felder (2006) report that attempts to foresee the increases in payroll tax rates to cover German health care costs give estimates with range as wide as between 16.5% and 39.5% in 2050. The lower figure stems from simulations using demographic change alone, while the higher one incorporates progress in medical technology, which has shown to be highly cost increasing. Although many technological advances are efficiency enhancing and cost reducing—using medicine instead of surgery for a gastric ulcer, for example—until now it has been cost increasing (see Lindgren & Lyttkens, in press).

It turns out that the effect of aging on health care expenditure is extremely difficult to foresee. First of all, health care has an income-elastic demand, meaning that as income goes up, so does demand for health care. Expenditure on health care closely follows a trend: The higher the GDP, the higher the proportion spent on health care. Thus, at least until now, demography is not the main explanation for increases in spending on health care. Adding costs for increasing quality at the same rate as real wage growth would increase health care costs by a factor of around 3.5% in addition to keeping per capita cost constant up to year 2040 (Lindgren & Lyttkens, in press).

Health care has a greater weight in older people's utility and demand. Aging means that older people's influence increases, both as consumers and via the political process as voters. We can thus expect that expenditures on health care will increase and do so more than just in response to demographic change. Furthermore, Richard Disney (2007) shows that aging will be associated with a larger welfare state.

Pensions

In his seminal article, Paul Samuelson (1958) analyzes the problem of how to support oneself in old age. He uses an overlapping generations model with three coliving generations, two working and one retired (children are assumed to belong to the adults' families and are outside the analysis). To focus on the necessity of cooperation of generations, he assumes that nothing keeps; trade with nature is not possible, and there is no capital market. During the working periods, each person or generation produces one unit.

Samuelson (1958) shows that one way of solving the life cycle problem of smoothing the consumption possibilities, when working capacity does not suffice for all periods, is to make the two working generations pay a percentage of their incomes as a tax and use the revenue for payments to the old generation. One important conclusion from this setup of a contract between generations, a *pension system,* is that the rate of return on contributions paid equals the population growth rate in the economy. Remember that there is no capital in this economy and thus by assumption no productivity growth. With a positive population growth rate, the number of workers increases; with a fixed contribution rate, the sum of contributions increases, and so do the outgoing payments to the old.

This solves the life cycle problem. However, Samuelson concludes that this kind of system will not come into existence because older persons do not have a negotiatory position to persuade the working generations to accept such a system, nor do they have the power to enforce it because they are in the minority. He points to the fact that life cycle redistribution is a linear business, not a circular one. That is, if A (old) borrows from B (middle-aged) and C (young), A will not be around to repay B in the next period, when B is old and needs support. The solution suggested by Samuelson is a social contact between generations; B gives part of his or her income to A, being convinced that in the period when B is old, C, now being middle-aged, and the new generation, D, now young, will do the same for him or her. In this simple setting, Samuelson shows the workings of a pay-as-you-go pension system and also that the rate of return in such a system equals the growth rate in the economy.

All industrialized countries have public pensions systems, often supplemented with pensions negotiated between the parties in the labor market and with private pensions. In most countries, public pensions provide the major part of income during retirement and constitute a large part of public sector expenditure. These expenditures are forecast to increase substantially with aging; hence, reforming the existing pension systems has become a top priority on political agendas.

Old age pensions can be organized in a number of ways. The main choices to make are the following:

- Public or private
- Obligatory or voluntary
- Pay-as-you-go or funded
- Defined benefit or defined contribution
- Basic or earnings related
- Redistribution or actuarial
- Indexed with prices, growth, or interest rate (rate of return in the capital market) during contribution years and during benefit receiving years.

The specific design chosen has different effects on the distribution between generations, on the rate of return the system gives, and also on how robust the system will be in response to demographic changes.

Public pensions are more often than not obligatory, meaning that the individual is not free to choose a life cycle consumption pattern according to his or her preferences. If the restriction imposed by the pension system is binding, this means a loss in utility. The higher the level of the system, the higher the probability of a binding restriction, which is probably more binding in low-income groups than in high-income groups. The reasons put forward to justify an obligatory system and this loss are the threat of free riders, the fear of myopia among younger people, and the desire to use the pension system for redistribution among socioeconomic groups.

A pay-as-you-go system may be described by its budget restriction:

$$q \times w \times L = b \times R, \qquad (2)$$

where q is the contribution rate, w is the average wage, L is the labor force, b is the average benefit, and R is the number of retirees. The left-hand side shows the sum of contributions (in a time period, a year, for example) and the right-hand side shows outgoing expenditures in that same period—that is, to contemporary retirees. The character of a pay-as-you-go system to be an implicit social contract between generations becomes evident with this formulation.

For the system to be in balance, the equality sign has to hold. Assume that wages, the labor force, and the number of retirees are exogenous to the pension system. It is then obvious that with demographic changes like those expected in the future, either the contribution rate has to be increased or the benefit level decreased, or both, in order to maintain a balanced system.

Rearranging equation 2 shows even more lucidly the importance of demography in a pay-as-you-go system:

$$q = b/w \times R/L, \qquad (3)$$

where b/w is the replacement rate—that is, the benefit in relation to wages—and R/L is the dependency ratio.

Table 57.5 is to be read in the following way: With a dependency ratio, R/L, of 0.33, a contribution rate of 16.5% suffices for a replacement rate of 50%. If a higher replacement rate is wanted, for example 60%, then a contribution rate of 20% is needed. The combined information in Tables 57.3 and 57.5 leaves no doubt that aging will lead to pressure on pay-as-you-go pension systems.

The budget restriction shows the working of a pay-as-you-go system from society's point of view, but it can also be used to show it from an individual's life cycle perspective as well. With such a perspective, L may be seen as the number of years the individual works, say from 20 to 64 years of age, giving 45 working years. R is then the number of years in retirement, say from 65 to 80 years of age. Using these figures in equation 3 gives

$$q = b/w \times 15/45. \qquad (4)$$

Table 57.5 The Required Contribution Rate at Different Combinations (Assumptions) of the Replacement Ratio and the Old Age Dependency Ratio

	R/L 0.33[a]	R/L 0.40	R/L 0.50	R/L 0.60[b]
b/w 50%	16.5%	20.0%	25.0%	30.0%
b/w 60%	20.0%	24.0%	30.0%	36.0%

SOURCE: Author's calculations using equation 3.

(a) Corresponds to 45 years of work (ages 20 to 64) and 15 years as a retiree (ages 65 to 80).

(b) Compare the forecasts for Germany and Italy in 2050.

Assume that the individual wants a replacement rate of 60%. It is then obvious that the contribution rate has to be 20% (see also Table 57.5). The equation can be used to illustrate different changes. Assume, for example, that the individual wants to retire earlier, other things being equal, at 60 years of age. Then we get

$$q = b/w \times 20/40, \qquad (5)$$

with a replacement rate, b/w, of 60%, the contribution rate has to be increased to 30%. Evidently early retirement is very expensive.

A last example here is increases in longevity. Assume an increase of 5 years, other things being equal. This gives us

$$q = b/w \times 20/45. \qquad (6)$$

Again, with a b/w of 60%, the contribution rate to balance the system is 27%.

The effects of aging on pay-as-you-go systems made policy makers and pension experts recommend reforms to change from pay-as-you-go systems to funded ones (see, e.g., World Bank, 1994).

In a funded system, the contributions paid during working years are put into a fund, which may invest in the stock market or hold equities, government bonds, or both. The fund increases each year with new contributions and with compound interest earned by the fund. At the time of retirement, the fund can be used for buying an annuity, the size of which depends of course on its value at the time of retirement.

There are pros and cons with either way of organizing a pension system. Obviously, the rate of return differs; in a pay-as-you-go system, it equals (approximately) the economic growth rate, and in a funded system, it equals the rate of return in the capital market. Historically, and in the long run, the rate of return in the capital market has surpassed the growth rate. This led Martin Feldstein (1974), among others, to the conclusion that funded systems were to be preferred; the same benefit would be possible with lower contribution rates. Thus, both aging and an expected discrepancy between growth and the interest rate seem to favor a funded system. Feldstein's conclusion builds, however, on the assumption that funding—and the eventual increased capital supply—will not affect the rate of return. If a great number of countries were to follow the advice of transforming their pay-as-you-go systems into funded ones, it is hard to believe that there would not be a downward pressure on the interest rate. Furthermore, it is worth noting that funded systems, to a certain extent, are also sensitive to demographic changes; for example, with a funded system, when baby boomers enter retirement and sell their funds to buy annuities and the increased capital supply meets a smaller working generation, the price—that is, the rate of return—will most certainly go down. Axel

Börsch-Supan, Alexander Ludwig, and Joachim Winter (2006) show that demographic effect on the rate of return depends on the degree of funding as well as on the degree on international openness in the capital market.

It should be noted that both kinds of pension systems are exposed to risk; a pay-as-you-go system is exposed to the risk of a deteriorating economic performance and low growth, and a funded one is exposed to the risk of capital market crises. Thus, it may be a good idea to diversify, to use both devices.

Whether pay-as-you-go or funded, pensions are mainly life cycle savings with a smaller part being insurance. The insurance is in order to cover an extraordinarily long life— that is, the risk of outliving one's means. Insurance uses the law of large numbers, meaning that it is enough to have a buffer (savings) covering the average expected number of years as a retiree. With insurance, the risk of living longer than average life expectancy is pooled among the participants in the pension scheme. Because individuals have risk aversion, without insurance, the individuals would keep a too large buffer, which reduces expected utility.

The budget restriction of a pay-as-you-go system clarifies the difference between a *defined-benefit* (DB) and a *defined-contribution* (DC) system. In a DB system, the benefit (b) or the replacement rate (b/w) is fixed. Demographic and economic changes then have to be counterbalanced by changes in the contribution rate (q) in order to keep the system in balance. This means that the costs of adaptation to these changes fall on the working generation. As this discussion has shown, aging leads to a shrinking labor force; in a DB system, this requires raised contribution rates. In a DC system, the contribution rate is fixed and benefits are then determined by the sum of contributions divided by the number of retirees. Aging, in the form of increased life expectancy, means that yearly benefits decrease in proportion to the increase in the number of years as a retiree. In the last decade, there has been a trend away from DB to DC systems, indicating a shift in who bears the risk of increased life expectancy, from the working generation to the retired one (Whitehouse, 2007).

The natural index in a pay-as-you-go system is the growth rate (again, see Samuelson, 1958). However, many countries have chosen to index by prices, the reasons often stated to be economic. This implies, though, that the development of the pension system does not follow the development of the economy and will thus be exposed to economic changes because it does not adapt automatically. The standard of living of different generations will be determined by economic growth; with a high economic growth, the retirees' standard of living falls behind that of the working generation, and vice versa.

In an actuarial system, there is no redistribution ex ante. The sum of expected contributions equals the sum of expected benefits. Of course, there will be redistribution ex post; some people will end up as losers, living shorter than the expected average, and some as winners. If there are no systematic differences between people or socioeconomic groups, then the system is actuarial. Note that if unisex life tables are used, there is redistribution in favor of women. In an actuarial system, with the contribution rate determined as a percentage of the wage, the system will be earnings related. Because women have a different labor market performance from men, with market work interrupted for child rearing, earnings-related systems are sometimes assumed to be disadvantageous to women. However, this turns out not to hold generally; see Ann-Charlotte Ståhlberg, Agneta Kruse, and Annika Sundén (2005) for an analysis of gender and the design of pension systems.

The Political Economy of Public Pensions and Aging

Edgar Browning (1975) shows that in a democracy with majority voting, a pay-as-you-go system will expand beyond its optimal level. To show this, he uses an overlapping generations model with three generations, one young, one middle-aged, and one old. The young and middle-aged are working, earning y_y and y_m respectively. To introduce a pay-as-you-go system, they all vote on their most preferred tax or contribution level, knowing that the sum of contributions paid into the system is to be used for benefits to the contemporary old generation. The voters assume that the tax rate will not be changed in their lifetime.

Assume that the individuals maximize their lifetime utility. The old individual has only one remaining period left to live. This period is spent in retirement; the old person will not pay any contributions but will receive benefits. At the extreme—for example, neither taking the utility of children and grandchildren into account nor expecting negative incentive effects—the old person will vote for a tax and contribution rate of 100%, t^{old}. The young individual has his or her entire life ahead of him or her and will pay contributions during a whole working life and get benefits during retirement. The preferred contribution rate by the young will smooth the consumption path over the life cycle, maximizing utility. The young person's chosen contribution rate is thus the optimal one, t^*, as the entire life is taken into consideration. The middle-aged generation's most preferred tax rate will be between the old person's and the young person's. What the middle-aged generation has left is one period of working and contributing to the system and one period of getting benefits: $t^* < t^{middle-aged} < t^{old}$. With majority voting, the median voter casts the decisive vote, and the system will be greater than its optimal level. The outcome builds on rather simplified assumptions, for example, that the only aspect of voting is the level of the system and that voting takes place only once. Other researchers have qualified the Browning model and made assumptions closer to actual pension systems and more realistic voting procedures; even so, the Browning result holds well (see, e.g., Sjoblom, 1985).

This result is even reinforced by aging. Aging means that the age of the median voter increases. By the turn of

this century, the age of the median voter was well below 50 years of age; in 35 years, it will increase to 54 in Germany, 55 in Italy and Spain, and 56 in France, to mention a few countries with rapidly aging populations (Galasso, 2006; Uebelmesser, 2004). Figure 57.2 shows how the median voter's considerations change with increased age.

• **2000:**

E		M	EX		D
20		47	65		80

• **2035:**

E			M	EX		D
20			53	65		85

Figure 57.2   Age of Median Voter and Life Expectancy: An Example

Assume that voting takes place in the year 2000 and that the median age is 47, retirement age 65, and expected remaining lifetime 15 years. Contributions before the age of 47 are sunk costs. The median voter knows that he or she has another 18 years of contributions (compared to the 40 to 45 years a person entering the labor market has) and 15 years of benefits. It is assumed that the median voter's age has increased 35 years later to 53 years, the retirement age is the same, but the expected lifetime has increased by 5 years. Voting in 2035, the median voter now has 12 years of contributions and is expected to get benefits during 20 years. A high contribution rate will certainly give a high payoff.

Aging gives rise to an opposite effect as well by exerting a downward pressure on the growth rate in the economy—that is, a downward pressure on the rate of return in a pay-as-you-go system. Therefore, it may be attractive to downscale the pay-as-you-go system and replace it with a funded one. So far, according to empirical results, the former tendency seems to have been the stronger:

> The most striking result . . . lies in the strong and significant positive effect of median voter age on program size. . . . one year adds half a percentage point to the GNP share of social security benefits. (Breyer & Craig, 1997, p. 719)

This also implies that reforming a pension system in response to the strain aging puts on the systems is politically difficult. Reform efforts have been met with fierce political resistance, especially from the so-called gray panthers. This notwithstanding, there has been a plethora of reforms in a number of countries where aging has put the pension systems under strain. The reforms range from marginal retrenching changes to radical parametric ones (Galasso 2006; Martin & Whitehouse, 2008). Radical reforms are of course more difficult to accomplish. Hans-Werner Sinn and Silke Uebelmesser (2002) analyze the political possibilities of such a change in the German system and conclude that it will be possible until around 2015. After that date, Germany will turn into a gerontocracy, and such a change will not be politically feasible.

In Sweden, a radical reform was decided on in the middle of the 1990s. The system was changed from a DB to a DC system—the major part being kept as a pay-as-you-go system and a minor part transformed to a funded one—from price indexation to (in the main) wage indexation and with annuities depending on life expectancy. It is regarded as being a stable pension system despite the aging of the population (for a description see Kruse, in press; Palmer, 2006). Jan Selén and Ann-Charlotte Ståhlberg (2007) and Kruse conclude that the design of the transition rules was a crucial factor to form a majority in favor of the new system, together with high political competence. Other countries as well have implemented more or less similar reforms. Robert Holzmann and Edward Palmer (2006) thoroughly describe and analyze the pros and cons of these reforms.

Possible Remedies and Concluding Remarks

There is no doubt, first, that aging will occur with increased old age dependency ratios, and second that aging will affect the extent of resources channeled to the elderly as well as affecting the possibilities of financing these resources. The prognoses give an increasing gap between available resources and future demands due to aging, ceteris paribus. Furthermore, aging is not the only foreseen challenge; in combination with ongoing globalization, aging is supposed to increase the strain. However, the ceteris paribus assumption will not come true. If there is anything to learn from history, it is that economies are flexible, adapting to new circumstances. The adaptation may, however, be costly.

To close the gap between the increasing demands due to an increased number of older persons and decreasing support possibilities due to a shrinking workforce, a number of measures aiming at both the demand and the supply side will probably be called for.

Immigration is often suggested as a remedy against the decreasing number of people of working age. However, demographers show convincingly that immigration is not a remedy; see for example Tommy Bengtsson and Kirk Scott (in press). Calculations show that the amount of immigration needed in order to compensate for demographic change and aging by far surpasses what is deemed possible to accommodate. Furthermore, even if the only accepted immigration would be people in working ages, immigrants also eventually get old and needy. Besides, such immigration assumes a rather odd immigration policy.

Another possibility would be to increase fertility, for example by stimulating fertility by subsidizing child rearing, making it possible to combine market work and children. Such policies are assumed to have kept fertility rates at rather high levels in France and Sweden, for example, in comparison with Germany, Italy, and Spain. However, fertility seems to be difficult both to predict and to influence. Besides, more children will at least initially not diminish the gap. On the contrary, it will reduce market labor supply because time is an important input into child rearing.

To raise taxes would be another way to close the gap. However, taxes give rise to incentive effects, which may reduce the tax base and cause deadweight losses. The deadweight loss increases with the square of the increase in the tax rate, making it an expensive way to go. There are, however, tendencies of a reformed tax structure, much in response to globalization, but it may also facilitate the financing of the welfare state (Bergh, 2008; Hansson, in press). Examples are pension reforms with a tighter connection between contributions and benefits, for example in the French and German point systems and in the Swedish defined-contribution system. The Japanese and German old age care insurance systems are other examples. Such earmarked taxes reduce the distortive effect of a tax.

An increased labor supply seems to be many countries' most favored measure to meet the strain of aging. For a long time, the opposite was common, with a number of countries taking measures to facilitate early retirement (see Gruber & Wise, 1999). To meet the challenges of aging, a number of countries are now trying to reverse these measures. Mandatory retirement ages are increased, and ways for early exit have been closed. Again, a closer link between taxes or contributions and benefits gives incentives for working longer hours and postponing retirement. Increased labor supply may be the solution to the financing problem caused by aging. Policy measures to give incentives in this direction are thus called for.

References and Further Readings

Ando, A., & Modigliani, F. (1963). The "life cycle" hypothesis of saving: Aggregate implications and tests. *American Economic review, 53*(1), 55–84.

Bengtsson, T., & Scott, K. (in press). The aging population. In T. Bengtsson (Ed.), *Population aging and the welfare state.* New York: Springer-Verlag.

Bergh, A. (2008). A race to the bottom for the big welfare states? In A. Bergh & R. Höijer (Eds.), *Institutional competition* (pp. 182–201). Northampton, MA: Edward Elgar.

Börsch-Supan, A., Ludwig, A., & Winter, J. (2006). Aging, pension reform and capital flows: A multi-country simulation model. *Economica, 73,* 625–658.

Breyer, F., & Craig, B. (1997). Voting on social security: Evidence from OECD countries. *European Journal of Political Economy, 13,* 705–724.

Breyer, F., & Felder, S. (2006). Life expectancy and health care expenditures: A new calculation for Germany using the costs of dying. *Health Policy, 75,* 178–186.

Browning, E. K. (1975). Why the social insurance budget is too large in a democracy. *Economic Inquiry, 13,* 373–388.

Burtless, G. (2008, February). *The rising age at retirement in industrial countries* (CRR Working Paper No. 2008-6). Chestnut Hill, MA: Center for Retirement Research.

Cutler, D. M., Poterba, J. M., Sheiner, L. M., & Summers, L. H. (1990). An aging society: Opportunity or challenge? *Brookings Papers on Economic Activity, 21*(1), 1–73.

Disney, R. (2007). Population ageing and the size of the welfare state: Is there a puzzle to explain? *European Journal of Political Economy, 23,* 542–553.

Erlandsen, S., & Nymoen, R. (2008). Consumption and population age structure. *Journal of Population Economics, 21,* 505–520.

EU Economic Policy Committee. (2003, October). *The impact of aging populations on public finances: Overview of analysis carried out at EU level and proposals for a future work programme* (EPC/ECFIN/435/03 final). Brussels, Belgium: Author.

Feldstein, M. (1974). Social security, induced retirement, and aggregate capital accumulation. *Journal of Political Economy, 82*(5), 905–926.

Galasso, V. (2006). *The political future of social security in aging societies.* Cambridge: MIT Press.

Gruber, J., & Wise, D. A. (Eds.). (1999). *Social security and retirement around the world.* Cambridge, MA: National Bureau of Economic Research.

Hansson, Å. (in press). In this world nothing is certain but death and taxes: Financing the elderly. In T. Bengtsson (Ed.), *Population aging and the welfare state.* New York: Springer-Verlag.

Holzmann, R., & Palmer, E. (Eds.). (2006). *Pension reform: Issues and prospects for non-financial defined contribution (NDC) schemes.* Washington, DC: World Bank.

Kruse, A. (1997, February). Replacement rates and age specific public expenditure. In European Commission (Ed.), *Pension systems and reforms: Britain, Hungary, Italy, Poland, Sweden* (P95-2139-R, pp. 191–209). Budapest, Hungary: Phare ACE Programme.

Kruse, A. (in press). A stable pension system: The eighth wonder. In T. Bengtsson (Ed.), *Population aging and the welfare state.* New York: Springer-Verlag.

Lindgren, B., & Lyttkens, C. H. (in press). Financing health care: A Gordian knot waiting to be cut. In T. Bengtsson (Ed.). *Population aging and the welfare state.* New York: Springer-Verlag.

Martin, J. P., & Whitehouse, E. (2008, July). *Reforming retirement-income systems: Lessons from recent experiences of OECD countries* (OECD Social, Employment and Migration Working Paper No. 66). Paris: Organisation for Economic Co-operation and Development, Directorate for Employment, Labour and Social Affairs.

Organisation for Economic Co-operation and Development. (2002). *Policies for an aging population: Recent measures and areas for further reforms* (Macroeconomic and Structural Policy Analysis Working Paper No. 1). Paris: Author.

Organisation for Economic Co-operation and Development. (2008). *Employment outlook 2008.* Retrieved December 20, 2009, from http://www.oecd.org/document/25/0,3343,en_2649_33927_40 762969_1_1_1_37457,00.html

Palmer, E. (2006). What is NDC? In R. Holzmann & E. Palmer (Eds.), *Pension reform: Issues and prospects for non-financial defined contribution (NDC) schemes* (pp. 17–33). Washington, DC: World Bank.

Samuelson, P. (1958). An exact consumption-loan model of interest with or without the social contrivance of money. *Journal of Political Economy, 66*(6), 467–482.

Selén, J., & Ståhlberg, A.-C. (2007). Why Sweden's pension reform was able to be successfully implemented. *European Journal of Political Economy, 23,* 1175–1184.

Sinn, H.-W., & Uebelmesser, S. (2002). Pensions and the path to gerontocracy in Germany. *European Journal of Political Economy, 19,* 153–158.

Sjoblom, K. (1985). Voting for social security. *Public Choice, 45,* 227–240.

Sjögren Lindquist, G., & Wadensjö, E. (in press). The labour market for older workers in Sweden: Changes and prospects. *European Papers on the New Welfare.*

Söderström, L. (2008). *The economics of social protection.* Northampton, MA: Edward Elgar.

Ståhlberg, A.-C., Kruse, A., & Sundén, A. (2005). Pension design and gender. *European Journal of Social Security, 7*(1), 57–79.

Uebelmesser, S. (2004). Political feasibility of pension reforms. *Topics in Economic Analysis and Policy, 4,* 20.

United Nations. (2007). *World population prospects: The 2006 revision population database.* Retrieved December 20, 2009, from http://ecoglobe.ch/population/e/p2k07407.htm

Whitehouse, E. (2007, October). *Life-expectancy risk and pensions: Who bears the burden?* (OECD Social, Employment and Migration Working Paper No. 60). Paris: Organisation for Economic Co-operation and Development.

World Bank. (1994). *Averting the old age crisis: Policies to protect the old and promote growth.* Washington, DC: Author; Oxford, UK: Oxford University Press.

58

AGRICULTURAL ECONOMICS

PATRICIA A. DUFFY

Auburn University

Agricultural economics is an applied field of economics that focuses primarily on food and fiber production and consumption. Defining the boundaries of agricultural economics can be difficult, however, because issues outside these traditional areas have become increasingly important to the profession in recent years. Agricultural economists engage in work ranging from farm-level cost accounting to assessing the consumer impact of food safety and nutrition labeling to analyzing worldwide agricultural trade patterns and a host of other real-world issues. Accordingly, the Agricultural and Applied Economics Association (AAEA), the largest professional organization for agricultural economists in the United States, currently recognizes a variety of topic areas under the broad disciplinary umbrella, including community and rural development, food safety and nutrition, international trade, natural resources and environmental economics, consumer and household economics, markets and competition, agribusiness management, and production economics (AAEA, n.d.).

Because many other topics in applied economics, including natural resources and environmental economics, are handled separately in this volume, this chapter concentrates on the field of agricultural economics as it relates to the food and fiber sector. It is worthwhile to note, however, that within the profession, an increasingly large share of university and government agricultural economists focus their teaching, research, and outreach efforts on work outside this sector.

The broadening of the field of agricultural economics reflects changes in the national economy. Dramatic changes in agricultural technology over the course of the twentieth century have meant that fewer and fewer people have been needed to feed more and more people. According to the National Agricultural Statistics Service of the U.S. Department of Agriculture, production agriculture (e.g., farming) directly employs fewer than 3 million workers, including farm owners and operators, or about 1% to 1.5% of the total U.S. workforce, depending on how the workforce is measured. Even as far back as 1946, the Nobel Prize–winning agricultural economist Ted Schultz (1946) commented on the decreasing need for labor in production agriculture and the declining role of production agriculture in U.S. employment. However, the food and fiber system, which includes processing, agricultural input production, and retail sales of food and fiber products remains one of the largest sectors in the U.S. economy, accounting for about 12% of the total U.S. gross domestic product, and employing about 16% of U.S. workers (Edmondson, 2004.) Thus, agricultural economics addresses issues of importance to a variety of clientele groups in the United States, including but not limited to those directly involved in farming. As one popular bumper sticker phrased it, "If you eat, you are involved in agriculture."

Further, although production agriculture may not hold a large, direct share of the U.S. economy, in many developing nations, agriculture remains the largest employer, and trade in agricultural products is an important engine for economic growth. Organizations focusing on international development, such as the World Bank, the Food and Agricultural Organization of the United Nations, and the International Food Policy Research Institute are all strong employers of agricultural economists. The International Association of Agricultural Economists (IAAE, 2008) provides a worldwide network for the discipline, and professional societies for agricultural economists can be found in countries around the world. The wide scope of the field and its overall importance to both the U.S. economy and worldwide economic systems thus warrants the inclusion of this chapter in *21st Century Economics: A Reference Handbook.*

In this chapter, an overview of the field of agricultural economics is provided, focusing on the applications and contributions affecting the food and fiber sector. The chapter begins with a brief history of the field. Next, the underlying theoretical underpinnings are discussed. This theoretical section is followed by an outline of quantitative tools used in agricultural economics, then by short descriptions of a few major subfields of the discipline. Some notable agricultural economists and their contributions to the profession are then discussed, followed by a section on the future of the profession. Finally, this chapter concludes with a list of references and some suggested further readings for those wishing to gain a deeper knowledge of this topic.

Short History of Agricultural Economics

The field of agricultural economics traces its origins largely to the growing demand at the turn of the twentieth century for college-educated professionals who could address the special concerns of the agricultural sector. A seminal textbook, *Farm Management* by Cornell agricultural economist George F. Warren, was published in 1913. Shortly after, in 1919, the *Journal of Farm Economics* was launched by the American Farm Economics Association with the stated purpose of serving those interested in "economic forces and influences as they operate to affect the business of farming," ("Forward," 1919, p. 1). At the time the journal was launched, a sizable proportion (over 20%) of the population lived on farms. From the end of the Civil War to the mid-1930s, with the westward movement of population, farm numbers rose sharply from about 2 million to a peak of nearly 7 million. Farming and the related concerns of rural residents were of widespread interest in the early decades of the twentieth century, and a journal dedicated to farm economics would have had a strong appeal at this time.

The journal continues to operate to this day; however, in 1967, its name was changed to the *American Journal of Agricultural Economics,* reflecting the broadening of interests that occurred over that time. The association that sponsored the original journal also continues to this day, although its name has twice changed, once to the American Agricultural Economics Association, and more recently to the Agricultural and Applied Economics Association, again reflecting the increasing scope of activities for its members.

The premiere issue of the *Journal of Farm Economics* included a presidential address by G. A. Billings of the U.S. government's Office of Farm Management, an organization established in 1905 that later gave way to the Office of Farm Management and Farm Economics and, finally, in 1961, to the present-day Economic Research Service of the U.S. Department of Agriculture. In addition, the issue contained an article on farm labor outlook by Secretary of Agriculture G. I. Christie and an article by H. W. Hawthorne, also from the Office of Farm Management, on information obtained from farm surveys. Notable to a modern-day agricultural economist is that, even from its inception long before the era of high-speed computing, the field was data driven. Also, a focus on practical, real-word problems is clearly evident in these historical documents.

At around the same period, in the early years of the twentieth century, agricultural economics (often then called *farm economics* or *farm management*) became an area of study in universities across the nation. Land-grant universities, in particular, with their focus on agricultural and mechanical arts, were fertile grounds for the development of this field. At the Agricultural and Mechanical College of North Carolina at Raleigh (which later became North Carolina State University), for example, a course in agricultural economics was required of all students in the College of Agriculture as far back as 1897, although a separate department, at the time called Agricultural Administration, was not established until 1923 (Bishop & Hoover, n.d.). At Michigan State University, a course in farm management was offered for the first time in 1906. At the University of Minnesota, a department for agricultural economics was established in the College of Agriculture in 1909 (Shaars, 1972). At Auburn University, in Alabama, a department of agricultural economics was established in the College of Agriculture in 1928 (Yeager & Stevenson, 2000). Interested readers are also referred to Bernard Stanton's (2001) history of agricultural economics at Cornell and Willard Cochrane's (1983) history of the discipline at the University of Minnesota.

In the first half of the twentieth century, farm-level issues remained the primary concern of research, outreach, and teaching efforts. One important area of endeavor was calculation of the cost of production for agricultural commodities. Other work involved agricultural marketing, credit, and then, in the years following the Agricultural Adjustment Act in 1933, the increasingly important subfield of agricultural policy. A glance at the table of contents of the *Journal of Farm Economics* will show, however, that even as far back as the 1930s, there was widespread interest in international trade in agricultural products. The scientific study of factors affecting consumer demand for agricultural products also dates to this period.

The period following World War II saw an expansion of the agricultural economics field with universities increasing the size of their faculties and the government employing larger numbers of agricultural economists. Membership in the American Agricultural Economics Association peaked in the 1980s and has been declining since.

The decades after World War II saw a proliferation of professional associations and sponsored journals in which agricultural economists could publish an expanding array of papers related to research, teaching, and outreach. Regional associations differentiated themselves, to some degree, in terms of their concerns for agricultural problems specific to their geographic areas, based on either different agricultural practices and outputs or different regional institutions. In 1969, the Southern Agricultural Economics Association launched the *Southern Journal of Agricultural Economics.* This journal was renamed the *Journal of Agricultural and Applied Economics* in 1993, reflecting a trend away from regional identification and an increased emphasis on applied economic analysis outside the traditional agricultural sector. The Western Agricultural Economics Association began publishing the *Western Journal of Agricultural Economics* in 1977. From the outset, this journal specifically solicited articles on natural resource economics, along with those related to human resources, and rural development. In 1992, this journal changed its name to the *Journal of Agricultural and Resource Economics,* to emphasize its continued focus on the economics of natural resources and to remove its regional focus. In the same mode, the *Northeastern Journal of Agricultural Economics,* whose publication dates from 1984, was renamed in 1993 as the *Agricultural and Resource Economics Review.* The *North Central Journal of Agricultural Economics,* published from 1979 to 1990, was renamed as the *Review of Agricultural Economics* and then again renamed in 2010 as *Applied Economic Perspectives and Policy.* It is no longer associated with an individual regional association.

The number of international journals devoted to agricultural economics also expanded over a similar period. Currently, international journals include the *Canadian Journal of Agricultural Economics,* the *European Review of Agricultural Economics,* the *Australian Journal of Agricultural and Resource Economics,* the *ICFAI University Journal of Agricultural Economics* (India), and the *Journal of Agricultural Economics* (United Kingdom). The International Association of Agricultural Economists publishes *Agricultural Economics,* which was launched in 1986. The importance of the field internationally is also evidenced by the recent launch of the new journal, *China Agricultural Economics Review,* by faculty at the China Agricultural University in Beijing, China.

Another important change that has taken place over time involves the use of quantitative techniques. Although statistical and quantitative analyses were important in agricultural economics since the field's inception, the advent of computer technology has greatly expanded the methods that can be employed for the analysis of agricultural economic problems. Today, agricultural economists employ highly sophisticated statistical techniques, and most are adept at the use of a variety of computer software packages, from electronic spreadsheet programs to dedicated statistical software. Further discussion of quantitative techniques in agricultural economics follows later in this chapter.

Undergraduate Education

Education in agricultural economics has evolved considerably from its early twentieth-century roots in farm management. A search of the College Board (n.d.) Web site yielded a list of over 100 universities in the United States and Canada offering 4-year degrees in agricultural economics or the closely related major of agricultural business.

In addition to university-wide general educational requirements, students majoring in agricultural economics or agricultural business typically take foundations courses in business, usually in economics and accounting, as well as a sampling of courses in agricultural sciences, such as agronomy, horticulture, and animal sciences. Courses in the home department cover topics such as agricultural marketing, agricultural finance, agribusiness or farm management, natural resource and environmental economics, and policy and trade. Additionally, most universities require quantitative courses, such as calculus and statistics, for all undergraduate majors in this field.

Theoretical Underpinnings

As an applied field, agricultural economics combines basic theory, quantitative techniques, and institutional knowledge to explain or predict real-world phenomena. Thus, most agricultural economists use economic theory for generating hypotheses to be tested or as the basis for formulating a statistical model to be estimated. Microeconomic theory is the branch of theory most often used, although a few agricultural economists have applied theory from macroeconomics (see, e.g., Penson & Hughes, 1979). In addition to drawing heavily from the field of economics for its general theory and disciplinary home, agricultural economics also may draw on other business disciplines including finance, marketing, and management, depending on the problem at hand, although even in these cases, economic theory forms the foundation. Agricultural economics may also draw heavily on biologically based disciplines, engineering, or ecology. In Part II of this handbook, economic theory is discussed in considerable detail; hence, the material will not be repeated at length here. Rather, this section will instead focus on how agricultural economists use microeconomic theory in their applied work.

A theoretical economic model is an abstraction from reality. To be useful, it cannot be so simple as to ignore key interrelationships, but neither can it be so complex that it obscures these relationships. To formulate a good theoretical model, agricultural economists must be well versed in general economic theory and must understand the processes and institutions involved in the problem of interest. The best theoretical model in the world, for example, would be useless to a production economist who did not know the growing seasons or climate zones for the agricultural products of interest in the research problem.

When existing theory has not been sufficiently developed to provide necessary insights into an applied problem, agricultural economists have contributed to the theory in important ways. Two classic examples are Clark Edwards's (1959) work on asset fixity and supply and a work by James Houck (1964) on the relationship between the demand elasticity for joint products and the demand elasticity of the underlying commodity. Similarly, Zvi Griliches (1957) contributed greatly to the understanding of causes and consequences of technical change, beginning with his seminal paper on hybrid corn. A recent example of contribution to economic theory is the paper by Carlos Carpio, Michael Wohlgenant, and Charles Safley (2008), providing a framework in consumer decision making for distinguishing the effect of time as a resource constraint and time that provides enjoyment. Another recent paper extending economic theory is the Jeffrey LaFrance and Rulon Pope (2008) investigation of the homogeneity properties of supply functions in the Gorman class.

Production Theory

Production theory is used in farm management applications, estimations of productivity growth, and formulation of estimates of the response of agricultural output to changes in economic conditions. The basis of production theory in microeconomics is the production function, a systematic way of showing the relationship between inputs and outputs, in physical terms. To produce an agricultural output such as corn, for example, land, fertilizer, labor, and other inputs are required. Although some may view the estimation of production relationships as the work of the biologically based fields, agricultural economists were among the pioneers in this area. Articles dating from the 1940s in the *Journal of Farm Economics* tackle the estimation of physical production relationships (Heady, 1946; Tintner & Brownlee, 1944).

An important principle related to the production function is the law of diminishing marginal returns (often called just the *law of diminishing returns*). The engineering law states that as additional units of a variable input are used in combination with one or more fixed inputs, the amount of additional output per additional unit of variable input will begin to decline. The law of diminishing returns can be traced back to the concerns of early economists such as von Thünen, Turgot, Malthus, and Ricardo and was one of the first principles addressed by agricultural economists (see, e.g., Spillman, 1923). It remains an important concept to this day, especially in the area of farm management.

Agricultural economists have long been interested in estimating the supply curve for agricultural products. Neoclassical production theory maintains that firm behavior is characterized by the maximization of profits subject to a set of technical and institutional constraints. In the basic perfectly competitive model, where perfect knowledge is assumed and producers are said to be price takers (i.e., no individual producer can influence market price for either output or inputs), the profit function can be used to solve mathematically for quantities supplied. Without requiring the assumption of perfectly competitive output markets, an alternative specification involves minimizing the cost of producing a given amount of output.

Because prices are fairly transparent in the market, in recent years, applied economists have typically started with indirect profit or cost functions (e.g., functions specified in terms of prices and costs) and used these to generate the functional form of their subsequent estimations of output supply or input demand. Readers interested in the properties of the functional forms specified for the production function and how they relate to indirect profit or cost functions and the derived supply function or input demand equations are referred to Robert Chambers (1988) or to Bruce Beattie and C. Robert Taylor (1985). For a classic example of the use of an indirect profit function to specify input demand and output supply equations, readers may see C. Richard Shumway's (1983) article on supply response of Texas field crops. Readers are also referred to Christopher O'Donnell, Richard Shumway, and V. Eldon Ball (1999) for a discussion of using flexible functional forms to specify input demand equations.

Although the perfectly competitive model has been the basis of much useful work, modifications to this model have been made to address real-world issues. For example, many factors important to agricultural producers, such as the output price to be received in the future, are uncertain. Thus, the role of producers' price expectations and their effect on supply response was explored in a seminal work by Marc Nerlove (1956). Additionally, output is not perfectly predictable because factors outside the producers' control, such as weather or pests, may affect it. The basic profit-maximization decision model may thus be altered to reflect producers' aversion to highly risky enterprises. For an overview of how risk is incorporated into agricultural decision making, readers may see Richard Just and Rulon Pope (2002) or J. Brian Hardaker, Ruud Huirne, Jock Anderson, and Gudbrand Lien (2004).

In field crop supply estimation, another important modification is the inclusion of variables to account for farm program provisions, such as support prices or acreage reduction programs, which may influence producer decisions. A method of accounting for government program effects on supply was developed by James Houck and Mary Ryan (1972). A theoretical framework to consider both farm program provisions and the impact of risk on agricultural supply for field crops was developed by Jean-Paul Chavas and Matthew Holt (1990) as the foundation for the empirical estimation of the aggregate response of soybean and corn acreage to changes in price, policy provisions, and risk.

The pages of agricultural economics journals will provide many other examples of the use of production economic theory to formulate models for empirical work. In addition to the types of work already considered, production economists have also provided insight on innovation and structural change (see, e.g., Huang & Sexton, 1996) and the impact of research expenditures on productivity. Readers interested in a more advanced and extensive treatment of the work of agricultural economists in production economics are referred to the *Handbook of Agricultural Economics: Volume 1A: Agricultural Production* (Gardner & Rausser, 2001a).

Consumer Theory

Consumer theory is also used extensively in agricultural economics, notably in the formulation of market demand curves for agricultural products or in applied price analysis. The basic behavioral hypothesis is that the consumer, in deciding among the myriad of products to buy, selects that combination and quantity that maximizes his or her utility (happiness) subject to a budget constraint. The budget constraint includes the consumer's income and market prices, both of which are assumed to be beyond the immediate control of the consumer. Income may also be assumed fixed for analytical convenience and to focus on the main objects of choice—namely, the quantities of the various goods the consumer purchases.

In some instances of demand equation estimation, a specific functional form for the utility function is specified, as in the almost ideal demand system model (Deaton & Muellbauer, 1980). More often, in estimation of demand for agricultural products, utility theory is used to place restrictions on estimated elasticities and to reduce the number of price variables included in the model through the maintained hypotheses of weak separability and two-stage budgeting.

A difference between agricultural economics and general economics, in terms of applications of demand theory, is that basic agricultural products are more likely to be homogenous or largely indistinguishable from each other than are other products in the market. Thus, a generalized demand curve for eggs, milk, or catfish filets makes more intuitive sense than a generalized demand curve for automobiles, which are distinguished by brand name and other features. Outside the agricultural sector, there are far fewer examples of truly homogenous products, other than raw minerals or metal ore. Because many agricultural products are homogeneous and the farm firms producing them have no individual control over the output price, generic advertising and promotion programs have been employed by the industries. Agricultural economists have provided valuable information to these industries on the effect of these promotion efforts both in U.S. markets and in export markets (see, e.g., Forker & Ward, 1993; Nichols, Kinnucan, & Ackerman, 1990).

Even within the agricultural sector, the assumption of homogenous products may not apply. Sales of agricultural land, for example, would not fit the assumption of a homogenous product. Many factors, including location, would distinguish one parcel from another. In addition, the market for land is usually thin, so that individual buyers and sellers may influence price. Alternative theoretical models have been applied in situations when the assumptions of perfect competition do not fit. Hedonic pricing models, which relate the price of a product to its attributes, have been applied to products that are not homogenous, one of the earliest applications in agricultural economics being by Frederick Waugh (1928) for vegetables. In markets for land, methods to account for spatial factors have also been applied. Agricultural economists have also incorporated theory related to asymmetric information into their conceptual models and contributed to the development of this vein of work. Even for products typically considered homogeneous, such as wheat or cotton, distinctions may be made in international trade models with respect to country of origin.

Demand theory applied in agricultural economics has incorporated the links between the farm and retail sectors. Exploration of the factors affecting marketing margins, or the farm-to-retail price spread, has been a fruitful area of applied research. A notable example of a paper that contributed to economic theory in this area as well as provided useful empirical information is by Michael Wohlgenant (1989).

Finally, because prices are determined by the intersection of supply and demand, agricultural price analysis is a subfield that draws from both consumer and producer theory. Agricultural economists working under this general umbrella have made strong contributions to the analysis of futures markets, the economics of storage, the economics of food labeling and food safety, and spatial price analysis. A reader interested in a more extensive treatment of the applications of consumer theory and price analysis by agricultural economists is referred to the *Handbook of Agricultural Economics: Volume 1B: Marketing, Distribution and Consumers* (Gardner & Rausser, 2001b).

Equilibrium Displacement Models

One final concept is worth noting in this section. Elasticity of supply or demand relates the percentage change in a commodity's own price to the percentage change in the quantity supplied or demanded. Elasticities of demand and supply as well as price-transmission elasticities taken from previously published work can be used in applied analyses. These studies, often called *equilibrium displacement models*, trace the effects of a shock or shifter of either the demand or supply curve (or both) on market prices, quantities, and producer and consumer welfare. Complicated real-world linkages between retail and wholesale markets can be specified, with various degrees of market power assumed at different levels in the marketing chain. However, to provide good estimates of the likely effects of the shock, the elasticity estimates used in the equilibrium displacement model must be accurate. Hence, the professional standards for publication of supply and demand estimates, from which elasticities can be drawn, require that the researchers present both sound theoretical justification for the functional form of the model and employ appropriate quantitative methods to avoid introducing bias in the parameters upon estimation.

(For further discussion of the use of equilibrium displacement models in applied research, see Piggott, 1992.)

Quantitative Techniques in Agricultural Economics

Agricultural economics makes heavy use of quantitative methods. Statistical techniques used by agricultural economics generally fall under the heading of *econometrics,* discussed in Chapter 5 of this handbook. As such, they will not be presented in great detail here. In observational data, as opposed to experimental data, many things change at once. Statistical methods of overcoming the limitations of the available data have been employed by agricultural economists for decades. Most published articles by agricultural economists involve the use of sophisticated econometric techniques. An excellent, although fairly technical, discussion of the use of and problems with these techniques was provided by Just (2008) in his presidential address to the AAEA.

Operations Research Methods

Although not as widely used as econometrics, operations research techniques have been employed in agricultural economics almost since the development of these tools in the period during and following World War II. Techniques typically used by agricultural economists are of two general types: mathematical programming models and simulation models. Mathematical programming models have an objective function to be maximized or minimized, and simulation models generally do not.

Linear programming, one of the best-known operations research techniques, is widely used in farm management work and is often taught in undergraduate classes (see, e.g., Kay, Edwards, & Duffy, 2008, chap. 12). Linear programming models have a linear objective function to be maximized or minimized subject to linear inequality constraints. They can be useful models for firm-level analysis in agriculture, either in terms of profit maximization for the farm or in terms of calculating a least-cost diet for feeding livestock.

Even before the simplex method for solving linear programming models was formally developed by Dantzig in 1947, George Stigler (1945) investigated the problem of the minimum cost diet for human subsistence using approximation to solve the constrained minimization problem. The objective of the model in this paper was to minimize the cost of feeding a person, subject to keeping nutrient intake above or below certain levels necessary for health. Calculation of the thrifty food plan for the Food Stamp Program is a similar modern-day endeavor, although information on human nutrition and techniques to solve this sort of problem have improved vastly since Stigler's time.

Following the introduction of the simplex method of solution, linear programming was adopted rapidly in the agricultural economics profession so that by 1960, it was already well established (Eisgruber & Reisch, 1961). Earl Heady and Wilfred Candler (1958) contributed an influential and widely used textbook on this new technique, specifically geared toward uses in agriculture. Although most of the early applications were to farm management, the technique was also used for marketing and other areas.

With the advent of high-speed computers, feasible operations research methods in agricultural economics became more sophisticated. R. C. Agrawal and Earl Heady (1972), in an updated textbook, listed several extensions to the linear model, such as variable resource programming, integer programming, quadratic programming, nonlinear programming, and dynamic programming. Loren Tauer (1983) introduced Target MOTAD, an extension of linear programming that allowed for a theoretically consistent method of incorporating a producer's risk preferences into the decision framework.

Simulation, another operations research tool, also has early roots in the agricultural economics profession, tracing back at least as far as an article in the *Journal of Farm Economics* by Pinhas Zusman and Amotz Amiad (1965). An overview of early uses for simulation in agricultural economics was provided by Anderson (1974). Simulation models can be used at the firm level, to simulate, for example, the probable effects on output and income of alternative farm program proposals, or at the sector level, to simulate the probable impacts of technical change or changes in macroeconomic conditions. Models can incorporate real-world linkages and the probabilistic nature of some outcomes, such as weather events, farm yields, or prices. Some simulation models use econometric estimates as their core, and others are constructed from systematic observation of the important relationships.

Areas of Concentration

In a recent paper presented to the AAEA and subsequently published in *Applied Economic Perspectives and Policy,* Gregory Perry (2010) pointed out the proliferation in areas of concentration in the association, from 12 in 1966 to more than 80 today, and the decline in the primacy of the traditional fields of farm management and marketing. Of approximately 2400 members of the association listed in the current directory, only 114 chose farm management as one of their areas of specialization, and 141 members chose marketing. One traditional area, agricultural policy, retains a fair share of the membership, with 291 members listing it as one of their subfields.

Space does not permit a discussion of each area of concentration in agricultural economics, and many of these, such as diet, consumption, and health, overlap with other fields of applied economics. Hence, the following paragraphs are devoted to providing a quick summary of a few agriculturally focused subfields. Readers interested in a broader look at the work of agricultural economics are referred to John Penson, Oral Capps, C. Parr Roson, and Richard Woodward (2006).

Farm Management and Production Economics

Although these are separate areas of concentration, there is considerable overlap between the two. Farm management is the area in agricultural economics primarily concerned with the profitability of a farm firm. Farm management professionals develop both cost-of-production estimates (based on already realized outcomes) and planning budgets (projections for future outcomes) for various farm enterprises, such as cotton production or a cow-calf operation. They are concerned with topics such as optimal machinery size for a given farm, risk management, income tax management, and a host of other issues that directly or indirectly affect the profits of the farm. Because farm policies and natural resource protection policies affect farm profitability, there can be considerable overlap between the work of farm management professionals and those specializing in policy or natural resource and environmental economics.

Production economics has its roots in farm management. Factors that make an individual farm profitable or not profitable will also affect the overall supply of a commodity. Production economists are concerned with such topics as the impact of technical change on agricultural output, efficiency gains in the use of inputs, returns to agricultural research, and the aggregate impact in terms of output of farm and environmental policies. Farm management specialists and agricultural production economists will often engage in interdisciplinary or multidisciplinary work with production scientists, such as agronomists or animal scientists. It is not unusual for researchers in this field to coauthor work in the journals of these other disciplines. The *Agronomy Journal,* for example, lists economics as one of its target areas, and there are currently over 100 papers in the area of economics posted on this journal's Web site.

Agricultural Marketing and Prices

Agricultural marketing can involve any of the processes that move an agricultural commodity from the farm gate to the dinner plate. A specialist in agricultural marketing may direct efforts toward helping establish a farmers' market, for example, or study the relationship between the futures price of a commodity and its cash price. Food processing and distribution are also areas of interest inside this concentration, and in this respect, agricultural marketing can have considerable overlap with the agribusiness area. Although agricultural marketing has much in common with business marketing, agricultural marketing distinguishes itself in terms of a heavier reliance on microeconomic theory, a greater focus on homogenous products, and an emphasis on the marketing institutions related to agriculture, such as forward contracting and the commodity futures and options market. Interested readers are referred to Richard Kohls, Joseph Uhl, and Chris Hurt (2007).

The subfield of agricultural prices examines price determination for agricultural products. As such, it is concerned with the intersection of supply and demand. Determination of marketing margins and the impact of industry structure on price are topics of investigation in this concentration, as is price differentiation based on spatial or quality factors. Readers interested in learning more about agricultural price analysis are referred to William Tomek and Kenneth Robinson (2003) or John Goodwin (1994).

Agricultural Policy

Since the inception of agricultural policy in the 1930s, agricultural economists have been at the forefront of this focus area. The cost of the major provisions of the U.S. farm bill averaged more than $45 billion per year over the 2002 to 2007 period, including $15 billion in farm support payments and more than $29 billion in Food Stamp Program costs (Chite, 2008). Given the sizable outlays, it is not surprising that agricultural economists have been interested in the impact of these programs. Analysis of farm programs may involve their effect on farm profitability, farm structure, or choice of inputs and outputs. Readers interested in learning more about agricultural policy are referred to Ronald Knutson, J. B. Penn, and Barry Flinchbaugh (2007).

Agribusiness Management

The term *agribusiness* can be applied to any firm involved in the food and fiber industry, from a farm to a retail store or restaurant to an input supplier, such as a firm that manufactures fertilizer or tractors, to an agricultural service provider, such as a veterinary operation or an agricultural lender. As such, this area overlaps or subsumes several other areas. As a research category within agricultural economics, the term generally refers to studies dealing with input suppliers, processors, retailers, or other sectors beyond the farm.

Perry (2010) pointed out that a shift has occurred in undergraduate education, with a decline in the number of undergraduate degrees in agricultural economics since the early 1990s, largely offset by an increase in the number of degrees in agribusiness. Distinguishing the two degree programs, in terms of coverage, is quite difficult, and some programs that offer a degree in agricultural economics have an agribusiness option. Further complicating a clear definition of the term *agribusiness* is its use in other departments inside colleges of agriculture as an option within, for example, agronomy or animal science. Readers interested in learning more about agribusiness management are referred to Steven Erickson, Jay Taylor Akridge, Fred Barnard, and W. David Downey (2002).

Agricultural Finance

Agricultural finance is the subfield of agricultural economics that deals most explicitly with capital and the use of credit. Topics in this subfield would include such endeavors as investment analysis, the effects of debt load on farm survival and structure, taxation, capitalization, and interest rates. The farm credit system was established in 1916 as a source of funds for agriculture, and some of the work in agricultural finance has focused on this system and its impact on the agricultural sector. The line between agricultural finance and other subfields is not always easy to draw, however, because investment and the use of credit are important in farm management and agricultural marketing. Considerable work on risk and uncertainty in agriculture has originated from research focused on agriculture finance. A journal dedicated to agricultural finance, the *Agricultural Finance Review,* began publication in 1938 and continues to this day. For more information about agricultural finance, see Peter Barry, Paul Ellinger, John Hopkin, and C. B. Baker (2000).

Other Areas

Agricultural economists have made considerable contributions to development economics, with Ted Schultz, a notable agricultural economist, winning a Nobel Prize for his work in this area. Many agricultural economists specialize in resources or environmental economics. Others focus their work in the area of international trade. In recent years, agricultural economists have made contributions to the area of health economics, particularly concerning the link between diet and health. Given the large outlays from the U.S. Department of Agriculture for nutrition support programs, especially the Food Stamp Program, some agricultural economists have conducted studies to estimate the impact of these programs on the nutritional status or food security level of the recipients. In all of these endeavors, the line between agricultural economics, general applied economics, and consumer economics is almost impossible to draw.

A Handful of Notable Agricultural Economists

Those interested in a thorough study of the contributions of agricultural economists to the solution of applied problems affecting agriculture and related areas are referred to the list of fellows of the AAEA (n.d.). The Association began naming fellows in 1957, and short biographies of the fellows, including their major contributions to the field, are published in the December issues of the journal. Because of space limitations, only a handful of these notable agricultural economists can be discussed in this chapter.

Theodore Schultz (1964) received a Nobel Memorial Prize in Economics in 1979 in recognition for his work in development economics. As he pointed out in his acceptance speech, the majority of the world's people are poor, and most of the poor are involved in agriculture. He was also one of the pioneers in exploring human capital and its role in development. A slim volume, *Transforming Traditional Agriculture*, is an excellent starting point for understanding Ted Schultz's contributions to the literature on economic development.

Schultz is also known for his unwillingness to bow to political pressure within agriculture during a controversy over the wartime promotion of margarine, in place of butter, in a pamphlet by an Iowa State agriculture economist, Oswald H. Brownlee. Schultz, then department chair at Iowa State, resigned in protest and took a position at the University of Chicago when Brownlee was forced to retract his pamphlet. The incident also illustrates the role of agricultural economists in providing society with objective analyses of the benefits and costs of alternative programs, policies, and investments.

D. Gale Johnson (1947), a colleague of Ted Schultz at the University of Chicago, made significant contributions in the analysis of commodity price policy, including his seminal work *Forward Prices for Agriculture*. He also contributed work on the agricultural labor market and to theoretical and practical approaches to understanding agricultural supply, among other topics. In addition to his original research, he is renowned for his contribution to the field in terms of educating students. Collected papers of Johnson can be found in *The Economics of Agriculture: Volume 1: Selected Papers of D. Gale Johnson* (Antle & Sumner, 1996a). *The Economics of Agriculture: Volume 2: Papers in Honor of D. Gale Johnson* (Antle & Sumner, 1996b) contains tributes from his former students.

Heady (1952), a professor at Iowa State University, made enormous contributions to agricultural production economics and agriculture finance. His seminal work, *Economics of Agricultural Production and Resource Use,* laid the foundation for production economics efforts for the decades following its publication. He pioneered the use of operations research techniques in farm management and made significant contributions to analysis of risk and uncertainty in agriculture.

Cochrane (1958), a professor and dean at the University of Minnesota, made substantial contributions in the field of agricultural policy and prices. His book *Farm Prices: Myth and Reality* laid out his famous treadmill theory, under which rapid output-enhancing technological advances caused a long period of production disequilibrium with resulting low product prices in agriculture. In addition to his scholarly work, he served as an agricultural advisor during John Kennedy's 1960 presidential campaign and subsequently as the chief economics advisor to the Secretary of Agriculture.

John Kenneth Galbraith (1958, 1995), a two-time winner of the Presidential Medal of Freedom, is known both for his work as a political advisor in several administrations and for his best-selling works, including *The Affluent Society*. He also published a volume laying out his largely Keynesian monetary views, *Money: Whence It Came, Where It Went*.

Future of the Field

If the past is a predictor of the future, very likely there will be fewer agricultural economists working on a wider array of problems. Increasingly, departments and degree programs have adopted the name *applied economics* or *resource economics* or other designations, showing the shift away from a sole focus on agricultural issues. As Perry (2010) pointed out, most of these departments have not merged into the general economics department, and he predicts that the number of what he called *AE cluster* departments will not change greatly in the future but that even fewer of these departments will be known as agricultural economics.

Regardless of what their home department is called, agricultural economists will very likely continue to lend their talents to a variety of applied problems. Sandra Batie (2008) in her fellows address for the AAEA discussed "wicked problems": complex problems that do not lend themselves to the type of rational, linear approach typical of applied science. To remain relevant, she suggests that agricultural economists will need to work on these sorts of issues, stepping outside disciplinary bounds to do so. Agricultural economics, which by its nature is interdisciplinary, may be a field well placed to address "wicked problems."

In their principles of economics textbook, Paul Samuelson and William Nordhaus (2005), in a section titled "Cool Heads at the Service of Warm Hearts," stated, "The ultimate goal of economic science is to improve the living conditions of people in their everyday lives" (p. 6). As a field, agricultural economics has long embodied this view, whether the work falls under the traditional area of farm management or in one of the newer concentrations, such as health economics. A solid training in economic theory coupled with sound quantitative techniques will serve the profession well in the decades to come.

Author's Note: The author gratefully acknowledges the helpful comments of Henry Kinnucan, James Novak, Rachel Smith, and Michael Wetzstein on an earlier version of this chapter.

References and Further Readings

Agrawal, R. C., & Heady, E. O. (1972). *Operations research methods for agricultural decisions.* Ames: Iowa State University Press.

Agricultural and Applied Economics Association. (n.d.). *AAEA online.* Available at http://www.aaea.org

Anderson, J. R. (1974). Simulation: Methodology and application in agricultural economics. *Review of Marketing and Agricultural Economics, 42,* 3–55.

Antle, J. M., & Sumner, D. A. (Eds.). (1996a). *The economics of agriculture: Vol. 1. Selected papers of D. Gale Johnson.* Chicago: University of Chicago Press.

Antle, J. M., & Sumner, D. A. (Eds.). (1996b). *The economics of agriculture: Vol. 2. Papers in honor of D. Gale Johnson.* Chicago: University of Chicago Press.

Barry, P. J., Ellinger, P. N., Hopkin, J. A., & Baker, C. B. (2000). *Financial management in agriculture* (6th ed.). Upper Saddle River, NJ: Prentice Hall.

Batie, S. S. (2008). Wicked problems and applied economics. *American Journal of Agricultural Economics, 90,* 1176–1191.

Beattie, B. R., & Taylor, C. R. (1985). *The economics of production.* New York: John Wiley.

Bishop, C. E., & Hoover, D. M. (n.d.). *ARE history.* Retrieved December 30, 2008, from http://www.ag-econ.ncsu.edu/ARE_history.htm

Carpio, C. E., Wohlgenant, M. K., & Safley, C. D. (2008). A structural econometric model of joint consumption of goods and recreational time: An application to pick-your-own fruit. *American Journal of Agricultural Economics, 90,* 644–657.

Chambers, R. G. (1988). *Applied production analysis: A dual approach.* New York: Cambridge University Press.

Chavas, J.-P., & Holt, M. T. (1990). Acreage decisions under risk: The case of corn and soybeans. *American Journal of Agricultural Economics, 72,* 529–538.

Chite, R. M. (2008, January). *Farm bill budget and costs: 2002 vs. 2007. CRS report for Congress.* Retrieved January 5, 2009, from http://www.nationalaglawcenter.org/assets/crs/RS22694.pdf

Cochrane, W. W. (1958). *Farm prices: Myth and reality.* Minneapolis: University of Minnesota Press.

Cochrane, W. W. (1983). *Agricultural economics at the University of Minnesota 1886–1979.* St. Paul: University of Minnesota, Department of Agricultural and Applied Economics.

College Board. (n.d.). [College search]. Available at http://www.collegeboard.com

Deaton, A. S., & Muellbauer, J. (1980). An almost ideal demand system. *American Economic Review, 70,* 312–326.

Edmondson, W. (2004). Economics of the food and fiber system. *Amber Waves, 2*(1), 12–13.

Edwards, C. (1959). Resource fixity and farm organization. *Journal of Farm Economics, 41,* 747–759.

Eisgruber, L. M., & Reisch, E. (1961). A note on the application of linear programming by agricultural economics departments of land grant colleges. *Journal of Farm Economics, 43,* 303–307.

Erickson, S. P., Akridge, J. T., Barnard, A. F., & Downey, W. D. (2002). *Agribusiness management* (3rd ed.). New York: McGraw-Hill.

Forker, O. D., & Ward, R. W. (1993). *Commodity advertising: The economics and measurement of generic programs.* New York: Lexington Books.

Forward. (1919). *Journal of Farm Economics, 1,* 1–2.

Galbraith, J. K. (1958). *The affluent society.* Boston: Houghton Mifflin.

Galbraith, J. K. (1995). *Money: Whence it came, where it went.* Boston: Houghton Mifflin.

Gardner, B. L., & Rausser, G. C. (Eds.). (2001a). *Handbook of agricultural economics: Vol. 1A. Agricultural production.* New York: Elsevier North-Holland.

Gardner, B. L., & Rausser, G. C. (Eds.). (2001b). *Handbook of agricultural economics: Vol. 1B. Marketing, distribution and consumers.* New York: Elsevier North-Holland.

Goodwin, J. W. (1994). *Agricultural price analysis and forecasting.* New York: John Wiley.

Griliches, Z. (1957). Hybrid corn: An exploration in the economics of technical change. *Econometrica, 25,* 501–522.

Hardaker, J. B., Huirne, R. B. M., Anderson, J. R., & Lien, G. (2004). *Coping with risk in agriculture* (2nd ed.). Cambridge, MA: CABI.

Heady, E. O. (1946). Production functions from a random sample of farms. *Journal of Farm Economics, 28,* 989–1004.

Heady, E. O. (1952). *Economics of agricultural production and resource use.* Englewood Cliffs, NJ: Prentice Hall.

Heady, E. O., & Candler, W. (1958). *Linear programming methods.* Ames: Iowa State University Press.

Houck, J. P. (1964). A statistical model of the demand for soybeans. *American Journal of Agricultural Economics, 46,* 366–374.

Houck, J. P., & Ryan, M. E. (1972). Supply analysis for corn in the United States: Impact of changing government programs. *American Journal of Agricultural Economics, 54,* 184–191.

Huang, S., & Sexton, R. J. (1996). Measuring returns to an innovation in an imperfectly competitive market: Application to mechanical harvesting of processing tomatoes in Taiwan. *American Journal of Agricultural Economics, 78*(3), 558–571.

International Association of Agricultural Economists. (2008). [Home page]. Available at http://www.iaae-agecon.org

Johnson, D. G. (1947). *Forward prices for agriculture.* Chicago: University of Chicago Press.

Just, R. E. (2008). Distinguishing preferences from perceptions for meaningful policy analysis. *American Journal of Agricultural Economics, 90,* 1165–1175.

Just, R. E., & Pope, R. D. (Eds.). (2002). *A comprehensive assessment of the role of risk in U.S. agriculture.* Norwell, MA: Kluwer Academic.

Kay, R., Edwards, W., & Duffy, P. (2008). *Farm management* (6th ed.). New York: McGraw-Hill.

Knutson, R. D., Penn, J. B., & Flinchbaugh, B. L. (2007). *Agricultural and food policy* (6th ed.). Upper Saddle River, NJ: Prentice Hall.

Kohls, R., Uhl, J., & Hurt, C. (2007). *Marketing of agricultural products* (10th ed.). Upper Saddle River, NJ: Prentice Hall.

LaFrance, J. T., & Pope, R. D. (2008). Homogeneity and supply. *American Journal of Agricultural Economics, 90,* 606–612.

Nerlove, M. (1956). Estimates of the elasticities of supply of selected agricultural commodities. *Journal of Farm Economics, 38,* 496–509.

Nichols, J. P., Kinnucan, H. W., & Ackerman, K. Z. (Eds.). (1990). *Economic effects of generic promotion programs for agricultural exports.* College Station: Texas A&M University.

O'Donnell, C. J., Shumway, R. C., & Ball, V. E. (1999). Input demands and inefficiency in U.S. agriculture. *American Journal of Agricultural Economics, 81,* 865–880.

Penson, J. B., Jr., & Hughes, D. W. (1979). Incorporation of general economic outcomes in econometric projections models for agriculture. *American Journal of Agricultural Economics, 61,* 151–157.

Penson, J. B., Capps, O., Jr., Rosson, C. P., & Woodward, R. (2006). *Introduction to agricultural economics* (4th ed.). Upper Saddle River, NJ: Prentice Hall.

Perry, G. (2010). What does the future hold for departments of agricultural economics? *Applied Economic Perspectives and Policy, 32*(1), 117–134.

Piggott, R. (1992). Some old truths revisited. *Australian Journal of Agricultural Economics, 36,* 117–140.

Samuelson, P. A., & Nordhaus, W. D. (2005). *Economics* (18th ed.). New York: McGraw-Hill.

Schultz, T. W. (1946). Changes in economic structure affecting American agriculture. *Journal of Farm Economics, 28,* 15–27.

Schultz, T. W. (1964). *Transforming traditional agriculture.* New Haven, CT: Yale University Press.

Shaars, M. A. (1972). *The story of the Department of Agricultural Economics 1909–1972.* Retrieved December 10, 2008, from http://www.aae.wisc.edu/pubs/AAEStory.pdf

Shumway, R. C. (1983). Supply, demand, and technology in a multiproduct industry: Texas field crops. *American Journal of Agricultural Economics, 65,* 748–760.

Spillman, W. J. (1923). Application of the law of diminishing returns to some fertilizer and feed data. *Journal of Farm Economics, 5,* 36–52.

Stanton, B. F. (2001). *Agricultural economics at Cornell: A history, 1900–1990.* Ithaca, NY: Cornell University, College of Agriculture and Life Sciences.

Stigler, G. W. (1945). The cost of subsistence. *Journal of Farm Economics, 27,* 303–314.

Tauer, L. (1983). Target MOTAD. *American Journal of Agricultural Economics, 65,* 606–610.

Tintner, G., & Brownlee, O. H. (1944). Production functions derived from farm records. *Journal of Farm Economics, 26,* 566–571.

Tomek, W. G., & Robinson, K. L. (2003). *Agricultural product prices* (4th ed.). Ithaca, NY: Cornell University Press.

Warren, G. F. (1913). *Farm management.* New York: Macmillan.

Waugh, F. V. (1928). Quality factors influencing vegetable prices. *American Journal of Agricultural Economics, 10,* 185–196.

Wohlgenant, M. K. (1989). Demand for farm output in a complete system of demand functions. *American Journal of Agricultural Economics, 71,* 241–252.

Yeager, J. C., & Stevenson, G. (2000). *Inside Ag Hill: The people and events that shaped Auburn's agricultural history from 1872 through 1999.* Auburn, AL: Auburn University, College of Agriculture.

Zusman, P., & Amiad, A. (1965). Simulation: A tool for farm planning under conditions of weather uncertainty. *Journal of Farm Economics, 47,* 574–594.

59

REAL ESTATE ECONOMICS

ERICK ESCHKER

Humboldt State University

Real estate economics is the study of the markets for land and structures, including residential housing, commercial office space, and industrial warehouses. Although much theory has existed for decades regarding real estate markets, questions are being answered today regarding mortgage finance innovation, the rise of suburban business and residential centers, and the effects of zoning laws. The housing boom and bust of the first decade of the twenty-first century has meant that households, businesses, and governments have become more interested than ever in real estate and its effect on various aspects of the economy. In this chapter, the theory of real estate markets is first presented, including the relevance of real estate rental price, the heterogeneous nature of real estate, the importance of location, and the interaction with the macroeconomy. Next, various contemporary applications of real estate economics are discussed, followed by a description of government policy intervention in the real estate market. Finally, the housing boom and bust is presented along with areas for future research.

Theory of Real Estate Markets

Flow of Services, Rent, and Price

In many respects, real estate markets are similar to markets for other goods and services. There exist buyers who demand real estate by demonstrating a willingness and ability to pay for property. There are also sellers who supply real estate. One unique feature of real estate is that the goods in question—namely, land and structures—are long-lived. Consuming real estate does not result in the disappearance of the good as with, say, consuming a slice of pizza. Real estate can be purchased and enjoyed today and then sold again tomorrow. In fact, the vast majority of real estate sold in any year was previously owned. Because of this durability, the decision to buy or sell real estate must take a long time horizon into account.

Durable goods deliver a flow of services over time to the owner or user of that good. For example, a car lasts many years, and a car will deliver a flow of transportation services each year. Real estate delivers a flow of shelter services, in residential housing, and a flow of retail store space, in commercial real estate. The person who purchases a durable good takes current and all future flows of services into account when making the decision to purchase the good. This is true whether or not the buyer intends to use the services that flow from the durable good. For example, in the case of a car, although often the buyer intends to drive the car for a number of years after the purchase, car rental companies purchase large amounts of cars in order to charge rent to their customers. The same is true in real estate, where a large amount is owner occupied, while other people intend primarily to offer for rent the shelter or retail space to others. If the buyer intends to rent the real estate to others, then the buyer's willingness to pay will be based on the rent that can be earned, which is determined by renters and landlords in the rental market for real estate. Renters will be willing to pay rent that is at or below the value that the renter puts on the flow of services. In fact, the dollar value of rent is an easy-to-obtain measure of the dollar value of the flow of services from a property.

Purchasing a piece of real estate today gives the buyer the use of services this year and every year in the future. See James Hamilton (2005) for a good discussion about how the buyer may approach the decision of whether to buy a house. The willingness to pay for that stream of service flows is equal to its present discounted value. The present discounted value is the sum of the discounted values, where the appropriate discount rate reflects the buyer's opportunity cost of purchasing today. Typically, it is the mortgage interest rate, which may be adjusted for risk and taxes. Numerically, the present discounted value in year t, PDV_t, is as follows:

$$PDV_t = S_t + \frac{S_{t+1}}{(1+i)} + \frac{S_{t+2}}{(1+i)^2} + \cdots, \qquad (1)$$

where S_t is the flow of real estate services, i is the interest rate, and t is the year index. If the value of services grows at a constant rate g, and if $g < i$, then the above reduces to

$$PDV_t = \frac{S_t(1+i)}{(i-g)}. \qquad (2)$$

The present discounted value will rise with the value of the flow of services provided by the property and the growth rate of services, and it will fall when the interest rate rises. This last result is because an increase in the interest rate will not only raise the numerator but also raise the denominator more, thus lowering the ratio. The present discounted value of the flow of current and future services is referred to as the *fundamental value* of real estate. The fundamental value simply says that the most that people will pay for a piece of real estate is the present discounted value of the flow of services. This is a very intuitive way to think about real estate pricing and shows the link between the market for real estate rentals and the market for real estate purchases—the main driver of real estate prices is the value that the end user puts on the property and the discount rate. The fundamental value of real estate is essentially an arbitrage condition that says that if the market price of real estate is equal to the present discounted value of future rents, then there are no sure profits to be made through buying or selling real estate, and thus, the market price of real estate will not rise or fall unless there is a change to the fundamental value.

Demand and Supply

The price of real estate in the short run is determined by supply and demand in the real estate market. See Denise DiPasquale and William Wheaton (1996, chap. 1) for a rigorous exposition of this material. The market for real estate, where potential buyers and sellers meet, is different from the market for rental properties, where renters and landlords come together to rent buildings. This discussion focuses on the market for rental properties and considers how that market sets the price and influences the construction, or development, of new real estate. In the rental market, each potential renter has an individual willingness to pay. The market willingness to pay is the sum of the willingness to pay for all renters, and just as with any good, the sum of willingness to pay determines the market demand for the good. As the market rental price of real estate falls, more and more renters will rent, and this results in the typical downward sloping demand curve, as shown by line Demand₁ in Figure 59.1. Market demand is a function of the size and composition of the population, the local job market and incomes, local amenities, and other factors that are discussed later. Demand shifts come about when any of these factors change. The quantity or stock of real estate is fixed in the short run because it takes a relatively long time for new real estate to be built or developed, given permitting, zoning, and construction considerations. Figure 59.1 therefore shows supply, Supply₁, in the rental market as a vertical line equal to the stock of real estate.

Because real estate is long-lived, today's supply is based on how much property was developed in the past. The amount of real estate construction or investment in any year

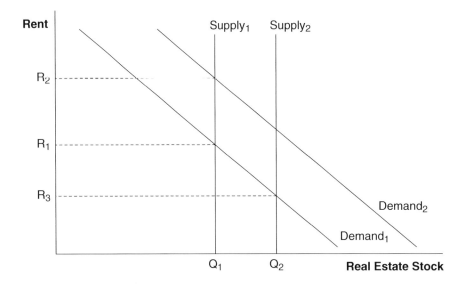

Figure 59.1　Real Estate Rental Market

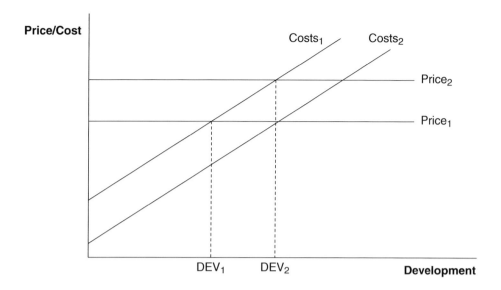

Figure 59.2 Real Estate Development

depends on the availability and cost of funds for construction, on construction costs and technology, and on zoning considerations. Construction costs include fixed and marginal costs, and an increase in these costs will lead to less investment. Investment also depends on the price of real estate at the time that the investment decision is made. All else the same, a higher price of real estate will induce more construction and will lead to a higher future stock of real estate. If the price of real estate is above construction costs, then developers will find it profitable to build, but if the current price of real estate is below construction costs, then property will not be developed. Figure 59.2 shows how real estate development is determined. Given the price of real estate, there is one level of development that will be obtained. In Figure 59.2, if the price is equal to $Price_1$, and if costs are represented by line $Costs_1$, then real estate development is equal to DEV_1. If this new construction is greater than depreciation, which is the erosion of the real estate stock due to normal wear and tear, then the supply of real estate in the rental market will be greater next period. Real estate is just like any capital good in that the stock of real estate grows only if the investment flow is greater than depreciation.

There is one rental price at which the quantity of real estate supplied is equal to the quantity demanded, and that is the market clearing or equilibrium rent. In Figure 59.1, if the initial demand is represented by the line $Demand_1$, and if the initial supply is represented by the line $Supply_1$, then the initial equilibrium rent is R_1. This current rent, along with the expected growth of rent and mortgage interest rates, will determine the present discounted value of future rents and the price that people are willing to pay to buy the real estate, and will it determine real estate development.

The equilibrium rent will change when demand or supply shifts. For example, suppose that population grows in a particular market. This will shift to the right the demand for real estate to $Demand_2$, pushing up the rent to R_2 in Figure 59.1. This increase in rent will lead to an increase in price to $Price_2$ in Figure 59.2 and will lead to increased construction level DEV_2. In the end, rent is higher, the price level is higher, and there is a larger stock of real estate. As another example, suppose that demand and price are back to their original positions and that credit becomes more easily available to developers. This will reduce construction costs to $Costs_2$ in Figure 59.2 and increase investment to DEV_2. The supply of real estate in Figure 59.1 will rise to $Supply_2$, which lowers the rent to R_3 and eventually lowers the price of real estate. In the end, the rent is lower, the price is lower, and there is a larger stock of real estate.

It is worth mentioning that although changes in the market price and the rental price of real estate are often positively correlated, as shown in the preceding two examples, one exception is when the mortgage rate changes. If the mortgage interest rate rises, this will decrease the present discounted value of future rents and lower the price. As a result, there will be less development, and the supply of real estate will fall in the rental market, which leads to higher rents.

Heterogeneity

Real estate is not a homogenous good in which each parcel of real estate is indistinguishable from another. Instead, each parcel has unique characteristics, including location, size, and amenities, and demand for these unique characteristics is determined in the market. The value for a particular real estate parcel is based on its unique characteristics. For example, people are generally willing to pay more to live near the ocean, and houses that are near the ocean have an ocean premium built into their market price. The more desirable features that a parcel has, the higher will be its market price. However, despite the uniqueness of each parcel, demand for a particular parcel is usually price elastic because other similar parcels are substitutes.

The demand and supply for a particular piece of real estate is composed of two distinct types of factors. The first is those characteristics that are unique to that parcel, such as exact location, number of rooms, size, land use zoning, and age of the structure. These unique characteristics will lead to different market prices among pieces of real estate. For example, commercial real estate that has better access to major road arteries will command a higher market rent and thus a higher market price, all else the same. But there are also factors that are common to all real estate within a certain market. In fact, one can define the market as all the real estate affected by these common factors. These common factors include the population, the local unemployment rate, and proximity to outdoor recreation activities, among others. These common factors will tend to raise or lower the market price of all properties but not change the relative prices. For example, if a large employer leaves the area, then this will decrease rents and lower the demand and prices for all real estate within the market.

Real Estate Value and Location

The theory of real estate value begins with the classic concept of Ricardian rent, which predicts that more desirable real estate will command a higher rent and market price as users compete for land. In the monocentric city model, distance to the single center of the city largely explains real estate prices. In urban residential real estate pricing, workers in a city must commute to their places of work, and they are willing to pay more for housing that is closer to their employers to avoid costs of commuting. Thus, land at the city center has a higher market price than land at the city edge. The price of all housing, which is made up of the price of the land and the price of the house, must be high enough to bid resources away from agricultural and physical structure uses. Thus, at the city edge, house prices must equal the sum of returns to agricultural land and construction costs of the house structure. But housing closer to the city center will have a higher price because people will pay to avoid the commute costs associated with greater distance from the city center. As commuting costs rise, prices in the city center rise relative to prices at the city edge. Users of urban land who differ based on their commuting costs, such as those with high wages and thus high opportunity costs of commuting time, will segregate themselves by location. Those with higher commuting costs will live closer to the city center, and if they earn higher wages, then segregation will appear along income levels. Because property closer to the city center has higher rent gradients associated with it, builders will often increase density to substitute structure for land, and residential real estate closer to the city center will be more densely populated.

The original city center was often built decades or centuries earlier and often has very low density. Redevelopment of the city center into higher density use will become profitable for developers once residents feel that reduced commute costs are large enough to outweigh the dislike of higher density living.

This monocentric model of urban development has many shortcomings, as outlined in Alex Anas, Richard Arnott, and Kenneth Small (1998). The most visible is the fact that many of today's cities are best described as multicentered, with suburban city centers surrounding the original city core. Industrial land often occupies land on the edge of the city where land rent is cheaper and truck access to roads is good. Both industrial and commercial land has gathered in new outlying clusters within larger metropolitan regions. These alternative city centers compete with the traditional city hub for workers, and there has been much employment growth in these alternative suburban centers. A strong incentive to pull firms outside the central city hub is lower wages in the suburbs, where more and more of its workforce lives and where commuting times and thus wages are lower. Economies of agglomeration refer to the reduced costs to firms by clustering near one another. These include access to a large pool of skilled workers, better communication between firms, and closer proximity to suppliers. Counteracting this migration to the suburbs are increased costs of isolation and the reduction in agglomeration economies. At some point, the draw to an alternative city center is greater than the loss of the agglomeration effects, and the firm leaves the city center. One expects firms with the largest economies of agglomeration to locate in the large city center, while firms with less economies of agglomeration will be found in the alternative city centers. Recent increases in information technology, such as the Internet, may reduce the benefits to firms of clustering near one another, but Jess Gaspar and Edward Glaeser (1998) suggest that telecommunications may be a complement for face-to-face interaction and promote city center growth.

Commercial real estate can profit by locating near customers, suppliers, roadways, or mass transit terminals. Retailers would also like to cluster near complementary retailers because consumers try to minimize travel costs and the number of trips and often prefer to shop at a single shopping center. However, retailers would like to be located farther from similar retailers, because that increases their market power and pricing ability. Shopping malls give retailers the chance to cluster together in a central location, which may benefit some retailers, although some retailers, such as those who sell lower priced, nondurable goods that are purchased frequently are often not found in central shopping malls. Thus, rent for retail and commercial space is based partly on the mix of businesses in the area and the likelihood that those businesses will draw customers to the firm. See Eric Gould, B. Peter Pashigian, and Canice Prendergast (2005) for a recent discussion of shopping mall pricing.

The Macroeconomy and Real Estate

The real estate market is both a determinant of the regional macroeconomic climate and a product of that climate. Land and buildings are inputs into the production process, whether those markets are for industrial, commercial, or residential purposes, and real estate prices affect costs of production. Exogenous increases in the supply of real estate, perhaps from the opening of new lands for development, reduce rents and reduce costs to firms in the region, which gives those firms a cost advantage over other regions of the state or country. Employment and wages in the region will increase. A very inelastic supply of real estate can inhibit demand-driven economic growth if increases in housing prices raise the cost of living sufficiently to keep real wages from rising and attracting new workers into a region. Economy-wide factors, such as an exogenous increase in labor supply due to immigration, will affect the real estate market. Immigration will increase employment and production because wages and costs to firms fall, and it will increase the demand for real estate, which raises real estate rents. An increase in the demand for goods produced in the region will lead to an increase in the demand and price of all factors of production, including real estate. If the supply of real estate is price elastic, real estate prices will increase less and real estate development will be more than if real estate supply is inelastic. Local real estate markets depend on the national economy, with recessions typically reducing the demand for most types of real estate. But regional differences matter too, and a local real estate market may suffer relatively less during a recession if the relative demand for the particular mix of goods and services produced in the region does not fall. Finally, real estate wealth is a large fraction of total household wealth, and Karl Case, Robert Shiller, and John Quigley (2005) find large impacts of housing wealth on consumption.

Applications and Empirical Evidence

Hedonic Prices

Richard Muth (1960) wrote an early paper on hedonic pricing. A hedonic price equation relates the price of a piece of real estate to various characteristics of the property, such as distance to city center, size measured in square feet, number of bathrooms, and neighborhood quality, which can be measured as either low quality (0) or high quality (1). This is an attempt to resolve the issue that real estate is not a homogeneous good. The hedonic price equation decomposes real estate into various characteristics and estimates prices for each characteristic. In the case of residential housing, an example is as follows:

$$Price = \alpha + \beta_1 DISTANCE + \beta_2 SIZE + \beta_3 ROOMS + \beta_4 NEIGHBORHOOD, \tag{3}$$

where α is a constant and the β s are the coefficients on each housing characteristic. Each β is the marginal impact of increasing the characteristic by one unit, in continuous variables such as distance, or the marginal impact of having that characteristic present, in binary characteristics such as neighborhood quality. One would expect that the coefficient on distance to the center of the city to be negative, because the amount of rent that people are willing to pay falls the farther the house is from the center of city, all else the same. One should note, however, that in very large metropolitan areas, some suburbs have developed into their own city centers, and distance to these new city centers may be just as important to house price as distance to the historic city center. James Frew and Beth Wilson (2002) present an empirical estimation of rent gradients in the multicentered city of Portland, Oregon. The coefficients on size, number of bathrooms, and neighborhood quality are expected to be positive because people are willing to pay greater rent for housing as these features increase, and thus, market real estate prices will be higher.

The coefficients in hedonic price equations are frequently estimated for both residential and commercial and industrial real estate parcels using ordinary least squares regression analysis or another estimation technique. There are typically many characteristics used to explain the price of real estate. In residential housing, these include local school quality, nearness to employment centers, proximity to amenities such as the ocean or recreational facilities, yard size, presence of a garage, and age of the house structure. In commercial or industrial property, these characteristics include nearness to major highways, airports, and rail lines; amount of pedestrian or car traffic; zoning considerations; nearness to suppliers, distributors, and customers; and parking availability, among others. Ioan Voicu and Vicki Been (2008) look at the effect of community gardens on property values in New York City and find a significant effect for high-quality gardens.

Demographics and Housing

The demand for residential real estate depends in the long run on characteristics of the population that move slowly over time. Gregory Mankiw and David Weil (1989) present a look at the implications of the baby boomers and the aging of the population on housing supply and demand. One factor is net household formation, which is the difference between newly created households and newly dissolved households in a year. A household, which is a group of related or unrelated individuals living at the same parcel of real estate, is a common unit of measurement by the Census Bureau. New households may be created when children leave their parents' residence and through divorce, for example, while the number of households may fall during marriage and death, for example. The average size of households, as well as the age, composition, and income of households, will influence the typical features found in newly constructed housing, because developers quickly respond to current market conditions.

Age, income, demographic mobility, and marital status also greatly influence whether the household rents or buys housing. According to the 2007 American Housing Survey (U.S. Census Bureau, 2008), 31% of households rent the houses that they live in, 24% own the houses outright, and 44% are making mortgage payments. Renters are on average younger and have lower incomes than nonrenters. Permanent, or long-run average income, appears to influence the decision on whether to buy more than current income. Transaction costs of buying and selling a house are large, and renters move much more frequently than owners. Getting married and having children appear to be big factors that explain the switch from renting to owning.

Housing vacancies are a closely watched measure in the housing market. For a given level of sales, as vacancies rise, the average time on the market increases. Increased time on the market will tend to lower market prices, because sellers face increased opportunity cost of funds if they cannot sell their houses. New house builders will also be more motivated to lower prices, and they will also respond to greater average time on the market by reducing new construction. Although vacancy rates are typically studied at the local market level, consider the recent drop in U.S. new housing demand. The U.S. Census Bureau (2009) reports that the U.S. homeowner vacancy rate increased very quickly over 2006, averaging 2.375 in 2006 compared to 1.875 in 2005. New house sales fell from 1.283 million in 2005 to 1.051 million in 2006. In December of 2005, there were 515,000 new houses for sale, and the median time for sale was 4.0 months, while in December of 2006, there were 568,000 new houses for sale, and the median time for sale was 4.3 months. The median price of new houses continued to rise for 2 more years, until falling from $247,900 in 2007 to $230,600 in 2008. Builders responded to these market changes, and from 2005 to 2006, housing starts fell from 2.068 million to 1.801 million units.

Mortgage Financing

Residential real estate typically sells for hundreds of thousands or even millions of dollars. This is greater than most households' annual incomes. Households typically do not save over many years to purchase housing but rather obtain financing to purchase residential real estate. Financing terms have changed considerably over the last 10 years and continue to change. Except for a short number of years in the first decade of the 21st century when houses could be bought with little or no down payment, down payments of 20% are common on loans. The down payment is subtracted from the sum of the purchase price and all fees and expenses to determine how much the buyer must finance. A mortgage is a residential real estate loan with the real estate itself as collateral. Most mortgages are fully amortizing, which means that the principal balance is repaid over the life of the loan, which is usually 30 years but

sometimes more or fewer, such as 40 or 15 years. A common question asked is why does the principal balance decline very slowly in the first years of the loan? To answer this, it is helpful to think of a mortgage as a loan that is to be repaid every month. After the first month of the loan, the interest due is extremely large, because the outstanding principal is large. As the number of months goes by, the interest due becomes less because the principal is being paid down. In the final months, the interest due is small because the principal is small.

Many residential mortgages do not have fixed mortgage interest rates over the lives of the loans but rather have a rate that rises and falls, within limits, along with the prevailing interest rate. These adjustable rate mortgages (ARMs) became more popular with lenders after the high inflation of the 1970s, when lenders were paying high interest rates on short-run liabilities (deposits) while receiving much lower interest rates on long-term assets (loans). Another recent change to mortgages has been the use of mortgages that do not fully amortize. These interest-only and even negative-amortizing loans allow the monthly mortgage payments to vary, within limits, such that the loan principal balances do not fall as they would with fully amortized loans. These pick-a-payment mortgages usually require full amortization to begin a few years after the loan begins.

Funding for mortgages is typically provided by commercial banks and thrifts, and these institutions, as well as mortgage brokers, typically issue mortgage loans to households. However, it is very common for these loans to be quickly sold on the secondary mortgage market to pension funds, insurance companies, and other investors. Mortgage-backed securities (MBSs) or mortgage bonds are sold to investors. Investment banks and the government-sponsored enterprises Fannie Mae and Freddie Mac package individual mortgages into these securities, which are sold on huge markets. The pooling of individual mortgages can reduce risk because only a small number of borrowers are expected to default. Fannie Mae and Freddie Mac also guarantee the payments on the securities that they process. Mortgages that conform to Fannie Mae and Freddie Mac standards, such as maximum loan to value, make up most of the secondary market, and the standardization of loans has allowed the market for these securities to grow. Conforming mortgage loan amounts must be below a threshold limit, adjusted to take average market price into account, or else the loans may be classified as jumbo loans, which have higher interest rates.

Government Policy

Tax Treatment of Housing

The federal government provides incentives to purchase housing to encourage home ownership. Government intervention is often justified on the grounds of positive externalities that result from home ownership, such as the idea that home owners will better maintain the exterior appearance of their houses than home renters or landlords. Glaeser and Jesse Shapiro (2003) lead an excellent discussion about the positive and negative externalities associated with home ownership. The mortgage interest deduction, whereby interest payments (not principal payments) are tax deductible, cost the federal government $67 billion in 2008, according to the Joint Committee on Taxation (2008). Additionally, local property taxes are deductible for federal income taxes. The marginal benefit to the owner of these tax deductions is equal to the deduction multiplied by the marginal tax rate. Because federal taxes allow a standard deduction, the housing tax incentives are relevant only if the household itemizes, but low- to moderate-income households often do not itemize. The evidence shows that federal tax treatment of housing has a more powerful effect in encouraging people to purchase larger houses rather than to purchase housing for the first time. Other tax incentives include a large exemption on housing capital gains and the mortgage interest deduction for state income taxes in many states. According to the Legislative Analyst's Office (2007) in California, the largest California income tax deduction is the mortgage interest deduction, which cost $5 billion in reduced revenue in 2007 to 2008. Various distortions are created by state tax treatment of housing, such as Proposition 13 in California, which discourages sales of existing houses because property taxes tend to be lower the longer one resides at an address.

Retail Development

In many towns, the location of newly developed retail space is a very sensitive political matter that often requires a vote by the city council or a voter referendum. This is because of the impact of new retailers on the sales of existing retailers. If a new shopping center is built, existing retailers will often lose sales and market pricing power. Of course, the total amount of retail sales may remain unchanged, with the new shopping mall simply taking sales from existing business, and sales in one town may rise at the expense of sales in a nearby town. In rural communities, a new shopping center may divert sales away from out-of-the-area retailers or Internet retailers. The rise of Internet retailing can reduce the overall demand for retail real estate while increasing the demand for warehouse real estate. It remains to be seen how demand for retail space, and retail rental prices, will be affected in the long run by the rise in Internet retailers. Elaine Worzala and Anne McCarthy (2001) present an early examination of Internet retailing on traditional retail location.

Zoning

Municipalities, counties, and special local governments, such as water districts, Indian tribes, and coastal commissions, set property tax rates and zone land for specific uses. They use this tax revenue and grants from the federal and state governments to administer public expenditures on items such as schools and infrastructure. These local governments usually have a much larger impact on real estate markets than do the federal and state governments. In the classic Tiebout model, the difference in spending levels by communities on public services, such as school quality and police protection, reflects differences in community preferences. Communities that value higher quality schools will spend more on school services than those communities that do not, and residents will segregate into locations that reflect differences in willingness to pay for public services. Because willingness to pay often depends on income, differences in public expenditures will also reflect differences in average income across communities.

When considering new land development for either residential or commercial purposes, local governments will ask whether the new development will make existing residents better or worse off. If the new development requires on average less expenditure and raises more in property taxes compared to existing developed land, then current residents will be better off. On the other hand, if the new development requires more expenditure and raises less in property taxes on average compared to existing development, then current residents will not be in favor of development. Property taxes are based on land value and are not directly proportionate to the number of households on a parcel. It is therefore likely that compared to existing housing, denser housing development will generate a demand for public services that is greater than the higher property tax revenue collected. As a result, many localities require a minimum lot size, which has the effect of keeping communities segregated by lot size and income.

Commercial and industrial real estate is also zoned by local governments. The big concern with nonresidential development is the impact on the character of the community. Households typically want to live near other households or amenities such as parks and prefer to not live near commercial or industrial sites. This is one reason property taxes tend to be set higher for nonresidential uses. Towns that are more willing to accept new tax revenue in exchange for an altered community character are more likely to have nonresidential real estate developed within their jurisdictions.

Zoning authority is typically justified by the externalities that land use imposes on other individuals in the market and by the need to provide public goods. Of course, zoning is a much-debated political matter, and there is no doubt that in practice, zoning considerations are often made that redistribute resources rather than improve the quality of living for citizens. Zoning will restrict the supply of new development and raise real estate prices. Glaeser and Joseph Gyourko (2003) find that in U.S. regions where zoning is more restrictive, such as coastal states, high housing prices are the result. Negative externalities resulting, for example, from industrial pollution, noise, odor, dilapidation, and increased parking congestion, can adversely impact residential, commercial, and industrial real estate values. Positive externalities such as brown field restoration or regular exterior house maintenance can increase real estate values. Transaction costs tend to make an optimal private market solution in the presence of externalities difficult to obtain, and a common economic solution is government intervention. Local governments extensively control or restrict land use to alleviate externalities. For example, a large city might require newly constructed apartments to have at least one on-site parking space per residential unit to reduce street parking congestion. Governments also turn toward market incentives that internalize the external costs, such as a large city charging car owners a fee for on-street parking permits. Another example of a serious negative externality from real estate is traffic congestion. Users of residential, commercial, and industrial real estate drive on existing roadways and can create substantial gridlock, especially at rush hour. This increases travel time for users, and estimates of the aggregate value of time lost can be substantial.

The City of London recently implemented a traffic congestion charge on cars during business hours, and the effect has been a substantial drop in congestion. Public goods, which once created are nonexcludable, face the well-known free-rider problem, which predicts underprovision of the good. Public goods include roads, parks, and footbridges. Local governments often zone real estate to provide for open space or tax residents to pay for road maintenance, for example. Richard Green (2007) finds that airports can help a region to experience economic growth. The optimum land use and government response to externalities and public goods will change over time. However, existing real estate usage is based on historical decisions, because real estate structures are typically long-lived, and governments may need to periodically revisit land use zoning.

Real Estate After 2000 and Future Directions

Housing Boom and Bust

Residential real estate prices began to climb very quickly in the early 2000s in many countries across the globe, and starting around 2006, prices began to decline. In the United States, nominal prices climbed 90% as measured by the Case-Shiller Index. The Case-Shiller Index is a repeat sales price index, which calculates overall changes in market prices by looking at houses that sold more than once over the entire sample period to control for differences in quality of house sold. In some regions, the median selling price of a house doubled in about 3 years from 2002 to 2005. Although regional real estate markets had previously experienced quick price increases, such as the Florida land boom of the 1920s, by all accounts this was the fastest increase in housing prices at the aggregate national level ever. As Shiller (2007)

shows, inflation-adjusted U.S. housing prices were remarkably consistent since 1890, with the 1920s and 1930s being the exception of years of low prices. But since the late 1990s, housing prices in the United States on average grew to levels not seen in any year in which data are available. This fast rise in house prices encouraged a great deal of investment into both residential and commercial real estate. Construction employment soared, as did the number of people working as real estate agents and mortgage brokers. By 2008, housing prices had fallen 21% from their peak levels, which was a greater fall, in inflation-adjusted terms, than during the Great Depression. Accompanying this massive drop in prices was a fall in new and existing house sales, an increase in foreclosures to record levels, a drop in construction spending and commercial real estate investment, massive drops in government tax collections, and a huge drop in jobs in construction, real estate, and the mortgage industry. Mortgage companies, banks, and financial firms that held real estate assets shut their doors, and there was massive contraction and consolidation in these industries. The U.S. recession that began in 2007 accompanied the collapse of the housing market.

It is important to explain both the boom and the bust of this historic housing cycle. Cabray Haines and Richard Rosen (2007) compare regional U.S. housing prices and find evidence that actual prices rose above fundamental values in some markets. The boom can be partly explained by the fact that mortgage interest rates were very low at the onset, which according to the fundamental value approach should raise house prices because lower interest rates will raise the present discounted value of future rents. But it seems that changes in mortgage financing may have been an even more important part of the explanation, and many economists characterize the housing boom as a manifestation of a credit bubble that saw simple measures such as the price-to-rent and price-to-income ratios rise to levels above historic averages. Housing affordability fell sharply in most of the country. The use of MBSs increased, and mortgage lenders greatly reduced holdings of their mortgages in the so-called originate-to-distribute model. Mortgage lending standards fell as more and more people fell into the subprime (poor credit history) or Alt-A (high loan to income value) borrowing categories and down payment and income documentation requirements were greatly reduced.

Both this increase in supply and the increase in demand for mortgage credit increased the demand for houses, which pushed prices to record highs. Starting in 2006, and particularly in 2007, the appetite for MBSs fell greatly as mortgage defaults increased across the country. The drop in available mortgage credit was a blow to new buyers, those refinancing, and those seeking to trade up or purchase second houses. The result was a huge drop in demand for housing. The U.S. Census Bureau (2009) reports that in the fourth quarter of 2008, the home ownership rate was 67.5%, the same level as the fourth quarter of 2000.

The Federal Reserve's (2009) Flow of Funds Accounts report that household percentage equity was lower than at any time in over 50 years of data. Government reaction to the housing bust has been unprecedented. In 2008, the U.S. Treasury Department and the U.S. Federal Reserve Bank tried to encourage consumer confidence in financial markets, brokered mergers between insolvent institutions and other companies, and committed hundreds of billions of dollars to help the financial industry and the U.S. economy at large. In September of 2008, Fannie Mae and Freddie Mac were placed into government conservatorship when their stock prices plummeted and they were unable to raise capital. A flurry of legislation passed that reduced income taxes for home buyers. At the federal level, first-time homebuyers in 2008 who were below the income limit received a credit on their taxes up to $7,500, which must be repaid over 15 years, while in 2009, there was a refundable tax credit equal to 10% of the purchase price of the house, up to $8,000. In California, a non-means-tested tax credit of 5%, up to $10,000, was available to all purchasers of newly constructed houses. Other states had their own home buyer income tax credits.

Areas for Future Research

One of the challenges of future research will be to better understand how financial product innovation contributed to the housing boom and what types of regulation would best fend off a similar future boom and bust cycle. Chris Mayer, Karen Pence, and Shane Sherlund (2008) point to zero-down-payment financing and lax lending standards as important contributors to the dramatic increase in foreclosures. Additionally, the difficulty of modifying mortgages and approving sales for a price lower than the outstanding principal balance (short sales) became evident with the diffuse ownership of mortgages through MBSs. In 2006, the Chicago Mercantile Exchange started issuing home price futures contracts with values based on the Case-Shiller Index for select cities. Like any futures contract, these are agreements between sellers and buyers to exchange housing contracts in the future at predetermined prices. If at the future date the actual contract price is higher than the agreed-upon price, then the buyer of the futures contract profits, while if at the future date the actual contract price is below the agreed-upon price, then the seller of the futures contract profits. An owner of residential real estate can use futures contracts to protect or hedge against price risk. For example, if the market price of a house falls, then the owner has a drop in net wealth. However, if an individual had sold a home price futures contract, then he or she may have earned a profit that cancelled the loss of owning housing. The ability of individuals, investors, and developers to protect themselves against price risk had been very limited before the introduction of these S&P/Case-Shiller Home Price futures, and it remains to be seen how well used these futures contracts will be.

Mark Bertus, Harris Hollans, and Steve Swidler (2008) show that the ability to hedge against price risk in Las Vegas is mixed.

An active literature has grown regarding housing and the labor market. Andrew Oswald (1996) shows that across countries, home ownership rates and unemployment rates are positively correlated. Jakob Munch, Michael Rosholm, and Michael Svarer (2006) find evidence that geographic mobility is decreased with home ownership, but home ownership appears to reduce overall unemployment. With more and more people having mortgage principals greater than the current market value of their houses, it seems that job mobility and wages will be negatively impacted.

Conclusion

This chapter reviewed the theory of real estate markets, including the important relationship of real estate rental price to selling price. Location is a key determinant of real estate rental price, but every parcel of real estate is unique, and hedonic pricing can determine the value that users place on individual characteristics of real estate. Most real estate is purchased with borrowed funds, and there have been important changes in mortgage financing over the last decade. The government treatment of real estate through taxation and zoning or land use restrictions will continue to be an important policy topic in the future. But perhaps the most visible issue in the short run is the impact of the real estate boom and bust. Future research will undoubtedly try to determine whether government policy can effectively prevent or mitigate the effects of similar episodes in the future.

References and Further Readings

Anas, A., Arnott, R., & Small, K. A. (1998). Urban spatial structure. *Journal of Economic Literature, 36*(3), 1426–1464.

Bertus, M., Hollans, H., & Swidler, S. (2008). Hedging house price risk with CME futures contracts: The case of Las Vegas residential real estate. *Journal of Real Estate Finance and Economics, 37*(3), 265–279.

Case, K. E., Shiller, R. J., & Quigley, J. M. (2005). Comparing wealth effects: The stock market versus the housing market. *B. E. Journals in Macroeconomics: Advances in Macroeconomics, 5*(1), 1–32.

DiPasquale, D., & Wheaton, W. C. (1996). *Urban economics and real estate markets*. Englewood Cliffs, NJ: Prentice Hall.

Federal Reserve. (2009). *Flow of funds accounts of the United States*. Available at http://www.federalreserve.gov/releases/z1/current/z1.pdf

Frew, D., & Wilson, B. (2002). Estimating the connection between location and property value. *Journal of Real Estate Practice and Education, 5*(1), 17–25.

Gaspar, J., & Glaeser, E. L. (1998). Information technology and the future of cities. *Journal of Urban Economics, 43*(1), 136–156.

Glaeser, E. L., & Gyourko, J. (2003, June). The impact of building restrictions on housing affordability. *Economic Policy Review*, 21–29.

Glaeser, E. L., & Shapiro, J. M. (2003). The benefits of the home mortgage interest deduction. *Tax Policy and the Economy, 17,* 37–82.

Gould, E. D., Pashigian, B. P., & Prendergast, C. J. (2005). Contracts, externalities, and incentives in shopping malls. *Review of Economics and Statistics, 87*(3), 411–422.

Green, R. K. (2007). Airports and economic development. *Real Estate Economics, 35*(1), 91–112.

Haines, C. L., & Rosen, R. J. (2007). Bubble, bubble, toil, and trouble. *Economic Perspectives, 31*(1), 16–35.

Hamilton, J. (2005). What is a bubble and is this one now? *Econbrowser.* Retrieved December 28, 2008, from http://www.econbrowser.com/archives/2005/06/what_is_a_bubbl.html

Joint Committee on Taxation. (2008). *Estimates of federal tax expenditures for fiscal years 2008–2012* (JCS-2-08). Washington, DC: Government Printing Office.

Legislative Analyst's Office. (2007). *Tax expenditures reviews.* Available at http://www.lao.ca.gov/2007/tax_expenditures/tax_expenditures_1107.aspx

Mankiw, N. G., & Weil, D. N. (1989). The baby boom, the baby bust, and the housing market. *Regional Science and Urban Economics, 19,* 235–258.

Mayer, C. J., Pence, K. M., & Sherlund, S. M. (2008). *The rise in mortgage defaults* (Finance and Economics Discussion Series Paper No. 2008-59). Washington, DC: Board of Governors of the Federal Reserve System.

Munch, J. R., Rosholm, M., & Svarer, M. (2006). Are homeowners really more unemployed? *Economic Journal, 116,* 991–1013.

Muth, R. F. (1960). The demand for non-farm housing. In A. C. Harberger (Ed.), *The demand for durable goods* (pp. 29–96). Chicago: University of Chicago Press.

Oswald, A. (1996). *A conjecture of the explanation for high unemployment in the industrialised nations: Part 1* (Research Paper No. 475). Coventry, UK: Warwick University.

Shiller, R. J. (2007). *Understanding recent trends in house prices and home ownership* (NBER Working Paper No. 13553). Cambridge, MA: National Bureau of Economic Research.

U.S. Census Bureau. (2008, September). *American housing survey for the United States: 2007.* Available at http://www.census.gov/prod/2008pubs/h150-07.pdf

U.S. Census Bureau, Housing and Household Economic Statistics Division. (2009). *Housing vacancies and homeownership.* Available at http://www.census.gov/hhes/www/housing/hvs/historic/index.html

Voicu, I., & Been, V. (2008). The effect of community gardens on neighboring property values. *Real Estate Economics, 36*(2), 241–283.

Worzala, E., & McCarthy, A. M. (2001). Landlords, tenants and e-commerce: Will the retail industry change significantly? *Journal of Real Estate Portfolio Management, 7*(2), 89–97.

60

Economics of Wildlife Protection

Rebecca P. Judge

St. Olaf College

conomics arrived late to wildlife protection. Although optimal timber harvest rates were first described by Martin Faustmann in 1849, and although Harold Hotelling had defined the parameters for profit-maximizing extraction of exhaustible resources like coal and petroleum by 1931, the problem of wildlife protection was ignored by the discipline until 1951. That year, Charles Stoddard (1951), a consulting forester working out of Minong, Wisconsin, urged fellow attendees at the North American Wildlife Conference to address the nation's "steady deterioration of wildlife habitat " with "an intensive development of a branch of knowledge devoted to the economics of wildlife management" (p. 248). The problem, according to Stoddard, was that wildlife production on private lands competed with more remunerative sources of income to landowners. For wildlife to recover, private landowners needed to be "provided with incentives, economic and otherwise, for producing wildlife crops" (p. 248).

But the discipline was slow to pick up on Stoddard's call. Although others joined in calling for public assistance to private landowners to promote increased investment in wildlife habitat on private lands, the economic problem of the optimal provision of wildlife remained largely ignored. The basic structure of the problem was obvious: Wildlife production on private lands competed with other uses, such as crop and timber production, for which the landowner received compensation. Therefore, although wildlife was certainly valued by society, the fact that private landowners were not reimbursed for their contributions to wildlife production meant that the supply of wildlife would be less than optimal. Following the economic logic first described by Arthur Pigou, wildlife production represented another case in which the marginal social value of a good exceeded

its marginal private value; the value of wildlife to society was greater than its value to the private landowner. Pigou (1932) notes that in response to these situations, "it is theoretically possible to put matters right by the imposition of a tax or the grant of a subsidy" (p. 381) that would, in effect, equate private returns with social returns. Stoddard's (1951) call for public subsidies to private landowners to increase wildlife production was a request for a Pigouvian subsidy for wildlife.

Although Pigou's work was widely accepted as having laid the theoretical foundation for government intervention in private markets, it took another 30 years for economists to overcome their reticence to use these theoretical insights to argue for public policies that, while benefiting some, would impose costs on others. Seminal contributions by Harold Hotelling, J. R. Hicks, and Nicholas Kaldor allowed the discipline to arrive at a basic consensus that economists could recommend policies that would change the distribution of income in society so long as the gains experienced by some members of society as a result of the policy were greater than the losses experienced by others. This allowed economists to return to Pigou's work, using it to ground an argument for the use of subsidies and taxes to promote social welfare. Practitioners of the new welfare economics set about describing the conditions that would determine when such intervention was warranted.

Social and private benefits differ when the production or consumption of a good creates externalities. An externality exists when an economic decision generates tangible benefits or costs that are not received or incurred by the economic decision maker but rather by some third party. In the case of wildlife, private landowners bear many of the costs associated with wildlife production. These costs may be deliberately incurred, as when a private landowner forgoes financially remunerative uses of the land to provide more suitable wildlife habitat, or they may be the unintended result of wildlife-related crop damage. Although private landowners bear the costs of wildlife production, they are seldom able to capture all of the benefits generated by wildlife. These benefits are instead enjoyed by hunters, hikers, bird-watchers, and other wildlife enthusiasts, as well as those who provide products like binoculars, camping gear, rifles, and vacation cabins to the wildlife enthusiasts. These benefits exist as externalities, and as such, they do not inform the landowner's land use decision.

When externalities exist, the resulting supply of the externality-producing good will differ from that associated with the maximization of net social benefits; the invisible hand of the free market will not lead all to the socially optimal result. In one of the earliest economic studies describing the value of wildlife, Hays Gamble and Ronald Bartoo (1963) estimated that the deer herd existing in Sullivan County, Pennsylvania, cost each farm in the county an average of $200 per year in crop damages, while simultaneously generating gross revenues to the county of about $546 per farm as a result of expenditures made in the county by hunters visiting the area. Although the county clearly had an interest in promoting the deer supply to attract more hunters to the area, the farmers, on whose land the herd depended, had an interest in reducing the herd's size. The presence of externalities caused the socially desirable outcome to deviate from that which occurred absent market intervention.

Despite the attractiveness of the Pigouvian argument, not all economists agree that externalities provide a sufficient rationale for government intervention in the market. These economists reject the Pigouvian solution of government taxes and subsidies in favor of a laissez-faire response best articulated by Ronald Coase. According to Coase and his followers, not only is the government's response likely to cause inefficiencies, but furthermore, government intervention is itself unnecessary. Absent government interference, the private parties affected by externalities and those creating the externalities will come to their own efficient solutions if the economic impact of the externality is sufficiently large. In the words of Harold Demsetz (1967), "Property rights develop to internalize externalities when the gains of internalization become larger than the cost of internalization" (p. 350). If the benefits of wildlife are significant enough, those who value the wildlife will do what it takes to see to it that wildlife is supplied. They can buy up land and convert it to wildlife reserves, or they can pay landowners to switch from crop production to wildlife production in exchange for the rights to enjoy the wildlife produced. According to the Coasians, if the benefits generated by the externality are not significant enough to warrant the internalization of these externalities, it follows that they are not significant enough to warrant government attention.

Although a discussion of the relative merits of the two positions is beyond the scope of this chapter, it is nonetheless a critical debate to those interested in the economics of

wildlife protection because it informs how one both frames and addresses the question of wildlife supply. According to the Pigouvians, government response to the chronic undersupply of wildlife requires subsidization to private landowners for those actions that contribute to the supply of wildlife and taxation of private landowners for those actions that diminish wildlife supply. This policy recommendation stands in sharp contrast to that resulting from a Coasian approach to wildlife protection. In this case, government should see to it that the property right—to the unrestricted use and enjoyment of private land or to a population or species of wildlife—is clearly established among private parties, and then the parties should be encouraged to negotiate private solutions.

The debate between the Pigouvians and the Coasians remains unresolved and has resulted in a lack of coherency in the policy recommendation offered by economics for wildlife and other goods (or bads) created as externalities. Given the lack of consensus among economists, the government met no concentrated opposition to its own particular approach to wildlife protection, which was to acquire even more land for wildlife habitat and refuge and to use legislation to prohibit activities on public or private lands that threatened to depress wildlife populations to the level of possible extinction. Between 1964 and 1994, land holdings of the U.S. Fish and Wildlife Service increased nearly fourfold, growing from 22.7 million acres to 87.5 million (*Federal Lands,* 1996). In 1973, Congress passed amendments to the Endangered Species Act of 1973, making it illegal, on public or private land, "to harass, harm, pursue, hunt, shoot, wound, kill, trap, capture, or collect" (Section 3) any species found to be in danger of extinction. Rather than solving the externality problem by creating habitat conservation incentives, via taxes and subsidies to private landowners, or staying out of the wildlife problem altogether, the government approached the problem of declining wildlife populations by making wildlife protection and production one of its responsibilities. By the end of the 1960s, the role of economics in wildlife protection had changed from debating the proper management tool to measuring and describing the extent to which the government's own policies had the potential to improve overall social welfare. With few exceptions, the economics of wildlife protection moved from policy prescription to the careful description, characterization, and quantification of benefits of government-provided wildlife conservation efforts.

Theoretical Foundations of Wildlife Protection: Wildlife and the Problem of Market Failure

Wildlife presents the economist with a near-perfect storm of exceptions to Adam Smith's argument that the invisible hand of individual self-interest will guide society to welfare-maximizing allocations of goods and services. Indeed, at least three characteristics of wildlife interfere with its optimal allocation. Economic theory predicts that because of (1) the particular characteristics of the production of wildlife benefits, (2) the particular characteristics defining access to these benefits, and (3) the particular characteristics of the benefits themselves, the market-generated supply of wildlife will fall short of the optimum. This makes wildlife supply and wildlife protection an interesting and perplexing problem for economists.

Market Failure in the Production of Wildlife Benefits

Wildlife is an ephemeral resource. Its nature is such that the very act of ownership transforms it to some other species of good. Thus, a wild deer becomes, on the act of extraction that is a precondition to ownership, someone's source of meat or potential trophy, pet, or unit of livestock. To be wildlife, or *ferae naturae*, is to be unowned and unownable. Once an animal is owned, it is no longer termed *wild*.

This concept, this metaphysical truth about wildlife, goes back at least as far as Roman law, which recognized wildlife as *res nullius*, literally, nobody's property. Wildlife differed in the Roman tradition from other natural resources, like water, which the Romans categorized as *res communis*, or common property, the property of everyone. The Roman government could claim for its people a property right to the waters within the empire's boundary, and it could protect that claim with force as necessary. It could not similarly claim for its people a property right to the wildlife that crossed international borders of its own will and according to its own tastes. Individuals could extract wildlife from the natural population to eat or domesticate, but that act of extraction changed the very nature of the extracted animal from *res nullius* to the property of the captor. Ownership removes the *wild* from *wildlife*.

The profound difference that exists between wildlife and owned animals constrains wildness and wildlife to exist as an externality. An animal cannot remain wildlife if it is produced as part of a deliberate breeding and management program. If a herd of buffalo exists as part of nature's endowment, it is wildlife, but if the herd exists as part of a rancher's assets, it is simply livestock. The valuable but ephemeral asset of wildness is diminished by the act of husbandry. Aldo Leopold (1986) noted, "The recreational value of a head of game is inverse to the artificiality of its origin, and hence in a broad way to the intensiveness of the system of game management which produced it" (p. 395). Perversely, attempts to address the externality of the wildlife benefit through the private management of the wildlife supply diminish the magnitude of the benefit itself.

Although the value attributable to the wildness of wildlife seems destined to exist as a nonexcludable externality generated by wildlife production, certain wildlife-associated benefits, such as those generated through the acts of hunting or viewing wildlife, are potentially excludable, because private landowners can limit entry to their private property. But even these excludable benefits are not likely to generate market compensation commensurate with the benefits generated. As a fugitive resource, wildlife does not necessarily reward those who practice good habitat management on their privately held land. Several characteristics of the wildlife production function, such as the magnitude of the land area typically involved in wildlife production, the fact that breeding habitat is often quite distinct and distant from grazing habitat, and the existence of chronobiologic phenomena like migration, mean that investments in wildlife-augmenting activities are unlikely to be able to capture the appropriate monetary recompense. If the wildlife population breeds and feeds on one parcel of land yet spends the hunting season on some other parcel, the owners of the breeding grounds cannot capture in hunting receipts the value of their contributions to wildlife production. Meanwhile, the owner of the prime hunting land potentially reaps an unearned profit. The inability to capture the benefits associated with the supply of wildlife means that wildlife will be undersupplied.

Market Failure and the Property Regime Controlling Access to Wildlife

Many wildlife populations exist under conditions of open access, which is to say their range is so broad or unpoliced that anyone wishing to exploit them for personal gain can do so. Open access resources are susceptible to overexploitation because those who employ the resource have no incentive to exercise restraint in doing so; like children grabbing up candy after the piñata has disgorged its contents to the floor, those who depend on an open access resource know that moderation receives no reward. Although the rational individual owner under a system of private property will extract only to the point where profits are maximized (i.e., to the point at which the marginal revenue generated by the extracted resource is equal to the marginal cost of extraction from the resource) and although the tribe or community extracting from a commonly held resource may develop means of regulating its use to preserve its benefit stream, exploitation under conditions of open access will continue so long as any positive profits remain to be earned from the resource. This is because profits, or net benefits, generated by extraction from the wildlife population will continue to lure others into the same enterprise so long as those profits exist. Thus, there is a greater rate of exploitation for a given population of wildlife under conditions of open access than would exist if access to the wildlife resource could be controlled as private property or as a regulated commons.

H. Scott Gordon (1954) first described this phenomenon with respect to the ocean fishery. Noting that "fishermen are not wealthy, despite the fact that the fishery resources of the sea are the richest and most indestructible available to man" (p.132), Gordon went on to explain the low returns to fishermen by considering how a profitable fishing grounds will continue to attract new entrants until such time as the potential entrants see no profit in exploiting the fishery. That is, entry continues into the fishery until all economic profits are exhausted. This is because those exploiting an open access resource have no reason to limit their extraction to promote the continued health of the fishery, because the benefits of any restraint will just go to some other fisherman. According to Gordon, "He who is foolhardy enough to wait for its proper time of use will only find that it has been taken by another" (p. 135). Open access explains the destruction of the North American buffalo herds, the near extinction of certain species of whales, and the precarious status of many species of African wildlife. The supply of a good existing under conditions of open access will be less than is economically efficient.

But even if access is limited to a tribe, licensed harvesters, or some other identifiable and closed group, collective ownership of a resource can lead to overexploitation, as Garrett Hardin (1968) describes in his paradigm-shifting article, "The Tragedy of the Commons." Overexploitation of the commons is the potential result of an asymmetry in the distribution of benefits and costs among those using a common property resource. Specifically, those who use the commons for their own purposes are able to capture for themselves the entire benefit associated with the use of the commons, while the costs that use imposes are shared by all who hold title to the commons. In the case of depredations on wildlife, although the hunter or trapper is able to gain the full benefit associated with capturing his or her prey (presumably by either selling the hide, consuming the carcass, or mounting its head on the library wall), insofar as extraction reduces the size of the wild population and requires, in turn, increased effort to extract the next animal from the population, this cost is divided among all who prey on the wild population. As such, the cost an individual bears when extracting a unit of resource from a commonly held population is less than he or she would bear as a result of extracting the same unit from a privately held population. The lowered perceived costs incurred by the individual extracting from a commonly held resource therefore results in more extraction for the same benefit function than would occur with a privately held property.

This is not to say that private ownership or management of wildlife would solve the problem of extinction. Indeed, as originally pointed out by Colin Clark (1973), extinction can be the efficient outcome for a renewable resource held by a profit-maximizing private owner. If revenues from exploiting a wild population (via hunting, fishing, or other extractive activity) exceed the costs associated with this effort and if the rate of growth of the species is less than the rate of return the owner could earn in some other investment, the owner has the economic incentive to convert the resource into cash to invest in the higher yielding asset. In other words, if the price a hunter can get for the last elephant tusk taken from the last elephant is greater than the costs the hunter incurs finding and killing this last elephant and if the rate of interest the

hunter could earn on the net revenues from the sale of that tusk is greater than the rate of growth of the elephant population, the profit-maximizing hunter would find it in his or her interest to kill that last elephant. Private ownership might result in efficient management of the wildlife resource, but it offers no guarantee of the resource's preservation.

Market Failure and the Benefits of Wildlife

The final factor contributing to the undersupply of wildlife concerns the public-good nature of many of the benefits wildlife generates. Public goods have two distinguishing characteristics. First, they are nonrival in consumption, meaning that more than one consumer may enjoy the same public good simultaneously. This differs from the rival nature of private good benefits, which can be enjoyed only by the single consumer possessing the good itself. The nonrival nature of the benefits generated by public goods means that a single unit of a public good bestows benefits simultaneously on all the consumers who are simultaneously consuming it. As a result, even if the benefits each individual derives from the provision of a unit of public good are very small, that unit can nonetheless contribute a very large amount to social welfare when its benefits are summed up over millions of individual consumers.

The other distinguishing characteristic of public goods is that their benefits are nonexcludable. Once a public good has been produced, it is impossible to restrict its consumption to a select group of individuals. This means that a public good cannot be rationed to those who pay for it. The inability to charge individuals for the use of public goods means that private producers will have no incentive to supply public goods to the market, because potential consumers will simply free ride and enjoy the goods' benefits without paying for them. Because those who do not pay for a public good enjoy the same level of benefit from the public good as those who do pay, public goods are unlikely to be produced and exchanged in a market economy. Government is necessary to ensure the production of public goods.

The public-good nature of the wildlife benefit entered the economic spotlight when John Krutilla (1967) published "Conservation Reconsidered." This seminal article changed forever the way economists, policy makers, and the general public characterized the services provided by environmental resources. Although economists since John Stuart Mill have used the existence of public goods to justify government provision of everything from lighthouses to national defense, Krutilla's essay expanded the list of public goods to include "some unique attribute of nature . . . a threatened species, or an entire ecosystem or biotic community essential to the survival of the threatened species" (p. 777). Krutilla based his argument on the assertion that the knowledge of the mere existence of these wild resources constitutes "a significant part of the real income of many individuals" (p. 778). By including the existence of a threatened species within the genre of public goods, Krutilla made the strongest economic case yet for the preservation of species and the conservation of wildlife habitat. If indeed the actuality of a species provided millions of people with some form of income, then that species' existence had a tangible economic value that would be irretrievably lost should society choose to allow development to proceed to the point that it resulted in the species' extinction.

Krutilla (1967) describes the basic contours of the benefits emanating from preservation of unique environmental assets as equal to the "minimum which would be required to compensate such individuals were they to be deprived in perpetuity of the opportunity to continue enjoying the natural phenomenon in question" (pp. 779–780). In the case of extinction, this compensation would need to reflect the amount individuals would have been willing to pay to retain an option to use or interact with the species, the expected value of what might have been learned or extracted from the species had it not gone extinct, the value individuals had placed on the species' contribution to "the mere existence of biological . . . variety" (p. 782), and the value of the benefit individuals would have derived from leaving the species as a bequest to their heirs. Because all of these benefits are nonrival and nonexcludable, the preservation of any particular species of wildlife represents a public good of potentially enormous economic value that nonetheless is not and cannot be reflected in market exchanges.

Krutilla's (1967) expansive view of wildlife benefits changed wildlife from prey to be managed for hunters to a resource capable of providing enjoyment to an entire nation, even the entire world. The recognition of the public-good benefits resulting from the mere existence of a species of wildlife provided needed justification for efforts to preserve endangered species and populations of wildlife across the globe. Wildlife protection after "Conservation Reconsidered" enlarged to include endangered species preservation as one of its key concerns.

Applications and Empirical Evidence

Economic solutions to the problems facing the supply of wildlife are largely limited to proposals of remedies for those attributes of the wildlife benefit and production functions that cause the market to fail to arrive at an efficient allocation of the wildlife good. That is, economists start by characterizing wildlife protection as an economic problem and then proceed to offer an economic solution to the problem. Although this seems to confirm Abraham Maslow's maxim that if one has only a hammer, one sees every problem as a nail, it also reflects the discipline's insistence on staying within its own area of expertise and imposing on itself its own standards for what constitutes advances in knowledge.

Some problems posed by wildlife are more amenable to economic solutions than others. For example, if wildlife is undersupplied because the market does not provide adequate compensation to those who incur the costs of wildlife production, a solution becomes both obvious and easy to implement, particularly for those benefits, like hunting and fishing, from which it is at least possible to exclude those who fail to pay.

But for other problems, the role of the economist in resolving issues pertaining to wildlife protection is less certain. It is one thing to point out the public-good nature of many of the benefits of wildlife protection; it is another thing entirely to arrive at estimates of preservation benefits and costs that allow the economist to describe for a given biome, ecosystem, or planet the optimal amount of preservation and extinction.

This section considers how economics has been used as a tool for informing optimal levels of wildlife protection. It begins with a review of economic solutions to the wildlife externality problem and continues to consider economic contributions to the understanding of how property regimes influence wildlife supply. This is followed by a description of how economics has contributed to both the understanding and the measurement of benefits flowing from wildlife. The section concludes with an examination of how economics has informed the question of endangered species preservation.

Addressing Market Failure in the Production of Wildlife: A Look at the Pigouvian and the Coasian Solutions

Even as the economics profession was slow to respond to Stoddard's (1951) call to develop a branch of the discipline devoted to the economics of wildlife protection, so too was Congress sluggish in its response to the call for subsidies to private landowners to encourage wildlife production. Indeed, over 30 years elapsed between Stoddard's article and congressional legislation authorizing subsidies to landowners for habitat conservation efforts. The 1985 farm bill, known as the Food Security Act of 1985, established a Conservation Reserve Program (CRP) that offered farmers rental payments of about $50 per acre per year for agricultural land taken out of crop production (Section 1231). Although initially designed as both a means of preventing soil loss on highly erodible land and a way to increase commodity prices through commodity supply reductions, the program is now viewed by the U.S. Department of Agriculture (USDA, 2007) as a primarily environmental program. Nearly 40 million acres of agricultural land are presently enrolled in the program, although the 2008 farm bill has reduced the target for future enrollments to 32 million (USDA, 2009). Additional landowner subsidy programs have been added to the mix—the Wetlands Reserve Program, the Environmental Quality Incentives Program, the Conservation Security Program, the Wildlife Habitat Incentives Program, and the Grasslands Reserve Program—which together add another 21 million acres of privately held land to those CRP lands managed with the goal of promoting wildlife habitat, according to the USDA. The total cost of these programs was estimated at $4.961 billion in 2008 (Cowan & Johnson, 2008).

The rationale for these subsidies, as introduced in the 1985 farm bill, sounds distinctly Pigouvian. Section 1231 of the 1985 legislation calls on the secretary of agriculture to enter into contracts with private landowners to encourage them "to conserve and improve the soil, water, and wildlife resources" (Food Security Act of 1985). However, insofar as the government makes no attempt to set the level of these subsidies to reflect the difference between the social and private welfare generated by conservation activities on private land, the subsidies fall far short of Pigou's suggested instrument. The informational demands of marginal benefits–marginal costs analysis make it practically impossible to estimate the requisite level of the Pigouvian subsidy, let alone arrive at an efficient means of taxing individuals for the benefits such a subsidy would generate. For this reason, Nobel Laureate James Buchanan (1962) criticized the Pigouvian solution as "not only politically unimaginable in modern democracy: it is also conceptually impossible" (p. 27).

Rather than tackling the unimaginable and impossible, applied economic research on subsidies to promote wildlife production has concentrated on evaluating the efficacy of the existing set of government programs. Although the CRP initially made no attempt to target cost-effective means of achieving conservation goals, later enrollments in the CRP have considered the ratio of environmental quality benefits to their costs, with salutary effects on program cost effectiveness (Osborn, 1993). However, because wildlife benefits appear to be uniformly distributed across CRP-eligible land, improving the overall cost effectiveness of the CRP enrollment appears to have little impact on the wildlife benefit generated by CRP participation (Babcock, Lakshminarayan, Wu, & Zilberman, 1996). Recent research on the cost effectiveness of government conservation subsidy programs compares the relative efficacy of land retirement programs like the CRP to programs like the Environmental Quality Incentives Program that keep the land employed while mandating landowner investment in ecosystem improvement. Here, the published evidence is somewhat mixed. Some (Polasky, Nelson, Lonsdorf, Fackler, & Starfield, 2005) have found the potential for significant savings is realized by satisfying a wildlife conservation goal through a mixed land use strategy that provides both wildlife habitat and crop production. Still others have obtained results that indicate that complete and total land retirement is a more cost-effective means of conserving

wildlife (Feng, Kurkalova, Kling, & Gassman, 2006). Clearly, this is an area where more research should prove both enlightening and productive.

Given the necessarily wild nature of wildlife, attempts to implement a Coasian solution to the wildlife undersupply problem are handicapped by an inability to assume away the problem by assigning property rights to the wildlife resource. The metaphysical essence of wildlife prevents it from becoming someone's property or herd. Coasian-inspired research has therefore focused on identifying the incentives that contribute to changes in the overall size of the wildlife population. These incentives can be directed at those whose actions affect the supply of wildlife as well as those responsible for changes in the demand for wildlife.

Regarding wildlife supply, Coasian-inspired analysis has examined how landowners respond to direct payments to create more wildlife habitat. Not surprisingly, research reveals consistently that landowners whose only interest in land is as a productive input to some market-related activity require higher payments to engage in habitat production than landowners whose interests in the land are not purely financial. Therefore, the somewhat expected result emerging from the analysis of landowner willingness to participate in wildlife conservation programs is that motives matter. Those landowners who exhibit an interest in wildlife or are not dependent on the land for their livelihoods require lower incentive payments than those who report no interest in wildlife or have only a financial interest in their own land holding. Whether this result would hold if habitat payments become standard across landowners is, of course, a matter of speculation. If government were to institute a large-scale program to pay landowners for their contributions to wildlife habitat, it could use its monopsonistic powers to discriminate among landowners based on these differences in wildlife habitat supply elasticity.

Coasian-inspired analysis of those factors that contribute to demand for the extractive use of wildlife focuses on the efficacy of trade bans as a means of reducing extractive pressure on a wildlife population. The desirability of the trade ban has been shown to depend on the ability of the state to protect the wildlife resource from illegal predations. If the police powers of the state are so extensive that the expected returns to poaching, given the probability of arrest, fines, or detention, are less than many would-be poachers could earn in their next-best income-generating opportunity, then trade bans should be discouraged because they reduce the returns to state-sponsored wildlife stewardship. That is, the state's incentives to protect its threatened wildlife are decreased under a trade ban, because the ban limits the potential for remuneration from the harvest of the protected species. On the other hand, if the police powers of the state are so nugatory that the species exists under what are essentially conditions of open access, import bans might be desirable because they lower the potential returns from exploiting the wildlife resource by restricting the size of its potential market. Mixed and muddled empirical results seem to confirm the theoretical ambiguity regarding the desirability of these bans. While Pigouvian subsidies will continue to be subjected to efficacy tests, Coasian attempts at limiting government intervention in wildlife exchanges and interactions will confront continued tests of their overall desirability.

Addressing Market Failure in the Access to Wildlife: Understanding the Role of Property Regimes

Perhaps the most well-known application of economic theory to address the wildlife access problem concerns the development and implementation of individual transferable quotas (ITQs). Like a license, which represents one way of regulating access under a common property regime, an ITQ is a government-granted right to extract a certain amount of a resource. But unlike a license, the individual possessing the ITQ can sell this right to another. By allowing sales, ITQs provide their owners with a means of capturing some of the benefits of conservation efforts. As the wild population increases in size, the ITQ increases in value because presumably less effort need be expended to harvest the same amount of resource. The ITQ addresses the open access problem by restricting access to the resource to only those individuals who possess licenses, and it attempts to solve the potential common property problem by rewarding restraint in resource extraction through increases in the value of the ITQ.

Unlike some economic policy suggestions, ITQs have an observable track record. New Zealand adopted the ITQ system as a means of regulating its fishery in 1986. A similar system was implemented 5 years later in Iceland. Studies evaluating the ITQ system give it relatively high marks for promoting economic efficiency. As predicted, the system allows the same amount of the resource extraction with less effort than is exerted under other systems regulating the commons (Arnason, 1991; Yandle, 2008). However, ITQs have admittedly undesirable distributional consequences, because those able to buy up ITQs can effectively close a regional fishery and thereby cause localized economic collapse and dislocation (Eythórsson, 2003).

Other empirically based research examines the effect of alternative property regimes on wildlife supply. Relying primarily on case studies in lieu of theoretical abstraction, the litmus test applied to the various property regimes is typically not whether a given ownership configuration is likely to promote economic efficiency so much as whether the ownership pattern will conserve the wildlife resource (Brown, 2000, p. 902). As such, these studies reflect what for some is a paradigm change in the economics of wildlife protection, because sustainability of the wildlife resource replaces efficiency as the norm about which property regimes are to be judged.

Addressing Market Failure and the Benefits of Wildlife

Convinced by Krutilla's (1967) argument that unique natural assets generate more benefits than are revealed through market transactions, economics developed a distinct typology of those benefits generated through interaction with the natural environment. Within this classification system, benefits sort into two main categories: use values and nonuse values. Those benefits generated as the result of direct in situ interaction with an asset are use values, while nonuse values are those that require no direct interaction with the environmental amenity. Hunting, bird-watching, nature photography, and fishing are all use values, while knowledge—of the existence of a wildlife population or a scenic wonder like the Grand Canyon—is a nonuse value.

The taxonomy of values includes a second tier of subordinate classifications. Use values can be consumptive or nonconsumptive, depending on whether they reduce the stock of the natural asset. Hunting and fishing represent consumptive uses of wildlife, while bird-watching and nature photography are nonconsumptive uses of the wildlife resource. Nonuse values are categorized on the basis of the type of knowledge generating the value. Knowledge that the resource exists to fulfill a potential future desire to interact with it contributes to the option value of the wildlife resource, while knowledge that the resource exists for the use and enjoyment of future generations contributes to its bequest value. Existence value is the monetized measure of satisfaction that one experiences from simply knowing that the wildlife population exists, independent of any desire to interact with it directly or save it as a bequest for one's heirs.

Benefit estimation techniques for these nonmarket goods differ according to whether one is estimating use or nonuse values. For a use value like bird-watching, even if the use itself is not allocated via markets, economists can estimate the value of the benefits it generates by observing how demand for complementary goods, like binoculars, changes with changes in the quantity of the nonmarket good consumed. From these changes, one can derive at least a minimum value for the nonmarket good. However, this technique is not available in the case of nonuse values, which we consume without leaving behind any "behavioral trail" (Smith, 1990, p. 875). Without market generated prices and quantities on which to base benefit calculations, economists have been forced to abandon their insistence on revealed preference and seek some other way of determining the value of these scarce goods that fail to exchange in markets. The contingent valuation method (CVM) is the invention to which this necessity gave birth.

Although initially a cause of great controversy within the discipline, CVM is now the orthodox method of quantifying nonuse values. In a CVM survey, individuals are asked to reveal their willingness to pay for the right to enjoy a particular environmental amenity or their willingness to accept payment to forgo the enjoyment of the amenity. Typically, a CVM survey describes an environmental asset and then proposes a scenario in which the quantity of the asset is changed. Survey respondents are asked to describe how much they value that change. Using individual responses to hypothetical changes in the quantity of an environmental asset, economists can estimate its value.

But even though CVM is now well accepted as a means of quantifying nonuse benefits, concerns remain. One persistent issue is whether to measure the respondents' willingness to pay (WTP) to acquire a certain amount of an environmental asset or to instead measure their willingness to accept (WTA) payment to forgo the use of the asset. Lest this seem like a merely semantic difference, consider the likely difference between the amount an individual might require from a cousin in exchange for the engagement ring a grandmother bequeathed to the individual and the amount the same individual would offer to purchase the identical ring from his or her cousin if the cousin had inherited the ring instead. Property rights matter. One's WTP is constrained by one's budget constraint, but no such constraint limits one's willingness to accept payment. As a result, WTA has been found to be higher, for certain goods, than WTP. But this is not solely a result of the effect of the budget constraint. Rather, even controlling for the income, the fewer the substitutes that exist for the good, the greater the difference between WTP and WTA. Although the price that would induce an individual to part with a grandmother's engagement ring might be significantly greater than what he or she would be willing and able to pay to purchase it from a cousin, one might expect that the price that would induce the same individual to part with his or her present refrigerator is similar to the price the individual would be willing to pay to purchase a similar one. There are many likely substitutes for a given refrigerator; there are no substitutes for a grandmother's engagement ring.

As concerns payments to conserve wildlife, contingent valuation surveys have evinced significant differences between WTP and WTA. Richard Bishop and Thomas Heberlein (1979) found that Wisconsin duck hunters required nearly five times more in payment to surrender their licenses than they were willing to pay to purchase the same license. David Brookshire, Alan Randall, and John Stoll (1980) found that elk hunters were willing to pay only one seventh as much to purchase a license from the state to hunt elk as they were willing to accept in payment for the retirement of a license that they had been given by the state. G. C. van Kooten and Andrew Schmitz (1992) discovered that Canadian landowners were willing to pay only

$3.90 per acre annually for a permit entitling them to drain wetlands but needed $26.80 per acre in compensation from the government to refrain from draining wetlands. These observed discrepancies between WTP and WTA lead to a conclusion that private activities that reduce the amount of wildlife impose a greater cost on society than is reflected in the measured WTP that appears in many CVM studies. In the words of Jack Knetsch (1990), the observed differences between WTA and WTP mean that "it is likely that, among other implications, losses are understated, standards are set at inappropriate levels, policy selections are biased, too many environmentally degrading activities are encouraged, and too few mitigation efforts are undertaken" (p. 227). If landowners had to pay the public for activities they engage in that diminish the wildlife resource, fewer of these activities would take place.

Contingent valuation studies have provided a set of estimates of interest to wildlife protection. Measured WTP for individual species ranges from a low of $8.32 annually (2006 dollars) to avoid the loss of the striped shiner to $311.31 per year (2006 dollars) to support a 50% increase in the saltwater fish population of western Washington and the Puget Sound (Richardson & Loomis, 2009). International visitors to China have a measured average WTP of $14.86 (1998 dollars) to conserve habitat for the giant panda (Kontoleon & Swanson, 2003). Citrus County, Florida, residents appear to be willing to pay a combined total of $194,220 (2001 dollars) per year to protect the Florida manatee (Solomon, Corey-Luse, & Halvorsen, 2004). As concerns the preservation of rare and endangered species, estimated WTP has increased over time (Richardson & Loomis, 2009). Evidence exists that WTP to protect a species grows at an increasing rate with the degree of perceived threat and at a decreasing rate as the population of a threatened species increases (Bandara & Tisdell, 2005).

WTP estimates reveal interesting and novel insights into wildlife conservation motives. Pennsylvania duck hunters were willing to pay more to avoid a reduction in duck populations resulting from global climate change than they were to avoid the same population reduction when caused by agricultural practices (Kinnell, Lazo, Epp, Fisher, & Shortle, 2002). A survey of Dutch households found that the respondents were willing to pay more to prevent reductions in the native seal population caused by oil spills than by a lethal, naturally occurring virus (Bulte, Gerking, List, & de Zeeuw, 2005). Economic research on payments for changes in wildlife populations continues to chip away at the margins, providing insight to many individual cases and refining and codifying survey techniques and statistical methods of analysis.

Economics has addressed the problems posed by the public-good nature of many wildlife benefits by developing new tools to measure these benefits. Once quantified, these values have been able to influence public policy through their inclusion in benefit-cost analysis. As such, although economics has not been able to solve the problem created by the existence of public goods, it has been able to propose partial remedies that are at least potentially welfare enhancing. Additionally, economic explorations into the differences between WTP and WTA have provided important insights into human behavior, even as they challenge the discipline to develop consistent theoretical explanations. Equally interesting and challenging for the discipline is the recent empirical evidence that WTP for wildlife conservation depends on the factors that make such payments necessary. Ducks threatened by agricultural practices are not the same as ducks threatened by climate change, and seals threatened by oil spills appear to be more valuable than seals threatened by a virus. Future research to explain these observed differences promises to both complicate and improve the discipline of economics.

Other Economic Contributions to Wildlife Protection: Economics of Species Preservation

Although economics has made great strides in helping provide information of value to policy makers as they make discreet decisions regarding wildlife conservation, the discipline has had difficulty developing a coherent and useful response to questions concerning wildlife preservation policy and strategy. This is largely because the benefits of biodiversity remain unknown and largely speculative, even though all agree that biodiversity is a good—and a pure public good, at that. Furthermore, while CVM might be reasonably effective at elucidating individual WTP to preserve a particular species under conditions of partial equilibrium, it has been unable to determine a WTP to preserve biodiversity in general. CVM estimates can be used to inform preservation decisions on a solely case-by-case basis and not as part of some overall preservation policy.

Economic contributions to the question of how much biodiversity to preserve include the controversial approach of recommending that all species be managed to preserve a population of sufficient size to avoid the threat of extinction. This minimally viable population size, known as the *safe minimum standard* (SMS), was originally described by Siegfried von Ciriacy-Wantrup in 1952. Ciriacy-Wantrup (1968) argued that conservation requires a collective choice rule that subjects "the economic optimum to the restriction of avoiding immoderate possible losses" (p. 88). This SMS functions as "an insurance policy against serious losses that resist quantitative measurement" (Ciriacy-Wantrup & Phillips, 1970, p. 28). As insurance, investments in the SMS should themselves be constrained; the SMS should be adopted unless the social costs of doing so are unacceptably large (Bishop, 1978). The abandonment of marginal analysis and the lack of rigor inherent in a policy based on judgments of what constitutes immoderate losses and unacceptably

large social costs inhibit widespread adoption of the SMS within the discipline of economics.

As a choice made under uncertainty, the SMS has been portrayed as a dominant strategy in a two-person game between society and nature. In this game, society chooses between development and preservation, while nature chooses whether to inflict a disease on society and whether to encode a cure for that disease within the species threatened with extinction. If the decision rule calls for minimizing the maximum possible loss, the game yields inconsistent results, depending on whether the source of the uncertainty is whether the disease outbreak will occur or whether the cure will be found in the species (Ready & Bishop, 1991). However, if the decision rule calls for society to minimize its regrets instead of its maximum possible losses, the game's results consistently favor the SMS. Under a regret-minimizing strategy, society makes choices that minimize the potential losses associated with being wrong. If society chooses development when it should have chosen preservation, the losses are greater than if society chooses preservation when it should have chosen development (Palmini, 1999). However, although regret minimization may well inform individual behavior, economists have not been able to make a case for regret minimization as an economic norm. Thus, the SMS may describe a human behavior but not an economic objective.

The SMS approach demands that the economic objective of welfare maximization be replaced by that of preservation whenever extinction is a real threat, and this demand inhibits its widespread adoption by the economics profession. By demanding a discrete policy regime shift from the pursuit of welfare enhancement to the pursuit of preservation, the SMS exposes itself to criticism of its inconsistency. Because the rationale for this shift has eluded any formal statement, the SMS enjoys only limited support as an economic norm. Applied economic research regarding the SMS has focused on measuring both the WTP for preservation and the threshold level for what constitutes excessive preservation costs, as revealed by empirical analysis of costs incurred in the preservation of endangered species.

At the heart of the dissatisfaction with the SMS is its inability to help inform the choice between preservation and development that is the core issue for endangered species policy. The SMS approach argues for the preservation of all species, and although this argument is certainly appealing and popular, it is not economics. As Gardner Brown (2000) wrote poignantly, "Economists know what many ecologists cannot bear to admit, that not all species can be saved in a world of scarce resources" (p. 908). Brown's remarks echo those of Andrew Metrick and Martin Weitzman (1998), who critically observe, "At the end of the day, all the brave talk about 'win-win' situations, which simultaneously produce sustainable development and conserve biodiversity, will not help us to sort out how many children's hospitals should be sacrificed in the name of preserving natural habitats. The core of the problem is conceptual. We have to make up our minds here what it is we are optimizing. This is the essential problem confounding the preservation of biodiversity today" (p. 21).

In place of the SMS, some economists have argued that preservation decisions should maximize biodiversity, subject to a budget constraint, by giving marginal preference to those species with no close substitutes as measured by the number of species within a genus. According to this model, the next dollar of preservation investment is more productively spent on a species with no close substitutes than on one that shares its genus with many other species. Of course, this assumes both that society has decided that biodiversity is the good whose production it values most and that the system of Linnaean taxonomy, an arguably human construct, accurately reflects the sort of biodiversity that society wishes to maximize. Economists remain frustrated by the inability of their discipline to help inform one of the central debates of our times.

Policy Implications

The immediate and obvious result of decades of economic inquiry into the challenges facing wildlife protection is that there is ample reason to believe that the present supply of wildlife is smaller than optimal and that government intervention is necessary to protect and augment it. Government intervention can be in the form of direct subsidies to private landowners, rearrangement of property regimes and the rules of access, trade bans, absolute prohibitions on activities that degrade the wildlife resource, and public acquisition of land and resources as necessary to augment the supply of wildlife.

Regarding government subsidies to private landowners providing habitat for wildlife, economic research indicates that the current practice of removing land from production might be improved by offering a mix of programs, some of which offer subsidies to encourage multiple uses of the land base. This promises to lower the costs of achieving some wildlife protection goals. As the relative cost effectiveness of these alternative land management regimes appears to differ with the particular characteristics of the landscape and its native wildlife, government should be prepared to tailor its incentive programs to arrive at the most cost-effective subsidy mix.

Government attempts to rearrange property regimes by providing a transferable right to wildlife extraction have succeeded in reducing the overall cost of the extractive effort and have thus promoted efficiency. However, although privatization of a publicly held good, like wildlife, might lead to more efficient exploitation of the resource, it might also lead to its extinction or to a smaller population size than would occur under a common property regime. If the goal of the property rights rearrangement is species conservation, there is little evidence supporting the efficacy of privatization as a means to realize this goal.

The overall impact of trade bans on endangered species populations has not been settled empirically. Because the trade ban reduces the market value of the traded species, it is not clear from the empirical evidence whether this in turn leads to reduced poaching or to reduced investment in species conservation. To be effective instruments of species preservation, trade bans might need to be coupled with direct payments to those bearing the costs of conservation efforts.

Both the policies resulting in absolute prohibitions on otherwise productive activities that threaten the wildlife stock and the use of government resources to promote conservation activities should be guided by a consideration of the benefits of these activities relative to their costs. In estimating the value of the benefits of the wildlife resource, policy makers need to be cognizant of the difference between WTP and WTA estimates of wildlife values. Insofar as wildlife belongs to the nation, reductions in wildlife are losses in the real income of a nation's citizens. Therefore, the correct measure of the loss is obtained by asking citizens how much they would be willing to accept as compensation for a reduction in the population level, or the extinction, of a species. However, if increasing the population of wildlife entails constraining actions on private property, respondents should be asked to consider how much they are willing to pay private property owners for the loss of a beneficial land use. Values obtained in this manner should be used to guide public appropriations to preservation efforts.

Although economics can be used to inform the level of welfare-enhancing preservation investment in individual species, public policy has eschewed using this information in its preservation decisions. Domestic endangered species policy is absolutist; the law requires that any species found to be in danger of extinction is to be protected, regardless of either the costs or the benefits associated with its preservation. This implies that society has embraced some version of the SMS, at least as a matter of public policy. However, empirical analysis of the listing process under the Endangered Species Act indicates that species protection is influenced by interest group participation in the rule-making process (Ando, 1999). Listing decisions have also been shown to be sensitive to the likely impact of species protection on the districts of key congressional stakeholders (Rawls & Laband, 2004). Policy makers wishing to depoliticize the preservation process might well consider including a consideration of the biodiversity benefits of a given preservation option as part of their deliberations prior to awarding protection to a species.

Future Directions

Trends in population growth, habitat modification, energy use, and waste production signal that wildlife populations will face increasing pressure in the future. Expanded use of the land base to meet the consumption needs of an ever-growing world population implies further that the opportunity cost of wildlife habitat is also likely to increase in the future. Finally, increasing political unrest in areas of the globe stressed by water shortages and climate change is likely to take its toll on native wildlife populations. In sum, the suboptimal supply of wildlife is likely to continue unabated and become more profound in the years to come.

Economics can contribute to ameliorating these problems with research concerning the most cost-effective means of providing wildlife habitat. This includes the development of spatially explicit landscape models linking conservation costs to the wildlife supply response across a variety of landscape types, thus allowing the manager to choose the least-cost method of achieving a particular conservation goal. Another line of research that holds promise for promoting conservation cost effectiveness examines incentives motivating landowner participation in conservation programs. Wildlife managers can use information gleaned from these studies to target those landowners most willing to participate in conservation efforts and therefore lower conservation costs.

An important area for new research involves developing mechanisms to reward those who engage in wildlife conservation efforts and compensate those who bear the costs of species preservation. This means identifying and addressing the perverse incentives to eradicate species that are created by preservation mandates that constrain traditional land uses and the use of private property. It also means continued research on the effects of divergent property regimes on conservation and wildlife protection.

Perhaps the most important contribution economics can make to the problems posed by wildlife protection is that of values discernment. Although existence values provide much of the economic basis for investment in wildlife preservation, they constitute a rather gross aggregation of the nonuse benefits accruing to individuals as a result of the preservation decision. These values need to be further refined and teased into their constituent parts if economists are to improve how they inform preservation decisions.

Although the public has consistently expressed both substantial interest in avoiding extinctions and measurable WTP to avoid them, economists need to develop better ways to help the public describe just what it is that they wish to avoid via these expenditures. The present disciplinary emphasis on maximizing biodiversity assumes that the public values genetic distance over, say, honoring an ethical commitment to stewardship or maintaining something wild in an increasingly tamed world. Would the public be less concerned with extinction if the science of cloning progresses to the point where animals can be recreated from saved genetic material? What distinguishes the value of a wild specimen from a particular species with an otherwise identical specimen living in a zoo? What are the valuable attributes of wildness? These are the questions that are likely to be addressed by future economics research, because these are the questions that need to be answered if preservation is going to be allocated by informed, transparent policy decisions.

Taken together, these future directions for wildlife economics imply a more interdisciplinary, more nuanced approach to research, which will increasingly rely on input from the natural sciences as well as other social sciences. Research teams including economists, biologists, psychologists, sociologists, political scientists, and soil scientists are likely to become both more common and more necessary as conservation and protection move beyond the wildlife reserve to lands devoted to other productive uses. Not only will economists increasingly rely on other disciplines in the conduct of their research, but they will also need to continue to improve upon methods of engaging in conversation with the public at large to elucidate the values informing the desire to engage in conservation efforts. Simple-minded, predictable Homo economicus will be replaced by sophisticated and complicated real human beings as the object of economic research on values and objectives for wildlife protection. How interesting and how ironic that in studying wildlife, economists end up learning more about being human.

Conclusion

The economics of wildlife protection has struggled over the years to incorporate a fugitive, unowned, and unownable natural asset into a discipline that is most comfortable describing exchanges of discretely bound goods in a market economy. Indeed, the nature of wildlife as an economic good is so unique that the discipline's early work in the field was devoted almost entirely to taxonomic descriptions of the benefits generated by wildlife and the property regimes that govern human interactions with the wildlife resource. These efforts were rewarded by a greater understanding of both what economists mean when they speak of value and the role property regimes play in determining resource conservation and exploitation.

Both wildlife protection and economics have benefited as a result of the development of this field of economic research. To the field of wildlife protection, economics has brought an explicit recognition of opportunity costs and their impact on the decisions of private landowners faced with deciding between promoting habitat conservation or development. Economics has emphasized the importance of understanding how distribution of costs and benefits flowing from wildlife conservation and extractive activities affect ultimately the rate of extraction, even the probability of extinction, of a wild population. Economics has expanded the number of stakeholders explicitly recognized by wildlife managers to include those who receive real but largely unobservable nonuse values from the wildlife resource.

Engagement with the questions and issues posed by wildlife protection has also benefited economics. The challenges confronted when working with such an unconventional subject have forced economics to grow beyond its regular confines. For a discipline accustomed to dividing the world into consumers and producers, the challenges posed when examining a system in which benefits can be enjoyed by millions, even billions, of persons, absent any act of consumption, and a system in which goods are supplied as part of a natural, replenishable endowment have proved both liberating and confounding. Disciplinary engagement with the problem posed by wildlife protection has revealed that welfare can be augmented or diminished independent of the act of consumption. Indeed, economics has shown that sometimes something as gossamer as the mere knowledge of a good's existence constitutes an important part of an individual's asset portfolio. This is a revolutionary concept for economics. Similarly, the idea of a supply function characterized by a range in which it irreversibly heads to zero has challenged the discipline to develop ways to consider whether and how to avoid treading into that range. This has in turn made the discipline more receptive to exploring alternatives to the private-property and market-oriented regimes as a means of attaining socially desired outcomes.

References and Further Readings

Ando, A. W. (1999). Waiting to be protected under the Endangered Species Act: The political economy of regulatory delay. *Journal of Law and Economics, 42*, 29–60.

Arnason, R. (1991). Efficient management of ocean fisheries. *European Economic Review, 35*(2–3), 408–417.

Babcock, B. A., Lakshminarayan, P. G., Wu, J., & Zilberman, D. (1996). The economics of a public fund for environmental amenities: A study of CRP contracts. *American Journal of Agricultural Economics, 78*(4), 961–971.

Bandara, R., & Tisdell, C. (2005). Changing abundance of elephants and willingness to pay for their conservation. *Journal of Environmental Management, 76*(1), 47–59.

Bishop, R. C. (1978). Endangered species and uncertainty: The economics of a safe minimum standard. *American Journal of Agricultural Economics, 60*(1), 10–18.

Bishop, R. C., & Heberlein, T. A. (1979). Measuring values of extramarket goods: Are indirect measures biased? *American Journal of Agricultural Economics, 61*(5), 926–930.

Brookshire, D. S., Randall, A., & Stoll, J. (1980). Valuing increments and decrements in natural resource service flows. *American Journal of Agricultural Economics, 62*(3), 478–488.

Brown, G. M. (2000). Renewable natural resource management and use without markets. *Journal of Economic Literature, 38*(4), 875–914.

Buchanan, J. M. (1962). Politics, policy, and the Pigovian margins. *Economica, New Series, 29*(113), 17–28.

Bulte, E., Gerking, S., List, J., & de Zeeuw, A. (2005). The effect of varying the causes of environmental problems on stated WTP values: Evidence from a field study. *Journal of Environmental Economics and Management, 49*(2), 330–342.

Ciriacy-Wantrup, S. (1968). *Resource conservation: Economics and policies* (3rd ed.). Berkeley: University of California Press.

Ciriacy-Wantrup, S., & Phillips, W. (1970). Conservation of the California tule elk: A socioeconomic study of a survival problem. *Biological Conservation, 3*, 23–32.

Clark, C. (1973). The economics of overexploitation. *Science, 181*(4100), 630–634.

Cowan, T., & Johnson, R. (2008). *Agriculture conservation programs: A scorecard* (CRS Report No. RL32940). Washington, DC: Congressional Research Service.

Demsetz, H. (1967). Toward a theory of property rights. *American Economic Review, 57*(2), 347–359.

Endangered Species Act of 1973, Pub. L. No. 93-205, § 3, 87 Stat. 884 (1973).

Eythórsson, E. (2003). Stakeholders, courts and communities: Individual transferable quotas in Icelandic fisheries 1991–2000. In N. Dolsak & E. Ostrom (Eds.), *The commons in the new millennium* (pp. 129–168). Cambridge: MIT Press.

Federal lands: Information on land owned and acquired: Testimony before the Subcommittee on Oversight and Investigations of the Senate Committee on Energy and Natural Resources, 104th Cong. (1996). (Testimony of Barry Hill). Retrieved from http://archive.gao.gov/papr2pdf/156123.pdf

Feng, H., Kurkalova, L., Kling, C., & Gassman, P. (2006). Environmental conservation in agriculture: Land retirement vs. changing practices on working land. *Journal of Environmental Economics and Management, 52*(2), 600–614.

Food Security Act of 1985, Pub. L. No. 99-198, § 1231, 99 Stat. 1354 (1985).

Gamble, H., & Bartoo, R. (1963). An economic comparison of timber and wildlife values on farm land. *Journal of Farm Economics, 45*(2), 296–303.

Gordon, H. (1954). The economic theory of a common-property resource: The fishery. *Journal of Political Economy, 62*(2), 124–142.

Hardin, G. (1968). The tragedy of the commons. *Science, 162*(3859), 1243–1248.

Kinnell, J., Lazo, J., Epp, D., Fisher, A., & Shortle, J. (2002). Perceptions and values for preventing ecosystem change: Pennsylvania duck hunters and the Prairie Pothole region. *Land Economics, 78*(2), 228–244.

Knetsch, J. (1990). Environmental policy implications of disparities between willingness to pay and compensation demanded measures of values. *Journal of Environmental Economics and Management, 18*(3), 227–237.

Kontoleon, A., & Swanson, T. (2003). The willingness to pay for property rights for the giant panda: Can a charismatic species be an instrument for nature conservation? *Land Economics, 79*(4), 483–499.

Krutilla, J. (1967). Conservation reconsidered. *American Economic Review, 57*(4), 777–786.

Leopold, A. (1986). *Game management.* Madison: University of Wisconsin Press.

Metrick, A., & Weitzman, M. (1998). Conflicts and choices in biodiversity preservation. *Journal of Economic Perspectives, 12*(3), 21–34.

Osborn, T. (1993). The Conservation Reserve Program: Status, future, and policy options. *Journal of Soil and Water Conservation, 48*(4), 271–278.

Palmini, D. (1999). Uncertainty, risk aversion, and the game theoretic foundations of the safe minimum standard: A reassessment. *Ecological Economics, 29*(3), 463–472.

Pigou, A. (1932). *The economics of welfare* (4th ed.). London: Macmillan.

Polasky, S., Nelson, E., Lonsdorf, E., Fackler, P., & Starfield, A. (2005). Conserving species in a working landscape: Land use with biological and economic objectives. *Ecological Applications, 15*(4), 1387–1401.

Rawls, R., & Laband, D. (2004). A public choice analysis of endangered species listings. *Public Choice, 121*(3–4), 263–277.

Ready, R., & Bishop, R. (1991). Endangered species and the safe minimum standard. *American Journal of Agricultural Economics, 73*(2), 309–312.

Richardson, L., & Loomis, J. (2009). The total economic value of threatened, endangered and rare species: An updated meta-analysis. *Ecological Economics, 68*(5), 1535–1548.

Smith, V. (1990). Can we measure the economic value of environmental amenities? *Southern Economic Journal, 56*(4), 865–878.

Solomon, B., Corey-Luse, C., & Halvorsen, K. (2004). The Florida manatee and eco-tourism: Toward a safe minimum standard. *Ecological Economics, 50*(1–2), 101–115.

Stoddard, C. (1951). Wildlife economics: A neglected tool of management. *Land Economics, 27*(3), 248–249.

U.S. Department Agriculture, Farm Service Agency. (2007). *Conservation Reserve Program: Summary and enrollment statistics FY 2006.* Retrieved December 29, 2009, from http://www.fsa.usda.gov/Internet/FSA_File/06rpt.pdf

U.S. Department of Agriculture. (2008). *FY 2009 budget summary and annual performance plan.* Retrieved April 28, 2009, from http://www.obpa.usda.gov/budsum/fy09budsum.pdf

U.S. Department of Agriculture, Economic Research Service. (2009). *Conservation policy: Background.* Retrieved December 29, 2009, from http://www.ers.usda.gov/Briefing/Conservation Policy/background.htm

van Kooten, G. C., & Schmitz, A. (1992). Preserving waterfowl habitat on the Canadian prairies: Economic incentives versus moral suasion. *American Journal of Agricultural Economics, 74*(1), 79–89.

Yandle, T. (2008). The promise and perils of building a co-management regime: An institutional assessment of New Zealand fisheries management 1999–2005. *Marine Policy, 32*(1), 132–141.

61

Environmental Economics

Jennifer L. Brown

Eastern Connecticut State University

On the political stage, environmental issues are usually placed at odds with economic issues. This is because environmental goods, such as clean air and clean water, are commonly viewed as priceless and not subject to economic consideration. However, the relationship between economics and the environment could not be more natural.

In its purest form, economics is the study of human choice. Because of this, economics sheds light on the choices that individual consumers and producers make with respect to numerous goods, services, and activities, including choices made with respect to environmental quality. Economics is able not only to identify the reasons that individuals choose to degrade the environment beyond what is most beneficial to society, but also to assist policy makers in developing environmental policy that will provide an efficient level of environmental quality.

Because environmental economics is interdisciplinary in nature, its scope is far-reaching. Environmental economists research topics ranging from energy to biodiversity and from invasive species to climate change. However, despite the breadth of the topics covered by the community of environmental economic researchers, a reliance on sound economic principles remains the constant.

This chapter outlines the basic concepts in environmental economics, including the ways in which environmental economists might estimate the value society holds for the natural environment. Further, the corrective instruments that environmental economists can employ to correct for situations in which markets fail to achieve an efficient outcome are closely examined. This chapter also stresses the important role economic analysis plays in today's most pressing environmental issues.

Theory

Environmental goods are those aspects of the natural environment that hold value for individuals in society. Just as consumers value a jar of peanut butter or a can of soup, consumers of environmental goods value clean air, clean water, or even peace and quiet. The trouble with these types of goods is that though they are valuable to most individuals, there is not usually a market through which someone can acquire more of an environmental good. This lack of a market makes it difficult to determine the value that environmental goods hold for society; although the market price of a jar of peanut butter or a can of soup signal the value they hold for consumers, there is no price attached to environmental goods that can provide such a signal.

To some, it may seem unethical to try to place a dollar value on the natural environment. However, there are plenty of cases in which ethics demands just that. Indeed, in cases of extreme environmental damage, such as the 1989 Exxon *Valdez* oil spill, an unwillingness to apply a value to environmental loss could be considered equivalent to stating that environmental loss represents no loss to society at all. Because of this, the assessment of appropriate damages, fines, or both, in cases such as this often depends on the careful valuation of varying aspects of the environment.

In the case of environmental policy development, insufficient evidence pertaining to the benefit that environmental goods provide to society could easily skew the results of a cost-benefit analysis (see Chapter 27: Cost-Benefit Analysis) against environmental protection. This would, in effect, undermine the value that society holds for environmental goods and could possibly lead policy makers to believe that certain environmental regulations are not worth the costs they impose on society when, in fact, they are.

For these reasons, as well as for other reasons that are covered later in this chapter, economists have long endeavored to develop methods of accurately determining the value of environmental goods to society. This effort has led to the development of several valuation techniques.

Valuing the Environment

Contingent Valuation

Contingent valuation, or stated preferences, is a seemingly simple method of valuation that involves directly asking respondents about their values for a particular environmental good. This method is particularly useful in determining the value of environmental goods that individuals have yet to experience or may never actually experience themselves.

The Exxon *Valdez* oil spill is an example of a case in which contingent valuation provided a useful tool of valuation (Goodstein, 2008). In this case, contingent valuation was used to determine, among other things, the value that individuals place on simply knowing that a pristine Alaskan wilderness exists, even though many respondents may never actually experience this wilderness for themselves (this value is defined as *existence value*). More generally, contingent valuation methods are often used in policy development to determine the amount respondents would be willing to pay for a new, higher level of environmental quality.

However, despite its simple concept, the contingent valuation method carries with it a host of complex problems that must be taken into account for the results of a survey to be considered credible. These problems usually stem from one or more of the following: information bias, strategic bias, hypothetical bias, and starting point bias (Tietenberg, 2007). Because any type of bias can hinder the usefulness of a contingent valuation survey, special care must be taken to ensure that any bias in the answers provided by survey respondents is minimized.

With information bias, hypothetical bias, and starting point bias, respondents unintentionally misrepresent the value that they hold for an environmental good. With information bias, respondents lack enough information to form an accurate response. To avoid this type of bias, surveyors will usually provide a great deal of information to respondents pertaining to the topic of the survey.

Hypothetical bias occurs because individuals tend to respond differently to hypothetical scenarios than they do to the same scenarios in the real world. One solution to this problem is to conduct the contingent valuation surveys in a laboratory setting (Kolstad, 2000). This solution provides the surveyor with an opportunity to remind respondents to consider the financial ramifications that their responses would produce in a real-world setting. It also allows the surveyor to use experimental techniques that mimic the conditions that respondents would face in a real-world situation.

Finally, starting point bias results when respondents are influenced by the set of responses made available to them by the contingent valuation survey. The solution to this problem requires significant pretesting of a survey to ensure that its design does not influence respondents to provide biased answers (Kolstad, 2000).

Unlike the other types of response bias that can occur in a contingent valuation survey, strategic bias occurs as respondents intentionally try to manipulate the outcome of a survey. It is not always possible to eliminate intentionally biased responses. However, in general, it is best to randomly survey a large number of individuals because this will decrease the likelihood that strategic bias will undermine the overall results of the survey.

Revealed Preferences

The revealed preferences method involves determining the value that consumers hold for an environmental good by observing their purchase of goods in the market that directly (or indirectly) relate to environmental quality. For example, the purchase of air fresheners, noise reducing materials, and water purification systems reveal the minimum amount individuals are willing to pay for improved air and water quality. This particular revealed preferences method is referred to as the *household production* approach.

Economists can also use revealed preferences to determine the value of clean air and clean water through differences in home prices across both pristine and polluted home locations. This particular revealed preferences method is referred to as the *hedonic approach* (Kolstad, 2000).

These approaches to valuing the environment have the advantage of relying on actual consumer choices to infer the value society holds for a particular environmental good, rather than relying on hypothetical scenarios. However, there are some environmental goods for which it can be nearly impossible to identify their value through market interactions. For example, using the revealed preferences method to determine the value that society holds for the survival of an endangered species would pose a tremendous challenge. In cases such as these, revealed preferences may not be the preferred method of valuation.

Valuation techniques are useful not only in cost-benefit analysis or in cases of extreme environmental damage but also in the more subtle cases of environmental degradation that occur as a result of market failure.

Market Failure

As was discussed in the previous section, individual consumers will often purchase goods with an environmental component to make up for their inability to directly purchase environmental goods, thus revealing the value they hold for certain aspects of environmental quality. For example, someone may buy a cabin on a lake in order to enjoy not only the home itself but also the pristine environment that comes with such a purchase. As long as this individual is able to exclusively incur the environmental benefits that come from owning a log cabin, the demand for log cabins will reflect the full value of both the home and the environmental goods it provides and the market for log cabins will be efficient.

Unfortunately, in the case of environmental goods, markets often fail to produce an efficient result because it is rare that any one individual can incur the full benefit (or cost) of a particular level of environmental quality. This is because environmental goods commonly suffer from the presence of externalities or a lack of property rights (see Chapter 22: Externalities and Property Rights).

There are two types of externalities: negative and positive. Negative externalities exist when individuals in society bear a portion of the cost associated with the production of a good without having any influence over the related production decisions (Baumol & Oates, 1988). For example, parents may be required to pay higher health care costs related to pollution-induced asthma among children because of an increase in industrial activity in their neighborhood.

Because producers do not consider these costs in their production decisions, they produce higher quantities of goods with negative externalities than is efficient, leading to more than the socially desirable level of environmental degradation.

As with negative externalities, positive externalities also result in inefficient market outcomes. However, goods that suffer from positive externalities provide more value to individuals in society than is taken into account by those providing these goods. An example of a positive externality can be seen in the case of college roommates sharing an off-campus apartment. Though a clean kitchen may be valued by all individuals living in the apartment, the person that decides to finally wash the dishes and scrub the kitchen floor is not fully compensated for providing value not only to himself or herself but also to the apartment as a whole. Because of this, the decision to clean the kitchen undervalues the benefits of such an action and the kitchen will go uncleaned more often than is socially desirable.

Such is the case with environmental quality. Because markets tend to undervalue goods that suffer from positive externalities, market outcomes provide a level of environmental quality that is lower than is socially desirable.

Corrective Instruments

Once the market inefficiency relating to a particular environmental good is understood, policy makers can correct for this inefficiency by employing any number of policy instruments. Regardless of the instrument, the goal is to provide incentives to individual consumers and firms such that they will choose a more efficient level of emissions or environmental quality.

Command and Control

Command and control is a type of environmental regulation that allows policy makers to specifically regulate both the amount and the process by which a firm is to reduce emissions. This form of environmental regulation is very common and allows policy makers to regulate goods where a market-based approach is either not possible or not likely to be popular. However, these regulations limit the choices that individual firms can make regarding their pollution levels. Because of this, they do not provide firms with an incentive to develop new pollution-reducing technologies (Kolstad, 2000).

The Coase Theorem

Ronald Coase developed the Coase Theorem in 1960, which, although not necessarily a regulatory framework, paved the way for incentive-driven, or market-based, regulatory systems. According to the Coase Theorem, in the face of market inefficiencies resulting from externalities, private citizens (or firms) are able to negotiate a mutually beneficial, socially desirable solution as long as there are no costs associated with the negotiation process (Coase, 1960). This result is expected to hold regardless of whether the polluter has the right to pollute or the average affected bystander has a right to a clean environment.

Consider the negative externality example given previously, in which parents face soaring health care costs resulting from increased industrial activity. According to the Coase Theorem, the firm producing the pollution and the parents could negotiate a solution to this externalities issue, even without government intervention. In this example, if the legal framework in society gave the firm the right to produce pollution, the parents with sick children could possibly consider the amount they are spending on medical bills and offer a lesser sum to the firm in exchange for a reduced level of pollution. This would save the parents money (as compared with their health care costs), and the firm may find itself more than compensated for the increased costs that a reduction in emissions can bring.

If it is the parents, instead, that have a right to clean, safe air for their children (this is more typically the case), then the firm could offer the parents a sum of money in exchange for allowing a higher level of pollution in the area. As long as the sum offered is less than the cost of reducing emissions, the firm will be better off. As for the parents, if the sum of money more than compensates the health care costs they face with higher pollution levels, they may also find themselves preferring the negotiated outcome.

Unfortunately, because the fundamental assumption of the Coase Theorem (costless negotiation) often falls short, this theorem is not commonly applicable as a real-world solution. Despite this fact, the Coase Theorem is an important reminder that even in the case of complex environmental problems, there may be room for mutually beneficial compromises. This theorem also sheds light on cases in which firms are willing to voluntarily comply with environmental regulations as well as on possible solutions to complex international environmental agreements.

Taxation

In 1920, Arthur C. Pigou (1920) developed a taxation method for dealing with the goods suffering from externalities. The idea behind his tax, now known as the *Pigouvian tax,* is to force producers to pay a tax equal to the external damage caused by their production decisions in order to allow the market to take into consideration the full costs associated with the taxed goods. This process is often referred to as *internalizing* an externality.

This concept can also be applied to goods that suffer from positive externalities. However, in this case, a negative tax (or subsidy) is provided to allow an individual to gain an additional benefit from providing the subsidized good. A common example of this type of subsidy can be seen each time an individual receives a tax break for purchasing an Energy Star appliance.

Of course, because the amount of the tax (or subsidy) must equal the value of the external environmental damage (or benefit) in order to correct for market inefficiencies, the valuation techniques detailed previously are crucial in the development of a sound tax policy.

Permit Markets

The concept of using a permit market to control pollution levels was first developed by John Dales (1968). Through this method of regulation, pollution permits are issued to firms in an industry where a reduction in emissions is desired. These permits give each firm the right to produce emissions according to the number of permits it holds. However, the total number of permits issued is limited to the amount of pollution that is allowed industry-wide. This means that some firms will not be able to pollute as much as they would like, and they will be forced to either reduce emissions or purchase permits from another firm in the industry (Barde, 2000).

Those firms able to reduce their emissions for the lowest possible cost benefit from this type of regulation. This is because these firms can sell their permits for an amount greater than or equal to the cost of their own emissions reduction, resulting in profits in the permit market. However, even firms for which it is very costly to reduce pollution experience a cost savings through this type of regulation because they are able to purchase pollution permits at a price that is less than or equal to the cost they would face if they were required to reduce emissions. Ultimately, permit markets make it less costly for an industry to comply with environmental regulations and, with the prospect of profits in the permit market, this type of regulation provides an incentive for firms to find less costly pollution reducing technologies.

Applications and Empirical Evidence

Valuing the Environment: Practical Applications

Both the methods of valuation and the corrective instruments described previously have been applied quite extensively to real-world environmental problems. In fact, according to Barry Field and Martha Field (2006), contingent valuation methods have been used to determine the amount respondents would be willing to pay for a myriad of environmental goods. For example, respondents have been surveyed to determine the value they would place on increased air visibility in places such as the White Mountains (located in New Hampshire) and the Grand Canyon (located in Arizona). Further, contingent valuation methods have been used to determine the value of old-growth forest preservation in the face of industrial expansion (Hagen, Vincent, & Welle, 1992).

Revealed preferences methods have increased in popularity in recent history and are commonly used by researchers to determine the value society holds for clean air and clean water. Though there are many recent cases in which researchers have used revealed preferences methods, Eban Goodstein (2008) provided a particularly useful example of the way in which this method has been used in a real-world setting.

The example given involves the decline in housing prices that occurred in the town of New Bedford, Massachusetts, in the early 1980s following severe contamination of the nearby harbor. Using the hedonic approach, economists were able to determine that those homes closest to the contamination experienced a $9000 reduction in value while the overall loss to homeowners in New Bedford was estimated to be approximately $36 million (Goodstein, 2008).

Although this type of analysis provides only a minimum value of the loss experienced due to the pollution of the harbor, it can be a valuable component in determining an appropriate fine for the firms responsible for the pollution. More generally, these results also shed light on the value that individuals place on clean water.

Corrective Instruments: Practical Application

Though many of the concepts in environmental economics predate the 1970s, the implementation of the Clean Air Act of 1970 represents the first major application of these concepts to government policy. Through these amendments, strict ambient air quality standards were set, and in some cases, specific technologies were required for compliance (Tietenberg, 2007). This regulatory framework is consistent with the command-and-control framework described previously.

However, since the Clean Air Act Amendments of 1990, pollution taxes and permit markets have taken center stage in terms of environmental regulation. In fact, though permit markets were used in the United States as early as the 1970s, the Clean Air Act Amendments of 1990 ushered in an era of increased popularity for this type of regulation by requiring the development of a nationwide permit market for sulfur dioxide emissions.

According to Jean-Philippe Barde (2000), the Environmental Protection Agency implemented a program in response to this requirement that was expected to result in a significant cost savings (20%–50%) as compared with other types of regulation. Further, Thomas Tietenberg (2007) asserted that the development of permit markets increased compliance with federally mandated pollution reduction requirements. (Chapter 14 of Tietenberg, 2007, provides a comprehensive overview of the effectiveness of a variety of pollution control policies.)

Additional programs have been used to reduce ozone-related emissions, including California's Regional Clean Air Incentives Market (RECLAIM), established in the Los Angeles basin, and the Ozone Transport Commission NO_X Budget Program, which spans approximately 10 states in the eastern United States. (Both of these programs were originally implemented in 1994. However, the NO_X Budget Program has since undergone several program modifications, including slight changes to the program name.)

The Ozone Transportation Commission program aimed to reduce nitrogen oxide emissions in participating states in both 1999 and 2003 (U.S. Environmental Protection Agency [EPA], n.d.). The results of this program, as reported by the Environmental Protection Agency, have included a reduction in sulfur dioxide emissions (as compared with 1990 levels) of over 5 million tons, a reduction in nitrogen oxide emissions (as compared with 1990 levels) of over 3 million tons, and nearly 100% program compliance (EPA, 2004).

In terms of taxation programs aimed at reducing pollution levels, Finland, Sweden, Denmark, Switzerland, France, Italy, and the United Kingdom have all made changes to their tax systems in order to reduce environmental degradation. Some of these changes include the introduction of new taxes, such as Finland's implementation of the 1990 carbon tax; other changes involve using tax revenue to increase environmental quality, such as Denmark's use of tax revenue to fund investment in energy-saving technologies (Barde, 2000).

In the United States, local grocery markets are at the center of a large tax system aimed at reducing environmental degradation: the deposit–refund system. This system effectively rewards individuals willing to return bottles and cans to an authorized recycling center. Such an incentive represents a negative tax (or subsidy) to individuals in exchange for recycling behavior that benefits society as a whole.

Policy Implications

The policy implications of work done by environmental economists are far-reaching. As countries deal with issues such as water quality, air quality, open space, and global climate change, the methodologies developed in environmental economics are key to providing efficient, cost-effective solutions.

Although command and control remains a common form of regulation, the previous sections detail the ways that countries have begun to use market-based approaches such as taxation and permit markets within the regulatory framework.

Examples of these types of programs continue to develop. For example, in an attempt to comply with the provisions of the Kyoto Protocol, which was implemented to control greenhouse gas emissions, the European Union has established a carbon dioxide permit market aimed at reducing greenhouse gases (Keohane & Olmstead, 2007).

Even the Coase Theorem comes into play as global environmental problems demand mutually beneficial agreements to be voluntarily negotiated across countries. In fact, the Montreal Protocol, which was implemented to control emissions of ozone-depleting chemicals, makes use of a multilateral fund that compensates developing countries for the costs incurred in phasing out ozone-depleting chemicals (Field & Field, 2006). This is very similar to the example in which parents in a community may find it beneficial to compensate a polluting firm in order to induce a reduction in emissions.

Future Directions

Because of the interdisciplinary nature of environmental economics, the discipline constantly presses forward in many directions. Many of the most pressing environmental issues involve both local and global pollutants. These range from local water quality issues to the reduction of greenhouse gas emissions.

In terms of local, regional, and national environmental issues, the application of currently available corrective instruments is quite feasible. However, an evaluation of the value of regulated environmental goods as well as the proposed regulatory instruments is still the topic of ongoing research.

In terms of global issues, such as global climate change, there is still much work to be done regarding the economic impact of changes to the earth's climate. In addition, solutions relying on government enforcement are less possible when it comes to global climate change. This means that there is likely to be more emphasis placed on voluntary compliance.

For example, in the wake of the Kyoto Protocol, there have been regional agreements that have been formed that have a reduction in greenhouse emissions as a primary goal. One such agreement, known as the Western Climate Initiative, was developed in February 2007. This initiative is a voluntary agreement between seven U.S. states and four Canadian provinces. Its goal is to reduce greenhouse gas emissions by 15% (as compared with 2005 emissions levels) by the year 2020 (Western Climate Initiative, n.d.).

Finally, countries have long suffered from the production decisions of their neighbors. However, since the availability of clean water in the border regions of developing countries remains an issue, solutions to these problems (and similar transborder problems) remain the focus of ongoing research.

Conclusion

Environmental economics provides a set of tools that are crucial in understanding today's most pressing environmental problems. Through the use of valuation techniques such as contingent valuation and revealed preferences, economists are able to estimate the value society holds for a variety of environmental goods. These values allow policy analysts to consider the impact that a proposed public policy might have on the natural environment. Economists are also able to use these techniques to provide an accurate description of the loss that occurs in cases of both extreme environmental damage and more subtle environmental degradation that occurs daily.

Environmental economics explains the role that externalities play in excessive environmental degradation because the failure of markets to capture the full value of environmental goods consistently results in the overproduction of those goods that can damage the environment and an underprovision of those goods that improve environmental quality. Further, through corrective instruments developed by economists such as Pigou (1920), Coase (1960), and Dales (1968), environmental economics has provided society with innovative solutions to excessive environmental degradation resulting from market failure.

Finally, the application of the techniques developed by environmental economists has become increasingly popular as concern over environmental issues has become a common staple in public policy. As environmental problems continue to become increasingly complex, environmental economists continue to press forward, applying the solutions provided by the fundamentals of economics to these problems.

References and Further Readings

Arrow, K. J., Cropper, M. L., Eads, G. C., Hahn, R. W., Lave, L. B., Noll, R. G., et al. (1996). Is there a role for benefit-cost analysis in environmental health and safety regulation? *Science, 272,* 221–222.

Barde, J.-P. (2000). Environmental policy and policy instruments. In H. Folmer & H. L. Gabel (Eds.), *Principles of environmental and resource economics: A guide for students and decision-makers* (2nd ed., pp. 157–201). Cheltenham, UK: Edward Elgar.

Baumol, W., & Oates, W. (1988). *The theory of environmental policy* (2nd ed.). New York: Cambridge University Press.

Coase, R. H. (1960). The problem of social cost. *Journal of Law and Economics, 3,* 1–44

Crocker, T. D. (1965). The structuring of atmospheric pollution control systems. In H. Wolozin (Ed.), *The economics of pollution* (pp. 61–86). New York: W. W. Norton.

Dales, J. H. (1968). *Pollution, property, and prices: An essay in policy-making and economics.* Toronto, Ontario, Canada: University of Toronto Press.

DeLong, J. V., Solow, R. M., Butters, G., Calfee, J., Ippolito, P., & Nisbet, R. A. (1981, March/April). Defending cost-benefit analysis: Replies to Steven Kelman. *Regulation,* 39–43.

Ellerman, A. D., Joskow, P. L., Schmalensee, R., Montero, J.-P., & Bailey, E. M. (2000). *Markets for clean air: The U.S. Acid Rain Program.* New York: Cambridge University Press.

Field, B. C., & Field, M. K. (2006). *Environmental economics: An introduction* (4th ed.). New York: McGraw-Hill.

Freeman, A. M., III. (2003). *The measurement of environmental and resource values* (2nd ed.). Washington, DC: Resources for the Future.

Goodstein, E. S. (2008). *Economics and the environment* (5th ed.). New York: John Wiley.

Hagen, D. A., Vincent, J. W., & Welle, P. G. (1992). Benefits of preserving old-growth forests and the spotted owl. *Contemporary Policy Issues, 10,* 13–26.

Keohane, N. O., & Olmstead, S. M. (2007). *Markets and the environment.* Washington, DC: Island Press.

Kelman, S. (1981, January/February). Cost-benefit analysis: An ethical critique. *Regulation,* 33–40.

Kolstad, C. D. (2000). *Environmental economics.* New York: Oxford University Press.

Kolstad, C. D., & Freeman, J. (Eds.). (2006). *Moving to markets in environmental regulation: Lessons from twenty years of experience.* New York: Oxford University Press.

Maler, K. G. (1974). *Environmental economics: A theoretical inquiry.* Baltimore: Johns Hopkins University Press.

Mitchell, R. C., & Carson, R. T. (1989). *Using surveys to value public goods: The contingent valuation method.* Washington, DC: Resources for the Future.

Pigou, A. C. (1920). *The economics of welfare.* London: Macmillan.

Sen, A. K. (1970). *Collective choice and welfare.* San Francisco: Holden-Day.

Shechter, M. (2000). Valuing the environment. In H. Folmer & H. L. Gabel (Eds.), *Principles of environmental and resource economics: A guide for students and decision-makers* (2nd ed., pp. 72–103). Cheltenham, UK: Edward Elgar.

Stavins, R. N. (2003). Experience with market based environmental policy instruments. In K. G. Maler & J. Vincent (Eds.), *Handbook of environmental economics* (Vol. 1, pp. 335–435). Amsterdam: Elsevier Science.

Stavins, R. N. (Ed.). (2005). *Environmental and natural resource economics* (6th ed.). Boston: Addison-Wesley.

Tietenberg, T. H. (1990). Economic instruments for environmental regulation. *Oxford Review of Economic Policy, 6*(1), 17–33.

Tietenberg, T. H. (1992). *Environmental and natural resource economics.* New York: HarperCollins.

Tietenberg, T. H. (2007). *Environmental economics and policy* (5th ed.). Boston: Pearson.

U.S. Environmental Protection Agency. (2004). *Acid Rain Program 2004 progress report.* Retrieved January 18, 2009, from http://www.epa.gov/airmarkets/progress/arp04.html

U.S. Environmental Protection Agency. (n.d.). *Overview of the Ozone Transportation Commission (OTC) NO_X Budget Program.* Retrieved January 18, 2009, from http://www.epa.gov/airmarkets/progsregs/nox/otc-overview.html

Western Climate Initiative. (n.d.). *U.S. states, Canadian provinces announce regional cap-and-trade program to reduce greenhouse gases.* Retrieved January 18, 2009, from http://www.pewclimate.org/docUploads/Sept%2023%20PR_0.pdf

62

ECONOMICS OF ENERGY MARKETS

STEPHEN H. KARLSON

Northern Illinois University

The improved living standards of the developed world rest on industrial processes that make intensive use of renewable and nonrenewable energy sources. Economists' attempts to understand that prosperity tend to focus on legal institutions and commercial practices rather than on resource endowments. As recently as the 1990s, David Landes's (1998) *The Wealth and Poverty of Nations* focuses on these institutions that enable people to contract with each other and to construct long-lived enterprises of large scale, rather than on resource endowments, including energy, as the foundations of that wealth. Thus, prosperity rests on division of labor, mechanization, and capital markets in a legal framework that enables people to coordinate their activities. Those elements were present in Adam Smith's (1776/1976) pin factory, which was supported by human and animal muscle power and wood. The energy source as contemporary economists understand it was not viewed as a constraint or as an opportunity in those days, although the limitations of existing sources of power imposed serious constraints on earlier economic powers.

Evolutionary biologist Matt Ridley summarizes the effect of those constraints:

> We saw a quintupling of cotton cloth output in two consecutive decades, in the 1780s and 1790s, none of it based on fossil fuels yet but based on waterpower. . . . At some point, you run out of dams. You run out of rivers in Lancashire to dam. (Bailey, 2009, pp. 50–51)

The British avoided the fate of previous economic powers by changing their power source to coal:

> By 1870 Britain is consuming the coal equivalent to 850 million human laborers. It could have done everything it did with coal with trees, with timber, but not from its own land. Timber was

bound to get more expensive the more you used of it. Coal didn't get more expensive the more you used of it. (Bailey, 2009, pp. 50–51)

A similar dynamic was at work in the United States, where Alfred Chandler (1977) claims, "Coal, then, provided the source of energy that made it possible for the factory to replace the artisans, the small mill owners, and putting-out system as the basic unit of production in many American industries" (p. 77). Those transitions were not inevitable. The term *horsepower* is a marketing comparison of the early steam era, used by advocates of steam power to highlight the advantages of their machinery over those using animal power, let alone human power or waterpower, as the primary energy source. Readers will see that the quest for energy efficiency neither implies nor is implied by quests for greater economic efficiency or greater prosperity.

Energy sources have contributed to episodes of technical progress and improvements in prosperity. A recent *Economist* report (Carr, 2008) notes,

> Many past booms have been energy-fed: coal-fired steam power, oil-fired internal combustion engines, the rise of electricity, even the mass tourism of the jet era. But the past few decades have been quiet on that front. Coal has been cheap. Natural gas has been cheap. The 1970s aside, oil has been cheap. The one real novelty, nuclear power, went spectacularly off the rails. The pressure to innovate has been minimal.
>
> In the space of a couple of years, all that has changed. (p. 3)

This chapter surveys the principal features of energy markets. Energy markets, like any other markets, are environments in which prices provide incentives for substitution, conservation, and invention. Those incentives, however, are subject to properties of markets that are the subject of advanced study, including the economics of exhaustible resources, the economics of large-scale enterprise including natural monopoly and economic regulation, the economics of common properties, and the economics of externalities. The usefulness of energy resources for industrialization and prosperity makes the resources the object of resource wars.

Daniel Yergin's *The Prize* (1991), a history of the oil business, identifies three defining influences on it. These influences—the emergence of industrial economies that use lots of energy, energy as a source of conflict, and the gains and losses from using nonrenewable energy—provide structure to his work. This chapter contains an overview of the role of energy in a modern economy, a more detailed look at the economics of exhaustible resources and of large-scale enterprises, and an examination of the public policy responses to the special problems those features pose. This chapter explores contemporary efforts to develop new sources of energy to cope with resource depletion and environmental damage. Noted also is the national security or strategic usefulness of energy supplies, without digression to the diplomatic and military consequences that are further removed from economic analysis.

History

Primary and Secondary Energy

The Industrial Revolution that Adam Smith and Karl Marx came to grips with is the use of machinery with some power source to augment muscle power. The term *energy* is a brief way of describing that power. The source can be what scholars and policy makers refer to as either primary or secondary energy. Primary energy refers to natural resources that can be used to provide energy, including human and animal power, wood and other combustible plants, water, wind, coal, oil, natural gas, and nuclear fission or fusion. Secondary energy refers to an energy source that requires conversion of a primary energy source. The most common form of secondary energy in the modern economy is electricity obtained from the use of fossil or nuclear fuels in a generating plant. The central steam heating plant of a university or hospital complex and the cogeneration by-product steam from a generating plant are also secondary energy sources.

Changing Fuel Sources

The first source of primary energy other than human, animal, or waterpower was wood. In the United States, coal emerged as a domestic source around 1850. It was the single largest source of power, providing approximately 20 quadrillion Btu (quads), equal to 21 trillion megajoules, per year from 1910 through World War II.

Petroleum emerged around 1900 and overtook coal in 1947. Current petroleum consumption is around 40 quads (42 trillion megajoules). Natural gas emerged as a source at about the same time and followed a similar growth curve, rising by around 1970 to 30 quads. Coal was not eclipsed by these new fuels. Current coal use is about 25 quads (U.S. Energy Information Administration [EIA], 2008, p. xx, Figure 5). The EIA expects coal use to exceed natural gas use as a primary energy source from 2015 on (Figure 6).

For 2007, the fossil fuels constitute 86.2 quads of primary energy used in the United States, comprising 22.8 quads from coal, 23.6 quads from natural gas, and 39.8 quads from petroleum. An additional 8.4 quads originate as nuclear electric power, with 6.8 quads provided by what the EIA (2008) classifies as renewable energy, aggregating "conventional hydroelectric power, biomass, geothermal, solar/photovoltaic, and wind." Annual energy consumption was 101.6 quads, of which industrial users consumed 32.3 quads, transportation 29.1, commercial enterprises 18.4, and residences 21.8 (EIA, p. 3, Diagram 1).

Energy Intensity Diminishes

Although industrialization means an increase in an economy's use of energy, the intensity with which an economy uses its energy tends to diminish. For instance, Natural Resources Canada (2009) reports that the aggregate energy intensity of Canadian industry was 13,000 Btu (13.6 megajoules) per 1997 dollar of gross domestic product in 1990, which falls to 11,000 Btu (11.3 megajoules) per 1997 dollar in 2006.

Declining energy intensity of industries and of entire economies is characteristic of most industries in most countries, although readers will see that energy prices or attempts to achieve greater energy efficiency are not necessarily driving these changes.

Na Liu and B. W. Ang (2007) evaluate the research on energy intensity in a paper that, although not explicitly a survey, includes references to numerous other surveys of the evidence. The most common outcome researchers identify is reduced energy intensity over time, accounted for either by industry-wide changes in energy intensity, which they refer to as intensity effects, or by changes in the mix of products within an industry, which can be a shift to a more or a less energy-intensive mix of products, which they refer to as structural effects. In Liu and Ang's review, the modal outcome is industry-wide reductions in energy intensity and a less energy-intensive mix of products, although many studies uncover a switch to a more energy-intensive mix of products that is offset by industry-wide reductions in energy intensity. The article focuses on improving index number techniques, leaving work on the sources of changing intensity, whether driven by prices or by factor-neutral technical change, for future research. Readers will see that such research will be of value for policy makers coping with resource depletion and environmental degradation as consequences of energy use.

Economic Theories for Modeling Energy Markets

Although energy markets offer economists ample opportunity to apply the traditional tools of supply and demand and those tools have been used to great effect in changing public policies, there are some features of energy markets where special models provide additional insight. Many primary energy sources are depletable, providing opportunities to use the theory of exhaustible resources. Many primary and secondary energy producers are large enterprises, where the theory of a natural monopoly is useful. Because energy markets sometimes involve competition of a few firms, for use of a common source or with pollution of a common sink, game-theoretic approaches (generally based on the prisoners' dilemma) help structure thinking about public policy. The large scale of energy enterprises is often a consequence of special equipment such as refinery vessels or turbogenerators, and energy users often make investments in special equipment, which in the home might be a refrigerator or an air conditioner or in the factory might be an energy management system or a new steel furnace. The common feature of all such special equipment is that it is lumpy (one can speak of a smaller refrigerator but not of half a refrigerator) and irreversible (that steel furnace cannot be turned into a slow cooker, and the resale market for steel furnaces is thin).

Exhaustible Resources

Energy consumers have recognized for some time that their primary energy sources can be depleted. Deforestation inspired an early generation of conservationists in the mid-nineteenth century. The current generation of environmentalists might be surprised to learn that fears of the extinction of the whales arose at about the same time (Yergin, 1991). Where capital markets and property rights exist, there are incentives for people to invest in replacing the stock that they take. Tomislav Vukina, Christiana Hilmer, and Dean Lueck (2001) study the price of Christmas trees in North Carolina using a model of those incentives to provide the hypotheses they test. The same model can be used to consider the replanting of trees, sugarcane, or corn to provide feedstock for biomass fuels. There is no generalization of the theory to the oceans, which is regrettable for the whales.

One of the changes Geoffrey Carr (2008) refers to in contemporary energy markets is the dawning fear that the oil reserves will be depleted. In popular parlance, the expression *peak oil,* coined by Shell Oil petroleum geologist M. King Hubbert, refers to that time at which more than half the world's proven reserves have been used or to

the time at which the cost of extracting the oil reserves begins to rise. One could speak of peak coal in the same way: That neither Ridley nor Chandler characterized coal as subject, with increased use, to rising prices reflects improvements in the technology for mining coal as well as price competition from other sources of primary energy, including oil and natural gas.

The theory of valuing an exhaustible resource provides both a logical structure to the peak oil problem and an explanation of the nondepletion of coal. The theory begins with Harold Hotelling's (1931) model. Although the mathematics (calculus of variations) proved daunting to economists of the day, the general principle is simple. A stock of an exhaustible resource is a capital asset. A wealth-maximizing holder of such an asset will use it in such a way as to be indifferent about the choice between consuming it now and holding it for later use. That indifference principle suggests the price of the resource will increase at the rate of interest, if the owner is in a competitive market. If the owner is a monopolist, the marginal revenue increases at the rate of interest. If extraction costs, either constant or contingent on the rate of depletion, are present, the argument becomes more complicated, but the general principle still applies. The results change in the presence of a backstop technology, which will replace the resource before it is depleted. Some models of exhaustible resources treat the time that a backstop technology becomes available as predetermined. The complementary problem, in which the Hotelling principle provides an incentive to develop the backstop technology, has not been investigated as intensively. Christopher Harris and John Vickers (1995) suggest a promising approach for such investigation.

Shantayanan Devarajan and Anthony Fisher (1981) revisit Hotelling's paper, identifying further improvements on the model and providing empirical extensions. Robert Pindyck (1980) proposes a number of extensions, based on uncertainty in the resource markets. Empirical tests are difficult, owing to difficulties obtaining the price at which the exhaustible resource itself trades, because the resource itself is often extracted by companies that transform it into some other product before selling it. That is true of vertically integrated oil companies, which is one reason the model has not been used to test the peak oil hypothesis empirically, although James Hamilton (2008) addresses peak oil in light of the Hotelling principle, and C.-Y. Cynthia Lin, Haoying Meng, Tsz Yan Ngai, Valeria Oscherov, and Yan Hong Zhu (2009) offer a theoretical explanation for what they characterize as trendless oil prices where technical progress is a possible response to rising energy prices. Readers will also see that the absence of a trend in the price of oil or coal reduces the incentive to develop a backstop technology.

Large-Scale Enterprise

A second component of the theory of energy markets is that of markets that cannot be described using the perfectly competitive model. The first large-scale enterprises of the Industrial Revolution included the coal mines, along with the canals and later the railroads that came into being to transport the coal. From the beginning, public policy makers had to choose whether to create public enterprises or to rely on private investment. The roads and canals were among the first public internal improvements of the United States and Britain. The railroads and the mines tended to be private enterprises at first, although that is not universally true. Public policy makers had to improvise new legal structures both to make possible and to restrain those enterprises. In energy markets, the institutions of antitrust, regulation, and public enterprise each play a role.

Antitrust

The coal economy tended to involve smaller, less vertically integrated firms in which the mining, transportation, and retailing were functions for distinct businesses. The rudimentary rules of contract and liability, perhaps supported by the inchoate intellectual basis there was for understanding a competitive economy, sufficed as an energy policy. That was not the case for the oil economy, in which the Standard Oil Trust became an early example of a vertically integrated firm, combining refining with pipeline transportation and retail distribution, as well as working with railroads to obtain more favorable prices for transporting its inputs and outputs than its smaller competitors could bargain for. The trust emerged as a producer and distributor of kerosene for lighting and cooking well before the diffusion of private automobiles, a development that offered the oil companies the opportunity to vertically integrate into operating service stations.

Yergin's (1991) *The Prize* provides a thorough overview of the emergence of the large oil companies. The worldwide extraction of crude oil, its refinement into fuels, lubricants, and petrochemicals, and its distribution to consumers led to firms of great scale and scope. In this expansion, entrepreneurs had many opportunities to get rich. The size of the stakes provided ample opportunities for corporations and governments to engage in acts of corruption and for owners to work together to take advantage of consumers.

Although the *Standard Oil Company of New Jersey v. United States* (1911) decision, which antitrust scholars call significant for its enunciation of the rule of reason as a general principle for enforcing United States antitrust laws, did not become the landmark case out of any special desire to make an example of the Standard Oil Trust, the legend of grasping and predatory oil barons the case inspires lives on to this day. John McGee (1958) interprets the evidence in the *Standard Oil* case to suggest that the oil trust, although clearly intending to monopolize sales of petroleum products, did so in such a way as to raise, rather than lower, its profits. He finds no evidence of the company selling at a loss to eliminate rivals.

The barons, however, more frequently operate in concert, rather than as a monopoly firm. In part, cooperative behavior is the only option in an industry where the dominant firm has been broken up by antitrust action. Cooperation, however, is a logical outcome for competing firms making common use of oil fields or pipelines. A similar logic applies to natural gas producers, and electricity producers share a common electricity transmission grid. Where firms have strong incentives to cooperate, government's best response might be to supervise the competition, or it might be to operate the energy companies itself. The Organization of Petroleum Exporting Countries turns out to be an attempt by multiple governments to cooperate in such supervision.

Regulation

Establishing ownership of crude oil is not easy. An oil pool might extend under several parcels of property or under a national boundary. Common-law methods such as the rule of capture, which works for a hunter taking an animal on land, provide incentives for each oil producer to extract oil from under its property more rapidly, before somebody else pumps it out (Yergin, 1991). That rule also provides incentives for producers to engage in slant drilling, where the wellhead is on the producer's land but the well draws from oil under a neighbor's land. The consequence is uneconomic extraction of the oil, because additional wells dissipate the natural gas that provides pressure to push the oil to the surface. Some oil that would otherwise be extracted remains in the ground, and producers invest in pumps that they would otherwise not have to install. When the competition is between nations, drilling under national boundaries becomes a casus belli, as it did most recently in Iraq's 1990 invasion of Kuwait.

The Texas Railroad Commission pioneered the use of an independent regulatory commission to manage the output of an oil field. Under a policy known as prorationing, each existing well received a production quota worked out with the intent of obtaining the maximum economic value of the field but often with the effect of enriching the firms subject to that regulation (Wilcox, 1971).

A prorationing policy with well-informed regulators can match the resource extraction behavior of competitive producers drawing down the resource in a Hotelling-optimal way. Those regulators can also match the resource extraction behavior of a monopoly, in which the marginal revenue from extraction rises at the rate of interest. The two outcomes are of more than academic interest, because the common property problem (Hardin, 1968) and the cartel problem (Osborne, 1976) can both be interpreted as prisoners' dilemmas, in which the regulator can prohibit the individually rational but collectively suboptimal dominant strategy equilibrium, which is too rapid a depletion of the common property in the former but means lower prices for consumers in the latter. Yergin (1991) credits the Texas

Railroad Commission with providing the Organization of Petroleum Exporting Countries, commonly called a cartel, with a model for their production quotas.

The large-scale enterprise provides a second, different rationale for government regulation when the enterprise is sufficiently large relative to its market that it is a natural monopoly. Perhaps the natural monopoly arises because the duplication of facilities, such as electric or gas distribution lines in a community, implies investments whose costs exceed any benefits that consumers might get from competitive supply of the electricity or the gas. Or perhaps the infrastructure involves large sunk costs, such that competing firms engage in Bertrand price competition down to avoidable incremental costs, risking the long-term profitability of both companies. In economic theory, a natural monopoly is an industry in which the cost function is subadditive, meaning any division of the outputs among two or more firms involves higher costs than a single firm would incur, over outputs likely to be observed in the industry's market (Baumol, Panzar, & Willig, 1988). Where a single firm can serve the market more cheaply than two or more firms, that firm might be able to price like a profit-maximizing monopolist, with the attendant allocative inefficiencies.

The public utility concept, in which a company obtains a legal monopoly subject to supervision by an independent regulatory commission, emerged as a more flexible replacement for legislative or court supervision or for a public ownership that some policy makers viewed as ideologically suspect and others saw as subject to corruption. Before the Great Depression, most states had regulatory commissions, and by 1966, they had diffused to all the states (Phillips, 1969). As government agencies, however, regulatory commissions can be subject to the same public choice dynamics that confront public enterprises or governments themselves and make them imperfect instruments of control (Hilton, 1972).

Public ownership of the natural monopoly offers an alternative to direct regulation. Economic theory argues that natural monopoly is not a sufficient condition for monopolistic exploitation of consumers (Baumol et al., 1988, particularly chap. 8). These alternatives receive consideration in subsequent sections of the article.

Deregulation

Changes in the direct regulation of energy companies reflected both failures of the regulatory apparatus and improvements of market institutions. Alfred Kahn (1988, pp. xv–xvii) offers a useful summary of the events. Put briefly, regulatory failures in energy markets provided economists and policy makers with incentives to consider alternatives to direct regulation.

In natural gas, regulators had the responsibility of determining wellhead prices for natural gas, interstate transmission rates for common-carrier pipelines facing increasing returns to scale, and local delivery rates for consumers served by municipal gas mains that operated under canonical natural monopoly conditions. The outcome, however, was what Paul MacAvoy (1971) calls a "regulation-induced shortage" of natural gas. Because natural gas fields consist of multiple independently operated wells producing natural gas jointly with crude oil, standard formulas to price the output well by well or field by field broke down in administrative complexity. Today's regulatory structure, in which city distribution companies and interstate transmission companies (where natural monopoly arguments make some sense) remain regulated while the gas wells enjoy relative freedom to compete in price, emerged as a less cumbersome alternative.

In electricity, a combination of perceived difficulties in regulating the enterprises with improvements in the implementation of market pricing led to the partial or full deregulation of the electric utilities. George Stigler and Claire Friedland (1962) suggest that regulators had relatively little effect on the price of electricity because electric utilities had relatively little monopoly power. The cost and duration of regulatory cases led regulators to circumvent their own procedures with automatic fuel adjustment clauses that raised production costs (Gollop & Karlson, 1978). Subsequent empirical research could not reject the hypothesis that regulated electric utilities were charging monopolistic prices (Karlson, 1986). At the same time, theoretical work considered the possibility of competition for the right to operate a natural monopoly, which in the work of Harold Demsetz (1968) takes the form of an auction, with the bidder offering to operate the service for the lowest price obtained the franchise, and in the work of Baumol et al. (1988) and extensive follow-on research takes the form of sufficient conditions under which potential competition compels a natural monopoly to price efficiently.

Paul Joskow (1997) provides an overview of the changed circumstances leading to deregulation. The transition to a deregulated environment came with difficulties, the most famous of which is the California power crisis of early 2001. Severin Borenstein (2002) evaluates what went wrong and suggests some directions for future improvements of policy.

Public Enterprise

In much of the world, the energy industries are private enterprises simply as a matter of course, with no ideological statement intended by the government or understood by the citizens (Viscusi, Harrington, & Vernon, 2005, chap. 14; Wilcox, 1971, chap. 21). In the United States, nuclear electricity is a by-product of research into the use of nuclear fission for purposes other than weapons. Contemporary efforts to develop solar, wind, and biofuels involve federal subsidies and public–private partnerships. The effectiveness of many of these projects will provide term paper topics for students later in the century.

Irreversible Investments

Many investments involve irreversible commitments to purchase equipment that cannot be easily converted to other uses. Electricity generating plants are large examples of such investments. Home air conditioners and refrigerators are smaller examples. All three are technologies that have the potential to reduce the economy's energy intensity as new units replace older ones, in the first case by reducing the energy intensity of the generating system, in the second and third by reducing household energy use. All three have been the subject of economic research suggesting that investors hold out for returns on their investment that exceed the opportunity cost of capital.

That reluctance, in seeming defiance of all models of rational investment behavior, was observed so frequently among energy producers and energy users that it received a special name, the *energy paradox*. Kenneth Train (1985) offers an early survey of research that seems to identify a reluctance to invest. Kevin Hassett and Gilbert Metcalf (1993) suggest that investors in energy conservation technologies require a rate of return of about four times the cost of capital for the investments they make. In subsequent research, the same authors evaluate the quality of the data used in consumer studies to suggest that "the case for the energy paradox is weaker than has previously been believed" (Metcalf & Hassett, 1999, p. 516).

That reluctance to invest is neither necessarily suboptimal nor necessarily paradoxical. The act of making an irreversible investment involves the exercise of a real option—namely, to defer the investment until economic circumstances are more favorable, where favorable can mean a higher price for the electricity the generating capacity produces—or a higher price for the electricity used to power the refrigerator or air conditioner. Investor behavior is thus a manifestation of economic hysteresis. The general theory of irreversible investments has been the subject of extensive analysis, much of it specifically inspired by observed behavior in energy markets. Avinash Dixit's (1992) "Investment and Hysteresis" is a straightforward introduction to the topic. Dixit and Pindyck's (1994) *Investment Under Uncertainty* provides comprehensive treatment of several different models of irreversible investment, with energy applications that will reward careful study.

The recent (late-2007 to mid-2009) swings in crude oil prices call for such research. A permanently higher price, or a price rising at or with the interest rate, is a stronger incentive to work on a replacement technology. A falling price weakens that incentive. In the irreversible investment models, greater price volatility also weakens the incentive. Where there is currently no backstop technology available, delayed invention has the potential to leave an economy with a depleting resource and no replacement in development.

Energy and the Environment

The interaction between energy uses and environmental consequences presents researchers and policy makers with substantial challenges. On one hand, worldwide economic development means improved living standards for people whose parents or grandparents might have lived their entire lives in extreme poverty. On the other hand, that development involves additional demands for the stocks of nonrenewable resources, additional pollution from the use of the carbon-based and nuclear primary energy sources, and additional pressures on water and land that has uses other than as energy sources.

That global development is substantial. Thomas Friedman (2008) uses the expression *Americum* to refer to "any group of 350 million people with a per capita income above [U.S.] $15,000 and a growing penchant for consumerism" (p. 50). That figure once described to two populations, primarily in North America and western Europe. There are at least two more today, one each in India and in China, and an environmental consultant Friedman cites expects a world of eight or nine Americums, which Friedman characterizes as "America's carbon copies." That's an ironic expression, referring to the potentially adverse economic and environmental consequences of that development.

There are several trade-offs at work. First, reductions in the energy intensity of the world economy are not necessarily improvements in the efficiency or the prosperity of the world economy. One does not have to contemplate a return to the less energy-intensive world economy of 1700, when living conditions were worse for everyone. The economic model of substitution in production provides the explanation for today's economy: Allocative efficiency is the equating of marginal products scaled for input prices. A firm that reduces its energy use irrespective of the opportunity cost of other inputs, or a public policy that mandates reductions in energy use without regard to those opportunity costs, reduces output and the allocative efficiency of the economy. Adam Jaffe, Richard Newell, and Robert Stavins (1999) describe several differing visions of lowered energy intensity. Three are relevant to this chapter. First, there is a technologist's optimum, in which economic efficiency is irrelevant as long as energy efficiency is increased. From an economic perspective, that outcome ignores the opportunity costs of the inputs that produce the outputs from which the derived demand for energy arises. Second, there is a theoretical social optimum, in which the cost of implementing energy-efficiency policies is irrelevant but the opportunity cost of other inputs is relevant. From an economic perspective, that outcome abstracts from the frictions of developing and implementing public policy. Third, they suggest a true social optimum, comprising those corrective policies that pass a cost-benefit test. The paper includes a useful list of references that supplements those noted in this chapter. The authors suggest that "market signals are effective for advancing [diffusion]" of new technologies, but imposition of minimum standards for energy efficiency, such as automotive fuel economy requirements, may not be. The market signals, however, can be incentives to adopt a technology because of its potential to lower the adopting firm's costs (a process technical change) rather than because of the energy savings it promises (a price-induced technical change). For example, Gale Boyd and Stephen Karlson (1993) suggest that the process incentive, rather than the price incentive, induced steel companies to install new steel-making technologies.

The achievement of any form of energy efficiency is more difficult because energy use produces negative non-pecuniary externalities. Completing energy markets, by taxation or regulation to address those externalities, is therefore likely to be a long-lived project for researchers and for policy makers. Such market completion might foster development of replacements for nonrenewable energy resources. It also changes the incentives energy consumers will face. The business that seeks all profitable opportunities to conserve on fuel use, for instance, currently faces prices that do not reflect the mortality or morbidity of a smoggy city or of proximity to a uranium mine or a nuclear waste pile, let alone the potential lost output that would follow a melting of the polar ice caps. The cost-benefit test that yields the true social optimum of Jaffe et al. (1999) requires somebody, or some collectivity, to determine what benefits and costs make up that test.

More recent research contemplates policy mixes to achieve compliance with tighter environmental standards, such as the Kyoto Protocol targets, while reducing the economic welfare or efficiency losses that compliance might imply. William Pizer (2002) simulates several policy changes looking forward to 2010. He suggests that policy makers combine mitigation policies, rather than rely on emissions targets or corrective taxes alone, to achieve greater efficiency gains. Bob van der Zwaan, Reyer Gerlagh, Ger Klaassen, and Leo Schrattenholzer (2002) introduce endogenous technical change, perhaps induced by environmental policies, into several macroeconomic simulations to suggest that improvements in technologies other than fossil-fuel-using technologies are more promising at reducing carbon emissions. The results of these simulations are not surprising, although they suggest opportunities for research on the actual evolution of new energy sources and new energy-conserving technologies in 2010 and beyond, perhaps in combination with work on irreversible investments and improved trading regimes for pollution permits.

Second, efforts to mitigate climate change without returning world standards of living to those of 1700 involve additional equity and efficiency trade-offs. Mitigation in an equitable way poses problems that may not be the comparative advantage of economists. Richard

Tol (2001) summarizes the challenge: The poorer countries, as measured by their low energy use, also face the greater harm from climate change. "Greenhouse gas emissions and vulnerability to climate change show a strong negative correlation. This is the moral issue at the heart of the climate problem" (p. 71). He describes his paper as "academic constructs" with the potential to "help to inform further thinking about how to handle the enhanced greenhouse effect" (p. 84).

Third, although renewable energy sources provide a way around depletion of the nonrenewable sources, those sources also involve trade-offs. Fuels that make use of biomass, including ethanol and vegetable oils, are carbon compounds. The act of growing the plants can serve as a carbon sink, but the net carbon balance need not be positive. Waterpower cannot escape the running out of rivers to dam. Reservoirs pose a common property problem in which maintaining sufficient depth for electricity or other industrial use means holding water back from downstream drinkers or recreational users. Wind power requires a connection to the electric transmission grid. The most reliable winds are in sparsely settled parts of the United States, and the power grids are where the people are. Thomas Ackermann (2005) provides a comprehensive survey of the technical challenges facing wind-power producers. Finally, land occupied by solar collectors is sometimes not available for other uses. Each of these technologies further involves an irreversible investment facing competition from exhaustible resources whose prices neither follow Hotelling paths nor incorporate the effects of negative externalities.

Conclusion

Energy markets allocate the primary and secondary energy sources that have relaxed the constraints of human and animal power on creating, producing, and exchanging. Those markets have also called for economic analysis using models other than the standard perfectly competitive model. Those models have suggested public policy reforms and reforms to those public policies. The use of primary energy requires that producers, consumers, and policy makers deal with resource depletion and environmental degradation. The challenges of these problems will continue to provide economists with theoretical and empirical research opportunities.

References and Further Readings

Ackermann, T. (Ed.). (2005). *Wind power in power systems*. Chichester, UK: John Wiley.

Bailey, R. (2009). Chiefs, thieves, and priests. *Reason, 40*(9), 49–54.

Baumol, W. J., Panzar, J. C., & Willig, R. D. (1988). *Contestable markets and the theory of industry structure* (rev. ed.). San Diego, CA: Harcourt Brace Jovanovich.

Borenstein, S. (2002). The trouble with electricity markets: Understanding California's restructuring disaster. *Journal of Economic Perspectives, 16*(1), 191–211.

Boyd, G. A., & Karlson, S. H. (1993). The impact of energy prices on technology choice in the United States steel industry. *Energy Journal, 14*(2), 47–56.

Carr, G. (2008, June). The power and the glory. *Economist, 387,* 8585.

Chandler, A. D., Jr. (1977). *The visible hand: The managerial revolution in American business.* Cambridge, MA: Harvard University Press.

Demsetz, H. (1968). Why regulate utilities? *Journal of Law and Economics, 11*(1), 55–65.

Devarajan, S., & Fisher, A. C. (1981). Hotelling's "economics of exhaustible resources": Fifty years later. *Journal of Economic Literature, 19*(1), 65–73.

Dixit, A. K. (1992). Investment and hysteresis. *Journal of Economic Perspectives, 6,* 107–132.

Dixit, A. K., & Pindyck, R. S. (1994). *Investment under uncertainty.* Princeton, NJ: Princeton University Press.

Friedman, T. L. (2008). *Hot, flat, and crowded: Why we need a green revolution and how it can renew America.* New York: Farrar, Straus and Giroux.

Gollop, F. M., & Karlson, S. H. (1978). The impact of the fuel adjustment mechanism on economic efficiency. *Review of Economics and Statistics, 60*(4), 574–584.

Hamilton, J. D. (2008). *Understanding crude oil prices* (UCEI Energy Policy and Economics Working Paper No. 023). Retrieved January 29, 2009, from http://www.ucei.berkeley.edu/PDF/EPE_023.pdf

Hardin, G. (1968). The tragedy of the commons. *Science, 162*(3859), 1243–1248.

Harris, C., & Vickers, J. (1995). Innovation and natural resources: A dynamic game with uncertainty. *RAND Journal of Economics, 26*(3), 418–430.

Hassett, K. A., & Metcalf, G. (1993). Energy conservation investment: Do consumers discount the future correctly? *Energy Policy, 21,* 710–716.

Hilton, G. R. (1972). The basic behavior of regulatory commissions. *American Economic Review Proceedings, 62*(2), 47–54.

Hotelling, H. (1931). The economics of exhaustible resources. *Journal of Political Economy, 39*(2), 137–175.

Jaffe, A. B., Newell, R. G., & Stavins, R. N. (1999). *Energy-efficient technologies and climate change policies: Issues and evidence* (Resources for the Future Climate Issue Brief No. 19). Washington, DC: Resources for the Future.

Joskow, P. A. (1997). Restructuring, competition, and regulatory reform in the U.S. electricity sector. *Journal of Economic Perspectives, 11*(3), 119–139.

Kahn, A. E. (1988). *The economics of regulation: Principles and institutions.* Cambridge: MIT Press.

Karlson, S. H. (1986). Multiple-output production and pricing in electric utilities. *Southern Economic Journal, 53,* 73–86.

Landes, D. S. (1998). *The wealth and poverty of nations: Why some are so rich and some so poor.* New York: W. W. Norton.

Lin, C.-Y. C., Meng, H., Ngai, T. Y., Oscherov, V., & Zhu, Y. H. (2009). Hotelling revisited: Oil prices and endogenous technical progress. *Natural Resources Research, 18*(1), 29–38.

Liu, N., & Ang, B. W. (2007). Factors shaping aggregate energy intensity trend for industry: Energy intensity versus product mix. *Energy Economics, 29,* 609–635.

MacAvoy, P. A. (1971). The regulation-induced shortage of natural gas. *Journal of Law and Economics, 14,* 167–199.

McGee, J. S. (1958). Predatory price cutting: The Standard Oil (N. J.) case. *Journal of Law and Economics, 1,* 137–169.

Metcalf, G. E., & Hassett, K. A. (1999). Measuring the energy savings from home improvement investments: Evidence from monthly billing data. *Review of Economics and Statistics, 81,* 516–528.

Natural Resources Canada, Office of Energy Efficiency. (2009, January). *Industrial energy intensity by industry.* Retrieved January 25, 2009, from http://oee.nrcan-rncan.gc.ca/corporate/statistics/neud/dpa/tableshandbook2/agg_00_6_e_1.cfm?attr=0

Osborne, D. K. (1976). Cartel problems. *American Economic Review, 66*(5), 835–844.

Phillips, C. F., Jr. (1969). *The economics of regulation* (Rev. ed.). Homewood, IL: Richard D. Irwin.

Pindyck, R. S. (1980). Uncertainty and exhaustible resource markets. *Journal of Political Economy, 88*(6), 1203–1225.

Pizer, W. A. (2002). Combining price and quantity controls to mitigate global climate change. *Journal of Public Economics, 85,* 409–434.

Posner, R. A. (1969). Natural monopoly and its regulation. *Stanford Law Review, 21*(3), 548–643.

Smith, A. (1976). *An inquiry into the nature and causes of the wealth of nations.* Chicago: University of Chicago Press. (Original work published 1776)

Stigler, G. J., & Friedland, C. (1962). What can regulators regulate? The case of electricity. *Journal of Law and Economics, 5,* 1–16.

Tol, R. S. J. (2001). Equitable cost-benefit analysis of climate change policies. *Ecological Economics, 36,* 71–85.

Train, K. (1985). Discount rates in consumers' energy-related decisions: A review of the literature. *Energy, 10,* 1243–1253.

U.S. Energy Information Administration. (2008, April). *Annual energy review 2007.* Washington, DC: Department of Energy. Retrieved January 24, 2009, from http://www.eia.doe.gov/emeu/aer/contents.html

van der Zwaan, B. C. C., Gerlagh, R., Klaassen, G., & Schrattenholzer, L. (2002). Endogenous technical change in climate change modelling. *Energy Economics, 24,* 1–19.

Viscusi, W. K., Harrington, J. E., Jr., & Vernon, J. M. (2005). *Economics of regulation and antitrust* (4th ed.). Cambridge: MIT Press.

Vukina, T., Hilmer, C. E., & Lueck, D. (2001). A Hotelling–Faustmann explanation of the structure of Christmas tree prices. *American Journal of Agricultural Economics, 83*(3), 513–525.

Wilcox, C. (1971). *Public policies toward business.* Homewood, IL: Richard D. Irwin.

Yergin, D. (1991). *The prize: The epic quest for oil, money, and power.* New York: Simon & Schuster.

63

POLITICAL ECONOMY OF OIL

YAHYA M. MADRA

Gettysburg College

In contrast to more narrow economic analyses of oil, where the focus lies on the price formation and the conditions under which the "right" price for this nonrenewable resource can be obtained, political economy of oil studies the conditions and consequences of the production, appropriation, distribution, and consumption of oil (and oil-related products) by taking into account social relations of power (at local, regional, and global scales), cultural codes of consumption, institutional structures of surplus extraction, and ecological impacts of human activity. In this sense, again in contrast to economics of oil, political economy of oil is decidedly interdisciplinary—moving beyond economics, it draws upon political science and international politics, sociology and cultural studies, geology and geography, and ecology. In what follows, the contours of a political economy approach (as distinct from the standard neoclassical approach) to oil will be outlined. Beginning with the status of oil as a nonrenewable resource, the chapter will discuss the nature of the global demand for oil and will offer a historical account of the concrete socioeconomic processes (including the processes of price making, market maintenance, and state formation) within which the price of oil is determined. In the process, a general political economy framework will be developed to explain why the increases in the price of oil may not result in the changes in production technologies and consumption patterns that are necessary to move beyond petroleum. In short, the chapter will argue that not only producer but also consumer petro-states suffer from the so-called oil curse.

Oil as a Nonrenewable Resource: Malthusianism and Its Limits

Oil is a fossil fuel, 150- to 300-million-year-old "solar energy" buried underground. Up until the Industrial Revolution, most of the world's energy was supplied from renewable sources. But with the Industrial Revolution and the depletion of wood in England in the early eighteenth century, the transition to technologies that run on nonrenewable sources of energy occurred as production and transportation began to rely increasingly on coal (Mitchell, 2009). Earlier in the twentieth century, we observe another shift to a new nonrenewable resource pioneered first by the introduction of battleships that run on oil to the Royal Navy and then by the mass production of cars in the 1920s (Yeomans, 2004; Yergin, 1991). Today, our highly industrialized, and predominantly capitalist, world economy continues to be heavily dependent on this nonrenewable energy source.

This state of dependence inevitably begs the question of the exhaustion of this nonrenewable resource. How far is it? How much oil is in the ground? What is the rate at which new oil reserves are found? How difficult is to extract them? How reliable is the reserve-to-production ratio that indicates the length of time the remaining oil reserves will last if the production will continue at the current levels? What is the rate at which the consumption of oil is growing? Even though the answers to these questions are heavily contingent upon the assumptions one is willing to make in calculations, if one were to accept the "optimistic" predictions of the International Energy Agency (from the 2004 edition of their *World Energy Outlook*) regarding the possibility of reaching peak production sometime between 2013 to 2037, it will be probably safe to assume that the current reserve-to-production ratio of 42 years (reported in the 2009 edition of British Petroleum's *Statistical Review of World Energy*) will not improve drastically in the coming decades.

Nevertheless, the picture is not that simple. For instance, it is important to recognize that what makes the geological approach to peak oil so powerful in the minds of the general public and research community is Hubbert's

(1956) success in predicting the U.S. (a limited territory) peak in 1970. Yet, in order to extend the argument to the world scale and to claim that the future production rate depends linearly on the unproduced fraction (Deffeyes, 2006, p. 40), a number of assumptions must be made. For instance, to assume that the aggregation of all regional annual oil production distribution fits a bell curve is to assume that the future path of global oil production will inversely mirror its past trajectory where a cheap and expanding oil supply will be followed beyond the peak by an expensive and decreasing one (Caffentzis, 2008, p. 315). One underlying assumption is that the larger and easily accessible fields will be depleted earlier than smaller and more difficult to extract fields (e.g., Klare, 2008a, p. 42). Nevertheless, for this to be true, one also has to assume the existence of a fully competitive market where the price of crude oil net of extraction costs grows steadily at a rate equal to the rate of interest (Hotelling, 1931). Yet, if one were to make these assumptions, as it will be shown below, there would be no reason to worry about oil depletion: The world economy, in response to price increases, will change its production technology and consumption patterns gradually, moving away from oil and instead substituting alternative, less scarce, resources.

Nevertheless, Hubbert's (1956) calculations did not take price into account (Deffeyes, 2006, p. 41). But more important, even if one were to take the price of oil into account, one would have to do so by acknowledging that historically, it has never been determined in competitive markets and that it has not been growing along an efficient extraction path. On the contrary, the long-run secular path of the price of oil reflects either the fall in costs brought about by technological progress or the various historical transformations and shifts in the market structure and the geopolitics of global oil production (Roncaglia, 2003). Moreover, the relatively high level of prices since the 1970s has allowed for the exploitation of expensive and difficult to extract oil fields (e.g., North Sea), whereas large and easy to extract fields continue to remain relatively underexploited (Roncaglia, 2003, p. 646f). And finally, in the past three decades, in part due to more effective exploration technologies and in part due to the high price of oil, the oil reserves have increased steadily, bringing the reserve-to-production ratio from 29 years in 1980 to 42 years in 2008 (British Petroleum, 2009).

Without doubt, the growing body of research and popular literature on "peak oil" has generated an increasing literacy among the general public about the coming end of the oil era. Nevertheless, the effects of this literature on the public perception have so far been mixed. On one hand, the dissemination of this particular kind of geological "petro-knowledge" increased the social legitimacy of high energy prices in the eyes of the general public. It is worthwhile to note that international oil companies, in 1971, as soon as it became clear that the formation of the Organization of the Petroleum Exporting Countries

(OPEC) and the nationalization of oil in the Middle East would limit their control over the flow of oil and lead to increases in the price of crude oil, "abruptly abandoned their cornucopian calculations of oil as an almost limitless resource and began to forecast the end of oil" (Bowden, 1985; cf. Mitchell, 2009, p. 419). On the other hand, the often apocalyptic and Malthusian tone of the books and documentary films in the genre make it a daunting task for ordinary citizens to tackle this complex issue. In short, while simple geological analyses of "peak oil" provide a necessary baseline in beginning to think about the political economy of oil, they fail to do justice to the complexity of the political, economic, and cultural processes that shape the exploration, production, distribution, and consumption of oil.

Oil as a Means of Consumption and Exploitation: Global Oil Demand

President Franklin Delano Roosevelt's meeting with King Abd al-Aziz Ibn Saud aboard an American ship in the Suez Canal in 1945 marks the beginning of a very important transition in the history of oil as a strategic commodity. Until the end of the World War II, the Middle East remained under British control. Nevertheless, as the war was drawing to a close, the United States decided to replace Great Britain as the leading Western military power in the region, fully aware not only of the wartime strategic importance of crude oil (recall that Hitler's two big defeats came in El-Alamein and Stalingrad, both on his way to the sources of oil, the Arabian peninsula and Baku, respectively) but also of the necessity of this strong source of energy for the postwar reconstruction (in Europe) and demand-led economic growth (in the States). In a sense, given the fact that the construction of new roads was a centerpiece of the New Deal even before the war (Yeomans, 2004, pp. 43–44), Roosevelt's courtship with King Ibn Saud and the oil-for-protection agreement between the United States and Saudi Arabia in the postwar era should not have come as a surprise. Today, the United States is the largest consumer of crude oil in the world, accounting for a quarter of the total consumption, followed by the European Union and China (British Petroleum, 2009).

The process of the gradual but secular growth of the U.S. demand for oil began in the 1920s, with the rapid adoption of motorcars as the individualized means of transportation and the first wave of suburbanization that it made possible. This "new mobile American way of life" came to an early grinding halt with the 1929 stock market crash and the onset of the Great Depression (Yeomans, 2004, p. 43). In this sense, the New Deal and the subsequent post–World War II Keynesian demand-led growth strategy transformed this incipient mode of organization of daily life into one of its central components. In the 1950s, the second wave of suburbanization and the construction of the interstate highway system made the American auto industry the driving force of postwar economic growth.

This particular macroeconomic role of the suburban and mobile lifestyle made the demand for oil highly insensitive to changes in price. American consumers' dependence on oil was not limited to their demand for gasoline to fuel their cars with which they drive to work, to school, and to the shopping mall or to their demand for heating oil to keep their increasingly bigger suburban houses warm. The entire infrastructure of the mass production and transportation of (agricultural and industrial) consumer goods was also dependent upon increased mechanization and therefore upon increased demand for oil and oil-based products (e.g., petrochemical feedstocks, lubricants).

The relatively low price elasticity of demand for oil means that the consumers are highly dependent on oil in their consumption and cannot easily reduce their demand or switch to substitutes when its unit price increases (Cooper, 2003). Nevertheless, it is important to understand the historically dynamic nature of the price elasticity of demand. For instance, in the late 1970s and early 1980s, when the real price of oil increased dramatically due to supply disruptions caused by the Iranian Revolution in 1978 and the start of the Iran-Iraq War in 1980, the demand for oil declined by 16%. On the other hand, a similar increase in the price of oil during the 2000s did nothing to affect the steady growth of the U.S. consumption of oil (Hamilton, 2008). A possible explanation is that during the earlier price hike, consumers in the United States were able to substitute away from the nontransportation uses of oil, whereas in the current price hike, consumers had much more limited substitution possibilities in transportation uses of oil. In other words, the price inelasticity of the American demand for oil may be increasingly becoming a function of its suburban and mobile lifestyle.

Nevertheless, it is important not to reduce the growing and highly inelastic demand for oil to a mere effect of consumerist and materialistic "American way of life." Industrialization and the mechanization of the production process as a secular and global tendency throughout the twentieth century may be the underlying factor that drives the secular growth of the demand for oil. A number of commentators who investigate the matter from the perspective of Marxian political economy argue that the increasing reliance on nonrenewable sources of energy itself is an unintended consequence of the political and economic struggles of the working classes throughout the twentieth century (Caffentzis, 2008; Midnight Notes Collective, 1992). Viewed from this perspective, both the social Keynesianism of the post–World War II era and the increasing mechanization of the labor process throughout the century are seen as responses of the capitalist states and enterprises to the demands and resistance of the working classes (see also Mitchell, 2009). According to Marxian labor theory of value, human labor is the only new value-creating energy, and the capitalist system and its

social institutions (the state, the corporations, the legal system, the ideological processes, etc.) have evolved through the past two centuries, in part, to manage and maintain the continual production, appropriation, and distribution of the surplus value by the working classes. These commentators, by noting the fact that "most energy derived from oil in capitalist society is involved in producing and transporting commodities and reproducing labor power [i.e., the consumption of consumer goods]" (Caffentzis, 2008, p. 318), argue that ever-growing demand for resilient and labor-saving nonrenewable resources in modern capitalist societies is an effect of the increasing difficulty of maintaining this system of exploitation.

Indeed, the gradually increasing demand for oil in newly industrialized countries such as China and India suggests that the driving cause may not simply be the "American way of life" but rather the class antagonism and the endless search for higher rates of surplus value extraction that propel both the increasing mechanization of the labor process and the increasing commodification of the reproduction of human capacity to labor. After the energy crisis of the 1970s, the U.S. economy went through a "neoliberal" restructuring, which led more and more American companies to outsource their production of consumer goods to developing countries such as China, where the value of labor power is significantly cheaper (Harvey, 2005). Today, a significant portion of the growing demand for oil in China (and other developing economies such as India and Brazil) is fueled by increased industrial production for the U.S. (and other advanced capitalist economies') consumer goods market (Gökay, 2006, p. 141). These cheap consumer products, in turn, made it possible for the increasingly precarious U.S. working class to continue to afford an increasing standard of living despite the fact that the real wages have remained stagnant since the early 1980s (Resnick & Wolff, 2006).

Oil as a Strategic Commodity: Price Formation and "Scarcity" Maintenance

The standard neoclassical theory of the optimal pricing of exhaustible resources was established by Harold Hotelling in 1931 during a period when oligopolistic arrangements over the exploration, production, transportation, refinery, and distribution of oil were being struck both in the United States and in the Middle East to prevent the price of oil from falling below its cost of production (Bromley, 1991, pp. 95–98; Yergin, 1991, pp. 244–252). In this essay, Hotelling (1931) theoretically demonstrated that, under competitive conditions (and under very stringent, and unrealistic, assumptions pertaining to information, preferences, and technology), the price of an exhaustible resource, net of the cost of extracting the marginal unit of the resource, must grow along an efficient extraction path at a rate equal to the rate of interest (see also Devarajan & Fisher, 1981; Solow, 1974). While the price grows along the efficient extraction path, the output (facing a stable demand) will decline asymptotically toward zero (Devarajan & Fisher, 1981, p. 66). Hotelling's analysis included a discussion of how under monopoly the price of oil will be initially higher but rise less rapidly and, accordingly, the depletion of oil reserves will be retarded. One important underlying presupposition of this analysis, as noted above, is that the price increases will "provoke changes in both production technologies and the consumption structure leading to substitution of the scarce resource with other, relatively less scarce, resource" (Roncaglia, 2003, p. 646).

While Hotelling's (1931) analysis is very useful in demonstrating the sheer impossibility of realizing competitive optimal outcomes in concrete, real economies, it has very little to offer in explaining the institutional complexity and historical trajectory of the political economy of the formation of the price of oil. In contrast to the abstract analyses of increasing "extraction" costs and optimizing firms found in the neoclassical tradition, the political economy approach offers an analysis of the oil industry as a multilayered process that involves the exploration, production, transportation, refinery, and distribution of oil (Bromley, 1991, pp. 87–90). In fact, it is possible to trace the history of the global oil industry and the changing institutional arrangements of price formation as different ways of organizing this multilayered process in response to shifting political, cultural, economic, and natural conditions.

Throughout its first century, the oil industry has been organized through the oligopolistic collusion of vertically integrated, large international oil companies (IOCs) that mobilized expert knowledge and expansive technology at all layers of this multilayered process, ranging from "upstream" activities such as exploration and production to "downstream" activities such as refinery, trade, and marketing. Under the "concession" system, which reigned until the early 1970s, IOCs used to purchase from sovereign states the rights to explore and exploit natural resources in return for fixed royalties. During the 1920s and 1930s, British Petroleum, various offshoots of the divided-up Standard Oil, and Royal Dutch/Shell controlled the oil industry, signing up "Red Line Agreements" among themselves to coordinate their activities in what used to be the Ottoman Middle East (Kurdistan, Iraq, Trans-Jordan, Arabian peninsula, and Gulf region; Yergin, 1991, pp. 184–206). But beginning with the 1950s, the anticolonialist, working-class struggles along with the emerging nationalist sentiments in oil-rich countries (e.g., antiracist labor strikes in Saudi Arabia, Baathist Arab socialism in Iraq, Iranian nationalism, Bolivarianismo in Venezuela) led to the formation of OPEC in 1960 in order to claim ownership of their resources and to enable oil-rich nation-states to exert greater control over the international oil market (Bromley, 1991; Mitchell, 2002, 2009; Vitalis, 2009). Nevertheless, the emergence of OPEC and the increasing role that national oil companies (NOCs) take in controlling

the "upstream" of the industry did not necessarily lead to the demise of IOCs. On the contrary, as the industry shifted from an era of "free flow" to that of "limited flow" after 1974, they continued to remain highly profitable: They not only continued to account for nearly 10% of the net profits of the entire U.S. corporate sector (even better than their heyday in the 1930s), but also the rates of return of the large, U.S.-based IOCs remained above that of the *Fortune* 500 average—the dominant sector of the U.S. capital (Nitzan & Bichler, 2002, pp. 220–223). This is, in part, because IOCs have continued to work with the governments and the NOCs of the resource-rich nation-states by entering into upstream joint ventures and by continuing to control downstream business. But this is also because the costs of expanding the oligopolistic coalition are borne by the consumers of petroleum (as a means of both consumption and production): In comparison to the free-flow era (1920–1973), the average price of crude oil has tripled during the limited-flow era (1974–2008), from $15 to $45 (in 2008 dollars) (British Petroleum, 2009). Because resource-rich countries do not always have the necessary wherewithal to explore and exploit their resources, they tend to be dependent upon the expert knowledge and financial power of IOCs.

While oil production in an individual oil field, in contrast to the exploration for oil, tends to be predicated upon a basic level of technology, relatively high fixed costs, and economies of scale, neoclassical economists argue that the overall oil production at the level of the industry betrays increasing costs: "The more is produced, the more must one draw upon higher-cost sources" (Adelman, 1972, p. 5). Nevertheless, as noted above, historically, the areas that are exploited first have not necessarily been the easily accessible ones. In fact, the peculiar oligopolistic institutional configurations of the oil industry and the relatively extended periods of high prices have enabled relatively low-cost fields (such as those in Saudi Arabia due to its role as a "swing" producer) to remain underexploited while making relatively expensive fields (such as those in the North Sea, United Kingdom) economically viable for exploitation.

To appreciate why this is so, it is necessary to recall that, while there is a finite amount of oil under the surface of earth, within the myopic temporal horizon of the oil market, the problem historically has been the surplus, rather than the scarcity, of oil. The case of East Texas in 1930, when the price of a barrel of crude oil dropped to 10 cents per barrel as a result of uncontrolled competition and collapsing aggregate demand due to the Great Depression, is a well-known example of such cases of sudden flooding of the market with cheap oil in the absence of coordinated price fixing and sales regulation. Nevertheless, the surplus problem, or this tendency for overproduction in the oil industry, is more structural than it may initially appear. To begin with, at any given moment, given the nature of the industry, there is always an easily accessible excess reserve of oil (both above and under ground). This gives the producers the opportunity and incentive to overproduce and increase their revenues in the short run by undercutting competition (e.g., governments that wish to finance an accelerated military buildup, the individual companies that wish to increase their market share or cash flow or both). In this precise sense, the historical trajectory of the price of oil can be read as a series of shifting institutional (oligopolistic) arrangements, based on a shifting and changing balance of power between petro-states and multinational corporations that collude to keep competitive impulses at bay.

The first thoroughly global configuration of the oil industry can be traced back to the 1930s. In the United States, the Texas Railroad Commission intervened in the East Texas "collapse" and divided the demand among the producers in proportion to their production capacity ("pro-rationing") and stabilized the domestic supply of oil. In the Middle East, the so-called Red Line Agreement of July 1928 and the infamous Achnacarry Agreement inaugurated the particular mode of oligopolistic arrangement that would regulate the allocation of the concessions among the Seven Sisters (Exxon, Mobil, Socal, Gulf, and Texaco from the United States and Royal Dutch/Shell and British Petroleum form Europe) until the 1970s. The oligopolistic domination of the Seven Sisters entailed the presence of a sizable surplus profit (monopoly rent) in the oil sector over a very long period of time. The concessions granted complete control over production across extensive areas for 60 to 90 years with complete control over pricing. And because the global price was determined according to the high-cost Texas crude as the benchmark, the Seven Sisters earned windfall profits from their low-cost production in the Middle East until the arrival of OPEC (Bromley, 1991).

Increasing demands for the nationalization of the local subsidiaries of IOCs that began in the 1950s and 1960s (e.g., Iran in 1951, Kuwait in 1960, Saudi Arabia in 1960, Iraq in 1964) culminated in the gradual nationalization of Aramco and a series of price increases in 1973–1974 in response to the 1973 Arab-Israel War and the United States' support of Israel. From this point onward, first Saudi Arabia and then OPEC as a whole began to play the role of the "swing" producer in the global oil market. A swing producer is defined by its capability to maintain an unused excess capacity of oil that can be switched on and off to discipline producers who may be tempted to undercut competition by producing above their allotted quotas. For an individual producer to be an effective swing producer, it has to have large enough and easily accessible (low-cost) excess capacity (Mitchell, 2002).

In the 1980s, in response to the price hikes of the late 1970s, the global demand for oil slumped, and OPEC, led by Saudi Arabia, played the role of the swing producer by cutting the production levels to adjust the global supply to the declining global demand. Nevertheless, as if making a demonstration of the structural tendency of the oil industry to overproduce, non-OPEC producers continued to increase their production rather steadily until stabilizing at 55% market share in 2004—even though OPEC continues to control three quarters of the proven oil reserves (British Petroleum, 2009). Today, Saudi Arabia continues to be the largest producer of oil, with 13.1% of the total oil production, and is followed by Russia (12.4%), a non-OPEC producer (British Petroleum, 2009). Some projections suggest that "total OPEC capacity is likely to fall significantly short—by the upwards of 5 million barrels per day—in the next decade" (Nissen & Knapp, 2005, p. 3) and that the Saudi Arabian production with 1.5 to 2 million spare capacity will not be able to make up for the difference, leaving "the global oil market with no institutional mechanism to control the upside of oil pricing" (Nissen & Knapp, 2005, p. 4). Nevertheless, significant evidence demonstrates that recent increases in the price of crude oil (U.S.$97 per barrel in 2008) cannot be simply explained by increasing global demand (its rate of growth has slowed down as the prices began to increase in 2005) or by supply problems or shortages (the proven oil reserves have been growing faster than consumption growth in recent years, and a number of low-cost substitutes, such as oil sands and oil shales, have become economically viable) (Hamilton, 2008; Wray, 2008).

A more realistic explanation suggests that the price increases are caused by "index speculation" that takes place in the futures markets for crude oil (Wray, 2008). Since the mid-1980s, actual negotiations and deliveries of oil contracts have been made based on the price of crude oil determined in spot and futures markets—where traders buy and sell futures contracts to either hedge against price fluctuations or to, plain and simple, speculate. The regional base price of the New York Mercantile Exchange (NYMEX) is represented by West Texas Intermediate—the type of crude that flows into the United States from its main ports on the Texas Gulf Coast. In contrast, the regional base price of the Singapore exchange is that of the Dubai crude. Even though the volume of trade in these markets may be very high, only a fraction of all trades ends up being realized, whereas most transactions are either "compensated" before expiration or rolled into newer futures contracts (Roncaglia, 2003, p. 655). While traditional speculative activity takes "the price risk that hedgers do not want," index speculators take only long positions by buying and holding a basket of commodities futures. Because these baskets are based on one of the commodity futures indexes (SP-GSCI and DJ-AIG), such speculative activities are named "index speculation" (Wray, 2008, pp. 63–64). But because these indices are based on the aggregation of different commodities (e.g., cotton, copper, corn, wheat, crude oil, natural gas) with varying weights (petroleum-related products account for 58% of the weighted average of SP-GSCI and DJ-AIG), the index speculators are insensitive to individual prices; they are only interested in the value of the index. As index speculation as an activity became popular (practiced by hedge funds, pension funds, university endowments, life insurance companies, sovereign wealth funds, banks, and oil companies themselves), the volume of money that flowed into the indexes grew from U.S.$50 billion in 2002 to U.S.$300 billion in 2008, and along with the influx, the price of crude oil has increased dramatically (Wray, 2008, pp. 66–67). Without doubt, increasing prices may have also encouraged further index speculation—but it is important to acknowledge the role that speculative activity plays in determining the price of oil in the short run (Hamilton, 2008).

Increasing importance of spot and futures markets in determining the price of crude oil might give the impression that, provided that the speculative excesses of traders are regulated, the oil markets are becoming more and more competitive and the price is approximating toward the market-clearing equilibrium price. Yet, it is equally possible to interpret the increasing importance of futures markets both as a smokescreen to distract the general public from the enduring collusive arrangement between OPEC NOCs, IOCs, and the governments of oil-consuming, advanced capitalist economies, "allowing them all to bypass antitrust regulations," and as a mutually agreed upon mechanism for price formation, which would limit price competition among producers (Roncaglia, 2003, p. 656). To the extent that the supply of oil continues to be controlled by OPEC and the global demand for oil continues to grow at a secular pace, the futures markets, at their best, merely reflect these underlying oligopolistic forces (see also Hamilton, 2008).

Moreover, while the high oil prices driven by the speculative activity in commodities markets may bring windfall profits for both NOCs and IOCs, in the long run, high oil prices are not necessarily the best configuration for the economic interests of oil-producing economies either: Sustained high prices tend to provoke consumers to substitute away from oil-based sources of energy, slowing down the demand growth and rendering the market susceptible, once again, to overproduction. In fact, price instabilities caused by speculative activities have adverse effects on the macroeconomic stability of both net-exporter and net-importer economies. In short, the post-1970s reconfiguration of the oligopolistic control of the oil industry is not necessarily a stable one and requires continuing attention, maintenance, and management—if necessary, by means of military intervention and occupation (Moran & Russell, 2008).

Even the division of labor struck between NOCs and IOCs, where the former controls exploration and production and the latter refinery and distribution, is not a stable arrangement. Even though IOCs seemed to have survived the nationalization wave of the 1970s unscathed, retaining their profitability, they nonetheless produce only 35% of their total sales and own only a mere 4.2% of the total reserves. For this reason, they have continuing incentives, along with the U.S. government, which has historically supported them, to reestablish their control over the upstream end of the industry (Bromley, 2005, p. 252). In this regard, the new Iraqi Oil Law of 2007, which marginalizes the role of Iraqi National Oil Company by opening nearly two thirds of the oil reserves to the control of IOCs, constitutes an instance in which the IOCs and the U.S. government explore the possibility of tilting the balance of power within the post-1970s oligopolistic arrangement in their favor.

Petro-States: Democracy, Economic Growth, and Class Conflicts

The term *petro-state* designates not only the "energy-surplus" oil-producing states but also "energy-deficit" oil-consuming states (Klare, 2008b; Mitchell, 2009). Economic growth and political stability of both producer and consumer states depend upon the uninterrupted and stable flow of oil between them. For the oil-producing states, the steady flow of oil provides a steady flow of revenues with which they can undertake public investments in infrastructures, purchase weapons and military technologies, induce economic growth through fiscal policy and transfer payments, redistribute income, invest in and incubate nonextractive sectors to replace the oil industry once the resources are depleted, or invest in international financial markets (sovereign wealth funds). For the energy-deficit advanced industrial states, the steady flow of "reasonably priced" oil can facilitate the smooth flow of transactions within the economy, sustaining a stable macroeconomic system, low unemployment levels, low levels of inflation, and sustained economic growth (in terms of the rate of growth of gross domestic product [GDP]).

Nevertheless, because there is a wide range of diversity among producer petro-states, it would be wrong to offer an ahistorical, general theory of state formation in petroleum-dependent economies. For instance, the dramatic failure of Nigeria's national project of petroleum-led development (Watts, 2006) cannot be lumped together with Venezuela's recent efforts to redistribute oil revenues to historically marginalized and impoverished sectors of the population (in particular, the urban poor and the indigenous populations). Similarly, while both the United States and China are energy-deficit petro-states that are dependent upon a steady flow of oil, the former is a global military power that has explicitly declared that it is ready to use "any means necessary, including military force" to protect its access to petroleum (the Carter Doctrine of 1980), whereas the latter is a fast-growing, export-oriented, state-controlled capitalist economy whose most important trade partner is the United States (Klare, 2004). Despite this internal diversity, it is still meaningful to suggest that a distinctive feature of the political economy approach to petro-states is to study the question of state formation in petroleum-dependent (producer or consumer) economies by analyzing the historical evolution of the political institutions, economic mechanisms, and social technologies as petro-states navigate, negotiate, govern, and manage their internal socioeconomic contradictions and class conflicts within the continuously realigning international geopolitical and economic context.

It is argued that energy-surplus countries tend to suffer from a deficit of democracy. Underlying this widespread perception is the assumption that oil revenues provide antidemocratic, authoritarian governments with the wherewithal to either buy off or repress political dissent (e.g., Ross, 2001). "Dutch disease" is the economic version of such "oil curse" arguments. Here the argument turns around the assumption that a booming natural extractive sector leads to stagnation or even deindustrialization in the manufacturing sector, leading to an imbalanced economic growth (e.g., Sachs & Warner, 1995). While such analyses of the "oil curse" may initially seem to capture some of the salient features of political economies of energy-rich oil states, they tend to obscure more than they reveal.

Political versions of the "oil curse" tend to represent the antidemocratic and authoritarian nature of these governments as a natural development, one that is bound to emerge given a presupposed natural human proclivity toward rent seeking in the absence of well-established property rights and competitive markets. Nevertheless, recent studies of the historical trajectories of state formation in producer petro-states suggest that antidemocratic, authoritarian governments emerge not because of oil revenues but rather to generate oil revenues in the first place. For instance, the emergence of Saudi Arabia as an authoritarian and sovereign oil state is intimately bound up in a history of repression of the antiracist, anticolonialist labor movement among petroleum workers (in particular, throughout the 1940s and 1950s; Vitalis, 2009) and the gradually increasing reliance of oil production on precarious immigrant workers (Midnight Notes Collective, 1992). Similarly, economic "Dutch disease" arguments tend to abstract from the international context within which economic policies are usually devised and implemented in many of the oil-rich yet underdeveloped economies. For instance, to be able to study the political economy of Nigeria as a failed state, it is necessary to look beyond the bureaucratic corruption and understand not only how the exploitation of oil from the Niger Delta has historically been based upon the oppression of indigenous peoples and cultures but also how the structural adjustment policies implemented throughout the 1980s and 1990s under the guidance of the International Monetary Fund (IMF) and World Bank have destroyed the social (multiethnic) and political (federal) fabric of the country by dismantling the welfare state through privatization and austerity programs (Midnight Notes Collective, 1992; Watts, 2006).

In contrast to energy-surplus countries, consumer petro-states appear to be much more democratic (with the exception of China). Nevertheless, there are two ways in which this assumption needs to be questioned. The first is the growing importance of economics and economic expertise in shaping the various aspects of the way states govern the "ordinary business of life." As discussed above, beginning with the Great Depression, the development and deployment of social Keynesianism (in the form of aggregate demand management policies) and New Deal liberalism (taking the shape of Great Society programs in the postwar era), which emerged as "a response to the threat of populist politics" during the 1930s, provided "a method of setting limits to democratic practices and maintaining them" (Mitchell, 2009, p. 416; see also Caffentzis, 2008–2009; Hardt & Negri, 1994). Second, throughout the postwar era, the United States consistently acted as an imperialist power conducting covert interventions in producer petro-states (hence shaping their formation) to protect the interests of the Seven Sisters (e.g., Iran in 1953, Iraq in 1963, Indonesia in 1965; Vitalis, 2009). As the Keynesian demand-led economic growth strategy (where wage increases followed productivity increases), along with the cold war geopolitical strategy of communist containment, became increasingly dependent on maintaining the free (and cheap) flow of oil through neocolonialist practices, the U.S. military began to gain increasing importance, gradually transforming the United States into an advanced national security state (Nitzan & Bichler, 2002). In the process, the sphere of democratic politics ended up being either usurped by the increasingly technical nature of economic expertise or regularly suspended by the concerns of national security (including ones pertaining to energy security).

As the era of free-flowing oil came to a close in the mid-1970s, the scope of democratic decision making in advanced capitalist social formations began to be limited with increasing vigor. The oil crisis came at a moment when the Keynesian regime of accumulation was not able to contain the working-class demands for an increased share of the social surplus (beyond the productivity increases), and the high price of oil quickly became an excuse for subsequent wage cuts (Caffentzis, 2008–2009). The attendant economic liberalism, which had been brewing at the Institute of Economic Affairs in London, the Mont Pelerin Society, and the Economics Department of the University of Chicago since the end of the World War II, emerged "as an alternative project to defeat the threat of populist democracy" (Mitchell, 2009, p. 417). Under the neoliberal regime of accumulation, the relationship between the state and the market was radically reconfigured, where the latter began to pursue a policy of active economization of the social life through marketization of social relations, privatization of the public sector, commodification of the commons, liberalization of trade, and financialization of daily life (Harvey, 2005). As life became more and more governed through market relations or market-based solutions, the postwar accord between the capitalist and the working classes broke down, wages ceased to increase in lock-step with productivity increases, and the tax cuts that were sanctioned by supply-side economics meant the dismantling of the welfare state and the reduction of government involvement in the economy to military Keynesianism (Resnick & Wolff, 2006). For the working classes of the consumer petro-states, the neoliberal deal meant, on one hand, stagnant wages, increasing work hours (and productivity), and increasing labor market insecurity (the decline of full-time employment and the rise of precarious forms of labor) and, on the other hand, lower income taxes (but higher social security taxes), cheaper goods (trade liberalization), and increasing access to credit (financial deregulation) (Wolff, 2009). As if this was not enough to limit and diffuse the threat of democratic populism, after the attacks on September 11, 2001, and the subsequent invasion of Afghanistan and Iraq, neoliberalism took a neoconservative turn and further limited the sphere of democratic politics in the name of national security. To conclude, as we enter the twentieth-first century, given the fact that the petroleum-based modernization strategies of both producer and consumer states are in deep, structural crises, it may be useful to entertain the hypothesis that the "oil curse" is a disease that inflicts not only producer but also consumer petro-states.

Conclusion: The "Real" Cost of Oil

Much of what has been discussed in this chapter so far has aimed at elaborating a political economy approach (as distinct from the standard neoclassical approach) to explain the concrete social and natural processes that make up the political economy of oil: the social construction of its natural limits; the social construction of the global oil demand; the social, economic, and political institutions that produce the price of oil; and the question of state formation in petroleum-dependent economies. An important assumption of the standard neoclassical approach is that, as the price of oil increases, over time, the world economy will gradually adjust its production technology and consumption patterns, substituting away from oil to alternative, less scarce resources. The political economy approach elaborated in this chapter suggests that there are a number of reasons why this may not be the case.

Let us leave aside for a moment the fact that the price of oil has historically been determined through oligopolistic arrangements (even when the buyers and sellers refer to spot and futures markets) and let us ask whether the windfall profits of the oil industry (shared between the oil-producing petro-states and their NOCs and IOCs) are invested in the research and development of viable alternatives to oil. Historically, petro-dollars have been extended as credits to developing countries (leading to the debt crises of 1980s), have enabled exploitation of more high-cost offshore fields (thereby delaying the need to develop alternatives), have been used to finance military buildups (the Middle East became the leading consumer of weapons and military equipment), have been used to invest in alternative business lines (e.g., the "financial sector" in Dubai, the "knowledge economy" in Qatar), and have been used to invest in financial markets (Davis, 2006). To say the least, none of these and other potential uses of the oil revenues necessarily facilitate the development of an alternative to oil. Moreover, the

neoliberal tendency to try to solve all social and economic problems within the short-term horizon of market-based solutions makes it difficult to initiate and coordinate a concerted effort for the development of alternatives and the transformation of the production technology and consumption patterns at a global scale. Such a concerted effort requires a public recognition of the "real" costs of oil—namely, the human and real economic costs of energy wars, the ecological costs of the use of carbon-based sources energy, the social and economic costs of the distributional conflicts that are caused by climate change, the social costs of the "oil curse" both in producer and consumer petro-states, and the social and economic costs of economic crises that are triggered by the speculation-driven price of oil. For this precise reason, the main task of the political economy of oil in the twenty-first century should be to generate a widespread public recognition of the "real" costs of oil.

References and Further Readings

Adelman, M. A. (1972). *The world petroleum market.* Baltimore: Johns Hopkins University Press.

Adelman, M. A. (1995). *The genie out of the bottle: World oil since 1970.* Cambridge: MIT Press.

Bowden, G. (1985). The social construction of validity in estimates of U.S. crude oil reserves. *Social Studies of Science, 15*(2), 207–240.

British Petroleum. (2009). *Statistical review of world energy.* Available at http://www.bp.com/statisticalreview

Bromley, S. (2005). The United States and the control of the world's oil. *Government and Opposition, 40,* 225–255.

Bromley, S. L. (1991). *American hegemony and world oil: The industry, the state system and the world economy.* University Park: Pennsylvania State University Press.

Caffentzis, G. (2008). The peak oil complex, commodity fetishism, and class struggle. *Rethinking Marxism, 20,* 313–320.

Caffentzis, G. (2008–2009). A discourse on prophetic method: Oil crises and political economy, past and future. *The Commoner, 13,* 53–71.

Cooper, J. C. B. (2003). Price elasticity of demand for crude oil: Estimates for 23 countries. *OPEC Review, 27*(1), 1–8.

Davis, M. (2006). Fear and money in Dubai. *New Left Review, 41,* 47–68.

Deffeyes, K. S. (2006). *Beyond oil: The view from Hubbert's peak.* New York: Hill and Wang.

Devarajan, S., & Fisher, A. C. (1981). Hotelling's "Economics of exhaustible resources": Fifty years later. *Journal of Economic Literature, 19,* 65–73.

Gökay, B. (Ed.). (2006). *The politics of oil: A survey.* London: Routledge.

Hamilton, J. H. (2008). *Understanding crude oil prices* (NBER Working Paper No. 14492). Cambridge, MA: National Bureau of Economic Research.

Hardt, M., & Negri, A. (1994). *Labor of Dionysus: A critique of the state-form.* Minneapolis: University of Minnesota Press.

Harvey, D. (2005). *The new imperialism.* New York: Oxford University Press.

Hotelling, H. (1931). The economics of exhaustible resources. *Journal of Political Economy, 39,* 137–175.

Hubbert, M. K. (1956, Spring). Nuclear energy and the fossil fuels. *American Petroleum Institute Drilling and Production Practice Proceedings,* pp. 5–75.

International Energy Agency. (2004). *World energy outlook.* Available at http://www.worldenergyoutlook.org/2004.asp

Klare, M. (2004). *Blood and oil: The dangers and consequences of America's growing dependency on imported petroleum.* New York: Metropolitan Books.

Klare, M. (2008a). Petroleum anxiety and the militarization of energy security. In D. Moran & J. A. Russell (Eds.), *Energy security and global politics: The militarization of resource management* (pp. 38–61). London: Routledge.

Klare, M. (2008b). *Rising powers, shrinking planet: The new geopolitics of energy.* New York: Metropolitan Books.

Midnight Notes Collective. (Ed.). (1992). *Midnight oil: Work, energy, war: 1973–1992.* New York: Autonomedia.

Mitchell, T. (2002). McJihad. *Social Text, 20*(4), 1–18.

Mitchell, T. (2009). Carbon democracy. *Economy and Society, 38,* 399–432.

Moran, D., & Russell, J. A. (2008). Introduction: The militarization of energy security. In D. Moran & J. A. Russell (Eds.), *Energy security and global politics: The militarization of resource management* (pp. 1–17). London: Routledge.

Nissen, D., & Knapp, D. (2005). Oil market reliability: A commercial proposal. *Geopolitics of Energy, 27*(7), 2–6.

Nitzan, J., & Bichler, S. (2002). *The global political economy of Israel.* London: Pluto Press.

Resnick, S. A., & Wolff, R. D. (2006). *New directions in Marxian theory.* London: Routledge.

Roncaglia, A. (2003). Energy and market power: An alternative approach to the economics of oil. *Journal of Post Keynesian Economics, 25,* 641–659.

Ross, M. L. (2001). Does oil hinder democracy? *World Politics, 53,* 325–361.

Sachs, J. D., & Warner, A. M. (1995). *Natural resource abundance and economic growth* (Development Discussion Paper No. 517a). Cambridge, MA: Harvard Institute for International Development.

Solow, R. M. (1974). The economics of resources or the resources of economics. *American Economic Review, 64*(2), 1–14.

Vitalis, R. (2009). *America's kingdom: Mythmaking on the Saudi oil frontier.* London: Verso.

Watts, M. (2006). Empire of oil: Capitalist dispossession and the scramble for Africa. *Monthly Review, 58*(4), 1–17.

Wolff, R. (2009). *Capitalism hits the fan: The global economic meltdown and what to do about it.* New York: Olive Branch Press.

Wray, L. R. (2008). Money manager capitalism and the commodities market bubble. *Challenge, 51*(6), 52–80.

Yeomans, M. (2004). *Oil: Anatomy of an industry.* New York: New Press.

Yergin, D. (1991). *The prize: The epic quest for oil, money, and power.* New York: Simon & Schuster.

64

TRANSPORTATION ECONOMICS

ANTHONY M. RUFOLO

Portland State University

To begin, transportation economics covers a broad range of issues. There are differences between personal and freight transportation, among transportation modes, and between the fixed and variable parts of the transportation system. Analysis of personal transportation tends to focus on commuting and choice of mode, although there is also substantial interest in other personal transportation choices, such as time of day for travel and grouping of trips. For freight, the issues are primarily related to the cost of freight movement and the damage that heavy vehicles do to roads. Each mode has similarities and differences in the issues to be analyzed. For virtually all transportation systems, there is a large, typically publicly owned, infrastructure and a variable, often privately owned, set of vehicles that use that infrastructure (Dean, 2003). The financing systems are often complex, and the incentives that they offer may generate further issues that need to be addressed in evaluating transportation systems.

In discussions of transportation, there is near universal agreement that there are problems. Each mode has different problems. For automobiles, increasing congestion, difficulty in financing construction and maintenance, and concern over the environmental effects are major issues. For public transportation, a long-term downward trend in share and rising costs are the key concerns. For freight, competition and cooperation among the modes, capacity of the freight system, and allocation of cost are among the important topics.

This chapter starts with a discussion of the demand for transportation services and the factors that are important in analyzing the choices made from the perspective of the user of the transportation system. Then, of course, supply of transportation is evaluated. Because the market for transportation services is not the typical market system, the method of funding and the incentives for efficient use of the system are then discussed, along with the role of government in regulating the transportations system. The chapter concludes with a discussion of some of the important policy debates regarding transportation.

Demand for Transportation Services

The trend for personal travel has been for increasing use of the automobile and reduced reliance on alternative modes. One result has been increased levels of congestion and delay on the road system and increasing subsidies for the transit system. From an economic perspective, many of the perceived problems occur because people do not pay the appropriate price for travel. Hence, it is important to understand the demand for transportation and the methods of finance because the latter determines the perceived price.

There are two important distinctions between the demand for transportation and the demand for most goods and services. The first is that transportation is typically classified as a derived demand; most travel is not consumed for itself. Rather, it is a method to achieve other goals. The second is that for personal transportation, the person's time must be used, and the value of this time is part of the cost of transportation. Thus, time and the value of time are very important issues in discussions of transportation. In fact, transportation economists often differentiate between the cost of transportation services and the cost of transportation, which includes the opportunity cost of the time used in making the trip. The latter is typically referred to as *generalized cost*. This distinction is very important when analyzing the demand for transportation services because the differences in time cost often have substantial impacts on the choice of mode for travel.

The next step in analyzing the demand for personal transportation refers to elasticity of demand. In addition to the common discussion of price elasticity of demand, the income elasticity of demand and cross-price elasticity of demand are important in analyzing transportation choices.

Cost and the Value of Time

The most common example of the distinction between the generalized cost and the monetary cost of different choices is the choice of mode for commuting. If one looks only at the monetary cost, then mass transit would be a bargain, compared to driving, for most people. The transit fare is typically a fraction of the cost of using an automobile, especially if the person driving must also pay for parking. Despite the price differences, the vast majority of commuters in the United States choose the automobile over mass transit. A major reason is that the auto commute is typically much shorter than the transit commute, and people value the time savings. A broad generalization often used in transportation analysis is that people value time in commuting at about half of their wage rate, but there is substantial variation in people's willingness to pay to save time. This valuation also varies by how the time is being used. Time spent waiting for a transit vehicle costs more than time spent in the vehicle, and time spent driving in congestion is viewed as being much more costly than time driving at free flow. More recent research also finds that there is considerable variation across individuals in the value they place on time (Small, Winston, & Yan, 2005).

Another aspect of the value of time is the reliability of the system. Although average travel time is very important, the variation in travel time may be equally important to many people. Getting to the destination either early or late may impose costs on the traveler. The cost might be being late for work or a meeting, or it might be having extra time before work starts. The greater the variation in travel time, the more of a cushion is needed to be reasonably certain of getting to the destination at a specific time. One method of describing this is to look at the probability distribution of trip times. For example, the average trip time may be 20 minutes, but because of wide variation in congestion, the traveler may have to leave 30 minutes before the desired arrival time to have a 90% probability of arriving on time. In general, higher levels of congestion are associated with higher levels of uncertainty in addition to the longer travel time. This may make it difficult to identify the value of time for the traveler, and there is evidence that people place a separate value on improved reliability compared to reduced travel time (Lam & Small, 2001).

Time is also of importance in freight transportation, although it is typically less a factor than for personal transportation choices. Some items are perishable, so the value of time is obvious, but the use of overnight express and similar services show that saving time in the movement of freight can also be valuable. In addition, many firms have come to rely on timely delivery of inputs as a method to reduce the need to hold large inventories of the items that they use in the production process. Because late delivery can disrupt the production process, both time and reliability are important for these freight services.

Elasticities

There are a variety of elasticities that are important in understanding transportation economics. The price elasticity of demand is the one most commonly discussed in economics, and it is very relevant for transportation. However, two other elasticities are important in analyzing transportation choices: the income elasticity of demand, which relates to changes in demand as income changes, and the cross-price elasticity of demand, which relates to the way demand for one good changes when the price of another good changes.

Price Elasticity

For transportation, the price elasticity of demand is complicated because there is either the ordinary price elasticity of demand, based on monetary price, or the generalized cost elasticity of demand, based on monetary and time cost. Where the time needed for travel does not change, the ordinary price elasticity of demand is evaluated. In general, the price elasticity of demand for transportation is fairly low in the short run; people do not appear to be overly sensitive to price in deciding whether to make a trip. For example, the general rule of thumb is that the price elasticity of demand for transit is about 0.3. Hence, a 10% increase in transit fare is expected to lead to a 3% reduction in the number of riders. However, the estimates of the elasticity of demand cover a wide range (Holmgren, 2007). Elasticity of demand for a particular mode or at a particular time may be higher or lower than the average because there will be different opportunities to substitute other modes, routes, or times, and the availability of substitutes makes demand more elastic. A variety of other price elasticities are sometimes discussed, such as the elasticity of demand for gasoline. The elasticity for gasoline is found to be very low in the short run (Congressional Budget Office, 2008), but this is largely because the cost of gasoline is only a part of the cost of the trip. Any given percentage increase in the price of gasoline will be a much smaller percentage of the cost of the trip, and the full cost of the trip is the more relevant consideration.

Income Elasticity

Another very important elasticity is the income elasticity of demand. It compares the change in the demand for a good or service at fixed prices with the change in income.

The demand for most goods and services is expected to increase with income. However, if the demand decreases as income increases, it is labeled an inferior good. Generally, inferior goods are goods that have a higher quality substitute available, and as income rises, people shift to the higher quality substitute.

In transportation, one sees that the demand for automobiles is highly income elastic. Both within countries and across countries, one sees rising demand for automobile ownership as income rises. This, of course, affects the demand for using transit, which is typically seen as an inferior good. There are many factors other than income that affect the demand for different types of transportation, but the general trend is consistent. The demand for more transit increases over some income ranges, but over most levels of income, the demand for transit decreases as income increases, everything else constant.

Cross-Price Elasticity of Demand

Another important elasticity concept is the cross-price elasticity of demand. It refers to how the demand for one good changes when the price of another good changes. This is the typical method to identify complements and substitutes. If the price of one good rises, people tend to use less of it. If as a consequence they buy more of some other good, that other good is a substitute. However, if the goods are complementary, then the reduction in the purchase of one good would also lead to a reduction in the purchase of its complements. Transit advocates argue that providing more transit services or reducing transit fares would reduce the number of automobile trips. This is an argument that the two are substitutes, and the amount of substitution then depends on the cross-price elasticity of demand. This is an empirical parameter, and it will differ among areas and over time. The evidence in the United States is that in most cities, the cross-price elasticity of demand between transit and automobiles is very low, if not zero. This means that lowering transit fare does very little to get people out of their automobiles. As noted earlier, the price elasticity of demand for transit is fairly low. This implies that lowering fares is not extremely effective in getting people to use transit, and some of the increase in transit usage is caused by an increase in trips taken or diversion from other modes, for example, carpooling, walking, or biking, rather than a diversion from trips in automobiles.

The other factor of importance with respect to cross-price elasticity is the relative shares of the substitutes. For example, if transit carries 10% of the trips and automobiles carry the other 90%, then even if all new transit trips represent a shift from automobiles, a 10% increase in transit usage (to 11%) would decrease auto use by only about 1% (to 89%). This means that transit-oriented policies are likely to have noticeable effects on auto use only in areas that already have large amounts of transit use.

Supply of Transportation Services

Just as the analysis of the demand for transportation had to take account of the unique characteristics of transportation services, the supply analysis is affected by them as well. Much of transportation infrastructure is large scale. In the United States, roads, transit, and airports are typically provided by the public sector, although there is increasing interest in private ownership and provision. Economies of scale in providing the infrastructure and the combination of passenger and freight transportation are two of the more important issues in the supply of transportation services.

Economies of Scale

Economies of scale relate to the relationship between the cost per unit and the number of units being produced. Economies of scale are often important in transportation, but the focus is typically somewhat different than for most goods and services. For example, mass transit requires many users for it to be cost effective. However, there are different ways to measure scale; one is simply system size, and the other relates to service over given segments of the system. The distinction is between the size and the density of the network. Density relates to the number of people wanting to make a particular trip, typically from a common set of origins to a common set of destinations. As more people want to make the same trip, the cost of providing that trip per person is often reduced, although the range of scale economies may be somewhat limited. If one considers simply the size of the system, then adding more routes would increase scale, but it is less likely there will be economies of scale using this measure.

In addition to the number of people wanting to make essentially the same trip, one also must consider the options that are available for a trip. In this case, the network becomes an important consideration. The network refers to the places that one can get to on the transportation system. For the automobile, the network is essentially any place that has a road, but for other transportation systems, the network is typically much more constrained. For a mass transit system, one might consider the network to be simply the areas within easy walking distance of stations or stops.

Another way to think about network effects is to consider each trip as composed of three separate functions. These are typically defined as collection, line haul, and distribution. First, the passenger must get to the transportation system. Then there is typically a relatively high-speed movement to some other point in the system, from which the traveler must get to the ultimate destination. For air travel, the three functions would be getting to the airport, the plane trip, and then getting to the ultimate destination. For commuting by car, each segment tends to be done in the vehicle, although there may be a walk to the vehicle at the beginning and the end. For transit, the collection phase may involve simply walking to a transit stop, but it may also involve driving or biking to a transit stop or using a feeder service to get to the main transit stop. Historically, collection was typically associated with walking to transit, and many residential areas developed around streetcar or other transit services. Once the passengers are on the transit vehicle, the majority of the distance is covered. This may be on local service or some form of express service. Finally, when the passengers leave the transit vehicle, they must get to their destination, typically by walking.

Economies of Scope

Another issue in the cost of providing transportation services is the ability to provide different types of transportation services. Using the same facilities to provide different types of transportation service is called *economies of scope*. The largest distinction in this area is between personal transportation and freight transportation. For example, both automobiles and heavy trucks typically use the same roads. This makes sense only if there are economies of scope in the provision of roads, and most studies conclude that this is indeed the case. In other words, it would be possible to have a separate network of roads for trucks and for automobiles, and occasionally there are such separate facilities. However, they are rare. There are disadvantages of mixing automobile and truck traffic on the same road. For example, roads must be built to higher standards to withstand the damage done by heavy vehicles, so a road built solely for automobiles could have thinner pavement. Safety concerns, speed differences, and the discomfort some drivers feel near large vehicles are also associated with mixing the vehicles. On the other hand, there are benefits to mixing the traffic. Roads with two lanes in each direction can carry more than twice as many vehicles as roads with only one lane in each direction because they allow easier passing and other operational improvements. Separate roads would also have to have separate fixed costs, like shoulders. It also seems that there are some benefits related to time of usage, with automobiles having more usage during peak congestion periods and trucks often showing greater flexibility to use the roads at less congested times (de Palma, Kilani, & Lindsey, 2008).

Passenger rail and freight rail are much less compatible. For passenger rail service, time is very important, but for freight rail service, the emphasis is on keeping the cost low. Hence, freight trains are often large and slow moving. Because it is difficult to pass another train, passenger and freight traffic tend to interfere with each other. If the volume of traffic is low, the economies of scale in sharing track may make combined service the least costly option, but as volume increases, the diseconomies of scope typically cause separation of the activities.

Mode Choice

Mode choice is important both for personal travel and for freight movement. Mode choice for commuting has received substantial interest because of the growth in the share of single-occupant vehicles and the decline in share for transit, carpooling, and other modes. Although the mode shares differ substantially across countries, the trend tends to be fairly universal. To some extent, this is the result of rising incomes and people placing a higher value on saving time, but there are also substantial concerns about whether people are making those choices based on full information regarding the cost differences.

Location Patterns

If one thinks about the commute in terms of the collection, line haul, and distribution phases, it becomes apparent that changes in location patterns over time have had a substantial impact on the ability of transit to serve these functions for commuters. As population decentralized, development moved away from concentration around transit stops, but transit could still serve effectively if people could get to the system and employment was concentrated around transit. Hence, park and ride became a viable option for people with a car available. The increased ownership of automobiles over time made this a possible method to use transit for many people. However, the decentralization of employment has proven to be more problematic. Although people are willing to take cars that were purchased primarily for personal use and let them sit in a parking lot while at work, they typically are not willing to purchase a car to be used to get from the transit station to work. Hence, a commuter often can still use transit if his or her residence is not located near a transit stop, but it is more difficult if his or her employment is not near a stop. Hence, employment location patterns have become an important issue for the viability of using transit.

Components of Cost

Another important consideration in mode choice is the cost perception on the part of the person making the decision. Economic theory tells us that the efficient decision depends on the decision maker's facing of the full marginal cost. However, it is seldom the case that the person making a commute decision will face that cost. The distinction between fixed cost, marginal cost, and external cost is helpful in understanding the potential distortion. In making a decision between auto and transit commuting, the person is likely to take account of both fixed and variable costs, but once the choice to use an auto is made, only variable costs enter the decision for a particular trip. Further, certain costs may be paid indirectly or by someone else and will not enter into the decision.

If one does not own a car for other reasons, then the full cost of purchase and maintenance will enter into the mode choice decision. Once the automobile is purchased and other fixed costs, such as insurance, are paid, only the variable cost of using it for a particular trip will be taken into account. The income elasticity of demand for automobiles has affected the relative cost of using transit and cars based on the marginal cost comparison. As income increases, people who are transit users may still find that the automobile is very convenient for recreation and household use. Yet once the vehicle is purchased, the cost of using it for commuting is only the variable cost, and this will shift the commute mode choice decision. There have been some experiments associated with converting some fixed cost of auto use into variable mileage costs to see how behavior would change (Abou-Zeid, Ben-Akiva, Tierney, Buckeye, & Buxbaum, 2008), and people do seem to drive less when the mileage charge is higher (Rufolo & Kimpel, 2008).

Aside from the difference between fixed and variable costs, automobile users, especially at peak times, do not pay all of the cost associated with automobile usage. Some costs are simply paid indirectly or by others. Parking is often cited in this category because relatively few employees pay for parking at their places of work (Shoup, 2005). Other costs are paid by the drivers, but those costs do not reflect the full marginal cost. Congestion falls into this category because the cost of increased delay with congestion is imposed on drivers, but the marginal cost of one more driver exceeds the average cost paid by the driver. This complex subject is covered in detail in a later section. Finally, automobile usage generates substantial negative externalities in the form of pollution and related costs, and these costs are not paid by automobile users (Parry, Walls, & Harrington, 2007).

Transit users typically do not face efficient prices either. Large subsidies keep the fare charged substantially below the marginal cost of providing service, although a later section shows that there is some disagreement about the optimal transit subsidy. Peak-period transit fares typically should be higher than off-peak fares to reflect the fact that the need for capital stock is determined by the peak usage. In addition, fares should be higher for longer trips, and there should be a variety of other adjustments to reflect cost differences. Few transit agencies follow any of these principles, so commuters by transit also tend to pay substantially less then the optimal charge. One effect of the pricing system is that there is likely to be too much consumption of all transportation services relative to the optimum.

Congestion

Road congestion is a significant and growing problem in most countries. Economists typically define the effect of congestion as an external effect of using the transportation system. There are actually several different causes of congestion. The first relates to bottlenecks. Bottlenecks reflect a reduction of capacity. A reduction in the number of lanes can certainly create a bottleneck; however, in transportation, they can occur for a variety of reasons. For example, places where traffic enters and leaves a limited-access road may have reduced capacity even though the number of lanes is unchanged, and the bottleneck is defined by the reduction in capacity. Next, there is congestion caused by incidents. These may be accidents or simply stalled vehicles or animals on the road. Finally, there is systemic congestion. This occurs based on the number of vehicles trying to use a road, and it can best be thought of as an effect that each driver has on all other drivers. For safety, there must be some distance between vehicles. As more vehicles try to use the same road, the distance between vehicles becomes compressed. The crowding forces traffic to slow. Because the slowing is associated with the number of vehicles on the road rather than some vehicles slowing others, it is typically analyzed as being caused equally by all users of the road.

Economists have concluded that there is a substantial difference between the additional time that each driver must take and the effect that having one more vehicle on the road creates for the whole system. To help see this, consider the following example. Suppose that if 1,000 cars per hour try to use the road, there is completely free flow, and each driver takes 10 minutes to complete his or her trip. However, if 1,001 cars per hour try to use the road, the slight slowing causes each driver to take 10 minutes and 1 second for the trip. The total travel time for 1,000 cars is 10,000 minutes, but the total travel time for 1,001 cars is slightly more than 10,026 minutes. Thus, although each driver sees a travel time of a little over 10 minutes, the total travel time for all drivers has increased by over 26 minutes. Because any one of the drivers could reduce the total by 26 minutes by not making the trip, it is clear that none of them are considering the full effect that their using the road has on the entire system.

Congestion Pricing

The effect of most types of congestion is that the cost to individual drivers is less than the cost to the system. As the example shows, someone who values the trip enough to make it if the time cost were as high as 15 minutes would, if faced with the full 26-minute cost imposed on the system, decide not to make the trip. Economists propose that all drivers be charged the difference between the cost that they face and the cost that their use of the system imposes on the whole system. This is known as congestion pricing.

It can be formally demonstrated that the idealized system of pricing would generate net benefits for society through more efficient use of the road system. However, drivers have been strongly opposed to such pricing systems. The basic reason is that to make the system work, most drivers must be made worse off than they are with the so-called free system. It may seem paradoxical that there is an improvement if most drivers are worse off. The reason is that under congestion, drivers pay with time, but under a toll, they pay with money. The time that they waste in congestion is a cost to them but provides no benefit to anyone. The toll that they pay is also a cost to them, but it is just a transfer of money to the toll agency. This money can be used to lower other taxes or provide additional benefits. Hence, the individual drivers are worse off, as they are with any tax or fee, but the transfer of money allows for some offsetting benefits to be created, while the wasting of time does not.

There are a variety of types of congestion pricing. State Route 91 (SR91) in California has two lanes in each direction that are priced and four lanes in each direction that are unpriced. The price is changed as often as every hour, but the rates are set in advance. The disadvantage of prices set in advance is that the demand for using the road varies randomly to some extent. The prices that are set in advance may have to be high on average so as to generate free flow most of the time. This could lead to less usage than would be efficient. With the fixed charges, drivers then have the choice of paying and saving some time or not paying and facing congestion. Studies of the usage of SR91 find that relatively few drivers use it every day, with many drivers using it occasionally. The explanation is that it may be worth it to save time on some days but not on others, for example, if parents are late to pick up their children.

Interstate 15 in California has two reversible lanes that are free for high-occupancy vehicles (HOV) and charge a price that is varied as frequently as every 6 minutes for other cars so as to maintain free flow. The benefit of the dynamic pricing is that it allows more vehicles to use the lanes in periods of low demand while still maintaining free flow during periods of very high demand. The disadvantage for drivers is that they do not know until they arrive at the entrance what the price will be. The price is displayed on an electronic sign, and they have a short time to decide whether to take the priced road or to stay on the free one.

A number of cities have adopted a system of charging vehicles either for entry into an area or for any driving in that area. Singapore is widely cited as the first city to use this system, but London has received substantial interest for instituting its system. London charges a flat fee for any vehicle that drives within the designated zone and designated times. The fee varies with type of vehicle and for a variety of other reasons, but the basic fee is a flat charge. The fee is enforced with a system of video license plate recognition.

There is one additional drawback to congestion pricing. It costs money to collect and administer the charge. For example, one study of the London system concluded that the cost to administer the system was so high that it offset the benefits from better traffic flow (Prud'homme & Bocarejo, 2005). Reductions in the cost of the equipment needed to impose charges, along with improvements in the

administrative capability to collect revenue, cause these issues to decline in importance over time, but they must be taken into account when evaluating the net benefits of using pricing to manage congestion.

Hypercongestion

Congestion can become so severe that there is actually a reduction in the number of cars that get through to their destinations in each time period. The easiest way to illustrate that would be to think of complete gridlock, the ultimate congestion. In this case, no vehicle gets to its destination. There is some disagreement about when congestion gets bad enough to cause an actual reduction in the flow of vehicles. For many years, it was thought that a speed of about 30 to 35 miles per hour maximized flow, but recent research suggests that flow may be reduced when speeds drop below free flow. Where hypercongestion exists, congestion management has the potential to increase both speed of travel and the number of vehicles traveling (Varaiya, 2005).

Congestion Policy

Although economists recommend pricing that varies by time of day to manage congestion, there is relatively little support for this approach. Most congestion policy relates to other methods to relieve congestion. Congestion caused by too many people trying to use the road can be addressed only by changing their demand to use the road. Pricing is the most effective way to do this, but other types of demand management also can be effective. The most common is the use of ramp metering to manage the number of vehicles entering a restricted access road. Ramp meters can improve the flow on the metered roads, but they have some drawbacks as well. They can cause backups onto surface streets, and they favor vehicles making long trips over vehicles making short trips. Responses to other types of congestion may differ. For example, the best response to congestion caused by incidents seems to be to work to rapidly clear the incident. Many states now have operations to do precisely this. They encourage people in fender benders to move to the side of the road and may have service vehicles to help clear accidents or stalls.

Latent Demand

As the time cost of a trip increases, people make various adjustments to their travel plans. With respect to peak period congestion, the term *triple convergence* is often discussed (Downs, 2004). Anthony Downs argues that when faced with increased congestion, some people respond by changing their time of travel to less congested periods, others change mode of travel, and still others change the route of travel. Another possibility is to choose not to make the trip. These changes reduce the maximum peak congestion from what it would be if people had not changed their behavior, but it also means that adding capacity has less impact on the maximum amount of congestion than it would if people did not change their behavior. As congestion decreases, people will shift back to their preferred times, routes, and modes. Hence, the triple convergence then offsets some of the benefits of the increased capacity.

With triple convergence, people may now be traveling closer to their ideal times, taking a more direct route, or traveling by a preferred mode, but these shifts then mitigate the effect on peak congestion that the increased capacity generates. To be sure, there are substantial benefits to these shifts, and the period of peak congestion is likely to be smaller. However, some see these shifts and argue that there is no benefit to building additional road capacity because it simply gets used up. They term the increase in usage as being *latent demand*. Although the convergence of travel times does mitigate the benefits of the capacity expansion, it is a serious mistake to conclude that there are no benefits. Nevertheless, understanding triple convergence and latent demand gives us more capability to accurately predict the impact of transportation investments.

Mass Transit

The long-term trend for transit is a declining share of personal transportation. Most transit in the United States was privately owned and largely funded from fares until about the 1960s. Since then, most systems have been converted to public ownership and rely heavily on public subsidies for funding. Critics contend that this has caused substantial inefficiencies in transit operations (Lave, 1994), while supporters argue that transit provides offsetting benefits. Hence, the important economic concerns are how the organization of transit affects efficiency and the arguments for public subsidies.

Economics of Transit

As noted earlier, two key issues for transit are the economies of density and the network characteristics. John Meyer, John Kain, and Martin Wohl (1965) are credited with first analyzing the relative cost of different methods of urban transportation. They did not consider the value of time, so they were just considering monetary cost. Their conclusion was that the automobile was the low-cost alternative for low density of use and that buses were then the low-cost alternative, except for very high density, when rail would have the lowest cost. Although actual density has increased in most cities over time, the density of transportation demand often has not. The transit system economies occur when a large number of people want to make the same trip at the same time. Decentralization of first residences and then employment has often reduced the density of trips, making transit more costly despite the increase in overall density. In addition, the outward spread of most urban areas has reduced the percentage of residences

and places of employment that are within the transit network. Finally, the increased value of time associated with rising incomes has increased the generalized cost of transit relative to auto travel.

The issue of public versus private provision generates substantial controversy. A number of other countries, including England, have moved toward more privatization of their transit systems. In the United States, some transit systems contract with private providers for service. Supporters of privatization argue that the competition leads to lower cost and improved efficiency, and the evidence seems to support this conclusion.

Transit Fares

Transit has peak demand that is similar to that for automobiles. Economists typically argue that prices should be set to reflect the cost of providing the service. From an economic perspective, the cost of providing peak transit service is higher than the cost of providing off-peak service. This seems counterintuitive to most people. The large number of people using the system during the peak means that the cost of running the vehicle is spread over more passengers than in the off-peak hours, but the number of vehicles needed by the system is determined by the peak usage. Thus, more of the cost of the system is attributed to the peak than to the off-peak usage.

The counterargument is that each person who uses transit actually creates a benefit for other users (Mohring, 1972). The basis for this conclusion is that as more people use the system, more service is provided and average wait time decreases. Average wait time for transit is somewhat dependent on the frequency of service. If people arrive randomly at the transit stop, then the average wait is half of the time between vehicles. So increasing the number of vehicles leads to reduced average wait time, and this means that the efficient fare would be lower than the marginal cost of providing the service because as more people use the system, wait time for others is reduced, creating an external benefit that justifies a subsidy. Despite this argument, Charles Lave (1994) finds that the subsidies have largely resulted in inefficient production rather than more service.

Although economists argue about whether subsidies promote or hinder efficiency in transit, the popular argument for transit subsidies is that the lower fare can be used to entice people out of their automobiles. However, the evidence on very low cross-price elasticity of demand between transit and automobiles means that this argument is largely incorrect for most cities.

Regulation

There is a long history of regulation of the transportation industry. Many types of regulation relate to issues such as safety, but there has also been substantial economic regulation of the various modes. For many years, the federal government set prices for airlines, railroads, and trucks. Although the intent was to protect consumers, the effect of deregulation of these industries has been substantial improvements in productivity and reduction in prices (Winston, 1998). To be sure, many of the improvements are viewed negatively by some. For example, under regulation, railroads were required to maintain substantial amounts of service where the cost exceeded the revenue, but they were then able to compensate by charging higher prices on service in high-demand areas. Under deregulation, prices declined in the high-demand areas, and much of the service to low-demand areas was discontinued. This is an improvement in efficiency, but it is negative from the perspective of those losing service.

Taxi regulation is one area of transportation regulation where there does not seem to be much prospect for reform. Many cities restrict the number of taxi licenses that they grant. From an economic perspective, the restrictions on entry are likely to cause prices to increase and service to be concentrated in the most profitable areas. More competition is expected to improve service and result in reduced prices. Yet experience with taxi deregulation has been problematic. This may be because certain types of competition are not allowed in the deregulated markets. For example, most airports require that passengers take the taxi at the front of the line. There is no opportunity for one farther back to offer the service at a lower price. Hence, deregulation may still not allow much competition. One study concludes that a whole new regulatory structure is needed for all parts of the transit and taxi system (Klein, Moore & Reja, 1997).

Issues

Funding for transportation has received substantial attention. For example, Congress created two separate commissions to study and make recommendations on transportation finance: the National Surface Transportation Policy and Revenue Study Commission and the National Surface Transportation Infrastructure Financing Commission. Each concluded that existing finance mechanisms were insufficient and recommended changes. The method of funding and the level of funding are both sources of controversy. In personal transportation, there are disputes about whether auto users or transit riders pay the appropriate costs. In addition, there is substantial concern that both highways and transit face substantial challenges with respect to finance.

Highway Finance

In an economist's ideal world, prices for vehicles using the road system would be set to reflect the cost the vehicle imposes on the system (Winston & Shirley, 1998). The economic system works most efficiently when price is equal to marginal cost. For cars and other light vehicles, the primary determinant of the efficient price would be the level of congestion on the road in use. Where congestion is heavy, the price would be high, and a low price would be charged for travel on uncongested roads or during off-peak times. The high price would discourage use during the peak (Rufolo & Kimpel, 2008) and induce more use of alternative modes, including carpooling. The substantial decline in the number of true carpools has caused some people to argue that carpooling will not occur because people value their time highly and carpools impose a time cost for formation. However, there has been spontaneous carpool formation where there is an incentive, such as reduced travel time for those in carpools (Spielberg & Shapiro, 2001). The revenue generated from pricing would also serve to guide new investment. Where revenue is high, the value of added capacity will also be high, so the price serves as a sign that more investment should be considered.

For heavy vehicles, the price should vary with the road damage done and congestion. Heavy vehicles do substantially more damage to roads than light vehicles, and the damage is largely related to the weight per axle of the vehicle. Oregon charges a weight-mile tax that varies with both weight and number of axles for heavy trucks, because spreading a given weight over more axles reduces road damage (Rufolo, Bronfman, & Kuhner, 2000); however, most states and the federal government raise road revenues from heavy vehicles through fuel taxes and registration fees. Raising revenue with efficient prices also serves to manage the use of the system. It is expected that efficient management would reduce the amount of road capacity required to meet any level of demand.

In the absence of better management of the road system, there are ongoing predictions of the need for massive investments. Although a pricing system would reduce the required investment as well as generate revenue, the large growth in demand for transportation over time indicates that more capacity will have to be added to the system. How that new capacity will be financed is a contentious issue. Although there is more consideration of pricing and tolling as finance mechanisms, they still represent a small percentage of the existing revenue sources.

Most revenue for the road system in the United States comes from fuel taxes and other charges to vehicle users, although there is substantial disagreement about whether road users pay the full cost of the system. Some of the disagreement comes from disagreement about what is a user cost. Fuel taxes are viewed as user charges by most, but some critics consider fuel tax revenue that goes to road construction and maintenance as a subsidy. More substantive disagreement occurs about items like property tax revenue used for local roads. Some view this as a subsidy for roads while others argue that local roads are primarily of use to local landowners. Other disagreements relate to how general-purpose taxes on vehicles should be counted (Dean, 2003). Virtually all economists agree that vehicles should be charged for the externalities that they generate; however, there is disagreement about what the charge should be (Delucchi, 2007).

Cost allocation studies are done by both the federal government and a variety of states to determine whether different classes of vehicles are paying their proportionate shares of the cost of building and maintaining the road system. This is another area of substantial controversy, but the complexity of the issue precludes going into it in detail here.

Whether vehicles pay the full cost or not, there is agreement that the current method of funding the road system faces serious problems. The fuel tax has been a major source of road finance at both the state and federal levels; however, growing fuel efficiency and the prospect of alternative fuel vehicles raise questions about the adequacy of this source over time. In addition, the tax is typically set at a rate per gallon, so the purchasing power decreases with inflation, and there has been substantial resistance to increasing this tax. Because of the concerns about fuel taxes, there has been increased interest in more directly pricing the use of roads, either with a simple charge per mile (a vehicle miles traveled [VMT] tax) or some form of congestion pricing. An important drawback to these alternatives is the cost of collecting the revenue. As these costs decline over time, there is likely to be more extensive use of these alternative revenue sources.

One effect of improved ability to collect tolls or impose other prices is that it becomes more feasible for private firms to build roads, operate roads, or both. The concern with private firms operating roads is that the price that optimizes the use of the road may not coincide with the profit-maximizing price. Rather than having too much traffic because drivers are not paying the full cost of using a congested road, the road may be underused because of the high monopoly price.

The use of pricing has also raised questions regarding whether uniform pricing is the most efficient approach. HOV lanes are problematic. Their intent is to encourage carpooling, but they often appear to be underused or ineffective. When demand is relatively low compared to capacity, the total vehicle flow may be substantially reduced relative to general use of the lanes. A number of HOV lanes have been modified to allow non-HOV drivers to use them and pay a toll (high occupancy vehicle toll lanes are called HOT lanes). Effectively, solo drivers have the choice of congested but no-charge lanes or paying a fee for better conditions. This raises the question of whether such charging systems are more efficient than leaving all lanes unpriced and whether more than two prices might be efficient (Small & Yan, 2001). Because the value of saving time differs across people and for the same person under different circumstances, a better

understanding of this distribution and of the effect of segregating lanes on traffic flow is needed. However, improvements in technology are likely to make complex pricing more feasible over time.

Transit

As noted earlier, transit is often criticized for being costly and ineffective, with costs rising rapidly over time and transit's share of travel declining. The share trend can be affected by items like high prices for fuel, but increased ridership is likely to increase cost more than revenue and place further financial pressure on the system. There seems to be little likelihood of transit in the United States becoming self-sufficient. Hence, the major issue for transit is whether subsidies will keep up with rising costs or whether some changes in the way transit services are provided will improve efficiency (Klein et al., 1997). If congestion pricing is implemented, then demand for transit service will increase and reduced congestion will make bus service less costly and more reliable. Under these circumstances, the economics would argue for higher fares and lower subsidies, but much of the discussion related to making congestion pricing more acceptable to the public regards increasing transit service, as was done in London.

Freight

Rapid growth in freight movement has placed strains on various parts of the freight system. The Federal Highway Administration (2007) identifies road congestion, intermodal transfer facilities, and capacity constraints on railroads as important issues. For trucks, the issues are very similar to the ones for automobiles in terms of congestion and financing the roads, although freight concerns are more concentrated on the need for improvements at specific bottlenecks.

Efficient pricing of roads would charge vehicles on the basis of their axle loadings and damage to roads. On the other hand, in the absence of such price incentives, regulations limiting weight per axle may also be inefficient. There is evidence that at least some truckers would be willing to pay for the extra damage if allowed to carry heavier loads (Rufolo et al., 2000). Expanding capacity for railroads that require additional construction would be at best a long-term solution given the high cost and other constraints on adding rail capacity. However, the railroads have shown significant ability to improve productivity since deregulation, and they may find other methods to address the capacity constraint.

Conclusion

Transportation economics is a complex field that has received relatively little attention. However, the growing divergence between demand for travel and the resources available to finance transportation infrastructure is focusing attention on both the methods of finance and the efficiency incentives. Transportation economists argue that more effective pricing of transportation would improve operation of the existing system while also providing funding for improvements. However, direct pricing faces technical, political, and public acceptance issues. Ongoing experiments and demonstration projects are likely to lead to gradual increases in the use of pricing, but a major shift does not appear likely in the near future. Hence, further increases in congestion on roads and financial pressure on transit systems seem inevitable.

References and Further Readings

Abou-Zeid, M., Ben-Akiva, M., Tierney, K., Buckeye, K. R., & Buxbaum, J. N. (2008). Minnesota pay-as-you-drive pricing experiment. *Transportation Research Record, 2079,* 8–14.

Congressional Budget Office. (2008, January). *Effects of gasoline prices on driving behavior and vehicle markets.* Available at http://www.cbo.gov/ftpdocs/88xx/doc8893/01-14-GasolinePrices.pdf

Dean, T. B. (2003). Policy versus the market: Transportation's battleground. *Transportation Research Record, 1839,* 5–22.

Delucchi, M. (2007). Do motor vehicle users in the U.S. pay their way? *Transportation Research Part A, 41,* 983–1003.

de Palma, A., Kilani, M., & Lindsey, R. (2008). The merits of separating cars and trucks. *Journal of Urban Economics, 64,* 340–361.

Downs, A. (2004). *Still stuck in traffic: Coping with peak-hour traffic congestion.* Washington, DC: Brookings Institution.

Federal Highway Administration. (2007, January). *Financing freight improvements.* Available at http://ops.fhwa.dot.gov/freight/publications/freightfinancing/index.htm

Flyvbjerg, B., Skamris Holm, M., & Buhl, S. (2002). Underestimating costs in public works projects: Error or lie? *APA Journal, 68*(3), 279–295.

Forkenbrock, D. J. (2008). Policy options for varying mileage-based road user charges. *Transportation Research Record, 2079,* 29–36.

Gómez-Ibáñez, J.A., Tye, W. B., & Winston, C. (Eds.). (1999). *Essays in transportation economics and policy: A handbook in honor of John R. Meyer.* Washington, DC: Brookings Institution.

Holmgren, J. (2007). Meta-analysis of public transport demand. *Transportation Research Part A, 41,* 1021–1035.

Klein, D., Moore A. T., & Reja, B. (1997). *Curb rights: A foundation for free enterprise in urban transit.* Washington, DC: Brookings Institution.

Lam, T. C., & Small, K. A. (2001). The value of travel time and reliability: Measurement from a value pricing experiment. *Transportation Research Part E, 37,* 231–251.

Lave, C. (1994). It wasn't supposed to turn out like this: Federal subsidies and declining transit productivity. *Access, 5,* 21–25.

Leape, J. (2006). The London congestion charge. *Journal of Economic Perspectives, 20*(4), 157–176.

Mackie, P. (2005). The London congestion charge: A tentative economic appraisal. A comment on the paper by Prud'homme and Bocarejo. *Transport Policy, 12,* 288–290.

Meyer, J. R., Kain, J. F., & Wohl, M. (1965). *The urban transportation problem,* Cambridge, MA: Harvard University Press.

Mohring, H. (1972). Optimization and scale economies in urban bus transportation. *American Economic Review, 62*(4), 591–604.

Parry, I. W. H., Walls, M., & Harrington, W. (2007). Automobile externalities and policies. *Journal of Economic Literature, 45,* 373–399.

Portney, P. R., Parry, I. W. H., Gruenspecht, H. K., & Harrington, W. (2003). The economics of fuel economy standards. *Journal of Economic Perspectives, 17*(4), 203–217.

Prud'homme, R., & Bocarejo, J. P. (2005). The London congestion charge: A tentative economic appraisal. *Transport Policy, 12,* 279–287.

Rufolo, A. M., & Bertini, R. L. (2003). Designing alternatives to state motor fuel taxes. *Transportation Quarterly, 57*(1), 33–46.

Rufolo, A. M., Bronfman, L., & Kuhner, E. (2000). Effect of Oregon's axle-weight-distance tax incentive. *Transportation Research Record, 1732,* 63–69.

Rufolo, A. M., & Kimpel, T. J. (2008). Responses to Oregon's experiment in road pricing. *Transportation Research Record, 2079,* 1–7.

Shoup, D. C. (2005). *The high cost of free parking.* Chicago: Planners Press, American Planning Association.

Small, K. A., Winston, C., & Yan, J. (2005). Uncovering the distribution of motorists' preferences for travel time and reliability. *Econometrica, 73*(4), 1367–1382.

Small, K. A., & Yan, J. (2001). The value of "value pricing" of roads: Second-best pricing and product differentiation. *Journal of Urban Economics, 49,* 310–336.

Spielberg, F., & Shapiro, P. (2001). Slugs and bodysnatchers: Adventures in dynamic ridesharing. *TR News, 214,* 20–23.

Varaiya, P. (2005). What we've learned about highway congestion. *Access, 27,* 2–9.

Winston, C. (1998). U.S. industry adjustment to economic deregulation. *Journal of Economic Perspectives, 12,* 89–110.

Winston, C., & Shirley, C. (1998). *Alternate route.* Washington, DC: Brookings Institution.

65

URBAN ECONOMICS

JAMES D. BURNELL

College of Wooster

The field of urban economics was developed based on the observation that population and economic activity are concentrated in geographic space. Thus, one can define the field of urban economics as the study of the spatial relationships between individuals, households, and firms from an economic perspective. Much of urban economic analysis extends the maximizing behavior of individuals and firms from microeconomics to include how location affects this behavior. A focal point of urban economic analysis is how distance affects maximizing behavior. The fact that there is increased population and employment density at certain points in geographic space indicates that there are advantages of clustering of activity at certain locations. The concentration of activity also has consequences, both positive (i.e., enhanced productivity) and negative (i.e., increased congestion), and urban economists also consider these consequences.

Urban economics had its origins in the area of location theory and regional economics. The foundation was the role transport costs played in location decisions (Richardson, 1979), the hierarchy of trading areas, the system of cities (Christaller, 1933; Lösch, 1940), and the theory of land rent (von Thunen, 1966). The inclusion of geography in the decisions made by economic agents set the stage for urban economics to become a separate field in economics in the 1960s. A major reason was the important contributions of William Alonso (1964), Richard Muth (1969), and Edwin Mills (1967, 1972) in presenting theoretical and empirical analysis on the organization of urban space. The 1960s were also a period in which there was a significant focus on problems associated with the current spatial organization. Problems of poverty and social unrest experienced by large central cities made cities the focal point in the media, in public policy, and in academia.

The application of urban economic analysis has extended to subareas of the field, such as urban transportation, housing and real estate, and urban public finance. The field has evolved as the structure of urban areas has evolved. The focus of transport costs on location decisions has diminished and been replaced with the analysis of the impact of agglomeration economies on the size and composition of urban areas. The Alonso-Muth-Mills focus on monocentric urban areas has evolved to incorporate the growing multicentric nature of urban areas and the relatively rapid rate of urban sprawl. The empirical approach to analyzing urban economic phenomena has also evolved with the development of spatial econometric techniques that allow empirical modeling to account for the influences of the contiguity of urban space.

The remainder of this chapter is organized as follows. First, the concept of the urban area is considered from the economist's viewpoint. Next, a discussion of the elements that affect urban areas in an interurban context is presented. This section considers dominant explanations for the productivity of urban areas. The following section considers the intraurban relationships that exist and how they explain the urban spatial structure that exists in metropolitan areas. In particular, this section considers the monocentric model of urban land use as well as growing suburban and multicentric land use patterns. Finally, some outcomes and issues related to modern urban spatial structure are considered. The focus of this section is how urban economists address the spatial pattern of households.

The Concept of an Urban Area From an Economist's View

Undergraduate urban economics textbooks typically provide different definitions of urban areas that reflect a hierarchy of urban areas, usually incorporating the definitions used by the Bureau of the Census. Currently, the Census defines an urban area as a community with a population of 2500 or more. A micropolitan area is an area with an urban core population of between 10,000 and 50,000 people, while a metropolitan area has an urban core of at least 50,000. The Census defines the spatial reach of these areas in terms of one or more counties that have a high degree of economic and social interaction with the urban core.

The urban core refers to an important city that is the focal point of the interactions with the areas outside the city. Cities are defined by political boundaries: the legal boundaries that define the political authority of these areas. Edwin Mills and Bruce Hamilton (1989) point out that to economists, political boundaries are less important than the market forces that contributed to the increased density of individuals and firms. The market forces that define the economic concept of an urban area can be considered from two perspectives: interurban and intraurban. These perspectives can be examined in terms of the location decisions made by households and firms.

One may consider interurban analysis as the study of competition across urban areas. Interurban analysis considers location decisions and their consequences for different urban areas. Households and firms evaluate the locational advantages of different urban locations. For example, a manufacturing firm may be assessing the productivity of the labor force for the type of workers it needs between the St. Louis and Minneapolis metropolitan areas. A household may evaluate which urban area to locate in based on the availability of employment, the cost of living, or the existence of desirable amenities. The economic concept of urban area in this case transcends the existence of the political boundaries of cities. The consequences of these decisions affect the growth and income-creation ability of the area.

Intraurban analysis addresses the location decisions and their consequences within urban areas. Once an urban area is chosen, both firms and households will then decide where within the area to locate. The market allocation of land among households and firms within an urban area was the focus of the Alonso-Muth-Mills monocentric model. Although the existence of political boundaries does not necessarily define the overall urban area in an economic sense, decentralization of households and employment within urban areas suggested that political boundaries do have some influence. The increasing fragmentation of urban areas since the middle of the twentieth century gave rise to a large number of suburban jurisdictions that could compete for households and firms based on their tax and service packages and their ability to use zoning to influence land market outcomes. The consequences of intraurban location decisions by households and firms and the existence of interjursidictional competition affect the fiscal viability of large central cities, the distribution of employment opportunity, and the distribution of income and minority groups throughout the urban area.

Interurban Analysis: The Urban Hierarchy

The focus of interurban analysis is on the process of urbanization, in which economic activity concentrates at particular locations, and the factors that contribute to the extent of this concentration. The starting point of the urbanization process is location theory, whereby the profit-maximizing decisions of firms specifically considered how location affected profitability. Although location theory could explain the location decision of individual firms, urbanization also meant that there were other factors that would influence the size and growth of urban areas. Early explanations were based on central place theory, which described a hierarchy of urban places in a system of urban areas based on the market area for goods and services (Christaller, 1933; Lösch, 1940). The most recent emphasis on explaining the process of urbanization is on the importance of agglomeration economies, factors external to the firms that provide advantages of clustering economics activity (Fujita, Krugman, & Venables, 1999; Rosenthal & Strange, 2004).

Location theory includes transportation costs as well as the costs of inputs in the cost functions of firms. To illustrate the importance of transport costs in location decisions, the basic model assumed labor and capital costs were equal across space and the firm used a raw material input that was available at one location while the market for the firm's product occurred at a different location. Thus, the firm would have to choose whether to transport the raw material to the market location to produce its product or to locate at the raw material site and transport the product. The firm's profit-maximizing location would be that which minimized transport costs. The usefulness of this simple location decision was that it introduced the concept of an economic location weight that was determined not only by the physical weight but also by the unit transport cost per mile (O'Sullivan, 2009). Traditional examples include weight-gaining and weight-losing production processes. Weight-gaining processes include products that gain physical weight, such as water added in the beverage industries, or products whose transport costs are high because of their fragile nature. Weight-losing processes include mining and lumber.

Relaxing the assumption that the costs of other inputs used by the firm are equal across space allowed the spatial variation in cost and productivity of inputs to influence the location of the firm. Inputs prices that are generally considered to vary across space include labor, capital, land, energy, and raw materials. Another factor considered important by firms is the impact of the tax and service package that can be offered by these governments as they compete among themselves for firms to locate within their boundaries.

Location theory could explain why firms choose among different locations, but it could not effectively address the fact that urban areas varied in size and in their ability to grow. Central place theory developed by Walter Christaller (1933) and August Lösch (1940) provided explanations for the location of market-oriented firms and the resulting hierarchy of urban areas that results.

The basic assumptions of the theory were that consumers were evenly distributed across space and transportation costs were equal in all directions. A firm existed at a particular location to serve the population. Consumers would travel to the firm to obtain the good, and the effective price paid by the consumer would be the price established by the firm plus transportation costs. The firm's market area would stretch to the point that the good's effective price was such that consumers were no longer willing to purchase the product from the firm. If the firm earned an economic profit, other firms producing the product would enter at another location.

As firms continued to enter, the market area of existing firms would decrease as consumers encountered lower effective prices due to closer proximity to firms. Firms would continue to enter only until normal profits were made and spatial equilibrium was reached. Each firm would have a spatial monopoly over a particular area, creating a spatial network for that product. Networks of different sizes for different goods would exist based on the size of the market area for the product. Smaller order goods are goods with small geographic market areas, and higher order goods have larger geographic market areas. A central place would be a location where one or more networks locate. The size of the urban area would be determined by the market area of the product with the largest geographic reach—the highest order good present at that location—and would contain all successively lower order goods. The market reach of its highest order good would define an urban area's position in the hierarchy. As an example, consider medical services. Small places would be expected to have a number of general practitioners and basic medical testing services. More specialized medical services would be found in a larger place. This establishes a hierarchical spatial link whereby residents of smaller places are linked to large places to obtain higher ordered services.

Central place theory's value in urban economics is primarily in its explanation of the pattern of retail activity. Other approaches to explaining the size and growth of urban areas also developed. Economic base theory posited that an area's economy was composed of two sectors. The basic sector was composed of firms that exported their product beyond the area's boundaries. The local sector was composed of firms that provided products to the area's residents. The growth of the area was determined by the export demand for the area's products. As income flowed into the area from exporting basic sector goods, a fraction of this income would be spent in the local sector through successive rounds of spending. The successive rounds of spending defined the multiplier effect—a dollar's worth of income would generate a larger amount of total income, depending on the size of the multiplier. The size of the multiplier was dependent on how much of the basic sector income was spent locally (McDonald & McMillen, 2007).

Economic base theory explains that the growth of an urban area is dependent on the change in the export demand for the area's basic sector products and how well developed the local sector is in providing goods and services for the area's population. This simple theory of urban growth has found wide practical application in the area of economic impact analysis, in which predictions are made regarding the impact of the attraction or departure of a key economic activity on the local area's economy.

The most recent emphasis in research on the process of urbanization has been on the advantages of the clustering of economic activity. This recent emphasis was stimulated by the emergence of the new economic geography based on the work of Paul Krugman (1991) in the area of international trade, but it has found much theoretical application in explaining the clustering of economic activity in urban areas (Fujita et al., 1999). Masahisa Fujita and Tomoya Mori (2005) describe the new economic geography as being a general equilibrium approach that specifically considers agglomeration in explaining the pattern and structure of urban areas. A primary consideration of the new economic geography is the specific incorporation of economies of scale and imperfect competition.

Scale economies are a fundamental requirement for increases in employment density in geographic space, since larger production facilities allow efficiencies that reduce average costs as output produced rises, and larger facilities lead to more workers locating in proximity to their jobs. The advantages of clustering are attributed to the existence of agglomeration economies, which are external benefits to firms that reduce their average costs at all levels of output.

Alfred Marshall (1920) originally identified three sources of agglomeration economies. One source is input sharing, in which final product firms purchase intermediate inputs from a specialized provider who is able to use economies of scale because of increased demand resulting from the clustering of the final product firms. Stuart Rosenthal and William Strange (2006) refer to input sharing as a form of local outsourcing. For example, computer hardware firms may locate near a computer chip manufacturer. The concentration of hardware firms allows the chip manufacturer to realize economies of scale that result in lower chip prices for the hardware firms.

A second source of agglomeration economies is labor pooling, which occurs when firms are able to draw from a large pool of specialized labor. The concentration of high-tech computer firms in Silicon Valley and biotech firms in the Boston metropolitan area reflect a large pool of highly educated individuals that offer small startup computer or biotech firms a labor force with requisite skills. This benefits not only firms who have a large demand for specialized labor, but also the workers who have other job opportunities if some of the small startups fail.

The third source is attributed to knowledge spillovers, whereby the presence and interaction of those with specialized knowledge about their products and production processes will stimulate a higher rate of innovation. The interaction of highly educated workers in Silicon Valley and Boston and the existence of (well-known) research universities increase the likelihood of innovation.

Agglomeration economies are classified according to the type of firm receiving the external benefit. Localization economies are external to the firm but internal to the industry, since they occur based on the extent of the presence of firms in the same industry. Urbanization economies are external to both the firm and industry and are attributed to the size of the area. Larger areas have a diverse set of firms and labor, which allows firms across industries to benefit.

The existence of agglomeration economies contributes to the size and growth of urban areas. Agglomeration economies increase the productivity of the area, which results in higher rates of growth. Increased demand for the area's products leads to higher labor demand. In areas realizing agglomeration economies, the existence of this greater productivity also provides a self-reinforcing effect. As production increases to meet the increased demand, there is an additional pull of firms who would benefit (O'Sullivan, 2009).

The consideration of the self-reinforcing effects of agglomeration suggests that agglomeration economies can be dynamic as well as static. Static agglomeration economies relate to the industrial and geographic dimensions of the effect of agglomeration economies on firms and the urban area and help explain why some urban areas are larger than others. The industrial dimension relates to the industries experiencing the benefits of localization or urbanization economies. The geographic dimension relates to the proximity of establishments in industries experiencing agglomeration economies and the diminishing effect of the agglomeration advantage as proximity between establishments decreases (Rosenthal & Strange, 2004). Static agglomeration economies refer to a one-time cost reduction associated with the clustering of firms (McDonald & McMillen, 2007).

Dynamic agglomeration economies relate to a time dimension of the impact and help explain not only the growth of particular urban areas but also the rate of growth. Dynamic localization economies cause continual reductions in the firm's average costs as the size of the industry in the area increases. Dynamic urbanization economies yield continual reduction in a firm's average costs as the size of the area increases compared to static agglomeration economies that are considered a one time reduction in cost (McDonald & McMillan, 2007). Rosenthal and Strange (2004) attribute dynamic agglomeration economies to knowledge spillovers whereby the acquisition and transfer of knowledge between firms occurs over time, resulting in cost advantages realized in the future.

Much empirical work has been done to determine the impact of agglomeration economies on the urbanization process. Rosenthal and Strange (2004) provide a comprehensive review of the empirical literature regarding agglomeration economies. The empirical literature follows a number of approaches to test various aspects of the impact of agglomeration economies on urban productivity. These include the testing for the importance of localization and urbanization economies, identifying the appropriate geographic level, and using a microbased versus an aggregate approach to estimating productivity effects. A brief representation of the empirical literature is considered here.

Edward Glaeser, Hedi Kallal, Jose Scheinkman, and Andrei Shleifer (1992) consider the role of knowledge spillovers on the growth of industry employment in the largest 170 cities. They test for three potential impacts of knowledge spillovers on industry growth. The first two relate to localization economies whereby within-industry knowledge spillovers lead to higher rates of growth, and the difference between them centers on the degree of local competition within the industries. On one hand, less competition allows innovating firms to realize the gains of the innovation internally and provides an incentive to innovate. On the other hand, greater local competition within the industry stimulates innovation as firms try to stay ahead of their competitors. The third potential impact of knowledge spillovers reflects urbanization economies. The more diverse the representation of industries, the greater the interchange of ideas across firms, which leads to faster growth.

The empirical model of Glaeser et al. (1992) considers the growth rate of employment in the six largest industries in 170 of the largest cities as a function of variables that measure the three potential impacts of knowledge spillovers, controlling for regional and natural characteristics that might affect local growth. Their findings show that growth is faster in cities where local industry competition is greater and where industry diversity is greater.

Rosenthal and Strange (2001) consider the three sources of localization economies to determine the level of geography at which the sources are important in explaining the concentration of industry employment. The authors hypothesize that the impact of the agglomeration advantages may be influenced by the spatial concentration of industry activity.

Some sources of agglomeration may be more important at close proximity, while others may be important over a larger area. They regress an index of spatial concentration for an industry on variables that measure input sharing, labor market pooling, and knowledge spillovers, controlling for transport cost and natural advantage. Versions of the model are estimated for the zip code, county, and state levels. The results provide evidence that labor market pooling is an important agglomerative source at all three levels of geography, input sharing was important at the state level but not lower levels of geography, and knowledge spillovers were important only at the zip code level.

J. Vernon Henderson (1986) addresses the importance of localization versus urbanization economies. From an industry location view, the difference is whether areas that specialize in particular industries have greater advantages or whether it is the size of the area that provides the greatest impact on productivity. Henderson employs a production function approach, where industry output is a function of inputs. He uses local industry employment as a measure of localization economies and urban size as a measure of urbanization economies. From his empirical results, Henderson concludes that there is strong evidence of localization economies for almost all industries considered and that the localization effects were large. He finds almost no evidence of urbanization economies. He also finds evidence that the agglomeration effects diminish for larger urban areas.

One of the empirical issues regarding estimating the effect of agglomeration economies has been the level of aggregation of the industry data. For example, Henderson (1986) used the two-digit level to define the industry. A more recent work by Henderson (2003) estimates plant-level production functions using panel data to provide a microlevel assessment of the effect of localization and urbanization economies and the ability to capture dynamic localization economies. Plant-level data is desirable since it is the plant that realizes the agglomeration economies at its particular location. Henderson considers the effect of localization economies and urbanization economies on what he identifies as machinery industries and high-tech industries. He also considers whether the plants are single plant or multiplant; single plants are more reliant on the local economic environment than plants that are affiliated with a corporation since the operation of these plants reflects the internal linkages determined by corporate decisions.

Henderson (2003) estimates plant-level production functions as a function of plant-level inputs plus measures to account for localization and urbanization economies. The number of plants in the same industry in the same county is used to measure localization economies and a measure of diversity of manufacturing employment for urbanization economies. Dynamic localization economies are measured by lagging the localization economies measure. The results indicate that localization economies are important for plants in high-tech industries but not for machine industries. The impact of localization economies

is stronger for single plant versus multiplant affiliates. High-tech single plant firms also benefit from dynamic localization economies. There is no evidence that urbanization economies had an influence for either high-tech or machinery industries.

Rosenthal and Strange (2003) also use a microlevel approach with a focus on the birth of new establishments for six industries. They hypothesize that the presence of agglomeration economies results in new establishments clustering around existing establishments, while a dispersed pattern of new establishment locations would occur if there were no agglomeration economies. The sample used is composed of data measured at the zip code level, which is a departure from earlier analysis that typically used metropolitan areas as the geographic reference point. This allowed the authors to test for whether the effects of agglomeration economies diminish as distance from existing establishments increases. The authors focus on six industries that represent both innovative (e.g., software) and traditional (e.g., machinery) industries. The number of new establishments or the amount of new establishment employment in a zip code is regressed against variables that include the number of establishments per worker in the industry and outside the industry as a measure of competitiveness and diversity of economic activity.

Measures of urbanization and localization economies are also included. Urbanization economies are measured as employment outside the industry, while localization economies are measured as employment within the industry. To test whether the impact of the agglomeration economies diminishes with distance, Rosenthal and Strange (2003) include within- and outside-industry employment in a series of concentric rings around the initial zip code. The results are that localization economies are important for five of the six industries, while there is little evidence that urbanization economies matter. The results also indicate that the impact of localization economies diminishes with distance.

The review of interurban analysis indicates that many factors affect the location of economic activity across geographic space. The recent focus on the role of agglomeration economies is important given the changing nature of the economic base in many urban areas. As urban governments try to influence the location of firms to generate growth within their boundaries, the understanding of the type of agglomeration economies and the geographic extent of these economies become important information for policy makers.

Intraurban Analysis: Urban Spatial Structure

Intraurban analysis considers how space is organized within an urban area. Historically, the development of urban areas was such that the intensity of land use was much greater at the urban core, generally referred to as the central business district (CBD) and diminished as distance from the CBD increased. The urban land market is the mechanism by which land is allocated to the competing residential and business users. Residential and business users establish their willingness to bid for a certain location based on the location's value in terms of utility for residents or profit for business. Competition in the land market would allocate space to the highest bidder.

The origin of the land allocation process was the theory of land use developed by Johann von Thunen (1966). His contribution was to consider the competition for land use among users who valued proximity to a central location, and he developed the concept of the land rent function, whereby agricultural land users who desired to minimize the costs of producing and transporting their outputs to the market would bid for locations in close proximity to the market. Bids would decline for sites farther from the market center to account for the increase in transportation costs. A land rent existed based on the value that users place on the scarce locations surrounding the desired central location.

The modern version of the land allocation process is generally labeled the Alonso-Muth-Mills approach. Alonso (1964), Muth (1969), and Mills (1967) formally developed the theory of spatial equilibrium in the land market. The Alonso-Muth-Mills approach considers a competitive urban land market in which the demand for urban land is based on the utility-maximizing decisions of households and the profit-maximizing decisions of firms in a monocentric city. Firms value CBD locations since the CBD contains the transport node where firms export their products. A CBD location would reduce the cost of transporting products to the export node. For households, the CBD is the location of employment, and households value proximity to the CBD to reduce commuting costs. The value that firms and households place on proximity to the CBD defines their bid-rent function, which is the willingness of a user to pay for a location at a particular location from the CBD.

For firms, the bid-rent function is based on the profits of the firm:

$$\text{Profit} = pq - cq - txq - Rs, \tag{1}$$

where p is product price, c is unit cost, q is quantity sold, t is the transport cost per unit of distance, s is the size of the site, and R is the rent bid per unit of site size. R is the amount the firm is willing to pay at distance x, holding the level of profit constant. Assuming competitive equilibrium where profits are zero and solving for R yields the firm's rent bid function:

$$R = \frac{pq - cq - txq}{s}. \tag{2}$$

As distance from the CBD increases, the firm will reduce its bid by the increase in transport cost incurred for shipping its product to the CBD. The slope of the bid rent function,

$$-\frac{tq}{s}, \tag{3}$$

represents the reduction in land costs necessary to compensate for increased transport costs as distance from the CBD increases, and it measures the value of accessibility to the CBD. As compared with firms that have smoother bid-rent curves, firms with steeper bid-rent functions assign greater value to accessibility since the reduction in rent bid will be greater in order to compensate for the higher level of transport costs.

For households, the utility-maximizing decision defines the concept of the bid-rent function. Household utility depends on the consumption of housing services and other goods, and households face a budget constraint where income is spent on other goods, housing services, and commuting costs. Holding income and expenditures on other goods constant, consider the expenditures on housing services and commuting costs, which depend on distance to the CBD:

$$Rh + tx, \tag{4}$$

where R is the rent bid per unit of housing services, h is the amount of housing service, t is the commuting cost per unit of distance, and x is distance from the CBD. Spatial equilibrium requires that utility is constant at different distances. This means that expenditures on housing and commuting must remain constant for a constant level of utility. As distance from the CBD increases, households will change their bids to compensate for the change in commuting costs:

$$\Delta Rh + t\Delta x = 0. \tag{5}$$

The slope of the household's bid-rent function is

$$\frac{\Delta R}{\Delta x} = -\frac{t}{h}, \tag{6}$$

and it represents the amount rent bid will go down as distance increases.

Land market equilibrium requires that land goes to the highest bidder and that neither firms nor households can gain profits or utility by moving to a different location. The graphical representation of the urban land market is depicted in Figure 65.1. The slopes of the bid-rent curves reflect the value of accessibility to the three users. Commercial firms have the greatest value of accessibility to the CBD and outbid resident and manufacturing firms.

The Alonso-Mills-Muth model has been useful in explaining patterns of urban land use evident in American cities. The declining importance of the CBD and the increased presence of population and employment in the suburbs can be explained by a reduction in transport costs,

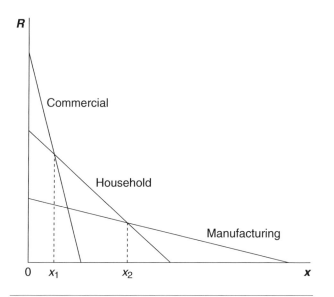

Figure 65.1 The Urban Land Market

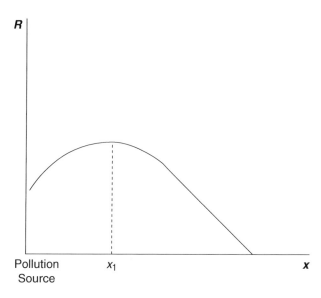

Figure 65.2 Disamenities and the Household Bid-Rent Curve

which leads to flatter sloped bid-rent curves. The model also provided an explanation for the fact that lower income groups lived in the central city and higher income groups lived in the suburbs. Both Alonso (1964) and Muth (1969) consider this in their formulations of the monocentric model. The explanation is based on the income elasticity of demand for housing relative to the income elasticity of commuting. If the income elasticity of demand for housing were greater than the income elasticity of commuting, then high-income populations would locate in the suburbs where housing prices are lower and the amount of land available for housing is greater.

The Alonso-Mills-Muth model can be extended to consider other factors related to the characteristics of urban areas. Douglas Diamond and George Tolley (1982) incorporate the concept of amenities to determine their impact on households' bid-rent functions. Amenities are location-specific characteristics that yield utility to households but are not purchased directly. Diamond and Tolley incorporate amenities as an additional component of the household's utility function. The resulting utility-maximizing outcomes determine the values households place on amenities and yield bid-rent functions that can be positively as well as negatively sloped functions. As depicted in Figure 65.2, the positive-sloped portion of the function would represent proximity to a negative amenity, such as pollution, in which households would need to be compensated for locating at or near the source of the negative amenity. As the distance from the source increases, the effect of the negative amenity on the household diminishes, resulting in higher bids as distance from the negative amenity increases. This occurs up to x_1. Beyond x_1, the effect of pollution has dissipated, and compensating for commuting costs now dominates the bids made.

The Alonso-Mills-Muth model and its variations provided a theoretical structure for empirical work on urban spatial structure. Empirical approaches have included the estimation of population and employment density functions. Here, population and employment density are regressed against the distance from the CBD to determine the intensity of land use, with the monocentric model predicting that density decreases as distance from the CBD increases. Estimation of a hedonic housing price function is another empirical tool used to measure the value that households place on characteristics that comprise housing services. These characteristics typically include structural characteristics such as size of the dwelling and the number of rooms, quality characteristics such as the age of the dwelling, neighborhood characteristics such as crime rate or school quality, and proximity characteristics such as distance to the CBD or to particular amenities (Sirmans, MacPherson, & Zietz, 2005).

Early empirical work estimated population and employment density functions to test the predictions of the monocentric model of decreasing population and employment density as distance from the CBD increases. The early evidence provided by Muth (1969) and Mills (1972) supported these predictions. Even recent estimation of population density functions indicates population density is negatively related to distance from the CBD (McDonald & McMillen, 2007). Glaeser (2007) estimates the relationship between housing prices and distance from the Boston CBD and also finds support for the monocentric model.

Although the monocentric focus of the Alonso-Muth-Mills model remains the basis of much of the analysis of urban spatial structure, there has been recognition that the decentralization of population and particularly employment represents a transformation of the urban landscape (Glaeser & Kahn, 2003). Although the recent estimation of population functions and housing price gradients suggest that there is still the negative relationship between density and distance from the CBD, the empirical results suggest that the explanatory power of the monocentric model is relatively low.

Population decentralization has been attributed to factors such as poorer quality housing and the concentration of minority groups and low-income groups in the central city that act to divert middle- and upper-income groups to the suburbs (Anas, Arnott, & Small, 1998). The politically fragmented nature of urban areas has also contributed to this decentralization through a Tiebout (1956) process, whereby households have the ability to match their preferences for local public services to particular communities.

Alternative explanations of the decentralization of employment have also been offered. In considering the intraurban location decisions of firms, Glaeser and Kahn (2003) offer three potential explanations of the draw to suburban locations. The first reflects the development of transportation infrastructure in the suburbs that offers savings in transportation costs compared to CBD locations. The second is that there may be differences in productivity between central locations and the suburbs. Knowledge and information spillovers are more likely to occur in the dense CBD areas, and this creates a productivity advantage for what Glaeser and Kahn refer to as idea firms—those that require high human capital and computers. The third explanation is that firms that do not benefit from these spillovers may find other cost advantages, such as proximity to workers, at suburban locations. They postulate that firms may follow the population to the suburbs. Based on their empirical research, Glaeser and Kahn conclude that the extent of decentralization in an urban area is greater when the presence of manufacturing firms in the area's industry mix is greater, that knowledge spillovers are important for idea-intensive industries, and that the labor force location has a strong influence on firm location.

The increasing focus on decentralization in urban areas suggests that there has been an evolution in the spatial structure such that many urban areas are considered polycentric. This relates to the observation that in many metropolitan areas, there exist edge cities (Garreau, 1991) that contain a concentration of office and commercial activity compared with other locations throughout the urban area. The existence of subcenters reflects agglomeration advantages away from the traditional CBD. In part, the technological advances of communication and the existence of the transportation infrastructure in suburban areas have contributed to this concentration of activity.

A major contributor to subcenter formation is also a contributor to the importance of monocentric city: agglomeration economies. Both localization and urbanization economies provide clustering advantages at locations away from the central business district. Robert Helsley and Arthur Sullivan (1991) and Denise DiPasquale and William Wheaton (1996) suggest that the advantages of these dispersed locations are enhanced by the increase in commuting costs associated with an increasingly dense monocentric city and by the existence of public infrastructure. Increased commuting costs necessitate higher wage costs for central business district firms to attract workers. Dispersed locations offer lower wages and land costs. The existence of public

infrastructure at these dispersed locations provides an additional locational advantage for firms to cluster at particular locations. All of these factors enhance the external economies that occur as firms cluster at these sites.

Much work has been done to determine what empirical evidence exists for the existence of the polycentric form of urban areas. Three examples will be considered here. Kenneth Small and Shunfeng Song (1994) estimate polycentric employment and population density functions for the Los Angeles metropolitan area for the years 1970 and 1980. They find that the polycentric functions have greater explanatory power for the density patterns compared with the monocentric estimates. Daniel McMillen and John McDonald (1998) estimate employment density functions for Chicago for 1980 and 1990 to determine the effect of agglomeration economies on the existence of subcenters. They hypothesize that the presence of highway interchanges and commuter rail contributes to increased density at the subcenters. They also include proximity to subcenters as a measure of agglomeration economies. They find evidence that the agglomeration effects of shared transportation infrastructure and information and shopping externalities associated with subcenters contribute to higher employment density at these locations. Last, McMillen and Stefani Smith (2003) consider the number of subcenters in a metropolitan area. They consider the characteristics of 62 metropolitan areas and find that the number of subcenters increases as the population and commuting costs of an area increase.

The Spatial Patterns of Residents

An important aspect of research in the urban economics field is the spatial pattern of the location of particular groups in urban areas and the consequences of this pattern. The spatial pattern that exists in most metropolitan areas is the centralization of low-income and minority groups in the central city or inner-ring suburbs. This spatial pattern evolves from household decisions to rent or own and from institutional factors such as lending and insurance practices and community land use policies.

Housing is important from an urban economics perspective because it is fixed in location and is a major component of housing services in the residential utility functions in the Alonso-Muth-Mills model. Along with a residential location decision, households must also decide whether to purchase or rent, which is referred to as *tenure choice.* Housing is also a durable good. The durability affects homeowners in two ways. First, housing deteriorates over time, and homeowners must decide on maintenance and repair. Second, homes generally appreciate in value over the length of ownership; thus, housing can represent an important asset to the owner. In the process of deciding to own a home, the household will require access to mortgage institutions. Housing market outcomes have important implications for the distribution of population groups throughout the urban area. Different income and racial groups are affected by the availability of affordable housing, the preferences individuals have for neighborhood racial composition, and the existence of discriminatory behavior by institutions that facilitate home ownership.

The tenure choice decision of the household is based on the costs of homeownership versus renting. One element of the costs of home ownership is the mortgage payment. Mortgage payments are based on ability to obtain a loan and the resulting terms of the loan. The ability to obtain a loan is affected by the income and wealth of the household, the household's credit risk, and the value of the property. Lack of wealth has been a factor for low-income households generally; it has also affected the home ownership rates of African Americans (Charles & Hurst, 2002; Gyourko, Linneman, & Wachter, 1999; Wachter & Megbolugbe, 1992).

Racial segregation is a feature of the residential living patterns in metropolitan areas. The concern for racially segregated living patterns is the impact that segregation has on the outcome of minorities who live in more centralized neighborhoods. These outcomes include living in neighborhoods with poorer housing quality, lower quality educational opportunities, and restricted job opportunities (Cutler & Glaeser, 1997; Ross, 1998).

The preferences of racial subgroups are incorporated in residential location choice models by considering composition of a neighborhood as one of the neighborhood characteristics that affect the household's utility. In the case where a racial subgroup has an aversion to living with other racial subgroups, this will lead to segregated outcomes in housing markets. Analysis of racial preferences indicates that whites have the greatest aversion to living with nonwhites, particularly African Americans (Charles, 2005).

Another area that has been the focus of segregated living patterns has been the role of racial discrimination in housing and mortgage markets. In the case of housing markets, the analysis of how discrimination occurs centers on the behavior of real estate agents who provide information on housing and mortgage availability that may steer clients to neighborhoods of a particular racial composition (Yinger, 1995). The most recent empirical analysis to determine the existence and extent of racial discrimination in housing markets was sponsored by the Department of Housing and Urban Development in 2000 (Turner, Ross, Galster, & Yinger, 2002). Researchers used paired testing methodology, whereby equally qualified white and minority home seekers and renters interact with real estate and rental agents to determine whether they receive the same treatment in their housing search. Compared to the results of an identical study conducted in 1989, the evidence showed that African American and Hispanic home seekers and renters suffered from discrimination, but the incidence of discrimination was lower for African American home seekers and renters and Hispanic home seekers compared to 1989. Hispanic renters faced the same incidence of discrimination as they did in 1989.

Access to mortgage credit also plays an important role in the tenure decision. There is growing research interest in the question of how decisions by financial institutions affect urban residents. Much of the interest has centered on whether financial institutions provide access to mortgage credit based on the creditworthiness of the household rather than the household's membership in a particular income or racial group. Since the 1990s, a dual mortgage market has developed. The prime market is composed of low-risk borrowers who obtain loans with lower interest rates compared to borrowers in the subprime market. The subprime market is composed of those considered to be high-risk borrowers, and as a result, they pay higher mortgage interest rates than prime borrowers (Apgar & Calder, 2005). Mortgage discrimination occurs when borrowers are denied credit or are channeled to the higher rates in the subprime market or when the financial institution bases its decision by incorporating group membership as an additional determinant of the loan decision. The consequences are not restricted to the influence on the tenure decision of a minority or low-income household, but also include the increased risk of foreclosure.

The empirical research in mortgage lending discrimination typically shows that there are racial differences in mortgage lending outcomes, but it is more difficult to conclude that these differences are attributed to discrimination on the part of lenders. Alicia Munnell, Geoffrey Tootell, Lynn Browne, and James McEneaney (1996) provided a detailed analysis of factors that contribute to mortgage loan denials in Boston. Their empirical model includes variables that reflect the mortgage applicant's risk and cost of default, loan characteristics, and personal characteristics, with race as one of the personal characteristics. The results showed that African American and Hispanic applicants had a greater likelihood of being denied a mortgage loan than whites. Stephen Ross and John Yinger (2002) and Anthony Yezer (2006) discuss the criticisms of this approach, which range from exclusion of relevant variables that reflect creditworthiness to inability to account for the interaction of the applicant with the loan originator. The conclusion from these criticisms is that the results on the race variables will be biased.

A more recent approach applies the paired-testing methodology to the mortgage market. Ross, Margery Austin Turner, Erin Godfrey, and Robin Smith (2008) apply the paired-testing methodology to the pre-application process, whereby potential applicants interact with loan originators to obtain information regarding various types of loan products. The sample is composed of 250 paired tests in the Los Angeles and Chicago metropolitan areas. The results showed that African American and Hispanic testers in Chicago were less likely to be provided information, or they received information on fewer products than white testers. The results for Los Angeles did not show a statistical difference in the treatment between African Americans, Hispanics, and whites. The implications for their results in Chicago are that minorities may have limited access to prime sources of mortgage credit, and this may lead qualified applicants to rely more heavily on the subprime market.

Conclusion

As the presentation of this chapter demonstrates, the field of urban economics concerns itself with the location decisions of firms and households and how those decisions affect the population who live in densely populated urban areas. Urban economics addresses the circumstances and consequences of living in metropolitan areas. Its emergence as a separate field in the 1960s coincided with the changing urban spatial structure—the decentralization of households and employment and the centralization of poverty and minority households—and the consequences of these changes on central city and suburban residents.

Urban areas have evolved from being largely centers of manufacturing activity to having more service- and information-oriented activity as important components of their economic bases. The focus on the role of agglomeration economies has important policy implications for areas undergoing the restructuring of their economic base. Policy makers trying to retain or attract new firms need to be aware of the important contributions of agglomeration economies that exist in their areas.

Research in the field has also addressed the change in urban spatial structure that has occurred within metropolitan areas over the past 40 years. The theory of monocentric urban areas remains the foundation of understanding how the role of distance affects the location decisions of firms and households within urban areas. Extensions of the theory have been used to explain the development of multicentric urban areas and urban sprawl. Urban economics has also developed a number of subfields. Real estate economics and finance extend theoretical and empirical approaches to real estate markets. Governmental issues such as jurisdictional fragmentation and competition, land use policy, and urban fiscal issues are widely addressed. Policy makers interested in the future outcomes of their local areas need to be aware of the interaction that occurs between the pattern of increasing suburbanization and sprawl and its consequences not only for newly formed suburban communities but also for the central city, which may bear the burden of being home to an immobile population.

There are a number of areas that will be pursued in future research. As the national economy continues to undergo structural change, the impact of these changes on the productivity of urban areas will be explored. Much of the literature on agglomeration economies has focused on manufacturing. Future research should extend to the growing service sectors to determine the consequences of this restructuring on the size and viability of urban areas. The development of geographic information data by local governments and the development of spatial econometric software will become an increasingly important component of future research. These developments allow inclusion of spatial spillover effects and their influence on firm and household decisions. Finally, future research will also explore the consequences of urban sprawl and political fragmentation for metropolitan areas. An increasingly important area in urban policy is the concept of regionalism, where metropolitan governments may supersede particular decisions of local governments. Future research should develop a theoretical approach to consider cooperative decision making in metropolitan areas.

References and Further Readings

Alonso, W. (1964). *Location and land use.* Cambridge, MA: Harvard University Press.

Anas, A., Arnott, R., & Small, K. A. (1998). Urban spatial structure. *Journal of Economic Literature, 36,* 1426–1464.

Apgar, W., & Calder, A. (2005). The dual mortgage market: The persistence of discrimination in mortgage lending. In X. Briggs (Ed.), *The geography of opportunity: Race and housing choice in metropolitan America* (pp. 101–126). Washington, DC: Brookings Institution.

Arnott, R. J., & McMillen, D. P. (Eds.). (2006). *A companion to urban economics.* Malden, MA: Blackwell.

Brueckner, J. (2001). Urban sprawl: Lessons from urban economics. In W. G. Gale & J. Rothenberg Pack (Eds.), *Brookings-Wharton papers on urban affairs 2001* (pp. 65–98). Washington, DC: Brookings Institution.

Brueckner, J. (2006). Strategic interaction among governments. In R. J. Arnott & D. P. McMillen (Eds.), *A companion to urban economics* (pp. 332–347). Malden, MA: Blackwell.

Carlino, G. A., Chatterjee, S., & Hunt, R. M. (2007). Urban density and the rate of invention. *Journal of Urban Economics, 61,* 389–419.

Charles, C. Z. (2005). Can we live together? Racial preferences and neighborhood outcomes. In X. Briggs (Ed.), *The geography of opportunity: Race and housing choice in metropolitan America* (pp. 45–80). Washington, DC: Brookings Institution.

Charles, K. K., & Hurst, E. (2002). The transition to homeownership and the black-white wealth gap. *Review of Economic Statistics, 84,* 281–297.

Christaller, W. (1933). *Central places in southern Germany.* London: Prentice Hall.

Cutler, D. M., & Glaeser, E. L. (1997). Are ghettos good or bad? *Quarterly Journal of Economics, 112,* 827–872.

Diamond, D. B., & Tolley, G. S. (1982). The economic roles of urban amenities. In D. B. Diamond & G. S. Tolley (Eds.), *The economics of urban amenities* (pp. 3–54). New York: Academic Press.

DiPasquale, D., & Wheaton, W. C. (1996). *Urban economics and real estate markets.* Englewood Cliffs, NJ: Prentice Hall.

Fischel, W. (2001). *The homevoter hypothesis: How home values influence local government taxation, school finance, and land-use policies.* Cambridge, MA: Harvard University Press.

Fujita, M., Krugman, P., & Venables, A. J. (1999). *The spatial economy: Cities, regions, and international trade.* Cambridge: MIT Press.

Fujita, M., & Mori, T. (2005). Frontiers of the new economic geography. *Papers in Regional Science, 84,* 377–405.

Garreau, J. (1991). *Edge city: Life on the new frontier.* New York: Doubleday.

Glaeser, E. L. (2007). *The economic approach to cities* (NBER Working Paper No. 13696). Cambridge, MA: National Bureau of Economic Research.

Glaeser, E. L., Hanushek, E. A., & Quigley, J. M. (2004). Opportunities, race, and urban location: The influence of John Kain. *Journal of Urban Economics, 56,* 70–79.

Glaeser, E. L., & Kahn, M. E. (2003). *Sprawl and urban growth* (NBER Working Paper No. 9733). Cambridge, MA: National Bureau of Economic Research.

Glaeser, E. L., Kallal, H. D., Scheinkman, J. A., & Shleifer, A. (1992). Growth in cities. *Journal of Political Economy, 100,* 1126–1152.

Gyourko, J., Linneman, P., & Wachter, S. (1999). Analyzing the relationships among race, wealth, and home ownership in America. *Journal of Housing Economics, 8,* 63–89.

Helsley, R., & Sullivan, A. (1991). Urban subcenter formation. *Regional Science and Urban Economics, 21*(2), 255–275.

Henderson, J. V. (1974). The sizes and types of cities. *American Economic Review, 64,* 640–656.

Henderson, J. V. (1986). Efficiency of resource usage and city size. *Journal of Urban Economics, 19,* 47–70.

Henderson, J. V. (2003). Marshall's scale economies. *Journal of Urban Economics, 53,* 1–28.

Kain, J. (1968). Housing segregation, negro employment and metropolitan decentralization. *Quarterly Journal of Economics, 82,* 175–197.

Krugman, P. R. (1991). *Geography and trade.* Cambridge: MIT Press.

Lösch, A. (1940). *The economics of location.* New Haven, CT: Yale University Press.

Marshall, A. (1920). *Principles of economics.* London: Macmillan.

McDonald, J. F., & McMillen, D. P. (2007). *Urban economics and real estate: Theory and policy.* Malden, MA: Blackwell.

McMillen, D. P., & McDonald, J. F. (1998). Suburban subcenters and employment density in metropolitan Chicago. *Journal of Urban Economics, 43,* 157–180.

McMillen, D. P., & Smith, S. C. (2003). The number of subcenters in large urban areas. *Journal of Urban Economics, 53,* 321–338.

Mills, E. S. (1967). An aggregative model of resource allocation in a metropolitan area. *American Economic Review, 57,* 197–210.

Mills, E. S. (1972). *Studies in the structure of the urban economy.* Baltimore: Johns Hopkins University Press.

Mills, E. S., & Hamilton, B. W. (1989). *Urban economics* (4th ed.). Glenview, IL: Scott, Foresman.

Mills, E. S., & Lubuele, L. S. (1997). Inner cities. *Journal of Economic Literature, 35,* 727–756.

Munnell, A. H., Tootell, G. E. B., Browne, L. E., & McEneaney, J. (1996). Mortgage lending in Boston: Interpreting HMDA data. *American Economic Review, 86,* 25–53.

Muth, R. (1969). *Cities and housing.* Chicago: University of Chicago Press.

O'Sullivan, A. (2009). *Urban economics.* Boston: McGraw-Hill.

Richardson, H. W. (1979). *Regional economics.* Urbana: University of Illinois Press.

Rosenthal, S. S., & Strange, W. C. (2001). The determinants of agglomeration. *Journal of Urban Economics, 50,* 191–229.

Rosenthal, S. S., & Strange, W. C. (2003). Geography, industrial organization and agglomeration. *Review of Economics and Statistics, 85,* 377–393.

Rosenthal, S. S., & Strange, W. C. (2004). Evidence on the nature and sources of agglomeration economies. In J. V. Henderson & J. F. Thisse (Eds.), *Handbook of urban and regional economics* (Vol. 4, pp. 2119–2171). Amsterdam: Elsevier North-Holland.

Rosenthal, S. S., & Strange, W. C. (2006). The micro-empirics of agglomeration economies. In R. J. Arnott & D. P. McMillen (Eds.), *A companion to urban economics* (pp. 7–23). Malden, MA: Blackwell.

Ross, S. L. (1998). Racial differences in residential and job mobility: Evidence concerning the spatial mismatch hypothesis. *Journal of Urban Economics, 43,* 112–135.

Ross, S. L., Turner, M. A., Godfrey, E., & Smith, R. R. (2008). Mortgage lending in Chicago and Los Angeles: A paired testing study of the pre-application process. *Journal of Urban Economics, 63,* 902–919.

Ross, S. L., & Yinger, J. (2002). *The color of credit: Mortgage discrimination, research methodology, and fair-lending enforcement.* Cambridge: MIT Press.

Sirmans, G., MacPherson, D. A., & Zietz, E. (2005). The composition of hedonic pricing models. *Journal of Real Estate Literature, 13,* 3–43.

Small, K. A., & Song, S. (1994). Population and employment densities: Structure and change. *Journal of Urban Economics, 36,* 292–313.

Tiebout, C. (1956). A pure theory of local expenditures. *Journal of Political Economy, 64,* 416–424.

Turner, M. A., & Ross, S. L. (2005). How racial discrimination affects the search for housing. In X. Briggs (Ed.), *The geography of opportunity: Race and housing choice in metropolitan America* (pp. 81–100). Washington, DC: Brookings Institution.

Turner, M. A., Ross, S. L., Galster, G. C., & Yinger, J. (2002). *Discrimination in metropolitan housing markets: National results from phase 1 of HDS 2000.* Washington, DC: Department of Housing and Urban Development.

von Thunen, J. H. (1966). *The isolated state* (P. Hall, Ed., & C. M. Wartenberg, Trans.). Oxford, NY: Pergamon Press. (Original work published 1826)

Wachter, S. M., & Megbolugbe, I. F. (1992). Racial and ethnic disparities in homeownership. *Housing Policy Debate, 3,* 333–370.

Yezer, A. M. (2006). Discrimination in mortgage lending. In R. J. Arnott & D. P. McMillen (Eds.), *A companion to urban economics* (pp. 197–210). Malden, MA: Blackwell.

Yinger, J. (1995). *Closed doors, opportunities lost: The continuing costs of housing discrimination.* New York: Russell Sage.

66

Economics of Gambling

Douglas M. Walker

College of Charleston

Gambling refers to placing something of value at risk on the outcome of an uncertain event. Often, it is money being put at risk (in a bet), and the event can be anything: a flip of a coin, a football game, a roll of the dice, a poker hand, a lottery, or a horse or greyhound race. Games of chance can be divided into skilled and unskilled, the distinction being dependent on the extent to which random chance determines the outcome of the wager. In coin tosses, slot machines, and lotteries, for example, the outcomes are based entirely on random luck; the behavior of the bettor has no impact on the outcome. Games of skill, on the other hand, are those where the decisions and actions of the bettor can impact the results. These types of games would include poker and blackjack, for example.

There are a number of interesting policy and economic issues surrounding different forms of gambling, and this chapter introduces many of these, with a focus on gambling in the United States. Since legal gambling is a relatively recent phenomenon, especially in the case of casino gambling outside Nevada, readers can find many other interesting questions that have yet to be addressed by economic researchers. One reason that gambling represents an interesting case study is that it is almost always subject to strict government regulation. Throughout much of the twentieth century, most forms of gambling were banned by most state governments. Gambling has often been seen by many as an unsavory or immoral activity. The reversing of these bans is a relatively recent phenomenon, and with most states having some form of legalized gambling, the so-called moral opposition to gambling has largely subsided. The result is an enormous expansion in legalized gambling industries in the United States. Indeed, as of 2008, approximately 38 states had lotteries, 40 had horse racing, 17 had greyhound racing, 12 had commercial casinos, and 29 had tribal casinos (American Gaming Association, 2008; Walker & Jackson, 2008). The growth of legalized gambling, led recently by casinos, has increased significantly worldwide. The economic downturn that began in 2007, however, has hit the gambling industry very hard.

The most interesting gambling sectors for economists are lotteries and casinos, although Internet gambling has seen a dramatic increase in popularity over recent years, and recent legal roadblocks have brought this type of gambling into the spotlight. Although pari-mutuels (e.g., greyhound racing and horse racing) have a longer history in the United States, these industries are not as large as the casino industry and contribute much less to state governments than lotteries or casinos do, so this chapter does not focus on pari-mutuel betting.

Like other service industries, the gambling sector can be expected to have a variety of impacts on local and regional economies. In the next section, this chapter discusses theoretical issues surrounding the economic effects of gambling, as well as the limited empirical evidence that is available. Next is a discussion of policy issues that can be informed by economic research and suggestions for future research topics. The focus of this chapter is on casinos primarily and lotteries secondarily; this is because they are the highest volume industries and have been the focus of most of the economic research in the gambling literature. Readers who are interested in smaller gambling sectors, such as greyhound racing, will find that many of the issues discussed in this chapter are directly applicable to those other sectors. Overall, the emphasis in this chapter is outlining what is currently understood among gambling researchers. Since this is still a relatively young area in economic research, with only a handful of individuals focusing on gambling, there is still very little empirical evidence on the economics of gambling.

What makes the gambling sector unique is that it must be specifically legalized by state governments. Unlike other everyday goods and services that anyone is free to produce and sell, state governments determine the types of gambling that can be offered, the sizes of the venues, who may offer them, and the taxes that will be levied.

Economic Impacts of Gambling

This chapter first addresses the benefits that are usually cited as reasons to adopt legal gambling. These effects include government revenues, which is the primary argument for lotteries and a major one for casinos; employment; consumer variety benefits; and complementary industry effects. Then this chapter discusses some of the potential negative impacts of legal gambling. These include regressivity of taxes, problem gambling, and a substitution effect with other industries. The discussion in this section includes an outline of theoretical issues, as well as a brief description of the available empirical evidence.

Benefits

Consumer Benefits

As with other industries, one of the major benefits of the gambling sector is that it results in increased mutually beneficial transactions. That is, since both the buyer and seller of the product, in this case a lottery ticket or a casino game, receive benefits from their transaction, generally there is an increase in the overall well-being in society. Such transactions are the source of economic growth, since both parties are enriched by them. One need not emphasize the benefits to the seller (i.e., the casino owner or the state government offering the lottery), because the profits earned by the industries are quite visible, and the fact that the sellers earn profits is not unique to the gambling industry.

Some people find it surprising that the consumers also benefit from gambling, even if they do not win. To understand this, it is necessary to discuss in more detail the nature of consumer transactions in a free market. Gambling is similar to other goods and services in that something of value is exchanged for money. For example, when someone purchases a $3 box of cereal from the grocery store, the grocery store prefers the $3 to the box of cereal—if the posted price is $3, then it means the store would rather have the $3 than the box of cereal. The cereal cost the store less than $3, and the difference is the store's profit. On the consumer side of the transaction, the benefits are slightly more difficult to see. Generally, consumers' willingness to pay must be at least as high as the market price for the consumer to be willing to buy the product. In the case of the cereal, the shopper will buy the cereal only if he or she believes the cereal will yield at least

$3 worth of benefits. For a consumer who really enjoys this particular brand of cereal, the expected benefit might be $10. In this case, the consumer receives a profit of $7, which is the difference between the value of the cereal to the consumer, or his or her willingness to pay ($10) and the price ($3). As shown in this example, both the buyer and seller receive a profit from the transaction. In economics, the seller's profit is referred to as *producers surplus,* while the benefit to the consumer is called *consumers surplus.*

Now turning to gambling as a service, one can see that transactions for gambling services are similar to that for the box of cereal. In the case of a lottery ticket, the price is $1. The state that sells the lottery ticket will, on average, return about 50¢ of each dollar to ticket buyers in the form of prizes and jackpots (Garrett, 2001). The remaining 50¢ is kept by the state to cover the costs of administering the lottery, with the remainder being kept as revenue for the state government to spend as it sees fit. (The costs section discusses lottery ticket revenues by the state in more detail.) The consumer pays $1 for the lottery ticket. The expected value of each ticket is around 50¢. That is, on average, the customer can expect to receive a 50% return on each dollar spent on the lottery. This is perhaps the worst bet of any legal form of gambling, in terms of the expected value. Aside from that, the odds against winning the jackpot are astronomical. Why, then, would anyone buy a lottery ticket? The reason is that the customers are not simply buying a return on their purchase prices. What are the benefits to lottery ticket buyers? Quite simply, enjoyment or entertainment. Many people find it entertaining and exciting to play the lottery. They enjoy the anticipation of seeing the winning numbers. They enjoy imagining what they would do if they won $200 million. Different people will value this experience differently.

Gambling at a casino is conceptually similar to the lottery. Almost all of the bets available in U.S. casinos have negative expected values. The casino makes its money by paying less than the true odds on winning bets. Typically the house edge is not that great, ranging from 1% to 15%, depending on the game. If a blackjack player bets and plays smart, the house edge is less than 5%. This means that for every $100 bet, the player should expect to lose less than $5. For slot machines, the house edge is higher, usually around 10%. As with lottery tickets, casino bets have negative expected value. The fact that millions of people go to casinos and play the games shows that they must receive some benefits from the experience. As with playing the lottery, casinos can be entertaining and fun. Gambling at a casino is also a more social experience than playing the lottery. The point here is many people enjoy the activity of gambling, and the benefits they receive from the activity (entertainment, excitement, etc.) apparently outweigh the price they pay (the house edge or the revenue from the lottery). This is similar to going to see a football game: Spectators expect to enjoy the experience enough to make it worth the price of the football ticket. Unfortunately, it is extremely difficult to estimate the amount of consumer benefits from gambling.

It might seem unnecessary to take such effort to explain why gambling might be beneficial for consumers. Surprisingly enough, the consumer benefit of legalized gambling is rarely cited as one of the benefits to support the legalization or expansion of gambling. Yet there is little doubt that consumer benefits are the largest benefit to be gained from having legal gambling (Walker, 2007b, p. 622). There is any number of reasons that may explain this common oversight. It may be that since politicians legalize gambling with their sights on government revenue, they are not so concerned with consumer benefits. It may also be due in part to the fact that a small percentage of consumers develop a gambling problem (i.e., addiction). The problems faced by these individuals may overshadow the benefits that accrue to the vast majority of gamblers who do not have a problem with the activity.

Empirical evidence on the consumer benefits from gambling is astonishingly rare. Several studies have been performed in a few countries, such as Australia (Australian Productivity Commission, 1999) and the United Kingdom (Crane, 2006), but no really comprehensive empirical studies have been performed in the United States to date. Some researchers have at least been attempting to keep the consumer benefits issue in the debate over gambling, but this benefit often gets lost in all the talk about tax benefits, employment, and the social costs of gambling.

Government Revenues

By far, the most obvious and commonly cited potential benefit from legalized gambling is revenue to the government. As discussed previously, the revenues from state lotteries can be substantial. Similarly, casinos can contribute a large amount of money to state government coffers. The government revenues from gambling are a strong argument for lotteries and casinos. However, the government revenue is one of the only arguments for the lottery. Casinos, as discussed in a subsequent section, may provide other economic benefits to a state that legalizes them.

Unfortunately, the issue of tax revenues it not as simple as it might first seem. Lottery revenues, for example, are often designated for supporting education. In states such as Georgia and South Carolina, lottery revenues are used to subsidize students' tuition. This additional funding for education may encourage legislators to designate less for education discretionary spending. That is, lottery-supported education may crowd out other education spending. The net impact of the lottery on education spending need not be positive. In fact, through lottery advertising, the state may imply that overall education spending has increased with the lottery, even if it has not. This would occur if nonlottery education expenditures were cut in an amount greater than the lottery-financed education spending. Unlike lotteries, tax revenues from legal casinos are not commonly designated for causes such as education. Such revenues are used to fund the oversight organization and sometimes for help for problem gamblers, with much of the tax revenue going into states' general funds.

Another interesting consideration for government revenues from legal gambling is that they represent voluntary taxes. That is, it is very easy for consumers to avoid paying these taxes; they can simply not buy lottery tickets or go to a casino. This argument is most commonly heard with the lottery, since nearly 50% of its sales represent tax revenues. One can argue that given government must raise revenue, consumers and taxpayers may prefer that the revenue be raised in ways in which it is easy to avoid paying the tax. Taxes on specific goods and services, like the lottery tax and taxes on casino gambling, fit this characteristic nicely.

As the states continue to face ever-worsening fiscal situations, they will continue to search for alternative ways of raising revenues. Raising more revenue using voluntary taxes is politically easier than cutting spending (benefits) or raising income taxes, property taxes, general sales taxes, or other unpopular taxes.

The total government revenues raised from gambling can be significant. As the American Gaming Association (AGA, 2008) reports, commercial casinos contribute a lot of money to the states, a total of $5.8 billion in the 12 states that had commercial casinos in 2007. Lotteries provide much more revenue. The North American Association of State and Provincial Lotteries (2009) reports that in fiscal year 2008, U.S. state lottery sales were about $60 billion, with net profits to the states around $18 billion. However, it is not clear that overall gambling revenue to the states more than offsets losses in other types of state revenues. The crowding-out issue has not been fully addressed by researchers. One recent empirical study on this topic suggests that gambling's net contribution—considering casinos, lotteries, greyhound racing, and horse racing—to states' budgets are relatively modest when they are positive (Walker & Jackson, in press). With respect to lotteries specifically, Thomas Garrett (2001) finds that state lotteries are designed to maximize the states' revenues from the lottery.

Employment Effects

Another potential benefit of casinos is that they may have positive impacts on local labor markets. First, if a new business opens, it increases the demand for labor, which should push average wages higher. This benefits not only casino employees, but also other workers in the region surrounding the casino. Second, since a casino requires a major capital investment to build, the labor force required to build the facilities can be significant. Even once the building phase is completed, the casino will also need a significant workforce for its everyday operations. Often, a casino represents a major employer in its region. In this case, aside from simply putting upward pressure on wages and perhaps providing jobs for the currently unemployed, the opening of a casino could increase the total number of jobs available.

Casinos may divert consumer spending away from other options, just as any new business is likely to do. But compared with many other businesses, casinos are rather labor intensive. That is, they tend to have more workers than other types of business. Consider a movie theater, for example. Given an equal number of customers, a casino would require many more employees than a movie theater would to operate effectively. The implication here is that even if there is a substitution effect whereby casinos divert spending and employment from other industries, it is certainly possible—and perhaps likely—that the casino will have a net positive impact on wages and employment. Unfortunately, the extent to which this occurs has not been addressed in much depth by economists.

Legalized gambling can have a significant impact on employment, but such cases will be limited. For lotteries and Internet gambling, for example, there is little or no employment effect. Horse and greyhound racing may have a modest employment effect but will probably not have as significant an impact as the average casino.

There have been very few econometric studies of how gambling affects employment and labor markets. Most of what has been written comes from the casino industry itself, and it amounts to a listing of employment data. The AGA (2008) provides a wealth of data and shows that commercial casinos do, in fact, hire a large number of employees. But as critics have suggested that some of those jobs may come at the expense of jobs in other industries, so the net effect of casinos on employment is unclear. One study that has addressed the issue rigorously is by Chad Cotti (2008). This paper examines casinos nationwide at a county level. Cotti finds that counties that introduce casinos tend to find increased employment is a result, but there is no measurable effect on average earnings. This is one of the first published studies to empirically address the employment effects of casinos.

Complementary Industry Benefits

A final potential benefit from legalized gambling is the effects that the industry may have on complementary industries. As with employment, this issue is probably most relevant for casinos. The most successful casino model has proven to be the destination resort. Most casinos have an attached hotel, and patrons often stay, gamble, and dine in the same hotel-casino. Everything a vacationer needs is in one place. Despite the fact that often casinos can be resorts unto themselves, casinos can often do more business by agglomerating, or situating themselves near each other. This helps explain the great success of the Las Vegas strip. Many people go to Las Vegas instead of some other casino market because they know that there is a huge variety of casino resorts in Las Vegas. This variety provides important options for visitors.

Even though competition often represents a negative for a particular business, in some cases, nearby competition can be beneficial.

Aside from any agglomeration effects that may benefit nearby casinos, a particular casino may also have a positive impact on other, noncasino industries. In Detroit, for example, there are three commercial casinos downtown. Casinos that draw tourists or even locals can provide business for the casinos, but visitors may also decide to patronize other area businesses. These businesses then may benefit from the casinos' existence. As discussed previously, the casino might have the opposite effect, substituting business away from other industries. Which effect is stronger is an empirical question that is going to vary by individual market conditions. As with other aspects of legalized gambling, there is scant empirical evidence on this issue. One recent paper to address this issue is by Cotti (2008). He finds that related industries see positive employment impacts and earnings spillovers from casinos. The other side of the coin (the substitution effect), however, has been studied more. Again, it is worth noting here that this issue applies mostly to casinos, less to racing, and not really at all to lotteries.

Costs

Substitution Effect

The previous discussion mentioned the possibility that casinos, in particular, may have complementary effects on neighboring businesses. On the other hand, casinos do act as a competitor to many types of business. In such cases, those industries will lose revenue and perhaps employment as the casino draws in customers. The state could in turn see a decrease in tax receipts. This substitution effect has been cited as a potential reason to avoid legalizing casinos, if the casino will cause more harm to other businesses than the benefits it creates. Consider an example in which casino revenues are taxed at the same rate that retail sales are taxed. Then, if casino spending were substituted dollar-for-dollar away from other industries, there would be no net tax effect from casinos. The same example could be applied to employment, so that the casino effect on employment would be neutral.

One might expect that as an entertainment industry, legalized gambling—whether the lottery, casinos, or horse racing—might impact different industries in different ways. This is fundamentally the case; in some cases, legalized gambling may act as a complement, and in others it is a substitute. It should be emphasized that the effects of a particular casino may be unique to that market. Simply because one sees a particular experience in one casino market does not mean that the same result would follow in another market.

Critics of casino gambling have long argued that gambling will not create new or better jobs because any jobs casinos create will be at the expense of other industries.

But it is not clear that this is the case. If employees actively seek casino jobs, it suggests that the casino job is the best opportunity available to them. However, if the casino causes other area businesses to close and those jobs disappear, then workers may have no option but to seek employment at the casino. Which case applies would depend on local economic conditions.

Regressive Tax

Vertical equity is one of the basic principles of tax theory. It says that individuals with higher income levels can generally afford to pay more in taxes and that they should be expected to pay more for fairness reasons. For this reason, many people expect the government to raise tax revenues disproportionately for higher income individuals. Such a tax is called *progressive:* The proportion of taxes paid to income rises as a person's income level rises. However, if the proportion of tax paid to income rises as income falls, economists call this a *regressive* tax. Most people see such a tax as unfairly burdening the poor. (A tax for which the proportion of tax paid to income remains constant as income changes is called a *neutral* or *flat* tax.)

As an example, if a person with $10,000 income pays $1,000 in taxes, while a person earning $100,000 income pays $8,000, then this is a regressive tax: The poor person is paying 10% in taxes, while the rich person is paying only 8%. If the rich person were paying $10,000 in taxes, one would call this a flat tax, and if he or she were paying $12,000, for example, it would be a progressive tax. (Often *regressive* and *progressive* are terms applied to marginal tax rates, but this chapter is ignoring those for simplicity.)

Lotteries gained popularity with the states following New Hampshire's legalization of them back in 1964. Lotteries in the various states have raised an enormous amount of revenue for state governments. However, questions have arisen over who bears the burden of these taxes. If poor people buy a disproportionate share of the lottery tickets, then they will bear a disproportionate share of the taxes raised by the state-sponsored lottery.

One of the main areas of debate over lotteries is whether the lottery represents a regressive tax. Evidence has shown that poor people do, in fact, spend a larger share of their incomes on lottery tickets than wealthier individuals do. The lottery is sometimes referred to as a tax on people who are poor or bad at math. The first part—the poor—is due to the fact that poor individuals spend a disproportionate amount of their incomes on the lottery than relatively rich people. The second part—bad at math—is referring to the fact that the lottery is by far one of the worst legal bets available anywhere. Casino games, pari-mutuel betting, and even poker all carry higher expected values, in general, than playing the lottery. Thus, the lottery may prey on those who are unaware of the odds against them—people who are bad at math. The general consensus is that lotteries do represent a regressive tax. This issue has not been studied for casinos or other forms of gambling, however. The issue has surfaced for casinos, but

it has not been analyzed. The regressivity issue has not really been a concern among researchers with respect to other forms of gambling.

One could argue that if state governments or voters were concerned about placing a disproportionate tax burden on poor people, this effect could be offset if the revenue raised were spent on helping those individuals who paid the tax. However, in many states, the lottery revenue is earmarked for subsidizing college students' educations. College students usually come from families with above average income. So even considering how the lottery revenue is spent, the lottery is generally believed to be regressive.

One issue to emphasize, however, is that the lottery tax is voluntary. That is, if poor people—or anyone else—would prefer not to pay the tax, they can simply not buy lottery tickets. According to this argument, then, the tax burden of lottery and casino taxes may not be a big concern. Of course, proponents of this argument might be sympathetic with the plight of the poor, and they might even believe that poor people would be better off if they spent their money on other goods and services, rather than on lottery tickets.

Problem Gambling

Consumer theory in economics suggests that individuals are generally best off when they are sovereign and have freedom to choose how to spend their money. The economics of consumer behavior is based on individuals attempting to maximize their utility or benefits from consumption, subject to some monetary budget that they can spend on goods and services. Given that consumers see decreasing marginal utility from consumption, then their optimal or utility-maximizing bundle of goods and services is that for which $MU_a/P_a = MU_b/P_b = \ldots = MU_z/P_z$, for all the z goods that they have the option of buying. Basically, this equation implies that consumers should spend each dollar on that good or service that will yield the most utility. Then when all the money is spent, they will have maximized utility. Theoretically, then, if the consumer has always chosen the best item to purchase, then the price-adjusted marginal utility for all items should be equal. Otherwise, the consumer could have purchased less of some goods (with relatively low MU/P) and more of others (with higher MU/P), resulting in a higher total utility. This behavior describes the typical consumer exhibiting rational behavior as it is taught in most intermediate microeconomics textbooks. In essence, the theory simply suggests that individuals make wise consumption choices based on prices and their estimates of potential benefits and costs from consumption. But perhaps gambling is different, or more precisely, perhaps some people behave differently when they gamble, compared with their behavior toward most other types of goods.

Psychologists, sociologists, and medical researchers have been studying gambling behavior, and over the past 20 years, the understanding of gambling problems has advanced greatly. Just as some individuals may develop addictions to alcohol or drugs, the same can happen with gambling. That is, some people may become so-called problem gamblers. (There is actually a wide range of different severity of gambling problems, but the discussion here will not distinguish among them.) This behavioral disorder is similar to alcoholism or drug addiction. It is characterized by gambling too much—to such an extent that careers, relationships, and families are significantly harmed by the behavior or its effects. It is fairly easy to imagine how a person spending all of his or her time and money gambling would cause other problems in life. The American Psychiatric Association (1994) has estimated that between 1% and 3% of individuals develop gambling problems to varying degrees. As a result, these individuals sometimes engage in socially costly behavior. Some will commit crimes to get money for gambling. Others will default on debts, be less productive, or skip work. Problem gambling has even been blamed for breakups of marriages, bankruptcy, and suicide.

Estimating the costs of such effects of problem gambling is difficult at best. A first step is estimating how many people are affected by their gambling problems. Then the researcher must somehow estimate dollar values for the various negative impacts from problem gambling. This dollar value is multiplied by the estimated number of problem gamblers in order to arrive at a social cost estimate. Empirical estimates of the social costs of gambling are fraught with methodological problems, and there is an ongoing debate among researchers over how to deal with these issues (Walker, 2007b). Because of this ongoing debate and the uncertainty surrounding the social costs of gambling, it would be irresponsible to suggest that a specific cost estimate is correct. On the other hand, it is very simple to point to errors in the various social cost estimates that have been published or publicized. The youngness of this area of research is evident from the fact that social cost estimates have ranged anywhere from $800 to over $13,000 per problem gambler per year. These estimates have been derived, in many cases, from a variety of arbitrary assumptions. As a result, such empirical estimates must be taken with a grain of salt. At a state or national level, of course, if 1% of the population exhibits problem gambling behaviors, then the social costs of gambling can be significant. Simply because at this time the empirical estimates are of poor quality does not mean that the costs, unmeasurable as they seem to be, are not important and significant.

Looking Forward: Policy Implications and Future Research

As is apparent from the discussion in the previous section, the research on the economic effects of gambling is still in the early stages of development. When empirical studies have been performed, their scope has usually been limited to small markets, to very short time periods, by unreliable data, or by some combination of these flaws. Therefore, it is very difficult to argue that there is some well-established empirical truth regarding how legalized gambling will affect a particular economy. At this time, the only thing one can say with certainty is that the economic effects of gambling will vary by location and region-specific characteristics. Obviously, much more research in this area is needed. Nevertheless, the political debates surrounding the economic effects of gambling have not waited on researchers to provide insight. Politicians and voters must deal with propositions to legalize or expand gambling or to change regulations. Often, the political debate is shaped by gambling proponents and opponents, with little support from economic research.

The policy implications with respect to lotteries are of limited importance at this time. Since most states already have some type of lottery, and for the most part, the states are extremely dependent on that money, there are few, if any, changes proposed in the status of lotteries. For example, it would be extremely surprising if any state that currently has a lottery were proposing to eliminate the lottery. Rarely will government simply cut off one of its revenue sources, especially during times of fiscal crisis. It is true, of course, that there is general agreement that the lottery represents a regressive tax. Even when the expenditures of the revenue are considered, the benefits of the lottery fall disproportionately on the relatively well-to-do, while the relatively poor pay a relatively large share of the burden. Although politicians and voters may be concerned with this type of redistribution of wealth, there is little chance that much will be done to change this.

Commercial casinos are a completely different story. During the past 20 years, these have been the source of intense debate in numerous states. As mentioned previously, 12 states currently have commercial casinos. Several others are actively working on legislation to allow them or have already had voted on casinos. For example, Kansas has approved casinos but is having trouble getting them started. Kentucky and Massachusetts have both already voted down casinos, but one can expect new proposals in the coming years until casinos are eventually approved.

Perhaps one should expect to see the most debate and the strongest push to adopt commercial casinos in those states that already have flourishing tribal casinos. This is because state governments receive limited revenues from tribal casinos. Since Native American nations are sovereign, their casinos are not governed by U.S. federal law or by state laws. However, tribes are required to sign compacts with their hosting states before tribal casinos can be offered. Often, such agreements include payments to the state for its agreeing to allow casino gambling. For example, the tribal casinos in Connecticut pay 25% of the slot machine revenue to the state's government. But the state could potentially do even better for itself if it were to allow commercial casinos too. Other states that have tribal casinos are going to be tempted to introduce commercial casinos, which they would have the power to regulate and tax. This temptation is going to become even stronger as economic conditions around the country worsen. State governments are strapped for cash, and any opportunity to raise revenues will help politicians avoid even more difficult decisions.

Cost-Benefit Analysis

When states have considered the introduction of casinos, a debate surrounding cost-benefit analysis typically ensues. One of the most common tools employed by state governments in evaluating the likely effects of introducing casinos is a cost-benefit analysis (CBA). These studies may be performed to a variety of degrees of technicality, but they almost always include the same components. The benefits and costs typically cited are those discussed earlier in this chapter. The exception is consumer benefits, which are rarely mentioned in such studies, and which are often ignored by politicians. The important benefits cited are usually tax revenues and employment. The costs focus almost entirely on social costs attributable to problem gamblers. These may include theft, bankruptcy, and decreased productivity on the job, as previously discussed.

The primary goal in CBA is to produce a concise summary of how legal casinos will affect a state's budget and economy. The simplicity of these studies—that their results can be summarized in one simple number, such as a net benefit of $10 million per year or a net cost of $10 million per year—makes them particularly attractive to politicians and even to voters. Policy makers may already know whether they wish to support casinos before seeing a CBA, but still the results of a CBA give them a piece of concrete data that they can cite to support their position. As discussed previously, however, in the context of social costs and consumer benefits, many of the costs and benefits associated with gambling are difficult, if not impossible, to measure. So even though politicians do rely on these types of studies to inform their decisions, they may be better advised not to, at least until this area of research improves significantly.

Other Considerations

Although the debate over legalized gambling is often couched in terms of expected costs and benefits such as tax revenues, employment, and economic development, there are arguably more important, fundamental considerations that have been largely ignored in the debate. Obviously, it is important that voters and policy makers be aware of the potential consequences of their actions. So a good understanding of the potential costs and benefits of legalized gambling is critical. The uncertainty of monetary estimates—that some of the costs and benefits are inherently unmeasurable—necessarily makes any cost-benefit analysis arbitrary to some extent. Even if this were not the case, the more basic issues of consumer sovereignty, and the role of government in a free society should be acknowledged and contemplated.

As mentioned previously, economists generally assume that consumers make rational consumption decisions, acting in ways that they see as improving their welfare. Whether it is gambling at a casino or buying lottery tickets or football tickets, consumers expect the benefits from their consumption choices to outweigh the costs. But with gambling, there is the potential that some consumers may become addicted. The same is true of other goods and services, and numerous goods and services can be harmful if consumed in excess. Generally, in a free country, consumers are given the right to make their own choices, even if they may harm themselves. This is an important right in a free society. Yet with gambling and many other consumer goods, people's freedom is restricted. The extent to which consumer choice should be restricted is obviously debatable. But this fundamental issue receives little attention in the political debate over gambling.

Another important issue that should arguably be given additional consideration is the question of what the role of government in a free society should be. Should government restrict consumer choice for the good of consumers? Proponents of such a paternalistic role of government will point to drugs, alcohol, and other potentially dangerous goods as clear cases for which government regulation is necessary. On the other hand, staunch libertarians who view individual freedom as critically important will argue that there are many cases in which individuals may cause harm to themselves but that government cannot and should not attempt to protect everyone from their potentially bad decisions. The majority probably is more sympathetic with those who view regulation of gambling as justified. Still, a discussion of these issues should accompany policy debates. Unfortunately, gambling is seen by most as simply a tax issue.

Directions for Future Research

Despite the growth of gambling industries worldwide, there is still relatively little economic research being performed. Of the different sectors of the gambling industry, lotteries have by far received most of the research attention. The focus has been primarily on the regressivity of the lottery tax, as well as on how the revenues are spent. There appears to be a general consensus in the literature that on net, the lottery is a mechanism that transfers wealth from lower income groups to higher income groups. Despite this undesirable outcome, governments are unlikely to abandon lotteries, since they are seen as providing easy money for the cash-strapped states.

The research on pari-mutuels has focused on how greyhound racing and horse racing are affected and how they affect other industries. There has been particular interest in the United States in the effect of allowing slot machines at racetracks. Racetrack owners have argued that allowing slots at tracks, so-called racinos, help keep the tracks competitive with the growing number of casinos. Overall, the racing industry appears to be fairly stagnant. Still, some research is published on this industry regularly. But there are generally not many policy debates surrounding racing, other than whether to allow slots, so one should not expect much additional research on racing in the near future.

Internet poker has recently become the focus of significant attention since it was the target of recent legislation in the United States. Legal scholars can be expected to analyze what the effects of that law have been. As with lotteries, however, there are not many economic issues to debate with regard to Internet poker and online gambling. These appear to be mostly issues of consumer choice and regulation.

Casino gambling is by far the area in which most new research should be expected. Since casinos first spread in the United States beyond Nevada, data availability for testing the various economic effects of casino gambling has increased significantly. Among the issues that still need empirical research are the effects of casinos on state revenues, the effects of casinos on other gambling industries and other nongambling industries, the extent to which casinos in different states affect each others' revenues, the extent to which gambling availability contributes to problem gambling, the social costs of gambling (defining, measuring, and creating monetary estimates), and many more. In fact, almost any conceivable issue surrounding the economic effects of casinos would represent a significant contribution to the literature.

A handful of researchers dedicate much of their research effort on legalized gambling. As such work gets published and as policy makers look for more reliable evidence to support their policy decisions with respect to legalized gambling, one should expect more researchers to look at this fascinating industry.

Conclusion

The economics of gambling is a wide-ranging subject, but most of the interesting issues under this topic are related to lotteries, horse and greyhound racing, and casinos. In terms of their revenues and contributions to state governments and the amount of academic and political debate they have inspired, casinos and lotteries are the most significant of the gambling sectors. This chapter focuses on those two industries, primarily.

Lotteries are important revenue sources for many states. Politicians like the lottery because it is a source of revenue, without which they might be forced to raise other taxes, cut spending, or some combination of both of those unpopular options. Despite the political attractiveness of lotteries, there has been some controversy in the economics literature over the extent to which lotteries raise their revenues at the expense of poor people. Empirical studies have confirmed that even considering how the states' lottery revenues are spent (e.g., many states use the revenues to subsidize college students' tuition), the lottery effectively transfers wealth from lower income to higher income individuals. Even considering this negative aspect of lotteries, there has been little push by voters or politicians to do away with lotteries. Of all the gambling sectors, economists' understanding of the effects of this one is the greatest. The lottery has been subject to numerous studies. There have not been too many new issues that have required the attention of researchers.

Casinos are receiving growing attention from researchers, but there is much work to be done. Casinos are the subject of intense political and academic debate, since many constituents have a strong interest in the outcomes of the debates. Among the issues that have been examined with respect to casinos are how casinos affect other industries within particular states, the effects casinos have on state-level employment and wages, and the net change in state revenues resulting from the introduction of casinos. Yet there are many issues for which empirical evidence simply does not exist. Since casinos began to spread across the United States in 1989, economists now have much more data on casinos and their effects. This will make empirical analysis possible. It is to be hoped that more researchers will become interested in the industry.

The literature on the economics of gambling focuses mainly on economic development effects of introducing casinos, for example. These benefits must be viewed alongside the potential social costs that may also come with gambling. Each jurisdiction's experience with legal gambling is likely different. Unfortunately, there has not been much empirical analysis of the economic effects of gambling. Even the relatively simple cost-benefit analyses that have been performed are potentially fraught with measurement errors. Gambling research is still young and is not very reliable yet. This suggests that researchers need to examine individual markets as well as more general relationships between gambling industries and other variables. There is much work to be done. The gambling industry is one that has been largely ignored by researchers. It is to be hoped that this is starting to change as the industry continues to grow.

References and Further Readings

American Gaming Association. (2008). *State of the states: 2008.* Washington, DC: Author. Retrieved from http://www.americangaming.org/assets/files/aga_2008_sos.pdf

American Psychiatric Association. (1994). *Diagnostic and statistical manual of mental disorders* (4th ed.). Washington, DC: Author.

Australian Productivity Commission. (1999). *Australia's gambling industries* (Report No. 10). Canberra, Australia: AusInfo.

Becker, G. S., & Murphy, K. M. (1988). A theory of rational addiction. *Journal of Political Economy, 96,* 675–700.

Clotfelter, C. T., & Cook, P. J. (1991). *Selling hope: State lotteries in America.* Cambridge, MA: Harvard University Press.

Collins, P. (2003). *Gambling and the public interest.* Westport, CT: Praeger.

Coryn, T., Fijnaut, C., & Littler, A. (Eds.). (2008). *Economic aspects of gambling regulation: EU and US perspectives.* Boston: Martinus Nijhoff.

Cotti, C. (2008). The effect of casinos on local labor markets: A county level analysis. *Journal of Gambling Business and Economics, 2,* 17–41.

Crane, Y. (2006). *New casinos in the United Kingdom: Costs, benefits and other considerations.* Unpublished doctoral dissertation, University of Salford—UK.

Eadington, W. R. (1999). The economics of casino gambling. *Journal of Economic Perspectives, 13,* 173–192.

Friedman, M., & Savage, L. J. (1948). The utility analysis of choices involving risk. *Journal of Political Economy, 61,* 279–304.

Garrett, T. (2001). The leviathan lottery? Testing the revenue maximization objective of state lotteries as evidence for leviathan. *Public Choice, 109,* 101–117.

Goodman, R. (1995). *The luck business.* New York: Free Press.

Grinols, E. L. (2004). *Gambling in America: Costs and benefits.* New York: Cambridge University Press.

Jackson, J. D., Saurman, D. S., & Shughart, W. F. (1994). Instant winners: Legal change in transition and the diffusion of state lotteries. *Public Choice, 80,* 245–263.

Kearney, M. S. (2005). State lotteries and consumer behavior. *Journal of Public Economics, 89,* 2269–2299.

McGowan, R. A. (2001). *Government and the transformation of the gaming industry.* Northampton, MA: Edward Elgar.

Morse, E. A., & Goss, E. P. (2007). *Governing fortune: Casino gambling in America.* Ann Arbor: University of Michigan Press.

National Gambling Impact Study Commission. (1999). *Final report.* Retrieved January 8, 2009, from http://govinfo.library.unt.edu/ngisc/index.html

National Opinion Research Center. (1999). *Gambling impact and behavior study: Report to the National Gambling Impact Study Commission.* Available at http://cloud9.norc.uchicago.edu/dlib/ngis.htm

National Research Council. (1999). *Pathological gambling: A critical review.* Washington, DC: National Academic Press.

North American Association of State and Provincial Lotteries. (2009). *Sales and profits.* Available at http://www.naspl.org

Smith, G., Hodgins, D., & Williams, R. (Eds.). (2007). *Research and measurement issues in gambling studies.* New York: Academic Press.

Thalheimer, R., & Ali, M. M. (1995). The demand for parimutuel horse race wagering and attendance. *Management Science, 41,* 129–143.

Walker, D. M. (2007a). *The economics of casino gambling.* New York: Springer.

Walker, D. M. (2007b). Problems in quantifying the social costs and benefits of gambling. *American Journal of Economics and Sociology, 66,* 609–645.

Walker, D. M., & Barnett, A. H. (1999). The social costs of gambling: An economic perspective. *Journal of Gambling Studies, 15,* 181–212.

Walker, D. M., & Jackson, J. D. (1998). New goods and economic growth: Evidence from legalized gambling. *Review of Regional Studies, 28,* 47–69.

Walker, D. M., & Jackson, J. D. (2008). Do U.S. gambling industries cannibalize each other? *Public Finance Review, 36,* 308–333.

Walker, D. M., & Jackson, J. D. (in press). The effect of legalized gambling on state government revenue. *Contemporary Economic Policy.*

Wynne, H. (Ed.). (2003). The socioeconomic impact of gambling: The Whistler Symposium. *Journal of Gambling Studies, 19*(2), 111–121.

67

Economics of HIV and AIDS

Roy Love

Health Economics Consultant

The economics of HIV and AIDS is a strange creature. There is no so-called economics of mumps or economics of appendicitis. It is of course associated with sex, but then so are syphilis and gonorrhea, yet there is no economics of syphilis or even an economics of sexually transmitted infections. The difference lies in not only the fact that the virus is most often transmitted through sexual intercourse, an activity intrinsic to our humanity and therefore of universal interest, but also the fact that its presence is not always obvious, the consequences if untreated are fatal within only a few years, and there is as yet no known cure. It is therefore alarming in both its mode of transmission, striking at the very heart of one of our most intimate and pleasurable activities, and its catastrophic impact at the personal level. Because it affects adults who in many cases will be key household income earners, it also has profound social implications. Its impact on labor morbidity, productivity, medical and insurance costs, and public health expenditures affects business efficiency and a number of macroeconomic variables such as savings, labor and capital productivity, and private and public borrowing, and it raises important issues of the role of the state in prevention, care, and treatment. When the behavioral aspects of the risks of infection are included, then it is clear that it is a topic of considerable interest to economists.

To say that HIV is transmitted primarily through sexual intercourse is a reflection of its most common mode of transfer. More generally, the virus is transferred from one person to another by means of one person's bodily fluids entering another's bloodstream. It has a brief survival period out of the body and cannot be transferred via normal healthy skin contact, saliva, perspiration, or mosquito bites. The most common means are through heterosexual intercourse, homosexual intercourse, intravenous drug (IVD) ingestion by infected needles, and occasionally through contaminated blood products in a hospital or clinic environment. By far, the most common of these globally is the first, with a predominance in Africa, especially southern Africa where adult prevalence rates of above 20% are common, though IVD is an increasingly important source in former eastern bloc countries of Europe, central Asia, and India. In North America and western Europe, heterosexual, homosexual, and IVD have roughly equal weight as sources of infection but collectively amount to less than 1% of the relevant adult populations.

It is useful, before proceeding to a review of economic analysis in the area, to summarize the main characteristics of the disease. Only from 4 to 6 weeks following infection, and sometimes up to about 3 months later, can the presence of the HIV virus be detected. During this period, there will be no outward symptoms apart from a brief flulike illness, but the victim will be highly infectious. There then follows a period of 5 to 7 years when the HIV virus eats away at the infected person's immune system. As this process develops, the individual becomes gradually weaker, in due course becomes highly prone to opportunistic infections such as TB and pneumonia, and if left untreated, will generally die within about 10 years. In the context of the developing world, death tends to occur sooner because of poorer general nutrition and greater environmental health hazards. For biological reasons, women are more likely to be infected than men (that is, the transfer from an infected man into the vagina is more probable than the reverse). Morbidity and mortality thus tend to follow infection after a lag of some 5 to 10 years, making for a complex epidemiological cycle.

There is no cure, but a number of drug combinations are available that when taken regularly and continuously for life will raise and keep the individual's immune system at a level such that his or her life expectancy is considerably extended, though the individual will always remain HIV positive. Often, there are side effects that entail a shift to what are termed *second line* drugs, which tend to be more expensive. There is also around a 30% probability that a child born to an infected woman will be HIV positive. Treatment through intake of antiretroviral drugs can be costly, and there are important debates on international trade in pharmaceuticals concerning the rules of the WTO regarding which patent rights may be protected and when producers of generic supplies may legitimately trade. The chapter returns to this in a subsequent section.

For economists, all this gives rise to three broad areas of interest. One is the impact of HIV and AIDS on the economy at the macro, sectoral, or individual business level. The second concerns the choices made by individuals that expose them to the risk of infection and the consequences at household level, and the third is concerned with the whole area of public response, the role of the state, and the potential impact on public expenditure and taxation. A number of other issues arise from these, including the role of the social and institutional environments, the availability and cost of the drugs on which treatment depends, and the impact of stigma. The existing literature is composed of a very large number of heterogeneous papers, from which only a small representative selection is possible here. Although there are few classics specific to HIV and AIDS, most analysis draws on mainstream theory and its classic works.

Impact on the Economy

This is a disease that principally affects sexually active adults, and to the extent that they are disabled by it, there is an impact on labor productivity and economic output. A simple list includes reduced productivity while at work through fatigue, increased absenteeism, higher than normal attrition rates and costs of recruitment, loss of skills, and time off to attend funerals, care for sick family members, and attend them in the hospital. Intergenerational effects will also appear as children in many poor communities are withdrawn from school and adult skills are not passed on (Bell, Devarajan, & Gersbach, 2004). At the macroeconomic level, these microeffects manifest themselves in reduced savings levels, reduced size of labor force (varying by sector and skill level), impact on public health expenditure, inflation due to increased business costs (group medical insurance, taxation, frequent recruitment), and possibly increased government borrowing, leading in turn to increased imports, balance of payments, and exchange rate problems. It is clear that in countries such as South Africa, Botswana, Zimbabwe, and Zambia,

where HIV prevalence rates have exceeded 20% of adults between the ages 15 and 49 for most of the twenty-first century to date, the macroeconomic impact is likely to be considerable.

The most common ways in which attempts have been made to measure the macroeconomic impact of HIV and AIDS are either by cross-country econometric estimation or by application of macroeconomic models of varying degrees of complication (for reviews, see Haacker, 2004a, and Booysen, Geldenhuys, & Marinkov, 2003). Econometric estimation takes the form of including an HIV variable among others conventionally seen as affecting economic growth, such as savings rates, private investment, and education levels of the labor force. This approach, although able to produce statistically significant results (e.g., McDonald & Roberts, 2006), is less satisfactory as an explanatory or predictive tool than macroeconomic growth models that contain behavioral equations. The simplest of the latter start from the traditional textbook Cobb-Douglas type of production function, where output is a function of capital and labor (taking a variety of mathematical forms entailing different assumptions). These use aggregate data on capital stock (by value) and labor and insert assumptions on the impact of HIV and AIDS on these input factors to estimate the effect on productivity and output, thus having two basic growth scenarios: with HIV and AIDS and without. The basic model can be extended to include several skill levels of labor and, important in the case of many developing countries, the formal and informal labor markets. The following is a simplified version of an example from an application in Botswana, a country with one of the highest rates of HIV infection in the world:

$$Y = \gamma^t E s^{\beta s} E u^{\beta u} K^{(1-\rho)},$$

where Y is output, Es and Eu represent labor supplies of skilled and unskilled labor, respectively, and K is the capital stock. The shares of output attributable to each factor are $\beta s,$ $\beta u,$ and $\rho = 1 - \beta s - \beta u$. An exogenous technological trend is represented by γ^t (Econsult, 2006; Jefferis, Kinghorn, Siphambe, & Thurlow, 2008). The authors then explore the principal ways in which HIV and AIDS are likely to affect the labor supply and the capital stock and feed this into the model. The impact on labor supply will be affected by the degree of availability of antiretroviral treatment (ART), which requires additional assumptions. Other assumptions underlie the validity of such models in representing economic behavior. They assume, for instance, that the economy responds to changes in factor prices and that markets will clear, but they also usually assume constant returns to scale and a fixed rate of factor substitution. The authors of this study on Botswana concluded that the annual growth rate of GDP at market prices from 2001 to 2021 would be 4.5% in the absence of AIDS, 2.5% with AIDS, and 3.3% with AIDS plus ART (Econsult, 2006, p. 55, Table 5.3).

An interesting extension of this approach is where the concept of health capital is introduced as an additional capital variable. McDonald and Roberts (2006), for instance, incorporate (in an augmented Solow model) technological change and labor, plus physical, education, and health capital. Health capital itself is defined in a reduced-form equation as a function of lagged per capita income, education capital, nutritional status, HIV and AIDS prevalence, and proportion of the population at risk of malaria in a cross-country analysis. Proxies for health capital (the dependent variable) are life expectancy at birth and infant mortality rate. The results of the statistical analysis for the African sample indicated that a 1% increase in the HIV prevalence rate was related to a 0.59% decrease in income per capita. For the world sample, the decrease in income per capita was 0.5%, and for the developing world sample, it was 0.8%, each case having been brought up by a suspect high rate for Brazil.

An alternative means of estimating the impact of HIV and AIDS on the macroeconomy, which attempts to deal with the more complex and more realistic situation where the economy is broken down into a number of interacting sectors, emerged during the second part of the twentieth century in the form of computable general equilibrium (CGE) models for forecasting macroeconomic outcomes. As the name indicates, these models are (or claim to be) computable and hence testable versions of general equilibrium models of an economy. That is, they are versions of mathematical models in which the macroeconomy is the product of a number of behavioral decisions by consumers and producers at the microlevel of supply and demand in individual markets. The theoretical foundations of such models are found in the work of Walras, Arrow, Debreu, and others in the early and mid-twentieth century and are reflected in a substantial literature on the conditions that determine the possibility and existence of a general equilibrium in which demand equals supply across all markets freely and simultaneously. From this body of theory and the development of increasingly powerful computer capacity, economists working in economies where there is an abundance of current and historical data have been able to evolve ever more sophisticated computable models based on this theoretical foundation.

In practice, however, the degree to which many applications do in fact adequately recognize and incorporate the variety of experience at a microeconomic level has been questioned (Booysen et al., 2003; Johnston, 2008; Mitra-Khan, 2008). The focus in most applications of specific country forecasts of macroeconomic growth rates and associated variables (for example, by the IMF and World Bank) leads unavoidably to the primacy of macroeconomic and aggregated sectoral data sources, most frequently in the form of a social accounting matrix (a matrix representation of the national accounts of a nation, indicating the flow of activities from one sector to another). Even at this level, the data demands are considerable, and for many of

the countries most affected by AIDS, the data are inadequate. Botswana is one of the better-off in this respect, and in the study referred to previously, the results of a CGE model with 26 productive sectors, 5 occupational categories, 3 regional areas, and a male–female breakdown are that the rate of growth of GDP from 2003 to 2021 would be 4.6% in the absence of AIDS, 3.0% with AIDS, and 3.4% with AIDS plus ART (Econsult, 2006, p. 101, Table 9.2).

Much of the work on applying CGE models to the macroeconomic impact of HIV and AIDS on an economy has taken place in South Africa, where the availability of data and local economic expertise, combined with levels of HIV prevalence above 20%, have stimulated much activity with the appearance of a number of such models. Some of these are demand-side driven, some are supply-side driven, and others have used a human capital approach. In a detailed review by Frederik le Roux Booysen et al. (2003) two of these (by ING Barings and the Bureau for Economic Research) are shown to forecast not only a difference in annual real growth of the South African GDP between an AIDS and no-AIDS scenario of –0.5 to –0.6 percentage points, but also a difference in predicted average annual growth in real per capita GDP of 0.9 percentage points in each model. The latter, in other words, is saying that real per capita growth in GDP is 0.9% higher in the presence of HIV and AIDS than without it. This seemingly perverse conclusion is created where the population growth rate is lower, as a result of HIV and AIDS, than growth in GDP. On the other hand, a CGE application to the Indian economy in 2006 concluded that the real GDP per capita growth rate between 2002 to 2003 and 2015 to 2016 was 6.13% with AIDS and 6.68% in the no-AIDS scenario. Real GDP itself was predicted to grow at 7.34% with AIDS, compared with 8.21% without AIDS, a difference of 0.87 percentage points (Ojha & Pradhan, 2006, Table 1). The latter is slightly higher than the corresponding figures for the growth rates with AIDS and without AIDS in South Africa, but too much should not be made of the differences since they will reflect different assumptions and specifications in the models and differences in the respective economies themselves.

Although these various models exhibit a high degree of mathematical sophistication, their output depends nevertheless on the quality of the data that is inputted. This includes the accuracy of existing measures of HIV prevalence (by which is usually meant the percentage rate of infection among adults aged between 15 and 49), which in most countries can be estimated from only a number of indicators since not all those infected will have come forward to be tested. In many developing countries, moreover, testing facilities are few and far between, and causes of death are often put down to an opportunistic disease such as TB or malaria. The most reliable figures historically have tended to come from testing of pregnant women at antenatal clinics, from which extrapolation, based on various assumptions, is made to the adult population as a whole. The introduction of mobile testing equipment has enabled more accurate prevalence rates to be gathered through house-to-house surveys, but accurate measurement still remains a problem in many countries, especially if there is a recent history of civil disorder.

Such data uncertainty also makes it difficult to forecast the epidemiological progress of the disease and hence the likely impact on the labor force, especially when possible behavioral changes in response to public-awareness-raising campaigns are taken into account. Equally uncertain is the timing of the appearance of AIDS, which will depend on the degree to which ART is likely to be available in 10 to 20 years' time, its adherence rates, and the likely costs to the public health services. There is also in many countries a relative absence of reliable and relevant microeconomic information, such as the effect of HIV and AIDS on labor morbidity and productivity, for the purposes of the macroeconomic models. Will labor productivity be reduced by 20%, 30%, or even 50% by the HIV epidemic in certain countries? Assumptions very often have to be made on the basis of very little empirical evidence, and conclusions must be tested for their sensitivity to different assumed values.

The accuracy of the forecasts of such models on the macroeconomic impact of HIV and AIDS has also been questioned on the grounds that the division of labor in many countries is heavily genderized and that the impact at household level differs depending on whether an adult man or an adult woman (and in either case, a household head) is hit by AIDS. Evidence suggests that a higher proportion of female nonagricultural workers in sub-Saharan Africa are in the informal sector than the corresponding figure for men, and thus, that to the extent that women tend be more susceptible to HIV, the impact on the informal sector (which is substantial in many developing countries) will be understated by models that do not recognize the gendered segmentation of the labor market. On the other hand, where the burden of maintaining household production falls on women, their productivity is likely to increase, and hence, the negative impact will tend to be overstated (Johnston, 2008). This example illustrates the importance of understanding institutional and cultural constraints at microlevel.

Moreover, in addition to these obvious direct monetary costs of an epidemic, including both internal and external, there are welfare losses that are less easily measurable. For an individual infected by HIV who doesn't receive treatment, there will be not only a loss of income earning ability but also the loss of years of life and quality of remaining years. Nicholas Crafts and Markus Haacker (2004) illustrate this in a standard utility curve diagram in which expected lifetime utility is a function of annual income and life expectancy. The effect of HIV infection is to move the individual to a lower utility curve, at a point where both income and life expectancy are lower than before. Thus, the fall in income alone does not capture the

total welfare loss to the infected individual. The authors then develop this model algebraically and use estimates of the value of a statistical life (VSL) to estimate the welfare effect of increased mortality across a sample of AIDS-affected countries. The VSL is a concept that measures the value of a variation in the risk of death and has been frequently estimated by surveys on individual willingness to pay for a given reduction in that risk. Given some qualifications regarding the paucity of data to estimate VSL in many developing countries, the authors show that the total welfare loss to countries such as South Africa, Zambia, and Botswana could range from 67% to 93% of each country's GDP (Crafts & Haacker, 2004, Table 6.2). Other theoretical work on welfare includes highly mathematical models (such as overlapping generations models) on the optimum control problem of social planners as they allocate limited resources in an economy to control an HIV epidemic at the cost of reduced levels of consumption (Shorish, 2007).

Choices and Behavior of Individuals

As the discussion in the previous section indicated, any model of general equilibrium, or one that explicitly recognizes the links between consumers and producers at the microeconomic level and their aggregate impact in macroeconomic terms, must begin with assumptions about microlevel behavior. The common theoretical benchmark of a perfectly competitive equilibrium depends on a number of structural axioms, such as each consumer and producer having perfect knowledge, being a price taker, and striving to maximize either utility (satisfaction) or profits; diminishing marginal utility and diminishing marginal rates of substitution between goods demanded by the consumer and between factors of production used by the producer prevail (that is, indifference curves and isoquants are concave and production functions are convex); resources being perfectly mobile; and transaction costs being zero. Many if not most of these require modification to reflect real-life situations. The sort of rational individual they imply is traditionally referred to in the literature as *homo economicus*, or economic man, an expression criticized by many feminist economists as much for its conceptual roots as for its terminology.

The relevance of this to individual behavior in the context of HIV and AIDS may not be immediately obvious, but a moment's reflection shows that the sexual relationship is one in which each person concerned is making a choice between alternatives that have a number of possible outcomes. One set of outcomes in particular may affect the individual's health and hence future lifetime income. A common starting point for analysis at this microlevel is provided by human capital models in which individuals invest in education and health in order to enhance their future stock of health capital (and hence income earning opportunities) and the general quality of their own lives and those of partners and near relatives. In doing so, they are forced to make choices between work and leisure, between activities that improve health or that have the potential to reduce it, and between more medical insurance and reduced current consumption and vice versa. These all lend themselves to traditional analysis of utility maximization, duly time discounted and adjusted for uncertainty, and many models of this type derive from original work by Michael Grossman (see Folland, Goodman, & Stano, 2007, for a summary). In the case of HIV, uncertainty takes the form of ignorance about a partner's HIV status, of the probability that they may be seropositive, and of the risk of becoming infected through a single act of intercourse. Unless the partner is in an advanced stage of AIDS, it is impossible to tell visually if he or she is infected, and hence, the exchange takes place in a context of incomplete information. In economic welfare terms, and somewhat unromantically and at its simplest, mutually agreed sexual intercourse involves an exchange of access to the most intimate parts of one's body in order to achieve an anticipated sensual satisfaction, whether or not money is present, and as such has the potential to be Pareto improving, except for the fact that complete information is absent in one or both of the parties to the exchange (Gaffeo, 2003).

Various mathematical models of microlevel behavior have been proposed and typically consider the numbers of people (or an individual) uninfected at the beginning of a period, the probability of becoming infected in each act of intercourse with an infected person, the number of partners during the period (though not always whether they are sequential or overlapping), and the probability that any one partner is infected. In one version, the trade-off then faced by an individual is the current benefit from more sexual activity and partners versus the costs involved if he or she becomes infected, where the infection is irreversible (Auld, 2003). In this example, the author predicts that where an epidemic is expected to get worse, certain individuals may actually increase their risky sexual activity, with the obvious policy implication that it may not be wise for governments to publicize the worst-case scenario as a means of reducing risky behavior. Another example constructs a lifetime model of utility from sex that takes account of the risks of infection and the relative pleasures from risky versus nonrisky sex, summed and discounted over an expected lifetime, from which the extent of the epidemic is determined significantly by the sensual difference between sex with or without condoms (corresponding to non-HIV risk and HIV risk) (Levy, 2002).

Underlying the development of such models is the interesting area of apparent dissonance between the predictions of rational decision making as conventionally understood in mainstream economic theory, as presumed in the human capital model, for instance, and the seemingly irrational behavior of individuals continuing to engage in HIV-risky sex despite knowing of its fatal consequences. It is unsatisfactory, however, to dismiss such deviance from the rational

model of "economic man" as irrational and hence somehow outside the range of economic analysis. There are also parallels with persistent smokers, overeaters, and dangerous drivers, for all of whom knowledge of the outcomes of their actions is not sufficient in itself to bring about a change of behavior. In the case of an epidemic such as HIV where the status of a casual partner is unlikely to be known, plus the knowledge that the virus is not transmitted in every instance of intercourse, a person may be prepared to take the chance. There is some evidence that in the face of average figures on risk, many people are risk takers in that they feel that the risk to themselves is less than the average, leading to unrealistic optimism (Gold, 2006). Many—especially young people—have confidence that it won't happen to them. In such cases, a rational calculation is still being made. This is similar to the cognitive dissonance approach of George Akerlof and William Dickens (1982) in which choice is being made between beliefs such that a favored outcome can be justified.

It is also sometimes argued that in certain developing countries where life expectancy is already low because of general poverty, the future is heavily discounted in favor of short-term pleasures, especially if AIDS is known to not take effect for several years. This may also be associated with a fatalistic outlook. Evidence on the extent of this view is scarce, however. A factor often overlooked is alcohol consumption prior to sex. Social drinking of alcohol is a widely accepted phenomenon in many societies, including those in southern Africa where the HIV prevalence rate is exceedingly high. It is well known that among the immediate effects is confused thinking, but this does not imply totally random behavior. It does tend to mean that the gratification of immediate pleasures comes to the fore and that the future consequences of one's actions are again heavily discounted. Other possibilities suggest that an individual may decide in advance to avoid a risky activity, but when the opportunity arises or if the social context encourages it, the decision is reversed, in a form of situational rationality. In consumer theoretic terms, one thus has the phenomenon of preference reversal with implications for discounting models.

Some examples of indulgence in risky sex are entirely rational in the context of the individual at the time. Thus, many women are forced into transactional sex by economic circumstances and are in a weak position to negotiate safe sex. This may also be the case of many women in regular relationships including marriage. For others of either sex, the availability of ART may lead to an increase in risky sex, as may explain the positive correlation between the availability of ART and HIV incidence in the United States in the early 2000s (Lakdawalla, Sood, & Goldman, 2006). For others, the stage of the epidemic may be an influence: If it is believed that it will get worse in the future, then this may lead to an increase in the number of partners in the present for people so inclined. Alternatively, as the chance of any one partner being infected increases, the marginal risk from an additional partner may be viewed as irrelevant.

What these examples all point to is that the challenge of changing behavior through public policy (such as campaigns for ABC: abstain, be faithful, condomize) is considerable, though there is evidence that condom use by sex workers has increased in many countries, sexually active people are having fewer partners in other countries, and young people (where they are free to do so) are delaying marriage and avoiding sex before marriage. This raises the question of the role of governments in prevention, care, and treatment of HIV and AIDS, discussed in the next section.

Public Intervention

The usual arguments made for government intervention to limit the spread of the epidemic is that there is market failure in that incomplete and asymmetric information exists between the parties and that the externalities of spreading infection are not readily internalized. In theory, in the absence of this failure, the individual would be able to take his or her own informed action to avoid infection (that is, make rational choices that maximize his or her health capital), and any third party affected would be able either to negotiate compensation or to pay for the infection not to be transmitted (the theoretical context here is that of the Coase Theorem, which is explained in most intermediate microeconomics textbooks). A simple example of the latter is the cost of a condom, and an example of the former is the higher price charged by a commercial sex worker for sex without a condom. Information shortfalls refer not only to information about the nature of the disease but also to the HIV status of each partner, as known both of themselves and of the other. The consequences of this ignorance on wider society—that is, on the expansion of the epidemic and on the externalities of public health costs, taxation, economic productivity, and diversion of public expenditure from other social welfare priorities—are likely in the case of HIV and AIDS to be substantial, from which it follows that state intervention to preempt the growth of an epidemic and minimize the extent of related externalities is likely to be socially cost effective, though this still requires justification via cost effectiveness analysis of alternative strategies.

One approach is to encourage the internalization of the externality—that is, to eliminate it by having its probability contained in the transactional arrangement between the two people directly involved in an exchange. An example is through state subsidy in the provision of condoms, commonly known as social marketing. Other examples include the wide distribution of information about HIV and AIDS, including myths leading to stigma; establishment of national AIDS agencies; and increased availability and subsidy of voluntary counseling and testing. An interesting,

if somewhat controversial, consequence of the last of these is that in a number of African societies, it is increasingly expected that couples intending to get married will undertake HIV tests (in subsidized clinics). These are examples of public intervention to internalize potential externalities. In general, such market-based compensatory negotiations, as theory suggests, between the two parties to an exchange will not be practical in instances of sexual trading, and in order to forestall or mitigate the potential impact of an epidemic on the wider community, the economy, and the public health services, there is a strong argument for state intervention.

The closest to a market solution tends to be found in treatment through private medical insurance, which in principle could cover physician fees, medication, hospital care, and loss of earnings but also contains the classic problems in the economics of insurance of adverse selection and moral hazard. The first refers to the tendency for those most likely to make a claim to seek to be members of an insurance scheme, and the second refers to the tendency of those within a scheme to maximize their claims income. In response to problems of this kind, insurance companies have adopted a variety of controlling regimes. In the case of HIV and AIDS, many require a statement of HIV status from new members and will charge a supplementary premium if the applicant is seropositive. This can have the effect, of course, of excluding those on low incomes, and in such cases, there are often publicly funded schemes that can step in. States in the United States provide HIV and AIDS treatment under the AIDS Drug Assistance Program (ADAP) for those otherwise unable to afford ARVs. To underline the point made about the social differences in the impact of HIV, it should be noted that in 2008, 59% of beneficiaries were African Americans and Hispanics and that only 35% were non-Hispanic whites (Kates, Penner, Carbaugh, Crutsinger-Perry, & Ginsburg, 2009), with an uneven geographic distribution. In most of the poorer developing countries, in which the highest rates of HIV prevalence are found, per capita disposable incomes are insufficient either to fund an adequate public health service through taxation or to purchase private health insurance. Only very few are able to afford private purchase of ART, which is often subsidized by international aid.

Market solutions are also constrained by social practices and institutions and tend to overlook relative positions of power. Of course, these can be taken as givens within which markets can be made as efficient as practically possible. However, it is not satisfactory, for instance, to take many traditional gender relationships simply as givens. Equalizing knowledge of HIV and AIDS does not equalize negotiating strengths between men and women when it comes to use of condoms or mutually agreed sex. In many societies, women also have fewer legal rights than men, fewer employment opportunities, and lower levels of education than men, all of which reduce women's scope for economic independence and hence their market power relative to men. The same may be said of people with disabilities or certain minority ethnic groups. Care should be taken in assuming that vulnerability to HIV and AIDS is a function only of poverty or inequality. Botswana has one of the highest prevalence rates in the world and yet has one of the highest per capita GDPs in Africa, with universal primary education, high levels of literacy, and an extensive public health service. The trigger for the HIV pandemic appears to have been rapid social change associated with increased urbanization and rising social aspirations.

All such factors are present in decisions by governments to intervene to mitigate the spread and impact of HIV and AIDS. These may be national governments informing and supporting their own populations out of domestic taxation, but in many cases, they are also likely to be augmented by international aid from bilateral and multilateral donors whose concern is partly humanitarian and partly motivated by a broader agenda of civil stability, promotion of democracy, sustainable economic growth, and international security, in which the HIV and AIDS pandemic is seen as a threat. Governments also respond to private lobbying, often religious, which favors certain moral positions regarding sexual relations. In this field, economic calculus is only one factor among many that politicians have to consider when formulating policy.

HIV and AIDS and Social Capital

Because of the way in which HIV affects working adults and, in many cases, heads of households, support within the immediate family is put under considerable strain, and help is often sought from members of extended families, neighbors, or the local community in general. Affected household members, in other words, draw on what has been termed their social capital for the additional resources needed to care for or treat an infected member or for help in holding the household together. Social capital is a concept that has been defined variously in the past and has been used loosely across a number of social science disciplines. A typical definition is found in the OECD Glossary of Statistical Terms (Organisation for Economic Co-operation and Development, n.d.), where it is described as "the norms and social relations embedded in the social structures of societies that enable people to co-ordinate action to achieve desired goals." It has also been defined as the "social structure which facilitates cooperative trade as an equilibrium" (Routledge & von Amsberg, 2003, p. 167) in which it is a means of reducing transaction costs in the absence of complete and enforceable contracts between individuals. As such, these definitions are also associated with a perception that social capital has an important positive role to play in the economic growth process, where in addition to the usual inputs of labor and physical (or monetized) capital, it becomes necessary to include norms of behavior, social networks, and trust as part of the informal institutional environment that supports most economic activities.

To the extent that HIV and AIDS damage social networks and trust within organizations and hence productivity, they also negatively affect economic growth (and are often implicit in the macroeconomic models discussed above). For example, additional work contracts may be required to cover absenteeism, or delays may appear in delivery of goods and services as informal personal links are weakened. In the HIV and AIDS context, social capital is also often brought into play at the microlevel, as indicated in the opening lines of the previous paragraph. A simple example of this would be an individual who helps a sick neighbor to purchase food, or it could be a group of neighbors who may help a struggling family with various farming tasks. However, the nature of HIV and AIDS is such that without ART, the pressures on the household are unremitting as time goes on, and the calls on the goodwill of extended family and neighbors eventually become resented. Another way of putting this is that the household's social capital is gradually used up. Furthermore, the stigma associated with AIDS can immediately restrict the amount of social capital available to a stricken individual or household.

It is, of course, extremely difficult to quantify social capital and hence to put a monetary value on it, and accordingly, it is common to use proxy indicators. An example is the measure of trust within communities, as gathered by the World Values Survey, for instance, which may then be taken as a dependent variable indicative of the level of social capital present in a range of countries. This can then be regressed statistically against assumed determinant independent variables including governance indexes, inequality data, and the prevalence rate of HIV and AIDS (David, 2007). The results show that a one standard deviation increase in HIV prevalence is associated with a 1% decline in the trust measurement index. And other things being equal, a country with a very high HIV prevalence rate would have a social capital level some 8% lower than one with a low rate (David). However, such studies are faced with serious methodological problems, largely deriving from the nebulousness of the concept of social capital and hence the characteristics of the dependent variable, plus problems of collinearity among the independent variables.

There are also a number of social norms, formally and informally institutionalized, that have a differentiating effect on the extent and type of social capital on which an individual can draw. In many developing countries, for instance, widows have fewer inheritance rights than men, and hence, their ability to survive independently is diminished, which may mean their reserves of social capital are both lower and used up more speedily. Orphans likewise may find that their inheritance rights are lost through family manipulation.

Economics of Antiretroviral Drugs

The availability of medication for treatment of HIV and AIDS has been a contentious area since the emergence of effective antiretroviral drugs that can control the immune deficiency created by the virus (though they cannot as yet eliminate it from the body). These drugs allow people infected by HIV to live active lives for many years, but they are demanding in terms of physician monitoring, side effects, and periodic regime changes caused by diminishing individual effectiveness. Initially, these drugs, usually now given in triple combinations, were very expensive but have come down substantially in price, especially for generic equivalents and, with international donor support, have enabled a gradual rollout in the most affected developing countries. There is no space here to go into the various regimes and their relative costs, but it is important to note that the regimes' provision and availability is part of the wider issue of drug supply and demand, in which several major economic problems are present.

The large pharmaceutical corporations that supply drugs tend also to be major researchers into the development of new drugs, but they argue that the opportunity to recover the costs of development would be compromised if competitors were able to reproduce the new drug too quickly. In more general terms, this is an issue of intellectual property rights. Since the nineteenth century, most industrialized countries have approached the problem by providing patent protection for a limited number of years, based on a patent registration scheme. Is this a case where the market has therefore failed? There are those who argue that the discoverer of a new drug has the advantage of being first in the field and that it is only because of effective political lobbying that patent laws have come into being, simply permitting excessive monopolistic profits to be made by beneficiary corporations. Evidence of this is difficult to come by and to interpret: For instance, profits higher than the industrial average will be defended as essential for the finance of research and development of new drugs. An alternative would be for more publicly funded research in universities or specialist research institutions. Underlying such proposals is the belief that medical research and its products are merit goods, having positive social externalities similar to the provision of literacy in the population, and that if left to individual choice, then the generated supply would be socially insufficient. Hence, a political decision is taken to support production either from taxation or, in the case of innovations, by patent laws. In the latter case, it will be the immediate consumer who provides the subsidy, which has some justice since the consumer is the direct user, but of course in social terms, this will tend to exclude the less well-off.

In most countries today, some form of patent protection exists, and it is relevant here to examine briefly how it is implemented and policed, especially in the context of a global economy and the ability of private sector companies in countries like India, Brazil, and China to reproduce, at considerably lower cost, many of the most advanced drugs developed by the larger, usually Western-based, pharmaceutical corporations. These nonpatent suppliers are generally referred to as *generic* producers in that they manufacture from a generic formula and sell products identical to the branded version of the original innovating company. In some cases, the original patent may have expired, but in others, this is not so. In the international market, this is clearly a threat to the ability of those companies that originally patented the drugs to receive the return they anticipated, and the problem becomes one of international trade regulation, in which the World Trade Organization (WTO) plays a central role. Following from the Uruguay Round trade talks (1986–1994) in which the Agreement on Trade-Related Aspects of Intellectual Property Rights (TRIPS) emerged, the Doha Declaration on the TRIPS Agreement and Public Health was produced at the fourth ministerial meeting in 2001, in which the conditions were laid out under which a member country would be permitted short-term acquisition of generic drugs, usually in the context of a national emergency. The agreement made specific reference to HIV and AIDS, tuberculosis, malaria, and other epidemics, and to members' right "to promote access to medicines for all" (WTO, 2001, ¶ 4). This directive contained a condition that generic production (under what is termed a *compulsory license*) should be for domestic consumption only, but this clearly left the position of those countries without production facilities out of the picture. Consequently, the general council of the WTO amended the TRIPS agreement in December 2005 to waive the domestic consumption requirement so that (the UN-defined) least developed countries would be able to import drugs from generic suppliers abroad. This amendment contains a number of conditions to prevent cheaper generic products from being reexported to nonqualifying countries. To participate, of course, each member country needs to have in place an appropriate legal structure regarding patents and drug registration.

What this account of the complexities of international trade in medical drugs, including HIV antiretrovirals, illustrates is that it has evolved into a highly regulated market, both domestically within any country and internationally, and that any analysis has to pay attention to the considerable political lobbying power of transnational pharmaceutical corporations (*big pharma*, as critics tend to refer to them) and to the competitive nature of nation states in protecting their own citizens. Insights in this area are to be gained through analysis as much by political economy and institutional economics as by traditional theory. Nevertheless, the more successful the branded producers are in protecting their markets with higher prices, the more likely, given their limited resources, are many poor countries and their citizens to look to generic suppliers one way or another to meet their demands. In such a context, another characteristic of the market in health provision—namely, asymmetric information about complex products—allows charlatans and counterfeiters to operate in the market, and there is evidence that the latter is occurring on a major international scale (see Web sites of the U.S. Food and Drug Administration and of the World Health Organization). In such an international environment, the ability of many developing countries to provide ART to all those infected by HIV is a major challenge that for the foreseeable future can be approached only with the support of international aid and technical assistance.

Conclusion

In this necessarily short paper, it has been impossible to do justice to the very many applications of economic analysis to individual country studies of the impact, at national, sectoral, and household levels, of HIV and AIDS and of the cost effectiveness of various forms of treatment and care that have emerged over the last 20 years or so. This is a very rich field with many papers produced or sponsored by multilateral agencies, international NGOs, and private or academic research institutes, not all of which subsequently appear in journals. Limited space has also led to a concentration on HIV infection by means of heterosexual activity, since this is by far the most common means of transfer in those countries worst affected. The points covered, however, have an applicability to other means of acquiring infection, principally through homosexual activity and intravenous drug use, in which for the latter, at least, there are particular problems of adherence to ART, and in all cases, including heterosexual transmission, continuing problems of societal stigma.

References and Further Readings

Akerlof, G. A., & Dickens, W. T. (1982). The economic consequences of cognitive dissonance. *American Economic Review, 72,* 3.

Auld, C. M. (2003). Choices, beliefs, and infectious disease dynamics. *Journal of Health Economics, 22,* 361–377.

Bell, C., Devarajan, S., & Gersbach, H. (2004). Thinking about the long-run economic costs of AIDS. In M. Haacker (Ed.), *The macroeconomics of HIV/AIDS* (pp. 96–133). Washington, DC: International Monetary Fund.

Booysen, F. le R., Geldenhuys, J. P., & Marinkov, M. (2003, September). *The impact of HIV/AIDS on the South African economy: A review of current evidence.* Paper presented at the TIPS/DPRU conference on the challenge of growth and poverty: The South African economy since democracy. Retrieved from http://www.tips.org.za/files/685.pdf

Canning, D. (2006). The economics of HIV/AIDS in low-income countries: The case for prevention. *Journal of Economic Perspectives, 20*(3), 121–142.

Crafts, N., & Haacker, M. (2004). Welfare implications of HIV/AIDS. In M. Haacker (Ed.), *The macroeconomics of HIV/AIDS* (pp. 182–197). Washington, DC: International Monetary Fund.

David, A. C. (2007, June). *HIV/AIDS and social capital in a cross-section of countries* (Policy Research Working Paper No. 4263). Washington, DC: World Bank.

Econsult. (2006). *The economic impact of HIV/AIDS in Botswana: Final report.* Available at http://www.unbotswana.org.bw

Folland, S., Goodman, A. C., & Stano, M. (2007). *The economics of health and health care* (5th ed.). Upper Saddle River, NJ: Prentice Hall.

Francis, A. M. (2008). The economics of sexuality: The effect of HIV/AIDS on homosexual behavior in the United States. *Journal of Health Economics, 27,* 675–689.

Gaffeo, E. (2003). The economics of HIV/AIDS: A survey. *Development Policy Review, 21*(1), 27–49.

Gold, R. S. (2006). Unrealistic optimism about becoming infected with HIV: Different causes in different populations. *International Journal of STD & AIDS, 17,* 196–199.

Haacker, M. (2004a). HIV/AIDS: The impact on the social fabric and the economy. In M. Haacker (Ed.), *The macroeconomics of HIV/AIDS* (pp. 41–94). Washington, DC: International Monetary Fund.

Haacker, M. (Ed.). (2004b). *The macroeconomics of HIV/AIDS.* Washington, DC: International Monetary Fund.

Jefferis, K., Kinghorn, A., Siphambe, H., & Thurlow, J. (2008). Macroeconomic and household-level impacts of HIV/AIDS in Botswana. *AIDS, 22,* S113–S119.

Johnston, D. (2008). Bias, not error: Assessments of the economic impact of HIV/AIDS using evidence from micro studies in sub-Saharan Africa. *Feminist Economics, 14*(4), 87–115.

Kates, J., Penner, M., Carbaugh, A., Crutsinger-Perry, B., & Ginsburg, B. (2009, April). *The AIDS drug assistance program: Findings from the National ADAP Monitoring Project annual survey.* Retrieved from http://www.kff.org/hivaids/upload/hiv040709 pres.pdf

Lakdawalla, D., Sood, N., & Goldman, D. (2006, August). HIV breakthroughs and risky sexual behavior. *Quarterly Journal of Economics, 121*(3), 1063–1102.

Levy, A. (2002). A lifetime portfolio of risky and risk-free sexual behaviour and the prevalence of AIDS. *Journal of Health Economics, 21*(6), 993–1007.

Markos, A. R. (2005). Alcohol and sexual behaviour. *International Journal of STD & AIDS, 16,* 123–127.

McDonald, S., & Roberts, J. (2006). AIDS & economic growth. *Journal of Development Economics, 80*(1), 228–250.

Mitra-Kahn, B. H. (2008). *Debunking the myths of computable general equilibrium models* (SCEPA Working Paper No. 2008-1). New York: Bernard Schwartz Center for Economic Policy Analysis.

Ojha, V. P., & Pradhan, B. K. (2006). *The macro-economic and sectoral impacts of HIV and AIDS in India: A CGE study.* New Delhi, India: United Nations Development Programme.

Organisation for Economic Co-operation and Development. (n.d.). *Glossary of statistical terms.* Retrieved from http://stats.oecd.org/glossary/search.asp

Routledge, B. R., & von Amsberg, J. (2003). Social capital and growth. *Journal of Monetary Economics, 50*(1), 167–193.

Shorish, J. (2007). *Welfare analysis of HIV/AIDS: Formulating and computing a continuous time overlapping generations policy model* (School of Economics Discussion Paper No. 0709). Manchester, UK: University of Manchester.

World Trade Organization. (2001, November). *Declaration on the TRIPS agreement and public health.* Retrieved from http://www.wto.org/english/thewto_e/minist_e/min01_e/mindecl_trips_e.pdf

68

ECONOMICS OF MIGRATION

ANITA ALVES PENA AND STEVEN J. SHULMAN

Colorado State University

The economics of migration is a sizable topic area within economics that encompasses broadly defined studies of the movement of people within and across economies. Studies of intranational, or internal, migration focus on movements within a country's borders, whereas studies of international migration (emigration and immigration) focus on movements across international boundaries. The economics of migration spans several subdisciplines within economics. Both microeconomists and macroeconomists are interested in how migration affects markets for labor, other factors of production, and output. Labor economists are particularly interested in migration as it is an important determinant of labor market outcomes such as wages and employment. Public economists and public policy makers are interested in the effects of migration on the social surplus and in the interrelationships between migration and public policy instruments. Economists studying economic development and international economics are interested in how migrations affect economic outcomes in the developing world and in the global economy broadly.

This chapter outlines the key theoretical elements of microeconomic and macroeconomic models of migration and presents empirical evidence from representative applied studies of intranational and international migration to date. Special attention is given to the debate about immigration into the United States and its consequences for both natives and immigrants.

Microeconomic Theory

Economic Benefits and Costs

In his classic article, "A Pure Theory of Local Expenditures," Charles Tiebout (1956) hypothesized that people "vote with their feet" by migrating to localities with public expenditure characteristics that best fit their personal preferences. Tiebout's model illustrates, for example, how residential decisions are related to taxation and expenditure characteristics such as local tax rates and the quality and quantity of publicly provided goods such as education and local amenities.

In microeconomic models of migration, "voting with one's feet" is generally modeled by assuming that individuals make decisions regarding remaining at a current location versus moving to a preferable location. In its simplest form, the model may be described by agents maximizing net present value of lifetime earnings and engaging in migration if the difference in lifetime earnings between a potential destination and the agent's origin is positive and greater than migration costs. Thus, agents make investments in their human capital by moving to where their economic opportunities, as measured by lifetime earnings net of migration costs, are improved (Sjaastad, 1962).

Agents in these migration models are assumed to maximize their welfare by comparing net economic benefits (benefits minus costs) at an origin and at alternative locations in a large set of potential destinations. The decision therefore is not only whether to migrate but also where to migrate if a migration is to be undertaken. Economic benefits and costs are not the same thing as financial or accounting benefits and costs. Instead, economists use surplus areas (e.g., consumer and producer surplus) to define these concepts. In addition to accounting costs, opportunity costs are included to form the cost definition, and welfare is measured relative to some status quo.

In extensions to the basic model, agents take into account factors that influence economic and psychic benefits and costs such as labor market variations, public policy and environmental attributes of various locations, and personal characteristics and circumstance. Furthermore, expected benefits and costs may differ depending on whether an individual will be migrating with or without family, legally or illegally, and so on. To complicate this further, precise values of economic benefits and costs often are unknown, and thus agents are thought to make decisions based on *expected* net benefits, instead of deterministic ones. Expected values take into account probabilities of uncertain outcomes.

If agents are assumed to be utility maximizers, then agents maximize expected utility by choosing to migrate to a destination from their set of potential destinations (which includes a stay at origin option) that maximizes expected net benefits where expected incomes and costs are mapped into utility terms. Expected net benefit to a person from making a migration is the difference between that agent's expected utility at the destination and his or her expected utility at the origin plus expected migration costs.

On the benefit side, expected income/utility may include both expected wage earnings and expected supplementary nonwage income such as public aid payments. More broadly, economists may include value of factors such as participation in public schooling and environmental amenities. Since both wage and nonwage income are expected measures, the probability of employment (and likewise the probability of receiving aid) should be included in the calculation. Agents compare these expected benefit values for each potential destination to expected utility at the origin, where again this may depend on probabilities of employment and of nonwage income as well as differences in generosities.

On the cost side, expected costs may be thought to be a function of monetary, opportunity, and psychological costs. An agent's total expected monetary cost of migration includes direct travel expenses. Opportunity costs of migrating to the United States include any foregone income at the origin and account for travel time and distance. Expected psychological costs associated with migration may include elements such as leaving family or one's homeland and may depend on travel distance and time. If a migrant intends to return to the sending location, then expected costs should represent round-trip costs. In the case of illegal migration, expected costs may include probabilities of apprehension and deportation and related costs (e.g., court costs, opportunity costs of time, and additional psychological costs) and any monetary payments to agents such as border smugglers for assistance in the trip.

All values on both benefit and cost sides may depend on a particular time of migration given varying political and economic contexts. Several locational attributes should also influence the propensity to choose one destination over another. High unemployment rates and other negative indicators of labor market conditions, for example, should be associated with decreases in the probabilities of employment at the destination and origin. Increases in average wages of similar workers and potential values received from social service programs, hospitals, and educational systems should be positively related to expected incomes. For those migrating illegally, border patrol intensity and the political economy of immigration policy may affect benefits and costs of migration. Furthermore, personal and professional networks may increase the probability that one crosses successfully and of employment at a destination. Networks also may increase the probability of receiving public aid benefits if experienced friends and family members help in the application process and may decrease both the monetary and unobserved psychological costs of crossing.

These considerations can shed light on applied questions such as the determinants of illegal immigration from Mexico into the United States. While the magnitude of illegal immigration cannot be known with certainty, it has clearly increased significantly over the past 30 years. By some estimates, the inflow of illegal immigrants has increased by a factor of five since the 1980s.

What can explain this long-term trend of increasing illegal immigration? Large wage differentials encourage illegal immigration (given limits on legal immigration) while enforcement of immigration law discourages it. These factors alone, however, cannot explain its long-term rise. One explanation is that migration is encouraged by the spread of social networks. When migrants from Mexico arrive in the United States, they are able to find friends and family from Mexico who welcome them, help them find jobs and housing, and otherwise facilitate their adaptation to the United States. Illegal immigration is thereby self-sustaining. It tends to grow over time because it spreads and deepens the social networks that facilitate it. (It is also worth noting that this growth of illegal immigration explains the increasing intensity of the controversy over it, a point we return to below.)

Macroeconomic Theory

Gravity Models

Gravity models, used in migration and trade flow literature, are used by economists to assess and predict aggregate migrant flows between pairs of locations. This is in contrast to the individual migrant decision-making models above. Gravity models borrow techniques from physics, and the applicability of a gravity model of migration depends on the relevance of the assumption that migrations of people follow laws similar to gravitational pulls. In gravity models, migration is assumed to move inversely with distance and positively with the size of an economy (squared), often measured by population size.

Modified gravity models characterize the recent literature following this technique. For example, Karemera, Oguledo, and Davis (2000) add sending and receiving country immigration regulations to the traditional gravity framework, and Lewer and Van den Berg (2008) include a measure of relative destination and sending country per capita income and show how the effects of supplementary variables on immigration to the traditional gravity model can be estimated in an augmented framework.

Applications and Empirical Evidence

Econometric discrete choice modeling, a type of multiple regression, is a common technique used by economists to quantify determinants of migration for various populations of study, and econometric selection models have been used to study the effects of migration on economic outcomes. Some of these applications will be discussed here.

Intranational Migration

Literature on the determinants of intranational migration suggests that life cycle considerations (e.g., age, education, family structure) and distance are key predictors of internal migrant flows (Greenwood, 1997). A complication to the unitary model of migration is that family units often migrate together, and therefore migration decision making may occur at the family level as opposed to the individual. Specifically, families may maximize family welfare as opposed to individual welfare with some family members suffering losses as the result of migration and others realizing offsetting gains.

In addition, locational attributes and amenities (disamenities), both environmental and those that are the result of public policy and market conditions, have been shown to attract (repel) internal migrants. Significant effort in economics literature has been made to examine the possibility of welfare migration or migration in response to differences in public aid availability and generosity across locations. McKinnish (2005, 2007), for example, in her examination of internal migration between U.S. counties, finds that having a county neighbor with lower welfare benefits increases welfare expenditures in border counties relative to interior counties. Welfare migration may occur among both those native to a country and new to it.

International Migration

The Immigration Debate in the United States

Intranational migration is rarely controversial. In contrast, international migration often arouses heated controversies and inflammatory rhetoric. That may seem odd in the context of the United States since we like to think of ourselves as a

"nation of immigrants." Why are there such passionate arguments about people who seem to like our country so much that they want to move here?

It is worth taking a moment to address this question since it puts the more technical issues in a larger, interpretive framework. The most direct answer concerns the sheer number of people who come to the United States each year. Since 2000, an average of about one million legal immigrants (Department of Homeland Security, 2008) and about 700,000 illegal immigrants (Passel & Cohn, 2008a) have entered the United States each year. About 300,000 foreigners have left the United States each year (Shrestha, 2006). Thus, net immigration has been directly increasing the U.S. population by 1.4 million persons per year. Net immigration then has indirect, subsequent effects on population growth due to immigrant fertility.

Taken together, the direct and indirect impacts of immigration on the U.S. population are startling. The Census Bureau projects that the total U.S. population will grow to 439 million by 2050, an increase of 157 million, or 56%, since 2000. To put this in concrete terms, this is equivalent to adding the entire populations of Mexico and Canada to today's (2009) population of the United States. According to Passel and Cohn (2008b), over four fifths of that growth will be due to immigrants and their descendents. Thus, immigration is dramatically increasing the number of people living in the United States.

Rapid population growth puts stress on society, on the environment, on the economy, on schools and neighborhoods, and on government. More people means more pollution, more crime, more crowding, and more need for government services. Americans take pride in their immigrant history, but they are also concerned about the impact of large-scale immigration, particularly when much of it seems to be illegal and uncontrollable. They are empathetic with immigrants, but they also are concerned about their own citizens and their own national identity. That conflict explains the intensity of the debate about U.S. immigration policy. Americans are caught between competing ideals, and neither side of the debate is obviously right.

Of all the concerns raised by mass immigration, its economic impact is perhaps the most complicated. Immigration has both good and bad effects on the economy and the workers of the host country that can be difficult to separate out. On one hand, immigration adds to labor resources and thus to the capacity for economic growth. Growth increases national income and potentially raises living standards. Immigrants "take jobs that Americans do not want" (as it is commonly said) and produce goods and services that otherwise would not be produced; that generates income for Americans as well as for immigrants. The capacity for immigration to increase the incomes of natives will be especially strong for the employers who hire the immigrants and for the more highly educated native workers whose skills complement the immigrants (in effect, the two groups establish a division of labor that benefits both). This is one basis for the claim that immigration is beneficial for the host country.

On the other hand, large-scale immigration can also harm native workers. It is a classic labor supply shock: It increases the competition for jobs and thus drives down employment and wages for native workers, especially those whose skills are most similar to those of the immigrants. Figure 68.1 illustrates a labor supply shock corresponding to large-scale immigration. In response to the shock on the labor supply side only, equilibrium labor increases from L_1 to L_2 while wages decrease from w_1 to w_2. Immigration, however, may have unpredictable effects on wages if labor demand also changes. Panel (a) of Figure 68.1 illustrates where a demand increase less than offsets the negative wage effect from increased labor supply. The final wage, w_3, is lower than the initial equilibrium wage, w_1, despite the demand increase. Panel (b) shows that the same model under different conditions, however, may yield the opposite.

Because immigrants (especially illegal immigrants) to the United States are likely to have low levels of education—one third of foreign-born persons in the United States and almost two thirds of persons born in Mexico lack a high school degree (Pew Hispanic Center, 2009)—they compete most directly with native workers who have not attended college and especially with those who have not completed high school. These native workers are likely to earn low wages and to be on the bottom of the income distribution. African Americans, Hispanic Americans, and immigrants are especially likely to fall into this category. Thus, immigration tends to be most harmful for low-wage native workers and ethnic minorities.

Of course, immigration can simultaneously increase both job competition and economic growth. Because the former tends to harm low-income natives and the latter

tends to help high-income natives, the result is an increase in inequality. In other words, immigration can have regressive effects on the income distribution of natives. The economy may grow, but the benefits of that growth flow away from the bottom and toward the top.

Because the rise in income for some natives is offset by the decline for others, the aggregate effects can wash out. These countervailing tendencies are typical of immigration. Consider the impact on productivity: Immigration can increase productivity growth if it stimulates economic activity and investment, but it can reduce productivity if the surplus of low-wage workers discourages the substitution of capital for labor. Or consider the impact on government budgets: Immigrants decrease budget deficits because they pay taxes, but they increase budget deficits because they use services. Because immigration can have contradictory effects that can cancel each other out, it may be more revealing to focus on its impact on specific groups of natives rather than on the United States as a whole.

Immigration and Job Competition

Perhaps the key issue at stake in the debate about immigration is the degree of job competition. The claim that immigrants "take jobs that Americans do not want" reflects a misunderstanding of microeconomics. The extent to which Americans want jobs (the labor-leisure trade-off) is a function of their pay. If labor supply shocks created by immigration drive down the wages in these jobs so that native workers leave them, it does not follow that Americans do not want these jobs. In the absence of immigration, wages would rise and American workers would be drawn back into them.

One way of examining this issue is to compare the occupational distribution of immigrants to natives. The

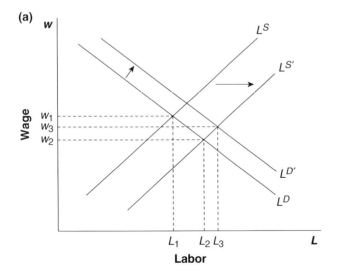
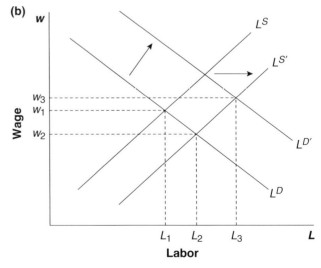

Figure 68.1   Effects of Immigration on Equilibrium Wages

NOTES: (a) Case where labor demand increase does not offset negative wage effects from increased labor supply. (b) Case where labor demand increase more than offsets negative wage effects from increased labor supply.

two show significant overlap. According to the Pew Hispanic Center (2009), fewer than 1 in 20 foreign-born Hispanics are in agricultural or related occupations. While illegal Hispanic workers are likely undercounted in these estimates, this still suggests that the common perception that most Hispanic immigrants work in the fields—the classic "jobs that Americans do not want"—is mistaken. Most Hispanic immigrants work in occupations that native workers also hold. For example, approximately 1 in 3 foreign-born Hispanics are in construction and maintenance occupations. Their occupational distribution is more skewed toward low-wage work than non-Hispanics, but there is still considerable occupational overlap, particularly with respect to low-wage jobs. This is not consistent with the notion that immigrants and natives are in separate labor markets (a difficult notion to reconcile with the high degree of mobility and fluidity in the U.S. labor market).

To the extent that the skills and occupations of immigrant and Hispanic workers overlap, the employment and wages of native workers will be depressed by competition with immigrant workers. That is the finding of a number of researchers, most notably George Borjas (2003, 2006) and Borjas and Katz (2007). These authors find that a 10% increase in the labor supply created by immigration (about equal to the increase from 1980 to 2000) depresses the wages of all native workers by about 3% and depresses the wages of native workers without a high school degree by about 8%. These percentages are economically significant, and Borjas (2003) concludes that "immigration has substantially worsened the labor market opportunities faced by many native workers" (p. 1370).

Borjas (2003) describes his results as consistent with the simple textbook model of wage determination. However, other researchers have concluded that immigration has virtually no impact on the wages of native workers. David Card (2005) shows that the wages of native high school dropouts have not declined relative to the wages of native high school graduates since 1980, as one would expect if immigration had had the most negative impact on the wages of the least educated American workers. He concludes that "the evidence that immigrants harm native opportunities is slight" (p. F300).

Card's (2005) evidence is indirect. Instead of looking at the impact of immigration on the wages of native workers without a high school degree, he looks at their wages relative to the wages of native workers with a high school degree. The finding that their relative wages have not declined is surprising given that nationally, the real hourly wage of male and female high school dropouts fell from 1990 to 2005 while it rose for all other educational groups (Mishel, Bernstein, & Shierholz, 2009).

Card (2005) speculates that native workers are not displaced by immigrants because firms grow and invest in labor-intensive technologies in response to the availability of immigrant workers. Firms may be more likely to move to cities with large immigrant populations that make it easy to hire low-wage workers. As a result, labor demand can increase and offset the immigrant-induced increase in labor supply. Panel (b) of Figure 68.1 illustrates this case. In the figure, a demand increase more than offsets the negative wage effect from increased labor supply. The final wage, w_3, is higher than the initial equilibrium wage, w_1. Of course, depending on the magnitude of the demand shift, cases in which wages remain below w_1 (but are greater than w_2) also are possible.

This argument illustrates the capacity of the economic system to mitigate the impact of shocks over time. Immigration drives down wages over the short run by boosting labor supply, but that effect dissipates over the long run due to offsetting increases in labor demand. Other long-run adjustments demonstrate the same tendency. For example, native workers who face increasing job competition from immigrants may respond by moving to places where there are fewer immigrants. That will reduce labor supply and thus the measured impact of immigration on wages in the cities that the native workers have left (by 40% to 60% according to Borjas, 2006). Also, the native workers most marginally connected to the labor force may drop out of the labor force in response to competition from immigrants (Johannsson, Weiler, & Shulman, 2003). That takes the lowest wage native workers out of the sample, thereby raising the average wage of the workers who remain (this is similar to the argument made by Butler & Heckman [1977] about the impact of welfare on average black labor force participation and wages).

It is important to note that the capacity of the economic system to adjust to shocks over the long run does not negate the losses that have occurred and accumulated over a succession of short-run states. The short-run losses continue to occur as immigrant inflows continue. These inflows tend to rise and fall with the state of the economy and the degree of enforcement of immigration law; nonetheless, they are projected to continue in large part indefinitely. If that projection proves to be true, the "short-run" losses from immigration-induced labor supply shocks will never cease even if each shock tends to diminish over time. In this sense, both Card and Borjas can be right.

Immigration, Growth, and Inequality

In the United States, immigration lowers the wages and employment of low-wage workers, but it also increases economic growth and national income. The recipients of this additional income—aside from the immigrants themselves—are the employers of the immigrants and the workers whose skills are complementary to the immigrants or who provide services to the immigrants. Since these tend to be high-skill, high-wage workers and since large employers typically have high incomes, it follows that many beneficiaries of immigration to the United States are relatively affluent.

Much of the above analysis refers to the immigration of low-skill workers. Of course, many other immigrants are highly skilled. Immigrants are almost as likely as natives to hold a bachelor's degree and are somewhat more likely to hold a graduate degree (Pew Hispanic Center, 2009). Highly skilled immigrants bring technical and entrepreneurial skills into the United States that add to productivity, innovation, and growth. One study shows that a 1% increase in the share of immigrant college graduates in the population raises patents, relative to population, by 6% (Hunt & Gauthier-Loiselle, 2008). However, high-skill immigrants can create job competition for high-skill natives, just as low-skill immigrants can create job competition for low-skill natives. Borjas (2005) estimates that a 10% immigration-induced increase in the supply of doctorates lowers the wages of comparable natives by 3%.

Immigration also affects prices, and that also should be factored into the discussion of its overall economic consequences. Although the low wages earned by the majority of immigrants can harm the workers who compete with them, this lowers the prices of the goods and services they produce. This unambiguously benefits native consumers. Cortes (2008), for example, finds that a 10% increase in the share of low-skilled immigrants in the labor force decreases the price of immigrant-intensive services (e.g., housekeeping and gardening), primarily demanded by high-income natives, by 2%. This is suggestive of surplus gains resulting from depressed prices as an additional result of immigration.

Immigration thus has a variety of both positive and negative effects on U.S. natives. Since the negative effects tend to be concentrated among low-income natives, and since the positive effects may be concentrated among high-income natives, there are two overall consequences. First, immigration may increase inequality along with other trends such as technological change, the decline in unions, international competition, and deindustrialization. The extent (and existence) of that increase in inequality is a matter of dispute, as one would expect from the corresponding dispute about the impact of immigration on the wages of low-skill native workers. Borjas, Freeman, and Katz (1997) conclude in a widely cited paper that immigration accounts for a quarter to a half of the decline in the relative wages of low-skill native workers. That would make it a significant factor in the increase in inequality between low-wage and high-wage workers. In contrast, a more recent paper by Card (2009) concludes that immigration does not significantly increase wage inequality.

Second, the gains and losses from immigration may approximately cancel out in the aggregate. This can be understood in two ways. First, the gains that accrue to affluent Americans are offset by the losses to low-income Americans; second, the benefits created by high-skill immigrants are offset by the losses created by low-skill immigrants. Consequently, the estimates of the aggregate impact of immigration are small relative to the size of the U.S. economy. The study of immigration conducted by the National Research Council (1997) concluded that immigration adds at most about 0.1% to gross domestic product (GDP).

Even that small benefit gets wiped out by the net fiscal costs imposed by immigration. Immigrants are disproportionately likely to have low incomes and large families. Thus, they have relatively high needs for social services (particularly schools) but pay relatively little in taxes. The fiscal balance is positive at the federal level because the federal government receives the Social Security taxes of immigrants but provides little in the way of services or Social Security benefits; however, it is negative at the state and local levels, substantially so in the locales most heavily affected by immigration. The negative effect outweighs the positive effect by a small amount. The study just cited showed that the current fiscal burden imposed by immigration is only about $20 per household as of the mid-1990s, but added up over all households, it amounts to an overall loss of about the same amount as immigration adds to economic growth. It therefore seems safe to conclude that the overall economic effect of immigration is approximately zero. In this sense, both sides of the immigration debate (one claiming that immigration is an economic disaster and the other claiming that immigration is an economic necessity) are wrong.

These conflicting considerations do not lend themselves to simple conclusions about the impact of immigration. Overall judgments will depend upon which group we view with most concern. For example, immigrants clearly benefit from immigration, so those who care most about the well-being of immigrants will support a more expansionist approach to immigration. Those who care most about low-income natives would support a more restrictionist approach. Those who care most about the business sector would support a more expansionist approach. Other policy combinations could arise as well. For example, those who care about both immigrants and low-income natives might support a more expansionist approach combined with government assistance to the adversely affected natives. Or those who care most about both immigrants and low-income natives might support a more restrictionist approach combined with government foreign aid to raise standards of living and reduce the incentive to emigrate from sending countries. These complicated ethical and political judgments cannot be resolved just by recourse to the economic evidence.

Immigrant Assimilation

In addition to the economic effects on U.S.-born workers, another area of debate concerns economic assimilation or whether immigrants' earnings distributions approach those of natives as time elapses within a host country. Recent empirical evidence generally does not support full economic assimilation by immigrants. Cross-sectional regressions in the early literature predicted rapid increases in immigrant earnings upon arrival in the United States. Borjas (1985), however, found that within-cohort growth is significantly smaller than previous estimates using cross-sectional techniques. In a follow-up, Borjas (1995) found evidence that increases in relative wages of immigrants after arrival in the United States are not enough to result in wages equivalent to those of like natives. Instead, immigrants earn 15% to 20% less than natives throughout most of their working lives.

There also are mixed results regarding assimilation across generations. Some authors argue that intergenerational assimilation may be faster than assimilation of migrants themselves. Card (2005), for example, argues that while immigrants themselves may not economically assimilate completely, children of immigrants will join a common earnings path with the children of natives, and thus assimilation is an intergenerational process. Therefore, intergenerational assimilation may be faster than assimilation of immigrants themselves. Smith (2003) finds that each successive generation of Hispanic men has been able to decrease the schooling gap, and this has translated into increased incomes for subsequent generations. On the other hand, some authors have argued that Mexican immigrants have slower rates of assimilation in comparison to other immigrants. Lazear (2007), for example, argues that immigrants from Mexico have performed worse and become assimilated more slowly than immigrants from other countries. He argues that this is the result of U.S. immigration policy, the large numbers of Mexican immigrants relative to other groups, and the presence of ethnic enclaves.

Immigrant Locational Choice

A number of state economic and demographic conditions and state policy instruments can be hypothesized to affect the locational distribution of immigrants. Bartel (1989) studies the locational choices of post-1964 U.S. immigrants at the city level and finds that immigrants are more geographically concentrated than natives while controlling for age and ethnicity and that education reduces the probability of geographic clustering and increases the probability of changing locations after arrival in the United States. Jaeger (2000) finds that immigrants' responsiveness to labor market and demographic conditions differs across official U.S. immigrant admission categories, including admission based on presence of U.S. relatives, refugee or asylee status, and employment or skills. Employment category immigrants, for example, are more likely to locate in areas with low unemployment rates. Other determinants of locational choice are wage levels and ethnic concentrations. A growing literature has examined how information networks affect migration decisions and outcomes conditional on arrival. Munshi (2003), for example, finds that Mexican immigrants with larger networks are more likely to be employed and to hold a higher paying nonagricultural job.

As in studies of internal migration, the possibility of welfare migration has been another theme in economic literature on the effects of international migration. If immigrants choose locations based on welfare availability and generosity, there may be fiscal consequences to certain communities. Like the literature on the effects of immigration overall, the literature on immigrant welfare migration is characterized by debates over appropriate data sources, econometric methods, and ultimate results.

Borjas (1999) presents a model of whether welfare-generous states induce those immigrants at the margin (who may have stayed home or located elsewhere in the absence of welfare) to make locational decisions based on social safety net availability. He examines whether the interstate dispersion of public service benefits influences the locational distribution of legal immigrants relative to the distribution of U.S.-born citizens. In this framework, he demonstrates that immigrant program participation rates are more sensitive to benefit-level changes than native participation rates are. Conclusions here, however, are sensitive to specification and the particular data source used. While some other authors find strongly positive, significant relationships between legal immigration flows and welfare payment levels (e.g., Buckley, 1996; Dodson, 2001), others conclude the opposite (e.g., Kaushal, 2005; Zavodny, 1999). Whether immigrants locate based on welfare generosity and availability is still a subject of academic debate within economics.

Effects on Sending Countries: Brain Drain, Remittances, and Intergenerational Effects

The effects of immigration on sending and receiving countries depend on how income distributions compare and whether immigrants come from the high or low end of the skill distribution within the sending economy (Borjas, 1987). If immigrants come from the high end of the skill distribution, then we may characterize this phenomenon as positive selection. Likewise, if immigrants come from the low end of the skill distribution, then we would refer to this as negative selection. Positive or negative selection may result from differences in the rate of return to skill across locations. If immigrants are positively selected from the sending country, then economists would describe the country as experiencing brain drain.

Recent studies have suggested positive, not negative, effects on sending countries overall. Beine, Docquier, and Rapoport (2001), for example, describe two effects of migration on human capital formation and growth in a small, open developing economy. First, migration leads to increases in the demand for education as potential migrants predict higher returns abroad, and second, brain drain occurs as people actually migrate. The net effect on the sending country depends on the relative magnitudes of these effects, and cross-sectional data for 37 developing countries suggest that the first effect may dominate the second. Stark (2004) presents similar results from a model where a positive probability of migration is welfare enhancing in that it raises the level of human capital in the sending country.

In addition to changing the skill distribution in host and sending countries, migrants may affect the cross-country income distribution by remitting portions of their income abroad to family members in the sending country. These remittances may decrease the prevalence of poverty in some locations in the sending country and therefore represent additional welfare improvements. The quantity of remittances, however, may be interrelated with the presence of brain drain. Faini (2007), for example, finds evidence that brain drain is associated with a smaller propensity to remit. Although skilled migrants may make higher wages in the second country, they are empirically found to remit less than do unskilled migrants.

Other areas of literature relating to the economics of immigration examine intergenerational effects of migration. Of particular interest, increasing research has focused on the effects of immigration on subsequent generations both in host and sending countries.

Illegal Immigration and Repeat Migration

As may be expected, research on undocumented or illegal immigration is plagued by a lack of reliable and representative data. Estimates on the aggregate size of the illegal foreign-born population generally rely on residual methodology. Passel (2006a, 2006b) estimates that 11.1 million illegal immigrants were present in the United States in March 2005. This estimate is up from 9.3 million in 2002 (Passel, 2004) and 10.3 million in 2003 (Passel, Capps, & Fix, 2005). Of this total, approximately 6.2 million (56%) were from Mexico. In terms of spatial distribution within the country, 2.5 to 2.75 million illegal immigrants resided in California, followed by Texas (1.4–1.6 million), Florida (0.8–0.95 million), New York (0.55–0.65 million), and Arizona (0.4–0.45 million). These five states account for more than 50% of the estimated total. Furthermore, some immigration streams are characterized by repeat migration where, for example, migrants work for a short period (sometimes a season) before returning to their country of origin and repeat this cycle several times. Seasonal agricultural work in the United States, for example, takes this pattern where migrants (particularly from Mexico) work a season, return to their country of origin, and then return the following year.

Evidence on whether border enforcement affects the locational distribution of illegal immigrants is mixed. Some authors conclude that border enforcement causes migrants to make several attempts to cross the border as opposed to deterring migration, that the composition of illegal migrants may respond to increases in border patrol, and that the distribution of destinations may be sensitive to border patrol intensity. Others do find a deterrence effect. Orrenius (2004), for example, considers preferred border crossing sites at the state and city levels and concludes that enforcement has played an important role in deterring Mexican migrants from crossing in California. Gathmann

(2008) and Dávila, Pagán, and Soydemir (2002) present results supporting this conclusion. Hanson (2006) summarizes existing literature on illegal immigration from Mexico to the United States and points to areas for future research, particularly that pertaining to policies to control labor flows.

Policy Implications

History of U.S. Immigration Policy and Current Reform Proposals

Recent U.S. immigration debates have included proposals for legalization or amnesty of long-term undocumented immigrants. The Comprehensive Immigration Reform Act of 2006 (CIRA), for example, suggested the admission of undocumented immigrants present in the United States more than 5 years, subject to the condition that these persons pay fines and back taxes. Those with 2 to 5 years of U.S. tenure would be allowed to remain in the country for 3 years, after which they would return to their countries of origin to apply for citizenship. In addition, CIRA proposed new guest worker programs. The 1986 Immigration Reform and Control Act (IRCA) was similar. IRCA included a general program (I-687) granting legal status on the basis of continuous U.S. residence for the 5 years leading up to the program and the Seasonal Agricultural Worker (SAW) program (I-700) for farm workers employed at least 90 days in the previous year. Applications for amnesty totaled 1.8 million under I-687 and 1.3 million under I-700, and a total of 2.7 million received legal permanent residency. Applicants were first granted temporary resident status, followed by permanent residency after passing English-language and U.S. civics requirements.

Understanding the effects of legal status on worker outcomes is crucial to anticipating potential effects of a new amnesty program. Several studies document a wage gap between documented and undocumented immigrants. Borjas and Tienda (1993), using administrative data for IRCA amnesty applicants, construct wage profiles by legal status and find that documented immigrants earn 30% more than undocumented immigrants with like national origins. Rivera-Batiz (1999), using a short panel of IRCA amnesty recipients, finds that average hourly wage rates of Mexican documented immigrants were approximately 40% higher than those of undocumented workers at the time amnesty was granted. Decomposing this wage differential into explained and unexplained parts, he finds that less than 50% of this gap is attributable to differences in observed worker characteristics. Furthermore, he confirms that undocumented immigrants who received amnesty in 1987 or 1988 had economically and statistically significant increases in earnings of the order of 15% to 21% by the follow-up survey in 1992. Less than 50% of this increase can be explained by changes in measured worker characteristics over this time period. Kossoudji and Cobb-Clark (2002) find the wage penalty for being undocumented to be in the range of 14% to 24% and estimate that the wage benefit that accrued to those legalized under IRCA was around 6%. Pena (2010) estimates wage differentials between legal and illegal U.S. farm workers to be on the order of 5% to 6%. Whether workers would realize this full gain as a result of legalization, however, depends on a number of general equilibrium characteristics and is unlikely.

Amnesties have been controversial because they seem to reward lawbreaking and because they can create incentives for more illegal immigration. Although CIRA passed the U.S. Senate in May 2006, it failed to pass the House of Representatives. Alternatives to amnesty include continued increases in border security via border enforcement efforts and extensions to temporary work permit programs. These alternative proposals suggest areas for future research regarding predicted effects of immigration reform on U.S. labor markets.

Conclusion

The economics of migration is an application of microeconomic and macroeconomic theory. Still, given the complexity of interrelationships between host and sending countries, many questions of migration dynamics and of the causes and effects of internal and international migration are empirical ones and are the subject of debates over data sources, methodology, and conclusions. Empirical arguments such as these are hardly unusual in the social sciences. Far from being a reason for cynicism, scholarly debates are progressive—some issues get resolved while others emerge and continue to be debated—and are necessary for rational policy making. Yet it is important to note their limitations as well. The economic analysis of migration cannot answer some of the basic questions at the heart of the public debates about immigration, such as which and how many people should be allowed into a country, how their interests should be balanced against the interests of natives, and how and to what extent national identity should be preserved. These ethical and political issues can be informed by economic analysis, but ultimately they cannot be resolved by it.

References and Further Readings

Bartel, A. P. (1989). Where do the new U.S. immigrants live? *Journal of Labor Economics, 7,* 371–391.

Beine, M., Docquier, F., & Rapoport, H. (2001). Brain drain and economic growth: Theory and evidence. *Journal of Development Economics, 64,* 275–289.

Borjas, G. J. (1985). Assimilation, changes in cohort quality, and the earnings of immigrants. *Journal of Labor Economics, 3,* 463–489.

Borjas, G. J. (1987). Self-selection and the earnings of immigrants. *American Economic Review, 77,* 531–553.

Borjas, G. J. (1995). Assimilation and changes in cohort quality revisited: What happened to immigrant earnings in the 1980s? *Journal of Labor Economics, 13,* 201–245.

Borjas, G. J. (1999). Immigration and welfare magnets. *Journal of Labor Economics, 17,* 607–637.

Borjas, G. J. (2003). The labor demand curve is downward sloping: Examining the impact of immigration on the labor market. *Quarterly Journal of Economics, 118,* 1335–1374.

Borjas, G. J. (2005). The labor-market impact of high-skill immigration. *American Economic Review, 95*(2), 56–60.

Borjas, G. J. (2006). Native internal migration and the labor market impact of immigration. *Journal of Human Resources, 41,* 221–258.

Borjas, G. J., Freeman, R. B., & Katz, L. F. (1997). How much do immigration and trade affect labor market outcomes? *Brookings Papers on Economic Activity, 1,* 1–90.

Borjas, G. J., & Katz, L. (2007). The evolution of the Mexican-born workforce in the United States. In G. J. Borjas (Ed.), *Mexican immigration to the United States* (pp. 13–55). Chicago: University of Chicago Press.

Borjas, G. J., & Tienda, M. (1993). The employment and wages of legalized immigrants. *International Migration Review, 27,* 712–747.

Buckley, F. (1996). The political economy of immigration policies. *International Review of Law and Economics, 16,* 81–99.

Butler, R., & Heckman, J. (1977). The government's impact on the labor market status of black Americans: A critical review. In L. Hausman, O. Ashenfelter, B. Rustin, R. F. Schubert, & D. Slaiman (Eds.), *Equal rights and industrial relations* (pp. 235–281). Madison, WI: Industrial Relations Research Association.

Card, D. (2005). Is the new immigration really so bad? *The Economic Journal, 115*(507), F300–F323.

Card, D. (2009). *Immigration and inequality* (NBER Working Paper No. 14683). Cambridge, MA: National Bureau of Economic Research.

Cortes, P. (2008). The effect of low-skilled immigration on U.S. prices: Evidence from CPI data. *Journal of Political Economy, 116,* 381–422.

Dávila, A., Pagán, J. A., & Soydemir, G. (2002). The short-term and long-term deterrence effects of INS border and interior enforcement on undocumented immigration. *Journal of Economic Behavior and Organization, 49,* 459–472.

Department of Homeland Security, Office of Immigration Statistics. (2008). *2007 yearbook of immigration statistics.* Washington, DC: Author.

Dodson, M. E., III. (2001). Welfare generosity and location choices among new United States immigrants. *International Review of Law and Economics, 21,* 47–67.

Faini, R. (2007). Remittances and the brain drain: Do more skilled migrants remit more? *The World Bank Economic Review, 21,* 177–191.

Gathmann, C. (2008). Effects of enforcement on illegal markets: Evidence from migrant smugglers along the southwestern border. *Journal of Public Economics, 92,* 10–11, 1926–1941.

Greenwood, M. J. (1997). Internal migration in developed economies. In M. R. Rosenzweig & O. Stark (Eds.), *Handbook of population and family economics* (pp. 647–720). Amsterdam: North-Holland.

Hanson, G. H. (2006). Illegal migration from Mexico to the United States. *Journal of Economic Literature, 44,* 869–924.

Hunt, J., & Gauthier-Loiselle, M. (2008). *How much does immigration boost innovation?* (NBER Working Paper No. W14312). Cambridge, MA: National Bureau of Economic Research.

Jaeger, D. A. (2000). *Local labor markets, admission categories, and immigrant location choice.* Unpublished manuscript, College of William & Mary, Williamsburg, VA.

Johannsson, H., Weiler, S., & Shulman, S. (2003). Immigration and the labor force participation of low-skill workers. In S. Polachek (Ed.), *Worker well-being and public policy: Research in labor economics* (Vol. 22, pp. 291–308). New York: JAI.

Karemera, D., Oguledo, V. I., & Davis, B. (2000). A gravity model analysis of international migration to North America. *Applied Economics, 32,* 1745–1755.

Kaushal, N. (2005). New immigrants' location choices: Magnets without welfare. *Journal of Labor Economics, 23,* 59–80.

Kossoudji, S. A., & Cobb-Clark, D. A. (2002). Coming out of the shadows: Learning about legal status and wages from the legalized population. *Journal of Labor Economics, 20,* 598–628.

Lazear, E. P. (2007). Mexican assimilation in the United States. In G. J. Borjas (Ed.), *Mexican immigration to the United States* (pp. 107–122). Cambridge, MA: National Bureau of Economic Research.

Lewer, J. J., & Van den Berg, H. (2008). A gravity model of immigration. *Economics Letters, 99,* 164–167.

McKinnish, T. (2005). Importing the poor: Welfare magnetism and cross-border welfare migration. *Journal of Human Resources, 40,* 57–76.

McKinnish, T. (2007). Welfare-induced migration at state borders: New evidence from micro-data. *Journal of Public Economics, 91,* 437–450.

Mishel, L., Bernstein, J., & Shierholz, H. (2009). *The state of working America 2008–2009.* Ithaca, NY: Cornell University Press.

Munshi, K. (2003). Networks in the modern economy: Mexican migrants in the U.S. labor market. *Quarterly Journal of Economics, 118,* 549–599.

National Research Council. (1997). *The new Americans: Economic, fiscal and demographic effects of immigration.* Washington, DC: National Academy Press.

Orrenius, P. M. (2004). The effect of U.S. border enforcement on the crossing behavior of Mexican migrants. In J. Durand & D. S. Massey (Eds.), *Crossing the border: Research from the Mexican Migration Project* (pp. 281–298). New York: Russell Sage Foundation.

Passel, J. S. (2004). *Undocumented immigrants: Facts and figures.* Washington, DC: Urban Institute, Immigration Studies Program.

Passel, J. S. (2005). *Unauthorized migrants: Numbers and characteristics.* Washington, DC: Pew Hispanic Center.

Passel, J. S. (2006a). *Estimates of the unauthorized migrant population for states based on the March 2005 CPS.* Washington, DC: Pew Hispanic Center.

Passel, J. S. (2006b). *The size and characteristics of the unauthorized migrant population in the U.S.: Estimates based on the March 2005 Current Population Survey.* Washington, DC: Pew Hispanic Center.

Passel, J. S., Capps, R., & Fix, M. (2005). *Estimates of the size and characteristics of the undocumented population.* Washington, DC: Pew Hispanic Center.

Passel, J. S., & Cohn, D. (2008a). *Trends in unauthorized immigration: Undocumented inflow now trails legal inflow.* Washington, DC: Pew Hispanic Center.

Passel, J. S., & Cohn, D. (2008b). *U.S. population projections: 2005–2050.* Washington, DC: Pew Hispanic Center.

Pena, A. A. (2010). Legalization and immigrants in U.S. agriculture. *The B. E. Journal of Economic Analysis & Policy, 10*(1), Article 7.

Pew Hispanic Center. (2009). *Statistical portrait of the foreign-born population in the United States, 2006.* Washington, DC: Author.

Rivera-Batiz, F. L. (1999). Undocumented workers in the labor market: An analysis of the earnings of legal and illegal Mexican immigrants in the United States. *Journal of Population Economics, 12,* 91–116.

Shrestha, L. (2006). *The changing demographic profile of the United States* (CRS Report RL 32701). Washington, DC: Congressional Research Service.

Sjaastad, L. A. (1962). The costs and returns of human migration. *Journal of Political Economy, 70*(5), 80–93.

Smith, J. P. (2003). Assimilation across the Latino generations. *American Economic Review, 93,* 315–319.

Stark, O. (2004). Rethinking the brain drain. *World Development, 32,* 15–22.

Tiebout, C. M. (1956). A pure theory of local expenditures. *Journal of Political Economy, 64,* 416–424.

Zavodny, M. (1999). Determinants of recent immigrants' locational choices. *International Migration Review, 33,* 1014–1030.

69

HEALTH ECONOMICS

SHIRLEY JOHNSON-LANS

Vassar College

Health economics is widely understood to encompass the study of the demand and supply for medical services (physician services, services provided in hospitals and independent laboratories, pharmaceuticals, etc.) and for health insurance, as well as comparative studies of different health care systems. It also includes the study of the determinants of demand for health itself, global public health problems, and the nonmedical inputs into health, such as a decent living standard, education, physical and social environment, and personal lifestyle choices, to the extent that they are exogenous (e.g., independent of one's health status). Although the nonmedical factors are increasingly realized to be important in achieving a healthy community at an affordable level of expenditure, most courses in health economics are primarily concerned with the provision of medical care and with health insurance that primarily covers medical care. This chapter will adhere to that tradition since expenditure on medical care, insurance, and research represents such a high proportion of gross domestic product (GDP), especially in the United States, and a proportion that is increasing in all high-income industrialized nations. We also focus on medical care as an input into health because it provides no benefits other than its contribution to health, unlike diet, recreation, and exercise.

Medical care also differs from most other expenditures, even those that we think of as human capital investments, because much of it occurs as a result of negative shocks to health that are largely unanticipated. It is the combination of the degree of uncertainty about one's future health state and the high cost of medical care (relative to household budgets) that makes the transferring of risk to a third-party payer through insurance such an important phenomenon

in the market for health care. For this reason, the role of health insurance will be discussed before the analysis of markets for other health care services.

The last several sections of this chapter are devoted to policy concerns. Before considering possible reforms of the U.S. health care system, a brief overview of several other countries' health care systems will be provided.

Methodology Used in Health Economics Research

The methodology of health economics research includes the following two categories.

Statistical Techniques

In health economics, experimental laboratory conditions rarely can be created. Therefore, once a hypothesis has been formulated and sample data have been gathered, statistical techniques must be used to isolate and estimate the effects of particular factors. Economists most commonly "remove" the other effects by using the techniques of multivariate correlation and regression analysis. Whenever possible, researchers use "difference-in-difference" estimators, where changes in a control group are compared with changes in a treatment group.

In isolating the effect of a change in policy or environment, one needs to have a control group to compare with a treatment group. In some cases, "natural experiments" are provided by the environment. For example, quasi-experimental conditions were provided when Tennessee raised its rate of Medicaid remuneration for physician visits while a neighboring state,

Maryland, did not. This enabled researchers to estimate the effect of fees on willingness of physicians to treat Medicaid patients. Physicians in Maryland were the control group.

Researchers occasionally are able to undertake experiments in which large numbers of subjects are randomly assigned to different groups. An example is the RAND Health Insurance Experiment, conducted over 1974 to 1982. More than 2,000 households were randomly assigned to a variety of insurance plans that offered differing degrees of coverage. This freed the research from the problem of selection bias that results when people systematically choose different insurance plans based on their expected use of medical care. Today an opportunity for a new experiment has been provided by a decision of Medicaid in Oregon to establish a lottery to randomly choose people from the eligible pool who will receive coverage for medical care.

Cost-Benefit and Cost-Effectiveness Analysis

Cost-benefit analysis is a strategy for comparing benefits with costs. It compares marginal benefits and marginal costs and employs the rule that one should devote resources to a use until the extra or incremental cost of the last unit just equals the incremental benefit of that unit. *This rule assumes that marginal benefits are declining and marginal costs are either constant or rising.* The underlying assumption is that people are rational and thus want to maximize benefits relative to costs. This approach is used to answer whether an activity is worth undertaking or continuing. It can be used only if we can measure both costs and benefits in the same metric. We can only decide whether the cost of a medical treatment is worth it if we can establish a monetary value for the benefit. For example, when considering whether to undergo heart surgery, the probable effects of the heart surgery are usually stated in terms of an estimated improvement in length of life and/or quality of remaining life years. To use cost-benefit analysis, one must assign a monetary value to a year of life or to a given quality-of-life improvement.

When it is not possible to establish monetary values for benefits, cost-effectiveness analysis may be used to compare marginal costs, expressed in monetary terms, with incremental benefits, expressed in natural units, such as amount of improvement in life expectancy or degree of reduction in blood pressure. Cost-effectiveness analysis can never establish whether some course of action is worthwhile, but it can be used to compare different treatment methods in terms of their relative effectiveness. This analysis can only provide unambiguous results when one alternative provides at least as good an outcome using fewer resources or a better outcome using the same level of resources. It is a better indicator of a rational use of resources than just cost, whether we are considering decision making of individuals or of societies.

The Demand for Health

It is important to clearly distinguish between health and health care. Health can be considered a form of human capital (like education), and medical care and other components of health care are inputs into the production of health. Spending on health is more appropriately treated as an investment in a stock of health (capital) rather than an item of current consumption. The formal model of investment in health, developed by Michael Grossman, employs a marginal efficiency of health capital function (MEC), which we can think of as a quasi-demand function for health (Grossman, 1972). The MEC is specific to an individual in that different people are endowed with different initial stocks of health and also suffer different shocks to their health status over time. It is downward sloping because it assumes diminishing returns to marginal inputs into the production function. Grossman distinguished between gross and net investment in health since there is depreciation in health capital that must be overcome as well as net investment in improvements in the health stock.

Things that augment the value of healthy days will increase the demand for health. Thus, an increase in the wage rate will shift the demand function. Education has also been found to be positively associated with the demand for health, although just why is still under investigation. Education may shift the demand for health because of a taste or preference change, and/or it may increase the productivity of the inputs into health.

This model can easily be accommodated to incorporate risk or uncertainty. The role of uncertainty in the demand for health and health care is very important. Uncertainty about one's future state of health, uncertainty about what kind of treatment to pursue, and uncertainty about the cost of treatment all contribute to the importance of insurance, or "third-party payment" in the market for health care services. Uncertainty has implications not only for the role of insurance but also for the relationship between patients and their health care providers, particularly their physicians (Arrow, 1963). Patients consult physicians in large part because of the latter's expertise. Asymmetry of information thus introduces the classic principal/agent set of problems that will be discussed later.

Health Insurance

Insurance is a mechanism for assigning risk to a third party. It is also a mechanism for pooling risk over large groups, which in the case of health insurance involves transferring benefits from healthy to ill individuals within a pool. Health insurance may be either private insurance, purchased by individuals or groups, or social insurance, provided by governments out of tax revenues.

The Demand for Private Health Insurance

Why is health insurance so widely purchased? The demand exists because people desire to protect themselves against potential financial losses associated with the treatment of illness. Why don't they self-insure themselves by saving money when they are well to use in times of illness? There are a number of reasons, including the fact that many people could never save or borrow enough to pay for potential catastrophic levels of medical expenditure. However, even people who have extensive wealth usually buy insurance. The reason is that most people want to avoid risk—that is, they are "risk averse." Economists define risk aversion as a characteristic of people's utility functions. Attitudes toward risk depend on the marginal utility of an extra dollar (lost or gained). If the marginal utility of an extra dollar is decreasing as wealth increases, a small probability of a large reduction in wealth entails a larger loss of utility than the certain loss of a smaller amount of wealth (the cost of the insurance) when the probability weighted or "expected value" of the two alternatives is equal. This is what is meant by being "risk averse." Risk-averse people will be willing to pay for insurance even though the cost of the insurance premium is more than the expected value of loss due to illness. (Insurance companies are willing to supply insurance when this excess over expected payouts allows them to cover administrative costs, build up a reserve fund, and, in the case of for-profit insurance firms, make a profit.)

Structure of Private Health Insurance Contracts

Insurance policies are commonly structured as indemnity contracts, where individuals are compensated by a certain amount in the event of an adverse event. Historically, most health insurance policies covering hospitalization and other health care services were modified indemnity contracts in which a certain portion of fee-for-service costs of covered services was reimbursed.

Deductibles and co-payments are used by insurance companies to try to limit the degree of moral hazard associated with insurance coverage. *Moral hazard* is the phenomenon of a person's behavior being affected by insurance coverage. The main way in which moral hazard operates in the health insurance market is through the tendency for the insured to use a greater quantity of medical care since insurance lowers its cost to the individual. Breadth of coverage increases moral hazard since more "discretionary" services are included. Moral hazard is greater where the price elasticity of demand for the service is greater.

Most private health insurance in the United States is provided on a group basis at one's place of employment. This type of health insurance has been favored by workers and firms since the 1950s in part because of the favorable tax treatment it receives in the United States. The cost of employment-based health insurance is not considered taxable income to employees but can be deducted by firms as labor expense. It is also favored because larger insurance pools usually involve lower premiums.

The problem of *adverse selection* is a feature of insurance markets in which there are multiple insurance pools. A pool suffers from adverse selection if it is composed of older, sicker, or other individuals more prone to use medical services. Insurance companies will, if legally allowed, charge higher premiums to higher risk individuals, families, or groups or avoid insuring them altogether. In some cases, regulation requires insurers to use community rating (e.g., charge the same premium to all subscribers for the same coverage), regardless of risk factors such as age or medical histories. Group health insurance is one means of dealing with adverse selection since risk factors are pooled for the group and community rates are charged to all members of the group.

In the past 20 years, health insurance policies have also evolved to incorporate aspects of "managed care," a variety of features instituted by third-party payers to contain costs and provide greater efficiency in the provision of services.

An important innovation in managed care is the sharing of risk not only with consumers of health care (through deductibles, co-payments, lifetime payout limits, etc.) but also with providers of health care (by entering into contracts with them that set the amount of reimbursement per treatment or by paying a fixed amount per subscriber).

In some cases, individuals join health maintenance organizations (HMOs), which provide integrated health care services and require subscribers to use in-network providers. In HMOs, primary care physicians act as "gatekeepers"; subscribers must get referrals from them to be reimbursed for other specialized services. The most common form of managed care contract in the United States today is the preferred provider organization (PPO). In this arrangement, consumers face lower prices if they use "in-network" providers but also receive some reimbursement for other services, although these usually have higher co-payments and are subject to deductibles. The PPO is a hybrid between the traditional indemnity contract and an HMO. In PPOs, the gatekeeper function of a primary care physician is not imposed.

In managed care contracts, there are usually requirements that patients receive precertification (e.g., obtain permission from the insurance company) before surgery, diagnostic tests, and so on, and physicians and hospitals are often subject to utilization review of treatments prescribed.

As health care costs have risen over time, insurance premiums have also risen. Employers, particularly those with smaller groups of workers, have tended to cut back on coverage, require employees to pay higher proportions of premiums, and in some cases discontinue coverage. Workers, even in jobs that provide options for group insurance, have also tended, in increasing numbers, to fail to subscribe to group plans as their required contributions have risen. Thus today, the ranks of the uninsured include many workers as well as people who are unemployed, not in the labor force, or self-employed.

Social Insurance

Social insurance, in addition to pooling risk, usually has a redistributive function since it is financed out of taxes, so one pays an amount dependent on income but receives benefits in accordance with need. In the United States, social insurance covers only certain groups: those over 65 years of age, most of whom are covered by Medicare; a portion of low-income persons who are covered by Medicaid; children of low-income families, who may be covered by the State Child Health Insurance Program (SCHIP); Native Americans living on reservations; and veterans who can receive health care services through the Veterans Administration. Certain other people with approved disabilities may also be eligible for social insurance. Federal employees, including members of Congress, are also covered by public insurance.

The two largest programs, Medicare and Medicaid, came into being in 1965 as amendments to the Social Security Act. Medicare Part A, which covers all senior citizens who are Social Security eligible, covers part of hospital bills and is financed federally out of payroll taxes paid jointly by employees and employers. Medicaid Parts B and D are voluntary and require contributions out of Social Security retirement benefit checks but are heavily subsidized. Medicaid is jointly financed by federal and state tax revenues. States administer Medicaid and are required to finance their portion of their programs or the federal contribution is reduced.

The financial solvency of Medicare is vulnerable not only to rising health care costs but also to shifts in the age distribution of the population since it is financed on a pay-as-you-go basis, which means that contributions from current workers are used to pay benefits to current beneficiaries. The financial solvency of Medicaid, which is means tested, is vulnerable to cycles in economic activity since during recessions, tax receipts fall and eligibility roles swell. The problem is exacerbated by the fact that states are required to balance their budgets annually.

Both Medicare and Medicaid originally reimbursed physicians and hospitals on a fee-for-service basis. However, both programs have adopted some of the same managed care strategies used by private insurance companies, and in fact, Medicare pioneered a prospective payment system of hospital reimbursement based on fixed payments per diagnosis. This diagnostic-related group (DRG) method has been copied by many private insurers. Physicians' payments are also set according to a scale (RBRVS) that determines reimbursement rates for different types of physician visits, factoring in the input resources (effort) used and the costs (based on capital intensity of an office practice, number of years of training required for a specialty, etc.).

Medicare and Medicaid both contract out to some private HMOs and other managed care insurers. Medicare Parts B and D contain options for subscribers to assign their premiums to private third-party payers. The intent is to provide competition in the social insurance market. Currently, the government is subsidizing the Medicare Advantage Programs (private options), paying more per beneficiary than for traditional Medicare Part B. Some states require Medicaid beneficiaries to receive services from an HMO.

The United States is nearly unique among high-income industrialized countries in not having universal health insurance coverage. About 15% of the U.S. population currently has no health insurance. It should be noted, however, that universal coverage does not mean universal social insurance coverage. Proposals for increasing insurance coverage of Americans involve various combinations of social and private insurance.

Markets for Physicians and Nurses, Hospitals, and Pharmaceuticals

Supply and Demand for Physicians and Registered Nurses

Physicians

The supply of professionals, whether physicians, nurses, engineers, attorneys, or accountants, depends on the willingness of people to undertake training to enter these professions. This investment in human capital is determined, at least in part, by the expected financial return compared with the cost of training. Assuming that people make rational, utility-maximizing decisions, the decision to invest in training will involve estimating the returns over a lifetime and comparing these returns with the costs of the training This model of human capital investment helps explain such questions as why the United States has so many medical specialists compared to general practitioners. The simple answer is that the net financial returns to specialties such as orthopedic surgery are higher than the returns to primary care physician practices. Public policy has attempted to change this somewhat. For example, Medicare's RBRVS method of determining reimbursements to physicians now provides relatively higher payments to primary care physicians than formerly. Nonetheless, a wide difference in incomes of physicians in different specialties, even when adjusted for years of training, still remains. However, over time, the net return to medical training as a whole, compared with many other professions, has declined. This is due in no small part to the growth of managed care in both private and public insurance.

In understanding the market for physician services, it is also necessary to look at the demand side. Demand for medical services has increased with improvements in medical technology, which make it possible to accomplish more improvements in health. This will be discussed further later in this chapter. Medicare (and Medicaid) also brought about a huge increase in the demand for physicians as elderly and low-income Americans could afford more medical care.

This led to a shortage of physicians. Medical schools received more government subsidies. The student loan program for medical training was expanded. Medicare began to heavily subsidize resident training in hospitals. Immigration and licensing laws were changed to make it easier for internationally trained physicians to immigrate to the United States and to become licensed practitioners once here.

Registered Nurses

Training to become a registered nurse (RN) also involves human capital investment, although one that requires fewer years of training. Because of chronic shortages of registered nurses, measured by persistent chronic vacancy rates in hospital nursing positions, there has been a great deal of subsidization of nurse training programs over the years. Although health policy planners still find a shortage of nurses, the nurse/physician ratio as well as the nurse/population ratio in the United States increased until the mid-1990s. Since then, the enrollment in nurse training programs has been declining. One reason for this is that there are now more professions open to women, including becoming an MD.

The market for nurses has been analyzed as a classic case of monopsony. Monopsony exists when there is monopoly power on the part of employers (hospitals) and an upward-sloping supply curve of nurses. It is manifested by a disequilibrium in the form of a gap between supply and demand at a given wage. There is considerable evidence of monopsony in the nurse market between 1940 and 1960. Whether it still exists today is a bit more problematic.

In the absence of monopsony, one expects a shortage to be resolved by a rise in wages until an equilibrium is reached. If shortages persist and wages do not rise, the logical explanation, in the absence of governmental intervention to control wages, is that there is monopsony. In that case, employers find that the marginal return to raising wages is not equal to the marginal cost of hiring more workers, even when there is a gap between demand and supply, such as persistent vacancy rates in positions for hospital nurses. Note that the supply curve is, to the employer, the *average factor cost curve,* whereas the real cost of hiring more workers is the *marginal factor cost.* The marginal factor cost rises faster than the average factor cost because when additional nurses are hired, wages of those already employed have to be raised to create parity. This is the reality of the workplace where productivity will decline if new hires are paid more than other employees doing comparable work.

The Physician–Patient Relationship

Although the proportion of total expenditure on medical care devoted to physician payments is less than 25%, physicians are of central importance in the provision of medical care in that they organize and direct the path of treatment. Because of asymmetry of knowledge between patients and physicians, patients delegate authority to physicians. This is a good example of a principal-agent relationship in which there is always the possibility of imperfect agency since physicians can substitute their own welfare for that of the patient. Since professional standards forbid this, we can assume that physicians experience

some disutility in behaving as imperfect agents and will therefore only do so if there are offsetting benefits from this behavior, such as enhancement of income.

The way in which physicians are paid for their services will have no effect on their treatment of patients if they are perfect agents. But in the case of imperfect agency, physicians paid on a fee-for-service basis may be tempted to recommend greater treatment intensity than is in the patient's best interest. Thus, there may be "physician-induced demand." On the other hand, if payment is on a capitation basis, where physicians agree to treat patients in return for a fixed fee per year, they may be tempted to skimp on the amount of treatment offered in order to handle a larger patient load. A risk-averse physician, worried about the possibility of accusations of malpractice, might also order unnecessary tests. Note that all of these examples apply only to an established patient-physician relationship. If a physician locates an office practice in a wealthy neighborhood in order to attract patients who will pay higher fees, this is not considered imperfect agency, although it may be done to enhance income.

Conventional models treat independent physician practices as monopolistically competitive firms with downward-sloping demand curves since physicians, even those practicing in the same subspecialty, are not perfect substitutes for each other and may have considerable market power based on reputation. A newer model, developed by Thomas McGuire (2000), applies particularly well to a post-managed-care world. In this model, physicians may not be able to set the price, but they can vary the quantity of service provided. McGuire substitutes the notion of a net benefit function for a demand curve. In this framework of analysis, there are substitutes (though imperfect ones) for physicians, and patients will only remain under the care of a given physician if he or she provides a service (net benefit) equal to or greater than some minimum level. Since patients have imperfect knowledge, they may want less treatment than a caring and conscientious physician thinks optimal. So, a patient might leave a physician, even if he or she were behaving as a perfect agent. However, this model can also explain the limits of either physician-induced demand or skimping on service that a patient will permit, in the case of a physician who is an imperfect agent.

Hospitals

Hospitals are complex organizations. The modern acute-care hospital is a multiproduct firm providing a variety of different in- and outpatient services. The most common form of hospital in the United States is the private nonprofit community hospital, although there are also public (government) hospitals and for-profit private hospitals. Public hospitals tend to have a higher proportion of patients of lower socioeconomic status, and most elite teaching hospitals, associated with medical schools, are private, not-for-profit institutions.

Theories of hospital management are derived from theories of the modern corporation, in which the function of manager and owners is usually separated. They focus on the behavior of the decision makers and differentiate between hospitals in which the CEOs are nonmedical professional managers (Newhouse, 1970), hospitals that are run by physicians (Pauly & Redisch, 1973), and those in which there is shared management by business managers and physicians who may have differing objectives (Harris, 1977). In all cases, the models assume that managers behave so as to maximize their utility.

In theory, managers of nonprofit organizations would be expected to emphasize quality over quantity or cost minimization compared with managers of for-profit hospitals since they do not distribute profits to owners. However, empirical research finds little difference between for- and not-for-profit hospitals. Studies that compare different ownership types of acute-care hospitals find that there is not much difference, on average, in prices charged, intensity of care, or patient outcomes. With respect to nursing homes and psychiatric hospitals, for-profit institutions are more prevalent but also may provide lower quality care.

Many communities have only one or two hospitals serving the area. Hospitals may be viewed as monopoly firms, particularly when we consider their relationships with employees. Hospitals may in some situations be natural monopolies. A natural monopoly is a firm characterized by long-run economies of scale (a downward-sloping cost curve) over the whole range of its demand. In this case, adding additional firms within the same market will result in higher costs (and prices). However, more commonly we use oligopoly models to analyze the behavior of hospitals as sellers of services since there is usually some degree of competition within a region, and natural monopoly characteristics do not seem to pertain beyond certain capacity levels.

Oligopolies often compete on some basis other than price. This was certainly true of hospitals, at least until the 1990s. This led to the notion of the "medical arms race," where hospital managers compete to have the best facilities and equipment. When one hospital acquires some new technology or opens a new department, other hospitals in the region are forced to follow suit. In this case, competition in a region leads to higher prices and duplication of facilities. The belief that hospital competition is not in the public interest led to the passage of certificate of need (CON) laws. CON laws require government approval to add facilities. The study of effects of CON laws has found some evidence that CON laws provide barriers to entry and lead to higher prices (Salkever, 2000). Moreover, in the post-managed-care era, there is evidence that hospitals do engage in price competition, faced with cost-conscious insurers who themselves have a good deal of market power.

Hospitals are well known to engage in price discrimination. They charge different prices to different third-party payers, public and private, and they may charge lower prices or provide free charity care to the uninsured. The latter is probably based on altruism, although it may be good public relations as well, and nonprofit hospitals are usually required by law to provide a certain amount of charity care. But price discrimination is consistent with a profit-maximizing model of the firm in which higher prices charged to customers whose price elasticity of demand is lower leads to greater profits.

Price discrimination does not necessarily involve cost shifting. The issue of the degree of cost shifting (e.g., charging more to certain consumers *in response to* lowered prices to others) is still not resolved, but there is less evidence of cost shifting than the general public assumes. There is, however, a good deal of cost shifting from individual patients to taxpayers who ultimately pay for much of the subsidized care that hospitals provide.

Pharmaceuticals

The market for pharmaceuticals is extremely complex. The pharmaceutical industry is heavily regulated, with many countries having some body similar to the U.S. Food and Drug Administration that rules on safety and efficacy of new products. Large drug companies are often thought to be oligopolies, but as the pharmaceutical industry has become global and smaller biotech companies have entered the market, it may be more accurate to think of the pharmaceutical industry as monopolistically competitive. However, drug companies do have some degree of temporary monopoly power in individual product markets when they obtain patents on new drugs. Patent protection is important in providing incentives to innovate. In the drug industry, patents are limited to 20 years, including time when the drug is being developed but is not yet on the market. The pharmaceutical industry, unlike many other industries characterized by rapid technological change (such as computers), is characterized by very high development costs compared with production costs (i.e., the marginal cost of an additional bottle of pills). An implication of this is that consumers in countries that have pharmaceutical industries that innovate are likely to experience higher prices for new drugs since the high cost of discovering the new drug, clinically testing it, and bringing it to market must be recouped, and only a small fraction of new innovations turn out to be marketable at a profit.

There is also a great deal of price discrimination, with cross-country differences in price, within-country price differences between brand-name and generic versions of drugs, and different prices charged depending on the negotiating power of third-party payers. Although on-patent brand-name drug prices tend to be higher in the United States than in many other countries, generic versions of drugs are often cheaper.

Comparative Health Care Systems: Brief Overviews

Canada

At approximately the same time that Medicare and Medicaid were enacted in the United States, Canada adopted a universal social health insurance system that covers most medical care for all citizens and permanent residents. Also called Medicare, it is a "single-payer" system in which the government acts as insurer. It is financed out of tax revenues. There is a separate Medicare budget for each province, jointly funded by the federal and provincial governments, but health insurance is portable throughout Canada. The medical care system is similar to that in the United States in that physicians are reimbursed on a fee-for-service basis and patients are free to choose their own doctors and are not subject to a gatekeeper system.

However, in Canada, global budgets determine how much health care is available, and physicians and hospital associations have to negotiate with the government, which sets rates of remuneration for providers. Technology is less widely diffused. For instance, there are many fewer magnetic resonance imaging (MRI) machines per 10,000 population.

In Canada, there is no option to the public system. Services that are covered by Medicare cannot be purchased privately. Supplementary private insurance can be used only to pay for services not covered by Medicare or to pay co-payments charged by Medicare.

United Kingdom

After World War II, the National Health Service (NHS) was enacted in the United Kingdom. It differs from the Canadian system in that it is a national health system, not a nationwide universal insurance system. Doctors who participate in the NHS are employees of the government and are paid by a mix of salary and capitation. Originally, hospitals contracted directly with the district health authorities who paid them for their services. In the early 1990s, the system was altered to give hospitals and physician practices some degree of autonomy. Hospitals are now often organized as trusts. Large regional groups of physicians are given their own budgets to manage. However, the source of funding is still the government, and therefore global budget caps apply. The United Kingdom is well known for high-quality care but long waits for all but emergency services, known as "rationing by queuing." In the United Kingdom, unlike Canada, there is the option to "go private" and purchase services outside the NHS system. These services are paid for out of pocket or by private insurance. Physicians in private practice are paid on a fee-for-service basis.

Germany

Germany has a system of many competing "sickness funds" that are nonprofit insurers. Most workers join sickness funds through their place of employment, though unions and other community organizations also provide access to the funds. The sickness fund system is social insurance in that premiums are financed through a payroll tax, which, like the Medicare Social Security tax in the United States, is jointly paid by workers and employers. It is, however, much higher than in the United States. Retired persons and the self-employed are also enrolled in sickness funds and contribute in proportion to their pensions or self-employment earnings. Only the very wealthy may opt out

of this social insurance system. About 95% of all German citizens are members of the sickness funds.

Since the sickness fund system is a not a single-payer system, there is the problem of adverse selection. To offset this, government regulation requires sickness funds to cross-subsidize each other so that those that have a more expensive pool of members receive payments from other funds whose expenses are lower.

Physicians associations negotiate fees with the sickness funds served by their members. The German government has imposed global caps on different components of the medical budget. If a group of physicians serving a particular sickness fund exceeds their budget cap, every member of the physician group is subject to a reduction in the rate of remuneration (fee schedule).

Reforms in the German system have increased co-payments and have introduced a degree of competition in that individuals or worker groups may choose which sickness fund to join and may shift their membership if they are dissatisfied. The German system has, historically, been very generous in its coverage of services. Physician visits are still free, although some fees are now charged for prescription drugs, eyeglasses, and so on.

In each of these countries, demand for medical services is rising, and the public systems, all of which have global budgets, are finding their finances strained. Services have to be rationed, by queuing up for nonemergency care, by charging fees for formerly free services, or by denying certain kinds of treatment. In Germany and the United Kingdom, it is possible to purchase services through the private market. In Canada, this can be done only by crossing the border and purchasing medical care in the United States.

Public Health Care in the Developing World

Although it is difficult to generalize about low-income nations in different parts of the world, there are certain common characteristics. Communicable diseases represent a higher proportion of the populations' sickness. A smaller proportion of the GDP is generally devoted to health care. Rural areas are often disproportionately lacking in health care facilities. And even countries that have recently experienced dramatic rates of economic growth, such as India and China, do not provide adequate free public health care, even to the poor. International agencies such as UNICEF and nongovernmental organizations (NGOs) play an important role in providing health care and medicine to the developing nations. This is particularly important in Africa, given the high incidence of HIV/AIDS.

Leading Proposals for Reform in the United States

The proportion of national income spent on health care in the United States is greater than in any other industrialized country. It is now in excess of 15%. Our medical technology, measured in terms of such indices as number of MRI units per 10,000 population, also exceeds that of other comparable countries. Yet, aggregate statistics (averages) of health outcomes place the United States far from the top of a list of comparable (Organisation for Economic Co-operation and Development) nations in life expectancy, both at birth and at 60 years of age, and U.S. infant mortality rates are discouragingly high. The United States is also the only high-income industrialized nation that does not have universal health insurance coverage for its citizens and permanent residents. More than 15% of families were without health insurance coverage in 2009. The fact that health insurance and medical care costs are increasing much more rapidly than the consumer price index, although not unique to the United States, also leads to the conclusion that the system needs reforms both with respect to its efficiency and its equity.

Incremental Reforms

Improvements in efficiency could be defined as those that result in the same quality of care provided at lower cost and/or better patient outcomes provided at no higher cost.

Use of Information Technology to Provide Better Records

Using information technology (IT) to provide comprehensive patient records would both reduce medical errors, such as prescribing drugs that are counterproductive, given patient allergies or when combined with other medications, and provide cost-savings by eliminating unnecessary duplication of diagnostic tests.

Another use of IT is the expansion of health care provider report cards. Although critics fear that providers will attempt to avoid treating the most difficult cases that might spoil their records, risk/adjustment applied to reporting can largely overcome this difficulty, and public support for making such information available is now widespread.

The use of IT to simplify and standardize insurance claim forms is also broadly advocated. A related proposal requiring that all health insurance contracts cover certain basic services is more controversial. Critics argue that this would curtail freedom of choice if "consumer-driven" insurance options were ruled out. However, proponents of regulation believe that most consumers would benefit from requirements that all plans cover a broad range of medically necessary treatments and not exclude any on the basis of preexisting health conditions.

Better Management of Care for Chronic Diseases

Another widely accepted reform is better ongoing care for patients with chronic illnesses. This would be facilitated by more continuity in health care provision as well as better recordkeeping over the lifetime of patients. Critics of employment-based health insurance see it as a stumbling block to long-term management of chronic conditions in a world in which there is so much mobility between jobs and in which employees are subject to employers' decisions to change insurance carriers based on cost considerations. Proposals for reforms that involve greater portability of health insurance address this problem. Advocates of a "single-payer" universal insurance system believe that this and other inefficiencies associated with the fragmented insurance system in the United States would be best overcome by having the government act as third-party payer for all citizens and residents.

Promoting Wellness

A third widely accepted reform is a health care system that provides incentives for a healthier lifestyle. Advocates favor promoting, through subsidies, types of preventive care that have been shown to be effective. This includes both screening for disease and programs that promote a healthier lifestyle.

Reforming the Tax Treatment of Employment-Based Health Insurance

This has been advocated for a number of decades by many economists who regard treating all employment-based health insurance premiums as tax-free income to be both inefficient and inequitable in that it encourages workers to demand excessive insurance coverage, which in turn promotes cost insensitivity and the use of health care services with low marginal value. It also benefits high-income workers disproportionately since they benefit more from the tax subsidy. Proposed reforms include capping the level of health insurance premiums that will receive favorable tax treatment and completely removing the tax-free status of insurance premiums.

Broadening Insurance Coverage

Although most people who advocate universal health insurance coverage in the United States are primarily concerned with equity or fairness, there are also inefficiencies associated with having approximately 47 million people currently uninsured. These include the inappropriate use of hospital emergency rooms by the uninsured who have no access to physician office visits and the postponing of treatment until advanced stages of disease. However, covering the uninsured would not be, at least in the short run, cost free (Institute of Medicine, 2003).

The Access Problem

There is a widespread belief in the United States that all residents should have access to affordable health insurance, but there is no general agreement on the best way to achieve this goal. Several main proposals are espoused by health economists, although the details differ. Some involve incremental change, building on our combination of existing employment-based private insurance and social insurance programs. Other plans would provide more dramatic changes by replacing employment-based health insurance altogether. Victor Fuchs and Ezekiel Emanuel (2005) have grouped reforms of the health care system into three main categories: (1) incremental reforms, such as expanding SCHIP or expanding Medicare to cover 55- to 65-year-olds, or individual or employer mandates, which create new insurance exchanges and provide subsidies to low-income families but do not radically alter the structure of the current health care system; (2) single-payer plans that would eliminate the private insurance market and have the government act as third-party payer; and (3) voucher-based reforms, which they advocate (Furman, 2008, chap. 4). Although they do not explicitly consider health savings accounts (HSAs), this is a fourth option that we need to include in a complete menu of proposed reforms.

1a. *Expand Medicare.* This can be accomplished by allowing people to buy into the Medicare program. One way to do this would be to allow anyone to pay a standard premium and buy Medicare as an alternative to private insurance. More ambitious proposals would gradually phase out Medicaid and other forms of social insurance, subsidizing low-income families' Medicare premiums and reducing the co-payments for them. There might, however, have to be some kind of subsidy from the federal government if Medicare suffered from adverse selection, compared with employment-based private insurance.

1b. *Mandate Individual Health Insurance Coverage: The Massachusetts Plan as Blueprint.* Massachusetts has instituted a plan for statewide universal health insurance coverage, achieved through a mandate that individuals must have health insurance or pay a fine. This plan involves a combination of private and public health insurance coverage, with Medicare, Medicaid, and SCHIP remaining in place. Low-income families that are not currently covered by social programs receive subsidies to cover all or part of their health insurance premiums. Most workers who currently have employment-based insurance are expected in the short run to remain with these plans. However, they have the option to acquire health insurance through the Commonwealth Connector, a market clearinghouse through which insurance providers can offer portable health plans that function like employment-based plans of large employers. To make the system work, the portable plans must be subject to the same tax treatment as employer-based plans. Other states are considering similar plans. Jonathan Gruber (2000) is the architect of a national health insurance system based on Massachusetts's plan.

2. *Single-Payer System.* Universal health insurance in the form of a single-payer system, modeled on Canadian Medicare, has been proposed (e.g., Rice, 1998) but has generally not been considered politically feasible, although it has had the support of some presidential candidates and members of Congress. Even though the U.S. Medicare program is more cost-efficient than most private health insurance, and the simplicity of a Canadian-type single-payer system is appealing and removes the problem of adverse selection, there is widespread belief in the United States that government- run programs have no built-in mechanisms that ensure efficiency and are likely to be subject to corruption. Moreover, Medicare itself in its present form is no longer a single-payer system since Parts B and D allow beneficiaries to assign their benefits to private insurers.

3. *A Voucher System* (Fuchs & Emanuel, 2005). All U.S. residents would receive a health care voucher that would cover the cost of an insurance plan with standard benefits. In the short run, those who are currently insured through Medicare, Medicaid, SCHIP, and so on would have the option of remaining in those plans or switching to the voucher plan. However, the existing forms of social insurance would gradually be phased out, and employment-based insurance would be discontinued. The latter would lose its attractiveness since part of the reform plan is to discontinue the favorable tax treatment of employment-based group insurance.

The voucher has no cash value but gives the recipient the right to enroll in a health plan with standard benefits. National and regional health boards, modeled on the Federal Reserve System, would regulate insurance plans with respect to both their finances and their provision of adequate networks of providers. Although the system would be universal, third-party payers would be private. People could choose insurance programs or, if they failed to do so, be assigned to one. The system assumes that private insurance companies would have an incentive to remain in the market and compete for subscribers. In that sense, it is not unlike the managed competition model of health insurance markets (Enthoven, 1993). The Fuchs and Emanuel (2005) plan would be financed by a value-added tax on consumption, but a voucher plan could also be financed out of an income tax.

4. *Health Savings Accounts (HSAs).* HSAs, whose advocates often structure the plans as forms of tax-free income, are not insurance per se. They are personal savings accounts, similar to 401K or 403B retirement accounts, and employers could contribute to them instead of supporting group health insurance. One of the earliest advocates of HSAs was Martin Feldstein (1971). An advantage of HSAs is that they encourage judicious use of health care since individuals are paying the bills themselves out of their own savings. A disadvantage is the loss of pooling of risk across individuals. What is retained is the individual's or family's ability to smooth expenditure on medical care over periods of health and illness. For such plans to constitute anything close to a universal system, low-income families would need to have their HSAs heavily subsidized. HSAs could be limited to medical care after retirement, in which case they would be an alternative to Medicare, or they could replace employment-based

health insurance as they have in Singapore. Singapore's HSAs are supplemented by social health insurance for catastrophic health expenses.

Conclusion

The United States is widely acknowledged to need health care reform. More than 47 million people without insurance is considered unacceptable by most people. Changes in the nature of the labor market have made employment-based health insurance less appropriate than it was when long-term employment with the same firm was usual. It provides job lock and reduces the competitiveness of U.S. firms. The proportion of the GDP devoted to health care is much higher than in other countries without better patient outcomes. A well-conceived reform plan could significantly lower health care costs and provide much greater equity (access). However, technological advances in medical care and demographic trends will almost inevitably lead to a continued upward trend in the proportion of the budget devoted to medical care (Newhouse, 1992). This is, however, not unique to the United States but is a problem facing all industrialized nations.

References and Further Readings

Arrow, K. (1963). Uncertainty and the welfare economics of medical care. *American Economic Review, 53,* 941–973.

Berndt, E. R. (2002). Pharmaceuticals in U.S. health care: Determinants of quantity and price. *Journal of Economic Perspectives, 26,* 45–66.

Currie, J., & Gruber, J. (1996). Health insurance eligibility, utilization of medical care, and child health. *Quarterly Journal of Economics, 111,* 431–466.

Cutler, D., & McClellan, M. (2001). Is technical change in medical care worth it? *Health Affairs, 20,* 11–29.

Cutler, D., & Zeckhauser, R. K. (2000). The anatomy of health insurance. In A. J. Culyer & J. P. Newhouse (Eds.), *Handbook of health economics* (Vol. 1A, pp. 563–643). Amsterdam: Elsevier.

Enthoven, A. C. (1993). The history and principles of managed competition. *Health Affairs, 10,* 24–48.

Feldstein, M. S. (1971). A new approach to national health insurance. *Public Interest, 23,* 93–105.

Finkelstein, A. (2007). The aggregate effects of health insurance: Evidence from the introduction of Medicare. *Quarterly Journal of Economics, 122,* 1–37.

Fuchs, V. R., & Emanuel, E. J. (2005). Health care vouchers: A proposal for universal coverage. *New England Journal of Medicine, 352,* 1255–1260.

Furman, J. (Ed.). (2008). *Who has the cure? Hamilton Project ideas on health care.* Washington, DC: Brookings Institution Press.

Glied, S. A. (2000). Managed care. In A. J. Culyer & J. P. Newhouse (Eds.), *Handbook of health economics* (Vol. 1A, pp. 707–753). Amsterdam: Elsevier.

Glied, S. A. (2001). Health insurance and market failure since Arrow. *Journal of Health Economics, 26,* 957–965.

Grossman, M. (1972). On the concept of health capital and the demand for health. *Journal of Political Economy, 80,* 223–255.

Gruber, J. (2000). Health insurance and the labor market. In A. J. Culyer & J. P. Newhouse (Eds.), *Handbook of health economics* (Vol. 1A, pp. 645–706). Amsterdam: Elsevier.

Gruber, J. (2008). Taking Massachusetts national: Incremental universalism for the United States. In J. Furman (Ed.), *Who has the cure? Hamilton Project ideas on health care* (pp. 121–141). Washington, DC: Brookings Institution Press.

Harris, J. E. (1977). The internal organization of hospitals: Some economic implications. *Bell Journal of Economics, 8,* 467–482.

Institute of Medicine. (2003). *Hidden costs, value lost: Uninsurance in America.* Washington, DC: National Academy of Sciences.

Johnson-Lans, S. (2006). *A health economics primer.* Boston: Pearson/Addison-Wesley.

Kremer, M. (2002). Pharmaceuticals and the developing world. *Journal of Economic Perspectives, 16,* 67–90.

McGuire, T. G. (2000). Physician agency. In A. J. Culyer & J. P. Newhouse (Eds.), *Handbook of health economics* (Vol. 1A, pp. 461–536). Amsterdam: Elsevier.

Newhouse, J. P. (1970). Toward a theory of nonprofit institutions: An economic model of a hospital. *American Economic Review, 60,* 64–74.

Newhouse, J. P. (1992). Medical care costs: How much welfare loss? *Journal of Economic Perspectives, 6,* 3–22.

Newhouse, J. P., & the Insurance Experiment Group. (1993). *Free for All? Lessons from the RAND Health Insurance Experiment.* Cambridge, MA: Harvard University Press.

Pauly, M. V. (2001). Making sense of a complex system: Empirical studies of employment-based health insurance. *International Journal of Health Care Finance and Economics, 1,* 333–339.

Pauly, M. V., & Redisch, M. (1973). The not-for-profit hospital as a physicians' cooperative. *American Economic Review, 63,* 87–100.

Reinhardt, U. E. (1972). A production function for physician's services. *Review of Economics and Statistics, 54,* 55–65.

Rice, T. (1998). Can markets give us the health system we want? In M. A. Peterson (Ed.), *Healthy markets: The new competition in health care* (pp. 61–103). Durham, NC: Duke University Press.

Salkever, D. S. (2000). Regulation of prices and investment in hospitals in the United States. In A. J. Culyer & J. P. Newhouse (Eds.), *Handbook of health economics* (Vol. 1B, pp. 1489–1535). Amsterdam: Elsevier.

70

ECONOMICS OF HEALTH INSURANCE

AMY M. WOLAVER

Bucknell University

Despite the fact that the United States spends more money per capita than any other nation, not everyone is insured. Perhaps even more surprising, when one adds the various government indirect subsidizations of health care through the tax code to the direct expenditures on Medicare, Medicaid, and other programs, the total dollars spent per capita by the *government* on health care is also higher than any other industrialized nation, in which all achieve universal coverage (Woolhandler & Himmelstein, 2002).

Because financing of health care in the United States is achieved through a mix of public and private insurance, the system is complex. Health insurance markets are riddled with market failures, which have important implications for who is covered and how coverage is achieved. Other industrialized countries are able to achieve universal coverage, even in systems that also mix public and private coverage. What are the market problems in health insurance that lead to gaps in coverage we experience in the United States?

This chapter will focus on the economics underpinning the market for health insurance in the United States. The primary goal of the chapter is to understand the impact of the market failures in the financing of care. First we will model demand for insurance and outline the market failures in insurance. We will examine some of the market and policy solutions to these market failures. We will briefly examine the history of health insurance coverage in the United States and how tax policy affects where Americans obtain their coverage. We will outline some of the major features of the forms of publicly provided health insurance, Medicare and Medicaid/State Child Health Insurance Program (SCHIP). We will examine the characteristics of the uninsured population in the United States in relation to the institutions and

market failures outlined in the chapter. We conclude with a case study on HIV/AIDS to illustrate some of the complexities in achieving health insurance coverage.

The Demand for Health Insurance

The perfectly competitive model in economics assumes perfect information, but in reality, there are many gaps in our information set. Kenneth Arrow's (1963) article, the cornerstone of health economics, beautifully describes the problem of uncertainty. We cannot know the future, and we face the possibility of loss of income and assets from health problems. The loss of income and assets comes through lost work time and from medical bills. At the same time, most of us would prefer to not face this risk of loss. This feature of our preferences, risk aversion, arises because most people have decreasing marginal utility in wealth or income. That is, the increase in utility from the first dollar of income you receive is higher than the increase in utility from your hundredth dollar and so on. Because of this feature, we dislike losing a dollar more than we like gaining a dollar. In economic terms, the decrease in utility from losing a dollar is bigger than the increase in utility from a dollar.

Economists model planning in the face of uncertainty by using probabilities and expected values. Suppose you know you have a 10% chance of having a health problem that will cost you $10,000, and normally your income is $50,000. Therefore, 90% of the time, your income is $50,000, and 10% of the time, it is $40,000. Your expected income (E[income]) for the year is therefore

$$E[\text{income}] = 0.90 * \$50,000 + 0.10 * \$40,000 = \$49,000.$$

The expected loss in this case is the probability of loss times the amount of the loss. In this case, $E[\text{loss}] = 0.10 * \$10,000 = \$1,000$.

However, economists believe that it is expected utility that matters when you are planning for the future, not expected income. Because of risk aversion, expected utility with that uncertain 10% chance of a $10,000 loss is different from the utility one would have with a 100% chance of a loss of $1,000, even though the losses in expected income are equivalent. Let us assume that we can characterize the utility function as $U = \sqrt{I}$, where U is utility and I is income. This is a simple function that is consistent with risk aversion; in other words, there is a decreasing marginal utility of income. Table 70.1 shows the level of utility for each of the possible levels of income with this function.

Expected utility with the 10% chance of loss is

$$E[\text{utility}] = 0.10 * 200 + 0.90 * 223.6 = 221.24.$$

Compare the expected utility with an uncertain loss to the utility with certain income of $49,000. Utility in the latter case is 221.4, higher than the expectation with loss. We will not place any direct interpretation on what one unit of utility means; the important feature is that you would have higher utility losing $1,000 every year with 100% certainty than you have with a 10% chance of losing $10,000 each year. This decrease in utility is risk aversion. Because of risk aversion, consumers are willing to pay someone to take away some of the financial uncertainty; this product is insurance. The discomfort from risk aversion increases with the level of uncertainty (risks that are closer to 50/50 rather than 0% or 100% risks). The discomfort also increases with the possible loss. Insurance has therefore traditionally been more likely to cover high ticket expenses that are uncertain.

What Is Insurance?

Given that we dislike risk, the following question then arises: Is there a market to pay someone to take the risk for us? The answer is yes; this market is insurance. Essentially, insurance is a product where consumers pay a price, the premium, to some other entity, the insurer, who then assumes the financial risks. After the policy is purchased, if the consumer in our example has a lucky year, with no loss, the income available to spend on other things or to save is $50,000 minus the premium. In an unlucky year, where the consumer becomes ill and has $10,000 in medical bills, the insurance company pays the bills for the consumer. Disposable income remains $50,000 minus the premium for the insurance.

Assume for simplicity's sake that there is an entire population of people just like our hypothetical consumer, with a 10% chance of a loss of $10,000. From the insurer's perspective, if the premium they charge is $1,000, and they sell 10 policies, on average, they will collect $10,000 in premiums and pay out one claim of $10,000, and they break even. However, this scenario ignores the administrative costs of running an insurance company. The company incurs administrative costs in selling the policies, in paying claims, and in designing their policies. Given these costs, to make normal (zero economic) profits, the insurance company must charge a premium equal to the expected loss plus the administrative costs, also known as a loading factor.

Because of the gap in the expected utility of taking our chances with a loss and the expected utility with a constant loss, consumers are willing to pay a loading factor, up to a certain point. However, the analysis becomes more complicated when we realize that different people face different chances of illness and medical-related losses.

Types of Insurance

The market for insurance has evolved into many different forms. The traditional form of insurance is fee-for-service, where health care providers are reimbursed for each service performed. Because of the fast growth in expenses in the health care sector, insurers have experimented with other forms of insurance. Managed care organizations (MCOs) are one market response to this growth in expenses. These organizations may take many forms, including health maintenance organizations (HMOs), preferred provider organizations (PPOs), and point-of-service (POS) plans. Cost savings are achieved through a variety of mechanisms. One mechanism is the use of monopsony (buyer) power to lower fees paid to the providers (hospitals, doctors, pharmacies, etc.). Because the insurer represents multiple potential patients, they may have market power to achieve price discounts. Another is capitated (prepayment) reimbursement mechanisms, which give incentives to providers to reduce the amount of care given. Other mechanisms are to emphasize preventive care and make use of information technologies to reduce the more expensive hospital care.

Market Failures in Insurance

To introduce the two main market failures in insurance, let us begin with an anecdote. Steve has a Mustang convertible, and the radio has been stolen. While shopping for a

Table 70.1   Utility at Different Incomes

Income	Utility
$40,000	200
$49,000	221.4
$50,000	223.6

new radio, he finds a store with a 100% theft guarantee; if someone steals the radio, the store will replace it for free. Steve happily purchases the radio and begins to leave the top down on the car when he parks. After the third time the new radio is stolen, the store refunds his money and refuses to replace it again.

Steve's story illustrates the two major problems facing both profit-maximizing insurance companies and the efficient working of the market: adverse selection and moral hazard. The replacement guarantee on the radio is a form of insurance; Steve no longer had to worry about the risk of loss. Since his radio had been stolen once before, Steve knew he had a high risk of theft, and therefore this insurance had more value to him than many other consumers. However, Steve was not one of the customers the electronics store would have preferred; they would prefer customers with a low risk of theft. The first part of the story is an example of adverse selection; the consumers with the highest demand for insurance at any given premium/price are those with the highest risk/expected losses, assuming that income and ability to pay are not an issue.

Once Steve had purchased the radio, his behavior changed. He began to leave the top down on the car because the guaranteed replacement meant he faced lower marginal cost of having his radio stolen. This behavior is indicative of moral hazard; the presence of insurance alters our incentives at the margin.

Market Failure 1: Adverse Selection

Translating this anecdote to the general issue of health insurance markets, we must first ask, how can adverse selection exist? The underlying problem is one of asymmetric information; one party in the transaction has more information than the other party. In this case, the consumer has more information about his or her risk than the seller (the insurer) does. The insurer cannot know with certainty the expected losses facing any individual, and the individual has an incentive to hide this information to avoid paying a higher premium for coverage. This type of market also has been termed a "lemons" market, by George Akerlof (1970), who coined it from the used car market.

When hidden differences in health risks exist between individuals, insurers have to figure out the profit-maximizing response. To examine this problem further, ignore the administrative costs and risk aversion for a moment and assume that one third of the population has a 15% chance of a $10,000 loss, another third has a 10% chance of the same loss, and the final third of the population has a 5% chance of loss. If an insurer offers a policy to cover the $10,000 loss based on the average population risk, the premium will be

$$\text{Average population loss} = (0.05 * \$10,000 + 0.10 * \$10,000 + 0.15 * \$10,000)/3 = \$1,000.$$

A consumer compares his or her expected losses without insurance to the premium he or she must pay to avoid the losses. If the premium is less than or equal to the consumer's expected losses (remember, we are ignoring risk aversion at the moment), he or she will purchase the insurance; otherwise, he or she will not. Consumers with the 5% loss have an expected loss of only $500, so they will not purchase insurance, but the consumers with the two higher levels of risk will.

The insurance company will have negative profits. Half of their policies were sold to consumers with a 15% risk and half to consumers with a 10% risk. They collect $1,000 in premiums per person but make average expected payouts of $(0.15 * \$10,000 + 0.10 * \$10,000) \div 2 = \$1,250$, for a per person loss of $250. If we imagine the company executives do not realize the problem of adverse selection and analyze their first profits, they might assume that the problem was that they miscalculated the population risk initially and feel they have better data now. In the following period, they might charge $1,250 in premiums. However, since consumers behave rationally, only those with a 15% chance of the loss will purchase the policies at the new price, resulting in still more losses for the insurer. As the cycle continues, the insurer will continue to raise premiums and insure fewer people, until the market itself might disappear. This process of increasing premiums and decreasing coverage has been called a death spiral and in extreme circumstances could lead to the disappearance of the entire market. Because of risk aversion, the lack of a market for insurance will decrease welfare (Arrow, 1963).

Solutions to Adverse Selection

Of course, insurers are not as naive as our above scenario would suggest. They are well aware of the problem of asymmetric information and the resulting adverse selection. The source of the death spiral is the free entry and exit of consumers in this market, combined with their hidden information. While you as a consumer do not have perfect information about your health risks, you do have more information about your own behaviors, family history, and so on than an insurer does. Because consumers are utility maximizing, the consumers who find it worthwhile to purchase insurance are the relatively high-risk consumers in this free entry and exit model. Insurers, consumers, and the public have developed mechanisms to at least partially solve the problems caused by adverse selection. We explore several of the most important solutions below, although this list is not exhaustive.

Market Solution 1: Group Insurance and Risk Pooling

If insurers could find a way to have a pool of consumers with both high and low risks, they could continue to make normal profits, and everyone would have access to insurance. Low-risk individuals would pay a higher premium than their average expected losses, and high-risk individuals would pay a lower premium than their average expected losses.

This risk pooling mechanism is essentially group insurance. In the United States, the grouping mechanism traditionally has been employers, for reasons we will explore more fully below. If we now remember that there are administrative costs to add to the premium, we can find one additional advantage above that of risk pooling to group insurance. Administrative costs decrease rapidly with the size of the group. If a salesperson contracts to insure a group of 250 employees, he or she has, in essence, sold 250 policies in one fell swoop, a less expensive alternative to selling 250 separate policies to 250 consumers. The employer offers the insurance to all employees as a work benefit.

Why would a low-risk individual be willing to, in effect, subsidize a high-risk individual through coverage at work? Several reasons exist; first, because of risk aversion, everyone is willing to pay something more than the value of their expected losses. Second, the cost of purchasing a dollar's worth of health insurance at work is less than a dollar because of the tax treatment of these benefits and because of the lower administrative costs. Third, a low-risk individual today might be a high-risk individual tomorrow, and there might be barriers to purchasing insurance later. In this situation, workers will find it to their advantage to obtain coverage early.

Market Solution 2: Benefit Design and Risk Segmentation

Insurers can also offer multiple types of policies designed to make individuals "signal" their risk level by which policy they choose to purchase. In essence, insurers separate risks and price the policies appropriate to the risk level. They also make use of observable characteristics correlated with health care expenses in setting the availability of the product. To discuss these options, let us first define several characteristics or terms related to health insurance coverage.

The premium is the price the consumer pays in exchange for the insurance coverage. If the consumer has a loss, he or she makes a claim and is reimbursed, or providers are paid directly. Deductibles are exemptions from reimbursement for the first dollars of losses. As an example, someone with a $500 deductible and a $750 medical bill will pay the first $500 out-of-pocket (himself or herself), and the insurance company will pay the next $250. Coinsurance is an arrangement where the insurance company pays a certain percentage of the claims and the consumer pays the remaining percentage out-of-pocket. A co-payment is either a fixed-dollar payment made by the consumer or the actual out-of-pocket payment by the consumer resulting from a coinsurance arrangement.

As an example of how benefit design can separate risks, insurers may increase the premiums but also increase the level of benefits by decreasing the deductibles, co-payments, and coinsurance rates. Compared to a policy with a low premium but high deductibles and co-payments, the premiums of both policies can be designed jointly with the benefits so that relatively high-risk individuals will find one policy more attractive and relatively low-risk individuals will find the other policy more attractive.

Insurers also spend considerable effort identifying observable characteristics (age, gender, etc.) that are correlated with higher risks and pricing the policies accordingly, as young, unmarried males purchasing automobile insurance can certainly attest. These factors include past medical conditions and other risk behaviors such as smoking. In addition to charging different premiums to different groups, insurers have written in a number of preexisting conditions clauses that exempt coverage from medical bills related to health problems that have already been diagnosed.

All of these efforts at risk segmentation add considerable costs to the loading factor associated with health insurance. These costs are one reason why the administrative costs for private insurance in the United States are considerably higher than the administrative costs in Canada, which has universal coverage (Woolhandler, Campbell, & Himmelstein, 2003). These costs are partly incurred by the insurers themselves in their benefit design and pricing mechanisms, but they also add administrative costs to the providers, who must deal with multiple payers with different reimbursement mechanisms.

Policy Solutions to Adverse Selection

The underlying problem with asymmetric information is that healthy consumers opt out of policies, leaving sicker consumers in the pool. Insurers are wary of the very consumers who are most likely to want to purchase insurance. If everyone in the community is covered, however, and opting out can be prevented, then the problem of adverse selection is alleviated. Several policies can be used to address this problem. We will focus on three: individual mandates, employer mandates, and single-payer plans. The recent extensive health care reforms in Massachusetts rely in part on the use of both types of mandates, although the subsidization of risk pools for individuals and small groups is another feature of this plan.

Mandates essentially require individuals to purchase insurance and/or employers to offer insurance to their workforce. In this case, everyone is now forced to demand insurance, and the willingness to purchase insurance is no longer a signal of hidden high risk to the insurer. Single payer, where the government is the insurer, is an option where the entire population is in one risk pool.

Policy Solution 1: Individual Mandates

Minimum requirements for automobile insurance are one example of individual mandates. Car insurance differs from mandated health insurance, however, in that if one cannot afford to purchase the policy, one can simply not drive. Health insurance mandates, in contrast, require everyone to purchase a policy. Unlike driving, one cannot simply forego medical treatment in all cases because emergency rooms are required to give treatment in cases of potentially life-threatening health problems. Thus, policy proposals that include mandates typically also include some form of subsidization of coverage through the tax code and/or increased access to public insurance as part of the plan. Creating or fostering risk pools outside of the existing group market is another feature that enhances the success of individual mandates. Penalties for not purchasing insurance under a mandate plan are also typically enacted through the income tax code. But because everyone is required to purchase insurance, low-risk individuals cannot opt out of the pool. The desire to purchase insurance is no longer an indicator of adverse selection.

Policy Solution 2: Employer Mandates

Employer mandates differ from individual mandates in several ways. First, employers are typically required to offer insurance, but individuals are not necessarily required to accept, or "take up," that offer. Individuals may have alternative access to insurance through a spouse, for example. Firms that do not offer coverage are expected to pay a financial penalty, which is then by the government to subsidize public provision of health insurance to individuals without access to employer-provided insurance. By forcing the expansion of the group market, more consumers will get access to the benefits of risk pooling.

Employer mandates will certainly have additional impacts outside of health care on the market for labor. A simple theoretical analysis of mandates is presented in Summers (1989). Figure 70.1 shows one possible outcome in the labor market of an employer mandate. Requiring employers to provide insurance to their workers adds to the cost of hiring labor, which will reduce demand from $D_{no\ insurance}$ to $D_{insurance}$. However, providing access to insurance at work may also increase the supply of labor from $S_{no\ insurance}$ to $S_{insurance}$. The overall impact on the market will be to lower wages to cover some fraction of the added costs of insurance.

As in any market where there is a simultaneous decrease in demand and increase in supply, the impact on the equilibrium number of workers hired is ambiguous. The new equilibrium could fall anywhere in the shaded area. Where exactly the new equilibrium falls depends on whether labor supply increases more, less, or the same amount as the decrease in demand for labor. If supply increases at the same rate as the demand decreases, the number of employed workers would remain unchanged and the wage offset exactly equals the cost of providing insurance. If supply increases *more* than demand decreases, which occurs if workers value the insurance more than it costs the employer to provide the insurance, the equilibrium quantity of workers could even increase. This latter effect could exist because of the benefits in risk pooling through group insurance in combination with the preferential tax treatment of health insurance purchased at work, which is described in more detail below.

Policy Solution 3: Single-Payer Financing

Even with mandates, adverse selection problems may remain, however, in the sorting of consumers and groups into different policies. Some insurers could attract relatively high-risk pools while others low-risk pools, reducing some of the subsidization of the high-risk individual. Mandates are not a complete answer to the market failure caused by asymmetric information. A single-payer system is one in which the public sector takes on the role of the

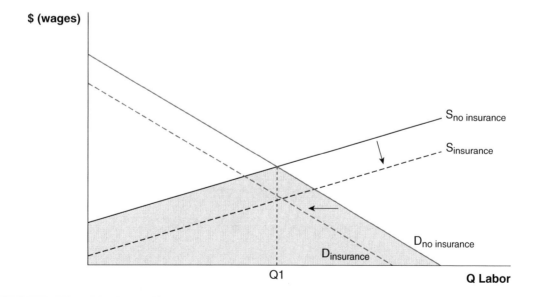

Figure 70.1 Possible Theoretical Impacts of Mandating Employer-Provided Insurance

only insurer. Financing of the care is typically through income taxes in which the healthy and wealthy subsidize the sick and poor. Universal health coverage is achievable without single-payer financing, but single payer has the advantage of virtually eliminating the problem of adverse selection, depending on how comprehensive the benefits associated with this form of financing are.

The Canadian health care system is one example of single-payer financing that retains private markets for the health care providers. In contrast, in the United Kingdom, the public sector is both the main financer and provider of health care. In the United States, Medicare is a single-payer financing mechanism for the elderly and disabled. In each of these examples, some private financing of health care coverage occurs through out-of-pocket payments by the patients themselves and the existence of supplementary insurance.

Market Failure 2: Moral Hazard

We now turn to the second major market failure in insurance: moral hazard. Remember Steve's behavior after he purchased the radio? He was less careful about securing the car when he knew the radio would be replaced if stolen. Economists characterize this behavior as moral hazard. Economists do not generally view the problem of moral hazard in health insurance as being primarily related to the idea that people engage in riskier activities because they are insured, although this behavior could be one aspect of moral hazard. Rather, the main problem with moral hazard in health insurance is that once an individual is insured, the marginal private cost of receiving care is reduced from the true marginal resource (social) cost of production of that care. The price facing the insured patient could even be zero; in other cases, the price is reduced from the full cost to a modest co-payment or coinsurance rate.

The efficiency, or welfare, costs of moral hazard are shown in Figure 70.2 for a sample market of doctor visits.

To keep things simple, we will assume constant marginal costs, which represent the true, social resource costs of production. In perfectly competitive markets, the equilibrium market price will also be equal to the marginal cost of production. The uninsured, whether their demand curve is represented by $D1$ or $D2$, pay the full marginal costs of care, and the quantity demanded for this group is $Q1$, where the market price (MC curve) intersects the demand curve. This point is the efficient level of production. Again for simplicity's sake, assume for the moment that insurance is full coverage—there are no deductibles or co-payments.

Whether a deadweight loss from moral hazard exists depends on the elasticity of demand for health care. Figure 70.2 shows both scenarios; $D1$ represents the perfectly inelastic demand case, and $D2$ represents an elastic demand curve. Full insurance moves the marginal personal cost (price facing the individual) from the market price to zero. If demand is perfectly inelastic, the quantity demanded of health care remains the same, $Q1$, and the efficient level of consumption is maintained. When demand is elastic, the rational, utility-maximizing individual will optimally consume doctor visits up to $Q0$, where the demand curve intersects the x-axis. As is evident, $Q0$ is greater than $Q1$, and the individual is consuming an inefficiently high amount of medical care. The efficiency losses from moral hazard are greater the more elastic the demand for medical care.

What determines the elasticity of demand for health care? Demand tends to be more elastic for goods that are not considered necessities and goods with substitutes. Different types of medical care are likely to differ in their elasticity; one might have more elastic demand for the doctor with a sore throat versus a heart attack, for instance. With some sore throats, one can rest, use over-the-counter remedies, and eat chicken soup without significantly worse outcomes than one would receive from a doctor's visit.

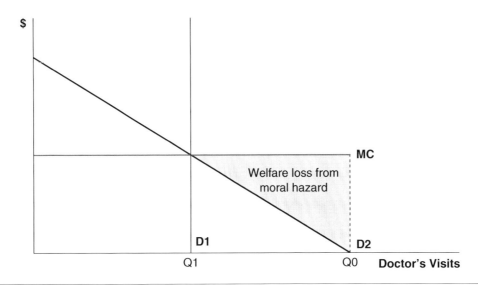

Figure 70.2 The Welfare Economics of Moral Hazard

Even if it is a strep throat, which requires a prescription for antibiotics, consumers with no insurance may wait for a bit to determine whether the sore throat will get better on its own. Consumers with insurance are more likely to go to the doctor sooner, and in some of those cases, the doctor's care is unnecessary because the illness would have resolved by itself. Because heart attacks are more life threatening and there are not many true substitutes to medical care, demand for cardiac care is likely to be more inelastic. The RAND health insurance experiment (discussed below) provides some evidence on the elasticity of demand for different types of health care services.

The overconsumption from moral hazard is rational for the individual, who receives positive marginal benefits from the additional care. The welfare problem is that his or her marginal benefits are less than the true resource cost of production. From a society's view, this behavior is undesirable; the resources used to produce those doctor visits could be going to producing other goods with higher marginal benefits in other markets. The amount of the efficiency loss can be measured if the marginal benefits of care are known. The deadweight loss of moral hazard is shown by the area of the shaded triangle in Figure 70.2. The welfare losses are not equal to the full resource costs of production because we still do count the marginal benefits accruing to the individual.

Market Solution: Benefit Design

The problem of moral hazard can be minimized by patient cost-sharing mechanisms. If designed well, the addition of deductibles and coinsurance can reduce the amount of welfare loss produced by insurance by returning some of the costs back to the patient. The introduction and encouragement of consumer-directed health care is an example of a market solution intended to combat moral hazard. These plans are typically a very high deductible catastrophic insurance plan. These insurance policies are then priced more cheaply than more generous coverage. The deductibles in these plans force the patient to face the full marginal cost of the first few thousand dollars of care. Presumably, consumers will then be less likely to go to the doctor for minor problems like colds and to think about less expensive options for other types of care.

The success of patient cost sharing at reducing use of health care presupposes that the consumers know the true marginal benefits of the health care and that they fully direct their health care expenses. The problem with these assumptions is that there is asymmetric information in the health care markets as well. Physicians and other health care professionals have considerably more technical knowledge than patients, and patients therefore rely on them to be good agents when prescribing care. In addition, can the average patient distinguish between the medical problems that require medical intervention from those that will resolve on their own? The heart attack example is illustrative; perhaps the symptoms experienced by the

patient are nothing more than heartburn, but without medical personnel to assess the patient, the consumer really does not know. To the extent that physicians direct the consumption of medical care, this limits the responsiveness of consumers to price. Patients may not be presented with a range of options for a particular health problem or may not possess the information to adequately assess the different costs and benefits of different options.

Cost containment mechanisms such as deductibles and coinsurance are common in the United States but rarer and/or more modest in other countries. While there is evidence that co-payments do reduce the quantity of care demanded, in a global sense, they seem to be fairly ineffective at reducing costs for the entire health care sector. Other countries, which rely more on cost containment strategies directed at the supply of health care, have lower per capita health care costs than the United States.

Income Taxes and Moral Hazard

The problem of moral hazard may be exacerbated by the differential treatment of health insurance "purchased" at work. In essence, total compensation received by workers in efficient markets is equal to the marginal revenue product that worker brings to the firm (his or her productivity). Workers could receive compensation in the form of wages or other benefits, including health insurance, pensions, and so on. To receive health insurance, workers must exchange wages for that benefit. The worker pays for the insurance directly through the employee share of the premium and indirectly in the form of lower raises and reduced wages.

The growth in employer-provided group health insurance in the United States has been fueled in part by the differential treatment of health insurance compensation versus wage and salary compensation. We are taxed on the latter but not the former at the federal and some state levels. This disparate handling in the tax code is rooted in the wage and price controls imposed during World War II. Having a large military mobilization increased both the domestic demand for goods and the domestic labor demand. Policy makers recognized that both factors would likely lead to considerable inflation. In the wartime environment, the government took a much more active role in regulating the economy, and one policy was the wage freeze. However, firms still required some means of trying to attract more workers in the tight labor market and began to offer additional, nonwage, fringe benefits. These were allowed and not considered part of the wage/salary freeze. This circumstance led to some questions about how nonwage compensation would be taxed. In 1954, the Internal Revenue Service (IRS) issued a judgment that these parts of compensation were not part of taxable income.

As a result, individuals who receive insurance at work pay less than a dollar for a dollar's worth of coverage. In effect, the treatment acts like a tax deduction; it reduces taxable income by the value of the insurance. In addition, it reduces payroll taxes. Policies such as this one are termed *tax expenditures;* they represent foregone tax revenues for the government. How much the tax bill is reduced for the family depends on which tax bracket the household falls into. The value of a deduction is equal to the premium multiplied by the highest marginal tax rate the household faces.

Because of the artificial lowering of the price of health insurance at work, workers may demand more of their compensation in the form of health insurance than is optimal. Insurance policies traditionally covered rare, catastrophic events; now they often cover routine, smaller ticket items. In essence, health insurance now takes on an additional role beyond that of taking away uncertain risks; it becomes the predominant form of financing for health care.

Welfare and Equity Implications

If no market failures existed in health insurance, the special tax treatment would artificially reduce the price of health insurance and cause inefficiently high levels of health insurance coverage. However, asymmetric information does exist. Increasing the quantity of health insurance in this context may imply that the tax treatment improves efficiency. Second, equity considerations are also considered to be relevant. Society may view access to health care as being a special good that should not be allocated by the market. Many believe that low income should not prevent access to health care. If the tax treatment of health insurance improves access to health care for disadvantaged groups, society may value that outcome even if some efficiency costs exist in increasing the equity of outcomes (Okun, 1975). The tax treatment, however, does not appear to be accomplishing the goal of increasing equity of coverage.

Efficiency Impacts

Critics argue that the favorable tax treatment of employer-provided health insurance has led to an inefficiently high level of coverage. Health insurance has become less health insurance and more health care financing, with benefits including small, regular expenses such as checkups, in addition to the coverage of big-ticket, uncertain expenses. More generous benefits lead in turn to more potential for moral hazard, as patients become increasingly insulated from the full marginal cost of care. As discussed above, the amount of inefficiency caused by this moral hazard depends on how elastic the demand for medical care is.

What is the evidence on elasticity of demand for health care? Estimating the elasticity of demand for health care by varying the levels of co-payments patients pay is subject to selection bias since, as we have described above, individuals choose their level of coverage based in part on their health status. In other words, consumers who are relatively unhealthy are more likely to opt for fuller insurance coverage with lower patient out-of-pocket expenses. The RAND health insurance study provides the cleanest estimates of the elasticity of demand for health care. In this study, individuals were randomized to different levels of health insurance coverage, and their medical care use was tracked, so their level of insurance was uncorrelated with their health status. For most services, the estimated demand elasticities were quite inelastic (Newhouse & the Insurance Experiment Group, 1993). Inelastic demand for medical care then implies relatively small losses from moral hazard.

Equity Considerations

How the tax treatment affects access to disadvantaged groups (the poor or the sick, for instance) is another societal concern. The tax benefits are highly inequitably distributed and make the relative access to private health insurance worse. The reasons for the inequity are twofold. Workers must first have an offer of insurance from their employer to take advantage of the tax subsidy. In addition, the size of the tax subsidy depends on the marginal tax rate facing the household receiving the insurance. Because the U.S. income tax structure is progressive, higher income households receive a higher tax subsidy for the same policy relative to a lower income household. Sheils and Haught (2004) estimate that the bulk (71.5%) of the benefits of this tax expenditure goes to families with incomes of $50,000 or more, relative to the rest of the population. Looking at the data in a different way, the average benefit for families with incomes of $100,000 or more is $2,780, compared to a mere $102 on average for families with less than $10,000 in annual income.

A horizontal inequity is also created by the policy. Otherwise similar individuals are treated differently, depending on where they access health insurance. While self-employed individuals are also now able to deduct their insurance, the treatment for individuals purchasing insurance in the nongroup market is quite different. Individuals who have medical expenses exceeding 7.5% of their adjusted gross income may deduct these expenses from their taxes; insurance premiums may count as part of these medical expenses. In other words, individuals must have substantial expenses before they are able to take advantage of this deduction. In addition, the employer-provided health insurance exemption reduces individuals' payroll tax (FICA) contributions, while the deduction for individual purchases of health insurance does not, reducing the relative value of the latter.

Public Insurance in the United States

Now that we have a better sense of the workings of the health insurance market, we turn our attention to the public insurance policies in the United States. The U.S. system of financing is a mix of private and public coverage. While there are a variety of government-run and funded health programs, including coverage for military personnel and veterans, this chapter will focus on the three main programs: Medicare, Medicaid, and SCHIP.

Medicare

Medicare, established in 1965, is the public coverage for individuals age 65 and older, individuals younger than age 65 with disabilities, and anyone with end-stage renal failure. In essence, for most recipients, it is a single-payer-type plan. The "traditional" Medicare policy is composed of two parts: Part A, essentially catastrophic coverage for inpatient hospital care and some temporary, limited coverage for hospice and long-term care coverage. These benefits are not subject to a premium. The second part, Part B, covers some outpatient and doctor's services. Beneficiaries contribute premiums for this coverage. Other funding is from payroll taxes and general tax revenues.

Individuals can also opt out of traditional Medicare coverage and choose Part C, aka "Medicare Advantage" plan, which could be an HMO, PPO, or a private fee-for-service plan. The government pays the premium for the individual, and the private insurance plan takes over the insurance role. With the passage of the Medicare Modernization Act of 2003, prescription drug coverage was added in 2006. Part D includes some premiums for individuals. In addition to this basic level of coverage, elderly individuals may purchase supplemental, or gap, insurance to cover expenses that are not covered by Medicare. Retiree health insurance plans often fill this role, as does Medicaid coverage for the elderly poor. Individuals who receive both Medicare and Medicaid coverage are called dual eligibles.

Medicaid and State Child Health Insurance Program

Medicaid and SCHIP are means-tested programs to provide insurance for the very poor. They are jointly state and federally funded and administered insurance for the poor. Eligibility for Medicaid varies by state, with the federal government establishing minimum criteria. As a means-tested program, individuals must have incomes below a specific cutoff based on the federal poverty line and hold limited assets to qualify for the benefits. The income eligibility cutoffs also vary by characteristics of the individual, with higher thresholds for infants, children, and pregnant women, for example. Individuals with very high medical expenses may qualify under the medically needy category; Medicare dual eligibles often qualify through this route.

The Uninsured

Not everyone in the United States has access to coverage. Given the market failures and the structure of public coverage, it is possible to predict characteristics that will be associated with lack of insurance. Individuals with preexisting conditions who do not have access to the group market will be particularly vulnerable. The elderly receive coverage through Medicare, so the uninsured will be found among the nonelderly. Means-tested programs cover the very poor, and to receive health insurance compensation through an employer, the worker's marginal revenue product must be high enough to pay for the insurance in lower wages.

The uninsured are by and large in families with one or more full-time workers and in families that are under or near the poverty line. They earn too much income to qualify for Medicaid/SCHIP or do not take up Medicaid, but they do not have enough income to purchase health insurance on their own. Since the benefits of risk pooling increase with the size of the group, uninsured workers are more likely to be employed at smaller firms, in occupations and industries with considerable job turnover, and in low-wage occupations.

The Evolution of HIV/AIDS and Insurance Coverage

On June 5, 1981, the Centers for Disease Control (CDC) reported a small cluster of deaths in Los Angeles from a form of pneumonia that was rarely fatal. After long investigations, the underlying cause was determined. Acquired immune deficiency syndrome (AIDS) was identified, an infectious disease caused by a retrovirus named human immunodeficiency virus (HIV). In the early years of the epidemic, HIV was a virtual death sentence, and until a blood test was approved by the Food and Drug Administration (FDA) in 1985, most cases were not identified until late in the disease stage, when the immune system had already been so compromised that opportunistic infections had already attacked the system. The disease has a long latency period, on average 6 to 10 years, in which the individual is infected with the virus before developing full-blown AIDS. During the latency period, the individual may show few or no debilitating symptoms. An individual develops AIDS when his or her CD4 cell count (an important component of the immune system) drops below 200 and/or begins to contract opportunistic infections.

In the beginning of the epidemic, treatment of the opportunistic infections was the only course of action available until the introduction of azidothymidine (AZT), which inhibits the replication of the virus itself. However, because of HIV's quick replication rate and high rate of mutations, AZT alone only temporarily extended the life expectancy of those infected before the virus developed resistance to the pharmaceutical. For many during this period, life expectancy was extended only a few months. It was not until the development of highly active antiretroviral therapy (HAART) in 1995 that medicine was able to significantly extend the life expectancy of HIV-positive individuals and the death rate from AIDS began to fall. HAART is characterized by treatment with more than one drug; each drug targets a different aspect of the viral infection and replication process. Success of the regimen depends on the strict adherence to the treatment; treatment cannot be stopped once started, or the virus may gain resistance, and the disease progression will resume.

The evolution of treatment for HIV/AIDS and the characteristics of the disease itself provide an important policy problem within the United States for the study of health insurance. As we have examined above, insurance "for insurance's sake" should be focused on catastrophic (high-cost), unexpected health problems. AIDS fit this model quite well early on in the epidemic since it was an acute problem, although the outcome was often death and not recovery. It was not until the development of effective medical therapies that HIV/AIDS changed to a chronic condition with important implications for the financing of health care for HIV-positive individuals.

Once started, to be effective, the drugs must be taken daily for the rest of the patient's life, to prevent the development of drug resistance. However, once an individual has become diagnosed with HIV, the level of uncertainty about the amount and costs of medical care required by the individual drops. One faces *certain* medical expenditures for many, many years. The HAART treatments alone are quite expensive, averaging $12,000 to $24,000 per year, not counting other treatments for opportunistic infections and toxicity-related side effects of the drugs themselves.

Individuals who have tested positive for HIV experience enormous difficulties in obtaining private coverage in the individual market. The presence of the virus is a preexisting condition with known, large current and future expenses. Pollitz, Sorian, and Thomas (2001) surveyed nongroup market insurers about premiums and policy restrictions for a set of hypothetical patients. In this study, even individuals who only had hay fever as a preexisting condition faced higher premiums and fewer offers of "clean" coverage (coverage without additional restrictions on the benefits); the hypothetical HIV-positive consumer received no offers of coverage at any price in any of the markets. To receive access to private group coverage, an individual must be able to work, find a job/employer that offers coverage, and be able to afford the employee share of the premium. If HIV/AIDS results in a disability for the individual, employment will become difficult or impossible.

The typical routes to public financing for HIV/AIDS care are through either Medicare under the low-income, disabled eligibility category or Medicaid as a low-income welfare, medically needy, or as a dual-eligible Medicare disability recipient. To qualify as a person with disabilities, one must have an employment history and wait for 2 years after the development of the disabling condition to become eligible. Once on the HAART therapy, HIV/AIDS can become less disabling, which then may disqualify the person from eligibility for the public coverage. If public coverage is lost, the patient may stop taking the drugs, become

disabled again, and can then regain coverage. From a public health perspective, this on-again/off-again financing of care could contribute to the rise of drug resistance in the virus, a significant negative externality. See Laurence (2001) for further analysis of the policy debate.

Given the market solutions to adverse selection and the strong tie of private insurance to employment, one would expect to find a lower rate of private insurance coverage among the population of HIV-positive individuals. This trend away from private coverage toward public coverage should increase over time, as medical technology has transformed HIV/AIDS into a chronic, albeit often debilitating, disease model. Data in Goldman et al.'s (2003) analysis confirms this picture, as half of all HIV-positive individuals in the study are insured by Medicaid, Medicare, or both. The importance of the public sector as a safety net for persons living with HIV has disadvantages. During recessionary time periods, states face pressure to cut back on their outlays for Medicaid, which can hurt access to care for this population. Ghosh, Sood, and Leibowitz (2007) find that one state strategy for cutting costs, decreasing the income threshold to qualify for Medicaid, increases the rate of uninsurance and decreases the use of HAART.

Stability of coverage is another issue of great importance for HIV-positive individuals. To what extent do HIV-positive individuals move from being insured to losing coverage? How often do they switch from private to public coverage or vice versa? Do these transitions affect the quality of medical care received by this population? Fleishman (1998) provides some evidence from the 1990s; most individuals who changed coverage status were those who went from no insurance to public insurance; individuals who had developed AIDS were more likely to make such a switch. Relatively few individuals in this sample lost private coverage, perhaps reflecting the increase in the effectiveness of HAART therapy at keeping individuals from developing disabling symptoms. More recent evidence in Kelaher and Jessop (2006) in New York City also shows the same pattern. However, some individuals do lose coverage, which has important implications for their ability to afford therapy.

Conclusion

Health insurance markets do not fit the standard market model of perfect competition. They exist because of the information problem of uncertainty, in combination with our risk aversion. Once created, they face the market failure of asymmetric information. Being insured may alter the consumption of health care in inefficient ways through moral hazard. All of these problems have real consequences for who gets covered and how they are covered. When analyzing these markets, society considers not only the efficiency of the market, but because insurance finances health care, equity concerns are also prominent in the debate on the appropriate policy response.

References and Further Readings

Akerlof, G. A. (1970). The market for 'lemons': Quality uncertainty and the market mechanism. *Quarterly Journal of Economics, 84,* 488–500.

Arrow, K. J. (1963). Uncertainty and the welfare economics of medical care. *American Economic Review, 53,* 941–973.

Centers for Disease Control. (1981). Pneumocystis pneumonia—Los Angeles. *Morbidity and Mortality Weekly Reports, 30,* 250–252.

Cutler, D. M., & Gruber, J. (1996). Does public insurance crowd out private insurance? *Quarterly Journal of Economics, 111,* 391–430.

Fleishman, J. A. (1998). Transitions in insurance and employment among people with HIV infection. *Inquiry, 35,* 36–48.

Ghosh, A., Sood, N., & Leibowitz, A. (2007). The effect of state cost containment strategies on the insurance status and use of antiretroviral therapy (HAART) for HIV infected people. *Forum for Health Economics & Policy, 10*(2), Article 3. Retrieved February 24, 2009, from http://www.bepress.com/fhep

Goldman, D. P., Leibowitz, A. A., Joyce, G. F., Fleishman, J. A., Bozzette, S. A., Duan, N., et al. (2003). Insurance status of HIV-infected adults in the post-HAART era: Evidence from the United States. *Applied Health Economics and Health Policy, 2*(2), 85–91.

Kelaher, M., & Jessop, D. J. (2006). The impact of loss of Medicaid on health service utilization among persons with HIV/AIDS in New York City. *Health Policy, 76,* 80–92.

Laurence, L. (2001, March 13). Special report: Medicaid's catch-22. *Kaiser Daily HIV/AIDS Report.* Retrieved February 24, 2009, from http://www.kaisernetwork.org/daily_reports/rep_index.cfm?DR_ID=3349

Medicare Payment Advisory Commission (MedPAC). (2008, December 5). *Medicare advantage program.* Paper presented at the MedPAC Public Meeting, Washington, DC.

Newhouse, J. P., & the Insurance Experiment Group. (1993). *Free for all? Lessons from the RAND health insurance experiment.* Cambridge, MA: Harvard University Press.

Okun, A. (1975). *Equality and efficiency: The big tradeoff.* Washington, DC: Brookings Institution.

Pollitz, K., Sorian, R., & Thomas, K. (2001). *How accessible is individual health insurance for consumers in less-than-perfect health?* Retrieved February 24, 2009, from http://www.kff.org/insurance/upload/How-Accessible-is-Individual-Health-Insurance-for-Consumer-in-Less-Than-Perfect-Health-Report.pdf

Sheils, J., & Haught, R. (2004). The cost of tax-exempt health benefits in 2004. *Health Affairs.* Available at http://content.healthaffairs.org/index.dtl

Summers, L. H. (1989). Some simple economics of mandated benefits. *American Economic Review: Papers and Proceedings, 79,* 177–183.

Woolhandler, S., Campbell, T., & Himmelstein, D. U. (2003). Costs of health care administration in the United States and Canada. *New England Journal of Medicine, 349,* 768–775.

Woolhandler, S., & Himmelstein, D. U. (2002). Paying for national health insurance–and not getting it. *Health Affairs, 21*(4), 88–98.

71

ECONOMICS OF INFORMATION

VIKTAR FEDASEYEU

Boston College

As Francis Bacon once noted, knowledge is power. The need to acquire and process information is a tremendously important part of human interactions. Economic interactions are no exception. Investors buying stocks or other securities need to analyze the quality and reliability of information supplied to them. Employers must evaluate qualifications of job applicants prior to starting a working relationship with them. Insurance companies must set premiums based on the perceived risks of the insured. Examples of this sort abound in any field of economics.

The purpose of this chapter is to show that the structure of the information environment can have significant consequences for how the markets and the whole economy operate. Standard theories of competitive equilibrium usually avoid these issues by assuming that all agents have costless access to the same information. The recognition that this is a very limiting assumption is what has fueled research in information economics.

Information, unlike other goods that interest economists, has several unique characteristics:

- Information is a public good: Learning does not prevent others from learning.
- Information cannot be unlearned; that is, the decision to acquire information is irreversible once it has been acquired.
- Information is asymmetric: Different people know different things.

It is conceptually easy to understand the public-good nature of information. The other two characteristics require further clarification. The fact that information cannot be unlearned complicates the process of information production. Unlike other goods, information cannot be sampled or returned for a refund: Once the decision has been made to learn something, it is virtually impossible to reverse it after obtaining information. It is of course possible to forget information. Forgetting, however, will not reimburse one for the efforts expended to obtain information.

Information asymmetry, the third property listed above, will be the primary focus of this chapter. The idea that people have different knowledge seems almost obvious. Its implications for market equilibrium, however, had not been recognized for a long time. It was usually assumed that in competitive markets, knowledge heterogeneity will be small and will not affect the equilibrium in any significant way. Contrary to this common belief, Akerlof and Yellen (1985) showed that even small deviations can have significant effects.

George Stigler is often regarded as the father of economics of information for it was he who focused economists' attention on the role of information in economic decision making. Stigler (1961) analyzed the dispersion of prices and noted that while it is often convenient to assume that all agents are endowed with perfect information about preferences and technologies, the very existence of price dispersion contradicts this simple view. He explained the persistence of such dispersion by the presence of search costs: Obtaining information requires time, which is a valuable resource. He then suggested that in equilibrium, the marginal benefit of the search for information must equal its marginal cost.

While Stigler's (1961) paper was a breakthrough that gave birth to a new field in economics, it treated information in very much the same way that the economists were treating other goods. Information, however, is different in many respects. It is these differences, and information asymmetry in particular, that will be the focus of our attention.

Information Asymmetry

The Problem of Asymmetry

Information is valuable, and its value is often determined by the number of people who know it. The fact that some people know more than others is referred to as information asymmetry. The examples of asymmetry are numerous: A job applicant knows more about his or her abilities and work ethics than the potential employer, an entrepreneur seeking a loan from the bank knows more about the viability of his or her business than the loan officer, and a person buying health insurance knows more about his or her health than the insurance company. Asymmetry is a departure from the model of perfect markets, and it creates challenges and problems.

While the problems of information asymmetry had been realized by early economists, Akerlof (1970) was the first to rigorously analyze the problem of private information. He showed that information asymmetry is crucial to understanding how markets operate.

Consider the market for used cars, which is the example discussed in Akerlof (1970). Assume that a car can be of either good or bad quality with equal probability ($\frac{1}{2}$)—that is, there are as many good cars as there are bad cars. Further assume that for the sellers, a good car is worth $800 and a bad car is worth $50. For potential buyers, on the other hand, a good car is worth $1,000 and a bad car is worth $100. What is the equilibrium clearing price in this market? As it turns out, the answer depends on who knows what.

First, consider the case when neither sellers nor buyers can differentiate between good and bad cars. The expected value to the seller of not selling the car is $425 = ½ × $800 + ½ × $50. The expected purchase value to the buyer is $550 = ½ × $1,000 + ½ × $100. Thus, at a price between $425 and $550, cars of all qualities will be traded in this market.

Now assume that sellers know the quality of their cars while buyers do not, which seems quite realistic. Notice that there is no credible way sellers can communicate their knowledge since every seller would try to claim that he or she has a good car. The $425 to $550 range no longer works in this case because sellers with good cars will be unwilling to sell them for less than $800. Therefore, only bad cars will be brought to the market. The buyers understand this and will only pay $100 or less since this is the value of bad cars to them. Notice that many welfare-enhancing trades will be forgone in the above equilibrium. A market breakdown occurs.

Adverse Selection and Moral Hazard

The applicability of Akerlof's (1970) result is very wide. Research that followed his seminal paper identified two major types of problems that arise from information asymmetry: adverse selection and moral hazard. The problem that Akerlof originally described in his work is a special case of adverse selection. It is now often associated with insurance markets, although it is far more general.

Consider the problem of selling health insurance. Different people have different degrees of health risks, and most important, they are likely to know more about their health than insurance companies. Notice that consumers with higher risks will value insurance more and will be more likely to buy it. As a result, the proportion of less healthy people in the pool of actual insurance buyers will be larger than their fraction in the general population. It is the more risky consumers who self-select themselves into buying the product—hence the term *adverse selection.* It is, of course, the opposite of what insurance companies would want.

Moral hazard refers to the inappropriate behavior of agents whose actions cannot be perfectly monitored. A person who has car insurance may be less vigilant about the car than he or she would have been without insurance. In this case, the insurance company has less information about future actions of the person than the person himself or herself. The principal-agent problem is a special case of moral hazard: As long as the principal cannot monitor the agent perfectly, the latter has an incentive to engage in behaviors inconsistent with the principal's interest. A simple albeit extreme example will illustrate this. Imagine a principal who hires an agent to manage retirement savings and agrees to pay the latter a fixed salary no matter what. It is obvious that the agent's optimal behavior would be to do nothing at all and simply collect the salary without effort.

Government welfare policies may sometimes create moral hazard problems. Unemployment benefits are one example: As long as a person is qualified to receive them, he or she may be less willing to search for a job. Another example is government bailouts. An expectation that the government will help some companies in bad times may create an implicit guarantee. As a result, such companies may undertake projects that they would have considered too risky had there been no implicit guarantee. While in many instances, letting a business entity fail may have catastrophic consequences, policy makers and students of economics should be aware of moral hazard implications and take them into account in their decision making.

Akerlof's (1970) pioneering work outlined the problems that can arise in markets with asymmetric information. It did not, however, look at how the markets can address these problems. Later research by Michael Spence and Josef Stiglitz suggested two elegant approaches: signaling and screening.

Signaling

Henceforth in our discussion, we will refer to agents with private information as the informed party, while their counterparty will be called the uninformed party.

Spence (1973) introduced the concept of signaling. While his original paper discussed a job market signaling model, its general idea can be applied in a wide variety of settings. The premise of Spence's reasoning is that informed agents can behave in a way that sends a "signal" to the uninformed party. This behavior can be used to reveal information about product quality, a person's qualification for the job, and so on. The signal, however, must be credible. Credibility is usually associated with costs for the informed party: If there are no costs involved, everyone would try to send the signal with the most favorable information, and the Akerlof-type market breakdown is likely to occur. The costs must be high enough to prevent some types of agents from sending the signal and low enough to make signaling worthwhile for other types. If this condition is met, signaling will separate agents based on their types and thus reveal information.

In Spence's (1973) original paper, schooling is used by potential employees to signal the level of their ability. Assume that there are two types of workers: those who are highly qualified for the job and those who are less qualified. The employer is unable to differentiate them a priori. The workers, however, are aware of their ability level. In a competitive labor market with complete information, every worker's wage will be determined by his or her marginal productivity. In the incomplete information case, on the other hand, the employer is unable to perfectly determine the worker's marginal product prior to hiring and must take into account the probability that the worker is unskilled.

The critical assumption in Spence (1973) is that marginal costs (monetary and mental) of schooling are greater for workers with less ability. As a result, the level of schooling is positively correlated with ability. What makes the signal credible is the fact that beyond a certain level of education, less able workers will find it unjustified to continue acquiring more schooling: Their costs will exceed potential benefits from higher wages. It is only the more able applicants who will find it worthwhile to pursue further education. Thus, additional investment in education will differentiate applicants based on their ability.

The cost of schooling in Spence's (1973) model is dissipative: Education does not bring any benefits beyond signaling the worker type. And since highly qualified workers have to privately bear the costs of education, total welfare declines relative to the full-information case. It is likely that other benefits of education may affect marginal productivity directly. In particular, even less skilled applicants can acquire necessary qualifications through education. These benefits are clearly important, but they may not solve the asymmetry problem since more able workers may still remain more qualified compared to the less able applicant with the same level of schooling.

Screening

Although conceptually similar to signaling, screening is a slightly different device used by the uninformed party to extract information. The uninformed agent may offer a menu of options to the informed party, whose choices out of that menu reveal information that the uninformed agent is seeking. Notice that this menu must be somewhat restrictive since letting the informed party choose whatever actions they prefer will not alleviate the problem.

Rothschild and Stiglitz (1976) developed a classical screening model for insurance markets. People who buy insurance usually know more about the risks they are facing. They will, therefore, self-select into buying insurance for the kinds of losses that are likely to occur to them. Insurance companies must account for this in the premiums they charge. In particular, premiums must be higher than they would have been had every person bought insurance regardless of his or her risk level because the proportion of high-risk individuals in the general population will be lower than among those who actually buy insurance. These higher premiums, however, will attract even fewer low-risk individuals and will only exacerbate the self-selection problem. Rothschild and Stiglitz show that competitive insurance markets can only be in equilibrium if insurance companies compete on both price and quantity—that is, they offer contracts that specify both price and quantity of insurance that can be purchased for that price. This is different from the usual competitive market equilibrium where the seller offers a price and the buyer determines the quantities he or she is willing to obtain.

Do real-life insurance markets behave in a way that is consistent with above conclusions? They do. In particular, insurance companies offer various quantities of coverage by using deductibles and caps. A deductible is the amount that the insured person must cover himself or herself, while any damage beyond that amount is paid by the insurer. A cap is the maximum possible amount of insurance that the company agrees to pay. Individuals facing higher risks will prefer lower deductibles and higher caps, while low-risk people will be willing to buy insurance with higher deductibles and lower caps. As one might expect, the magnitude of the deductible and the cap a person is willing to accept affect premiums very significantly.

Rothschild and Stiglitz (1976) show that under certain circumstances, insurance markets can have no equilibrium. If feasible equilibrium exists, however, it can only be separating. In a pooling equilibrium, people of all risk types buy the same contract, and screening is unnecessary. In a separating equilibrium, on the other hand, every type buys the contract geared specifically to that type's risk profile. Separating equilibria are usually welfare inferior to pooling equilibria because of screening costs. Rothschild and Stiglitz show that low-risk people are left underinsured compared to the full-information case. This fact prompted policy makers to advocate mandatory insurance to mitigate the adverse selection problem. The reasoning goes as follows. If everyone is required to purchase insurance, people will no longer have the option to self-select based on their risk characteristics. Insurance companies will know that people buying the contracts were required to do so regardless of their risk characteristics and may be willing to lower the rates to reflect the expected average level of risk. This average level of risk will be lower than without mandatory insurance since people of different risk types are required to participate. The effectiveness and fairness of this approach is an important part of current policy debates.

It should also be clear that insurance markets might have other problems that may diminish the effectiveness of this policy. In particular, Rothschild and Stiglitz (1976) forego a detailed discussion of the incentives of insurance companies themselves, mainly because of the lack of theoretical guidance in that respect.

Applications: Financial Markets

Credit Rationing and Screening With Interest Rates

One of the puzzling features of economic reality is the fact that credit is rationed. In simple terms, credit rationing is the situation when credit markets do not clear (i.e., the demand for funds exceeds their supply at the prevailing interest rate). As Stiglitz and Weiss (1981) note, when the price mechanism works well, rationing should not exist: If demand for credit were to exceed supply, prices (i.e., interest rates) would rise and lead to an appropriate increase in the supply of funds. In Stiglitz and Weiss, it is information asymmetry that may be responsible for credit rationing.

Interest rates may affect the riskiness of the pool of potential borrowers, in which case the problems of adverse selection and moral hazard arise. The observation that high interest rates may drive away the safest borrowers dates back to Adam Smith. Those who are willing to accept higher interest rates may be, on average, of higher risk to the bank since they may be willing to borrow at higher rates precisely because they perceive their repayment probability as being low. In addition, higher interest rates may lead to moral hazard and change the behavior of the borrowers: Stiglitz and Weiss (1981) show that higher interest rates lead firms to undertake projects with lower probabilities of success but higher payoffs conditional on success. As a result, the bank's expected profits may decline after a certain cutoff interest rate. It is conceivable that at this cutoff rate, the demand will still exceed supply, but banks will be unwilling to lend due to the moral hazard and adverse selection problems.

Information Asymmetry Problems in Corporate Finance

Signaling With Capital Structure

Capital structure is a focal problem in corporate finance. Academics have for a long time been concerned with why firms choose a particular mix of debt and equity financing. The very fact that firms opt to manage their capital structure is puzzling from the standard viewpoint of competitive markets. Modigliani and Miller (1958) showed that in a frictionless world, the choice of debt over equity should not matter. Empirical studies, on the other hand, have documented several stylized facts about leverage, and these facts required explanation. Several theories and a strand of empirical papers testing those theories emerged (for an incomplete list, see Graham, 2000; Rajan & Zingales, 1995; Titman & Wessels, 1988).

Myers and Majluf (1984) discuss corporate structure decisions in a setting of incomplete information: The firm's insiders know more about the firm's assets than outside investors. Assume that the firm has a profitable investment opportunity and must raise outside financing in order to pursue it. Also assume that the management acts in the interest of existing shareholders. Due to information asymmetry, the market will at times undervalue the firm relative to insiders' private information. If new equity is issued, existing shareholders will be diluted since they will have to share profits with new shareholders. The extent of this dilution will be large if the insiders have very favorable information about the firm relative to the market's assessment. Sometimes this dilution will be sufficiently large to result in a wealth loss for existing shareholders.

A numerical example will make this argument clear. Imagine that the market values Firm A at $1,100,000 while insiders observe the true value of $2,500,000. Firm B has the same market valuation, but insiders value it at $1,500,000. Assume that both firms have access to identical projects that cost $320,000 and will create a net value of $180,000 next period (the gross value of the project is therefore $500,000). Also assume that information asymmetry will be resolved next period regardless of whether the project is implemented. If both firms implement the project, Firm A will be worth $3,000,000, and Firm B will be worth $2,000,000. The a priori market valuation, however, is different because of asymmetry: It is $1,600,000 for both firms. Thus, outside investors will be willing to provide $320,000 in exchange for a 20% stake in either company ($320,000/$1,600,000 = 0.20). Notice, however, that from the insiders' point of view, if the project is implemented, a 20% stake is worth $600,000 and $400,000 in Firm A and Firm B, respectively. Insiders are diluted in both cases, but Firm A insiders are clearly worse off.

It is, however, incorrect to assume that offering a stake will result in a wealth loss in both cases. Consider Firm B: Without the project, it will be worth $1,500,000. With outside financing, current shareholders will own 80% of a bigger $2,000,000 firm, for a total of $1,600,000. This is clearly greater than $1,500,000 they would have should they decide to forgo the project and raise no equity. Thus, even though they are forced to sell equity below its true value, the greater future value of the firm will compensate them for that. This is not the case for Firm A, however. After issuing equity and implementing the project, its current shareholders will be left with 80% of a $3,000,000 company, which translates into $2,400,000. This is less than the $2,500,000 standalone value of current assets. Thus, Firm A will refrain from issuing equity and forego the investment.

In essence, not issuing stock is a good signal to the market since it implies that insiders have very favorable information relative to the market's assessment. To obtain a more precise intuition for this result, we provide a semiformal discussion of a simplified example in the spirit of Myers and Majluf (1984).[1]

The assumptions are:

1. Agents are risk neutral.
2. Insiders (managers) have private information about the true value, π, of the firm's existing assets. π can have the value of either H or L:

$$\pi \in \{H, L\}, \ H > L > 0.$$

3. The firm obtains access to a value-enhancing project, which will yield cash flow C at Time 1. The firm needs external financing I to undertake the project. Assume that equity is the only available option to raise funds. In principle, we could relax this assumption and decrease the amount of required investment. In other words, one can interpret I as the amount of required equity financing in excess of other sources available. If the firm does not issue new equity, the new project is not implemented since other sources are assumed to have been depleted.
4. Since the project has a positive net value, its cash flows must exceed cash flows obtained from comparable passive investments, or equivalently, $C > I(1 + r)$, where r is the return on comparable investment opportunities. For simplicity, we let r equal the risk-free rate.

Agents make their decisions at Date 0 after observing their private signals and the firm's actions. At Date 1, asymmetry is resolved, and cash flows are distributed. We should be careful not to attach any calendar meaning to Date 0 and Date 1 since it may take weeks or even months for asymmetry to be resolved. At Date 0:

- Insiders observe the realization of π, and outsiders observe only a probabilistic distribution $P(\pi = L) = p$ or, equivalently, $P(\pi = H) = 1 - p$.
- Insiders now offer fraction s, $(0 \leq s \leq 1)$, of the firm's shares to outside investors, in return for the amount I.

After observing s, outside investors may accept or reject the offer.

If investors reject the offer:

- Investors' payoff is $I(1 + r)$.
- Insiders' payoff is p.

If investors accept the offer:

- Investors' payoff is $s(\pi + C)$.
- Insiders' payoff is $(1 - s)(\pi + C)$.

There are two types of equilibria in this game: the pooling and the separating equilibria. We will discuss them below. While we do not formally define the equilibrium concept used here, it may be useful to know that we are describing pure-strategy perfect Bayesian equilibria. Informally, this concept requires that actions of each agent are an optimal response to *equilibrium* actions of the other players and that in equilibrium, actions are consistent with agents' beliefs (i.e., if everyone believes a firm to be of high quality, it should take actions that a high-quality firm is supposed to take rather than mimic some other firm type).

In a pooling equilibrium, investors' probability assessment of the firm being type L remains unchanged after observing

$$P(\pi = L|s) = P(\pi = L) = p.$$

Equivalently,

$$P(\pi = H|s) = P(\pi = H) = 1 - p.$$

In this case, both types of firms offer s, which is accepted by the investors.

What are the conditions under which this equilibrium can exist? Intuitively, all parties must be satisfied with the equilibrium outcomes and beliefs and be unwilling to deviate. More formally, investors' participation constraint (they must be no worse buying equity than investing in the risk-free asset) is as follows:

$$s[pL + (1 - p)H + C] \geq I(1 + r). \tag{1}$$

Insiders' optimality requirement (they expect to be no worse off after dilution than before; notice that while their holdings are diluted after the issuance, the firm is worth more because of the profitable investment):

$$(1 - s)(\pi + C) \geq \pi \Rightarrow s \leq \frac{C}{\pi + C} \text{ for } \pi \in \{H, L\}$$

This translates into

$$s \leq \frac{C}{L + C}, \tag{2a}$$

$$s \leq \frac{C}{H + C}. \tag{2b}$$

Equation 2b is the stronger condition (since $H > L$), and Equation 2a can therefore be ignored since it is automatically satisfied as long as Equation 2b holds. Combining Equations 1 and 2b yields the necessary condition for equity issuance to occur in a pooling equilibrium:

$$\frac{I(1 + r)}{pL + (1 - p)H + c} \leq \frac{c}{H + c}. \tag{3}$$

It is easy to see that when p is small (close to zero), Equation 3 is almost always satisfied, and a pooling equilibrium is feasible. The intuition behind this result is straightforward. Notice that in a pooling equilibrium, type H firms subsidize type L firms because every company gets the same average valuation, so that type H firms are undervalued while type L firms are overvalued. In essence, by participating in a pooling equilibrium, type H firms accept lower valuations and thus transfer part of their value to type L firms. For equity issuance to occur, the cost of subsidizing the type L firm must be compensated by the benefit of a higher firm value from the new project, which would otherwise have to be abandoned.

If p is high enough (i.e., the likelihood of encountering a type L firm is high), the pooling equilibrium is no longer feasible. It is obvious that if a separating equilibrium exists, it is the type L firm that makes stock issuance since costs of issuance are higher for type H firms. In a separating equilibrium, therefore, the market must correctly anticipate this and update the probability of firm type based on observed behavior: If the firm announces an issuance, investors set the probability of it being type L equal to 1 or, equivalently, $P(\pi = H \mid \text{Issuance announcement}) = 0$.

In such equilibrium, the type L firm issues equity with

$$s' = \frac{I(1+r)}{L+C}$$

(i.e., Equation 1 is satisfied as an equality, with $p=1$). Investors accept this offer since they are no worse off than investing in the riskless asset. Type H firms do not issue stock and do not undertake the project since issuing stock and diluting current shareholders will reduce their wealth beyond what could be compensated by profits from the new investment.

Notice that in this equilibrium, only the type L firm implements the project. As a result, social welfare declines since some firms have to forego profitable investment opportunities. To avoid such a scenario, firms may accumulate what Myers and Majluf (1984) call "financial slack"—that is, retained earnings and the capacity to issue riskless debt: If issuing new shares has dilutive effects and may prevent the firm from investing, it may use internal funds to undertake the investment when outside financing is unattractive.

The model above explains why share prices, on average, drop when new stock issuance is announced (Mikkelson & Partch [1986] document a 3% to 4% price decline in the 2-day window around the stock issuance announcement). Myers and Majluf propose what is now called the pecking order theory of capital structure: When possible, firms should use their retained earnings to finance projects; if internal funds do not suffice, firms should issue debt, while equity financing is the option of last resort.

Dividends

Dividends are another type of corporate financial policy that is difficult to explain in terms of frictionless markets. If a firm has profitable investment opportunities, the managers should pursue them and thus maximize the total firm value. Distributing dividends to shareholders may indicate the lack of such investment opportunities. Surprisingly, however, corporations issue dividends and obtain external financing at the same time, thus distributing funds to their shareholders and making investments at the same time. Miller and Rock (1985) address this problem by considering the information content of dividends. Dividends are a signaling device because of the commitment associated with them: Dividends must be paid at regular intervals and therefore effectively restrict free cash flows of the firm. In equilibrium, firms with relatively high cash flows can afford to pay dividends, and thus dividend announcements can be used to signal firm value.

Market Efficiency

Stock prices communicate information about the firm's expected future performance. Determining the amount of information that a stock price contains is therefore tremendously important since it underlies capital allocation decisions in the economy. The question is, "What does the stock price really tell us?"

Fama (1965) advocated the concept of informationally efficient financial markets, meaning that stock prices reflect all information currently available. Efficiency does not assume that prices do not change over time or that they correctly reflect true intrinsic values of securities. It does assume that prices are the best guesses about intrinsic values currently available. In a later paper, Fama (1970) distinguished three different forms of the efficient market hypothesis: the weak, semi-strong, and strong market efficiency. Weak efficiency states that future stock prices cannot be predicted from past prices or returns, semi-strong efficiency exists when prices quickly reflect all available public information, and strong-form efficiency implies that both private and public information is reflected in the current stock price. Fama argues that in modern financial markets, many analysts try to extract information about stocks. It is the competition between them that leads to new information being incorporated into prices quickly: If somebody perceives that there are profitable trades to be made, those trades will be executed. Fama (1970) lists the following sufficient conditions for markets to be fully informationally efficient:

1. There are no transaction costs.
2. All available information is costlessly available to all market participants.
3. Everyone agrees on the implications of current information for the current price and the distribution of future prices.

While Fama (1970) concedes that these conditions are extreme and are likely to be violated in real markets, he states that they need to hold to a "sufficient" degree to ensure efficiency.

To make the model of efficient markets empirically testable, it must be given statistical content. Usually, market efficiency has been associated with the random walk hypothesis, which states that successive price changes (or returns) are independently and identically distributed. Empirical evidence accumulated from the 1960s to 1990s was generally supportive of the efficient market hypothesis, at least in its semi-strong form. In particular, successive price changes were found to be almost independent, corroborating the random walk hypothesis. More recent evidence, however, is mixed. For example, low price-to-earnings stocks tend to outperform other stocks in a demonstration of what appears to be inconsistent with even the weak-form efficiency.

The primary problem with tests of market efficiency, which Fama (1991) acknowledges, is the joint hypothesis test: Efficiency can only be tested relative to a normative model of stock price behavior. In the absence of such a model, it is virtually impossible to statistically determine whether it is the model that is incorrect or the market that is inefficient.

Grossman and Stiglitz (1980) challenge the assumptions underlying the efficient markets hypothesis. They develop an equilibrium theory that explains why prices cannot at all times reflect all information available to market participants. They show that what Fama (1970) lists as conditions sufficient for efficiency are also the conditions necessary for it to exist. Below we provide a simplified version of their argument.

In a world where the search for information is costly, an investor would only expend effort to acquire it if he or she can earn compensation for doing so. Thus, the very decision to obtain information is endogenous and depends on the information content of prices. If prices always reflect all available information, searching for information elsewhere does not provide any value and cannot be justified. On the other hand, if nobody is trying to acquire information beyond prices, these prices cannot reflect all available information by definition, and thus abnormal profits can be made. As a result, what Grossman and Stiglitz (1980) call an "equilibrium degree of disequilibrium" arises, where prices transmit information available to arbitrageurs but only partially, so that the efforts to obtain private information are justified.

Financial Intermediation

The student of economics may wonder why financial institutions play such a crucial role in modern economic systems: In the end, it is the real productive capacity of the economy that matters. What is the role of financial intermediaries that makes them so indispensable? To address this question, we need a specific definition of an intermediary. For the purposes of this discussion, it is an institution that holds one class of securities and sells securities of other types. One example is a bank taking deposits and providing loans; another would be a company holding individual mortgages and selling bonds backed by those

mortgages (the so-called asset-backed securities) to outside investors.

Financial intermediation can arise because of transaction costs: It may be difficult for ultimate borrowers to deal with lenders directly because of search and evaluation costs. However, simple transaction costs have failed to explain the magnitude of financial intermediation: While clearly present, these costs just do not seem to be large enough. Leland and Pyle (1977) suggest that information asymmetry may be the primary reason financial intermediation exists.

There are classes of assets, such as mortgages and insurance, for which it is possible to obtain private information by expending effort. A loan officer evaluating a mortgage applicant may be able to obtain quite extensive documentation about his or her financial situation, for example. In the presence of economies to scale, it may be beneficial to create organizations that specialize in collecting information about particular asset types. Reselling this information to ultimate lenders, however, can be problematic. As Leland and Pyle (1977) note, two problems arise in this case:

1. Information is a public good, so the collector will be able to capture only a fraction of its value to potential buyers.
2. Selling information is related to the credibility of that information.

The second problem is arguably more severe: The Akerlof-type market breakdown can occur. If potential buyers of information cannot distinguish between good and bad information, they will be willing to pay only the price that would reflect the average quality of information. Thus, providers of high-quality information will be unwilling to participate, and the quality of information supplied will further decline.

These problems can be overcome if the information-gathering entity becomes an intermediary, holding assets on its own balance sheet. In this case, the returns to information collection will be captured in the returns to the portfolio of assets and will therefore be privatized. The asymmetry problem can be solved by signaling, and Leland and Pyle (1977) suggest a particular type of signal that can be used in this case: Insiders can hold a relatively large share of their own firm to signal its quality. Their argument is straightforward: Risk-averse insiders would like to diversify their holdings, and it is therefore suboptimal for them to hold large shares of their own company unless they have favorable information about it.

Reputation

Reputation may be viewed as another endogenous response to asymmetric information. It arises in a repeat-business context, with the idea that repeated interactions can support equilibria impossible in a static transaction. In a dynamic game, it may be possible to create a punishment code severe enough so that deviating from trustworthiness is unprofitable. Creating such codes has been a challenging game-theoretic problem: The difficulty arises because the punishment code must be severe enough to prevent deviations, but at the same time, it must be credible so that those who threaten to use it will actually do so (in terms of economic rationality, it is not a good idea to hurt someone else and suffer at the same time). Abreu, Pearce, and Stacchetti (1990) develop a general treatment of this problem and show how optimal punishment codes can be constructed.

The idea of reputation in a repeat-business context is intuitively appealing. Consider a bank that tries to attract deposits. If its only interest is the transaction at hand, the optimal policy is to expropriate the depositor to the largest extent possible (within legal bounds). On the other hand, if the bank is interested in inviting future transactions from its clients, it must maintain reputation of a fair dealmaker. If potential future benefits exceed the profit foregone by not expropriating clients today, the bank has incentives to heed to reputational concerns. In essence, the possibility of profitable future interactions may compel the informed agent not to expropriate the uninformed party and may therefore alleviate the problem of asymmetry.

Information Production and Innovation

So far in this chapter, we have been mostly concerned with how information is interpreted in various economic settings. With few exceptions (Grossman & Stiglitz, 1980, being a notable one), the models discussed above say little about the actual process of acquiring new information. In most cases, the discussion of equilibrium starts by assuming the presence of private information. In this section, we intend to address the problem of information production.

The way information is produced and disseminated can have significant consequences for the economy. Sometimes changes in information production can trigger a total overhaul of incentive structures in a certain business field. The way credit rating agencies are compensated is one example: Until the 1970s, the agencies were paid by the users of financial information, while today most of them are being paid by the issuers of bonds these agencies rate. Many economists believe this creates conflicts of interest, but it may be interesting to note that the compensation structure was changed when photocopying technologies became widely available. In effect, disseminating ratings after obtaining them from the agencies became less costly. As a result, rating agencies found it difficult to privatize returns to their efforts. Other factors may have been responsible for the change, of course, but the availability of technology is likely to have played a role.

Since information is a public good, private production of information may sometimes be insufficient or even impossible. In cases when information is very valuable, the markets have found ways to cope with the problem by creating special structures and institutions that enable private information production. Financial intermediation discussed above is one example. Quite surprisingly, however, there are public institutions and mechanisms such as patent protection designed to safeguard private information.

Why is it necessary to create mechanisms that protect private information even as this may lead to information asymmetries and the associated problems? The answer is far more difficult than it may seem. We live in a world where scientific discovery and innovation drive technological progress. Many economists acknowledge that it is the rate of technological progress that stimulates economic growth more than any other factor. Since innovation is impossible without producing information, it is difficult to underestimate the importance of creating incentives to acquire information. The problem, however, is how much and what kind of information needs to be produced to ensure economic progress.

One may argue that due to the public-good nature of information, it is government-financed institutions that must perform most information production. Since benefits of information are often public, the public should be responsible for financing the production of this information. Even a cursory observation of economic realities, however, leads one to conclude that the share of private funding for research is far from trivial. The Organisation for Economic Co-operation and Development (2009) performs biannual surveys of science and technology indicators, which suggest that more than two thirds of research and development is performed by corporations. Apparently, publicly funded research may be associated with problems that go beyond the public-good nature of information.

One problem with public research is its remoteness from economic realities. Since the amount of information that can potentially be discovered is virtually unbounded, limited research funds and efforts must be allocated in a way that produces more or less tangible benefits. Aghion, Dewatripont, and Stein (2005) developed a theory to address the problem of research allocation between corporations and academic institutions. They assume that the primary difference between academic and private research is the degree of scientific freedom: In academia, a scientist may pursue whatever direction he or she finds interesting, while in the private sector, he or she will have to work on a specific project mandated by the management. Aghion et al. show that in this case, it is optimal to originate fundamental research in academia and delegate later stages to corporations (by later stages, they mean stages close to actual product implementation). They also show that there exists an optimal transfer point prior to which private sector research may inhibit innovation. Thus, the structure of incentives in social institutions may be suitable for some kinds of research and detrimental to others. Monopolistic information production within public entities is, therefore, suboptimal.

The debate about patent protection and whether it promotes or inhibits innovation is ongoing. This debate, however, is not the focus of our discussion. Our purpose is to show that it is impossible to create a single mechanism that would address all issues related to information production.

Conclusion

Information economics is a growing field with high potential for future research. This chapter was intended to give an incomplete overview of the main themes in the literature and discuss their applicability to various economic problems. Our hope was to show that the structure of information environment has far-reaching consequences for economic behavior.

When information is asymmetric, a market breakdown can occur because of adverse selection and moral hazard: People will try to adjust their behavior to use the information available to them. Other agents anticipate this behavior and will either demand compensation or will refuse to participate in market transactions that will leave them at a disadvantage. Screening and signaling are two ways to deal with the problem of asymmetry. With signaling, the informed party behaves in a way that reveals private information. A credible signal can separate different types of informed agents: Some types of informed agents find signaling costly enough not to engage in it, while others find it profitable enough to send the signal. Screening is a device used by the uninformed party to extract information from informed agents. It translated into a menu of options, which are catered to different types of informed agents.

Screening, signaling, and information asymmetry have applications in various fields of economics. We discussed examples from the theory of credit rationing, corporate finance literature, insurance markets, literature on market efficiency, financial intermediation, and reputation. Each of these topics has important implications for policy debates.

Health care and medical insurance are one example. Some countries and states develop universal systems of health care, in effect requiring mandatory medical insurance from their residents. Sometimes such systems fail (as in some post-Soviet countries) while sometimes they seem to be very successful (as in France). The reasons why the results may be so different are not yet well understood, and the debate is likely to continue.

Private information and concerns about its use in financial markets led to continuous attempts on behalf of the governments to increase market transparency and design optimal systems of financial regulation. While progress has been made, economic crises of the past and the recent 2008 global financial meltdown are evidence that much still needs to be done. The structure of financial intermediation and the role of reputational capital are a major topic for academic research and policy debates.

The development of e-commerce also stimulates reputation research since online identities are often easy to change, and reputation may be one of the ways to deal with unscrupulous deal making.

We also briefly discussed information production. This is a growing area of research, with information technology affecting every facet of our lives. We showed that it might be challenging to design optimal systems of information production. There are entire countries that place emphasis on public research, Russia being one example, while other governments favor a more laissez-faire approach to scientific discovery. The difference in these approaches may be in part responsible for why fundamental research succeeds in some places while applied research succeeds in others. Explaining and detailing such differences may be invaluable for future policy decisions.

There are many topics we had to leave untouched, such as the role of information in designing optimal compensation, dissemination of information through social networks, and many others. The student is referred to the list of suggested readings for further details on some of the topics.

Note

1. In writing this section, I benefited from discussions and notes from Tom Chemmanur's corporate finance theory class at Boston College.

References and Further Readings

Abreu, D., Pearce, D., & Stacchetti, E. (1990). Toward a theory of discounted repeated games with imperfect monitoring. *Econometrica, 58,* 1041–1063.

Aghion, P., Dewatripont, M., & Stein, J. C. (2005). *Academic freedom, private-sector focus, and the process of innovation* (NBER Working Paper No. 11542). Cambridge, MA: National Bureau of Economic Research.

Akerlof, G. (1970). The market for lemons: Qualitative uncertainty and the market mechanism. *Quarterly Journal of Economics, 84,* 488–500.

Akerlof, G. A., & Yellen, J. L. (1985). Can small deviations from rationality make significant differences to economic equilibria? *American Economic Review, 75,* 708–720.

Bikhchandani, S., Hirshleifer, D., & Welch, I. (1992). A theory of fads, fashion, custom, and cultural change as informational cascades. *Journal of Political Economy, 100,* 992.

Ellison, G., & Fudenberg, D. (1995). Word-of-mouth communication and social learning. *Quarterly Journal of Economics, 110,* 93–125.

Fama, E. F. (1965). The behavior of stock-market prices. *Journal of Business, 38,* 34.

Fama, E. F. (1970). Efficient capital markets. *Journal of Finance, 25,* 383–421.

Fama, E. F. (1991). Efficient capital markets: II. *Journal of Finance, 46,* 1575–1617.

Graham, J. R. (2000). How big are the tax benefits of debt? *Journal of Finance, 55,* 1901–1941.

Grossman, S. J., & Stiglitz, J. E. (1980). On the impossibility of informationally efficient prices. *American Economic Review, 70,* 393–408.

Hall, B. J., & Liebman, J. B. (1998). Are CEOs really paid like bureaucrats? *Quarterly Journal of Economics, 113,* 653–691.

Jensen, M. C., & Murphy, K. J. (1990). Performance pay and top-management incentives. *Journal of Political Economy, 98,* 225.

Leland, H. E., & Pyle, D. H. (1977). Informational asymmetries, financial structure, and financial intermediation. *Journal of Finance, 32,* 371–387.

Mikkelson, W. H., & Partch, M. M. (1986). Valuation effects of security offerings and the issuance process. *Journal of Financial Economics, 15*(1/2), 31–60.

Miller, M. H., & Rock, K. (1985). Dividend policy and asymmetric information. *Journal of Finance, 40,* 1031–1041.

Modigliani, F., & Miller, M. (1958). The cost of capital, corporation finance and the theory of investment. *American Economic Review, 53,* 433–443.

Myers, S., & Majluf, N. (1984). Corporate investment and financing decisions when firms have information that investors do not have. *Journal of Financial Economics, 13,* 187–221.

Organisation for Economic Co-operation and Development (OECD). (2009). *Main science and technology indicators* (Vol. 2008/2). Paris: Author.

Rajan, R. G., & Zingales, L. (1995). What do we know about capital structure? *Journal of Finance, 50,* 1421–1460.

Rothschild, M., & Stiglitz, J. (1976). Equilibrium in competitive insurance markets: An essay on the economics of imperfect information. *Quarterly Journal of Economics, 90,* 629–649.

Spence, M. (1973). Job market signaling. *Quarterly Journal of Economics, 87,* 355–374.

Stigler, G. J. (1961). The economics of information. *Journal of Political Economy, 69,* 213.

Stiglitz, J. E., & Weiss, A. (1981). Credit rationing in markets with imperfect information. *American Economic Review, 71,* 393–410.

Titman, S., & Wessels, R. (1988). The determinants of capital structure choice. *Journal of Finance, 43,* 1–19.

72

FORENSIC ECONOMICS

LAWRENCE M. SPIZMAN

State University of New York at Oswego

The National Association of Forensic Economics (NAFE) defines forensic economics as "the scientific discipline that applies economic theories and methods to the issue of pecuniary damages as specified by case law and legislative codes" (National Association of Forensic Economics, n.d.-a). During the litigation process, economists determine the value of economic damages, testify, and critique the opposing experts' economic analysis.

The purpose of this chapter is to provide a general overview of the economic issues in a typical personal injury and wrongful death litigation tort, which is a private or civil wrong. The chapter also discusses the ethical issues involved when using different methodologies to estimate damages.

Economic damages typically are presented to the trier of fact (which can be a jury or judge) as the last phase of a trial. The importance of this should not be underestimated. Before there can be any award for economic damages, the plaintiff (the one suing for damages) must show that the defendant (the one being sued) is liable. If an attorney offers a meticulous case for liability but the economist presents unrealistic damage estimates, then the initial favorable impression of the trier of fact may be reversed if the opinions of the last expert to testify are perceived as bogus.

Before a trial, the plaintiff and defendant participate in settlement negotiations. During these negotiations, the plaintiff will present the demands for economic damages while the defendant might have a counteroffer. The plaintiff will usually retain an economist to estimate the economic damages. The plaintiff's economist will be identified and will have to present a report showing how the results were derived. In federal cases as well as in some state jurisdiction cases, the economists may be deposed and asked a series of questions to find out how damages were estimated. This information will later be used at a trial. The defense may or may not list an economist as an expert to counter the claims of the plaintiff. However, the defense often will retain a consulting expert to help prepare and critique the plaintiff's economic analysis. The defense does not disclose who the consulting expert is, nor does the consultant testify. The plaintiff's economic expert will not know if there is a defense expert critiquing and checking the results of his or her analysis. If the case settles before trial, the expert's work is complete. Even though most cases settle before trial, it is prudent for the testifying expert to estimate damages assuming that a trial will occur. A testifying expert is sworn to tell the truth. Therefore, the economic analysis must be based on accurate information even if there is only a remote chance that a trial will occur. Spizman (1995) discussed the negotiating strategy process between the plaintiff and defendant given the small probability of a trial occurring.

Forensic economics as a formal academic discipline began in 1986 with the formation of NAFE. NAFE started publishing the first journal devoted exclusively to forensic economics, the *Journal of Forensic Economics,* in 1988. NAFE also published the journal *Litigation Economic Digest* for several years before it ceased publication. In addition, NAFE sponsors sessions devoted to forensic economics at the major economic conferences. The American Academy of Economics and Financial Experts started publishing the *Journal of Legal Economics* in 1991. The American Rehabilitation Economics Association began publishing *The Earnings Analyst* in 1998.

Arguably the most important book in forensic economics is by Martin (2009). First published in 1988, it had 21 annual supplements and includes special sections written by more than 40 leading forensic economists.

Kaufman, Rodgers, and Martin (2005) published a compilation of major articles dealing with personal injury or wrongful death. Ireland et al. (2007) and Brookshire, Slesnick, and Ward (2007) discussed the major issues of forensic economics.

Ethics and Assumptions of Damage Models

The discipline of forensic economics is unique in economics because most academic forensic economists are also consultants to the legal community. Since forensic damage models are based on assumptions that may favor one side in litigation, practitioners are confronted with ethical issues dealing with the impact of their models' assumption on litigants. Consequently, forensic economists must go beyond the simplifying assumptions made in introductory economics classes and understand the consequences of the models' assumptions. Because experts are not advocates for either the plaintiff or defendant (attorneys are), it is crucial that their assumptions be consistent and not change depending on which side retains them. Neutrality can be difficult to maintain when the marketplace rewards those providing opinions beneficial to the retaining side. The ethical consistency dilemmas are real and not abstract. Different sections in this chapter will address these ethical consistency issues. However, it is important to realize that each case is unique and that research and new data may warrant changing methodology on specific issues. Changes must be defended if they differ from past practices.

Law

Each state, as well as the federal government, has different laws pertaining to estimating economic damages. Nevertheless, the methodology of estimating damages within the legal parameters is remarkably consistent from one jurisdiction to another. The purpose of estimating damages is to restore the plaintiff's economic condition to what it was prior to the tort, or to make the plaintiff whole.

Life, Work Life, and Healthy Life Expectancy

Each component of damages depends on how long the loss lasts. Lost earnings depend on work life expectancy, which is the number of years the plaintiff would have worked if not injured or deceased. Long-term health care resulting from an injury and pension losses depend on the plaintiff's life expectancy. Other losses such as household services last as long as the plaintiff is healthy enough to provide those services. Skoog and Ciecka (2003) provide work life expectancy

tables, while Arias (2005) generates life expectancy tables. *Healthy Life Expectancy* (Expectancy Data, 2010) provides tables for healthy life expectancy. All these tables are broken down by various demographic characteristics such as age, gender, race, and educational levels.

Because all expectancy tables are based on the age of the plaintiff, an important issue in determining expectancies is whether to use the plaintiff's age on the date of the incident or on the date of the trial. Using the age on the date of trial extends an individual's work life and life expectancy beyond what it would be if using the date of the incident. Thus, the number of years the loss continues is increased. Damages should commence based on the plaintiff's age on the date of the incident rather than on the date of trial, unless the laws of a specific jurisdiction require otherwise. Ethical consistency requires that the forensic economist not choose one starting date for the plaintiff in order to have a longer life or work life expectancy and another starting date for the defense to get lower expectancies.

Although the trial date is generally not used to determine expectancies, it is used to delineate past losses from future losses. This is important because future losses, not past losses, are discounted to present value.

Life Expectancy

Life expectancy is the number of years an average person would have lived but for the tort. Life expectancy is relevant if the plaintiff requires lifetime medical care and has a lifetime-defined benefit pension plan. Pain and suffering, which is awarded by the trier of fact and not calculated by an economist, also can be awarded for life. Arias (2005) presents life expectancy by age, gender, and race. The use of race-neutral tables to determine life expectancy is often required by case law. If the law does not specify race-neutral life expectancy tables, then the forensic economist should not choose to use race tables when those tables favor one side and use race-neutral tables when it favors another side. For example, suppose black males have lower life expectancies than white males and the all-male life expectancy category is what is normally used. The black male category should not be used when the plaintiff is black in order to get a lower life expectancy if the defendant is estimating damages. If the black male was a physician, would his life expectancy be any different than a white male physician? Switching life tables to benefit one side over the other raises the ethical consistency issue.

The plaintiff's age on the date of the incident should be used to determine life expectancy. Suppose a female was 35 at the time she was involved in an accident and the trial occurred 3 years after the accident. The correct work life should be for a 35-year-old female. Using the work life for a 38-year-old female would add more years to the work life. The probability of the plaintiff living from 35 to 38 is

100% since she is already 38 years old. If losses continue for 30 more years, adding one additional year to work life can significantly increase losses when the effects of 30 years of compounding damages are considered. The last extra year will be the largest yearly loss. Ethical consistency requires using the same methodology for the plaintiff and defendant.

Another potential problem in estimating damages occurs with partial years of loss. The first and last year loss is usually a partial year unless the tort commenced on January 1 or ended on December 31. For example, if an injury occurred May 4, 2009 (2009.34), the first year's loss is only 66% of the year since 34% has already occurred. If the loss continues until the plaintiff's work life expectancy year 2045.3, then the loss is only for 30% of the year 2045. Sometimes, the first year and last year are rounded to complete years with the false claim that they offset each other. The final year's loss is the highest because of growth and compounding, and the first year's loss is the lowest, and thus they cannot offset each other. Rounding to full years in one case and using partial years in another to get a loss favorable to either the defendant or plaintiff would be ethically inconsistent.

Work Life Expectancy

Smith (1982) used the increment-decrement Markov model, which considers the probability of an individual's movement from being active to inactive in the labor force. Smith (1986) updated these tables using 1979 data. The Department of Labor stopped publishing work life tables but continues providing data through the Current Population Survey, allowing economists to keep work life tables up-to-date. One of the most recent tables was published by Skoog and Ciecka (2003).

Work life tables show the number of years, on average, a person will be working or actively looking for work throughout his or her life. The tables do not tell us when an individual retires from the labor force. For example, a 42-year-old female with a bachelor's degree who is currently employed has, on average, 19.03 years of working or actively looking for work for the remainder of her life. Her work life is to age 61.03. This does not mean she will retire at age 61.03; rather, it tells us the number of continuous years she can be expected to either work or look for work. The tables take into account a worker's being out of the labor force for various reasons. In essence, work life frontloads the person's remaining years in the labor force because she may still be working past her work life. Thus, if a female is out of the labor force for childrearing purposes, that is factored into her work life expectancy. For example, if a worker leaves the labor force to get a degree in business administration or is injured temporarily and later returns to work, then that is factored into the work life tables.

To properly use work life tables, you need to know whether the plaintiff was active or inactive at the time of the injury. Age, gender, and levels of education also determine work life. Because work life tables frontload the loss, some forensic economists use the life, participation, and employment (LPE) method. This method takes the probabilities of participation in the labor force, survival, and unemployment to determine the expected value of future earnings.

Healthy Life Expectancy

Some damages such as household services may not continue for life because as a person's health normally deteriorates with age, the amount of household services he or she is able to perform diminishes. To account for this deterioration, *Healthy Life Expectancy* (Expectancy Data, 2010) publishes tables showing the number of years a person considers his or her health to be excellent without any limitations to activities. Even though a person's health may decline, he or she is still capable of performing household services. *Healthy Life Expectancy* also has tables of full-function life expectancy (FFLE), which has fewer years than life expectancy but more than healthy life expectancy (HLE). The ethical consistency issue requires the use of either HLE or FFLE to determine the number of years household services would have continued but for the tort. Using one table for the plaintiff and another for the defendant would be inconsistent and therefore unethical.

Wage and Salary Loss

Past and future earning losses resulting from an injury or death are recoverable. Legal parameters determine whether expected earnings (earnings the plaintiff expected to earn prior to the tort) or earning capacity (earnings the plaintiff had the ability to earn prior to the tort) are to be used. Upon establishing preinjury earnings, postinjury earnings (residual earnings) have to be determined and deducted from lost earnings. In wrongful deaths, there are no residual earnings. Vocational rehabilitation experts usually determine the future earnings potential given the impaired condition of the plaintiff.

Since 1040 tax forms can show additional income (such as spouse's income, business income, and royalties), the best sources for preinjury earnings are W-2 tax forms. The Social Security Administration also provides yearly earnings that can easily be obtained if the plaintiff's W-2 forms are unavailable.

When the plaintiff's work history is well documented, it is easier to establish the base earnings necessary to estimate future earning losses. If earnings vary from year to year, average earnings can be used to determine the base earnings. It is debatable how many prior years to use in establishing the average, but 3 to 5 years should be appropriate. Past earnings should be in current dollars (constant dollar equivalents) before taking an average. For example, if using average earnings from 2003 through 2008, then 2003 earnings should grow by the rate for 5 years, and 2004 earnings grow by 4 years, 2005 by 3 years, and so forth. The average is based on the current dollar earnings.

Earning capacity can be used in the absence of earning records. Earning capacity considers those occupations that an individual is capable of entering. Earnings for broad occupational categories are found in National Occupation and Wage Estimates (U.S. Department of Labor, 2007b) and State Occupational Employment and Wage Data (U.S. Department of Labor, 2007c).

If the plaintiff is an injured child or a recent graduate, then a broader category of average earnings is required. One such category is educational attainment. Wages for different age, gender, and race cohorts can be found in the U.S. Census Bureau (2007) and Expectancy Data (2008, 2009, 2010).

When broad statistical averages are required, then median (not mean) earnings should be used. For example, if 9 of 10 workers in the sample earn $50,000 and one earns $250,000, mean earnings are $70,000. One high-salaried worker skews the average upward. If the sample size is small, this becomes all the more important. Median earnings are $50,000 because half the workers earn more and half earn less. Since median earnings are less than mean earnings, the ethical consistency issue requires that the mean not be used if retained for the plaintiff and the median if retained for the defense.

Union or professional dues should be deducted from lost earnings because they are a cost to the plaintiff's job maintenance. Even though union dues are small, ethical consistency issues require that you be consistent when choosing to deduct union dues.

Growth of Earnings

Once the plaintiff's current wage or salary is established, the future growth rates of wages have to be determined. If past employment records are available, then average past growth rates can be used to project future increases. When employment records are not available or suitable, then the use of general wage or price indexes such as the Consumer Price Index (CPI) or Employment Cost Index (ECI) can be used for estimating wage growth rates. The implied assumption when using the CPI to determine wage growth rates is that the plaintiff's wages will only increase by the level of the CPI, which shows the increase in the price level for goods and services. An index that gives a broader measure of wage and salary increases is the ECI. The ECI not only shows the historical growth rate for all workers but also allows tailoring the growth rates to a specific industry group. In addition to showing straight time salary and wage rates, the ECI includes earning incentives, cost of living adjustments, and production and earning bonuses. In addition, the ECI has an index for employee-provided benefits.

The number of past years required to establish the average growth rate is not universally agreed upon and should be justified. However, to avoid the ethical consistency issue, the same number of years to estimate the average should be used for both plaintiffs and defendants rather than using one number that provides a higher growth rate for the plaintiff and then using a different number that provides a lower growth rate for the defense.

The compounding of growth rates can magnify the total value of losses when there is what appears to be a small percentage difference. The longer the timeframe growth is, the greater the loss.

Fringe Benefit Losses

Employer-provided fringe benefits that are lost due to the injury have value that the plaintiff or the plaintiff's family can recover. It is important not to double count fringe benefit losses. For example, if the plaintiff received 3 weeks of paid time off annually and the plaintiff is already being compensated for 52 weeks of lost earnings, then including another 3 weeks of earnings for time off would be double counting the loss.

The two largest components of fringe benefit losses are often health insurance and retirement benefits. When employee fringe benefits are well established, then those benefit amounts should be used as a basis for lost fringe benefits. When it is unclear what the benefits are or if fringe benefits have not been established, then statistical averages of fringe benefits as a percentage of total earnings can be used.

One data source that provides fringe benefits as a percentage of earnings is *Employer Costs for Employee Compensation* (U.S. Department of Labor, 2008). Growth rates for fringe benefits can be determined from the *Employment Cost Index* (U.S. Department of Labor, 2009a).

Employee Benefits in Private Industry (U.S. Department of Labor, 2007a) provides information on the participation of workers receiving different types of fringe benefits and the frequency of benefit use. The *Employer Health Benefits Annual Survey* (Kaiser Family Foundation, 2009) provides information about the cost of employer-provided health insurance. Some state health insurance departments provide health cost by local jurisdictions.

If general statistical data are used, it is important to be familiar with both the data source and the actual data. For example, the *Employer Costs for Employee Compensation* (U.S. Department of Labor, 2008) tables data show the percentage of fringe benefits to the total compensation package. However, the total compensation package already includes fringe benefits so the percentage provided in the data should not be used. Instead, the economist should calculate fringe benefits as a percentage of wages and salaries and use that amount in estimating damages. The tables provide different categories of fringe benefits so for each case the appropriate benefit can be used. Another source of general data of fringe benefits is the U.S. Chamber of Commerce's annual *Employee Benefits Study*. However, there are many statistical issues about the Chamber of Commerce study that should raise red flags about its use. Spizman (2008) suggests not using this study because of its bias and extremely small self-selected sample size.

Health Insurances

There are several ways to calculate the loss to the plaintiff or the plaintiff's family for medical insurance. No one method is absolutely correct, so the best method depends on the facts of each case. The first method is to award the plaintiff the cost of the employer's medical insurance premium. However, this may not allow the plaintiff to purchase comparable insurance because an employer's group rates are often lower than individual rates. A second approach is to get price quotes for health insurance to replace the coverage for comparable medical insurance. Some states' insurance departments provide comparable rates by state regions. Since employer-provided insurance benefits are well defined, it is critical to find the replacement value for similar coverage. Online price quotes simplify the process of getting costs. However, often online policies provide minimum coverage that would not make the plaintiff whole.

A third method of estimating insurance costs is used when it is not clear whether the plaintiff received or would have received medical insurance in the future. For example, when a minor child or a recent graduate is injured before entering the labor market, what value should be placed on lost health insurance? If a worker has an entry-level job without medical insurance but future employment opportunities would provide health insurance, how is that future insurance valued? Given these circumstances, general statistical data that take the average percentage cost of health insurance may be appropriate to use in estimating lost health insurance. Several issues should be considered when using statistical averages. Suppose that, on average, health insurance is 12% of wages and salaries. Consequently, a worker earning $30,000 a year with family coverage will be allocated $3,600 a year ($300 per month) for health insurance losses. If the replacement cost is $12,000 a year, then the plaintiff is undercompensated by $8,400. If the plaintiff is an executive receiving the same coverage for the same price but earning $200,000 a year, then losses would include $24,000 a year for health insurance, thus overcompensating the plaintiff by $12,000. Health insurance is a quasi-fixed labor cost and should be valued the same for all employees; that is, it is fixed per worker no matter how much workers earn or how many hours a week they work.

Regardless of how health insurance losses are determined, the employee's preinjury contribution to health insurance should be deducted from any loss because that is an expense before the plaintiff incurred the loss.

Pension Loss

There are two types of pensions that workers usually participate in: a defined contribution and a defined benefit. A defined contribution is a percentage amount that an employer contributes to the employee's 401k or similar plan. The employer's contribution is the loss to the plaintiff. If an employee contributes to his or her own retirement plan, then that contribution should not be counted as a loss because the percent contribution is already being replaced from earnings; to replace it again would double count the loss. Since many employee pension contributions are tax deferrals, it is important to use Medicare earnings rather than Social Security reported earnings. Medicare earnings are higher because Social Security earnings are reduced by pension deferrals.

A defined benefit is often based on a formula that takes the number of years of employment multiplied by a final average salary multiplied by some percentage amount. Any pensions that accumulated before the injury should be deducted from the pension the plaintiff would have accumulated if not for the injury. For example, if a plaintiff had not been injured and would have received a monthly $1,500 pension but instead, as a result of the injury, only received a $400 pension monthly, the loss is $1,100 a month. If a plaintiff starts receiving the $400 a month pension before his or her normal retirement age, that amount is part of the offset against the full pension he or she would have received if not injured.

Other types of fringe benefits losses that may be considered are premiums paid by the employer on a life insurance policy and the use of a company car or cell phone for personal use.

Social Security and Fringe Benefits

Federal Insurance Contributions Act (FICA) taxes are divided between employees and employers, with each paying 7.65% of the employees' salaries. The Social Security benefits portion of FICA is 6.2% on the first $106,800 (2009 rates) of an employee's income. This includes 5.3% for Old Age Survivors and .9% for disability insurance. The Medicare tax portion of FICA is 1.45% of every dollar of earnings, with no limit on earnings. Whether or not Social Security benefits should be included as part of fringe benefits losses is a controversial issue. If a claim is being made for lost Social Security, then the 5.3% for Old Age Survivors should be used, not the full 7.65% employer contribution. Including Medicare and disability benefits as a loss would be double counting since they would be forthcoming to the injured plaintiff. One reason many economists do not include FICA taxes as part of lost fringe benefits is because taxes are ignored in most jurisdictions.

A more compelling reason not to include the plaintiff's portion of FICA as a loss is that the plaintiff no longer has to make a matching contribution to FICA, which offsets the employer's contribution.

Rodgers (2000) shows that using a percent loss for Social Security is a poor estimate of lost Social Security benefits. If there are any losses of Social Security, in most circumstances they are small. However, it is important to recognize that the circumstances of each case (e.g., an injured young child) can alter the approach used in determining whether FICA should be included as a part of fringe benefits losses.

Household Service Losses

Household services are those activities performed outside the paid marketplace that have pecuniary value that can be quantified by an economist. Household services provided by the plaintiff that he or she is no longer capable of doing because of the accident are economic damages. Household services may include cleaning, cooking and cleaning up, doing laundry, shopping, maintaining the home and vehicles, managing the household, providing transportation for the household, caring for children, and other types of services unique to the plaintiff.

Household services are not a loss if the plaintiff never performed them in the past and if there is no evidence to support that he or she would have performed them in the future. A method to determine the pre- and postinjury hours of household services is to have the plaintiff fill out a questionnaire asking how many hours were spent doing specific household work before and since the accident. The difference between the two is the reduction of household services, which would then be valued. The potential for self-reporting bias has to be recognized. However, the purpose of the survey is to show that a foundation for losses does exist. Without a foundation, it may be difficult to claim lost household services.

The *Dollar Value of a Day* (*DVD;* Expectancy Data, 2009) provides general statistical averages that estimate the hours of household services performed categorized by age, number of children, marital status, and gender. The *DVD* relies on the latest government data and is widely used. The DVD provides national average hourly wages for household services with adjustments for different geographic areas within each state.

It is important to remember that the role of the economist is to provide guidance to the trier of fact with respect to valuing losses. The trier of fact can increase or decrease losses based on the testimony of the plaintiff or the plaintiff's survivors. The *DVD* provides an excellent starting point for determining the number of hours of household services. While there are other sources and methods for computing household services, ethical consistency requires that the economist not choose one source for the plaintiff and another for the defense. Consistency and neutrality are important.

Healthy Life

The aging process limits a person's ability to perform the same level of household services when older compared to when he or she was younger and healthier. Consequently, it may not be appropriate to use a person's life expectancy to project future losses of household services. The publication *Healthy Life Expectancy* (Expectancy Data, 2010) considers the diminution of household services because of aging by providing tables showing how many remaining years of healthy life expectancy an individual has based on age, race, and gender. The publication also provides full-function life expectancy tables, anticipating that household activities will be reduced rather than eliminated when an individual is sick.

Personal Consumption Deduction

Wrongful death requires that a deduction be made for the income the decedent would have used for his or her personal consumption of items such as food, clothing, and personal care. Some states allow for personal maintenance rather than personal consumption. Personal maintenance is the amount that would have been spent by the decedent to maintain himself or herself to attain his or her earning capacity. The percent deduction for the decedent's personal consumption can be found in Ruble, Patton, and Nelson (2007). The percentage deduction changes as family size and income change.

There is some difference of opinion as to whether fringe benefits should be reduced for personal consumption since the survivors would not have received the dollars the deceased would have spent on maintenance had he or she lived. Consequently, as a result of the plaintiff's death, the survivors did not lose these dollars. A personal consumption deduction may or may not be appropriate when dealing with household services. If the trier of fact determines that the decedent's household services cannot be split between members of the household, then it may not be appropriate to deduct personal consumption from household services. One solution is to estimate lost household services in death cases both with and without the personal consumption deduction.

There are situations when personal consumption deductions are made for personal injury. For example, a severely injured person may have to spend the rest of his or her life in an extended-care facility that provides all services that the plaintiff formerly performed for himself or herself. If there is a claim for damages for the cost of the extended-care facility, then to count household services losses (which are being provided by the facility) would be double counting that loss.

Present Value

Since future dollars are worth less today, future losses must be discounted to present value. Each jurisdiction has different rules about discounting. Some states do not discount, while others specify what the discount rate should be. Because of the inverse relationship between discount rates and present values, choosing the appropriate discount rate can be a very contentious issue. That being said, what is widely accepted is that low risk and safety should be the guiding principle in choosing discount rates. This usually means U.S. government bonds. Kaufman et al. (2005) present the different approaches used to determine discount rates. Historical averages of some instruments, spot rates at the time of the analysis, short-term versus long-term rates, and net discount rates (the difference between the growth rate and the discount rate) can also be used. Because small differences in the discount rate (as well as growth rates) can affect total damages, justifying the rate being used for discounting is important. Bloomberg.com (n.d.) and *Federal Reserve Statistical Release* (n.d.) provide current rates.

Ethical consistency issues become most noticeable when determining the discount rate because lower discount rates favor the plaintiff while higher rates favor defendants. Whether retained by the plaintiff or defendant, the same discount rate should be used. It is considered unethical to choose a low rate for the plaintiff and a high rate for the defendant. Since court testimonies are a matter of record and prior economic reports are often seen and saved by opposing experts, it is not difficult to find inconsistencies in methodological approaches between plaintiff and defense cases that are not looked upon favorably by the courts.

Life Care Plan

Catastrophic injuries and disabilities to children or adults often require lifetime health and personal care. Life care planners provide plans that show the different components of care that the plaintiff will require in the future. Examples are prescription and nonprescription drugs, future medical care, and future attendant care. The life care plan presents the required care, the length of care, the frequency of care, and the current cost of the care. Once this information is provided, the economist then estimates the future cost of the life care plan. Each component of the life care plan grows by the appropriate inflation rate associated with the historical average from the Medical Care Price Index subsection of the CPI. Communications between the life care planner and economist to match the life care component to the medical care index component are useful. Items from the life care plan such as transportation are matched to the appropriate transportation index of the CPI. Double counting between the life care plan and other elements of damages must be avoided. For example, if the life care plan provides for all future medical care, then lost medical insurance should not be an element of damages. If a special van is required for transportation, then only the additional cost of modifying the van is a loss and not the full cost of the van, since the plaintiff would have bought transportation regardless of the accident. If the life care plan includes funding for certain household services, care must be taken not to double count lost household services. If the jurisdiction where the trial is occurring requires discounting, the present value of the life care plan should be made.

Collateral Source Payments

Collateral sources are payments the plaintiff receives due to the injury from a third party from insurance or the government. Collateral sources are ignored and not deducted from any loss if the payment is made by an entity that is not the defendant. The reason is that the third party who is paying the plaintiff can have a lien on any recovery from the lawsuit. Thus, if that amount is deducted from the loss, the remaining award will not be large enough to cover damages, and the defendant will benefit because he or she has to pay less in damages. However, if the defendant paid for insurance, then he or she is entitled to deduct that amount from the award. Collateral sources are often a confusing aspect of damages, and legal guidance may be required.

Taxes

Deducting federal and state income taxes from any estimated loss depends on the jurisdiction in which the case is being tried. Taxes are generally ignored in most states and are deducted in federal jurisdictions. Nevertheless, it is important to find out how the court's jurisdiction treats taxes.

Conclusion

This chapter addressed the key issues of forensic economics while stressing the interrelationships between law and economics when dealing with wrongful death and personal injury litigation. Because forensic economics is intricately tied to changes in both statutes and common law, there is tremendous potential for future research and growth in the area. Many ethical dilemmas confronting a practitioner were highlighted. Most of the topics discussed in this chapter are developed more fully in Martin (2009) and the book of readings by Kaufman et al. (2005).

References and Further Readings

American Academy of Economic and Financial Experts. (n.d.). *Journal of Legal Economics.* Index. Available at http://www.econ.unt.edu/jle

American Rehabilitation Economics Association. (n.d.). *The Earnings Analyst.* Available at http://www.a-r-e-a.org/journal.shtml

Arias, E. (2005). United States life tables. *National Vital Statistics Reports, 58*(10). Available at http://www.cdc.gov/nchs/data/nvsr/nvsr56/nvsr58_10.pdf

Bloomberg.com. (n.d.). *Government bonds.* Available at http://www.bloomberg.com/markets/rates/index.html

Brookshire, M., Slesnick, F., & Ward, J. (2007). *The plaintiff and defense attorney's guide to understanding economic damages.* Tucson, AZ: Lawyers & Judges Publishing.

Expectancy Data. (2008). *Full-time earnings in the United States: 2007 edition.* Shawnee Mission, KS.

Expectancy Data Inc. (2009). *The dollar value of a day: 2008 valuations.* Shawnee Mission, KS: Author.

Expectancy Data Inc. (2010). *Healthy life expectancy: 2004 tables.* Shawnee Mission, KS: Author.

Federal Reserve Statistical Release: Selected Interest Rates (Daily). (n.d.). Available at http://www.federalreserve.gov/Releases/H15/update

Ireland, T., Horner, S., Rodgers, J., Gaughan, P., Trout, R., & Piette, M. (2007). *Expert economic testimony: Reference guides for judges and attorneys.* Tucson, AZ: Lawyers & Judges Publishing.

Ireland, T., & Ward, J. (2002). *Assessing damages in injuries and deaths of minor children.* Tucson, AZ: Lawyers & Judges Publishing.

Ireland, T. R., & Depperschmidt, T. O. (1999). *Assessing family loss in wrongful death litigation: The special roles of lost services and personal consumption.* Tucson, AZ: Lawyers & Judges Publishing.

Kaiser Family Foundation and Health Research Family Trust. (2009). *Employer Health Benefits Annual Survey.* Available at http://ehbs.kff.org/pdf/2009/7936.pdf

Kaufman, R., Rodgers, J., & Martin, G. (Eds.). (2005). *Economic foundations of injury and death damages.* Cheltenham, UK, Northampton, MA: An Elgar Reference Collection.

Martin, G. (2009). *Determining economic damages.* Costa Mesa, CA: James Publishing.

National Association of Forensic Economics. (n.d.-a). Home page. Available at http://nafe.net/default.aspx

National Association of Forensic Economics. (n.d.-b). *Journal of Forensic Economics.* Back issues. Available at http://nafe.net/JFE/Forms/AllItems.aspx

National Association of Forensic Economics. (n.d.-c). *Journal of Forensic Economics.* Index of articles. Available at http://www.econ.unt.edu/jle/JLEBackissues19912008.pdf

National Association of Forensic Economics. (n.d.-d). *Litigation Economic Digest.* Back issues. Available at http://nafe.net/LER/Forms/AllItems.aspx

Rodgers, J. (2000). Estimating loss of Social Security benefits. *The Earnings Analyst, 3,* 1–28.

Ruble, M., Patton, R., & Nelson, D. (2007). Patton-Nelson personal consumption tables 2005–2006. *Journal of Forensic Economics, 20*(3), 217–225.

Skoog, G. R., & Ciecka, J. E. (2003). The Markov (increment-decrement) model of labor force activity: Extended tables of central tendency, variation, and probability intervals. *Journal of Legal Economics, 11,* 23–87.

Smith, S. (1982). *Tables of working life: The increment-decrement model* (Bulletin 2135). Washington, DC: Bureau of Labor Statistics.

Smith, S. (1986). *Work life estimates: Effects of race and education* (Bulletin 2254). Washington, DC: Bureau of Labor Statistics.

Spizman, L. (1995). The defense economist's role in litigation settlement negotiations. *Journal of Legal Economics, 5*(2), 57–65.

Spizman, L. (2008). Sample selectivity bias of the U.S. Chamber of Commerce employee benefits study. *The Earnings Analyst, 10,* 49–63.

U.S. Census Bureau. (2007). *Educational attainment—people 18 years old and over, by total money earnings in 2007: Work experience in 2007, age, race, Hispanic origin, and sex* (PINC-04). Available at http://pubdb3.census.gov/macro/032008/perinc/toc.htm

U.S. Department of Labor, Bureau of Labor Statistics. (2007a). *Employee benefits in private industry.* Available at http://www.bls.gov/ncs/ebs/sp/ebsm0006.pdf

U.S. Department of Labor, Bureau of Labor Statistics. (2007b). *National occupation and wage estimates.* Available at http://www.bls.gov/oes/current/oes_nat.htm

U.S. Department of Labor, Bureau of Labor Statistics. (2007c). *State occupational employment and wage data.* Available at http://www.bls.gov/oes/current/oessrcst.htm

U.S. Department of Labor, Bureau of Labor Statistics. (2008). *Employer costs for employee compensation.* Available at http://stats.bls.gov/schedule/archives/ecec_nr.htm and http://www.bls.gov/news.release/pdf/ecec.pdf

U.S. Department of Labor, Bureau of Labor Statistics. (2009a). *Employment cost index.* Available at http://data.bls.gov/PDQ/outside.jsp?survey=ci

U.S. Department of Labor, Bureau of Labor Statistics. (2009b). *Employment cost index compensation component.* Available at http://data.bls.gov/PDQ/outside.jsp?survey=ec

U.S. Department of Labor, Bureau of Labor Statistics. (n.d.). *Consumer Price Index: All urban consumers* (Current Series). Available at http://data.bls.gov/PDQ/outside.jsp?survey=cu

73

ECONOMICS OF CRIME

ISAAC EHRLICH

State University of New York at Buffalo

The persistence of "crime" in all human societies and the challenges it imposes for determining how to enforce laws enjoining it have attracted the attention of scholars throughout human history, including, in particular, utilitarian philosophers and early economists such as Beccaria, Paley, Smith, and Bentham. Indeed, in view of its empirical regularity, sociologists such as Durkheim adopted the view that "crime, in itself, is a normal social phenomenon," rather than an aberration of human nature. It was not until the late 1960s, especially following the seminal work by Becker (1968), however, that economists reconnected with the subject in a systematic fashion, using the modern tools of economic theory and applied econometrics.

The essence of the economic approach, as restated by Becker (1968), lies in the assumption that potential offenders respond to incentives and that the volume of offenses in the population can therefore be deterred or prevented through an optimal allocation of resources to control crime. The objective of social policy is specified as minimization of the aggregate social loss from crime and law enforcement. Based on this criterion, Becker derived a comprehensive set of behavioral propositions and optimal enforcement strategies involving the certainty of apprehending and convicting offenders, the severity of punishment to be imposed on those convicted, and the selection of optimal instruments of punishment. The "deterrence hypothesis," as stated by Ehrlich (1973, 1975b, 1982, 1996), expands the scope of the relevant incentives by which offenders can be motivated or controlled. It highlights the relative roles and limitations of "negative" incentives such as the prospect of apprehension relative to conviction and punishment, whether by public law enforcement or private self-protection efforts, as well as

"positive" incentives such as opportunities for gainful employment for workers at the lower end of the earnings distribution or education and rehabilitation efforts as deterrents to criminal activity. In this approach, the analysis of crime shares some formal similarities with that of occupational choice in labor-theoretic settings.

For this approach to provide a useful approximation to the complicated reality of crime, it is not necessary that all offenders respond to incentives, nor is the degree of individual responsiveness prejudged; it is sufficient that a significant number of potential offenders so behave on the margin. By the same token, the theory does not preclude a priori any category of crime, as offensive or heinous as it may be, or any class of incentives. Indeed, economists have applied the deterrence hypothesis to a myriad of illegal activities, from tax evasion, corruption, and fraud to robbery, murder, and terrorism.

Theory

The economic approach to criminal behavior can be summarized by the following syllogism: "People respond to incentives. Offenders are people too. Therefore, offenders respond to incentives." Crime, in turn, inflicts material and emotional harm on both individual victims and on society as a whole and disrupts the foundations of civil society and efficient resource allocation. This is true even in the case of petty theft, which entails just a small redistribution of wealth from victim to offender. Theft involves a net social loss by virtue of the fact that thieves spend their time and energy on effecting a redistribution of wealth instead of creating new wealth. In addition, individuals and society spend resources on protection of property and avoidance of emotional loss, as well as the potential loss of life and limb from being victims of serious crime, which is another significant drag on the economy and the pursuit of happiness. Therefore, theft, let alone more serious crime, entails a significant social cost, and society has a strong incentive to resist it in various forms.

In Becker's (1968) analysis, equilibrium volume of crime reflects the interaction between offenders and the law enforcement authority, and the focus is on optimal probability, severity, and type of criminal sanction—the implicit "prices" society imposes on criminal behavior to minimize the aggregate income loss from crime. This thesis has powerful implications concerning the choice of an optimal level of resources to be devoted by society to combat crime, as well as the optimal combination of law enforcement instruments to be imposed—the probability of apprehending and convicting offenders, the magnitude of the punishment to be meted out for crimes of different severity, and the form of the sanction to be imposed: imprisonment or monetary compensation (see Becker, 1968; Stigler, 1970).

Subsequent work has focused on more complete formulations of components of the criminal justice system, especially the supply of offenses, the production of specific law enforcement activities, and alternative social welfare criteria for producing optimal law enforcement strategies. Another methodological evolution has expanded the basic analytical setting of the Becker (1968) model by addressing the interaction between potential offenders (supply), consumers and potential victims (private "demand" for illegal goods or "derived demand" for protection), and deterrence and prevention (government intervention). This "market model" applies not just in the case of transactions involving direct demand for illegal goods and services, such as illicit drugs and prostitution, but also theft, robbery, and murder, for which the "demand" side derives from the private demand for individual safety. In this setting, government intervention works as a form of both demand and supply management, which can in principle combine elements of pure deterrence, such as monetary fines, with methods of individual control, such as incapacitation (retention, imprisonment, or confiscation of illegal goods) and rehabilitation of convicted offenders. This virtual market for offenses (Ehrlich, 1981, 1996) has later been extended to include interactions of crime with the general economy as well, including the prospect that crime could harm creative economic activity and thus economic growth and development. These extensions are discussed in greater detail in the following sections. For specific articles on which the following discussion is based, see Ehrlich and Liu (2006).

Supply

The extent of participation in crime is generally modeled as an outcome of the allocation of time among competing legitimate and illegitimate activities by potential offenders acting as expected-utility maximizers. While the mix of pecuniary and nonpecuniary benefits varies across different crime categories, which attract offenders of different attitudes toward risk and proclivities ("preferences") for crime, the basic opportunities affecting choice are identified in all cases as the perceived probabilities of apprehension, conviction, and punishment, the marginal penalties imposed, and the differential expected returns on competing legal and illegal activities. Entry into criminal activity and the extent of involvement in crime is shown to be related inversely to deterrence variables and other opportunity costs associated with crime and directly to the differential return it can provide over legitimate activity as well as to risk aversion. Contrary to the perception that criminals constitute a "noncompeting group" in classical labor jargon, by which all of them are completely specialized in the pursuit of criminal activities as members of gangs or organized crime, the labor-theoretic approach to participation in illegitimate activities expects many offenders to be "part-time" offenders, pursuing legitimate endeavors as well, and criminal enterprises to be typically small organizations, partly to diversify excessive risk bearing, given the prospect of detection, apprehension, and punishment (see Ehrlich, 1973, and the extensive empirical evidence documented by Reuter, MacCoun, & Murphy, 1990).

The theory yields not just general qualitative propositions about the way offenders respond to incentives but also discriminating implications about the relative magnitudes of responses to different incentives. For example, a 1% increase in the probability of apprehension is shown to exert a larger deterrent effect than corresponding increases in the conditional probabilities of conviction and punishment. Essentially due to conflicting income and substitution effects, however, sanction severity can have more ambiguous effects on active offenders: A strong preference for risk may weaken or even reverse the deterrent effect of sanctions, and the results are even less conclusive if one assumes that the length of time spent in crime, not just the moral obstacle to entering it, generates disutility. The results become less ambiguous at the aggregate level, however, as one allows for heterogeneity of offenders due to differences in employment opportunities or preferences for risk and crime: A more severe sanction can reduce the crime rate by deterring the entry of potential offenders even if it has little effect on actual ones. In addition to heterogeneity across individuals in personal opportunities and preferences, the literature has also addressed the role of heterogeneity in individuals' perceptions about probabilities of apprehension, as affected by learning from past experience. As a result, current crime rates may react, in part, to past deterrence measures. A different type of heterogeneity that can affect variations in crime across different crime categories and geographical units may stem from the degree of social interaction, which can partly explain why urban crime rates generally exceed rural rates.

This theory also yields testable propositions about the way participation in criminal activity varies across states, over the life cycle, and across different crime categories. Ehrlich's work identifies inequality in the distribution of income, especially at the lower tail of the income distribution, as having a powerful impact on participation in all felonies, essentially because those with lower skills have poorer prospects for entry into legitimate occupations and lower opportunity costs of imprisonment. In contrast, area wealth provides higher gains from property crimes. Also, educated workers who earn relatively high salaries in legitimate occupations can be expected to avoid especially street crimes, which require low skills, but this is not necessarily the case with white-collar crimes, which do require education and legitimate skills. Evidence from prison data and self-reported crimes confirms these propositions (Ehrlich, 1973, 1975a; Lochner, 2004).

Private "Demand"

The incentives operating on offenders often originate from, and are partially controlled by, consumers and potential victims. Transactions in illicit drugs or stolen goods, for example, are patronized by consumers who generate a direct demand for the underlying offense. But even crimes that inflict pure harm on victims are affected by an indirect (negative) demand, or "derived demand," which is derived from a positive demand for safety, or "self-protection." This term has been used in the economic literature to indicate individual efforts aimed at reducing the probability of being afflicted by hazards to their economic or physical well-being (Ehrlich & Becker, 1972). The hazard of becoming a victim to crime is a natural application of the concept. By their choice of optimal self-protective efforts through use of locks, safes, Lojacks, private guards and alarm systems, or selective avoidance of crime-prone areas, potential victims lower the marginal returns to offenders from targeting them and thus the implicit return on crime to the offender. And since optimal self-protection generally increases with the perceived risk of victimization (the crime rate), private protection and public enforcement will be interdependent. Thus, even in the absence of public enforcement of laws, the incidence of crime in the population can be contained or "equilibrated" through private self-protection. At the same time, however, private protection can also generate both positive and negative externalities (i.e., spillover effects) of considerable magnitudes, which makes it both necessary and expedient to resort to the power of the state to play the major role in protecting life and property and ensuring law and order.

Public Intervention

Since crime, by definition, causes a net social loss, and crime control measures are largely a public good, collective action is needed to augment individual self-protection. Public intervention typically aims to "tax" illegal returns through the threat of punishment or to "regulate" offenders, via incapacitation and rehabilitation programs. All control measures are costly. Therefore, the "optimum" volume of offenses cannot be nil but must be set at a level where the marginal cost of each measure of enforcement or prevention equals its marginal benefit.

To assess the relevant net social loss, however, one must adopt a criterion for public choice. Becker (1968) and Stigler (1970) have chosen maximization of variants of "social income" measures as the relevant criterion, requiring the minimization of the sum of social damages from offenses and the social cost of law enforcement activities. This approach leads to powerful propositions regarding the optimal magnitudes of probability and severity of punishments for different crimes and different offenders or, alternatively, the optimal level and mix of expenditures on police, courts, and corrections. The analysis also reaffirms the classical utilitarian proposition that the optimal severity of punishment should "fit the crime" and thus be set according to its overall deterrent value, essentially because applying the more severe sanctions on, say, petty theft would induce offenders to go for grand larceny. Moreover, it makes a strong case for the desirability of monetary fines, when feasible, as a deterring sanction: Since fines are essentially a transfer payment that does not require use of real resources to punish offenders as do imprisonment, confinement, deportation, and banishments, they are "socially costless." However, fines cannot be relied upon as the dominating form of sanctions since optimal crime control requires the reliance on incapacitating offenders with a high risk of recidivism or providing them opportunities for rehabilitation through training programs oriented to bolster legitimate skills (Ehrlich, 1981).

Another aspect of optimal law enforcement where the income-maximizing, or cost-minimizing, criterion has a natural appeal is the choice of the optimal way to produce enforcement or security services. This is inherently a "supply-side" issue since optimal enforcement services need not be produced by government agencies—they could be delivered by private enforcers or private suppliers of security and protection services whose task can be to detect legal infractions, help prosecute offenders, or administer legal sanctions. Optimal public law enforcement involves setting up rules of compensation to maximize the efficiency of the supply of enforcement and protection services, including private provision of detention, imprisonment, and rehabilitation services (see, e.g., Becker & Stigler, 1974; Benson, 1998; Landes & Posner, 1975).

Different criteria for public choice, however, yield different implications regarding the optimal mix of law enforcement strategies. An important example is the optimal mix of probability and severity of apprehending and punishing offenders, as is the case when the social welfare function is expanded to include concerns for "distributional consequences" of law enforcement on offenders and victims in addition to aggregate income. These considerations can be ascribed to aversion to risk, as in Polinsky and

Shavell (1979), or to an alternative concept of justice, as proposed in Ehrlich (1982). Furthermore, a positive analysis of enforcement must address the behavior of the separate agencies constituting the enforcement system: police, courts, and prison authorities. For example, Landes's (1971) analysis of the courts, which focuses on the interplay between prosecutors and defense teams, explains why settling cases out of court may be an efficient outcome of many court proceedings.

The optimal enforcement policy arising from the income-maximizing criterion can be questioned from yet another angle: a public-choice perspective. The optimization rule invoked in the preceding papers assumes that enforcement is carried out by a social planner. In practice, public law enforcement can facilitate the interests of rent-seeking enforcers who are amenable to malfeasance and bribes. Optimal social policy needs to control malfeasance by properly remunerating public enforcers (Becker & Stigler, 1974) or setting, where appropriate, milder penalties (Friedman, 1999).

Market Equilibrium

In Ehrlich's (1981) "market model," the equilibrium flow of offenses results from the interaction between aggregate supply of offenses, direct or derived demand for offenses (through self-protection), and optimal public enforcement, which operates like a tax on criminal activity. Some behavior classified as crime, such as prostitution and consumption of illicit drugs, involves the interaction between suppliers and consumers in an explicit market setting. But even crimes against persons and property can be analyzed by reference to a virtual market that involves the interaction between offenders and potential victims through the latter's demand for self-protection and thus a negative demand for crime. This analysis identifies more fully the interaction between crime, private self-protection, and public law enforcement and the limitations of alternative means of crime prevention. One important application concerns a comparison of deterrence, incapacitation, and rehabilitation as instruments of crime control. This is because the efficacy of deterring sanctions cannot be assessed merely by the elasticity of the aggregate supply of offenses schedule, as it depends on the elasticity of the private demand schedule as well. Likewise, the efficacy of rehabilitation and incapacitation programs cannot be inferred solely from knowledge of their impact on individual offenders. It depends crucially on the elasticities of the market supply and demand schedules, as these determine the extent to which successfully rehabilitated offenders will be replaced by others responding to the prospect of higher net returns. This market setting has also been applied in works by Schelling (1967), Buchanan (1973), and Garoupa (2000), for example, to analyze various aspects of organized crime.

The "market model" has been developed largely in a static, partial-equilibrium setting in which the general economy affects the illegal sector of the economy but not vice versa. More recently, the model has been extended to deal with the interaction between the two under dynamic settings as well. Specific applications focus on the interaction between crime and income distribution and the relation between bureaucratic corruption and economic growth over the process of economic development (Ehrlich & Lui, 1999; Imrohoroglu, Merlo, & Rupert, 2000).

Applications and Empirical Evidence

Scope

Largely due to the paucity of theoretically relevant data, little has been done thus far to implement a comprehensive market model of illegitimate activity. Many researchers have attempted, however, to implement a simultaneous equation model of crime and law enforcement activity consisting, typically, of three sets of structural equations originally proposed in Ehrlich (1973): supply-of-offenses functions linking the rate of offenses with deterrence variables and other measurable incentives; production functions of law enforcement activity linking conditional probabilities of arrest, conviction, and punishment with resource inputs and other productivity measures; and demand-for-enforcement functions linking resource spending with determinants of public intervention. Attempts to address other aspects of the market model of crime include measuring the effect of law enforcement on the net return from crime, as in Viscusi (1986), and simulating a general equilibrium model that focuses on the interaction between the legal and illegal sectors of the economy (Engelhardt, Rocheteau, & Rupert, 2008; Imrohoroglu et al., 2000). Other applications concern modeling organized crime or "victimless crimes," for which there is direct demand by consumers and patrons, and analyses of the general criminal justice system (see, e.g., Buchanan, 1973; Garoupa, 2000; Reinganum, 1993).

A number of studies have focused instead on specific components of the market model. Some have examined various forms of private self-protection, including use of guards, flight from high-crime neighborhoods into suburbs, and carrying concealed guns as a possible means of self-protection against crime. Other studies have focused on the effects of specific measures of law enforcement, such as the federal sentencing guidelines, enhanced police presence, and the two- and three-strike legislation in California. Another set of papers focuses on crime and various aspects of the labor market. Studies related to these applications by Bartel (1975, 1979); Ayres and Levitt (1998); Cullen and Levitt (1999); Lott and Mustard (1997); Duggan (2001); LaCass and Payne (1999); Gould, Weinberg, and Mustard (2002); Raphael and Winter-Ebmer (2001); Shepherd (2002); and Lochner (2004) are surveyed in Ehrlich and Liu (2006, vols. 2 and 3). See also Kling (2006) and Evans and Owens (2007).

The bulk of the empirical implementation, especially over the past two decades, tested the deterrence hypothesis against data from different population aggregates and different types of crime. The first set explores data on individual offenders, juveniles, females, urban areas, and different countries, such as Canada, the United Kingdom, Italy, Finland, and Germany. The second set includes data on specific crime categories, ranging from aircraft hijacking, drugs, drunk driving, antitrust violations, corporate fraud, and federal fraud. Early and recent papers on these topics (e.g., Bartel, 1975, 1979; Block, Nold, & Sidak, 1981; Corman & Mocan, 2000; Glaeser & Sacerdote, 1999; Karpoff & Lott, 1993; Landes, 1971; Levitt, 1997; Waldfogel, 1995; Witte, 1980; Wolpin, 1978) are also surveyed in Ehrlich and Liu (2006, vols. 2 and 3). Also see the recent study by Drago, Galbiati, and Vertova (2009).

Methodological Issues and Major Findings

The econometric applications via regression analyses have been hampered by a number of methodological problems. Federal Bureau of Investigation (FBI) crime reports are known to understate true crime rates, and related errors of measurement in estimated punishment risks may expose parameter estimates to biases and spurious correlations. The inherent simultaneity in the data, whereby the relation between crime and deterrence variables may reflect different directions of causality corresponding to supply, demand, or production relationships, requires systematic use of identification restrictions to ensure consistent estimation of structural parameters. In testing offenders' responsiveness to incentives, the deterrent effect of imprisonment must be distinguished from its incapacitating effect. Efficient functional forms of structural equations must be selected systematically. And there is the ubiquitous possibility that regression estimates would be affected by "missing variables" and sample selection biases. Most of these problems have been recognized and addressed in the literature from the outset, but more attention has been paid to these problems in recent studies.

In particular, and as the "market model" of crime suggests, higher crime rates, and thus risks of victimization, should increase the willingness of potential victims and law enforcement agencies to spend resources on crime prevention and deterrence, which could bias the estimated association between crime and enforcement variables in a direction contrary to the one predicted by the deterrence hypothesis. In contrast, the "crowding effect" on existing law enforcement resources that can be produced by unexpected surges of crime, as well as errors of measurement in crime counts, are likely to produce the opposite bias (Ehrlich, 1973). To overcome such statistical biases, researchers must try to identify instrumental variables that are not affected by the concurrent incidence of crime but otherwise raise the public willingness to enforce the law or the efficiency of law enforcement efforts. Examples of

variables identified by researchers as "instrumental variables" include "political cycles" that bring to power politicians running on strengthening law and order (see, e.g., Levitt, 1997, although successful campaigns may also reflect previously high and persisting crime rates) and the stock of legal decisions stemming from constitutional principles, especially by the Supreme Court, which make it either easier or more difficult to convict those apprehended and charged by police (see, e.g., Ehrlich & Brower, 1987). Another important research challenge concerns the separation of deterrence from incapacitation effects since law enforcement, by way of detention, incarceration, and imprisonment, can reduce the incidence of crime by incapacitating actual offenders rather than deterring would-be ones. The deterrence hypothesis applies only to the latter effect. The incapacitation effect can be assessed theoretically, since it depends largely on the level of the risks of apprehension and imprisonment rather than changes in these variables (Ehrlich, 1982), but the two effects can also be isolated empirically by estimating a set of interrelated crimes simultaneously: For example, higher prison terms for burglary cannot have incapacitating effects on those committing robbery, but they may deter would-be robbers (Kessler & Levitt, 1999). Helland and Tabarrok (2007) provide further evidence on the existence of pure deterrence effects based on California's "three-strike" law.

Use of different types of data can also affect the researcher's ability to measure the effects of "positive incentives." For example, cross-sectional data on variations in unemployment rates may be affected by an area's industrial composition, unemployment compensation level, and the age and skill composition of the area's labor force rather than involuntary layoffs. Time-series data that span business cycles are more likely to reflect involuntary layoffs and thus the opportunities for gains from legitimate labor market activities. Studies based on time-series and panel data are therefore more likely to reflect the force of legal employment incentives—the effect of the unemployment rate specifically—and the deterrence hypothesis.

The overwhelming volume of studies following systematic econometric applications, which were applied to alternative regions, population groups, and different crime categories, has produced similar findings: Probability and length of punishment are generally found to lower crime rates, with elasticities of response of crime rates to probability of punishment often exceeding those with respect to severity of punishment (see, e.g., the early studies by Ehrlich and the recent study by Drago et al., 2009). Also, the estimated elasticities of crime with respect to the risk of apprehension are generally found to exceed those with respect to the conditional risks of conviction and punishment. Crime rates are also found to be directly related to measures of income inequality and community wealth (proxy measures of relative gains from crime). Estimates of unemployment effects are somewhat ambiguous, however, depending, in part, on whether they are derived from time-series or cross-section data (see the surveys by Ehrlich, 1996; Freeman, 1983), but more recent studies (e.g., Raphael & Winter-Ebmer, 2001) have confirmed the existence of deterrent effects of employment opportunities using instrumental variable techniques.

Not all past research appears to be consistent with the deterrence hypothesis. For example, some studies report a positive association between police expenditure and crime, although this relationship may represent positive demand for public protection from crime. Critics have argued that the estimated deterrent effects may mask a crowding effect of crime on punishment rather than vice versa (Blumstein, Cohen, & Nagin, 1978). However, recent studies provide evidence corroborating the deterrence hypothesis by using effective instrumental variables and panel data techniques to isolate and identify the effect of deterrence variables. Some studies have also estimated a system of interrelated crimes to separate deterrence from incapacitation effects of imprisonment (e.g., Ehrlich & Brower, 1987; Ehrlich & Liu, 1999; Kessler & Levitt, 1999; Levitt, 1997).

The applicability of the economic approach to the crime of murder, and whether the death penalty constitutes a specific deterrent have raised greater controversy. The center of debate has been Ehrlich's (1975a, 1977) studies based on time-series and cross-state data, in which deterrence variables, including the risk of execution as well as the probability and length of punishment by imprisonment, were found to lower murder rates (see Blumstein et al., 1978; and the response in Ehrlich & Mark, 1977). The controversy has generated additional empirical research, which is still ongoing, some inconsistent with the deterrence hypothesis (e.g., Avio, 1979; Hoenack & Weiler, 1980; McManus, 1985) but others strongly corroborative of not only the direction of the deterrent effect of the probability of execution but even the quantitative impact of this extreme penalty as originally estimated (e.g., Dezhbakhsh, Rubin, & Shepherd, 2003; Ehrlich & Liu, 1999; Layson, 1983, 1985; Mocan & Gittings, 2003; Wolpin, 1978). The studies by most economists have been motivated by scientific curiosity concerning the issue of deterrence, for if severity of punishment matters, as is overwhelmingly documented by studies following a rigorous econometric methodology, why wouldn't the most severe legal sanction impart a deterrent effect as well? Many critiques have been motivated, however, by a normative concern about the desirability of executions as a legal sanction, an issue that should be divorced from the issue of its effectiveness. Indeed, if murderers respond to incentives, alternative sanctions can be effective as well.

Policy Implications

The principle of minimizing the aggregate income loss from crime, while involving a narrow efficiency criterion involving material losses, nevertheless has powerful implications concerning optimal crime control policies. It suggests the need to employ differential punishments for different types of offenses, to "fit the crime," as well as for different types of offenders in proportion to their deterrent and incapacitating or rehabilitating values. It also implies that although government intervention in the economy is necessitated to avoid a suboptimal reliance on private self-protection, which creates both external economies (thus too little private protection) and diseconomies (too much emphasis on the protection of individual interests as opposed to society as a whole), the production of means of crime control need not be done just by government agencies and may involve outsourcing the production of desirable security services to private firms (e.g., bail bonding services, legal firms, private prisons, and training centers).

The relative desirability of specific means of crime control cannot be determined just by their relative efficacy or cost-efficiency; it also depends on their relative social costs and on the welfare criteria invoked as a justification for public law enforcement. For example, if the welfare objective is to maximize social income, then the social cost of purely deterring sanctions, such as fines, would be close to zero because as transfer payments, fines are free of the deadweight losses associated with imprisonment, house arrests, probation, and other intermediate punishments. An optimal enforcement strategy may then involve raising such fines to their maximal feasible level (consistent with a convict's wealth constraint) while lowering the probability of apprehension and conviction to its minimal level. Even under this (narrow) efficiency criterion, however, it would be optimal to use imprisonment and intermediate punishments along with fines for those crime categories where the added incapacitation value of imprisonment justifies its added costs.

The enforcement strategy would be different if the social welfare function were broadened to include distributional objectives as well. These include, for example, a preference for promoting equality of individuals under the law, reducing the legal error of convicting the innocent, or lowering the corollary prospect of letting the guilty go free. For example, since the probability of apprehension and punishment is substantially less than 1, penalties are in fact applied through a lottery system. Offenders who are caught and punished are subjected to ex post discrimination under the law because they "pay" not just for their own crime but also for offenders who get away with crime. The degree of such ex post discrimination rises as the penalty becomes more severe or if the probability of punishment is very low. Such concerns help explain why severity of punishment is often traded on the margin for a higher probability of apprehension and conviction. It also helps explain why the justice system introduces numerous safeguards to protect the rights of the accused and why the opposition to capital punishment tends to increase when the penalty is applied infrequently and capriciously (Ehrlich, 1982).

Incorporating concerns for equality and legal error in the social welfare function raises not just the marginal social cost of severity of punishment but that of any strategy of enforcement (as long as the probability of being arrested and punished for a crime is low) relative to its cost under the narrower efficiency criterion. The implication is that more crime would be tolerated as a result of a trade-off between equity and efficiency in enforcement—a trade-off typical of social choice in general.

Another common mistake is the argument that higher severity of punishment makes juries less inclined to convict or punish severely or that more public law enforcement will necessarily lower private protection. There is, however, no mechanical substitution relationship between severity of penalty and probability of conviction and punishment, and the association, or simple correlation, between these two variables could be both positive and negative since it depends on the underlying factors that generate their observed co-variation. If the more severe punishment is considered in cases where optimal severity should be lower, as is the case when the crime is less severe or the penalty is less likely to deter because of the offender's age or mental capacity, then indeed, juries would be less inclined to convict. However, if severity of punishment is justified by the greater severity of the offense or a higher risk of victimization in the community, the more severe penalty could be associated with a greater tendency to convict (see Ehrlich & Gibbons, 1977).

This analysis is applicable to crime control strategies concerning the use of positive incentives as well. The market model implies that a lower disparity in the distribution of earning opportunities in legitimate markets will deter offenders on the margin by reducing their differential gains from criminal activity. This provides a justification for public policies aimed at equalizing educational and employment opportunities partly as means of reducing crime. However, since these policies, unlike conventional law enforcement, cannot be targeted specifically at actual or potential offenders, they may entail relatively high social costs as means of crime control. The positive implications of the market model and some corroborating empirical evidence concerning the relative efficacy of deterrence versus incapacitation and rehabilitation for many crimes suggest a direction of reform of the criminal justice system through greater reliance on general incentives and purely deterring sanctions. Forcing offenders to pay fines through work release programs (including direct restitution to their victims) may in many cases be as effective a means of crime prevention as the more costly incapacitating penalties—especially in the case of many theft crimes or transactions in illicit goods and services. The dramatic growth in the proportion of those imprisoned for drug offenses in the past few decades appears to be inconsistent with this implication of optimal enforcement.

"Intermediate punishments," including work release programs and probation, can also provide effective substitutes to imprisonment and incapacitation through the force of incentives, as implied by the general "deterrence hypothesis."

Future Directions

The application of the economic approach to crime in the analysis of some of the main components of the criminal justice system has been done primarily under a partial equilibrium setting in which the criminal sector of the economy has been analyzed separately from the general economy. The analysis has revolutionized previous literature on the causes and consequences of criminal activity by identifying new factors that account for the diversity of the incidence of criminal behavior across geographical areas, across population groups, and over time, as well as by predicting and measuring their empirical importance. Much remains to be done, however, to improve both the analytical rigor and econometric accuracy of the relevant behavioral relations and clarify their implications for public policy. On the analytical part, the complete application of the market model, which exposes more fully the interaction of crime with both private and public protection efforts, is still a challenge to be addressed, partly through better collection and utilization of the relevant data. Moreover, the development of a general equilibrium setting that identifies more fully the interaction between the legal and illegal sectors of the economy and their feedback effects at a point in time, over the business cycle, and over the long run are still challenges to be met. Indeed, macroeconomic and growth accounting still misses a satisfactory assessment of the role played by the illegal sector of the economy, the underground economy in particular, on the behavior of the full economy and its dynamic movements. I expect the next wave of works on crime to delve into these challenging areas of inquiry through the application of general equilibrium models and numerical analyses under both static and dynamic settings.

Also, a disproportionate work on illegal activity has focused so far on felonies and street crime and less on white-collar crimes because of the paucity of relevant statistical data on the latter: At this point, there is little information available on the actual volume of these legal infractions independently of clearance and arrest statistics. The relatively little attention paid so far to fraud, digital counterfeiting, and violations of fiduciary obligations in business endeavors may have been partly the result of unjustified belief in the power of competitive market forces to eliminate these economically and socially harmful behaviors, but the recent worldwide financial crisis implies that the study of these illegal infractions deserves closer attention. The greater reliance in recent decades on victimization studies and comprehensive population surveys could offer opportunities for systematic applications of the economic approach in studying white-collar crimes and their economic impact.

Furthermore, most of the studies on crime have relied on within-country data. The application of the economic approach in studying variation in criminal activity across countries and different legal systems is still a major challenge to be met, largely because of differences in the definition, interpretations, and methods of reporting crime. The role of the legal system itself (e.g., the common law, the Islamic Sharia, or the Napoleonic Code) is yet to be revealed through rigorous analyses.

Conclusion

The economic approach to crime has provided one of the important revolutions in the social sciences by applying the rigorous tools of economic analysis and econometric methodology to offer a unified approach for understanding illegal behavior as part of human behavior in general. It has also offered significant insights about the relative efficiency and desirability of different means of crime control and different components of the law enforcement system.

The economic approach and the "market model" specifically, however, are still a work in progress. It is still too early to assess the degree to which the various econometric studies have produced accurate estimates of critical behavioral relationships underlying variations and trends of crime. While a strong consensus is emerging in the economic literature regarding the power of the economic approach to explain criminal behavior and the validity of the "deterrence hypothesis," future progress will depend on better data and more complete implementations of the comprehensive model of crime.

The economic approach, however, has not been equally embraced outside of economics. This is partly due to healthy interdisciplinary competition. Criminologists have also tended to produce theories of crime in which the economic and social environments and institutions, rather than individual incentives and enforcement efforts, play the major role in explaining the phenomenon. This, however, does not contradict the economic approach, which assigns an important role to institutions as well, often as an endogenously evolving part of the comprehensive market system. A common misconception about the broad meaning of the "deterrence hypothesis" is that it applies only to negative incentives, while positive incentives may hold a greater promise for solving the crime problem. Another often heard claim is that we don't need to know more about punishment because punishment does not eliminate crime. Both claims are inappropriate. The deterrence hypothesis and its logical extension—the market model—rely on the marginal efficacy of both positive and negative incentives and on the interaction between market demand and supply forces to explain the observed variability in the frequency of offenses across space and time. The empirical evidence developed in most econometric applications is consistent with the hypothesis that punishment and other general incentives exert a deterrent effect

on offenders. This suggests, for example, that there is no need to rely exclusively on harsh or incapacitating sanctions to achieve efficient crime control. A better understanding of what does work, however, calls for more rather than less research into the general deterrence hypothesis and the market model based on it.

References and Further Readings

Avio, K. L. (1979). Capital punishment in Canada: A time-series analysis of the deterrent hypothesis. *Canadian Journal of Economics, 12*, 647–676.

Ayres, I., & Levitt, S. D. (1998). Measuring positive externalities from unobservable victim precaution: An empirical analysis of Lojack. *Quarterly Journal of Economics, 113*, 43–77.

Bartel, A. P. (1975). An analysis of firm demand for protection against crime. *Journal of Legal Studies, 4*, 433–478.

Bartel, A. P. (1979). Women and crime: An economic analysis. *Economic Inquiry, 17*, 29–51.

Becker, G. S. (1968). Crime and punishment: An economic approach. *Journal of Political Economy, 76*, 169–217.

Becker, G. S., & Landes, W. M. (Eds.). (1974). *Essays in the economics of crime and punishment.* New York: Columbia University Press.

Becker, G. S., & Stigler, G. J. (1974). Law enforcement, malfeasance, and compensation of enforcers. *Journal of Legal Studies, 3*, 1–18.

Benson, B. (1998). *To serve and protect: Privatization and community in criminal justice.* New York: New York University Press.

Block, M. K., & Heineke, J. M. (1975). A labor theoretic analysis of the criminal choice. *American Economic Review, 65*, 314–325.

Block, M. K., Nold, F. C., & Sidak, J. G. (1981). The deterrent effect of antitrust enforcement. *Journal of Political Economy, 89*, 429–445.

Blumstein, A., Cohen, J., & Nagin, D. (Eds.). (1978). *Deterrence and incapacitation: Estimating the effects of criminal sanctions on crime rates.* Washington, DC: National Academy of Science.

Buchanan, J. M. (1973). A defense of organized crime? In *The economics of crime and punishment: A conference sponsored by American Enterprise Institute for Public Policy Research* (pp. 119–132). Washington, DC: American Enterprise Institute for Public Policy Research.

Clotfelter, C. T. (1977). Public services, private substitutes, and the demand for protection against crime. *American Economic Review, 67*, 867–877.

Cook, P. J. (1975). The correctional carrot: Better jobs for parolees. *Policy Analysis, 1*, 11–55.

Corman, H., & Mocan, H. N. (2000). A time-series analysis of crime, deterrence, and drug abuse in New York City. *American Economic Review, 90*, 584–604.

Cullen, J. B., & Levitt, S. D. (1999). Crime, urban flight, and the consequences for cities. *Review of Economics and Statistics, 81*, 159–169.

Dezhbakhsh, H., Rubin, P. H., & Shepherd, J. M. (2003). Does capital punishment have a deterrent effect? New evidence from postmoratorium panel data. *American Law and Economics Review, 5*, 344–376.

Drago, F., Galbiati, R., & Vertova, P. (2009). The deterrent effects of prison: Evidence from a natural experiment. *Journal of Political Economy, 117,* 257–280.

Duggan, M. (2001). More guns, more crime. *Journal of Political Economy, 109,* 1086–1114.

Ehrlich, I. (1973). Participation in illegitimate activities: Theoretical and empirical investigation. *Journal of Political Economy, 81,* 521–565. Reprinted with supplements in Becker and Landes (1974).

Ehrlich, I. (1975a). The deterrent effect of capital punishment: A question of life and death. *American Economic Review, 65,* 397–417.

Ehrlich, I. (1975b). On the relation between education and crime. In F. T. Juster (Ed.), *Education, income, and human behavior.* Cambridge, MA: National Bureau of Economic Research.

Ehrlich, I. (1977). Capital punishment and deterrence: Some further thoughts and additional evidence. *Journal of Political Economy, 85,* 741–788.

Ehrlich, I. (1981). On the usefulness of controlling individuals: An economic analysis of rehabilitation, incapacitation and deterrence. *American Economic Review, 71,* 307–322.

Ehrlich, I. (1982). The optimum enforcement of laws and the concept of justice: A positive analysis. *International Review of Law and Economics, 2,* 3–27.

Ehrlich, I. (1996). Crime, punishment, and the market for offenses. *Journal of Economic Perspectives, 10,* 43–67.

Ehrlich, I., & Becker, G. S. (1972). Market insurance, self-insurance, and self-protection. *Journal of Political Economy, 80,* 623–648.

Ehrlich, I., & Brower, G. D. (1987). On the issue of causality in the economic model of crime and law enforcement: Some theoretical considerations and experimental evidence. *American Economic Review, Papers and Proceedings, 77,* 99–106.

Ehrlich, I., & Gibbons, J. (1977). On the measurement of the deterrent effect of capital punishment and the theory of deterrence. *Journal of Legal Studies, 6,* 35–50.

Ehrlich, I., & Lui, F. T. (1999). Bureaucratic corruption and endogenous economic growth. *Journal of Political Economy, 107*(Pt. 2), S270–S293.

Ehrlich, I., & Liu, Z. (1999). Sensitivity analyses of the deterrence hypothesis: Let's keep the econ in econometrics. *Journal of Law and Economics, 42*(Pt. 2), 455–487.

Ehrlich, I., & Liu, Z. (2006). *The economics of crime* (3 vols.). Cheltenham, UK: Edward Elgar.

Ehrlich, I., & Mark, M. R. (1977). Fear of deterrence. *Journal of Legal Studies, 6,* 293–316.

Engelhardt, B., Rocheteau, G., & Rupert, P. (2008). Crime and the labor market: A search model with optimal contracts. *Journal of Public Economics, 92,* 1876–1891.

Entorf, H., & Spengler, H. (2000). Socioeconomic and demographic factors of crime in Germany: Evidence from panel data of the German States. *International Review of Law and Economics, 20,* 75–106.

Evans, N., & Owens, E. (2007). Cops and crime, *Journal of Public Economics, 91,* 181–201.

Forst, B. E. (1976). Participation in illegitimate activities: Further empirical findings. *Policy Analysis, 2,* 477–492.

Freeman, R. B. (1983). Crime and unemployment. In J. Q. Wilson (Ed.), *Crime and public policy* (pp. 89–106). San Francisco: Institute for Contemporary Studies.

Freeman, R. B. (1996). Why do so many young American men commit crimes and what might we do about it? *Journal of Economic Perspectives, 10,* 25–42.

Friedman, D. (1999). Why not hang them all: The virtues of inefficient punishment. *Journal of Political Economy, 107* (Pt. 2), S259–S269.

Garoupa, N. (2000). The economics of organized crime and optimal law enforcement. *Economic Inquiry, 38,* 278–288.

Glaeser, E. L., & Sacerdote, B. (1999). Why is there more crime in cities? *Journal of Political Economy, 107*(Pt. 2), S225–S258.

Gould, E. D., Weinberg, B. A., & Mustard, D. B. (2002). Crime rates and local labor market opportunities in the United States: 1979–1997. *Review of Economics and Statistics, 84,* 45–61.

Grogger, J., & Willis, M. (2000). The emergence of crack cocaine and the rise in urban crime rates. *Review of Economics and Statistics, 82,* 519–529.

Hannan, T. H. (1982). Bank robberies and bank security precautions. *Journal of Legal Studies, 11,* 83–92.

Helland, E., & Tabarrok, A. (2007). Does three strikes deter? A non-parametric investigation. *Journal of Human Resources, 42,* 309–330.

Hoenack, S. A., & Weiler, W. C. (1980). A structural model of murder behavior. *American Economic Review, 70,* 327–341.

Imrohoroglu, A., Merlo, A., & Rupert, P. (2000). On the political economy of income redistribution and crime. *International Economic Review, 41,* 1–25.

Karpoff, J. M., & Lott, J. R., Jr. (1993). The reputational penalty firms bear from committing criminal fraud. *Journal of Law and Economics, 36,* 757–802.

Kessler, D., & Levitt, S. D. (1999). Using sentence enhancements to distinguish between deterrence and incapacitation. *Journal of Law and Economics, 42*(Pt. 2), 343–363.

Kling, J. R. (2006). Incarceration length, employment, and earnings. *American Economic Review, 96,* 863–876.

LaCass, C., & Payne, A. A. (1999). Federal sentencing guidelines and mandatory minimum sentences: Do defendants bargain in the shadow of the judge? *Journal of Law and Economics, 42*(Pt. 2), 245–269.

Landes, W. M. (1971). An economic analysis of the courts. *Journal of Law and Economics, 14,* 61–107.

Landes, W. M., & Posner, R. A. (1975). The private enforcement of law. *Journal of Legal Studies, 4,* 1–46.

Layson, S. (1983). Homicide and deterrence: Another view of the Canadian time-series evidence. *Canadian Journal of Economics, 16,* 52–73.

Layson, S. (1985). Homicide and deterrence: A reexamination of the United States time-series evidence. *Southern Journal of Economics, 52,* 68–89.

Levitt, S. D. (1997). Using electoral cycles in police hiring to estimate the effect of police on crime. *American Economic Review, 87,* 270–290.

Liu, Z. (2004). Capital punishment and the deterrence hypothesis: Some new insights and empirical evidence. *Eastern Economic Journal, 30,* 237–258.

Lochner, L. (2004). Education, work, and crime: A human capital approach. *International Economic Review, 45,* 811–843.

Lott, J. R., & Mustard, D. B. (1997). Crime, deterrence, and right-to-carry concealed handguns. *Journal of Legal Studies, 26,* 1–68.

McManus, W. S. (1985). Estimates of the deterrent effect of capital punishment: The importance of the researcher's prior beliefs. *Journal of Political Economy, 93,* 417–425.

Mocan, H. N., & Gittings, R. K. (2003). Getting off death row: Commuted sentences and the deterrent effect of capital punishment. *Journal of Law and Economics, 42,* 453–478.

Philipson, T. J., & Posner, R. A. (1996). The economic epidemiology of crime. *Journal of Law and Economics, 39,* 405–433.

Phillips, L. (1981). The criminal justice system: Its technology and inefficiencies. *Journal of Legal Studies, 10,* 363–380.

Polinsky, A. M., & Shavell, S. (1979). The optimal trade-off between the probability and magnitude of fines. *American Economic Review, 69,* 880–891.

Raphael, S., & Winter-Ebmer, R. (2001). Identifying the effect of unemployment on crime. *Journal of Law and Economics, 44,* 259–283.

Reinganum, J. F. (1993). The law enforcement process and criminal choice. *International Review of Law and Economics, 13,* 115–134.

Reuter, P., MacCoun, R., & Murphy, P. (1990). Money from crime: A study of the economics of drug dealing in Washington, D.C. *Contemporary Drug Problems, 18,* 713–716.

Sah, R. K. (1991). Social osmosis and patterns of crime. *Journal of Political Economy, 99,* 1272–1295.

Schelling, T. C. (1967). Analysis of organized crime. In *Task force report: Organized crime. The President's Commission on Law Enforcement and Administration of Justice* (pp. 114–126). Washington, DC: Government Printing Office.

Shepherd, J. M. (2002). Fear of the first strike: The full deterrent effect of California's two- and three-strikes legislation. *Journal of Legal Studies, 31*(Pt. I), 159–201.

Stigler, G. J. (1970). The optimum enforcement of laws. *Journal of Political Economy, 78,* 526–535.

Van den Haag, E. (1975). *Punishing criminals.* New York: Basic Books.

Viscusi, W. K. (1986). The risks and rewards of criminal activity: A comprehensive test of criminal deterrence. *Journal of Labor Economics, 4*(Pt. I), 317–340.

Wadycki, W. J., & Balkin, S. (1979). Participation in illegitimate activities: Forst's model revisited. *Journal of Behavioral Economics, 8,* 151–163.

Wahlroos, B. (1981). On Finnish property criminality: An empirical analysis of the postwar era using an Ehrlich model. *Scandinavian Journal of Economics, 83,* 553–562.

Waldfogel, J. (1995). Are fines and prison terms used efficiently? Evidence on federal fraud offenders. *Journal of Law and Economics, 38,* 107–139.

Witte, A. D. (1980). Estimating the economic model of crime with individual data. *Quarterly Journal of Economics, 94,* 57–84.

Wolpin, K. I. (1978). Capital punishment and homicide in England: A summary of results. *American Economic Review, Papers and Proceedings, 68,* 422–427.

74

ECONOMICS OF PROPERTY LAW

RICHARD D. COE

New College of Florida

Property law is the body of law that establishes the rules governing ownership rights over scarce resources. Ownership rights are multifaceted—often referred to as a "bundle of rights"—but in general such rights encompass three broad areas of control over a specific resource: the right to exclude (the ability of the owner to prevent others from using the resource), the right to use (the ability of the owner to use the resource in the manner he or she sees fit), and the right to transfer (the ability of the owner to assign ownership rights to the resource to another). The economic analysis of property law is primarily concerned with the effect of various property rules on the allocation of resources and whether such effects conform to the economic concept of efficiency.[1] Equity issues are also addressed but to a lesser degree.

The Economics of the Right to Exclude

Ownership rights to a resource grant to the owner the ability to exclude others from using the resource. In contrast, an open-access resource, often labeled common property, is one that an individual has a right to use but cannot exclude others from using. The ability to exclude is probably the most commonly associated aspect of ownership—"that's mine; you can't use it." A derivative power of the excludability right is that the owner can determine which other persons can use the property, either now or in the future, via some form of permission, such as a rental or licensing agreement.

The Minimization of Conflict Costs

Economists distinguish between goods and resources that are characterized by rival consumption (or use) and goods

and resources that are characterized by nonrival consumption (or use). Rival consumption exists when consumption by one individual physically precludes consumption by another individual, such as the eating of an apple. Nonrival consumption exists when consumption by one person does not preclude consumption by others, such as the viewing of a fireworks display.

A world of scarce resources characterized by rival use will inevitably lead to disputes over the control of such resources. If ownership rights are uncertain, costly conflicts arise in an attempt to gain or defend use of the resource. Resources are expended (including lives lost) in the actual conflict as well as in preemptive protective measures against attack. Conflict costs are particularly detrimental in that they are unproductive from a societal standpoint. Nothing new is produced; worse yet, existing valuable resources are destroyed—a negative-sum game. Thomas Hobbes (1651/1963) was one of the earliest political philosophers to emphasize the costs of a lawless "state of nature," where ownership rights were determined by the private use of force. A well-defined system of ownership rules can reduce the uncertainty and attendant conflict costs regarding who controls scarce resources. While it requires resources to establish and enforce a system of property rights, a state-enforced system has substantial economies of scale over a system where each individual is responsible for establishing and defending his or her ownership rights.

In contemporary society, most ownership rights are acquired via transfer from the (previous) legal owner of the resource. However, property law is regularly called upon to resolve ownership rights in resources that have no prior owner. *Pierson v. Post* (1805) is a legendary case on this issue. Post was leading a fox hunt. As the target was in sight, Pierson—not a member of the party—shot the fox and claimed the corpse. Post sued for ownership. The court awarded ownership to Pierson, establishing (or reinforcing) the legal rule that (with respect to wild animals) ownership rights are bestowed on the person who first "possesses" the animal.

The "rule of first possession" is a common rule for resolving ownership disputes over previously unowned resources (Rose, 1985). The rule has been defended on efficiency grounds as a low-cost method of establishing rights, in that possession is often an unambiguous phenomenon (as in *Pierson v. Post*), providing a clear demarcation for establishing who owns a specific resource. However, the cost-benefit calculus does not always favor first possession, as issues of difficulty in determining possession, wasteful expenditures in the race to first possession, and possible disincentives to productive efforts, among other issues, may favor more finely tuned rules for establishing ownership to previously unowned resources (Lueck, 1995). Economic analysis of alternative rules for establishing initial ownership claims has focused on the cost of establishing such claims versus the benefits from the right to exclude (for an example with respect to the whaling industry, see Ellickson, 1989).

The Prevention of Resource Depletion

It is a fundamental proposition in economics that an open-access resource will be used beyond the point of efficiency in the short run and quite likely to the point of depletion in the long run—the famous "tragedy of the commons" (Hardin, 1968). Hardin (1968) used the example of open grazing rights to village pastures that were a common arrangement in seventeenth-century England. The cost of using the pasture was zero to any individual herder; therefore, each herder had an incentive to graze his or her livestock as long as some return could be gained, that is, as long as some grass (or other grazing material) remained. This individual-maximizing behavior had two consequences. One, it reduced the current productivity of the pasture for other herders, as their livestock now had less grazing material. Two, it reduced the future productivity of the pasture, as it would be unable to regenerate itself.[2] This outcome results from rational individuals following their own self-interest and maximizing their individual productivity, a behavioral characteristic that in the world of Adam Smith results in beneficial social outcomes. Furthermore, it is of no consequence if a specific individual user (e.g., a herder) recognizes the seeds of the tragedy and attempts to avert the outcome by refraining from using the resource. His or her place would be taken by another user following his or her own maximizing instincts, and the tragedy would continue to its inexorable conclusion.

The crux of the tragedy lies not in the self-interested maximizing behavior of individuals but rather in the institutional setting in which such behavior is allowed to operate. In order to defeat the tragedy, an institutional setting must be found so that access to the resource can be limited. One possibility is to establish private ownership rights in the resources, with the accompanying ability to exclude. If the commons can be privatized, then maximizing incentives for the private owner will be in line with the socially efficient condition for resource utilization, as the profit-maximizing private owner will use the resource to the point where marginal revenue product equals marginal (factor) cost.

The tragedy of the commons, unfortunately, is no mere theoretical construct; rather, its destructive outcome is characteristic of some of the more serious problems currently facing the world's environment. Ocean fisheries serve as a textbook case of the tragedy of the commons in action, as open access has resulted in a state of near collapse for several species. The shrinking of tropical rain forests is another prominent example of the overexploitation of an open-access resource.

Securing Returns From Investment

The act of investment requires incurring costs today in order to earn a return in the future. Such acts are unlikely without confidence in the ability to claim a future return, that is, without the ability to exclude others from the return to the investment. "Open access is associated with depletion and disinvestment rather than with accumulation and economic growth" (Eggertsson, 2003, p. 77). A system of private property rights can ensure that an owner who undertakes an investment today can secure the gains from that investment, thus eliminating the disincentive to investment that exists with an open-access resource.

The grant of exclusive rights to the use of the product of investment activities is to grant a form of monopoly power—the owner is the sole seller of the product. Such a grant creates no efficiency issues when the product is sold in a competitive market. Thus, if a wheat farmer is granted exclusive rights to the crop produced in his or her field, there will be no inefficiency if the wheat is sold in a competitive wheat market. The ownership right provides an incentive for efficient investment, and competitive markets will guarantee the efficient level of wheat production and consumption.

However, the scope of ownership rights—the power to exclude—can raise serious efficiency issues when such rights result in the creation of substantial monopoly power in product markets. These issues arise most notably when rights of exclusion are granted to the inventors of new products and the authors of creative works. This is the realm of intellectual property rights—patents and copyrights. The efficient level of output occurs when price, a measure of the social benefit from additional units of the good, equals the marginal cost of production, a measure of the opportunity cost to society of producing an additional unit of the good. A monopolist will set price higher than marginal cost, thus denying access to the good for consumers whose benefit from additional units of the good (as indicated by the price they are willing to pay) exceeds the cost of producing additional units. Furthermore, monopoly prices will most likely result in extra-normal (monopoly) profits, resulting in a transfer of income from consumers to monopoly producers.

The economic justification for granting such monopoly power is that without the expectation of high returns, inventors and authors have little incentive to undertake the risky process of discovering and developing new products and expressive works. The benefits to society of having the new invention or creative work outweigh the costs of restricting its use. The specific provisions of patent and copyright law, such as the duration of the ownership rights and exceptions such as the "fair use" provision of the copyright law, attempt to strike a balance in the trade-off between incentives to create and monopoly inefficiencies. Changes in the parameters, which determine the magnitude of this trade-off, result in pressure to change the legal rules governing this area of property law.[3]

Recently, a more fundamental challenge has been leveled against the degree of monopoly power granted by patents and copyrights. Rather than promoting the creation of new products and creative works, the web of legal restrictions established by patent and copyright law may actually hinder discovery, innovation, and creative expression by creating substantial barriers to using the knowledge and ideas contained in existing protected works to develop new products and expressive works—an example of the "tragedy of the anticommons." The tragedy of the anticommons occurs when numerous individual property rights to a resource result in underutilization of that resource—the opposite outcome of the overutilization inherent in the tragedy of the commons (Heller, 1998).

The Economics of Use Rights

If resources are scarce, then a society must answer the question of how those resources will be used. In a society characterized by private property rights, individuals who hold the ownership rights to the resources control the answer to that question, subject to the laws governing the use of their property. This freedom granted to private resource owners—"ownership sovereignty," if you will—reflects a fundamental tenet of economics—that individuals are the best judges of their own well-being and should be free to choose how to use their resources so as to maximize that well-being. Broad use rights conferred on individual owners are consistent with the underlying normative justification for a competitive market system—that the pursuit of individual self-interest in a competitive market system will result in a socially efficient allocation of resources.

Externality Problem: When Use Rights Conflict

However, user rights are not unlimited. The conclusion that the decisions of rational, self-interested utility maximizers will result in a socially efficient allocation of resources rests on several assumptions. One key assumption is the absence of negative externalities. A negative externality exists when the activity of Person A imposes costs on Person B, and such costs are not reflected in the price Person A must pay to undertake the activity. It is a well-established principle in economics that the existence of negative externalities can result in a suboptimal allocation of resources.[4] Property law has likewise recognized the problems created by negative externalities, as perhaps best illustrated by the common law maxim "*sic utere tuo ut alienum non laedas*," which translates to "use your own (property) in such a way that you do no harm to another's."

A straightforward example of the externality problem is presented by the case of *Orchard View Farm v. Martin Marietta Aluminum* (1980). The defendant's aluminum plant had emitted fluoride into the atmosphere, which damaged the plaintiff's orchards. From an economic standpoint, such emissions may be inefficient if the benefit from the emissions is less than the harm to the orchards (or, alternatively, the cost of reducing the emissions is less than the benefit to the orchard from reduced emissions). Assume that the harm to the orchards reduced the plaintiff's profits by $500, an amount that represents the net benefit to society (price paid by consumers minus cost of production) of the lost output. Assume further that the defendant could reduce the emissions to a nonharmful level by reducing output, with an accompanying loss of profits (representing again the net benefit to society of the foregone output of aluminum) equal to $300. Under this scenario, the reduction in aluminum output and the resulting increase in the output of the orchard would represent a more efficient allocation of resources, as the increased orchard output is more valuable to society than the reduction in aluminum output. However, the aluminum producer has no incentive to reduce output unless some corrective action is taken to "internalize" the external cost imposed on the orchard.

Property law provides one method to internalize the external costs—the award of compensatory damages for the harm done, often in a complaint of nuisance or trespass. (The *Orchard View Farms* case was a trespass action.) In the above hypothetical, if the court found the defendant liable for damages of $500, then the defendant would have an incentive to reduce output to the nonharmful level, as the $300 in lost profits would be less than the $500 in damages it would have to pay if it did not reduce output. The externality would be internalized, and the allocation of resources would be more efficient. (If the numbers in the above hypothetical were reversed, then the defendant would continue to produce at the same level and pay the damages, which would be the efficient result.)

The award of compensatory damages was one of several mechanisms that property law provided to deal with negative externalities. This mechanism was in line with traditional economic theory, which most often suggested the imposition of taxes (or fines) on the negative externality-generating activity. However, the publication of Ronald Coase's (1960) seminal article "The Problem of Social Cost" dramatically changed the way economists analyzed the question of negative externalities.

The Coase Theorem

Instead of viewing negative externalities as a situation where Person A's activity imposed a cost on Person B, Coase (1960) recast the situation as one in which the two parties were vying over the use of a scarce resource in which no ownership rights had yet been established. If Person A were allowed to use the resource, then a cost would be imposed on Person B, who would not be able to use the resource. However, Coase argued that the converse was also true—if Person B were allowed to use the resource, a cost would be imposed on Person A, who would not be able to use the resource. In effect, externalities were reciprocal in nature, in that one party's use of the resource precluded the other party's use. In the *Orchard View Farms* case, the two parties were competing over the (incompatible) use of the atmosphere, to which neither (prior to the legal decision in the case) had an established property (use) right. The defendant's emissions imposed a cost on the plaintiff, but if the plaintiff were successful in preventing the defendant from releasing emissions, a cost would be imposed on the defendant. The question of which party is harming the other—that is, which party is creating the negative externality—cannot be determined until it is decided who has the right to use the resource in question.[5]

Drawing on this basic insight, Coase (1960) developed the famous Coase theorem: In the absence of transactions cost, the allocation of resources will be efficient regardless of the assignment of property rights. Placing the *Orchard View Farms* case in the idealized world of no transactions costs, the Coase theorem states that an efficient allocation of resources will result regardless of whether the plant is given the right to emit fluoride or whether the orchard is given the right to be free from fluoride emissions. To state the point more starkly, it does not matter, with respect to efficiency, what the court decides, as long as it decides something!

What is the logic behind this remarkable conclusion? It was concluded above that if the owners of the orchard were given the right to be free from harm from the emissions (via compensatory damages), the defendant would reduce output so as to avoid paying damages—the efficient outcome. If, instead, the owners of the plant were given the right to emit, then the orchard owners would have an incentive to offer the owners of the plant a payment, say $400, to reduce the emissions. The plant owners would agree to do so, as the $400 payment is greater than the

$300 in decreased profit resulting from reducing emissions. As long as there are no obstacles to reaching this agreement—that is, there are no transactions costs—the efficient result is reached. The offer of payment by the orchard owners internalizes the cost of the emissions to the plant owners, as the refusal to accept the offer represents an opportunity cost to them.

This example illustrates the *strong* version of the Coase theorem, which states that allocation of resources will be *identical* (and efficient) regardless of the assignment of property rights. But identical allocational outcomes may not result, even in the absence of transactions costs. Efficiency requires that resources go to their most highly valued use. But "value" can be measured in two distinct ways—by how much one is *willing to pay* to acquire a resource (i.e., to buy) and by how much one is *willing to accept* to give up a resource (i.e., to sell). These two amounts may differ. It may require more to compensate a person for the loss of the right to a resource than the person would be willing to pay to acquire the right to that resource. For example, it may take $8,000 to compensate an individual who owns a beachfront cottage with beautiful sunset views to give up that right so that an oil well, which obstructs the view, can be drilled. However, that same individual, perhaps due to income constraints, may only be willing to pay $2,000 to prevent the oil well from being drilled. If there exists a divergence between willingness to pay and willingness to accept (i.e., if endowment effects exist), then the initial assignment (endowment) of the property right may result in a different allocation of resources.[6] However, regardless of the outcome, the resultant allocation of resources will be efficient, *given the property right assignment*. In other words, the resource will go to the most highly valued use regardless of the assignment of the right, but the most highly valued use may differ due to endowment effects stemming from the different assignment of the right.[7] This is the *weak* version of the Coase theorem: In the absence of transactions cost, the allocation of resources will be efficient (but not necessarily the same), regardless of the assignment of property rights.[8]

The Coase theorem is a fascinating and provocative proposition. Despite the fact that transactions costs are likely never zero, it has several implications for property law. One, the law should strive to reduce transactions costs so as to facilitate private agreements to resolve externality conflicts. A clear delineation of property rights is a key step in this process. Negotiations are likely to be particularly acrimonious if the parties believe their rights are being violated. Two, in cases where transactions costs are low, the courts do not have to burden themselves unduly worrying about the efficiency effects of their (clear) assignment of the property right in question, as bargaining will eventually result in an efficient outcome. The courts can focus on other possibly important aspects of their decision, such as the distributional or "fairness" implications. Third, when transactions costs are high, the court should assign the resource in question to the most highly valued use. If transactions costs are high and the resource is assigned to the lower valued use, it is unlikely that a transfer to the more highly valued use will occur, thus resulting in an inefficient allocation of resources. This proposition is dependent on two key assumptions: one, that allocative efficiency is the primary objective of the legal system and, two, that the identification of the most highly valued use is clear and is not subject to possible endowment effects.

The Economics of the Right to Transfer

The rules of property law are part of the set of rules that determine how resources can be passed from one user to another, that is, the right of alienability.[9] This transfer can include the transfer of all rights of use for all time or can be limited in both type of use and length of use. Full voluntary transference of rights can be done by sale, gift, or bequest. A partial transfer of rights can be done in a variety of legal forms, including licensing and leasing arrangements.

Voluntary Transfers

It is a bedrock principle of economics that a voluntary transfer of resources between two reasonably informed parties improves the well-being of both parties, thus representing a Pareto superior reallocation of resources. This is perhaps the fundamental justification for a market-based economy. One prominent role of property law is to facilitate such transfers, primarily by clearly specifying property rights so that uncertainty over ownership can be removed from the market transaction.

But in some instances, the legal system explicitly restricts rather than facilitates the transfer of a property right. The restriction may be complete, as in the case of the right to vote, which can neither be sold nor given away. More often, however, the restraint on alienability is in the form of a prohibition on the sale of the resource, that is, the transfer of the resource in exchange for compensation. For example, it is illegal in most countries to sell one's bodily organs, such as a kidney, for purposes of transplantation, although the transfer of such via a donation is not only legal but often encouraged. Several economic justifications have been advanced in support of inalienability, among them the existence of negative externalities, poor information regarding the consequences of a sale, and myopic behavior (see Rose-Ackerman, 1985). While these justifications may be valid in certain situations, none address the fundamental question of why uncompensated transfers are allowed. The suspicion is that society fears that the offer of compensation will distort the owner's valuation of the resource—that is, that the lure of financial compensation will tempt the owner to transfer the resource when such transfer is not really in the owner's best interest. This is the classic paternalism argument. The argument is

often applied most directly to lower income people, who may be particularly susceptible to an offer of financial compensation. Such temptation has been characterized in such adverse terms as "exploitation" of the poor, as if the provision of compensation is actually detrimental to the welfare of the poor. Paternalistic arguments violate the basic assumption in economics that individuals are the best judge of their own well-being, and thus restrictions on alienability based on such arguments are often criticized by economists as inefficient.

Questions have arisen as to exactly when and what ownership rights are given up in the process of a voluntary transaction, particularly when the transaction involves body tissue. In *Moore v. Regents of the University of California* (1990), the plaintiff agreed to the removal of his diseased spleen, which, unbeknownst to him, contained unique cells. Defendants, through genetic engineering, developed a highly lucrative line of pharmaceutical products based on the plaintiff's cells, without informing plaintiff. The patient claimed ownership; the defendant argued that all ownership rights to the spleen and cells therein were voluntary transferred at the time of the operation. The court ruled that the patient had forfeited his ownership right in the spleen once it was voluntarily removed from his body.[10]

Involuntary Transfers

Adverse Possession (Private Taking)

Adverse possession is the rule of law that transfers ownership of property from the current owner to another private party, without the permission of or compensation to the owner. Adverse possession can be invoked when the owner has not objected to the "open and notorious use" of his or her property by another. For example, if a person builds a garage that encroaches five feet onto the adjacent property of another, and if, over an extended period of time, the owner of the adjacent property makes no attempt to claim ownership, then ownership of that part of the property may pass to the person who built the garage under a claim of adverse possession. The economic justification for such involuntary transfers is twofold. One, the property is moving to the person who values it more highly, on the presumption that the lack of objection by the owner indicates a very low valuation of the property by the owner. Two, adverse possession can discourage ownership claims based on occurrences in the distant past.

Eminent Domain (Public Taking)

Eminent domain is the power of the government to take private property to pursue a government function. The Fifth Amendment of the U.S. Constitution states, "No property shall be taken for public use without just compensation." Public works projects often require the acquisition of multiple parcels of private property, allowing the possibility of one or more owners to "hold out" in an attempt to capture a larger share of the gains from the project. Assume that the government plans on building a hospital, with estimated net benefits (excluding property acquisition costs) of $100 million. The hospital is to be built on 10 identical parcels of private property, each with a market value of $1 million. Thus, the project is economically efficient, with net social benefits of $90 million. Assume the government engages in voluntary market transactions to acquire 9 of the 10 parcels at their aggregate market value of $9 million. The last parcel is now worth up to $91 million to the government, although no other buyer would pay more than $1 million. The owner of the last parcel is in a position to extract an enormous gain by refusing to sell—"holding out"—unless the government pays a substantial premium over the market price. The government may refuse to pay the premium, thus scuttling the project. If more than one of the owners of the 10 parcels attempts to follow this strategy, the problem is confounded. The power of eminent domain eliminates such strategic behavior, allowing the government to acquire property at (preproject) market value, which presumably represents the true opportunity cost of the property to society. The owner is left no worse off, and efficient projects can go forward.

Actual compensation is in accordance with the Pareto test for efficiency but is not required under the more widely used Kaldor-Hicks potential compensation test. However, the "just compensation" requirement promotes efficiency by forcing the government to more explicitly weigh the benefits of a proposed project against the actual costs, an incentive that is not as great if the government can simply take property without compensation. On equity grounds, the compensation requirement results in no one citizen bearing an unduly large cost of providing a public benefit—the general public will bear the cost through the taxation necessary to pay the compensation.

In principle, as well as practice, "fair market value" is considered the standard measure of "just compensation." However, market value—a willingness-to-pay measure of value—may not reflect the amount necessary to induce the owner to sell the property, that is, the amount necessary to fully compensate the owner for his or her loss. As discussed with respect to the Coase theorem, a property owner's willingness to accept may be greater than his or her willingness to pay. This is not unusual when the property in question is the owner's private residence—his or her home. In such a situation, the exercise of the power of eminent domain with "just compensation" based on fair market value may result in a reallocation that does not meet either the strict Pareto test for efficiency or even the weaker potential compensation test for efficiency.

The Fifth Amendment states that the government can acquire property for "public use." If title to the acquired property is transferred to the government and the property is available for use by the public, such as a park or a highway, the public use requirement is clearly fulfilled. The question has arisen, however, concerning the limits on the public use requirement. In *Kelo v. City of New London* (2005), the plaintiff challenged the city government's proposed taking of her house (with compensation at market value), the property to be converted to a parking lot for a private corporation in accordance with a comprehensive economic development plan formulated to reverse the city's declining economic fortunes. In a 5–4 decision, the Supreme Court ruled that the "public use" requirement was fulfilled, as the proposed development plan could provide substantial benefits to the general public.

Regulatory Takings

The police power of the state enables the government to pass laws and regulations to protect the "health, safety, and welfare"[11] of the public. Such regulations may reduce the value of affected property, but the government is generally not required to compensate property owners for the reduced value. For example, the government can restrict the playing of outdoor music at a nightclub if the noise disturbs the peace and quiet of local residents without compensating the owner of the nightclub for any reduction in the value of his or her property resulting from reduced profits or even the closing of the business. Can such regulations so restrict the use of property that in effect the government has "taken" the property, even though title remains with the private owner? In *Lucas v. South Carolina Coastal Council* (1992), the defendant adopted a setback rule prohibiting construction on coastal property within a certain distance from the water, justifying the regulation as necessary to mitigate coastal erosion and to protect the coastal environment. The rule prevented the plaintiff from carrying out plans to build a house on each of his two coastline properties (purchased for $975,000). The plaintiff sought compensation for the significant reduction in the value of his properties, arguing that the regulation in effect constituted a "taking" under the Fifth Amendment. The Court held that if a new government regulation "deprived the owner of virtually all economic benefit" from his property and was not inherent "in the common law traditions of the state," then the regulation resulted in a government taking, requiring compensation under the Fifth Amendment.

The legal issue of whether a government regulation is a legitimate use of the state's police power with no compensation required for any resulting losses or whether the regulation is a taking requiring compensation remains unresolved. From an economic perspective, the analysis echoes the discussion above regarding the Coase theorem and the theory of externalities. As a logical proposition, it is equally correct to state, with reference to the *Lucas* case, that the property owner would harm the coastal environment if he built on the property (i.e., impose a negative externality) or, alternatively, that he would benefit the coastal environment if he did not build (i.e., confer a positive externality).[12] As with the Coase theorem, the assignment of property right must be decided (presumably the role of the court) before the appropriate characterization of the externality can be determined.

Protecting Property Rights

The primary remedies for the protection of property rights are injunctions and damages. An injunction is a court order requiring the defendant to cease the behavior that violates the plaintiff's property right in order to prevent "irreparable harm" to the plaintiff in the future. If the defendant violates the injunction, he or she can be held in contempt of court and face large fines or possible incarceration. The plaintiff can agree to have the injunction lifted if an agreement is reached with the offending party.

Damages are intended to compensate the holder of a property right for the damages that have resulted from the violation of his or her property right. As such, they are backward looking.[13] Damages and injunctions are not mutually exclusive remedies—a court may grant an injunction against future harms while awarding damages for past harms.

In their seminal article, Calabresi and Melamed (1972) highlighted a key difference between injunctions and damages as remedies. An injunction prevents another party from using (harming) the property of the owner (assuming that large fines and the threat of incarceration are effective deterrents). Damages, on the other hand, allow the offending party to use (harm) the property of another, as long as compensation is paid. Returning to the *Orchard View Farms* case, an injunction against emissions from the plant would result in the orchard being free from emissions. If damages were awarded (without an injunction), emissions could continue as long as the orchard owners were compensated for their losses. Calabresi and Melamed classified this distinction as protection by a *liability rule* (damages) and protection by a *property rule* (injunction).

Following the logic of the Coase theorem, in a world of zero transactions cost, the type of remedy should not affect the allocation of resources. Reversing the numbers in the *Orchard View Farm* hypothetical above, assume that profits from the plant are increased by $500 if emissions are released while damage to the orchard from the emissions equals $300. If the court awards damages, the plant owners will continue to allow the emissions and pay damages of $300, thus gaining $200. (Note that this represents an efficient allocation of resources.) On the other hand, if the court issues an injunction prohibiting future emissions, the plant owners have an incentive to offer the orchard owner an amount between $300 and $500 (say, $400) to lift the injunction and allow the emissions (again, the efficient outcome), an offer that the orchard owner would presumably accept. The choice of remedy does not affect the allocation of resources, only the distribution of the resultant efficiency gain.

As with the Coase theorem, the equivalency result relies on the key assumption that transactions costs are sufficiently low so that the two parties are able to reach an agreement. If transactions costs are high, then granting an injunction against the plant owners will result in the plant being forced to eliminate emissions, an inefficient outcome. In this situation, the award of damages (a liability rule) would lead to the efficient result, as the plant owners would continue to emit and pay the damages. As a general proposition, if transactions costs are low, an injunction is the preferred solution, as the parties can negotiate their own (efficient) agreement without the court undertaking the costly task of determining actual damages. However, if transactions costs are high, damages are the preferred solution so as to allow for the resource to be used by the more highly valued user, if that user is not awarded the property right.[14]

Future Directions

The above discussion has touched on certain issues that will challenge the established rules of property law. Some form of property-like exclusionary rights must be established to currently open-access natural resources, or else such resources will soon face extinction. As new life-saving pharmaceutical products are developed, the ability of patent holders to restrict access via monopoly prices will become ever more costly to society. Medical advances in organ transplantation practices combined with increasing life expectancies of a healthier population will make the inalienability of bodily organs increasingly inefficient. The broader issue of property rights in one's bodily tissue, cell line, and genetic code will need to be addressed if the full benefits of scientific advances in biotechnology and genetic engineering are to be realized. In the area of government takings, the courts must decide how broadly the concept of "public use" will be defined and in what circumstances government regulations become so restrictive as to require compensation. But it should not be forgotten in the midst of these weighty national and global issues that one of the most important functions of property law is to decide conflicts over the appropriate uses of one's property that constantly arise at the most local of levels—disputes between neighbors.

Conclusion

Economic efficiency requires that scarce resources are not exploited to the point of depletion, that they are employed in their most valuable use, and that productive investments are undertaken in order for the resource base to grow. Property law plays a key role in the successful obtainment of these objectives by establishing exclusion rights, use rights, and transfer rights to resources and then protecting those rights with appropriate remedies. Ownership rights grant to the owner of a resource the legal authority to exclude others from access (without permission) to the resource, thus providing an incentive against overutilization and depletion as well as for productive investment in the growth of the resource. An owner has broad discretion to put the resource to the use that he or she deems most utility enhancing, thus promoting efficiency. However, that use may impinge on another's resource, and property law determines the extent to which an owner can use his or her resource in a manner that interferes with the property of another (the externality issue). By facilitating negotiations between the affected parties and, in situations in which negotiations are not feasible, by assigning use rights to the most highly valued use, the legal system can contribute to an efficient allocation of resources. A well-functioning system of property law will enable the voluntary transfer of resources between parties on mutually agreeable terms so that resources are moved to their most highly valued use. In situations where voluntary agreements may be difficult to achieve, the legal rules governing the involuntary transfer of ownership rights—adverse possession and government takings—can move resources to more highly valued uses, if properly structured. In a dynamic market economy, the effectiveness of established property law is constantly challenged by changing preferences of individuals, changing production technologies, and changes in the institutional arrangements governing society. The economic analysis of property law is aimed at evaluating how effective the current legal rules that govern ownership rights, as well as proposed changes to such, are in promoting an efficient and equitable allocation of resources in an ever-changing world.

Notes

1. The Pareto test and the Kaldor-Hicks potential compensation test are the two standard concepts of economic efficiency (see Coleman, 1988).

2. More formally, an open-access resource will be used to the point at which the *average* revenue product of utilization equals the *marginal* cost of utilization, which is greater than the socially efficient level of utilization where *marginal* revenue product equals marginal cost.

3. For example, advances in file-sharing technology, which greatly lowered the cost of reproducing recorded music, have fueled the legal battle by the recording industry against the "pirating" (i.e., unauthorized reproduction) of copyrighted music (see *A&M Records v. Napster*, 2001).

4. Standard economic theory concludes that too many resources will be devoted to the negative externality-generating activity because individuals will not take account of the full cost of their activities, ignoring the external costs imposed on others.

5. If the reader is unconvinced by this reasoning, consider the following scenario. The aluminum plant has been a long-established business whose fluoride emissions created no harm on the surrounding people. The orchard owner purchases the land adjacent to the plant and proceeds to plant relatively delicate trees that are harmed by the emissions and then sues to have the emissions stopped. Whose actions impose a cost on whom?

6. The reader can trace out the different outcomes under an alternative assignment of the property right in the cottage owner/oil well example, assuming that the profits from drilling the oil well are $5,000.

7. This result is equivalent to the conclusion in welfare economics that a competitive market economy will generate an efficient allocation of resources, with the actual allocation dependent on the initial distribution of income and wealth (endowments). Change the initial distribution of endowments and the resulting allocation of resources will (presumably) change yet still be efficient

8. The distribution of economic welfare will, of course, change with the changing distribution of initial endowments.

9. Other fields of the law, most notably contract law and estate and trust law, play a prominent role in determining the conditions under which the transfer of ownership rights can occur.

10. The court did hold that defendant had violated other rights of the plaintiffs' (e.g., informed consent).

11. Protecting the "morals" of the public is sometimes added to this list of objectives for the police power.

12. In his majority opinion in the *Lucas* case, Justice Scalia stated, "A given restraint will be seen as mitigating 'harm' to the adjacent parcels or securing a 'benefit' for them, depending on the observer's evaluation of the relevant importance of the use that the restraint favors" (*Lucas v. South Carolina Coastal Council,* 1992, p. 1025).

13. "Permanent" damages, intended to compensate for anticipated future harms, can be awarded.

14. Kaplow and Shavell (1996) present a detailed economic analysis of the alternative remedies.

References and Further Readings

A&M Records v. Napster, 239 F. 3d 1004 (2001).

Anderson, T. L., & McChesney, F. S. (Eds.). (2003). *Property rights: Cooperation, conflict, and law.* Princeton, NJ: Princeton University Press.

Barzel, Y. (1997). *Economic analysis of property rights* (2nd ed.). New York: Cambridge University Press.

Calabresi, G., & Melamed, A. D. (1972). Property rules, liability rules, and inalienability: One view of the cathedral. *Harvard Law Review, 85,* 1089–1128.

Coase, R. H. (1960). The problem of social cost. *Journal of Law and Economics, 3,* 1–44.

Coleman, J. (1988). *Markets, morals, and the law.* Cambridge, UK: Cambridge University Press.

Demsetz, H. (1967). Toward a theory of property rights. *American Economic Review, 57,* 13–27.

Eggertsson, T. (2003). Open access versus common property. In T. L. Anderson & F. S. McChesney (Eds.), *Property rights: Cooperation, conflict, and law* (pp. 73–89). Princeton, NJ: Princeton University Press.

Ellickson, R. C. (1989). A hypothesis of wealth-maximizing norms: Evidence from the whaling industry. *Journal of Legal Studies, 5,* 83–97.

Ellickson, R. C., Rose, C. M., & Ackerman, B. A. (2002). *Perspectives on property law* (3rd ed.). New York: Aspen.

Epstein, R. A. (1985). *Takings: Private property and the power of eminent domain.* Cambridge, MA: Harvard University Press.

Fischel, W. (1995). *Regulatory takings: Law, economics, and politics.* Cambridge, MA: Harvard University Press.

Gordon, H. S. (1954). The economic theory of a common property resource: The fishery. *Journal of Political Economy, 62,* 124–142.

Hardin, G. (1968). The tragedy of the commons. *Science, 162,* 1243–1248.

Heller, M. A. (1998). The tragedy of the anticommons: Property in the transition from Marx to markets. *Harvard Law Review, 111,* 621–688.

Hobbes, T. (1963). *Leviathan.* In J. Plamenatz (Ed.), *Thomas Hobbes: Leviathan.* Cleveland: The World Publishing Company. (Original work published 1651)

Kaplow, L., & Shavell, S. (1996). Property rules and liability rules: An economic analysis. *Harvard Law Review, 109,* 713–790.

Kelo v. City of New London, 545 U.S. 469 (2005).

Landes, W. M., & Posner, R. A. (2003). *The economic structure of intellectual property law.* Cambridge, MA: Harvard University Press.

Lucas v. South Carolina Coastal Council, 505 U.S. 1003 (1992).

Lueck, D. (1995). The rule of first possession and the design of the law. *Journal of Law and Economics, 38,* 393–436.

Miceli, T. J., & Sirmans, C. F. (1995). An economic theory of adverse possession. *International Review of Law and Economics, 15,* 161–173.

Michelman, F. I. (1982). Ethics, economics and the law of property. In J. R. Pennock & J. W. Chapman (Eds.), *Ethics, economics and the law* (pp. 3–40). New York: New York University Press.

Moore v. Regents of the University of California, 793 P.2d 479 (1990).

Nash, C. A. (1983). The theory of social cost measurement. In R. Haveman & J. Margolis (Eds.), *Public expenditure and policy analysis* (3rd ed., pp. 56–79). Boston: Houghton Mifflin.

Orchard View Farm v. Martin Marietta Aluminum, 800 F. Supp (Oregon) (1980).

Pierson v. Post, 3 Cai. R. 175, 2 Am Dec. 264 (1805).

Rose, C. M. (1985). Possession as the origin of property. *University of Chicago Law Review, 53,* 73–88.

Rose-Ackerman, S. (1985). Inalienability and the theory of property rights. *Columbia Law Review, 85,* 931–969.

Sax, J. (1971). Takings, private property and public rights. *Yale Law Journal, 81,* 149–186.

Yandle, B. (1998). Coase, Pigou and environmental rights. In P. J. Hill & R. E. Meiners (Eds.), *Who owns the environment?* (pp. 119–152). Lanham, MD: Rowman and Littlefield.

75

QUEER ECONOMICS

Sexual Orientation and Economic Outcomes

RICHARD R. CORNWALL

Middlebury College

Queer economics looks at a particular example of the tight connection between markets and the emergence and shaping of social identities. What makes it "queer" is focusing on the role markets have played in the birth of lesbian-gay-bi-transexual identities with particular interest in how certain identities are queered (i.e., their social valuation is switched across a social boundary between straight-respectable and gay-abjected). Queer economics also goes the other direction— namely, from perceptions of sexual orientations in markets to the behavior of individuals and businesses in markets resulting, for example, in inequality in earnings according to sexual orientation.

Conventional Economic Thinking

An economist ignorant of queer theory might imagine measuring the economic impact of queer culture on the circular flow of national output/consumption by measuring how many units of currency per year of queer culture are bought and sold. But then, does one count only sales of new lesbian, bisexual, gay, transgender, queer/questioning (LBGTQ) books, art, movies, television, radio, theater, receipts at gyms, Internet sex sites, sex clubs, and bars? Does one include phenomena deriving from LBGTQ cultures but aiming at mainstream culture such as dance clubs, Madonna videos, sexy couture, and even very mainstream clothing such as Abercrombie & Fitch's with a gay esthetic permeating its marketing through, especially, Bruce Weber's photos (McBride, 2005, chap. 2)? How should

one account for designs created by LBGTQ people or sales by stores catering to LBGTQ consumers but also selling to straight folks?

This type of conventional thinking would see "the queer economy" as a distinct part of a nation's gross domestic product. Yet this approach fails since boundaries for LBGTQ cultures do not exist, and this conventional thinking is challenged by the new field of queer political economy (Cornwall, 1997). LBGTQ cultures are more like queer glasses: They transform how people view *all* culture since they change what is permitted, what is valued, what is disparaged, and how we conceptualize our economic lives.

We begin then by looking historically at the queering of social identities. This took place especially at the rollover from the nineteenth to the twentieth centuries simultaneously with the redefinition of boundaries between classes and genders. This *ver/mischung* of the codifications of class, sexuality, and gender is of fundamental importance for queer political economy.

Part I: Markets Contribute to Creation of Identities Based on Sexual Orientations: The Rise of LBGTQ Identities

In the beginning, there were no sexual identities! Well, a bit more carefully, excluding earlier urban and cloistered, single-sex environments (e.g., see Boswell, 1980, on ganymedians in the eleventh century), there was no space in language and in thinking for what we label

LBGTQ. As D'Emilio (1983/1993) notes describing colonial North America,

> There was, quite simply, no "social space" in the colonial system of production that allowed men and women to be gay. Survival was structured around participation in a[n extended] nuclear family. There were certain homosexual acts—sodomy among men, "lewdness" among women—in which individuals engaged, but family was so pervasive that colonial society lacked even the category of homosexual or lesbian to describe a person. It is quite possible that some men and women experienced a stronger attraction to their own sex than to the opposite sex—in fact, some colonial court cases refer to men who persisted in their "unnatural" attractions—but one could not fashion out of that preference a way of life. Colonial Massachusetts even had laws prohibiting unmarried adults from living outside family units. (p. 470)

In the nineteenth century in the United States, a bit earlier in Britain, a bit later in some countries and continuing in many places today, has been a transformation from, on one hand, an economic system where most people live and work in kinship groups in agriculture to, on the other hand, the market system with individualized wage labor and with more urban living. This transformation was engendered by and simultaneously contributed to reduced costs of transportation and communication resulting in the spread of concentrated factory production sites and the spread of wage labor. This, in turn, enabled people to be able to conceive of being economically independent from their kin and from agricultural activities. It allowed LBGTQ individuals to move to urban areas and to meet each other and to discover their often hidden (from themselves) same-sex erotic interests as they participated as customers of boarding houses, molly houses, bathhouses, coffee shops, and cruising spots in, for example, England in the eighteenth century. Somewhat similarly, though changed by the filter imposed by gender in Western cultures, lesbians emerged as a self-aware and socially distinguished group in the nineteenth and twentieth centuries (see Cornwall, 1997, for references).

A tight cognitive link between biological sex, gender, and sexuality (Rubin's [1975] "sex/gender system"; see also Escoffier, 1985), from our vantage, appears to have been hegemonic until approximately the end of the nineteenth century. It was taken for granted, as "natural," that sexual object preference was determined by gender: "In the dominant turn-of-the-century cultural system governing the interpretation of homosexual behavior, especially in working-class milieus, one had a gender identity rather than a sexual identity or even a 'sexuality'; one's sexual behavior was thought to be necessarily determined by one's gender identity" (Chauncey, 1994, p. 48). In other words, the concept of gender consisted of the dichotomy of "male" versus "female," and this included sexual object choice. This tendency to focus on "gender" economized on cognitive categories, which simplified thinking by

avoiding the ambiguities that can be expected in cases where there are small numbers of examples encountered by people as was certainly the case in rural settings.

The turn from the nineteenth to the twentieth century was a time not only of increasing urbanization in the United States but also of radical changes in the roles and extent of markets and the organization of production. The rise of wage labor in this country occurred early in the nineteenth century (e.g., "daughters of failing small farmers in the Northeast" began working in textile mills at Lowell; Amott & Matthaei, 1991, p. 295) and was followed in the second half of the century by dramatic growth of sex-segregated labor markets (Amott & Matthaei, 1991, pp. 315–348; Matthaei, 1982). Further and equally socially momentous was the rise of factories with thousands of workers under one roof, which led to enormous social upheaval as new codes for thinking about "productive" activities were developed.

Interaction Between Shaping Class Boundaries and Sexuality Borders

This blender of changing social roles created a vortex of changing social identities:

> Working-class men and boys regularly challenged the authority of middle-class men by verbally questioning the manliness of middle-class supervisors or physically attacking middle-class boys. . . . [One contemporary] recalled, he had "often seen [middle-class cultivation] taken by those [men] of the lower classes as 'sissy.'" The increasingly militant labor movement, the growing power of immigrant voters in urban politics, and the relatively high birthrate of certain immigrant groups established a worrisome context for such personal affronts and in themselves constituted direct challenges to the authority of Anglo-American men as a self-conceived class, race and gender. (Chauncey, 1994, p. 112)

These struggles over where to map key social boundaries led

> politicians, businessmen, educators, and sportsmen alike [to protest] the dangers of "overcivilization" to American manhood. . . . Theodore Roosevelt was the most famous advocate of the "strenuous life" of muscularity, rough sports, prizefighting, and hunting. . . . The glorification of the prizefighter and the workingman bespoke the ambivalence of middle-class men about their own gender status . . . a "cult of muscularity" took root in turn-of-the-century middle-class culture. . . . Earlier in the nineteenth century, men had tended to constitute themselves as men by distinguishing themselves from boys. . . . But in the late nineteenth century, middle-class men began to define themselves more centrally on the basis of their difference from women . . . gender-based terms of derision [e.g., sissy, pussy-foot] became increasingly prominent in late-nineteenth-century American culture. (Chauncey, 1994, pp. 113–114)

This oversimplifies and ignores resistance to this respecification of gender ("They wonder to which sex I belong": Matthaei, 1995; Vicinus, 1992), but this recoding of masculinity seems to have been powerful at this time.

Closely tied to this redefinition of "male" in the 1890s was redefinition of class:

> Men and women of the urban middle class increasingly defined themselves as a class by the boundaries they established between the "private life" of the home and the rough-and-tumble of the city streets, between the quiet order of their neighborhoods and the noisy, overcrowded character of the working-class districts. The privacy and order of their sexual lives also became a way of defining their difference from the lower classes. (Chauncey, 1994, p. 35)

Just as a new "face" was being put on not-male (i.e., not-male became "female" instead of "boy"), so "middle-class" became "clean-face-and-well-laundered/mended-clothes" versus the "dirty" faces of slums. A quickly judged face was put on people living in slums: "The spatial segregation of openly displayed 'vice' in the slums had . . . ideological consequences: it kept the most obvious streetwalkers out of middle-class neighborhoods, and it reinforced the association of such immorality with the poor. . . . Going slumming in the resorts of the Bowery and the Tenderloin was a popular activity among middle-class men (and even among some women), in part as a way to witness working-class 'depravity' and to confirm their sense of superiority" (Chauncey, 1994, p. 26).

This simultaneous redefinition of gender, class, and occupations spilled over, "infected," the definition of sexual orientation that was occurring at the turn of the century:

> In a culture in which becoming a fairy meant assuming the status of a woman or even a prostitute, many men . . . simply refused to do so. . . . The efforts of such men marked the growing differentiation and isolation of sexuality from gender in middle-class American culture. . . . The effort to forge a new kind of homosexual identity was predominantly a middle-class phenomenon, and the emergence of "homosexuals" in middle-class culture was inextricably linked to the emergence of "heterosexuals" in the culture as well. If many workingmen thought they demonstrated their sexual virility by playing the "man's part" in sexual encounters with either women or men, normal middle-class men increasingly believed that their virility depended on their exclusive sexual interest in women. Even as queer men began to define their difference from other men on the basis of their homosexuality, "normal" men began to define their difference from queers on the basis of their renunciation of any sentiments or behavior that might be marked as homosexual. (Chauncey, 1994, p. 100)

Furthermore, "the queers' antagonism toward the fairies was in large part a *class* antagonism . . . the cultural stance of the queer embodied the general middle-class preference for privacy, self-restraint, and lack of self-disclosure" (Chauncey, 1994, p. 106).

Thus, it is no accident that this social earthquake of a lingual transformation in American culture, creating as "pervert" the distinct person now known as lesbigay, coincided with the rise of wage labor markets. John D'Emilio (1983) and Jeffrey Weeks (1979) have sketched this well for gaymen: how gender segregation in workplaces and in institutions for living and for social interaction such as clubs, baths, bars, and access to "public" spaces facilitated the evolution of notions of sexual identities. Especially important was the growth of wage labor in urban areas allowing gaymen to support themselves outside of traditional, kin-based agricultural networks,[1] and this, in turn, fed the rise of gay bars, baths, and so on, which, again in turn, made urban labor markets increasingly alluring for gaymen.

As Julie Matthaei (1995) notes, D'Emilio's "argument is much stronger for men than for women" (pp. 31–32, note 11; see also Chauncey, 1994, p. 27). The very different values that evolved for women compared to men in the last half of the nineteenth century in American culture (D'Emilio & Freedman, 1988) and the very different earnings levels resulting from the sex segregation of labor markets (Matthaei, 1995, p. 13) led to rather different manifestations of same-sex eroticism for women than for men. Thus, Matthaei (1995, pp. 12–14) offers tangible accounts of women whose transgendered performances in prominent public careers were "masterful" for their entire adult lives. Women passed as men, and their partnerships passed as marriage at a time when apparently few men exhibited similar reasons for living in drag. Analogously, while two women (neither transgendered) could be referred to as living in a "Boston marriage," no comparable term seems to have been used for two men living together. Thus, it seems important for socioeconomists to allow for the possibility of a (general equilibrium type of) simultaneity or interdependence in the social articulation of gender, sexuality, and labor and product markets.

What is "lesbian" and what is "gay" are fluid and are historically contingent on other social constructions. This poses a danger for economists who are as mentally conditioned as any other market players to seek discrete, firm economic identities that can be captured by yes/no decisions (zero/one dummy variables) across history. Although it may appear very likely (I conjecture, at our 2009 stage of imperfect "knowledge") that Sappho, Jane Addams, and Willa Cather may have shared a chromosomal structure differentiating them (with "statistical significance") from the chromosomal structures of more than 90% of the women who have lived on planet Earth, to then jump from conjectured or measured chromosomal patterns to inferences about the constructed trait now labeled "lesbianism," not to mention observed market behavior or even erotic activity, seems foolish if lesbianism and, indeed, sexuality in general are linguistically based and are as fluid over time and place as lingual structures are easily observed to be. Thus, Jane Addams was able in the 1890s to exhibit market behavior that a cliometrician might take for clear evidence of lesbian "identity"—that is, arranging in advance on her speech-making travels that each hotel provide a room with just one double bed for her and her "devoted companion," Mary Rozet Smith (Faderman, 1991, pp. 25–26)—yet a few decades later, Willa Cather kept her relation with her partner, Edith Lewis, of almost 40 years private until her death (O'Brien, 1987, p. 357). In between, the notion of "romantic friendship" had been replaced in Euro-based lingual cultures by the psychiatric diagnosis/identity-disorder of lesbianism.[2]

Queer Theory's Perspective on Social Boundaries: Articulating What Is Unspeakable, Unthinkable

The term *queer theory* was first used by Teresa de Lauretis (1991) to describe "the conceptual and speculative work involved in discourse production, and . . . the necessary critical work of deconstructing our own discourses and their constructed silences" (p. iv). This focus on the use of language—on what is explicit and what remains hidden—studies people's discourse as a window into how these humans think and, especially, into how we (often unconsciously) categorize people and actions.

Humans depend on their linguistic communities to think, that is, to perceive, categorize, and articulate our desires (with erotic desires having an almost lexicographic priority). de Lauretis (1991) aimed to "problematize . . . to deconstruct the silences of history and of our own discursive constructions" (pp. iii, xvi). Judith Butler (1993) has noted,

> The construction of gender operates through *exclusionary* means, such that the human is not only produced over and against the inhuman, but through a set of foreclosures, radical erasures, that are strictly speaking, refused the possibility of cultural articulation. (p. 8)

The object of study in queer theory is the social articulation of same-sex eroticism and why, in recent centuries in Western-dominated cultures, this human interaction has been articulated as queer, as abject Other. The subtlety and complexity of this articulation led many, most notably Michel Foucault, who were searching for an analytical handle in this domain of socioeconomic inequality to the notion of discursive structure. I describe this as a mental structuring of concepts, each of which has an "aroma" of connotations, where these concepts are linked via physically developed neurological links that guide, often in a probabilistic and certainly in a nonconscious way (Damasio, 1994, p. 215), how we make inferences about what is "true"—hence, Foucault's (1972, p. 191; 1994, pp. 13, 68, 89) term *épistémè*. In short, discursive structures are (largely) linguistic cognitive structures—physically instantiated as ready-to-fire neural

pathways in our brains—which develop as we learn our mother tongues and as we learn to understand, to map, our social embedment. Central to this queer thinking are the concepts of disgust, abjection, and Otherness.

The Social Roles of Disgust, Abjection, and Otherness

> [I]n colonial America, [convicted] sodomites were more often than not lower-class servants, and the shoring up of patriarchal power was imbricated in nascent class divisions. One has only to look to other colonial situations of the time to see that that was not the only way the category of sodomy was being mobilized; the Spaniards, for instance, prone to see sodomites among the Moors in Spain, saw native cultures as hotbeds of irregular sexual practices. (Goldberg, 1994, p. 7)

Stallybrass and White (1986) note, "The bourgeois subject continuously defined and re-defined itself [as a way of distinguishing itself and its social legitimacy vis-à-vis the nobility and landed gentry] through the exclusion of what it marked out as 'low'—as dirty, repulsive, noisy, contaminating. Yet that very act of exclusion was constitutive of its identity. The low was internalized under the sign of negation and disgust" (p. 191). Slightly earlier, Stallybrass and White summarized this: "[Social] *differentiation . . . is dependent upon disgust*" (p. 191, emphasis added).

The ideas of abjection and of Otherness require careful explanation. The process of abjection gets started in the preverbal, deepest learning and mental formatting occurring when we are babies, and we develop perceptions of most-feared horrors that we may conflate with excrement, which is threateningly close to, even part of, ourselves. Since Freud and Lacan, there has been significant storytelling about such overarching psychic events shaping us. Julie Kristeva's (1982) formulation of how we transfer the symbolic and emotional meaning of these early experiences into verbal (and oneiric) articulations throughout the rest of our lives has been especially useful in queer theory.

Reading "Otherness" as mere difference, as simply being a mathematical reflection across an arbitrary and rather inconsequential boundary, is easy when transgenders such as RuPaul appear so sleekly, so *easily* on MTV. This is how most of the students in my queer studies classes who are not lesbigay first read "Other." Those who have not been subjected to the shame of being named faggot/dyke and of baring what they have (synecdochically) learned are their "most private," most individualizing parts of themselves before taunting gym classmates do not instantly jump to what queer scholars such as Judith Butler, Foucault, and de Lauretis or even writers such as Jean Genet and Dorothy Allison have grappled with. It is not enough to recite that the bloodiest hate crimes appear to be linked to the Levitical teaching about abomination, teaching that is carried out explicitly or implicitly by almost all churches that, *at best,* merely tolerate those lesbigays who adopt the pose of synthetic straight (i.e., desiring "marriage" and all the other trimmings of liberal respectability we have inherited). It is not sufficient to point out how these teachings seem to encourage some people to follow a metanorm (Axelrod, 1986) to shoot/stab/bind-and-push-off-quarry-in-February-in-Vermont faggots and dykes. Reciting these episodes of brutality seems to communicate nothing of what Other describes.

So let's proceed didactically: "A *performative* is that discursive practice that enacts or produces that which it names" (Butler, 1993, p. 13). An example of a performative speech act is the creation of "currency": The inscription "This note is legal tender for all debts, public and private" is exactly what makes currency legal tender. Performatives gain collective credibility only through constant *reiteration.* Thus, currency *gains currency* only through its reiteration and its *anticipated* reiteration by juridical institutions and by private traders.

Another familiar performative is the utterance "I pronounce you man and wife." When certain institutionally designated people say this is a fact, then it becomes a fact, and it remains a fact to the extent that the husband and wife and their social interactions reiterate it. Similarly, "the norm of sex takes hold to the extent that it is 'cited' as such a norm, but it also derives its power through the citations that it compels" (Butler, 1993, p. 13). It does this by naming us, sexing us with culturally assigned connotations that place us in social space. Indeed, "the subject, the speaking 'I,' is *formed* by virtue of having gone through such a process of assuming a sex" (Butler, 1993, p. 3, emphasis added).

This assignment of gender roles gives us not only gender but also what we now call sexuality. This social process shaping female/male identities is the discursive means by which the heterosexual imperative enables certain sexed identifications *and forecloses and/or disavows other identifications.* This exclusionary matrix by which subjects are formed thus requires the simultaneous production of a domain of abject beings, those who are not yet "subjects" but who form the constitutive *outside* to the domain of the subject (Butler, 1993, p. 3).

"Abjection (in latin, *ab-jicere*) literally means to cast off, away, or out. . . . [T]he notion of *abjection* designates a degraded or cast out status within the terms of sociality. . . . [It] is precisely what may not reenter the field of the social without threatening psychosis, that is, the dissolution of the subject itself . . . ('I would rather die than do or be that!')" (Butler, 1993, p. 243, note 2).

In particular, Foucault (1990a and especially 1988 & 1990b) has sketched how Western discursive structures since late antiquity have very slowly evolved to make the male-female *couple* the social-civic atom (Foucault, 1988, p. 153). This evolution also made monogamy, "sexual monopoly" (Foucault, 1988, p. 149), a hegemonic doctrine and obliterated awareness—people stopped taking for granted—that there are good reasons for erotic intercourse other than procreation (Foucault, 1984/1990b, p. 181). Finally, Foucault (1978/1990a) most forcefully initiated linguistic study of the "exclusionary matrix by which subjects are formed" (i.e., the social process through which one's gender became more rigidly linked to the sex of her or his erotic partners).

Foucault (1978/1990a, p. 103) argued that this occurred through the development of the concept of sexuality. The breadth of Foucault's vision and of what might be involved in understanding the formation of social identities can be glimpsed from his careful analysis of what he saw as a change in the way "truth" is discovered/revealed (épistémè) from the seventeenth to the nineteenth centuries (Foucault, 1966/1994, 1972) *plus* his identification of "four great strategic unities which, beginning in the eighteenth century, formed specific mechanisms of knowledge and power centering on sex" (Foucault, 1978/1990a, p. 103) and were developed and "applied first, with the greatest intensity, in the economically privileged and politically dominant classes . . . the 'bourgeois' or 'aristocratic' family" (Foucault, 1978/1990a, p. 120).

1. "[T]he first figure to be invested by the deployment of sexuality, one of the first to be 'sexualized,' was the 'idle' woman" (Foucault, 1978/1990a, p. 121). This was the wife of the bourgeois market player.

2. The alarms about overpopulation economists associated with Robert Malthus brought about a "socialization of procreative behavior: . . . 'social' and fiscal measures brought to bear on the fertility of couples" (Foucault, 1978/1990a, pp. 104–105). This use of taxes/prohibitions to promote (for some governments) or restrain fecundity (some rapidly growing countries) continues to be a frequently employed and debated type of public policy.

3. "A psychiatrization of perverse pleasure: the sexual instinct was isolated as a separate biological and psychical instinct; a clinical analysis was made of all the forms of anomalies by which it could be afflicted" (Foucault, 1978/1990a, p. 105). Thus arose in the late nineteenth century the diagnosis of the pathological condition (identity) of being homosexual.

4. "As for the adolescent wasting his future substance in secret pleasures, the onanistic child who was of such concern to doctors and educators from the end of the eighteenth century to the end of the nineteenth, this was not the child of the people, the future worker who had to be taught the disciplines of the body, but rather the schoolboy, the child surrounded by domestic servants, tutors, and governesses, who was in danger of compromising not so much his physical strength as his intellectual capacity, his moral fiber, and the obligations to preserve a healthy line of descent for his family and his social class"

(Foucault, 1978/1990a, p. 121). Laqueur (2003, e.g., p. 13) has confirmed Foucault's view, noting how historically striking is this sudden social focus on masturbation: For well over a millennium and a half, masturbation was viewed as a minor theological infraction of good behavior, but in the eighteenth century, it suddenly reared up in Western social imagination as an especially heinous sin, perhaps the MOST heinous sin. It only gradually started to fade in importance in the twentieth century after the newly developed rainbow of erotic sins (the "psychiatrization of perverse pleasure"), ranging from homosexualities to diverse heterosexualities (heterosexuality was initially coined to label a particular variant of psychosexual "disease"), had grabbed the imagination of social facilitators: especially doctors and also, later, psychologists, reformers, ministers, and lawyers.

These newly positioned social facilitators, enunciators of *norms of respectability,* abjected so-called homosexual identities as exemplars of Other. The bourgeoisie "must be seen as being occupied, from the mid-eighteenth century on, with creating its own sexuality and forming a specific body based on it, a 'class' body with its health, hygiene, descent, and race" (Foucault, 1978/1990a, p. 124) This "queering" of certain behaviors and individuals, labeling them egregious transgressors of respectability, led those so labeled to react by adhering more strongly to each other as a distinct group, even flaunting the condemned behavior. Thus, the queer imprecations were queered by being embraced by their targets in newly evolving niches in labor, housing, and entertainment markets.

> Somewhat similar to the way in which, at the end of the eighteenth century, the bourgeoisie set its own body and its precious sexuality against the valorous blood of the nobles, at the end of the nineteenth century it sought to redefine the specific character of its sexuality relative to that of others, . . . tracing a dividing line that would set apart and protect its body. (Foucault, 1978/1990a, pp. 127–128)

Thus, Foucault conjectured that the social construction of the identities that we now term *lesbian, gay, bisexual,* and *transgendered* was part of, intimately tied to, the emergence of markets in Western societies. As noted above, George Chauncey (1994, pp. 13, 27, 111–126), Lillian Faderman (1991), John D'Emilio and Estelle Freedman (1988), and David Greenberg (1988) trace some of the details of this lingual construction of class boundaries as well as the coevolution of concepts of sexuality with institutions such as markets, churches, military training, and professional networks of doctors, social workers, artists, businesspeople, educators, professors, research people, and so on in the United States. This process leads to people generally investing heightened importance to categories we now label LBGTQ but had often hitherto seemed not worthy of much public notice.

Part II: Perceptions of Sexual Orientations Affect Markets

This construction of LBGTQ identities is the lingual heritage of those growing up and learning to think in market-dominated cultures. This lingual inheritance determines in large part what we can think by determining the vocabulary of notions and connotations that are encoded in the neural circuits in our brains. It is these "flavors"/"smells" (i.e., connotations) of social identities that influence our perceptions of social labels and so enable us to articulate ideas about them. We grow axons and dendrites on neurons to connect neurons through their generation of and reception of neurotransmitters and thereby create these neural circuits (Panksepp, 1998, pp. 65, 85, 182–184). This physical embodiment of connotations in our brains makes the association of certain traits (e.g., "disgusting") with a social identity "automatic" and almost instantaneous. It precedes and provides the basis for "thinking," for deliberative cognition.

For just one example, this social language (and associated values and connotations) has made certain erotic desires and activities unspeakable, especially for politicians, and so has determined what data on erotic preferences and activity are (*not*) publicly funded and are (*not*) available as we seek to design public health measures to deal with human immunodeficiency virus (HIV) or to ascertain inequality in earnings (Badgett, 1995; Klawitter & Flatt, 1998).

Inequality in Earnings by Sexual Orientation

Part I sketched the intensity of "antigay animus" (Badgett, 2007, p. 25), but is there any evidence that this animus actually affects markets? This evidence is important even if we accept the prevalence of antigay animus because it is often argued that markets can act to discipline would-be discriminators who would refuse to hire LBGTQ people or who would pay them less than other equally qualified people for the same work. Indeed, this is a standard economic argument since

1. the would-be discriminator is giving up profit by paying more than needed to accomplish the firm's hiring goals by not hiring less expensive and/or more qualified workers who happen to be LBGTQ and
2. competitive markets drive profits down to the minimum required to stay in business so this firm would be driven out of business.

This is the conventional neoclassical argument that, however, has been empirically refuted for, just for example, racial inequality, by Jim Heckman and Brook Payner's (1989) demonstration that passage of the 1964 Civil Rights

Act had an immediate effect on hiring black employees in textile mills in South Carolina. What blocks this neoclassical competitive-markets argument from dissolving inequality in employment is social norms that impose costs on those who violate them, as Heckman and Payner argued.

Badgett (2007, p. 27, Table 2.1) summarizes 12 econometric studies of inequality beginning with her pioneering work in 1995: "[Almost] every study using US data has found that gay/bisexual men earn less than heterosexual men, with a range of 13 percent to 32 percent" (p. 29). In particular, earnings for gay and/or bisexual men in the United States and the United Kingdom are estimated to range from 2% to 31% lower than for comparable straight men with similar human capital characteristics (education, age, region of country, partnership status, and, sometimes, occupation). Lesbians and bisexual women, on the other hand, in similar studies earn 3% to 27% more than straight women in most studies, although 3 of the studies found lesbians and bisexual women earning slightly less than straight women. As Badgett notes, "Lesbians do not earn less than heterosexual women, at least not when controlling for our imperfect measures of experience and human capital" (p. 32). And lesbians *do* earn less than straight men with similar productivity characteristics.

The preceding evidence of inequality tied to sexual orientation suggests that there might be an ameliorative role for antidiscrimination laws. The effects of local laws, however, are not entirely clear. The first study of them (Klawitter & Flatt, 1998) found "no impact on average earnings for people in same-sex couples" (Carpenter & Klawitter, 2007, p. 279) compared to straight couples. Carpenter and Klawitter's (2007) more recent study ends with a very weak conclusion on this potential ameliorative effect of legislation: "Policymakers should not abandon efforts to adopt and enforce policies that prohibit labor market discrimination against sexual minority individuals on the belief that they are ineffective" (p. 288). This tepidness results from their having found significant positive parameters for the effects of local antidiscrimination laws (in the presence, also, of a state law banning such discrimination) on gay-bisexual male earnings only for the effects of laws banning discrimination by *private employers* on the earnings of *government workers!* For female government workers, laws banning discrimination both by private employers and by public employers had a significant positive effect on earnings, but for both gay and lesbian employees of private employers, there was no significant effect.

What seems to be going on are two key selection effects:

1. Selection by LBG people to live/work in safer areas with protection against discrimination: A much higher fraction of the survey's LBG people (compared to straights) lived in localities with laws banning discrimination on the basis of sexual orientation (Carpenter & Klawitter, 2007, p. 283,

Table 19.1), and also a higher fraction of LBG people lived in these areas than lived in areas with no laws banning discrimination. Badgett (2007) also notes that gay and bisexual men are choosing occupations where their coworkers will have less hostility toward them "or are going into more heavily female occupations than are heterosexual men" (p. 30).

2. Selection of which localities adopt laws banning discrimination against LBG people: Localities with nondiscrimination laws have higher earnings for all individuals, both straight and LBG, than do localities without such laws. This suggests that more prosperous and urban areas are more likely to adopt such laws and also provide a more welcoming locale for LBGTQ people (Carpenter & Klawitter, 2007, p. 285).

The work by Carpenter and Klawitter (2007) is one of the few studies using data from a large survey (California Health Interview Survey [CHIS] of 40,000 households in California in 2001 and 2003) where sexual orientation is determined by respondents' own reports ("Do you think of yourself as straight-heterosexual, gay (lesbian), or bisexual?" Carpenter & Klawitter, 2007, p. 281). This is one of the few direct sources of data on respondents' sexual orientation in the United States, so researchers have had to be very ingenious to tease this out of earlier data sources.

The first econometric work on LBGTQ inequality in earnings by Badgett (1995) used the General Social Survey (GSS) and inferred respondents' sexual orientation from their relative lifetime frequency of same-sex behavior since age 18. The GSS gives a rather small sample for each year, which is overcome by the 1990 and 2000 U.S. censuses where, however, there is no direct question on sexual orientation; rather, same-sex behavior is inferred for people who indicate they have an "unmarried partner" of the same sex. But even here, Badgett and Rogers (2002) found that 13% of couples in one survey of "cohabiting same-sex couples" (Badgett, 2007, p. 22) and 19% in another survey of such couples did not choose the "unmarried partner option" in the 2000 U.S. census, with this propensity not to respond being biased according to income: *Lower income couples were less likely to choose this option on the census.* This would tend to bias upwards resulting estimates of LBGTQ incomes, which means that the inequality in earnings according to sexual orientation is even *stronger* than indicated above, especially for gaymen.

The confusion on measuring the effects of local antidiscrimination laws might be due in part to the market impact of antigay animus being hidden by operating indirectly through a wage premium paid to married employees, all of which, until very recently, had to be in straight marriages. As Carpenter (2007) notes, "Employers who are uncertain about a worker's sexual orientation might plausibly use marriage as a signal for heterosexuality" (p. 77). He finds, again using CHIS data on cities in California, that the male marriage premium in California is large (18% after allowing for earnings differences due to age, ethnicity, education, urbanicity, and occupation) and, indeed, it is largest in San Francisco, which has the highest percentage (28.4%) of adult men younger than age 65 say they are gay or bisexual. The premium is lowest in Riverside, which has the lowest percentage (4.5%) of adult men who are gay or bi. The marriage premium is also found to increase nonlinearly with age, as we would expect since an unmarried man age 50 is less likely to be straight than is an unmarried man age 20.

Markets Segmented by Sexual Orientation

A response by profit-seeking business to the emergence of distinct LBGTQ people was to aim products (e.g., club clothes, bars and clubs, books, music and periodicals, Internet sites) to them. This formation of queer market niches gave these businesses a degree of brand-name distinctness and hence market power by which to earn monopoly profits. Of course, this evolution of markets reinforces the social cohesion of self-identifying participants in queered markets, but it can also seduce non-queer, self-imagined non-homophobic people ("metrosexuals") as well as not-gay-self-identified LBGTQ people who discover a certain pleasure (perhaps of tweaking norms of respectability) gotten when consuming these newly queered goods (e.g., going to LBGTQ dance clubs). This evolution suggests to marketers-producers that they can enlarge profits by aiming at self-conceived "sophisticated" heterosexuals.

Thus, we might argue that LBGTQ identities get doubly queered by markets: They act as a social blender by mixing and matching body-costume-identity parts across whatever social identities currently exist. This both reifies boundaries between identities (e.g., queering previously straight products like music/dance venues) and also dissolves these cultural boundaries ("queering" LBGTQ product niches by seducing non-LBGTQ people to join LBGTQ consumers and so making this product less queer). Thus, queering is like negation: Double queering results in un-queering.

Conclusion

Queer political economy shares with feminist and race theory interest in the social articulation of cognitive codes (what in psychology are termed *schemas*) that stigmatize bodies with certain traits and so amplify social inequality. This interest in the perception of bodies differs from both neoclassical analysis and classical Marxian analysis, which have constructed analytical methods that ignore "desiring bodies" and instead model the interaction in markets of bodiless actors whose "desires" have been largely erased. See Cornwall (1997) for detail on the erasure of preferences from economics.

Microeconomic analysis that ignores the interactions between social labeling and the operation of markets distorts our economic policy making, including, for example, marketing, land use planning, and fecundity projections. In particular, it blinds us to substantial inequality in earnings and occupational choice and the evolution of market niches by sexual orientation.

Notes

1. See also Chauncey (1994), who notes that urban areas also offered "relatively cheap accommodations and the availability of commercial domestic services for which men traditionally would have depended on the unpaid household labor of women" (p. 135).

2. Cather indicated sensitivity to this lingual transformation occurring during her young adulthood: "When [Cather] confessed to Louise [Pound, her first big love while a student at the University of Nebraska] that she thought it unfair that feminine friendships were 'unnatural,' she used a loaded word which reveals that certain intense female friendships were being defined as deviant—as lesbian—by the dominant culture. In the 1890s, *unnatural* was a code word . . . that meant 'deviant,' 'aberrant,' or 'homosexual'" (O'Brien, 1994, pp. 58–59).

References and Further Readings

Amott, T., & Matthaei, J. (1991). *Race, gender, and work: A multicultural economic history of women in the United States.* Boston: South End.

Axelrod, R. (1986). An evolutionary approach to norms. *American Political Science Review, 80,* 1095–1111.

Badgett, M. V. L. (1995). Wage effects of sexual orientation discrimination. *Industrial and Labor Relations Review, 48,* 726–739.

Badgett, M. V. L. (2007). Discrimination based on sexual orientation: A review of the literature in economics and beyond. In M. V. L. Badgett & J. Frank (Eds.), *Sexual orientation discrimination: An international perspective* (pp. 19–43). New York: Routledge.

Badgett, M. V. L., & Frank, J. (Eds.). (2007). *Sexual orientation discrimination: An international perspective.* New York: Routledge.

Badgett, M. V. L., & Rogers, M. (2002). *Left out of the count: Missing same-sex couples in census 2000.* Amherst, MA: Institute for Gay and Lesbian Strategic Studies.

Blandford, J. (2003). The nexus of sexual orientation and gender in the determination of earnings. *Industrial and Labor Relations Review, 56,* 622–642.

Boswell, J. (1980). *Christianity, social tolerance, and homosexuality: Gay people in Western Europe from the beginning of the Christian era to the fourteenth century.* Chicago: University of Chicago Press.

Butler, J. (1993). *Bodies that matter: On the discursive limits of "sex."* New York: Routledge.

Carpenter, C. (2007). Do straight men "come out" at work too? The heterosexual male marriage premium and discrimination against gay men. In M. V. L. Badgett & J. Frank (Eds.), *Sexual orientation discrimination: An international perspective* (pp. 76–92). New York: Routledge.

Carpenter, C., & Klawitter, M. (2007). Sexual orientation-based antidiscrimination ordinances and the earnings of sexual minority individuals. In M. V. L. Badgett & J. Frank (Eds.), *Sexual orientation discrimination: An international perspective* (pp. 277–292). New York: Routledge.

Chauncey, G. (1994). *Gay New York: Gender, urban culture, and the making of the gay male world, 1890–1940.* New York: Basic Books (HarperCollins).

Cornwall, R. R. (1997). Deconstructing silence: The queer political economy of the social articulation of desire. *Review of Radical Political Economics, 29,* 1–130.

Damasio, A. R. (1994). *Descartes' error: Emotion, reason, and the human brain.* New York: Putnam.

de Lauretis, T. (1991). Queer theory: Lesbian and gay sexualities. An introduction. *differences: A Journal of Feminist Cultural Studies, 3,* iii–xviii.

D'Emilio, J. (1983). Capitalism and gay identity. In A. Snitow, C. Stansell, & S. Thompson (Eds.), *Powers of desire: The politics of sexuality* (pp. 100–113). New York: Monthly Review Press. (Reprinted in *The lesbian and gay studies reader,* by H. Abelove, M. A. Barale, & D. Halperin, Eds., 1993, pp. 467–476. New York: Routledge)

D'Emilio, J., & Freedman, E. B. (1988). *Intimate matters: A history of sexuality in America.* New York: Harper & Row.

Escoffier, J. (1985). Sexual revolution and the politics of gay identity. *Socialist Review, 15,* 119–153.

Faderman, L. (1991). *Odd girls and twilight lovers: A history of lesbian life in twentieth-century America.* New York: Columbia University Press.

Foucault, M. (1972). *The archaeology of knowledge and the discourse on language* (A. M. Sheridan Smith, Trans.). New York: Pantheon.

Foucault, M. (1988). *The care of the self: Vol. 3. The history of sexuality* (R. Hurley, Trans.). New York: Vintage (Random House). (Original work published 1984)

Foucault, M. (1990a). *The history of sexuality: Vol. 1. An Introduction.* New York: Vintage (Random House). (Original work published 1978)

Foucault, M. (1990b). *The use of pleasure: Vol. 2. The history of sexuality* (R. Hurley, Trans.). New York: Vintage (Random House). (Original work published 1984)

Foucault, M. (1994). *Les mots et les choses: Une archéologie des sciences humaines* [The order of things: An archaeology of the human sciences]. New York: Vintage (Random House). (Original work published 1966)

Frank, J. (2007). Is the male marriage premium evidence of discrimination against gay men? In M. V. L. Badgett & J. Frank (Eds.), *Sexual orientation discrimination: An international perspective* (pp. 93–103).New York: Routledge.

Goldberg, J. (Ed.). (1994). *Reclaiming Sodom.* New York: Routledge.

Greenberg, D. F. (1988). *The construction of homosexuality.* Chicago: University of Chicago Press.

Heckman, J. J., & Payner, B. S. (1989). Determining the impact of federal antidiscrimination policy on the economic status of blacks: A study of South Carolina. *American Economic Review, 79,* 138–177.

Klawitter, M. M., & Flatt, V. (1998). The effects of state and local antidiscrimination policies on earnings for gays and lesbians. *Journal of Policy Analysis and Management, 17,* 658–686.

Kristeva, J. (1982). *Powers of horror: An essay on abjection* (L. S. Roudiez, Trans.). New York: Columbia University Press.

Laqueur, T. W. (2003). *Solitary sex: A cultural history of masturbation.* New York: Zone Books.

Matthaei, J. (1982). *An economic history of women in America: Women's work, the sexual division of labor, and the development of capitalism.* New York: Schocken.

Matthaei, J. (1995). The sexual division of labor, sexuality, and lesbian/gay liberation: Towards a Marxist-feminist analysis of sexuality in U.S. capitalism. *Review of Radical Political Economics, 27,* 1–37.

McBride, D. (2005). *Why I hate Abercrombie & Fitch: Essays on race and sexuality.* New York: New York University Press.

O'Brien, S. (1987). *Willa Cather: The emerging voice.* New York: Oxford University Press.

O'Brien, S. (1994). *Willa Cather.* New York: Chelsea House.

Panksepp, J. (1998). *Affective neuroscience: The foundations of human and animal emotions.* New York: Oxford University Press.

Rubin, G. (1975). The traffic in women: Notes on the "political economy" of sex. In R. R. Reiter (Ed.), *Toward an anthropology of women* (pp. 157–210). New York: Monthly Review Press.

Stallybrass, P., & White, A. (1986). *The politics and poetics of transgression.* London: Methuen.

Vicinus, M. (1992). "They wonder to which sex I belong": The historical roots of the modern lesbian identity. *Feminist Studies, 18,* 467–498.

Weeks, J. (1979). *Coming out: Homosexual politics in Britain, from the nineteenth century to the present.* New York: Quartet Books.

76

Economics and Religion

Carmel U. Chiswick

University of Illinois at Chicago

The last two decades of the twentieth century saw an explosion of empirical as well as theoretical research into the relationship between religion and economic behavior. For the most part, this research ignores theological differences, focusing instead on behavioral differences associated with different religious identities. The causation runs both ways: Some studies analyze the effects of religious identity on various economic activities, and others analyze the effects of economic incentives on religious observances and institutions. Both of these lines of research have yielded strong results and have dramatically affected our understanding of the relationship between economics and religion. Prices and incomes are powerful incentives that invariably influence the actions of individuals, and the human capacity for creative rationalization contributes to the widespread evasion of costly behaviors, including costly religious strictures.

Before economics became a modern social science, casual observation generated many stereotypes about differences between religious groups regarding economic success, differences that were often attributed to differences in religious teachings. Today these arguments are viewed with skepticism. Some are based on stereotypes that do not stand up to empirical scrutiny. Others are based on an imperfect understanding of the religious teachings to which they refer. Recent research suggests that some of the most important differences between religious groups can be explained not directly, by the religious strictures themselves, but indirectly by intervening variables that affect the economic incentives faced by individuals.

To provide an overview of this subject, this chapter begins with a consideration of the economic incentives affecting a consumer's decisions in the religious marketplace—that is to say, the demand for "religion." It will then look at how this demand affects religious institutions and generates a supply of religious goods and services. Other topics will include the structure of this religious marketplace, the related "marketplace for ideas" in a religiously pluralistic society, and religious human capital. Finally, there will be a brief discussion of empirical findings for the effects of religious affiliation and intensity of belief or practice on selected economic behaviors.

The Demand for Religion

From the perspective of an individual consumer, religious expression is an economic good that must compete with all other goods for a share of the resource budget. It is not a good in the material sense but rather an intangible for which people express a preference by their willingness to spend time and money on its acquisition. Nor is it a good that can be purchased in a consumption-ready form. It belongs to the category of economic goods that must be self-produced by each individual. The consumer may buy goods and services that contribute to this end but must spend his or her own time to use them in a way that creates a religious experience.

The theological aspects of any particular religion may be thought of as its technology, a set of "recipes" or blueprints for behaviors, expenditures, and beliefs that will produce the desired results. This gives the consumer a production function that converts time and money—that is, labor and capital—into an output that can be called "religious experience." The substance of this theology is generally irrelevant for an economic analysis, much as the theory of the firm can analyze its behavior without specifying the particular good it produces or the specifics of its production. What follows here is a similar abstraction, an analytical framework that can be applied to good effect for deepening our understanding of many different religious behaviors.

In their seminal work on this subject, Azzi and Ehrenberg (1975) suggest that religion is best thought of as a bundle of three distinct but interrelated goods. First there is spirituality, the desire for which seems to be a primal human impulse that finds some sort of expression in every society from the earliest times to the present. Then there is the fact that religion always seems to have a collective dimension—an individual "joins" or "belongs to" a particular religion and observes various rituals as a "member" of this group, typically in conjunction with other adherents. These two aspects of religion are sometimes referred to as its "spiritual good" and its "social good," respectively. Religion also addresses the dilemma of human mortality, the frightening inevitability of death and its implications for the meaning of life. This is usually referred to as the "afterlife good," although not every religion speaks to this need by positing an explicit life after death. In most religions, these three "goods" are bundled into a single product called "religion," but since their economic attributes differ, it is useful to consider them separately.

Supernatural Being(s): The Spiritual Good

For many people, the search for spirituality is at the heart of any religious experience. Not everyone feels deeply about this—preferences vary, just as they do when the subject is ice cream or toys or fashionable clothing. Regardless of the priority placed on it, however, for most people spirituality is the central quality that effectively defines an experience as religious.

Spirituality is a classic example of a self-produced good. It is very, very personal and can never be acquired without intimate involvement of the individual consumer. The religious technology (theology) provides a guide for behaviors that will achieve this, religious rituals and their associated objects are designed to facilitate the process, and religious professionals are there to support and direct these activities. Yet in the end, it is the individual alone who has this spiritual experience at a deeply personal level. Like other dimensions of human capital, it cannot occur without the individual's participation, and once it has occurred, it is inalienable from that person.

Although the spiritual impulse seems to be a basic human need, the extent to which a person chooses to indulge in it is certainly affected by its price. Using a basic two-factor production function approach, the full price of this good is the direct cost of purchased goods and services and the indirect cost of the time spent in pursuit of spirituality. Some religions make heavy demands on consumers' incomes, but many of the most popular can be practiced with little direct expenditure. The search for spirituality thus tends to be a relatively time-intensive

activity, and its full price is therefore sensitive to the value of a consumer's time.

Time is valued at its opportunity cost, and a consumer's budget is allocated optimally when the marginal value of time is the same in every alternative use. It is conventional to use the wage rate as a first approximation of this value, whether the actual wage for those who participate in the labor force or the shadow wage for those who do not. The full price of a time-intensive religious activity is thus positively related to the wage rate. Full income is also positively related to the wage rate, especially for people in the positively sloped region of their labor supply curve. The effect of higher wages on the demand for spirituality is thus ambiguous: A higher full price reduces the quantity demanded, but the higher income shifts the demand curve to the right. Empirical studies suggest that for most Americans, the price effect dominates the income effect so that higher wages are associated with less time spent in religious activities seeking spirituality.

In the production process, a relatively high cost of labor is an incentive to "economize" by becoming more capital intensive. In the search for spirituality, this takes the form of religious practices that substitute money for time. A high-wage person, for example, might purchase expensive religious objects but spend little time using them, might donate generously to causes associated with godliness, or might hire a substitute to engage in specific religious rituals on his or her behalf. Expensive time is also an incentive for innovations that raise its marginal product, whether by investing in skills relevant for the production of spirituality or by altering the religious environment in ways more suitable for (complementary to) the reduced time inputs.

This model has implications that result in testable hypotheses that appear to be consistent with the behavior of American consumers. Wealthy consumers often donate large amounts of money to religious causes even though they may not devote much of their own time to religious activities. Congregations with less time-intensive religious practices, like shorter services or fewer holy days, tend to attract disproportionately congregants at the upper end of the wage distribution. American religious institutions have also been innovative in adapting to the spiritual needs of consumers with a high value of time, for example, with services conducted in the English language or sermons applicable to a busy lifestyle.

Belonging: The Social Good

In contrast with the search for spirituality, which is an intensely personal activity, adopting a specific religion implies participating in a group of similarly inclined individuals. This aspect of the demand for religion is analyzed as a "club" good, drawing on an extensive economics literature on club theory. Like other self-produced goods, a club good cannot be purchased directly but must be produced with the consumer's own time and effort. A club good, however, cannot be produced by a single consumer in isolation. The productivity of resources that one individual devotes to making this good depends on the resource allocations made by other members of the club. For example, joining the church choir has different implications for a consumer's religious experience depending on how many others join the choir and with what intensity of religious participation.

Although all religions contain some measure of this characteristic, they vary in the way in which it is displayed. At one extreme, it may be possible to "buy" a membership, either directly or indirectly by making a large donation. Such a group would lack spiritual content and thus raises the question as to whether it is truly a religion. Most religions, however, require some participation in group rituals related to worship, to life cycle celebrations, or to obtaining or demonstrating merit by performing good deeds. In each case, the religious experience a consumer obtains as output depends not only on the effective use of his or her own resources but also on their complementarity with the resources devoted by other participants in the group.

Because of this interaction, clubs are a "quasi-public" good in the sense that they have some but not all properties of a public good. Like a true public good, a consumer can belong to a religion without diminishing its availability to other consumers. Unlike a true public good, however, a club can devise means of limiting membership and thus excluding potential consumers. This can be done by charging a membership fee or by specific criteria such as age, gender, race, profession, national origin, or place of residence. Although some religious groups use such means of restricting entry, these are generally eschewed by most American religions on the basis of theological, social, or political principles.

A club with important interpersonal complementarities that does not limit entry is faced with the classic "free-rider" problem. Since the productivity of a consumer's resources is enhanced by the resources devoted to the club by its other members, he or she has an incentive to choose a group where the other members spend more than he or she does. In effect, individuals try to economize on their own resources by substituting the resources of others. But it is mathematically impossible for everyone in the group to spend below the average. People spending more than the average are getting less output for their resources and have an incentive to seek another group where they could obtain a greater benefit from the same resource expenditure. When these people leave the original group, it begins an immiserating spiral that makes it increasingly unable to attract new members.

In a classic paper, Iannaccone (1992) considers this free-rider problem in the context of religious groups. He points out that many religions impose implicit taxes on their members as a means of supporting the religious group itself. This can take the form of tithing, of requiring the purchase of expensive religious articles, or of social pressure to donate money. There can also be a "tax" on time if membership requires volunteering for time-intensive ritual or charitable activities. Even in the absence of such taxes, however, many religions require a "sacrifice" of goods or time by which is meant a donation that is actually destroyed as part of a religious ritual. A sacrifice does not contribute directly to the support of the group itself, but from the individual's perspective, it is similar to a membership fee. It thus serves to discourage people from joining if their resource contributions would otherwise be lower than the value of the required sacrifice. By discouraging participation by people whose commitment to the group is low, a large sacrifice can raise the average level of commitment and thus benefit the remaining group members indirectly. A religion may also impose nonmonetary requirements to discourage adherents who might otherwise leave the group. Requirements such as those affecting clothing, appearance, or diet serve to identify adherents as committed members of the group but would be stigmatizing in the world of nonadherents. Both sacrifice and stigma are commonly observed characteristics of religion that serve to limit the problem of free riders in the religious community.

An Unusual Investment: The Afterlife Good

Mortality is at the heart of the human condition, and religion is an important way in which people deal with the uncertainties and loss associated with their own death and that of their loved ones. Religions typically address this issue by embedding the relatively short life span of a human being in a larger picture of eternal life. There are various ways in which a theology deals with this question, but one that is very common is to posit a more or less explicit life that a person will experience after his or her own death. As long as an action during a person's current life on earth will have consequences for his or her circumstances in this afterlife, there is an incentive to alter current behavior with a view toward this long-run future. The benefits of good behavior induced by this theology are summarized by the term "afterlife" good.

A religious theology posits afterlife rewards to people who spend their time and money on "good" behaviors and afterlife punishments to those who spend their resources on "bad" behaviors. To the extent that this causes a consumer to alter his or her spending patterns, it trades present utility for future rewards after death. In this respect, it is best thought of as an investment rather than a consumption good, and as such, it can be treated analytically like any other investment. Other investments, however, are typically designed to yield their rewards at a later point in a person's lifetime, whereas the afterlife good pays off only after the investor is dead. The optimal strategy is thus to invest first in prospects that mature earlier and postpone this late-pay-off investment until later in life. This is consistent with the observation that older people tend to spend more time and money on religious participation than do youngsters, and it reinforces any tendency for people to become more concerned with the afterlife as they face their own mortality.

The Supply of Religion

Since religious experience is a self-produced good, there is no explicit market for it and so no supply curve in the usual sense. Yet there is a market for religious goods and services, and there is a large sociology literature that views the religious sphere as having a "marketplace of ideas" (Warner, 1993). In this marketplace, religious groups compete with each other for adherents in much the same way that firms compete for customers, and individuals seek out a religious congregation to join in much the same way as they shop for other goods and services. Much of this sociology literature is concerned with the structure of this market, highly competitive in the United States but more like a monopoly in countries with a state religion. This analogy has contributed much to a new understanding of the economic aspects of religion.

A fundamental requirement for a market to be competitive is free entry of new firms and free exit of firms that are unsuccessful. Religious "startups" are characteristic of the American religious scene. New congregations frequently appear within established religious denominations, and entirely new religions can and do emerge. Most of these new religions are small, and many of them eventually disappear for lack of followers, but some—like the Church of the Latter-day Saints (Mormon) and Christian Science—have been very successful and grew into established religions.

Unlike religious monopolies that are licensed (and funded) by the government and typically managed by a religious hierarchy or bureaucracy, competitive religious markets are characterized by independent congregations that hire their own clergy. The clergy in a competitive market are responsible directly to their congregants and thus tend to be more sensitive to their religious needs. Also unlike a religious monopoly structure, congregationalism finds it more efficient to conduct nonritual religious functions (e.g., charities or proselytizing) in a separate set of para-religious organizations. It is also common for congregations within the same religious denomination to form an umbrella organization (analogous to an industry group) to represent their common interests in the larger society.

Each of these types of religious organization is characteristic of the United States, a pluralistic society in which religious markets are highly competitive. In countries with one or more state religions, however, the government-sanctioned religious body typically carries out all of these religion-related functions. As an indication of how distinctive American religious pluralism actually is, the separation of function associated with religious pluralism is frequently described as a symptom of "Americanization" in a religious group.

Religious Human Capital

Most people think of themselves as having been born into a religion, suggesting that perhaps they have no choice as to where they belong. While it is true that a person may be born into a family that practices a certain religion, it is not true that this religion is innate in a newborn child. In fact, religious education and training are an important part of a child's upbringing, often from a very young age. The consequence of this training is that youngsters accumulate human capital—skills, knowledge, memories, sensations— specific to a particular religion, denomination, or perhaps even congregation. The more religious human capital a person has, the more efficiently he or she can obtain a religious experience from any given amount of resources. Religious education is an important activity for the community as a whole as well as for its individual members, and it is the core function of any proselytizing undertaken by a religious group.

A human capital approach provides additional insights into the workings of a competitive religious market for adults. Each religion may be thought of as having its own religion-specific human capital, the formation of which is characterized by the usual positively sloped marginal cost curve. Each person may be thought of as accumulating religion-specific human capital until the (shadow) marginal rate of return to religious education approaches the marginal rate of return to other types of human capital. If a person were to convert to a different religion, the human capital specific to the "old" religion would lose its productive value, and human capital specific to the "new" religion would need to be acquired. The economics of religious switching is formally analogous to occupational change or to international migration, a new investment that would be attractive only if the benefits outweigh the costs. The incentives are such that conversion is less likely to occur the greater the human capital intensity of either the "old" or the "new" religion, and it is most likely to occur between denominations with similar human capital where religious skills are highly transferable as, for example, among mainline Protestant denominations in the United States. Religious switching is also more likely among young adults who have not yet made heavy religion-specific investments.

Religion and Socioeconomic Behavior

Religions differ with respect to the compatibility of their teachings with other aspects of the society to which their adherents belong. This can be analyzed as the degree of complementarity between religious and other forms of human capital and the mutual complementarity among different kinds of human capital investments (Chiswick, 2006). People whose religious teachings complement the public school curriculum, for example, would have higher rates of return to both types of education and therefore an incentive to invest in both religious and nonreligious human capital. Adherents of these religions tend to have high levels of education, better health, lower fertility, and marriage patterns that tend to go along with these attributes.

In contrast, people whose religious teachings are anti-complementary (i.e., contradictory) to a public school curriculum would have an incentive to specialize in either religious or nonreligious investments in human capital. Those who invest more heavily in religious human capital would face lower rates of return to investments in secular education, for example, and those who choose to invest in nonreligious forms of human capital would have less incentive to invest in religious education. In these denominations, adherents who are very religious tend to have low levels of education and health, high fertility, and marriage patterns associated with their consequent low socioeconomic status, and adherents with greater secular achievements would tend to have lower levels of religious observance.

Empirical Evidence

Empirical analyses of economic and demographic behaviors in the United States suggest that religion is an important factor in many decisions related to education, health, fertility, marriage, and divorce. This literature distinguishes between religious affiliation, on one hand, and the degree of religiosity, on the other. Whether or not a person identifies himself or herself as belonging to a particular religion or denomination seems to be less important than the intensity of religious observance and the degree of commitment to the group. Some of these findings fit conventional stereotypes, but some do not.

Data on Religion and Economics

Empirical analyses of the effect of religion on economic and demographic behaviors are constrained by the paucity of data. Data collected by the U.S. government generally do not have a question on religion. A few economic surveys ask respondents to self-identify as Protestant, Catholic, Jew, or Others, categories that are too heterogeneous for testing hypotheses about religious behavior. The National Survey of Religious Identity (NSRI) and the American Religious Identity Survey (ARIS) have nationwide random samples with considerable detail for self-identified religion. A number of other sets of data are available from the Web site of the Association of Religion Data Archives (ARDA; http://www.thearda.com), which also have questions about religion, some more detailed

than others, but few of these data sources have information on employment or wage rates that would be useful to test economic hypotheses. Newer surveys are beginning to address this problem, but in the meantime, only a few of the existing data sets can be used to study the influence of economic factors on religious behavior.

Studies that use economic data to analyze the effects of religious identification on economic and demographic behaviors find that the usual religion categories—Protestant, Catholic, Jew, Other—are too heterogeneous to be very useful. The aggregation principles for religious groupings should be analogous to those used for aggregating factors of production or industrial output. Religions can be grouped together into a single category if they are close substitutes with each other or if their respective types of religious human capital have similar complementarity properties with respect to nonreligious human capital. Religions should be separated into different groupings if neither of these conditions holds. The so-called Mainstream Protestant denominations can be grouped together because they typically have very similar religious human capital. Fundamentalist Protestant denominations can be grouped together because they typically share a strained relationship between religious human capital and some of the nonreligious human capital of mainstream America. In contrast, Mainstream Protestants and Fundamentalist Protestants should not be grouped with each other because they differ with respect to both religious human capital and its complementarity with nonreligious human capital.

Empirical results are much clearer when religious identification variables are classified according to these principles. It has become conventional to distinguish between "fundamentalist" and "mainstream" Protestant denominations. If the data permit, it is also useful to split the Mormons and the "African" Protestant denominations into separate categories. The Other category includes a number of very small groups, but whenever possible, the people reporting no religion (including agnostics and atheists) should be separated from those identifying with small religious groups (e.g., Greek Orthodox, Buddhists, Hindus, Moslems).

Variables relating to the degree of religiosity—that is, to the intensity of religious observance without regard to the particular religion—also need to be interpreted with caution. Some of the most common questions ask about the frequency of attendance at religious services and donations of money (and sometimes of time) to religious organizations. Other questions may ask about beliefs: whether there is a supernatural deity (God), whether there is life after death, or whether the words of the Bible are to be taken literally. These questions are reasonably good indicators of religiosity for Protestant religions and perhaps for Christians in general, who usually comprise the large majority of American respondents. For other religions, however, they may be less apt. The concept of God, for example, may be different for some of the Asian religions than it is for the monotheistic religions of Judaism, Christianity, and Islam. As another example, intensely religious Jews may interpret the Bible literally only in its original Hebrew language, subject not only to variations in translation but also to a variety of possible interpretations of its original intent. Such differences reduce the effectiveness of these questions as general indicators of religiosity, although the problems are assumed to be small for samples with mainly Christian respondents.

As an increasing number of immigrants bring with them a religion that is relatively new to the United States, another issue arises with regard to intensity of religious practice. This occurs when a religion is specific to a particular ethnic group, as is the case for Jews, Greeks, Armenians, and Russians. (It was also the case for Roman Catholics in an earlier era, when immigrants from Ireland, Italy, Germany, and Poland attended separate churches, but their descendants today are no longer deeply divided along ethnic lines.) The distinction between ethnicity and religion is not always clear in such cases, and survey respondents might indicate belonging to a religion when in fact their identity is primarily with the ethnic group. Even if their actual beliefs are similar to those of agnostics or atheists, the fact that they observe religious rituals as part of their ethnic activity may lead them to self-identify otherwise.

Some Preliminary Findings

With these considerations in mind, a number of empirical studies have investigated the effects of religion and religiosity on economic and demographic behaviors (Lehrer, 2009). The evidence for the United States is generally consistent with the predictions of economic theory, but for the most part, the particular religion to which a person belongs does not seem to matter as much as the fact that a person belongs to some religion rather than none. It is possible that this arises because people ignore religious teachings (theology) when making human capital investment decisions. It is possible, however, that in a pluralistic society, religion would have low explanatory power for statistical reasons. For example, suppose people tend to choose an affiliation compatible with their nonreligious human capital portfolio, and suppose religious groups tend to adapt practices and even teachings to be compatible with the characteristics of their members. The data would then show that people are sorted into religious groups by their socioeconomic characteristics, and there would be little additional explanatory power for religion after controlling for the usual determinants of a human capital investment.

The empirical evidence for the United States also suggests that the degree of religiosity has a very important effect on investments in nonreligious human capital. Measures of religiosity describe an individual's commitment to religious practices (e.g., church attendance) and the intensity of his or her belief in its theology. For at least some of the socioeconomic outcomes, religiosity seems to

have a nonlinear effect. For example, education levels tend to rise with religiosity up to a point, but people with very high levels of education tend to have low levels of religiosity. This pattern is consistent with predictions of the human capital model outlined above. People whose religious human capital is complementary with secular investments would exhibit a positive relationship between religiosity and, say, education, while those with anticomplementary religious human capital would combine high religiosity with low education levels or low religiosity with high education levels.

Institutional Change

Americans affiliate with religions that have adherents in other parts of the world. Some of these are international, with a leadership established somewhere in its "world headquarters," while others are rooted in a single country to which adherents look for inspiration and guidance. In either case, however, the adherents living in the United States typically alter their observances (and even sometimes their beliefs) to better fit the American socioeconomic scene in a process that is labeled "Americanization." This may be perceived as a falling off of religious observance, yet the evidence suggests that Americans are among the most religious people in the modern world.

Economic analysis suggests an alternative interpretation in which Americanization is seen not as rampant materialism but rather an adaptive response to different economic circumstances. High American wage rates provide an incentive to substitute goods for time in the production of any religious experience—hence the observed tendency toward "materialism"—but they also provide an incentive to improve the efficiency of time spent in religious observance. In a competitive religious marketplace, people seek the religious community most compatible with their personal preferences, and clergy have an incentive to be sensitive to the religious needs of their congregants. Religious education also adapts to the relatively high education level of American congregants, and human capital formation is another means of raising the efficiency of time spent in religious activity. As Americans adapt their consumption patterns to changes in their economic environment, their religious consumption patterns and even theologies also change, and their congregations change along with them.

This institutional adaptability goes a long way toward explaining why religion continues to play an important role in American life despite all predictions to the contrary. Karl Marx characterized religion as "the opiate of the masses" that should disappear with economic development—it has not. Others believed that religion could not survive the scrutiny of science and would disappear among people with high levels of secular education—it has not. Instead, evidence for the United States suggests that when wages and wealth are held constant, religious participation actually increases with the level of education. By placing religion and religiosity in their economic context, it is possible to obtain a deeper appreciation of the social importance of religion and its ability to thrive in many different circumstances.

References and Further Readings

Azzi, C., & Ehrenberg, R. (1975). Household allocation of time and church attendance. *Journal of Political Economy, 83,* 27–56.

Chiswick, C. U. (2006). An economic perspective on religious education: Complements and substitutes in a human capital portfolio. *Research in Labor Economics, 24,* 449–467.

Iannaccone, L. R. (1990). Religious practice: A human capital approach. *Journal for the Scientific Study of Religion, 29,* 297–314.

Iannaccone, L. R. (1992). Sacrifice and stigma: Reducing free-riding in cults, communes, and other collectives. *Journal of Political Economy, 100,* 271–291.

Kosmin, B. A., & Keysar, A. (2006). *Religion in a free market: Religious and non-religious Americans.* Ithaca, NY: Paramount.

Lehrer, E. L. (2009). *Religion, economics, and demography: The effects of religion on education, work, and the family.* New York: Routledge.

Warner, R. S. (1993). Work in progress toward a new paradigm for the sociological study of religion in the United States. *American Journal of Sociology, 98,* 1044–1093.

77

ECONOMICS AND CORPORATE SOCIAL RESPONSIBILITY

MARKUS KITZMUELLER

University of Michigan

Corporate social responsibility (CSR) constitutes an economic phenomenon of significant importance. Today, firms largely determine welfare through producing goods and services for consumers, interest for investors, income for employees, and social and environmental externalities or public goods affecting broader subsets of society. Stakeholders often take account of ethical, social, and environmental firm performance, thereby changing the nature of strategic interaction between profit-maximizing firms, on one hand, and utility-maximizing individuals, on the other hand.

Hence, CSR is referred to as "one of the social pressures firms have absorbed" (John Ruggy, qtd. in *The Economist,* January 17, 2008, special report on CSR) and considered to "have become a mainstream activity of firms" (*The Economist,* January 17, 2008; Economist Intelligence Unit, 2005). Many (inter)national firms strive to achieve voluntary social and environmental standards (e.g., ISO14001), and the number of related certifications in Organisation for Economic Co-operation and Development (OECD) countries as well as in emerging market economies is constantly growing. Broad access to the Internet as well as comprehensive media coverage allow the public to monitor corporate involvement with social ills, environmental degradation, or financial contagion independent of geographical distance. A 2005 U.S. survey by Fleishman-Hillard and the National Consumers League (*Rethinking Corporate Social Responsibility*) concludes that technology is changing the landscape in which consumers gather and communicate information about CSR and that Internet access has created a "more informed, more empowered consumer . . . searching for an unfiltered view of news and information."

In light of (a) such "empowered" market participants able to discipline firms according to their preferences and (b) the public good nature of business "by-products," policy makers must reevaluate the border between public and corporate social responsibility. In this context, Scherer and Palazzo (2008) note that "paradoxically, today, business firms are not just considered the bad guys, causing environmental disasters, financial scandals, and social ills. They are at the same time considered the solution of global regulation and public goods problems" (p. 414). In sum, CSR opens up a wide array of economic questions and puzzles regarding firm incentives behind voluntary and costly provision of public goods as well as the potential welfare trade-off between their market and government provision. While economic research had initially addressed the question of whether CSR possesses any economic justification at all, it has recently shifted to how it affects the economy, stressing the need of analytical machinery to better understand the mechanisms underlying CSR as well as its interaction with classical public policy. Therefore, the objective of this chapter is to identify, structure, and discuss essential economic aspects of CSR.

At first sight, CSR appears to be at odds with the neoclassical assumption of profit maximization underlying strategic firm behavior. Corporate social performance often means provision of public goods or reduction of negative externalities (social or environmental) related to business conduct. As public goods and externalities entail market failure in the form of free riding or collective action problems, government provision through direct production or regulation may be most efficient, a concept generally known as Friedman's classical dichotomy. If firms still decide to engage in costly social behavior beyond regulatory levels (i.e., CSR), then why would they voluntarily incur these costs, and is this behavior overall economically efficient?

The attempt to answer these questions leads to the firm's objective—maximizing shareholder value—and its dependence on the nature of shareholders' and stakeholders' preferences. Shareholders and investors can be profit oriented and/or have social and environmental preferences. The same is true for consumers, while workers may be extrinsically and/or intrinsically motivated. This heterogeneity in preferences (i.e., the presence of nonpecuniary preferences alongside classical monetary ones) is able to shed light on CSR within standard economic theory.

Another important issue intrinsically related to CSR concerns information asymmetries between firms and stakeholders. Reputation and information are important determinants of consumer, investor, employee, or activist behavior and, therefore, firm profits. Hence, many firms proactively report on their CSR activities and consult governments, international organizations, nongovernmental organizations (NGOs), and private auditors to earn credibility. In short, firms seek to build and maintain social or environmental reputation in markets characterized by information asymmetry and socially or environmentally conscious agents.

While information economics, contract, and organization theory provide a suitable framework to analyze the motivations and strategies beneath CSR, public economics and industrial organization may enhance the understanding of how the underlying "social pressures" might affect market structure, competition, and total welfare. The remainder of this chapter is organized as follows: The second section defines CSR and discusses the classical dichotomy between the public and private sectors in light of CSR. The third section outlines the crucial role of preferences in explaining and conceptualizing CSR. The fourth section gives a structured overview of distinctive theoretic explanations of strategic CSR in light of some empirical evidence. The fifth section concludes.

What Is CSR? From Definition to Analysis

Before entering economic analysis, the stage has to be set by defining *corporate social responsibility*. In practice, a variety of definitions of CSR exists. The European Commission (2009) defines corporate social responsibility as "a concept whereby companies integrate social and environmental concerns in their business operations and in their interaction with their stakeholders on a voluntary basis." The World Bank (n.d.) states,

> CSR is the commitment of businesses to behave ethically and to contribute to sustainable economic development by working

with all relevant stakeholders to improve their lives in ways that are good for business, the sustainable development agenda, and society at large.

A notion similar to "voluntary behavior" can be found in definitions that refer to either "beyond compliance," such as those used by Vogel (2005) or McWilliams and Siegel (2001), who characterize CSR as "the fulfillment of responsibilities beyond those dictated by markets or laws," or to "self-regulation," as suggested by Calveras, Ganuza, and Llobet (2007), among others.

These attempts to define CSR reveal two basic conceptual features: First, CSR manifests itself in some observable and measurable behavior or output. The literature frequently refers to this dimension as corporate social or environmental performance (CSP or CEP). Second, the social or environmental performance or output of firms exceeds obligatory, legally enforced thresholds. In essence, CSR is corporate social or environmental behavior beyond levels required by law or regulation. This definition is independent of any conjecture about the motivations underlying CSR and constitutes a strong fundament for economic theory to investigate incentives and mechanisms beneath CSR. Note that, while Baron (2001) takes the normative view that "both motivation and performance are required for actions to receive 'the CSR label,'" it is proposed here that linking a particular motivation to the respective performance is required for the action to receive "the correct CSR label" (e.g., strategic or altruistic). From an economic point of view, the "interesting and most relevant" form of CSR is strategic (i.e., CSR as a result of classical market forces), while McWilliams and Siegel's (2001) definition would reduce CSR only to altruistic behavior.

The logical next step is to build the bridge from definition to economic analysis. CSR often realizes as a public good or the reduction of a public bad. Hence, revisiting the classical dichotomy between state and market appears to be important. Relevant works that relate CSR with public good provision include Bagnoli and Watts (2003) and Besley and Ghatak (2007), who explicitly define CSR as the corporate provision of public goods or curtailment of public bads. Firms may produce a public good or an externality jointly with private goods, either in connection with the production process of private goods (e.g., less polluting technology such as in Kotchen [2006], or safe/healthy working conditions) or linked to the private good/service itself (e.g., less polluting cars or energy-saving light bulbs). This perspective on CSR relates directly to earlier work by J. M. Buchanan (1999), who referred to such joint provision of a public and private good as an "impure public good," and relevant insights such as those derived by Bergstrom, Blume, and Varian (1986) in their seminal paper on the private provision of public goods, which can be readily translated into the CSR framework. For example, Bergstrom et al. focused on the interaction between public and private (individual) provision of the public good and the effect on overall levels of provision and con-cluded that public provision crowds out its private coun-terpart almost perfectly. Along these lines, Kotchen (2006) compares joint corporate provision of private and public goods in "green markets" (where the private good is produced with an environmentally friendly production technology) and separate provision of either, leading to the similar conclusion that the very same crowding out takes place between corporate provision and individual provision and may even lead to an overall reduction in the level of the public good. More precisely, Besley and Ghatak (2001) notice that public goods provision has dra-matically shifted from public to mixed or complete private ownership in recent years, while Rose-Ackerman (1996) phrases the problem as the "blurring of the analytically motivated division between for-profit, nonprofit and pub-lic sectors in reality." To explain these observations, Besley and Ghatak suggest that in the presence of incom-plete contracts, optimal ownership is not a question of public versus private provision but simply should involve the party that values the created benefits most. Another interesting rationale provided by Besley and Ghatak (2007) identifies economies of scope (i.e., natural com-plementarities between private and public goods produc-tion, leading to cost asymmetries/advantages on the firm side) to be the decisive variable in determining the effi-ciency of impure public goods. The conclusion states that if economies of scope are absent, tasks should be segre-gated into specialized organizations (i.e., governments provide public goods and firms private ones). Otherwise, CSR might very well be optimal if governments or not-for-profit providers are unable to match CSR levels of public good provision due to opportunism, cost disadvan-tages (= economies of scope argument), or distributional preferences. All these findings are of immediate impor-tance to those authorities involved in the mechanism design of public good provision.

Assuming that private and public good production is naturally bundled, the major trade-off between government regulation and CSR can be summarized as follows: While government regulation of firms may entail the production of optimal or excessive levels of public goods, the alloca-tion of costs and benefits may be suboptimal due to the uniformity of public policy tools (i.e., firms have to charge higher prices and cannot sell to those consumers without sufficient willingness to pay for the impure public good anymore; this also denies those consumers the acquisi-tion of the pure private good under consideration). On the other hand, CSR may achieve second best levels of the public good combined with distributional optimality inher-ent in the working of markets. Under special circumstances (e.g., if a government foregoes regulation because an absolute majority of voters does not have preferences for the public good), CSR can even Pareto improve total wel-fare by serving the minority of "caring" consumers (Besley & Ghatak, 2007). In sum, policy makers should take into account the systemic constraints of both public and corporate provision of public goods.

While analyzing CSR through a "public economics lens" offers important insights into welfare implications, effi-ciency, and comparative and normative questions regarding CSR and public policy, it does not shed sufficient light on the motivations behind CSR. Therefore, the next section develops a categorization of CSR along motivational lines and across theoretical frameworks. In short, CSR can be subclassified as either *strategic,* market-driven *CSR,* which is perfectly compatible with profit maximization and Milton Friedman's view of the *socially responsible firm,* or as not-for-profit CSR that comes at a net monetary cost for share-holders. However, foregone profits (note that Reinhardt, Stavins, & Vietor [2008] define CSR in this spirit as *sacri-ficing profits in the social interest*) due to costly CSR need not be at odds with the principle of shareholder value maxi-mization and do not automatically constitute moral hazard by managers if shareholders have respective intrinsic (social or environmental) preferences that substitute for utility derived from extrinsic (monetary) sources. Hence, any microeconomic explanation of CSR builds upon the recent advancement of new concepts of individual behavior in eco-nomics and the related departure from the classical *homo oeconomicus* assumption. In other words, the economic rationalization of CSR is closely linked to the extension of traditional individual rational choice theory toward a broader set of attitudes, preferences, and calculations.

From *Whether* to *Why:* Economics and the Evolutionary Understanding of CSR

Initial research into CSR was dominated by the question of *whether* firms do have any social responsibility other than employing people, producing goods or services, and max-imizing profits. However, firms increasingly engaged in CSR activities that, at first sight, seemed to be outside its original, neoclassical boundaries. Hence, research shifted focus to why firms actually do CSR. Both questions, whether and why CSR, are intimately related and will be jointly addressed in this section.

Should firms engage in CSR? And if so, why (not)? In this respect, Milton Friedman (1970) examined the doc-trine of the social responsibility of business and concluded that the only responsibility of business is to maximize profits (i.e., shareholder value), while goods or curtailment of bads based on public preferences or social objectives should be provided by governments endowed with demo-cratic legitimation and the power to correct market ineffi-ciencies (such as free riding or collective action problems). Based on the assumption of perfect government, this view suggested that CSR was a manifestation of moral hazard by managers (firm decision makers) toward shareholders and not only inefficient but also inconsistent with the neo-classical firm's profit orientation. But rather than putting the discussion about CSR to a halt, Friedman's thoughts provoked the search for an economic justification of CSR in line with neoclassical economics. The breakthrough came with the idea that CSR may actually be a necessary part of strategy for a profit-maximizing firm. In other words, profit maximization can be a motivation for CSR.

But how may CSR be integrated into the objective function of the profit-maximizing firm? The answer to this question builds upon the existence of preferences that are beyond those of the classical *homo oeconomicus.* Stakeholders as well as shareholders often are socially or, in general, intrinsically motivated, a fact that profit-maximizing firms cannot ignore as it directly affects demand in product markets and/or supply in labor markets. Furthermore, such preferences may induce governments to intervene in the market via regulation or taxation while fishing for votes (as stakeholders are at the same time voters and thereby determining who stays in power/government). In sum, social stakeholder preferences translate into some sort of action or behavior relevant to corporate profits. Therefore, CSR qualifies as part of a profit-maximizing strategy. CSR induced by demand side pressures or as a hedge against the risk of future regulation has been termed *strategic CSR* by Baron (2001), while McWilliams and Siegel (2001) refer to the same underlying profit orientation of CSR as a *theory of the firm perspective.*

If shareholders have preferences allowing them to derive intrinsic utility equivalent to extrinsic, monetary utility, any resulting social or environmental corporate performance will constitute a nonstrategic form of CSR that is equally consistent with Friedman's (1970) view of the firm. Here, the objective of the firm reflects the preferences of its owner(s) and therefore might involve a reduction of profits or even net losses without breaking the rule of shareholder value maximization. So Friedman's concept of CSR being equal to profit maximization has been confirmed and enriched by taking account of a new set of stakeholder and shareholder preferences. The result is a bipolar conception of CSR being either strategic or not for profit with varying implications for the financial performance of a firm. Figure 77.1 summarizes the four basic combinations of stakeholder and shareholder preferences and their implications for CSR. If shareholders are purely profit oriented, the firm should act strategically, maximize profits, and engage in CSR efforts only if stakeholders demand it. On the other hand, if shareholders care about corporate environmental and social conduct, CSR will always act as a corporate channel of contributing to public goods independent of stakeholder preferences. In this case, profit maximization is not the target, and nonstrategic firms may forego profits or incur losses to be borne by shareholders. The size of these losses depends, however, on stakeholders' willingness to pay for and general attitude toward CSR.

At this point, a general discussion of the crucial role of individual preferences in the economic analysis of CSR is in order.

It was again Friedman (1970) who explicitly pointed out that to understand any form of social responsibility, it is essential to notice that *society is a collection of individuals and of the various groups they voluntarily form* (i.e., incentives, preferences, and motivations of individual share- and stakeholders determine organizational behavior). Stiglitz (1993, 2002) talks about new concepts to be taken into account when modeling individual behavior. Becker (1993) proposes an "Economic Way of Looking at Behavior," stressing the importance of a richer class of attitudes, preferences, and calculations for individual choice theory. What Friedman, Stiglitz, and Becker have in mind is a new class of psychological and sociological ideas that

	SHAREHOLDER/OWNER PREFERENCES	
PREFERENCES Social/Environmental	Social/Environmental	Purely Monetary
STAKEHOLDER	Not-for-Profit CSR Mixed Effects on Profits	Strategic CSR Profit Maximization
Purely Monetary	Not-for-Profit CSR Negative Effect on Profits	No CSR Profit Maximization

Figure 77.1 Typology of CSR

SOURCE: Kitzmueller (2008).

recently entered microeconomic theory in general and the individual agent's utility function in particular. Standard motivational assumptions have been expanded, and a literature on intrinsic (nonpecuniary) aspects of motivation has emerged. As the behavioral economics literature is rather extensive, only a few selected contributions that are believed to improve the understanding of CSR will be reviewed.

Three general determinants of individual utility can be distinguished. Contributions by Benabou and Tirole (2003, 2006) as well as Besley and Ghatak (2005) identify (1) extrinsic (monetary) preferences and (2) intrinsic (nonmonetary) preferences as two main categories driving individual behavior via utility maximization. The intrinsic part of utility can be further divided into a (2.1) direct, nonmonetary component determined independently of how others perceive the action or payoff and (2.2) an indirect component determined by others' perception of respective action. (2.2) is frequently referred to as *reputation*. Assuming that individuals do derive utility from these three sources, economic theory can contribute to the analysis of strategic firm behavior such as CSR.

A first important insight is that intrinsic motivation can act as a substitute for extrinsic monetary incentives. Depending on the degree of substitutability, this affects both pricing through a potential increase in consumers' willingness to pay as well as "incentive design" in employment contracting (subject to asymmetric information). In sum, when pricing products, firms may be able to exploit intrinsic valuation of certain characteristics by charging higher prices, while salaries might be lower than usual if employees compensate this decrease in earnings by enjoying a social or environmentally friendly workplace, firm conduct, or reputation in line with their expectations and personal preferences. Relevant theoretic works include Benabou and Tirole (2006), who find that extrinsic incentives can crowd out prosocial behavior via a feedback loop to *reputational signaling concerns* (2.2 above). This concern reflects the possibility that increased monetary incentives might negatively affect the agent's utility as observers are tempted to conclude greediness rather than social responsibility when observing prosocial actions. Here the signal extraction problem arises because agents are heterogeneous in their valuation of social good and reputation, and this information is strictly private. Such considerations could influence not only employees, consumers, and private donors but also social entrepreneurs. Social entrepreneurs are individuals ready to give up profits or incur losses by setting up and running a CSR firm. (The opposite would be the private entrepreneur, who creates a firm if and only if its market value exceeds the capital required to create it.) CSR here expands the "social" individual's opportunity set to do "good" by the option to create a CSR firm. Summing up, agents are motivated by a mixture of extrinsic and intrinsic factors, and therefore potential nonintended effects due to crowding between extrinsic and intrinsic motivators should be taken into account when designing optimal incentives (salaries, bonus payments, taxes, etc.).

So stakeholders demand CSR in line with their intrinsic motivation, and the key question that follows, this time with respect to alternative private ways of doing social good, asks why this *corporate channel* of fulfilling one's need to do public good is used at all if there are alternatives such as direct social contribution (e.g., charitable donations or voluntary community work). From a welfare perspective, there should be some comparative advantage of CSR, something that makes it more efficient than other options. In an important paper, Andreoni (1989) compares different ways to contribute to social good and asks whether they constitute perfect or rather imperfect substitutes. Although the initial version compares public and private provision of public goods, the same analysis can be extended to compare various ways of private provision such as corporate and individual social responsibility. The answer then is straightforward. If *warm glow* effects (Andreoni, 1990) of individual (direct) altruistic giving exist, then investment into a CSR firm, government provision of public goods, and direct donations will be imperfect substitutes in utility and therefore imperfectly crowd out each other. In other words, a socially responsible consumer might not derive the same utility from buying an ethical product and from donating (the same amount of) money to charitable organizations directly. However, this analysis is unable to explain in more detail why individuals allocate a share of their *endowment to do social good* to CSR. A reasonable conjecture might be that people must or want to consume certain private goods but derive intrinsic disutility (e.g., bad conscience) from being connected to any socially stigmatized, unethical behavior or direct negative externality related to their purchase, seller, and/or use of the good or service. Furthermore, one should notice that social or environmental goods do not always directly or physically affect consumers but rather are feeding through to individual utility indirectly via intrinsic, reputational concerns (e.g., Nike's connection to child labor in Asian sweatshops). However, these conjectures have yet to be sufficiently tested empirically.

A final economic puzzle worth thinking about is the one of causality between preferences and CSR—that is, opposite to the above assumed causality from preferences to firm behavior, CSR often has been connected with advertisement or public relations of firms, thereby suggesting that CSR eventually could determine or change preferences and ultimately individual behavior over time. While the management literature has approached these issues via the concept of corporate social marketing (Kotler & Lee, 2004), economists have been more cautious when it comes to *endogenous preferences*. As far as preference formation is concerned, Becker (1993) concluded that "attitudes and values of adults are . . . influenced by their childhood experiences." Bowles (1998) builds the bridge from Becker's "family environment" to markets and other economic institutions influencing the evolution of values, preferences, and motivations. Simon (1991) was among the first to argue that agency problems may be best overcome by attempting to change and ideally align preferences of workers and principals. The following real-world example shall illustrate the key issue here. Empirical evidence from the 1991 General Social Survey (outlined in Akerlof & Kranton, 2005, p. 22) suggests that workers strongly identify with their organization (i.e., employer's preferences). In theory, this finding can be a result of matching (selection), reducing cognitive dissonance (psychology), or induced convergence of preferences (endogenous preferences). Given these alternatives, CSR could be either interpreted as a signal leading to matching of firms and individuals with similar preferences or alternatively used to align agents' preferences over time. While the latter suggestion lacks theoretic or empirical treatment, the former potential matching role of CSR has been analyzed and will be outlined below.

It can be seen that a lot of open questions need to be answered when it comes to the mechanics of intrinsic motivation and social preferences within the human mind. Hence, further discussion of CSR focuses on strategic interaction between firms and stakeholders and treats the existence of intrinsic preferences as exogenously given.

Six Strategies Behind Strategic CSR

Six relevant economic frameworks within which strategic CSR can arise are discussed and linked to empirical evidence at hand: (1) labor markets, (2) product markets, (3) financial markets, (4) private activism, (5) public policy, and (6) isomorphism.

Labor Economics of CSR

CSR may alter classical labor market outcomes. Bowles, Gintis, and Osborne (2001) address the role of preferences in an employer-employee (principal-agent) relationship. The main idea is that employees might have general preferences such as sense of personal efficacy that are able to compensate for monetary incentives and therefore allow the employer to induce effort at lower monetary cost. Besley and Ghatak (2005) establish a theoretic framework to analyze the interaction of monetary and nonmonetary incentives in labor contracts within the nonprofit sector. They refer to not-for-profit organizations as being mission oriented and conjecture that such organizations (e.g., hospitals or universities) frequently are staffed by intrinsically motivated agents (think of a doctor or professor who has a nonpecuniary interest in the hospital's or university's success, i.e., saving lives or educating students). The main conclusion from their moral hazard model with heterogeneous principals and agents is that

pecuniary, extrinsic incentives such as bonus payments and the agents' intrinsic motivation can act as substitutes. In other words, a match between a mission-oriented principal and an intrinsically motivated agent reduces agency costs and shirking (i.e., putting lower effort when the principal cannot observe the work effort given by the agent but only the outcome of the work) and allows for lower incentive payment. As today many firms adopt missions (such as CSR activities) in their quest to maximize profits, this analysis may directly carry over to the private sector.

As opposed to Friedman's (1970) concern that CSR is a general form of moral hazard (here moral hazard refers to managers or employees not acting in the best interest of shareholders or firm owners), Brekke and Nyborg (2004), based on Brekke, Kverndokk, and Nyborg (2003), show that CSR can actually reduce moral hazard in the labor market context. More precisely, CSR can serve as a screening device for firms that want to attract morally motivated agents. This view on CSR as a device to attract workers willing to act in the best interest of the principal is again based on the same substitutability of motivation due to CSR and related firm characteristics valued by the employees and high-powered incentives such as bonus payments.

Another labor market context that involves CSR and corporate governance is explored by Cespa and Cestone (2007). They conjecture that inefficient managers can and will use CSR (i.e., the execution of stakeholder protection and relations) as an effective entrenchment strategy to protect their jobs. CEOs and managers engage in CSR behavior in face of a takeover or replacement threat in order to then use such "personal" ties with stakeholders to bolster their positions within the firm (in other words, such managers establish themselves as key nodes linking the firm with strategic stakeholders, thereby gaining value independent of their true managerial capacity and performance). This discussion of the effect of corporate governance institutions on firm value leads to the conclusion that institutionalized stakeholder relations (as opposed to managers' discretion) close this "insurance" channel for inefficient managers and increase managerial turnover and firm value. This finding clearly provides a rationale for the existence of special institutions such as ethical indices or social auditors and increased interaction between social activists and institutional shareholders in general. A similar approach to CSR is taken by Baron (2008), who links managerial incentives and ability with the existence of socially responsible consumers. He concludes that, given that consumers value CSR, when times are good, a positive correlation emerges between CSR and financial performance via the fact that high-ability managers tend to contribute more to CSR than low-ability ones, and the level of both, CSR and profits, is increasing in managers' ability. In bad times, however, shareholders are not supporting social expenditure (for profits) anymore, high-ability managers become less likely to spend money on CSR as compared to low-ability ones, and the correlation between CSR and profits becomes negative. Baron's work gives a first idea of the importance of consumer preferences in the determination of CSR efforts, which will be the subject of the following subsection.

CSR and Product Markets (Socially Responsible Consumption)

With regard to whether consumers really care about CSR, there is substantial empirical evidence supporting this assumption. Consumer surveys such as the Millennium Poll on Corporate Social Responsibility (Environics International Ltd., 1999) or MORI (http://www.ipsos-mori.com/about/index.shtml) reveal that consumers' assessment of firms and products as well as their final consumption decisions and willingness to pay depend on firms' CSR records. In this respect, Trudel and Cotte (2009) find the equivalent to loss aversion in consumers' willingness to pay for ethical products. According to their findings, consumers are willing to pay a premium for ethical products and buy unethical goods at a comparatively steeper discount. So there exists a channel from preferences and demand to CSR and/or vice versa.

Consumer preferences may translate into demand for CSR and alter the competitive environment of firms as CSR can either act as product differentiation or even trigger competition with respect to the level of CSR itself. Bagnoli and Watts (2003) analyze competitive product markets with homogeneous, socially responsible consumers and find that CSR emerges as a by-product and at levels that vary inversely with the degree of competitiveness in the private goods market (competitiveness is reflected through both number of firms and firm entry). Bertrand (price) as opposed to Cournot (quantity) competition forces firms to reduce markups and hence limits their ability to use profits to increase CSR. This leads to reduced competitiveness in terms of product differentiation via CSR and hence to reduced overall CSR activity. In sum, there exists a trade-off between efficient provision of the private good and public good (i.e., Bertrand competition entails lower prices and lower levels of CSR than Cournot competition).

A more general framework is provided by Besley and Ghatak (2007), who find that Bertrand (price) competition in markets with heterogeneous demand for CSR leads to zero profits—that is, prices equal marginal costs and second best (suboptimal) levels of public good provision equivalent to results obtained in models of private provision (e.g., Bergstrom et al., 1986). Their analysis further allows validation of a whole array of standard results from the screening and public goods literature, among which, (a) the maximum sustainable level of CSR (under imperfect monitoring by consumers) is achieved when the firms' incentive compatibility constraint binds—that is, at such a public good level the profits from doing CSR and charging

a price premium are equivalent to profits from not producing the public good and still charging a price premium (cheating), given any probability (between 0 and 1) of being caught cheating and severely punished. (b) An exogenous increase of public good supply (e.g., by a government through regulation or direct production) perfectly crowds out competitive provision of CSR. (c) In the absence of government failure, governments are able to implement the first best Lindahl-Samuelson level of public good (i.e., the Pareto optimal amount, which is clearly above the levels markets can provide via CSR). (d) However, when governments fail (e.g., due to corruption, capture, relative production inefficiencies, or distributional bias), CSR might generate a Pareto improvement vis-à-vis no production or government production of public good, while CSR and provision by nonprofits (e.g., NGOs) are identical unless one or the other has a technological (cost) advantage in producing the public good. (e) Finally, a small uniform regulation in the form of a minimum standard (on public good levels) would leave the level of CSR unchanged and redistribute contributions from social to neutral consumers, while large regulatory intervention can raise supply of the public good to or above its first best level given that neutral consumers are willing to pay higher (than marginal cost) prices for the private good. These results highly depend on respective consumer preferences and their related willingness to pay for the private and public good (CSR) characteristics of the consumption good.

Arora and Gangopadhyay (1995) model CSR as firm self-regulation (i.e., voluntary overcompliance with environmental regulation) and assume that although consumers all value environmental quality, they vary in their willingness to pay a price premium for CSR, which is positively dependent on their income levels. Firms differentiate by catering to different sets of consumers; here choice of *green* technology acts as product positioning similar to the choice of product quality, and CSR is positively correlated with the income levels of either all consumer segments or the lowest income segment. If a minimum standard is imposed into a duopoly, it will actually bind on the less green firm while the other firm will overmeet the standard. CSR subsidies can have the same effect as standards, while ad valorem taxes (i.e., taxes on profits) always reduce output and CSR efforts by all firms.

An example of empirical work in this subfield is provided by Siegel and Vitaliano (2007), who test and confirm the hypothesis that firms selling experience or credence goods—that is, the good's quality can only be observed after consumption (by experience, e.g., a movie) or is never fully revealed (credence, e.g., medical treatment or education)—are more likely to be socially responsible than firms selling search goods (i.e., goods where characteristics such as quality are easily verified ex ante). This lends support to the conjecture that consumers consider CSR as a signal about attributes and general quality when product characteristics are difficult to observe. From the firm perspective, CSR then can be used to differentiate a product, advertise it, and build brand loyalty. The advertising dimension of CSR is especially strong when social efforts are unrelated to business conduct. In Navarro (1988), corporate donations to charity are identified as advertisement, and CSR is meant to transmit a positive signal about firm quality/type. However, according to Becker-Olsen and Hill (2005), this signal might not necessarily be positive, as consumers are able to identify low-fit CSR as advertisement and tend to negatively perceive such CSR efforts as greediness of firms rather than genuine interest in social or environmental concerns.

CSR and Financial Markets (Socially Responsible Investment)

Investors also care about CSR, and firms competing for equity investment in stock markets will have to take that into account. Geczy, Stambaugh, and Levin (2005) put forward strong evidence of the increasing importance of CSR in financial markets. A new form of investment, so-called *socially responsible investment* (SRI), has come into being. SRI is defined by the Social Investment Forum (SIF, 2009) as *an investment process that considers the social and environmental consequences of investments, both positive and negative, within the context of rigorous financial analysis.* Social investors today include both private and institutional ones. More precisely, the U.S. Social Investment Forum (figures are taken from SIF, 2006) reports 10.8% of total investment under professional management in 2007 to be socially responsible (i.e., using one or more of the three core socially responsible investing strategies: screening, shareholder advocacy, and community investing). In Europe, the European Sustainable and Responsible Investment Forum (EuroSIF) identifies 336 billion euros in assets to be SRI. The trend points upward in most financial markets (e.g., in the United States, where SRI assets grew 4% faster than total assets and more than 258% in absolute terms between 1995 and 2005).

Recalling the typology of CSR (Figure 77.1), we know that investors either have or do not have social preferences. Neutral investors just have their monetary return on investment in mind and hence just care about firm profits. It follows that such investors will use SRI as an investment strategy only if SRI actually translates into higher returns on investment. So, SRI by neutral investors signals a comparative advantage in corporate financial performance (CFP). This conjecture and the related question of correlation and causality have attracted a lot of attention in the scarce empirical literature on CSR. A comprehensive survey is provided by Margolis and Walsh (2003). Taking into account 127 published empirical studies between 1972 and 2002, they find that a majority of these studies exhibit a statistically significant and positive correlation between CSR and CFP in both directions (i.e., causality is running from CFP to CSR and vice versa). However, there exist sampling problems, concerns about the validity of CSR and CFP measures and

instruments, omitted variable bias, and the ultimate (and still unanswered) question of causality between CSR and CFP. A first attempt to address inconsistency and misspecification is the work by McWilliams and Siegel (2000), who regress firm financial performance on CSR and control for R&D investment. It follows that the upwards bias of the financial impact of CSR disappears and a neutral correlation emerges. In sum, further studies will have to clarify whether neutral investors should put their money into SRI and the underlying CSR effort qualifies as *strategic.*

Alternatively, SRI can be a way for social investors to enforce their preferences through a demand channel similar to the one consumers use. The group of social investors, however, can again be heterogeneous in the sense that there might be those for whom corporate giving is a close substitute for personal giving and those for whom it is a poor substitute (Baron, 2005). Small and Zivin (2005) enrich this setup by deriving a Modigliani-Miller theory of CSR, where the fraction of investors that prefers corporate philanthropy over private charitable giving drives CSR by firms attempting to maximize their valuation. A share constitutes a charity investment bundle matching social and monetary preferences of investors with those of the firm's management. The main conclusion is that if all investors consider CSR and private charity as perfect substitutes, share prices and the aggregate level of philanthropy are unaffected by CSR. If they are imperfect substitutes and a sufficiently large fraction of investors prefers CSR over private charity (e.g., to avoid corporate taxation), a strictly positive level of CSR maximizes share prices and hence the value of a corporation.

CSR and Private Politics (Social Activism)

The existence and impact of social or environmental activists is intimately related with information asymmetries between companies and the outside world. The rationale of *social activism* is that the threat of negative publicity (revelation of negative information) due to actions by an unsatisfied activist motivates CSR. As soon as the activist is credible and has the ability to damage a firm's reputation or cause substantial costs to the firm, the existence of such an activist is sufficient to integrate CSR as part of corporate strategy. The logic is comparable to the one of "hedging" against future risk in financial markets, but here the firm insures itself against a potential campaign by an activist. Baron (2001) explicitly adds this threat by an activist, who is empowered with considerable support by the public, to the set of motivations for strategic CSR. CSR is referred to as corporate redistribution to social causes motivated by (1) profit maximization, (2) altruism, or (3) threats by an activist. However, it can be argued that the existence of activism qualifies CSR as an integral part of profit maximization (i.e., motivation 3 fuses into 1).

The main insights from the analysis of CSR and social activism can be summarized as follows: First, CSR and private politics entail a direct cost effect depending on the competitive environment (i.e., the degree of competition is positively correlated with the power of an activist boycott and strengthens the ex ante bargaining position of the activist). On the other hand, CSR can have a strategic effect that alters the competitive position of a firm. What is meant here is that CSR can act as product differentiation (lower competition), take the wind out of the sails of any potential activist, and reduce the likelihood of being targeted in the future. This result roots in the assumption that the activist also acts strategically and chooses "projects" that promise to be successful (i.e., weaker firms are easier targets). Finally, the existence of spillover effects from one firm to other firms or even the whole industry can act as an amplifier to activist power, on one hand, and motivation for concerted nonmarket action by firms in the same industry, on the other (e.g., voluntary industry standards).

Baron (2009) assumes that citizens prefer not-for-profit (morally motivated) over strategic CSR. If signaling is possible, morally motivated firms achieve a reputational advantage, and social pressure will be directed toward strategic firms. If citizens are not distinguishing, morally motivated firms are more likely targeted as they are "softer" targets in the sense that an activist is more likely to reach a "favorable" (i.e., successful from activist objective's point of view) bargain with such a firm. However, the distinction between strategic and not-for-profit CSR can be extremely difficult, subtle, and based on perception rather than facts. Recent work by marketing scholars lends support to this proposition. Becker-Olsen and Hill (2005) find that consumers form their beliefs about CSR based on perceived fit and timing of related efforts (i.e., a high fit between CSR and the firm's business area as well as proactive rather than reactive social initiatives tend to align consumers' beliefs, attitudes, and intentions with those of the strategic firm). Finally, if activists differ in ability, Baron shows that high-quality activists attract greater contributions and then are more likely to identify and target strategic firms, while the opposite holds for low-quality activists.

CSR and Public Politics (Regulation)

CSR is defined as corporate social or environmental effort beyond legal requirements. Then how can public politics and laws actually stimulate CSR? This time, it is the threat of future laws and regulations and the adjustment costs and competitive disadvantage they could entail that act as an incentive to hedge against such an event and build a strategic "buffer zone" via CSR. Again, by doing CSR, firms not only are "safe" in the event of regulation but also might discourage government intervention. This last point has been addressed under the label of *crowding out*. The analysis here focuses on whether market provision of public goods and public provision are substitutes or complements and how they might interact (Bergstrom et al., 1986). From a policy perspective, it seems to be important not only to understand interaction between public provision and CSR but also to consider CSR itself as a potential target for novel policies aiming to stimulate corporate provision of public goods.

Calveras et al. (2007) study the interplay between activism, regulation, and CSR and find that private (activism) and public (regulatory) politics are imperfect substitutes. It is emphasized that when society free rides on a small group of activist consumers, loose formal regulation (voted for by the majority of nonactivists) might lead to an inefficiently high externality level, where activist consumers bear the related cost via high prices for socially responsible goods. This conclusion draws attention to another relevant correlation—namely, between regulation and political orientation. Consumers are also voters, and not only firms but also governments want to signal their type (i.e., whether they value environmental or social public goods). As governments signal their future intentions and policy stances through legislation or regulation and firms through CSR, the potential competition and related interaction between regulation and CSR constitute an important subject of further investigation.

Empirically, Kagan, Gunningham, and Thornton (2003) address the effect of regulation on corporate environmental behavior. They find that regulation cannot fully explain differences in environmental performance across firms. However, "social license" pressures (induced by local communities and activists) as well as different corporate environmental management styles significantly add explanatory power. In sum, regulation matters, but variation in CSR is also subject to the antagonism between social pressure and economic feasibility.

Isomorphism

Here, the incentive to do CSR roots in isomorphic pressures within geographic communities or functional entities such as industries. Community isomorphism refers to *the degree of conformity of corporate social performance in focus, form, and level within a community*. It is the institutional environment and commonly (locally) accepted norms, views, and values that might discipline firms into certain social behavior. Institutional factors that are potentially shaping the nature and level of CSR in a community include cultural-cognitive forces, social-normative factors, and regulative factors. Marquis, Glynn, and Davis (2007) use an institutional theoretic setting and identify community isomorphism as a potential explanatory variable for empirical observations concerning CSR. Isomorphic pressures may also arise within industries and may lead to industry-wide self-regulatory activities.

Conclusion

From an economic point of view, a fundamental understanding of CSR is emerging. Based on a new set of social or environmental stakeholder preferences, CSR can be fully consistent with a profit- and/or shareholder value-maximizing corporate strategy. It qualifies as strategic behavior if consumers, investors, or employees have relevant social or environmental preferences and if these preferences translate into action with direct or indirect monetary effects for the firm. Direct consequences include the firm's ability to charge price premia on CSR comparable to premia on product quality, as well as the potential lowering of wages for "motivated" employees, who substitute the utility they gain from working for and within a responsible firm/environment for monetary losses due to lower salaries. Firms' profits may be indirectly affected by CSR in the sense that CSR can help avoid competitive disadvantages or reputation loss arising in situations where stakeholder action (consumption or activism) depends on social or environmental corporate conduct. Empirical evidence lends support to most of these incentives for strategic CSR; however, rigorous statistical analysis is still in an infant state and subject to various problems, including measurement error, endogeneity, and misspecification.

Author's Note: Portions of this chapter appeared in different form in Kitzmueller (2008).

References and Further Readings

Akerlof, G. E., & Kranton R. E. (2005). Identity and the economics of organization. *Journal of Economic Perspectives, 19,* 9–32.

Andreoni, J. (1989). Giving with impure altruism: Applications to charity and Ricardian equivalence. *Journal of Political Economy, 97,* 1447–1458.

Andreoni, J. (1990). Impure altruism and donations to public goods: A theory of warm-glow giving. *The Economic Journal, 100,* 464–477.

Arora, S., & Gangopadhyay, S. (1995). Toward a theoretical model of voluntary overcompliance. *Journal of Economic Behavior and Organization, 28,* 289–309.

Bagnoli, M., & Watts, S. G. (2003). Selling to socially responsible consumers: Competition and the private provision of public goods. *Journal of Economics and Management Strategy, 12,* 419–445.

Baron, D. P. (2001). Private politics, corporate social responsibility, and integrated strategy. *Journal of Economics and Management Strategy, 10,* 7–45.

Baron, D. P. (2005). *Corporate social responsibility and social entrepreneurship* (Stanford GSB Research Paper No. 1916). Stanford, CA: Stanford University Press.

Baron, D. P. (2008). Managerial contracting and CSR. *Journal of Public Economics, 92*(1–2), 268–288.

Baron, D. P. (2009). A positive theory of moral management, social pressure and corporate social performance. *Journal of Economics and Management Strategy, 18,* 7–43.

Becker, G. S. (1993). Nobel lecture: The economic way of looking at behavior. *Journal of Political Economy, 101,* 385–409.

Becker-Olsen, K. L., & Hill, R. P. (2005). The impact of perceived corporate social responsibility on consumer behavior. *Journal of Business Research, 59,* 46–53.

Benabou, R., & Tirole, J. (2003). Intrinsic and extrinsic motivation. *Review of Economic Studies, 70,* 489–520.

Benabou, R., & Tirole, J. (2006). Incentives and pro-social behavior. *American Economic Review, 96,* 1652–1678.

Bergstrom, T., Blume, L., & Varian, H. R. (1986). On the private provision of public goods. *Journal of Public Economics, 29,* 25–49.

Besley, T., & Ghatak, M. (2001). Government versus private ownership of public goods. *Quarterly Journal of Economics, 116,* 1343–1372.

Besley, T., & Ghatak, M. (2005). Competition and incentives with motivated agents. *American Economic Review, 95,* 616–636.

Besley, T., & Ghatak, M. (2007). Retailing public goods: The economics of corporate social responsibility. *Journal of Public Economics, 91,* 1645–1663.

Bowles, S. (1998). Endogenous preferences: The cultural consequences of markets and other economic institutions. *Journal of Economic Literature, 36,* 75–111.

Bowles, S., Gintis, H., & Osborne, M. (2001). Incentive-enhancing preferences: Personality, behavior and earnings. *American Economic Review, 91*(2), 155–158.

Brekke, K. A., Kverndokk, S., & Nyborg, K. (2003). An economic model of moral motivation. *Journal of Public Economics, 87,* 1967–1983.

Brekke, K. A., & Nyborg, K. (2004). *Moral hazard and moral motivation: Corporate social responsibility as labor market screening* (Memorandum N025). Oslo, Norway: Department of Economics, University of Oslo.

Buchanan J. M. (1999). *The demand and supply of public goods.* Indianapolis, IN: Liberty Fund. Retrieved from http://www.econlib.org/Library/Buchanan/buchCv5c1.html

Calveras, A., Ganuza, J. J., & Llobet, G. (2007). Regulation, corporate social responsibility, and activism. *Journal of Economics and Management Strategy, 16,* 719–740.

Cespa, G., & Cestone, G. (2007). Corporate social responsibility and managerial entrenchment. *Journal of Economics and Management Strategy, 16,* 741–771.

Economist Intelligence Unit. (2005, January). *The importance of corporate responsibility* (White paper). Retrieved from http://graphics.eiu.com/files/ad_pdfs/eiuOracle_Corporate Responsibility_WP.pdf

Environics International Ltd. (1999, September). Millennium poll on corporate responsibility, in cooperation with The Prince of Wales Trust.

European Commission. (2009). *Corporate social responsibility (CSR).* Available at http://ec.europa.eu/enterprise/policies/sustainable-business

Fleishman-Hillard & the National Consumers League. (2005). *Rethinking corporate social responsibility.* Retrieved from http://www.csrresults.com/FINAL_Full_Report.pdf

Friedman, M. (1970, September 13). The social responsibility of business is to increase its profits. *The New York Times,* pp. 32–33, 122, 126.

Geczy, C., Stambaugh, R., & Levin, D. (2005). *Investing in socially responsible mutual funds* (Working paper). Philadelphia: Wharton School of Finance.

Kagan, R. A., Gunningham, N., & Thornton, D. (2003). Explaining corporate environmental performance: How does regulation matter? *Law and Society Review, 37,* 51–90.

Kitzmueller, M. (2008). *Economics and corporate social responsibility* (EUI ECO Working Paper 2008–37). Available at http://cadmus.eui.eu

Kotchen, M. J. (2006). Green markets and private provision of public goods. *Journal of Political Economy, 114,* 816–845.

Kotler, P., & Lee, N. (2004, Spring). Best of breed. *Stanford Social Innovation Review,* pp. 14–23.

Margolis, J. D., & Walsh, J. (2003). Misery loves companies: Rethinking social initiatives by business. *Administrative Science Quarterly, 48,* 268–305.

Marquis, C., Glynn, M. A., & Davis, G. F. (2007). Community isomorphism and corporate social action. *Academy of Management Review, 32,* 925–945.

McWilliams, A., & Siegel, D. S. (2000). Corporate social responsibility and financial performance: Correlation or misspecification? *Strategic Management Journal, 21,* 603–609.

McWilliams, A., & Siegel, D. S. (2001). Corporate social responsibility: A theory of the firm perspective. *Academy of Management Review, 26,* 117–127.

Navarro, P. (1988). Why do corporations give to charity? *Journal of Business, 61,* 65–93.

Reinhardt, F. L., Stavins, R. N., & Vietor, R. H. K. (2008). *Corporate social responsibility through an economic lens* (NBER Working Paper 13989). Cambridge, MA: National Bureau of Economic Research.

Rose-Ackerman, S. (1996). Altruism, nonprofits and economic theory. *Journal of Economic Literature, 34,* 701–728.

Scherer, A. G., & Palazzo, G. (2008). Globalization and corporate social responsibility. In A. Crane, A. McWilliams, D. Matten, J. Moon, & D. Siegel (Eds.), *Oxford handbook of corporate social responsibility* (pp. 413–431). Oxford, UK: Oxford University Press.

Siegel, D. S., & Vitaliano, D. F. (2007). An empirical analysis of the strategic use of corporate social responsibility. *Journal of Economics and Management Strategy, 16,* 773–792.

Simon, H. A. (1991). Organizations and markets. *Journal of Economic Perspectives, 5*(2), 25–44.

Small, A., & Zivin, J. (2005). A Modigliani-Miller theory of altruistic corporate social responsibility. *Topics in Economic Analysis and Policy, 5*(1), Article 10.

Social Investment Forum. (2006). *2005 report on socially responsible investing trends in the United States.* Retrieved from http://www.socialinvest.org/pdf/research/Trends/2005%20 Trends%20Report.pdf

Social Investment Forum. (2009). *The mission in the marketplace: How responsible investing can strengthen the fiduciary oversight of foundation endowments and enhance philanthropic missions.* Available at http://www.socialinvest.org/resources/pubs

Stiglitz, J. E. (1993). Post Walrasian and post Marxian economics. *Journal of Economic Perspectives, 7,* 109–114.

Stiglitz, J. E. (2002). Information and the change in the paradigm in economics. *American Economic Review, 92,* 460–501.

Trudel, R., & Cotte, J. (2009). Is it really worth it? Consumer response to ethical and unethical practices. *MIT/Sloan Management Review, 50*(2), 61–68.

Vogel, D. (2005). *The market for virtue: The potential and limits of corporate social responsibility.* Washington, DC: Brookings Institution Press.

World Bank. (n.d.). *Financial and private sector development.* Retrieved from http://www.ifc.org/ifcext/economics.nsf/content/ csr-intropage

78

POLITICAL ECONOMY OF VIOLENCE

SHAWN HUMPHREY

University of Mary Washington

Long-term economic prosperity requires the existence of secure property rights. A resource, in the possession of an individual, can be characterized as secure property if that individual can exclude others from exploiting its use. So, as the fundamental instrument of exclusion, who should have recourse to violence? In a world where violence is a recognized margin of competitive adjustment available to all community members, a world of *unorganized* violence, an individual's exclusive right to use a resource is determined in large part by his or her ability to use naked violence to protect that resource from others. This fact creates an incentive for all community members to allocate scarce effort away from production and toward protection and/or predating on others—both of which undermine a community's potential for prosperity.

A solution to this inefficient outcome is to structure a world of *organized* violence, a world where violence is managed and access to it is limited to a subset of the community. In other words, community members can choose to structure a political economy. One such example is the state. In its simplest form, the state consists of a third party (e.g., a prince, king, queen, prime minister, and/or president) and constituents. The fundamental exchange undergirding the state involves constituents surrendering their autonomy, forgoing their rightful recourse to violence, and providing some sort of compensation (e.g., tax revenue) to the third party in exchange for secure property rights. Decisions regarding the projection of violence are reserved for the third party. Structuring a political economy also includes deciding on the number, character, and composition of those that the third party can call upon to violently enforce property rights (e.g., citizens militias, police, military and/or paramilitary forces). However, when deciding how to organize violence, the members of any community confront a dilemma. Centralizing too much violence potential in too few hands can be an inefficient alternative to a world of *unorganized* violence. The power disparity between the third party and its constituents can create an incentive for the third party to predate on its constituents and consequently destabilize its own property rights regime. Constituents can confront this challenge by dissipating the third party's violence potential. This can be accomplished by choosing a more decentralized organization of violence—for example, one in which access to violence is granted to more individuals other than the third party and his or her forces (e.g., a citizens militia). However, this organization can weaken the third party and invite external and internal rivals to challenge the established order, thereby also destabilizing property rights. In other words, economic prosperity requires the presence of a third party that is powerful enough to establish and enforce property rights but not so powerful that its presence destabilizes these rights. This tension is known as the credible commitment dilemma. Successfully managing this tension is pivotal to secure property rights and hence economic prosperity.

Theory

Violence and Economic Prosperity

The fundamental purpose of this chapter is to explore the role that violence plays in the determination of a community's economic prosperity. We begin by acknowledging the fact that we live in a world of scarcity. There are simply not enough resources available to satisfy every want. We also reside in a world populated by individuals with a multiplicity of desires, wants, and preferences. Alternative uses are envisioned for some, if not most, and maybe all scarce resources. Competition—two or more individuals placing simultaneous demands upon the same resource—is our constant companion. In general, if one individual currently possesses something that another desires to allocate toward an alternative use, there is one of two ways that such a conflict of interest can be resolved. The individual who does not currently possess the resource can trade away something he or she does possess in exchange for that which he or she desires, or the individual can forcibly take it. Whether this interaction results in attempted trading or taking is contingent on whether or not possession, by the individual who currently holds the resource, translates into exclusive ownership. In other words, does this individual have secure property rights over this resource? Property rights, in a world of scarcity and competition, are only as exclusive as others around you allow them to be. Those around you have to decide whether or not to respect your rights. Respect can be earned by your ability to personally exclude the encroachments of others and/or bestowed by your community. The latter is most conducive to a voluntary value-creating rearrangement of resources and therefore economic prosperity.

Among neighboring individuals, violence has been and continues to be a fundamental way of deciding issues of ownership—this is mine and this is yours. Within the confines of this chapter, *violence* is defined as the use or threatened use of scarce resources for the sake of imposing physical costs on others. We will define *unorganized violence* as a context in which violence is a widely recognized and practiced method of establishing exclusivity. As you may expect, unorganized violence is inimical to economic prosperity. It can lead to the absolute destruction of resources and productive assets (e.g., the killing and maiming of people and livestock and the destruction of infrastructure—including roads, bridges, hospitals, and schools). It can also create an incentive for individuals to redirect their efforts from otherwise growth-augmenting endeavors—specifically taking the steps to enhance their individual productivity.

Productivity—how much output an individual can produce in one hour of his or her time—is the key to economic prosperity. An individual's productivity is a function of the degree of specialization in his or her community and his or her access to capital (both physical and human) and technological innovations. Choosing to specialize, gaining access to capital, and taking advantage of technological innovations are investments that the members of a community must be willing and able to take. Investments, however, entail a trade-off. The individual must forgo some level of current consumption and other alternative uses of his or her time in exchange for enhanced future productivity and returns. For some extended period of time, this person is tying up today's scarce resources in the pursuit of future returns. Returns that lie in the future are returns that can never be guaranteed. Indeed, the longer that resources are tied up in a particular investment, the greater risk of

conditions changing and thereby threatening his or her returns. Every investment, necessarily, is a risky action that not everyone will find worthwhile to take.

Ubiquitous violence only makes making investments more risky. For example, knowing that everyone else, like you, has recourse to violence, you confront a fundamental trade-off when attempting to arrive at an income-maximizing allocation of effort. Namely, in the context of unorganized violence, your exclusivity over resources is determined in large part by your comparative advantage in violence. Necessarily, every unit of effort invested in enhancing your productivity raises your opportunity cost of allocating effort toward violence. Enhancing your productivity dissipates your comparative advantage in violence. Indeed, your enhanced income-producing potential combined with your diminished willingness to enforce an exclusive claim to that income (it has simply become more costly to exclude) makes you a more lucrative target. Your investment in the future motivates those around you to predate upon you. Looking forward to this possible outcome, you may choose against this act. Indeed, you may enjoy relatively more secure property rights—albeit over limited property and diminished income streams—by being less productive. Choosing relative poverty may insure you against being victimized.

Beyond adversely influencing the level of investment in the economy, unorganized violence induces a number of other growth-discouraging dynamics. For example, you may enjoy a higher standard of living by simply protecting what you already have from your neighbors or by predating upon them. Necessarily, you may have an incentive to invest scarce time and effort into enhancing your protective and/or predatory potential. These investments include the development of your potential to impose physical costs on others by investigating new techniques and/or training in traditional techniques of violence. These investments can also include the steps taken to diminish the potential of competitors to impose costs on you by building fortifications, training dogs, and finding hiding places for your wealth. Protective measures can also include shying away from interacting with others—which is not conducive for the creation markets.

A market exists whenever a buyer and seller of a particular good or service conclude that their interaction is mutually beneficial. The extent of a market for a particular good or service is determined by the number of mutually beneficial exchanges that occur between buyers and sellers. Necessarily, any force that diminishes these mutual benefits—the gains from trade—threatens the existence and extent of markets. A number of forces can influence the gains from trade. We are concerned with transaction costs—the cost of engaging in exchange—which include search, bargaining, and enforcement costs. Our focus is on enforcement costs. In particular, before the conclusion of an exchange, a buyer may ask, "Will I get what I paid for?" Conversely, the seller may ask, "Will I get paid?" An exchange environment that is characterized by mutual trust and hence low enforcement costs allows both to answer the aforementioned questions affirmatively and capture the gains from trade. However, in the context of unorganized violence, where mutual trust is lacking, enforcement costs will be significant. Consequently, in this exchange environment, the gains from trade will fall, fewer and fewer exchanges will be concluded, and markets will either shrink or fail to exist.

This is important because the returns that attend all three aforementioned productivity-enhancing investments are positively associated with the existence and extent of markets. If markets do not exist, then there is no opportunity to make investments. Even if markets exist, if their extent is limited, then the returns for these investments may be too low to make them worthwhile.

Unorganized violence also creates an incentive for you to manage your possessions and resources in such a way so as to maximize their liquidity. You can accomplish the latter by not tying up your resources in investments whose benefits are delayed. Your neighbors confront the very same trade-offs. In consequence, market size will be reduced, and what property is possessed will remain portable to enhance its liquidity. Incentives are such that it may be individually rational to forgo specialization, productivity-enhancing pursuits, and potentially mutually advantageous exchanges with others. Either way no one individual in the community is taking the costly and risky steps toward becoming a productivity-enhancing specialist short-circuiting the emergence of markets and disabling the fundamental engine of economic prosperity.

Why the State Is Necessary for Economic Prosperity

Social order, the opposite of unorganized violence, is widely recognized as a necessary condition for long-term economic prosperity. Order exists when community members find it worthwhile, given their expectations about the actions of others, to respect and defend the rules that delineate claims of ownership. By adhering to a set of rules and agreeing not to predate upon each other, members can reduce the amount of resources allocated toward protective purposes. By agreeing to punish predators in their midst, the returns to predation fall, hence discouraging this activity. Moreover, by working together, they may be able to realize a higher level of exclusivity at lower cost. All possibilities free up scarce resources for productivity-enhancing pursuits and allow for the value-creating rearrangement of resources to take place through trade as opposed to violent struggles. Yet, how does a community of rational self-interested individuals realize social order?

As opposed to the status quo (unorganized violence), social order provides an opportunity for mutually beneficial interactions. Necessarily, there will be a demand for some property rights to govern the community's interactions. It is

the supply, monitoring, and enforcement of these rights that are the fundamental hurdles to the emergence of order (Ostrom, 1990). The supply of a set of rules that yields social order will make the whole better off; however, the rules may not make everyone equally better off. Disagreements, necessarily, may emerge over which set of rules to put in place. Even in the case of symmetric benefits, the costs of supplying these rules may not be borne equally by all members. Moreover, supplying a new set of rules is a public good. Individual members have an incentive to secure these benefits without bearing any cost. Ignoring these difficulties, whether or not a set of rules yields benefits above and beyond those that attend unorganized violence, is contingent on whether or not those subscribing to them actually abide by them. It is here that additional difficulties arise.

One way to realize social order is by some or all individuals making up a community to choose to cooperate in a mutual defense pact, which obligates everyone to respect and defend the rights of others. Respecting the rights of others is costly. It requires one to accept the way in which ownership is defined and structured. The individual bears all these costs—the forgone benefits one could have enjoyed by simply taking what he or she deemed desirable—yet enjoys only a share of the benefits that attend the consequent stability. Similarly, when defending the rights of another, an individual bears fully the opportunity cost of the resources allocated toward this task but enjoys only a share of the benefits. In both cases, the community at large enjoys the remaining share. Respecting and defending the rights of others are public goods. Every member of the community has an incentive to free ride on the effort of others. Everyone in the group is susceptible to this temptation. Everyone in the group knows that everyone in the group is susceptible to this temptation. No one member of the mutual defense pact can truly trust that others will abide to the agreement. This heightens the temptation to renege even more—all choose to be violent. It is their dominant strategy.

This outcome can be avoided if everyone commits to respecting the rules. The idea here is that by committing to respect the rules, you can effectively alter others' expectations concerning your behavior, and by altering their expectations, you can alter the behavior of those around you. They expect you to respect and defend the rules, which in turn favorably alter their marginal net return to respecting and defending the rules. The process of committing yourself and the group may be as simple as you and the group asking each other, "Will you abide by the rules?" The question is whether or not your respective replies, "I will abide" and "We will abide," are believable. Will they alter your expectations concerning their behavior? Will you change their expectations concerning your behavior? They may not believe you. They may not be telling you the truth. Your respective replies lack credibility for the simple reason that they go against rationality.

Rationality dictates that an individual should ex ante promise to abide by the rules and ex post renege when everyone has invested costly effort into productive pursuits. The cost of a promise is negligible. And if everyone else cooperates, you can enjoy a share of the output they produce by predating upon them. It is possible that other members of the group will attempt to monitor your actions and, if necessary, exclude you from the benefits that attend order; however, two things make it possible for your strategy to be successful. Like the supply of rules, monitoring is a public good. It will be undersupplied by the rest of the group. Moreover, even if you were caught attempting to predate, you could expect not to be punished. Enforcement is also a public good. It will not be supplied, by the group, at the efficient level. This logic holds for every member of the group. They all can enjoy the benefits of order without bearing the costs. Commitments, without effective monitoring and enforcement, lack credibility (Ostrom, 1990). Neither your expectation concerning their behavior nor their expectations concerning your behavior will change. Consequently, forward-looking individuals, expecting both services to be undersupplied, may find it worthwhile to continue to invest in protecting what they have. Indeed, it may be worthwhile to continue to encroach, take, rob, and steal. Prospective members are also cognizant of the fact that when conditions change, those who agree to be bound by the rules today may find it worthwhile to break them tomorrow. Given the aforementioned difficulties, we would not expect a collective of rational self-interested individuals to be capable of supplying order and self-regulate violence in their community. Even if one member of the group were willing to bear solely the cost of supplying a set of rules, looking forward, he or she would expect that commitments lack credibility. Consequently, any effort this individual would allocate toward structuring a set of rules would be a fruitless endeavor (Ostrom, 1990). Unorganized violence, however, does not characterize all communities (Molinero, 2000). In the following sections, we review the conditions that can yield credible and noncredible commitments and how changes in these conditions are intimately related to the emergence of the state.

Order can arise by voluntary agreement when groups are small for two reasons. With the benefits of supplying social order shared among a smaller number of individuals, the net advantages of doing so may be positive (Olson, 1965). Even in the presence of the positive externality, individuals may still be willing to respect and defend others' property rights. Smaller numbers also facilitate one's ability to supply order. Individuals in smaller communities are for the most part related to each other through blood, marriage, or both (Diamond, 1999). When a conflict does arise, the parties to the conflict will share many kin who have the ability to intervene, adjudicate, and apply pressure for a nonviolent resolution (Diamond, 1999). Moreover, the relationships among members of small communities are not characterized by one-shot interactions—they are repeated. If one member of the collective is deciding whether or not to act against the prevailing order,

the lost opportunity of no longer engaging in trade with the rest of the community can be a forceful constraint (Axelrod, 1985).

The larger share of benefits enjoyed coupled with the familiarity and repeated play that characterizes small communities are favorable conditions for the emergence of order; however, they can be ephemeral. The rising living standards that accompany social order, including increased life expectancy and decreased mortality rates, translate into population growth. Population growth brings opportunities and challenges. Additional community members, with their unique preferences and abilities, can allow for the introduction of new goods and services and the lowering of transformation costs, through competition and economies of scale. Capturing them, however, is contingent on the successful conclusion of an increased number of exchanges with multiple trading partners. It is here where difficulties crop up. An increase in the number, and maybe the diversity, of exchange partners increases the complexity of the economic-exchange environment. These new exchange partners may require monitoring because having another exchange partner(s) limits the need to return again and again to a previous exchange partner. Forward-looking exchange partners recognize that it may be worthwhile for the partner in trade to renege. Consequently, more monitoring will be required, and exchanges may become more costly to transact, limiting the potential to capture the aforementioned gains that attend population growth.

It is also reasonable to assume that beyond a certain population threshold, social order begins to break down (Olson, 1965). Large numbers erode the familiarity and repeated play that characterized earlier interactions. They also diminish the share of the benefits that attend supplying order. Both forces adversely influence the net advantages of this activity. Knowing that others like you are unmotivated to supply, monitor, and enforce order, individual maximization predicts that if one's interests are better served by breaking the predominant order, then one will do just that. Necessarily, conflicts of interests become more frequent. Moreover, even if you wanted to monitor and enforce order, your ability to do so may be handicapped by the simple fact that you may no longer know both sides to a disagreement. Commitments begin to lose their credibility. Conflicts become more frequent and can escalate if either one or both parties to a dispute summon friends and family members to aid them in an armed threat or attack on the other. The community's ability to self-regulate violence begins to erode.

Unorganized violence, however, may not return. It can be forestalled by the community splintering (Molinero, 2000). One or more subgroups simply relocate and set up independent albeit smaller communities. Splintering forestalls the descent into chaos by reducing the population of the group to the point at which it once again is possible to leave the supply of order to the group as a whole. Each subgroup forgoes the benefits of a large population and relatively more complex economic environment. Smaller numbers and simpler economies, however, insure it against internecine chaos. Splintering, as a conflict resolution technique, seems possible as long as resources are relatively free and abundant, property rights are nonexistent, and emigration costs are low (Molinero, 2000). Splintering allows social order to return as commitments once again gain credibility. Social order results in population growth. Continued population growth allows conflicts once again to arise. This pattern of spin-off and population growth continues. At some point, however, some or all of these communities conclude that they are either unwilling or unable to splinter any further. Our analysis, which began its focus on a community of independent individuals, is now focused on a neighborhood of autonomous communities—none of which, in the presence of the others, has an incentive to limit its population growth. The search for an alternative source of credible commitment begins.

Solution: Statehood

The state can provide a solution to the difficulties of organizing order. The fundamental exchange underlying the state involves a third party and constituents. In exchange for an exclusive share of the output that attends order, constituents forsake violence as an income-maximizing strategy and centralize violence into the hands of the third party (which can be either an individual or a group of individuals). The state, consequently, is defined as an organization with a comparative advantage in violence extending over a geographical area (North, 1979). Why would the third party take on this task? It is because of the residual—which is the difference between the output that order makes possible to be produced and the sum of output promised to constituents (Alchian & Demsetz, 1972). This difference, guaranteed to the third party by constituents, is maximized when the third party allocates the efficient level of effort toward monitoring and enforcing property rights. This is a problem that the community found difficult to solve previously. Now, when constituents turn to each other and commit to respecting each other's property rights, the third party's presence lends them credibility. Indeed, if anyone were to encroach on the rights of another, the third party is willing and able to punish this behavior. No longer feeling the need to maintain or invest in their violence potential so as to deter or otherwise predate on others, scarce effort is freed up and can be allocated toward enhancing their productivity. One of the fundamental advantages of having a third party structure and enforce property rights is that economies of scale attend this particular form of specialization or monopolization of this task. It is simply less costly for the state to provide these services rather than the overlapping and redundant actions of community members. In other words, the same degree of exclusivity may be realized at a lower cost or a higher degree of exclusivity at the same cost. By endowing the third party with the motive (i.e., ownership of the residual) and the means (i.e., monopoly on violence) to monitor and enforce property rights, each constituent's dominant strategy becomes cooperation; thus, the gains from social order can be captured.

Why the State Is Not Sufficient for Economic Prosperity

The value of the state lies in the fact that its representatives have an incentive to supply, monitor, and enforce a set of property rights. Indeed, the state is a mechanism by which citizens can credibly commit to recognizing and respecting the rights of others. However, when contemplating the value of citizenship, an individual considers not only the way in which property rights are structured, which stipulates his or her exclusive right to the gains that attend order, but also their stability. One way to express the idea of stability is to consider it from the perspective of a prospective constituent. Stability is realized if, upon entering the state, no other constituent has an incentive to allocate scarce effort toward violently restructuring your rights in the hopes of realizing a more favorable outcome. Enforcement, of course, is the key concern here. Is the third party willing and able to exclude other constituents and rivals to his or her rule? Because of the residual, we know the third party is definitely willing. Moreover, because of his or her monopoly on violence, the third party is also able to do so. Stable property rights, therefore, are intimately related to the third party's comparative advantage in violence. The lower the opportunity cost he or she confronts when projecting violence, the less costly is it for him or her to exclude others, and the more secure are property rights. However, there is a trade-off. By centralizing violence and in essence volunteering to be coerced, constituents transfer from themselves onto the third party the incentive to employ violence as an opportunistic income-maximizing strategy. Having given up their arms and made the costly investments to enhance their productivity, constituents have become lucrative targets for predation. The third party has the motive (income maximization) and the means (comparative advantage in violence) to act opportunistically and restructure property rights in his or her favor. Indeed, our history is resplendent with countless occurrences of the state using its monopoly on violence to override the very rights it is organized to protect. In other words, while constituents are able to credibly commit to recognizing and respecting each other's property rights, the third party is incapable of such a credible commitment. This is a source of instability whose consequences include prospective constituents reconsidering statehood. Indeed, rational individuals would never agree to a contract that made it incumbent upon them to give up their right to defend themselves when it is possible that once they enter into the contract, another may prey upon them. Necessarily, stability is a function of the third party's willingness and ability to not only enforce but also credibly commit to property rights.

Making the State a Sufficient Condition for Economic Prosperity

Barzel (2002), in his theory of the state, addresses the third party's inability to credibly commit and offers the following solution. Prospective constituents, before inviting another individual or group of individuals to take on the role of the third party, construct a "collective action mechanism" with which to protect themselves against the consequent differential in power. Barzel, however, does not provide an explicit example of such a collective action mechanism. North and Weingast (1989) arrived at this conclusion a decade earlier. In their case study of seventeenth-century England, they concluded that power-sharing rules that give rise to political "veto players" can check the king's incentive to arbitrarily restructure property rights. Barzel acknowledges that mechanisms along the lines of North and Weingast are at times incomplete guarantees against the abuse of power; however, he does not address the fact that if prospective constituents are capable of looking ahead and recognizing that the third party is incapable of credibly committing to property rights, then why are they not just as capable of looking ahead and addressing the limitations of their chosen collective action mechanism?

Humphrey (2004) extends Barzel's (2002) analysis by providing an example of such a collective action mechanism. Constituents recognize that by dissipating the third party's comparative advantage in violence, they can diminish the returns that attend predation and thereby blunt the third party's incentive to prey upon them. They can accomplish this by choosing to organize state-sponsored violence in a way that purposively increases the cost of motivating and coordinating the community's scarce resources toward violent ends. For example, they could choose a more decentralized organization of violence that increases the number and changes the character and composition of those who have access to violence (e.g., a citizens militia). Such an organization will increase the third party's costs of employing violence as an opportunistic strategy. Moreover, if the costs are greater than the returns, then it is worthwhile for the third party to commit. Rationality dictates that he or she does. Indeed, his or her commitment is credible. Consequently, stability is also negatively related to the third party's comparative advantage in violence.

The implementation of such a collective action mechanism, however, is attended by a significant trade-off. Indeed, the problem is more complex than originally framed. Earlier we discussed how our original community could use splintering as a conflict mitigation mechanism. Over time, splintering will result in a neighborhood of communities. These communities also confront the same world of scarcity and competition. Realizing a cooperative solution in this context,

however, is much more difficult. The conflict mitigating mechanisms of small groups are less effective between groups—for the same reasons enumerated above within a community. Unorganized violence is the likely state of affairs among independent communities. Therefore, when it comes to enumerating those individuals whose actions can influence the stability of a prospective constituent's property rights, we must add to that list external rivals to the third party's rule. Consequently, actively dissipating the third party's comparative advantage in violence can signal weakness to its rivals—enticing them to predate. Although willing to enforce property rights, the third party may no longer be able.

Stability will only be realized when the third party's rivals (both internal and external) recognize and respect his or her constituents' property rights. Prospective constituents must reconsider allowing the third party to maintain a monopoly on the community's violence potential. However, as we already know, this may induce the third party to renege. The risky step centralizing violence will not be acted upon until another collective action mechanism, one that can be substituted for the decentralized organization of violence, can be implemented. For example, instead of the third party unilaterally deciding when, where, and upon whom to project violence, one solution to this tension would be to introduce politics into these decisions. This can be accomplished by increasing the number of individuals who have a say in the use of violence and manipulate their character (popularly elected or appointed) and composition (bicameral or unicameral system). If these constitutional innovations are adopted, then the community can feel comfortable proceeding with the centralization of violence. Moreover, by simultaneously choosing to centralize violence and decentralize the decision to employ violence, the third party may now be capable of signaling strength to his or her rivals and weakness to his or her constituents. Consequently, managing the credible commitment dilemma requires paying attention not only to the number, character, and composition of those who have recourse to violence but also to the number, character, and composition of those who have a say in its use.

Applications and Empirical Evidence

England's Glorious Revolution of 1688 furnishes an opportunity to evaluate the claims of the aforementioned discussion. North and Weingast (1989) have already demonstrated the role of the Glorious Revolution in establishing the conditions under which the state can credibly commit to property rights. However, there is more to the story—namely, Article VI of the Bill of Rights. Per Article VI of the Bill of Rights, William III, in exchange for the crown, surrendered to Parliament one of the king of England's historical prerogatives: absolute decision-making authority over England's military establishment. The Glorious Revolution, by giving Parliament sovereignty over state-sponsored violence, created conditions under which the state could raise and maintain a standing army without threatening property rights. Thus, the emergence of Parliamentarians, whose bundle of political rights included a "veto" over military-related decisions, played a pivotal role in enhancing security by allowing the state to place instruments of violence continuously, even in times of peace, in the hands of professionals, thus allowing the state to realize the efficiency-enhancing benefits of a flexible, immediate, and overwhelming response to property right–destabilizing challenges from rivals inside and outside the state—without threatening its own constituents. Pamphlets, authored by political activists during this period of history, provide evidence that constituents were cognizant of the tension surrounding the choice of how to organize violence, of the inadequacies of collective choice mechanisms alone as credible commitment devices, and how their attempts to address this tension had a measurable influence on the political-military structure of their community (Humphrey & Hansen, 2010).

Future Directions

In economics, we have a definition of the state. The state is an organization with a comparative advantage in violence that extends over a geographic area. For the most part, economists are in agreement regarding the valuable role that the state plays realizing social order. Economists, however, have not adequately explained the process by which the state emerges. That is, we do not fully understand how an individual or group of individuals centralizes and thereby creates a comparative advantage in violence. In theories of the state, the third party is either simply assumed or the story usually told is that self-interested individuals (some subset or the entire population of a community) recognize the aforementioned benefits of centralizing violence in some entity and invite either one of their own or an outsider to specialize in this role. Indeed, looking forward, these individuals recognize that if the conditions are right (the third party has a sustained monopoly on violence), then favorable forces are put into play, which provide the third party with an incentive to not only regularize his or her rate of taxation but also supply ancillary public goods that further facilitate economic growth (North, 1979; Olson, 1993). A number of scholars, however, argue against this process of state formation. Economic agents, they argue, are inherently jealous of their autonomy. The idea that self-interested individuals would willingly subject themselves to a third party is fanciful. In addition, as we have already discussed, prospective citizens will forgo membership until the state can credibly commit to the rules it created. Yet, with respect to social organization, the long-term historical trend has been an increase in the centralization of violence potential. Olson (2000) was correct when he informed us of who the bandits (the "violent

entrepreneurs") were—they were the ones "who can organize the greatest capacity for violence" (p. 568). We need to open up the hood of this comment. Is it a function of their ability to finance the minimum efficient scale of military operations? We are not sure. Does one's capacity for violence stem from their physical attributes? In this case, we know the answer is no. It is a biological fact that the weakest can kill the strongest and/or a subset of the weakest can collude and kill the strongest (Molinero, 2000). The process of organizing organized violence—and, in consequence, accumulating and centralizing political authority—still needs to be explored. Here are some things to consider:

1. Collusion among a subset of the weakest requires some degree of cooperation; however, given that we are talking about small groups, the costs of acting collectively—in particular the costs of monitoring each others' behavior—are minimized. Understanding the conditions that allow for and frustrate the emergence of cooperation in the collective act of projecting violence may provide insight into the conditions that allow for and frustrate the emergence of the third party.

2. Earlier we discussed how unorganized violence creates a disincentive to make productivity-enhancing investments. However, it is important to note that those who become more productive may now be able to purchase the violence potential of others. In other words, the relatively more prosperous can also be deadly by co-opting predators into becoming protectors. A constraint on this possibility is that there must exist a low transaction cost environment in the market for violence. Those who are now in the position to purchase the violence potential of others must be able to answer yes when they ask, "Will I get what I paid for?" Conversely, those who are selling their violence potential must be able to answer yes when they ask, "Will I get paid?" Issues of credibility once again arise. The market for violence needs to be explored.

3. Among competing states, war can be a selection mechanism—selecting for survival those states that structure and enforce a system of political and economic property rights that capture the gains from cooperation. Changes in the complexity of the instruments and/or tactics of warfare will require concomitant changes in the organization of state-sponsored violence. For example, in the later part of the seventeenth century, England's citizens militias were coming under increasing criticism for their numerous weaknesses—including disorganization, poor leadership, and outdated tactics and weaponry. All of these defects could in some way be traced back to the militia's extreme decentralization. There were 52 autonomous county militias. These critiques were being leveled while continental powers (in particular, France) were centralizing military power by organizing standing armies in response to changes in military technology and tactics (e.g., the rise

of firearms and the consequent changes in military formations to take advantage of this technology). Political pamphleteers in England argued that survival would require an organizational innovation—that is, a standing army. Adaptations such as these, however, will have an influence on the state's comparative advantage of violence and hence its ability to credibly commit. Concomitant changes may have to take place in the political arena if credibility is to be restored. Necessarily, there may be a link between changes in military technology and constitutional innovations.

In general, understanding the process by which organized violence becomes organized and the factors that influence this process gives us a glimpse into the font of state power and also a glimpse into the ways in which we can tweak said power toward creating credibility.

Conclusion

Unorganized violence destabilizes property rights, strips individuals of their current wealth and property, and creates an incentive for community members to redirect their efforts from productive growth-augmenting endeavors— for example, specialization and trade—into predatory and/or protective activities. Necessarily, the task set before a community is finding a way to self-regulate the use of violence within its boundaries. If there is an opportunity for mutually beneficial interactions, then individuals will be motivated to take the costly steps to make it happen. In other words, there will be a demand for some rules to govern the use of violence. It is the supply, monitoring, and enforcement of rules that are the fundamental hurdles to the emergence of these rules. A key variable is the willingness and ability of each community member to commit to be bound by the rules. The supply of rules, even under the best conditions (one agent is willing and able to finance the cost of supplying the rules), will be in vain if their commitments lack credibility. The likelihood of accomplishing this task is pretty good when the community is small, homogeneous, and characterized by repeated interactions.

These traits, however, are the very opposite of those traits that characterize a commercial society and form the bedrock of economic prosperity—namely, large numbers, heterogeneous population, a high degree of specialization, and complex trade across space and time. Necessarily, the new task set before the community is to allow for the emergence of an accountable, honest, and responsible individual or group of individuals into whose hands violence is centralized (i.e., organized). It is the state that is usually tasked with providing protection services. Indeed, the value of the third party lies in its willingness and ability to enforce the rules and thereby allow community members to credibly commit to recognizing and respecting each other's property rights. However, in this arrangement, the inability to credibly commit is simply transferred from constituents to the third party. Prospective constituents are aware of this dilemma and will be resistant to monopolizing violence within the third party until they settle upon and introduce mechanisms by which the third party can credibly commit. Until that time, they will forgo the benefits that attend economic prosperity.

The third party's ability to renege and predate is fundamentally a function of his or her violence potential relative to that of his or her constituents. A credible commitment can be engineered by manipulating this power differential through choosing an organization of violence that increases the third party's costs of coordinating and motivating the resources that are set aside for violence (labor, tools, and entrepreneurial spirit). Yet, herein lies a tension. Choosing an organization of violence that is too decentralized, while yielding a credible commitment, makes the third party too weak and may invite insurrection and/or invasion. Choosing an organization of violence that is too centralized, while efficient, makes the third party a threat. A solution to this dilemma requires a constitutional innovation (e.g., Article VI) designed to simultaneously provide for defense while protecting property rights. For example, settle upon a relatively more centralized organization of violence (signal strength to rivals within and outside)—but invest the decision to deploy violence into the hands of political veto players (signal impotence to constituents). Both require manipulating the number, character, and composition of those who have access to violence and those who have a voice in the political arena. Settling upon a particular number, character, and composition in each arena is shaped not only by the dynamic interaction between the third party and constituents but among the third party, his or her constituents, and rivals inside and outside the state.

Successfully managing the credible commitment dilemma, structuring a self-enforcing politico-military settlement, is pivotal to secure property rights. Therefore, truly ascertaining the conditions that underlie economic prosperity requires us to ask the following questions: How do political economies, in response to their strategic environment, organize *organized* violence, and what are the ramifying consequences of their choices? In particular, how do the number, character, and composition of those who have access to violence change in response to a political economy's strategic environment? And, in turn, how do these changes influence the number, character, and composition of those with decision-making authority over a political economy's organization of violence?

References and Further Readings

Alchian, A., & Demsetz, H. (1972). Production, information costs and economic organization. *American Economic Review, 62,* 777–795.

Andrzejewski, S. (1954). *Military organization and society.* London: Routledge and Paul.

Axelrod, R. (1985). *The evolution of cooperation.* New York: Basic Books.

Barzel, Y. (2002). *A theory of the state: Economic property rights, legal rights and the scope of the state.* Cambridge, UK: Cambridge University Press.

Bates, R. (2001). *Prosperity and violence: The political economy of development.* New York: W. W. Norton.

Collier, P. (2007). *The bottom billion: Why the poorest countries are failing and what can be done about it.* Oxford, UK: Oxford University Press.

Diamond, J. (1999). *Guns, germs and steel: The fates of human societies.* New York: W. W. Norton.

Hirschleifer, J. (1994). The dark side of the force. *Economic Inquiry, 32,* 1–10.

Hobbes, T. (1968). *Leviathan.* London: Penguin. (Original work published 1651)

Humphrey, S. (2004). Protecting your protection in a violent world: The link between a state's organization of violence and its constitutional design. *Homo Oeconomicus, 21,* 117–152.

Humphrey, S., & Hansen, B. (2010). Constraining the state's ability to employ force: The standing army debates, 1697–99. *Journal of Institutional Economics, 6*(2), 243–259.

Miller, G. (1992). *Managerial dilemmas: The political economy of hierarchy.* Cambridge, UK: Cambridge University Press.

Molinero, J. M. S. (2000). The origins of the state from reciprocity to coercive power. *Constitutional Political Economy, 11,* 231–253.

North, D. (1990). *Institutions, institutional change, and economic performance.* Cambridge, UK: Cambridge University Press.

North, D. C. (1979). A framework for analyzing the state in economic history. *Explorations in Economic History, 16,* 249–259.

North, D. C. (1981). *Structure and change in economic history.* New York: W. W. Norton.

North, D. C., & Weingast, B. (1989). Constitutions and commitments: The evolution of institutions governing public choice in 17th century England. *Journal of Economic History, 49,* 803–832.

Nye, J. V. C. (1997). Thinking about the state: Property rights, trade, and changing contractual arrangements in a world with coercion. In J. N. Drobak & J. V. C. Nye (Eds.), *The frontiers of the new institutional economics* (pp. 121–142). New York: Academic Press.

Olson, M. (1965). *Logic of collective action: Public goods and the theory of groups.* Cambridge, MA: Harvard University Press.

Olson, M. (1993). Dictatorship, democracy, and development. *American Political Science Review, 87,* 119–138.

Olson, M. (2000). *Power and prosperity: Outgrowing communist and capitalist dictatorships.* New York: Basic Books.

Ostrom, E. (1990). *Governing the commons: The evolution of institutions for collective action.* Cambridge, UK: Cambridge University Press.

Schofield, N. (2000). Institutional innovation, contingency, and war: A review. *Social Choice and Welfare, 17,* 1–17.

Turney-High, H. H. (1971). *Primitive war: Its practice and concepts.* Columbia: University of South Carolina Press. (Original work published 1949)

Umbeck, J. (1981). Might makes rights: A theory of the formation and initial distribution of property rights. *Economic Inquiry, 19,* 38–59.

79

The Economics of Civil War

Marta Reynal-Querol

Pompeu Fabra University

Different social sciences have adopted different perspectives in the study of conflict. Most economists have approached this issue using a theoretical perspective and the tools of game theory. During the past two decades, some economists have constructed theoretical models to explain why individuals and groups become involved in a conflictive situation. For an outstanding review on the theoretical literature of the economics of conflict, I strongly recommend reading Garfinkel and Skaperdas (2007).

However, the empirical approach to this topic is still in its early stages. Recently, some researchers have stressed the importance of economic factors in the study of civil war. This chapter will provide a brief overview of the most relevant empirical papers that address this topic from an empirical point of view. This is not an overview of the main empirical literature on civil war but a summary of the most important papers, as well as the evolution and state of the art on this topic, for undergraduate readers.

Introduction to the Empirical Analysis of Civil Wars

Civil wars have only recently been recognized as one of the main impediments for economic development. Their effects are not only related to the destruction of infrastructure or human life but also to the elimination of the rule of law, the generation of an uncertain environment for future foreign investment, and the destruction of institutions. Empirical research has used different approaches to deal with the explanation of the basic elements of civil wars. Researchers have analyzed the onset of civil wars, the incidence of civil wars, and the duration of civil wars.

These indicators are related but measure different concepts. The probability of onset is the conditional probability of being in state A (war) at time t given that it was in state B (peace) at time $t - 1$.

The incidence is the unconditional probability that we observe state A at time t. The hazard function measures the probability of being in state A between period t and $t + 1$ given that it was in state A in period t. The duration measures the units of time in state A for each event. Obviously, these three analyses are complementary but deal with different sides of the civil war phenomenon.

We can create an analogy with the analysis of macroeconomic cycles. Researchers in that field distinguish between shocks and their propagation mechanism as two different and independently interesting issues. For instance, a cycle could be caused by a productivity shock that is propagated through many alternative mechanisms. In the case of civil wars, the situation is similar, although identification is more difficult.

For instance, in many situations, civil wars start by random acts, which trigger, given a particular propagation mechanism, full-fledged conflicts.

A crucial issue in this topic is understanding the process of conflict.

In order for a conflict to exist, not only do we need an origin that brings about conflict but also a propagation mechanism that allows conflict to exist and propagate. Conflict onset is a highly unpredictable event. In many conflicts, the onset is related to some unpredictable shocks, such as the original trigger of the genocide in Rwanda or the events of 2005 in France (the burning of vehicles during November 2005). All countries receive unexpected shocks, but not all of them enter into conflict.

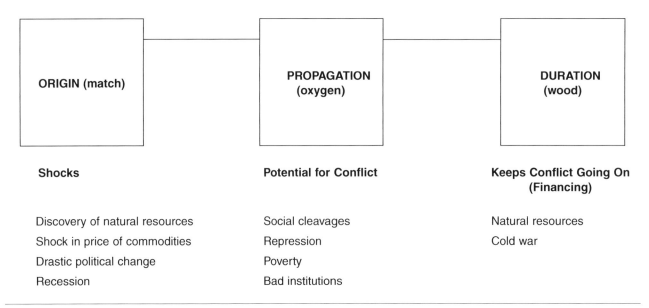

Figure 79.1 Conflict (Fire)

The countries that do not have potential for conflict—that is, do not have the propagation mechanism for conflict—are the ones that are safe. Therefore, given the process of conflict (shocks, propagation mechanism, and financing), three types of policies could be applied to reduce the probability of conflict: policies that try to avoid shocks (e.g., diversification policies), policies that try to reduce the propagation mechanism (e.g., institutions that try to reduce the intensity of social cleavages), and policies that try to cut the source of financing (e.g., the Kimberly process).

Since onset of conflict is usually produced by unexpected shocks, trying to find measures to prevent them is an impossible task, given the unexpected characteristics of shocks. While diversification can protect countries against shocks concerning the price of some products, it is not possible to predict and avoid unexpected shocks, such as the terrorist attacks on September 11, 2001. Also, policies that address the financing are policies with a very short-term effect because rebel groups look for other alternative sources of financing.

Some of this evidence is explained in the work of Michael Ross (2002), who describes this phenomenon very well with an example of Angola:

Before the end of the Cold War, successful rebel groups in the developing world were typically financed by one of the great powers. Since the Cold War ended, insurgent groups have been forced to find other ways to bankroll themselves; many have turned to the natural resources sector. . . . In Angola, for example, UNITA (National Union for the Total Independence of Angola) was backed by the United States and South Africa for most of the 1970s and 1980s. But the end of the Cold War, and the end of the apartheid in South Africa, left UNITA with no outside sponsors; as a consequence, it began to rely much more heavily on diamond revenue to support itself. (p. 20)

This is indicative that policies that try to avoid conflict by cutting the sources of financing are policies that have a short-term effect. Therefore, if we want to find measures to prevent conflict in the long run, we need to look for policies that address the propagation mechanism for conflict.

If we want to analyze the cause of civil wars, we need to be aware of what onset, incidence, and duration are capturing, either in panel or cross-sectional data. For example, if we want to analyze the effect of variables that are invariant over time, the most appropriate specification would be to use a cross section of countries.

But before describing the main literature on this topic, we need to clarify what we mean by conflict. Many phenomena can be classified as conflict: riots, demonstrations, coups d'état, political assassinations, terrorist attacks, civil wars, genocide, and mass killing. The empirical literature on the causes of all these conflicts is very recent. This is basically due to the lack of reliable data on conflict. Recently, there has been a huge effort in trying to obtain good data on civil war. We will basically concentrate on the empirical studies that work with civil war data. But then, what is a civil war? A traditional source for data on civil wars is the Armed Conflict Dataset, a joint project between the Department of Peace and Conflict Studies at Uppsala University and the Center for the Study of Civil War at the International Peace Research Institute, Oslo (PRIO). An armed conflict is defined as a contested incompatibility that concerns government and/or territory where the use of armed force between two parties, of which at least one is the government of a state, results in at least 25 battle-related deaths. This source also provides information on civil war with a threshold of 1,000 battle-related deaths per year.

Empirical Analysis of the Causes of Civil Wars

The empirical analysis of civil war is very recent and basically concentrates on the analysis of the causes of civil war from a macroeconomic perspective. In particular, the relationship between poverty and civil war from a macroeconomic perspective has been one of the main topics under discussion in the empirical literature on civil war. Now there is a growing emerging literature that addresses these issues from a microeconomic point of view. In this chapter, we will concentrate only on the most developed literature on the causes of civil war from a macro point of view and raise the state of the art on the new development on the microeconomic literature that has just started being developed.

Relationship Between Poverty and Civil War: The Seminal Work

One of the most robust results in the civil war literature is the correlation between per capita income and civil war. Some studies have interpreted this correlation as causality, but the potential reverse causality and omitted variable problems indicate that we should consider these results with caution. In this section, we will examine the main papers that discuss these issues.

One of the most influential papers in the empirical literature on the relationship between poverty and civil war is Collier and Hoeffler (2004). This essay develops an econometric model that tries to predict the probability of civil war. It focuses on the initiation of conflict, the onset of civil wars. The article argues that any rebellion needs a motive and an opportunity. The political science approach offers an account of conflict in terms of motive: Rebellion occurs because of grievances. The economic approach, inspired by Herschell Grossman (1994) and Jack Hirshleifer (1989, 1991), models rebellion as an industry that generates profits from looting. Such rebellions are motivated by greed. The political science and the economic approaches to rebellion have assumed different motivations: greed versus grievances. Collier and Hoeffler test empirically both models. One of the questions that arises here is how to measure empirically opportunity and grievance.

Opportunities to finance rebellion can be divided into different types: first, natural resources (diamonds, etc.), which are captured by the ratio of primary commodity exports to gross domestic product (GDP); second, diasporas, where the size of a country's diasporas is captured by its emigrants living in the United States; and third, subventions from hostile governments. The proxy for the willingness of foreign governments to finance military opposition to the incumbent governments is cold war. During cold war, each super power supports rebellions in countries allied to the opposing power.

Moreover, recruits must be paid. Rebellions may occur when income is unusually low. Therefore, the paper proxies this opportunity with the mean income per capita, the male secondary schooling, and the growth rate of the economy.

Finally, another opportunity for rebellion is when the conflict-specific capital is cheap. The study uses the time since the most recent previous conflict to proxy this. Because this captures the legacy of weapons stock and so forth, another dimension of opportunity is weak government military capability, which can be captured with the idea that some terrain may be favorable to rebels, such as forests and mountains. Therefore, Collier and Hoeffler (2004) use the following variables to capture these terrain characteristics: percentage of terrain that is forest, percentage of terrain that is mountain, and the dispersion of the population.

Another source of rebel military opportunity is social cohesion. A newly formed army may need social cohesion and can therefore constrain recruitment to a single ethnic group. Therefore, a diverse society might then reduce the opportunity for rebellion.

Collier and Hoeffler (2004) consider different dimensions of grievances: ethnic or religious hatred; political repression (traditional measures of democracy [Polity III]); political exclusion, a measure that captures whether the largest ethnic group constitutes between 45% and 90% of the population; and economic inequality, which is captured by the Gini index.

In the empirical analysis, Collier and Hoeffler (2004) try to predict the risk that a civil war will start during a 5-year period, through a logit regression, during 1965 to 1999. In all of the analysis, the dependent variable is a dummy that has value 1 if a civil war started during the period and zero otherwise. Ongoing wars are coded as missing observations.

The independent variables included to capture economic conditions are per capita income or male schooling. First, Collier and Hoeffler (2004) test the two models separately and then test them together just taking the significant variables. One result of this study is that exports of primary commodities are highly significant. Once primary commodities are disaggregated into different types of commodities (e.g., oil vs. non-oil), the findings are that low levels of oil dependence are less risky than other commodities, and high levels of dependence are more risky. The most significant variables in predicting the probability of civil wars are male secondary education, per capita income (initial period), and growth rate (average of the 5 previous years).

However, we should consider these results with caution since we have endogeneity problems due to reverse causality and omitted variable problems. For example, it could be that the poverty path and civil war path may be caused by some historical determinants, which are missing in the regression. If this is the case, the relationship we observe could be simply spurious.

The best way to address these issues would be to run instrumental variable (IV) regressions for economic growth and per capita income and to include country fixed effects. This is done by other studies that we will describe in the next section.

The second most influential article on civil war that has stressed the relationship between poverty and civil War is Fearon and Laitin (2003). The main question this article tries to answer is, "Why do some countries have more civil wars than others?" Fearon and Laitin use their own definition of civil war, which includes anticolonial wars. One important hypothesis is that financing is one determinant of the viability of insurgency. The authors argue, however, that economic variables such as per capita income matter primarily because they proxy for state administrative, military, and police capabilities. The interpretation is the following: Where states are relatively weak and capricious, both fears and opportunities encourage the rise of would-be rulers who supply a rough local justice while arrogating the power to "tax" for themselves and often for a large cause. Following this argument, the authors test the following hypothesis, which I have summarized directly from Fearon and Laitin's article:

H1: Measures of a country's ethnic or religious diversity should be associated with a higher risk of civil wars.

H2: The effect of ethnic diversity on the probability of civil war should increase at higher levels of per capita income (a proxy for economic modernization).

The idea is that more modernization should imply more discrimination and thus more nationalist contention in culturally divided societies.

H3: Countries with an ethnic majority and a significant ethnic minority are at greater risk of civil war.

To capture all these hypotheses, the article uses the following variables: the ethnolinguistic fractionalization index (ELF, which is basically the fragmentation index using the Atlas Narodov Mira data set), the share of the population belonging to the largest ethnic group, the number of different languages spoken by groups exceeding 1% of the country's population, and the religious fractionalization index.

H4: Measures of political democracy and civil liberties should be associated with the lower risks of civil war onset.

H5: Policies that discriminate in favor of a particular language or religion should raise the risk of civil war onset in states with religious or linguistic minorities.

H6: Greater income inequality should be associated with higher risks of civil war onset.

In this article, the idea is that to explain why some countries have experienced civil wars, one needs to understand the conditions that favor insurgency, which are largely independent of cultural differences between groups.

The idea is that these conditions should be understood in the logic of insurgency. The story explained in the article is the following: The fundamental fact about insurgency is that insurgents are weak relative to the government they are fighting. If the government forces knew who the rebels are and how to find them, they would capture them. Because of the weakness of the insurgents, to survive, the rebels must be able to hide from government forces. Therefore, the following hypotheses are tested:

H8: The presence of
• rough terrain, poorly served by roads and at a distance from centers of state power, should favor insurgency and civil war.

So should the availability of

• foreign, cross-border sanctuaries and
• a local population that can be induced not to denounce the insurgents to government agents.

Insurgents are to survive and prosper better if the government and military they oppose are relatively weak (badly financed).

H9: A higher per capita income should be associated with a lower risk of civil war onset because

• it is a proxy for a state's overall financial, administrative, police, and military capabilities, and
• it will mark more developed countries with terrain that is more "disciplined" by roads and rural society that is more penetrated by central administration.

They argue that there is another reason why a lower per capita income should favor the technology of insurgency, which is that

• recruiting young men to the life of a guerrilla is easier when the economic alternatives are worse.

It is difficult to find measures to distinguish among these three mechanisms associating a low per capita income with civil war onset. In any case, the main argument provided in the article is that the results of the relationship between per capita income and civil war onset are basically due to the channel of weak states. Fearon and Laitin (2003) believe this occurs because the relationship between the percentage of young males and male secondary schooling rates and civil war is not strong. The empirical analysis uses annual data between 1945 and 1999. The dependent variable is the onset variable, which is a dummy variable that has a value of 1 for the years in which civil war started and zero otherwise (peace and ongoing civil wars). The main results of this study indicate that per capita income, population, and mountains are significant variables, while ethnic fractionalization is not insignificant.

As before, the endogeneity problems due to reverse causality and omitted variable problems imply that we need to be very cautious in the interpretation of these results. Moreover, interpreting why per capita income affects civil war should be solved by analyzing the microeconomics of civil war.

From these two studies, the two main ideas that have emerged and translated into the policy arena are that poverty (per capita income) is the main cause of conflict and that ethnic diversity and democracy do not play any role.

However, these studies have important econometric shortcomings that could reverse the results, once addressed:

1. The current consensus, which emerges from those analyses, is that poverty is the single, most important determinant of civil wars. However, this result could be an artifact of simultaneity problems: The incidence of civil wars and poverty may be driven by the same determinants, some of which are probably missing in the typical econometric specifications. In the next section, we will show what happens once we consider endogeneity problems.
2. They do not address the endogeniety problems between institutions and civil wars.
3. This literature does not use the appropriate index to capture the potential for conflict. Theoretical models of conflict suggest that polarization measures could be better proxies than fractionalization measures. In the next section, we will see what happens once we change the measure to capture ethnic diversity.

All of these three concerns have been recently addressed by the literature. We briefly describe below the strategy followed and the main findings.

Poverty and Civil War: Addressing Endogeneity Problems

More recently, three studies have begun to address the main concerns regarding the relationship between income and civil wars. We will briefly describe the main innovations of two such studies here (Djankov & Reynal-Querol, in press; Miguel, Satyanath, & Sergenti, 2004) and one in the next section (Besley & Persson, 2008) since they also address the role of institutions.

The first study to address the endogeneity problems between economic variables and civil wars is Miguel et al. (2004). I briefly describe the main innovations and the strategy followed by this study. Therefore, this part is basically based on extracts from Miguel et al.

This article is concerned with civil wars in sub-Saharan African countries. The main motivation for the authors is that the literature highlights the association between economic conditions and civil conflict. However, this literature does not adequately address the reverse causality problem of economic variables to civil war and therefore does not convincingly establish a causal relationship. Also, omitted variables (e.g., institutions) may be driven by both economic outcomes and conflict.

Miguel et al. (2004) use exogenous variation in rainfall as an instrumental variable for economic growth to estimate the impact of economic growth on civil conflict.

They very reasonably argue that weather shocks are plausible instruments for growth in domestic product in economies that largely rely on rain-fed agriculture, do not have extensive irrigation systems, and are not heavily industrialized.

The nature of the econometric identification strategy allows them to focus on short-term economic fluctuations that "trigger" conflicts, but it is not as well suited for understanding conflict duration. But why sub-Saharan African countries? As they argue, "Only one percent of the cropland is irrigated in the median African country, and the agricultural sector remains large. The paper finds that weather shocks are in fact closely related to income growth in Sub-Saharan African countries. This identification strategy is not appropriate for other regions of the world, because weather is not sufficiently closely linked to income growth. The IV approach allows addressing another problem: The measurement error in African national income figures, which are thought to be unreliable" (p. 726).

The econometric specification is basically focused on the incidence of civil war. The dependent variable, incidence, is constructed in the following way: All country-year observations with a civil conflict that has at least 25 battle deaths per year are coded as 1; otherwise, they are coded as zero. The analysis also considers the onset definition (coded 1 for the year in which a civil war starts) since the impact of income shocks on conflict may theoretically differ depending on whether the country is already experiencing conflict. Data on civil war come from Uppsala/PRIO as described above.

The main innovation of this article is to analyze the relationship between economic growth and civil war using an instrumental variable approach. Rainfall is used as an instrumental measure of economic growth. The authors use the Global Precipitation Climatology Project (GPCP) database of monthly rainfall estimates as a source of exogenous weather variation.

There is information on rainfall estimates for each point at which latitude and longitude degree lines cross. This data set measures a latitude-longitude degree node point p in country i during month m of year t : R_{ipmt}.

The average rainfall across all points p and months m for that year is R_{it}. The principal measure of a rainfall shock is the proportional change in rainfall from the previous year,

$$(R_{it} - R_{it-1})/R_{it-1},$$

denoted as ΔR_{it}.

Weather variation, as captured in current and lagged rainfall growth (ΔR_{it} and ΔR_{it-1}), is used to measure per capita economic growth ($growth_{it}$) in the first stage, with other country characteristics (X_{it}) controlled for.

Country fixed effects (a_i) are included in some regressions to capture time-invariant country characteristics that may be related to violent conflict (sometimes also country-specific time trends to capture additional variation).

The main specification of Miguel et al. (2004) is the following:

$$growth_{it} = a_{1i} + X_{it}b_1 + c_{1,0}\Delta R_{it} + c_{1,1}\Delta R_{i,t-1} + d_{1i}year_t + e_{1it}.$$

The main results indicate that current and lagged rainfall growth are both significantly related to income growth. The story behind these results is that positive rainfall growth typically leads to better agricultural production since most of sub-Saharan Africa lies within the semiarid tropics and is prone to drought.

Results for the reduced-form equation estimate the effect of rainfall growth on civil conflict. Higher levels of rainfall are associated with significantly less conflict in the reduced-form regression for all civil conflicts. This indicates that better rainfall makes civil conflict less likely in Africa.

A second-stage equation estimates the impact of income growth on the incidence of violence:

$$conflict_{it} = \alpha_{2i} + X_{it}\beta_2 + \gamma_{2,0}growth_{it} + \gamma_{2,1}growth_{it-1} + \delta_{2i}year_t + \varepsilon_{2it}.$$

One way of looking at the endogeneity problem is to run an instrumental variable estimation for civil wars, disregarding the fact that this is a 0–1 variable that is an IV–two-stage least square (2SLS). Angrist (1991) shows that if we ignore the fact that the dependent variable is dichotomous and use the instrumental variables approach, the estimates are very close to the average treatment effect obtained using a bivariate probit model. Moreover, following Angrist and Krueger (2001), the IV-2SLS method is typically preferred even in cases in which the dependent variable is dichotomous.

The main results of the ordinary least squares (OLS) and Probit analyses indicate that that lagged economic growth rates are negatively but not statistically significantly correlated with the incidence of civil war with country controls. However, the IV results indicate that lagged economic growth has a negative and statistically significant effect on the incidence of civil war (using the definition of more than 25 deaths per year). Moreover, contemporaneous economic growth has also a negative and statistically significant effect on the incidence of civil war (more than 1,000 deaths per year).

Let us now provide some discussion on the exclusion restriction, which Miguel et al. (2004) raised in their article:

> While it is intuitive that rainfall instrument is exogenous, it must also satisfy the exclusion restriction: Whether shocks should affect civil conflict only through economic growth.

> Can we think of a possible channel through which rainfall shocks affect conflict apart from economic growth? It could be that high levels of rainfall might directly affect civil conflict independently of economic conditions. For example, floods may destroy roads and then make it more costly for government troops to contain rebellion. Since in the reduced form we observe that higher levels of rainfall are empirically associated with less conflict, then we should not worry too much about this possibility. (p. 745)

Also, it could be that rainfall may make it more difficult for both government and rebel forces to engage each other in combat and to achieve the threshold number of deaths that constitutes a conflict. To explore this possibility, they estimate the impact of rainfall shocks on the extent of the usable road network and do not find a statistically significant relationship.

In the main conclusions of their article, Miguel et al. (2004) argue that the results support previous findings on the literature, particularly the results of Collier and Hoeffler (2004) and Fearon and Laitin (2003), who argue that economic variables are often more important determinants of civil wars than measures of grievances. "Collier and Hoeffler stress the gap between returns from taking arms relative to those from conventional economic activities, such as farming, as the causal mechanism linking low income to the probability of civil war. Fearon and Laitin argue that individual opportunity cost matters less than state military strength and road coverage. They argue that low national income leads to weaker militaries and worse infrastructure and thus make it difficult for poor governments to repress insurgencies" (Miguel et al., 2004, p. 728). Miguel et al. argue that the results are consistent with both explanations, and they view the opportunity cost and the repressive state capacity as complementary rather than competing explanations.

However, the analysis by Miguel et al. (2004) is on shocks, changes of per capita income on conflict, not on the relationship between poverty (level) and civil war. Djankov and Reynal-Querol (in press) address the relationship between poverty and civil war. They find that their correlation is spurious and is accounted for by historical phenomena that jointly determine income evolution and conflict in the post–World War II era. In particular, the statistical association between poverty, as proxied by income per capita, and civil wars disappears once we include country fixed effects. Also, using cross-sectional data for 1960–2000, they find that once historical variables such as European settler mortality rates, population density in the year 1500, and European settlement in 1900 are included in the civil war regressions, poverty does not have an effect on civil wars. These results are confirmed using longer time series for 1825 to 2000. The results are in line with Krueger and Malecková (2003), who provide evidence that any relationship between poverty and terrorism is indirect. Abadie (2006) also shows that terrorist risk is not significantly higher in poorer countries once the effect of other country-specific characteristics, such as the level of political freedom, is taken into account.

These results can be consistent with Miguel et al. (2004), who find that sudden changes in income growth affect the probability of conflict. They analyze the effect of one component of income growth, transitory shocks caused by the change in rainfall. One can imagine a situation where a sudden (and exogenous) hit in consumption drives people to violence. Once various such effects cumulate to increase or reduce the level of income, the effect on civil war seems to disappear. The relationship is similar to the relationship between income and democracy, as well as economic growth and democracy. Acemoglu and Robinson (2001), for example, emphasize that regime changes are more likely during recessionary periods because the costs of political turmoil, both to the rich and to the poor, are lower during such episodes. This is analogous to the results of Miguel et al. However, Acemoglu and Robinson also find that "holding inequality and other parameters constant, rich countries are not more likely to be democratic than poor ones" (p. 949). This is analogous to the result in Djankov and Reynal-Querol (in press).

In Djankov and Reynal-Querol's (in press) recent study, the explanatory variables follow the basic specifications of the literature on civil war, particularly Collier and Hoeffler (2004) and Fearon and Laitin (2003). Collier and Hoeffler consider population size an additional proxy for the benefits of a rebellion since it measures potential labor income taxation. Fearon and Laitin indicate that a large population implies difficulties in controlling what goes on at the local level and increases the number of potential rebels that can be recruited by the insurgents.

The basic specification used in Djankov and Reynal-Querol (in press) is therefore

$$cw_{it} = \alpha ly_{i(t-1)} + \beta lpop_{i(t-1)} + X'_{i(t-1)}\gamma + \delta_t + \lambda_i + \varepsilon_{it},$$

where cw_{ti} is a dummy that has a value of 1 if there is a civil war in the country and zero otherwise, $ly_{i(t-1)}$ is the lagged value of the natural log of per capita income, $lpop_{i(t-1)}$ is the lagged value of the log of population, X is a vector of all other potential covariates, and δ_t denotes the full set of time effects that capture common shocks or trends to the civil wars of all countries. They include a full set of country dummies in λ_i. Finally, ε_{it} is an error term.

The standard regression in the literature (see previous section) usually omits country fixed effects (λ_i). In this context, these dummies capture any time-invariant country characteristics that affect the probability of civil war. This is important in the study of the relationship between per capita income and civil war, as some determinants that affect the condition for conflict may at the same time be the condition for economic development.

Djankov and Reynal-Querol (in press) first replicate the results reported in the previous literature. They perform a pooled OLS estimation of the effect of per capita income

on the incidence and onset of civil war, using panel data from 1960 to 2000. They use three definitions of civil war. First, they use the definition of the incidence of civil war, which corresponds to more than 25 battle-related deaths per year; the definition of the onset of civil war from the Armed Conflict Dataset, which corresponds to more than 1,000 battle-related deaths in at least one year; and the 1,000-death threshold for the definition of the incidence of civil wars. All regressions include time dummies, and all have robust standard errors clustered at the country level. The results are in line with the literature and show that per capita income has a negative and significant effect on the probability of civil war, whether they use the incidence variable or the onset variable. Also, the results are robust to the use of different thresholds for the definition of civil wars. Then they perform the same analysis but control for time-invariant country-specific variables. Results show that the relationship between per capita income and civil war disappears once fixed country effects are included.

The results using fixed country effects indicate that the relationship between income and civil war is possibly spurious. It is likely that the colonization strategies brought by Europeans were important determinants for the economic development and political stability paths taken by colonies. Using a cross section of countries from 1960 to 2000, they show that while the effect of per capita income on civil war is robust to the inclusion of some contemporaneous variables, its effect disappears once they include historical variables that capture colonization strategies. In the cross-sectional specification, the dependent variable is a dummy that has a value of 1 if the country suffered a civil war during 1960 to 2000 and zero otherwise. In order to reduce the endogeneity problems between per capita income and civil war, the independent variables are taken at the beginning of the period. The specification is

$$cw_{i60-00} = \alpha + \beta_1 \lg dp_{i60} + \beta_2 lpop_{i60} + X'_{i60}\phi + \varepsilon_i,$$

where cw is a dummy variable that has a value of 1 if the country had a civil war during 1960 to 2000 and zero otherwise, α is a constant, $\lg dp$ is the log of real per capita income in 1960, $lpop$ is the log of the population of the country in 1960, and X is a set of covariates, some of which are time invariant. All regressions have robust standard errors.

All these results indicate that the correlation between poverty and civil war could be accounted for by historical phenomena that jointly determine income evolution and conflict in the post–World War II era. A plausible explanation for the results found in the literature is that some determinants favor both economic development and peaceful negotiations, which are absent in the traditional specification. If this is the case, then OECD countries are peaceful not because they are rich but because historically they have benefited from circumstances that have favored negotiated settlements and economic development at the same time.

The historical variable could be a proxy of this historical phenomenon that jointly determines the income and conflict path of countries. In another study, explained below, Djankov and Reynal-Querol (2007) propose that institutions, determined by historical variables, could be the channel that determines the path that countries follow.

Poverty, Institutions, and Civil War

To date, very few and recent studies in economics link economic development, institutions, and civil wars. Djankov and Reynal-Querol (2007) investigate whether the quality of economic institutions has played a role in sustaining peace. In particular, they test the hypothesis that when governments cannot enforce the law and protect property rights, conflict emerges. The idea that strong institutions prevent conflict derives from the theoretical literature of conflict: Haavelmo (1954), Grossman (1994; Grossman & Kim, 1996), Skaperdas (1992, 1996), Garfinkel (1990), and Hirshleifer (1995), among others. The Djankov and Reynal-Querol (2007) study is also related to the extensive empirical literature that has investigated the role of institutions in development that shows a positive relationship between institutions and various proxies for development. Their empirical approach is closely related to this literature. The common idea in the literature is that some historical roots are based on the European influence during colonization that explain institutional development and have nothing to do with contemporaneous factors—in our case, civil wars. They follow the work of Acemoglu et al. (2001), who propose a theory of institutional differences among countries colonized by Europeans, based on the role of settler mortality in shaping local institutions. Consistent with Acemoglu et al., they also study institutional differences between British colonies and colonies from the other major imperial powers (France, Spain, and Portugal).

The results indicate that a lack of secure property rights and law enforcement is a fundamental cause of civil war. Moreover, once institutions are included in the regression analysis, income does not have any direct effect on civil war. This suggests that the direct effect of per capita income found in previous literature may have simply captured the effect of institutions.

Recently, Besley and Persson (2008) have provided a theoretical and empirical framework for the study of the causes of conflict. The aim of this study is to develop a theoretical model on the economic and institutional determinants of civil war and to use this model to interpret the evidence on the prevalence of civil conflict across countries and its incidence within countries over time. This work is a first step along an iterative path where the development of theory and empirical work in this area is joined together. The main empirical contribution of this study is that it looks at the incidence of conflict, controlling for unobserved causes behind the uneven incidence of civil war across countries and time by fixed country effects and fixed year effects. One of the main results of this study is that country-specific price indices constructed for agricultural products, minerals, and oils have considerable explanatory power in predicting the within-country variation of conflict. Preliminary results indicate that higher prices of exported commodities raise the probability of observing conflict. The same result is found for a higher process of imported commodities. This seems to depend on the institutional framework of the country.

Besley and Persson (2008) build a model that serves as a useful guide for how observable economic and political factors determine the probability of violent domestic conflict. This model gives a transparent set of predictions on how parameters of the economy and the polity affect the incidence and severity of conflict.

Besley and Persson (2008) develop a simple microfounded model to illustrate how prices of importable and exportable commodities affect wages and natural resource rents and hence the incidence of civil war over time. The story is as follows: A higher price of the imported raw material lowers the wage, which raises rents in the export sector and hence the prize for winning conflict. The lower wage also has a direct positive effect on the probability of observing conflict by lowering the opportunity cost of fighting and hence conflict. The economic intuition behind these results is that higher prices for exported commodities have a direct effect on civil war by increasing rents. The effect of higher imported commodity prices comes from the fact that they reduce the demand for labor in the importable sector and hence put downward pressure on the wage.

This study also estimates panel regressions with a binary civil war indicator as the dependent variable and with fixed country effects. In this way, the analysis can identify the effect of resource rents and real income on the incidence of civil war exclusively from the within-country variation of these variables. This is in contrast to the existing empirical literature that does not usually include country fixed effects.

Besley and Persson (2008) wish to exploit changes in commodity prices in world markets to generate exogenous time variation in resource rents and real incomes. They construct country-specific export price and import price indices. Given the prediction of the model, they interpret a higher export price index as a positive shock to natural resource rents, as well as a higher import price index as a negative shock to income. The empirical results indicate that both export and import indices for agricultural and mineral products are positively and significantly correlated with the incidence of civil war. They also show that the effects of the world market process are heterogeneous, depending on whether a country is a parliamentary democracy or has a system of strong checks and balances.

Ethnic Diversity and Civil War

As we explain above, the literature on the study of the relationship between ethnic diversity and conflict uses ethnic fractionalization measures to capture the effect of ethnic grievances on civil war. The findings are that ethnic diversity has no effect on civil war (using ethnic fractionalization measures).

Several authors have stressed the importance of ethnic heterogeneity in the explanation of growth, investment, and the efficiency of government for civil wars. Easterly and Levine (1997) find empirical evidence to support their claim that the very high level of ethnic diversity of countries in Africa explains a large part of their poor economic performance. Several authors have interpreted the finding of a negative relationship between ethnic diversity and growth as being a consequence of the high probability of conflict associated with a highly fractionalized society. For this reason, many studies use ELF as the indicator of ethnic heterogeneity. The raw data for this index come from the *Atlas Narodov Mira* (Bruck & Apenchenko, 1964) compiled in the former Soviet Union in 1960. The ELF index was originally calculated by Taylor and Hudson (1972). In general, any index of fractionalization can be written as

$$FRAG = 1 - \sum_{i=1}^{N} \pi_i^2,$$

where π_i is the proportion of people who belong to the ethnic (religious) group i, and N is the number of groups. The index of ethnic fractionalization has a simple interpretation as the probability that two randomly selected individuals from a given country will not belong to the same ethnic group.

However, many authors have found that, even though ethnic fractionalization seems to be a powerful explanatory variable for economic growth, it is not significant in the explanation of civil wars and other kinds of conflicts. These results have led many authors to disregard ethnicity as a source of conflict and civil wars. Fearon and Laitin (2003) and Collier and Hoeffler (2004) find that neither ethnic fractionalization nor religious fractionalization has any statistically significant effect on the probability of civil wars.

However, it is not clear to what extent an index of diversity could capture potential ethnic conflict. In principle, claiming a positive relationship between an index of fractionalization and conflict implies that the more ethnic groups there are, the higher is the probability of a conflict. Many authors would dispute such an argument. Horowitz (1985), who is the seminal reference on the issue of ethnic groups in conflict, argues that the relationship between ethnic diversity and civil wars is not monotonic: There is less violence in highly homogeneous and highly heterogeneous societies and more conflicts in societies where a large ethnic minority faces an ethnic majority. If this is so, then an index of polarization should better capture the likelihood of conflicts or the intensity of potential conflict than an index of fractionalization.

Montalvo and Reynal-Querol (2005) argue that one possible reason for the lack of explanatory power of ethnic heterogeneity on the probability of armed conflicts and civil wars is the measure for heterogeneity. In empirical applications, researchers should consider a measure of ethnic polarization, the concept used in most of the theoretical arguments, instead of an index of ethnic fractionalization.

$$\text{Polarization} = RQ = 1 - \sum_{i=1}^{N} \left(\frac{0.5 - \pi_i}{0.5} \right)^2 \pi_i$$

The original purpose of this index, constructed by Reynal-Querol (2002), was to capture how far the distribution of the ethnic groups is from the $(1/2, 0,0, \ldots 0,1/2)$ distribution (bipolar), which represents the highest level of polarization. This type of reasoning is frequently present in the literature on conflict. Montalvo and Reynal-Querol (2005) show how to obtain the RQ index from a pure contest model, particularly on ethnic conflict. Esteban and Ray (1999) show, using a behavioral model and rather a general metric of preferences, that a two-point symmetric distribution of population maximizes conflict.

Montalvo and Reynal-Querol (2005) analyze the empirical support for the link between ethnicity and conflict. They pursue this objective by reexamining the evidence on the causes of civil wars using alternative indices to measure ethnic diversity. The empirical section of this article shows that the index of ethnic polarization is a significant explanatory variable for the incidence of civil wars. This result is robust to the use of other proxies for ethnic heterogeneity, alternative sources of data, and the use of a cross section instead of panel data. Therefore, it seems that the weak explanatory power of ethnic heterogeneity on the incidence of civil wars found by several recent studies is due to the use of an index of fractionalization instead of an index of polarization.

Montalvo and Reynal-Querol (2005) estimate a logit model for the incidence of civil wars as a function of polarization and fractionalization measures of ethnic and religious heterogeneity. The sample includes 138 countries from 1960 to 1999 and is divided into 5-year periods. The endogenous variable is the incidence of a civil war. The data on civil wars come from the PRIO data set, particularly the definition of intermediate and high-intensity civil wars of PRIO.

In the empirical analysis, the explanatory variables for the core specification of the incidence of civil wars include the log of real GDP per capita in the initial year (LGDPC), the log of the population at the beginning of the period (LPOP), primary exports (PRMEXP), mountains (MOUNTAINS), noncontiguous states (NONCONT), and the level of democracy (DEMOCRACY).

Results show that the index of ethnolinguistic fractionalization (ETHFRAC) has no statistically significant effect on the incidence of civil wars, following the results of the previous literature. This result is consistent with Fearon and Laitin (2003) and Collier and Hoeffler (2004). However, once they substitute the index of ethnic fractionalization with the RQ index of ethnic polarization, ETHPOL, they find a positive and statistically significant effect on the incidence of civil wars. These results are robust to the inclusion of alternative measures of heterogeneity such as ethnic dominance or a large ethnic minority. Besides the indices of fractionalization and polarization, the literature has proposed some other indicators of potential ethnic conflict. Collier (2001) notices that ethnic diversity could not only be an impediment for coordination but also an incitement to victimization. Dominance, or one ethnic group in the majority, can produce victimization and therefore increase the risk of a civil war. Therefore, the effect of ethnic diversity will be conditional on being measured as dominance or fractionalization. In principle, fractionalization should make coordination more difficult and, therefore, civil wars will be less probable since it will be difficult to maintain cohesion among rebels. The empirical results reported by Collier seem to indicate that a good operational definition of dominance implies a group that represents between 45% and 90% of the population. However, Collier and Hoeffler (2004) find that dominance, defined as mentioned above, has only a weak positive effect on the incidence of civil wars. When ethnic dominance is included with the RQ index, its coefficient is not significant, while ethnic polarization continues being a significant explanatory variable on the probability of civil wars. Caselli and Coleman (2006) propose another indicator, which is the product of the largest ethnic group (ETHLRG) by primary exports (PRIMEXP). This variable has a coefficient that is not significantly different from zero. The index of polarization is significant even when the product of the largest ethnic group by primary exports is included as an explanatory variable. Finally, the article could also have included the size of the largest minority (LARGMINOR) as another way to proxy polarization. The coefficient of this new variable is not statistically significant, while ethnic polarization continues to be significant even in the presence of this new variable.

The results of Montalvo and Reynal-Querol (2005) are robust to including dummy variables for the different regions of the world. They are also robust to the elimination of regions that are considered especially conflictive, the use of different operational definitions of civil war, the use of alternative data sources to construct ethnic polarization, and the use of cross-sectional samples. Given the nature of the ethnic measures, which are time invariant, they perform regressions in a cross section. In this case, the dependent variable now takes the value of 1 if a country has suffered a civil war during the whole sample period (1960–1999) and zero otherwise.

Future Development

The study of the economic causes of civil war is still in its early stages. The main studies have been from a macroeconomic perspective, and more has to be done to understand the mechanisms that explain why, for example, income shocks affect conflict. This line of research is little explored, but Dube and Vargas (2008) have taken an important step in this direction in a recent manuscript titled *Commodity Price Shocks and Civil Conflict: Evidence From Colombia*. They try to answer how income shocks affect armed conflict. This article exploits exogenous price shocks in international commodity markets and a rich data set on civil war in Colombia to assess how different income shocks affect conflict. Also, more research needs to be done on the institutional and social mechanism and its interaction with economic shocks that are related to violence.

References and Further Readings

Abadie, A. (2006). Poverty, political freedom, and the roots of terrorism. *American Economic Review Papers and Proceedings, 96*(2), 50–56.

Acemoglu, D., Johnson, S., & Robinson, J. A. (2001). The colonial origins of comparative development: An empirical investigation. *American Economic Review, 91,* 1369–1401.

Acemoglu, D., & Robinson, J. (2001). A theory of political transition. *American Economic Review, 91,* 938–963.

Angrist, J. D. (1991). *Instrumental variables estimation of average treatment effects in econometrics and epidemiology* (NBER 0115). Cambridge, MA: National Bureau of Economic Research.

Angrist, J. D., & Krueger, A. B. (2001). Instrumental variable and the search for identification: From supply and demand to natural experiments. *Journal of Economic Perspectives, 15,* 69–85.

Besley, T., & Persson, T. (2008). *The incidence of civil war: Theory and evidence* (NBER Working Paper 14585). Cambridge, MA: National Bureau of Economic Research.

Bruck, S. I., & Apenchenko, V. S. (Eds.). (1964). *Atlas Narodov Mira* [Atlas of the people of the world]. Moscow: Glavnoe Upravlenie Geodezii i Kartografii,

Caselli, F., & Coleman, W. J., II. (2006). *On the theory of ethnic conflict* (NBER Working Paper 12125). Cambridge, MA: National Bureau of Economic Research.

Collier, P. (2001). Implications of ethnic diversity. *Economic Policy, 16,* 127–166.

Collier, P., & Hoeffler, A. (2004). Greed and grievances in civil wars. *Oxford Economic Papers, 56,* 563–595.

Djankov, S., & Reynal-Querol, M. (2007). *The causes of civil war* (World Bank Policy Research Working Paper No. 4254). Washington, DC: World Bank.

Djankov, S., & Reynal-Querol, M. (in press). Poverty and civil war: Revisiting the evidence. *Review of Economics and Statistics.*

Dube, O., & Vargas, J. (2008). *Commodity price shocks and civil conflict: Evidence from Colombia.* Unpublished manuscript, Harvard University, Cambridge, MA.

Easterly, W., & Levine, R. (1997). Africa's growth tragedy: Policies and ethnic divisions. *Quarterly Journal of Economics, 112,* 1203–1250.

Esteban, J., & Ray, D. (1999). Conflict and distribution. *Journal of Economic Theory, 87,* 379–415.

Fearon, J., & Laitin, D. (2003). Ethnicity, insurgency, and civil war. *American Political Science Review, 97,* 75–90.

Garfinkel, M. R. (1990). Arming as a strategic investment in a cooperative equilibrium. *American Economic Review, 80,* 50–68.

Garfinkel, M. R., & Skaperdas, S. (2007). Economics of conflict: An overview. In T. Sandler & K. Hartley (Eds.), *Handbook of defense economics* (Vol. II, pp. 649–709). Amsterdam: North-Holland.

Grossman, H. I. (1994). Production, appropriation, and land reform. *American Economic Review, 84,* 705–712.

Grossman, H. I., & Kim, M. (1996). Predation and accumulation. *Journal of Economic Growth, 1,* 333–351.

Haavelmo, T. (1954). *A study in the theory of economic evolution.* Amsterdam: North-Holland.

Hirshleifer, J. (1989). Conflict and rent-seeking success functions: Ratio vs. difference models of relative success. *Public Choice, 63,* 101–112.

Hirshleifer, J. (1991). The paradox of power. *Economics and Politics, 3,* 177–200.

Hirshleifer, J. (1995). Anarchy and its breakdown. *Journal of Political Economy, 103,* 26–52.

Horowitz, D. (1985). *Ethnic groups in conflict.* Berkeley: University of California Press.

Keen, D. (1998). *The economic functions of violence in civil wars* (Adelphi Paper 320). London: International Institute of Strategic Studies.

Krueger, A., & Malecková, J. (2003). Education, poverty and terrorism: Is there a causal connection? *Journal of Economic Perspectives, 17,* 119–144.

Le Billon, P. (2001). The political ecology of war: Natural resources and armed conflicts. *Political Geography, 29,* 561–584.

Miguel, E., Satyanath, S., & Sergenti, E. (2004). Economic shocks and civil conflicts: An instrumental variables approach. *Journal of Political Economy, 112,* 725–753.

Montalvo, J. G., & Reynal-Querol, M. (2005). Ethnic polarization, potential conflict, and civil wars. *American Economic Review, 95,* 796–816.

Reynal-Querol, M. (2002). Ethnicity, political systems and civil war. *Journal of Conflict Resolution, 46,* 29–54.

Ross, M. (2002). *Natural resources and civil war: An overview with some policy options.* Retrieved from http://siteresources.worldbank.org/INTCPR/1091081-1115626319273/20482496/Ross.pdf

Skaperdas, S. (1992). Cooperation, conflict, and power in the absence of property rights. *American Economic Review, 82,* 720–739.

Skaperdas, S. (1996). Contest success functions. *Economic Theory, 7,* 282–290.

Taylor, C., & Hudson, M. C. (1972). *The world handbook of political and social indicators* (2nd ed.). New Haven, CT: Yale University Press.

80

Economic Aspects of Cultural Heritage

Leah Greden Mathews

University of North Carolina at Asheville

Cultural heritage is universal in that every culture has a heritage, but that heritage is unique to each culture or community. A building that may be slated for replacement in one region because it is mundane or out of date may be revered in another due to the cultural meaning attached to the building's heritage. As a result, different preferences for cultural goods arise from the differences in culture. In addition, one rarely hears that we have "too much" cultural heritage; more heritage is universally desired, but protecting and creating cultural heritage is costly. Thus, there are many reasons for the study of the economics aspects of cultural heritage, including a desire to study the values that people have for cultural heritage as well as to inform the efficient management of cultural heritage assets.

The economics of cultural heritage is, like many applied economic fields, the result of the application of microeconomic and macroeconomic concepts to the study of a particular facet of our lives, cultural heritage. Cultural heritage has both tangible and intangible aspects, and thus the economics of cultural heritage invokes methodologies used to study both market and nonmarket goods and services.

This chapter begins with a definition of cultural heritage and discussion of the scope of the economics of cultural heritage and next provides an overview of the primary theoretical issues addressed by the economics of cultural heritage. The chapter then moves to discuss empirical examples and applications and policy implications. The fifth section offers emerging trends in the economics of cultural heritage and identifies gaps in the literature where opportunities for significant contributions to the economics of cultural heritage

exist for twenty-first-century researchers. The final section offers a summary.

What Is the Economics of Cultural Heritage?

Definition

Cultural heritage includes stories, collections, and other artifacts that are used to define and convey the specific attributes of a culture. Thus, cultural heritage is the set of tangible and intangible assets that help to uniquely define a community or nation. Vaughan (1984) indicated that a nation's cultural heritage included three distinct types: the artistic, the natural, and the historical. Some heritage assets are constructed; these include architecture, archaeological sites, and monuments, which are tangible assets, as well as cultural goods such as art, songs, dance, and stories that may be intangible or ephemeral. In addition, some heritage assets are natural assets such as trees imbued with cultural meaning such as the California redwoods; these assets would exist without human intervention, but the values assigned to them are humanly constructed and help to define a culture. Thus, we may think of a country's or region's cultural heritage as a type of capital asset that includes both natural (trees or landscapes) and built assets (monuments or archaeological sites), some of which are tangible (buildings) and some of which are intangible (customs).

A significant challenge exists for those studying the economics of cultural heritage since the definition of cultural heritage not only is broad but also likely includes distinctly subjective elements. As a result of the diversity of heritage assets and the fact that they are, by definition, uniquely defined for each region, the methodologies used to study the economics of cultural heritage are also diverse.

The Scope of the Economics of Cultural Heritage

The economics of cultural heritage is often situated as a theme in the cultural economics subdiscipline, which includes the study of cultural industries such as the art and music markets and the consumption and production of cultural goods such as film, art, music, and books. Both cultural economics and the economics of cultural heritage investigate the role of government in the provision of cultural assets, including the study of subsidy, tax, and other policies in the provision or protection of these assets. The economics of cultural heritage also has many overlaps with the environmental and natural resource economics literature due to the nature of the assets being studied (unique, place based), the methodologies used to study them (nonmarket valuation), and the shared characteristics of public goods and externalities that motivate a role for government intervention in both cases.

Outside of economics, the economics of cultural heritage has several important links to sociology and anthropology, especially the sociology of art, which studies how cultures create value. Due to the fact that many cultural heritage sites are historic in nature, the economics of cultural heritage rubs elbows with the fields of history and historic preservation, architecture, and urban planning. And because many heritage sites are tourist attractions, the economics of cultural heritage also often finds itself aligned with tourism studies.

Theory

Throsby (1997) provides an excellent overview of the core concerns in the economics of cultural heritage. At its most basic level, the first step for any study in the economics of cultural heritage is to clearly define the good that is being studied. In the case of cultural heritage, this is less straightforward than in many other applied economic fields. Once defined, the central theoretical concern in the economics of cultural heritage is clearly the question of the value of cultural heritage. Because of the public goods nature of cultural heritage assets, the role of government intervention is an important theme as well. To study these elements, researchers in the economics of cultural heritage apply several different theoretical constructs from economics.

The Nature of Cultural Heritage

Public Goods

Many cultural heritage assets have been identified as having the public good characteristics of nonexclusion and shared consumption. Nonexclusion implies that it is difficult if not impossible to exclude nonpayers from enjoying the benefits of the good. In the case of many monuments and buildings with architectural elements relevant to cultural heritage, it is clear that nonexclusion applies. Shared consumption means that multiple consumers can enjoy the same good simultaneously without reducing the benefit to any one individual. This, too, is relevant for some cultural heritage assets as many consumers can enjoy viewing the exterior façade of the Cathedral of Notre Dame or an archaeological site at the same time.

The economics of market failure tells us that due to the rational free-riding behavior of consumers when public goods are present, these goods will not be provided in socially optimal levels by markets. It is this market underprovision that invokes a potential role for the government provision of public goods. The appropriate role of government in the provision and protection of cultural heritage is thus a key topic for the economics of cultural heritage. Questions regarding whether the destruction of cultural heritage assets should be regulated are studied by cultural heritage economists, as is the determination of the socially optimal amount of investment in a region or nation's cultural heritage assets. Once government has invested in cultural heritage assets as theory predicts, another question for the economics of cultural heritage is whether that investment actually provides social benefits that outweigh the costs of the protection.

Externalities

Externalities are said to exist when economic actors other than those directly involved in the market transaction are affected by the production or consumption of the good. Second-hand smoke is a classic example of a negative externality since innocent bystanders are negatively affected from the actions of the smoker. When negative externalities are present, market outcomes are not efficient since the market provides more than the socially optimal amount of the good. Positive externalities also exist when bystanders receive benefits from the actions of others. When positive externalities are present, the market will provide less than the socially optimal amount of good.

There are many cases where positive externalities exist with cultural heritage assets. One example can be found in the protection of architectural elements in historic districts that lead to the increased prices of neighboring properties. Similarly, if an individual has protected an old mill or barn from destruction by maintaining the property on his or her own land, the entire community will benefit from that protection since the cultural heritage asset is being maintained as a visual reminder of the historic, symbolic, and perhaps aesthetic values of regional culture.

Many cultural heritage assets are provided by private parties, of course. Private parties regularly maintain cultural heritage sites such as cemeteries without the assistance of government intervention. And in addition to fine examples of architectural heritage that may be owned by private individuals, Native American rock drawings and burial grounds may be found on what is now private property, due to the history of land transfers. The protection of those assets may be optimal for the collective good, but private individuals will tend to under invest in their protection given the nature of externalities. As a result, the inventory of cultural heritage assets may decline over time.

Government intervention in markets where externalities are present comes in many forms. One form of government intervention is the regulation of activities that promote positive externalities or discourage negative externalities. In the instance of cultural heritage, governments regulate historic districts and prohibit the destruction, sale, or commercial use of certain kinds of cultural artifacts. However, it is difficult to regulate cultural heritage if governments are not aware of the assets, as is sometimes the case when the heritage assets are completely contained on private property.

Another form of government intervention in markets with externalities is to use fiscal policy to encourage (or discourage in the case of negative externalities) the activities. Subsidies for some historic preservation work exist in the form of government grants, and tax credits are granted for renovations and protection work in federally designated historic districts.

The Value of Cultural Heritage

By far and away the most central concern of the economics of cultural heritage has been the study of the value of cultural heritage. The treatment of value in economics has an interesting evolution, as succinctly described by Throsby (2001, pp. 20–23). A good's market price is typically considered the most effective indicator of economic value that we can identify. The so-called paradox of value, which questions why diamonds, a nonessential luxury, are more expensive than water, a necessity, points to an important caution for relying on market prices as indicators of value. It is clear that for many goods, values other than economic value are not likely to be reflected in market prices; these include cultural values. As a result, a student of the economics of cultural heritage must recognize that market prices cannot directly measure the total value of a cultural heritage asset.

A holistic measure of the value of a cultural heritage asset would include all elements of its cultural value— that is, its historic, aesthetic, spiritual, social, symbolic, and authenticity values (Throsby, 2001) in addition to its economic value. The *historic values* associated with a cultural heritage asset may be readily conveyed by its mere existence, which provides a direct connection with a community or individual's past. For example, singing songs that are traditional to one's culture provides a tangible link to earlier members of one's community, even though the asset itself is intangible. This connection will create historical value. *Authenticity values* are generated when a cultural heritage asset is a genuine artifact of the culture; the value associated

with this authenticity is distinct from the other cultural values that may be associated with the asset. Communities may derive *aesthetic values* from a cultural heritage asset due to its beauty or design or the placement of the heritage asset in the landscape, such as the façade of a cathedral or the arrangement of boulders at Stonehenge. Some cultural heritage assets may take on *symbolic* or even *iconic values,* such as the cedar tree in Lebanon that adorns their flag. The cedar tree is not just a tree for the Lebanese but rather a cultural symbol of strength and longevity. *Spiritual values* may be derived from cultural heritage assets such as cathedrals and churches whose sites invoke connection to one's spiritual identity or connectedness with other members of the same spiritual community. The aspects of culture that are defined by shared values and beliefs will generate *social values* for communities and provide a sense of connection with others in the community.

Other types of values may be assigned to cultural heritage assets as well. Borrowing from the literature in natural resource and environmental valuation, *bequest values* are those values that we hold for assets merely because we wish to be able to pass them on to our heirs. Cultural heritage assets may generate significant bequest values due to their historic, symbolic, and authenticity values.

Markets are not likely helpful in determining these cultural values for two reasons. The first reason is that many heritage assets are not exchanged in markets, and thus market prices do not exist that might serve to proxy or provide a fractional estimate of the total value of a cultural heritage asset. The second reason is that even when there is a market for cultural heritage asset (or an attribute of it), the market price will likely not reflect the cultural value assigned to that asset due to the nature of cultural heritage assets as public goods and/or those exhibiting positive externalities. As a result, nonmarket valuation techniques such as contingent valuation are frequently used in the economics of cultural heritage. Later in the chapter, we'll see that some methods will be incapable of measuring the cultural values of heritage sites, which has implications for the empirical work in the economics of cultural heritage.

The previous discussion has implied that economic values are likely less than the total value of a cultural heritage asset that includes its cultural values. The relative weight of economic and cultural values in total value is an empirical question, although it is likely to vary by type of cultural heritage asset. It may be that for many cultural heritage assets, the economic (market) value of a particular heritage asset is low, while the cultural heritage values are high. For example, an old industrial site may have great cultural value for its ability to tangibly depict the historical importance of a particular manufacturing technique or way of life, but it may have a very low property value.

One might ask whether it is appropriate to concern ourselves with the individual components of value, when the total value is what is effectively useful for the study of the economics of cultural heritage. Insofar as these values are unable to be represented in market prices, it is important to catalog them so that we can create a more holistic picture of the overarching or total value for the cultural heritage asset in question. This will be helpful for managers of heritage assets and policy makers who are determining the policies that provide support for such assets.

It may also be that by deconstructing the value of a cultural heritage asset into its composite elements and querying consumers about them, we can learn more about the importance of that asset while also learning about how and why consumers formulate preferences. The estimation of willingness to pay (WTP), discussed more thoroughly in the next section, is presumed to be a proxy for value, and it is hypothesized that the factors that influence WTP include the presence or absence of the cultural values described above. While neoclassical economics has traditionally been uninterested in the preference formation process, instead presuming that we have a well-defined set of preferences a priori, it is clear that additional knowledge about consumer preference formation will benefit the discipline as a whole. Models of consumer behavior, for example, would be enriched by including models of preference formation.

Cultural Heritage as a Capital Asset

Because cultural heritage is effectively a bundle of assets, the valuation of those assets is a core concern of the economics of cultural heritage. Learning how much citizens value historic monuments is one way of measuring the value of cultural heritage capital assets. Another is to ask how much they would be willing to pay to preserve those assets or to protect them from quality degradation. The answers to these questions are essential to understanding the amount of wealth that a nation has, how a citizen's quality of life is affected by the presence or absence of such assets, and the role of heritage assets in economic activities. In addition, a valuation of cultural heritage assets is an essential input into policy questions regarding the level of investment and regulation of cultural heritage assets.

As previously indicated, cultural heritage assets may be tangible or intangible, built or natural, permanent or ephemeral. This cultural heritage capital is thus uniquely differentiated from the physical capital, human capital, and natural capital that are typically studied by economists. However, there are similarities with other forms of capital, especially with regards to the decisions that are made that affect their quantity and quality. In theory, cultural heritage capital will continue to accumulate over time as a culture evolves, and we can encourage the accumulation of cultural capital to accelerate this growth. If this type of policy is pursued, the aggregate value of a region's cultural heritage assets will increase over time.

However, some forms of cultural heritage capital (monuments, architecture) must also be maintained to ensure that the asset does not deteriorate over time. Of course, it is likely that the condition of the heritage capital will determine

some or all of the values that people hold for those assets, a testable hypothesis for researchers in the economics of cultural heritage. If a historic barn or church is left to disintegrate into the landscape, then eventually there may be no remnants of the site that induce cultural value. As a result, assessing the condition of heritage capital, as well as the change in that condition, is required just as it is essential to measure depreciation for other capital assets. The decisions regarding the accumulation, maintenance, and deterioration of cultural heritage capital assets are shared by individuals and government, as described in the previous section. Concerns about intergenerational equity are inherent in the management of cultural heritage assets since costs and benefits may not be evenly distributed across time or space.

Applications and Empirical Evidence

Valuation Studies

The value of cultural heritage can be estimated using several different methods. The appropriate choice of method will be determined by the type of cultural heritage asset that is to be valued such as whether it is fixed in a given geographic location, whether it draws visitors, whether it is tangible or intangible, and whether significant cultural values are believed to exist for the asset. This section will explore the diverse types of methods used to estimate the value of cultural heritage empirically and issues associated with this applied valuation work in the economics of cultural heritage.

The most frequently applied method for valuing cultural heritage has been the contingent valuation method (CVM). The CVM is a *nonmarket valuation technique,* a name given to the set of methodologies for valuing goods and services that are not exchanged in markets. Nonmarket valuation (NMV) techniques were developed to estimate the benefits associated with the attributes of the environment and natural resources that do not have market exchanges to determine price, such as clean air and water or recreation that is not marketed. The most common NMV technique, CVM, asks beneficiaries directly about their willingness to pay for a particular good or service. The method has been openly criticized because the method presumes a hypothetical, rather than actual, market and risks introducing biases without careful study design. The reliability of the CVM was thoroughly investigated by a National Oceanic and Atmospheric Administration (NOAA) panel, which concluded with a cautious stamp of approval for the use of CVM in natural resource damage assessment (NOAA, 1993). Since then, thousands of CVM studies have been used to estimate the value of natural resource and environmental amenities, due in part to the fact that it is a flexible method that can be applied to virtually any good or service. It is for this reason that CVM has been used in the estimation of cultural heritage values. CVM has been used to estimate many cultural heritage assets, including museum sites, cathedrals, the medina in Fes (Morocco), and monasteries, among others. Because of its inherent flexibility, the CVM has also been frequently used to estimate the value of additional protection or preservation for cultural heritage assets. Navrud and Ready (2002) provide a sampling of such studies.

Another nonmarket valuation method that can be used to estimate some of the values of cultural heritage assets is the travel cost method. The travel cost method (TCM) uses recreational trip costs as a proxy for site value, and thus it is only a relevant method for those heritage sites that generate recreational visitation. Because the travel cost method presumes that nonvisitors have no value for the site, it is a less than perfect method for many heritage sites that will be valued by individuals who do not actually visit them. One of the first studies to use the travel cost method to value a cultural heritage site was Poor and Smith (2004), who estimated the value of historic St. Mary's City of Maryland.

As in the environmental and natural resource literature, studies of the economics of cultural heritage have combined the travel cost and contingent valuation methods. The advantage of combining the two methods is that actual price information revealed in travel costs can serve to mitigate the hypothetical nature of the contingent valuation exercise. Alberini and Longo (2006) combined travel cost and contingent behavior methods to study the value of cultural heritage sites in Armenia.

Choice modeling is another nonmarket valuation method that has been used to estimate the value of cultural heritage as an element in the overall valuation of a heritage site. In a choice modeling study, respondents are asked to simultaneously value the various attributes of a good or service by selecting from various bundles of characteristics for the asset in question. For example, respondents could be asked about different scenarios for a particular heritage site that are defined by varying levels of protection for cultural sites, differing levels of monetary contribution, and varying levels of access to the heritage asset. Choice modeling has been used to investigate the value of aboriginal cultural heritage sites (Rolfe & Windle, 2003) and the heritage values associated with farmland in western North Carolina (Mathews & Bonham, 2008).

Because some cultural heritage values are likely to be embedded in property values, the hedonic price method has also been applied to uncover the value of cultural heritage. The hedonic price method examines market prices for a good such as housing as a function of its component characteristics, including both housing characteristics (number of bedrooms and bathrooms, etc.) and other characteristics, including attributes such as air quality and proximity to amenities, recreation sites, or heritage assets. Rosato, Rotaris, Breil, and Zanatta (2008) use the hedonic method to explore whether housing prices in the Veneto region of Italy vary due to proximity to built heritage sites such as historical palaces, fortresses, and religious buildings; the variation in housing prices represents a value of cultural heritage.

While several methods can be used to estimate the value of cultural heritage, each of them is imperfect. The limitations of the travel cost method dictate that it will underestimate cultural values by assuming that only site visitors have value for them. The hedonic method can capture the component of cultural value that may be embedded in property values, but it is likely that many cultural values that we hold for heritage sites are accruing to individuals who do not own property proximate to them, and thus the hedonic method, too, will provide an underestimate of the total value of cultural heritage. Choice models more closely mimic market transactions than the contingent valuation method, but they are challenging to design due to their complex nature and may be confusing for respondents to complete. The contingent valuation method is the only method that is likely to be able to capture the full value that we have for cultural heritage assets (economic + cultural values), which is likely why we have seen relatively more CVM conducted than any other method. Additional methodological advances in the valuation of cultural heritage, perhaps by strengthening the field's connection with environmental and natural resource economics, would help resolve some of the issues noted here.

The Economic Impact of Cultural Heritage

Most studies estimating the value of cultural heritage have investigated built sites such as monuments and historic buildings. Because these historic sites can attract visitors, and because those visitors expend scarce dollars to experience the heritage assets at the site that benefit communities in the form of sales and tax revenue, there have been many studies estimating their economic impact. The economic impact studies provide what might be considered a lower bound value for the sites since they cannot provide an accounting of the cultural values ascribed to the sites. However, it is likely that the cultural values that consumers hold for these sites are a factor in the demand for visits and thus an important underlying preference.

Until recently, most studies of the economics of cultural heritage were studies estimating the economic impact of tangible or built heritage assets such as monuments and architecture. A vast majority of these studies have been done outside the United States, in both Europe and developing countries. This may be because the portfolio of cultural heritage assets is richer for countries with longer histories than the United States or because the widespread public interest in those heritage assets provides a rationale for their study.

The role that cultural heritage plays in attracting tourists has led to several tourism studies of cultural heritage sites. These studies have implications for both their economic impact and the management of the sites themselves. Cuccia and Cellini (2007) examined the preferences of tourists visiting Scicli, a Sicilian town known for its baroque heritage, and found that cultural heritage was not among the most important reasons for visitors making their trip. Other studies have examined the behaviors of tourists at cultural heritage sites with the aim of providing recommendations for tourism management (de Menezes, Moniz, & Vieira, 2008; Kolar & Zabkar, 2007) and whether or not World Heritage Site listing increases tourism (Tisdell & Wilson, 2002).

In addition to studies estimating the economic impact of visitation to heritage sites, the economic impact of construction and maintenance expenditures for cultural heritage assets has been investigated. In the European Union, for example, it has been estimated that 50% of all construction activity is related to building restoration work (Cassar, 2000). Thus, the protection of cultural heritage assets can provide a significant contribution to a region's economy.

Cultural Heritage and Economic Development

The more general question of the relationship between cultural heritage and economic development is, as one might expect, also a concern for the economics of cultural heritage. For example, Murillo Viu, Romani Fernandez, and Surinach Caralt (2008) investigated the impact of the Alhambra on the economy of Grenada, Spain. Additional studies of heritage sites' role in economic development have been predominantly focused on developing countries, due in part to the role that institutions such as the World Bank have had in developing place-based economic development strategies that include protection of cultural heritage sites.

Policy Implications

Government Provision of Cultural Heritage

Because the public goods nature of cultural heritage will lead to the underprovision of heritage by markets, there is a motivation for the government provision of cultural heritage. Several studies have examined whether public support exists for additional government activities to protect cultural heritage. The outright, direct provision of cultural heritage is frequently pursued by governments as evidenced by the Smithsonian Institution in the United States and in national parks, monuments, and historic sites across the globe. An infrequently pursued but perfectly applicable empirical investigation for the economics of cultural heritage is cost-effectiveness analysis of these government investments in cultural heritage.

Government intervention is also prescribed if the provision of cultural heritage assets has spillover benefits (positive externalities) since the market will also tend to provide fewer heritage assets than would be optimal for society in this case. Governments frequently use subsidies and tax policy to promote private provision and/or preservation of heritage assets. In addition, regulation is frequently used by governments, despite the fact that it is often the economist's least favorite tool. Historic districts that restrict design and construction and even color of homes are commonly used to promote or ensure the provision of cultural heritage by private individuals.

Another interesting question that has been identified for the economics of cultural heritage is the question of who benefits from government investment in cultural heritage and who pays (Throsby, 1997). Social benefit-cost analyses of cultural heritage projects have not been widespread, although it is hypothesized that the benefits are not as well distributed as costs. While we might expect that everyone benefits equally from the existence of cultural heritage, since individuals with higher education and income levels are more likely to visit or otherwise consume certain types of cultural heritage, it is not clear that the distribution of costs and benefits is coincident. Additional studies on the distribution of the costs and benefits of providing cultural heritage will greatly enrich the field.

Emerging Opportunities in the Economics of Cultural Heritage

The economics of cultural heritage has up to now positioned itself as many other applied fields in economics, where conventional methodologies (economic impact analysis, nonmarket valuation techniques, welfare analysis) are applied to new settings. While the value of cultural heritage will likely continue to reign as the primary investigative theme for some time to come, several emerging opportunities indicate the field may be approaching an adolescence of sorts. If these opportunities are pursued, the economics of cultural heritage may very well push the boundaries of economics into exciting new territory in the twenty-first century.

One opportunity for researchers that has yet to be realized is to study in depth the nature of cultural heritage as cultural capital. In particular, one interesting question would be to investigate the change in the value of heritage assets over time. In theory, if we construe cultural heritage as another form of capital asset, then the value of these assets, if maintained, should rise over time. Exploring the rate of appreciation of these assets, especially with the aim of making comparisons with other assets in which the government may invest, is a fruitful direction for future research that could yield significant implications for government policy. This line of inquiry requires both a benchmark valuation for cultural heritage capital and a commitment to regular investigation of a specific asset, and thus it will be more likely that we would see this type of research conducted with tangible heritage assets that are easier to define and monitor than intangible heritage assets.

Another opportunity for the economics of cultural heritage is to strengthen its link with natural resource and environmental economics by increasing the recognition and importance of natural assets in defining cultural heritage. To date, very few economic studies have been conducted that define cultural heritage via a region's natural assets. One such study investigated the value of Armenia's Lake Sevan as a unique symbol of Armenian cultural heritage (Laplante, Meisner, & Wang, 2005). However, there are many cases around the globe where natural assets are important components of a region's cultural heritage that would provide interesting and significant case studies for the economics of cultural heritage. One example exists in Lebanon, where the cedar tree, which adorns the Lebanese flag, is an important part of Lebanese cultural heritage. These trees, some as much as 3,000 years old, have been nominated as one of the Seven Wonders of the World and are currently under threat due to global climate change. Investigating the value of protecting these cultural heritage assets, as well as other forms of heritage that exist in natural resources, would both advance the work of the economics of cultural heritage and environmental valuation methodologies.

Along these lines, it would be interesting to know how the global citizenry values iconic cultural heritage assets such as UNESCO-designated World Heritage Sites. To date, most studies have focused on estimating the values that regional citizens or visitors hold for their proximate cultural heritage assets. Learning the values held by the global population could assist in designing effective policies for their long-term survival.

A related opportunity is to more intentionally situate the study of the economics of cultural heritage in a given geographic space. Although much of our heritage is specifically embedded in a particular geographic location or place, very few studies have intentionally incorporated the use of geographic information systems and other spatial methods to better understand the value of cultural heritage assets. One example is the interdisciplinary Farmland Values Project that investigates the values that four communities in western North Carolina have for farmland. One of the methodologies used in the study had participants describe the places that were culturally important to them using a widely and freely available mapping software, GoogleEarth, and rate places they had located on the map for their heritage and other attributes. The exercise yielded a community-defined map of culturally important places that is intentionally embedded in place. Additional work in the economics of cultural heritage could serve to strengthen the methodologies for both collecting and spatially organizing cultural heritage valuation data and work toward building a bridge between economics, geography, and other fields such as ethnobotany and cultural anthropology that have more intentionally place-based modes of inquiry.

At the outset of the chapter, the definition of cultural heritage included intangible elements such as customs, yet no studies have investigated the value of cultural customs, ways of life, or other intangible aspects of cultural heritage. Investigations in this area would be an excellent bridge between the traditionally quantitative methods of economics and the more qualitative methods of anthropology and sociology. Thus, in addition to broadening the repertoire of the economics of cultural heritage, research in this area could help to push the boundaries of the economic discipline by gathering information on how and why consumers formulate preferences for intangible goods and services.

Conclusion

The economics of cultural heritage is an emerging subfield in economics that has the ability to both serve academic audiences outside of economics (sociology, anthropology, history, political science) and push the boundaries of the economics discipline as a whole. The development of the field has been closely linked with cultural economics and shares with it the importance of incorporating knowledge from disciplines that traditionally have not been rigorously studied by economists, including history, architecture, and the arts. The future of the economics of cultural heritage looks bright as there are numerous opportunities for the field to make significant advances in the valuation of cultural heritage and for pushing the boundaries of economics. Some of these include a more intentional incorporation of interdisciplinary methods and more complex studies to evaluate the full set of values that we hold for our cultural heritage, including the truly intangible elements.

References and Further Readings

Alberini, A., & Longo, A. (2006). Combining the travel cost and contingent behavior methods to value cultural heritage sites: Evidence from Armenia. *Journal of Cultural Economics, 30,* 287–304.

Cassar, M. (2000, September). *Value of preventive conservation.* Keynote lecture at the European Preventive Conservation Strategy Meeting, Institute of Art and Design, Vantaa, Finland. Retrieved January 3, 2008, from http://www.ucl.ac.uk/sustainableheritage/keynote.htm

Cuccia, T., & Cellini, R. (2007). Is cultural heritage really important for tourists? A contingent rating study. *Applied Economics, 39,* 261–271.

de Menezes, A. G., Moniz, A., & Vieira, J. C. (2008). The determinants of length of stay of tourists in the Azores. *Tourism Economics, 14,* 205–222.

Ginsburgh, V., & Throsby, D. (Eds.). (2006). *Handbook of the economics of art and culture* (Vol. 1). Amsterdam: Elsevier, North-Holland.

Hutter, M., & Rizzo, I. (Eds.). (1997). *Economic perspectives on cultural heritage.* New York: St. Martin's.

Kolar, T., & Zabkar, V. (2007). The meaning of tourists' authentic experiences for the marketing of cultural heritage sites. *Economic and Business Review, 9,* 235–256.

Laplante, B., Meisner, C., & Wang, H. (2005). *Environment as cultural heritage: The Armenian diaspora's willingness-to-pay to protect Armenia's Lake Sevan* (Policy Research Paper, WPS 3520). Washington, DC: The World Bank.

Mathews, L. G., & Bonham, J. (2008, June). *Pricing the multiple functions of agricultural lands: Lessons learned from the Farmland Values Project.* Paper presented at the annual meeting of the Western Agricultural Economics Association, Big Sky, MT.

Murillo Viu, J., Romani Fernandez, J., & Surinach Caralt, J. (2008). The impact of heritage tourism on an urban economy: The case of Granada and the Alhambra. *Tourism Economics, 14,* 361–376.

National Oceanic and Atmospheric Administration (NOAA). (1993). Report of the NOAA panel on contingent valuation. *Federal Register, 58,* 4602–4614.

Navrud, S., & Ready, R. C. (Eds.). (2002). *Valuing cultural heritage: Applying environmental valuation techniques to historic buildings, monuments and artifacts.* Cheltenham, UK: Edward Elgar.

Poor, P. J., & Smith, J. M. (2004). Travel cost analysis of a cultural heritage site: The case of historic St. Mary's City of Maryland. *Journal of Cultural Economics, 28,* 217–229.

Richards, G. (Ed.). (2007). *Cultural tourism: Global and local perspectives.* New York: Haworth.

Rizzo, I., & Towse, R. (Eds.). (2002). *The economics of heritage: A study in the political economy of culture in Sicily.* Cheltenham, UK: Edward Elgar.

Rolfe, J., & Windle, J. (2003). Valuing the protection of aboriginal cultural heritage sites. *Economic Record, 79,* S85–S95.

Rosato, P., Rotaris, L., Breil, M., & Zanatta, V. (2008). *Do we care about built heritage? The empirical evidence based on the Veneto House Market* (Working Paper 2008.64). Milan, Italy: Fondazione Eni Enrico Mattei.

Throsby, D. (1997). Seven questions in the economics of cultural heritage. In M. Hutter & I. Rizzo (Eds.), *Economic perspectives on cultural heritage* (pp. 13–30). Basingstoke, UK: Macmillan.

Throsby, D. (2001). *Economics and culture.* Cambridge, UK: Cambridge University Press.

Tisdell, C., & Wilson, C. (2002). World heritage listing of Australian natural sites: Tourism stimulus and its economic value. *Economic Analysis and Policy, 32,* 27–49.

Towse, R. (Ed.). (2003). *A handbook of cultural economics.* Cheltenham, UK: Edward Elgar.

Towse, R. (Ed.). (2007). *Recent developments in cultural economics.* Cheltenham, UK: Edward Elgar.

Vaughn, D. R. (1984). The cultural heritage: An approach to analyzing income and employment effects. *Journal of Cultural Economics, 8,* 1–36.

81

MEDIA ECONOMICS

GILLIAN DOYLE

Centre for Cultural Policy Research, University of Glasgow

Media economics combines the study of media with economics. The term *media* is usually interpreted broadly and includes sectors such as television or radio broadcasting plus newspaper, magazine, or online publishing; communications infrastructure provision; and also production of digital and other forms of media content. Media economics is concerned with unravelling the various forces that direct and constrain choices made by producers and suppliers of media. It is an area of scholarship that has expanded and flourished in departments of economics, business, and media studies over the past two decades.

A number of reasons explain why media economics has advanced quite significantly in popularity and status over recent years. The increasing relevance of economics has been underlined by the so-called digital revolution and its effect in reshaping media businesses while, at the same time, accelerating related processes of convergence and globalization. Deregulation of national media industries is another major trend that has shifted attention on the part of media policy makers and also academics from political toward economic issues and questions. So although media economics—the application of economics theories and concepts to all aspects of media—is still at a relatively early stage of development as a subject area, its importance for industry, policy makers, and scholars is increasingly apparent.

The earliest studies of economics of mass media can be traced back to the 1950s, and these looked at competition among newspapers in the United States. Competition and concentrations of ownership are still key and constant themes within media economics, notwithstanding the many shifts and changes that have redrawn the competitive landscape over time. Other early work that marked out economics of

media as being a distinctive field includes studies of competitive programming strategies (i.e., of the different program content strategies used by competing broadcasters).

Some landmark studies in media economics owe their existence to the needs of policy makers who have asked for work on, for example, competitive conditions within specific sectors of industry or questions around market access or issues such as spectrum pricing. A very good example is the Peacock (1986) report, commissioned by the U.K. government ahead of the 1990 Broadcasting Act. As the first systematic economic assessment of the U.K. television industry, this report was to have seminal influence over subsequent broadcasting policy in Britain. More recently, a wave of interest, initially sparked by Richard Florida's (2002) work on urban economics, has fuelled demand for work by economists on "creative industries" (which include media content production). Studies in this area (see, e.g., Hutton, O'Keefe, Schneider, Andari, & Bakhshi, 2007) are frequently concerned with the capacity for creative industries to drive forward growth in the wider economy.

The origins and approaches evident in economic studies of the media are varied. Some work has been theoretical, seeking to build on approaches within mainstream economics and, occasionally, to develop specialized models that take account of the special contingencies of the media industry. Much work so far in this subject area has tended to be in the applied tradition, looking at specific markets and firms under specific circumstances.

Generally, the broad concern is how best to organize the resources available for provision of mass media. Economists specializing in media economics have explored whether firms are producing the right sorts of goods and services and whether they are being produced efficiently.

Some (frequently drawing on an industrial organization approach) have examined the association between the markets media firms operate in and their strategies or their performance or their output. Another common concern, especially in work on broadcasting, has been what role the state should play in ensuring that the organization and supply of media output matches societal needs.

While research within the tradition of media economics has spanned across all aspects of all media sectors, including film, television, radio, newspapers, magazines, and the Internet, it is worth noting that an overlap exists between this and the related area of "cultural" economics. Cultural economics has a wider ambit; covering arts and heritage as well as media and cultural economics has developed as a separate field with its own concerns (such as subsidies for the arts). But there is some common ground, for instance, concerning the economics of creativity or optimal levels of copyright protection. Research into international trade in films, for example, can be regarded as equally at home in either of these fields.

As well as what might be termed *mainstream economic research into mass media,* the field of media economics is also strongly populated by work that emerges from political economy traditions. The "critical" political economy approach links sociopolitical with economic analysis. It adopts a more normative approach to the analysis of economic actors and processes, rather than focusing simply on, say, questions of efficiency. A number of influential thinkers in media and communications, such as Bagdikian, Garnham, and McChesney, have emerged from the critical political economy tradition. One such is Douglas Gomery (1993), who points out that "studying the economics of mass communication as though one were simply trying to make toaster companies run leaner and meaner is far too narrow a perspective" (p. 198).

So, media economics is a diverse and lively area of scholarship that draws on many different sorts of approaches. Those coming new to the subject will find a number of textbooks on hand to provide a basic understanding of economic concepts and issues in the context of media. The emergence of such books was traced recently by Robert G. Picard (2006), one of the leading figures in this subject. The first textbook appeared in French back in 1978 (Toussaint-Desmoulins), followed by a Spanish-language text in the mid-1980s (López, 1985) and, later, the first German text (Bruck, 1993). Picard himself wrote the first introductory textbook in media economics in the English language (1989) and, in surveying later contributions from the United States, he (2006, p. 21) draws attention to textbooks by Alexander, Owers, and Carveth (1993); Albarran (1996); and Owen and Wildman (1992). Also highlighted is a textbook by a U.K.-based author (Doyle, 2002) that blends traditional economics along with political economy perspectives.

Helpful though textbooks are, the depth and diversity of the field can only be fully appreciated through acquaintance with the growing range of scholarly books, journal articles, monographs, research reports, and studies that focus on economic aspects of media. A rich and diverse body of literature has emerged over the years from a variety of sources, and as the subject grows, media economics continues to expand both in its ambitions and popularity.

This chapter introduces some key themes that are characteristic of media economics and have shaped the development of the field. This survey is not exhaustive, and although the discussion is broken into sections, in reality there are numerous overlaps and interconnections between topics and concerns central to this area of scholarship. In highlighting core issues that students working in the area of media economics are likely to encounter, the main aim here is to provide an introductory overview and a sense of what is special and interesting about this particular subfield within economics.

Economics of Media Is Different

One of the main attractions as well as a key challenge of carrying out work on economics of media stems from the fact that media are a bit "different" from other commodities. It is sometimes said that media operate in dual-product markets—generating not only media output (i.e., content or messages) but also audiences (i.e., the viewers or readers who are attracted by the output) (Picard, 1989, pp. 17–19). The peculiarities of media as a commodity relate mostly to first sort of product: media content.

Collins, Garnham, and Locksley (1988) were pioneers in explaining the economic peculiarities of the broadcasting commodity. These authors flag up a similarity between broadcast output (e.g., a program broadcast on television) and other cultural goods insofar as "the essential quality from which their use-value derives is immaterial" (p. 7). Many cultural goods share the common characteristic that their value for consumers is tied up in the messages or meanings they convey, rather than with the material carrier of that information (the radio spectrum, CD, or the digital file, etc). Because messages or meanings are intangible, media content is not "consumable" in the purest sense of this term (Albarran, 1996, p. 28). Because of the "public good" characteristic of not being used up or not being destroyed in the act of consumption, broadcast material exhibits the peculiarity that it can be supplied over and over again at no extra cost. If one person watches a TV broadcast or listens to a song, it does not diminish anyone else's opportunity to view or listen. In this respect, media seem to defy one of the very basic premises on which the laws of economics are based—scarcity.

The various insights offered by Collins et al. (1988) about, for example, the nonrivalrous and nonexcludable nature of broadcast output were an important early landmark in the development of thinking about how the economic characteristics of mass media differ from other industries. But later work by Richard Caves (2000) again highlighted the requirement for any understanding of the economics of creative industries, of which media are a part, to be based around an appreciation of the peculiarities of that sector. His influential work on "art and commerce" (Caves, 2000) applies economic analysis to the special characteristics of creative activities (e.g., uncertainty of demand, incentives and motivations guiding artistic and creative "talent") and, in so doing, explores various aspects of the organization and behavior of creative industries.

Students and researchers cannot escape the challenges that derive from the distinctive nature of their area of enquiry. One such, in media economics, is the difficulty of measuring or evaluating the impacts that arise from a decision to allocate resources in one fashion rather than another. Communicating with mass audiences, as an economic activity, is inextricably tied up with welfare impacts. And media economics seeks to play a role in showing how to minimize the welfare losses associated with any policy choices surrounding media provision. But, as prominent economist Alan Peacock (1989, pp. 3–4) observed some years ago, welfare impacts are and still remain very difficult to measure convincingly.

Another problem is that, whereas notions of economic "efficiency" and assessments of whether efficiency is being achieved depend on clarity about objectives, the circumstances surrounding cultural provision often militate against such clarity. The perceived objectives associated with media provision are varied and at times contradictory, with some organizations operating in the nonmarket sector (Doyle, 2002, p. 11). So, when it comes to analyzing media, the application of all-embracing models based in conventional economic theory often proves inadequate. Thus, as many have observed, an ongoing concern for economists specializing in media is to build on and develop suitable and coherent overarching theories and paradigms for the study of this as a particular subject area (Fu, 2003; Gomery, 1993; Lacy & Bauer, 2006; Wirth & Bloch, 1995).

Other special challenges that media economists are faced with stem from, for example, the uncertainties, risks, and irrationalities associated with producing creative output or from seeking to analyze production, distribution, and consumption in an ever-changing technological environment for mass media (Doyle & Frith, 2006). The business of supplying ideas and information and entertainment to mass audiences is different from supplying other ordinary commodities such as baked beans, but the complexities that go along with this are central to the legitimacy as well as to the unique appeal of media economics as a distinctive subject area.

Audiences and Advertising

The business of media is about supplying audiences as well as forms of content, and indeed, many mass media are supported largely through advertising revenue. So, not surprisingly, work on audiences and their behavior and around advertising has featured strongly in media economics research and scholarship to date. The vast influence that patterns of advertising activity exert over the fortunes of the media industry has been underlined by the 2008 banking crisis and associated economic recession where a diminution in expenditure on advertising in newspapers, magazines, and broadcast channels has prompted wide-scale closures and job losses across the media in the United States and Europe. Work on the economics of advertising has addressed questions around the relationship between economic wealth and advertising, cyclicality in advertising, the economic role played by advertising, and the impact it exerts over competitive market structures and over consumer decision making (Chiplin & Sturgess, 1981; Schmalensee, 1972; Van der Wurff, Bakker, & Picard, 2008).

Audiences are another focus of interest. A number of studies have examined the nature of audiences (or of access to audiences) as a commodity, audience ratings, and how demand among advertisers for audience access is converted into revenue streams by media enterprises (Napoli, 2003; Webster, Phelan, & Lichty, 2000; Wildman, 2003). Audience fragmentation, although present as an issue in early work about television audiences (Barwise & Ehrenberg, 1989), has risen to greater prominence in recent studies. As Picard (2002) suggests, fragmentation of mass audiences is "the inevitable and unstoppable consequence of increasing the channels available to audiences" (p. 109). In a recent study, Webster (2005) concludes that, despite ongoing fragmentation, levels of polarization among U.S. television audiences are modest so far. Nonetheless, the continued migration of audiences toward digital platforms and associated processes of fragmentation raises important questions for future work in media economics (and in media sociology too).

Media Firms, Markets, and Competition

Although some studies of the relationship between the economy and advertising are macroeconomic, most work by economists interested in media fits within the category of microeconomics. A central focus of interest is firms and how they produce and supply media and also the markets in which media organizations operate and levels of competition.

The concept of a media firm covers many different sorts of actors, but what they all have in common is an involvement somehow in producing, packaging, or distributing media content. Of course, all media firms are not commercial organizations. The prevalence, initially within broadcasting but now across digital platforms too, of nonmarket organizations devoted to providing public service content means that standard assumptions about profit maximization that are central to the theory of firms become questionable in the context of media. Another complicating factor is that ownership of media such as national newspapers is sometimes motivated by concerns that have little to do with economics, such as, especially, the pursuit of political influence. So firms are important within media economics research, but standard economic theories about the behavior of firms have their limitations in this context.

Be that as it may, the industrial organization (IO) model, which is based on the theory of firms, offers an analytical framework that has frequently proven useful to economists working on media firms or industries (Hoskins, McFadyen, & Finn, 2004, pp. 144–156). The IO model (and associated structure-conduct-performance or SCP paradigm) suggests that the competitive market structure in which firms operate will, in turn, affect how they behave and subsequently their performance. Although some doubts have been cast on the causal links of the SCP in recent years, it remains that many media economists have profited from the broad insights offered by IO theory about how, in practice, media firms behave under different market structures and circumstances.

Approaches toward analyzing media firms and markets sometimes take as their starting point the concept of the "value chain" approach first developed by Michael Porter (1998). The media industry can be broken up into a number of broad stages, starting first with production or creation of content (which usually, though not always, brings initial entitlement ownership of intellectual property), then assembling content into services and products (e.g., a newspaper or television channel), and finally distribution or sale to customers. Definitions of markets and sectors in media economics studies are often implicitly or explicitly informed by this conceptual framework. All of the stages in the vertical supply chain are interdependent, and this has important implications for the kinds of competitive and corporate strategies media firms will pursue.

A notable feature of the economics of media is that firms in this sector tend to enjoy increasing marginal returns as their output—or, more properly, *consumption* of their output—expands. The prevalence of economies of scale is strongly characteristic of media industries, and the explanation for this lies in the "public good" nature of the product and how it is consumed. Because the cost of producing a newspaper or supplying a television service is relatively unaffected by how many people choose to consume that output, it follows that these activities will enjoy increasing returns to scale. Plentiful studies exist that confirm the tendency toward high initial production costs in the media sector accompanied by low marginal reproduction costs. The cost of producing a feature film, a music album, or a television program is not affected by the number of people who are going to watch or listen to it. "First-copy" production costs are usually high, but then marginal reproduction or distribution costs are low and, for some media suppliers, zero.

Another important feature is the availability of economies of scope. Economies of scope are generally defined as the savings available to firms from multiproduct production or distribution. In the context of media,

economies of scope are common, again because of the public good nature of media output and the fact that a product created for one market can, at little or no extra cost, be reformatted and sold through another. Because the value of media output is contained in messages that are intangible and therefore do not get used up or "consumed" in the traditional sense of the word, the product is still available to the supplier after it has been sold to one set of consumers to then sell over and over again. The reformatting of a product intended for one audience into a "new" one suitable to facilitate additional consumption (e.g., the repackaging of a celebrity interview into a television news package, a documentary, a radio transmission, etc.) releases savings for the firm and therefore generates economies of scope (Doyle, 2002, pp. 4–15).

In any industry where economies of scale and scope are present, firms will be strongly motivated to engage in strategies of expansion and diversification that capitalize on these features. This is certainly true of media. Concentrations of ownership within and across sectors of the media are a highly prevalent feature of the industry. As a result, many scholars working in the area of media economics have taken an interest in questions about sustaining competition and diversity, measurement of concentration levels, and more generally around how strategies of expansion affect the operation, efficiency, and output of media suppliers.

The link between ownership patterns and diversity within the output offered by media firms is one area of enduring interest. Theories of program choice, the early versions of which are reviewed in Owen and Wildman (1992), are concerned with under what conditions—including the number of competing channels and ownership of broadcast channels—the marketplace will offer similar as opposed to different sorts of programming, or cheap as opposed to expensively produced programs, and so on. The connection between diversity of ownership and output has also been studied in the context of the music industry and the film industry.

Some studies (e.g., Albarran & Dimmick, 1996) have focused on defining and measuring concentration levels within media markets using either the Herfindahl-Hirschman Index (HHI) or a "concentration ratio" such as CR4 or CR8. Others are more concerned with analyzing the economic motivations that underlie strategies of expansion and diversification by media firms. Sánchez-Tabernero and Carvajal (2002) and others have analyzed advantages and also risks associated with a variety of growth strategies, including horizontal, multimedia (cross-sectoral), and international expansion.

A great deal of work in media economics has concerned itself with changing market structures and boundaries within the media. Economics provides a basic theoretical framework for analyzing markets based on the clearly defined structures of perfect competition, monopolistic competition, oligopoly, and monopoly. In practice, many media firms have tended to operate in markets whose contours are strongly influenced by technological factors, state regulations, or both. In addition, most media have tended to operate in very specific geographic markets and to be closely linked to those markets by the nature of their product and through relationships with advertisers. These factors have restrained levels of competition in the past. But times are changing, and this is reflected in much more fluid boundaries and competitive market structures.

Whereas, at the outset of broadcasting, market access was constrained by spectrum limitations, the structure of the television and radio industries has been transformed by the arrival and growth of new forms of delivery for television such as cable, satellite, and digital platforms. Many studies over the years have focused on the effect of channel proliferation and additional competition, as well as increased sectoral overlap between broadcasting and other forms of communications provision (Picard, 2006). Likewise, major changes in the economic organization of print media industries and their impact on production costs, market access, and levels of competition are frequently the subject of interest in media economics texts and studies.

Not only have the avenues for distribution of media been expanding, but also changes in technology and in state policies have opened up national broadcasting systems and contributed to a growing trend toward internationalization of operations by media companies. The process of globalization of media has been propelled forwards by digital technologies (Goff, 2006) and the growth of the Internet, which has created a major impetus in the direction of global interconnectedness. Much recent research work has addressed strategic responses on the part of firms both to common trends generally affecting the media environment, such as globalization and convergence (Kung, 2008), and to changes that are very specific to individual media markets, such as internationalization of Norwegian newspapers (Helgesen, 2002), deregulation of broadcasting in Finland (Brown, 2003), or the role of domestic quotas in the success of Korean films (Lee & Bae, 2004).

Business Strategies

Media economics concerns itself with a wide range of strategies and behaviors that reflect the distinctive features and circumstances of this industry. Hoskins, McFadyen, and Finn (1997) have examined some key economic and managerial challenges facing firms in the television and film production industries, for example, the need to ensure that creative and business inputs function effectively alongside each other—an issue that has also been tackled in some depth by Caves (2000). Hoskins et al. explain how risks and uncertainties associated with producing high-cost audiovisual output are offset, for example, by the use of sequels and series that build on successful formats and through the "star" system, which helps to build brand loyalty among audiences and therefore promote higher and more stable revenue streams.

Strategies of risk spreading are important in media because of uncertainty surrounding the success of any new product. Production is expensive, and while market research may prove helpful, these are essentially hit-or-miss businesses. The factors that determine whether films, books, and music albums will prove popular (including fads, fashions, and the unexpected emergence of "star" talent) are difficult to predict. So strategies that counteract or mitigate risk are essential.

In television and radio, the fact that what is transmitted on any single channel is usually a whole range of products (a full schedule of programs) allows for some of the risks inherent to broadcasting to be reduced (Blumler & Nossitor, 1991, pp. 12–13). Control over a range of products greatly increases a broadcaster's chances of making a hit with audience tastes and therefore covering the cost of producing the whole schedule or "portfolio" or programs. In the twenty-first century, digital compression techniques and more channel capacity have extended the opportunities for broadcasters to engage in portfolio strategies because, as well as offering variety within the schedule of an individual channel, many television companies have become multichannel owners offering variety across a range of related services (MTV1, MTV2, etc.).

The success of the Hollywood majors in counteracting risk and dominating international trade in feature films has been of enduring interest for scholars working in media economics, including De Vany (2004), Hoskins et al. (1997), Steemers (2004), and Waterman (2003). The key to risk reduction for Hollywood producers is again to be found in control over distribution and the ability to supply audiences with a range of product. The ability to support and replenish a large portfolio of output is dependent on being able to fully exploit new and old hits but, as with the music industry, this is now potentially under threat from illegal copying.

Many of the strategies for economic advancement adopted by media firms are based on sharing content and therefore exploiting intellectual property assets as fully as possible. "Networking" is a good example. In broadcasting, a network is an arrangement whereby a number of local or regional stations are linked together for purposes of creating or exploiting mutual economic benefits (Owen & Wildman, 1992, p. 206). Usually the main benefit is economies of scale in programming. Because they are based in different localities, local or regional stations that form part of a network can successfully share a similar or identical schedule of programs, thereby reducing per-viewer costs by spreading the cost of producing that service across a much bigger audience than would otherwise be possible.

A similar sort of logic is at work in, for example, the affiliations or networks of international publishing partners that may be involved (e.g., under franchise agreements) in publishing several different international versions of the same magazine title (Doyle, 2006). The ability to share content and images across the network means that the cost of originating copy material can be spread across a much wider readership, and each partner benefits from access to more costly elements of content (e.g., celebrity interviews) than could be afforded if the magazine were a stand-alone operation. Aside from reaping economies on content, being part of a network may also confer benefits in terms of shared deals on advertising sales.

The translation or reformatting of content from one media platform to another makes increasing economic sense in the context of globalization and digitization, especially so in times of economic recession when revenues are under pressure. This process, referred to by Murray (2005, p. 420) as "content streaming," involves the coordinated distribution of strongly branded content across multiple delivery formats. The aim is to reap economies not by using content that appeals to a single mass audience but rather through building and leveraging brand loyalties among specific target audience segments.

For media content suppliers, profit maximization depends on the full and effective exploitation of intellectual property rights across all available audiences. So a crucial concept in the economics of supplying media content is "windowing" (Owen & Wildman, 1992). This refers to maximizing the exploitation of content assets by regarding primary, secondary, and tertiary audiences (e.g., on free vs. pay channels) as "windows" and by selling your products not only through as many windows or avenues as possible but also in the order that yields the maximum possible return. The idea behind windowing is to carefully arrange the timing and sequence of releases so as to maximize the profit that can be extracted from the whole process, taking into account factors such as audience size, profit margin per head, risks of piracy, and so on.

When Owen and Wildman (1992) explained the practice of windowing, it was in the context of releasing programs via pay and free television and video outlets in the United States and overseas markets. Approaches toward exploiting content have evolved considerably since then, with many media operators now adopting "blended" distribution strategies and operating a "360-degree" approach to commissioning (Pennington & Parker, 2008). In other words, product is created with the intention of selling it across numerous different delivery platforms, not just television but also mobile and Internet. In an increasingly cross-platform or converged production context, the need to devise and execute strategies for effective and full economic exploitation of intellectual property assets has become more pressing and more complex. So windowing remains an important theme in media economics, with potential to offer useful theoretical and practical insights for all media content suppliers.

Media Economics and Public Policy

It is usually assumed in economics that free markets will work better to allocate resources than centralized decision making by government, but intervention is sometimes called for to counteract deficiencies arising from the free operation of markets. This might be, for instance, because a "market failure" has occurred. A concern that is often at the root of work carried out in media economics is what role the state should play in ensuring that the organization and supply of media output matches societal needs. Which sorts of policies and what forms of intervention and regulation are needed to correct market failures and/or improve the allocation and usage of resources devoted to media provision?

So generally speaking, the most important economic reasons why state intervention might be needed are because of a need to address market failures, deal with the problem of "externalities," or restrict or counteract the use of monopoly power. But it is worth noting that governments can and do very often intervene in media markets for noneconomic reasons too. Because of the sociocultural and political influence that accompanies the ability to communicate with mass audiences, media and communications tend to be much more heavily regulated than other areas of economic activity, with special provisions covering, for example, protection of minors, balance and impartiality, and so on.

Broadcasting—still the largest sector of the media in economic terms—is, as evident from much of the literature of media economics, seen as especially prone to market failure. An example of failure is that broadcasting would not have taken place at all in the first place if left up to profit-seeking firms reliant on the conventional mechanism of market funding (i.e., consumer payments) because at the emergence stage in radio and television, there was no way to identify and/or charge listeners and viewers.

But many failures stem partly from the public good characteristics of the broadcasting commodity already mentioned. With any good or service that is "nonexcludable" (i.e., you cannot exclude those that do not want to pay) and where customers do not have exclusive rights to consume the good in question, free rider problems are virtually inevitable. Being a public good, broadcast output also has the characteristic of being "nonexhaustible"—typically, there are zero marginal costs in supplying the service to one extra viewer. Thus, it can be argued that "restricting the viewing of programmes that, once produced, could be made available to everyone at no extra cost, leads to inefficiency and welfare loss" (Davies, 1999, p. 203). Another cause of market failure relates to the problem of asymmetric information. Graham and Davies (1997) summarize this by explaining that "people do not know what they are 'buying' until they have experienced it, yet once they have experienced it they no longer need to buy it!" (p. 19).

Another source of market failure is externalities. These are external effects imposed on third parties when the internal or private costs to a firm of engaging in a certain activity (pollution, for example) are out of step with costs that have to be borne by society as a whole. Broadcasting can have negative external affects when, for example, provision of violent content imposes a cost on society (through increasing fear of violence among viewers). Because the cost to society is not borne by the broadcaster, there arises a market failure in that broadcasters may well devote more resources to providing popular programs with negative external effects than is socially optimal. And this needs to be corrected through some form of public policy intervention.

Externalities in the media are by no means always negative. It is generally recognized that some forms of media content confer positive externalities (e.g., documentaries, educational and cultural output) and, equally, that such output may be undersupplied under free-market conditions.

Although advances in technology have gone some way toward correcting initial causes of market failure (e.g., absence of mechanisms for direct payments), there are still a number of ways in which it might be argued that when it comes to broadcasting, a completely unregulated market might fail to allocate resources efficiently. (Setting aside efficiency problems, some would say broadcasting is, in any event, too important in sociocultural terms to be left up to free market—a separate argument.) The most commonly used tools to correct failures have been regulation (e.g., content rules that apply to commercial television and radio operators) and public ownership. Much important research work carried out in the area of media economics over the years has focused on questions around market failure and the merits or otherwise of public ownership as a solution. Economists have put forward different sorts of evidence and arguments concerning how best to advance "public purposes" associated with broadcasting.

For some, the public good characteristics of broadcasting (nonexcludability and nonexhaustability) suggest it would best be supplied by the public sector at zero price, using public funds (Davies, 1999). And indeed, most countries have some sort of publicly funded and state-owned broadcasting entity to provide public service broadcasting (PSB). But in an era of increased choice and when the technology to allow viewers to make payments directly for whatever services they want is well established, others argue that the use of public funds to finance broadcasting is no longer appropriate (Elstein, 2004).

Aside from public ownership, other ways in which state authorities can encourage the dissemination of particular forms of output include provision of public subsidies directed not at organizations but rather at encouraging production or distribution of whatever sort of content is favored. Special support measures that encourage greater supply and consumption of media content that confers positive externalities are very common and have frequently been the subject of analysis in media economics research work.

Policy interventions designed to support media content generally take two forms. Some interventions are essentially protectionist and help domestic producers by restricting the permitted level of imports of competing nondomestic television or feature film content. Work on international trade in audiovisual content, as well as on the dominance of U.S. suppliers and the efficacy of policy measures to counter this, has been a staple in media economics over many years (Noam & Millonzi, 1993). The affect of tariffs, quotas, and trade disputes in the audiovisual sector have received attention from numerous economists, most notably Acheson and Maule (2001) and Hoskins et al. (1997, 2004).

An alternative approach, rather than imposing tariffs or trade barriers, is to provide grants and subsidies for content producers. European countries such as Germany and France have a long tradition of providing grants to television and film producers to boost indigenous production levels. Work in media economics has helped explain how production grants allow the positive gains to society arising from the availability of, say, indigenously made audiovisual content to be internalized by the production firm, thus correcting the failure of the market system to provide an adequate supply of such content. But the dangers that grants may encourage deviations from profit-maximizing behavior and promote a culture of dependency among local producers are also well covered in media economics texts.

One other very significant concern that arises from the free operation of markets and is frequently a focus in work by media economists is monopolization—the accumulation and potential for abuse of excessive market power by individual media firms and organizations. The prevalence of economies of scale and scope in media, as discussed above, creates an incentive toward expansion and diversification by media firms and, in turn, a natural gravitation toward monopoly and oligopoly market structures. So concentrations of media ownership are a widespread phenomenon, and notwithstanding ongoing technological advances affecting distribution, questions about how policy makers should deal with these have long been of interest to those working in media economics.

A key question is the extent to which media expansion strategies give rise to useful efficiency gains and how much they result in the accumulation of excessive market power within and across media industries. A tricky problem facing policy makers is that sometimes expansion and mergers in the media sector will result in both of these outcomes (i.e., expansion makes possible greater efficiency), but at the same time, it facilitates market dominance and therefore poses risks for competition (Doyle, 2002, p. 166). Concerns about the potential for exercise of monopoly power and about suitable measures to accommodate the development of media firms, while enabling competition, remain important themes in policy making that media economics specialists can help shed light on.

Impact of Technological Change

Because media industries are heavily reliant on technology, a recurring theme for work in media economics is the impact of technological change. From the arrival of the printing press to the era of wireless Internet, processes of media production and distribution have been heavily dependent on and shaped by technology. For media firms, the need to understand, participate in, and capitalize effectively on technological advancements is a constant challenge. For regulators, the task of protecting and promoting public interest concerns associated with mass communication is greatly complicated by ongoing technological change. So a great deal of work in media economics is about, in one way or another, exploring the implications of recent technological advances.

The introduction of digital technology and the growth of electronic infrastructures for delivery of media have been major forces for change in recent years. The spread of digital technology has affected media production, distribution, and audience consumption patterns with knock-on implications for advertising. In the United Kingdom, the Internet accounted for "nearly one in every five pounds of advertising in 2007" (Ofcom, 2008, p. 27).

In broadcasting, digital compression techniques have multiplied the potential number of channels that can be conveyed. Digital technology has allowed for improved and enhanced television and radio services and for a more efficient usage of available spectrum. Much recent work in media economics has examined the implementation of digital broadcasting, looking at, for example, systems of incentives to encourage broadcasters and/or audiences to migrate from analog to digital, as well as at the economic implications and advantages of redeployment of radio spectrum post-digital switchover.

Digitization has facilitated a greater overlap or convergence in the technologies used in broadcasting, telecommunications, and computing and has opened up opportunities for the development of multimedia and interactive products and services. Convergence is encouraging more cross-sectoral activity and conglomerate expansion, raising new questions about the blurring of traditional market boundaries and barriers. Shaver and Shaver (2006, p. 654) observe that, whereas scholars have tended to focus on individual media industries in the past, the challenges posed by cross-media development will require more evolved approaches in future decades.

The Internet is based on digital technology, and its expansion over recent years has had a seismic impact on the whole media industry. Media content is ideally suited to dissemination via this digital infrastructure. But the question of how much the Internet will revolutionize competition in media content provision is debatable. Graham (2001, p. 145) notes that, despite changing technology and widening market access, the economics of content provision and the importance of reputation (or strong brands)

favor the predominance of large players. Goodwin (1998) similarly has argued that these fundamental economic characteristics and features that favor the position of large diversified media enterprises remain largely unchanged because of the arrival of digital technology.

However, for large media content suppliers just as much as small ones, the question of how best to take advantage of digital delivery platforms remains problematic, even a decade into the twenty-first century. Newspaper publishers, having followed their readers and advertisers online and adjusted to a more cross-platform approach, have not found it easy to convert their Web-based readership into revenues (Greenslade, 2009). Notwithstanding the growing popularity of online services based on user-generated content, social networking sites, and search engines and the increasing propensity for advertisers to invest in online rather than conventional media, concerns about the economic viability of Internet-based media provision still abound.

Internet-based television opens up the prospect of a further significant widening of market access to broadcast distribution, albeit that poor or unreliable reception and an uncertain legal environment for Internet-based television have to some extent served as deterrents to new market entry (Löbbecke & Falkenberg, 2002, p. 99). Be that as it may, few broadcasters are ignoring the growth of the Internet (Chan-Olmsted & Ha, 2003). As the infrastructure of the Internet continues to improve, research into organizational responses to new delivery technology in the television industry represents another important area for emerging work in media economics.

Some studies have paved the way in exploring how the Internet has affected mass media (Kung, Picard, & Towse, 2008) and problems that media enterprises have faced in establishing viable business models for Internet-based content provision services. However, in a climate of rapid technological evolution, further economic research work is needed to build our understanding of the transformative effect of this interactive delivery platform.

Ever-expanding avenues for distribution and the growth of interactive and cross-platform products and services have increased overall demand for attractive and high-profile content. At the same time, digital technology has reduced audiovisual production costs, opened up more possibilities for user-generated content, and generally made it more economically feasible to produce content aimed at narrow audience segments. But digitization and the growth of the Internet have also introduced new threats. The possibility of widespread intermediation of data (i.e., for reassembling or repackaging content lifted from other Web sites) is a significant threat for online publishers.

Copyright is an important topic affecting the economics of creation and supply of media output. A number of scholars working in the area of cultural economics have provided useful analyses of systems of incentives for authors to produce creative output that copyright provides. Prominent among these is Ruth Towse (2004), who explains that "ownership of copyrights is likely to be concentrated in enterprises with excessive market power" (p. 60), but on the other hand, potentially high rewards are needed to offset the risks and heavy initial costs involved in supplying creative works.

Digitization and the scope, created by the Internet, for widespread illegal reproduction and dissemination of copyright protected work have made it more difficult for rights owners to capture all the returns due to them. So far, this has affected the music industry more than others, albeit that recent declines in the revenues earned by record companies are attributable to factors other than piracy. Nonetheless, audiovisual material and indeed any information goods that can be conveyed in a digital format are also now increasingly fallible to large-scale electronic piracy. This poses significant potential challenges, for example, to film distributors. For all content creators and rights owners, electronic piracy or illegal reproduction of copyright protected works is now a major concern. Thus, identifying sustainable revenue models for the future represents a major challenge for many media suppliers, as indeed for economists working in this area.

Conducting scholarly work in the area of media economics can be problematic, not least because, on account of the industry's reliance on technology, it is a sector that is almost always in a state of flux. Rather than deterring interest, however, such challenges are a source of attraction that continues to inspire innovative and exciting research work where the tools of economics are deployed in analyzing media issues and problems.

References and Further Readings

Acheson, K., & Maule, C. (2001). *Much ado about culture.* Ann Arbor: University of Michigan Press.

Albarran, A. (1996). *Media economics: Understanding markets, industries and concepts.* Ames: Iowa State University Press.

Albarran, A., & Dimmick, J. (1996). Concentrations and economies of multiformity in communication industries. *Journal of Media Economics, 9*(4), 41–50.

Alexander, A., Owers, J., & Carveth, R. (Eds.). (1993). *Media economics: Theory and practice.* Mahwah, NJ: Lawrence Erlbaum.

Barwise, P., & Ehrenberg, A. (1989). *Television and its audience.* London: Sage.

Blumler, J., & Nossitor, T. (Eds.). (1991). *Broadcasting finance in transition.* Oxford, UK: Oxford University Press.

Brown, A. (2003). Different paths: A comparison of the introduction of digital terrestrial television in Australia and Finland. *International Journal on Media Management, 4,* 277–286.

Bruck, P. (1993). *Okonomie und Zukunft der Printmedien* [Economics and the future of print media]. Munich: Fischer.

Caves, R. (2000). *Creative industries: Contracts between art and commerce.* Cambridge, MA: Harvard University Press.

Chan-Olmsted, S., & Ha, L. (2003). Internet business models for broadcasters: How television stations perceive and integrate the Internet. *Journal of Broadcasting and Electronic Media, 47,* 597–617.

Chiplin, B., & Sturgess, B. (1981). *Economics of advertising.* London: Advertising Association.

Collins, R., Garnham, N., & Locksley, G. (1988). *The economics of television: The UK case.* London: Sage.

Davies, G. (Chairman). (1999). *The future funding of the BBC: Report of the Independent Review Panel.* London: DCMS.

De Vany, A. (2004). *Hollywood economics: How extreme uncertainty shapes the film industry.* London: Routledge.

Doyle, G. (2002). *Understanding media economics.* London: Sage.

Doyle, G. (2006). Managing global expansion of media products and brands: A case study of FHM. *International Journal on Media Management, 8*(3), 105–115.

Doyle, G., & Frith, S. (2006). Methodological approaches in media economics and media management research. In A. Albarran, S. Chan-Olmsted, & M. Wirth (Eds.), *Handbook of media management and economics* (pp. 553–572). Mahwah, NJ: Lawrence Erlbaum.

Elstein, D. (2004). *Building public value: The BBC's new philosophy.* London: Institute of Economics Affairs.

Florida, R. (2002). *The rise of the creative class: And how it's transforming work, leisure, community and everyday life.* New York: Basic Books.

Fu, W. (2003). Applying the structure-conduct-performance framework in the media industry analysis. *International Journal on Media Management, 5,* 275–284.

Goff, D. (2006). Global media management and economics. In A. Albarran, S. Chan-Olmsted, & M. Wirth (Eds.), *Handbook of media management and economics* (pp. 675–689). Mahwah, NJ: Lawrence Erlbaum.

Gomery, D. (1993). The centrality of media economics. *Journal of Communication, 43,* 190–198.

Goodwin, P. (1998). Concentration: Does the digital revolution change the basic rules of media economics? In R. Picard (Ed.), *Evolving media markets: Effects of economic and policy changes* (pp. 173–190). Turku, Finland: Business Research and Development Centre.

Graham, A. (2001). The assessment: Economics of the Internet. *Oxford Review of Economic Policy, 17,* 145–158.

Graham, A., & Davies, G. (1997). *Broadcasting, society and policy in the multimedia age.* London: John Libbey.

Greenslade, R. (2009, January 5). Online is the future–and the future is now. *Guardian,* p. 4.

Helgesen, J. (2002). The internationalisation of Norwegian newspaper companies. In R. Picard (Ed.), *Media firms: Structures, operations and performance* (pp. 123–138). Mahwah, NJ: Lawrence Erlbaum.

Hoskins, C., McFadyen, S., & Finn, A. (1997). *Global television and film: An introduction to the economics of the business.* Oxford, UK: Clarendon.

Hoskins, C., McFadyen, S., & Finn, A. (2004). *Media economics: Applying economics to new and traditional media.* Thousand Oaks, CA: Sage.

Hutton, W., O'Keefe, A., Schneider, P., Andari, R., & Bakhshi, H. (2007). *Staying ahead: The economic performance of the UK's creative industries.* London: The Work Foundation.

Kung, L. (2008). *Strategic management in the media.* London: Sage.

Kung, L., Picard, R., & Towse, R. (2008). *The Internet and the mass media.* London: Sage.

Lacy, S., & Bauer, J. (2006). Future directions for media economics research. In A. Albarran, S. Chan-Olmsted, & M. Wirth (Eds.), *Handbook of media management and economics* (pp. 655–673). Mahwah, NJ: Lawrence Erlbaum.

Lee, B., & Bae, H.-S. (2004). The effect of screen quotas on the self-sufficiency ratio in recent domestic film markets. *Journal of Media Economics, 17,* 163–176.

Löbbecke, C., & Falkenberg, M. (2002). A framework for assessing market entry opportunities for Internet-based TV. *International Journal on Media Management, 4*(2), 95–104.

López, J. T. (1985). *Economia de la communicación de masas* [Economics of mass communications]. Madrid, Spain: Grupo Zero.

Murray, S. (2005). Brand loyalties: Rethinking content within global corporate media. *Media, Culture and Society, 27,* 415–435.

Napoli, P. (2003). *Audience economics: Media institutions and the audience marketplace.* New York: Columbia University Press.

Noam, E., & Millonzi, J. (Eds.). (1993). *The international market in film and television programs.* Norwood, NJ: Ablex.

Ofcom. (2008). *The international communication market 2008.* London: Author.

Owen, B., & Wildman, S. (1992). *Video economics.* Cambridge, MA: Harvard University Press.

Peacock, A. (Chair). (1986). *Report of the committee on financing the BBC.* London: HMSO, Cmnd. 9824.

Peacock, A. (1989). Introduction. In G. Hughes & D. Vines (Eds.), *Deregulation and the future of commercial television* (David Hume Institute Paper No. 12, pp. 1–8). Aberdeen, UK: Aberdeen University Press.

Pennington, A., & Parker, R. (2008, November 19). Multiplatform commissioning. *Broadcast,* p. 11.

Picard, R. (1989). *Media economics: Concepts and issues.* Newbury Park, CA: Sage.

Picard, R. (2002). *The economics and financing of media companies.* New York: Fordham University Press.

Picard, R. (2006). Comparative aspects of media economics and its development in Europe and the USA. In H. Jurgen & G. Kopper (Eds.), *Media economics in Europe* (pp. 15–23). Berlin: VISTAS Berlag.

Porter, M. (1998). *Competitive strategy: Techniques for analyzing industries and competitors.* New York: Free Press.

Sánchez-Tabernero, A., & Carvajal, M. (2002). *Media concentrations in the European market, new trends and challenges, media markets monograph.* Pamplona, Spain: Servicio de Publiciones de la Universidad de Navarra.

Schmalensee, R. (1972). *The economics of advertising.* Amsterdam: North-Holland.

Shaver, D., & Shaver, M. A. (2006). Directions for media management research in the 21st century. In A. Albarran, S. Chan-Olmsted, & M. Wirth (Eds.), *Handbook of media management and economics* (pp. 639–654). Mahwah, NJ: Lawrence Erlbaum.

Steemers, J. (2004). *Selling television: British television in the global marketplace.* London: BFI.

Toussaint-Desmoulins, N. (1978). *L'economie de medias* [The media economy]. Paris: Presses Universitaires de France.

Towse, R. (2004). Copyright and economics. In S. Frith & L. Marshall (Eds.), *Music and copyright* (pp. 54–69). Edinburgh, UK: Edinburgh University Press.

Van der Wurff, R., Bakker, P., & Picard, R. (2008). Economic growth and advertising expenditures in different media in different countries. *Journal of Media Economics, 21,* 28–52.

Waterman, D. (2003). Economic explanations of American trade dominance: Contest or contribution? *Journal of Media Economics and Culture, 1*(1).

Webster, J. (2005). Beneath the veneer of fragmentation: Television audience polarization in a multichannel world. *Journal of Communication, 15,* 366–382.

Webster, J., Phelan, P., & Lichty, L. (2000). *Ratings analysis: The theory and practice of audience research* (2nd ed.). Mahwah, NJ: Lawrence Erlbaum.

Wildman, S. (2003). Modeling the advertising revenue potential of media audiences: An underdeveloped side of media economics. *Journal of Media Economics and Culture, 1*(2), 7–37.

Wirth, M., & Bloch, H. (1995). Industrial organization theory and media industry analysis. *Journal of Media Economics, 8*(2), 15–26.

82

MICROFINANCE

SHANNON MUDD

Ursinus College

Over the past several decades, microfinance, broadly defined as financial services to poor and low-income clients, has become an increasingly important tool for governments, multilateral agencies, and nongovernmental organizations (NGOs) to address poverty. Initially, for example, with Banco Sol in Bolivia, the Grameen Bank of Bangladesh, and Bank Rakyat of Indonesia, microfinance was focused primarily on microcredit, small loans to poor people. The basic idea was to extend credit to poor people who do not have access to finance, enabling them to help themselves. In designing products for the poor, the industry has made substantial innovations in the practices used in lending. In addition, some microfinance institutions (MFIs) now offer a range of financial services, including savings vehicles, money transfers, and insurance specifically designed to meet both the needs and specific situations of poor people. Broad recognition of microfinance as a development strategy came with the United Nations (UN) declaring 2005 The International Year of Microcredit and with the awarding of the 2006 Nobel Peace Prize jointly to Mohamed Yunus and to the Grameen Bank, which he founded.

In this chapter, we examine some of the economic questions associated with microfinance, particularly credit.[1] At the most basic level is the question of why the poor have not had access to finance in the past. A surprising outcome of the "microfinance revolution," as it was referred to by Marguerite Robinson (2001), is evidence that poor people, despite their impoverished situation, are good credit risks. Poor people borrowing small amounts of money almost always repay their loans, including sometimes fairly steep interest charges, and do it on time. This suggests that they find productive uses for the funds ("Economics Focus," 2009). But if they are good credit

risks, why haven't banks been operating in this sector in the past—that is, what is the market failure? To answer this, we look at how banks function as a response to problems of asymmetric information. Over the past several centuries, banks have developed a number of common practices to address these problems, such as the use of collateral, restrictive covenants in binding loan contracts, credit registries, and so on. However, many of them are not applicable to poor people. The innovative practices developed by microfinance institutions serve as alternative, innovative responses to this same problem.

Some Brief General Statistics

Before looking directly at the economic questions of microfinance, it is helpful to look at some statistics from the industry. There has been substantial and sustained growth in the microfinance industry. Between 1997 and 2005, the number of microfinance institutions increased from 618 to 3,133. The number of borrowers increased from 13.5 million to 113.3 million, with 84% of them being women (Daley-Harris, 2006). This works out to an average annual increase of nearly 20%. Gonzalez and Rosenberg (2009) find a lower value when adjustments are made to data sources that incorporate institutions for the first time as if their number of borrowers are all new when in fact the institution has had years of history and borrowers. Still, their adjusted figure of an average growth rate of 12% is substantial, although they do note a recent slowing.

The Gonzalez and Rosenberg (2009) data provide some other interesting results. For example, while microfinance is often associated with NGOs, they show that in 2004, these institutions accounted for only 24% of borrowers (financial cooperatives are not included as there was not sufficient representation in the sample to analyze). Licensed private banks and finance companies accounted for a further 17%, while state-owned institutions accounted for 30%. The remaining 29% was accounted for by the large number of borrowers in Indian self-help groups. As these Indian self-help groups are mostly financed through state banks, adding them to share from state-owned institutions indicates that government-financed organizations account for well over 50% of all borrowers. Note, however, that these statistics exclude financial cooperatives for which there was not sufficient representation in the sample to analyze.

Survey data from Lapenu and Zeller (2001) indicate that only a small percentage of microfinance institutions use the group lending methodology that has been so closely associated with microlending, while most microfinance institutions use individual-based lending. Yet, the 16% of institutions using group lending account for more than two thirds of the actual microfinance borrowers.

Gonzalez and Rosenberg (2009) also report on the profitability, concentration, and geographic distribution of microfinance. Measured by number of borrowers, South Asia dominates with 67 million of the 94 million borrowers in the database. East Asia and the Pacific comprise another 21 million. Sub-Saharan Africa and Latin America comprise 6 and 5 million, respectively. Because of a relatively late start, the regions of the Middle East/North Africa and Eastern Europe/Central Asia have relatively little microfinance. Because advanced economies have wealthier populations and well-developed financial systems, borrowers are a very small percentage of their population.

South Asia is very populous, but even on a per capita basis, it has twice as much microcredit as any other region with nearly 2.25% of the population having microfinance loans. The regions of East Asia and the Pacific and of Latin America have just over 1%, with sub-Saharan Africa slightly lagging.

One of the biggest debates in microfinance in recent years has been the issue of sustainability, the ability of a microfinance organization to maintain its operations without donor funds or subsidization. While most MFIs are not profitable, 44% of borrowers work with profitable MFIs. Interestingly, they find that MFIs tend to be more profitable than the commercial banks operating in the same country, although the data set does not include many tiny MFIs, which would tend not to be profitable. Not surprisingly, profitable MFIs in the database grow faster than those that are not profitable.

Like many industries, especially in developing countries, microfinance tends to be highly concentrated. Within a country, the median share of the largest MFI is one third of the entire market. The median share of the top five microfinance institutions in a country is 81%, and for the top 10 MFIs, it is 95%. This high level of concentration

also extends to the world market. Nine percent of the MFIs account for 75% of all microfinance borrowers.

Microfinance as a Response to Information Asymmetries

"Only those with money are able to borrow it." —Proverb

Asymmetric Information in the Banking Sector

Like many a proverb, there is some wisdom within. To understand why this proverb rings true as a description of the way finance often works, consider a basic problem of finance, *information asymmetry.* Information asymmetry arises when the agent on one side of a transaction has more information than the agent on the other side *and* the agent with more information cannot easily and credibly convey that information to the other party even if he or she tries.

While standard examples of markets with asymmetric information include the used car market and markets for insurance, we also find the problem of asymmetric information in finance. Consider one of the basic functions of a financial sector, *financial intermediation.* Financial intermediation is the process in which an organization gathers funds from those who do not have immediate productive use for it and channels these funds to those who can use it productively. Banks, the most important financial intermediary, take in deposits and then use these funds to make loans to individuals, businesses, and governments. Traditionally, the banks earn income from the interest rate spread (i.e., the difference between the interest paid to their depositors and the interest earned on loans). Like any firm, they seek to ensure revenues cover their costs. Their costs include not only the interest paid on deposits but also the costs of screening, monitoring, and enforcing loan agreements with borrowers; the costs of providing additional services to clients; overhead expenses; and so on. Banks also incur losses from unpaid loans. To deal with the risk of unpaid loans, the interest rates charged to borrowers reflect the level of *credit risk* (i.e., the risk that the borrower will not pay back the loan).

Consider the two types of credit risk associated with business loans. First, credit risk arises because there is uncertainty about the income the borrower is able to generate from its activities. The borrower may not pay back the loan because of a bad outcome of those activities; for example, demand for a redesigned product may not be as large as expected. The higher the probability of a bad outcome, the higher the probability the borrower will be unable to make its payments and default and the lower the expected income from the loan. Banks charge a higher interest rate to reflect this credit risk.

Second, credit risk stems from asymmetric information because the borrower's actions are not completely observable. The borrower always knows more about his or her activities than the bank and may engage in behaviors that would negatively affect the bank. For example, suppose Joe the plumber receives a bank loan to purchase a new piece of plumbing equipment that will enable Joe to expand his business and earn greater income. The first type of behavior of concern for the bank is that Joe may simply break the promise to pay back the loan. Another behavior of concern would be if Joe decided not to work as hard once he received the loan. Furthermore, Joe may engage in more risky activities than the bank would desire, for example, by not using the money to purchase new plumbing equipment but instead purchasing a share in a racehorse that his neighbors own. These examples are of behaviors that occur *after* the loan has been made and are referred to as problems of *moral hazard*. Once the loan is made, the incentives for the borrower such as Joe to do what he said he would do may no longer be as strong. If the bank cannot monitor the borrower's behavior, the borrower may, for example, prefer to work less hard since it is now the bank's money at risk, and he can try to renegotiate the payment schedule of the loan claiming he is unable to pay because of a bad economy beyond his control rather than because he did not work hard. If the problem of moral hazard is great, banks may choose not to lend, and there is market failure from this information asymmetry.

The problem of information asymmetry *before* the loan occurs can result in *adverse selection* or the "lemons problem" (Akerlof, 1970). A potential borrower knows more about his or her intentions of keeping a promise than the lender. Because the lender does not know whether a given borrower represents a high risk of breaking its promise, the bank will charge an interest rate that represents the expected level of risk determined by the bank's assessment of the proportion of high-risk and low-risk applicants for loans. However, those who know they are low-risk borrowers may not be willing to pay such a high interest rate and may drop out of the market. As the low-risk applicants drop out, the probability of a loan applicant being high risk increases, the expected risk is higher, and the bank will charge a higher interest rate. This causes even more low-risk applicants to drop out of the market. Thus, there is "adverse selection": The low-risk applicants select themselves out of the market, and only high-risk applicants remain.

As banks generally prefer not to lend to high-risk borrowers, at the extreme, they may stop lending. In this case, the market fails (i.e., there is no lending) because low-risk borrowers cannot credibly identify themselves in this situation of asymmetric information. In a less extreme outcome, banks may choose not to charge high interest rates and instead ration credit to try to avoid asymmetric information problems (Stiglitz & Weiss, 1981). Although it is not complete market failure, it still presents problems for access to finance, especially to the poor. If banks are rationing credit, one must ask what determines who receives the limited amount of loans.

Standard Banking Responses to Problems of Asymmetric Information

Over time, banks have developed a number of mechanisms of screening, monitoring, and enforcement to try to mitigate problems of adverse selection and moral hazard. These mechanisms are explored here while the following section describes the alternative mechanisms microfinance has developed specifically for the poor.

To deal with the adverse selection problem, banks become experts both in analyzing information produced by the firm and in the further production of information about firms. This enables them to better assess risk and screen out good risks from bad risks. Established firms seeking a loan provide formal accounting data for the bank to assess. However, banks may gather additional information on the background of potential borrowers to determine, for example, if they had been involved in criminal activities in the past. Banks may also seek to collect information on the credit history of potential borrowers to find out whether they have failed to fulfill past promises or been unable to meet payment obligations such as rent, utility bills, credit card payments, and so on. Banks may also gather information about previous business activities to assess the business acumen of the potential borrower. They may also look at the market in which the potential borrower is operating to better assess the borrower's business plans and projections of future costs and sales.

Banks also often require *collateral,* a valuable asset that is surrendered to the bank if the borrower is not able to fulfill its promise to repay the loan (remember the proverb!). Collateral requirements reduce adverse selection as high-risk borrowers who know they are unlikely to pay off the loan are less willing to risk giving up a valuable asset and may choose not to apply. Furthermore, collateral helps to mitigate the costs of adverse selection to the bank when a high-risk borrower defaults. However, even if the bank were to take possession of the collateral, there are likely to be significant costs involved for the bank, and it may not be able to recover the full value of the loan.

To further reduce the other problems of asymmetric information, moral hazard problems, banks engage in monitoring and write debt contracts with restrictive covenants that limit the behavior of borrowers. For example, banks may monitor borrowers by requiring them to regularly report sales volumes, maintain bank accounts at the lending bank, and so forth. They may have a contract that limits how the funds can be used, for example, to purchase a certain type of equipment. These contracts are enforceable through the courts and provide the bank with recourse should the borrower try to use the money for other types of activities that the bank would deem undesirable. Bank loan officers may choose to visit the borrower to check that the funds are being used as agreed. Of course, collateral also serves to reduce the problem of moral hazard. The loss of the valuable asset continues to provide an incentive to borrowers to fulfill their promise to repay.

Note that these responses to the problems of asymmetric information are standard in "arm's-length" banking systems. An alternative response is "relationship banking," which is more common in Asian countries. In these banking systems, banks develop strong ties to groups of firms, for example, through cross-ownership. Because of the close ties, banks have more intimate knowledge of borrowers and often some control, lessening the problems of information asymmetry. Both systems have advantages and disadvantages. For example, arm's-length banking systems do not work well in countries that do not have strong judicial systems to enforce contracts. The relationship banking system may lead to problems of transparency, due to a lack of information production or because the close ties can lead to cronyism and noneconomic decision making. For further discussion, see Rajan and Zingales (1998).

The Microfinance Innovation

While, generally, the poor are considered bad credit risks because they lack net worth that might be used to pay off a loan in the event of a bad outcome of a business activity, perhaps more important is the problem that many of the standard responses to the problems of asymmetric information mentioned above are not appropriate for microloans to the poor, particularly in developing countries. First, the poor lack easily valued, marketable assets that could serve as collateral. Furthermore, especially in developing countries, the poor are less likely to engage in activities that would provide relatively accessible background information about them (credit cards, utility payments, etc.). Their business activities may be more informal and lack financial records or business plans. Many developing countries may also not have a well-functioning legal system to enforce contracts. For example, according to the 2008 Doing Business Report, the time required to settle a contract dispute in India is 1,420 days. This is nearly three times the average of Organisation for Economic Co-operation and Development (OECD) countries and represents a significant cost to any party trying to enforce a contractual obligation.

Microfinance has developed a number of innovative practices that serve as alternative responses to asymmetric information problems. These include group lending, dynamic incentives, regular repayment schedules, collateral substitutes, and lending targeted toward women. These are discussed individually below.

Group Lending

Once every week in villages throughout Bangladesh, groups of forty villagers meet together for half an hour or so, joined by a loan officer from a microfinance organization. The loan officer sits in the front of the group (the "center") and begins his business. The large group of villagers is subdivided into eight five-person groups, each with its own chairperson, and the eight chairs, in turn, hand over their group's passbooks to the chairperson of the center, who then passes the books to the loan officer. The loan officer duly records the individual transactions in his ledger, noting weekly installments on loans outstanding, savings deposits, and fees. Quick arithmetic on a calculator ensures that the totals add up correctly, and, if they do not, the loan officer sorts out any discrepancies. Before leaving, he may dispense advice and make arrangements for customers to obtain new loans at the branch office. All of this is done in public, making the process more transparent and letting the villagers know who among them is moving forward and who may be running into difficulties.

This scene is repeated over 70,000 times each week in Bangladesh by members and staff of the Grameen Bank, and versions have been adapted around the world by Grameen-style replicators. Other institutions instead base their methods on the "solidarity group" approach of Bolivia's BancoSol or the "village bank" approach operated by microlenders in seventy countries through Africa, Latin America, and Asia (including affiliates of FINCA, Pro Mujer, and Freedom from Hunger). For many, this kind of "group lending" has become synonymous with microfinance. (Armendariz de Aghion & Morduch, 2005, p. 85)

In his innovative, seminal venture into microfinance, Mohammed Yunus recognized that the very low income of the potential borrowers he was targeting meant that collateral, the standard tool used in lending in developed banking systems, was not a mechanism he could use to reduce the basic lending problems of adverse selection and moral hazard. Instead, he devised a way to use the social ties among a group of borrowers to help avoid these problems.

In the traditional Grameen model of group lending, loans are administered to groups of five borrowers who form voluntarily. Loans might be used for rice processing, the raising of livestock, traditional craft materials, and so on. The process of lending starts with two members of the group receiving funds. After these two start making regular payments, loans are gradually extended to two additional members and eventually to the fifth member. In the Grameen model, the group meets with their lender weekly, along with seven other groups, so that a total of 40 group members participate. In this way, the program builds a sense of community, or *social capital,* as well as individual self-reliance. However, just as important is a "joint responsibility" rule in forming the group that if any one member of the group of five defaults, all of the members will be blocked from future access to loans from the lender. Some group lending programs are even more restrictive, requiring "joint liability." In this type of program, group members may be required to make payments in the case of nonpayment or default by one of its members.

Group lending works to avoid the problem of asymmetric information by taking advantage of local information in screening, monitoring, and enforcement. Group members often know each other and can monitor each other relatively easily. The joint responsibility rule ensures that it is in all group members' interest that each member meet his or her obligations. The group may also serve as a localized enforcement mechanism, able to threaten social isolation (or even physical retribution). Together, these provide a powerful antidote to moral hazard problems. To ensure obligations are met, the group may also serve as an informal insurance contract so that if one member has a bad outcome, such as becoming sick, the others may make the sick member's payments until he or she can return to work.

Local knowledge may also help address the problem of adverse selection. Potential borrowers may be able to distinguish who among them are inherently risky borrowers and who are relatively safe borrowers. If banks knew this information, they could charge higher interest rates to the more risky borrowers to reflect the greater risk of default. By allowing groups to form voluntarily, potential borrowers can sort themselves into groups of relatively risky and relatively safe borrowers. Safe borrowers will seek to stick together. Risky borrowers will have no choice but to form groups with other risky borrowers. Because risky borrowers will have more instances of default, the joint liability rules ensure that they make more payments to cover other members of their group when their risky ventures do not succeed. Members thus effectively pay a higher interest rate than the safe borrowers in their separate groups. This sorting helps transfer the risk from the banks to the risky borrowers. And this occurs without the bank itself uncovering the information and without different contracts for different groups (Armendariz de Aghion & Morduch, 2005; Ghatak, 1999; Morduch, 1999).

However, there may be some drawbacks to group lending when social ties are too strong between friends or relatives, worsening repayment rates. Higher levels of social cohesion may lead to collusion among borrowers to cheat the microfinance lender. In addition, group lending may not work as well for larger loan amounts.

Dynamic Incentives

A common practice of microfinance institutions is dynamic incentives in extending an initial loan to a borrower for only a small amount but increasing the loan amount over time with successful repayment (Besley, 1995). This is sometimes referred to as "step lending" or "progressive lending." For the borrower, the increasing access to funding provides an incentive to continue to meet obligations and so reduces moral hazard. Furthermore, the repeated aspect of these transactions establishes a long-term relationship between the borrower and the lender, facilitating the MFI's gathering of "soft information" about the borrower.

The effectiveness of dynamic incentives is limited when borrowers are mobile and when there are competing lenders in the area. If a borrower changes location, the advantage of the established relationship is lost, and the borrower no longer has an incentive to pay back the loan to gain a larger subsequent loan. Thus, the value of such dynamic lending may be low in more urban areas in which mobility is high and other lenders are available in neighboring areas. Borrowers who default may find it relatively easy to move to another area and start a new relationship with a lender who is unaware of the previous default. In some areas, MFIs are working to share information to reduce this problem.

Regular Repayment Schedules

In developed banking systems, the common practice in small business lending is for payment in full (a lump-sum payment) of principal and interest at the end of the loan period. In contrast, microfinance institutions often issue loans with frequent payment schedules that begin soon after the loan is disbursed. For example, the terms for an annual loan may consist of 50 weekly payments of principal and interest that begin 2 weeks after the initial disbursement. Such a regular repayment schedule provides several advantages in dealing with information asymmetries. First, the process serves to screen out undisciplined borrowers who recognize their inability to manage their funds to keep such a schedule of payments. The practice also helps with monitoring of the borrower, by the MFI or by the peer group borrowers, who quickly learn about cash flow issues and can address problems at an early stage.

There may be an additional benefit to the borrower of the commitment mechanism of frequent payments unrelated to asymmetric information. Poor households often have difficulty amassing funds over time due to a number of different types of diversions, including other demands on funds, requests from relations who are aware of the household's availability of funds, and also theft (Rutherford, 2000). This limits the ability of households to collect funds over a longer time to make large payments. The frequent payments force the household to prioritize its funds and help limit the diversions that may have prevented it from amassing the savings, which otherwise would have obviated the need for borrowing.

However, the practice of frequent payments has some drawbacks. The early payments will tend to create a bias in lending to those households who have additional sources of cash income, especially when loan proceeds are used for investments that do not generate immediate cash flows. This problem is particularly apparent in agricultural lending for fertilizer and seeds for crops that will not produce cash flow until a future harvest. As Morduch (1999) points out, the MFI is effectively lending against the household's steady diversified income stream rather than on the project itself and its particular riskiness. This will limit the usefulness of this mechanism for certain populations. (Some MFIs have loan products specifically designed for agriculture and other seasonal industries, such as tourism. The repayment schedule is adjusted to take into account the repayment capacity of the borrower, e.g., repayment may be due only at harvest.)

Collateral Substitutes

Microfinance loan terms may include collateral or partial collateral in a number of different forms. For example, Grameen Bank required all borrowers to contribute to an "emergency fund" in an amount proportional to the loans received (0.5% beyond a set minimum). This fund serves as insurance for group members against death, disability, and default, with payouts related to the length of membership. In addition, loan disbursements were subjected to a 5% group tax paid into a group fund account. Up to half of this fund could be accessed by members, with unanimous group consent, as a zero-interest loan. While initially not allowed, Grameen Bank now allows these funds to be withdrawn by members who are leaving the group. Although the term *collateral* may not be used, these funds function as partial collateral, and the group fund serves as a form of forced savings.

Some microfinance institutions explicitly require collateral—for example, Bank Rakyat Indonesia's *unit desa* program. While some may point to the fact that collateral is rarely collected to show its relative unimportance, noncollection of collateral does not mean the threat of its collection did not have a big effect on the borrower's repayment behavior and that it does not serve as an important enforcement mechanism. However, it is difficult to parse the influence of collateral from the influence of other practices of a microfinance institution, such as dynamic lending.

Lending Targeted Toward Women

One interesting practice of many microfinance institutions is to focus on lending to women. While for some MFIs, this may be connected to gender issue goals, such as increased empowerment for women, for many the simple fact that repayment rates for women tend to be higher goes far to explain this focus. However, there is substantial debate about why women are more likely to repay loans than men. Some explanations are quite simplistic, stating that women are simply more reliable and less likely to use funds for nonessential leisure purposes, including tobacco and alcohol. Looking deeper into gender differences, some assert that women are more sensitive to negative reactions of fellow members and loan officers when payment difficulties arise. Another explanation that may be more consistent with information problems is that women are simply more likely to be close to the home and thus more easily located and more easily pressured. Men may work away from the home and may more easily remove themselves from difficult situations, making it more difficult to monitor them.

Other explanations of the difference in repayments behavior hinge on societal differences. For example, in many societies, men, but not women, have alternative sources of credit, whether formal or informal. This access to additional credit beyond the MFI means men are less affected by the removal of access to credit by the MFI. For

them dynamic incentives (i.e., step lending) will have less of an impact. A further societal difference is that, in some societies, women may be more involved with the type of small trade that can most effectively use and service microfinance loans.

A Potential Concern About Competition

The innovations reported above can all be viewed as alternative responses to problems of asymmetric information from the practices employed by the commercial banking industry. There is another information problem that may arise as the industry grows.

As competition in microlending becomes stronger, there is a risk that competitors may poach borrowers. The issuance of a loan from one microlender can serve as a signal to another lender that a borrower is a good credit risk. This can serve as an inexpensive screening mechanism of borrowers. Like the problems of information asymmetry, this information problem can also lead to a market failure. The poaching of clients from other MFIs may reduce the incentive for MFIs with sustainability goals to incur the initial costs of screening a new borrower, meaning competition may lead to reduced lending (Peterson & Rajan, 1995).

Empirical Findings on Alternative Practices Used in Microfinance

Microfinance has developed a number of innovative lending practices to deal with problems of asymmetric information and the particular situations of the poor. But given there are both drawbacks as well as benefits to the different innovations, which types are most effective? Within each type of innovation, which aspects of the practices are most important? And what is it that makes them work? These are some of the economic questions that arise in examining microfinance innovations.

To answer these questions, ideally, researchers would set up an experiment with a large group of households receiving microfinance using different types of contracts and compare the outcomes. This is difficult to do in the field, especially since MFIs tend to specialize in the types of lending terms they use. While poverty outcomes are certainly the primary interest, repayment rates have been the primary focus of empirical research, with many of the studies looking specifically at the effectiveness of group lending.

Some researchers have conducted experiments in a lab setting to better understand how group lending works (Abbink, Irlenbusch, & Renner, 2006). A key question is the importance of social ties on repayment rates. The experiment compared outcomes when groups were formed randomly to outcomes when groups were self-selected, presuming that the latter were largely among people with preexisting social ties. The results indicate that the groups with stronger social ties performed no better (and sometimes worse) in terms of repayment rates than groups with no social ties.

This result seems counter to the standard description of group lending that relies on social ties for selection, monitoring, and imposing social sanctions as an enforcement mechanism. However, field studies of group lending in Guatemala (Wydick, 1999) and in Thailand (Ahlin & Townsend, 2003) are consistent with the experimental results, finding that strong social ties have little or even a negative impact on repayment rates. In contrast, studies of "social capital" in Peru (Karlan, 2007) and "social cohesion" in Costa Rica (Wenner, 1995) find positive effects of their increase. It appears that the definitions of social ties used may be key to the findings. While Wydick (1999) found a negative impact of increased social ties (friendship), his measure of social cohesion, proxied specifically by living proximity or knowing each other prior to joining the group, had a positive impact. This is consistent with the earlier mentioned problem that social ties that are too close may be counterproductive.

Note that even with what seem to be good data, evaluating the effects of various microfinance practices is difficult because of selection and other problems. Armendariz de Aghion and Morduch (2005) specifically point out the difficulties of assessing group lending by discussing in more detail the Gómez and Santor (2003) study of two Canadian microlenders that make loans both individually and in groups. Because most microfinance is targeted to the poor in developing countries, to some extent, these programs differ from the norm. With much more developed financial systems, legal systems, and so on, microfinance in more developed countries operates in a very different paradigm, as can be seen by default rates much higher than usually reported. Still, both the methodology and the findings are instructive.

In the two programs studied, while interest rates and fees are similar, there are substantial differences in the populations and loan sizes between the portfolio of individual-based loans and the portfolio of group lending loans. Individual loans tend to be larger ($2,700 vs. $1,000). Group borrowers tend to be female, Hispanic, and immigrant while individual borrowers tend to be male, Canada born, and of African descent. A comparison of the two portfolios shows that group lending loans are more likely to be repaid with 20% default rates versus 40% default rates for the individual loans. However, before attributing the differences in repayment rates to the loan methodology, it is important to take into account the differences in the populations.

The approach taken by Gómez and Santor is to follow the "matching method" approach of Rosenbaum and Rubin (1983). Using a sample of almost 1,400 borrowers, the method involves first pooling all of the data and estimating the likelihood that a borrower will have a group loan (rather than a standard individual loan). Determinants include age, income, neighborhood, education level, and ethnicity. The estimates yield an index of the probability of taking a group loan, with the important feature that borrowers within the same level of the index also have similar observed characteristics. Reliable comparisons are thus achieved by comparing only borrowers with similar levels of the index. . . . Using this method, Gomez and Santor find that borrowers under group contracts repay more often. The result, they argue, arises both because more reliable borrowers are more likely to choose group contracts and because, once in the group contracts, the borrowers work harder. (Armendariz de Aghion & Morduch, 2005, pp. 104–105)

However, as Armendariz de Aghion and Morduch (2005) point out, this methodology only works if the variables used to develop the index are the only variables that matter in the choice of contract. If there are important omitted variables, the method will not produce consistent results. For example, suppose that borrowers who are higher risk tend to have a relative preference for individual loan contracts as opposed to group lending programs. If so, more of the high-risk borrowers would end up borrowing with individual loan contracts. If these high-risk borrowers are more likely to default, then individual loan contracts will have higher default rates. However, this would not be because of the contract design but because of the selection bias in the type of borrower who chooses the individual loan contract. In this case, if unable to identify high-risk from low-risk borrowers, an interpretation of results from an econometric model that indicates group lending increases repayment rates would be spurious.

Interestingly, further results from the experiments of Abbink et al. (2006) find that groups had higher repayment rates than would be expected if loans were to individuals. They also find that larger groups do worse.

As to the effectiveness of other practices, results are fewer. However, Abbink et al. (2006) do find that women are more reliable.

Evaluating the Impact and Effectiveness of Microfinance

The experiments and field studies just detailed shed some light on the effectiveness of group lending and other practices on MFI performance, particularly repayment rates. However, the ultimate question for microfinance is not about MFI performance but about how the lives of poor people are affected. At the most basic level, economists ask what are the full social costs and benefits of using microfinance as a development strategy targeted toward the poor. In terms of benefits, how has microfinance affected the lives of borrowers and their families? Does the use of microfinance services lead to increased income and standards of living? Perhaps just as important, does it lead to less vulnerability to negative shocks/bad events, especially those out of their control (weather, job loss, illness, family death)?

Although microfinance institutions provide many examples of borrowers who are doing quite well, these stories are only anecdotal. A more complete assessment is needed as even on the anecdotal side, there are concerns. For example, Montgomery (1996) worries that group lending puts such high pressure to repay on poor households that it may actually make them worse off in the event of a negative outcome, compelling them to pay even when difficulties arise beyond their control. Examples of how households can be harmed include stories of forced seizure of household utensils, livestock, and so forth of defaulting members.

To fully assess the benefits, one must understand the goals of the microfinance sector. Unfortunately, not all participants agree. While the issues of income or standard of living raised above are certainly an important area of concern, some MFIs view their role as more than just providers of financial services. Their goals may extend to providing health education, increasing the education of children, improving health and nutrition, empowering women, basic business training, and so on. Given the multiple goals, assessment of the success of a microfinance program involves more than an examination of repayment rates and requires a variety of data.

Measurement Issues

The number of good, academic studies of the impact of microfinance on poor people is few but growing, and some are discussed below. Importantly, the industry itself is making an effort to improve impact assessment. Hashemi, Foose, and Badawi (2007) present the efforts of the Social Performance Task Force, which met in Paris in 2005 and agreed on five Dimensions of Social Performance to guide them in designing standards for reporting to better analyze the success of microfinance in positively affecting people's lives. The difficulty of such an assessment is apparent in the list itself. The five dimensions are as follows:

1. *Intent and Design.* What is the mission of the institution? Does it have clear social objectives beyond providing access to credit and other financial services to poor people?
2. *Internal Systems and Activities.* What activities will the institution undertake to achieve its mission? Are systems designed and in place to achieve those objectives?
3. *Output.* Does the institution serve poor and very poor people? Are the products designed to meet their needs?
4. *Outcome.* Have clients experienced social and economic improvements?
5. *Impacts.* Can these improvements be attributed to institutional activities?

For a microfinance institution to collect data on all five dimensions is a large task. MFIs have increased their

reporting capabilities on the financial side to gain greater access to both donor and commercial funding. However, this is concentrated only in the first three dimensions. The last two dimensions necessary to evaluate their social performance are much more difficult. Data collection is expensive, and an MFI may find it hard to justify expending its limited funds on this activity when the apparent need among its potential borrowers is so great. However, to fully attribute any impacts on households of borrowing and other financial and nonfinancial services, researchers must collect data on other household factors that can affect outcomes as well as from other similar households that did not use microfinance services. Surveys to collect such data require careful design and can be expensive to implement. While the industry's efforts will surely provide more extensive data to analyze questions, it is likely that academic and donor-sponsored surveys will continue to be key to assessment of the industry's effectiveness in combating poverty.

The Debate on Sustainability

As noted, data collection to assess financial performance has greatly improved, especially as many MFIs have sought access to private capital. Private capital requires a return on its investment, and to attract this type of funding, MFIs must show that their activities are sustainable (i.e., that borrower repayments are sufficient to be able to repay invested funds). However, there is continuing controversy about whether microfinance institutions should have as a goal to cover all their economic opportunity costs.

For example, Richard Rosenberg (2008) discusses an actual debate at the World Microfinance Forum in Geneva in 2008 between Mohamed Yunus and Michael Chu, a former investment banker and president of ACCION, one of the larger microfinance institutions, and now on the faculty at Harvard Business School:

> The debaters argued about whether commercialization (let's define it as the entry of investors whose primary motive is financial rather than social) is good for microfinance. Yunus thinks that it's immoral to make money off the poor, and that the only kinds of investors needed in microfinance are ones who are willing to accept very limited profits for the sake of keeping as much money as possible in the pockets of the borrowers. Michael thinks that we can't meet the worldwide demand for poor people's financial services unless we can draw in private, profit-oriented capital, and that eventual competition can be counted on to bring interest rates and profits down to consumer-friendly levels in most markets.

In terms of social performance, to the extent that MFIs are profitable and self-sustaining, the need for a full assessment may not be necessary. Even those that rely on volunteer donations may not need a full assessment of costs and benefits if the anecdotal stories of how microfinance loans have improved the lives of borrowers are enough to satisfy potential donors. However, much of the sector continues to exist with the help of grants and government/taxpayer subsidies. Given scant resources from institutional donors and governments, it is important to determine whether the benefits outweigh the costs and whether these funds are well allocated or could produce a better outcome deployed on some other type of poverty reduction program.

Empirical Findings

The amount of well-designed studies on social performance is few, but an increasing number of good ones are providing interesting results. One important series of studies is based on a survey of 1,800 households in Bangladesh. For example, Pitt and Khandker (1998) find a number of positive impacts of microlending to households. Interestingly, the impacts differ by whether the loan is made to women or men. One important measure to assess is how consumption is affected. Pitt and Khandker find that household consumption increases by a substantial 18 taka for every 100 taka lent to women. However, the increase in household consumption when the loans are made to men is only 11 taka for every 100 taka lent. Part of the difference is due to how labor choices are affected. While lending has no effect on labor supply by women, men choose to increase their consumption of leisure (i.e., work less). Results on the schooling of children indicate that schooling increases for boys no matter the gender of the borrower. However, whether schooling for girls increases when women borrow depends on the lending program, perhaps an indicator that the nonfinancial emphasis of microfinance programs can have an important affect on their impacts. McKernan (2002) finds that nonfinancial aspects of microfinance programs do have an impact. She finds that the provision of the loan itself only accounts for about half of the measured increase in self-employment income from borrowings. She attributes the other half of the increase to improved borrower discipline, empowerment, and even shared information from the social network that arises from the social development programs accompanying the borrowing, such as vocational training and education about health and other issues. Pitt and Khandker (2002) also find that lending helps households to smooth consumption across seasons, indicating that entry into the programs may be motivated by insurance concerns.

However, the results are not unanimous. For example, Morduch (1999) reports on results using a subset of the same data limited to what he considers comparable households. He finds no effects on consumption or education, although his findings do indicate lending helps with consumption smoothing. Importantly, Pitt (1999) has mounted a strong defense of their original methodologies and results.

Fortunately, as noted before, there are substantial efforts to increase the availability of standardized data from microfinance institutions as well as surveys to better distinguish the effects of different types of contracts, nonfinancial program aspects, and so on on poor household outcomes. Future studies using this and other data will be able to provide additional evidence on the impact and effectiveness of microfinance in addressing issues of poverty. The industry is relatively young and still evolving. The impacts of microfinance may not be fully apparent during the relatively short time periods of most studies. As more data become available, the prospects for future research in this area are great.

For additional information on developments in microfinance there are a number of excellent Web sites devoted to the industry. For example, the UN created a Web site in conjunction with its Year of Microcredit (www.yearofmicrocredit .org). The Consultative Group to Assist the Poor (CGAP) maintains both a general Web site (www.cgap.org) and one that is targeted toward the microfinance community (www.microfinancegateway.org). The Microfinance Information Exchange (MIX) provides analysis and data (www.themix.org). The Grameen Foundation has created measures to facilitate microfinance institutions in working with their clients, the Progress Out of Poverty Index (www.progressoutofpoverty.org). A documentary on microfinance produced by PBS, "Small Fortunes," along with other material, is available at www.pbs.org/kbyu/small fortunes. In addition, two periodicals focused on microfinance are available online, the Asian Development Bank's *Finance for the Poor* and the Microfinance Information Exchange's *The Microbanking Bulletin*.

Note

1. For a more thorough analysis of the many economic aspects of microfinance and empirical evidence its effectiveness, see the excellent and accessible Armendariz de Aghion and Morduch (2005).

References and Further Readings

Abbink, K., Irlenbusch, B., & Renner, E. (2006). Group size and social ties in microfinance institutions. *Economic Inquiry, 44,* 614–628.

Ahlin, C., & Townsend, R. (2003). Using repayment data to test across models of joint liability lending. *Economic Journal, 107,* F11–F51.

Akerlof, G. (1970). The market for "lemons": Quality uncertainty and the market mechanism. *Quarterly Journal of Economics, 84,* 488–500.

Armendariz de Aghion, B., & Morduch, J. (2005). *The economics of microfinance.* Cambridge: MIT Press.

Asian Development Bank, *Finance for the Poor,* quarterly newsletter of Microfinance (note selected bibliography in each issue): http://www.adb.org/Documents/Periodicals/Microfinance/default.asp

Asymmetric Information discussed in the context of the work of the three 2001 Nobel Prize laureates in economics: http://www.nobel.se/economics/laureates/2001/public.html

Besley, T. (1995). Savings, credit, and insurance. In T. N. Srinivasan & J. Behrman (Eds.), *Handbook of development economics* (Vol. 3A, pp. 2125–2207). Amsterdam: Elsevier.

CGAP Consultative Group to Assist the Poor: http://www.cgap .org/p/site/c

CGAP's Microfinance Gateway: http://www.microfinancegate way.org

Daley-Harris, S. (2006). *State of the Microcredit Summit Campaign report 2006.* Washington, DC: Microcredit Summit Campaign.

Economics focus: A partial marvel. (2009, July 18). *The Economist,* p. 76.

Ghatak, M. (1999). Group lending, local information and peer selection. *Journal of Development Economics, 60,* 27–50.

The Global Development Research Center: http://www.gdrc.org/icm

Gómez, R., & Santor, E. (2003). *Do peer group members outperform individual borrowers? A test of peer group lending using Canadian micro-credit data* (Working Paper 2003–33). Ottawa, Ontario: Bank of Canada.

Gonzalez, A., & Rosenberg, R. (2009). *The state of microfinance: Outreach, profitability, poverty, findings from a database of 2600 microfinance institutions.* Retrieved from http://ssrn .com/abstract=1400253

Hashemi, S., Foose, L., & Badawi, S. (2007). *Beyond good intentions: Measuring the social performance of microfinance institutions* (CGAP Focus Note No. 41). Washington, DC: CGAP.

Hermes, N., & Lensink, R. (2007). The empirics of microfinance. *Economic Journal, 117,* F1–F10.

IFC Doing Business Report (cross-country comparisons of various measures of the ease of doing business, from setting up a firm, to trading across borders, to hiring and firing employees, to obtaining credit): http://www.doingbusiness.com

Karlan, D. (2007). Social connections and group banking. *Economic Journal, 117,* F52–F84.

Lapenu, C., & Zeller, M. (2001). *Distribution, growth and performance of microfinance institutions in Africa, Asia and Latin America* (FCND Discussion Paper 114). Washington, DC: International Food Policy Research Institute (IFPRI).

McKernan, S.-M. (2002). The impact of micro-credit programs on self-employment profits: Do non-credit program aspects matter? *Review of Economics and Statistics, 84,* 93–115.

Microfinance Information Exchange (MIX), *The Microbanking Bulletin,* semi-annual: www.themix.org/microbanking-bulletin/microbanking-bulletin

Microplace.com: http://www.microplace.com

MIX Markct—Global Microfinance Information Platform: http://www.mixmarket.org

Montgomery, R. (1996). Disciplining or protecting the poor? Avoiding the social costs of peer pressure in micro-credit schemes. *Journal of International Development, 8,* 289–305.

Morduch, J. (1999). The microfinance promise. *Journal of Economic Literature, 37,* 1569–1614.

PBS Small Fortunes Documentary and Accompanying Web site: http://www.pbs.org/kbyu/smallfortunes

Peterson, M., & Rajan, R. (1995). The effect of credit market competition on lending relationships. *Quarterly Journal of Economics, 110,* 407–443.

Pitt, M. (1999). *Reply to Jonathan Morduch's "Does microfinance really help the poor? New evidence from flagship programs in Bangladesh* (Unpublished mimeo). Retrieved from http://www.pstc.brown.edu/~mp/reply.pdf

Pitt, M., & Khandker, S. (1998). The impact of group-based credit on poor households in Bangladesh: Does the gender of participants matter? *Journal of Political Economy, 106,* 958–996.

Pitt, M., & Khandker, S. (2002). Credit programs for the poor and seasonality in rural Bangladesh. *Journal of Development Studies, 39*(2), 1–24.

Progress Out of Poverty Index, Grameen Foundation: http://www .progressoutofpoverty.org

Rajan, R., & Zingales, L. (1998). Which capitalism: Lessons from the East Asian financial crisis. *Journal of Applied Corporate Finance, 11*(3), 40–48.

Robinson, M. (2001). *The microfinance revolution.* Washington, DC: The World Bank.

Rosenberg, R. (2008, October 14). Muhammad Yunus and Michael Chu debate commercialization [Web log post]. Available at http://www.microfinance.cgap.org

Rutherford, S. (2000). *The poor and their money: An essay about financial services for poor people.* Delhi: Oxford India Paperbacks and the Department for International Development. Retrieved from http://www.uncdf.org/mfdl/readings/ PoorMoney.pdf

Stiglitz, J., & Weiss, A. (1981). Credit rationing in markets with imperfect information. *American Economic Review, 71,* 393–410.

UN International Year of Microcredit: http://www.yearofmicro credit.org

Wenner, M. (1995). Group credit: A means to improve information transfer and loan repayment performance. *Journal of Development Studies, 32,* 263–281.

Wydick, B. (1999). Can social cohesion be harnessed to repair market failures? Evidence from group lending in Guatemala. *The Economic Journal, 109,* 463–475.

83

LATIN AMERICA'S TRADE PERFORMANCE IN THE NEW MILLENNIUM

MARITZA SOTOMAYOR

Utah Valley University

Latin America has witnessed impressive economic growth since 2003. The average annual growth of the gross domestic product (GDP) for Latin America has been 5% for the 2003–2007 period, the highest in three decades. Trade performance has been one of the essential factors in explaining this growth. The purpose of this article is to analyze the main elements of Latin America's trade performance from the 1990s until recent years and to explain whether global demand and economic reforms of the 1990s helped strengthen the role of the region's trade sector.

Latin American countries have had both a positive and negative relationship with the global economy. After their independence around the beginning of the nineteenth century, most of them were involved in the first period of globalization. During this first era of globalization, Latin America based its economic growth on trade of basic commodities with Europe (for some countries, exports represented more than 60% of GDP). With World War I and the Great Depression, international prices of commodities fell, affecting the Latin American countries. An inward-looking economic model known as import substitution industrialization (ISI) was pursued to eliminate industry's growing dependence on imports and the negative impacts of external shocks from the global economy. Although ISI was crucial in the construction of a manufacturing industry for countries such as Mexico, Brazil, and Argentina, there were also inconsistencies in industrial and trade policies. In the end, this had consequences for the whole economy. After three decades of ISI, it was clear for Latin American governments that it was not possible to uphold an industry based on a growing demand for imported inputs relying on foreign debt.

Throughout the 1970s, Latin America obtained low-interest loans. However, after the oil crisis in 1973 and the economic depression through those years, real interest rates increased. As a consequence, Latin American countries entered into a decade of debt crisis. The period 1980–1989 is known as *the lost decade* because of Latin America's poor economic performance, increase in poverty, and lack of viable solutions.

Latin American countries began a process of trade liberalization after several stabilization programs. The positive numbers in the trade account (exports minus imports) during the first years of the twenty-first century were the result of two factors. The first was the economic reforms whereby exports were again the growth engine during the 1990s. The second factor was the fact that the positive global economic conditions enhanced commodity prices, which made Latin America again dependent on the volatilities of the foreign market.

This second era of globalization set new challenges for Latin America. The current global economic conditions with the financial crisis will very likely slow down the region's economic growth. However, it can be seen as a juncture to reevaluate Latin America's trade specialization in the global economy. This change would imply diversification of export destinations, increase the participation of manufacturing products in exports, and consolidate efforts for regional economic integration.

This chapter consists of three sections: (1) trade liberalization process, which reviews the main aspects of economic reforms in the 1990s; (2) trade performance in Latin America 2000–2007, which includes analyses of statistics referring to exports and imports (since demand of exports from China has been an important element in trade performance, there is a subsection regarding the trade between Latin America and China); and (3) the financial crisis of 2008 and trade performance, which evaluates how the global economy's slowdown would affect the region.

Trade Liberalization Process

This section covers the main elements of Latin America's trade liberalization process that started for most countries in the 1990s. It will give a perspective on how economic reforms transformed the trade sector where exports had become the main engine of growth.

Theory

Regarding the potential benefits of trade liberalization, Krugman and Obstfeld (2000) stated that an economic opening through tariff reduction eliminates distortions for consumers and producers with the consequent increase in national welfare. An increase in competition through the supply of imported goods in the domestic market pushes prices down with direct benefits for consumers. Dornbusch (1992) pointed out that trade liberalization brings potential dynamic benefits, for example, through the introduction of a new method of production, the opening of a new market, or the carrying out of new production methods. With the same approach, Rodrik (1999) affirmed that benefits from opening markets are not on the side of exports but rather on the side of imports. According to him, developing countries can benefit from imports of capital and intermediate inputs that are too expensive to produce locally.

One of the main criticisms of free trade and its application to developing countries has been that models of free trade suppose perfect competition in the market. However, Latin America's industries are imperfect market structures. Therefore, selective tariffs on industries can prevent additional distortions in the economy. This is referred to as the market failure justification for infant industry protection (Krugman & Obstfeld, 2000).

This argument against trade liberalization in Latin America was used to emphasize its potential negative effects on local industry. If the speed of trade liberalization were too fast (i.e., the tariff reduction is not gradual), the industry would not have time to adjust to upcoming competition after a period of high protection. The results would be the loss of jobs and wiping out of small and medium enterprises that probably could not compete with multinational corporations.

According to Ffrench-Davis (2005), the competitiveness of the industrial sector should not be based on low wages, government subsidies, or tax exemptions. Industrial policies should aim to increase productivity in the export sector. The export sector promoted by these policies should generate value added and spillovers to the rest of the economy (activities such as the *maquiladoras,* where the value added and spillovers are small, could not be part of these efforts).

These different points of view about benefits and cost of trade liberalization provide an introduction for Latin America's economic policies during the 1990s.

Economic Reforms of the 1990s

Most Latin American economies used different stabilization programs as a result of the debt crisis. The decade of the 1980s was known as *the lost decade* because of the severe impact on GDP per capita (the average annual percentage change of real GDP per capita was –0.4% for the region), inflation (Argentina: 385% and Brazil: 228% both in 1985 or Bolivia: 2,252% for the 1980–1985 period), and the increase of poverty (39% of Latin America's population lived in poverty in 1990 compared with 35% in 1980; Helwege, 1995). At the end of the 1980s, most of Latin America engaged in economic reforms that had exports as the main engine of economic development. A second era of globalization began with economic reforms that included privatization (reducing the role of the state in the economy) and trade liberalization (opening the economy).

These economic reforms were part of what is now termed the "Washington Consensus" reforms or the neoliberal policies (free-market approach). Williamson (1990) summarized in an article the 10 policy instruments that institutions such as the U.S. Treasury, the International Monetary Fund (IMF), the World Bank, and the Inter-American Development Bank (all of them located in Washington, D.C.) advised as the most significant economic reforms for Latin America. These were fiscal discipline, reordering public expenditure priorities, tax reform, liberalizing interest rates, a competitive exchange rate, trade liberalization, liberalization of foreign direct investment (FDI), privatization, deregulation, and property rights (Williamson, 1990).

Throughout this period, several Latin American countries entered into a period of democratic processes (e.g., elected presidents Alfonsin in Argentina, Siles in Bolivia, Collor in Brazil, and Belaunde in Peru), which helped with the implementation of these economic policies. Besides reduction of the role of the state, economic policies pursued an increase in international trade's participation and promotion of private investment. Argentina followed closely the Washington Consensus recommendations. However, this country suffered from a peso crisis and a reduction of GDP (as a consequence, unemployment levels reached record levels of 20% in 1995; Hofman, 2000). Countries such as Brazil decided not to follow the neoliberal approach. It established a middle path with changes in a slow pace with different stabilization plans (heterodox reforms).

Trade Performance in Latin America 2000–2007

Main Economic and Social Characteristics

Table 83.1 summarizes the main economic and social characteristics of Latin American economies for recent years. These data offer an outlook on similarities and differences among these nations.

Generally speaking, Brazil and Mexico account for more than half of the total region's population. Latin America's land area is bigger than the size of the United States and Canada together. The land areas range from El Salvador with 8.1 thousand square miles to Brazil with 3.3 million square miles. Natural resources are diverse because of geographical and geological conditions. The Andes cross South America from north to south where mineral resources are relatively abundant in countries such as Chile, Peru, and Bolivia. The tropical climate of Colombia is suitable for coffee production, while the conditions of Argentina's plains are good for the cattle industry.

As can be seen in Table 83.1, Argentina, Brazil, and Mexico together explain three quarters of Latin America's

Table 83.1   Basic Economic and Social Indicators for Latin America

	Population 2007 (in Thousands of Persons)	Land Area (in Thousands of km²)	Share of Regional GDP 2000–2007 (%)	GDP Growth 2003–2007 (%)	GDP Per Capita 2007 (in 2000 U.S. Dollars)	Urban Population % Total Population 2005	HDI 2006 (%)[1]
Argentina	39,356	2,767	13.28	8.83	9,396	91.80	0.860 (46)
Bolivia	9,828	1,099	0.42	4.13	1,090	64.23	0.723 (111)
Brazil	192,645	8,512	31.79	3.93	4,216	83.40	0.807 (70)
Chile	16,604	757	3.89	4.99	6,127	86.56	0.874 (40)
Colombia	46,116	1,139	4.85	5.90	2,843	76.62	0.787 (80)
Costa Rica	4,475	51	0.83	6.54	5,085	62.61	0.847 (50)
Cuba	11,248	111	n.d.	8.02	4,173	76.15	0.855 (48)
Dominican Republic	9,749	49	1.22	5.89	3,464	65.49	0.768 (91)
Ecuador	13,601	248	0.85	4.79	1,624	62.82	0.807 (72)
El Salvador	7,108	21	0.64	3.21	2,252	57.84	0.747 (101)
Guatemala	13,344	109	0.86	4.00	1,665	49.97	0.696 (121)
Haiti	9,602	28	0.16	0.83	392	41.75	0.521 (148)
Honduras	7,176	112	0.38	5.88	1,420	47.83	0.714 (117)
Mexico	106,448	1,958	30.36	3.32	7,094	76.50	0.842 (51)
Nicaragua	5,603	130	0.20	3.95	885	56.99	0.699 (120)
Panama	3,337	77	0.61	7.80	5,206	65.77	0.832 (58)
Paraguay	6,120	407	0.35	4.40	1,467	58.50	0.752 (98)
Peru	27,894	1,285	2.77	6.47	2,751	72.66	0.788 (79)
Uruguay	3,332	177	0.91	7.01	7,255	91.95	0.859 (47)
Venezuela RB	27,460	912	5.65	7.92	5,789	92.77	0.826 (61)
Latin America	**561,046**	**19,949**	**100.00**	**4.94**	**4,723**	**77.84**	**0.810**[2]

SOURCES: Based on data from Economic Commission for Latin America and the Caribbean (ECLAC), CEPALSTAT Databases and Statistical Publications (http://www.eclac.cl/estadisticas/default.asp?idioma=IN) and Statistical Update (http://hdr.undp.org/en/media/HDI_2008_EN_Tables.pdf).

NOTES: 1. Human Development Index (HDI) was developed by United Nations Development Programme (UNDP) in 1990. According to them, it "is a new way of measuring development by combining indicators of life expectancy, education attainment and income into a composite human development index. The HDI sets a minimum and a maximum for each dimension, called goalposts, and then shows where each country stands in relation to these goalposts expressed as a value between 0 and 1." Numbers in parentheses show the country's ranking. 2. Includes the Caribbean.

GDP, which justifies why these economies share a central role in the region's economic performance. One of the most notable aspects in Latin American economies has been their GDP growth for the 2003–2007 period (with the exception of Haiti with a GDP growth of less than 1%). In Table 83.1, many economies show percentages of growth above 5%, while the percentage for the 1999–2002 period was only 1%. The rapid increase in commodity prices is among the factors that explain this performance, due to an increase in demand by countries such as China and India. Although the region is not homogeneous in per capita income, Argentina and Uruguay have one of the highest levels of income per capita. Haiti is among the lowest income per capita countries in Latin America with severe poverty. Overall, Central America and the Caribbean countries have the worst poverty. This assessment turns out to be more evident with the Human Development Index (HDI) indicator proposed by the United Nations Development Programme (UNDP) in 1990. The index's objective is to add social aspects such as life expectancy, education attainment, and income to the existing economic indicators to give a broader measure of economic development. The HDI goes from 0 to 1, and countries are ranked according to this index (UNDP, 1990). The last column of Table 83.1 includes the HDI and the country's ranking in parentheses for 2006. According to this index, Chile, Argentina, and Uruguay have shown high levels of economic development. Even though Uruguay is a small country in comparison with the rest of the region, this country can be considered as developed in terms of its HDI. Then again, although Brazil has a big economy, its HDI was below average for the overall region. As can be inferred from Table 83.1, Latin America is not a homogeneous region in social and

economic terms. The trade liberalization process initiated in the 1990s allowed these countries to participate in the global economy. However, the results from that experience have not always translated into an increase in living standards.

Tariff Reduction and Regional Trade Agreements

One of the policy tools used in the trade liberalization process was the reduction of tariff rates. Figure 83.1 shows Latin America's simple average tariff for manufacturing products for the 1980–2006 period and for selected countries.

Protectionist measures taken throughout ISI led to an increase in tariff rates that lasted for several decades. In 1980, Brazil had an average tariff for manufactured imports of 99.4%, while the rest of Latin America averaged a rate of 50%. The exception was Chile since this country started opening its economy in the mid-1970s. This opening process implied for some countries joining the General Agreement on Tariffs and Trade (GATT), which in 1995 became the World Trade Organization (WTO). As members, they have to limit their tariff rates. In consequence, for 2006, the tariff rates fluctuated around 10% or less.

During the 1990s, there was a revival effort for regional economic integration as an element of trade liberalization in Latin America. The first experiences with regional trade integration occurred in the 1960s. However, attempts to form regional integration arrangements did not reach the expected results. One of the first integration experiments took place when some Central American countries (Costa Rica, El Salvador, Honduras, Nicaragua, and Guatemala)

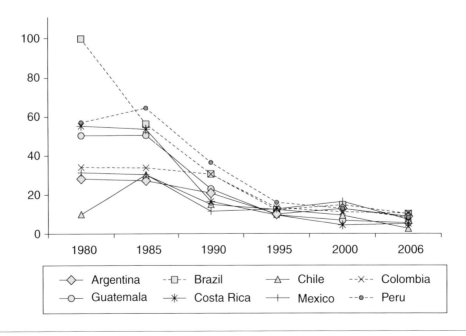

Figure 83.1 Simple Average Tariff for Manufacturing Products in Latin America 1980–2006 (%)

SOURCES: Based on data from the United Nations Conference on Trade and Development (UNCTAD, 2008); World Trade Organization, *World Tariff Profiles,* various years; Gwartney and Lawson (2008); and data from http://www.freetheworld.com.

together formed the Central American Common Market (CACM) in 1960. It was created as a "custom union." A "custom union" is a free trade area with a common external tariff for nonmembers. According to Bulmer-Thomas (2003), one of CACM's problems was the size of its market and the inward-looking industrial policies that hurt exports of manufacturing products.

The Andean Community treaty was signed in 1969. Its objective was to build a common market between Bolivia, Colombia, Ecuador, Peru, Venezuela, and Chile. The Andean Community has been in place for four decades. It has not reached the stage of a common market. It has faced problems of coordination, and the institutions have not worked properly.

Other experiences with common markets occurred when the Caribbean countries formed the Caribbean Community and Common Market (CARICOM) in 1973, signed by all Caribbean countries. The Latin American Integration Association (LAIA) was formed in 1980 as a free trade area with most South American countries (Argentina, Bolivia, Brazil, Chile, Colombia, Ecuador, Paraguay, Peru, Uruguay, and Venezuela), as well as Cuba and Mexico.

The first regional integration agreement of the 1990s was formed with Argentina, Brazil, Paraguay, and Uruguay as members of the Southern Cone Common Market (SCCM or MERCOSUR, acronym in Spanish) in 1991. The same year, the CACM reconstructed its trade agreement with the creation of the Central American Integration System (CAIS), adding Panama and Belize as well as one country from the Caribbean, the Dominican Republic. The Group of Three (G3) was signed by Colombia, Mexico, and Venezuela in 1995 as a free trade area. All of these regional economic integration agreements were understood as part of Latin America's trade policy to diversify their markets and gain from specializations among the region.

Among experiences that have been successful, it is important to mention MERCOSUR. The group has expanded with the inclusion of Venezuela in 2003 and Chile as an observer member. The intra-industry trade between members has grown, particularly for Paraguay, which increased its trade from 30% in 1990 to 50% in 2005. Uruguay's intra-industry trade increased also; more than a third of its trade is made between bloc members. However, Yeats (1997) indicated that trade barriers with third countries have affected the comparative advantages in capital goods due to high trade restriction with nonmembers of the bloc.

In addition, there have been other bilateral agreements with countries outside the region such as Mexico with the United States and Canada (North American Free Trade Agreement [NAFTA]) in 1994, Peru and the United States in 2009, or between regional groups such as MERCOSUR with the European Union (still in the process of signing an agreement).

Openness Indices

Tariff reductions and regional trade integration agreements were two significant factors for an increase in the participation of external trade (exports plus imports) as a percentage of GDP. This participation is measured as an openness index. It has been used as an indicator of the trade sector's significance in an economy. Figure 83.2 shows the openness indices for selected Latin American countries.

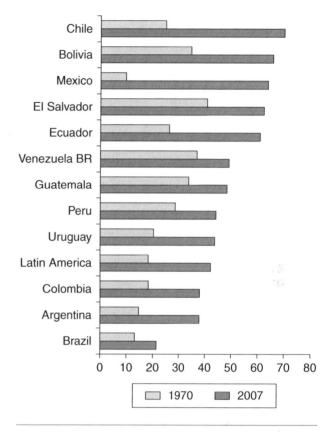

Figure 83.2 Openness Indices (%)

SOURCE: Based on data from UNCTAD (2008).

Figure 83.2 shows the indices for 2 years, 1970 and 2007. This figure can give an overview of how extensive the external sector is now for Latin American economies. On one hand, the average share of external trade as part of GDP for the region was situated between 10% and 20% in 1970. Some small countries' trade participation in the economy was 40% (El Salvador) or 34% (Guatemala). On the other hand, some countries moved slowly toward opening their economies. In this case, Brazil's trade sector was 13% and Argentina's just 14% of the GDP. Currently, Latin America is one of the most open regions in the world. As can be seen from Figure 83.2, many economies surpassed the 40% mark in 2007. In most cases, it was the increase of exports in the total trade that explained the relative performance.

Structure of Exports

Trade liberalization had as one of its objectives the increase of manufacturing goods exports as a percentage of total trade. Figure 83.3 shows the structure of exports for Latin America for selected years.

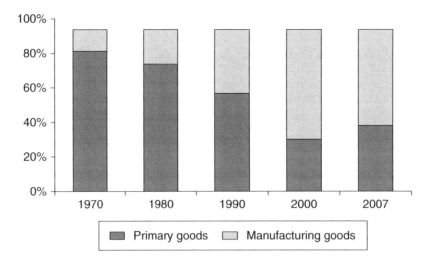

Figure 83.3 Structure of Exports (%)

SOURCE: Based on data from Economic Commission for Latin America and the Caribbean (ECLAC, 2008).

This figure illustrates how until the 1980s, primary goods were the main export products. The structure of exports started to transform in the 1990s. Manufacturing goods exports were 37% for 1990 and increased to 60% in 2001. Parts and components have played a significant role in increasing manufacturing products, particularly for Brazil and Mexico, as well as exports of finished vehicles. The participation of primary goods began to intensify again in 2003 due to the rise in commodity prices (crude oil was 14.5% of total exports in 2005). In 2006, the exports of manufacturing products were just 48%.

A closer look of leading export products reveals the significance of commodities for the 1970s and the 1980s. In more recent years, there are more manufacturing products exported, particularly those from the automotive industry. The increase of manufacturing goods export has international vertical specialization as one explanation. This trade specialization began in the 1970s with multinational corporations. They established labor-intensive production stages in developing countries to reduce labor costs. The in-bond industry or *maquiladora* is one example of this type of manufacturing production. The maquiladora was a program initiated in 1965 in Mexico along its northern border with the United States. It was backed by a specific tariff scheme between these two countries. It allowed the imports of parts and components from the United States without duties for assembly in Mexico and subsequent export as final product for the U.S. market.

Feenstra (1998) coined the process as integration of trade and disintegration of production. As a result, there is an increase in exports of parts and components, but for countries such as Brazil and Mexico, the export of finished vehicles has become the third most important product.

Recent growth in the demand for commodity products from China and India has caused a rise in prices. On one hand, some Latin American countries (Bolivia, Chile, Peru, and Venezuela) have benefited from this important source of income. The GDP's performance for the 2003–2007 period

has as one of its determinants the increase in the demand for commodity products. On the other hand, income revenues from commodity exports have created overvalued pressures on real exchange rates. An overvalued pressure exists when the supply of foreign currency in the economy is greater than the demand. In consequence, the local currency increases in value. An overvalued exchange rate becomes an anti-export bias for noncommodities exports. In addition, inflation pressures have affected the region due in part to the commodity price boom. The average inflation rate for Latin America was 6% for the 2006–2007 period and increased to 9% in 2008. The slowdown in global economic activity due to the international financial crisis will reduce inflationary pressures. The Economic Commission for Latin America and the Caribbean (ECLAC, 2009b) predicted that Latin America's GDP growth rate would fall off to 1.7%.

Origin and Destination of Exports and Imports

The origin and destination of exports and imports for Latin American countries can be seen in Table 83.2.

Table 83.2 Exports and Imports Main Partners, 1980–2007

	Exports		Imports	
	1980	*2007*	*1980*	*2007*
United States	35.4	40.3	36.9	34.7
European Union	26.8	14.3	20.6	14.8
Latin America	15.9	17.8	14.4	20.8
China	0.7	5.9	0.3	7.7
Other countries	21.3	21.7	27.8	22.0

SOURCE: Data from Economic Commission for Latin America and the Caribbean (ECLAC, 2008).

Table 83.2 shows the composition of exports and imports in 1980 and 2007 for trade with selected partners. Regarding exports, the U.S. market has been significant for Latin American exports. In 1980, the region sent 35% of its total exports to the United States, 27 years later increasing that percentage to 40%. The European Union market was important for some manufacturing products (automotive goods) in the 1980s but has gradually lost participation as a destination of Latin American exports (from 27% in 1980 to half of that percentage in 2007). Latin America has also been a destination for exports from members of the region. However, the composition between 1980 and 2007 has not changed significantly (16% in 1980 to 18% in 2007). China has become an important partner for some Latin American countries, particularly for the supply of commodities. Since 2003, China has become the second most important trading partner for Mexico. This performance has meant an increase in its participation as a destination market from 1% in 1980 to 6% in 2007.

The main trade partners for imports of products demanded by Latin American countries can be seen in Table 83.2. The import composition shares similarities with exports. The United States and European Union were significant as sources for imported products. Even though the participation of the European Union has decreased, there are still significant trade ties between both regions. There has been an increase in the import demand from members of the Latin American region from 14% in 1980 to 21% in 2007. Since 2003, China has increased exports to Latin America; so far, the trade balance has been positive for most Latin American countries, but the demand for Chinese products has increased steadily.

Trade With China

Trade with China has been an important factor for overall trade performance of Latin American economies in the past 5 years. The main goods demanded from this country are primary goods, particularly ores and metals. Figure 83.4 shows the main products imported from Latin America for 1995 and 2006. The economic growth of China since the 1980s has demanded imports of primary products for expanding its industrial base and of some agricultural products that appeal to the more sophisticated Chinese population (e.g., by-products from cattle farming).

Some Latin American countries have consolidated their trade relations with China through bilateral trade agreements. Chile was the first Latin American country to sign a free trade agreement (FTA) with China in 2005. Peru initiated negotiation toward an FTA the same year, signing an agreement in 2008. Rosales and Kuwuyama (2007) pointed out that the benefits of trading with China have been uneven for the region. South American countries have gained from an increase in terms of trade (export prices/import prices), while Central American countries have been hurt by the competition of Chinese products in the U.S. manufacturing market.

Mexico has seen its share of manufactured products decrease in the U.S. market (textiles and apparel) due to an increase in imports from China. Chiquiar, Fragoso, and Ramos-Francia (2007) calculated that Mexico lost comparative advantages (Mexican exports vs. world exports to the U.S. market) in the textile and apparel sectors because of competition by Chinese products. Even though Mexico enjoyed free-market access to the U.S. market with NAFTA, the low cost of Chinese manufacturing as well as changes in the WTO regulations explain the increase of

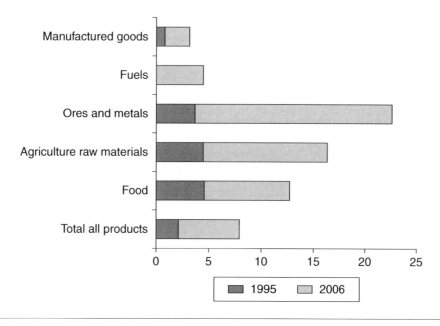

Figure 83.4 China: Main Products Imported From Latin America (%)

SOURCE: Based on data from United Nations Conference on Trade and Development (UNCTAD, 2008).

Chinese goods in the U.S. market. Gallagher, Moreno-Brid, and Porzecanski (2008) stated that Mexico has lost competitiveness in 15 non-oil-exported products in the U.S. market due to Chinese competition. Their measurement indicates that industries that depend on unskilled labor are the most threatened.

Effects on GDP

Finally, we analyze the possible links between trade performance and its effects on GDP, employment. and industrial production. There is some argument about the positive effects of trade performance on economic growth. Empirical evidence for the 1990s has not been conclusive about this relationship (Giles & Williams, 2000). Furthermore, one of the most debated issues at that time was the slow economic growth that accompanied the posttrade liberalization period. Latin America's per capita GDP growth rate for 1990–2004 was 0.9%, a much lower rate than the period of ISI (2.6% for 1950–1980). This rate was lower than for the East Asian countries for the 1990–2000 period (3.95%) and for the world (1.2%).

Ffrench-Davis (2005) reviewed the different approaches to explain the low economic growth of the 1990s. Some of his focus was on the stabilization programs during the 1980s and the lack of complementary reforms to support manufactured exports. For example, Dijkstra (2000) affirmed that trade liberalization effects on industrial development were mixed depending on the level of development of the industrial base in Latin American countries. He found that industrial structural changes in Chile and Brazil were explained by domestic demand and exchange rate factors rather than an increase in exports. Other studies criticized the Washington Consensus reforms and their failure to deliver the expected benefits of an open economy. This disappointment with the neoliberal economic reforms has been one of the reasons for recent trends toward more state intervention in the economy. Countries such as Venezuela, Bolivia, and Ecuador have distanced themselves from the Washington Consensus policies.

Figure 83.5 shows some indicators of growth, per capita GDP, and exports for the 2000–2008 period for Latin America.

The GDP per capita and the value-added manufacturing and total export rates of growth are depicted in the left axis, and the urban open unemployment rate is depicted in the right axis. As can be seen in the figure, the per capita GDP has grown steadily since 2003, with percentages that the region has not experienced since the ISI period (around 5%). The performance of total exports varied over this period, since between 2001 and 2003, there was a decline in the rate of growth, but it has started to increase since 2003 due to an important increase in primary product exports (more than 15% since 2004). Besides, it is important to take into consideration that during this same period, primary product exports explained more than 10% of the total GDP. As mentioned before, the international demand for these products

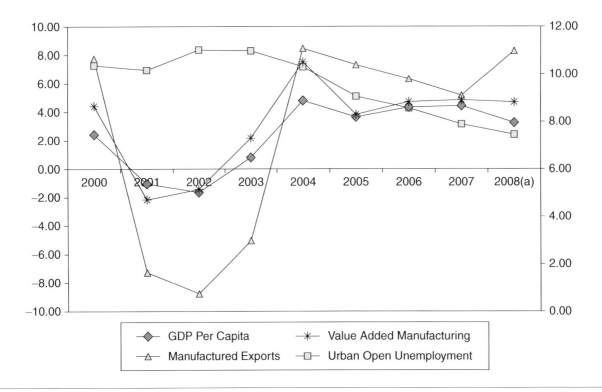

Figure 83.5 Exports Growth Rates and Economic Performance (%)

SOURCES: Based on data from United Nations Conference on Trade and Development (UNCTAD, 2008) and Economic Commission for Latin America and the Caribbean (ECLAC, 2008).

NOTE: (a) Estimated figures.

and the favorable terms of trade have helped to shape these results. Since 2004, the value added for manufacturing products grew at rates close to 5% until 2008. One of the results of the positive performance of the economies can be seen in a reduction of unemployment. From 8% in 2000, it was reduced to close to 5% in 2008. However, the international financial crisis of 2008 affected the economic performance of the following years for the region, as we will discuss in the next section.

Financial Crisis of 2008 and Trade Performance

Latin American countries began to experience the slow-down of the global economy in 2008, particularly during the last quarter of the same year, when major problems in the U.S. financial crisis could not be solved and spread over European and Japanese financial markets. This financial crisis was a result of the real estate market's collapse and the damage to the related financial system. The immediate consequence was a reduction in consumer spending, which brought an increase in unemployment. According to the National Bureau of Economic Research (NBER), the U.S. economy officially entered into a period of recession on December 1, 2007 (NBER, 2008).

Dealing with financial crises is not new for Latin American economies. For example, the Great Depression of the 1930s and the debt crisis of the 1980s had lasting negative consequences for many economies and took several years to stabilize. For Latin America, the main transmission channels of the global economic crisis could come from the reduction in export demand, decline in prices of commodity goods, and therefore a reduction in terms of trade as well as remittances and restrictions in financial credit sources (World Bank, 2008).

According to a number of analyses (ECLAC, 2008; International Development Bank [IDB], 2008; World Bank, 2008), most of Latin America is better prepared than before to confront external shocks due to improved management of macroeconomic policies. During the 1990s and, to a major extent, in the beginning of the twenty-first century, these countries have reduced their external debt, increased FDI flows, limited fiscal spending, and followed semi-flexible exchange rates. These macroeconomic measures should reduce the possibility of an economic crisis of big proportions. Also, the decline in foreign demand would reduce inflationary pressures that increase external demand caused during 2008 in some countries of the region such as Peru, Argentina, or Bolivia. In general terms, ECLAC (2009a) has projected a negative growth of –0.3% for Latin America and the Caribbean for 2009 and a decline of 15% in the region's terms of trade.

The effects of the financial crisis will not be homogeneous in the region. First, it is expected that countries with commercial ties to the U.S. market will experience a sharp decline in demand for their exports. That is the case of Mexico, in which more than 60% of total exports go to the U.S. market. The Mexican economy also depends on the flow of remittances from Mexican workers living in the United States, so if those decrease, that could worsen the trade account. A reduction in remittances was expected for the rest of 2009. It could have an impact on the Mexican GDP since the remittances account for 3% of the total GDP. Moreover, ECLAC estimates a reduction of –2.0% in total GDP in 2009 (ECLAC, 2009a). The Central American countries face similar economic perspectives. The U.S. market is significant for Central America's maquiladora products; a reduction in demand would affect these economies. Remittances also are significant for countries such as El Salvador (30% of GDP) and Honduras (20% of GDP).

The economies of South America are more diversified in terms of export destinations. Even though the U.S. market is considerable for their products, there is an important growing trade with Asian countries and intra-regional trade with countries in South America. Since the increase in demand for commodity products originates in Asian countries, particularly from China, the fall of commodity prices will have an effect on volume of exports. However, the export performance predictions for South America are not worrisome (with the exception of Argentina) since it is expected that demand of goods from countries such as China and India will continue, and these countries will maintain economic ties with South America to secure sources of primary goods for their own economic growth, although not at the same pace as during the past 5 years.

Conclusion

Trade liberalization began during the 1990s for most Latin American countries. After decades of inward-looking economic policies and the struggles to develop a strong industrial base, countries such as Brazil, Mexico, and Argentina are considered today to be emerging economies with competitive industrial sectors.

However, the economic reforms of the 1990s have proven to be a challenge for the region since the eruption of several macroeconomic collapses such as in Argentina in 2001. For that reason, there have been criticisms of the Washington Consensus approach. In fact, the discontent with the market fundamentalism of the Washington Consensus has been the reason for the conception of a new path of development in Latin America. Under a different approach, the state again is taking a role in the economy, as in Venezuela, Bolivia, and Ecuador and, to a lesser measure, in Brazil and Argentina.

In general, the first years of the twenty-first century have been relatively successful for Latin American countries. After almost two decades of stabilization programs, the region has started to experience steady economic growth from 2003 until 2007. The impact on GDP growth has been considerable, around 5% per year for the same period, a percentage that the region has not seen since three decades earlier. This performance has been explained by the rapid increase in primary goods prices. However, economic reforms from the 1990s have been a factor in the development of its external trade sector.

One of the results of trade liberalization has been a transformation in the composition of exports, with an increase of manufactured goods as a share of total exports. However, trade performance has not been homogeneous for the whole region. While Mexico's exports are concentrated in manufactured products (including products from the maquiladora program) directed to the U.S. market, countries from South America are more diversified in terms of their export destination and share a significant intraregional trade. MERCOSUR plays an important role for the region as well as the Andean Community.

The rise of China in the global economy has been a turning point for Latin American primary goods. Since 2003, these countries have become one of the main origins of exports as well as destinations for imports coming from China. In industrial sectors such as textiles, China has been a serious competitor with Mexico and Central American countries in the U.S. market.

The financial global crisis of 2008 will have an important impact on Latin American economies. At the beginning of 2008, the economic growth rate prediction for the region was around 3%. At the beginning of 2009, that percentage was dropped to –0.1%. Latin America faces the current global financial crisis as a new test of how it can manage an external shock without entering a recession (such as in the 1930s or the 1980s). The crisis will hit countries that depend on the U.S. market for their exports more severely, such as in Mexico and Central America. Moreover, incomes from remittances also will diminish during this period. Meanwhile, South America will experience the impact of financial restrictions and the decline in the demand for primary goods. The crisis will also help countries such as Peru to cope with imminent inflation problems.

In the second era of globalization, Latin American countries are much better prepared to face external shocks. The region has stronger institutions with significant international reserves as well as fiscal and monetary discipline that will help to ease negative impacts. The financial crisis has been analyzed as evidence of market failures. For this reason, Latin America is taking this time to reassess, searching for a new path of economic development. It includes the structural economic characteristics without the need for protectionist policies or inward-looking economic policies.

The global financial crisis can be seen as an opportunity for a change in trade pattern specialization. First, a diversification of the destination of exports can reduce the dependence of demand of one country (i.e., the U.S. market). Second, increasing intra-industry trade between members of the region and efforts toward regional integration can increase the trade in manufacturing goods. Third, even though Latin American countries have a comparative advantage in primary products, there are industrial sectors that have been proven successful in the international arena, such as the automotive industry in Brazil and Mexico. Therefore, Latin America could increase the share of manufacturing products in total trade and reduce the volatilities of prices of primary goods. All of the above could result in a new role in the international economy for the region.

References and Further Readings

Balassa, B. (1971). Regional integration and trade liberalization in Latin America. *Journal of Common Market Studies, 10,* 58–78.

Bulmer-Thomas, V. (2003). *The economic history of Latin America since independence* (2nd ed.). Cambridge, UK: Cambridge University Press.

Cardoso, E., & Helwege, A. (1997). *Latin America's economy: Diversity, trends and conflicts.* Cambridge: MIT Press.

Chiquiar, D., Fragoso, E., & Ramos-Francia, M. (2007). *La ventaja comparativa y el desempeño de las exportaciones manufactureras mexicanas en el periodo 1996–2005* [Comparative advantage and the performance of the Mexican manufactured export during 1995–2005 period] (Working Paper 2007–12). Mexico DF: Banco de Mexico.

Dijkstra, G. (2000). Trade liberalization and industrial development in Latin America. *World Development, 28,* 1567–1582.

Dornbusch, R. (1992). The case for trade liberalization in developing countries. *Journal of Economic Perspectives, 6,* 69–85.

Economic Commission for Latin America and the Caribbean (ECLAC). (2008). *Latin America and the Caribbean in the world economy, 2007: Trends 2008.* Santiago de Chile: Author.

Economic Commission for Latin America and the Caribbean (ECLAC). (2009a, April). *Economic growth in Latin America and the Caribbean will fall to –0.3% in 2009* (Press release). Santiago de Chile: Author.

Economic Commission for Latin America and the Caribbean (ECLAC). (2009b, December). *El comercio internacional en América Latina y el Caribe en 2009. Crisis y recuperación.* Santiago de Chile: Author.

Edwards, S. (2004). *Crisis and reform in Latin America: From despair to hope.* Washington, DC: World Bank.

Feenstra, R. C. (1998). Integration of trade and disintegration of production. *Journal of Economic Perspectives, 12*(4), 31–50.

Ffrench-Davis, R. (2005). *Reforming Latin America's economies: After market fundamentalism.* New York City: Palgrave-Macmillan.

Flam, H., & Grunwald, J. (1985). *The global factory: Foreign assembly in international trade.* Washington, DC: The Brookings Institution.

Franco, P. (2007). *The puzzle of Latin American economic development.* Lanham, MD: Rowman & Littlefield.

Frieden, J., Pastor, M., Jr., & Tomz, M. (Eds.). (2000). *Modern political economy and Latin America: Theory and policy.* Boulder, CO: Westview.

Gallagher, K., Moreno-Brid, J. C., & Porzecanski, R. (2008). The dynamism of Mexican exports: Lost in (Chinese) translation? *World Development, 36,* 1365–1380.

Giles, J., & Williams, C. (2000). Export-led growth: A survey of the empirical literature and some non-causality results. *Journal of International Trade & Economic Development, 9,* 261–337.

Gwartney, J., & Lawson, R. (with Norton, S.). (2008). *Economic freedom of the world: 2008 annual report*. Vancouver, British Columbia, Canada: The Fraser Institute.

Helwege, A. (1995). Poverty in Latin America: Back to the abyss? *Journal of Interamerican Studies & World Affairs, 37*(3), 99–123.

Hofman, A. (2000). *The economic development of Latin America in the twentieth century*. Northampton, MA: Edward Elgar.

International Development Bank. (2008, October). *The fiscal impact of the international financial crisis on Latin America and the Caribbean* (Technical note). Washington, DC: Author.

Krugman, P., & Obstfeld, M. (2000). *International economics: Theory and policy* (5th ed.). Reading, MA: Addison-Wesley Longman.

Lederman, D., Olarreaga, M., & Perry, G. (Eds.). (2009). *China's and India's challenge to Latin America: Opportunity of threat*. Washington, DC: World Bank.

Lora, E. (2001). *Structural reforms in Latin America: What has been reformed and how to measure it* (Research Department Working Paper Series No. 466). Washington, DC: Inter-American Development Bank.

Lustig, N. (1994). *México. Hacia la Reconstrución de una Economía* [Mexico: The remaking of an economy]. México DF: El Colegio de México, Fondo de Cultura Económica.

National Bureau of Economic Research (NBER). (2008). *Determination of the December 2007 peak in economic activity*. Cambridge, MA: Business Cycle Dating Committee, NBER.

Rodrik, D. (1999). *The new global economy and developing countries: Making openness work* (Policy Essay No. 24). Washington, DC: Overseas Development Council.

Rosales, O., & Kuwuyama, M. (2007). Latin America meets China and India: Prospects and challenges for trade and investment. *Cepal Review, 93,* 81–103.

Santiso, J. E. (2007). *The visible hand of China in Latin America*. Paris: OECD.

United Nations Conference on Trade and Development (UNCTAD). (2008). *Handbook of statistics 2008*. New York: Author. Retrieved from http://stats.unctad.org/Handbook/TableViewer/tableView.aspx

United Nations Development Programme (UNDP). (1990). *Human development report 1990: Concept and measurement of human development, UNDP*. Oxford, UK: Oxford University Press.

Williamson, J. (1990). What Washington means by policy reform. In J. Willianson (Ed.), *Latin American adjustment: How much has happened?* (pp. 7–20). Washington, DC: Institute for International Economics.

World Bank. (2008). *Global economic prospects: Commodities at crossroads 2009*. Washington, DC: Author.

Yeats, A. (1997). *Does Mercosur's trade performance raise concerns about the regional trade arrangements?* (World Bank Policy Research Working Paper 1729). Washington, DC: World Bank.

PART VII

EMERGING AREAS IN ECONOMICS

84

BEHAVIORAL ECONOMICS

NATHAN BERG

University of Texas–Dallas

Behavioral economics is the subfield of economics that borrows from psychology, empirically tests assumptions used elsewhere in economics, and provides theories that aim to be more realistic and closely tied to experimental and field data. In a frequently cited survey article, Rabin (1998) describes behavioral economics as "psychology and economics," which is a frequently used synonym for behavioral economics. Similarly, Camerer (1999) defines behavioral economics as a research program aimed at reunifying psychology and economics.

Definitions and Naming Problems

Reunification is a relevant description because of the rather tumultuous relationship between psychology and economics in the arc of economic history. A number of preeminent founders of important schools of economic thought, including Adam Smith, wrote extensively on psychological dimensions of human experience and economic behavior, while later economists sometimes sought explicitly to exclude psychology from economic analysis. For example, Slutsky (1915/1952), whose famous equation is taught to nearly all upper-level microeconomics students, sought to erect a boundary excluding psychology from economics: "If we wish to place economic science upon a solid basis, we must make it completely independent of psychological assumptions" (p. 27).

Although historical accounts vary, one standard narrative holds that in the twentieth century, neoclassical economists made an intentional break with psychology in contrast to earlier classical and institutional economists who actively integrated psychology into their writings on economics (e.g., Bruni & Sugden, 2007). In twentieth-century economics' break with psychology, one especially important source is Milton Friedman's (1953) essay. In it, Friedman argues that unrealistic or even obviously untrue assumptions—especially, the core assumption used throughout much of contemporary economics (including much of behavioral economics) that all behavior can be modeled as resulting from decision makers solving constrained optimization problems—are perfectly legitimate, so long as they produce accurate predictions. Friedman put forth the analogy of a billiards player selecting shots "as if" he or she were solving a set of equations describing the paths of billiards balls based on Newtonian physics. We know that most expert billiards players have not studied academic physics and therefore do not in fact solve a set of equations each time they set up a shot. Nevertheless, Friedman argues that this model based on manifestly wrong assumptions should be judged strictly in terms of the predictions it makes and not the realism of its assumptions.

In contrast to Friedman's professed lack of interest in investigating the realism of assumptions, behavioral economists have made it a core theme in their work to empirically test assumptions in economic models and modify theory according to the results they observe. Despite this difference with neoclassical economists such as Friedman, behavioral economists frequently use as-if arguments to defend behavioral models, leading some methodological observers to see more similarity than contrast in the behavioral and neoclassical approaches (Berg & Gigerenzer, in press).

Bounded Rationality

The term *bounded rationality,* coined by Nobel laureate Herbert Simon (1986), is strongly associated with behavioral economics, although there appears to be far less agreement on the term's meaning. The neoclassical model assumes that economic man, or *homo economicus,* is infinitely self-interested, infinitely capable of processing information and solving optimization problems, and infinitely self-disciplined or self-consistent when it comes to having the willpower to execute one's plans—whether those plans concern how much junk food to eat or how much to save for retirement. In contrast, much of behavioral economics focuses on limits, or bounds, on one or more of these three assumptions. Thus, bounded self-interest, bounded information-processing capacity, and bounded willpower are three guiding themes in the behavioral economics literature.

Bounded self-interest enjoys widespread appeal in behavioral economics, which has proposed numerous models of so-called social preferences to address a number of observations from human experiments that appear to falsify the assumption that people maximize their own monetary payoffs. A decision maker with social preferences cares about the material or monetary payoffs of others as well as his or her own, although the manner in which concern for others' payoffs is expressed can take a variety of forms. For example, a person with social preferences might be happier when others are worse off, which is sometimes described as spite; be happier when others are better off, which is sometimes described as altruism; prefer equal over unequal allocations of money, which is sometimes described as inequality aversion; prefer allocations in which the sum of all people's payoffs is maximized, which is sometimes described as a preference for social welfare; prefer allocations in which the least well-off person has a larger payoff, which is sometimes described as a Rawlsian preference; or prefer allocations of resources in which his or her payoff is large relative to others, which is sometimes described as a competitive preference (Charness & Grosskopf, 2001). Common to all these variations and many other forms of social preferences is that people are not generally indifferent between two allocations of payoffs for all members in a group just because their own monetary payoff is the same. This violates the common neoclassical assumption that people are infinitely self-interested because it would imply that people are indifferent so long as their own material payoffs are held constant.

Bounded information-processing capacity is another active area within behavioral economics, which would have looked very much out of place in the mainstream economics literature only three decades ago. Topics in this area include limited memory, limited attention, limited number of degrees of perspective taking in strategic interaction, limited perceptual capacity, distorted beliefs, and decision and inference processes that violate various tenets of logic and probability theory (see Camerer, 2003, for examples).

Bounded willpower, often described as time inconsistency or dynamic inconsistency, is another large and growing part of the behavioral economics research program. In the neoclassical optimization model, decision makers choose a sequence of actions through time by selecting the best feasible sequence, with virtually no mention of the costs associated with implementing that plan over the course of people's lives. If there is no new information, then the neoclassical intertemporal choice problem is decided once and for all before the first action in the sequence is taken. Unlike the neoclassical model's assumption that acting on the optimal plan of action through time is costless, behavioral economists studying bounded willpower focus squarely on the tension between what a person wants himself or herself to do tomorrow versus what he or she actually does. This tension can be described as subjective inconsistency concerning what is best for oneself at a specific point in time, which, contrary to the neoclassical assumption, changes as a function of the time at which the decision is considered. One can think of planning now to start working on a term paper tomorrow but then tomorrow deciding to do something else instead—and regretting it after the fact.

Empirical Realism

Proponents of bringing psychology more deeply into economics argue that it is necessary to depart from the assumptions of *homo economicus* to achieve improved empirical realism (i.e., more accurate descriptions of economic behavior and better predictions following a change in policy or other economic conditions). In an article published in the *Journal of Business* titled "Rationality in Psychology and Economics," Simon (1986) writes,

> The substantive theories of rationality that are held by neoclassical economists lack an empirically based theory of choice. Procedural theories of rationality, which attempt to explain what information people use when making choices and how information is processed, could greatly improve the descriptive and forecasting ability of economic analysis. (p. S209)

Improving the empirical realism of economic analysis is a primary and ongoing motivation in behavioral economics, frequently stated in the writings and presentations of behavioral economists.

Example of Reference Point–Dependent Utility Functions

Similarly to Simon, Rabin (1998) argues that theories and experimental results from psychology enrich mainstream economics. But Rabin's idea about how behavioral economists can bring more empirical realism into economics is much more narrowly circumscribed than Simon's, with Rabin essentially arguing that behavioral economics should proceed within the utility maximization model of neoclassical economics. Despite their occasional claims to radical or revolutionary methodological innovation, many behavioral economists side with neoclassical economists in viewing constrained optimization as a non-negotiable methodological tenet that defines and distinguishes economics from other disciplines. Rabin says that the new empirical content that behavioral economists bring to bear will help economics as a whole to more realistically describe people's utility functions.

For example, as mentioned earlier in the discussion of the neoclassical model's assumption of unbounded self-interest, this assumption is often interpreted to mean that consumers care only about their own levels of consumption and that workers care only about their own income, irrespective of what others are consuming or earning. Behavioral economics models, in contrast, allow utility to depend on the *difference* between one's own level of consumption or income and a reference point level. The reference point level might reflect what one is accustomed to or reflect a social comparison made with respect to the average level within a social group.

Thus, a worker with a behavioral reference point–dependent utility function might prefer an annual salary of $90,000 at a company where the average worker earns $50,000 over a salary of $95,000 at a company where the average worker earns $200,000. In the standard economic model, only the worker's own payoffs should determine the ranking of job opportunities, holding all else equal, and not the comparison of one's own income with that of other workers. The reference point–dependent utility function tries to reflect the observation that many normal, healthy, and socially intelligent people do in fact care about their own payoffs relative to others. For some workers, it may be worthwhile to trade off a few thousand dollars of their own salary for a work environment where the relative pay structure is more to their liking (e.g., a feeling of relative high status in the $90,000 job being subjectively worth more than the extra $5,000 of income at the $95,000 job). It should be mentioned, however, that reference point–dependent theories in behavioral economics are not entirely new. One finds interpersonal comparisons in Veblen's (1899/1994) concept of conspicuous consumption from his classic *The Theory of the Working Class* and even earlier among some classical economists.

Debates About the Realism of Assumptions in Economic Models

There is active debate between behavioral and nonbehavioral economists—and among behavioral economists—about the extent to which empirical realism is being achieved by the behavioral economics research program. These two distinct layers of debate need to be untangled to appreciate the different issues at play and how behavioral economics is likely to influence public policy now that the Obama administration has recruited among its top advisers a number of behavioral economists, including Richard Thaler, Cass Sunstein, and Daniel Kahneman.

When trying to convince neoclassical economists who are skeptical about the need for behavioral economics, behavioral economists point to the improved ability of their psychology-inspired models to fit data collected from a variety of sources, including experimental, macroeconomic, and financial market data. Skeptics from outside behavioral economics have questioned whether the deviations from neoclassical assumptions have any important consequences for the economy as a whole, suggesting that they might perhaps "average out" in the aggregate. Skepticism about the relevance of experimental data remains strong, with many doubts expressed about whether the college students who participate in economic experiments can be relied upon to teach us anything new about economics and whether anything learned in one laboratory experiment can be generalized to broader populations in the economy—the so-called problem of external validity. Experimentalists have responded that the reason they carefully incentivize decisions by making subject payments dependent on their decisions is to make it costly for them to misrepresent their true preferences. Experimentalists have addressed the issue of external validity by going into the field with so-called field experiments and by conducting experiments among different subpopulations, such as financial market traders, Japanese fishermen, and other groups of adult workers (e.g., Carpenter & Seki, 2006).

Within behavioral economics, a different debate takes place. Among behavioral economists, despite a shared commitment to borrowing from psychology and other disciplines, there remains tension over how far to move away from constrained optimization as the singular organizing framework of neoclassical theory and in much of behavioral economics, too. An alternative approach, advocated by a minority of more psychology- and less economics-inspired behavioral economists, seeks to break more substantially with neoclassical economics, dispensing with optimization theory as a necessary step in deriving equations that describe behavior. Constrained optimization, whether in behavioral or neoclassical economics, assumes that decision makers see a well-defined choice set; exhaustively scan this set, plugging each possible action into a scalar-valued objective function, which might include parameters intended to capture psychological phenomena; weigh the costs and benefits associated with each action, which includes psychic costs and benefits; and finally choose the element in the choice set with the highest value according to the objective function. There is very little direct evidence of people making decisions—especially high-stakes decisions, such as choosing a career, buying a house, or choosing whom to marry—according to the constrained optimization process just described. In many real-world decisions such as those just mentioned, the choice set is impossibly large to clearly define and exhaustively search through. In other settings such as choosing a life partner or whom to marry, constrained optimization would be seen by some to violate important social norms.

Instead, critics such as Gigerenzer and Selten (2001) attempt to base theory directly on empirical description of actual decision processes. Like other economists, these critics use equations to describe behavior. However, their behavioral equations skip the step of deriving behavioral equations as solutions to constrained optimization problems. To these researchers, theorizing and observing how decision makers deal with the overwhelmingly high-dimensional choice sets they face, quickly searching for a good-enough action and discarding the rest, is a fundamental scientific question of primary importance. Herbert Simon (1986) referred to such threshold-seeking behavior as *satisficing* as distinct from *optimizing*.

Methodological Pluralism

Another theme in behavioral economics derives from its willingness to borrow from psychology and other disciplines such as sociology, biology, and neuroscience. To appreciate why methodological pluralism is characteristic of behavioral economics, one should recall that in neoclassical economics, there is a singular behavioral model applied to all problems as well as a number of prominent efforts in economic history to expunge influence from other social sciences such as psychology and sociology. Although the structure of choice sets and the objective functions change depending on the application, contemporary economists typically apply the maximization principle to virtually every decision problem they consider. Consumer choice is modeled as utility maximization, firm behavior is modeled as profit maximization, and the evaluation of public policy is analyzed via a social welfare function whose maximized value depends systematically on parameters representing policy tools. In contrast, commitment to improved empirical description and its normative application to policy problems motivates behavioral economists, in many cases, to draw on a wider set of methodological tools, although the breadth of this pluralism is a matter of debate, as indicated in the previous section.

Naming Problems

The term *behavioral economics* is often associated with the pioneering work of George Katona (1951). Behavioral economists sometimes joke that the name of their subfield is redundant since economics is a social science in which the objects of study depend directly on human behavior. "Isn't all economics supposed to be about behavior?" the quip goes. Despite the appearance of a "distinction with no distinction" inherent in its name, proponents of behavioral economics argue that there is good reason for the explicit emphasis on accurate description of human behavior, as indicated by the word *behavioral* in behavioral economics.

In psychology, there is a sharp distinction between the terms *behaviorist* and *behavioral*. Behaviorism refers to research and researchers that draw on the work of B. F. Skinner in hypothesizing that most behavior can be explained in terms of adaptation to past rewards and punishments. Behaviorism rejects investigation of mental states or other psychic determinants of behavior. Thus, behaviorism is more similar to neoclassical economics because both schools of thought rely on a singular story about what underlies observed behavior while expressing overt antipathy toward the inclusion of mental states, cognitive processing, or emotion in their models. One frequently finds mistaken references to behavioral economists as "behaviorists" in the popular press, whereas "behavioralists" would be more accurate.

Behavioral Economics and Experimental Economics

Strong connections between behavioral and experimental economics can be seen in behavioral economists' reliance on experimental data to test assumptions and motivate new theoretical models. There nevertheless remains a distinction to be made (Camerer & Loewenstein, 2004). Some experimental economists do not identify with behavioral economics at all but rather place their work firmly within the rational choice category, studying, for example, the performance of different market institutions and factors that enhance the predictions of neoclassical theory. Experimental economics is defined by the method of experimentation, whereas behavioral economics is methodologically eclectic. The two subfields have subtly different standards about proper technique for conducting lab experiments and very different interests about the kinds of data that are most interesting to collect. Therefore, it is incorrect to automatically place experimental work under the heading of behavioral economics. In the other direction, there are many behavioral economists working on theoretical problems or using nonexperimental data. Thus, although behavioral and experimental economists frequently work complementarily on related sets of issues, there are strong networks of researchers working in the disjoint subsets of these subfields as well.

Frequently Discussed Violations of Internally Consistent Logic

This section describes several well-known violations of the rational choice model based on reasoning that allegedly suffers from internal inconsistency. The following example about deciding where to buy a textbook illustrates the kind of inconsistencies that are frequently studied in behavioral economics. Readers are encouraged to decide for themselves how reasonable or unreasonable these inconsistencies in fact are.

Suppose you are shopping for a required textbook. A bookstore across the street from where you work sells the book for $80. Another bookstore, which is 15 minutes away by car or public transportation, sells the book for only $45. Which do you choose: (A) Buy the book at the nearby store for $80, or (B) Buy the book at the farther away store for $45?

Just as standard theory does not prescribe whether it is better to spend your money buying apples versus oranges, so, too, standard economic theory takes no stand on which choice of stores is correct or rational. But now consider a second choice problem.

Suppose you are buying a plane ticket to Europe. The travel agent across the street from where you work sells the ticket for $1,120. Another travel agency, which is 15 minutes away by car or public transportation, sells the same ticket for $1,085. Which do you choose: (C) Buy the ticket from the nearby agency for $1,120, or (D) Buy the ticket at the farther away store for $1,085?

Considered in isolation, either A or B is consistent with rationality in the first choice problem, and either C or D can be rationalized in the second choice problem—as long as these problems are considered alone. Internal consistency requires, however, that a rational person choosing A in the first problem must choose C in the second problem and that a rational person choosing B in the first problem must choose D in the second problem.

Based on extensive data from pairs of choices like the ones just described, many people prefer B in the first problem (i.e., the $35 saved on the cheaper textbook justifies spending extra time and money on the 30-minute round-trip commute) while preferring C in the second problem (i.e., the $35 saved on the cheaper airline ticket does not justify spending extra time and money on the 30-minute round-trip commute). According to axiomatic rationality, this pair of choices is inconsistent and therefore irrational. Yet many competent and successful people, without any obvious symptoms of economic pathology, choose this very combination of allegedly irrational (i.e., inconsistent) decisions.

One explanation is that some people weigh the $35 savings in percentage terms relative to total price. An $80 textbook is more than 75% more expensive than a $45 textbook, whereas a $1,120 planet ticket is less than 5% more expensive than a $1,085 ticket. Nevertheless, the logic of the cost-benefit model of human behavior at the core of rational choice, or neoclassical, economics regards dollars saved—and not percentages saved—as the relevant data.

Choosing A over B, in the eyes of a neoclassical economist, reveals an algebraic inequality:

utility of saving $35 > disutility of a
30-minute round-trip commute.

Choosing D over C reveals another algebraic inequality:

utility of saving $35 < disutility of
a 30-minute round-trip commute.

Thus, choosing B over A and C over D leads to inconsistent inequalities, which violate the axiomatic definition of a rational preference ordering. One may justifiably ask, so what? Skepticism over the importance of such violations of axiomatic rationality is discussed in a subsequent section under the heading "Rationality."

Endowment Effect

Suppose you walk into a music store looking for a guitar. The very cheap ones do not produce a sound you like. And most of the guitars with beautiful sounds are priced thousands outside your budget. You finally find one that has a nice sound and a moderate price of $800. Given the guitar's qualities and its price, you are almost indifferent between owning the guitar and parting with $800, on one hand, versus not owning it and hanging on to your money, on the other. You go ahead and buy the guitar. After bringing it home, enjoying playing it, and generally feeling satisfied with your purchase, you receive a phone call the very next day from the music store asking if you would sell the guitar back. The store offers $1,000, giving you an extra $200 for your trouble. Would you sell it back?

According to the standard cost-benefit theory, if you were indifferent between the guitar and $800, then you should be more than happy to sell it back for anything over $800—as long as the amount extra includes enough to compensate for the hassle, time, and transport costs of returning it to the store (and also assuming you haven't run into someone else who wants to buy the guitar and is willing to pay a higher price). Hoping to bargain for a higher offer from the music store, you might demand something far above $800 at first. But after bargaining, when facing a credible take-it-or-leave-it last offer, anything that gives you $800 plus compensation for returning to the store should leave you better off than holding onto the guitar.

Based on data showing the prevalence of the endowment effect, however, behavioral economists would predict that you probably will choose to hang onto the guitar even if the guitar store's offer climbed well over $1,000. The endowment effect occurs whenever owning something shifts the price at which one is willing to sell it upward to a significantly higher level than the price at which the same person is willing to buy it. In the neoclassical theory taught in undergraduate textbooks with demand curves and indifference curves, an important maintained assumption that is not frequently discussed in much depth is that, for small changes in a consumer's consumption bundle, the amount of money needed to just compensate for a reduction in consumption is exactly equal to the consumer's willingness to pay to acquire that same change in consumption. In a related experiment, Carmon and Ariely (2000) showed that Duke University students who win the right to buy sports tickets in a university lottery valued these tickets—which they became the owner of by chance—roughly 14 times as much as students who had entered the lottery but did not win. Some researchers have linked the endowment effect to loss aversion, which refers to the phenomenon by which the psychic pain of parting with an object one currently owns is greater than the psychic gain from acquiring it. Thus, rather than ownership shifting the pleasure derived from a good or service upward, some experimental evidence suggests that an increase in pain at dispossessing oneself of a good or service generates the gap by which willingness to accept is significantly higher than willingness to pay.

Preference Reversals

Lichtenstein and Slovic (1971) and Thaler and Tversky (1990) produced evidence that shook many observers' confidence in a fundamental economic concept—the preference ordering. These and other authors' observed preference reversals, which call into question the very existence of stable preferences that neoclassical analysis depends on, occurred in a variety of contexts: gamblers' valuations of risky gambles at casinos, citizens' valuations of public policies aimed at saving lives, firms' evaluations of job applicants, consumers' feelings toward everyday consumer products, and savers' attitudes toward different savings plans.

In a typical experiment, a group of subjects is asked to choose one of two gambles: (A) win $4 with probability 8/9, or (B) win $40 with probability 1/9. When asked to choose between the two, the less risky gamble A, which provides a high probability of winning a small amount, is typically chosen over B, which pays slightly more on average but pays off zero most of the time. Next, another group of experimental subjects is asked to assign a dollar value to both gambles, A and B, stating the amount of money they would be willing to pay for A and B, respectively. Most subjects typically choose A over B when asked to *choose.* But most subjects place a larger dollar valuation on gamble B when asked to *evaluate* in terms of money. Choosing A over B, while valuing B more highly than A in dollar terms, is a preference reversal. In neoclassical theory, a person with a stable preference ordering should produce identical rankings of A and B whether it is elicited as a pairwise choice or in terms of dollar valuations. A preference reversal occurs when two modes of elicitation theorized to produce the same implicit rankings actually produce rankings that reverse one another.

One explanation is that when asked to choose, people focus on the risk of getting zero. Gamble A provides a lower risk of getting zero and therefore dominates B by this criterion. When asked to give a dollar valuation, however, people tend to focus on the amounts or magnitudes of payoffs more than the probabilities of their occurrence. Focused on the magnitude of the largest payoff, gamble B's 40 dominates gamble A's 4. These different thought processes—prioritizing risks of getting zero or prioritizing the magnitude of the largest payoff, respectively—might be very reasonable approaches to decision making

in particular contexts. Nevertheless, they violate the norms defined by the standard definition of a rational preference ordering (see Brandstätter, Gigerenzer, & Hertwig's [2006] alternative explanation based on their *priority heuristic*).

Measuring Risk and Time Preferences

Innovative techniques for measuring preferences along a number of dimensions have emerged as an interesting subset of behavioral and experimental economics. Given the widespread reach of expected utility theory in economics in and outside behavioral economics, Eckel and Grossman (2002, 2008) and Holt and Laury (2002) have designed experimental instruments for quantifying the extent to which people are risk averse or risk loving. The Eckel-Grossman instrument has proven useful in capturing interpersonal variation of risky choice in a wide variety of populations, including those with very limited experience interpreting numerical risk measures, thanks to its remarkable simplicity. Together with a parameterized expected utility function, their instrument produces quantifiable ranges for an individual's risk aversion parameter based on a single choice from among six binary gambles, where each gamble has only two possible outcomes, each of which occur with 50% probability. Reconciling possible inconsistencies among risk measures generated by different instruments and exploiting information about subjects whose preferences appear inconsistent is an active area of ongoing research (Berg, Eckel, & Johnson, 2009; Dave, Eckel, Johnson, & Rojas, 2007).

Behavioral economists have also established commonly used techniques for measuring time preferences. In the standard formulation, a person's time preference, or impatience, can be identified as the extent to which he or she trades off larger cash flows arriving in the more distant future in favor of smaller cash flows that arrive earlier. Impatience is frequently quantified in terms of the subject discount rate, although this depends on auxiliary assumptions about the utility function.

Biased Beliefs

In contrast to the violations of internally consistent logic discussed in the previous section, this section introduces another broad theme in behavioral economics concerning subjective beliefs that are objectively incorrect. The gap between a subjective belief about the probability that an event will occur and the objective probability of its occurrence (assuming an objective probability exists) is referred to as bias. The very notion of biased beliefs depends on how well calibrated subjective perceptions are to external benchmarks (i.e., objective frequencies of occurrence in the world), whereas the rationality assumptions discussed earlier are based solely on internal consistency and make no reference to external normative benchmarks when describing what it means to make a good decision. Studies of biased beliefs confront surprisingly subtle challenges, first, in measuring people's subjective beliefs and, second, in establishing the existence of proper benchmarks (in the form of objective probabilities) against which subjective beliefs can be compared.

"All the Kids Are Above Average" Not as Crazy as It Sounds

One sometimes hears people who should know better mistakenly claim that, if most people's beliefs about an attribute of theirs is different from the average value of that attribute, then people's beliefs must be systematically wrong (e.g., nearly everyone reporting that they are better-than-average drivers in terms of safety). In a bell-curved or other symmetric probability distribution, gaps between what most people believe—the modal response—and the average might justifiably be interpreted as evidence of bias. However, in many real-world probability distributions, such as traffic accidents (where a few bad drivers are responsible for most of the accidents) or annual income (where a small number of very high-earning individuals pull average income well above median income), the sample average is surprisingly nonrepresentative of most people.

Consider a society comprising 999 people who have nothing and one person—call him Bill Gates—who owns $1 billion in wealth. The average person in this society is a millionaire, with average wealth = $1,000,000,000/1,000 = $1 million. Nearly everyone in this society is poorer than average. Thus, when the modal belief about how wealthy a person is turns out to be significantly lower than average wealth, it implies no bias in beliefs. Realizing this, researchers attempt to carefully elicit beliefs about medians and other percentiles that pin down the value of some variable X below which a known percentage of the population falls (e.g., Camerer & Hogarth, 1999).

Bias Implies Existence of Normative Benchmarks

Bias in econometrics is defined as the difference between the expected value of an estimator and the true value of the number(s) being estimated. In econometrics as well as in everyday usage, asserting that there is a "bias" implies having made an unambiguous commitment to what the true or correct value is. The term *bias* is ubiquitous in behavioral economics, and much of its empirical and theoretical work concerns deviations from normative benchmarks that implicitly assert how people ought to behave. Given the observation that people deviate from a benchmark (typically an axiomatic definition of rationality or formal logic), there are at least two distinct reactions to consider.

Most behavioral economists have interpreted observed deviations from the assumptions of neoclassical economics as bias, implicitly asserting that neoclassical assumptions are undisputed statements defining what good, or smart,

economic behavior ought to be. According to this view, people who deviate from the neoclassical benchmarks are making mistakes, which is equivalent to saying they are biased. This, in turn, motivates some authors to recommend prescriptive policy changes aimed at de-biasing the choices we make, inducing us to more closely conform to the axioms of economic rationality. Alternative interpretations of observed deviations from neoclassical norms have been put forward by those who question whether the neoclassical model provides sound guidance for how we ought to behave and by those who fear the paternalistic implications of policies aimed at de-biasing choice. One alternative interpretation takes its point of departure from the observation that people who systematically violate neoclassical assumptions are also surviving quite successfully in their respective economic environments—they are going to college, holding down jobs, having children and grandchildren, and so on. If this is the case, then social scientists should abandon neoclassical benchmarks as normative guideposts in favor of more meaningful measures of economic performance, happiness, health, longevity, and new measures of adaptive success that have yet to be proposed.

Social Preferences

The standard assumption of unbounded self-interest is often described as a hypothesis holding that people only care about their own monetary payoffs and are completely indifferent among allocations of payoffs to different people in a group as long as their own payoff is the same. Challenging this assumption, behavioral economists seeking to study the extent to which people care about the overall allocation of payoffs among participants in a strategic interaction have described their alternative hypothesis as "social preferences." Researchers studying social preferences have sought to remain as close to the standard utility maximization framework as possible, modeling and testing the implications of social preferences by introducing utility functions that depend on other people's monetary payoffs as well as one's own payoff. Two of the most famous experiments in behavioral economics, the dictator game and the ultimatum game, are discussed below. These are formulated as extremely simple two-player games in which the hypothesis that people maximize their own monetary payoff makes a clear prediction. After hundreds of experimental tests in many places and in the presence of different contextual factors, there is widespread consensus that real people's behavior typically violates the hypothesis of own-payoff maximization.

Dictator Game

In the dictator game, one player is handed a resource endowment, say $10, and then decides how to split or allocate it between himself or herself and the other player. The other player has no choice to make. There is typically no communication, although both players see the entire structure of the game, which means they know the other's payoffs and how different combinations of actions lead to different payoffs. The game is played anonymously and one time only to avoid motivating players to try appearing "nice" in the expectation of future reciprocation. The player making the decision, referred to as the dictator, can keep all $10 for himself or herself and give the other player $0. The dictator can also choose a $9–$1 split, an $8–$2 split, a $5–$5 split, and so on. In versions of the game with unrestricted action spaces, the dictator can keep any amount for himself or herself K, $0 \leq K \leq 10$, leaving the other player with a monetary payoff of $10 - K$. The theory that players of games maximize their own monetary payoffs without regard for other people's payoffs makes a clear prediction in the dictator game: Dictators will choose to keep everything, maximizing their own monetary payoff at $K = 10$ and allocating zero to the other player.

However, when real people play this game, the most common choice by dictators is a 50–50 split, even when playing versions of the game with much larger monetary payoffs. This is a clear violation of the hypothesis that people maximize an objective function that depends only on one's own monetary payoffs, and it is typically interpreted as evidence in favor of social preferences. In other words, the gap between the predictions of standard economic theory and the data observed in experiments implies (although this point is open to alternative interpretations) that people care about the monetary payoffs of others. Note that caring about the payoffs of others does not imply altruism or benevolence, so that spiteful preferences that register increased psychic gain based on the deprivation of others is also a form of social preferences.

Ultimatum Game

In the ultimatum game, a proposer receives an endowment, say $10, and then makes a proposed allocation. Reusing the symbol K to represent the amount the proposer proposes to keep, the proposed allocation looks similar to the allocation in the dictator game: K for the proposer, $0 \leq K \leq 10$, and $10 - K$ for the other player, sometimes referred to as the responder. Unlike the dictator game, however, the responder has a binary decision to make in the ultimatum game: whether to accept the proposer's proposal or not. If the responder accepts, then payoffs follow the proposal exactly. If the responder declines the proposal, then both players receive zero. Once again, this game is typically played anonymously and only one time to limit the expectation of future reciprocation as a confounding motive when interpreting the results.

As long as the proposal includes any positive payoff for the responder, a responder who maximizes his or her own monetary payoff will choose to accept because even a small amount is better than zero according to the money maximization hypothesis. The subgame perfect equilibrium is for the proposer to offer the smallest positive amount possible to the responder and for the responder to accept. For example, if payoffs are restricted to integer values, the strict subgame perfect equilibrium is uniquely defined by a proposal in which the proposer keeps $9 and the responder receives $1, and the responder accepts this proposal even though it is far from an even split.

Contrary to the theoretical prediction of proposers offering a $9–$1 split and responders accepting it, the most common proposal in the ultimatum game is an even (or nearly even) 50–50 split. The responder's behavior is especially interesting to students of social preferences because responders typically reject unfair offers even though it leaves them with zero as opposed to a small positive amount. It is this willingness of responders to choose zero by rejecting "unfair" offers of $9–$1 and higher that provides one of the most decisive pieces of evidence for social preferences. A common interpretation is that the responder receives more utility from punishing the proposer for having made an unfair proposal than he or she would get by accepting $1 and leaving the proposer's unfair offer unpunished. This shows that the responder does not make decisions solely on the basis of his or her own payoff but is considering the payoffs of the other player.

Extending Utility Theory to Incorporate Social Preferences

A well-known approach to modeling social preferences (Fehr & Schmidt, 1999) extends the neoclassical utility function (which typically depends only on one's own monetary payoffs) to include three components: utility from one's own payoff (as one finds in a neoclassical utility function), utility from the positive deviation between one's own payoff and other players' payoffs (i.e., the pleasure of doing better than others), and a third term placing negative weight on negative deviations from other players' payoffs (i.e., displeasure of doing worse than others). Some authors have introduced models that add similar "social preferences" terms to the utility function, for example, placing negative weight on highly unequal allocations, weighted by a parameter referred to as inequality aversion.

Critics of the social preferences program draw on distinct points of view. Binmore and Shaked (2007) argue that the tools of classical and neoclassical economics can easily take social factors into account and need not be set off from neoclassical economics under distinct "social preferences" or "behavioral economics" labels. Although Binmore and Shaked are correct that, in principle, neoclassical utility theory does not preclude other people's payoffs from entering the utility function, the assumption of unbounded self-interest is indeed a key tenet of neoclassical normative theory. The no-externalities assumption (i.e., people care only about their own payoffs, and their actions affect each other only indirectly through market prices) is crucial to the validity of the fundamental welfare theorem, which states that competitive markets are socially efficient. It is difficult to overstate the role that this theoretical result has enjoyed in guiding public policy toward private versus government provision of services such as health care. Critics rightly point to this theory's reliance on the unrealistic assumptions of no externalities and no information asymmetries.

Rationality

In the popular press, behavioral economics is often portrayed as a branch of economics that points to systematic irrationality in human populations and in markets in particular. Titles such as *Irrational Exuberance* (Shiller, 2000), *Predictably Irrational* (Ariely, 2008), and much of Nobel laureate Daniel Kahneman's work documenting deviations from axiomatic definitions of rationality make it easy for nonexperts to associate behavioral economics with irrationality. Indeed, many behavioral economists in their writing, especially when describing their results verbally, use *rational* as a synonym for behavior that conforms to standard economic theory and *irrational* as a catch-all label for behavior that deviates from standard neoclassical assumptions.

One prominent voice in behavioral economics, David Laibson, advocates to aspiring behavioral economists that they avoid describing behavior as "irrational" and avoid the ambiguous term *bounded rationality*. Laibson's admonition is, however, very frequently violated, leading to subtle paradoxes regarding the normative status of the neoclassical model within behavioral economics (Berg, 2003).

In neoclassical economics, a rational preference ordering is defined as any ranking scheme that conforms to the axioms of completeness and transitivity. In choice under uncertainty, many economists—including the seminal contributor Leonard Savage—argue for a strong normative interpretation of what has now become the dominant tool in economics for modeling choice under uncertainty (Starmer, 2005): expected utility theory. The normative interpretation of expected utility theory asserts that choices over probabilistic payoff distributions that can be rationalized as having maximized any expected utility function are rational, and those that admit no such rationalization are irrational.

In choice problems that involve trade-offs over time, choices that can be rationalized as maximizing a time-consistent objective function are frequently referred to as "rational" and those that cannot as "irrational." An important intuitive problem arises in these uses of the term *rationality*—namely, that all parties in a strategic interaction in which more than one party is playing an allegedly "irrational" strategy may be strictly better off than would be the case if each party accepted economic "rationality" as a prescription for action.

Two distinct problems arise. First, there is behavior that conforms to axiomatic rationality but is manifestly bad or undesirable in many people's views. Second, there is behavior that is very reasonable to many people because it achieves a high level of performance, which nevertheless violates axiomatic rationality. Thus, axiomatic rationality is both too strong and too weak. Too strong because it rules out reasonable behavior as irrational, and too weak because it allows for behavior whose consequences for well-being are intuitively bad in many people's views.

Rational preferences impose the requirement of self-consistent choice but typically say nothing about how well choices work in the real world, a distinction that psychologists Hastie and Rasinski (1988) and Hammond (1996) describe as coherence (internally consistent) versus correspondence (well calibrated to the world) norms. Thus, dropping out of college, walking past a pile of cash on the ground, becoming addicted to drugs, or even committing suicide can be rationalized (and regularly have been in the economics literature) as maximizing a rational preference ordering because they can be made to satisfy internal coherence. Economic rationality here imposes nothing more than consistency.

A rational person can walk past $100 lying on the sidewalk, revealing (within the rational choice framework) that his or her disutility of stopping to lean over and pick up the money is greater than the benefit of the money. Rationality requires only that the person is consistent about this ranking, never stopping to pick up money on the sidewalk when the amount is $100 or less. In the other direction, a person who drops out of college and then—without anything else in his or her life circumstances changing significantly—decides to reenroll is regarded as inconsistent and therefore irrational, even though many parents would no doubt regard this as, on the whole, good economic behavior.

In expected utility theory, a decision maker can be completely averse to risk or love risk taking, but not both. The requirement of rationality is that all risky choices are consistent. Thus, someone who always takes risks and perhaps is regarded by many as foolish and imprudent would pass the consistency requirement, conforming squarely with axiomatic rationality based on consistent foolishness. In the other direction, a person who buys health insurance (revealing himself or herself to be risk averse) and also decides to start a new business (revealing himself or herself to be risk loving) cannot easily be rationalized within expected utility theory because of the appearance of inconsistent choices in risky settings.

In time trade-off decision problems, consistency allows for both infinite impatience and infinite patience, but not in the same person. A person who, every payday, throws a party and spends all his or her money and then starves until next payday passes the consistency test and is therefore rational. Consistently strange behavior (e.g., blowing one's paycheck and starving thereafter until the next paycheck) can be rationalized, but inconsistent behavior—even when it seems to reflect a positive step in a person's maturing or taking responsibility for his or her well-being—is labeled irrational because it violates consistency. If the person who previously blew his or her paycheck every payday decides to start saving money for his or her retirement, this would be inconsistent, although very reasonable to most people. These cases illustrate tension between what most people regard as sensible economic behavior and the surprising simultaneous tightness and looseness of rational choice as it is defined in economics as a criterion for normative evaluation.

Behavioral Economics: Prospects and Problems

The origins of behavioral economics are many, without clear boundaries or singularly defining moments (Hands, 2007; Heukelom, 2007). And yet, even a cursory look at articles published in economics today versus, say, 1980 reveals a far-reaching behavioral shift. One can cite a number of concrete events as markers of the emergence of behavioral economics onto a broader stage with wide, mainstream appeal. One might imagine that such a list would surely include Herbert Simon's Nobel Prize in 1978. But prior to the 1990s, behavioral work appeared very infrequently in flagship general interest journals of the economics profession. A concise and, of course, incomplete timeline of milestones in the recent rise of behavioral economics would include Richard Thaler's "Anomalies" series, which ran in the *Journal of Economic Perspectives* starting in 1987; hiring patterns at elite business schools and economics departments in the 1990s; frequent popular press accounts of behavioral economics in *The Economist, New York Times,* and *Wall Street Journal* in the past 10 years; and the 2002 Nobel Prize being awarded to experimental economist Vernon Smith and psychologist Daniel Kahneman. The 1994 Nobel Prize was shared by another economist who is an active experimenter and leading voice in game theory and behavioral economics, Reinhardt Selten.

A striking element in the arguments of those who have successfully brought behavioral economics to mainstream economics audiences is the close similarity to Friedman's as-if methodology. In prospect theory, behavioral economics adds new parameters rather than psychological realism to repair and add greater statistical fit to an otherwise neoclassical weighting-and-summing approach to modeling choice under uncertainty. In the social preferences approach, behavioral economics adds parameters weighting decision makers' concern for receiving more, or less, than others do to an otherwise neoclassical utility function. In intertemporal choice, behavioral models of time inconsistency add discounting parameters with non-exponential weighting schemes while hanging onto the assumption of maximization of a time-separable utility function. Frequently billing itself as a new empirical enterprise aimed at uncovering the true preferences of real people, the dominant method in the most widely cited innovations to emerge from behavioral economics can be perhaps better described as filtering observed choices through otherwise neoclassical constrained optimization problems, with augmented utility functions that depend on new functional arguments and parameters.

Behavioral economists' attempts to filter data through more complexly parameterized constrained optimization problems suggest more similarity than difference with respect to neoclassical economics. It will be interesting to see whether moves in the direction of neuroeconomics based on brain imaging data portend more radical methodological shifts (Camerer, Loewenstein, & Prelec, 2005) or rather a strengthening of the core methodological tenets of neoclassical economics (Glimcher, 2003). There is a route not taken, or not yet taken, following Herbert Simon's call to abandon universalizing, context- and content-free characterizations of rational choice in favor of models that explicitly consider the interaction of decision processes and the different environments in which they are used—that is, ecological rationality (Gigerenzer, Todd, & the ABC Research Group, 1999).

Criticisms notwithstanding, a number of new and practical suggestions for designing institutions and intervening to help people change their behavior have emerged from the behavioral economics literature of recent decades. These include plans that encourage greater levels of retirement savings (Benartzi & Thaler, 2004), higher rates of organ donation (Johnson & Goldstein, 2003), controlling the amount of food we eat (Wansink, 2006), and new tools for encouraging greater levels of charitable giving (Shang & Croson, 2009). One recent example of behavioral economics being put into practice is President Obama's tax cut, which is disbursed as a small reduction in monthly tax withholding, thereby increasing workers' monthly take-home pay by a small amount each month instead of arriving in taxpayers' mailboxes as a single check for the year. In the rational choice theory, taxpayers' decisions about how much of the tax cut to spend should not depend significantly on whether one receives, say, 12 paychecks with an extra $50 or a single check for $600 for the entire year. But behavioral economists such as Richard Thaler have advised the Obama administration that, to induce immediate spending (which is what most economists call for in response to a recession), it is important that taxpayers view tax cuts as an increase in income rather than wealth—in other words, that taxpayers put the tax cut proceeds into a "mental account" from which they are relatively more likely to spend (Surowiecki, 2009).

All indications suggest that more empirical findings and theories from behavioral economics will make their way into public policy and private organizations aiming to influence the behavior of workers and consumers. Whether these tools will be regarded as benevolent interventions that make our environments better matched to our cognitive architecture or an Orwellian shift toward psychology-inspired paternalism is currently under debate (Berg & Gigerenzer, 2007; Thaler & Sunstein, 2003). There would seem to be genuine cause for optimism regarding behavioral economists' widely shared goal of improving the predictive accuracy and descriptive realism of economic models that tie economics more closely to observational data, while undertaking bolder normative analysis using broader sets of criteria that measure how smart, or rational, behavior is.

References and Further Readings

Ariely, D. (2008). *Predictably irrational.* New York: HarperCollins.

Benartzi, S., & Thaler, R. (2004). Save more tomorrow: Using behavioral economics to increase employee saving. *Journal of Political Economy, 112,* 164–187.

Berg, N. (2003). Normative behavioral economics. *Journal of Socio-Economics, 32,* 411–427.

Berg, N., Eckel, C., & Johnson, C. (2009). *Inconsistency pays? Time-inconsistent subjects and EU violators earn more* (Working paper). Dallas: University of Texas–Dallas.

Berg, N., & Gigerenzer, G. (2007). Psychology implies paternalism? Bounded rationality may reduce the rationale to regulate risk-taking. *Social Choice and Welfare, 28,* 337–359.

Berg, N., & Gigerenzer, G. (In press). "As-if" behavioral economics: Neoclassical economics in disguise? *History of Economic Ideas.*

Binmore, K., & Shaked, A. (2007). *Experimental economics: Science or what?* (ELSE Working Paper 263). London: ESRC Centre for Economic Learning and Social Evolution.

Brandstätter, E., Gigerenzer, G., & Hertwig, R. (2006). The priority heuristic: Making choices without trade-offs. *Psychological Review, 113,* 409–432.

Bruni, L., & Sugden, R. (2007). The road not taken: How psychology was removed from economics, and how it might be brought back. *Economic Journal, 117*(516), 146–173.

Camerer, C. (1999). Behavioral economics: Reunifying psychology and economics. *Proceedings of the National Academy of Sciences of the United States of America, 96,* 10575–10577.

Camerer, C. (2003). *Behavioral game theory: Experiments in strategic interaction.* New York: Russell Sage Foundation.

Camerer, C., & Hogarth, R. (1999). The effects of financial incentives in experiments: A review and capital-labor-production framework. *Journal of Risk and Uncertainty, 19*(1–3), 7–42.

Camerer, C., & Loewenstein, G. (2004). Behavioral economics: Past, present and future. In C. Camerer, G. Loewenstein, & M. Rabin (Eds.), *Advances in behavioral economics.* Princeton, NJ: Princeton University Press.

Camerer, C., Loewenstein, G., & Prelec, D. (2005). *Neuroeconomics: How neuroscience can inform economics. Journal of Economic Literature, 43,* 9–64.

Carmon, Z., & Ariely, D. (2000). Focusing on the forgone: How value can appear so different to buyers and sellers. *Journal of Consumer Research, 27*(3), 360–370.

Carpenter, J., & Seki, E. (2006). Competitive work environments and social preferences: Field experimental evidence from a Japanese fishing community. *Contributions to Economic Analysis & Policy Berkeley Electronic Press,* 5(2), Article 2.

Charness, G., & Grosskopf, B. (2001). Relative payoffs and happiness: An experimental study. *Journal of Economic Behavior and Organization, 45,* 301–328.

Dave, C., Eckel, C., Johnson, C., & Rojas, C. (2007). *Eliciting risk preferences: When is simple better?* (Working paper). Dallas: University of Texas–Dallas.

Eckel, C., & Grossman, P. (2002). Sex differences and statistical stereotyping in attitudes toward financial risk. *Evolution and Human Behavior, 23,* 281–295.

Eckel, C., & Grossman, P. (2008). Forecasting risk attitudes: An experimental study using actual and forecast gamble choices. *Journal of Economic Behavior and Organization, 8*(1), 1–17.

Fehr, E., & Schmidt, K. (1999). A theory of fairness, competition and cooperation. *Quarterly Journal of Economics, 114,* 817–868.

Friedman, M. (1953). *Essays in positive economics.* Chicago: University of Chicago Press.

Gigerenzer, G. (2008). *Rationality for mortals.* New York: Oxford University Press.

Gigerenzer, G., & Selten, R. (2001). *Bounded rationality: The adaptive toolbox.* Cambridge: MIT Press.

Gigerenzer, G., Todd, P. M., & ABC Research Group. (1999). *Simple heuristics that make us smart.* New York: Oxford University Press.

Glimcher, P. W. (2003). *Decisions, uncertainty and the brain: The science of neuroeconomics.* Cambridge: MIT Press.

Güth, W. (2008). (Non-) behavioral economics: A programmatic assessment. *Journal of Psychology, 216,* 244–253.

Hammond, K. R. (1996). *Human judgment and social policy: Irreducible uncertainty, inevitable error, unavoidable injustice.* New York: Oxford University Press.

Hands, D. W. (2007). *Economics, psychology, and the history of consumer choice theory.* Retrieved from http://ssrn.com/abstract=988125

Hanemann, W. M. (1991). Willingness to pay and willingness to accept: How much can they differ? *American Economic Review, 81,* 635–647.

Hastie, R., & Rasinski, K. A. (1988). The concept of accuracy in social judgment. In D. Bar-Tal & A. W. Kruglanski (Eds.), *The social psychology of knowledge* (pp. 193–208). New York: Cambridge University Press.

Heukelom, F. (2007). *Kahneman and Tversky and the origin of behavioral economics* (Tinbergen Institute Discussion Papers 07–003/1). Rotterdam, the Netherlands: Tinbergen Institute.

Holt, C., & Laury, S. (2002). Risk aversion and incentive effects. *American Economic Review, 92,* 1644–1655.

Johnson, E. J., & Goldstein, D. G. (2003). Do defaults save lives? *Science, 302,* 1338–1339.

Jolls, C., & Sunstein, C. R. (2006). Debiasing through law. *Journal of Legal Studies, 35,* 199–241.

Kahneman, D., Knetsch, J., & Thaler, R. (1991). The endowment effect, loss aversion, and status quo bias. *Journal of Economic Perspectives, 5*(1), 193–206.

Katona, G. (1951). *Psychological analysis of economic behavior.* New York: McGraw-Hill.

Lichtenstein, S., & *Slovic, P.* (1971). Reversals of preference between bids and choices in gambling decisions. *Journal of Experimental Psychology, 89,* 46–55.

Loewenstein, G., & Thaler, R. (1989). Intertemporal choice. *Journal of Economic Perspectives, 3*(4), 181–193.

Plott, C., & Zeiler, K. (2007). Exchange asymmetries incorrectly interpreted as evidence of endowment effect theory and prospect theory? *American Economic Review, 97,* 1449–1466.

Rabin, M. (1998). Psychology and economics. *Journal of Economic Literature, 36,* 11–46.

Shang, J., & Croson, R. (2009). Field experiments in charitable contribution: The impact of social influence on the voluntary provision of public goods. *Economic Journal, 119,* 1–17.

Shiller, R. (2000). *Irrational exuberance.* Princeton, NJ: Princeton University Press.

Shogren, J. F., Shin, S. Y., Hayes, D. J., & Kliebenstein, J. B. (1994). Resolving differences in willingness to pay and willingness to accept. *American Economic Review, 84*(1), 255–270.

Simon, H. (1986). Rationality in psychology and economics. *Journal of Business, 59,* S209–S224.

Slutsky, E. E. (1952). Sulla Teoria del Bilancio del Consonatore. In G. J. Stigler & K. E. Boulding (Eds.), *Readings in price theory* (pp. 27–56). Homewood, IL: Irwin. (Original work published 1915)

Starmer, C. (2004). *Friedman's risky methodology* (Working paper). Nottingham, UK: University of Nottingham.

Starmer, C. (2005). Normative notions in descriptive dialogues. *Journal of Economic Methodology, 12,* 277–289.

Surowiecki, J. (2009, January 26). A smarter stimulus. *The New Yorker.* Available at http://www.newyorker.com

Thaler, R. H., & Sunstein, C. R. (2003). Libertarian paternalism. *American Economic Review, 93,* 175–179.

Thaler, R. H., & Sunstein, C. R. (2008). *Nudge: Improving decisions about health, wealth, and happiness.* New Haven, CT: Yale University Press.

Thaler, R., & Tversky, A. (1990). Preference reversals. *Journal of Economic Perspectives, 4*(2), 201–211.

Veblen, T. (1994). *The theory of the leisure class.* New York: Dover. (Original work published 1899)

Wansink, B. (2006). *Mindless eating: Why we eat more than we think.* New York: Bantam.

85

EXPERIMENTAL ECONOMICS

SEDA ERTAÇ
Koç University

SANDRA MAXIMIANO
Purdue University

Being able to test theories and understand the underlying mechanism behind observed phenomena is crucial for scientific progress in any discipline. Experimentation is an important method of measurement in the natural sciences as well as in social sciences such as psychology, but the use of experiments for gathering economic data is a much more recent endeavor. Economics has long been regarded as a nonexperimental science, which has to rely on observations of economic behavior that occur naturally. Experiments, however, have found their way into the economist's toolkit in the past few decades and are now being employed commonly in mainstream economics research in many diverse subfields such as game theory, industrial organization, labor and development economics, and, more recently, macroeconomics.

The very first experiment in economics is known to have been conducted by Bernoulli on the St. Petersburg's paradox in 1738 (see Kagel & Roth, 1995, for more on the history of experimental economics). However, more formal experimentation started in the 1930s with individual choice experiments and flourished especially with the advent of game theory with the work of von Neumann and Morgenstern (1944) on the theory of decision making and games. Also around that time, the first "market experiments" were run by Chamberlin (1948) to test competitive equilibrium. Gradually, experiments started being used more and more widely in many areas of economics, and the number of experimental research papers published in economics journals has been growing rapidly and is now on par with more "classical" fields such as economic theory. The development of experimental economics as a field has also been parallel to advances in the field of "behavioral economics." Behavioral economics aims at integrating insights obtained from psychology into economic models, frequently uses experiments as a method for collecting data and finding out patterns of behavior that are inconsistent with standard theory, and builds new models that can explain the observed behavior in experiments. The most evident recognition of the importance of experimental and behavioral economics was the 2002 Nobel Prize in economics, which was awarded to Daniel Kahneman and Vernon Smith for their contributions to behavioral and experimental economics, respectively.

But why and when do economists need experiments? One of the main goals of empirical analysis in economics is to understand how different models of economic decision making fare in understanding observed economic behavior and outcomes and therefore test the predictive success of economic theories. However, it is not always possible to conduct proper tests of theories or to measure the effects of different economic policies using naturally occurring data because of at least three reasons. First, naturally occurring data may simply not exist. For example, in testing models of strategic interaction, oftentimes it is important to know what people think or believe about other people's actions, and although actions are observable, beliefs are not. Similarly, reservation wages and workers' outside options are also not observed in naturally occurring data but are important to understand agents' behavior in labor markets. Laboratory experiments, on the other hand, allow us to collect data on these unobservables.

Second, experiments allow *randomization* into treatments of interest, reducing selection bias and giving the researcher the proper counterfactual for causal inference. Consider the following example. Suppose that we are interested in the effects of tournament-type compensation schemes (where one's wage depends on his or her performance relative to others) versus piece-rate compensation schemes (one's wage depends only on his or her own performance) on worker productivity. If we collect real worker productivity data from firms that use each of these two types of incentive schemes and make a direct comparison, we cannot be sure whether any productivity differential we observe comes from the true effect of incentives or from firms or workers' unobservable differences that are correlated with productivity. For example, more able and more ambitious workers may think that they have better prospects in a firm that uses tournament incentive schemes, and this motivation differential will bias the estimates of the "treatment effect" of incentives on productivity. That is, the samples under the two incentive schemes are "selected" and not directly comparable, and this incomparability will blur any type of inference we can make. Although econometricians have been devising methods that could alleviate some of these problems (such as instrumental variables and matching techniques), having direct control over the data-generating process makes inference much simpler. In the context of the incentives example, by assigning workers randomly into two treatments, one where they work under a tournament incentive scheme and one under the piece-rate scheme, it would be possible to measure the "true" effect of incentive schemes on productivity. This is possible because random assignment acts as a control for individual characteristics, considering the fact that if you have a sufficient number of subjects, the two groups will look sufficiently alike along dimensions such as ambition, ability, and so on, which we would like to control. By assigning subjects randomly into "treatments" that differ along the dimension of interest, experiments take care of the selection problem through randomization and can accurately isolate the effect of the focus variable.

Likewise, in a controlled experiment, which variables are exogenous and which are endogenous is clearly known, and this allows the experimenter to make causal inferences about the association between the variables, whereas with natural data, there are usually many factors changing at the same time, making it hard to disentangle the effect of a certain factor on the variable of interest. Another rationale for using experiments, perhaps of more theoretical interest, is that it may be difficult to test theories of one-shot interactions with naturally occurring data since factors such as reputation are oftentimes present because interactions naturally take place mostly in repeated settings. All these advantages suggest that experimentation can be a very valuable tool for gathering data on economic decision making.

While economic experiments have generally used the laboratory as their setting and university students as subjects, "field experiments" have been receiving much attention recently. By testing behavior in a setting that is more "natural" on several dimensions, field experiments provide insight on the "external validity" or generalizability of the results from laboratory experiments and complement lab experiments in improving our understanding of economic phenomena. According to Harrison and List (2004), experiments may differ in the nature of (a) subject pool, (b) information and experience that the subjects bring to the task, (c) the commodity being transacted, (d) task and institutional rules, and (e) the environment that subjects operate in. These five factors are used to determine the field context of an experiment and result in the following taxonomy: (a) *conventional lab experiments,* which use a standard subject pool of university students, abstract framing (e.g., choices are labeled A, B, C, etc., rather than with words that suggest context), and an imposed set of rules; (b) *artifactual field experiments,* which are conventional lab experiments but with a nonstandard subject pool (e.g., actual workers from a firm rather than university students); (c) *framed field experiments,* which are artifactual field experiments but with field context in the task, commodity, information, or environment (e.g., rather than trading a "virtual" commodity on the computer, subjects trade a real commodity in a real field context); and (d) *natural field experiments,* which are framed field experiments in which subjects are not aware that they are in an experiment.

In what follows, we will first provide a discussion of some of the main methodological issues involved in experimental research and then provide a selective account of the main areas of application where experiments have been employed in economics. Because of space issues, we are bound to leave out many important domains and applications, so our treatment here should be taken as an illustrative approach that provides examples of how experiments can contribute to our understanding of economic behavior.

The Methodology of Experiments

The goal of the experimenter is to create a setting where behavior can be measured accurately in a controlled way. This is usually achieved by keeping constant as many variables as possible and varying others independently as "treatment variables." To achieve as much control as possible, the experimental method in economics is based on "inducing preferences" by using appropriate monetary incentives that are tied to the consequences of decisions made during the experiment. A typical economics laboratory experiment involves recruiting subjects, who are usually university students, and paying them a fixed show-up fee for their participation, plus the amount they earn during the experiment. The amount they earn during the experiment, in turn, is tied to the payoff consequences of the decisions they make. This feature of economics experiments, in fact, is a main characteristic that distinguishes economics experiments from psychology experiments, where decisions are often hypothetical and not incentivized.[1]

For properly inducing preferences, the experimenter should have control over the preferences of the subjects and should know what the subject is trying to attain. For example, in a game theory experiment, we would like the numbers in the payoff matrix of the game to represent the players' utilities, and we therefore pay subjects according to the payoffs in the matrix. Naturally, however, there may be unobservable components of utility affecting subjects' behavior. For instance, if one runs a 100-period experiment with the same type of choice being repeated every period, subjects might get bored and start acting randomly. Alternatively, some subjects might have preferences over other subjects' monetary earnings, and if they know the payoff distribution among the participants, this might affect their behavior in ways that are unrelated to the hypothesis of interest. To make the effects of these unobserved factors minimal, one should make monetary rewards as strong as possible. Having salient monetary rewards will also ensure that subjects are motivated to think carefully about the decision, especially when the decision task is cognitively demanding. Attaching strong monetary consequences to decisions reduces the occurrence of random decisions and minimizes the errors and outliers that would otherwise be observed more often in the data.

On the basis of these general ideas, Nobel Prize winner Vernon Smith (1982) put forward the following precepts for achieving proper control:

- *Nonsatiation*: This means that individuals should prefer more of the reward medium used in the experiment (usually money) to less of it.
- *Saliency*: This assumption means that the reward medium is suitably associated with the choices in the experiment—for example, if one wants action A to be a better action for the individual than action B, then action A should be associated with a higher monetary payoff than B.
- *Dominance*: This means that the reward structure should dominate other factors associated with participation in the experiment (e.g., boredom). High monetary stakes can help achieve this.
- *Privacy*: Individuals' utility functions may have unobservable components that depend on the utility or payoffs of others. For example, a subject's decisions may depend on how much others are earning, if he or she cares about "fairness" of payoffs across subjects. By withholding information about other subjects' payoffs and giving subjects information about their own payoffs only, this potential issue can be mitigated, and better control of preferences can be achieved.

While inducing preferences is very important for experimental control, there are some cases in which experimenters do not want to induce preferences but are interested in obtaining information on the natural ("homegrown") preferences of subjects. For example, we may be interested in knowing how much an individual values a certain object (e.g., the item for sale in an auction). Likewise, we may be interested in knowing the beliefs of the individual. As mentioned before, the latter can be especially important in testing game-theoretic models, where subjects' beliefs about others' possible actions are important in shaping optimal strategies. Experimental economists have devised incentive-compatible mechanisms to elicit subjects' true valuations for an object (e.g., the maximum amount of money they would be willing to pay to buy the object) and use various techniques to elicit subjects' beliefs truthfully. While discussion of these methods in detail is beyond the scope of this chapter, it is important to note that these methods have allowed economists to obtain crucial information that is not available in the field.

One last principle that is relevant for running a "good" experiment is "design parallelism" (Smith, 1982). This principle refers to the need for laboratory experiments to reflect naturally occurring environments to the extent possible. This is very much related to the concept of "external validity" of the experiment, in other words, how much the experimental decision resembles decisions that individuals face in the "real world," which will affect the extent to which the experimental results can be extrapolated to natural economic environments. Although the external validity of an experiment is important, it should be noted that adding more and more complexity to an experiment to increase external validity could result in loss of control and compromise the "internal validity" of the experiment, making the data useless. One should therefore be careful in choosing an experimental design that can be as realistic as possible while still maintaining proper control and avoiding confounds.

Applications of Experimental Methods in Economics

Individual Decision-Making Experiments

The experiments conducted in this area analyze nonstrategic decision making by a single individual, in a context with no interaction between the subjects in the experiment. The goal is to understand the decision-making process of the individual and the motivation behind the observed behavior. The topic is strongly related to the psychology of judgment and illustrates the interdisciplinary aspect of experimental methods quite well. In fact, as we will explain below, this strand of the experimental economics literature has collected quite a large body of observations that are inconsistent with standard economic theory and has been an important part of the research in behavioral economics.

Experiments of individual decision making investigate choice in different contexts: over time, under static uncertainty, under dynamic uncertainty, and so on. A very important set of experiments here concerns decision making under uncertainty and provides tests of the relevant standard economic theory, which posits that individuals are expected utility maximizers. As mentioned before, this means that individuals maximize the expected value of utility, defined as the sum of utility from different possible outcomes, each multiplied by the respective probability that that outcome occurs. Anomalies, or observations violating expected utility theory in these experiments, have been frequent. For example, a well-known departure from the predictions of expected utility is the Allais paradox. Consider the following example, with two decision tasks (Kahneman & Tversky, 1979):

Decision 1:
- Option A: $3,000 for sure
- Option B: $4,000 with 80% chance, $0 with 20% chance

Decision 2:
- Option C: $3,000 with 25% chance
- Option D: $4,000 with 20% chance

A vast majority of subjects select Option A in Decision 1 but Option D in Decision 2, which is inconsistent with expected utility theory since the lotteries in Decision 2 are equivalent to Decision 1 (when one divides all the winning probabilities of Decision 1 by 4, Decision 2 is obtained, and this across-the-board reduction in winning probabilities should not affect the choice according to expected utility theory).

Choices in such lottery choice experiments have also pointed to a "reflection effect": While individuals make risk-averse choices when the choices involve gains (e.g., a lottery that pays $100 with 50% chance and $0 with 50% chance vs. a sure gain of $40), they act as if they are risk loving when the choices involve losses (e.g., a lottery that involves a $100 loss with 50% chance and no loss with 50% chance vs. a sure loss of $40). That is, losses and gains are treated differently, which is again inconsistent with expected utility theory.

The laboratory evidence that highlights such anomalies has stimulated the development of alternatives to expected utility theory. A well-known alternative, called "prospect theory," was proposed by Kahneman and Tversky (1979). Prospect theory allows for loss aversion, reference dependence, reflection effect, and probability miscalculations and can explain a significant amount of the anomalous findings in the lottery choice experiments. Through its modeling of reference dependence and loss aversion, prospect theory can also explain a phenomenon called the "endowment effect," which refers to the observation in experiments that there is a discrepancy between individuals' valuations of a good, depending on whether they own it or not. That is, the minimum amount of money that individuals are willing to accept in order to part with a good they own (e.g., a coffee mug that has been given to them in the experiment) is higher than the maximum amount they

would be willing to pay for the same good when they do not own it, which is inconsistent with standard theory.

Although many experimental results in individual decision-making experiments point to deviations from the predictions of standard economic theory, there is also some evidence that market experience and large monetary stakes can improve the alignment of observed behavior with standard predictions. For example, John List (2006) finds, in a field experiment involving traders in an actual market for sports memorabilia, that inexperienced traders display a strong endowment effect, but experienced traders who have been engaging in market activities for a long time do not. This might suggest that these anomalies or biases might be less prevalent in actual markets, where individuals self-select into economic roles and gain experience through repeated transactions.

One methodological point to be made here is that the type of individual lottery choice tasks mentioned above can also be used to measure subjects' risk preferences in the laboratory. In many different experiments involving a wide range of economic decisions, it is useful to know the risk preferences of individuals. For example, risk-averse and risk-neutral individuals are predicted to bid differently in auctions, and having information on risk preferences allows economists to obtain better insight into behavior. One such method to measure risk preferences is the "Holt-Laury mechanism" (Holt & Laury, 2002), which involves giving subjects a series of choices between a risky lottery (that has a large spread between the good and bad payoff) and a safe lottery (that has a small spread between the good and the bad payoff), which differ in the likelihood of the good payoff. As the probability of the good payoff increases, the attractiveness of the risky lottery increases. By looking at when the subject switches to the risky lottery as the good payoff probability increases, it is possible to get a measure of the risk aversion of the subject.

Game Theory Experiments

Most of modern microeconomics research involves models of strategic interaction. Since the work of John von Neumann and Oskar Morgenstern (1944) and later of John Nash, game theory has become the fundamental approach in microeconomics, replacing the Walrasian and Marshallian models of consumption, production, and exchange in which individuals take decisions in response to exogenous prices by models of strategic interaction. The theory of games has been used to analyze strategic behavior in coordination games, public good contribution games, auctions, analysis of oligopolies in industrial organization, and so on. In general, game-theoretic models assume that individuals are rational and have stable preferences over outcomes and correct beliefs as to how choices affect the relative probability of possible outcomes. They are assumed to maximize their own expected payoff given their preferences and beliefs and take into consideration material and informational constraints that may exist.

There are two main criticisms to game theory. First, individuals may not be able to be as forward looking as game theory predicts. They may not always behave rationally or may not perceive others to be rational. Second, people do not behave "selfishly" in all situations and may not expect others to behave in that way either. Experimental methods help economists explore how important these issues are. In experiments, information and incentives are held constant, which allows us to accurately test how well game-theoretic principles predict behavior and understand in which situations individuals do behave in line with the theory and in which cases they deviate from it.

Many of the experiments on game theory have tested (a) the rationality assumption or the depth of strategic reasoning and (b) the assumption of "selfishness," which posits that individuals' utility is dependent on their own monetary payoffs only. In the following discussion, we will focus on games that have attempted to clearly test these two postulates of standard economic theory. First, we will illustrate the effects of limits on rationality through experiments on limited strategic thinking. Second, we will discuss social preferences experiments that test the assumption of selfishness and exclusively money-maximizing behavior.

Illustration 1: Why Aren't We All Chess Players? Experiments on Limited Thinking

We will illustrate tests of rationality through a discussion of the "guessing game." An important recent set of experiments that has provided a great way to test the depth of players' reasoning is "guessing games" or "beauty contest games." (This name is based on John Maynard Keynes's likening of the stock market to a newspaper beauty contest where readers' aim is to guess the most beautiful lady, as determined by the population. Keynes noted that in such games, it would be important to guess how others think, how others think others think, and so on.) In the canonical version of the guessing game (Nagel, 1995), a group of players is asked to choose a number from a given range (e.g., [0, 100]). The average of all numbers submitted is taken, and 2/3 (or any fraction smaller than 1) of that average becomes the "target number." The person whose chosen number comes closest to this target number wins a fixed prize. In other words, the goal is to correctly guess 2/3 of the average guess. The prediction of game theory in this game is that all players will submit a guess of zero. In fact, this solution can be achieved by a process called "iterated elimination of dominated strategies," which proceeds as follows: If I am rational, I should realize that since the maximum possible number is 100, the target number can never be more than 66. Therefore, any guess above 66 is a "dominated" action—no matter what others might be doing, I should not submit a guess more than 66. But if I

know that everyone is rational, I should also realize that no one will submit a guess above 66, which makes any guess above 44 dominated for me because I know the target number cannot be more than 44. Continuing in this fashion, it is possible to reach the unique equilibrium outcome of everyone guessing zero. Experimental results, on the other hand, show that very few people submit guesses of zero and that there are clusters of observations around points such as 33 and 22. Researchers have provided the following type of model to account for these deviations from the prediction of game theory: Suppose that individuals differ in their "depth of reasoning" and are classified as "Level k thinkers," where k is the number of rounds of iterated reasoning they can engage in. For example, a Level 0 person just guesses randomly, without any strategic thought. A Level 1 person, on the other hand, thinks that everyone else is Level 0 and best responds to that—meaning, a Level 1 person will assume that on average the guess will be 50 and therefore chooses a number that is 2/3 of that, 33. A Level 2 person thinks that everyone else is Level 1 and therefore the average guess will be 33 and takes 2/3 of that to submit his or her guess. The experimental data show that most people are within three levels of thinking. Although this game may seem of theoretical interest, in fact it highlights mechanisms that are important in many economic settings, such as the stock market, where it is important to guess what others think about the value of a stock and how rational they are in their behavior.

Illustration 2: Do We Care Only About Ourselves? Experiments on Social Preferences

As mentioned before, another important focus of game theory experiments has been testing the assumption of "pure self-interest," which we define as preferences that depend only on our own monetary earnings, independently of what others earn. A very interesting set of results in this literature comes from experiments that highlight "social preferences."

The concept of social preferences refers to the concern (positive or negative) for others' well-being. We distinguish between two types of social preferences. The first type refers to *outcome-oriented social preferences.* Here, individuals care about the distribution of payoffs, and this encompasses pure altruism, inequality aversion, and possibly a concern for efficiency. The second type of social preferences concerns *intention-based reciprocity* (i.e., individuals care about the intentions that drive other players' actions). Here an individual is willing to sacrifice his own material payoffs in order to reciprocate, either rewarding kind (fair) or punishing unkind (unfair) behavior.

Research in experimental economics has helped us understand the nature of attitudes toward social preferences and how these attitudes interact with self-interest.

An important workhorse that is used for studying social preferences is simple games in which subjects have to decide on an allocation of money between themselves and an anonymous other subject. Experiments on social preferences generally study such games, which include the so-called ultimatum game, dictator game, trust game, gift exchange game, prisoner's dilemma, public good game, and modifications to these canonical settings. Subjects make decisions usually for a certain number of periods and are usually rematched with different subjects every period, which enables economists to think about this as a one-shot interaction and abstract from repeated game effects. In the past three decades, a vast number of experiments on social preferences have been conducted either to check the existence of social preferences (in the lab) or to test the robustness of results to different subject pools, stakes, framing, number of players, and other design and procedural variables. More recently, field experiments have been conducted to test the external validity of lab experiments and to obtain insight on the strength of social preferences in the field. In the following, we first describe classical experiments on social preferences and some extensions. We then discuss the related field experiments.

Ultimatum and Dictator Games

The ultimatum bargaining game has been one of the most widely studied games in the past 25 years. In the basic version of this game (Güth, Schmittberger, & Schwarze, 1982), two subjects bargain over the division of a "pie." The first player (the proposer) has an endowment of money and decides on the amount X to send to an anonymous partner (the responder), who then decides whether to accept it or not. If accepted, both players get their agreed-upon shares. If rejected, both receive nothing. While the rational solution predicts that the proposer should offer the smallest possible share and the responder should accept it, Güth et al. (1982) find that, on average, proposers offer 37% of the pie and that low offers are frequently rejected. Since then, numerous other experiments using the ultimatum game have been conducted, and many possible methodological explanations (stakes, subject pool, nature of the game) for the gap between theory and empirical results have been tested. Results are robust: (a) The modal and median ultimatum offers are usually 40% to 50%, and mean offers range from 30% to 40%; (b) very low offers (0%–10%) and "too fair" offers (51%–100%) are rarely observed; and (c) offers below 20% are rejected half the time.

The equilibrium in the ultimatum game is easy to compute and is exempt from bounded rationality or confusion as possible explanations for the results, which makes the ultimatum game one of the most common experimental designs used for inference about individuals' social preferences. For instance, when a responder rejects a positive offer, this means that his or her utility function has more than only a monetary argument. For example, a rejection of

a positive but low offer could reveal a concern for negative reciprocity, as the responder is willing to sacrifice his or her own monetary payoff to punish the proposer's action. When the proposer makes a higher offer, however, it could mean a preference for fairness, a fear of rejection, or both. Further experiments using the so-called dictator game disentangle the two explanations and show that both have some explanatory validity. Forsythe, Horowitz, Savin, and Sefton (1994) conducted a dictator experiment that mainly removes the responder's move from the standard ultimatum game—proposers have the power to decide on the allocation of the pie, and the responder cannot reject. In this game, offers are found to be less generous than in the ultimatum game (the mean allocation is about 20% of the pie), but there is still a significant fraction of people who give positive amounts of money to the other party.

Trust and Gift Exchange Games

Trust and gift exchange games are both sequential prisoner's dilemma games, and they represent situations where contracts are necessarily incomplete, allowing for a controlled study of the nature and effectiveness of trust and reciprocity in economic interactions. The trust game (Berg, Dickhaut, & McCabe, 1995), which is also called the investment game, considers a situation in which one individual (the investor) transfers to another (the trustee) the power to make a decision that affects the utility of both. More specifically, the investor has an initial endowment A and decides the amount X of A to invest. The money invested is multiplied by r and transferred to the second player, who decides the amount Y of rX to return to the investor. The trustee, therefore, plays a dictator game with an endowment decided by an initial investment made by the recipient. The investor receives $A - X + Y$, and the trustee receives $rX - Y$.

When players are entirely selfish and only interested in maximizing their own monetary payoffs, the second player would never return any positive amount of rX. Given that the investor knows that the second player will behave selfishly and he or she will receive nothing in return, Player 1 invests nothing, keeping A for himself or herself. Although it yields a socially inefficient outcome (the total payoffs would be maximized if the investor transferred everything), this "subgame perfect" equilibrium of zero investment holds because (a) players cannot sign binding and irrevocable contracts before the beginning of the game, and the trustee cannot be punished for not sending a positive amount back to the investor, and (b) the game is played only once or with different partners, so there is no role for reputation formation and strategic behavior on the part of the trustee.

In Berg et al. (1995), each player was matched only once with another player, and subjects' anonymity among themselves as well as anonymity from the experimenter was guaranteed. Parameters used in their experiment consisted of $10 for investor's endowment, and any amount passed to the trustee was tripled by the experimenter. The results deviate substantially from standard predictions, supporting both the hypothesis of pure trust on the investors' side and the hypothesis of trustworthiness on the trustees' side. With respect to investors' behavior, the average amount sent was 5.2, with only 2 of 320 investors sending zero, but the amount sent varied substantially across subjects. The trustees returned on average 4.6 (about 1/3 of the tripled amount), and the amount repaid was highly heterogeneous also, with 50% of trustees returning less than $1. The trust game has been often replicated with different subjects and with a fair amount of variation in experimental procedures, either to test for the robustness of the Berg et al. results or to infer about the effectiveness and nature of trust and trustworthiness in different settings with incomplete contracts.

While the first player's behavior in the trust game allows us to infer whether the investor trusts his or her experimental partner, it is less obvious what we can infer about the trustworthiness of the second player. If the trustee chooses to send a positive amount back, it can signal either altruism (a pure concern for the investor's payoffs) or positive reciprocity (the desire to be kind to someone who was kind). Comparing the amount sent back in the trust game with dictator allocations of comparable size endowments, James Cox (2004) found support for both altruism and intention-based positive reciprocity. Further experiments have been conducted on the importance of intentions using a similar game to the trust game, called the "gift exchange" game.

As in the trust game, the gift exchange game (Fehr, Kirchsteiger, & Riedl, 1993) represents a situation where contracts are incomplete. It represents the interaction between an employer and a worker, and it was designed to test efficiency wage theory (Akerlof, 1982), according to which firms will offer higher than market clearing wages, expecting that workers will work harder in return. Workers then compare the wage received with a norm they consider fair and choose whether to increase their effort or not, resulting in a positive wage effort relationship.

In the most basic version of the gift exchange game, the employer first decides on an unconditional wage transfer. After observing the wage that he or she will earn, the worker subsequently decides how much effort to supply. Effort increases the profits to the employer, but is also (increasingly) costly to the worker. As an example, suppose that firms earn $(q - w)e$ and workers earn $w - c(e)$, where $c(e)$ is a convex effort cost function over effort levels that range from 0.1 to 1.0. Fehr et al. (1993) implement this experiment in a labor market where there is an excess supply of workers (eight workers for six employers). The market is organized as a one-sided posted offer, in which workers accept or reject offers in a random order. Therefore, if the worker is entirely selfish, he or she will not supply any effort at all, irrespective of the actual wage offered. Anticipating this entirely flat wage effort schedule, the employer offers the lowest possible wage that satisfies the worker's participation constraint.

Experimental findings sharply contrast these theoretical predictions. Workers are typically willing to supply more effort when a higher wage is offered, yielding a significantly positive correlation between wages and effort, which can be interpreted as positively reciprocal behavior. Results in these games have been highly replicated and appear to be robust and found in various versions of the standard gift exchange game.

In general, the robustness of laboratory results on social preferences has led to the extrapolation of prosocial behavior to a large number of real-world situations. As pointed out by Levitt and List (2007), however, behavior in the laboratory may differ from that observed in real economic environments, depending on the presence of moral and ethical considerations, the nature and extent of scrutiny of one's actions by others, the stakes of the game, self-selection of the individuals making the decisions, and the context in which the decision is embedded. In general, real-world situations tend to be far more complex than those created in simple laboratory games—for example, workers in reality work in large firms with many other workers, at different hierarchical levels and within a complex payment structure. The possible dependence of fairness and reciprocity considerations on the features of such complex environments could invalidate the direct generalizability of laboratory experimental results to natural markets.

More recently, field experiments have been conducted to address such issues of generalizability and to explore the external validity of laboratory experiments on social preferences. One important example of this endeavor is field experiments on gift exchange. Findings from these field experiments appear to be mixed in terms of their support for social preferences. To capture gift exchange in the field, List (2006) conducted a series of field experiments in a sports card fair, where buyers and sellers of sports cards interacted. The buyer asked the seller for a card of a certain (unverifiable) quality and offered either a high or a low price, and the seller chose the quality of card to provide after seeing this offer. When there was no possibility of reputation building, List did not find reciprocal behavior by sellers: The average card quality provided by nonlocal dealers (who had no incentives to build reputation) was the same for both the buyers who offered a high price and the buyers who offered a low price. On the other hand, in a charity donation context, Falk (2007) found that a small gift included in solicitation mails significantly increases charitable donations.

Another issue that has been explored by field experiments is the time dimension of social behavior, which is a dimension of labor interactions largely ignored in laboratory experiments. Gneezy and List (2006) tested the gift exchange hypothesis in two actual spot labor markets, a library data entry job and a door-to-door fundraising job, and investigated the effect of the duration of the task. Both experiments consisted of a control group that was paid according to the promised wage and a treatment group that was told after recruitment that the wage was raised to a higher level than promised. The authors found that paying more than market-clearing wages had a positive effect on the effort exerted but that the effect was short-lived in both tasks. In particular, treated workers logged more books and raised more money in the initial hours of the tasks, but no significant differences were observed in later hours. Placing the labor relation within a firm instead of a spot labor market, however, Bellemare and Shearer (2009) got different results. They conducted a field gift exchange experiment within a tree-planting firm where workers received a surprise bonus. Here, reciprocity seems to play a role, as workers' average daily productivity increased by 10%. Moreover, workers' reciprocal behavior persisted several days after the gift. The mixed results obtained from gift exchange field experiments suggest that reciprocal behavior may be less important in spot markets and more relevant in economic settings where norms of giving apply such as employment relationships and charitable giving.

Market Experiments

Market experiments, for which Vernon Smith received his Nobel Prize, have been very important in the development of experimental economics since these marked one of the first rigorous uses of experiments to understand economic behavior. One main motivation for running market experiments is to test the predictions of competitive equilibrium (the equilibrium price realizes where the demand curve intersects the supply curve), the equilibration process and speed, and market efficiency (the question of whether all potential gains from trade can actually be exploited). Another motivation is to study different "market institutions," which are specifications of the rules of trading. For example, a retail market could be organized as a "posted-offer" market where one side of the market (e.g., sellers) posts prices. An alternative market institution is a "double-auction mechanism," where both buyers and sellers could post bids and asks, and all participants can see the highest outstanding bid and the lowest outstanding ask. The design of a typical market experiment provides a direct illustration of induced values. In these experiments, subjects are assigned the roles of buyers and sellers and trade a virtual object. Buyers are assigned "valuations" for the object, whereas sellers are assigned "costs" of selling the object. A buyer's profit, if he or she buys, is his or her valuation minus the transactions price, and a seller's profit, if he or she sells, is the price minus his or her cost. The major finding from market experiments is that competitive equilibrium works (i.e., the trade price realizes at the intersection of the induced demand and supply curves) even with only a few buyers and sellers.

Another sales mechanism that has been analyzed extensively using experiments is auctions. These experiments test bidding behavior under different auction formats such as first-price, second-price, English, and Dutch auctions. The usual experimental design involves assignment of valuations to bidders randomly and the bidders submitting bids to win an experimental object in the auction. The profit of the winner is determined according to the auction format—for example, when the auction is a first-price auction, the

winner gets an amount equal to his or her valuation minus his or her bid. The experimental auction literature to date has found some robust results regarding bidding behavior, such as bidders overbidding with respect to the risk-neutral Nash equilibrium prediction in first-price auctions, and different models of behavior have been considered to explain these results, such as risk-averse bidding, or bidders who obtain additional utility when they win ("joy of winning," see Kagel and Levin [2008] for a review). Auction experiments also highlight the feedback between theory and experiments: Experiments test existing theories of bidding, and the results obtained could suggest new models that can more appropriately predict behavior in auctions.

It should also be noted that experiments are also being conducted in fields such as development economics and macroeconomics. Randomized field experiments in development economics have been very useful to test the effectiveness of different policies, such as the use of monetary incentives to increase school performance and attendance (for a review, see Duflo, 2006). Likewise, experimental macroeconomics research has yielded some important insights about the process of equilibration, equilibrium selection, and coordination problems (for a review, see Duffy, 2008).

Years of experimental economics research have also uncovered some differences in behavior driven by individual characteristics. One of these factors is gender. Although men and women behave similarly in many settings, there are some contexts that produce interesting and gender differences. One important context is decision making under risk: Women are found in several studies to be more risk averse than men (Croson & Gneezy, 2008). Likewise, there is some evidence that women are more averse to competitive situations (such as working under a tournament incentive scheme as opposed to an incentive scheme that only depends on one's own performance) than men (Niederle & Vesterlund, 2007), but whether these differences come from biological (nature explanation) or social factors (nurture explanation) is not determined conclusively yet, and this has been an active area of research in recent years (Gneezy, Leonard, & List, 2009).

Another exciting field of research that adds one other layer to experimental methods in economics is neuroeconomics. Neuroeconomic research allows economists to get at the neural basis of economic decision making, which is especially helpful when there are competing models of behavior that make different assumptions about the decision-making process. In this interdisciplinary field that is rapidly growing, subjects' brain activity is measured while they make decisions during an experiment. The predominant method of measurement is functional magnetic resonance imaging (fMRI), although positron emission tomography (PET) and electro-encephalography (EEG) have also been employed. The regions of the brain that are "activated" while making a certain choice can provide economists with direct data that can help them understand the motivations behind the observed behavior. An example of this type of result that has received much interest is one that establishes the source of "non-selfish" preferences in the brain. In an ultimatum game study by Sanfey, Rilling, Aronson, Nystrom, and Cohen (2003), subjects presented with unfair offers have been found to have different activation patterns in their brain, depending on whether the offer is coming from another human or a computer. In particular, brain areas associated with negative emotion such as anger "light up" when one faces an unfair offer, and this activation correlates with the subsequent decision to reject the offer. Neuroeconomics research can therefore shed light onto what kinds of decision processes are involved in economic choice and can help economists build models that have assumptions that have a "basis" in the brain.

Conclusion

Given that naturally occurring data are not always sufficient for measuring economic behavior or inference about a variable of interest, controlled experiments provide an invaluable tool for the economist for gathering data. Experimental data can be used for testing existing economic theories, and the results can direct the creation of new ones. For example, many theories of social preferences today have been built to explain experimental findings, and these new models are being increasingly widely applied in areas such as organizational and personnel economics. With the use of field experiments in conjunction with laboratory experiments, it is possible to test economic behavior in a realistic way, obtain insights that can tell us something about the economic behavior of real agents interacting in natural settings, and evaluate the potential effectiveness of different economic policies. We therefore believe that experimentation is likely to continue to establish itself as a standard method of empirical economic research in the years to come.

Note

1. It should be noted, as an aside, that although some of the topics studied are common (e.g., decision making), the norms of experimental methodology in the two disciplines can be quite different. Another such major difference of economics experiments from psychology experiments is a norm against deception—economists think that having been given misleading information would lead subjects to mistrust and try to second-guess the experimenter in future experiments, which would result in loss of control and contaminate the data in the long run.

References and Further Readings

Akerlof, G. A. (1982). Labor contracts as partial gift exchange. *Quarterly Journal of Economics, 97,* 543–569.

Bellemare, C., & Shearer, B. (2009). Gift giving and worker productivity: Evidence from a firm-level experiment. *Games and Economic Behavior, 67,* 233–244.

Berg, J., Dickhaut J., & McGabe, K. (1995). Trust, reciprocity, and social history. *Games and Economic Behavior, 10,* 122–142.

Camerer, C. (2002). *Behavioral game theory: Experiments in strategic interaction.* Princeton, NJ: Princeton University Press.

Chamberlin, E. H. (1948). An experimental imperfect market. *Journal of Political Economy, 56*(2), 95–108.

Cox, J. C. (2004). How to identify trust and reciprocity. *Games and Economic Behavior, 46,* 260–281.

Croson, R., & Gneezy, U. (2008). Gender differences in preferences. *Journal of Economic Literature, 47*(2), 1–27.

Duffy, J. (2008). Experimental macroeconomics. In S. N. Durlauf & L. E. Blume (Eds.), *The new Palgrave dictionary of economics* (2nd ed.). New York: Palgrave Macmillan.

Duflo, E. (2006). Field experiments in development economics. In R. Blundell, W. K. Newey, & T. Persson (Eds.), *Advances in economics and econometrics* (pp. 322–348). New York: Cambridge University Press.

Falk, A. (2007). Gift exchange in the field. *Econometrica, 75,* 1501–1511.

Fehr, E., Kirchsteiger, G., & Riedl, A. (1993). Does fairness prevent market clearing? An experimental investigation. *Quarterly Journal of Economics, 108,* 437–459.

Forsythe, R., Horowitz, J. L., Savin, N. E., & Sefton, M. (1994). Fairness in simple bargaining experiments. *Games and Economic Behavior, 6,* 347–369.

Gneezy, U., Leonard, K. L., & List, J. A. (2009). Gender differences in competition: Evidence from a matrilineal and a patriarchal society. *Econometrica, 77,* 1637–1664.

Gneezy, U., & List, J. A. (2006). Putting behavioral economics to work: Testing for gift exchange in labor markets using field experiments. *Econometrica, 74,* 1365–1384.

Güth, W., Schmittberger, R., & Schwarze, B. (1982). An experimental analysis of ultimatum bargaining. *Journal of Economic Behavior & Organization, 3,* 367–388.

Harrison, G. W., & List, J. A. (2004). Field experiments. *Journal of Economic Literature, 42,* 1009–1055.

Holt, C. (2006). *Markets, games and strategic behavior.* Reading, MA: Addison-Wesley.

Holt, C. A., & Laury, S. K. (2002). Risk aversion and incentive effects. *American Economic Review, 92,* 1644–1655.

Kagel, J. H., & Lewin, D. (2008). Auctions (experiments). In S. N. Durlauf & L. E. Blume (Eds.), *The new Palgrave dictionary of economics* (2nd ed.). New York: Palgrave Macmillan.

Kagel, J. H., & Roth, A. E. (1995). *The handbook of experimental economics.* Princeton, NJ: Princeton University Press.

Kahneman, D., & Tversky, A. (1979). Prospect theory: An analysis of decisions under risk. *Econometrica, 47,* 313–327.

Levitt, S. D., & List, J. A. (2007). What do laboratory experiments measuring social preferences reveal about the real world? *Journal of Economic Perspectives, 21*(2), 153–174.

List, J. A. (2006). The behavioralist meets the market: Measuring social preferences and reputation effects in actual transactions. *Journal of Political Economy, 114,* 1–37.

Nagel, R. (1995). Unraveling in guessing games: An experimental study. *American Economic Review, 85,* 1313–1326.

Niederle, M., & Vesterlund, L. (2007). Do women shy away from competition? Do men compete too much? *Quarterly Journal of Economics, 122,* 1067–1101.

Sanfey, A. G., Rilling, J. K., Aronson, J. A., Nystrom, L. E., & Cohen J. D. (2003). The neural basis of economic decision-making in the ultimatum game. *Science, 300,* 1755–1758.

Smith, V. (1982). Microeconomic systems as an experimental science. *American Economic Review, 72,* 923–955.

von Neumann, J., & Morgenstern, O. (1944). *Theory of games and economic behavior.* Princeton, NJ: Princeton University Press.

86

COMPLEXITY AND ECONOMICS

TROY L. TASSIER

Fordham University

Complex systems research is a growing field in economics as well as other social and natural sciences. Complex systems research aims to understand underlying phenomena that regularly occur across various complex systems, whether those systems occur in physics, chemistry, biology, social sciences, or any other discipline. Thus, throughout the field, one finds models and methodologies being shared across disciplines. For instance, one finds statistical mechanics methods from physics applied to the study of infectious diseases in epidemiology. The study of economics from a complex systems or complexity perspective is closely tied to the study of complex systems in general.

Defining what is meant by a complex system or complexity can be a difficult task. When one looks up the root word *complex* in a dictionary, one will read something similar to "made up of complicated interrelated parts" or "involved and intricate." These definitions give one a start in defining how the word *complexity* is used in the sciences, but one needs a bit more. A complex system is made of interacting parts (usually many), but those parts do not always need to be complicated. Sometimes, seemingly simple systems produce complex behavior. Further, an understanding of each of the constituent parts individually does not lead to an understanding of the entire system. Thus, complex systems research in economics and elsewhere often constitutes a holistic approach to understanding economic systems. It encompasses understanding not only how individual constituent parts (such as individuals or firms) operate or behave but also how those operations or behaviors aggregate to create a system (such as a market outcome or dynamic time series).

What Makes a System Complex?

There are several common features of systems that are associated with complex behavior. These are diversity, structured interactions, bounded rationality, adaption and learning, dynamic systems, and lack of centralized authority. These features are inherently associated with many of the systems that economists often study. It is not the case that all complex systems contain all of the elements listed above, but most contain several of these features. In the next section, this chapter describes these common features of a complex system and gives relevant examples from economics.

Diversity or Heterogeneity

Complex systems frequently are composed of diverse or heterogeneous elements. Elements of a system may be diverse simply because they perform different functions in systems, individuals, firms, and governments, for example. But even agents or objects within a given group or class in a complex system tend to behave, learn, or organize in a multitude of ways. In economics, at the lowest level, the constituent parts are individuals. Individuals in economic systems differ in so many ways it is difficult to count or list them all. Sometimes, this variety is based on characteristics that an agent is born with, such as race, ethnicity, gender, age, or religion. Other characteristics are primarily choices of the agent. Some of these include training and education, residential location, or specialization in a profession, to name a few. Of course, some of these items are interlinked. For instance, one may be born into a Catholic family but convert to another religion. Further, some of the choice characteristics are constrained choices, where the constraints may vary across individuals. For instance, one's opportunity to acquire education and human capital are constrained by one's ability to pay college tuition or by the educational opportunities provided by one's caregivers in the home, and one's choice of residential location is constrained by the income and wealth that one attains or inherits. Finally, in many economic models, agents are assumed to have homogeneous preferences or tastes. Very few economic models consider that individuals may have different preferences or objectives, yet if one asked each individual in a group of 1,000 to name a favorite restaurant, flavor of ice cream, time to awaken in the morning, and number of hours to relax in a day, one would probably get 1,000 different answers. In summary, there is a great number of ways in which individual economic agents differ, and complex systems models in economics often embrace this diversity.

Structurally Interacting Agents or Parts

In many complex systems models, there exists a specified structure on which interactions occur. Sometimes, this is based on geography; other times, the interactions are a function of some other structural constraint such as the neurological connections in the human body. In sum, there is some network architecture central to the interactions of agents.

Although this is currently changing, most traditional economic models assume that agents interact without attention to the details of the interaction. In some cases, agents interact only through a market mechanism like a traditional Walrasian auctioneer. In other instances, agents are supposed to interact through random meetings, as though in a so-called Walrasian soup. For instance, most labor market search models have random meetings between potential employers and employees. Agents then optimize their choice to accept employment if offered a job, based on their expected waiting time for other (preferably better) job opportunities to randomly arrive at or above a reservation wage. However, it is common for individuals to learn of job opportunities through family and friends. In fact, around 50% of jobs are found in this manner (Granovetter, 1995). Further, individuals base many of their decisions on information gained from friends, such as recommendations on which products or brands of products to buy, what restaurants to try when visiting a new city, or what theater performances or movies to attend.

There are multiple ways that one can think of this idea of network architecture and the influence of social contacts playing a role in economic outcomes. The first is probably the least controversial: Network structures can act as constraints on the decisions of agents. If information travels through social contacts, then the contacts of an agent help to determine what information that agent holds, whether it is about jobs, products, or another item of economic interest. Second, one may also view the social contacts of an agent in helping to determine one's behavior through a traditional

externality perspective. For instance, if all of one's friends own Apple computer products, it is more beneficial to own an Apple than if all of one's friends own PC-based products because of direct reasons such as the (legal or illegal) sharing of software or because of less direct reasons such as troubleshooting when operational problems arise. Third, one can be influenced just by the actions of friends through conformity effects. Rationally, it may be advantageous to attend movies that one's peers attend just so that one can fit in and engage in conversations about these movies. Perhaps less rationally, one can imagine a lemminglike scenario where one attends movies just because his or her friends attended these movies. In any case, the interactions with one's social contacts help determine behavior and decision making either through a traditional constraint-based approach or through less traditional conformity effects.

These social contacts may be exogenously given (e.g., family) or endogenous; they may be a constrained choice of the agent, such as the friendships formed at school. One gets to choose one's friends from the set of other agents that one meets. But this choice is constrained by the opportunities that one has (geography) and, in some cases, by the willingness of other agents to reciprocate the interaction (friendships). In other cases, reciprocation is not needed. For instance, one can pass on some infectious diseases, such as influenza, without asking permission of the recipient agent.

Finally, since each individual has a unique set of friends and family, each person has a unique set of social contacts. Thus, social contacts are yet another way in which agents are diverse.

Bounded Rationality

Again, as in the discussion of structured interaction, traditional economic models often make simplifying assumptions that are unrealistic. This occurs again when one considers the rationality of agents. Many economic models assume that the agents that populate them can compute the answers to very complicated problems almost instantly. Even before the interest by economists in complex systems-style economics, this überrationality was already being challenged by numerous economists, resulting in the development of a boundedly rational economics model (Rubinstein, 1998). This literature took several directions, and a few of them are discussed here.

Limited Cognition

Most individuals do not often perform complicated calculations like inverting a large matrix in their heads in a matter of seconds. Thus, some boundedly rational economics models simply assume that economic agents do not have the capacity to easily perform some calculations. There have been a variety of ways in which to implement nonrational agents. Perhaps one of the most notable is the "satisficing" approach of Herbert Simon (1996). Here, agents accept a solution to a problem or an alternative that yields an acceptable but perhaps not optimal solution or alternative.

Rational to Be Irrational

In some cases, the primary constraints on optimization and rationality concern the ability to gather information as opposed to the ability to process this information. For instance, if one wants to find the best price on a common consumer good, say a specific make and model of shoes, in a large city, one could potentially check every retail establishment that sells shoes. But the time cost required to do so may make it irrational to actually complete this comprehensive search for the optimal price. Thus, consumers may find it optimal to simply accept a reasonable price once found. Similarly, in labor economics, many models assume that agents search for jobs and calculate the optimal search behavior, given knowledge about the distribution of offers that exist; they ask themselves if they should accept the jobs offered or wait for better ones, given that they know the distribution of jobs that are available. This line of research still assumes that agents act rationally and also that agents solve a rather complicated optimization problem.

Limited Information Due to Network Constraints

Recall the previous discussion about the transfer of information across social networks. If the majority of information needed to solve a problem or to maximize utility or profits must be obtained from an information source that depends on some contact structure, then agents may optimize, but they do so with potential information constraints. The cognitive abilities of agents may be very powerful, but the agents can act only on the information that is available to them through the given interaction structure. In this scenario, agents may act rationally, given their information, but the actions may appear irrational to outsiders because of the limited information held by an agent. A simple example of this process is contained in the information cascades literature. Here, agents must choose between two similar goods, where one good is superior to the other. Agents receive a private noisy but informative signal about the quality of two goods and observe the choices of other agents choosing prior to them. Through the other agents' actions and the agent's own private signal, the agent rationally calculates the likelihood of each good being the superior one and chooses that good. Even though agents act rationally, it is possible that the agents may coordinate on a bad equilibrium where the agents all choose the inferior good. (See Holt, 2007, for simple examples.)

Adaption or Learning

Central to the idea of bounded rationality is the fact that agents must face some constraint on their ability to optimize. The constraint may be limited cognitive abilities, limited information, or limited time. All of these items force an agent to act in a way that does not guarantee optimization. In some of the cases described, agents simply act rationally given the constraint. But since many if not most economic models include a dimension of time, an alternative and increasingly popular approach is to allow agents to learn over time. The learning often takes on two different dimensions that this chapter calls *experiential* and *imitative* learning. With experiential learning, the agent uses his or her past experiences to try to improve on economic outcomes. This approach may include some type of trial-and-error learning where agents apply a heuristic to a given problem and view the results. Then when faced with the same problem, or a similar problem, the agent adjusts his or her behavior to attempt to reach a better outcome. Or it may proceed according to a more traditional economics approach where agents use a rational cognitive model where an optimal decision is made according to the available information at a given time. Then as more information is revealed, the agent reoptimizes according to the new information. With imitative learning, agents use the experiences of others around them to try to improve their outcomes. For instance, one might copy the strategy of a neighbor who has fared well in a labor market in one's own search for a job. Imitative learning often takes on many dimensions. For instance, one can copy the actions of neighbors or the strategies of neighbors. This distinction must be considered carefully especially in light of the fact that actions are often more observable than strategies.

There are several common methods for incorporating either form of learning. Most involve some type of error or mutation process that allows agents to improve. For instance, suppose that one observes the outcomes of a selection of agents in a population (an agent's neighbors). One method of learning would be for the agent to simply replicate the agent he or she observes who has the best outcome. Another would be for the agent to replicate the best agent in most cases but sometimes make a mistake and, when doing so, replicate another randomly chosen agent. Or in another method yet, an agent could choose another agent to replicate as a function of the other agent's performance; better performing agents are more likely to be replicated than poorly performing agents, but all agents have some positive likelihood of being replicated. The ability of agents to make mistakes often allows the population and the individual agent to improve on their outcomes in the long run. For instance, suppose that every agent can observe the outcome of every other agent in a population. If every agent copies the best agent, then all agents will have the same strategy in the next time period, and no additional learning can result. This is fine if the best agent was acting optimally, but if the agent was not acting optimally, then the population will never act optimally. Thus, one can get stuck with a suboptimal strategy. Replication of some subperforming agents can maintain diversity, which may allow the population to reach a better long-term outcome. Another component common in many learning models is the ability of agents to simply make mistakes or errors. Similar to not always replicating the best agents, errors can allow for continued diversity in a population and the ability to more fully explore the set of possible solutions to a problem or game. It is common for learning models to incorporate both of these elements. For instance, a genetic algorithm mimics the reproduction found in nature (Holland, 1995). Better performing agents are more likely to be reproduced. But when an agent does reproduce, it does not produce an exact copy of himself or herself; mutations to strategies occur, and sometimes, strategies of agents are combined (as in genes of an offspring being a combination of parents' genes). Finally, there is also a literature that discusses things like optimal rates of learning and optimal rates of errors. Further, it is sometimes best for rates of error to change across time. One may want a high rate of error early on in order to explore and cover a large range of the possible solution space, but once so-called good solution regions are identified, it may be best to begin to limit errors so that these good regions can be better and more fully explored. (See the discussion of simulated annealing in Miller & Page, 2007.) Thus, there can be a balance between the amount of exploration and exploitation in problem solving (March, 1991).

Dynamic, Complex Adaptive System

Models in complex systems are almost always dynamic. The preceding paragraph listed various ways in which agents learn. Learning is inherently a dynamic phenomenon. But dynamic properties of complex systems are not limited to this area. It is common that agents in a complex system model are changing in some way. Sometimes this change includes learning. But it may also include change in the form of new interactions for the agents, revelation of new strategies, or the creation of new types of agents, firms, or institutions in an economic or social system. Thus, not only are individual agents often evolving but the systems that guide the agents also are changing or evolving. Of course, this produces feedbacks between the system and the agents that make up the system. A strategy or action that does well today may not be the best strategy tomorrow or next year.

As an example, consider Brian Arthur's (1994) "El Farol Bar Problem." In the problem, individual agents in a population of fixed size must decide whether to attend an event (an Irish music night at a local bar, in the original example). If more than $x\%$ of agents attend the event, each agent that attends receives less utility than if he or she stayed home; the event is too crowded. But if less than or equal to $x\%$ of agents attend, then each agent attending receives more utility than if he or she had stayed home. The dilemma here is that if all agents use the same strategy, then everyone attends or no one does. More importantly for this discussion, the best choice for each agent depends on the choices of all other agents. Thus, an agent's best strategy today may not be a successful strategy tomorrow if other agents learn and adapt to the system. For instance, suppose that agents rely on their friends to report attendance at the event to them in order to project attendance in the following week. If $x = 75$ and 50% of agents attend this

week and honestly tell their friends that they had a great time, then one might expect to get more than 75% attending next week. This may lead agents to develop more sophisticated strategies that may include misinforming other agents. Further, the organizers of the event may also have an incentive to report attendance figures that may or may not be accurate in order to maximize attendance according to a profit function. The important thing to note is that even some simple scenarios or games can easily lead to complex behavior.

Lack of Top-Down Administration

In most examples of complex systems, there does not exist a central authority that is responsible for overseeing and coordinating activities of the various agents in the system. Thus, outcomes in the system occur as a result of ex ante uncoordinated actions. Coordination may occur in the system, but coordination does not occur as a result of an exogenously specified central authority. (It is possible, though, that such an authority may emerge from the activities of the system.) Thus, complex systems modeling is sometimes referred to as social science from the bottom up (Epstein & Axtell, 1996).

Economic Outcomes From a Complex System Perspective

One of the hallmark features of most complex systems is that one cannot understand the whole by independently understanding the sum of the parts. For instance, one can understand the incentives of buyers and sellers participating in a market as well as the rules or laws that define a market but still not fully understand the aggregate behavior of the market. In traditional economics, one might focus on something like a price as a market outcome and take this observation as an indicator of market performance or behavior. The study of complex systems embraces a larger goal of also understanding how the market emerges, how relationships between participants may form and fail, and how institutions, laws, consumer strategies, and firm organization change over time.

One of the reasons that complex systems are difficult to understand is because the interactions between system components tend to create complicated feedbacks and nonlinear relationships between various parts of the system. Another hallmark feature of many complex systems is the existence of multiple feedback relationships in the system. Feedback can be positive or negative. Positive feedback exists in a system if a change in variable x causes the system to respond to the change by creating further change in x in the same direction. Negative feedback exists in a system if a change in variable x causes the system to respond to the change by reversing the direction of the change in x. As an example of positive feedback, consider the juvenile crime rate in a neighborhood. Suppose that this crime rate is affected by the number of businesses in the neighborhood. More business activity leads to more jobs for young people, which lowers the crime rate. But a lack of businesses leads to fewer job opportunities and more crime. Further suppose that businesses are adversely affected by high crime rates. Now suppose that an exogenous change occurs in the system and several new businesses open in a neighborhood. By the relationships described, crime rates would decrease; this would lead to even more businesses entering the neighborhood and a further reduction in crime rates. As an example of negative feedback in the same example, suppose that the decrease in the crime rate is met by a decrease in enforcement of laws. This lax enforcement might then lead to an increase in the crime rate.

Of particular importance, positive feedbacks can lead to there being multiple equilibria in a system. As another example of positive feedback, suppose that there are two competing operating systems for a computer, X and Y. Further, suppose that the value to an agent of using a given operating system increases in the number of other agents who use the same system. Thus, if a large percentage of consumers use System X, the value of an agent's using System X is higher than if a small percentage were using System X. One can think of the same scenario with Operating System Y coming to dominate the market. Thus, an equilibrium could be reached where there are a large percentage of Operating System X users and a small percentage of Operating System Y users. Or one could have the opposite scenario, with a large percentage of System Y users and a small percentage of System X users.

Understanding Complex Systems: Theory and Policy

The possibility of multiple equilibria in a complex system makes the issue of equilibrium selection even more important. For instance, in the simple supply and demand model taught in introductory economics courses, there is only one equilibrium and thus one prediction for the outcome of that model. But if a system has a multitude of equilibria, how does one make predictions? Further, how does one understand the process of selecting and attaining a specific equilibrium?

To begin answering these questions, one needs to consider that not all equilibria are created equal. An equilibrium that is associated with positive feedback is inherently unstable, while an equilibrium that has negative feedback surrounding it is stable. As an example, consider the following equilibrium: a pencil perfectly balanced on its end. This is an equilibrium for the pencil: As long as no one changes the conditions around the pencil by perhaps blowing on it or shaking the table on which it is balanced, the pencil will stay balanced as it is. But if the pencil tips just a bit, the positive feedback introduced by gravity will lead the pencil to tip a little further and eventually fall over. Positive feedback in any one direction away from an equilibrium can result in forces that drive a system away from the equilibrium. On the other hand, negative feedback is associated with stability. Consider the simple supply and demand

model of an introductory economics course. In this model, prices act as negative feedback. If the price deviates from equilibrium, perhaps by dipping too low, the shortage created in the market acts to push prices upward and back to equilibrium. On the other hand, if prices increase, the surplus created in the market will pull prices back down toward the equilibrium. So if prices deviate in any direction away from equilibrium, the negative feedback in the system acts to restore the system to the equilibrium.

One way to predict which of the many equilibria in a system will occur is to consider whether an equilibrium is stable or unstable. Like the pencil balanced on its end, any unstable equilibrium requires very specific conditions to occur. If any of these conditions deviate slightly, the system leaves that equilibrium. As an example, throw a pencil in the air and let it land on the desk 100 times; how many times does it land balanced perfectly on its point? Unstable equilibria are almost never observed. Thus, when predicting which equilibrium will occur in a system, one can rule out any unstable equilibria as good predictors for the system.

However, one may still be left with many stable equilibria in a system. Which equilibria will be attained is another focal point for complex systems research, and many angles have been taken in addressing this issue. There are formal theoretical interests such as measuring the size of the basin of attraction of an equilibrium. (The basin of attraction for a given equilibrium is the set of states that lead to the equilibrium.) A larger basin of attraction should imply that the equilibrium will be attained more often.

More interesting from an empirical perspective, different methods of learning or behavior can lead to a different equilibrium. For example, consider the following simple situation. An agent wants to meet a friend for lunch and knows that they are going to meet at one of two restaurants, A or B, in 10 minutes, but the agent's phone is broken, and he or she cannot contact the friend to coordinate on which restaurant. So the agent chooses one of the restaurants. Suppose that the agent fails to coordinate with the friend, who chose the other restaurant, so the agent eats alone. Now suppose that the next day the same situation occurs. What should the agent do? What strategy does he or she follow? One option is to follow a pure best response to what happened in the previous period. This strategy would lead the agent to choose the opposite restaurant from the last time. If the friend follows the same strategy, they will fail to coordinate again. On the other hand, suppose that the agent plays a best response to the entire history of the friend's choices. The agent chooses according to the fraction of times the friend chooses each restaurant. Thus, as the agent keeps choosing the wrong restaurant time after time, his or her frequency of visiting each one approaches one half. Thus, choosing Restaurant A 50% of the time and Restaurant B 50% of the time, the agent will be able to meet the friend for lunch in 50% of the cases. (One quarter of the time, both choose A; one quarter of the time, both choose B; one quarter of the time, the agent chooses A and the friend chooses B; and one quarter of the time, the agent chooses B and the friend chooses A.) But one could do even better in this case by weighting the more recent choices more strongly.

Then as chance meetings occur, the probability of another chance meeting increases. But recall that one can't go too far. If one plays a pure best response to only the last period, one will return to the possibility of never coordinating. As a side note here, suppose that one prefers Restaurant A and the friend prefers restaurant B. One could also analyze this game from the perspective of an altruist and an egoist strategy. An egoist chooses the restaurant that he or she prefers all the time, and an altruist chooses the restaurant that his or her partner prefers all the time. If two altruists or two egoists (again with conflicting restaurant preferences) play the game, they never coordinate. But if one of each plays the game, they always coordinate. Thus, there can be situations where diversity of preferences, tastes, or types can lead to better outcomes than if diversity is lacking.

Equilibrium selection may also be a function of path dependence (Page, 2006). For instance, in an example given previously, once Operating System X is chosen over Y by a majority of the population, it may be very hard to break out of this equilibrium. Further, even if X and Y start out equal in terms of quality, it may be the case that one comes to dominate the market. But if the minority technology makes improvements and becomes the superior choice, it may be hard to get the population to switch to the better equilibrium. Simply put, history can matter. Further, institutions matter too. As a simple example, there may be a role for the government to help push the public toward coordinating on a superior equilibrium if the population is stuck at an inferior equilibrium. Public policy can be used as a lever to push systems toward or away from one equilibrium or another, depending on the best interest of society.

Understanding Complex Systems: The Tools

There are a variety of tools used to understand complex systems. Traditional analytical modeling and statistical and econometric techniques are sometimes helpful in understanding complex systems. But their use is often limited by the severe nonlinearity of many of the systems. As mentioned previously, the nonlinearity results from the multiple interdependent relationships and feedback effects common in complex systems models. Because mathematical and statistical methods for dealing with nonlinear systems are limited, computational simulations and particularly agent-based computational experiments are commonly used in the study of complex systems (Miller & Page, 2007).

An agent-based model begins with assumptions about the preferences and behavior of individual agents, firms, and institutions and the interrelationships among them. After specifying the initial conditions (agent endowments of wealth, firm endowments of capital, etc.), a group of artificial agents is set forth and studied. Economists can then vary conditions in the model, changing, say, initial wealth endowments or different learning rules and perform a controlled experiment of the computational system. Such computational models are already common in many natural sciences—physics, for example. Use of these methods in economics is beginning to take hold, and there are a growing number of researchers engaged in agent-based computational economics (ACE). (See Leigh Tesfatsion's Web site for a great overview of the current literature.)

As ACE grows, there are opportunities for complex systems research to merge and collaborate with the equally exciting and emerging field of experimental economics. Experimental economists use populations (usually small) of human subjects to engage in controlled experiments of economic relevance, perhaps risky gambles where individual risk preferences can be uncovered. One limit to human subject experiments is the scale to which the experiments can be run. Typical experiments may have dozens or sometimes a couple hundred participants. An agent-based computational experiment does not suffer from this limit. In fact, it is the goal of one group of economists using agent-based methods to build a model of the entire U.S. economy with one artificial agent for each person and firm residing in the United States. Of course, one strong limit of agent-based models is the fact that the agents are artificial, not real people. Thus, there is fertile ground that can be covered by using agent-based models to scale up human subject experiments and to use human subject experiments to add realism to artificial agent experiments.

An Example: Schelling's Residential Segregation Model

As an example of a simple complex systems model in economics, consider Thomas Schelling's (1978) residential segregation model. The model is so simple that one may be surprised that it generates segregation at all. To begin, assume that there is a town where all houses are located along one street like the one below:

x x x x x x x x x

Further assume that some of the homes are inhabited by people from the land of p, some are inhabited by people from the land of k, and some of the homes are vacant. The vacant homes are denoted with a v.

k p v v p p k p k

In this example, there are nine homes, seven families (four p families and three k families), and two vacant homes. Now assume that all houses have the same value to all families and that a family can swap its house for a vacant one at any time. Further assume that a family is satisfied with its home as long as one of the neighbors is of the same type as the family; a p is satisfied as long as he or she has one p neighbor, and a k is satisfied as long as he or she has one k neighbor. Thus, in this example, the only two families that are happy are the two p families at the fifth and sixth homes. All the other five families are unhappy about their current living conditions.

Now introduce dynamic movement into the model as follows. Take the citizens in order of location from left to right and ask each if he or she is satisfied at his or her current location. If the resident is not satisfied, ask if he or she would be satisfied at any of the homes currently vacant. If the resident prefers a vacant home to the current home, move him or her there. If there are two homes the resident would prefer to the current home, move him or her to the home nearest to the current location. If the resident is not satisfied but there is no vacant home in which he or she would be satisfied, the resident waits until the next opportunity to move and checks the vacant homes again. Thus, one would start with the family at the first home. This is a k family with one neighbor, who is a p. The resident is not satisfied with the current home. There are two locations vacant (third and fourth homes), but neither of these locations has a k neighbor. Thus, the resident would be unsatisfied at both of these locations as well and remains at the first home. Now move to the family at the second home. This is a p family with one k neighbor and one vacant neighbor. Since this family does not have a p neighbor, it is not satisfied either. Thus, it will move if it can find a vacant home with a p neighbor. The fourth home fits this criterion. Thus, the family at the second home moves to the fourth. One now has as follows:

k v v p p p k p k

The next three occupied homes (fourth, fifth, and sixth) are all satisfied. Thus, they remain at their current locations. The family at the seventh home is not satisfied since it has two p neighbors. But it could move to the second home and be satisfied. Thus, one now has as follows:

k k v p p p v p k

At the eighth home, there is a p family that is not satisfied. There are two locations this family could move to in order to be satisfied, the third and seventh home, and they move to the closest one, the seventh.

k v k p p p p v k

Finally, there is a k family at the ninth home that is not satisfied. It can move to the third home and become satisfied. This move yields the following:

k k k p p p p v v

If one checks all of the families again, one sees that they are all satisfied. And what one also may notice is that the neighborhood has become completely segregated with three k's and four p's all living next to each other. Note that this high level of segregation occurs even though the families required only that one of their neighbors be similar to them. Even with these modest preferences, the model generated a large amount of segregation.

Note that perfect segregation is not the only outcome in the model. The following configuration would be an equilibrium as well:

p p k k k p p v v

And there are other equilibria similar to this that would not be perfectly segregated. However, what one sees in this simple model is that even modest preferences for wanting to have neighbors similar to oneself can lead to large amounts of homogeneity within neighborhoods and large amounts of segregation.

One can make the model slightly more complex by introducing more dimensions to the neighborhood. Assume that there is a population of individuals that live in Squareville. Squareville is a set of 36 residential locations like the one below:

x x x x x

x x x x x

x x x x x

x x x x x

x x x x x

x x x x x

Again, one can populate the neighborhood with a set of agents of two types and some vacant locations. Again, let the families be satisfied if at least one half of their neighbors are of the same type as them. This time, take each family in a random order and check to see if it is satisfied. If it is, leave the family there. If it is not, look for the nearest location where the family can be happy and move it there. (Break ties with a flip of a coin.)

One can do this in the following way: Take 24 coins and place them on a grid like the one above. Place 12 of the coins on the grid heads up and 12 of the coins on the grid tails up at random locations. Now roll a six-sided die two times. Let the first number be the row and the second number be the column. Thus, if one rolls a two and then a three, look at the coin located at row two and column three. If there is not a coin there, roll again. If there is a coin there, determine if that coin is satisfied or unsatisfied. If it is satisfied, roll again. If it is unsatisfied, find the nearest location where the coin would be satisfied and move it there.

What one will notice is that as one proceeds with this algorithm, patches on the grid begin to develop where there are mostly heads and others where there are mostly tails. And eventually one will reach a point where every coin is satisfied, and in a majority of the cases, there is a very large degree of segregation. Even though each coin would be satisfied if it had only one half of its neighbors like it, many of the coins have only neighbors like them. The grid will have patches of heads only and tails only, with some borders in between.

One can also try this model with different parameters. What happens if families require only one third of their neighbors to be the same as them? What about three quarters? What if there are more vacant spaces? Fewer vacant spaces? What one will find is that the details of the outcomes will vary (for example, the location of the tails and heads neighborhoods on the grid), but the amount of segregation will still be surprisingly high. For instance, if one sets the tolerance parameter to be one third, significantly more than one third of a family's neighbors will be the same as the family. (In addition to the exercise described, there are several simulation applets available on the Web that can be found in a quick search with such terms as *Schelling segregation model simulation.* One of the simplest to use is the NetLogo Schelling segregation model.)

This simple example displays many of the previously described characteristics of a complex system. The system is dynamic. There are multiple equilibria in the location choices of residents. The coordination on a given equilibrium may have very little to do with the preferences of agents; it may be a product of historical chance. Positive feedback results as neighborhood composition changes. For instance, a decrease in one neighborhood of type p individuals makes it less likely that other type p individuals will remain in the neighborhood. It may not be obvious from understanding the individual incentives and preferences of the agents that large amounts of segregation are likely to result. Simple agent motives lead to complex behavior and outcomes. Neighbors result from a specified interaction structure, in this example a line or a grid, but more complicated structures can incorporate actual neighborhood structures. Finally, even though the model is simple, diversity exists both in the types of agents and in the neighbor of a specified location.

Conclusion

This chapter has outlined the emerging field of complex systems in economics. All of the hallmark aspects of complex systems are present in almost all economic contexts. Complex systems are generally composed of boundedly rational, diverse agents and institutions who interact within a specified structure in a dynamic environment. Further, these agents and institutions often learn and update their behaviors and strategies and lack a centralized authority that oversees control of the system. These characteristics make the study of economics from a complex systems perspective natural.

Once one embraces a complex systems thinking within economics, many new avenues and tools for research open for one's consideration. There is a rich history in fields such as physics that customarily deal with the nonlinear nature of complex systems models. As such, tools from disciplines such as nonlinear mathematics, computational simulations, and agent-based computational experiments are becoming more and more common in economics. These tools help economists to work through the complicated feedbacks and existence of multiple equilibria that are common in many complex systems.

In addition, it should be recognized that the complex systems approach to economics considers many tools from a variety of approaches that are already common in economics. For instance, learning models are not unusual in contemporary economics, nor are interactions across social networks or diversity. But as with the idea of complexity, the sum of combining many of these constituent parts often leads to a more rich environment and understanding than the analysis of these parts individually.

References and Further Readings

Anderson, P. W., Arrow, K. J., & Pines, D. (1988). *The economy as an evolving complex system.* Reading, MA: Addison-Wesley.

Arthur, W. B. (1994). Inductive reasoning and bounded rationality. *American Economic Review (Papers and Proceedings), 84,* 406–411.

Arthur, W. B., Durlauf, S. N., & Lane, D. A. (1997). *The economy as an evolving complex system 2.* Reading, MA: Addison-Wesley.

Axelrod, R. (1997). *The complexity of cooperation: Agent based models of competition and collaboration.* Princeton, NJ: Princeton University Press.

Blume, L. E., & Durlauf, S. N. (2006). *The economy as an evolving complex system 3.* Oxford, UK: Oxford University Press.

Epstein, J. M., & Axtell, R. (1996). *Growing artificial societies from the bottom up.* Washington, DC: Brookings Institution.

Fudenberg, D., & Levine, D. K. (1998). *The theory of learning in games.* Cambridge: MIT Press.

Granovetter, M. (1995). *Getting a job: A study of contacts and careers.* Chicago: University of Chicago Press.

Holland, J. (1995). *Hidden order: How adaptation builds complexity.* Reading, MA: Helix Books.

Holland, J. (1998). *Emergence: From chaos to order.* Reading, MA: Helix Books.

Holt, C. A. (2007). *Markets, games and strategic behavior.* Boston: Pearson.

Jackson, M. O. (2008). *Social and economics networks.* Princeton, NJ: Princeton University Press.

March, J. G. (1991). Exploration and exploitation in organizational learning. *Organization Science, 2*(1), 71–87.

Miller, J. H., & Page, S. E. (2007). *Complex adaptive systems: An introduction to computational models of social life.* Princeton, NJ: Princeton University Press.

Page, S. E. (2006): Essay: Path dependence. *Quarterly Journal of Political Science, 1,* 87–115.

Page, S. E. (2007). *The difference: How the power of diversity creates better groups, firms, schools, and societies.* Princeton, NJ: Princeton University Press.

Rosser, J. B., Jr. (Ed.). (2004). *Complexity in economics.* Northampton, MA: Edward Elgar.

Rubinstein, A. (1998). *Modeling bounded rationality.* Cambridge: MIT Press.

Schelling, T. C. (1978). *Micromotives and macrobehavior.* New York: W. W. Norton.

Simon, H. A. (1996). *The sciences of the artificial* (3rd ed.). Cambridge: MIT Press.

Tesfatsion, L. (2008). *Agent-based computational economics.* Available at http://www.econ.iastate.edu/tesfatsi/ace.htm

Waldrop, M. M. (1992). *Complexity: The emerging science at the edge of order and chaos.* New York: Simon & Schuster.

87

ETHICS AND ECONOMICS

VICTOR V. CLAAR

Henderson State University

Can markets and market interactions be viewed as ethical? This is a crucial consideration inasmuch as it calls into question the entire discipline of economics and every human action within each market. Markets might very well afford individuals opportunities to choose among a variety of options and to choose rightly. If so, then markets are neither moral nor amoral, yet they create occasions for each individual to make ethical decisions.

But markets are more than this from the viewpoint of the broader society. Although it is true that an individual market participant may be thinking of only his or her own family in deciding whether to purchase a quart of milk, individual participation in market interactions nevertheless leads to outcomes that—over time—lead to the mutual benefit of all, even to those not directly involved in the exchange component of given market trade. This was the point made when Adam Smith conducted his inquiry into what leads to the growing wealth of nations. Though it is no one person's job to make sure that societal wealth and opportunities evolve, improve, and grow over time, market systems accomplish it anyway. And in the view of Smith and his successors, this great feat of the enrichment of humanity can hardly be thought unethical—though individuals may nevertheless be tempted by and succumb to occasional fits of pure selfishness. Moreover, in Smith's view, indeed it is individuals' own self-interest that leads them to behave in ways that are for the betterment of others, inasmuch as they value the esteem of others in their reference groups. So self-interest can reinforce rightful actions, letting individuals measure up in their own eyes as well as in the eyes of others.

Yet critics of markets and market systems accuse markets themselves of rewarding only selfish behaviors. In this brutish view, the most selfish person gets farthest ahead, at the expense of others. And according to this story, a sort of market Darwinism happens wherein those who quickly appreciate that the system rewards the selfish and opportunistic will adapt, behave still more selfishly, and eventually dominate the others as the natural selection process unfolds. This is also why some charge that the study of economics leads to more selfishness: Better understandings and appreciations of markets systems—so the argument goes—lead to more selfish thoughts and actions.

Even in the face of these doubts about markets and the science of their study—economics—most economists are hopeful that markets enrich the lives and work of everyone, including governments, private citizens, nongovernmental organizations, places of worship, and private organizations of all kinds. Indeed, the most rapid path out of poverty and early death is one that passes through a system of law that treats each human being as an equal and one that leads to a fully flourishing system of markets.

To stay on task, this chapter is organized in the following manner. The next section summarizes linkages between economics and ethics prior to Adam Smith, a period influenced by ancient philosophers such as Aristotle, as well as Scholastics trained in the tradition of St. Thomas Aquinas.

Next, the chapter turns to the modern era in economics, using the writing of Adam Smith as the threshold. Building on the tradition of Aristotle and the Scholastics, Smith explicitly linked the interactions of markets to the ethical motivations of human beings, making the case that morals and markets need each other for the good of all members of society.

Following a careful accounting of this period, which persists into the present day, the chapter summarizes critiques of modern economic thinking where ethics is concerned.

Critics of modern economic thinking, on ethical grounds, come from both inside and outside the profession. Outsiders are often theologians and moral philosophers who attempt to knock down an unfair characterization of modern economics, misunderstanding what economics says (and does not say) about human motives and not firmly grasping Smith's position on self-interest. Further, the theologians often claim the moral high ground, inasmuch as they have been to seminary while most economists have not.

Finally, because one of the accusations leveled at modern economics is that studying it leads to more self-interested behavior on the part of its students, this chapter examines this charge. There is limited empirical evidence on this question, though, and the findings are mixed.

Early Economists and Ethicists

Since the very beginning, economic thinking has been closely linked to ethical thinking. This linkage derives from the intellectual backgrounds and interests of the first economists. Beginning with early philosophers such as Aristotle, the first economic thinkers were also moral philosophers. Centuries later, Scholastics—educated in the tradition of Thomas Aquinas—brought their expertise as moral theologians to the choices people face and the decisions they eventually make. Throughout most of this rich, historical tradition—entwining morals and market considerations—economic decision making and behavior simply were not thought to be in conflict with ethical conduct. On the contrary, for both Aristotle and the Scholastics, human actions and choices within markets make living a good life possible.

Plato and Aristotle

Little regarding economics and ethics exists prior to Plato (ca. 427 B.C.E.–327 B.C.E.). In his defining and best-known work, *The Republic,* Plato outlines both his understanding of economics as well as his personal insights into the ethical limitations of trade. *The Republic* analyzes both political and economic life, and in it, Plato outlines his views of economy. According to Robert Ekelund and Robert Hébert (1990), though, Plato stopped short of developing any sort of economic theory of exchange; he was more concerned with the resulting distribution of wealth, rather than any specific theory behind trading goods or services. In Plato's view, trading was likely to be a zero-sum game, rather than a means through which the mutual benefit of all might result.

Because Plato saw all profit-seeking activities as potentially corrosive to society, Plato championed a significant role for the state as a regulator and administrator in chief. The state would need to intervene in order to maintain civility, as well as to oversee the resulting distribution.

Though Aristotle was foremost among Plato's students, Aristotle's conception of humanity and its place in the world differed considerably from that of his teacher. For Aristotle, humanity's highest aspiration is to live a good life: a life that is moral and one that thus requires the exercise of virtue.

In his writings, Aristotle outlines a collection of social sciences that he calls *practical sciences,* ones that lead to living a good life. Included among Aristotle's practical sciences are both ethics and economics.

Ricardo Crespo (2008) provides a particularly clear linking of economics, *oikonomike,* and ethics in Aristotle's writings. Where economics is concerned, it may simply be thought of as the study of the ways in which individuals use the things around them in their pursuit of a good life. Inasmuch as individuals take actions in pursuit of a good life, there can be nothing necessarily immoral about such behaviors. In fact, one might regard each action taken in pursuit of a good life as a moral action, inasmuch as pursuing the good life is indeed moral.

To not oversimplify, it is worth considering Crespo's (2006) earlier essay, in which he spells out four different possible meanings for *oikonomike* as used by Aristotle. According to Crespo, *the economic* is actually an analogical term, meaning that it has multiple interpretations, though one of the meanings is central and forms a core around which other related meanings for the same term may be identified. Crespo sees the central meaning of the economic as the human actions taken with the eventual goal of a leading a virtuous—that is, so-called good—life.

Surrounding this central definition of *oikonomike* as human action lie three other orbital definitions, according to Crespo. First, the economic can refer to one's capacity, ability, or talent for the pursuit of good things. Second, the economic can also refer to the habits individuals develop in their pursuit of virtue. That is, through their repeated practice of individual moral actions, each develops a discipline to practice virtue. And third, the economic may also be the practical science of economics itself: the study of human actions in the pursuit of good lives.

As a consequence, then, Aristotle envisioned a much smaller role for the state: one that is limited in scope, predictable, and reliable in relation to the choices made by individuals. A heavy-handed state, such as that suggested by Plato, would steal from each individual the freedom and opportunity to exercise wise judgment in the pursuit of lives that are good. Thus, Aristotle championed private property among all classes of humanity, operating within a market-based economy in which each individual engages in trades that prove beneficial to both parties in a voluntary exchange. In this way, society will become more efficient in its use of resources, enjoy peace and civility, and develop good moral habits.

This is not to say that Aristotle favored no government at all. On the contrary, civil institutions potentially could play two very important roles. First, institutional arrangements could reassure citizens that they were truly equal under the law, regardless of class. An important role of the state, then, is to establish the rights to private property, as well as to ensure that all property transfers are exclusively voluntary. In this way, society's economic habits are free to emerge, and one will thus be able to study the economic as a practical social science. Second, a predictable and reliable institutional arrangement enhances efficiency. One need only consider any of the modern nations governed by ruthless and arbitrary dictatorial regimes to appreciate that economies do not grow and flourish when the people do not have reasonable assurances about what really belongs to them. Working hard to create even a little wealth might be a terrible bet if the ruling class can take whatever it likes from the rest.

When one puts together Aristotle's thinking on economics and ethics, it is easy to conclude that Aristotle's vision for economic life is one in which actors have sufficient freedom to make their own moral decisions in hopes of living virtue-filled lives. Freedom itself gives each individual constant opportunities to choose well and to develop well-formed habits of doing so.

The Scholastics and Natural Law

Europe during the Middle Ages bore a much stronger resemblance to the Platonic view of a hierarchical order and state than to the world Aristotle envisioned in which all were equal under the law and the primary role of the state was to establish and maintain the rights to private property. Indeed, Ekelund and Hébert (1990) describe the period as one in which most people belonged to (a) the peasant class, (b) the military, or (c) the clergy. Because it was the clerics who spent time in solitude and contemplation, thinking deep thoughts about the moral order of things, it was these clergy—working throughout a period from roughly 1200 to 1600—who advanced Aristotle's thought linking ethics to economics. As men of faith who were also well-educated men of letters, the Scholastics quite naturally brought their theological and moral thinking to all parts of life.

Ekelund and Hébert (1990) identify five clerics who exemplify the Scholastic tradition that linked Aristotle's economic and ethical thinking to moral thinking in Catholic Europe: Albertus Magnus (ca. 1206–1280), Thomas Aquinas (ca. 1225–1274), Henry of Friemar (ca. 1245–1340), Jean Buridan (ca. 1295–1358), and Gerald Odonis (ca. 1290–1349). Llewellyn Rockwell (1995) extends this list to include late Scholastics from the School of Salamanca. In sixteenth-century Spain, the University of Salamanca served as the center of Scholastic thought. Key economic thinkers from the School of Salamanca include Francisco de Vitoria (1485–1546), Martin de Azpilcueta Navarrus (1493–1586), Diego de Covarrubias y Leiva (1512–1577), and Luis de Molina (1535–1601).

Playing a key role in the linkage of the thinking of the Scholastics to Aristotle is a concept known as *natural law.* Though Aristotle is sometimes viewed as the father of natural law, it is not a term he explicitly used himself.

Nevertheless, it is clear that his thinking informed the concept of natural law for the Stoics and later the Scholastics.

The natural law tradition holds that there are certain moral rules or obligations, established in the fundamental nature of things, that apply to all individuals at all times and in all places. These universal truths govern all men and women and cannot be usurped by the laws of humankind. They are inviolable and establish the basic ground rules with which human beings are to conduct themselves in their dealings with each other. In this tradition, all men and women are equal under the natural law. One could think of natural law as an undeniable, unavoidable force like gravity: Regardless of wealth or lineage, if one jumps from a tall building, one is just as likely as anyone else to get seriously injured.

To further illustrate the notion of natural law, it is helpful to refer to the famous second sentence of the Declaration of Independence of the United States. Its authors were surely writing in the natural law tradition when they wrote, "We hold these truths to be self-evident, that all men are created equal, that they are endowed by their Creator with certain unalienable Rights, that among these are Life, Liberty and the pursuit of Happiness." For the framers of the Declaration, it required no argument that "all men are created equal" or that each individual is born with some fundamental human rights that cannot be sold or taken away. These claims were thought to be entirely obvious to all: They were "self-evident."

Natural law ideas are clearly present in the writing of Aristotle, though not explicitly stated. Instead, Aristotle contrasts particular laws that might be written by humankind with common laws that have bearing everywhere. And certainly the equality of humans and their right to private property in the pursuit of a moral life may be viewed as part of the common—rather than particular—law.

Because the Scholastics served as the moral umpires for the church during the period, their main interest in economics derived largely from its potential to distribute justice. That is, the Scholastics were more interested in the potential for justice following from economic actions than they were in any specific details about exchange mechanisms. So they employed their reason in the search for universal, transcendent ideas that govern everyone. And certainly economic laws govern individuals' interactions with each other and also apply equally to all people in all places. So the Scholastics' study of economics was driven by their desire to discern universal truths—natural law—that give insight into the nature of the universe in which individuals live and interact. Of course, although Aristotle did not ascribe the origin of natural law to a higher being, it was easy and obvious for the Scholastics to read Aristotle and see God as the ultimate source of the natural law under which everyone lives, and economic forces as part of God's natural law. So the Scholastics studied economics in order to better understand God's created order.

Given that the Scholastics followed in the natural law tradition begun by Aristotle, they also viewed all humans as equal, both in the sight of God and in the sight of each other. And viewing economic forces as ones that are blind to the specific plight of a given person, the Scholastics followed Aristotle's lead and viewed economic decisions and actions as opportunities to act morally. Thus, like Aristotle, the Scholastics viewed the proper role of civic institutions as a limited one designed to defend, predictably and reliably, the fundamental rights of all.

Rockwell (1995) gives a few specific examples of the economic thought of the late Scholastics, illustrating how the work of the School of Salamanca clearly follows from Aristotle and also anticipates well the modern study of economics that begins with Adam Smith. Each is especially intriguing in light of modern antipathy from theologians toward economics and economists, which is discussed later in the chapter.

According to Rockwell (1995), Luis de Molina was among the first of the Scholastics in the Jesuit order to think very carefully about theoretical topics in economics. In his defense of private property, he simply pointed to the commandment that says, "Thou shalt not steal." But Molina went farther and began to explore modern economic arguments for private property, including what is now called the *tragedy of the commons:* that when everyone owns a resource, then no one has the correct incentive to care for it. Good stewardship of a resource comes only when the steward is also the owner; only then are incentives correctly aligned. Molina also saw government—the king—as capable of great moral sin against the good of the people when government's powers are either broad or arbitrarily applied.

Covarrubias took private property ownership to the extreme, making the case that the owner of a piece of land is the only person who has the moral right to decide what to do with its fruits. In fact, Covarrubias claimed that government could not intervene even if a landowner were growing some kind of medicine but refused to sell. If the landowner were forcibly made to do something against his or her will with property he or she rightly owned, even if it might be beneficial to others, such an action would constitute violation of the natural law.

Orthodox Views of Ethical Behavior Within Markets

Adam Smith, *Wealth of Nations,* and *Theory of Moral Sentiments*

Modern thought on ethics and economics begins with the work of Scottish professor Adam Smith (1723–1790). All students of economics should spend at least some time reading Smith in order to see for themselves what Smith says—and what he does not say—regarding self-interest,

selfishness, and the market. In particular, students should be sure to look closely at Smith's best-known work, *An Inquiry Into the Nature and Causes of the Wealth of Nations* (1776/1981), as well as his earlier *Theory of Moral Sentiments* (1759/1982). As this chapter shows, Smith did not view morals and markets as conflicting forces. On the contrary, Smith viewed market behavior and moral behavior as cooperative activities, following from similar views regarding what motivates each individual to action or inaction. Although many practicing modern mainstream economists have forgotten much of Smith's thinking on ethical behavior, remembering instead only his treatment of self-interest in *The Wealth of Nations,* modern economics nevertheless gets exactly right the Smithian conclusion regarding markets and their tremendous potential for improving the good of all.

Smith represented the synthesis of the natural law tradition begun by Aristotle, then articulated by the Stoics, the Scholastics, and later the French Physiocrats, following the tradition of their countryman and forebear Pierre le Pesant de Boisguilbert. The Physiocrats, led by François Quesnay, had believed that the natural law served as a reflection of the creator. In their view, then, natural law needed to take precedence over laws created by humankind. Further still, the laws of humans were certainly not as good as the natural laws of the creator. After all, the creator is the Supreme Being. In this light, the Physiocrats thought that the laws enacted by humans (called *positive law*)—flawed as they are—should be kept to a minimum. Society would be much healthier and in greater harmony with the mind of the creator if it learned to lean on natural law more and on positive law less.

In this light, the stage had been set for the laissez-faire (natural liberty) views articulated by Smith in his writings. And to grasp clearly how Smith integrated ethics, economics, and natural law to form a seamless natural theology—which owes much indeed to the natural law tradition—one must consider together *The Wealth of Nations* and *The Theory of Moral Sentiments.* To focus on only *The Wealth of Nations,* which is certainly what most economists do (if they read it at all), is to miss the primary articulation of Smith's natural theology. Indeed, *The Theory of Moral Sentiments* is a theory of how and why individuals each act in a largely moral way in their affairs. *The Wealth of Nations* is merely an extension of Smith's theory to individuals' interactions in markets and the power of each of those actions to have a cumulatively beneficial impact on society as a whole. Or to state it another way, *The Theory of Moral Sentiments* is Smith's statement of his ethics; *The Wealth of Nations* is the application of Smith's ethics to economics.

But this discussion begins the way most students of economics begin: first with *The Wealth of Nations* (henceforth *WN*), then working back to Smith's earlier *Theory of Moral Sentiments* (henceforth *TMS*). In looking at *WN,* the main goal is to grasp accurately what Smith said—and did not say—about the role of self-interest (or self-love) in *WN* and whether it is indeed ethical to afford a role to self-interest in people's economic dealings with each other. Then, in looking at *TMS,* this chapter attempts to work out what has been referred to as the *Adam Smith problem:* that the same fellow who articulated the role of self-interest in economic dealings had put forward an entire theory of our moral feelings and actions just 17 years earlier.

Although much of *WN* is widely known (e.g., the pin factory as an illustration of the production efficiency gains possible from specialization of tasks and the division of labor), the concern here is with only the passages relevant to the relationship between ethics and economics. The most famous idea relevant to the present purpose is the role that self-interest plays in market dealings. And unfortunately, the most common telling of the story of self-interest misses much of Smith's point. To clarify, this chapter first reviews this common telling that mischaracterizes Smith's articulation of the role of self-interest in markets.

The common story proceeds like this. Economic agents—people and firms—are self-interested; they like to be happier (or wealthier or both). Seeking greater happiness, they pursue opportunities that leave them happier than they currently are. And in a decentralized market system with no central planner, potential trading partners will discover each other and execute trades that leave them both better off. These mutually beneficial exchanges improve the lot of both traders; if this were not the case, they would not trade, because trade is voluntary. Also, no one—neither the traders nor any bystander—is harmed as a result (in most circumstances). Much as in Aristotle's view, each person is at liberty to pursue a personal course of action leading to a good life as he or she sees it, and mutually beneficial trades are small steps making the good life possible. Even greater still, when many such actions are repeatedly taken over time, across an entire society, the end result is a better life for all. Indeed, markets and their workings help build the wealth of nations, even though no central planner or planning committee is in charge.

What this story leaves out is what Smith actually wrote in *WN.* True, Smith did make the final point in the preceding paragraph: Decentralized, mutually beneficial exchange ultimately grows the wealth of nations. But a common misunderstanding (or misrepresentation) of Smith is the role that self-interest plays in a market transaction. To consider this more carefully, look at the key passage in *WN,* found in Chapter 2 of Book 1. Smith writes,

> In civilized society [man] stands at all times in need of the co-operation and assistance of great multitudes, while his whole life is scarce sufficient to gain the friendship of a few persons. In almost every other race of animals each individual, when it is grown up to maturity, is intirely independent, and in its natural state has occasion for the assistance of no other living creature. But man has almost constant occasion for the help of his brethren, and it is in vain for him to expect it from their benevolence only. He will be more likely to prevail if he can

> interest their self-love in his favour, and shew them that it is for their own advantage to do for him what he requires of them. . . . It is not from the benevolence of the butcher, the brewer, or the baker, that we expect our dinner, but from their regard to their own interest. We address ourselves, not to their humanity but to their self-love, and never talk to them of our own necessities but of their advantages. (Smith, 1776/1981, pp. 26–27)

Reading this passage makes clear what many—including many economists—misunderstand about Smith's view of the role of self-interest. Suppose, for example, that one feels a strong need to acquire some pencils in the progress toward a good life. Without market exchange, how could one get them? Well, one could try to make some pencils, but as Leonard Read (1958/1999) makes thoroughly clear, one person working alone might not be able to complete even one pencil in a lifetime, if one must rely on no one but oneself for every single input and production step required.

Assuming one needs pencils relatively soon, or at least before death so that they can be of some help in a good life, what other possibilities are there? A second avenue might be to become great friends with someone who currently possesses some pencils and hope that the friend's affection is so great that he or she will simply give away some pencils. But again, working at sufficiently ingratiating oneself with another person so that he or she will give one gifts requires time, effort, and energy. Moreover, attempting to acquire all of the goods and services one needs throughout one's life in this way—appealing to the good nature of others in the hope of receiving gifts—is a dubious undertaking indeed.

A third possible strategy for obtaining pencils would be simply to beg for them—and to beg for everything else one needs for a good life. One could go around town on bended knee, with a tin cup in hand, and beg, attempting to convince anyone one meets that one's need for pencils is more pressing or more important than the pencil owner's needs are. But as Robert Black (2006) points out, begging for what one needs would clearly violate the idea of natural law. Begging is dehumanizing and reduces the value and sense of self-worth of the beggar. One who has even a single experience of begging in one's life probably remembers how miserable it felt to be forced by life's circumstances into that situation. In the natural law tradition, all human beings are of equal value, regardless of class, and are entitled to maintain their dignity as human beings.

A fourth option is force. One could simply steal pencils. But that option falls short because it involves taking another person's property, which is clearly at odds with the natural law tradition.

Having exhausted (a) making pencils, (b) ingratiating one's self with others who have pencils, (c) begging for pencils, and (d) stealing pencils, what remains? For Smith, only one possibility remained that maintained the dignity of all, and it also smoothly and quickly moved goods and services from less- to more-valued uses. If a person wants pencils, it might be simplest for him or her to appeal to the self-interest (self-love) of those who have pencils or make pencils and convince them how much better off they would be if they traded away some of their pencils. That is, a highly efficient way to get others to do things one wants, which also lets everyone keep their dignity, is to appeal to others' self-interest. If individuals do this well, then others will happily trade with them, thereby making the individuals' lives happier and easier also.

Simply put, it is not mere selfishness that makes one better off in Smith's view; it is one's appeal to the self-interest of others. In fact, everyone's lives depend on it.

Having clarified what Smith said and did not say in *WN* regarding self-interest, this chapter turns to the reconciliation of *WN* with Smith's earlier *TMS*. As discussed previously, scholars have struggled for many years with the Adam Smith problem: reconciling Smith's moral theory in *TMS* with the role of self-interest in *WN*.

James Otteson (2002) provides one of the clearest answers to the Smith problem. For Otteson, both *TMS* and *WN* share a common theme: Natural law and self-love work together as a powerful force to explain and predict human behaviors and interactions, whether those interactions are in the marketplace or in social settings. Either way, even with no one person in charge of either markets or morality, there is a natural ordering that results when men and women everywhere have the freedom to live a good life. In markets, people engage in trades that prove mutually beneficial to both parties. And in relationships with each other, people learn to act in ways that are humane and that preserve the dignity of everyone.

By what mechanism does one discover what is appropriate in social contexts? Smith argues in *TMS* that everyone craves sympathy of feeling from others. People want others to share in their joys, sorrows, pleasures, and pain. People want to be viewed with dignity at all times and to be taken seriously as fellow human beings. So Smith makes the case that just as individuals and firms can learn through market interactions which goods and services are valuable in the marketplace, individuals also learn, through social interactions, which behaviors will be rewarded with sympathy of feeling in the social realm.

Consider two specific examples from *TMS,* in which someone might misunderstand how to express appropriately his or her feelings to others in a social setting: someone who wails over some small hurt and another who laughs inappropriately long at a joke. In both cases, Smith (1759/1982) suggests that others will like the person less because the behaviors are out of proportion to the circumstance:

> If we hear a person loudly lamenting his misfortunes, which, however, upon bringing the case home to ourselves, we feel, can produce no such violent effect upon us, we are shocked at his grief; and, because we cannot enter into it, call it pusillanimity and weakness. It gives us the spleen, on the other hand, to see another too happy or too much elevated. . . . We are

> even put out of humour if our companion laughs louder or longer at a joke than we think it deserves; that is, than we feel that we ourselves could laugh at it. (p. 16)

What hope is there, then, for each of us—even social clods—to learn how to behave appropriately in society? How can one learn to behave in ways that others will find appropriate yet remain true to one's own inalienable rights? Smith's answer is that throughout people's entire lives, even when they are young, they all are students at the school of self-command. And people are in class at the school of self-command anytime they find themselves interacting with other human beings. So for example, if people are in the bad habit of laughing too long at a joke, presumably they will catch on from the feedback they receive (eye rolling, fewer social invitations, gentle admonitions from friends) about their inappropriate behaviors and modify them, throughout their lives, accordingly.

> A very young child has no self-command; but . . . [w]hen it is old enough to go to school, or to mix with its equals, it . . . naturally wishes to gain their favour, and to avoid their hatred or contempt. Regard even to its own safety teaches it to do so; and it soon finds that it can do so in no other way than by moderating, not only its anger, but all its other passions, to the degree which its play-fellows and companions are likely to be pleased with. It thus enters into the great school of self-command, it studies to be more and more master of itself, and begins to exercise over its own feelings a discipline which the practice of the longest life is very seldom sufficient to bring to complete perfection. (Smith, 1759/1982, p. 145)

And who is to help give instruction and guidance to each individual? Smith (1759/1982) envisioned that each person has a conscience, an "impartial spectator" who recalls all of the lessons one has learned during study at the school of self-command and holds one accountable for all of those lessons:

> The man of real constancy and firmness . . . has never dared to forget for one moment the judgment which the impartial spectator would pass upon his sentiments and conduct. He has never dared to suffer the man within the breast to be absent one moment from his attention. With the eyes of this great inmate he has always been accustomed to regard whatever relates to himself. This habit has become perfectly familiar to him. He has been in the constant practice, and, indeed, under the constant necessity, of modelling, or of endeavouring to model, not only his outward conduct and behaviour, but, as much as he can, even his inward sentiments and feelings, according to those of this awful and respectable judge. He does not merely affect the sentiments of the impartial spectator. He really adopts them. He almost identifies himself with, he almost becomes himself that impartial spectator, and scarce even feels but as that great arbiter of his conduct directs him to feel. (pp. 146–147)

Thus, just as market order is spontaneously driven by people's appeals to others' self-love, a mutually beneficial social system can result spontaneously as long as individuals crave sympathy of feeling with others and desire to hold personal views that are in accord with those of others. Barring the occasional clod or sociopath who simply cannot learn from the school of self-command, humans learn from each other how to behave appropriately and, more to the point, they learn how to behave morally in regard to others, while nevertheless doing so out of their own self-love: their desire to be liked and esteemed by others. Further, their personal impartial spectator is ever present, reminding them of all of the lessons they have studied over the years at the school of self-command and exhorting them to choose rightly in all things.

Putting *WN* together with *TMS* leads to a fascinating solution to the Adam Smith problem: Smith's overarching view is that human interactions, though motivated by self-love, can nevertheless lead to thoroughly pleasing outcomes, whether the outcomes are economic or social. As long as the dignity of humankind is preserved in the freedom to make choices, individuals will all ultimately be motivated to actions that not only benefit themselves but also benefit the other individuals they know and encounter; with time, society's overall economic wealth will grow, as will its capacity for great moral good.

Ethics and Economics Since Adam Smith

Even though economics has deepened in terms of economic understanding and broadened in terms of the range of topics it explores, economics has never tossed out Smith's famous invisible hand: By constantly directing resources from less- to more-valuable uses, market forces lead to the eventual betterment of all, even though all individuals are primarily focused on living good lives for themselves, their families, and their friends.

If there is tension in modern economics along ethical lines, it comes mainly from the distinction between efficiency and fairness in the allocation of resources. Efficiency in the allocation of resources refers to *Pareto efficiency,* named for Italian economist and sociologist Vilfredo Pareto (1848–1923). According to the Paretian standard of efficiency, economists describe an allocation of resources as efficient when it is impossible to make one person better-off without harming someone else in the process. Economists are always on the lookout for Pareto-improving possibilities: situations in which one or more persons may be made better-off (in whatever sense that means to them) at no expense to others.

The Paretian standard of efficiency is not in conflict with the market system described by Smith, because an obvious way to make two people better-off without harming others is to let the two people execute any voluntary trades they like. Once all possible potentially Pareto-improving trades in a society have been exhausted, then there will be no way to improve the lot of one without causing another to surrender something involuntarily. Because the Paretian standard is difficult to argue against on moral grounds and because it is consonant with Smith's self-love and natural law ideas, Pareto efficiency is the primary way in which allocations of resources are assessed in welfare economics.

Yet some argue that in its simplicity, Pareto efficiency leaves something out: fairness. That is, they contend that market outcomes, even if Pareto efficient, may not be fair if the outcomes are too unequal. So economists working in welfare economics consider alternative measures of societal welfare besides the Paretian standard. The two most common are utilitarianism (following the work of Jeremy Bentham and other utilitarian thinkers) and Rawlsianism (named for Harvard philosophy professor John Rawls). Because these two alternative measures of society's well-being lie beyond the scope of this chapter, they are not discussed in detail here. Nevertheless, it is important to note that though drawn from different ideological starting points, both utilitarianism and Rawlsianism yield the same clear policy recommendation: Regardless of the unfettered market outcome, all resources need to be redistributed until each member of society is equally well-off. To do otherwise would not be fair. Of course, because such redistributions (a) reduce incentives for high-income earners to create more jobs that lead to greater societal wealth (i.e., a slower growing pie), (b) may prove very costly to administer and control, and (c) encroach on the rights of individuals to maintain private property and surrender it voluntarily, most economists prefer efficiency to fairness as an assessment tool. If nothing else, the Paretian standard is clearly defined. In contrast, fairness is always murky; what appears fair to one usually depends on where one happens to be sitting.

Modern Suspicions and Critiques of Ethical Views in Economics

Owing largely to the shifting focus from Smith's companion views of morals and markets to one centered on mere human self-interest—frequently misinterpreted as selfishness—modern critiques of economics have come from both within the profession and without. Most critics who are economists try to gently point out that the profession needs to expand its focus to remember what Smith really said. They care deeply and passionately about the great issues of our day, especially global poverty, the environment, and basic human rights. Amartya Sen and William Easterly represent the very best of this movement in modern economics.

But the harshest attacks on economics come from outside the profession. These attacks are mounted on ethical grounds, charging that the models, theories, and policy prescriptions of the social science are driven by a view that selfish, greedy behavior is both perfectly acceptable and to be expected. Stated another way, these critics are somewhat guilty of setting up a straw-man argument: critiquing a caricature of modern economics, rather than economics as economists actually think about it and talk about it among themselves. And these critics attempt to position themselves as coming from morally high ground—perhaps from out of theology or from the environmental movement.

The remainder of this section considers briefly the interactions of theologians with economics since Smith. And as this section shows, the antipathy of theologians toward economics and economists is a relatively recent phenomenon. Until at least the mid-nineteenth century, clergymen—at least in the United States—embraced economics and its study as a powerful tool to uplift humanity. The late Paul Heyne (2008) gives an excellent overview of this period in Part 4 of *Are Economists Basically Immoral?*, a posthumously published volume of his works.

According to Heyne (2008), in the years before 1800, Christian thinkers had not fully integrated economics and their faith. True, Smith had followed in the natural law tradition of the Christian Scholastics in his thinking on economics and the moral order. Yet Smith was hardly more than a deist: someone who believes that a supreme being created the universe and its natural laws, set the universe in its course, yet left humankind to do what it will.

But the publication of the Reverend Francis Wayland's (1837) *Elements of Political Economy* united the laissez-faire economics of Smith with a distinctly Christian articulation of the natural-law tradition. Wayland's book, which became the most widely used economics textbook in the United States on its publication, echoed *WN*. Wayland claims that the rules for wealth accumulation were part of God's providence (a gift) and that individuals who honestly worked toward improving their own lots would thereby promote the welfare of humanity. Heyne (2008) argues that Wayland and other Christian thinkers were inclined to link the optimism of Smith to their own faith inasmuch as markets gave great promise for dramatic improvement of the human condition. And Heyne considers the Reverend Arthur Latham Perry, professor of history and political economy at Williams College, as the clergy's foremost defender of laissez-faire economics during the period. Indeed, when the American Economic Association was founded in 1885, several Protestant clergy were among its charter members.

Yet as the century drew to a close—and as the association quickly shook off its Christian roots—the clergy quickly grew critical of the promise of markets to do much of the heavy lifting in the transformation of society. Such a quick reversal, from an embrace of economic thinking by the clergy to full-throated criticism of it, is indeed puzzling. By way of explanation, Heyne (2008) posits that it is no coincidence that academic clergy began to grow tired of Smithian economics at the same time that the surrounding academic culture began to grow critical as well. For Heyne, prevailing political and academic cultural winds, far more than any deeply informed change of course, were the main reason that academic clergy moved from fans to foes of the promise of markets.

Lamentably, this division between economics and theologians persists into the present day, and finding theologians who are critical of modern economics is not a difficult task. And more often than not, their criticisms are likely to be founded on a caricature of economics, rather than a richer depiction of it. For example, William Cavanaugh (2008) writes this regarding scarcity:

> The standard assumption of economists that we live in a world of scarce resources is not based simply on an empirical observation of the state of the world, but is based on the assumption that human desire is limitless. In a consumer culture we are conditioned to believe that human desires have no end and are therefore endless. The result is a tragic view of the world, a view in which there is simply never enough to go around, which in turn produces a kind of resignation to the plight of the world's hungry people. (p. xii)

Similarly, Christine Hinze (2004) states, "When they reduce the meaning and purpose of 'economy' to market exchange, or human agents to self-interest-maximizing Homo economicus, mainstream economists fall prey to a category mistake bound to distort both analysis and policy recommendations" (p. 172).

And D. Stephen Long (2000) claims, "As a discipline, economics has increasingly developed an anti-humanistic mode. . . . [E]conomics has become an increasingly abstract—mathematical—science" (p. 9). For two spirited book-length debates between market advocates and market critics, see Doug Bandow and David Schindler (2003) and Donald Hay and Alan Kreider (2001).

Yet many of today's thinking clergy continue to have tremendous faith in markets both as mechanisms that can transform the lives of the global poor living in material poverty and mechanisms that afford individuals a wealth of occasions in which to choose to act morally. Particularly notable is the work of Father Robert Sirico, president of the Acton Institute in Grand Rapids, Michigan, as well as that of Michael Novak (1982), author of *The Spirit of Democratic Capitalism*. Though not theologians, Victor Claar and Robin Klay (2007) defend—from a faith perspective—the power of markets to effect tremendous good.

Does Studying Economics Change One's Ethics?

A final intersection of ethics and economics concerns whether instruction in economics leads students and eventual economists to think or act in more self-interested ways, as some of the profession's critics might assume. First, there does seem to be some evidence, including a study by Robert Whaples (1995), that taking even an introductory economics course influences students to view market outcomes as more fair. Whaples finds the strongest change in attitudes among women.

Second, empirical evidence concerning whether studying economics leads to changes in one's behavior is mixed. For example, using laboratory-based experiments, John Carter and Michael Irons (1991) find little actual change in behavior between freshman and senior economics students, suggesting that studying economics did not change them. If so, perhaps students who gravitate to the study of economics are already different from other students when they arrive. This finding has been reinforced more recently by Bruno Frey and Stephan Meier (2005) and by Meier and Frey (2004). This more recent work calls into question the earlier finding of Robert Frank, Thomas Gilovich, and Dennis Regan (1993) that economics majors were less likely to cooperate in prisoners' dilemma games than students in other majors. Further, Harvey James and Jeffrey Cohen (2004) find that including an ethics component in an economics program can reduce the tendency to not cooperate in laboratory games.

Nevertheless, there is considerable hope that students and practitioners of economics may perform at least as nobly as others in settings that are not known to be experimental. For example, one of the findings of Carter and Irons (1991) is that economics students stated they would be more likely to keep money that had been lost. Yet in a follow-up experiment using actual money, Anthony Yezer, Robert Goldfarb, and Paul Poppen (1996) discover that students of economics were significantly more likely to return money they had found. In the experiment, $10 was put inside stamped, addressed envelopes, and then the envelopes were dropped into economics classrooms, as well as classes in other disciplines. To return the money, all that was required was to seal an envelope and mail it. Though only 31% of envelopes were returned in business, history, and psychology classes, economics students returned 56% of the envelopes. And David Laband and Richard Beil (1999) find that practicing economists were less likely to cheat on their professional membership dues than professional political scientists and—especially—professional sociologists, suggesting practicing economists behave significantly more ethically than other professional social scientists.

of living for all. And the personal liberty available in a market system gives each individual ongoing opportunities to make wise moral and ethical choices. Moreover, in a market-based economy, the fastest way for individuals to make life better for themselves and their families is to meet the needs of others. Indeed, perhaps even without human feeling for another, each individual will nevertheless act humanely toward another, because the very means by which people enrich their own lives is by enriching the lives of others. And according to Smith, such relationships are borne out in the social realm as well: People behave decently to others in order to earn others' respect and sympathy of feeling in exchange.

Though most modern theologians are critical of economics and economists, instead hoping for the arrival of a more so-called moral allocative system than the one Smith envisioned, their criticism is a relatively recent phenomenon. Even 400 years ago, Scholastics were working out an economic theory, in the belief that economic laws were among the natural laws given by their creator. They studied economic laws in order to better understand and appreciate their world. Only since the close of the eighteenth century have academic clergy grown harshly critical of the wisdom and ethics of market economics and economic science, perhaps owing to the influence of similar suspicions growing contemporaneously in other parts of academe. Yet the work of market-minded modern theologians such as Michael Novak and Father Robert Sirico of the Acton Institute have begun to renew the faith of the clergy in the power of markets to bring dramatic transformation of society, especially where global poverty is concerned.

Students of economics may perhaps be less cooperative than others, but the empirical evidence is mixed. Further, students selecting economics may already be different from others, suggesting that any perceived differences may be attributable to a selection effect, rather than to any specific treatment effect of studying economics. Further, in nonexperimental settings, recent empirical evidence suggests that both students of economics and professional economists behave more ethically than their counterparts from other disciplines.

Conclusion

To this day, Adam Smith's moral theory advanced in *The Theory of Moral Sentiments* and applied to economic interactions in his later *Wealth of Nations* constitutes the foundation and nucleus of all moral and ethical thinking in economics. Barring instances of market failure, market-based exchanges lead to Pareto improvements, because some members of society are made better-off through market exchange, and none are harmed as a result. Further, markets are the most powerful mechanism available for the perpetual redirection of society's resources from less- to more-desired uses, leading to eventual transformation of entire nations as the resulting wealth accumulation leads to a higher standard

References and Further Readings

Bandow, D., & Schindler, D. L. (Eds.). (2003). *Wealth, poverty, and human destiny.* Wilmington, DE: ISI Books.

Black, R. A. (2006). What did Adam Smith say about self-love? *Journal of Markets & Morality, 9,* 7–34.

Broome, J. (1999). *Ethics out of economics.* Cambridge, UK: Cambridge University Press.

Carter, J. R., & Irons, M. D. (1991). Are economists different, and if so, why? *Journal of Economic Perspectives, 5*(2), 171–177.

Cavanaugh, W. T. (2008). *Being consumed: Economics and Christian desire.* Grand Rapids, MI: William B. Eerdmans.

Claar, V. V., & Klay, R. J. (2007). *Economics in Christian perspective: Theory, policy and life choices.* Downers Grove, IL: IVP Academic.

Crespo, R. F. (2006). The ontology of "the economic": An Aristotelian perspective. *Cambridge Journal of Economics, 30,* 767–781.

Crespo, R. F. (2008). Aristotle's science of economics. In I. R. Harper & S. Gregg (Eds.), *Christian theology and market economics* (pp. 13–24). Cheltenham, UK: Edward Elgar.

Ekelund, R. B., & Hébert, R. F. (1990). *A history of economic theory and method* (3rd ed.). New York: McGraw-Hill.

Frank, R. H., Gilovich, T., & Regan, D. T. (1993). Does studying economics inhibit cooperation? *Journal of Economic Perspectives, 7*(2), 159–171.

Frey, B., & Meier, S. (2005). Selfish and indoctrinated economists? *European Journal of Law and Economics, 19,* 165–171.

Graafland, J. J. (2007). *Economics, ethics, and the market: Introduction and applications.* New York: Routledge.

Harper, I. R., & Gregg, S. (Eds.). (2008). *Christian theology and market economics.* Cheltenham, UK: Edward Elgar.

Hay, D. A., & Kreider, A. (Eds.). (2001). *Christianity and the culture of economics.* Cardiff, UK: University of Wales Press.

Heyne, P. (2008). *"Are economists basically immoral?": And other essays on economics, ethics, and religion* (G. Brennan & A. M. C. Waterman, Eds.). Indianapolis, IN: Liberty Fund.

Hinze, C. F. (2004). What is enough? Catholic social thought, consumption, and material sufficiency. In W. Schweiker & C. Mathewes (Eds.), *Having: Property and possession in religious and social life* (pp. 162–188). Grand Rapids, MI: William B. Eerdmans.

James, H. S., Jr., & Cohen, J. (2004). Does ethics training neutralize the incentives of the prisoner's dilemma? Evidence from a classroom experiment. *Journal of Business Ethics, 50,* 53–61.

Journal of Markets & Morality: Scholarship for a humane economy. (n.d.). [Various issues].

Knight, F. H. (1997). *The ethics of competition.* New Brunswick, NJ: Transaction. (Original work published 1935)

Krelle, W. E. (2003). *Economics and ethics 1.* Berlin, Germany: Springer.

Laband, D. N., & Beil, R.O. (1999). Are economists more selfish than other "social" scientists? *Public Choice, 100,* 85–101.

Long, D. S. (2000). *Divine economy: Theology and the market.* London: Routledge.

Meadowcroft, J. (2005). *The ethics of the market.* New York: Palgrave Macmillan.

Meier, S., & Frey, B. (2004). Do business students make good citizens? *International Journal of the Economics of Business, 11,* 141–163.

Novak, M. (1982). *The spirit of democratic capitalism.* New York: Touchstone.

Nozick, R. (1974). *Anarchy, state, and utopia.* New York: Basic Books.

Otteson, J. R. (2002). *Adam Smith's marketplace of life.* Cambridge, UK: Cambridge University Press.

Read, L. E. (1999). I, pencil: My family tree as told to Leonard E. Read. *Library of Economics and Liberty.* Retrieved June 26, 2009, from http://www.econlib.org/library/Essays/rdPncl1.html (Original work published 1958)

Rockwell, L. H. (1995, September). Free market economists: 400 years ago. *Freeman, 45*(9). Retrieved June 5, 2009, from http://www.thefreemanonline.org/featured/free-market-economists-400-years-ago

Roth, T. P. (2002). *The ethics and the economics of minimalist government.* Northampton, MA: Edward Elgar.

Sacks, J. (1999). *Morals and markets.* London: Institute of Economic Affairs.

Sen, A. (1988). *On ethics and economics.* Malden, MA: Blackwell.

Smith, A. (1981). *An inquiry into the nature and causes of the wealth of nations.* Indianapolis, IN: Liberty Fund. (Original work published 1776)

Smith, A. (1982). *The theory of moral sentiments.* Indianapolis, IN: Liberty Fund. (Original work published 1759)

Tamari, M. (1987). *"With all your possessions": Jewish ethics and economic life.* New York: Free Press.

U.S. Catholic Bishops. (1986). *Economic justice for all: Pastoral letter on Catholic social teaching and the U.S. economy.* Retrieved June 5, 2009, from http://www.osjspm.org/economic_justice_for_all.aspx

VanDrunen, D. (2006). *A biblical case for natural law.* Grand Rapids, MI: Acton Institute.

Wayland, F. (1837). *The elements of political economy.* New York: Leavitt, Lord.

Whaples, R. (1995). Changes in attitudes about the fairness of free markets among college economics students. *Journal of Economic Education, 26,* 308–313.

Yeager, L. B. (2001). *Ethics as social science: The moral philosophy of social cooperation.* Cheltenham, UK: Edward Elgar.

Yezer, A. M., Goldfarb, R. S., & Poppen, P. J. (1996). Does studying economics discourage cooperation? Watch what we do, not what we say or how we play. *Journal of Economic Perspectives, 10*(1), 177–186.

88

FEMINIST ECONOMICS

GILLIAN HEWITSON

University of Sydney

During the nineteenth and early twentieth centuries, in Western countries such as the United States and Britain, women's economic situation was largely dictated by the legal framework within which economic activity took place. Some examples include the legal requirement, embedded within the common law of marriage, for wives to provide housework, childrearing, and sexual services to their husbands, in return for at least a minimal subsistence. Husbands were legally entitled to the wage earnings of working wives. Wives were, in effect, legal chattels. Women's labor supply decisions were restricted by "protective legislation" with respect to total hours worked, which hours, and in which occupations. Sex discrimination was legal, and women's wages were determined not by their productivity but by socially accepted norms, such as the widespread belief that women worked for "pin money" rather than for economic necessity, which allowed employers to pay them badly. Indeed, working-class women were frequently unable to support themselves, making marriage an attractive economic proposition. Furthermore, women had limited opportunities, if any, to attend university, and they could not own property in their own names. Despite the restrictions of marriage, then, most women married because their access to economic independence was so limited. Women were assumed to be actual or future wives, and the legal and economic environment ensured that this would be so. Even in the mid-twentieth century, women in certain occupations were terminated if they got married; if a wife had a bank account in her own name, her husband had access to it, and a married woman could not borrow money without her husband's consent.

However, by the 1970s, most, if not all, of the legal restrictions on women's economic activity mentioned above had been eliminated in modern Western countries.

Most countries have ratified the Convention on the Elimination of Discrimination Against Women. And now there are laws in place that make it illegal to discriminate against women in employment, hours, earnings, and lending. Indeed, the first piece of legislation signed by President Obama was the Lily Ledbetter Act, which widens the scope of women's access to the courts upon discovering wage discrimination on the basis of sex. Wives own their own earnings. Women have become prime ministers and presidential candidates, and they have entered the boardrooms of *Fortune* 500 companies. And, in the United States, women make up nearly half the labor force. This environment, in which women appear to have the same ability as men to determine their own economic fates, sometimes makes young people question the relevance of feminist economics in today's world. As this chapter shows, however, the economic system remains a gendered system, and most women's economic outcomes are related to the fact that they are women. This is true both domestically in the United States and in other Western countries, as well as globally.

Feminist economics is the area of research and practice within which the gendered economic system is analyzed.[1] Feminist economists argue that gender is central to understanding the allocation of economic opportunities, rewards, and punishments, and therefore gender is a key determinant of individual economic outcomes. They use a variety of feminist perspectives to understand and change the social and economic institutions and policies that reinforce the economic subordination of women. In common with other schools of heterodox economics, such as ecological economics, (old) institutionalism, and social economics, feminist economics is critical of the discipline's mainstream, also known as neoclassical, orthodox, free-market, or neoliberal economics. Feminist economists, however, make the specific claim that orthodox economics naturalizes women's economic subordination and have also been critical of some other heterodox schools of thought, such as traditional Marxism, for the same reason.

A brief overview of some of the facts of economic inequality is in order.[2] In the United States, in 2007, full-time female workers earned 80 cents for every dollar earned by full-time male workers. In 2007, 12.5% of the U.S. population and 9.8% of all families lived in poverty. Single-parent households are more likely to be poor than two-parent households, and 85% of them are headed by women. Of those, 28.3% live in poverty. Of the 15% of single-parent households headed by males, only 13.6% live in poverty. Gender differentials in the global context are even more significant. Of the 1.3 billion people living in extreme poverty around the world, 70% are women. Globally, the average gender wage gap is 17%, but the range is from 3% to 51%. Two thirds of the world's working hours are performed by women, including the production of half of the world's food supply, but women receive only one tenth of the world's income and own 1% of the world's property.

However, globally and nationally, the differences between women can swamp the differences between men and women. For example, women in Botswana have a life expectancy of 33, but women in Hong Kong can expect to live until 86. When women work for pay in Georgia, they earn only 49 cents for every dollar earned by a Georgian man, while Maltese women earn 97 cents for every dollar earned by a Maltese man. In comparison to the earnings of full-time white male workers in the United States, full-time white female workers earn 79 cents for every dollar, full-time black female workers earn 68 cents, and full-time Hispanic female workers earn just 60 cents. Thus, many feminist economists are as concerned with the differences between women as they are with differences between men and women.

Feminist economists view these facts as problematic and symptomatic of an oppressive economic system that distributes economic rewards on the basis of gender, race, and ethnicity. They argue that mainstream economics plays an important role in the maintenance of this oppressive gender system through its various absences or silences around women and femininity, as well as race, class, and other signifiers of difference. Feminist economic research is both theoretical and empirical, but a piece of work cannot be called feminist economics if it does not support the feminist contentions that women are economically subordinate to men and that this is unacceptable. With this proviso in mind, one may exclude such classic economic tracts as Gary Becker's (1991) *Treatise on the Family,* which shows that, given a particular set of assumptions, it is efficient and hence, from a mainstream economic perspective, desirable for men to specialize in paid work and women in children and unpaid work. This understanding of the family is widespread among orthodox economists. Although there are many disagreements among feminist economists, all agree that Gary Becker's reductionist account of the sexual division of labor should not be included in any definition of feminist economics. Other mainstream economic treatments of women's economic status, even if sympathetic, also attribute most of the problem to women's choices, especially their innate desire to bear and rear children (a desire absent from men), and downplay the role of constraints on women's choices such as gender socialization and sex discrimination.

Given that feminist economists are united in their understanding of the current national and global distribution of economic rewards and punishments as gendered and as problematic, their primary aim is to improve the lives of women. But their research agendas can be very different, depending on the feminist perspective they take and their theoretical or empirical orientation. This plurality of approaches within feminist economics can, for convenience, be aggregated into two broad foci: research that uses gender as a theoretical variable and research that uses gender as an empirical variable. Those using gender as a theoretical variable are interested in the ways in which economic concepts and categories become gendered and in developing new theoretical perspectives on economic processes. Those feminist economists who undertake research in which gender is an empirical variable tend to be more practically minded, being interested in statistical analyses in which gender is a descriptive category and developing new statistical models to generate insights into the economic behavior of men and women.

Gender as Theory and Practice

When a feminist economist uses gender as a theoretical variable or a category of analysis, she or he is taking a critical stance in relation to the power of the discipline to shape the way we see the world. Typically, she or he sees mainstream economics as a discourse, or a set of practices and institutions that do not merely describe or reflect a given reality but rather have an important role in creating and naturalizing the categories through which we interpret the world. Thus, mainstream economics is viewed as deeply implicated in the creation and reproduction of the hierarchies across gender, race, ethnicity, and other classifications of difference that privilege white heterosexual Western men at the expense of others. This kind of research problematizes and reconstructs orthodox and heterodox economic concepts and categories of analysis. It is crucial to the feminist economic project: After all, if feminist economics was an empirical endeavor alone, it would simply consist of economists who work on gender, with no critical feminist insight into the discipline's gendered foundations (see Barker, 2005; Hewitson, 1999).

As well as revealing the ways in which economic theories, frameworks of analysis, concepts, and categories are gendered, feminist economists undertake empirical analyses that measure the real effects of theory, challenge existing empirical analyses justifying women's economic subordination, and offer new ways of examining theoretical issues. In these feminist economic works, gender is necessarily a descriptive rather than a theoretical variable—the aim of the work is to analyze and quantify the economic activities of actual men and women. Consider the following example of the two approaches. In the United States, women undertake most child care. Feminist economists using gender as a descriptive variable are interested in the impact of child care subsidies aimed at giving mothers access to the labor market on the same terms as those workers without child care responsibilities. Empirical analysis can provide estimates of the effects of the subsidy on mothers' labor supply behavior. A feminist economist might also develop an empirical model that includes variables not normally considered, such as state licensing requirements as a measure of quality. Furthermore, empirical feminist economists might advocate alternative ways of providing child care, such as mandated provision by employers (see Bergmann, 2005). In each case, the researcher is examining the economic activity of actual women, making gender an empirical category.

On the other hand, a researcher focusing on gender as a theoretical category might deconstruct the whole framework of analysis by examining the gendered meanings of the concepts of "mother" and "worker." The concept of mother has been historically and culturally constructed as someone who devotes herself to the well-being of her children. The concept of worker has been historically and culturally constructed as someone who devotes himself to a full-time job and a lifelong career, a breadwinner without domestic responsibilities that would reduce his work commitment. That is, mothers are women who care for children and do not work, while workers are male heads of households who undertake market work and not unpaid child care. This is not to say that men do not care for children or that mothers do not work for pay—it is an analysis of the concepts used in a debate about child care subsidies, and it would broaden that debate by questioning the institutions that reinforce the need for the "real worker" to be free of domestic responsibilities and therefore require that parenting be fitted into the workplace, rather than work fitted into parenting (see J. Williams, 2000). Both studies are vital: Empirical work provides essential information for policy decisions and brings theoretical work into the realm of economic practice, and theoretical work points to new ways of thinking about change and to new policies.

The following five sections review the key areas of theoretical and empirical research in feminist economics. Methodological concerns, reviewed in the first section, are crucial, as the methodology of a discipline dictates the authorized ways in which its practitioners go about producing the discipline's accepted knowledge. The second section deals with the rational economic agent, which is the foundational concept of mainstream economics, the concept upon which all its theories rely. Unpaid and paid work, those activities that structure most people's days, weeks, and years, are the subject of the third and fourth sections. In the final section, gender is examined within a global economic context.

Methodology

Methodology refers to the way in which knowledge is generated and justified—the methods used by economists to establish what they know. Orthodox economists typically assert that economics is a science and that economic knowledge is produced using the scientific method. The scientific method refers to the process of statistically testing hypotheses against the facts in ways that can be replicated by any practitioner in the discipline. Knowledge develops when the facts support the hypothesis. Neoclassical economists view facts as independent of the hypotheses: They believe, therefore, that facts, or reality, can be perceived by anyone, whatever their social situation or value system. If this is so, it follows that the knowledge produced using the facts as the arbiter of truth must necessarily be objective. This is the basis of the claim that neoclassical economics is a "positive science" or knowledge from which normative statements or values have been excluded.

Feminist economists have been highly critical of these methodological claims. Along with other heterodox schools of thought, feminist economists reject the idea that neoclassical economics is value free and deny its claims to scientific status. Critics of neoclassical economics argue that it is underpinned by a conservative set of values based on a belief in individualism, the efficiency of free markets, and a merit-based system of economic rewards. This value system is built into the very fiber of the neoclassical paradigm: its methods, categories, and analyses. Feminist economists are unique in focusing on gender: They argue further that the value system underpinning neoclassical economics reflects the needs and preferences of masculinity as they have been constructed within the history of science.

Modern scientific methods emerged during the Enlightenment, when philosophers constructed a series of dualisms in their quest to understand how knowledge is produced. Rene Descartes, for example, with the dictum that "I think, therefore I am," constructed a mind–body split in which the thinker could be conceptually separated from any particular embodiment: This is the "view from nowhere" that defines the objective stance of the scientific inquirer. To see this, consider the meaning of an alternative, such as "I feel, therefore I am"—the thinker in this case is necessarily embodied, and embodiment is necessarily sexually and racially specific, which means that the "view" or perspective of the "feeling thinker" is from somewhere and hence not objective. Francis Bacon wrote about the necessity of conquering and penetrating nature, thereby constructing a subject, the researcher, in opposition to the object of research, and in this can be seen the object–subject, mind–matter, and culture–nature distinctions. These distinctions were also gendered: The detached, objective observer with the "view from nowhere," the penetrator of passive matter, and the producer of scientific knowledge were associated with masculinity. Subjectivity, passivity, nature, the body, emotions, and materiality were associated, on the other hand, with femininity (see Nelson, 1993). These connections persist into the present day—one need only construct a list of contemporary stereotypical masculine and feminine characteristics.

The scientific method reflects a specifically *Western* as well as androcentric perspective. It was the European man, not just any man, who had the capacities of autonomy, independence, and objectivity that were necessary for scientific knowledge production. The scientific approach was becoming dominant over the seventeenth to nineteenth centuries, just when the West (or Europe) was discovering, conquering, and claiming as European territory the lands occupied by dark-skinned native peoples. Like nature, and women, these native peoples existed to be ruled by European men. They and their cultures were seen as passive, exploitable, primitive, and inferior, and science was used to justify their domination. The scientific method was used to establish the superiority of the colonizers and hence the unchallengeable supremacy of their perspective on the world. The power relations established by the use of the scientific method in economics continue to reverberate within economics. For example, in development economics, Western modernization via the extension of market relations is viewed as the solution to the lack of "progress" within the so-called less-developed world (see Olsen, 1994; R. M. Williams, 1993).

The dualisms and their gendered and racial associations created within this history of philosophical thinking define the way in which orthodox economists have understood the discipline's methodology—as scientific or positivist—from the late nineteenth century until today. Developments within the philosophy of science, particularly the rejection of the positivism espoused in every first-year economics textbook, have not undermined this self-perception. Feminist economists have drawn on feminist philosophy of science to argue that mainstream economists constitute a community of practitioners with a jointly held perspective and value system that underpins and structures the processes of knowledge production. Specifically, the perspective and value system is that of the middle-class, Western, white male who has historically dominated the discipline and who has been positioned by the scientific method as the source of unbiased knowledge. This value system is invisible within the mainstream, which is therefore incapable of recognizing its own gender and racial biases, and hence incapable of producing objective, or value-free, knowledge. But these biases powerfully shape, among the myriad of choices that are made by researchers

in any discipline, the identification of research issues, the questions asked, the facts viewed as relevant, the methods deemed appropriate, the choice between taking as given and questioning the various assumptions that necessarily underlie the analysis of a problem, the interpretation of empirical results, and the choice of statistical methods to decide between hypothesis verification or falsification. The methodological argument, then, is not simply that the mainstream is dominated by men but that its method imposes a symbolically masculine perspective of the world on its practitioners, whether they are men or women (see the introduction and reprinted essays in Volume 4 of Barker & Kuiper, 2009; Strassmann & Polanyi, 1995).

For example, mainstream economists explain the gender wage gap as a function of human capital variables. That is, they assume that individuals' wages are the result of utility-maximizing choices with respect to their skills and qualifications. Competition ensures that labor markets equilibrate where the wage is equal to the marginal productivity of labor. Therefore, if women earn lower wages than men, mainstream economists' first response is that women must have lower productivity as the result of their utility-maximizing choices. The unquestioned assumptions underlying this analysis are numerous: that the individual is the appropriate unit of analysis, that productivity is an individual characteristic and not a function of the requirements of the job, that productivity is a choice variable, that preferences and technology are exogenous, that competitive market forces determine wages, that the marginal product of labor is observable independently of wages, that women expect to have and make decisions on the basis of a marginal connection to the labor market, that the problem must be amenable to mathematical modeling and statistical analysis, and so on.

A feminist economic analysis of the gender wage gap rejects the neoclassical view that wage setting is a rational and efficient process undertaken by individuals within competitive markets. Instead of viewing wage setting as an application of the mainstream's timeless and universally applied economic laws, wage setting is situated with a historically and culturally specific analysis where constructions of gender are central to understanding how work and workers are valued. Waged work emerged in the nineteenth century, unions formed, and men fought for a family wage, or a wage sufficient to sustain a family. It was in this era that the low values attributed to the service and caring occupations, within which women were crowded, were established, a function not of some allegedly objective standard like the marginal product of labor but of dominant social views on what women should be doing and how they should be doing it. In fact, men's demands for a family wage spells out these social views: Women should be in the home, economically dependent on a breadwinner. Tracing the impact of this history on contemporary valuations of women's work exposes the mainstream's value system—in ignoring gender constructions, in assuming the primacy of the individual, in confining the analysis to the narrow limits of mathematical modeling, in viewing individuals as prior to society, and in assuming that preferences and technology are not shaped in relation to gender, among others. Mainstream economists can always justify sex wage differences as objectively determined differences in productivity, which are functions of individual preferences, because of what they carve off as irrelevant (see Figart, Mutari, & Power, 2002). An empirical feminist economic analysis challenges the neoclassical explanation within the data itself. The neoclassical story says that women expect to move in and out of the labor market because of their roles in the home and child rearing. It is therefore rational for them to choose to acquire human capital that retains its value during periods of absence from the labor market. It happens that these skills are also low-productivity ones, and hence, women earn less than men. Thus, we should expect to see different rates of depreciation of the education and skills required in male-dominated and female-dominated occupations. In fact, this hypothesis is not supported by the facts, but despite this, it remains a key plank in the neoclassical theory of wage differentials. Thus, the empirical approach, which adopts many of the methodological assumptions made by neoclassical economists, reveals the way in which the perspective of privileged white men shapes research agendas (see Blau, Ferber, & Winkler, 2010).

The mainstream's reliance on individual choices to explain social outcomes, such as the gender wage gap, occupational segregation, and women's poverty, is called methodological individualism. This method dictates that all analyses must be built on a foundation of the isolated individual, homo economicus. If society as a whole is simply the sum of isolated individuals, then the individual preexists that society, joining with other isolated individuals with a universal human nature and a fully formed set of preferences. Society has no role in creating individuals—as gendered and as raced—in this view; rather, society is a reflection of the universal human nature. In the next section, this human nature is discussed.

The Rational Economic Agent

An important focus of feminist economists who use gender as a category of analysis has been the model of the individual at the center of all neoclassical theorizing. Several assumptions construct this model. The economic agent is assumed to embody a timeless human nature consisting of a number of critical characteristics: Individuals maximize their utility; they are instrumentally rational, always choosing the least-cost means to meet their objectives; they are self-interested and uninterested in the well-being of others; and they are independent or entirely separate from others. Socially significant categories such as race or ethnicity, class, gender, nationality, or sexuality are irrelevant to this definition of the economic agent. The characteristics attributed to the economic agent are critical because, without them, the neoclassical edifice of the modeling of individual choices within a constrained environment becomes hopelessly entangled. For example, in neoclassical consumer theory, rational, self-interested, and independent consumers maximize their individual well-being by spending their incomes such that the marginal utility of the last dollar spent on each good or service is equal. The solution to each consumer's maximization problem can be found diagrammatically as a point of tangency between the budget constraint and the indifference curve or mathematically by setting the derivatives of the utility function equal to zero. Now imagine the impact of a different theory of the economic agent: What if consumers care about others, live within complex social arrangements and relationships, and use ethics, rather than self-interest, to determine their shopping cart contents? This interrelatedness of individuals means that the solution to the consumer's utility-maximizing problem is a function of many other people's utility, potentially billions (e.g., when shopping fair trade). No neat diagrammatic or mathematical solutions are available: The predictions of individual behavior, as well as the whole policy framework of free markets that is built on those predictions, collapse.

Feminist economists have developed numerous critical analyses of the assumptions supporting the neoclassical theory of human nature (see England, 1993). As mentioned, neoclassical economics claims that this human nature is universal and preexists any social arrangements. This is the basis of the mainstream use of the literary figure of Robinson Crusoe as the representative economic agent. Crusoe was a British slave trader who was shipwrecked on a deserted island, on which he lived alone for more than two decades, and who then rescued a native, whom he called Friday, from cannibals. To neoclassical economists, the facts of Crusoe's race, sex, and class; his socialization in seventeenth-century London; the importance of the slave trade to the story; his unusual living conditions, including the absence of women, children, and a family; and his assertion of ownership of the island and virtual enslavement of Friday to his will are irrelevant to the capacity of the figure of Robinson Crusoe, a white Western colonizing man, to function as an exemplar of the economic agent. It need hardly be said that economic agents begin life as helpless babies and often end life as helpless elders. Economic agents then can, in reality, exist only within particular social and familial relations, relations that entail a fundamental dependence on others and are completely absent from the paradigmatic neoclassical story of the individual. Neoclassical economics excludes all these aspects of Crusoe's story, leaving only the fantasy of the autonomous agent, independent of all others, seeking only his own self-interest within competitive market conditions, naturalizing and legitimizing the failure of the mainstream to consider gender, race, history, culture, power relations, and connections to others as absolutely essential to an understanding of the sexual, national, and global distribution of economic well-being (see Grapard & Hewitson, 2010).

Unpaid Work

Unpaid work, including child care, shopping, subsistence crop production, food preparation, cleaning, laundry, and collecting water and firewood, is essential for the functioning of the market economy, by creating workers and consumers on a daily basis. Unpaid work absorbs as many hours of work as paid work, and the majority is performed by women. Several groups of feminist economists work in this area. Those who used gender as a theoretical category include Marxist feminist economists, who, in the 1970s, pointed out that the home was a site of production as well as consumption. How to integrate the idea that domestic labor was economic production into the existing concepts of the Marxist framework was the subject of the so-called domestic labor debate. Others sought to understand how unpaid work had come to be excluded from mainstream definitions of economic activity and the implications of this exclusion. Unpaid work as productive economic activity is also vital to the research agendas of empirical feminist economists working in areas such as national accounting, development, and labor markets (see the introduction and reprinted essays in Volume 2 of Barker & Kuiper, 2009).

Although unpaid work is an important aspect of the neoclassical economics of the family and its explanations for women's inferior economic outcomes, it really plays a minor role within the discipline as a whole, being almost or completely ignored in most research fields. This is a function of the way in which unpaid work evolved as a feminine-gendered concept and as an activity that takes place outside the realm of the economy per se. The foundational constrained optimization problem of labor economics, for example, is the utility-maximizing choice between paid work and leisure. And recent macroeconomic policy and performance debates are completely silent on unpaid work, despite the fact that the value of the output of home production rivals the value of market sector output (see Ironmonger, 1996). Outside of first-year economics classrooms, gross domestic product (GDP), which is the annual value of the market sector's output, is treated as a direct measure of the health and well-being of a nation. Although these exclusions seem natural to many economists, they rely not on some inevitable way of organizing economic activity but on a particular historically and culturally specific set of theoretical creations.

Before the Industrial Revolution (1770–1830), which heralded the widespread development of capitalism in Europe, the wage labor system did not exist. The economic unit was the family, and family members as well as

any servants worked together to produce food, clothing, and perhaps some cash to buy things they could not make, such as tools. The family economy divided tasks by sex and age. For example, women might have been responsible for food preparation, milking, feeding livestock, and growing vegetables for home consumption; men for planting and harvesting grains (perhaps as a serf); and younger people for spinning and sewing. Task allocation varied by region, rather than being a set of male and female jobs common to all humanity. But the fact that people's work varied by sex and age did not imply a hierarchy of value. In the family economy, husbands and wives were equally essential for the survival of the family.

The spread of the capitalist mode of production, within which individuals sell their labor to employers and "go to work" at a central location, broke down the family economy and was the basis of the development of a hierarchical valuation of different types of work. A lot of the work undertaken by men left the house and attracted wage payments, while a lot of women's work did not. Work undertaken outside the home was often viewed as skilled work, while women's work was not—in fact, during the nineteenth century, women's work in the home lost its definition as work and became something that women did naturally and out of love for their families.

We see this transformation of unpaid work and the unpaid worker in the evolution of census categories during the nineteenth century. The censuses documented and categorized the population and its activities—in Britain, every 10 years from 1800. The categories used for this documentation were products of generally held views on gender, and men's and women's proper places, as well as the writings of economists. Early in the century, economists understood labor as the most important source of the wealth of nations; hence, the work that was undertaken by the population was of key significance. In the early decades of the census, those who worked in the home on domestic tasks were deemed to be economically occupied. Later in the century, however, economists excluded all nonmarket activities from their definition of economic activity, and by the end of the century, the census categories also reflected this new theoretical boundary of economic behavior. Thus, by the end of the century, women's work in British, Australian, and North American homes had no place within the census; rather, those undertaking domestic labor were categorized as economic dependents, or economically unoccupied (see Deacon, 1985; Folbre, 1991).

This particular history is responsible for many of the seemingly natural categories that are used to define and understand today's economies. For example, the labor force categories of employed, unemployed, and not in the labor force, as well as the national accounting system and GDP, are based on nineteenth-century census categories. Until 1993, the System of National Accounts (SNA), which generates estimates of the annual value of the productive activity in an economy, GDP, excluded unpaid work (see Waring, 1990). The production boundary, or the division between productive and unproductive activities, enclosed the market and excluded nonmarket activities. In 1993, the SNA was revised, and the production boundary was extended to all goods for household consumption, whether or not those goods had been acquired through markets (United Nations Development Fund for Women [UNIFEM], n.d.). Where possible, the value of unpaid work is published in a satellite account. This means that macroeconomics, which is the study of GDP (its definition, how it changes, how its changes affect inflation and unemployment, and how the government can manage it), continues to exclude about half the economic activity actually being undertaken.

This is significant for many reasons. Without knowing anything about the household sector, economists cannot make claims about the efficiency of resource allocation. They are also blind to the full impact of economic policy (see Sharp, 1999). Cutting the federal budget, for example, may simply generate additional, invisible, unpaid work to be shouldered by women. Structural adjustment policies within the development context have been especially problematic in this regard. A full understanding of the amount and distribution of unpaid work is also vital to a full understanding of equity and welfare issues. It might not seem equitable, for example, that people working the same number of hours over a lifetime receive very different economic rewards, because in men's case, two thirds of their work is for pay, while in women's case, only one third of their work is paid. Furthermore, unpaid workers in the household sector, although imperative to the market economy, do not attract the benefits of paid work, such as social security. Nor are they covered by legislation that protects paid workers, such as occupational health and safety. Finally, without a full accounting of economic activity, all manner of distortions can persist. For example, income produced in the home in the form of goods and services is tax free, while income deriving from market activities is taxed.

Research into the value of unpaid work has taken two approaches. The first applies market wages to the hours of work in the home, while the second uses the value of the output produced in the home. The market wage method of valuing unpaid work can use three different market wages. Specialist wages can be used to value time spent on specialist tasks. For example, the time cooking a meal would attract a chef's hourly rate, and the time counseling children would receive a psychologist's hourly rate. Alternatively, a generalist wage can be used to value all the time spent in domestic labor, whatever the particular tasks. Here the value of unpaid work is the number of hours times the hourly wage of a housekeeper. Finally, the opportunity cost wage, or the wage that is given up to free the time for unpaid work, can be used to value unpaid work. These market wage applications normally generate an estimate of approximately half the value of GDP. Feminist economists

have pointed out, however, that comparing the value of labor time in the home to GDP is like comparing apples to oranges. GDP is the sum of all incomes, not simply wages, and in particular, it includes the return to capital used up in the production process. Given the equality between GDP measured by incomes and GDP measured by the value of current production, comparing oranges to oranges requires that the value of the household sector be measured as the value of its output, or value added. When the economic activity of households is measured in this way, the value of the household sector is at least equal to the value of the market sector (see Beneria, 2003; Goldschmidt-Clermont, 1992; Ironmonger, 1996).

As noted, women undertake the majority of unpaid work. Feminist economists argue that the mainstream theory of this sexual division of labor personifies an ideal of the family and femininity that developed in post–World War II United States. With the growth of suburbia and the industrial war machine now manufacturing consumer goods, the 1950s saw the development of a powerful ideal of the modern suburban family with all the latest modcons, in which men had careers and women devoted their energies to keeping up with the Jones's, cleanliness, and helping their husbands' careers. It is this view of the family, reflected in television programs of the era such as *Leave It to Beaver,* which has been personified within the neoclassical theory of the family, primarily through the work of Gary Becker (1991). Becker's new home economics (NHE) modeled the household as a single unit, within which the wage earner is a benevolent dictator who seeks to maximize the household's well-being subject to constraints of time, wages, and prices. He can ensure, via distribution decisions, that each family member will concur with his wishes (maximize his utility). Benevolence guarantees that the household as a whole is as well off as it can be. Spouses exploit their comparative advantages, and hence husbands, rather than wives, will typically take on the role of benevolent dictator because men typically earn more than women. This is efficient because women can take advantage of economies of scale in childbearing and rearing—they can be pregnant while also caring for children.

Because NHE has been so influential and is the most widely used model of the household within the mainstream, feminist economists have attacked it vigorously (see Ferber, 2003). They have pointed out that the model relies on circular reasoning: Recall that husbands specialize in the labor market because they earn more, while wives specialize in domestic work because they earn less. But women earn less because they specialize in domestic work. To explain women's specialization in the home, look at women's lower wages. To explain women's lower wages, look at women's specialization in the home. This circular reasoning naturalizes women's role in the home and their lower labor market earnings by leaving out the possibility of labor market discrimination against women and the role of gender ideologies and gendered institutions in shaping and forming value assessments of women's work and skills.

Another major problem with NHE's vision of the family is its silence on power relations. But empirical evidence suggests that power relations exist—in particular, that the person earning the most money wages has the most bargaining power. For example, the more equal are the wages of a husband and wife, the more equal is the division of unpaid labor. Those women who specialize in the home are likely to experience declines in their bargaining power over time as their labor market skills decline. Once considerations of power differentials enter the analysis, the notion that the sexual division of labor is efficient becomes extremely questionable (see Ferber, 2003). Instead of NHE, some feminist economists have used bargaining models to explicitly incorporate the power relations within families as well as including a longer term perspective than what is possible in the static NHE model (see the introduction and reprinted essays in Volume 2 of Barker & Kuiper, 2009).

A third important critique of NHE is its heteronormativity, or its assumption that natural family relations are heterosexual and reproductive. Indeed, Becker (1991) defines anyone who does not fit into such a family as "deviant." According to NHE, deviants are inefficient because they do not take advantage of the complementarity of men and women in reproduction and production. Such deviants include homosexual people, "career women," "house-husbands," people who do not want children, people who cannot have children, and people who prefer to remain single. This critique is also one internal to feminist economics because the category of the family is mostly taken by feminist economists themselves to be self-evidently made up of a heterosexual couple. The naturalization of the conjugal family contributes tremendously to economists' and policy makers' inability to imagine economic activity being organized and work, income, and wealth being distributed differently (see Badgett, 1995; Danby, 2007; Hewitson, 2003).

Paid Work

Feminist economists argue that the gendered institutional structures that frame and reproduce the current organization of unpaid work also support women's economic subordination in the realm of paid work. Women's paid work often replicates their unpaid work, reflecting a gender ideology that maps femininity onto service work and work involving the support of men. Thus, women dominate in occupations such as maids and housekeeping cleaners, child care workers, elementary and primary school teachers, secretaries and administrative assistants, nurses, and receptionists. These jobs are both derivative of unpaid labor and often badly remunerated. Thus, the gender wage gap can also be traced to the sexual division of labor in paid work. NHE justifies this pattern of economic rewards but does not explain why, when women make up nearly half the labor force, they continue to be responsible for the majority of domestic labor and child care.

Interest in the interrelatedness of women's domestic role and their occupational distribution within the labor market has led to the development of a new category of analysis called *caring labor.* Caring labor refers to both paid and unpaid caring work, such as child care for pay and unpaid emotional support within the family. Feminist economists have found that caring occupations dominated by women tend to attract a "caring penalty," which can be linked to the lack of value attributed to unpaid work and the lack of esteem with which this work is generally viewed (see the introduction and reprinted essays in Volume 2 of Barker & Kuiper, 2009; Folbre, 1995).

Mainstream economists agree that there is a sexual division of labor in paid work and that there is a gender wage gap. However, as has been noted, they believe that these phenomena result from rational, utility-maximizing, individual choices. Early labor market studies within the orthodox school did not consider women at all. It was only in the 1960s, during an unprecedented movement of white wives into the formal labor market, that a female labor supply function was delineated, and because it referred to wives, it necessarily included the opportunity cost of women's time at work—not leisure but home-produced goods and services. Later, race and sex discrimination moved onto the mainstream agenda, though it was and continues to be argued that discrimination is an individual phenomenon ("I don't like black people or women"), analytically having nothing to do with larger social institutions such as the organization of unpaid work, gender ideologies, or the history of colonization, slavery, and associated racism. In the mainstream model, racists and sexists are punished by the market with lower profit than their competitors and hence go out of business.

There is an extensive empirical literature, which will not be reviewed in detail here, examining gender issues in the labor market from a feminist perspective (see Bergmann, 2005; Blau et al., 2010). Some key results will suffice. Feminist economists have found that sex discrimination plays a role in the gender wage gap. Women often earn less than men who are doing the same job and are promoted more slowly than equally or lesser qualified men. Women also hit a glass ceiling, so that in many occupations, the senior positions are largely taken by men, while women's careers have stopped progressing once they have reached some midway point up the ladder. Feminist economists also insist on the importance of "indirect discrimination," or the discriminatory impact of the gender system that shapes women's choices. When women choose to enter traditionally male occupations, they encounter the revolving door: Women enter, find the working environment hostile to women, and leave. Most occupations are dominated by either women or men, and this occupational segregation also accounts for some of the gender wage gap. But as already discussed, the evidence for women's low productivity is lacking, and in any case, women can earn less even with the same human capital investments. Experiments have shown that application letters from male (or white) applicants are evaluated more positively and lead to more invitations to an interview than application letters that are the same in every relevant respect but are presented as being from female (or black) applicants.

Because of women's work in the home, feminist economists are very interested in the ways in which these responsibilities fit with the institutional requirements of the labor market, for full-time attendance at a workplace, a 40-hour week, 6 p.m. meetings, and so on. Because the categories of work and the worker are gendered masculine, as the complement of the feminine gendered unpaid work and the housewife (discussed above), the worker is someone without domestic responsibilities. (This is a theoretical point about the concept of the worker rather than being a point about empirical men and women.) This way of viewing the worker—that is, as a gendered category—leads to a different perspective on the labor market. Such mechanisms as the mommy track, family-friendly policies, and unpaid maternity and paternity leave are ways in which mothers are added to or fitted into the labor market, leaving mothers, rather than work, as the problem. Fathers, because the notion of worker is already intrinsically dependent on the idea of male breadwinner, have been hesitant to make use of these mechanisms for fear that their commitment to work will be questioned. Indeed, holding other factors constant, men with children earn more than those without, while the opposite is true of mothers, revealing the assumptions regarding the work commitment of breadwinners versus mothers. In other words, anyone not fitting the identity of worker in the same way as unencumbered men is problematic. This points once again to the extent to which gendered institutions naturalize and reproduce an organization of work that is detrimental to women (see Barker, 2005; J. Williams, 2000).

Gender in a Global Perspective

In the early 1970s, Western feminists began to consider the role of women within Third World development. This literature came to be known as "women in development" (WID). It examined the ways in which Western modernization affected women's work, a topic neglected by earlier development specialists. Although the WID perspective added a much-needed voice to the development literature, which had thus far ignored the gendered impacts of development policies, it did so problematically. WID theorists viewed the women, men, and economies of "less-developed" countries (the global South) through Western concepts and categories. For example, they accepted that development meant the extension of markets and commodification but

did not recognize that equality in labor market participation, being a goal of Western feminists, did not necessarily improve women's status or well-being in non-Western countries (see the introduction and reprinted essays in Volume 3 of Barker & Kuiper, 2009).

The fact that women of the South are not the same as Western women seems fairly obvious. But at a theoretical level, this insight is very powerful. It means that the category of woman is a construct of theory. In particular, it emerges from the privileging of the perspective of the West, discussed above. Western feminists are positioned within the history of European theorizing of knowledge production as colonizers, as superior, civilized, and modern, compared to women of the South. A stay-at-home white mother married to a wealthy man living in the United States, for example, has very different experiences of womanhood than a poor woman working in an Asian export processing zone, and an analysis of the desires, opportunities, and constraints facing the stay-at-home mother cannot be assumed to apply equally to the Asian woman. This is not simply because the Asian woman's situation is so different but because the very meaning of woman is different in each case. One is not just a woman, but a woman with a race. Feminist economists who generalize from the experiences of white Western women are performing an act of violence, in that it enacts an imperial power relation of colonizer and colonized and therefore silences non-Western women with different histories and cultures (see R. M. Williams, 1993).

The inability of the category of woman to be universally applied is part of the postcolonial critique that has developed within feminist economics. Feminist economists have also problematized, as gender and race specific, such seemingly natural entities and concepts as the national economy as an object of economic control, development, progress, and less-developed or underdeveloped countries. The concept of the national economy as it has been integrated into mainstream economics is a gendered and racial concept that developed during the mid-twentieth century at the time macroeconomics and the national accounting framework emerged from the Keynesian revolution and just as former colonies became independent. The new national economies, no longer subject to the needs of their colonizers, were understood to be in need of Western-style modernization, which marginalized the unpaid subsistence work of women (see Bergeron, 2004). The concepts of development and progress are situated firmly within the European theories of race and human evolution, which justified the creation of European empires and colonized peoples by positioning European societies as the endpoint of civilization (see Bergeron, 2004; Olsen, 1994; Zein-Elabdin & Charusheela, 2004).

There are also many important empirical issues in the area of gender in the global context. For example, the economies of the South have been the object of surveillance and control by the World Bank and the International Monetary Fund, and many have been subjected to structural adjustment policies, which reorient the economy to the repayment of debt by minimizing the size of government and maximizing exports. But the full effects of structural adjustment programs were unknown because the subsistence and reproductive work mainly performed by women was not quantified or accounted for or integrated into the policies. In fact, however, increases in this work were critical for mediating the social costs of the policies, such as the loss of the safety net as governments cut their expenditures (see the introduction and reprinted essays in Volume 3 of Barker & Kuiper, 2009; Beneria, 2003).

The international sexual division of labor is another important area of research. Women make up the majority of workers in the factories of global corporations located in the South. They are paid poverty-level wages and lack basic protections such as occupational health and safety regulations and union membership. Global corporations will simply relocate should worker demands raise labor costs. Furthermore, hundreds of thousands of women from the South work as poorly paid domestics, maids, and nannies for wealthy women in the West and in wealthy Arab countries. Again we see the importance of the postcolonial critique and the emptiness of the assumption of some kind of global sisterhood (see Olsen, 1994).

Conclusion

This chapter has established that the field of feminist economics is necessary, that feminist economic researchers use two main approaches, each with its own important role to play in meeting the goal of ending the economic subordination of women, and reviewed five of the most important areas within which these researchers are working. Needless to say, many other important areas of theory and empirical work could not be covered for reasons of space (see Peterson & Lewis, 1999). Examples include the history of economic thought (where Pujol [1992] uses gender as a theoretical variable, while Dimand, Dimand, & Forget [2001] take an empirical approach); feminist perspectives on other heterodox schools of thought, such as post-Keynesian economics and institutionalism; integrating feminist thinking into the teaching of economics (see Bartlett, 1997); engendering government budgets and macroeconomic policy (see Sharp, 1999); and gender in emerging market economies. The five topics discussed above, however, capture the essence of feminist economics: They cover the main ways in which the economic experiences of men and women are shaped by gender, and they address the most central and problematic of the concepts and categories of the mainstream.

Notes

1. Feminist economics is quite recent. Its organization, the International Association for Feminist Economics, was formed in 1992, and its journal, *Feminist Economics,* began in 1995.

2. All statistics are from the United Nations Development Fund for Women (UNIFEM, n.d.) and the U.S. Census (n.d.).

References and Further Readings

Badgett, M. V. L. (1995). Gender, sexuality, and sexual orientation: All in the feminist family? *Feminist Economics, 1*(1), 121–139.

Barker, D. K. (2005). Beyond women and economics: Rereading "women's work." *Signs, 30,* 2189–2209.

Barker, D. K., & Kuiper, E. (Eds.). (2003). *Toward a feminist philosophy of economics.* New York: Routledge.

Barker, D. K., & Kuiper, E. (2009). *Feminist economics* (4 vols.). New York: Routledge.

Bartlett, R. L. (Ed.). (1997). *Introducing race and gender into economics.* New York: Routledge.

Becker, G. S. (1991). *Treatise on the family* (Rev. ed.). Cambridge, MA: Harvard University Press.

Beneria, L. (2003). *Gender, development and globalization.* New York: Routledge.

Bergeron, S. (2004). *Fragments of development.* Ann Arbor: University of Michigan Press.

Bergmann, B. (2005). *The economic emergence of women* (2nd ed.). New York: Palgrave Macmillan.

Blau, F. D., Ferber, M. A., & Winkler, A. E. (2010). *The economics of women, men and work* (6th ed.). Upper Saddle River, NJ: Prentice Hall.

Danby, C. (2007). Political economy and the closet: Heteronormativity in feminist economics. *Feminist Economics, 13*(2), 29–54.

Deacon, D. (1985). Political arithmetic: The nineteenth century Australian census and the construction of the dependent woman. *Signs, 11,* 27–47.

Dimand, R., Dimand, M. A., & Forget, E. (2001). *A biographical dictionary of women economists.* Aldershot, UK: Edward Elgar.

England, P. (1993). The separative self: Androcentric bias in neoclassical assumptions. In M. A. Ferber & J. A. Nelson (Eds.), *Beyond economic man* (pp. 37–53). Chicago: University of Chicago Press.

Ferber, M. A. (2003). A feminist critique of the neoclassical theory of the family. In K. S. Moe (Ed.), *Women, family and work* (pp. 9–23). Oxford, UK: Blackwell.

Ferber, M. A., & Nelson, J. A. (Eds.). (1993). *Beyond economic man.* Chicago: University of Chicago Press.

Ferber, M. A., & Nelson, J. A. (Eds.). (2003). *Feminist economics today.* Chicago: University of Chicago Press.

Figart, D. M., Mutari, E., & Power, M. (2002). *Living wages, equal wages.* New York: Routledge.

Folbre, N. (1991). The unproductive housewife: Her evolution in nineteenth century economic thought. *Signs, 16,* 463–484.

Folbre, N. (1995). "Holding hands at midnight": The paradox of caring labor. *Feminist Economics, 1*(1), 73–92.

Goldschmidt-Clermont, L. (1992). Measuring households' nonmonetary production. In P. Ekins & M. Max-Neef (Eds.), *Real-life economics* (pp. 265–283). New York: Routledge.

Grapard, U., & Hewitson, G. J. (Eds.). (2010). *Robinson Crusoe's economic man.* New York: Routledge.

Hewitson, G. J. (1999). *Feminist economics.* Cheltenham, UK: Edward Elgar.

Hewitson, G. J. (2003). Domestic labor and gender identity: Are all women carers? In D. K. Barker & E. Kuiper (Eds.), *Toward a feminist philosophy of economics* (pp. 266–283). New York: Routledge.

Ironmonger, D. (1996). Counting outputs, capital inputs and caring labor: Estimating gross household product. *Feminist Economics, 2*(3), 37–64.

Kuiper, E., & Sap, J. (Eds.). (1995). *Out of the margin.* New York: Routledge.

Nelson, J. A. (1993). The study of choice or the study of provisioning? Gender and the definition of economics. In M. A. Ferber & J. A. Nelson (Eds.), *Beyond economic man* (pp. 23–36). Chicago: University of Chicago Press.

Nelson, J. A. (1996). *Feminism, objectivity and economics.* New York: Routledge.

Olsen, P. (1994). Feminism and science reconsidered: Insights from the margin. In J. Peterson & D. Brown (Eds.), *The economic status of women under capitalism* (pp. 77–94). Aldershot, UK: Edward Elgar.

Peterson, J., & Lewis, M. (Eds.). (1999). *The Elgar companion to feminist economics.* Cheltenham, UK: Edward Elgar.

Pujol, M. A. (1992). *Feminism and anti-feminism in early economic thought.* Aldershot, UK: Edward Elgar.

Seguino, S., Stevens, T., & Lutz, M. A. (1996). Gender and cooperative behavior: Economic *man* rides alone. *Feminist Economics, 2*(1), 1–21.

Sharp, R. (1999). Women's budgets. In J. Peterson & M. Lewis (Eds.), *The Elgar companion to feminist economics* (pp. 764–770). Cheltenham, UK: Edward Elgar.

Strassmann, D., & Polanyi, L. (1995). The economist as storyteller: What the texts reveal. In E. Kuiper & J. Sap (Eds.), *Out of the margin* (pp. 129–150). New York: Routledge.

United Nations Development Fund for Women (UNIFEM). (n.d.). United Nations development fund for women. Available at http://www.unifem.org

U.S. Census. (n.d.) United States Census [Online]. Available at http://www.census.gov

Waring, M. (1990). *If women counted.* New York: HarperCollins.

Williams, J. (2000). *Unbending gender.* Oxford, UK: Oxford University Press.

Williams, R. M. (1993). Race, deconstruction, and the emergent agenda of feminist economic theory. In M. A. Ferber & J. A. Nelson (Eds.), *Beyond economic man* (pp. 144–153). Chicago: University of Chicago Press.

Zein-Elabdin, E., & Charusheela, S. (Eds.). (2004). *Postcolonialism meets economics.* New York: Routledge.

89

NEUROECONOMICS

DANTE MONIQUE PIROUZ

University of Western Ontario

ecision making is a fundamental part of human behavior. We all make decisions every day that influence our health, well-being, finances, and future prospects, among other things. Researchers have become increasingly interested in why we make the decisions we do, especially when, in many cases, these decisions do not appear to be rational or beneficial to us in the long run. While neoclassical economics has traditionally looked at how people *should* behave, other disciplines such as psychology and cognitive science have tried to answer the question of *why* people act the way they do.

A new discipline, referred to as neuroeconomics, has sought to meld theory and methodology from diverse areas such as economics, psychology, neuroscience, and decision theory to create a model of human behavior that not only explains but also predicts how people make decisions (Glimcher & Rustichini, 2004). Neuroeconomics research examines how people make choices and attempts to determine the underlying neural basis for these choices and decisions. This chapter examines some of the seminal studies in neuroeconomics, highlighting the public policy implications and offering areas of future research where neuroeconomics could be applied.

Theory

Traditional economic theory has maintained that humans are rational decision-making entities, that each individual has a clear sense of his or her own preferences, tries to maximize his or her own well-being, and makes consistent choices over time (Huang, 2005). However, this model is more often violated than upheld as people and animals attempt to outwit evolution

and destiny. Neuroscience gives researchers the opportunity to look into the "black box" of cognitive processing to reveal empirical indications of how the brain really processes choice, risk, and preferences. The goal is to create "a complete neuroeconomic theory of the brain" (Glimcher, 2003).

Decision theory integrates mathematics and statistics to better understand how decisions such as choices between incommensurable commodities, choice under uncertainty, intertemporal choice, and social choice are made. It has been assumed that agents respond rationally in forming their choices and preferences. This theory finds that any "normal" preference relation over a finite set of states can be expressed as an expected utility equation.

However, the introduction of prospect theory, which suggests the possibility that other factors may affect behavioral decision making for the individual, has generated an interest in understanding the underlying mechanisms of preference, judgment, and choice (Kahneman & Tversky, 1979). The significance of these findings can have important implications for the marketing discipline. To this end, a better understanding of the decision-making processes used by people is important to understanding the critical drivers of economic behavior.

Psychology has sought to investigate the inner workings of the human mind (Camerer, Loewenstein, & Prelec, 2005; Loewenstein, Rick, & Cohen, 2008). Cognitive psychology, and more recently cognitive neuroscience, has introduced new tools that allow researchers to capture and measure data from brain activity related to a specific function and behavior. This new type of data has led to new directions of research that combine neuroscience, psychology, and decision theory to better understand the complexities of human decision making.

Neuroscience looks at the structure, function, and development of the nervous system and brain, while cognitive neuroscience investigates how behavior and the nervous system work together in humans and animals. In other words, cognitive neuroscience is the study of the neural mechanisms of cognition (Gazzaniga, 2002). At the nexus of neuroscience, economics, and psychology, there is an area that has tentatively been coined *neuroeconomics*, which uses neuroscience techniques to look specifically at how human subjects make choices. Neuroeconomics is interested not only in exposing brain regions associated with specific behavior but also in identifying neural circuits or systems of specialized regions that control choice, preference, and judgment (Camerer et al., 2005; Loewenstein et al., 2008).

Techniques borrowed from neuroscience include brain imaging methods that may reveal how humans and animals use the neural substrates of the brain to process and evaluate decisions, weigh risk and reward, and learn to trust others in transactions. Brain imaging techniques that can be used on human subjects include electroencephalography (EEG), positron emission tomography (PET), magnetoencephalography (MEG), and functional magnetic resonance imaging (fMRI). EEG and MEG measure changes in electrical brain currents by placing electrodes on the scalp to measure electrical waves emitted from the cortex. PET scans measure changes in blood flow by capturing images of radioactive isotopes injected in the bloodstream. fMRI measures blood flow to neural regions by relying on the magnetic properties of oxygenated and deoxygenated blood in the brain.

Another technique borrowed from neuroscience is transcranial magnetic stimulation (TMS), which is used to produce a magnetic pulse that can temporarily interfere with normal brain activity. For example, TMS can produce sudden movements in motor areas. While it has not yet been used for neuroeconomic studies, TMS has been used successfully for cognitive neuroscience studies and could potentially be used in the future to study decision making. In addition, there are invasive techniques of monitoring brain activity in animals, including single-cell recording, wherein an electrode is passed through the skull into the brain and neural activity is recorded. Neuroeconomics studies can also use nonimaging techniques. For example, some studies have been conducted using patients with brain lesions that disable specific parts of the brain. In addition, to determine central nervous system (CNS) response, studies can measure hormone levels, galvanic skin response, sweat gland activity, and heart rate (Carter & Tiffany, 1999; Frackowiak et al., 2004).

Before these technologies made it possible to examine the neural mechanisms of cognition, much of economic theory relied on the rational choice model. This model posits that individuals have stable preferences and a clear understanding of the options facing them. Thus, people are assumed to make their choices based on careful, unemotional calculations that maximize the benefits and minimize the costs that they will incur. However, current models of decision making only partially explain real human behavior. Neuroeconomics examines higher level cognitive functions of personal choice and decision making, demonstrating how these are expressed at the neuronal and biochemical levels. The analysis of this newest form of data that more closely examines brain processing promises to bring us closer to answering questions as to why people consume, have addictions, save, and hoard; what drives preference and choice; and what makes people happy, risk seeking or risk adverse, and trusting or trustworthy.

Over the past 50 years, scientists have experimented with a number of hypothetical game scenarios to determine models of how people make choices in economic situations. Before imaging technology, it was not possible to accurately investigate the influence of emotions and cognition on these economic models of decision making. However, behavioral economists have begun to challenge the assumptions of the rational agent and have found that psychological and emotional factors do indeed play an important role in people's economic decision-making process. Essentially, neuroeconomics looks at two branches of choice: solitary choice and strategic choice (Zak, 2004).

In their article on neuroeconomics, Camerer et al. (2005) argue for the fundamental insights that neuroscience could offer economics. They maintain that economic theory has assumed that agents can "mentalize," or infer from the actions of others, what their preferences and beliefs are. However, accumulating evidence from individuals with autism, Asperger's syndrome, and brain lesions shows that mentalizing is a specialized skill modularized in specific brain regions. More important, the ability to mentalize exists in varying degrees from person to person.

Applications and Empirical Evidence

The Neuroscience of Game Playing

Games give neuroeconomists a useful way to isolate decision and choice variables in experimental studies. Most of these studies look at either behavior, autonomic reactions (such as hormone levels or heart rate), or brain activity while subjects are engaged in strategic games, thus revealing how the neuronal system processes fairness, reward, loss, trust, distrust, revenge, discounting, and choice. Specific brain regions have been implicated in how judgments are made about perceptual stimuli received from our environment (Adolphs, 2003). Some of these brain regions involved in judgment include the amygdala, which is central in the processing and memory of emotions; the insula, believed to be involved with feelings of disgust and unease; and the anterior cingulate cortex, which is implicated in reward anticipation, decision making, and empathy (Frackowiak et al., 2004).

Neural Calculations of Decisions

The idea that people seem prone to violate expected utility theory has led to the development of alternative models on how choices are made under risk. One such alternative, prospect theory, exhibits a series of effects that alter the value assigned to gains and losses (Kahneman & Tversky, 1979). Phenomena such as the certainty effect, which states that people are prone to undervalue probable versus certain outcomes, or the isolation effect, which finds inconsistent preferences for identical outcomes based on how the outcomes are framed, challenge the notion that utility theory holds in real-life cases of human judgment (Kahneman & Tversky, 1982). Interestingly, Camerer et al. (2005) make clear in their article on neuroeconomics that all the violations of the utility theory that humans commit have been replicated in animal studies. For example, rats have also committed the same patterned violations in addition to other expected utility properties (Kagel, Battalio, & Green, 1995). Probability is how animals and humans calculate associations between events and predict outcomes critical to survival and understanding their environment. For example, there is evidence that dopamine neurons of the primate ventral midbrain may act to predict reward by specifically coding errors (Fiorillo, Tobler, & Schultz, 2003). It was found that dopamine levels increase during gambling, which indicates that uncertainty may be the mechanism that induces this dopamine rush. This may explain the reward people feel when gambling, which cannot be explained by the monetary gain of gambling because losses usually outnumber gains.

Trust and Cooperation

Imaging studies have revealed more about how social interaction shapes neural response, allowing us to choose mutual cooperation and shared gains over self-interested choices to create a sense of stability in longer-term game scenarios (McCabe, Houser, Ryan, Smith, & Trouard, 2001). Increased activity in players who were more trusting and cooperative was shown in a brain area believed to be the locus of mentalizing, as well as in the limbic system, where emotions are believed to be processed (Camerer et al., 2005).

The trust game is often used in neuroeconomics studies and mimics the relationship between an investor and broker. The game is played in multiple rounds where a player is given an amount of money (e.g., $10) and then must decide how much of the money, if any, to send to a second player. The amount is tripled, and then the second player decides how much to send back to the first player. One study found that subjects who received the first "investment" violated the rational response, which would be to accept any amount of money offered to them by the first player or "investor" (McCabe, 2003). Interestingly, when a small amount of money was offered by a computer player instead of a human, the response by the investor was not as extreme. In other words, players were upset about receiving a low return only if they believed that another person was trying to take advantage of them. If they thought the small amount of money was from an impartial computer, investors were not as emotionally sensitive. In addition, half of the subjects in the study were characterized as cooperators and had a common pattern of divergent activation in the prefrontal cortex where simultaneous attention to mutual gains and inhibition of immediate gratification allow for cooperative choices.

Studies of fMRI brain scans found that when responders were offered low monetary amounts (e.g., $1 out of a maximum of $10), there was more activation in the prefrontal cortex, anterior cingulate, and the insula cortex (Sanfey, Rilling, Aronson, Nystrom, & Cohen, 2003). When monetary offers were low, the receivers had increased activity in the insula, which is often associated with feelings of pain and disgust (Wright, He, Shapira, Goodman, & Liu, 2004). The anterior cingulate cortex receives input from a number of other areas and is thought to resolve conflict among these areas. A player refusing an offer could be predicted by the level of activation in the insula. The author speculates that the insula may be the neural area responsible for distaste for inequality or unfair conditions.

The relationship between trust and hormones is another area of interest for researchers. Hormonal response in people was investigated during a series of trust games to determine whether there was a specific hormone that could be connected to feelings of trust and distrust (Zak, Kurzban, & Matzner, 2004). Participants' blood was tested after each round for levels of oxytocin, which has been associated in facilitating social behaviors, social recognition, maternal attachment, pair bonding, and the feeling of falling in love. The study found that when money was returned to the first player, oxytocin did indeed increase to twice the levels of the random draw. This means that if people felt they were being trusted, increased oxytocin levels made them more likely to trust back. Interestingly, ovulating women were less likely than nonovulating women or men to give money back even if they received the full amount from the other player. This, Zak (2004) believes, is due to the fact that progesterone, which increases during ovulation, binds with oxytocin to inhibit its affect. In looking at distrust, Zak looked at dihydrotestosterone and testosterone in both men and women to see if levels increased during low-trust games. The study found that testosterone did not significantly increase in either women or men, and dihydrotestosterone levels did not increase for women. However, there was a significant increase in the level of dihydrotestosterone in men when the other player signaled distrust. Zak hypothesizes that this may be related to the increased feelings of aggression that men reported when engaged in a low-trust game.

While cooperation is an important component in human society, the desire to punish is the flip side of cooperation, which may be how society is able to enforce social norms.

An interesting study that looked at the neural basis for altruistic punishment or revenge found that people feel a sense of satisfaction when punishing those who break what are considered social norms (de Quervain et al., 2004). Using PET scans, researchers found greater activation in the striatum, which is usually "implicated in the processing of rewards that accrue as a result of goal-directed actions." In addition, those with the strongest responses in the striatum were more likely to take on higher costs for the right to mete out punishment to those who deviate from societal norms.

Fairness

Humans tend to reject inequality even if it means walking away from a reward (Powell, 2003). In a study that looked at the neural substrates of cognitive and emotional processing, specifically fairness and unfairness activated during the ultimatum game, 19 subjects were scanned using fMRI (Sanfey et al., 2003). The ultimatum game is based on one player offering the other a split of a sum of money that the responder can either reject or accept. Players were paired with others who offered various split amounts of $10. The responders were scanned as they decided whether they would choose fair or unfair proposals. Previous behavioral research on the ultimatum game found that low offers are rejected 50% of the time even though a rational maximizing solution would be for the responder to accept any amount of money because some money should be better than no money. Subjects usually report that low offers are often rejected because it provokes an angry response. In Sanfey et al.'s (2003) study, brain imaging revealed that unfair offers activated the bilateral anterior insula, dorsolateral prefrontal cortex, and anterior cingulate cortex. The anterior insula is often implicated in negative emotional responses, more specifically in disgust (Krolak-Salmon et al., 2002; Wright et al., 2004). The dorsolateral prefrontal cortex is often implicated in executive function and goal maintenance, which may stem from the responder actively maintaining the cognitive goal of acquiring as much money as possible. Increased activation of the insula was biased toward rejection of the offer, and increased activation of the dorsolateral prefrontal cortex was biased to accepting the offer. The anterior cingulate cortex has been implicated in cognitive conflict and may be a result of conflict between emotional and goal motivation during the game. Interestingly, the experiment was also run with both human and computer partners who acted in offering the split. The response in these brain areas was stronger when unfair offers were made by the human partner versus the computer, suggesting that the response was not just to the monetary amount offered but also to the contextual factor that the unfair offer was made by another human.

Even monkeys seem to adhere to this notion of fairness. Brosnan and de Waal (2003) found that cooperation may have developed through evolution where individuals must compare their own efforts to the payoff they receive with those of others. Brown capuchin monkeys responded negatively when offered unequal rewards from experimenters and even refused to participate when they witnessed other monkeys receiving more attractive rewards for the same amount of effort. The researchers posit that this inequity aversion may have an evolutionary origin in our neurological development.

Reward and Loss

Kahneman and Tversky (1979) found that loss is judged by people as being more painful than an equivalent gain is pleasurable, as is evidenced in the convex utility curve for losses and concave utility curve for gains in the value function. How valuation of gain and loss is calculated in the brain is an area under investigation by neuroscientists. Montague and Berns (2002) have looked at a number of experiments to develop a computational model referred to as the predictor valuation model, which anticipates neural responses in the orbitofrontal cortex and striatum. Other brain imaging studies have found that the brain processes gains and losses differently (K. Smith, Dickhaut, McCabe, & Pardo, 2002). PET imaging has revealed that there are two separate but functionally integrated choice systems, both in anatomical structure and in processing, each sensitive to loss. The dorsomedial system processes loss when deliberating risky gambles. When subjects make a choice that results in loss, there is a greater use of the dorsomedial system, which serves to calculate the loss versus the visceral representations in the more primitive ventromedial system, which animals most likely use to make decisions. Choice processing seems to be centered in the more medial structures, with more ventral than dorsal distribution.

Animal studies, mainly using monkeys, are revealing new information about how animals estimate the value of specific actions. For example, in a series of experiments, Schultz (1998; Schultz, Dayan, & Montague, 1997) looked at the neuronal response in the substantia nigra and the ventral tegmental area of the monkey brain to determine activity when a monkey pressed levers for juice rewards. Another animal study looked at whether specific neuronal activation can be correlated to the probability that the animal expects gain (Platt & Glimcher, 1999). Another animal study looking at reward valuation has found that reward valuation in monkeys can be predicted in a model based on reward history that duplicates foraging behavior (Sugrue, Corrago, & Newsome, 2004).

How we respond to monetary reward has also been investigated using fMRI. The neural substrates of financial reinforcement overlap with areas that deal with primary reinforcers, such as food (Elliott, Newman, Longe, & Deakin, 2003). Gold (2003) has made an argument for reward expectation to be linked to the basal ganglia. Breiter, Aharon, Kahneman, Dale, and Schizgal (2001) have used fMRI to analyze the neural response to expectation and experience of gains and loss. The study found that that there may be a common circuitry of neurons that processes different types of rewards. In studies conducted with monkeys, it was found that the rhinal cortex was important for creating the associations between visual stimuli and their motivational significance (Liu, Murray, & Richmond, 2000; Liu & Richmond, 2000). Monkeys whose rhinal cortex had been removed were not able to adjust their motivation to changes in a reward schedule, while unaffected monkeys were able to adjust their motivation. The complexity of how motivation works to cause action is not clearly understood, but it is believed that a limbic-striatal-pallidal circuit forms the basis for the translation of motivation into action (Liu et al., 2000).

The neural substrate association with time discounting was investigated using fMRI, and it was found that human subjects use different regions in the brain to calculate short- and long-term monetary rewards (McClure, Laibson, Loewenstein, & Cohen, 2004). The limbic system associated with dopamine production tended to be activated when decisions that would bring immediate gratification were contemplated. On the other hand, the lateral prefrontal cortex and posterior parietal cortex were activated regardless of whether there was short or long intertemporal delay. There was greater frontal parietal cortex activity only when the choice made by subjects was longer term.

Risk

Aversion to risk is linked to the amygdala and is driven by the ancient fear response (Camerer et al., 2005). Cortical override of the fear response is demonstrated in animal studies using shock. Over time, the response will be "extinguished." However, when the connections between the amygdala and the cortex are severed in the animal, there is a tendency for the fear response to return. This demonstrates that the amygdala does not "forget" but that the cortex is suppressing the response.

Risky choice is different from risk judgment in that the subject must choose between risky gambles that force an interaction between cognition and affect. Patients with damage to the ventromedial prefrontal cortex seem to suffer from decision-making deficits. In a study that measured performance in gambling tasks, patients continued to make the wrong choice, resulting in higher losses even after knowing the correct strategy (Bechara, Damasio, Damasio, & Tranel, 1997). Normal subjects used the advantageous strategy even before they consciously realized which strategy worked best. In addition, normal subjects developed skin conductance responses when facing a risky choice even before they knew that the choice was actually risky. For the patients with prefrontal damage, these skin conductance responses never developed. This suggests that there might be a nonconscious, autonomic

bias that guides risky decision making based in the ventromedial prefrontal cortex, responding even before conscious cognition is aware of the risk. Bechara et al. (1997) hypothesize that this covert bias activation is dependent on past reward and loss experiences and the emotions that go with them, with damage to the ventromedial cortex interfering with access to this knowledge.

A study looked at how emotion affects perceptions of risk in investment behavior. Using patients with lesions in the brain areas associated with emotion, Shiv, Loewenstein, Bechara, Damasio, and Damasio (2005) compared investment decisions over 20 rounds to those made by patients with lesions in areas unrelated to emotion (control) and normal subjects. They hypothesized that the patients with damage to the emotional regions would be able to make better investment decisions because they would not be subject to emotional reactions that could lead to poor choices. This hypothesis was based on the case of a patient with ventromedial prefrontal damage who was able to avoid an accident on an icy road while others skidded out of control. The patient revealed later that because he felt a lack of fear, he was able to calmly react to the road conditions by thinking rationally about the appropriate driving response (Damasio, 1994). This led the researchers to wonder whether a lack of normal emotional reactions might allow people to make more advantageous decisions.

The study found that normal participants and control patients became more conservative in the investment strategy after a win or loss, whereas the lesion patients took more risk and, as a result, made more money from their investing choices (Shiv et al., 2005). Other studies have found that even low levels of negative emotions can result in loss of self-control, which can have less than optimal outcomes for the subjects. For example, as the result of myopic loss aversion, people exhibit high levels of loss aversion when gambles are presented one at a time rather than all at once (Benartzi & Thaler, 1995).

Addictive Behavior

Closely related to the question of reward is addiction. Neural activity drives the search for food in both animals and humans. These same neuronal networks may also drive behavior to seek other kinds of substances that rate high on the reward evaluation. When the brain is strongly activated by, for example, sugar, food, or drugs, it can lead to abuse, which is often called addiction (Hoebel, Rada, Mark, & Pothos, 1999). A critical issue in behavioral decision theory is the question of why people and animals would choose to engage in behavior that is detrimental or harmful. This issue is related to the question of addictive behavior and the endeavor to understand the neural underpinnings of reinforcement and inhibition of behavior. In an early neuroeconomic paper dealing with this issue, Bernheim and Rangel (2002a, 2002b) proposed a mathematical theory of addiction that sought to explain irrational addictive behavior in terms of decision theory and economics. The model is based on the idea that cognitive processes such as attention can affect behavioral outcomes regardless of initial preference. If a person is subject to "hot cognition" (or affect-laden thinking), for example, he or she may engage in consumption behavior that conflicts with preference because the focus is on usage and "the high" (Bernheim & Rangel, 2002a).

The theory of cue reactivity is another theory that might serve to explain why addiction levels remain high even though subjects self-report that they are striving to quit and they do not enjoy the consumption of their addictive substance (Carter & Tiffany, 1999; Laibson, 2001). In a recent study that used fMRI to analyze neural response in adolescents to alcohol-related imagery, researchers found that adolescents with even a short usage history of alcohol had significantly higher blood oxygen response in areas of the brain associated with reward, affect, and recall (Tapert et al., 2003).

Various types of addictive behaviors are under investigation by researchers. A type of consumption addiction involves the dispensation of products. The neural basis of collecting and hoarding in humans was analyzed using patients with prefrontal cortex lesions (Anderson, Damasio, & Damasio, 2005). In addition to judgments of use and consequences of discarding possessions, other cognitive processing going on at the time of the decision to save may be important. Compulsive hoarders appear to have a peculiar perspective with regard to possessions. When deciding whether to discard a possession, they spend most of their time thinking about being without the possession (the cost of discarding) and little time thinking about the cost of saving it or the benefit of not having it. This notion is similar to an observation made by J. P. Smith (1990) about animal hoarding. Smith speculated that the sight of a nut (by a squirrel) puts the squirrel "in touch with" the feeling of being hungry and without the nut. For the hoarders, the sight of the possession puts them "in touch with" the feeling of being without the possession and needing it. This feeling dominates their consideration of whether the possession should be discarded (Frost & Hartl, 1996).

Limitations

The fact that brain science offers insights into economic and behavioral phenomena is not necessarily a new concept. While not universally embraced by all economists, some behavioral economists have been using constructs from psychology to attempt to build more descriptive and realistic models of behavior (Huang, 2005). However, for the first time, imaging technology such as fMRI offers the type of tools that can effectively explore the subtleties of the human brain while being noninvasive, relatively safe for human subjects, and providing results that are robust and revealing.

However, fMRI studies have been questioned by critics because of, for example, use of small sample sizes (typically less than 40 subjects), ambiguity in human neuroanatomy mapping, lag time in the hemodynamic response, image distortion due to signal drop-off, motion artifacts, poor temporal resolution, and the debate over functional definitions of neural areas (Savoy, 1998, 1999; Savoy, Ravicz, & Gollub, 2000; Wald, 2005). Despite the limitations and difficulties in analyzing the results produced by fMRI, significant improvements in brain mapping, imaging power, and resolution (there are now 3T, 4T, and 7 T scanners being used to gain improved imaging resolution) have indicated that at least some of these shortcoming may be reduced with the next generation of equipment.

Policy Implications

An example of how neuroeconomics could be applied to an important research area deals with the question of consumption addiction. This is especially true in developing effective marketing communications for vulnerable consumers such as children and adolescents. Pechmann, Levine, Loughlin, and Leslie (2005) presented evidence from the addiction and neuroscience literature that adolescents were more vulnerable to advertising and promotions due to the unique structure of their neural development. This may indicate that the decision-making process for adolescents is significantly different from that of children and adults. While there has been evidence from empirical social psychology studies to support this assertion, increasing evidence based on neuroimaging studies has been developed by researchers from psychology, neuroscience, and medicine (Pechmann & Pirouz, 2007). This important development could offer a strong basis for research that seeks to investigate how and why adolescents respond to marketing communications and advertising differently. Furthermore, research could begin to develop ways to protect vulnerable adolescents from detrimental product categories such as cigarettes and alcohol, while enhancing the relevance and efficacy of marketing, such as health messages, targeted toward adolescents. In this way, neuroeconomics methods can offer researchers a valuable suite of methods that will allow a more refined and revealing understanding of the neural basis of choice for adolescents—a developmentally unique segment of the population.

Future Directions

A diverse array of questions can be addressed using neuroeconomic techniques and methods. Neuroeconomics could serve as an important new area for tackling many of the fundamental questions about decision making that have been difficult to explain theoretically. Neuroeconomics offers the potential for insights into the neurological processes that underlie human behavior. Using experimental methodologies combined with imaging and other neuroscience tools, neuroeconomics can better help us understand the mechanisms of decision making, including preference, risk behavior, valuation, biases, and conflict. While neuroeconomics as a field of study is in a relatively early phase, a growing number of researchers are establishing new theoretical constructs that could potentially inform economics, behavioral decision theory, management, marketing, and psychology.

Within neuroeconomics, a number of intriguing areas of research have not yet been fully explored and could prove of further interest. Such future areas of research might include the following:

- How do neural systems work together to create decision-making behavior?
- How does decision making vary for vulnerable populations such as adolescents or the elderly?
- What factors influence the development of addictive behavior, and what factors could act to discontinue these addictions?
- How can an understanding of the neural systems underlying decision making help people to make better decisions in their lives?

Conclusion

While the application of neuroscientific methods to economics and other related fields may cause continuing controversy and debate among scientists and the public, the results gleaned thus far from neuroeconomic research have revealed valuable insights into the neural substrates that affect human and animal decision making. It seems reasonable to think that these insights may allow for new, more revealing models of decision making that will take into account the underlying neurological mechanisms that drive behavior, emotion, and choice.

References and Further Readings

Adolphs, R. (2003). Cognitive neuroscience of human social behaviour. *Neuroscience, 4,* 165–178.

Anderson, S. W., Damasio, A. R., & Damasio, H. (2005). A neural basis for collecting behaviour in humans. *Brain, 128,* 201–212.

Bechara, A., Damasio, A. R., Damasio, H., & Tranel, D. (1997). Deciding advantageously before knowing the advantageous strategy. *Science, 275,* 1293–1295.

Benartzi, S., & Thaler, R. (1995). Myopic loss aversion and the equity premium puzzle. *Quarterly Journal of Economics, 110,* 73–92.

Bernheim, B. D., & Rangel, A. (2002a). *Addiction and cue-conditioned cognitive processes.* Cambridge, MA: National Bureau of Economic Research Program on Public Economics.

Bernheim, B. D., & Rangel, A. (2002b). *Addiction, cognition and the visceral brain.* Cambridge, MA: National Bureau of Economic Research Program on Public Economics.

Breiter, H. C., Aharon, I., Kahneman, D., Dale, A. M., & Schizgal, P. (2001). Functional imaging of neural responses to expectancy and experience of monetary gains and losses. *Neuron, 30,* 619–639.

Brosnan, S. F., & de Waal, F. B. M. (2003). Monkeys reject unequal pay. *Nature, 425,* 297–299.

Camerer, C. F., Loewenstein, G., & Prelec, D. (2005). Neuroeconomics: How neuroscience can inform economics. *Journal of Economic Literature, 43,* 9–64.

Carter, B. L., & Tiffany, S. T. (1999). Meta-analysis of cue-reactivity in addiction research. *Addiction, 94,* 327–340.

Damasio, A. (1994). *Descartes' error: Emotion, reason, and the human brain.* New York: HarperCollins.

de Quervain, D. J.-F., Fischbacher, U., Treyer, V., Schellhammer, M., Schnyder, U., Buck, A., et al. (2004). The neural basis of altruistic punishment. *Science, 305,* 1254–1258.

Elliott, R., Newman, J. L., Longe, O. A., & Deakin, J. F. W. (2003). Differential response patterns in the striatum and orbitofrontal cortex to financial reward in humans: A parametric functional magnetic resonance imaging study. *Journal of Neuroscience, 23,* 303–307.

Fiorillo, C. D., Tobler, P. N., & Schultz, W. (2003). Discrete coding of reward probability and uncertainty by dopamine neurons. *Science, 299,* 1898–1902.

Frackowiak, R. S. J., Friston, K. J., Frith, C. D., Dolan, R. J., Price, C. J., Zeki, S., et al. (2004). *Human brain function* (2nd ed.). San Diego: Elsevier Academic Press.

Frost, R. O., & Hartl, T. L. (1996). A cognitive-behavioral model of compulsive hoarding. *Behaviour Research and Therapy, 34,* 341–350.

Gazzaniga, M. (2002). *Cognitive neuroscience.* New York: W. W. Norton.

Glimcher, P. W. (2003). *Decisions, uncertainty and the brain.* Cambridge: MIT Press.

Glimcher, P. W., & Rustichini, A. (2004). Neuroeconomics: The consilience of brain and decision. *Science, 306,* 447–452.

Gold, J. I. (2003). Linking reward expectation to behavior in the basal ganglia. *Trends in Neurosciences, 26*(1), 12.

Hoebel, B. G., Rada, P., Mark, G. P., & Pothos, E. N. (1999). Neural systems for reinforcement and inhibition of behavior: Relevance to eating, addiction and depression. In D. Kahneman & N. Schwarz (Eds.), *Well-being: The foundations of hedonic psychology.* New York: Russell Sage.

Huang, G. T. (2005, May). The economics of brains. *Technology Review,* p. 74.

Kagel, J. H., Battalio, R., & Green, L. (1995). *Economic choice theory: An experimental analysis of animal behavior.* New York: Cambridge University Press.

Kahneman, D., & Tversky, A. (1979). Prospect theory: An analysis of decision under risk. *Econometrica, 47,* 263–292.

Kahneman, D., & Tversky, A. (1982). Judgement under uncertainty: Heuristics and biases. In D. Kahneman, P. Slovic, & A. Tversky (Eds.), *Judgment under uncertainty: Heuristics and biases.* Cambridge, UK: Cambridge University Press.

Krolak-Salmon, P., Henaff, M.-A., Isnard, J., Tallon-Baudry, C., Geunot, M., Vighetto, A., et al. (2002). An attention modulated response to disgust in human ventral anterior insula. *Annals of Neurology, 53,* 446–453.

Laibson, D. I. (2001). A cue theory of consumption. *Quarterly Journal of Economics, 116,* 81–120.

Liu, Z., Murray, E. A., & Richmond, B. J. (2000). Learning motivational significance of visual cues for reward schedules requires rhinal cortex. *Nature Neuroscience, 3,* 1307–1315.

Liu, Z., & Richmond, B. J. (2000). Response differences in monkey TE and perirhinal cortex: Stimulus association related to reward schedules. *Journal of Neurophysiology, 83,* 1677–1692.

Loewenstein, G., Rick, S., & Cohen, J. D. (2008). Neuroeconomics. *Annual Review of Psychology, 59,* 647–672.

McCabe, K. (2003). A cognitive theory of reciprocal exchange. In E. Ostrom & J. Walker (Eds.), *Trust and reciprocity: Interdisciplinary lessons from experimental psychology.* New York: Russell Sage.

McCabe, K., Houser, D., Ryan, L., Smith, V., & Trouard, T. (2001). A functional imaging study of cooperation in two-person reciprocal exchange. *Proceedings of the National Academy of Sciences USA, 98,* 11832–11835.

McClure, S. M., Laibson, D. I., Loewenstein, G., & Cohen, J. D. (2004). Separate neural systems value immediate and delayed monetary rewards. *Science, 306,* 503–507.

Montague, P. R., & Berns, G. S. (2002). Neural economics and the biological substrates of valuation. *Neuron, 36,* 265–284.

Pechmann, C., Levine, L. J., Loughlin, S., & Leslie, F. (2005, Fall). Self-conscious and impulsive: Adolescents' vulnerability to advertising and promotions. *Journal of Public Policy & Marketing,* pp. 202–221.

Pechmann, C., & Pirouz, D. (2007, June). *The dark side of attachment: Addiction.* Paper presented at Advertising and Consumer Psychology 2007: New Frontiers in Branding: Attitudes, Attachments, and Relationships, Santa Monica, CA.

Platt, M. L., & Glimcher, P. W. (1999). Neural correlates of decision variables in parietal cortex. *Nature, 400,* 233–238.

Powell, K. (2003). Economy of the mind. *PLoS Biology, 1,* 312–315.

Sanfey, A. G., Rilling, J. K., Aronson, J. A., Nystrom, L. E., & Cohen, J. D. (2003). The neural basis of economic decision-making in the ultimatum game. *Science, 300,* 1755–1758.

Savoy, R. (1998). *Introduction to designing fMRI-based experiments.* Boston: Massachusetts General Hospital, Martinos Center for Biomedical Imaging.

Savoy, R. (1999). Magnetic resonance imaging (MRI). In G. Adelman & B. H. Smith (Eds.), *Encyclopedia of neuroscience* (2nd ed.). Boston: Elsevier.

Savoy, R., Ravicz, M. E., & Gollub, R. (2000). The psychophysiological laboratory in the magnet: Stimulus delivery, response recording, and safety. In C. T. W. Moonen & P. A. Bandettini (Eds.), *Functional MRI.* Berlin: Springer.

Schultz, W. (1998). Predictive reward signal of dopamine neurons. *Journal of Neurophysiology, 80,* 1–27.

Schultz, W., Dayan, P., & Montague, P. R. (1997). A neural substrate of prediction and reward. *Science, 275,* 1593–1599.

Shiv, B., Loewenstein, G., Bechara, A., Damasio, A., & Damasio, H. (2005). Investment behavior and the negative side of emotion. *Psychological Science, 16,* 435–439.

Smith, J. P. (1990). *Mammalian behavior: The theory and the science.* Tuckahoe, NY: Bench Mark Books.

Smith, K., Dickhaut, J., McCabe, K., & Pardo, J. V. (2002). Neuronal substrates for choice under ambiguity, risk, gains, and losses. *Management Science, 48,* 711–718.

Sugrue, L. P., Corrago, G. S., & Newsome, W. T. (2004). Matching behavior and the representation of value in the parietal cortex. *Science, 304,* 1782–1787.

Tapert, S. F., Cheung, E. H., Brown, G. G., Lawrence, F. R., Paulus, M. P., Schweinsburg, A. D., et al. (2003). Neural response to alcohol stimuli in adolescents with alcohol use disorder. *Archives of General Psychiatry, 60,* 727–735.

Wald, L. (2005). Physics of NMR, MRI, functional MRI, and safety. In *Functional MRI visiting fellowship: A short course in fMRI.* Boston: Massachusetts General Hospital, Martinos Center for Biomedical Imaging.

Wright, P., He, G., Shapira, N. A., Goodman, W. K., & Liu, Y. (2004). Disgust and the insula: fMRI responses to pictures of mutilation and contamination. *NeuroReport, 15,* 2347–2351.

Zak, P. J. (2004). Neuroeconomics. *Philosophical Transactions of The Royal Society, 359,* 1737–1748.

Zak, P. J., Borja, K., Matzner, W. T., & Kurzban, R. (2005). The neuroeconomics of distrust: Sex differences in behavior and physiology. *Cognitive Neuroscience Foundations of Behavior, 95,* 360–363.

Zak, P. J., Kurzban, R., & Matzner, W. T. (2004). The neurobiology of trust. *Annals of the New York Academy of Sciences, 1032,* 224–227.

90

EVOLUTIONARY ECONOMICS

CLIFFORD S. POIROT JR.

Shawnee State University

Evolutionary economics has gained increasing acceptance as a field of economics that focuses on change over time in the process of material provisioning (production, distribution, and consumption) and the social institutions that surround that process. It is closely related to, and often draws on research in, other disciplines such as economic sociology, economic anthropology, and international political economy. It has important implications for many other fields in economics, including, but not limited to, growth theory, economic development, economic history, political economy, history of thought, gender economics, industrial organization, the study of business cycles, and financial crises.

Historically, evolutionary economics was the province of critics of the mainstream, neoclassical tradition. Both Marxist and original institutional economists (OIE) have long asserted the importance and relevance of understanding change over time and critiqued the standard competitive model for its abstract, ahistorical, and static focus. In recent years, however, the rise of the new institutional economics (NIE) as well as game theory has resulted in wider acceptance of evolutionary explanations by the mainstream (Hodgson, 2007b, pp. 1–15; North, 1990). Consequently, it is now possible to identify three major traditions in evolutionary economics: the Marxist (Sherman, 2006), the OIE (Hodgson, 2004), and the NIE (North, 1990). Each of these major traditions encompasses multiple strands within it. As a general rule, Marxists and OIEs seek to replace the standard competitive model of mainstream economics, while NIEs seek to complement the standard competitive model, although the growing acceptance of game theory may make this less of an important distinction. Despite their differences, it is possible to identify some common themes that are shared by each of these disparate traditions. For example, authors in each tradition have exhibited a concern with how the interaction of technology, social institutions, and ideologies leads to changes in economic and social organization over time.

The goal of this chapter is to introduce the reader to a few of the major concerns, themes, and important authors of each respective tradition. In doing so, it will first address some general issues in evolutionary economics, including its relationship to evolutionary biology as well as some conceptual, definitional, and taxonomic issues. It will then proceed to provide a brief overview of the evolution of each respective tradition. Unfortunately, the length of this entry precludes discussion of many worthy contributions to each tradition as well as important topics that can and should be addressed by evolutionary economics. For example, space does not permit a discussion of how evolutionary economics could be applied to gender economics or how economists who write on gender often incorporate the contributions of evolutionary economists. Nor will this entry attempt to assess the extent of empirical or conceptual progress in evolutionary economics within or between respective traditions. In addition, the reader should be aware that evolutionary economics itself is an evolving field and that the boundaries between the three traditions are often fluid.

General Issues

Relationship Between Theories of Biological and Sociocultural Evolution

Taken at face value, the word *evolution* simply means change. But Darwin's theory of gradual (step-by-step) evolution by variation of inherited characteristics and natural selection (differential survival based on the level of adaptation) removed both theological and teleological explanations from the process of biological evolution and placed humans firmly in the natural world. The modern neo-Darwinian synthetic theory of evolution combines Darwin's focus on gradual (step-by-step) change based on variation of inherited characteristics and natural selection with modern population genetics. Both Darwin's original theory and the modern synthetic theory of evolution explain change within a species, the rise of new species, and the more dramatic kinds of change such as the rise of mammals, primates, and eventually human beings as a result of the same step-by-step process (Mayr, 2001, 2004).

At the risk of oversimplifying slightly, it should be noted that the neo-Darwinian synthesis formulated by Thedosius Dobzhansky and Ernst Mayr in the 1950s has given rise to two sometimes opposing strands within the overarching frame of the synthesis (Mayr, 2004, pp. 133–138). One strand, exemplified by Richard Dawkins, who has written many widely read books on evolution, focuses on the role of genes in building organisms and on the tendency of natural selection to result in highly adapted organisms. This approach is sometimes referred to as the strong adaptationist program in evolutionary biology. It is closely related to fields such as sociobiology and evolutionary psychology, which explain many human behaviors in terms of their evolutionary origins.

Other evolutionary biologists have de-emphasized the role of natural selection and emphasize the importance of understanding biological evolution in terms of emergence, chance, path dependence, satisficing, and punctuated equilibrium. Richard Lewontin and the late Stephen J. Gould are two widely read authors who have advocated this position. Both Gould and Lewontin have been strongly critical of biologically based explanations for human behavior.

Although these two differing approaches to evolution are sometime viewed as rivals, they are in actuality complementary to each other. It is important to understand both aspects of biological evolution. In addition, biological evolution is a very complex process, and evolutionary biologists continue to push their field forward. Contemporary research in evolutionary biology focuses on the important interactions between genes, organisms, and their interaction with the environment in the process of development. Evolutionary biologists have also become more aware of the importance of lateral gene transfer and endo-symbiosis in bacteria evolution. However, there is still widespread consensus among evolutionary biologists that the synthetic theory of evolution is a true theory. Evolutionary biologists reject theories that incorporate teleological explanations or inheritance of acquired characteristics because these theories have been discredited empirically. Evolutionary biologists reject theories that are premised on or seek to find evidence of supernatural design as this adds nothing to the explanation and draws the focus of science away from understanding and explaining natural law.

Evolutionary economists often draw on and incorporate concepts developed by evolutionary biologists to explain how economic evolution occurs. For example, many evolutionary economists view economic evolution as a nondirected step-by-step process that is non-teleological (it lacks a specific goal or predetermined endpoint). Many, although not necessarily all, evolutionary economists agree that humans have at least some genetically based cognitive and social predispositions that are a result of genetic evolution. Some examples include the ability to learn a language, to learn social norms, to cooperate in groups, and to develop complex tool kits with which to transform nature into useable goods and services. In addition, the use of the Darwinian concepts of inheritance, variation, and selection as analogs to explain outcomes is pervasive in evolutionary economics. Evolutionary economists also distinguish between specific or microevolution (change that occurs within a sociocultural system) and general or macroevolution (change from one sociocultural system to another).

Some evolutionary economists view the market as natural and as an extended phenotype. Other evolutionary economists argue that evolutionary economics should be viewed as a generalization of the Darwinian concepts of variation, inheritance, and natural selection with each case specifying additional, relevant detail (Hodgson, 2007a; Hodgson & Knudsen, 2006). Others have argued that while Darwinian concepts often provide useful analogies for understanding sociocultural evolution, aspects of sociocultural evolution are distinctly non-Darwinian (Poirot, 2007). For example, in at least some instances, social and economic evolution results from the conscious decisions of groups of purposive agents who intentionally design or redesign human institutions. Also, in the process of sociocultural evolution, we can pass on cultural traits that we acquire through the process of learning. Biological evolution results in a branching pattern and barriers between different species. But human cultures can always learn from each other. The more emphasis that is placed on purposive design of social institutions and cultural learning as well as the abruptness (instead of the step-by-step nature) of social change, the less Darwinian a model of sociocultural evolution becomes. However, it would be difficult to identify anyone today who argued for a strong teleological concept of sociocultural evolution or who sought to explain sociocultural evolution in terms of divine or supernatural intervention.

Two other important concepts borrowed from the natural sciences, emergence and complexity, also play a key role in evolutionary economics. Emergence means that an observed system results from the complex interaction of the components of the subsystems. This process of interaction gives rise to patterns that would not be predicted from and cannot be reduced to the behaviors of the individual components. However, understanding the system still requires an understanding of its components and the interaction of the components. So it is important to understand what individuals do. And it is also important to understand how individual choices and habits interact with social institutions in a dynamic way. It is often easier to think in mechanical terms. But if we are careless with mechanical analogies, then we can be easily misled.

This raises the question of what it is that evolves in sociocultural evolution. In evolutionary biology, selection takes place at multiple levels but logically requires changes in the gene pool of a population over time (Mayr, 2004, pp. 133–158). This has led some evolutionary economists to suggest that institutions and/or organizational routines provide us with an analog to the gene. Others argue that there is not a precise analog. To understand this debate, we first have to understand what an institution is.

It is popular to define institutions as "rules of the game." This is a good start, but it confuses the function of institutions with a definition of institutions. A more extensive definition of *institution* defines an institution as any instituted process, or in other words a shared, learned, ordered, patterned, and ongoing way of thinking, feeling, and acting. Institutions may be tacit and informal or highly organized and structured. By this latter definition, modern firms, medieval manors, technology, nation-states, political ideologies, and even technology are all institutions. In other words, virtually everything that humans do is an instituted process. Institutions are component parts of a sociocultural system.

But to just call everything an "institution" can make it difficult to conduct analysis. So it is useful to draw a distinction between entities such as social ideologies (e.g., Calvinism and democracy), social institutions (e.g., class, caste, kinship, the family, the nation-state), organizations (e.g., the modern firm, the International Monetary Fund, the medieval manor), organizational routines of actors within specific organizations, and technology (the combined set of knowledge, practices, and tool kits used in production). So in that sense, everything in sociocultural systems is constantly evolving. There is no precise analog in sociocultural evolution to the gene pool of a population.

As suggested above, social institutions are part of more general wholes, which it is convenient to term *sociocultural systems.* A sociocultural system includes the direct patterns of interaction of a society with the ecosystem (its subsistence strategy, technology, and demographic patterns), its social institutions, and its patterns of abstract meaning and value. Many anthropologists classify sociocultural systems by their scale, complexity, and the amount of energy captured by their subsistence strategy. Standard classification includes bands, tribes, chiefdoms, agrarian states, and industrial states, each of which corresponds roughly to subsistence strategies of foraging, horticulture, pastoralism and fishing, settled agriculture, and modern industrial technology. This classification system provides a useful scheme with which to understand the rise of large agrarian empires in the neolithic era and, ultimately, the Industrial Revolution in northwestern Europe. It also provides a useful classificatory schema with which to

understand the interaction of multiple kinds of contemporary societies in a globalizing world. However, care must be taken to emphasize the multilinear and dynamic nature of sociocultural evolution rather than rigidly applying these concepts as a universal and unilinear schema (e.g., see Harris, 1997; Wolf, 1982).

The Scope and Methods of Evolutionary Economics

The evolutionary biologist Ernst Mayr (2004) argued that biologists who study genetic evolution ask "why" questions while biologists who study things such as biochemistry ask "how" questions. Similarly, many mainstream economists ask "how" questions while evolutionary economists ask "why" questions. While the study of evolutionary economics does not preclude the use of formal mathematical models or quantification, most of its practitioners employ qualitative and interpretive methods. Also, as suggested above, some evolutionary biologists focus on changes that occur at the level of species, while others focus on more dramatic kinds of change. Similarly, evolutionary economists are interested in the study of sociocultural evolution on a grand scale, such as the rise of agrarian empires or modern capitalism, as well more specific, micro-level evolution such as changes in the organizational routines of individual firms.

Consequently, the kinds of issues that evolutionary economists are interested in overlap with the focus of other social sciences and even, in some instances, with the fields of ecology and evolutionary biology. Evolutionary economics reflects a tendency to counter the fragmentation of political economy into disparate social sciences that occurred in the late nineteenth and early twentieth centuries. Evolutionary economists, like their counterparts in economic sociology, economic anthropology, and political economy, focus more directly on those institutions with the strongest, most immediate, direct relevance to the process of material provisioning. So there may still be a need for some division of labor in the social sciences. What is of direct relevance will vary according to what is being analyzed in any particular study. An economic historian studying the rise of capitalism may, following Weber, find an understanding of Calvinist theology to be essential. Someone studying financial innovation in twenty-first-century industrialized societies would most likely find the religious affiliation of modern banking executives to be of little interest or relevance.

Research Traditions in Evolutionary Economics

Evolutionary economics is composed of three rival but sometimes overlapping major traditions: the Marxist, the OIE, and the NIE. While there is some degree of ideological overlap between the schools, each of the respective schools tends to share a common overarching ideology. Marxists seek to replace capitalism, OIEs seek to reform capitalism, and NIEs generally view capitalism as beneficent. This is not, notably, to argue that the ideology necessarily *determines* the empirical and theoretical analysis. Also, as previously noted, Marxists and OIEs seek to replace the standard competitive model while NIEs seek to complement the standard model. However, the reader should be aware that the boundary between the three traditions is often fuzzy, and there is sometimes overlap between the three traditions. Similarly, each of these three schools is composed of multiple strands and has undergone significant change over time.

The remainder of this entry will focus on outlining in very broad terms a few of the significant themes and concerns of each respective tradition, how these traditions have changed over time, and the contributions of a few representative authors of each of the three traditions. The reader may note that despite the differences between the traditions, there is a strong interest in all three in understanding how technology, social institutions, and cognitive models interact in the process of sociocultural evolution. The division made between the three traditions may be of greater interest and relevance in the United States, where there is a strong correlation between specific organizations and schools of thought. For example, the Association for Evolutionary Economics (AFEE) has been the primary promoter of OIE in the United States. In contrast, the European Association for Evolutionary Political Economy (EAEPE) has a much wider umbrella. So there may be hope someday for a grand synthesis of the three respective traditions.

Marxist Models of Evolution

There are, of course, many different Marxist and quasi-Marxist models of sociocultural evolution. For the purposes of this entry, it is convenient to make the *differentia specifica* of a Marxist model of sociocultural evolution a focus on class struggle: the conflict between social groups defined in terms of differential access to the productive resources of a given society (Dugger & Sherman, 2000). This way of understanding sociocultural evolution is often referred to as historical materialism. While Darwinian reasoning may at times be employed in Marxist theories of sociocultural evolution, Marxists have generally emphasized the non-Darwinian aspects of sociocultural evolution as well as sharp discontinuities between human and infrahuman species. At the same time, it is hard to think of any academic Marxists writing today who would advocate Lysenkoism or Lamarckian theories of inheritance as valid explanatory concepts for understanding genetic evolution.

To understand historical materialism, we must begin with Marx's concept of the mode of production (for extended discussions, see Wolf, 1982, chap. 3, and also Fusfeld, 1977). A mode of production includes the techno-environmental relationships (e.g., agriculture based on a plough or factories using steam engines) and the social relationships of production (e.g., warlords and peasants or factory owners and workers) or, in Marxist jargon, the forces of production and the social relations of production, respectively. These relationships between groups of people in Marx's view are characterized by unequal relations of power, domination, subordination, and exploitation. This gives rise to social conflict over the terms of access to and the distribution of the productive resources of society. Social conflict requires the creation of a coercive entity to enforce the interests of the dominant social class (i.e., a state). In addition, human beings develop complex ideologies with which to justify their positions. Thus, the entire civilization (or what above is termed a *sociocultural system*) rests on a given mode of production, with the mode of production distinguished by the primary means of mobilizing labor (e.g., slavery, serfdom, wage labor).

In his analysis of Western history, Marx distinguished between the primitive commune, the slave mode of production of the ancient Roman Empire, the Germanic mode of production, the feudal mode of production of medieval Europe, and the modern capitalist mode of production. In analyzing Western history, Marx argued that each successive mode of production had produced technological advance, thus elevating the material level of human existence.

Capitalism, in Marx's view, is qualitatively different from extended commodity production. Capitalism requires that land, labor, and capital are fully treated as commodities. This means that labor is "free" in the sense of not being legally bound to perform labor for the dominant class and "free" in the sense that it has no claim to the resources needed to produce goods and services. Therefore, capital is used as a means to finance innovation in production, and labor is compelled by economic circumstances to sell its labor power. Because capitalism promotes endless accumulation of capital, it is thus far the most successful in a material sense. However, the dynamic of capitalist accumulation gives rise to periodic crises, and it is therefore unstable. In addition, it is often destructive of human relationships. So a relationship of apparent freedom is in actuality a relationship of power, subordination, and domination that will give rise to social conflict. The only way to end this conflict, in Marx's view, is to redesign social institutions so as to promote both development of the forces of production and social cooperation (i.e., replace capitalism with socialism). There is disagreement among scholars who study Marx as to whether Marx thought that the triumph of socialism over capitalism was inevitable.

Insofar as one seeks to explain the historical origins of capitalism and the Industrial Revolution, two historical epochs are of particular relevance. Marxist historians and Marxist economists (and many others) with a particular interest in economic history thus often refer to two transitions (one from antiquity to feudalism and the other from feudalism to capitalism) as giving rise to modern capitalism. Howard Sherman (1995, 2006), a well-known Marxist economist, has summarized and synthesized much of this existing literature.

Sherman traces Western economic history from tribal organization through the rise of modern capitalism. Sherman is a materialist who analyzes societies by starting with the material base of human existence and examines the interaction between technology, economic institutions, social institutions, and ideologies. Technology and technological innovation as well as social conflict between classes are key variables in Sherman's analysis. But overall, Sherman's schema is holistic and interactive, rather than mechanical or reductionist.

In analyzing the breakdown of feudalism, Sherman focuses on the tripartite class conflict between peasants, nobles, and monarchs and the ability of each of the respective classes to force an outcome on the other classes. As a consequence of this conflict, a new pattern of relationships based on private property and production for profit in a market, as well as increasingly organized around new sources of mechanical power, gave rise to a unique and extremely productive system referred to as capitalism. This system of production encourages constant cost cutting, innovation, and capital accumulation, thus leading to the potential for the progressive material elevation of human society.

However, capitalist society is still riven by conflict between property-less workers and property-owning capitalists. Because the capitalist has a monopoly over the productive resources of society, the capitalist is still able to compel the worker to produce a surplus for the capitalist. This creates social conflict between the capitalist and worker and also forces the capitalist into an ultimately self-defeating boom-and-bust cycle of rising profits and increasing concentrations of capital, followed by falling rates of profit, leading to cycles of recession and crisis. The institutional structure of capitalism also magnifies other social conflicts and problems such as environmental degradation and destruction, as well as relations between racial and ethnic groups and genders. The solution to this social conflict, in Sherman's view, is to replace the institutions of capitalism with economic democracy (i.e., democratic socialism).

Sherman, who has long been a critic of Stalinist-style socialism, also extends his analysis to change in Russia and the Soviet Union. The October Revolution of 1917 occurred because neither the czar nor the Mensheviks were able to satisfy the material aspirations of the vast majority of Russians. But industrialization in the Soviet Union became a nondemocratic, elite-directed process due primarily to the particular circumstances surrounding the Bolshevik Revolution, the ensuing civil war, and the problems of the New Economic Policy. In time, factions among the elites developed as the Soviet economy proved unable to satisfy the material aspirations of the majority of the Soviet population. This created new pressure for change as elites were able to capture this process. Due also to pressure from the West, change in the former Soviet Union took the direction of restoring capitalism rather than developing greater economic democracy.

It should be noted that the standard Marxist model of historical materialism focuses on the ability of capitalism to elevate the material *capacity* of human societies. This focus has been challenged by the rise of world systems and dependency theory. Theorists who follow this line of thinking focus on the uneven nature of development and the tendency of core economies to place boundaries on the development of formerly colonized areas of the world. Some theorists in this tradition have been justly accused of having a rather muddled conception of the term *capitalism,* insofar as they claim inspiration from Marx. The late Eric Wolf (1982), a well-known economic anthropologist, resolved many of these conceptual issues in his book *Europe and the People Without History.* So rather than assume that capitalism leads uniformly to material progress, Wolf extended the historical materialist model to analyze the process of uneven development in the world system as a whole. In their textbook on economic development, James Cypher and James Dietz (2004) provide an excellent history and exposition of classical Marxism, dependency theory, and extended analysis and discussion of the new institutional economics, original institutional economics, and modernization theory.

Original Institutional Economics

Thorstein Veblen (1898) was the founder of OIE, and his influence on OIE continues to be prevalent (Hodgson, 2004). Veblen was strongly influenced by Darwin's theory of biological evolution and held evolutionary science as the standard for the social sciences, including economics, to emulate. He was also deeply influenced by the evolutionary epistemology of the American pragmatists Charles Saunders Peirce and John Dewey. In addition, he incorporated the contrasting positions of nineteenth-century evolutionist anthropology, as exhibited by the work of Tylor and Morgan, and the historical particularism of Franz Boas. Although he was strongly critical of Marx and of Marxism, there are both parallels as well as differences in the writings of Marx and Veblen.

Like Marx, Veblen focused on the importance of understanding the interaction of changes in technology, social institutions, and social ideologies as well as social conflict. Veblen also had a stage theory of history, which he borrowed from the prevailing anthropological schemas of his day. However, where Marx focuses on concepts such as class and mode of production, Veblen focuses on instituted processes and the conflicts created by vested interests seeking to reinforce invidious distinctions. Veblen's model of sociocultural evolution is a conflict model in that it focuses broadly on social conflict that arises in the struggle for access to power, prestige, and property. But it is not a class-based model in the sense that Marxists use class.

In "Why Is Economics Not an Evolutionary Science?" (1898) and in "The Preconceptions of Economic Science" (1899), Veblen developed a critique of the mainstream economics of his day. In developing this critique, Veblen was critical of the abstract and a priori nature of much of mainstream economic analysis. In articulating this point, he contrasted the "a priori method" with the "matter of fact method." This particular aspect of Veblen's criticism has often led some to view both Veblen and later OIEs as "atheoretical." But this misses the point for at least two reasons.

Veblen did not eschew theoretical analysis per se. He was however, critical of theory that divorced itself from understanding actual, real-world processes of material provisioning. But most important, in Veblen's view, economics was not up to the standards of evolutionary science because economics continued to implicitly embrace the concepts of natural price and natural law by focusing on economics as the study of economizing behavior and the adjustment of markets to equilibrium. In contrast, Veblen argued that the process of material provisioning entailed a constant process of adaptation to the physical and social environment through the adjustment of institutions or deeply ingrained social habits based on instinct. Veblen's understanding of the term *institution* was broad enough to encompass any instituted process. Yet he drew a sharp distinction between institutions and technology. He was sharply critical of the former and strongly in favor of the latter.

When Veblen wrote about deep-seated and persistent social habits developing on the basis of genetically based instincts, he did in fact appear to mean something similar to contemporary theories of gene-culture evolution. Social habits are not consciously thought-through, purposive behaviors—they develop out of the complex "reflex arc" of enculturation based on genetically based propensities to act in the presence of environmental stimuli. Instincts are acquired through genetic evolution and social habits through enculturation. Both are inherited, vary in nature, and may therefore be selected for or against in the process of sociocultural evolution (Hodgson, 2004, Part III). However, Veblen also borrowed from Dewey a view of socialization in which individuals are active participants in socialization, a concept that was later more clearly articulated by Meade. In addition, Veblen also emphasized the ability of humans to conceptualize and engage in purposive behavior.

Veblen drew a sharp dichotomy between the instinct of workmanship and the instinct of predation. He associated the instinct of workmanship with a focus on adaptive, problem-solving, tinkering, and innovative behavior. In contrast, he associated predation with a focus on brute force, ceremonial displays of power, emulative behavior, conspicuous consumption, financial speculation, and the power of vested interests. Veblen argued that the instinct of workmanship arose in the primitive stage of human history (roughly corresponding to what contemporary anthropologists would term *bands* and *tribes*) and that the instinct of predation emerged during the stage of barbarism (roughly corresponding to the rise of chiefdoms). These instincts gave rise to deep-seated social habits. Both instincts continued to be present during the rise of civilization (agrarian states) and persisted in modern civilization (industrial states). But because modern civilization is based on the rise

and extensive application of machine technology, further progress would require the triumph of the instinct of workmanship over the instinct of predation.

But in Veblen's view, there was no reason to expect this would necessarily occur. Vested interests were often capable of instituting their power to reinforce the instinct of predation. Hence, institutions often served to encapsulate and reinforce the instinct of predation. The behaviors of predation were primarily exhibited by the new "leisure class" or, in other words, the robber barons of the late nineteenth century. In contrast, workmen and engineers often exhibited the instinct of workmanship. Consequently, Veblen tended to view institutions in general as change inhibiting and the instinct of workmanship as change promoting.

In later works, Veblen extended this kind of analysis to study other topics such as changes in firm organization and the business cycle. Veblen argued that as modern firms became larger and more monopolistic, a permanent leisure class arose, thus displacing technological thinking among this new class. In addition, increasing amounts of time and energy were channeled into financial speculation, leading to repeated financial crises. Emulative behavior in the form of conspicuous consumption and ceremonial displays of patriotism and militarism served to reinforce the instinct of predation. In his analysis of the rise of militarism in Prussia, Veblen noted the socially devastating impact of the triumph of the instinct of predation. Thus, Veblen tended to identify institutions with imbecilic behaviors that serve to block the triumph of technological innovations.

Veblen's focus on the conflict between the instinct of workmanship and predatory and pecuniary instincts is often referred to as the instrumental-ceremonial dichotomy. Ayres (1938) in particular reinforced the tendency of the OIE to focus on the past binding and ceremonial aspects of institutions and on the scientific and progressive nature of instrumental reasoning. This dichotomy was, at one point in time, a core proposition of the OIE.

Most contemporary OIEs, however, recognize and accept that at least some institutions can promote and facilitate progressive change and that technology itself is an institution. This rethinking of the ceremonial-instrumental dichotomy is also reflected in the incorporation of Karl Polanyi's (1944) dichotomy between habitation and improvement. Polanyi noted that the need for social protection may actually serve a noninvidious purpose. Some improvements destroy livelihoods and reinforce invidious distinctions while others promote the life process. So the distinction might better be thought of in terms of "invidious versus noninvidious."

One OIE who had a more positive understanding of the role of institutions is J. R. Commons (Commons, 1970; Wunder & Kemp, 2008). Commons in particular focused on the need for order in society and thus addressed the evolution of legal systems and the state. Commons's theory is primarily microevolutionary insofar as he focuses on the evolution of legal arrangements and shifting power alignments in modern industrial states. Commons is not as critical of existing arrangements as Veblen. Institutions, including the state, in Commons's view, are clearly both necessary and potentially beneficial. For example, with the rise of big business, labor conflict, and the problems inherent in the business cycle, there is a need for a strong state to manage this conflict. At the same time, Commons developed a theory of the business cycle that has strong elements in common with some of Keynes's analysis.

The Veblenian strand as expressed by Commons is, by the standards of American politics, moderately left of center in that it expresses support for much of the regulatory framework and expanded role of government in managing the business cycle that came out of the New Deal and the publication of Keynes's (1936) *The General Theory of Employment, Interest and Money*. Not surprisingly, a number of OIE economists have begun to attempt to synthesize OIE and Keynes, relying to a large degree on the work of Hyman Minsky (1982). This project, often referred to as PKI (post-Keynesian institutionalism), is microevolutionary in nature in that it focuses on the problems of financial instability created by financial innovation and deregulation. The goal of PKI is wisely managed capitalism (Whalen, 2008). PKI clearly has a focus on the possibility of designing effective institutions, which logically implies that at least some institutions can embody instrumental reasoning.

In contrast to the direction taken by some OIEs, Hodgson (2004) has argued that Veblen's focus on technological thinking and the Commons-Ayres trend in OIE was a wrong turn for OIE. He has sought to revivify OIE by reinterpreting Veblenian economics as generalized Darwinism. Generalized Darwinism, according to Hodgson, generalizes the basic principles of Darwin's biological theory of evolution (inheritance, variation, and selection) to sociocultural evolution. In Hodgson's view, the mechanisms of inheritance, variation, and selection are not just analogies or metaphors to explain outcomes in social evolution—they are ontological principles that describe any entity that evolves. As noted above, because institutions and organizational routines are inherited through cultural learning and vary, they are subject to selection. Social evolution is therefore a special case of the more general case of evolution.

However, Hodgson (2004) also acknowledges that human agents are purposive and that culture is an emergent phenomenon. So Hodgson is not seeking to biologize social inequality or to reduce the social sciences to genetic principles such as inclusive fitness. Indeed, as Hodgson states, "more is needed" than just the principles of inheritance, variation, and natural selection. This would appear to be an understanding of how social institutions, in concert with instincts and human agency, generate outcomes in a complex, emergent process of social evolution. To this end, Hodgson has incorporated some elements of structure agency theory into his analysis.

Hodgson's program could be taken as an injunction to OIEs to build models of change that incorporate both Darwinian principles as well as more complex concepts of structure and agency. Hodgson has used this model to explain how changes in firm organization can be selected

for or against by changes in market structure. So there are strong parallels between the work of Hodgson and that of Nelson and Winter (1982), who could notably be placed in either the OIE or NIE camp. As noted in the preceding section, Hodgson's view of evolutionary economics as "generalized Darwinism" is controversial, even among his fellow OIEs.

One competing strand of Veblenian economics is the radical strand as advocated by Bill Dugger (Dugger & Sherman, 2000). Dugger focuses on the role of technology, instrumental reasoning, and institutions as providing the capacity for improving the material condition of humans. The full application of instrumental reasoning, however, in Dugger's view is blocked by the key institutions of capitalism. These institutions are reinforced by ceremonial myths. Dugger also puts more emphasis on the social and ideological implications of the respective traditions and has been sharply critical of the NIE. He has also notably been instrumental in promoting dialogue between Marxists and OIEs and has often copublished works on sociocultural evolution with Howard Sherman. Dugger also tends to emphasize the non-Darwinian nature of sociocultural evolution.

The New Institutionalists

It can be fairly argued that Adam Smith was the first evolutionary economist, even though his contributions predate any significant consideration of biological evolution by naturalists. Adam Smith provides an account of how an increasingly complex society arises out of the natural propensity of humans to truck, barter, and exchange (Fusfeld, 1977; Smith, 1776/1937). Ironically, some of Smith's concerns with specialization and division of labor, as well as the writings of another political economist, Thomas Malthus, influenced Darwin. Many Social Darwinists in the late nineteenth century drew on Darwinian reasoning to explain how competitive markets work and to justify social inequality. Some twentieth-century theorists such as Frederick Hayek and Larry Arnhart have tended to view the market as a natural outgrowth of human genetic endowments.

Taken as a whole, however, evolutionary explanations fell out of favor among economists in the twentieth century. In the late nineteenth century, the social sciences became increasingly fragmented, and the new field of economics increasingly lost its evolutionary focus. With the triumph of the standard competitive model in the mid-twentieth century, economics became narrowly focused on providing formal mathematical proofs of narrowly defined "how" questions. However, there are some signs that the standard competitive model is in the process of being displaced by game theory. There is also widespread recognition that it is necessary to supplement the standard competitive model with an evolutionary account. These developments have led to an increased acceptance of evolutionary explanations among mainstream economists and renewed attention to the importance of institutions in framing economic outcomes.

Some strands of the NIE, particularly the version espoused by Coase (1974) and Williamson (1985), view institutions primarily as providing "solutions" to the problems of asymmetric information and transactions costs. This strand of NIE does not significantly challenge the standard competitive model or its underlying behavioral assumptions. To the contrary, it is a complement to the standard competitive model. It is also to a large degree a micro-oriented theory of sociocultural evolution.

A more dynamic view of economic evolution is that of Joseph Schumpeter (1908, 1950). Schumpeter focused on the individual entrepreneur and his role in promoting technological innovation. This technological innovation disturbs the equilibrium and leads to gales of creative destruction. However, with the rise of the modern, bureaucratically organized firm, the role of the entrepreneur was lessened, leading to a static and moribund organization. Schumpeter thought that this would eventually lead to the destruction of capitalism, an outcome that, in contrast to Marx, Schumpeter viewed in a negative way. Schumpeter, however, drew a strong distinction between statics, exemplified by the Walrasian model of his day, and dynamics, exemplified by theories of economic evolution. Thus, "dynamics" was intended to complement "statics" (Andersen, 2008). Many contemporary mainstream models of economic growth, often referred to as new growth theory, explicitly incorporate Schumpeterian analysis.

Some of the richness of Schumpeter's focus on technological innovation as gales of creative destruction has been recaptured by the economic historian Joel Mokyr (1990) in his masterful work on technological progress. Mokyr adapts Gould's concept of "punctuated equilibrium" to the history of technology. He also draws a distinction between invention (the rise of new techniques and processes) and innovation (the spread of these new techniques). The Industrial Revolution, in Mokyr's view, is ongoing but is nevertheless a clear instance of a dramatic change in technological and social organization. Similarly, the work of Nelson and Winter (1982), previously cited, which acknowledges the contributions of Veblen, can also be considered neo-Schumpeterian. There are, it should be noted, significant parallels between Marx, Schumpeter, and Veblen, as well as differences.

The most prominent and most successful NIE, of course, is Douglas North. North's career has spanned several decades, during which his contributions to multiple fields in economics have been voluminous. Notably, North's own views themselves have undergone significant evolution. North's (1981) earlier work on economic evolution was an application of the work of Coase (1974) and Williamson (1985) to the problem of economic evolution and did not significantly challenge the standard competitive model. North viewed economic evolution as taking place due to changing resource constraints in response to the growth in population as rational agents calculated the marginal costs and marginal benefits of shifting from foraging to farming.

North's later work (1990, 1991, 1994), however, has challenged many aspects of the standard competitive model. North has focused specifically on the role institutions play in cognitive framing of decision making. Notably, North has explicitly abandoned the theory of strong rational choice in favor of models of human behavior that focus on the limited ability of humans to obtain, process, and act on information. In most textbook models of market behavior, price is the primary means of providing information. But in North's view of markets, information encompasses much more than price. In addition, norms, values, and ideology can blunt the ability of humans to obtain and interpret some information. North is not arguing that humans are "irrational" as his approach still logically implies some degree of calculation and conscious decision making based on self-interest. But he has abandoned the strong view of rationality, which implies humans are lightning rods of hedonic calculation. In that sense, his view of human behavior is much closer to that of the Austrians in focusing on the purposiveness of human behavior.

For the most part, North tends to see institutions as constraints on human action, though he acknowledges that institutions can provide incentives both in terms of the things we actually do, as well as the things that we do not do. Thus, institutions that reward innovative behavior, risk seeking, and trade will lead to efficient outcomes. Institutions that reward rent seeking and prohibit innovation and trade will lead to inefficient outcomes. Once an institutional structure is set, there is a strong degree of inertia that perpetuates the existing institutional structure. In other words, evolutionary paths, in North's view, tend to be path dependent. Clearly, the kinds of institutions in North's view that promote efficient outcomes are those that clearly define the rules of the game in favor of the operation of markets. This does not necessarily imply laissez-faire as the state may still be necessary to perform multiple functions. It does serve to distinguish between states, such as Great Britain in the seventeenth and eighteenth centuries or South Korea in the past several decades, that were able to define an institutional framework that promoted innovation and growth as opposed to states such as Spain in the sixteenth and seventeenth centuries or in the Congo (Zaire) today that destroy any incentive for innovation and economic growth.

This raises two very interesting questions. How does a particular type of path become established, and how does it change? North's explanation is one that is rooted in a metaphor of variation and selection. Greater variation will allow for a higher probability that a particular path will be successful. Greater centralization will reduce variation and increase the chances that the state will adopt or promote institutions that blunt technological and social innovation. North explains the greater success of Europe versus the rest of the world as a result of the relative decentralization of Europe in the early modern period. Arbitrary authoritarian states that destroyed incentives for growth such as Spain existed. But Spain was unable to impose its will on Europe or on the emerging world market. Consequently, this enabled states such as England, where the power of the Crown became limited as Parliament enacted laws to protect commercial interests and innovation, to industrialize rapidly and emerge as world leaders. These contrasting paths were transferred to the New World. The United States inherited and successfully modified the institutional framework of Britain and therefore developed. Latin America inherited and failed to successfully modify the institutional framework of absolutist Spain and developed much more slowly.

Whither Evolutionary Economics?

Evolutionary economics clearly has a future. Economists in general are becoming more attuned to the importance of understanding how humans organize the economy through institutions and how institutions change over time. This entails extensive borrowing of concepts from evolutionary biology and a reconsideration of the underlying behavioral assumptions of mainstream economics. Understanding how institutions permit or inhibit changes in technology, as well as how changes in technology in turn require changes in institutions, is a concern of all three schools of evolutionary economics. As NIE economists push the boundaries of the mainstream, at least some have increasingly asked heterodox questions, and a few have been willing to acknowledge heterodox contributions. Some Marxist and OIE scholars have also begun to note that at least some versions of NIE, if not necessarily entirely new, are at least genuinely institutional and evolutionary. Any grand synthesis seems distant, but there is at least a basis for further argumentation and even dialogue.

References and Further Readings

Andersen, E. S. (2008). Appraising Schumpeter's "essence" after 100 years: From Walrasian economics to evolutionary economics. In K. K. Puranam & R. Kumar Jain B. (Eds.), *Evolutionary economics.* Hyderabad, India: ICFAI University Press.

Ayres, C. (1938). *The problem of economic order.* New York: Farrar and Rinehart.

Coase, R. H. (1974). The new institutional economics. *Journal of Institutional and Theoretical Economics, 140,* 229–231.

Commons, J. R. (1970). *The economics of collective action.* Madison: University of Wisconsin Press.

Cypher, J., & Dietz, J. (2004). *The process of economic development.* London: Routledge.

Dugger, B. (1988). Radical institutionalism: Basic concepts. *Review of Radical Political Economics, 20,* 1–20.

Dugger, B. (1995). Veblenian institutionalism. *Journal of Economic Issues, 29,* 1013–1027.

Dugger, B., & Sherman, H. (Eds.). (2000). *Reclaiming evolution: A dialogue between Marxism and institutionalism on social change.* London: Routledge.

Dugger, B., & Sherman, H. (Eds.). (2003). *Evolutionary theory in the social sciences: Vol. 1. Early foundations and later contributions.* London: Routledge.

Fusfeld, D. R. (1977). The development of economic institutions. *Journal of Economic Issues, 11,* 743–784.

Harris, M. (1997). *Culture, people, nature* (7th ed.). New York: Addison Wesley Longman.

Hodgson, G. M. (2004). *The evolution of institutional economics: Agency, structure and Darwinism in American institutionalism.* London: Routledge.

Hodgson, G. M. (Ed.). (2007a). *The evolution of economic institutions: A critical reader.* Cheltenham, UK: Edward Elgar.

Hodgson, G. M. (2007b). Introduction. In G. M. Hodgson (Ed.), *The evolution of economic institutions: A critical reader* (pp. 1–15). Cheltenham, UK: Edward Elgar.

Hodgson, G. M., & Knudsen, T. (2006). Why we need a generalized Darwinism and why a generalized Darwinism is not enough. *Journal of Economic Behavior and Organization, 61,* 1–19.

Keynes, J. M. (1936). *The general theory of employment, interest and money.* Cambridge, UK: Cambridge University Press.

Mayr, E. (2001). *What evolution is.* New York: Basic Books.

Mayr, E. (2004). *What makes biology unique?* Cambridge, UK: Cambridge University Press.

Minsky, H. (1982). *Can "it" happen again? Essays on instability and finance.* Armonk, NY: M. E. Sharpe.

Mokyr, J. (1990). *The lever of riches: Technological creativity and economic progress.* New York: Oxford University Press.

Nelson, R. R., & Winter, S. G. (1982). *An evolutionary theory of economic change.* Cambridge, MA: Harvard University Press.

North, D. (1981). *Structure and change in economic history.* New York: W. W. Norton.

North, D. (1990). *Institutions, institutional change and economic performance.* Cambridge, UK: Cambridge University Press.

North, D. (1991). Institutions. *Journal of Economic Perspectives, 5,* 97–112.

North, D. (1994). Economic performance through time. *American Economic Review, 84,* 359–367.

Poirot, C. S. (2007). How can institutional economics be an evolutionary science? *Journal of Economic Issues, 51,* 155–179.

Polanyi, K. (1944). *The great transformation.* New York: Farrar and Rinehart.

Schumpeter, J. (1908). *Das Wesen und der Haupterhault der theoretischen Nationolokonomie* [The nature and essence of theoretical economics]. Leipzig, Germany: Duncker und Humboldt.

Schumpeter, J. (1950). *Capitalism, socialism and democracy* (3rd ed.). New York: Harper.

Sherman, H. (1995). *Reinventing Marxism.* Baltimore: Johns Hopkins University Press.

Sherman, H. (2006). *How society makes itself.* New York: M. E. Sharpe.

Smith, A. (1937). *An enquiry into the nature and causes of the wealth of nations.* New York: Modern Library. (Original work published 1776)

Veblen, T. (1898). Why is economics not an evolutionary science? *Quarterly Journal of Economics, 12,* 373–397.

Veblen, T. (1899). The preconceptions of economic science. *Quarterly Journal of Economics, 13,* 121–150.

Whalen, C. J. (2008). Toward wisely managed capitalism: Post-Keynesianism and the creative state. *Forum for Social Economics, 37,* 43–60.

Williamson, O. E. (1985). *The economic institutions of capitalism.* New York: Free Press.

Wolf, E. (1982). *Europe and the people without history.* Berkeley: University of California Press.

Wunder, T., & Kemp, T. (2008). Institutionalism and the state: Founding fathers re-examined. *Forum for Social Economics, 37,* 27–42.

91

MATCHING MARKETS

THOMAS GALL

University of Bonn

A matching market assigns objects to individuals, or individuals to each other. Typically, the different objects are indivisible, and individuals differ in how much they value each of them, so that the assignment has important implications for the well-being of the individuals. Moreover, relevant applications involve markets where the use of monetary payments is limited or infeasible, such as public school choice, assignment of graduate students, or the exchange of live-donor kidneys for transplantation. In these markets, exhausting all opportunities for mutually beneficial exchange with the limited means available is important for the well-being and, in the case of the last example, the health of those involved. This chapter will demonstrate how economic theory can offer some guidance for the design of markets in order to solve such problems of assignment.

Several problems may arise in assignment problems that impede the attainment of a satisfactory outcome, where "satisfactory" could refer to Pareto efficiency or to other welfare criteria. Best understood among these problems are unraveling, strategic behavior and a failure to arrive at a stable allocation; they will be defined and discussed later in greater detail. Indeed, a growing body of economic research on market design is concerned with developing mechanisms that ensure that outcomes with desirable welfare properties are reached, while ensuring that individuals have adequate incentives to participate and to truthfully reveal their preferences over how much they value the objects to be assigned. Two such mechanisms, the Gale-Shapley mechanism and the top trading cycles mechanism, will be presented here, as well as applications to assigning students to colleges and schools and to the exchange of live-donor kidneys for transplantation.

This chapter is organized as follows. The next section gives an introduction to the theory of matching markets, discussing characteristics that typically distinguish matching from competitive markets, such as heterogeneity, indivisibility, and a lack of market prices. Then the concepts of stability, strategy-proofness, and optimality of an outcome are presented. Also, two algorithms that can be used to achieve outcomes with these properties are briefly discussed. To illustrate the practical relevance of matching markets, three applications of real-world assignment problems and the methods that have been employed to solve them are then described. A short discussion of policy considerations and a brief survey of further topics in matching market theory follow, and several areas for future research are reviewed that promise to eventually generate interesting and much-needed results. The chapter concludes with a summary. Also included is a detailed list of references for the interested reader.

Theory

The following gives a brief introduction in the theory of matching markets, with an emphasis on stable outcomes and methods to implement such outcomes, while ensuring that participants have no interest to misrepresent their preferences. This is demonstrated both in a marriage market model and a housing market setup.

Principles and Terminology

Assigning individuals to objects or, to a lesser extent, to other individuals appears to be a feature common to most markets. There are, however, some characteristics that typically differentiate matching markets from competitive markets in general. For one thing, objects and individuals in a matching market are usually heterogeneous and indivisible. This means that "goods" on a matching market (e.g., individuals) are typically supplied and demanded in quantities of 1 that cannot be further broken down. In a competitive market, a good that is demanded by many traders will be divided to satisfy the traders' demands at the market price.

Indeed, the use of the word *market* seems to imply that a market price will be used to equate demand and supply for goods or individuals. While this might often be a viable method of assignment (e.g., one used in auctions), there are a number of applications where reaching a market price might be infeasible. This is true, for example, when prices are regulated, as in the choice of public schools or of dormitories at a university where places are provided essentially for free and as in admission into certain professions with rigid wage-setting conventions. This is also true when prices and monetary payments cannot be used on ethical grounds, such as for exchanges of kidneys from live donors. Moreover, a market price may not be informative about preferences, for instance, when some participants in a matching market are subject to credit constraints, as in the cases of university choice and the job market. In an extreme case, when individuals have no access to loans but need to make a sizable investment in tuition fees or special training, personal wealth will at least partially determine individual rankings of schools or jobs. Absence or limitations of a market price and monetary payments is often referred to as a situation with *nontransferable utility*.

If a matching market is not cleared by the market price, its outcome, also referred to as the matching allocation, will depend crucially on the method used to assign individuals to objects. For instance, the order in which individuals are allowed to choose may matter, as earlier choosers have a better chance that their preferred match is still on the market (think of the drafts in American professional sports leagues). Hence, a relevant issue is how to evaluate and compare different conceivable outcomes of matching markets. One important concern is that a matching allocation should be final in the sense that all feasible profitable exchanges are exhausted and there is no mutually profitable opportunity for rematching among individuals. This property is called stability. If an assignment scheme violates stability, individuals who expect that they will have such a profitable rematching opportunity given an assignment might decide they are better off bypassing the assignment scheme, for instance, by attempting to secure a favorable match before the market takes place. This is known as unraveling of a matching market and can lead to quite unsatisfactory matching allocations (see, e.g., Li & Rosen, 1998; Roth & Xing, 1994).

Having identified a desirable property of allocations such as stability, the next step is to find an assignment scheme that actually reaches a stable outcome. Such an assignment scheme is often simply an algorithm specifying step-by-step instructions for the assignment based on the preferences of market participants. Because the algorithm is based on information announced by participants (i.e., their stated preferences), quality of outcomes can be evaluated only with respect to reported information. Therefore, it is of great importance to elicit truthful revelation of information by individuals. Devising algorithms, or mechanisms, that reach desirable outcomes from a social point of view while ensuring that agents do not benefit by strategically misrepresenting their preferences is the object of the field of market design (see Roth, 2002, for an overview).

Matching market mechanisms are usually centralized in the sense that assignments are generated by a central matchmaker or a clearinghouse. This is in contrast to what is typically the case in the literature on search and matching in the labor market. There matching is decentralized, often meaning that participants in the market meet and match randomly.

Two-Sided Matching Markets

The simplest instance of a matching market is the *marriage market* model. In a marriage market, economic agents belong to one of two different groups, called the *market sides* (e.g., men and women or students and colleges). Suppose, following the first example, that there are n women to be assigned to m men, such that every woman is matched to one man or stays solitary, and likewise every man is matched to one woman or stays solitary. That is, there are two disjoint market sides, and an individual on one market side can only be assigned to a member of the opposite market side. The restriction of allowable matches to those between two market sides is the defining characteristic of a *two-sided* matching market, as opposed to a *one-sided* matching market where there is only one market side in the sense that a priori any individual is free to match with any other individual. Furthermore, here each man is matched to at most one woman, and vice versa, so that matching is *one to one*. In the context of students and colleges, typically many students may be assigned to one college, so that matching is *many to one*.

Men and women have preferences in the form of complete rankings of all individuals from the other market side that they would prefer to be matched with over staying solitary. Suppose that preferences are strict, so that no individual is exactly indifferent between being matched with any two members of the opposite side (or between being matched with any member of the opposite side and staying solitary).

Stability of a Matching Allocation

As was mentioned above, a desirable property for an outcome of a matching market is that it is final in the sense that all mutually profitable matches have been exhausted.

To capture this, say that an outcome can be *blocked* if there is an individual or a pair of individuals who can make themselves strictly better off by altering their own assignment when mutual consent is required. More precisely, an outcome can be blocked by an individual, if he or she is assigned to somebody in the outcome but would prefer to stay solitary. An outcome can be blocked by a pair, if a pair of individuals, one from each side, is not assigned to each other in the outcome but would both strictly prefer this to their actual assignment in the outcome. Consequently, an outcome is called *stable* if there is neither an individual nor a pair that can block the outcome. That is, to borrow the image of a marriage market once more, given a stable outcome, no mutually desired marriage is left un-brokered, and nobody will demand a divorce. This illustrates well the appeal of a stable allocation: In a stable allocation, an individual cannot gain by choosing differently because all matches preferred to the current one would not accept a proposal. For this reason, stability is also sometimes said to eliminate justified envy, where envy is considered only justified when an envied match would actually accept a proposal.

The Gale-Shapley Algorithm

Fortunately, existence of a stable outcome in a marriage market is always guaranteed, as David Gale and Lloyd Shapley (1962) found. Since their proof is highly instructive for the understanding of a great variety of assignment problems, a sketch of it is given here. They prove existence constructively by proposing a very simple algorithm that never fails to achieve a stable matching allocation in a marriage market. A matching algorithm provides a detailed set of instructions for how to assign and possibly rematch individuals on both market sides. It proceeds sequentially in steps until a stopping condition is met, for instance, when there is no activity in the current step. Then it terminates, and the current assignment becomes the matching allocation. The *Gale-Shapley algorithm* is as follows:

Step 1

    (i) Each man proposes to his first choice, if this is preferred to remaining solitary. Otherwise, he does not propose.

    (ii) Each woman tentatively accepts the most preferred proposal made to her, or stays solitary if that is preferred, and rejects all other proposals.

Step k

    (i) Each man who has been rejected at step $k - 1$ proposes to his kth choice, if this is preferred to remaining solitary. Otherwise, he does not propose.

    (ii) Each woman tentatively accepts the most preferred proposal made to her (out of all proposals in the current step and her most recent previous tentative acceptance), or stays solitary if that is preferred, and rejects all other proposals (including the supplanted previous tentative acceptance if applicable).

End

    The algorithm stops when a step is reached in which no proposals are made. All tentative acceptances by women become permanent, and the resulting matches constitute the outcome.

The key characteristic of this algorithm is that women hold on to the best proposals they receive but are free to reject any previous proposal should a better one arrive later on. This means acceptances by the women are not binding as long the algorithm has not terminated. This is why this algorithm is also sometimes called the *deferred acceptance* algorithm.

To verify that a marriage market has a stable outcome, one can proceed in two steps: It has to be confirmed first that the algorithm always produces an outcome and second that the outcome produced is indeed stable. For the first statement, one simply notes that both men and women are finite in number. Therefore, after a finite time, the algorithm must have exhausted all entries in all individual rankings so that nobody proposes anymore, or, if not, there must have been a step when nobody proposed. Moreover, the outcome of the algorithm does not depend on the order in which men are allowed to propose in each step or on the order in which women are allowed to decide which proposals to reject. It does, however, depend on whether men or women propose, as will become clear below.

That the matching outcome produced by a Gale-Shapley algorithm must be stable can be seen as follows. Suppose there are a man and a woman who can block the outcome. Then, under the rules of the algorithm, the man must necessarily have proposed to the woman before and been rejected. But then, again according to the rules of the algorithm, the woman cannot prefer a match with this man to the match she is assigned in the outcome. Hence, the initial assumption that there is a pair that can block the outcome must be false. Neither can any individual block the outcome since men only propose to women if this is preferred to staying solitary, and women only hold on to such proposals that are preferred to staying solitary. Therefore, neither an individual nor a pair can block the outcome, and so the outcome of a Gale-Shapley algorithm is stable.

Optimal Matching Allocations

There may, however, be more stable outcomes than just the one arrived at by this algorithm. Furthermore, different stable outcomes may differ widely in how well-off the individuals find themselves. Gale and Shapley (1962) provide a useful result: There is always a stable outcome that is at least weakly preferred by all men to all other stable outcomes, which is typically called the *men-optimal* (or student-optimal in the case of college admission) stable outcome. Likewise, there is always a stable outcome that all women at least weakly prefer to all other stable outcomes, which is called the *women-optimal* stable outcome. Moreover, Gale and Shapley show that the men-optimal outcome is reached by a deferred acceptance algorithm in which the men propose (as outlined above) while, if instead the roles are reversed and women propose, such an algorithm reaches the women-optimal outcome.

This result has an immediate implication for how policy makers would want to implement the algorithm if one market side were of more concern than the other. For instance, suppose one market side consists of organizations rather than individuals—say, in a student-college interpretation of the marriage market, where men can be relabeled as students and women as colleges. Then the student-optimal outcome seems clearly desirable from a social point of view, when assuming that the well-being of colleges is not a crucial social concern. This suggests that it would be desirable from a social point of view to implement the algorithm such that it is the students who make the proposals.

Truthful Information Revelation

Using the Gale-Shapley algorithm, a social planner can implement a stable outcome and furthermore, simply by choosing which market side will play what role, can implement the stable outcome that is optimal for a given market side. However, the social planner must apply the algorithm on the basis of submitted preference rankings from both market sides. This means that the outcome that is reached will be stable only with respect to the stated preferences. If individuals do not report their preferences truthfully, however, the outcome might not be stable with respect to the true preferences, which may lead to Pareto inefficiency, secondary markets, or unraveling. Therefore, a further desirable property of any assignment mechanism is to ensure that individual participants cannot gain by misrepresenting their preferences. An assignment mechanism is called *strategy-proof* if it ensures that, for all possible combinations of individual strict preferences, participants at least weakly prefer to reveal information on their preferences truthfully. The interested reader may consult the textbook on two-sided matching by Roth and Sotomayor (1990) for a more exhaustive treatment of the following results and many others.

First, a negative result has to be mentioned: There is no assignment mechanism that generally implements a stable outcome in a marriage market and is strategy-proof (Roth, 1982). To see this, suppose men- and women-optimal outcomes do not coincide, and an algorithm is in place where men propose (as described above). Then all women prefer an outcome other than is reached by the algorithm. In particular, the following situation may arise. A woman misrepresents her preferences by eliminating her match in the men-optimal outcome from her submitted list. Then this man is rejected and tentatively assigned to another woman who prefers that man to her match in the men-optimal outcome. The newly rejected man in turn proposes to the first woman (who lied) and is tentatively accepted, if this woman prefers him to her match in the

men-optimal outcome. That is, women exchange men such that all participating women are better off and all exchanged men worse off. Because this possibility cannot be precluded in general, strategy-proofness cannot be ensured for both market sides.

Lester Dubins and David Freedman (1981) present a slightly more encouraging result in finding that a mechanism that yields the men-optimal outcome on a marriage market ensures that no man can gain by misrepresenting his true preferences. That is, such a mechanism is strategy-proof among the men. This must be the case because by misrepresenting preferences, a man may induce a different stable outcome, but the men-optimal outcome is preferred by all men among all stable outcomes. A similar property holds for a mechanism inducing a women-optimal outcome: It is strategy-proof among the women. This is in fact a very useful result in case one is interested in a matching market where participants on one market side can be considered to be not self-interested. This may be the case, for instance, when assigning pupils to schools, students to universities or courses, or airplanes to landing slots. Some caution is appropriate, however, when the matching is many to one, as the result on strategy-proofness for one market side holds only for the market side having one partner each. To illustrate this, consider a school choice problem where schools have multiple places. A matching mechanism yielding the pupil-optimal allocation is strategy-proof among the pupils, but a matching mechanism yielding the school-optimal allocation is not necessarily strategy-proof among the schools.

One-Sided Markets

In contrast to the two-sided marriage market discussed so far, an individual participating in a one-sided matching market may be assigned to any other individual participating in that market. Examples are team or group formation or marketplaces where indivisible objects are exchanged, such as markets for houses or dorm rooms. In these markets, every individual may initiate a trade with any other individual or group of individuals. The basic *housing market* model due to Lloyd Shapley and Herbert Scarf (1974) considers an exchange economy where n individuals trade in an indivisible good, say houses. Each individual owns one house when entering the market, has need of exactly one house, and possesses strict preferences over all existing houses. Potential matches in this market are between individuals and indicate house trades.

An outcome in this market is an allocation of houses among individuals such that each individual holds at most one house. That is, potential trades, or matches, among (groups of) individuals generate an allocation of houses to individuals, the market outcome. Note that also a school choice matching market could potentially be formulated as a one-sided market, if pupils are endowed with a place at certain school. Shapley and Scarf (1974) use the *core* as a solution concept to determine the outcome. An outcome is in the core if there is no group of individuals (of size one or greater) that could make every group member weakly and at least one strictly better off by reallocating the houses owned by group members among members of the group. This is equivalent to saying that an outcome exhausts all opportunities for mutually beneficial trade among any number of individuals (not only between pairs of members of opposing market sides).

The Top Trading Cycles Algorithm

When all individuals have strict preferences, there is always at least one matching allocation in the core (Roth & Postlewaite, 1977). Shapley and Scarf (1974) show that an outcome in the core can be reached by following a specific algorithm, the *top trading cycles* algorithm, which they attribute to David Gale. Before presenting the algorithm, it will be useful to explain what is meant by *cycles.* A cycle is a *sequence of individuals* such that each individual is followed by, or points to, the owner of his or her most preferred house, and the last individual in the sequence most prefers the first individual's house. A cycle may consist of one individual only. Note that, among a finite set of individuals who have strict preferences, there must always be at least one cycle. For cycles of more than one individual, if all members of a cycle give their houses to their successors in the sequence and the last individual to the first, all individuals in the cycle will be strictly better off. That is, cycles identify opportunities for mutually strictly beneficial trades in groups. The top trading cycles algorithm exhausts all such opportunities and works as follows.

Step 1

Let all individuals point to the owners of their most preferred houses. Identify all cycles, effect the implied exchange of houses, and remove the individuals in the cycles from the market.

Step k

Let all individuals that remain in the market after step $k-1$ point to the owners of their most preferred houses. Identify all cycles, effect the implied exchange of houses, and remove the individuals in the cycles from the market.

End

The algorithm stops when there are no more individuals in the market.

This means that the top trading cycles algorithm iteratively identifies all trading cycles, executes the trades, and removes the individuals in the cycles until the market is cleared. The outcome generated by this algorithm is in the core for all housing markets (Shapley & Scarf, 1974). That is, given a matching allocation resulting from this mechanism, there is no opportunity for mutually strictly beneficial exchange among any group of agents. This means the

outcome is Pareto efficient and essentially replicates the competitive equilibrium allocation (Roth & Postlewaite, 1977). Hence, from a social planner's perspective, outcomes of a top trading cycles mechanism on a housing market have highly desirable properties. Moreover, the mechanism does not require monetary payments and can therefore be deployed in situations in which competitive market prices may not be feasible. To make it a desirable mechanism, it should also ensure that participants have no incentive to misreport their preferences. Roth (1982) shows that this is indeed the case.

Applications

In the following, a number of real-world assignment problems are presented, along with the matching markets that have arisen in correspondence. The aim of the following presentation is twofold. On one hand, assignment mechanisms that have been employed on matching markets are described and analyzed with respect to shortcomings such as unraveling or preference misrepresentation. On the other hand, possible remedies, or policies, are presented to amend any such shortcomings identified in the analysis.

The Market for Medical Interns and Residents

The market for medical interns and residents in the United States is a two-sided matching market. On one side are colleges offering internship and residency positions, and on the other side are graduate students seeking such positions. Both colleges and students are very heterogeneous in academic quality, both are indivisible (as part-time employment is usually infeasible), and wages for students are fixed before the application process begins. Alvin Roth (1984) gives an account both of the problems encountered in this market and the theoretical reasons. Before a viable assignment mechanism was introduced in 1951, matching was conducted in a de-centralized manner by private initiatives of market participants. Because the number of positions exceeded that of students, colleges had an incentive to try to preempt competitors in securing good candidates by making offers earlier. Indeed, whereas students tended to obtain a position about half a year before graduation in the 1930s, they were typically offered a contract about 2 full years before graduation by 1944. Such early timing, of course, forgoes a lot of information on the quality of candidates, which is very likely to adversely influence the quality of the matches. This is an instance of unraveling. Others include markets for law clerks and gastroenterologists (see Avery, Jolls, Posner, & Roth, 2001; Niederle, Proctor, & Roth, 2006).

In 1945, an attempt was made to remedy the shortcomings by disclosing information on candidates only shortly before graduation. This prevented unraveling but created another problem, as offers and acceptances were binding.

It became costly for colleges to hold offers open for any amount of time because by the time an offer was rejected, the market was quite likely to be depleted. Not surprisingly, while offers remained open for 10 days in 1945, this time fell to about 10 minutes by 1950.

As this development was unsatisfactory, a clearinghouse was formed in 1951 that used a centralized mechanism, the National Internship Matching Program (NIMP). This mechanism works as follows. Students and colleges submit their preferences over the other market side in the form of rankings to the clearinghouse. An algorithm is then used to determine the matching outcome. The principal characteristic of the algorithm employed is that it uses deferred acceptance, as with the Gale-Shapley algorithm. Therefore, the outcome reached by the NIMP is stable with respect to the stated rankings by students and colleges (Roth, 1984). Hence, given the outcome, no participant can obtain a better match—that is, the allocation is envy free—and there should be no reason for a secondary market to emerge. This may explain why the program, although participation was voluntary, was quite successful. Indeed, the mechanism is still in use today, albeit renamed the National Residency Matching Program (NRMP) and in a slightly modified form. Some changes were designed to accommodate concerns such as differences in medical training programs and the desire of couples to end up in similar locations. More significantly, the algorithm was changed from a college-proposing to a student-proposing format to ensure student optimality of the matching outcomes after complaints arose that students had been treated badly. Potential gains to students from misrepresenting their preferences appear to be small in the NRMP, however (see Roth & Peranson, 1999, for further details).

Public School Choice

The assignment of pupils to public schools provides another informative real-world example of a two-sided matching market. In many U.S. school districts, the assignment mechanism used to match pupils and schools often fails to implement a stable outcome, which can generate incentives to misreport preferences. For instance, the city of Boston employed the following mechanism to assign pupils to public schools in the years 1999–2005. Parents submitted a ranking of their top schools. Schools assigned priority to pupils who lived within walking distance, higher priority to those who had a sibling already enrolled, and highest priority to pupils who satisfied both criteria. Further details can be found in the studies by Abdulkadiroglu and Sönmez (2003) and Ergin and Sönmez (2006). The so-called Boston Student Assignment Mechanism (BSAM) proceeds as follows.

Step 1

> For each school, pupils who have listed that school as their first choice are assigned in order of priority while the school still has free capacity. Ties are broken using a random procedure (such as flipping a coin).

Step k

> For each school, pupils who have not been matched to a school in a previous step and who have listed that school as their *k*th choice are assigned in order of priority while the school still has free capacity. Ties are broken using a random procedure.

End

> The algorithm stops, when either all pupils are assigned or there is no school left with remaining places.

The key feature of this algorithm is that assignments at each step are permanent—that is, when a school accepts a pupil, this acceptance is binding. Note that this is in contrast to deferred acceptance, which is characteristic of the Gale-Shapley algorithm. Ultimately, the fact that acceptances are permanent gives pupils an opportunity for strategic behavior. This implies in turn that the BSAM is not strategy-proof. This is because being rejected by one's top-ranked school may waste one's priority at another school if the other school is over-demanded and fills to capacity in a previous step. For example, if some pupil most prefers an over-demanded school at which he or she does not have priority but does have priority at his or her second most preferred school, it is strictly better for the pupil to list the second most preferred school in the first place on the submitted ranking to minimize the chances of being stuck with his or her third choice or worse. That is, under the BSAM, pupils can strictly gain by misrepresenting their preferences.

This observation has spawned a lively debate on possible implications for policy, in particular on whether to replace the existing mechanism by one that is strategy-proof, such as the Gale-Shapley algorithm. To offer theoretical guidance, Ergin and Sönmez (2006) investigate a game of school choice and find that the outcome of a pupil-optimal Gale-Shapley algorithm is more desirable from an efficiency perspective than the one of the BSAM (as long as the preferences of both market sides are strict). Furthermore, Adulkadiroglu, Pathak, Roth, and Sönmez (2006) and Pathak and Sönmez (2008) put forward the argument that a Gale-Shapley algorithm places lower cognitive and computational burden on participants than does the BSAM. This may be desirable, as evidence suggests that while some participants actually behave strategically, others announce their rankings sincerely. The BSAM systematically disadvantages these "naive" individuals if there are sophisticated players who behave strategically.

In 2006, public authorities changed the mechanism used in the assignment of pupils to public schools in Boston and introduced a version of the Gale-Shapley algorithm. New York City has also undergone a similar change in its assignment mechanism of pupils to high schools (see Abdulkadiroglu, Pathak, & Roth, 2005). There, a chief problem that had to be dealt with was strategic behavior of high schools.

Kidney Exchange

As a final example, consider the problem of assigning kidneys from live donors to patients in need of transplantation. Often, patients who are in desperate need of a kidney transplant have a willing donor. (It is perfectly possible to live a healthy life with only one kidney.) Several compatibility conditions need to be met, however, to make a transplant feasible, such as having common blood types. Suppose that a patient has found a willing donor but is incompatible with that donor. Finding another patient who is compatible with the first donor and who has a live donor who is compatible with the first patient would make both patients better off (and presumably the donors, too). Obviously, it is of tremendous interest to identify all possible opportunities for mutually beneficial exchange because forgone opportunities to exchange will very likely result in the loss of human life.

Alvin Roth, Tayfun Sönmez, and Utku Ünver (2004) provide a theoretical analysis of this matching market and propose a mechanism for the exchange of kidneys from live donors. The key insight is that the market for kidney exchange is a one-sided matching market, similar to the housing market presented above. For this type of matching market, a mechanism is known that achieves a Pareto efficient allocation—that is, a matching outcome that exhausts all possible profitable trades—and is strategy-proof: the top trading cycles algorithm outlined above. Because not all patients necessarily have a donor to bring to the market, the appropriate theoretical model is a housing market with existing tenants, as studied by Abdulkadiroglu and Sönmez (1999), who explicitly allow for a waiting list. Roth et al. (2004) extend this theoretical work by allowing for the possibility of a waiting list for kidneys from deceased donors and derive a top trading cycles and chains (TTCC) mechanism that is Pareto efficient and strategy-proof.

The number of live-donor kidney exchanges that are actually carried out appears to be quite small relative to that which could be achieved by exhausting all potential for mutually beneficial exchange, pointing to a clear need for a centralized matching institution. In 2005, a clearinghouse (the New England Program for Kidney Exchange) for gathering data on donors and patients and generating the actual assignment was founded in New England (Roth, Sönmez, & Ünver, 2005, 2007). By 2008, this clearinghouse had already enabled a substantial number of two-way and even some three-way kidney exchanges. A similar program has since been started in Ohio.

Further Issues

Recently, some further issues have been raised in public debate about some of the matching markets mentioned above. In the case of the market for medical residents, complaints have been made that the use of the NRMP depresses salaries for residents and fellows. An antitrust lawsuit in this matter was brought forward in 2002 but dismissed in 2004. Some theoretical support for the claim comes from Bulow and Levin (2006). They find that, when explicitly accounting for the fact that wage setting by colleges takes place before the matching market does, wages can indeed be depressed compared to the competitive outcome. Other studies (e.g., Kojima, 2007; Niederle, 2007) argue that this result hinges on particular assumptions that do not describe the real market for medical residents well.

As for school choice, recently it has been suggested that a version of the BSAM that modifies the random tie-breaking procedure would be able to better respect the intensity of pupils' preferences for different schools (see Abdulkadiroglu, Che, & Yasuda, 2008; Miralles, 2008). Thus, schools could be allocated to the pupils who have the highest valuations, which is different from merely ensuring that schools are assigned to pupils who prefer them to the next best school. This concern becomes more relevant when the pupils' preferences over schools are closely aligned, which seems to be the case in this market.

The cases mentioned above raise two additional issues. First, it is not clear whether the desirability of a mechanism is better judged based on whether it exhausts all potential mutually profitable exchanges or on whether it maximizes the sum of individuals' valuations of the outcome, that is, aggregate surplus. Aggregate surplus, also sometimes interpretable as output, may be a relevant criterion, for example, when analyzing economy-wide policies, such as labor market regulations and their effects on growth. Second, often there will be some means of compensation between partners, for instance, through the exchange of favors or gifts.

These issues have at least been partially addressed. When preferences are perfectly aligned—that is, the rankings of all individuals in the market agree—Becker (1974) shows that stable matching allocations need not maximize aggregate surplus when the possibility to compensate a partner in any form is completely excluded. Indeed, independently of which matching allocation maximizes aggregate surplus, a stable outcome in his model always assigns individuals whose attributes are more attractive to individuals or objects that have more attractive attributes. This is known as positive assortative matching. The general case, where compensation within a match is possible but costly in terms of surplus, has only recently been characterized. Legros and Newman (2002, 2007) provide conditions for assortative matching and confirm that stability and surplus maximization need not coincide.

When asymmetric information about individuals' attributes is a concern (e.g., concerning the productivity of firms and workers in labor markets), some form of segmentation and randomization of the matching within segments may be desirable (see, e.g., Jacquet & Tan, 2007; McAfee, 2002).

Directions for Future Research

While the design of matching markets is already sufficiently well understood to offer useful contributions in many important assignment problems, there are a number of issues in which further theoretical progress would appear to be highly valuable. A first topic worth mentioning for being understudied is the forming of and properties of individuals' preferences. In large markets, constructing a complete preference ranking over every member of the other market side may be extremely costly because all potential matches would first need to be evaluated. In the labor market, for instance, this would require time-consuming interviews and assessments of and by all individual applicants and employers. A possible alternative may consist of designing a mechanism with a prematching stage in which participants indicate a crude preliminary ranking based on easily observable information (e.g., grades, public rankings). Such a mechanism has been tried out in the entry-level job market for economists since 2007. Whether this is indeed the optimal approach remains an open theoretical question.

Second, note that most of the theoretical results presented above rely on strict preferences, meaning that market participants cannot be indifferent between any two matches. This is indeed a limitation because the assumption cannot be easily discarded without affecting the theoretical properties of the mechanisms yet seems unreasonable in many relevant contexts. Some work has been done in identifying strategy-proof mechanisms for situations in which individuals may be indifferent between multiple matches. In such cases, the manner of breaking the tie and choosing the actual match may affect incentives for strategic behavior (see, e.g., Abdulkadiroglu, Pathak, & Roth, 2009; Erdil & Ergin, 2008; Miralles, 2008). Exploiting the possibility of indifference through the use of stochastic mechanisms—that is, matching mechanisms that use random procedures for assignment—appears to be a very promising field for future research. This is because such mechanisms allow respecting the intensity of individuals' preferences over matches (e.g., by setting odds to obtain a certain match that are acceptable only for individuals with intense preference for that match).

A third limitation of the theory of matching markets is that many of the theoretical results described above do not necessarily apply when individuals care not only about the match they obtain (e.g., the instructor, school, university, firm) but also about who else obtains the same match. This is, for instance, the case when thinking about couples searching jointly for jobs in the labor market. Although evidence suggests that a hands-on approach to market design works well in the market for medical residents (see Roth & Peranson, 1999), sound theoretical guidance for generating mechanisms that can also account for preferences over the outcomes of individuals on the same market side would be very welcome.

Another important area for future research is analyzing the effects of the anticipated outcome of a matching market (possibly generated by a mechanism) on individuals' behavior before entering the market. Often the attributes that the preferences of market participants are based on are subject to individual choices and investments. For example, the choice of how much education to acquire appears to affect individual outcomes in the labor market quite substantially. Some recent work suggests that, when partners in a match cannot compensate each other without incurring a loss in efficiency or when there is asymmetric information concerning attributes, stable outcomes need not maximize aggregate surplus and may distort individuals' prematching choices when these are based on anticipating the matching outcome (Gall, Legros, & Newman, 2006; Hoppe, Moldovanu, & Sela, 2009).

Conclusion

There is a growing interest in and demand for applying economic theory to the design of mechanisms that solve real-world assignment problems. Cases in point are entry-level job markets, school choice, and exchange of live-donor kidneys. This chapter has presented an overview of such matching markets, typically characterized by heterogeneity and indivisibility of individuals and objects, as well as by limited possibilities for compensation of matching partners through side payments. A brief introduction to the theory of matching outlined important concepts such as stability of a matching allocation and strategy-proofness of an assignment mechanism. Two assignment mechanisms have been discussed in greater detail: the Gale-Shapley or deferred acceptance algorithm for two-sided matching markets and the top trading cycles algorithm for one-sided markets. Both algorithms satisfy two desired properties: stability of the resulting outcome and strategy-proofness.

The chapter proceeded to consider several real-world applications of matching markets in detail. In the market for medical residents and the choice of public schools, both two-sided matching markets, appropriate versions of the Gale-Shapley algorithm have been implemented with a high degree of success. An example of a one-sided matching market was provided in the exchange of kidneys for transplantation from live donors through a centralized facility using a version of the top trading cycles algorithm.

Further issues arise when it is in the social interest to choose a matching allocation that maximizes aggregate surplus. Because the stable outcome does not necessarily maximize aggregate surplus, a tension between surplus efficiency and stability may arise. In such cases, it is important to identify surplus-maximizing outcomes and to design and implement mechanisms that reliably reach such outcomes.

Finally, the chapter considered some relevant issues and questions that demand further investigation. The theory of matching markets needs to achieve higher levels of sophistication to provide results that are more applicable in empirically relevant situations, such as when individuals are indifferent between multiple matches or have preferences concerning who else obtains the same match as they do. This is needed to be able to devise adequate matching mechanisms that can be successfully employed to address a wider range of assignment problems. Promising directions for future research lie in the use of stochastic mechanisms, which may use fine-tuned random procedures for the assignment, and in considering the dynamic environment of an assignment problem to evaluate effects on choices made prior to entering the matching market, particularly those that affect attributes relevant for the resulting matching allocation.

References and Further Readings

Abdulkadiroglu, A., Che, Y., & Yasuda, Y. (2008). *Expanding "choice" in school choice* (Working paper). New York: Columbia University.

Abdulkadiroglu, A., Pathak, P., & Roth, A. E. (2005). The New York City high school match. *American Economic Review, 95*, 364–367.

Abdulkadiroglu, A., Pathak, P., & Roth, A. E. (2009). Strategy-proofness versus efficiency in matching with indifferences: Redesigning the NYC high school match. *American Economic Review, 99*, 1954–1978.

Abdulkadiroglu, A., Pathak, P., Roth, A. E., & Sönmez, T. (2006). *Changing the Boston school choice mechanism: Strategy-proofness as equal access* (NBER Working Paper 11965). Cambridge, MA: National Bureau of Economic Research.

Abdulkadiroglu, A., & Sönmez, T. (1999). House allocation with existing tenants. *Journal of Economic Theory, 88*, 233–260.

Abdulkadiroglu, A., & Sönmez, T. (2003). School choice: A mechanism design approach. *American Economic Review, 93*, 729–747.

Avery, C., Jolls, C., Posner, R. A., & Roth, A. E. (2001). The market for federal judicial law clerks. *University of Chicago Law Review, 68*, 793–902.

Becker, G. (1974). A theory of marriage: Part I. *Journal of Political Economy, 81*, 813–846.

Bulow, J., & Levin, J. (2006). Matching and price competition. *American Economic Review, 96*, 652–668.

Dubins, L. E., & Freedman, D. (1981). Machiavelli and the Gale-Shapley algorithm. *American Mathematical Monthly, 69*(3), 9–15.

Erdil, A., & Ergin, H. (2008). What's the matter with tie-breaking? Improving efficiency in school choice. *American Economic Review, 98*, 669–689.

Ergin, H., & Sönmez, T. (2006). Games of school choice under the Boston mechanism. *Journal of Public Economics, 90*, 215–237.

Gale, D., & Shapley, L. S. (1962). College admission and the stability of marriage. *American Mathematical Monthly, 69*(3), 9–15.

Gall, T., Legros, P., & Newman, A. F. (2006). The timing of education. *Journal of the European Economic Association, 4*, 427–435.

Hoppe, H., Moldovanu, B., & Sela, A. (2009). The theory of assortative matching based on costly signals. *Review of Economic Studies, 76*, 253–281.

Jacquet, N. L., & Tan, S. (2007). On the segmentation of markets. *Journal of Political Economy, 115*, 639–664.

Kojima, F. (2007). Matching and price competition: Comment. *American Economic Review, 97*, 1027–1031.

Legros, P., & Newman, A. (2002). Monotone matching in perfect and imperfect worlds. *Review of Economic Studies, 69*, 925–942.

Legros, P., & Newman, A. (2007). Beauty is a beast, frog is a prince: Assortative matching with nontransferabilities. *Econometrica, 75*, 1073–1102.

Li, H., & Rosen, S. (1998). Unraveling in matching markets. *American Economic Review, 88*, 878–889.

McAfee, P. (2002). Coarse matching. *Econometrica, 70*, 2025–2034.

Miralles, A. (2008). *School choice: The case for the Boston mechanism* (Working paper). Boston: Boston University.

Niederle, M. (2007). Competitive wages in a match with ordered contracts. *American Economic Review, 97*, 1957–1969.

Niederle, M., Proctor, D. D., & Roth, A. E. (2006). What will be needed for the new GI fellowship match to succeed? *Gastroenterology, 130*, 218–224.

Niederle, M., Roth, A. E., & Sönmez, T. (2008). Matching and market design. In S. N. Durlauf & L. E. Blume (Eds.), *The new Palgrave dictionary of economics* (2nd ed., Vol. 5, pp. 436–445). New York: Palgrave Macmillan.

Pathak, P., & Sönmez, T. (2008). Leveling the playing field: Sincere and sophisticated players in the Boston mechanism. *American Economic Review, 98*, 1636–1652.

Roth, A. E. (1982). The economics of matching: Stability and incentives. *Mathematics of Operations Research, 7*, 617–628.

Roth, A. E. (1984). The evolution of the labor market for medical interns and residents: A case study in game theory. *Journal of Political Economy, 92*, 991–1016.

Roth, A. E. (2002). The economist as an engineer: Game theory, experimental economics and computation as tools of design economics. *Econometrica, 70*, 1341–1378.

Roth, A. E., & Peranson, E. (1999). The redesign of the matching market for American physicians. *American Economic Review, 89*, 748–780.

Roth, A. E., & Postlewaite, A. (1977). Weak versus strong domination in a market with indivisible goods. *Journal of Mathematical Economics, 4*, 131–137.

Roth, A. E., Sönmez, T., & Ünver, U. (2004). Kidney exchange. *Quarterly Journal of Economics, 119*, 457–488.

Roth, A. E., Sönmez, T., & Ünver, U. (2005). A kidney exchange clearinghouse in New England. *American Economic Review, 95*, 376–380.

Roth, A. E., Sönmez, T., & Ünver, U. (2007). Efficient kidney exchange: Coincidence of wants in markets with compatibility-based preferences. *American Economic Review, 97*, 828–851.

Roth, A. E., & Sotomayor, M. (1990). *Two-sided matching: A study in game-theoretic modeling and analysis*. Cambridge, UK: Cambridge University Press.

Roth, A. E., & Xing, X. (1994). Jumping the gun: Imperfections and institutions related to the timing of market transactions. *American Economic Review, 84*, 992–1044.

Shapley, L. S., & Scarf, H. (1974). On cores and indivisibility. *Journal of Mathematical Economy, 1*, 23–37.

92

Beyond Make-or-Buy

Advances in Transaction Cost Economics

Lyda S. Bigelow

University of Utah

Thinking about problems of economic organization from a transaction cost economics point of view takes concerted effort. Once, however, a threshold of understanding is reached, the world of organization is "spontaneously" reordered. Applications abound. . . . The worldview of new students who get caught up in transaction cost reasoning is irreversibly altered.

Oliver E. Williamson (1985, p. x)

Although Ronald Coase is often credited with inspiring a line of economic inquiry that came to be known as transaction cost economics, it is the work of Oliver Williamson, which appeared some 40 years later, that laid the foundation and provided the theoretical apparatus that has allowed scholars in this field to make headway on fundamental problems in law, economics, and the study of organizations. The magnitude of this contribution earned Williamson the Nobel Prize in Economics in 2010. This chapter sets out to familiarize the reader with central ideas and contributions of transaction cost economics and to illustrate the ongoing research trajectories that have emerged since Williamson set forth to expand on the implications of Coase's famous 1937 article. In addition, this chapter is written with the purpose of identifying recent areas of research that offer students the opportunity to consider possible empirical and theoretical extensions of transaction cost reasoning. Clearly, given the space constraints of a chapter, this survey cannot be exhaustive but will provide a basic outline of central insights and reflect the author's own assessment of the most promising new areas. The reader is asked to keep this caveat in mind in reading the chapter material.

The chapter is organized as follows: The first section provides a summary of the initial formulation of transaction cost economics with an emphasis on the above-mentioned "reordering" of economic organization; the next introduces the concept of discrete structural alignment and assesses the empirical evidence in predicting firm boundaries; the third section discusses contributions to problems beyond make-buy, focusing on strategic alliances, international business, and performance; the fourth section highlights emerging areas of research and research opportunities in the areas of contracts, technological evolution, and industry dynamics and concerns related to measurement and methodological issues; and the fifth section summarizes and concludes.

Formulation of Transaction Cost Economics

Economics students are certainly aware of the Coase Theorem and the fact that Ronald Coase won the Nobel Prize for Economics in 1991. What they may not be aware of is the contribution Coase made to rethinking economic organization. In a seminal paper published in 1937, Coase proposed relaxing the assumption that transactions costs are zero, and once those costs are allowed to be positive, insights surrounding the efficacy of markets and the costs of bureaucracy are altered. Coase is among a group of economists, who, beginning in the 1960s, sought to better understand institutions and the reasons for why we observe different forms of exchange. In essence, if markets work so well, why is there a need for firms at all? Why are contracts between firms specialized? With the publication of *Markets and Hierarchies,* Oliver Williamson (1975) began laying the theoretical foundation for modern transaction cost economics. This and his later work (e.g., Williamson, 1985, 1991, 1996), as well as the work of other economists (e.g., Grossman & Hart, 1986; Hart & Moore, 1990; Klein, Crawford, & Alchian, 1978), focused on addressing fundamental questions of the structure of economic exchange and how firms resolve the risks inherent in exchange in a world where there are no perfect governance solutions. (Note that throughout this chapter, the term *governance* is used to refer to the structure of economic exchange. This is how the term is used in the transaction cost literature. It is assumed that economic agents can choose and create governance structures that best protect them from the hazards of opportunistic behavior on the part of others, but no governance solution offers complete protection. More on this in the second section.)

Williamson (e.g., 1985, 1996) in particular espouses the view that there is broad applicability of this perspective. For example, he builds the case for using transaction cost economics to understand organizational, institutional, and nation-state exchange issues ranging from the familiar problems of contracting hazards to more unique phenomena such as the presence of company towns and the utilization of franchising. As an individual scholar, his appointment to three departments—economics, business, and law—while at the University of California, Berkeley, reflects his embodiment of this broad applicability of his work, based as it is on an interdisciplinary approach.

To best appreciate the insight/contribution of transaction cost economics, it is useful to put its development/ appearance in historical context. Prior to the publication of *Markets and Hierarchies* in 1975, a dominant economic explanation for firms that used unusual strategies was to invoke a monopoly explanation. Indeed, Williamson (1985), in his introduction to *The Economic Institutions of Capitalism,* deploys the following quote from Coase (1972): "If an economist finds something—a business practice of one sort or another—that he does not understand, he looks for a monopoly explanation" (p. 67). Much of this focus was due to an era in which economists examined firm decisions with a high concern for antitrust and anticompetitive issues. Not surprisingly, this concern was driven, in part, by a period in which there were high levels of mergers and acquisitions. With the rise of the conglomerates in the 1960s, many economists, often those directly employed by the U.S. government antitrust divisions, sought to provide economic explanations for why these organization decisions led to anticompetitive practices revealed in unfair pricing, restraint of trade, and reduction

in choice. While the concern was certainly warranted, Williamson sought to correct an overreliance on such antitrust explanations for firm behavior. His work was groundbreaking at the time because it carefully examined the same cases that had been deemed anticompetitive and offered an explanation that revealed transaction cost economizing and thus competitive rather than anticompetitive logic. For example, in his discussion of cable TV franchise bidding, Williamson (1985) elaborated a host of contracting problems that could have explained the behavior of the firm just as well as anticompetitive explanations.

Thus, Williamson illustrates that, indeed, there is an alternate logic underlying much of the actions that firms undertake. In other words, much of what we observe, within firms and within institutions that support economic activity in capitalist systems, may be explained with the understanding that the objective is to economize on transaction costs.

And what are transaction costs? These costs may be thought of as the economic equivalent of friction in physical systems. They are the costs of considering, crafting, negotiating, monitoring, and safeguarding contracts. Another powerful insight developed and elaborated by Williamson was to consider that most economic exchange can be undertaken either within or between firms (and later hybrids). Either way, understanding the ability of firms to economize on transaction costs requires recognizing that they must choose between alternate modes of organizing and that this choice must take into account both the features of the economic exchange, or transaction, as well as the features of the governance structure. In one of the most important statements in Williamson's *Economic Institutions of Capitalism,* he states, "The underlying viewpoint that informs the comparative study of issues of economic organization is this: Transaction costs are economized by assigning transactions (which differ in their attributes) to governance structures (the adaptive capacities and associated costs of which differ) in a discriminating way" (p. 18).

Discrete Structural Alignment and Firm Boundaries

Beginning with his work in 1985 and perhaps best articulated in a paper that appeared in *Administrative Science Quarterly* in 1991, Williamson invoked the logic of discrete structural alignment. This is the theoretical apparatus that supports modern transaction cost theory. It begins with an understanding that there are different structural solutions to organizing economic exchange. These structural solutions, referred to as "governance," can be arrayed along a spectrum with markets on one end (arm's-length contracts, in which the identity of the parties to the exchange is not relevant—you can literally think of markets as the New York Stock Exchange) and hierarchy (a typical organization, e.g., a *Fortune* 500 company) on the other. Intermediate or hybrid forms of organization such as joint ventures, long-term contracts, and franchising fall somewhere in the middle between the market and hierarchy anchor points of this governance spectrum. The big differences between the two extremes have to do with the ability to adapt or coordinate action, the incentive intensity (i.e., the ability to motivate people), and the way disputes or disagreements are settled.

Because the theory adopts the premise that there is no such thing as a perfect governance solution (i.e., Williamson [e.g., 1985, 1996] emphasizes that there is little use in considering hypothetical ideals), there are trade-offs. Three dimensions constitute these trade-offs: incentives, adaptation, and dispute resolution (see Table 92.1). Note that markets enjoy high-powered incentives compared to hierarchy, hierarchy is better than markets when coordinated adaptation is required, and dispute resolution of last resort takes place in courts when market exchange is used, while hierarchy relies on internal mechanisms. From the table, it is clear that there is no form of governance that will score highly on all dimensions. Put differently, it is impossible to create a firm (hierarchy) that offers the dispute resolution and cooperative adaptation advantages as well as the high-powered incentive advantages reserved for markets. A common mistake managers make is to attempt to create just such governance structures. Williamson (1991) labels this problem "the folly of selective intervention."

The question of economic exchange thus becomes one of how to select the right governance structure. The answer to this question depends on the characteristics of the transaction. Transactions are differentiated based on three variables: asset specificity, uncertainty, and frequency (i.e., is this an exchange that you intend to repeat over time), of which asset specificity is deemed to be the critical factor. Williamson (1991) first identified three different types of asset specificity, but that list has now been expanded to six.

Table 92.1 Comparison of Attributes of Governance Structures

Attributes	Market	Hybrid	Hierarchy
Incentive intensity	++	+	0
Administrative control	0	+	++
Autonomous adaptation	++	+	0
Cooperative adaptation	0	+	++
Reliance on contract law	++	+	0

SOURCE: Adapted from Williamson (1991, p. 281).

NOTES: ++ = strong; + = semi-strong; 0 = weak.

They are physical asset specificity, human asset specificity, site specificity, brand-name specificity, dedicated assets, and temporal specificity. Think of asset specificity as the degree to which an asset has become specialized for a given exchange. Highly specific assets are those that are much more valuable to a firm in the context of a given transaction and whose value is negligible outside this exchange. For example, prior to agreeing to build components for General Motors (GM), Fisher Body had tool-and-die equipment that could be tailored to stamp out body parts for any automobile manufacturer. These industrial machines had little physical asset specificity. However, once Fisher Body agreed to produce parts for GM, these machines needed to be calibrated to technical specifications unique to the GM components. Now these same tool-and-die machines would be categorized as being highly asset specific. In other words, their value to anyone other than Fisher and GM would be their scrap value.

The central insight of transaction cost alignment is that with an increase in asset specificity (as well as uncertainty and frequency), the potential hazards of relying on market-like forms of exchange increase. Think about the risks to both GM and Fisher Body if one party decides—*after* the specific investment in the tool-and-die equipment is made—to alter the terms of the contract. Fisher Body might decide to raise the price of the components. If this occurs during a period of peak demand, GM will likely be hard-pressed to find another supplier, much less find another supplier quickly enough to meet demand. Alternatively, during a period of weak demand, GM might decide to lower the price it is willing to pay. Fisher Body would find itself in a poor bargaining position and thus may likely acquiesce to this change in terms.

Recognizing ahead of time that this sort of behavior might occur is a key insight of transaction cost economics. The theory is unusual in that it specifies two important behavioral assumptions: (1) Agents are far-sighted, boundedly rational decision makers, and (2) they will behave opportunistically. Combining an appreciation for (a) unwavering differences in governance structures; (b) an ability to measure the features of transactions, particularly the level of asset specificity; and (c) these behavioral assumptions, transaction cost economics generates the following testable hypotheses, the last of which is known as the "discriminating alignment hypothesis" (Williamson, 1991):

- As asset specificity rises, contracting hazards rise.
- As contracting hazards rise, transaction costs rise.
- Thus, as asset specificity rises, we are more likely to observe hierarchical modes of governance.

Williamson (1991) articulates that managers at both Fisher Body and GM, given those stated behavioral assumptions, would recognize that the idiosyncratic (asset-specific) investments required to stamp out customized components would lead to potential contracting hazards and thus increased transaction costs—costs that could not be remedied through pricing. Instead, as the third hypothesis above indicates, managers chose the governance structure that economizes on transaction costs. Recall that these are the costs that arise not only from the contracting hazards (e.g., the potential last-minute changes in pricing depending on external demand conditions) but also the costs of writing, monitoring, and haggling over contracts to try to prevent such opportunistic behavior. As a result, transaction cost economics predicts that the best form of governance, the form that is best able to economize on these costs, is hierarchy. And indeed, after several years of exchange, GM did adjust its governance structure accordingly and acquired Fisher Body, transforming it from an exchange partner to an embedded division within the GM organization.

As outlined in the introduction, transaction cost economics has had tremendous success in predicting the mode of organization or governance choice. According to recent reviews of the empirical literature (Boerner & Macher, 2000; Macher & Richman, 2008; Shelanski & Klein, 1995), more than 600 studies have been published, the majority of which support the primary hypotheses of the discriminating alignment argument. Consistent with theoretical predictions, high levels of asset specificity lead to an increased likelihood of firms relying on vertical integration.

Even today, the vast majority of the empirical studies that have been undertaken in transaction cost economics have tested the discriminating alignment hypothesis. But as we will highlight in the remaining sections of this chapter, this is reflective of the early timing of these papers, not the state of current empirical research. Nonetheless, to highlight the contributions of these early papers is warranted. Monteverde and Teece (1982) provided what is still seen as an archetypal study of vertical integration through a transaction cost lens. Using data on the two leading U.S. automobile producers, the authors found that, as predicted, as the level of asset specificity increased, the likelihood of vertical integration did as well. Asset specificity is measured in this paper as is still commonly done today: via surveying experts as to the degree of unique, idiosyncratic investment required to support the exchange. Generally, such surveys use multiple questions in combination as a proxy for asset specificity.

Although using surveys remains a popular measurement technique, not all studies rely on survey measures of asset specificity. For example, Joskow (1985, 1987, 1990) used the measurement of physical proximity when measuring site specificity. He finds that indeed as site specificity increases, power plants are more likely to use more hierarchical forms of exchange in accessing the coal needed for power generation.

While three variables—asset specificity, frequency, and uncertainty—are theorized to affect the choice of governance, it is interesting to note that most studies deal with either uncertainty or asset specificity, but few deal with frequency. To be sure, Williamson (1985, 1991) explains that absent asset specificity, the other two variables do not pose the same sort of governance concerns. Thus, studies that have examined uncertainty do so in conjunction with inclusions of controls for asset specificity (e.g., Anderson, 1985; Stump & Heide, 1996; Walker & Weber, 1987).

Beyond Make-Buy: Strategic Alliances, International Business, and Performance

Strategic Alliances

Transaction cost economics is a branch of economics best known for its contribution to the boundary of the firm literature, with particular emphasis on vertical integration (e.g., Williamson, 1975, 1985, 1996). As discussed in the preceding section, hundreds of studies (as many as 600) have largely corroborated the primary predictions of the theory (i.e., the discriminating alignment hypothesis) regarding the likelihood of integration under certain conditions. Few theoretical perspectives on the firm have been so richly supported by the empirical evidence. But transaction cost economics has made significant contributions to other research areas, contributions that may not be as well known. This section highlights the recent application of transaction cost logic to strategic alliances, international business, and performance.

The initial governance spectrum developed by Williamson was designed to illustrate the trade-offs of the two extreme forms, markets and hierarchy. Over time, researchers began to unpack the middle of the governance spectrum, what Williamson (1991, 1996) refers to as hybrid forms of governance. Given the prevalence of strategic alliances, these became the focus of much recent work on better understanding this particular hybrid form of governance.

While there had been a handful of studies that examined hybrid modes early on (e.g., Heide & John, 1990; Palay, 1984), it was not until Oxley (1999) that the field had a means for separating the features of hybrid modes. In her paper, Oxley provides evidence that these hybrid forms of organization are being used at an increasing rate, motivating interest in better understanding them. Furthermore, her work provides a spectrum to be used in conjunction with the initial governance spectrum outlined by Williamson, to guide research in determining how market-like or hierarchical a given hybrid mode is and thus what sort of trade-offs does this hybrid form offer.

Examining strategic alliances has gone beyond extensions of the discriminating alignment hypothesis as illustrated with the above research. For example, Reuer, Zollo, and Singh (2002) examine the evolution of strategic alliances, using data on biotech and pharmaceutical alliances. They specifically set out to determine whether collaborative agreements experience significant contractual alterations in the area of control or monitoring. Interestingly, while governance does change over time, it does so more often based on the experience of the strategic alliance partners, rather than in response to changes in conditions.

International

A review of the transaction cost empirical literature shows that it is only recently, over the past decade, that a sustained effort has been under way to expand the geographic scope of the theory. Due to both the spread of transaction cost research among scholars in institutions outside the United States as well as the research activities of U.S.-based scholars, real progress in examining issues related to international business through a transaction cost lens has been achieved. For example, work has analyzed foreign direct investment decisions, the sequence of such decisions (e.g., Delios & Henisz, 2003), the role of institutions in these decisions (e.g. Henisz, 2000), and the value created through these decisions (e.g., Reuer, 2001).

In an interesting paper that relates to both the strategic alliance and international literatures, Dyer (1996) compares the differences in governance structures used by U.S. and Japanese automobile manufacturers. He finds that U.S. firms use either end of the spectrum, relying on arm's-length contracting or vertical integration. In contrast, Japanese manufacturers rely heavily on hybrid forms of governance, especially long-term, relational contracting. The Japanese firms are able to thereby reap some of the benefits of hierarchy (e.g., they can manage higher levels of asset-specific investment) with markets (e.g., they are able to manage technical uncertainty better by switching suppliers as needs change). An important insight, however, is that it is due to the differences in the national-level institutional supports for exchange that allow the Japanese firms to be so successful. In other words, without such institutional support, U.S. firms cannot replicate the governance structure employed by their Japanese counterparts and achieve similar results.

Understanding the role of political or country-specific institutional factors in the decisions of large firms to enter new markets has been improved through the recent work of researchers working through a transaction cost lens. Henisz and colleagues (e.g., Delios & Henisz, 2000; Henisz, 2000; Henisz & Zelner, 2001) have found a method of better measuring political risk—an oft-cited rationale for the reluctance of large multinationals to enter these markets—and used it to predict not just the likelihood of entry but the likelihood of entry mode (i.e., what form of governance does the entering firm employ to offset the likely contractual hazards that may occur as a result of institutional factors). In addition to political risk, they measure the feasibility of adaptation in the institutional environment and find results that support their hypotheses

regarding the use of governance mode given more favorable institutional conditions.

Performance

As we have discussed, transaction cost economics adopts the view that firms can be thought of as bundles of transactions. And each transaction has an optimal (i.e., transaction cost economizing) way of being structured. The implication for strategy researchers is that firms that are the most optimally aligned (most efficiently structured) will outperform those that are not. The other big implication for strategy is that those firms that recognize the pitfalls of exchange will do better. These kinds of questions go beyond the basic likelihood of what governance structure is chosen by a firm. The question now becomes, if a firm does adhere to the discriminating alignment hypothesis, does it benefit as a result? Benefit, in this instance, meaning does it outperform its rivals?

Although the implications for firm performance of transaction cost economics have been of great interest to strategy scholars, the empirical demands of conducting actual tests of these potential performance hypotheses have been daunting (e.g., Masten, 1993). For example, in addition to collecting data at the microanalytic level (e.g., information on the asset specificity, uncertainty, and frequency of the transaction), as well as information on what governance mode is chosen, researchers also must collect data at the firm, industry, and/or economic levels (e.g., the performance of the firm, industry averages of performance, economic variables that might also affect performance). Note that there are also temporal differences in the nature of the data required. Researchers who study questions related to testing variations of the discriminating alignment hypothesis can use cross-sectional data. But strategy researchers interested in tracking the impact of firm decisions on performance require longitudinal data. This presents enormous empirical obstacles that must be overcome. As a result, it is only recently that progress has been made in this area.

Early studies in this area measured performance as something other than profitability. Nickerson and Bigelow (2008) summarize much of this initial performance research. They describe the finding that the transfer of technological knowledge is diminished as firms must rely on market governance given relatively high levels of asset specificity (Poppo & Zenger, 1998) while Leiblein, Reuer, and Dalsace (2002) find that the alignment of governance choice and contracting hazards ultimately improves technological performance. Using data on R&D alliances, Sampson (2004) finds that the alignment of transactions according to transaction cost predictions conferred collaborative benefits not found in transactions organized otherwise. Transaction cost economics has begun to amass a body of research that indicates that firms that achieve an efficient alignment enjoy performance benefits. However, none of these studies estimates economic performance in terms of profitability or cost savings.

The first study to provide estimates of economic performance at a transaction level was Masten, Meehan, and Snyder (1991). Their study found that cost savings in shipbuilding were achieved in conjunction with organizing governance structures as predicted by transaction cost theory. In developing their empirical estimates, they also used econometric methods that statistically remedied the endogeneity problem inherent in doing comparative analysis that accounts for the selection of discrete organizational forms. While this study offered a breakthrough in empirical transaction cost research by estimating cost savings, it still did not achieve the long-sought-after goal of estimating economic profits at the transaction level.

To date, the first and only study to provide estimates of profitability at a transaction level is Mayer and Nickerson (2005). Analyzing the contracts of an information technology company, the authors first test the discriminating alignment hypothesis. Then, using a two-stage switching regression model, they show that projects aligned according to the discriminating alignment hypothesis are, on average, more profitable than misaligned projects. Note that this is another econometric solution to the endogeneity problem endemic to transaction cost research that aims to study performance.

While measuring the impact of profitability and cost savings remains rare, researchers in this area have demonstrated creativity in adopting alternate proxies for financial performance. For example, Silverman, Nickerson, and Freeman (1997); Nickerson and Silverman (2003a, 2003b); and Argyres and Bigelow (2007) employ the duration and survivability of firms as substitutes for financial performance. The crux of the argument is that in competitive markets, firms that survive longer than their rivals must have greater profitability and/or access to financial resources. These studies find that consistent with transaction cost predictions, firms that use governance structures aligned with transaction characteristics are more likely to live longer and are less likely to fail than firms that do not organize efficiently.

Emerging Areas of Research: Opportunities in the Areas of Contracts, Technological Evolution, and Industry Dynamics

While there remain many opportunities to build on the areas of strategic alliances (and other hybrid governance structures), international business, and performance, at least two areas of research in transaction cost economics have emerged only recently: the study of contractual features and the role of technological evolution and industry dynamics.

Contracts

In a study designed to better understand the nature of contractual learning processes over time, Argyres, Bercovitz, and Mayer (2007) examine two categories of contractual provisions that are used to manage uncertainty and asset specificity. Using data from an information technology provider over an 18-year period, the authors find that certain contractual clauses related to contingency planning and task description did change over time. They suggest that time-dependent reputation advantages may have played a role, providing an effective and efficient safeguard against opportunistic behavior.

Other studies in the contracting area have focused on the role of trust not just as a complement but as a substitute for other contractual provisions. Gulati and Nickerson (2008) argue that trust acts as a shift parameter that lowers governance costs for all modes of governance whenever exchange hazards are present and thus enhances performance regardless of the mode of governance chosen. This lowering of governance cost arises because trust, which is less formal than either contracts or ownership, facilitates adaptation—exchange partners are more likely to avoid disputes or resolve them quickly when trust is present (Gulati, Lawrence, & Puranam, 2005). Gulati and Nickerson's (2008) theory also suggests that trust can lead to a substitution of less formal for more formal modes of governance because governance cost-reducing benefits of trust are greater for market than for hybrid and greater for hybrid than for hierarchy. These differences arise because trust proves a less useful safeguard when formal mechanisms such as contracts and ownership are used. The result of this differential impact is that the market mode of governance, with the addition of preexisting trust, may be used over a broader range of exchange hazards than can market sans trust, which in turn offers lower governance costs and enhances exchange performance. Also, a hybrid with preexisting trust can substitute over some range of exchange hazards for hierarchy, which enhances exchange performance. Drawing on a sample of 222 sourcing arrangements for components from two assemblers in the automobile industry, Gulati and Nickerson (2008) find broad support for both substitutive and complementary affects of interorganizational trust on qualitative measures of perceived exchange performance.

Other additional areas of recent interest include understanding the role of contractual features (e.g., Mellewigt, Madhok, & Weibel, 2007), the range of contractual provisions (e.g., Oxley & Wada 2009), and the development of contracting capabilities (e.g., Argyres & Mayer, 2004). Again, as in the performance area, the current obstacle to more research is accessing suitable data, not lack of interest.

Technical Evolution and Industry Dynamics

As stated earlier, in the section on performance, the ability to withstand selection pressures and survive longer than rivals as a result of adhering to the discriminating alignment hypothesis has been used in a handful of studies. A branch of this research is now focused on linking the selection environment to the evolution of the industry. Furthermore, this focus highlights the fact that selection environments change over time. Unfortunately, the presumption in transaction cost economics is that this selection pressure hinges on alignment and is made without a discussion of how factors such as the industry life cycle and degree of technological evolution might drive changes in this selection pressure.

Thus, important questions remain regarding the time required before selection pressures drive less efficient (i.e., transaction cost-economizing) firms from the industry as well as how the force of these selection pressures changes over time. Williamson (1985, p. 23) briefly suggests that efficient transaction cost economizing might occur over 5 to 10 years, though the timescale required to achieve efficient organization is rarely addressed in empirical studies. One exception is Nickerson and Silverman (2003a), who found that institutional constraints on firms in the U.S. trucking industry slowed their efforts to economize on transaction costs after deregulation.

Industry life cycle theories (e.g., Abernathy & Utterback, 1978; Klepper, 1996; Klepper & Miller, 1995) are of particular interest because they postulate general patterns in the waxing and waning of selection forces that may be and have been made subject to empirical confirmation. Thus, integrating theories of industry and technological evolution, as well as competitive intensity with transaction cost economics, may help address the need for estimating the selection pressures in operation in a given empirical context.

In the first study of this kind, Argyres and Bigelow (2007) integrate industry life cycle theory with transaction cost economics to examine the impact of organizational choice and firm survival over time. They find that firms that misalign transactions face increased risk of failure. However, this risk is mitigated by environmental selection pressures. Research on industry life cycles demonstrates that competitive pressures are more severe during the shakeout stage, which occurs later in the industry life cycle, than at other stages. Transaction cost theory, on the other hand, assumes generally competitive markets and does not address the industry life cycle. It therefore implies that transaction cost economizing is a superior firm strategy regardless of the stage of the life cycle. The authors find that, indeed, adhering to the discriminating alignment hypothesis is not a superior strategy under all time periods. Analyzing data from the early U.S. auto industry, they find that while transaction cost economizing did not have a significant impact on firm survival during the pre-shakeout stage, it did have a significant positive impact on survival during the shakeout stage. This suggests that applications of transaction cost theory, which assume uniformly severe selection pressures across the industry life cycle, could be misleading. It also suggests that theories of the industry life cycle could usefully take transaction costs into account along with production costs in their analyses of competition over the life cycle.

Discussion and Conclusion

The purpose of this chapter has been to familiarize the reader with the key insights and contributions of transaction cost economics as well as highlight the many potential applications of the theory. As chief architect, Oliver Williamson has combined ideas from economics (e.g., Coase, 1937), law (e.g., Macaulay, 1963), and organization theory (e.g., Simon, 1957, 1959, 1962). Over the past three decades, he has refined his thinking, and other researchers have extended the empirical and theoretical reach of the theory. With fair warning to readers, it should be noted that the author still remembers reading the quote that introduced this chapter as a graduate student in a seminar taught by Williamson himself and has indeed seen her worldview of organizations irreversibly altered as a result. Thus, although every effort was made to be even-handed in discussing the current state of viewing economic problems of organization through a transaction cost lens, the reader should be aware that there may be some inadvertent bias.

Recall that in brief, the transaction cost approach works as follows: The decision makers within a firm begin by (a) understanding the trade-offs between different modes of governance. This relies on thinking of governance as falling on a spectrum with markets (arm's-length contracts) on one end and hierarchy (a typical organization, e.g., Monsanto) on the other. Hybrid forms of organization such as joint ventures, long-term contracts, and franchising fall somewhere in the middle. The big differences between the two extremes have to do with the ability to adapt (coordinate), the incentive intensity (e.g., a manager's ability to motivate people), and the way disputes are adjudicated. The next step has to do with (b) understanding the characteristics of the transaction. The three characteristics we think are critical are uncertainty, frequency (i.e., is this an exchange that the firm intends to repeat over time), and the primary driver of governance choice—asset specificity. Asset specificity is the degree to which an asset has become specialized for a given exchange. The next step is to (c) outline the contracting hazards that may arise, depending on the nature of the transaction and the features of potential governance solutions. Finally, (d) choose the governance structure that economizes on transaction costs. These are the costs that arise not only from the contracting hazards but also the costs of writing, monitoring, and haggling over contracts.

So, the immediate implications of transaction cost economics are that (a) as asset specificity increases, contracting hazards intensify; (b) as asset specificity increases and/or contracting hazards intensify, managers are likely to find that a hierarchical mode of governance is more efficient; and (c) in application, no form of governance is perfect. There are always trade-offs. The role of managers, then, is to assess those trade-offs in a systematic way and anticipate the shifts in trade-offs that will occur over time as the nature of the underlying transaction changes over time.

One additional advantage of using a transaction cost economics approach: The theory forces researchers to be precise about what questions need to be asked, what the objectives of the exchange are, and what trade-offs can be tolerated.

Furthermore, note that even the oldest research puzzles are fair game for renewed discussion. For example, a recent series of papers revisiting Fisher Body–GM (e.g., Coase, 2000; Goldberg, 2008; Klein, 1988, 2007, 2008) suggests that debates regarding governance choices, contracting hazards, and transaction costs are far from settled. This does not mean that the theory itself is not valid. Quite the contrary, as the various literature reviews have documented. Instead, this renewed debate suggests that transaction cost theory remains a robust and active area of economics, law, and organization theory. It is hoped that the student of transaction cost economics will be inspired by this and, perhaps, contribute to the conversation.

Author's Note: I thank Nick Argyres, Jackson Nickerson, and Todd Zenger for helpful discussions. Nonetheless, this manuscript reflects my own biases, and thus any inadvertent errors or omissions are solely the responsibility of this author.

References and Further Readings

Abernathy, W. J., & Utterback, J. (1978, June–July). Patterns of industrial innovation. *Technology Review*, pp. 40–47.

Anderson, E. (1985). The salesperson as outside agent or employee: A transaction cost analysis. *Marketing Science, 4,* 234.

Argyres, N., & Bigelow, L. (2007). Does transaction misalignment matter for firm survival across all stages of the industry lifecycle? *Management Science, 53,* 1332–1345.

Argyres, N., & Mayer, K. (2004). Learning to contract: Evidence from the personal computer industry. *Organization Science, 15,* 394–410.

Argyres, N., & Mayer, K. (2007). Contract design as a firm capability: An integration of learning and transaction cost perspectives. *Academy of Management Review, 32,* 1060–1077.

Argyres, N. S., Bercovitz, J., & Mayer, K. J. (2007). Complementarity and evolution of contractual provisions: An empirical study of IT services contracts. *Organization Science, 18,* 3–19.

Boerner, C., & Macher, J. (2000). *Transaction cost economics: An assessment of empirical research in the social sciences* (Working paper). Washington, DC: Georgetown University.

Coase, R. H. (1937). The nature of the firm. *Economica, 4,* 386–405.

Coase, R. H. (1972). Industrial organization: A proposal for research. In V. R. Fuchs (Ed.), *Policy issues and research opportunities in industrial organization* (pp. 59–73). New York: National Bureau of Economic Research.

Coase, R. H. (2000). The acquisition of Fisher Body by General Motors. *Journal of Law & Economics, 43,* 15–31.

Delios, A., & Henisz, W. J. (2000). Japanese firms' investment strategies in emerging economies. *Academy of Management Journal, 43,* 305–323.

Delios, A., & Henisz, W. J. (2003). Political hazards, experience, and sequential entry strategies: The international expansion of Japanese firms 1980–1998. *Strategic Management Journal, 24,* 1153–1164.

Dyer, J. (1996). Does governance matter? Keiretsu alliances and asset specificity as sources of Japanese competitive advantage. *Organization Science, 7,* 649–666.

Goldberg, V. P. (2008). Lawyers asleep at the wheel? The GM–Fisher Body contract. *Industrial & Corporate Change, 17,* 1071–1084.

Grossman, S. J., & Hart, O. (1986). The costs and benefits of ownership: A theory of vertical and lateral integration. *Journal of Political Economy, 94,* 691–719.

Gulati, R., Lawrence, P. R., & Puranam, P. (2005). Adaptation in vertical relationships: Beyond incentive conflict. *Strategic Management Journal, 26,* 415–440.

Gulati, R., & Nickerson, J. A. (2008). Interorganizational trust, governance choice, and exchange performance. *Organization Science, 19,* 688–708.

Hart, O., & Moore, J. (1990). Property rights and the nature of the firm. *Journal of Political Economy, 98,* 1119–1159.

Heide, J., & John, G. (1990). Alliances in industrial purchasing: The determinants of joint action in buyer-supplier relationships. *Journal of Marketing Research, 27,* 24–36.

Henisz, W. J. (2000). The institutional environment for multinational investment. *Journal of Law, Economics & Organization, 16,* 334–364.

Henisz, W. J., & Zelner, B. A. (2001). The institutional environment for telecommunications investment. *Journal of Economics & Management Strategy, 10,* 123–147.

Henisz, W. J., & Zelner, B. A. (2005). Legitimacy, interest group pressures, and change in emergent institutions: The case of foreign investors and host country governments. *Academy of Management Review, 30,* 361–382.

Joskow, P. (1985). Vertical integration and long-term contracts: The case of coal-burning electric generating plants. *Journal of Law, Economics, and Organization, 1,* 33–80.

Joskow, P. (1987). Contract duration and relation specific investments: Empirical evidence from coal markets. *American Economic Review, 17,* 168–185.

Joskow, P. (1990). The performance of long-term contracts: Further evidence from the coal markets. *Rand Journal of Economics, 21,* 251–274.

Klein, B. (1988). Vertical integration as organizational ownership: The Fisher Body–General Motors relationship revisited. *Journal of Law, Economics & Organization, 4,* 199–214.

Klein, B. (2007). The economic lessons of Fisher Body–General Motors. *International Journal of the Economics of Business, 14,* 1–36.

Klein, B. (2008). The enforceability of the GM–Fisher Body contract: Comment on Goldberg. *Industrial & Corporate Change, 17,* 1085–1096.

Klein, B., Crawford, V., & Alchian, A. (1978). Vertical integration, appropriable rents, and the competitive contracting process. *Journal of Law and Economics, 21,* 297–326.

Klepper, S. (1996). Entry, exit, growth, and innovation over the product life cycle. *American Economic Review, 86,* 562–583.

Klepper, S., & Miller, J. (1995). Entry, exit, and shakeouts in the United States in new manufactured products. *International Journal of Industrial Organization, 13,* 567–592.

Leiblein, M. J., Reuer, J. J., & Dalsace, F. (2002). Do make or buy decisions matter? The influence of organizational governance on technological performance. *Strategic Management Journal, 23,* 817–834.

Macaulay, S. (1963). Non-contractual relations in business. *American Sociological Review, 28,* 55–70.

Macher, J. (2006). Technological development and the boundaries of the firm: A knowledge-based examination in semiconductor manufacturing. *Management Science, 52,* 826–843.

Macher, J., & Richman, B. (2008). Transaction cost economics: An assessment of empirical research in the social sciences. *Business and Politics, 10*(1), 1–63.

Masten, S. (1993). Transaction costs, mistakes and performance: Assessing the importance of governance. *Managerial and Decision Economics, 14,* 119–130.

Masten, S., Meehan, M., & Snyder, E. (1991). The costs of organization. *Journal of Law, Economics and Organization, 7,* 1–25.

Mayer, K. J., & Nickerson, J. A. (2005). Antecedents and performance implications of contracting for knowledge workers: Evidence from information technology services. *Organization Science, 16,* 225–242.

Mellewigt, T., Madhok, A., & Weibel, A. (2007). Trust and formal contracts in interorganizational relationships: Substitutes and complements. *Managerial & Decision Economics, 28,* 833–847.

Monteverde, K., & Teece, D. (1982). Supplier switching costs and vertical integration in the automobile industry. *Bell Journal of Economics, 13,* 206–213.

Nickerson, J. A., & Bigelow, L. S. (2008). New institutional economics, organization, and strategy. In J.-M. Glachant & E. Brousseau (Eds.), *New institutional economics: A guidebook* (pp. 183–208). Cambridge, UK: Cambridge University Press.

Nickerson, J., & Silverman, B. (2003a). Why firms want to organize efficiently and what keeps them from doing so: Evidence from the for-hire trucking industry. *Administrative Science Quarterly, 3,* 433–465.

Nickerson, J. A., & Silverman, B. S. (2003b). Why firms want to organize efficiently and what keeps them from doing so: Inappropriate governance, performance, and adaptation in a deregulated industry. *Administrative Science Quarterly, 48,* 433–465.

Oxley, J. (1999). Institutional environment and the mechanisms of governance: The impact of intellectual property. *Journal of Economic Behavior & Organization, 38,* 283–310.

Oxley, J., & Wada, T. (2009). Alliance structure and the scope of knowledge transfer: Evidence from US-Japan agreements. *Management Science, 55,* 635–649.

Palay, T. (1984). Comparative institutional economics: The governance of rail freight contracting. *Journal of Legal Studies, 13,* 265–288.

Poppo, L., & Zenger, T. (1998). Testing alternative theories of the firm: Transaction cost, knowledge-based, and measurement explanations for make-or-buy decisions in IT services. *Strategic Management Journal, 19,* 853–877.

Reuer, J. J. (2001). From hybrids to hierarchies: Shareholder wealth effects of joint venture partner buyouts. *Strategic Management Journal, 22,* 27–45.

Reuer, J. J., Zollo, M., & Singh, H. (2002). Post-formation dynamics in strategic alliances. *Strategic Management Journal, 23,* 135–152.

Riordan, M., & Williamson, O. E. (1985). Asset specificity and economic organization. *International Journal of Industrial Organization, 3,* 365–378.

Sampson, R. C. (2004). The cost of misaligned governance in R&D alliances. *Journal of Law, Economics & Organization, 20,* 484–526.

Shelanski, H., & Klein, P. (1995). Empirical research in transaction cost economics. *Journal of Law, Economics and Organization, 11,* 335–361.

Silverman, B., Nickerson, J. A., & Freeman, J. (1997). Profitability, transactional alignment, and organizational mortality in the U.S. trucking industry. *Strategic Management Journal, 18,* 31–52.

Simon, H. (1957). *Administrative behavior* (2nd ed.). New York: Macmillan.

Simon, H. (1959). Theories of decision-making in economics and behavioral science. *American Economic Review, 49,* 253–284.

Simon, H. (1962). New developments in the theory of the firm. *American Economic Review, 52,* 1–15.

Stump, R. L., & Heide, J. B. (1996). Controlling supplier opportunism in industrial relationships. *Journal of Marketing Research, 33,* 431–441.

Suarez, F., & Utterback, J. (1995). Dominant designs and the survival of firms. *Strategic Management Journal, 16,* 415–430.

Walker, G., & Weber, D. (1987). Supplier competition, uncertainty, and make-or-buy decisions. *Academy of Management Journal, 30,* 589–596.

Williamson, O. E. (1975). *Markets and hierarchies.* New York: Free Press.

Williamson, O. E. (1985). *The economic institutions of capitalism.* New York: Free Press.

Williamson, O. E. (1991). Comparative economic organization: The analysis of discrete structural alternatives. *Administrative Science Quarterly, 36,* 269–296.

Williamson, O. E. (1996). *The mechanisms of governance.* New York: Oxford University Press.

INDEX

Main topics and their page numbers are in **bold.** Page numbers referring to figures and tables are followed by (figure) and (table).

A.A. Poultry Farms, Inc. v. Rose Acre Farms, Inc. (1989), **1:**136
A&M Records v. Napster (2001), **2:**764n
Abadie, A., **2:**812
Abbink, K., **2:**842
ABC Research Group, **2:**870
Abdulkadiroglu, A., **2:**936, **2:**937, **2:**938
Abernathy, W. J., **2:**947
Ability-to-pay principle, **1:**369
Abou-Zeid, M., **2:**659
Abowd, J. M., **1:**157
Abreu, D., **2:**736
Absolute advantage, **1:**411. *See also* **International trade, comparative and absolute advantage, and trade restrictions**
Absolute purchasing power parity (PPP), **1:**437
Absolute uncertainty, **1:**315
Absorptive capacity of formalism, **1:**38–39
ACCION, **2:**844
Accumulationist view, of East Asian growth, **1:**488
Acemoglu, Daron, **1:**41, **2:**813, **2:**814
Acheson, K., **2:**833
Achnacarry Agreement, **2:**649
Ackerman, K. Z., **2:**601
Ackermann, Thomas, **2:**643
Acton Institute, **2:**898, **2:**899
Actual compensation, economics of property law and, **2:**761–762
Adam Smith Problem, Das, **1:**5, **2:**895
Adaption, complexity and economics, **2:**885, **2:**886
Addams, Jane, **2:**769–770
Addictive behavior, neuroeconomics and, **2:**917–918
Adelman, Irma, **1:**15, **1:**17, **1:**19, **1:**20, **1:**465n
Adelman, M. A., **2:**648
Adequate yearly progress (AYP), **2:**521
Adjustable rate mortgages (ARMs), **2:**612
Adjusted R^2, **1:**46
Administrative Science Quarterly, **2:**942
Adolphs, R., **2:**914
Adridge, Jay Taylor, **2:**604
Adverse selection, **2:**709
    economics of health insurance and, **2:**719–724
    economics of information and, **2:**730
    microfinance and, **2:**839
Advertising
    endorsements by athletes, **2:**547
    media economics and, **2:**829
Advisory Council on Intergovernmental Relations, **1:**372
Affluent Society, The (Galbraith), **2:**605

Africa
    economic history and, **1:**18–21
    economics of aging, **2:**586 (table)
    world development in historical perspective, **1:**456–457
African Americans, **2:**564–566
    average years of schooling, **2:**565 (figure)
    geographic distribution by race, **2:**566 (table)
    industrial employment distribution by race, **2:**567 (table)
    marital status by race, **2:**566 (table)
    median income, **2:**564 (figure), **2:**565
    See also **Economics and race**
Afterlife, economics and religion, **2:**779–780
Age of Discovery, **1:**18
Age of Imperialism, **1:**19
Agenda manipulation, **1:**240
Agent-based models, complexity and economics, **2:**888
Agglomeration economies, **2:**667–668, **2:**680
Aggregate demand and aggregate supply, 1:333–340
    applications and empirical evidence, **1:**336–337
    basic AD/AS model, **1:**333 (figure)
    enhanced AD/AS model, **1:**335 (figure)
    Lucas aggregate supply hypothesis, **1:**401–402
    policy implications, **1:**337–338
    theory, **1:**333–336
Aggregate demand/price adjustment model, **1:**326
Aggregate equilibrium demand curve, **1:**339
Aggregate expenditures model and equilibrium output, 1:319–331
    aggregate expenditures (AE), defined, **1:**319
    applications, refinements, policy, **1:**324–327
    history of the AE/Keynesian cross framework, **1:**327–330
    Keynesian cross diagram, **1:**322 (figure)
    theory, **1:**319–324
Aghion, P., **2:**736
Aging. *See* **Economics of aging**
Agrawal, R. C., **2:**602
Agreement on Trade-Related Aspects of Intellectual Property Rights (TRIPS), **2:**694
Agribusiness management, **2:**603–604
Agricultural Adjustment Act of 1933, **2:**598
Agricultural and Applied Economics Association (AAEA), **2:**597, **2:**598
Agricultural and Mechanical College of North Carolina, **2:**598
Agricultural and Resource Economics Review, **2:**599
Agricultural economics, 2:597–606
    areas of concentration, **2:**602–604
    economic analysis of the family and, **2:**580

economic history and evolution of, **1:**15

future of, **2:**605

history of, **2:**598–599

notable economists in, **2:**604–605

quantitative techniques in, **2:**602

theory, **2:**599–602

undergraduate education in, **2:**599

Agricultural Economics, **2:**599

Agricultural Finance Review, **2:**604

Agriculture, food production and economic methodology, **1:**25

Agronomy Journal, **2:**603

Aharon, I., **2:**916

Ahlin, C., **2:**843

Aid to Families with Dependent Children (AFDC), **1:**260

AIDS. *See* **Economics of HIV and AIDS**

AIDS Drug Assistance Program (ADAP), **2:**692

AIG, **1:**353

Air traffic controllers (PATCO), **1:**63

Akaike info criterion, **1:**53

Akerlof, George A.

economics and corporate social responsibility, **2:**790

economics of gender and, **2:**556

economics of health insurance and, **2:**719

economics of HIV/AIDS and, **2:**691

economics of information and, **2:**729, **2:**730

experimental economics and, **2:**879

microfinance and, **2:**839

new classical economics, **1:**407

Albarran, A., **2:**828, **2:**830

Alberini, A., **2:**823

Albrecht, J., **2:**559

Alchian, Armen, **1:**38, **1:**196, **2:**801, **2:**942

Aldrich, J. H., **1:**241

Aldy, Joseph, **1:**279

Alexander, A., **2:**828

Alexander, Donald L., **2:**535, **2:**539

Allan, G., **2:**538

Allegretto, S., **1:**63

Allen, D. W., **2:**582

Allison, Dorothy, **2:**770

Alm, J., **1:**253

Alonso, William, **2:**665, **2:**670, **2:**671

Alonso-Muth-Mills approach, **2:**670–672

Altig, D., **1:**376

Altonji, Joseph G., **2:**555, **2:**569

American Academy of Economics and Financial Experts, **2:**739

American Agricultural Economics Association, **2:**598

American Airlines, **1:**139

American Association of University Professors, **1:**146

American Civil War, **1:**17, **1:**56, **1:**133

American Clean Air Act, **1:**279

American Drugs, Inc. v. Wal-Mart Stores, Inc. (1993), **1:**139

American Economic Association, **1:**383, **2:**898

American Enterprise Institute, **1:**64

American exceptionalism, **1:**165

American Farm Economics Association, **2:**598

American Federation of Labor (AFL), **1:**56, **1:**60

American Federation of Labor and Congress of Industrial Organizations (AFL-CIO), **1:**167–168

American Gaming Association, **2:**677, **2:**679, **2:**680

American Institute for Economic Research (AIER), **1:**290

American Journal of Agricultural Economics, **2:**598

American Psychiatric Association, **2:**682

American Recovery and Reinvestment Act of 2009, **1:**148, **1:**367

American Rehabilitation Economics Association, **2:**739

American Religious Identity Survey (ARIS), **2:**781

Amiad, Amotz, **2:**602

Amott, T., **2:**768

Amsterdam Stock Exchange, **1:**17

"Analysis," "vision" *vs.,* **1:**34

Anarchy, **1:**245

Anas, Alex, **2:**610, **2:**672

Andari, R., **2:**827

Andean Community, **2:**851

Andersen, E. S., **2:**928

Anderson, B. M., **1:**327

Anderson, E., **2:**528, **2:**944

Anderson, J., **1:**360

Anderson, J. R., **2:**602

Anderson, Jock, **2:**600

Anderson, S. W., **2:**918

Anderson, Torben, **2:**568

Ando, Albert W., **2:**589, **2:**626

Ando, Faith, **2:**568

Andreoni, J., **2:**789

Ang, B. W., **2:**638

Angrist, J. D., **2:**812

"Antigay animus," **2:**772–774

Antiretroviral drugs, **2:**694–695

Antitrust laws

economics of energy markets and, **2:**640

imperfectly competitive product markets, **1:**133–134

Antle, J. M., **2:**604

Antonovics, Kate, **2:**566

Apenchenko, V. S., **2:**815

Apgar, W., **2:**673

A+ Plan for Education (Florida), **2:**521–522

Applebaum, Eileen, **1:**57, **1:**64

Applied Economic Perspectives and Policy, **2:**599, **2:**602

Appropriable quasi rent, **1:**198

Aquinas, Thomas, **1:**25, **2:**891, **2:**892, **2:**893

Arab-Israel War (1973), **2:**649

Arabian Peninsula, **1:**18

Aramco Oil, **2:**649

Arbitration, role of labor unions and, **1:**168

Arc elasticity, **1:**90

Are Economists Basically Immoral? (Heyne), **2:**898

Areeda, P., **1:**137

Arestis, R., **1:**316

Argonne National Laboratory, **1:**77

Argyres, Nick S., **2:**946–947, **2:**948n

Arias, E., **2:**740

Ariely, Dan, **1:**24, **2:**865

Aristotle, **1:**25, **1:**33, **2:**891, **2:**892–893, **2:**893, **2:**894, **2:**895

Arizona State University, **2:**548

Arkansas Unfair Trade Practices Act of 1937, **1:**139

Armed Conflict Dataset, **2:**808, **2:**813

Armendariz de Aghion B., **2:**840, **2:**841, **2:**845n

Arnason, R., **2:**623

Arnhart, Larry, **2:**927

Arnott, Richard, **2:**610, **2:**672

Aronson, J. A., **2:**881, **2:**915

Arora, S., **2:**791

Arrow, Kenneth J.

costs of production and, **1:**108

economics and race, **2:**567, **2:**569

economics of education and, **2:**516

economics of gender and, **2:**556

economics of health insurance and, **2:**717, **2:**719

economics of HIV/AIDS and, **2:**689

externalities and property rights, **1:**231

health economics and, **2:**708

public choice and, **1:**238

transaction cost economies and, **1:**195, **1:**196, **1:**199, **1:**201

Arrow-Debreu-McKenzie model, **1:**8

Arrow-Hahn-Debreu model, **1:**34

Arthur, Brian, **2:**886

Article VI of the Bill of Rights (England), **2:**802

Artifactual field experiments, **2:**874

Artis, M., **1:**479, **1:**480, **1:**483

Aschauer, D., **1:**314

Ashenfelter, Orley, **2:**516, **2:**556

Ashton, T. S., **1:**17

Asia

economic history and, **1:**18–21

economics of aging, **2:**586 (table)

world development in historical perspective, **1:**456–457

Asian Americans, **2:**570–572

average years of schooling, **2:**571 (figure)

geographic distribution by race, **2:**572 (table)

industrial employment distribution by race, **2:**573 (table)

marital status by race, **2:**572 (table)

median income, **2:**570 (figure), **2:**571 (figure)

See also **Economics and race**

Asset pricing models, 1:203–213

description of specific, **1:**207–210

empirical performance of, **1:**210–212

future directions, **1:**212–213

mean-variance opportunity set, **1:**208 (figure)

understanding risk and return, **1:**203–207

Asset specificity, defined, **1:**194, **1:**196–199

Assimilation, immigrant, **2:**702–703

Assimilationist view, of East Asian growth, **1:**488

Association for Evolutionary Economics (AFEE), **2:**924

Association of Religion Data Archives (ARDA), **2:**781

Assortative mating, **2:**578

Asymmetry, information, **2:**729, **2:**730–734

AT&T, **2:**568

Athletes. *See* **Earnings of professional athletes; Sports economics**

Atkinson, S. M., **2:**559

Atlas Narodov Mira, **2:**810, **2:**815

Auburn University, Alabama, **2:**598

Auctions, **1:**73

Audience, media economics and, **2:**829

Audit testing studies, **2:**557

Auerbach, Alan, **1:**313, **1:**357, **1:**376

Auld, C. M., **2:**691

Aumann, R. J., **1:**181

Australia, economics of aging, **2:**586 (table)

Australian Journal of Agricultural and Resource Economics, **2:**599

Australian Productivity Commission, **2:**679

Austria, gender wage gap in, **2:**555 (table)

Autocorrelated errors, **1:**49, **1:**50

Automatic stabilizers, **1:**360

Autonomous level of consumption, **1:**321

"Average," behavioral economics and, **2:**867

Average fixed cost (AFC), **1:**104

Average total cost (ATC), **1:**104

Average variable cost (AVC), **1:**104

Averch, Harvey, **1:**269

Avery, C., **2:**935

Avio, K. L., **2:**752

Axelrod, R., **2:**771, **2:**800

Axtell, R., **2:**886

Ayres, C., **2:**926

Ayres, I., **2:**750

Azpilcueta Navarrus, Martin de, **2:**893

Azzi, C., **2:**778

Baade, Robert, **2:**539

Babcock, B. A., **2:**622

Babcock, Linda, **2:**560

Backward induction, economics of strategy and, **1:**189–191

Bacon, C., **1:**510

Bacon, Francis, **2:**729, **2:**903

Badawi, S., **2:**844

Badgett, M. V. L., **2:**772, **2:**773, **2:**908

Bae, H.-S., **2:**831

Bagdikian, Ben H., **2:**828

Bagnoli, M., **2:**786, **2:**791

Bagues, Manuel, **2:**558

Bailey, R., **2:**637

Bailey, Ralph, **1:**183n

Bailey, T., **1:**64

Baird, S. B., **2:**559

Baker, C. B., **2:**604

Baker, H., **1:**219

Bakhshi, H., **2:**827

Bakker, P., **2:**829

Balance of payments (BOP), **1:**471–474

Balance of trade and payments, 1:419–429

balance of payments (2007), **1:**423 (table)

balance of payments and foreign exchange market, **1:**427–428

balance of payments (selected years, 1960–2005), **1:**424 (table)

capital account and savings-investment relationship, **1:**426 (figure)

classifications used in accounting of, **1:**419–421

current account and domestic savings-investment relationship, **1:**426–427

current account balance and capital account balance measures, **1:**423–425

foreign exchange market, **1:**427 (figure)

measures of overall balance of payments, **1:**421–423

national income accounting and components, **1:**425–426

national savings and capital account, **1:**427 (figure)

sample balance of payments transactions, **1:**421 (table)

Balanced budget

Balanced Budget Amendment, **1:**378

multiplier, **1:**364 (table)

rule, **1:**364–365

Balassa, Bela, **1:**412–**1:**413

Ball, Laurence, **1:**388

Ball, V. Eldon, **2:**600

Banco Sol (Bolivia), **2:**837, **2:**840

Bandara, R., **2:**624

Bandow, Doug, **2:**898

Banerjee, Abhijit, **1:**40

Bank of America, **2:**567

Bank of Canada, **1:**385

Bank of England, **1:**314, **1:**386, **1:**428

Bank of Japan, **1:**386, **1:**422

Bank of the United States, **1:**349

Bank Rakyat (Indonesia), **2:**837, **2:**842

Banking, microfinance and, **2:**838–842

Banz, Rolf, **1:**211

Barber, B., **1:**219

Barde, Jean-Philippe, **2:**634, **2:**635

Barilla, A. G., **2:**536

Barker, D. K., **2:**902, **2:**904, **2:**906, **2:**908, **2:**909, **2:**910

Barnard, Freddie, **2:**604

Baron, D. P., **2:**786, **2:**788, **2:**790–791, **2:**792, **2:**793

Barro, Robert

    aggregate expenditures model and equiibrium output, **1:**339

    East Asian economies and, **1:**489

    fiscal policy and, **1:**366

    government budgets, debt, deficits and, **1:**371, **1:**376

    macroeconomic models and, **1:**312

    new classical economies and, **1:**399, **1:**405, **1:**406

Barry, Peter, **2:**604

Bartel, A. P., **2:**703, **2:**750, **2:**751

Barth, Karl, **1:**60

Bartlett, R. L., **2:**910

Bartoo, Ronald, **2:**618

Barwise, P., **2:**829

Barzel, Yoram, **1:**195, **2:**802

BASF, **1:**130–1:131

Bassetto, Marco, **1:**371

Bateman, I. J., **1:**278

Batie, Sandra, **2:**605

Battalio, R., **2:**915

Battle of the Sexes (game), **1:**175 (figure)

Bauer, J., **2:**829

Baumann, Robert, **2:**539

Baumol, William J.

    economics of energy markets and, **2:**641

    environmental economics, **2:**633

    externalities and property rights, **1:**228

    measuring and evaluating macroeconomic performance, **1:**298, **1:**303, **1:**305

    predatory pricing and strategic entry barriers, **1:**139

    profit maximization and, **1:**123

    twentieth-century economic methodology and, **1:**35, **1:**36

Bayer, Patrick, **2:**519, **2:**522

Bayesian Game, normal-form table (game), **1:**179 (figure)

Bayesian Nash equilibrium, **1:**180

Beane, Billy, **2:**546

Bear market, **1:**300

Beattie, Bruce, **2:**600

Beccaria, Cesare, **2:**747

Becchetti, L., **1:**510

Bechara, A., **2:**917

Becker, Gary S.

    economic analysis of the family, **2:**577, **2:**579

    economic history and, **1:**14

    economics and corporate social responsibility, **2:**788, **2:**789

    economics and race, **2:**566–567, **2:**568

    economics of crime and, **2:**747–750

    economics of education and, **2:**515

    economics of gender and, **2:**555, **2:**556

    feminist economics and, **2:**902

    labor markets and, **1:**145

    matching markets and, **2:**907, **2:**937

    regulatory economics and, **1:**270, **1:**272

    sports economics and, **2:**538

    wage determination and, **1:**155–1:156, **1:**157, **1:**158

Becker-Olsen, K. L., **2:**792, **2:**793

Becker's model, **1:**272

Beckett Baseball Card Price Guide, **2:**568

Been, Vicki, **2:**611

Behavioral economics, 2:861–872

    biased beliefs, **2:**866–867

    definitions and naming problems, **2:**861–864

    HET and, **1:**10

    prospects and problems, **2:**870–871

    social preferences, **2:**867–870

    violations of internally consistent logic, **2:**864–866

Behavioral finance, **1:**218–219

Behaviorism, **2:**864

Beil, Richard O., **2:**626, **2:**899

Beine, M., **2:**703

Beinhocker, Eric D., **1:**24

Belgium, economics of aging, **2:**590 (table)

Belichick, Bill, **2:**537, **2:**546

Bell, C., **2:**688

Bell, C. R., **1:**200

Bellamy, Edward, **1:**441

Bellemare, C., **2:**880

Beller, A. H., **2:**556

Belonging, economics and religion, **2:**778–779

Benabou, R., **2:**789

Ben-Akiva, M., **2:**659

Benartzi, S., **2:**870, **2:**917

Benchmarks, behavioral economics and, **2:**867

Benefit design, economics of health insurance and, **2:**720, **2:**723

Benefit principle, **1:**369

Beneria, L., **2:**907, **2:**910

Bengtsson, Tommy, **2:**594

Ben-Ner, A., **1:**448

Bennett, J. T., **1:**170

Ben-Porath, Yoram, **1:**157

Benson, B., **2:**749

Bentham, Jeremy, **1:**79–1:80, **2:**747, **2:**897

Bercovitz, J., **2:**946

Berg, J., **2:**878–879

Berg, N., **2:**861, **2:**866, **2:**869, **2:**870

Berg, P., **1:**64

Bergeron, S., **2:**909

Bergh, A., **2:**594

Bergman, Barbara, **1:**145

Bergmann, B., **2:**556, **2:**903, **2:**908

Bergson, Abram, **1:**441, **1:**442

Bergstrom, T., **2:**786, **2:**791, **2:**793

Berlin, I., **2:**527

Berliner, Joe, **1:**441

Bernanke, Ben, **1:**313, **1:**353, **1:**354, **1:**382, **1:**385, **1:**386, **1:**398

Bernard, Andrew, **1:**416

Bernheim, B. D., **2:**917–918

Bernhein, B. Douglas, **1:**376

Bernoulli, Daniel, **1:**216, **2:**873

Berns, G. S., **2:**916

Bernstein, J., **1:**63, **2:**701

Bernstein, Jared, **1:**367

Bernstein, Peter, **1:**203

Bernstein, Richard, **1:**42

Berri, David J., **2:**536, **2:**537, **2:**547

Bertalanffy, Ludwig, **1:**40

Bertrand, Joseph, **1:**130, **1:**187, **1:**189, **1:**191

Bertrand, Marianne, **2:**569

Bertrand model, **1:**130, **1:**189
Bertus, Mark, **2:**615
Besley, T., **2:**786, **2:**787, **2:**790, **2:**791, **2:**811, **2:**814, **2:**841
Best Buy, **1:**129
Beyond make-or-buy: advances in transaction cost economics,
     2:941–948
     comparison of attributes of governance structures, **2:**943 (table)
     contracts, technological evolution, industry dynamics, **2:**946–947
     discrete structural alignment and firm boundaries, **2:**942–944
     formulation of transaction cost economics, **2:**941–942
     strategic alliances, international business, performance, **2:**944–946
     See also **Transaction cost economics**
Bhalla, S. S., **1:**494, **1:**496
Bias, behavioral economics and, **2:**866–867
Bichler, S., **2:**648, **2:**651
Biddle, J. E., **1:**4
Bienenstock, Elisa, **2:**570
Bigelow, L. S., **2:**945, **2:**946–947
Bilateral governance structure, **1:**199–200
Billings, G. A., **2:**598
Binmore, K., **2:**868
Biological evolution, evolutionary economics and, **2:**921–923
Bishop, C. E., **2:**598
Bishop, Richard C., **2:**624, **2:**625
Bismarck, Otto von, **1:**18
Björklund, A., **2:**559
Black, Duncan, **1:**238
Black, Fischer, **1:**211
Black, Robert A., **2:**895
Black, Sandra, **2:**556
Black Death, **1:**16
Black Sox, **2:**544
Black-white pay gap, **1:**158
Blanchard, Olivier J., **1:**367, **1:**399, **1:**480
Blanchflower, David, **2:**568
Blank, R., **2:**555
Blau, Francine D., **2:**554, **2:**555n, **2:**905, **2:**908
Blaug, Mark, **1:**4, **1:**27, **1:**37
Blinder, Alan S., **1:**298, **1:**303, **1:**305, **1:**313, **1:**363, **1:**367, **2:**557
Bloch, H., **2:**829
Block, M. K., **2:**751
Blocker, A. W., **1:**373
Bloomberg.com, **2:**745
Blume, L., **2:**786, **2:**791
Blumler, J., **2:**831
Blumstein, A., **2:**752
Board of Governors of the Federal Reserve System, **1:**367
Boardman, Anthony, **1:**268
Boas, Franz, **2:**925
Bocarejo, J. P., **2:**660
Boeing Company, **1:**198
Boerner, C., **2:**944
Boettke, Peter, **1:**245
Bok, D. C., **1:**163
Bok, Derek, **2:**574
Boland, Lawrence, **1:**37
Bolshevik Revolution, **2:**925
Bolton, P., **1:**135, **1:**137, **1:**138
Bonaparte, Louis Napoleon, **1:**17
Bonham, J., **2:**823
Bonin, John, **1:**448
Booth, A., **1:**163
Booysen, Frederik le Roux, **2:**688, **2:**689

Bordo, Michael D., **1:**433–**1:**434
Borenstein, Severin, **2:**641
Borjas, George, **2:**569, **2:**701, **2:**702, **2:**703, **2:**704
Bork, Robert H., **1:**136
Börsch-Supan, Axel, **2:**592
Boskin, Michael, **1:**304
Boston Globe, The, **2:**569
Boston Student Assignment Mechanism (BSAM), **2:**936
Boswell, J., **2:**767
Bottlenecks, **1:**325
Boudreaux, D., **1:**139
Boulding, Kenneth, **1:**38, **1:**40
Bound, John, **2:**565
Bounded rationality
     behavioral economics and, **2:**862, **2:**869–870
     complexity and economics, **2:**884–886
     defined, **1:**194–195
Bowden, G., **2:**646
Bowen, William, **2:**574
Bowles, G., **2:**531
Bowles, Samuel, **1:**58, **2:**789, **2:**790
Boyd, Gale, **2:**643
Boyer, Kenneth, **1:**272
Boyes, William, **1:**269
Bradbury, J. C., **2:**537
Bradford, D. F., **1:**261
Brain. *See* **Neuroeconomics**
"Brain drain," **2:**703–704
Brainard, Elizabeth, **2:**556
Brand-name capital specificity, defined, **1:**196
Brandstätter, E., **2:**866
Braverman, Harry, **1:**58, **1:**59
Breeden, Douglas, **1:**210, **1:**212
Breil, M., **2:**823
Breiter, H. C., **2:**916
Brekke, K. A., **2:**790
Brennan, Geoffrey, **1:**241, **1:**243
Brenner, Robert, **1:**16
Bretton Woods
     balance of trade and payments, **1:**422
     economics of fair trade, **1:**505
     European Monetary Union, **1:**477
     exchange rates, **1:**431, **1:**433
     international finance, **1:**475
     monetary policy and inflation targeting, **1:**383
     world development in historical perspective, **1:**453, **1:**457–459,
         1:464n, **1:**465n
Breyer, Friedrich, **2:**590, **2:**593
Britain
     cost-benefit analysis by, **1:**280–281
     Marx on Industrial Revolution of, **1:**59
     See also United Kingdom
British Empire, **1:**17
British Petroleum, **2:**645, **2:**646, **2:**648, **2:**649
Broadcasting, media economics and, **2:**831–832, **2:**834
Broadcasting Act of 1990, **2:**827
Broda, C., **1:**500
Brodley, J., **1:**135, **1:**137, **1:**138
Brody, D., **1:**57
Bromley, S. L., **2:**647, **2:**648, **2:**649, **2:**650
Bronfenbrenner, Kate, **1:**57, **1:**64
Bronfman, L., **2:**662
Brook, Stacey, **2:**535, **2:**537, **2:**547

Brooke Group Ltd. v. Brown and Williamson Tobacco Corp.
(1993), **1:**135, **1:**136, **1:**137, **1:**138
Brookshire, David, **2:**624
Brookshire, M., **2:**740
Broome, J., **1:**279
Brosnan, S. F., **2:**916
Brower, G. D., **2:**751, **2:**752
Brown, A., **2:**831
Brown, E. Cary, **1:**367
Brown, G. M., **2:**623
Brown, Gardner, **2:**625
Brown, K. H., **2:**536–537
Brown, M., **1:**510
Brown, S., **1:**445
Browne, Lynn E., **2:**569, **2:**673
Browning, Edgar, **2:**593
Brownlee, Oscar H., **2:**600, **2:**604
Bruck, S. I., **2:**815, **2:**828
Brumberg, R., **1:**328
Bruni, L., **2:**861
Buchanan, James M.
economics and corporate social responsibility, **2:**786
economics of crime and, **2:**750
economics of wildlife protection and, **2:**622
public choice and, **1:**237–**1:**238, **1:**241, **1:**243, **1:**244
public finance and, **1:**257
transaction cost economies and, **1:**196
twentieth-century economic methodology, **1:**35, **1:**36, **1:**38, **1:**40
Buckeye, K. R., **2:**659
Buckley, F., **2:**703
Budget lines, **1:**83–84
Budget set, **1:**83
Buffett, Warren, **1:**219
Buhl, S. L., **1:**281
Bull market, **1:**300, **1:**352
Bulmer-Thomas, V., **2:**851
Bulow, J., **1:**138, **2:**937
Bulte, E., **2:**624
Bundesbank, **1:**388n
Bureau for Economic Research, **2:**689
Bureau of Economic Analysis (BEA), **1:**299, **1:**302, **1:**422, **1:**424t
Bureau of Labor Statistics (BLS)
economic measurement and forecasting, **1:**289
labor markets and, **1:**145, **1:**146, **1:**147f, **1:**147t, **1:**149
measuring and evaluating macroeconomic performance, **1:**299, **1:**304
role of labor unions in labor markets and, **1:**166f, **1:**167f, **1:**169, **1:**170f, **1:**171f
Bureau of National Affairs (BNA), **1:**165–**1:**166, **1:**170
Bureaucracies, public choice and, **1:**242–244
Buridan, Jean, **2:**893
Burkhauser, R. V., **1:**159
Burns, A. F., **1:**289
Burns, Arthur, **1:**351, **1:**394
Burns, M., **1:**135
Burns, S., **1:**375
Burtless, Gary, **2:**588
Bush, George H. W., **1:**351
Bush, George W., **2:**521
Business cycle
economic measurement and forecasting, **1:**288 (figure)
economic measurement and forecasting and grouping economic indicators by, **1:**290 (table)

measuring and evaluating macroeconomic performance, **1:**302
monetary equilibrium approach to business cycle theory (MEBCT), **1:**399
real business cycle theory, **1:**312–313
timing, **1:**289–290
Business Cycle Dating Committee of the National Bureau of Economic Research, **1:**299, **1:**353
Business unionism, **1:**56
Buti, M., **1:**479
Butler, Judith, **2:**770, **2:**771
Butler, R., **2:**701
Buxbaum, J. N., **2:**659

Cabral, L., **1:**138
Caffentzis, G., **2:**646, **2:**647, **2:**651
Calabresi, G., **2:**763
Calcagno, P. T., **1:**243
Calculus of Consent: Logical Foundations of Constitutional Democracy, The (Buchanan, Tullock), **1:**238, **1:**244, **1:**257
Calder, A., **2:**673
Caldwell, Bruce, **1:**37, **1:**444
California Health Interview Survey (CHIS), **2:**773
Calveras, A., **2:**786, **2:**793
Calvo, Guillermo A., **1:**388n, **1:**433
Cambridge University, **1:**392
Camerer, C. F.
behavioral economics and, **2:**861, **2:**862, **2:**864, **2:**867, **2:**870
game theory and, **1:**178
neuroeconomics and, **2:**913, **2:**914, **2:**915, **2:**917
Cameron, D., **1:**479
Campbell, J. Y., **1:**211
Campbell, T., **2:**720
Canada
economics of aging, **2:**586 (table)
health economics and, **2:**712–713
monetary policy and inflation targeting, **1:**385
role of labor unions in, **1:**166–168
Canadian Journal of Agricultural Economics, **2:**599
Candler, Wilfred, **2:**602
Cao, S., **1:**486
Capital, aging and, **2:**589
Capital account balance, **1:** 423–424, **1:**426 (figure), **1:**427 (figure).
See also **Balance of trade and payments**
Capital asset, cultural heritage as, **2:**822
Capital asset pricing model (CAPM), **1:**207–209
consumption-based, **1:**210
intertemporal, **1:**209–210
Capital budgets, government, **1:**369–370
Capital inflow, **1:**424
Capital (Marx), **1:**6, **1:**58
Capitalism
comparative economic systems, **1:**441–448
economic history and evolution of, **1:**14–15
economic methodology and, **1:**25
labor and, in U.S., **1:**55–57
Marx and capitalist employment relationship, **1:**58–60
See also **Marxian and institutional industrial relations in U.S.**
Capitalism and Freedom (Friedman), **2:**519, **2:**528
Capps, Oral, **2:**603
Capps, R., **2:**704
Caralt, Surinach, **2:**824
Carbaugh, A., **2:**692
Card, David, **1:**159, **2:**518, **2:**574, **2:**701, **2:**703

Card Game, **1:**176 (figure)

Cardenas, Enrique, **1:**21

Cardoso, F. H., **1:**21

Caribbean Community and Common Market (CARICOM), **2:**851

Caring labor, **2:**908

Carlsson, Mangus, **2:**558

Carmon, Z., **2:**865

Carpenter, C., **2:**773

Carpenter, J., **2:**863

Carpio, Carlos, **2:**600

Carr, Geoffrey, **2:**637, **2:**638

Carson, R. T., **1:**278

Carter, B. L., **2:**914, **2:**918

Carter, Jimmy, **1:**351, **1:**396

Carter, John R., **2:**899

Carter Doctrine of 1980, **2:**650

Carvajal, M., **2:**830

Carveth, R., **2:**828

Case, A. C., **2:**569

Case, Karl, **2:**611

Caselli, F., **2:**816

Case-Shiller Index, **2:**614, **2:**615

Casey, B., **1:**478, **1:**484

Cash for Clunkers, **1:**148

Cassar, M., **2:**824

Cather, Willa, **2:**769–770, **2:**774n

Cavanaugh, William T., **2:**898

Caves, Richard, **2:**829, **2:**831

Celler-Kefauver Act, **1:**134

Cellini, R., **2:**823

Center for the Study of Civil War, **2:**808

Centers for Disease Control (CDC), **2:**725

Centipede Game, **1:**181 (figure)

Central American Common Market (CACM), **2:**851

Central American Integration System (CAIS), **2:**851

Central business district (CBD), **2:**670

Central place theory, **2:**667

Centre for Economic Policy Research (CEPR), **1:**480, **1:**482–**1:**483

CEO Confidence Survey, **1:**289

Certificate of need (CON), **2:**712

Cespa, G., **2:**790

Cestone, G., **2:**790

Chamberlain, E., **1:**138

Chamberlin, E. H., **2:**873

Chambers, Robert, **2:**600

Chan, Ping Ching Winnie, **2:**520

Chan-Olmsted, S., **2:**834

Chandler, Alfred D., Jr., **2:**637

Chang, C., **1:**166

Change in demand, **1:**69

Change in quantity demanded, **1:**69–70

Change in quantity supplied, **1:**71

Change in supply, **1:**71

Change to Win (CTW), **1:**167

Chari, V. V., **1:**407

Charles, C. Z., **2:**673

Charles, K. K., **2:**673

Charles, Kerwin, **2:**568

Charness, G., **2:**862

Charusheela, S., **2:**909

Chaudhuri, K. N., **1:**20

Chauncey, George, **2:**768, **2:**769, **2:**772, **2:**774n

Chavas, Jean-Paul, **2:**600

Che, Y., **2:**937

Chemmanur, Tom, **2:**737n

Chen, S., **1:**496

Chenery, H., **1:**108

Chiaravutthi, Y., **1:**138

Chicago Mercantile Exchange, **2:**615

Chicago Public Schools, **2:**520–521, **2:**522

Chicago school of thought, **1:**136–137

Chicago Tribune, **2:**569

Chicago White Sox, **2:**544

Chicken (game), **1:**175 (figure), **1:**181 (figure)

Children. *See* **Economic analysis of the family**

China

comparative economic systems and, **1:**447–448

East Asian economies and, **1:**485–491

economic history and, **1:**19–20

globalization and inequality, **1:**494

main products imported from Latin America, **2:**853–854, **2:**853 (figure)

China Agricultural Economics Review, **2:**599

China Agricultural University, Beijing, **2:**599

China Pharmaceutical Group, **1:**131

Chinese Communists, **1:**20

Chiplin, B., **2:**829

Chiquiar, D., **2:**853

Chiswick, Barry, **2:**572–574

Chiswick, C. U., **2:**781

Chite, R. M., **2:**603

Choice, when future consumption is uncertain, **1:**86

Christaller, Walter, **2:**665, **2:**666

Christian Science, **2:**780

Christie, G. I., **2:**598

Christofides, Louis, **1:**158

Chrysler, **1:**169

Chu, Michael, **2:**844

Church of the Latter-day Saints (Mormon), **2:**780

CIA World Factbook, **1:**374

Cialdini, Robert, **2:**548

Cicchetti, C. J., **1:**278

Ciecka, J. E., **2:**740, **2:**741

Ciriacy-Wantrup, Siegfried von, **2:**625

City of London, **2:**614

Civil Aeronautics Act of 1938, **1:**272

Civil Aeronautics Board, **1:**272

Civil Rights Act of 1964, **1:**160, **2:**517, **2:**564, **2:**574, **2:**772–773

Civil war. *See* **Economics of civil war**

Civil War, American, **1:**17, **1:**56, **1:**133

Claar, Victor V., **2:**898

Clairol, **1:**127

Clarida, Richard, **1:**383

Clark, Colin, **2:**620

Clark, Gregory, **1:**17

Clark, John B., **1:**7

Class-based typologies

comparative economic systems and, **1:**446

queer economics and, **2:**768–770

Class conflict, petro-states and, **2:**650–652

Class power, **1:**62–64

Class size, economics of education and, **2:**517–518

Classical linear regression (CLR) model, **1:**48–49, **1:**50

Classical school of thought, **1:**400

debates in macroeconomic policy, **1:**391–392

economic methodology and, **1:**24–27

HET and, **1:**5–6
IS-LM model and, **1:**344
See also **New classical economics**
Clawson, D., **1:**64
Clayton Act, **1:**134
  predatory pricing and, **1:**137
Clayton Act of 1914, **1:**134, **1:**136, **1:**137, **1:**159
Clean Air Act Amendments of 1990, **2:**634
Clean Air for Europe (CAFE), **1:**279
Clement, S., **1:**507
Climate change
  cost-benefit analysis and, **1:**280–281
  economic history and, **1:**15–16
  economics of energy markets, **2:**643
  gasoline consumption and, **1:**247–254
Clouatre, M., **1:**139
Clower, Robert W., **1:**344–**1:**345, **1:**346–**1:**347nn
Coase, Ronald
  advances in transaction cost economics and, **2:**941–942, **2:**947, **2:**948
  econometrics and, **1:**45
  economics of property law and, **2:**760
  economics of wildlife protection and, **2:**618
  environmental economics and, **2:**633, **2:**636
  evolutionary economics and, **2:**928
  externalities and property rights, **1:**234
  public finance and, **1:**256
  taxes *vs.* standards and, **1:**248
  transaction cost economics and, **1:**194, **1:**196, **1:**199
  twentieth-century economic methodology and, **1:**35, **1:**36, **1:**38
  See also Coase Theorem
Coase Theorem
  economics of HIV/AIDS and, **2:**692
  economics of property law and, **2:**760–761
  economics of wildlife protection and, **2:**621–623
  environmental economics and, **2:**633–634, **2:**635
  externalities and property rights, **1:**234
  public finance and, **1:**256–**1:**257, **1:**256–257
  sports economics and, **2:**536
Coate, S., **2:**569, **2:**574
Coates, D., **2:**537
Cobb, C. W., **1:**108
Cobb-Clark, D. A., **2:**705
Cobb-Douglas production function, **1:**108
Coca-Cola, **1:**129
Cochrane, John, **1:**210
Cochrane, W. W., **2:**604
Cochrane, Willard, **2:**598
Cohen, J., **2:**752
Cohen, J. D., **2:**881, **2:**913, **2:**915, **2:**917
Cohen, Jeffrey, **2:**899
Cohen, L., **2:**583
Cohn, D., **2:**699
Coincidental indicators, **1:**290
Colander, David, **1:**24, **1:**39, **1:**41, **1:**42, **1:**339
Colarelli, S. M., **2:**560
Cold War, **2:**808
Cole, Shawn, **2:**570
Coleman, James S., **2:**517, **2:**519
Coleman, R. H., **2:**764n
Coleman, W. J., II, **2:**816
Collateral, **2:**839, **2:**842
Collateral source payments, forensic economics and, **2:**745

Collective bargaining, **1:**164, **1:**168. *See also* **Role of labor unions in labor markets**
College Board, **2:**599
Collegiate sports, **2:**540
Collier, P., **2:**809, **2:**812, **2:**813, **2:**815, **2:**816
Collingwood, R. G., **1:**38
Collins, R., **2:**828
Collusion
  competition *vs.,* **1:**128–129
  economics of strategy and, **1:**188–189
Colonialism, economic history and, **1:**15
Columbia University, **1:**441
Columbus, Christopher, **1:**18
Comfort zone, **1:**386–387
Comiskey, Charles, **2:**544
Command and control (CAC) regulation, **2:**633
Command-and-control (CAC) regulation, **1:**248
Command economics, **1:**445
Commisariat Général du Plan, **1:**281
Commodity Price Shocks and Civil Conflict: Evidence From Colombia (Dube, Vargas), **2:**816
Common-pool resources, twentieth-century economic methodology and, **1:**34–35
Commons, John R., **1:**29, **1:**56, **1:**57, **2:**531, **2:**926–927
Commonwealth Connector, **2:**715
Communism, **1:**443–446
Communist Manifesto (Marx, Engels), **1:**59, **1:**144
Companion to the History of Economic Thought, A (Samuels, Biddle, Davis), **1:**4
Comparative advantage, **1:**411–412. *See also* **International trade, comparative and absolute advantage, and trade restrictions**
Comparative economic systems, 1:441–449
  China and, **1:**447–448
  class-based typologies, **1:**446
  origins of, **1:**441–443
  socialist controversy and, **1:**443–446
  transition economics, **1:**446–447
  in the twenty-first century, **1:**448
Comparative Economic Systems (Loucks, Hoot), **1:**441
Comparative health care systems, **2:**712–713
Competition
  media economics and, **2:**829–831
  microfinance and, **2:**842
Complements, **1:**70–71, **1:**72
Complexity and economics, 2:883–890
  defined, **2:**883–886
  economic outcomes, **2:**886–887
  Schelling's residential segregation model, **2:**888–890
  theory and policy, **2:**887–888
  tools of, **2:**888
Composite coincidental indicator (CCI), **1:**292
Composite Index of Leading (Economic) Indicators (LEI), **1:**299–300
Comprehensive Immigration Reform Act of 2006 (CIRA), **2:**704
Computable general equilibrium (CGE) models, **2:**689
Concentration ratio, **2:**830
Conditional expectation of wage, **1:**46
Conference Board, **1:**289, **1:**290–**1:**292, **1:**291t, **1:**299–**1:**300
Conference Board of Canada, **1:**385
Conflict. *See* **Economics of civil war**
Conflict (fire example), **2:**808 (figure)
Congestion, transportation economics and, **2:**659–660
Congress of Industrial Oranizations (CIO), **1:**56

Congressional Budget Office (CBO)
  fiscal policy, **1**:357, **1**:358f, **1**:359f, **1**:360
  government budgets, debt, deficits, **1**:374
  Impact of Ethanol Use on Food Prices and Greenhouse-Gas Emissions, The, **1**:77–78
  public finance, **1**:261
  supply, demand, equilibrium, **1**:77
  taxes *vs.* standards, **1**:252
  transportation economics, **2**:656
Consensus Forecasts, **1**:385
Conservation Reserve Program, **2**:621
Conservation Reserve Program (CRP), **2**:621–623
Conservation Security Program, **2**:622
Constant, **1**:46
Constant growth rate rules (CGRR), **1**:395
Consumer behavior, 1:79–87
  agricultural economics and, **2**:601
  consumer fallibility, **1**:251–252
  customer-based discrimination and race, **2**: 568
  demand and number of consumers, **1**:71
  diminishing marginal utility, **1**:79–80
  economics of aging and, **2**:587 (figure), **2**:589–594
  economics of fair trade and, **1**:508 (figure)
  forensic economics and, **2**:744
  macroeconomics and, **1**:9
  modern consumer theory, **1**:81–86, **1**:82 (figure)
  socially responsible consumption, economics of corporate social responsibility, **2**:791–792
  theory of the sports consumer, **2**:537–538
Consumer benefits, economics of gambling and, **2**:678–679
Consumer Confidence Index, **1**:289
Consumer Price Index (CPI), **1**:337, **2**:742
Consumer price index (CPI), **1**:304
Consumer Product Safety Commission, **1**:266
Consumer Sentiment Index, **1**:289
Consumption bundles, **1**:81–82, **1**:84
Content streaming, **2**:832
Continental Airlines, **1**:139
Contingent valuation method (CVM), **2**:623–625, **2**:632, **2**:822–823
Continuity, **1**:1
Contracts
  beyond make-or-buy: advances in transaction cost economics, **2**:946–947
  private health insurance, **2**:709–710
Convention on the Elimination of Discrimination Against Women, **2**:901
Conventional lab experiments, **2**:874
Coolidge, Calvin, **1**:101
Cooper, J. C. B., **2**:647
Cooperation, neuroeconomics and, **2**:915–916
Coordination Game (game), **1**:175 (figure)
Cordwainers, **1**:164
Corey-Luse, C., **2**:624
Corman, H., **2**:751
Corn market case study, **1**:77–78
Cornell University, **2**:598
Cornwall, R. R., **2**:767, **2**:768, **2**:774
Corporate Average Fuel Economy (CAFE), **1**:71, **1**:250–**1**:251, **1**:252, **1**:253
Corporate bonds, **1**:219–222
Corporate finance, information asymmetry and, **2**:732–734
Corporate social responsibility (CSR). *See* **Economics and corporate social responsibility**

Corrago, G. S., **2**:916
Correlated equilibrium, **1**:181
Correlation, in game theory, **1**:181–182
Correspondence testing studies, **2**:557
Corsetti, G., **1**:491
Cortes, P., **2**:702
Cost-benefit analysis, 1:275–283
  discounting, **1**:280–281
  economics of gambling and, **2**:683
  endowment effect and behavioral economics, **2**:865–866
  health economics and, **2**:708
  measuring benefits/costs for nonmarginal changes in quantity, **1**:277 (figure)
  present value of $1 million under different time horizons/discount rates, **1**:281 (table)
  sensitivity analysis, **1**:281
  social welfare, defined, **1**:276
  Stockholm congestion charging policy example, **1**:281–282, 282 (table)
  valuing benefits and costs, **1**:276–280
Cost curves, **1**:105 (figure), **1**:108–109
Costantino, M., **1**:510
Costs of production: short run and long run, 1:101–109
  applications and empirical evidence, **1**:108–109
  cost curves, **1**:105 (figure)
  short-run output–one variable input, **1**:103 (figure)
  shut-down decision, **1**:104–108
  theory, **1**:101–104
Cotte, J., **2**:791
Cotti, Chad, **2**:680
Couch, Jim, **1**:244
Couch, Kenneth A., **1**:157, **1**:158, **1**:159, **1**:160
Council for Mutual Economic Assistance, **1**:442, **1**:443
Council of Economic Advisors, **1**:313, **1**:367
Council of Ministers for Economic and Financial Affairs (ECOFIN), **1**:483–**1**:484
Count data, **1**:51
Cournot, Augustin
  Cournot model, **1**:129, **1**:187–188
  demand elasticities and, **1**:89
  economics of strategy and, **1**:187, **1**:188, **1**:189, **1**:191
  HET and, **1**:6, **1**:8
  imperfectly competitive product markets and, **1**:129, **1**:130
Covarrubias y Leiva, Diego de, **2**:893, **2**:894
Covered interest rate parity (CIP), **1**:435–436
Cowan, T., **2**:622
Cowen, Tyler, **1**:41
Cowie, J., **1**:56
Cox, James, **2**:879
Crafts, Nicholas, **2**:690
Craig, B., **2**:593
Crane, Y., **2**:679
Crawford, Robert, **1**:196
Crawford, V., **2**:942
Credibility of threat, **1**:133 (figure)
Credit rationing, economics of information and, **2**:732
Credits
  balance of trade and payments, **1**:419–420
  international finance and, **1**:472
Crespo, Ricardo F., **2**:892
Crime. *See* **Economics of crime**
Critically Low Performing Schools List, **2**:522
Crocker, Keith J., **1**:200

Crooker, John, **2**:539
Croson, Rachel, **2**:559, **2**:560, **2**:870, **2**:880
Cross, John, **1**:269–**1**:270
Cross-elasticity of demand, **1**:96–97
Cross Incentive Pricing Scheme, **1**:269–270
Cross-price demand curves, **1**:84–85
Cross-price elasticity, transportation economics and, **2**:657
Crotty, James, **1**:58
Crouch, C., **1**:484
Crowding out, **1**:338
    deficits and, **1**:375–377
    fiscal policy and, **1**:365–366
Crude oil, strategic importance of, **2**:646–647
Crusoe, Robinson, **2**:905–906
Crusoe, Robinson (literary figure), **2**:905
Crutsinger-Perry, B., **2**:692
Cuccia, T., **2**:823
Cullen, Julie, **2**:520, **2**:750
Cult of Statistical Significance, The (McCloskey), **1**:38
Cultural heritage. *See* **Economic aspects of cultural heritage**
Current account balance (CAB), **1**:423–424, **1**:471–474. *See also*
    Balance of trade and payments
Current budget constraint, **1**:370
Current Population Survey, **2**:741
Curtis, G., **1**:219
Cusatis, P., **1**:216
Customers. *See* **Consumer behavior; Labor markets; Wage**
    determination
Customs Union, Germany, **1**:18
Cutler, David M., **2**:569, **2**:588, **2**:589, **2**:673
Cvivil Aeronautics Act, **1**:272
CVS, **1**:132–**1**:133
Cycles, **2**:935
Cycles Research Institute (CRI), **1**:301
Cyclical indicator approach, **1**:299–300
Cyclical stocks, **1**:300
Cyclical unemployment, **1**:305–306
Cypher, James, **2**:925
Czech Republic, monetary policy and inflation targeting, **1**:386

Dae-jung, Kim, **1**:489
Dahl, Gordon, **2**:518
Dale, A. M., **2**:916
Dales, John, **2**:634, **2**:636
Daley-Harris, S., **2**:837
Dallas Cowboys, **2**:535
Dalsace, F., **2**:945
Daly, Mary, **1**:158, **1**:160
Damage models, forensic economics and, **2**:740
Damasio, A. R., **2**:770, **2**:917, **2**:918
Damasio, H., **2**:917, **2**:918
Danby, C., **2**:908
Dantzig, George, **2**:602
Darity, William A., Jr., **2**:556, **2**:557, **2**:570
Dark Ages, **1**:16, **1**:18
Darwin, Charles, **1**:25, **2**:921–922
Datta Gupta, N., **2**:560
Dave, C., **2**:866
David, A. C., **2**:693
Davidson, Paul, **1**:314, **1**:317, **1**:345
Davies, G., **2**:832
Dávila, A., **2**:704
Davis, Al, **2**:535

Davis, B., **2**:699
Davis, G. F., **2**:793
Davis, J. B., **1**:4, **1**:24
Davis, John, **1**:38, **1**:39, **1**:41, **1**:42
Davis, J. Ronnie, **1**:328
Davis, M., **2**:651
Davis, M. C., **2**:537
Davis, S., **1**:247
Davis, W. B., **1**:251
Dawkins, Richard, **2**:922
Dayan, P., **2**:916
De Alessi, Louis, **1**:268
De Lauretis, Teresa, **2**:770
De Menezes, A. G., **2**:824
De Palma, A., **2**:658
De Quervain, D. J.-F., **2**:916
De Vany, A., **2**:831
De Vries, Jan, **1**:16
De Vroey, M., **1**:10
De Waal, F. B. M., **2**:916
De Zeeuw, A., **2**:624
Deacon, D., **2**:906
Deadweight loss, **1**:121, **1**:265
Deakin, J. F. W., **2**:916
Dean, T. B., **2**:655, **2**:663
Deardorf, Alan, **1**:416
Deaton, A. S., **2**:601
Debates in macroeconomic policy, 1:391–398
    activism *vs.* laissez-faire, **1**:398
    classical tradition and, **1**:391–392
    Great Depression and Great Recession of 2007, **1**:397–398
    Great Inflation and "Volker Recession," **1**:396
    Keynes and the Great Depression, **1**:392–393
    Keynesian macropolicy in U.S. and, **1**:393–394
    postwar study of economic growth, **1**:393
    real business cycle models, **1**:396–397
    rebirth of economic growth theory, **1**:397
    Savings and Loan (S&Ls) crisis, **1**:397
    stagflation and conservative macroeconomics, **1**:394–396
DeBeers group, **1**:195
Debits
    balance of trade and payments, **1**:419–420
    international finance and, **1**:472
Debreu, Gerard, **2**:689
Debt repudiation, **1**:373–374
Decentralized economy
    economic methodology and, **1**:25–26
    Marxian and institutional industrial relations in U.S., **1**:64
    role of labor unions and, **1**:169
Decision making
    experimental economics and, **2**:875–876
    family decision making and labor market, **1**:145
    neuroeconomics and, **2**:915
Declaration of Independence, **2**:893
Dedicated asset specificity, defined, **1**:196
Deductive reasoning, **1**:24
Deductive reductionism, **1**:26
Defensive stocks, **1**:300–301
Deferred acceptance algorithm, **2**:933–934
Deffeyes, K. S., **2**:646
Deficit, defined, **1**:375
Deflation, **1**:289
Defranceschi, P., **1**:507

Delios, A., **2:**945
DeLong, B., **1:**313
Delors, Jacques, **1:**478
Delors Report, **1:**478
Delucchi, M., **2:**663
Demand
    change in demand, **1:**69–70
    change in quantity demanded, **1:**69–70
    changes in demand *vs.* changes in quantity demanded, **1:**70 (figure)
    curves, **1:**84
    defined, **1:**69–70
    demand-led growth, **1:**315
    demand shocks, **1:**336–338
    determinants of demand, **1:**70–71
    labor, **1:**142
    law of demand, **1:**69
    See also **Demand elasticities; Supply, demand, and equilibrium**
Demand elasticities, 1:89–100
    demand facing competitive firm with industry demand/supply and equilibrium price, **1:**94 (figure)
    demand for beef, **1:**91 (figure)
    demand for beef: elasticities along straight-line demand curve, **1:**92 (figure)
    demand schedule, **1:**90 (table)
    elasticities of steep *vs.* flat demand curves, **1:**92 (figure)
    Engel curve, **1:**96 (figure)
    other types of demand elasticities, **1:**97 (table)
    own price elasticities of demand, **1:**91 (table)
    price elasticity of demand, total revenue (expenditure) and marginal revenue, **1:**94 (table)
    technical rule for calculation of, **1:**89–99
DeMartino, G., **2:**530
D'Emilio, John, **2:**768, **2:**769, **2:**772
Democracy. *See* **Public choice**
Demographics
    changing world demographics, **1:**455 (figure) (*See also* **World development in historical perspective**)
    economic history and, **1:**14
    economic methodology and, **1:**25
    labor market and, **1:**144–145
    real estate economics, **2:**611–612
    See also **Economic analysis of the family**
Demsetz, Harold, **1:**36, **1:**231, **1:**268, **2:**618, **2:**641, **2:**801
Denmark, economics of aging, **2:**590 (table)
Density, of union membership, **1:**165–166, **1:**167 (figure)
Department of Homeland Security, **1:**261, **2:**699
Dependency ratios, **2:**585, **2:**586 (table), **2:**588 (table)
Dependency theory, **1:**21
Dependent variable, **1:**46
Depken, C. A., **2:**538
Deregulation
    economics of energy markets and, **2:**641
    regulatory economics and, **1:**272
    See also **Regulatory economics**
Desai, Padma, **1:**441
Descartes, René, **2:**903
Determinants of supply, **1:**71–72
Deterring entry by capacity decision, **1:**132 (figure)
Deutsche Mark, **1:**386
Devarajan, Shantayanan, **2:**639, **2:**647–648, **2:**688
Dewatripont, M., **2:**736
Dew-Becker, I., **1:**500

Dewey, Edward R., **1:**301
Dewey, John, **2:**925, **2:**926
Dezhbakhsh, H., **2:**752
Diagnostic testing, **1:**52
Diamond, Douglas B., **1:**138, **2:**671
Diamond, J., **2:**800
Diamond, Peter, **1:**259
Dickens, William, **1:**155, **2:**691
Dickhaut, J., **2:**878–879, **2:**916
Dictator game
    behavioral economics and, **2:**867–868
    experimental economics and, **2:**878
Diebold, F. X., **1:**293, **1:**471
Dietz, James, **2:**925
Digital technology, media economics and, **2:**834
Dijkstra, G., **2:**854
Dillard, D., **1:**330
Dimand, M. A., **2:**910
Dimand, R., **2:**910
Dimensions of Social Performance, **2:**844
Diminishing marginal rate of substitution (MRS), **1:**82
Dimmick, J., **2:**830
DiPasquale, Denise, **2:**608, **2:**672
Discontinuity, **1:**–2
Discounting, **1:**280–281
Discretionary spending, **1:**358
Discrimination
    discrimination alignment hypothesis, **1:**197
    economics and race, **2:**566–570, **2:**572–574
    economics of gender and, **2:**557–559
    economics of migration and, **2:**701–702
    queer economics and earnings inequality, **2:**772–774
    in sports, **2:**539–540
    wage determination, **1:**158–160
"Dismal science" designation, **1:**5
Disney, Richard, **2:**590
Displaced workers, wage determination and, **1:**156–157
Diversity, complexity and economics, **2:**883–884
Dividends, economics of information and, **2:**734
Divorce, **2:**583
Dixit, Avinash, **2:**642
Djankov, S., **1:**448, **2:**811–814
Dobb, Maurice, **1:**441
Dobzhansky, Theodosius, **2:**922
Docquier, F., **2:**703
Dodd, David, **1:**215–**1:**216, **1:**217, **1:**218
Dodds, D. E., **1:**229
Dodson, M. E., III, **2:**703
Doeringer, P., **2:**556
Doha Declaration on the TRIPS Agreement and Public Health, **2:**694
Doing Business Report, **2:**840
Dollar, D., **1:**496
Dollar Value of a Day, **2:**744
Domar, Evsey, **1:**393
Donohue, J. J., III, **2:**574
Dornbusch, R., **2:**848
Dot-com stock market bubble, **1:**352–353, **1:**367
Douglas, Dorothy, **1:**446
Douglas, Major, **1:**327
Douglas, P. H., **1:**108
Dow, Charles, **1:**217

Dow Jones Industrial Average (DJIA), **1:**139, **1:**217, **1:**223, **1:**352–353, **1:**355
Dow Theory (Rhea), **1:**217
Downey, W. David, **2:**604
Downs, Anthony, **1:**239, **1:**240–**1:**241, **2:**660
"Downstream" production, **2:**648
Doyle, G., **2:**828, **2:**829, **2:**830, **2:**832, **2:**833
Drago, F., **2:**751
Dreyfus, M. K., **1:**251
Dubai, **2:**649, **2:**652
Dube, O., **2:**816
Dubin, J. A., **1:**251
Dubins, Lester E., **2:**934
Dubner, S. J., **2:**577
Dubofsky, M., **1:**57, **1:**165
Duesenberry, J. S., **1:**328
Duffy, J., **2:**880
Duffy, P., **2:**602
Duflo, Esther, **1:**40, **2:**880
Duggan, M., **2:**750
Dugger, B., **2:**924, **2:**927
Dugger, W., **2:**531
Duguet, Emmanuel, **2:**558
Dundee School of Economics and Commerce, **1:**194
Dunlop, John T., **1:**56, **1:**57, **1:**136
Dupuit, Jules, **1:**80–**1:**81
Duration data, **1:**51
Durbin-Watson stat, **1:**53
Durkheim, Émile, **2:**747
Dusansky, R., **2:**533
Dutch East Indies Company, **1:**17
Dutch Republic, economic history and, **1:**17
Dye, R., **2:**539
Dyer, J., **2:**945
Dynamic time inconsistency, **1:**404–405

Earned Income Tax Credit (EITC), **1:**260, **2:**518
Earnings Analyst, The, **2:**739
Earnings of professional athletes, 2:543–551
    challenges, **2:**550–551
    evolution of athletes' endorsements and, **2:**547–549
    evolution of athletes' salaries, **2:**543–547
    global considerations and future directions, **2:**549–550
    sports economics and, **2:**533–542
Earnings per share (EPS), **1:**301
East Asian economies, 1:485–492
    Asian financial crisis, **1:**491
    China and imports from Latin America, **2:**853–854, **2:**853 (figure) (*See also* **Latin America's trade performance in new millenium**)
    demographics and growth, **1:**485–486
    growth determinants, **1:**488–491
    role of total factor productivity (TFP), **1:**487–488
    savings and investment, **1:**486–487
East Texas "collapse," **2:**649
Easterbrook, Frank H., **1:**136
Easterlin, R. A., **1:**464n
Easterly, William, **1:**40, **1:**465n, **2:**815, **2:**897
Eaton, Jonathan, **1:**416
Ebenstein, A., **1:**500
Eckel, C., **2:**866
Econometric modeling, **1:**292–293

Econometrica, **1:**30
Econometrics, 1:45–54
    classical linear regression model, **1:**48–49
    defined, **1:**45–46
    diagnostic testing, **1:**52
    illustrative regression results, **1:**52–53, **1:**53, **1:**53 (table)
    linear regression, **1:**46
    maximum likelihood, **1:**51
    maximum likelihood estimation, **1:**51 (figure)
    nonlinear regressions, **1:**50–51
    panel data, **1:**51–52
    robust estimation, **1:**52
    sampling distributions, **1:**46–48
    time-series data, **1:**52
    violating classical linear regression model assumptions, **1:**50
Economic analysis of the family, 2:577–584
    applications and empirical evidence, **2:**579–582
    family decision making and labor market, **1:**145
    future of, **2:**584
    marriage and market model, **2:**932
    policy and, **2:**582–584
    theory, **2:**577–579
Economic aspects of cultural heritage, 2:819–826
    applications and empirical evidence, **2:**822–824
    defined, **2:**819–820
    emerging opportunities in, **2:**824–825
    policy and, **2:**824
    theory, **2:**820–822
Economic base theory, **2:**667
Economic categories, **1:**289
Economic Commission for Latin America and the Caribbean (ECLAC), **2:**849 (table), **2:**852, **2:**852 (figure), **2:**852 (table), **2:**854 (figure), **2:**855
"Economic Focus," **2:**837
Economic growth
    causes of modern economic growth, **1:**13–15
    effects of modern economic growth, **1:**15–16
Economic history, 1:13–22
    causes of modern economic growth, **1:**13–15
    effects of modern economic growth, **1:**15–16
    future directions, **1:**21–22
    historical record of, **1:**16–21
    policy implications, **1:**21
    theory, **1:**13
Economic instability and macroeconomic policy, 1:349–355
    1990–1991 recession and start of U.S. housing boom, **1:**352
    collapse of housing bubble, **1:**353
    creation of Federal Reserve System and, **1:**349
    dot-com stock market bubble and 2001 recession, **1:**352–353
    fiscal policy and 2007 recession, **1:**354
    future of macroeconomic policy, **1:**355
    Great Depression and origin of macroeconomics, **1:**349–350
    Great Inflation (1970–1981), **1:**350–352
    monetary policy and 2007 recession, **1:**353–354
    rise/fall of Keynesian consensus (1961–1973), **1:**350
    U.S. national debt and foreign trade debt, **1:**354–355
Economic Institutions of Capitalism, The (Williamson), **1:**194, **1:**201, **2:**942
Economic measurement and forecasting, 1:287–295
    business cycle, **1:**288 (figure)
    combining information and predicting a turning point, **1:**291–294

economic indicators, **1:**289–291

economic indicators, defined, **1:**288

economic indicators and forecasting in twenty-first century, **1:**294

forecasting and, in twenty-first century, **1:**294

grouping, by business cycle timing, **1:**290 (table)

grouping economic indicators by business cycle timing, **1:**290 (table)

measuring and evaluating macroeconomic performance and, **1:**299

U.S. composite leading indexes, **1:**291 (table)

Economic methodology, 1:23–31

classical paradigm, **1:**24–27

Keynes, neoclassical synthesis, and monetarism, **1:**29–30

marginal/Marshalian methodology and rise of neoclassical, **1:**27–29

present state of, **1:**23–24

Economic Policy Institute, **1:**63

Economic Report of the President, **1:**298, **1:**302, **1:**357, **1:**375

Economic Research Service, **2:**598

Economic Stimulus Act of 2008, **1:**354

Economic Theory in Retrospect (Blaug), **1:**4

Economics (Stiglitz), **1:**34

Economics, etymology of, **1:**8, **2:**892

Economics: Principles, Problems and Policies (McConnell), **1:**326, **1:**330

Economics and corporate social responsibility, 2:785–795

CSR, defined, **2:**786–787

evolutionary understanding of CSR, **2:**787–790

strategic CSR, **2:**790–793

typology of CSR, **2:**788 (figure)

Economics and justice, 2:525–532

applications and policy implications, **2:**530–531

egalitarianism and heterodox economics, **2:**528–530

future directions, **2:**531–532

neoclassical economics, **2:**526–527

neoclassical economics, distribution, and justice, **2:**527–528

Economics and Philosophy, **1:**38

Economics and race, 2:563–576

African Americans: average years of schooling, **2:**565 (figure)

African Americans, data, **2:**564–566

African Americans: geographic distribution by race, **2:**566 (table)

African Americans: industrial employment distribution by race, **2:**567 (table)

African Americans: marital status by race, **2:**566 (table)

African Americans: median income, **2:**564 (figure), **2:**565

Asian Americans: average years of schooling, **2:**571 (figure)

Asian Americans, data, **2:**570–572

Asian Americans: geographic distribution by race, **2:**572 (table)

Asian Americans: industrial employment distribution by race, **2:**573 (table)

Asian Americans: marital status by race, **2:**572 (table)

Asian Americans: median income, **2:**570 (figure), **2:**571 (figure)

Asian Americans, research on discrimination, **2:**572–574

classical school and, **1:**5–6

discrimination and wage determination, **1:**158–160, **1:**159–160

discrimination in sports and, **2:**539–540

policy and, **2:**574

theories of discrimination, **2:**566–570

urban economics and, **2:**673–674

Economics and religion, 2:777–783, 2:898

demand for religion, **2:**777–780

empirical evidence, **2:**781–782

institutional change and, **2:**782–783

socioeconomic behavior and, **2:**780–781

supply of religion, **2:**780

Economics Department, University of Chicago, **2:**651

Economics of aging, 2:585–595

age of median voter and life expectancy, **2:**593 (figure)

aging populations, **2:**585–586

dependency ratios, **2:**585, **2:**585 (table)

dependency ratios, old age (2005 and 2050), **2:**588 (table)

intergenerational effects of immigration and, **2:**703–704

labor force participation and, **2:**587 (tablez)

life cycle and, **2:**586–587

life cycle income and consumption planning, **2:**587 (figure)

production and consumption patterns, **2:**589–594

production and labor supply, **2:**587–589

public expenditure on pensions, **2:**590 (table)

replacement ratio, **2:**591 (table)

wage determination and, **1:**157

Economics of Agricultural Production and Resource Use (Heady), **2:**604

Economics of Agriculture: Volume 1: Selected Papers of D. Gale Johnson (Antle, Sumner), **2:**604

Economics of Agriculture: Volume 2: Papers in Honor of D. Gale Johnson (Antle, Sumner), **2:**604

Economics of civil war, 2:807–817

conflict (fire), **2:**808 (figure)

empirical analysis of causes of civil wars, **2:**809–816

Economics of Control (Lerner), **1:**35

Economics of crime, 2:747–756

applications and empirical evidence, **2:**750–752

future of, **2:**753–754

policy and, **2:**752–753

theory, **2:**747–750

Economics of education, 2:515–523

in agricultural economics, **2:**599

economics of civil war and, **2:**809–811

education policy, **2:**519–522

education production function, **2:**517–519

optimal education level determination, **2:**516 (figure)

public school choice and matching markets, **2:**936–937

theory, **2:**515–517

wage determination and, **1:**155–156, **1:**159

Economics of energy markets, 2:637–644

environment and, **2:**642–643

history, **2:**638–639

theory, **2:**639–642

Economics of fair trade, 1:503–511

composite indicator price of green coffee, **1:**504 (figure)

consumer choice problem, **1:**508 (figure)

evidence, **1:**509–510

fair trade as price floor, **1:**509 (figure)

future of, **1:**510–511

history, **1:**503–508

theory, **1:**508–509

Economics of gambling, 2:675–685

economic impact of gambling, **2:**678–682

future of, **2:**682–684

Economics of gender, 2:553–562

economic analysis of the family and, **2:**577–584

economics of HIV/AIDS and, **2:**691–692

evidence of discrimination, **2:**557–559

evidence on gender differences in preferences, **2:**559–560

feminist economics and, **2:**901–910

gender wage gap, **2:**555 (table)

identifying discrimination in labor market, **2:**557

in labor market, **2:**553–555
theoretical explanations for differences in labor market,
    2:555–557
Economics of health insurance, 2:717–727
    demand for, **2:**717–724
    employer mandates, **2:**721 (figure)
    evolution of HIV/AIDS and insurance coverage, **2:**725–726
    forensic economics and, **2:**743
    health economics and, **2:**708–710
    public insurance in U.S., **2:**724–725
    uninsured and, **2:**725
    welfare economics of moral hazard, **2:**722 (figure)
    See also **Health economics**
Economics of HIV and AIDS, 2:687–695
    choices and behavior of individuals, **2:**690–692
    economics of antiretroviral drugs, **2:**694–695
    economics of health insurance and, **2:**725–726
    impact on economy, **2:**688–690
    public intervention, **2:**692–693
    social capital, **2:**693–694
    See also **Health economics**
Economics of information, 2:729–738
    applications, **2:**732–736
    information asymmetry, **2:**729, **2:**730–734
    information production and innovation, **2:**736–737
Economics of migration, 2:697–706
    applications and empirical evidence, **2:**699–704
    effects of, on equilibrium wages, **2:**700 (figure)
    macroeconomic theory, **2:**698–699
    microeconomic theory, **2:**697–698
    policy, **2:**704–705
Economics of property law
    externalities and, **1:**227–235
    future of, **2:**763
    property rights, defined, **1:**231–232
    protecting property rights, **2:**763
    right to exclude and, **2:**757–759
    right to transfer and, **2:**761–763
    twentieth-century economic methodology and, **1:**36
    use rights and, **2:**759–761
Economics of strategy, 1:185–192
    competitive market and competitive firms, **1:**185–186
    dynamic oligopoly and backward induction, **1:**189–191
    monopoly and monopolistic behavior, **1:**186
    Prisoner's Dilemma as strategic form game, **1:**188 (table)
    repeated strategic interaction, **1:**191
    static oligopoly and strategic interaction, **1:**186–189
Economics of wildlife protection, 2:617–629
    applications and empirical evidence, **2:**621–625
    future of, **2:**626–627
    policy and, **2:**626
    species preservation and, **2:**625–626
    theory, **2:**618–621
Economies of scale, **1:**107, **2:**657–658, **2:**667
Economies of scope, **2:**658
Economist, The, **1:**368, **1:**493, **1:**498, **2:**637, **2:**785, **2:**870
Econsult, **2:**688, **2:**689
Edgeworth, Francis Y., **1:**81, **1:**342
Edlin, A., **1:**138
Edmondson, W., **2:**597
Education Quality and Accountability Office, Ontario, **2:**520
Edwards, Clark, **2:**600
Edwards, R., **1:**58

Edwards, W., **2:**602
Effective-protection rate, **1:**499
Efficiency, **1:**47
    media economics and, **2:**829
    role of labor unions and, **1:**170
Efficiency wages, **1:**157
Efficient market hypothesis (EMH), **1:**218
Egalitarianism, **2:**528–530
Eggertsson, Gauti, **1:**367, **2:**758
Ehrenberg, A., **2:**829
Ehrenberg, R., **2:**778
Ehrlich, I., **2:**748, **2:**749, **2:**750, **2:**751, **2:**752, **2:**753
Eichengreen, B., **1:**479
Eighteenth Brumaire (Marx), **1:**60
Eisgruber, L. M., **2:**602
Ekelund, Robert B., Jr., **1:**89, **2:**892, **2:**893
"El Farol Bar Problem," **2:**886
Electric vehicles, **1:**250
Elements of Political Economy (Wayland), **2:**898
Elements of Pure Economics (Walras), **1:**80
El-Hodiri, Mohamed, **2:**535
Eliasson, J., **1:**281, **1:**282t
Ellickson, R. C., **2:**758
Ellinger, Paul, **2:**604
Elliott, Graham, **1:**291, **1:**294
Elliott, R., **2:**916
Elmendorf, Douglas, **1:**376
Elstein, D., **2:**833
Ely, Richard, **1:**56, **1:**57
Elzinga, K., **1:**135, **1:**137, **1:**138
Emanuel, Ezekiel J., **2:**715
Eminent domain, economics of property law and,
    2:762–763
Emission standards, **1:**234–235
Empirical evidence
    aggregate demand and aggregate supply, **1:**336–337
    asset pricing model, **1:**210–212
    costs of production: short run and long run, **1:**108–109
    demand elasticities and, **1:**99
    economic analysis of the family and, **2:**579–582
    economic aspects of cultural heritage, **2:**822–824
    economics and religion, **2:**781–782
    economics of crime and, **2:**750–752
    economics of migration and, **2:**699–704
    environmental economics, **2:**634–635
    fiscal policy and, **1:**366
    of gender discrimination in labor market, **2:**557
    Heckscher-Ohlin model, **1:**415
    imperfect competition model, **1:**416
    on inequality and trade, **1:**499–501
    labor market, **1:**144–145
    microfinance and, **2:**842–843, **2:**845
    new classical economics, **1:**402–406
    political economy of violence, **2:**802–803
    public finance and, **1:**260–261
    real estate economics, **2:**611–612
    specific factors (Ricardo-Viner) model, **1:**414
    twentieth-century economic methodology and, **1:**41
Empirical realism, behavioral economics and, **2:**862
Employee Benefits in Private Industry, **2:**742
Employee Benefits Study, **2:**743
Employer-based discrimination, race and, **2:**566–568
Employer Costs for Employee Compensation, **2:**742

Employer exceptionalism, **1:**62–64

Employer Health Benefits Annual Survey, **2:**742

Employment

economics of gambling and, **2:**679–680

economics of health insurance and, **2:**721

employment-based health insurance, **2:**714

immigration and job competition, **2:**700–701

urban economics and, **2:**668–669

Employment Act of 1946, **1:**305

Employment and Training Administration (ETA), **1:**148

Employment Cost Index (ECI), **2:**742

Employment relations, Marxian and institutional industrial relations
     in U.S., **1:**64–65

Endangered Species Act of 1973, **2:**618, **2:**626

Endogeneity, economics of civil war and, **2:**811–814

Endogenous preferences, **2:**789

Endorsements, by athletes, **2:**547

Endowment effect, behavioral economics and, **2:**865–866

Energy. *See* **Economics of energy markets**

Energy Independence and Security Act of 2007, **1:**77

Engel, C., **1:**471

Engel curves, **1:**84–85

Engelhardt, B., **2:**750

Engels, Friedrich, **1:**15, **1:**17, **1:**59, **1:**60

England, P., **2:**556, **2:**557, **2:**905

English East Indies Company, **1:**17

English Premier League, **2:**539

Enlightenment, feminist economics and, **2:**903–904

Enthoven, A. C., **2:**715

Entry game, **1:**180 (figure)

Environics International Ltd., **2:**791

Environmental economics, 2:631–636

applications and empirical evidence, **2:**634–635

economics of energy markets and, **2:**642–643

future of, **2:**635

policy, **2:**635

theory, **2:**631–634

Environmental Protection Agency (EPA), **1:**279

Environmental Quality Incentives Program, **2:**622

Epp, D., **2:**624

Epstein, J. M., **2:**886

Equal Employment Opportunity Commission (EEOC), **2:**574

Equal Pay Act of 1963, **1:**160

Equality of Educational Opportunity (Coleman), **2:**517

Equilibrium, **1:**7, **1:**73–76, **1:**73 (figure)

aggregate demand/supply and, **1:**336

algebra of demand and supply, **1:**73–74

changing prices and quantity, **1:**74–75

displacement models and agricultural economics,
     2:601–602

economic methodology and, **1:**23, **1:**24

economics of crime and, **2:**750

effects of a change on demand, **1:**74 (figure)

effects of a change on supply, **1:**75 (figure)

effects of price controls and, **1:**76

fiscal policy and, **1:**361

general, and modern consumer theory, **1:**86

in Keynesian cross diagram, **1:**322–323, **1:**325–326

labor, **1:**142–143

multiple equilibria, in complex systems, **2:**887–888

price controls: ceilings and floors, **1:**75–76

See also **Game theory; Imperfectly competitive product
     markets; Supply, demand, and equilibrium**

Equity in Education Tax Credit Act, **2:**520

Erdil, A., **2:**938

Ergin, H., **2:**936, **2:**938

Erickson, Steven, **2:**604

Erlandsen, Solveig, **2:**589

Ernesto Méndez, V., **1:**510

Error correlated with an explanatory variable, **1:**50

Escoffier, J., **2:**768

Essay on the Nature and Significance of Economic Science, An
     (Robbins), **1:**37

Esteban, J., **2:**815

Estenson, P., **1:**298, **1:**302

Esteve-Volart, Berta, **2:**558

Estimators, **1:**46–47

Ethics and economics, 2:891–900

forensic economics and, **2:**740

history, **2:**892–894

modern suspicions/critiques, **2:**897–898

orthodox views, within markets, **2:**894–897

study of economics and, **2:**898–899

Ethnicity

Classical School and, **1:**5–6

economics of civil war and, **2:**814–816

Ethnolinguistic fracionalization index (ELF), **2:**810

EU Economic Policy Committee, **2:**589, **2:**590t

Eugenia Flores, M., **1:**510

Euro, **1:**478, **1:**483 (figure)

Europe

economic history and, **1:**16–18

economics of aging, **2:**586 (table)

Europe and the People Without History (Wolf), **2:**925

European Association for Evolutionary Political Economy
     (EAEPE), **2:**924

European Central Bank (ECB), **1:**316, **1:**382, **1:**477,
     1:483, **1:**483f

European Commission, **1:**281, **2:**786

European Council, **1:**478

European Economic Community (EEC), **1:**477

European Journal of the History of Economic Thought, **1:**4

European Monetary Institute, **1:**478

European Monetary System (EMS), **1:**433, **1:**477

European Monetary Union, 1:477, 1:477–484

defined, **1:**477–478

future of EMU, **1:**483–484

monetary policy of ECB, **1:**480–483

M3, HICP, ECB main refinancing rate percentage changes,
     1:482 (figure)

output gaps, **1:**481 (figure)

real gross domestic product percentage changes, **1:**481 (figure)

unemployment and, **1:**478–480

U.S. dollar/euro exchange rates (1999–2004), **1:**483 (figure)

European Review of Agricultural Economics, **2:**599

European Sustainable and Responsible Investment Forum
     (EuroSIF), **2:**792

European System of Central Banks (ESCB), **1:**478

European Union, **1:**147, **1:**281, **1:**433, **1:**477, **1:**496, **2:**824, **2:**853

cost-benefit analysis by, **1:**281

economics of aging, **2:**587 (table)

European Monetary Union, **1:**477–484

See also individual names of countries

Eurostat, **2:**555n

Evans, N., **2:**750

Evolutionary economics, 2:921–929

general issues, **2:**921–923
    research, **2:**923–929
Exchange rate mechanism (ERM), **1:**477
Exchange rates, 1:431–439, 1:432–433
    defined, **1:**431–432
    determinants of, **1:**434–438
    history, **1:**432–434
    international finance and, **1:**467–475
    model of exchange rate determination, **1:**434 (figure)
    nominal and real exchange rates, **1:**438
    summary predictions of monetary approach to, **1:**438 (table)
Exchange-traded funds (ETF), **1:**221
Exclusive representation, role of labor unions and, **1:**169
Executive Order 10988, **1:**164
Executive Order 11246, **1:**160
Exhaustible resources, **2:**639, **2:**647–650
Expansionary fiscal policy, **1:**363–364
Expectancy Data, **2:**740, **2:**741, **2:**742, **2:**744
Expectations, **1:**71
Expected utility theory (EUT), **1:**216, **2:**748–749
Experimental economics, 2:873–881
    applications, **2:**875–877
    behavioral economics and, **2:**864
    limited thinking and, **2:**877
    methodology, **2:**874–875
    social preferences and, **2:**877–881
    See also **Game theory**
Explanatory variables, **1:**46
Explicit costs, **1:**106
Exports. *See* **Latin America's trade performance in new millenium**
Extensive form games
    defined, **1:**176
    economics of strategy and, **1:**189–190
External benefit, **1:**228
    economics of cultural heritage and, **2:**820–821
    media economics and, **2:**833
Externalities and property rights, 1:227–236, 2:759–760
    income and costs from open-access groundwater aquifer, **1:**233 (figure)
    policy implications, **1:**234–235
    private and socially efficient market equilibria, **1:**230 (figure)
    regulatory economics and, **1:**266
    theory, **1:**227–233
Exxon, **2:**649
Exxon *Valdez*, **2:**631–632, **2:**632
Eythórsson, E., **2:**623

Fabozzi, F., **1:**216
Fackler, P., **2:**622
Factor-based modeling, **1:**292–293
Factor costs, **1:**72
Factor Price Equalization Theorem, **1:**414
Faderman, Lillian, **2:**770, **2:**772
Faini, R., **2:**704
Fair Labor Standards Act, **1:**62, **1:**149, **1:**159
Fair rate of return, **1:**268
Fair trade. *See* **Economics of fair trade**
Fairlie, Robert, **2:**573
Fairlie, R. W., **1:**160
Fairness, neuroeconomics and, **2:**916
Fairtrade Foundation, **1:**507
Fairtrade Labeling Organizations International (FLO), **1:**507
Faletto, E., **1:**21

Falk, A., **2:**879
Falkenberg, M., **2:**834
Fallick, Bruce, **1:**157
Fama, Eugene F., **1:**36, **1:**211, **1:**212, **1:**215, **1:**218, **2:**734–735
Family decision making. *See* **Economic analysis of the family**
Family factors, economics of education and, **2:**518
Fannie Mae, **1:**353, **1:**397, **2:**612, **2:**615
Farm management, **2:**603
Farm Management (Warren), **2:**598
Farm Prices: Myth and Reality (Cochrane), **2:**604
Farmland Values Project, **2:**825
Faulkner (Arkansas) County Chancery Court, **1:**139
Fault-based divorce, **2:**583
Faustmann, Martin, **2:**617
Fearon, J., **2:**810, **2:**812, **2:**813, **2:**815
Federal Bureau of Investigation, **2:**751
Federal Deposit Insurance Corporation (FDIC), **1:**219, **1:**393
Federal Energy Regulatory Commission, **1:**266
Federal Funds Rate, **1:**289
Federal Highway Administration, **1:**247, **2:**663
Federal Insurance Contributions Act (FICA), **2:**743
Federal Lands, **2:**618
Federal Open Market Committee (FOMC), **1:**353, **1:**387, **1:**393
Federal Reserve Act of 1913, **1:**349, **1:**392
Federal Reserve Bank of Kansas City, **1:**313
Federal Reserve Board of Governors, **1:**148, **1:**353
Federal Reserve of New York, **1:**287, **1:**288, **1:**349, **1:**350–**1:**352, **1:**365, **1:**367, **1:**382–**1:**383, **1:**386, **1:**392, **1:**393, **1:**396, **1:**397, **1:**428, **2:**615
Federal Reserve Statistical Release, **2:**745
Federal Reserve System, **1:**289, **1:**292, **1:**294, **1:**299, **1:**349, **1:**374, **1:**382, **1:**392, **2:**615, **2:**715
    creation of, **1:**349, **1:**392
    on inflation, **1:**294
    monetary policy and inflation targeting, **1:**382–388
    See also **Debates in macroeconomic policy**
Federal spending, fiscal policy and, **1:**358 (figure)
Federal Trade Commission (FTC), **1:**76–**1:**77, **1:**134, **1:**137
Federal Trade Commission Act, **1:**134, **1:**159
    antitrust laws and, **1:**134
    gasoline case study and, **1:**76–77
Federal workers, role of labor unions in labor markets and, **1:**164–165
Federation, of unions, **1:**167
Feebates, **1:**250–251
Feenstra, Robert C., **1:**416, **1:**499, **2:**852
Fehr, E., **2:**868, **2:**879
Felder, Stefan, **2:**590
Feldstein, Martin S., **1:**313, **1:**376, **1:**495, **2:**592, **2:**715
Feminist economics, 2:901–911
    gender as theory and practice, **2:**902–903
    global perspective, **2:**909–910
    methodology, **2:**903–905
    paid work, **2:**908–909
    rational economic agent, **2:**905–906
    unpaid work, **2:**906–908
    See also **Economics of gender**
Feminist Economics, **2:**910n
Feng, H., **2:**622
Fenn, Aju, **2:**535, **2:**539
Ferber, M. A., **2:**905, **2:**907–908
Ferguson, D. G., **2:**535
Ferguson, Niall, **1:**17

Fernanco, F., **2:**522
Fernandez, Romani, **2:**824
Fertility
    aging and, **2:**585
    economic analysis of the family and, **2:**579
Fes, Morocco, **2:**823
Ffrench-Davis, R., **2:**848, **2:**854
Field, Barry C., **1:**234, **2:**634, **2:**635
Field, Martha K., **1:**234, **2:**634, **2:**635
Field crop supply estimation, **2:**600
Fifth Amendment, **1:**266, **2:**761–762
Figart, D. M., **2:**905
Figlio, David, **2:**522
Filer, R., **1:**170
Final goods, **1:**319
Finance
    agricultural, **2:**604
    financial markets and economics of information, **2:**732–734
    microfinance, **2:**837–845
    socially responsible consumption, economics of corporate social
        responsibility, **2:**792
    See also **Portfolio theory and investment management**
Finance Committee, U.S. Senate, **1:**360
Financial Accounting Standards Board, **1:**372
FINCA, **2:**840
"Fine tuning," **1:**363
Finegold, K., **1:**62
Finland, economics of aging, **2:**590 (table)
Finley, Charles, **2:**545
Finn, A., **2:**830, **2:**831
Fiorillo, C. D., **2:**915
Firm foundation theory, **1:**216–217
Firms
    competitive market and economics of strategy, **1:**185–186
    corporate finance and information asymmetry, **2:**732–734
    economics and corporate social responsibility, **2:**785–795
    ILE/IR and, **1:**60
    media economics and, **2:**829–831
    theory of the sports firm, **2:**534–537
    See also **Labor markets; Wage determination**
Fiscal policy, 1:357–368
    automatic stabilizers, **1:**360
    balanced budget multiplier, **1:**364 (table)
    balanced budget rule, **1:**364–365
    bias toward expansionary policy, **1:**363–364
    components of federal spending, **1:**358 (figure)
    components of federal tax revenue, **1:**359 (figure)
    components of mandatory spending, **1:**358 (figure)
    components of tax revenue, **1:**359 (figure)
    crowding out, **1:**365–366
    equiibrium output/income, **1:**361
    federal government spending, **1:**357–359
    federal tax revenue, **1:**359–360
    full-employment budget balance, **1:**365
    future of, **1:**367–368
    government spending multiplier, **1:**362 (table)
    market for loanable funds, **1:**365 (table)
    monetary policy and, **1:**366–367
    multiplier, **1:**361–363
    proportional tax multiplier, **1:**363 (table)
    Ricardian equivalence, **1:**366
    Social Security and Medicare, **1:**360
    state and local government spending and tax revenue, **1:**360

tax multiplier, **1:**362 (table)
temporary *vs.* permanent fiscal policy measures, **1:**363
theory, **1:**360–361
2007 recession and, **1:**354
Fischer, C., **1:**251
Fischer, Stanley, **1:**194, **1:**313, **1:**399
Fischhoff, B., **1:**279
Fisher, A., **2:**624
Fisher, A. C., **2:**647–648
Fisher, Anthony, **2:**639
Fisher Body, **2:**943–944, **2:**948
Fisher effect, **1:**311
Fix, M., **2:**704
Fixed exchange rates, **1:**428
Flatt, V., **2:**772, **2:**773
Fleishman, J. A., **2:**726, **2:**785
Flinchbaugh, Barry, **2:**603
Floating exchange rates, **1:**428
Flood, Curt, **2:**544
Flood v. Kuhn (1972), **2:**544
Florida, Richard, **2:**827
Florida Supreme Court, **2:**521
Flow of Funds Accounts, **2:**615
Flow of services, real estate economics and, **2:**607–611
Flynn, Joseph, **1:**269
Flypaper effect, **1:**261
Flyvbjerg, B., **1:**281
Folbre, N., **2:**906
Folland, S., **2:**691
Food and Agricultural Organization of the United Nations, **2:**597
Food Security Act of 1985, **2:**621, **2:**622
Food Stamp Program, **2:**602, **2:**603, **2:**604
Foose, L., **2:**844
Forbes, **1:**360
Ford, Henry, **1:**107
Ford Motors, **1:**169
Forecasting. *See* **Economic measurement and forecasting**
Foreign exchange market, **1:**427 (figure), **1:**467–469
Foreign trade debt
    economic instability and macroeconomic policy, **1:**354–355
    government debt and, **1:**377
    standard of living and, **1:**377–378
Forensic economics, 2:739–746
    collateral source payments, **2:**745
    ethics and assumptions of damage models, **2:**740
    fringe benefit losses, **2:**742–744
    growth of earnings, **2:**742
    household service losses, **2:**744
    law, **2:**740
    life, work life, healthy life expectancy, **2:**740–741
    life care plan, **2:**745
    personal consumption deduction, **2:**744
    present value, **2:**745
    taxes, **2:**745
    wage and salary loss, **2:**741–742
Forges, E., **1:**181
Forget, E., **2:**910
Forker, O. D., **2:**601
Formalism
    absorptive capacity of, **1:**38–39
    twentieth-century economic methodology and, **1:**37, **1:**38–39
Forsythe, R., **2:**878
Fort, Rodney, **2:**536

Fortune 500, **2:**648, **2:**901
Forward, **2:**598
Forward exchange rates, **1:**434–435, **1:**469
Forward Prices for Agriculture (Johnson), **2:**604
Foucault, Michel, **2:**770, **2:**771, **2:**772
Foundation for the Study of Cycles, **1:**301
Fourier, Charles, **1:**27
Fourth Circuit Court of Appeals, **1:**137
Frackowiak, R. S. J., **2:**914
Fragoso, E., **2:**853
Framed field experiments, **2:**874
France
    economic history and, **1:**17–18
    economics of aging, **2:**590 (table)
    gender wage gap in, **2:**555 (table)
Franchise bidding, government regulation and, **1:**268–269
Franco, D., **1:**479
Frank, Andre Gunder, **1:**15, **1:**21
Frank, Robert H., **2:**899
Frankel, J., **1:**434
Freakonomics (Levitt, Dubner), **2:**577
"Freakonomics," twentieth-century economic methodology and,
    1:41
Freddie Mac, **1:**353, **1:**397, **2:**612, **2:**615
Frederick, S., **1:**279
Free, Rhona, **1:**65n
Free agency, athletes' salaries and, **2:**544–547
Free choice, **2:**527–528
Free market thought, **1:**29
Free to Choose (Friedman), **2:**528
Freedman, David, **2:**934
Freedman, Estelle B., **2:**769, **2:**772
Freedom from Hunger, **2:**840
Freeman, A. M., **1:**278
Freeman, J., **2:**946
Freeman, R. B., **2:**702
Freeman, Richard, **1:**57, **1:**63, **1:**163, **1:**170, **1:**171, **2:**565
Free-rider problem, **1:**256
French, Kenneth, **1:**211, **1:**212
French Physiocrats, **1:**33, **2:**894
French Revolution, **1:**17
Frenkel, Jacob A., **1:**436
Freud, Sigmund, **2:**770
Frew, James, **2:**611
Frey, Bruno, **2:**899
Frictional unemployment, **1:**305–306
Friedan, B., **1:**158
Friedland, Claire, **1:**270, **2:**641
Friedman, Benjamin, **1:**384
Friedman, D., **2:**750
Friedman, Milton
    aggregate demand and aggregate supply, **1:**335, **1:**339
    aggregate expenditures model and equilibrium output, **1:**327,
        1:328–**1:**329
    behavioral economics and, **2:**861, **2:**870
    debates in macroeconomic policy and, **1:**393, **1:**394–**1:**395
    economic methodology and, **1:**30
    economics and corporate social responsibility, **2:**787, **2:**788,
        2:790
    economics and justice, **2:**525, **2:**528, **2:**530–532
    economics of education and, **2:**519
    exchange rates and, **1:**432
    fiscal policy, **1:**363

HET and, **1:**9
    macroeconomic models, **1:**311
    monetary policy and inflation targeting, **1:**382–**1:**383, **1:**388n
    new classical economics and, **1:**399–**1:**400, **1:**405
    profit maximization and, **1:**123
    role of labor unions in labor markets, **1:**163
    twentieth-century economic methodology and, **1:**35, **1:**37, **1:**38,
        1:41, **1:**42
Friedman, R., **1:**163, **1:**327, **2:**528
Friedman, Thomas L., **2:**642
Friedman's rule, **1:**311
Fringe benefit losses, forensic economics and, **2:**742–744
Frisch, Ragnar, **1:**406
Frith, S., **2:**829
Fromlet, Hubert, **1:**219
Frost, R. O., **2:**918
Frye, M. B., **2:**559
Fryer, Roland, **2:**569–570
F-statistic, **1:**53
Fu, W., **2:**829
Fuchs, Victor R., **2:**715
Fudenberg, D., **1:**136
Fuel
    changing fuel sources, **2:**638 (*See also* **Economics of energy**
        markets)
    economy, **1:**251–252
    See also **Political economy of oil**
Fujita, Masahisa, **2:**666, **2:**667
Full employment, **1:**309, **1:**325, **1:**365
Full unemployment, **1:**305–306
Fundamental analysis, firm foundation theory and, **1:**216–217
Fundamental transformation, **1:**198
Fundamental uncertainty, **1:**315
Funk, Jonas, **2:**540
Furman, J., **2:**715
Fusfeld, D. R., **2:**924, **2:**927
Futures, **1:**434–435
FX market, **1:**431

Gaffeo, E., **2:**691
Galasso, V., **2:**593
Galbiati, R., **2:**751
Galbraith, John Kenneth, **2:**605
Gale, David, **2:**933, **2:**935
Gale-Shapley algorithm, **2:**933
Gali, Jordi, **1:**383
Gall, Thomas, **2:**938
Gallagher, K., **2:**854
Gallant, Harmon, **2:**535
Gallaway, L. E., **1:**327
Galster, G. C., **2:**673
Gamble, Hays, **2:**618
Gambling. *See* **Economics of gambling**
Game theory, 1:173–184
    Battle of the Sexes (game), **1:**175 (figure)
    Bayesian Game, normal-form table (game), **1:**179 (figure)
    Card Game (game), **1:**176 (figure)
    Centipede Game, **1:**181 (figure)
    Chicken, correlation device, **1:**181 (figure)
    Chicken (game), **1:**175 (figure)
    cooperation, **1:**182–183
    Coordination Game (game), **1:**175 (figure)
    correlation, **1:**181–182

entry game, **1:**180 (figure)

entry game, normal form, **1:**180 (figure)

game solvable by iterative elimination of dominated strategies (game), **1:**179 (figure)

game where randomized strategy of player 1 is dominant (game), **1:**179 (figure)

game with dominant strategy for player 1 (game), **1:**179 (figure)

HET and, **1:**6, **1:**10

imperfectly competitive product markets and, **1:**130–133

Matching Pennies (game), **1:**175 (figure)

models, **1:**174–178

neuroscience of, **2:**914–918

Prisoner's Dilemma (game), **1:**175 (figure)

refinements, **1:**180–181

repetition, **1:**182

solutions, **1:**178–180

Three-Person Game (game), **1:**175 (figure)

Ultimatum Game (game), **1:**176 (figure)

Umbrella Game, normal-form table (game), **1:**178 (figure)

Umbrella Game (game), **1:**177 (figure)

See also **Experimental economics; Neuroeconomics**

Gangopadhyay, S., **2:**791

Ganguly, Chirantan, **1:**183n

Ganuza, J. J., **2:**786

Gardner, B. L., **2:**601

Garfinkel, M. R., **2:**807, **2:**814

Garnett, Kevin, **2:**549

Garnham, N., **2:**828

Garoupa, N., **2:**750

Garreau, J., **2:**672

Garrett, Thomas, **2:**678, **2:**679

Gasoline case study, **1:**76–77

Gasoline consumption, policies for the reduction of, **1:**247–254

Gaspar, Jess, **2:**610

Gassman, P., **2:**622

Gatewood, W. B., **2:**570

Gauthier-Loiselle, M., **2:**702

Gayer, Ted, **1:**263n, **1:**375

Gazzaniga, M., **2:**914

Geczy, C., **2:**792

Geldenhuys, J. P., **2:**688, **2:**689

Gelfand, Michele, **2:**560

Gender

discrimination in sports and, **2:**539–540

labor market and, **1:**144–145

male–female pay gap, **1:**158

microfinance targeted toward women, **2:**842

rise in world female labor force participation, **1:**455 (figure)

See also **Economics of gender**

General Agreement on Tariffs and Trade (GATT), **1:**464n, **2:**850

General-equilibrium (economy-wide) analysis, of inequality and globalization, **1:**497

General equilibrium theory, **1:**8

HET and, **1:**9–10

twentieth-century economic methodology, **1:**34

General Mills, **1:**128

General Motors, **1:**62, **1:**169, **1:**250, **2:**943–944, **2:**948

General Motors–United Auto Workers, **1:**169

General Social Survey, **2:**568, **2:**773, **2:**790

General Theory (Keynes), IS-LM model and, **1:**341–342

General Theory of Employment, Interest and Money (Keynes), **1:**9, **1:**307, **1:**319, **1:**326, **1:**327, **1:**328–**1:**330, **1:**338, **1:**341–**1:**346, **1:**350, **1:**355, **1:**361, **1:**366, **1:**392, **1:**399, **2:**927

Generalized least squares (GLS) estimator, **1:**50

Genet, Jean, **2:**770

Georgetown Law Journal, **1:**138

Geras, N., **2:**530

Gerking, S., **2:**624

Gerlagh, Reyer, **2:**643

Germany

economic history and, **1:**18

economics of aging, **2:**586 (table), **2:**587 (table), **2:**588 (table), **2:**590 (table)

economics of aging and, **2:**585

health economics and, **2:**713

Gersbach, H., **2:**688

Gershenkron, Alexander, **1:**15, **1:**18

Gertler, Mark, **1:**383

Gesell, Silvio, **1:**327

Gettmen, Hilary, **2:**560

Ghatak, M., **2:**786, **2:**787, **2:**790, **2:**791, **2:**841

Ghosh, A., **2:**726

Gibbons, J., **2:**753

Gibbons, Michael, **1:**212

Gibson paradox, **1:**311

Giffen, Robert, **1:**85

Gift exchange games, experimental economics and, **2:**878–880

Gigerenzer, G., **2:**861, **2:**864, **2:**866, **2:**870

Giles, J., **2:**854

Gilovich, Thomas, **2:**899

Gini coefficient, **1:**502 n1

Ginsburg, B., **2:**692

Gintis, H., **2:**531, **2:**790

Gittings, R. K., **2:**752

Glaeser, Edward L.

comparative economic systems and, **1:**448, **2:**569

economics and race, **2:**569

economics of crime and, **2:**751

real estate economics, **2:**610, **2:**613

twentieth-century economic methodology and, **1:**41

urban economics and, **2:**668, **2:**671, **2:**672, **2:**673

Glass, Gene, **2:**518

Glenn, A. J., **1:**159

Glimcher, P. W., **2:**870, **2:**913, **2:**916

Global oil demand, **2:**646–647

Global Precipitation Climatology Project (GPCP), **2:**811

Globalization and inequality, 1:493–502

athletes' salaries and, **2:**549–550

defining, measuring, evaluating, **1:**494–497

empirical evidence on inequality and trade, **1:**499–501

public finance and, **1:**262

sustainability of globalization, **1:**501–502

theory, **1:**497–499

Glorious Revolution of 1688 (England), **2:**802

Glynn, M. A., **2:**793

Gneezy, Uri, **2:**559, **2:**560, **2:**879, **2:**880

Godfrey, Erin, **2:**673

Goeree, J., **1:**138

Goff, D., **2:**831

Gökay, B., **2:**647

Gokhale, J., **1:**373

Goklany, I. M., **1:**16

Gold, J. I., **2:**916

Gold, R. S., **2:**691

Gold standard, **1:**433

Goldberg, J., **2:**770

Goldberg, P. K., **1:**501
Goldberg, V. P., **2:**948
Goldfarb, Robert S., **2:**673, **2:**899
Goldin, Claudia, **1:**494, **2:**556, **2:**558
Goldman, D., **2:**691
Goldman, D. P., **2:**726
Goldman, Marshall, **1:**441
Goldschmidt, Chanan, **1:**448
Goldschmidt-Clermont, L., **2:**907
Goldsmith, Andrew, **2:**570
Goldstein, D. G., **2:**870
Gollop, F. M., **2:**641
Gollub, R., **2:**918
Gomery, Douglas, **2:**828, **2:**829
Gomez, R., **1:**138, **2:**843
Gonzalez, A., **2:**837–838
Good-looking sampling distribution, **1:**47–48
Goodfriend, Marvin, **1:**407
Goodman, A. C., **2:**691
Goodman, W. K., **2:**915, **2:**916
Goodstein, Eban S., **2:**632, **2:**634
Goodwin, John, **2:**603
Goodwin, P., **2:**834
GoogleEarth, **2:**825
Gordon, D., **1:**58, **1:**62
Gordon, H. Scott, **2:**619–620
Gordon, R. J., **1:**401, **1:**406, **1:**407, **1:**500
Gossen, Herman Heinrich, **1:**80, **1:**84
Gossen's rule, **1:**80–81, **1:**84
Gottschalk, P., **1:**158
Gould, E. D., **2:**750
Gould, Eric, **2:**610
Gould, Stephen J., **2:**922, **2:**928
Gould, W., **1:**164
Governance, of labor unions, **1:**166–168
Governance structure
    as continuum, **1:**199–200
    defined, **1:**194–195
Government
    economic aspects of cultural heritage and, **2:**824
    economics of gambling and, **2:**679
    economics of HIV/AIDS and, **2:**692–693
    economics of property law and, **2:**762–763
    government spending multiplier, **1:**362 (table)
    HET and, **1:**4
    intervention of, and policies for the reduction of gasoline
        consumption, **1:**248
    Marxian and institutional industrial relations in U.S., **1:**61
    open-access resources and, **1:**234–235
    political economy of violence and, **2:**799–801
    public choice and, **1:**243–244
    public finance and, **1:**255–263
    theory of, **1:**256–257
    twentieth-century economic methodology and, **1:**33–36, **1:**40
    See also **Fiscal policy; Government budgets, debt, and deficits;**
        Monetary policy; Policy; **Regulatory economics;** Taxes
Government budgets, debt, and deficits, 1:369–379
    definitions and principles, **1:**369–373
    national debt and deficits, **1:**373–378
    ratio of U.S. federal gross debts to U.S. GDP, **1:**374 (figure)
Graham, A., **2:**832, **2:**833, **2:**834
Graham, Benjamin, **1:**215–**1:**216, **1:**217, **1:**218
Graham, J. R., **2:**732

Grameen Bank (Bangladesh), **2:**837, **2:**840, **2:**841
Gramm, P., **1:**326
Granger, Clive, **1:**291, **1:**294
Granitz, E., **1:**138
Granovetter, M., **2:**884
Grants, media economics and, **2:**833
Grapard, U., **2:**906
Graphs. *See* **Economic methodology**
Grasslands Reserve Program, **2:**622
Gravity model, **1:**416, **2:**698–699
Gray, G., **1:**216
Great Depression
    aggregate expenditures model and equilibrium output, **1:**327
    debates in macroeconomic policy, **1:**392, **1:**397–398, **1:**398
    economic history and, **1:**21
    economic instability and macroeconomic policy, **1:**349–**1:**350,
        1:355
    economic methodology and, **1:**29–**1:**30, **1:**29–30
    economics of energy markets and, **2:**641
    exchange rates and, **1:**433
    fiscal policy and, **1:**361, **1:**366–**1:**367
    globalization and inequality, **1:**501
    HET and, **1:**9
    imperfectly competitive product markets and, **1:**134
    IS-LM model and, **1:**341, **1:**344
    Keynes and debates in macroeconomic policy, **1:**392–393
    labor markets and, **1:**149
    Latin America's trade performance in new millenium and, **2:**847,
        2:855
    Marxian and institutional industrial relations in U.S., **1:**57,
        1:61–62, **1:**63
    measuring and evaluating macroeconomic performance,
        1:301, **1:**302
    monetary policy and inflation targeting, **1:**382
    origin of macroeconomics and, **1:**349–350
    political economy of oil and, **2:**646, **2:**648, **2:**651
    real estate economics and, **2:**614
    role of labor unions in labor markets and, **1:**164
    twentieth-century economic methodology and, **1:**37
    world development in historical perspective and, **1:**452, **1:**464
Great Inflation (1970–1981), **1:**350–352, **1:**396, **2:**647
Great Northern Railway, **1:**201
Great Recession of 2007, **1:**397–398
Great Society, **1:**393, **2:**651
Green, J., **1:**56, **1:**61
Green, L., **2:**915
Green, Richard, **2:**614
Green Book, **1:**281
Green coffee, composite indicator price of. *See* **Economics of fair**
    trade
Green Jobs Act, **1:**148
Green Revolution, **1:**20
Greenberg, David, **2:**772
Greene, D. L., **1:**251
Greenlees, J., **1:**304, **1:**305
Greenslade, R., **2:**834
Greenspan, Alan, **1:**287, **1:**304, **1:**352–**1:**353, **1:**355, **1:**381
Greenwald, Bruce, **1:**338
Greenwood, M. J., **2:**699
Grenada, Spain, **2:**824
Grier, Kevin, **1:**243, **1:**244
Griliches, Zvi, **2:**600
Grogger, Jeffrey, **2:**519, **2:**569

Gros, D., **1:**478

Gross domestic product (GDP), **1:**289
    aggregate demand/supply and, **1:**333–338
    aggregate expenditures model and equilibrium output and, **1:**319
    measuring and evaluating macroeconomic performance, **1:**298
    ratio of U.S. federal gross debts to U.S. GDP, **1:**374 (figure)
    System of National Accounts (SNA), **2:**906–907
    See also **Fiscal policy;** *individual macroeconomic topics;*
        individual names of countries and regions

Gross national product (GNP), role of labor unions and impact on,
    1:170

Grosskopf, B., **2:**862

Grossman, G. M., **1:**445, **1:**498, **1:**499, **1:**500

Grossman, Herschell I., **2:**809, **2:**814

Grossman, Michael, **2:**691, **2:**708

Grossman, P., **2:**866

Grossman, S. J., **2:**735, **2:**736, **2:**942

Group lending, microfinance and, **2:**840–841

Group of Three (G3), **2:**851

Groves, T., **1:**278

Growth stocks, **1:**301

Gruber, Jonathan, **1:**263n, **2:**587, **2:**594, **2:**715

Gruenspecht, H. K., **1:**252

G3 (U.S. Federal Reserve, ECB, Bank of Japan), **1:**386

Guatland BOP (2010), **1:**472 (table)

Gulati, R., **2:**946

Gulf Oil, **2:**649

Gundersson, M., **2:**556

Gunningham, N., **2:**793

Gupta, F., **1:**216

Gupta, Sonali Sen, **1:**183n

Guryan, Jonathan, **2:**568

Güth, W., **2:**878

Guthrie, W., **1:**326, **1:**330

Gwartney, J., **1:**238, **1:**244, **1:**246, **2:**850n

Gyourko, Joseph, **2:**613, **2:**673

Ha, L., **2:**834

Haacker, Markus, **2:**688, **2:**690

Haavelmo, T., **2:**814

Hadley, Larry, **2:**540n

Hagen, D. A., **2:**634

Hahn, Frank, **1:**40

Haines, Cabray, **2:**614

Hall, Robert E., **1:**324, **1:**326

Halvorsen, K., **2:**624

Hamermesh, D., **1:**170

Hamilton, Bruce W., **2:**666

Hamilton, Darrick, **2:**570

Hamilton, G., **1:**201

Hamilton, James, **2:**607, **2:**639

Hamilton, J. D., **1:**293

Hamilton, J. H., **2:**647, **2:**649, **2:**650

Hamilton, William Peter, **1:**217

Hammond, K. R., **2:**869

Handbook of Agricultural Economics: Volume IA: Agricultural
    Production (Huang, Sexton), **2:**601

Handbook of Agricultural Economics: Volume IB: Marketing,
    Distribution and Consumers (Gardner, Rausser), **2:**601

Hannan, Timothy, **2:**556

Hansen, Alvin, **1:**309–**1:**310, **1:**319, **1:**325–**1:**326, **1:**346

Hansen, Lars, **1:**211

Hanson, G., **1:**499

Hanson, G. H., **2:**704

Hanson, Philip, **1:**442

Hansson, Å., **2:**594

Hanushek, Eric, **2:**517, **2:**521

Happiness, quantity of, **1:**80

Harberger, Arnold, **1:**259

Harberger's Triangle, **1:**259

Harbison, F., **1:**56

Hardaker, J. Brian, **2:**600

Hardin, Garrett, **1:**232–**1:**233, **2:**620, **2:**640, **2:**758

Hardt, M., **2:**651

Harmonized index of consumer prices (HICP), **1:**480–484

Harrigan, James, **1:**415

Harrington, Joseph E., **1:**139, **1:**240, **1:**272, **2:**641

Harrington, W., **2:**659

Harrington, Winston, **1:**249, **1:**251, **1:**252

Harris, Christopher, **2:**639

Harris, J. E., **2:**712

Harris, M., **2:**923

Harrison, A., **1:**501

Harrison, G. W., **1:**279, **2:**874

Harrison, H., **1:**500

Harrod, Roy, **1:**393

Hart, O., **2:**942

Hartl, T. L., **2:**918

Hartman, Heidi, **1:**58

Harvard Business School, **2:**844

Harvard Clerical and Technical Workers, **1:**64

Harvard University, **1:**441

Harvey, D., **2:**647, **2:**651

Hashemi, S., **2:**844

Hassett, Kevin, **2:**642

Hastie, R., **2:**869

Haught, R., **2:**724

Hausman, Dan, **1:**38

Hausman, J. A., **1:**251

Hausman, William, **1:**268

Havelaar, Max, **1:**507

Haveman, R. H., **1:**278

Hawley-Smoot (1930), **1:**393

Hawthorne, H. W., **2:**598

Hawtrey, Ralph, **1:**329

Hay, Donald A., **2:**898

Hayek, Friedrich A. von, **1:**29, **1:**38, **1:**40, **1:**193, **1:**195, **1:**444,
    2:927

He, G., **2:**915, **2:**916

Heady, Earl O., **2:**600, **2:**602, **2:**604

Health economics, 2:707–716
    comparative health care systems, **2:**712–713
    demand for health, **2:**708
    health insurance, **2:**708–710
    markets for physicians, nurses, hospitals, pharmaceuticals,
        2:710–712
    methodology, **2:**707–708
    reform in U.S., **2:**713–716
    See also **Economics of health insurance; Economics of HIV**
        and AIDS; Forensic economics

Health insurance. *See* **Economics of health insurance**

Health maintenance organizations (HMOs), **2:**709–710

Health savings accounts (HSAs), **2:**715–716

Healthy Life Expectancy, **2:**740, **2:**741, **2:**744

HEATCO, **1:**279

Heberlein, Thomas, **2:**624

Hébert, Robert F., **1:**89, **2:**892, **2:**893

Hechanova, M. R., **2:**560

Heckelman, Jac, **1:**244

Heckman, James, **2:**516, **2:**557, **2:**574, **2:**701, **2:**772

Heckscher-Ohlin model, **1:**414–415

Hedonic approach, **2:**632

Hedonic prices, real estate economics, **2:**611

Heide, J. B., **2:**944

Heilbroner, Robert, **1:**4

Helgeson, J., **2:**831

Helland, E., **2:**751

Heller, M. A., **2:**759

Hellerstein, Judith, **2:**556

Helpman, Elhanan, **1:**416

Helsley, Robert, **2:**672

Helwege, A., **2:**848

Henderson, D., **1:**464n

Henderson, J. Vernon, **2:**669

Henisz, W. J., **2:**945

Henry of Friemar, **2:**893

Hepburn Act of 1906, **1:**272

Herbal Essences, **1:**127

Herfindahl-Hirschman Index (HHI), **2:**830

Heritage Foundation, **1:**63–**1:**64

Herring, C., **2:**570

Hertwig, R., **2:**866

Heterodox economics, **2:**528–530

Heterodoxnews.com, **1:**24

Heterogeneity
    complexity and economics, **2:**883–884
    real estate economics and, **2:**609–610

Heteroskedasticity, **1:**49, **1:**50

Heukelom, F., **2:**870

Hewitson, G. J., **2:**902, **2:**906, **2:**908

Heyne, Paul, **2:**898

Heywood, John, **2:**568

Hicks, John R., **1:**9, **1:**30, **1:**81, **1:**309–**1:**310, **1:**341–**1:**346, **1:**350, **2:**617

High benefits, **2:**578–579

High School and Beyond Survey, **2:**519

Hill, J., **1:**250

Hill, R. P., **2:**792, **2:**793

Hill Ore Lease, **1:**201

Hillard, M., **1:**63, **1:**64, **2:**785

Hilmer, Christiana, **2:**639

Hilton, G. R., **2:**641

Himmelstein, D. U., **2:**717, **2:**720

Hinze, Christine F., **2:**898

Hirsch, B., **1:**166f, **1:**167f

Hirschman, Albert O., **1:**38, **1:**170

Hirshleifer, Jack, **2:**809, **2:**814

History of analysis, **1:**1

History of Economic Analysis (Schumpeter), **1:**4, **1:**34, **1:**419

History of economic thought, 1:1–11, 1–11
    economic methodology and, **1:**27, **1:**29
    history of recent economics, **1:**10–11
    since 1925, **1:**8–10
    through 1925, **1:**4–8

History of Economic Thought: A Reader (Medema, Samuels), **1:**4

History of Economics Society, **1:**4

History of Political Economy, **1:**4

History of Standard Oil Company, The (Tarbell), **1:**135

Hitler, Adolf, **2:**646

HIV. *See* **Economics of HIV and AIDS**

Hobbes, Thomas, **1:**5, **1:**40, **2:**757

Hobsbawm, Eric, **1:**15, **1:**17

Hochschild, A., **1:**64

Hodgson, G. M., **2:**921, **2:**922, **2:**925, **2:**926, **2:**927

Hoebel, B. G., **2:**917

Hoeffler, A., **2:**809, **2:**812, **2:**813, **2:**815, **2:**816

Hoenack, S. A., **2:**752

Hoffer, Thomas, **2:**519

Hofman, A., **2:**848

Hofstede, Geert, **1:**448

Hogarth, R., **2:**867

Hold-up problem, **1:**198

Holland, J., **2:**886

Hollans, Harris, **2:**615

Holm, M. K., **1:**281

Holmgren, J., **2:**656

Holt, C. A., **1:**138, **2:**866, **2:**876, **2:**885

Holt, Matthew, **2:**600

Holt, R. P. F., **1:**24

Holzer, H. J., **2:**568, **2:**574

Holzman, Frank, **1:**441

Holzmann, Robert, **2:**594

Homma, Munehisa, **1:**215, **1:**217

Homo economicus, **2:**898

Hoot, J. Weldon, **1:**441

Hoover, D. M ., **2:**598

Hoover, Herbert, **1:**301, **2:**544

Hoover, K. D., **1:**399–**1:**400

Hopkin, John, **2:**604

Hoppe, H., **2:**938

Horioka, C., **1:**486

Horowitz, D., **2:**815

Horowitz, J. L., **2:**878

Horsepower, **2:**637

Hoskins, C., **2:**830, **2:**831, **2:**833

Hospitals, market for, **2:**710–712

Hotelling, Harold, **1:**239, **2:**617, **2:**639, **2:**646, **2:**647–648

Houck, James P., **2:**600

Household production approach, **2:**632

Household service losses, forensic economics and, **2:**744

Houser, D., **2:**915

Housing
    collapse of bubble, **1:**353
    1990–1991 recession and start of U.S. housing boom, **1:**352
    real estate economics and, **2:**611–615

Houthakker, H., **1:**473

Howe, S., **1:**58

Howland, J., **2:**564

Hoxby, Caroline, **2:**517–518

Huang, G. T., **2:**913, **2:**918

Huang, S., **2:**601

Hubbert, M. King, **2:**639, **2:**645–646

Hudson, M. C., **2:**815

Hughes, D. W., **2:**599

Huirne, Ruud, **2:**600

Human asset specificity, defined, **1:**196

Human capital
    economic history and, **1:**14
    economics of education and, **2:**515–517
    wage determination, **1:**155–158

Human Development Index (HDI), **2:**850

Human Development Report (United Nations), **1:**496

Human resource management (HRM), **1:**62
Hume, David, **1:**33, **1:**36, **1:**39, **1:**40, **1:**327, **1:**392, **1:**464n
Humphrey, S., **2:**802
Humphreys, Brad R., **2:**537, **2:**539
Hunt, J., **2:**702
Hunter, Jim "Catfish," **2:**545
Hurley, F., **1:**279
Hurst, E., **2:**673
Hurt, Chris, **2:**603
Hurwicz, Leonid, **1:**35
Husted, S., **1:**471
Hutchison, T. W., **1:**4, **1:**37
Hutton, W., **2:**827
Hypothesis testing, **1:**48

Iacobucci, E., **1:**138
Iannaccone, L. R., **2:**779
IBM, **1:**130, **1:**490
Ibn Saud, King Abd al-Aziz, **2:**646
Icfai University Journal of Agricultural Economics, **2:**599
Idson, Todd, **2:**537
Ihlanfeldt, Keith, **2:**568
ILE/IR
    Great Depression and expert group, **1:**57
    Marxian and institutional industrial relations and New Deal, **1:**57, **1:**62
    Marxian and institutional industrial relations in U.S., **1:**60–61
    See also **Marxian and institutional industrial relations in U.S.**
Illegal immigration, **2:**704
Illinois Standards Achievement Test, **2:**522
Illinois State Board of Education, **2:**522
Illustrative regression, **1:**52, **1:**53
Immigration, labor market and, **1:**149–150
Immigration Reform and Control Act (IRCA), **2:**704
Impact of Ethanol Use on Food Prices and Greenhouse-Gas Emissions, The (Congressional Budget Office), **1:**77
Imperfect competition model, **1:**416
Imperfect preference satisfaction, **2:**578
Imperfectly competitive product markets, 1:125–134
    antitrust laws, **1:**133–134
    changes in monopolist's total revenue resulting from price cut, **1:**126 (figure)
    deterring entry by capacity decision, **1:**132 (figure)
    examination of credibility of threat, **1:**133 (figure)
    labor market, **1:**143–144
    monopolistic competition, **1:**127–128
    monopoly, **1:**125–127
    oligopoly, **1:**128–133
    payoff matrix for firms choosing quantity of output, **1:**131 (figure)
    profit-maximizing quantity and price for a monopolist, **1:**126 (figure)
    short-run/long-run equilibrium under monopolistic competition, **1:**128 (figure)
    welfare loss due to monopoly, **1:**127 (figure)
Imperialism, economic history and, **1:**15
Implicit costs, **1:**106
Imports. *See* **Latin America's trade performance in new millenium**
Impulse mechanisms, **1:**406
Imrohoroglu, A., **2:**750
Income, **1:**70
    demand for health insurance and, **2:**717–718
    effect, **1:**79, **1:**85
    externality, and costs from open-access groundwater aquifer, **1:**233 (figure)

Income elasticity
    of demand, **1:**95–96
    transportation economics and, **2:**656–657
"Incredible threat," **1:**181
Independent variables, **1:**46
Index of Coincident Economic Indicators, **1:**300
Index of Consumer Expectations, **1:**300
Index of Lagging Economic Indicators, **1:**300
Index of Leading Economic Indicators, **1:**299
India
    East Asian economies and, **1:**485
    economic history and, **1:**20
    globalization and inequality, **1:**494
Indifference curves, **1:**82
Indifference maps, **1:**82–83
Individual assets, asset pricing model and, **1:**205
Individual behavior
    economic methodology and, **1:**24
    economics of HIV and AIDS and, **2:**690–692
    HET and, **1:**4, **1:**5
Individual transferable quotas (ITQs), **2:**623
Individuals, matching markets and, **2:**931–939
Industrial democracy, **1:**56–57
Industrial relations (IR). *See* **Marxian and institutional industrial relations in U.S.**
Industrial Revolution, **1:**56, **1:**465n, **2:**638, **2:**640, **2:**645, **2:**906, **2:**923, **2:**928
    in Britain and Europe, **1:**59, **2:**924
    economic history and, **1:**14, **1:**15, **1:**16, **1:**19, **1:**20
    HET and, **1:**5
Industrial unions, **1:**57
Industrial Workers of the World (IWW), **1:**165
Industrialization
    economic analysis of the family and, **2:**580
    economic history and evolution of, **1:**14–15
    See also Economic history
Industry, transaction cost economics and, **1:**200–201
Inequality. *See* **Globalization and inequality**
Inferior goods, **1:**70
Inflation
    economic measurement and forecasting, **1:**287
    HET and, **1:**9
    long-term trend in world inflation, **1:**461 (figure)
    measuring and evaluating macroeconomic performance, **1:**304
Inflation targeting (IT)
    implementing, **1:**383–385
    implementing and practice, **1:**385–388
    inflation targeting-time of adoption and target range, **1:**386 (table)
    real output growth and inflation volatility, **1:**387 (table)
Information. *See* **Economics of information**
Information asymmetry, microfinance and, **2:**838–842
Information sources, **1:**289, **1:**291
Information technology, health economics and, **2:**714
ING Barings, **2:**689
Ingrao, B., **1:**9
Input, **1:**102
    elasticity of demand for, **1:**98
    input-price shocks, **1:**337
    See also **Costs of production: short run and long run; Profit maximization**
Institute for Fiscal Studies (IFS), **1:**263n
Institute of Economic Affairs, **2:**651

Institute of Medicine, 2:714
Institutional Industrial Relations. *See* **Marxian and institutional industrial relations in U.S.**
Institutionalization, 1:61
Institutions
  economic history and, 1:14
  economics and religion, 2:782–783
  economics of civil war and, 2:814
  new institutionalists (NIE), 2:927–929
  original institutional economics (OIE), 2:925–927
  public choice and, 1:244–245
  See also **Evolutionary economics**
Instituto Brasileiro do Café (IBC), 1:504
Instrumental variable (IV) estimator, 1:50
Insurance Experiment Group, 2:724
Inter-American Development Bank, 2:848
Intercept, 1:46
Inter-Continental Exchange (ICE), 1:504
Interest rate parity, 1:435–436
Internal consistency of theory, 1:24
International Association for Feminist Economics, 2:910n
International Association of Agricultural Economists (IAAE), 2:597, 2:599
International Bank for Reconstruction and Development, 1:433
International Bank for Reconstruction and Development (IBRD), 1:433
International Coffee Agreement, 1:506, 1:509, 1:511
International Coffee Organization, 1:504f, 1:506
International Development Bank (IDB), 2:855
International Energy Agency, 2:645
International finance, 1:467–475
  balance of payments and models of current account behavior, 1:471–474
  economic history and, 1:15
  exchange rate behavior in short/long run, 1:469–471
  exchange rate regimes and regime choice, 1:474–475
  exchange rates and foreign exchange market, 1:467–469
  open-economy macroeconomics, 1:474
  selected exchange rates (January 12, 2009), 1:468 (table)
  2010 Guatland BOP, 1:472 (table)
International Food Policy Research Institute, 2:597
International Labour Office (ILO), 1:145
International Management Group, 2:548
International migration, 2:699–704
International Monetary Fund (IMF)
  balance of trade and payments, 1:421
  Bretton Woods and, 1:433
  East Asian economies, 1:491
  economics of fair trade, 1:505, 1:506
  exchange rates, 1:432, 1:433
  feminist economics, 2:909, 2:923
  globalization and inequality, 1:496
  international finance, 1:475
  Latin America's trade performance in new millennium, 2:848
  macroeconomic models, 1:313
  measuring and evaluating macroeconomic performance, 1:304
  monetary policy and inflation targeting, 1:386
  political economy of oil, 2:651
  structural adjustment, 1:505–506
  world development in historical perspective, 1:464n, 1:465n
International oil companies (IOCs), 2:648–649
International Peace Research Institute, Oslo (PRIO), 2:808

International trade, comparative and absolute advantage, and trade restrictions, 1:411–418
  costs and benefits of a tariff, 1:417 (figure)
  current topics in international trade theory, 1:416–417
  trade restrictions, 1:417–418
  trade theory and evidence, 1:411–416
International Trade Organization, 1:464n
International Year of Microcredit, 2:837
Internet, media economics and, 2:834
Interstate Commerce Act of 1887, 1:266, 1:272
Interstate Commerce Commission (ICC), 1:266, 1:271, 1:272
Intertemporal budget constraint (IBC), 1:370
Intertemporal choice, 1:85–86
Intertemporal substitution, 1:312–313, 1:406
Interurban analysis, 2:666–669
Intranational migration, 2:699
Investment, economics of property law and, 2:758–759
Investment Company Institute (ICI), 1:221
Investment management, defined, 1:219–222
  See also **Portfolio theory and investment management**
Investment Under Uncertainty (Dixit, Pindyck), 2:642
"Invisible hand," 1:8, 1:34–36
Involuntary transfers, economics of property law and, 2:761–762
Iowa Test of Basic Skills, 2:520
Iranian Revolution, 2:647
Iran–Iraq War, 2:647
Iraqi National Oil Company, 2:650
Iraqi Oil Law of 2007, 2:650
Irlenbusch, B., 2:842
Ironmonger, D., 2:906, 2:907
Irons, Michael D., 2:899
Irrational Exuberance (Shiller), 2:869
Irreversible investment, energy as, 2:642
Isenberg, D., 1:317
Islamic Empire, 1:18
Islamic Sharia, 2:754
IS-LM model, 1:341–347
  aggregate demand and aggregate supply, 1:339
  aggregate expenditures model and equilibrium output, 1:327
  development of, 1:342–343
  diagram, 1:344 (figure)
  HET and, 1:9
  Keynes's *General Theory* and, 1:341–342
  new Keynesian macroeconomics and, 1:313–314
  policy analysis, 1:344–346
  twentieth-century economic methodology and, 1:35
Isomorphism, 2:793
Isoquant curve, 1:106
Israel, G., 1:9
Italy
  economics of aging, 2:586 (table), 2:587 (table), 2:590 (table)
  economics of aging and, 2:585
  gender wage gap in, 2:555 (table)

Jackson, J. D., 1:243, 2:677, 2:679
Jacob, Brian, 2:520, 2:521
Jacobsen, J. P., 2:580, 2:582
Jacoby, Sanford, 1:56, 1:57, 1:62, 1:63, 1:65n
Jacquet, N. L., 2:937
Jaeger, D. A., 2:703
Jaffe, Adam B., 1:248, 2:642, 2:643
James, Harvey S., Jr., 2:899

Japan
    East Asian economies and, **1**:485
    economics of aging and, **2**:585, **2**:586 (table), **2**:587 (table),
        2:588 (table)
    gender wage gap in, **2**:555 (table)
Japanese Candlestick Charting Techniques (Nison), **1**:215
Jefferis, K., **2**:688
Jefferson, Gary, **1**:447
Jegadeesh, Narasimhan, **1**:211
Jenkin, Fleming, **1**:89
Jensen, J. Bradford, **1**:416
Jensen, Michael, **1**:211
Jepson, L. K., **2**:536–537
Jessop, D. J., **2**:726
Jevons, William Stanley, **1**:7, **1**:28, **1**:80, **1**:342
Job matching theory, **1**:157–158
Johannsson, H., **2**:701
John, G., **2**:944
Johnson, C., **2**:866
Johnson, David, **1**:388
Johnson, D. Gale, **2**:604
Johnson, E. J., **2**:870
Johnson, Harry G., **1**:263n, **1**:432, **1**:465n
Johnson, Jack, **2**:543
Johnson, James, **2**:570
Johnson, Leland, **1**:269
Johnson, Lyndon, **1**:160, **1**:393
Johnson, R., **2**:622
Johnston, D., **2**:689, **2**:690
Joint Committee on Taxation, **1**:261, **2**:613
Jolls, C., **2**:935
Jones, Charles I., **1**:339–**1**:340
Jones, Eric, **1**:19, **1**:20
Jones, J. C., **2**:535
Jones, Jerry, **2**:535
Jones, R. W., **1**:497, **1**:498
Jordan, B., **1**:217n, **1**:220n
Joskow, Paul A., **1**:200, **2**:641, **2**:944
Journal of Agricultural and Applied Economics,
    2:599
Journal of Agricultural and Resource Economics,
    2:599
Journal of Agricultural Economics, **2**:599
Journal of Business, **2**:862
Journal of Economic Literature, **1**:38, **2**:534
Journal of Economic Methodology, **1**:38
Journal of Economic Perspectives, **1**:38, **2**:870
Journal of Economic Theory, **1**:402
Journal of Farm Economics, **2**:598, **2**:600, **2**:602
Journal of Finance, **1**:216
Journal of Forensic Economics, **2**:739
Journal of Legal Economics, **2**:739
Journal of Sports Economics, **2**:533
Journal of the History of Economic Thought, **1**:4
Juglar, Clement, **1**:302
Juhn, Chinhui, **1**:158, **2**:557
Junakar, Pramod, **2**:573
Just, Richard, **2**:600, **2**:602
Justice. *See* **Economics and justice**

Kagan, R. A., **2**:793
Kagel, J. H., **2**:873, **2**:915

Kahane, Leo, **2**:537
Kahn, Alfred, **1**:272, **2**:641
Kahn, J. A., **1**:252
Kahn, Lawrence M., **2**:535, **2**:536, **2**:537, **2**:554, **2**:555n, **2**:568
Kahn, M. E., **2**:671, **2**:672
Kahneman, Daniel
    behavioral economics and, **2**:863, **2**:869, **2**:870
    cost-benefit analysis and, **1**:277
    experimental economics and, **2**:873, **2**:876
    neuroeconomics and, **2**:913, **2**:915, **2**:916
    portfolio theory and investment management,
        1:215, **1**:219
Kain, John D., **2**:517, **2**:568, **2**:569, **2**:661
Kaiser Family Foundation, **2**:742
Kaldor, Nicholas, **2**:617
Kaldor-Hicks criterion, **1**:276
Kalecki, Michal, **1**:316–**1**:317
Kalleberg, A., **1**:64
Kamp, B., **1**:139
Kanazawa, Mark, **2**:540
Kaplow, L., **2**:764n
Karemera, D., **2**:699
Karlan, D., **2**:843
Karlson, Stephen H., **2**:641, **2**:643
Karpoff, J. M., **2**:751
Kaserman, David, **1**:273
Kates, J., **2**:692
Katona, George, **2**:864
Katz, H., **1**:56
Katz, L. F., **1**:494, **2**:569, **2**:701, **2**:702
Kau, James, **1**:243
Kaufman, Bruce S., **1**:55, **1**:56, **1**:57, **1**:58, **1**:60, **1**:61, **1**:62, **1**:64,
    1:65n, **1**:170
Kaufman, P. J., **1**:201
Kaufman, R., **2**:740, **2**:745
Kaushal, N., **2**:703
Kay, R., **2**:602
Kehoe, P. J., **1**:407
Keith, V., **2**:570
Kelaher, M., **2**:726
Keller, R. R., **1**:244
Keller, S., **1**:139
Kellogg's, **1**:128
Kelo v. City of New London (2005), **2**:762
Kemp, T., **2**:926
Kennedy, John F., **1**:350, **1**:393
Kenney, Roy, **1**:195
Keohane, N. O., **2**:635
Kern, William, **2**:535, **2**:539
Kerr, Clark, **1**:56, **1**:57
Kesenne, Stefan, **2**:535, **2**:536
Kessler, D., **2**:751, **2**:752
Kessler-Harris, A., **1**:62
Keynes, John Maynard
    aggregate demand and aggregate supply, **1**:336, **1**:338
    aggregate expenditures model and equilibrium output, **1**:319,
        1:321–**1**:322, **1**:325–**1**:327, **1**:328–**1**:330
    critique of classical economics, **1**:307–308
    debates in macroeconomic policy and, **1**:392–**1**:393
    debates in macroeconomic policy and Great Depression,
        1:392–393
    demand elasticities and, **1**:89, **1**:99n

economic instability and macroeconomic policy, **1**:350
economic methodology and, **1**:29–**1**:30, **1**:31
emergence of macroeconomics and, **1**:9–**1**:10
evolutionary economics and, **2**:927
experimental economics and, **2**:877
fiscal policy and, **1**:361, **1**:366
HET and, **1**:11
IS-LM model, **1**:341–**1**:346
Keynesian economics, **1**:309
macroeconomic models, **1**:307–**1**:309, **1**:315–**1**:317
model represented as set of propositions,
    1:308–309
new classical economics and, **1**:399, **1**:401
portfolio theory and investment management,
    1:215, **1**:218
rise/fall of Keynesian consensus (1961–1973), **1**:350
twentieth-century economic methodology and, **1**:35
Keynes, John Neville, **1**:29, **1**:37
Keynes effect, **1**:334
Keynesian cross
  comparative statics of, **1**:324
  defined, **1**:321
  diagram, **1**:322 (figure), **1**:327–330
Keynesianism, **1**:9–10
  debates in macroeconomic policy and, **1**:393–394
  Keynesians, defined, **1**:309
  measuring and evaluating macroeconomic performance, **1**:301
Khan, Richard, **1**:345
Khandker, S., **2**:845
Kidney exchange, matching markets and, **2**:937
Kilani, M., **2**:658
Kilgore, Sally, **2**:519
Kilian, L., **1**:252
Kim, M., **2**:814
Kim, Y., **1**:471
Kimpel, T. J., **2**:659, **2**:662
Kindleberger, C. P., **1**:464
King, J. R., **2**:750
King, Robert, **1**:407
Kinghorn, A., **2**:688
Kinnell, J., **2**:624
Kinney Drugs, **1**:132–**1**:133
Kinnucan, Henry W., **2**:601, **2**:605n
Kirchsteiger, G., **2**:879
Kirsh, Lenny, **1**:441
Kitchin, Joseph, **1**:302
Kitheno River, Kenya, **1**:510
Kitzmueller, M., **2**:788f, **2**:794n
Klaassen, Ger, **2**:643
Klaeffling, Matt, **1**:387
Klare, M., **2**:646, **2**:650
Klawitter, M. M., **2**:772, **2**:773
Klay, Robin J., **2**:898
Klein, Benjamin, **1**:138, **1**:195, **1**:196, **1**:198, **2**:942, **2**:948
Klein, D., **2**:662, **2**:663
Klein, J., **1**:64
Klein, Lawrence, **1**:404
Klein, P. G., **1**:200, **2**:944
Kleit, A. N., **1**:251
Klepper, S., **2**:947
Kletzer, Lori G., **1**:157, **1**:500
Kling, C., **2**:622
Knapp, D., **2**:649

Knetsch, Jack L., **1**:277, **1**:278, **2**:624
Knight, Frank, **1**:35, **1**:37
Knights of Labor, **1**:165
Knowledge and Class (Resnick, Wolff), **1**:446
Knudsen, T., **2**:922
Knutson, Ronald, **2**:603
Kochan, Thomas, **1**:56, **1**:57, **1**:62, **1**:64, **1**:65n
Kohls, Richard, **2**:603
Kojima, F., **2**:937
Kolar, T., **2**:824
Koller, R., **1**:137
Kolstad, C. D., **2**:632, **2**:633
Kondratieff, Nikolai, **1**:302
Kontoleon, A., **2**:624
Koppl, Roger, **1**:41, **1**:42
Kortum, Samuel, **1**:416
Kossoudji, S. A., **2**:705
Kotchen, M. J., **2**:786, **2**:787
Kotler, P., **2**:789
Kotlikoff, Laurence J., **1**:373, **1**:375, **1**:376, **1**:378
Kraay, A., **1**:496
Kraft, **1**:509
Kramarz, F., **1**:157
Kranton, R. E., **2**:556, **2**:790
Krashinsky, Harry, **2**:566
Krasker, W., **1**:470
Krautmann, A. C., **2**:536
Kreider, Alan, **2**:898
Kreps, D. M., **1**:137, **1**:181
Kresteva, Julie, **2**:770
Krolak-Salmon, P., **2**:916
Kropp, David, **2**:516–517
Krueger, A. B., **1**:157, **1**:159, **2**:574, **2**:812
Krueger, Alan, **2**:518
Krueger, A. O., **1**:241
Krugman, Paul
  East Asian economies and, **1**:488, **1**:491
  exchange rates and, **1**:437
  international trade and, **1**:413, **1**:416
  Latin America's trade performance in new millenium and, **2**:848
  measuring and evaluating macroeconomic performance, **1**:298
  twentieth-century economic methodology and, **1**:39
  urban economics and, **2**:666, **2**:667
Krupnick, A., **1**:279
Kruse, Agneta, **2**:589, **2**:593, **2**:594
Krutilla, John, **2**:620–621, **2**:623
Kuhn, Bowie, **2**:544
Kuhn, Thomas, **1**:24, **1**:37, **1**:340
Kuhner, E., **2**:662
Kuiper, E., **2**:904, **2**:906, **2**:908, **2**:909, **2**:910
Kung, L., **2**:831, **2**:834
Kurani, K. S., **1**:251
Kurkalova, L., **2**:622
Kurtz, D., **1**:139
Kurzban, R., **2**:915
Kuwuyama, M., **2**:853
Kuznets, Simon, **1**:13
Kverndokk, S., **2**:790
Kydland, Finn E., **1**:10, **1**:384, **1**:399, **1**:404, **1**:405, **1**:406
Kyoto Protocol, **2**:635, **2**:643

La Croix, Sumner, **2**:568
La Porta, R., **1**:448

Laband, David N., **2:**626, **2:**899

Labor contracts, role of labor unions and, **1:**169

Labor-Management Reporting and Disclosure Act (LMRDA) of 1959, **1:**167

Labor markets, 1:141–151

applications and empirical evidence, **1:**144–147

capitalism and, in U.S., **1:**55–57 (*See also* **Marxian and institutional industrial relations in U.S.**)

economic methodology and, **1:**25

economics of aging and, **2:**587–588, **2:**587–589

economics of gender and, **2:**553–562

future directions, **1:**149–150

labor economics of corporate social responsibility, **2:**790–791

modern consumer theory, **1:**86

monopoly in, **1:**120–121 (*See also* **Profit maximization**)

monopsony labor market, **1:**144 (figure)

perfectly competitive market for labor and firm level employment, **1:**143 (figure)

policy implications, **1:**147–149

public finance and, **1:**260

role of labor unions and impact on, **1:**170

sports economics and, **2:**534, **2:**536–537

theory of labor market allocation, **1:**141–144

unemployment across industrialized countries, **1:**147 (figure)

U.S. unemployment rate (seasonalized) 16 years and over, **1:**147 (figure)

See also **Wage determination**

Labor "problems," **1:**58

"Labor question," **1:**56

Labor theory of value, **1:**26

Lacan, Jacques, **2:**770

LaCass, C., **2:**750

Lacy, S., **2:**829

Laffer, Arthur, **1:**352

Laffont, J., **1:**248

Lafontaine, F., **1:**201

LaFrance, Jeffrey, **2:**600

Lagging indicators, **1:**289

Lahiri, K., **1:**291

Laibson, David, **2:**869, **2:**917, **2:**918

Laidler, D. E. W., **1:**406

Laissez-faire, **1:**35, **1:**355, **1:**398

Laitin, D., **2:**810, **2:**812, **2:**813, **2:**815

Lakatos, Imre, **1:**37

Lakdawalla, D., **2:**691

Lake Sevan, Armenia, **2:**825

Lakshminarayan, P. G., **2:**622

Lam, T. C., **2:**656

Landes, David S., **1:**16, **1:**19, **2:**637

Landes, W. M., **2:**749–750, **2:**751

Landrum-Griffin Act, **1:**167

Landry, M., **1:**139

Lang, Kevin, **2:**516–517, **2:**569

Lange, Oskar, **1:**35, **1:**443, **1:**444, **1:**447, **1:**448

Lapenu, C., **2:**838

Laplante, B., **2:**825

Laqueur, T. W., **2:**772

Large-scale enterprise, energy markets, **2:**639–640

Larrick, R. P., **1:**251

Larsen, Andrew, **2:**539

Laski, Harold, **1:**464n

Latin American Integration Association (LAIA), **2:**851

Latin America's trade performance in new millenium, 2:847–857

basic economic and social indicators, **2:**849 (table)

China: main products imported from Latin America, **2:**853 (figure)

economic history and, **1:**18–21

exports growth rates and economic performance, **2:**854 (figure)

exports/imports main partners (1980–2007), **2:**852 (table)

financial crisis of 2008, **2:**855

openness indices, **2:**851 (figure)

simple average tariff for manufacturing products, **2:**850 (figure)

structure of exports, **2:**852 (figure)

trade liberalization process, **2:**848

2000–2007, **2:**848–855

world development in historical perspective, **1:**456–457

Laubach, Thomas, **1:**385

Laurence, L., **2:**726

Laurie, B., **1:**56

Laury, S. K., **2:**866, **2:**876

Lave, Charles, **2:**661

Law, forensic economics and, **2:**740

Law of demand, **1:**69

Law of one price, **1:**436–437

Law of supply, **1:**71

Lawrence, P. R., **2:**946

Lawrence, R. Z., **1:**500

Lawson, R., **2:**850n

Layson, S., **2:**752

Lazear, Edward P., **2:**518, **2:**703

Lazo, J., **2:**624

LBGTQ identities, **2:**767–768

Le Dressay, Andre, **2:**535

Leading indicators, **1:**290

Leadley, John, **2:**537

Leamer, Edward E., **1:**37, **1:**415, **1:**498

Leave It to Beaver (television series), **2:**907

Lee, B., **2:**831

Lee, N., **2:**789

Lee, Young, **2:**538

Leeds, Michael, **2:**535, **2:**540

Leeson, Peter, **1:**41

Legislative Analyst's Office, **2:**613

Legros, P., **2:**937, **2:**938

Lehfeldt, R. A., **1:**99

Lehman Brothers, **1:**353

Leiblein, M. J., **2:**945

Leibowitz, A., **2:**726

Leijonhufvud, Axel, **1:**344–**1:**345, **1:**346–**1:**347nn

Leland, H. E., **2:**735

Lenovo, **1:**490

Leonard, Jonathan, **1:**155, **2:**574

Leonard, Kenneth L., **2:**560, **2:**880

Leontief, Wassily, **1:**443

Leopold, Aldo, **2:**619

Lerner, Abba, **1:**35, **1:**94

Leslie, F., **2:**918

Lesser, J. A., **1:**229

Lester, Richard, **1:**57

Lettau, Martin, **1:**212

Letter to Bloch (Engels), **1:**60

Levenstein, M., **1:**139

Levich, Richard M., **1:**436

Levin, D., **2:**792

Levin, J., **2:**937

Levine, L. J., **2:**918
Levine, M. D., **1:**251
Levine, Phillip, **2:**568
Levine, Ross, **2:**567, **2:**815
Levinsohn, James, **1:**415
Levitt, Steven D.
    economic analysis of the family and, **2:**577
    economics and race, **2:**569–570
    economics of crime and, **2:**750, **2:**751
    economics of education and, **2:**520, **2:**521
    experimental economics and, **2:**752, **2:**879
    twentieth-century economic methodology and, **1:**41
Levkov, Alexey, **2:**567
Levy, A., **2:**691
Levy, D. M., **1:**5
Lewellen, Jonathan, **1:**213
Lewer, J. J., **2:**699
Lewis, Edith, **2:**770
Lewis, M., **1:**223, **2:**910
Lewis, Michael, **2:**546
Lewontin, Richard, **2:**922
LGBTQ. *See* LBGTQ identities
Li, H., **2:**932
Li, J., **1:**251
Li, Qi, **1:**158
Liberty Fund, **1:**4
Library of Economics and Liberty, **1:**4
Licht, Amit, **1:**448
Lichtenstein, N., **1:**56, **1:**57, **1:**61, **1:**62
Lichtenstein, S., **2:**866
Lichty, L., **2:**829
Lien, Gudbrand, **2:**600
Life care plan, forensic economics and, **2:**745
Life cycle
    economic analysis of the family and, **2:**577
    economics of aging and, **2:**586–587
Life expectancy, forensic economics and, **2:**740–741
Liggett Group, Inc. v. Brown and Williamson Tobacco Corp.
    (1992), **1:**137
Lily Ledbetter Act, **2:**901
Limited dependent variable, **1:**51
Limited thinking, experimental economics and, **2:**877
Lin, C.-Y. Cynthia, **2:**639
Lindert, P. H., **1:**15, **1:**17
Lindgren, Björn, **2:**589, **2:**590
Lindqvist, E., **1:**279
Lindsey, R., **1:**138, **2:**658
Linear average cost pricing, **1:**268
Linear marginal cost pricing, **1:**268
Linear regression, **1:**46
Linearity, **1:**48
Linneman, P., **2:**673
Lipset, S. M., **1:**165
Liquidity preference, **1:**334
List, John A., **1:**41, **2:**560, **2:**624, **2:**874, **2:**876, **2:**879
Literacy, **1:**455 (figure), **1:**460
Litigation Economic Digest, **2:**739
Litzenberger, Robert, **1:**212
Liu, F. T., **2:**748, **2:**750, **2:**751
Liu, Na, **2:**638
Liu, Y., **2:**915, **2:**916
Liu, Zhenjuan, **1:**158, **2:**752, **2:**917
Llobet, G., **2:**786

Loanable funds, market for, **1:**365 (table)
Löbbecke, C., **2:**834
Localization economies, **2:**668–669
Location theory
    economics of migration and, **2:**703
    location patterns and transportation economics, **2:**658
    urban economics and, **2:**667
Lochner, Lance, **2:**516, **2:**518, **2:**749, **2:**750
Locke, John, **1:**40, **1:**464n, **2:**528
Lockheed Aircraft Manufacturing Company, **1:**198
Locksley, G., **2:**828
Loewenstein, G., **2:**864, **2:**870, **2:**913, **2:**914, **2:**917
Log likelihood, **1:**53
Logan, J., **1:**63
Logrolling, **1:**240
Lomansky, Loren, **1:**241
Long, D. Stephen, **2:**898
"Long Boom," **1:**397–398
Long run equilibrium, **1:**106–108
    in Keynesian cross diagram, **1:**325–326
    under monopolistic competition, **1:**128 (figure)
    profit maximization in, **1:**116–117
Longe, O. A., **2:**916
Longitudinal data, **1:**51–52
Longley, N., **2:**537
Longo, A., **2:**823
Lonsdorf, E., **2:**622
Looking Backward (Bellamy), **1:**441
Loomis, J., **2:**624
López, J. T., **2:**828
Lopez-de-Silanes, F., **1:**448
Lopez Perez, Victor, **1:**387
Lösch, August, **2:**665, **2:**666
Loss, neuroeconomics and, **2:**916–917
Lott, John R., Jr., **1:**136, **2:**750, **2:**751
Loucks, William N., **1:**441
Loughlin, S., **2:**918
Loury, G. C., **2:**569, **2:**574
Low benefits, **2:**578–579
Lowenstein, Louis, **1:**219
Lucas, Robert E.
    asset pricing models and, **1:**210
    debates in macroeconomic policy and, **1:**394–**1:**395
    HET and, **1:**9
    macroeconomic models and, **1:**311–**1:**312
    new classical economics and, **1:**399, **1:**400, **1:**401–**1:**402, **1:**404,
        1:406
    twentieth-century economic methodology and, **1:**36, **1:**40
Lucas aggregate supply hypothesis, **1:**401–402
Lucas v. South Carolina Coastal Council (1992), **2:**762, **2:**764n
Ludvigson, Sydney, **1:**212
Ludwig, Alexander, **2:**592
Lueck, Dean, **2:**639, **2:**758
Lukes, S., **2:**530
Lundberg, S., **2:**569, **2:**574, **2:**582
Lutz, M. A., **2:**528
Lynch, D., **1:**139
Lynd, S., **1:**61
Lyttkens, Carl Hampus, **2:**589, **2:**590

Maastricht Treaty (Treaty on European Union), **1:**478
Macaulay, S., **2:**947
MacAvoy, Paul A., **2:**641

MacBeth, James, **1:**211
MacCoun, R., **2:**748
MacDonald, R., **1:**470
Macher, J., **2:**944
Machlup, Fritz, **1:**33
MacPherson, C. B., **2:**528
Macpherson, D. A., **1:**166f, **1:**167f, **2:**671
Macroeconomic models, 1:307–318
    economic methodology and, **1:**29–30
    evolution of macroeconomics since 1960s, **1:**309–310
    HET and, **1:**9–10, **1:**11
    Keynesian economics, **1:**309
    Keynes's critique of classical economics, **1:**307–308
    Keynes's model represented as set of propositions, **1:**308–309
    measuring and evaluating macroeconomic performance,
        1:297–306
    opposition to new classical (NC) economics, **1:**313–314
    performance, **1:**297–298
    post-Keynesian and new Keynesians (NK), **1:**316–317
    post-Keynesian economics, **1:**314–316
    rise of new classical (NC) economics, **1:**310–313
Macroeconomics
    aggregate demand and aggregate supply, **1:**333–340
    aggregate expenditures model and equilibrium output, **1:**319–331
    debates in, **1:**391–398
    economic instability and macroeconomic policy, **1:**349–355
    economic measurement and forecasting, **1:**287–295
    fiscal policy and, **1:**357–368
    government budgets, debt, and deficits, **1:**369–379
    IS-LM model, **1:**9, **1:**35, **1:**313–314, **1:**327, **1:**339, **1:**341–347
    macroeconomic models, **1:**307–318
    measuring and evaluating macroeconomic performance,
        1:297–306
    monetary policy and inflation targeting, **1:**381–389 (*See also*
        Monetarism)
    new classical economics, **1:**399–408
Maddison, Angus, **1:**15, **1:**19, **1:**459, **1:**464n
Madhok, A., **2:**946
Madison, James, **1:**40
Magee, Stephen, **1:**414, **1:**415, **1:**473, **1:**498
Magellan, Ferdinand, **1:**18
Magnus, Albertus, **2:**893
Majluf, N., **2:**732–733, **2:**734
Major League Baseball, **2:**534, **2:**544
Major League Baseball Players Association (MLBPA), **2:**544
Make-or-buy decision, **1:**196–199
Malecková, J., **2:**812
Malkiel, Burton, **1:**215, **1:**218
Malthus, Robert, **2:**771
Malthus, Thomas
    aggregate expenditures model and equilibrium output, **1:**327
    agricultural economics and, **2:**600
    economic history and, **1:**14
    economic methodology and, **1:**25–1:**26, **1:**27, **1:**31
    evolutionary economics and, **2:**927
    HET and, **1:**6
    IS-LM model and, **1:**342
    Malthusianism and political economy of oil, **2:**645–646
Managed care, **2:**709–710
Manchu China, **1:**19
Mandates, health economics and, **2:**715
Mandatory spending, components of, **1:**358 (figure)
Mandeville, Bernard, **1:**33

Mankiw, N. Gregory
    aggregate demand and aggregate supply, **1:**335, **1:**335f
    government budgets and, **1:**376
    macroeconomic models and, **1:**313
    measuring and evaluating macroeconomic performance, **1:**302,
        1:305
    new classical economics and, **1:**406, **1:**407
    real estate economics and, **2:**611
    twentieth-century economic methodology and, **1:**38
Mansfield, M., **1:**108
Manski, Charles, **2:**518
Manual of Political Economy (Pareto), **1:**81
Manufacturing products, Latin America, **2:**850 (figure)
Mao Zedong, **1:**447
Marcellino, Massimiliano, **1:**293
March, J. G., **2:**886
Marginal analysis, **1:**102–104
Marginal cost (MC) curve, **1:**105
Marginal efficiency of health capital function (MEC), **2:**708
Marginal labor cost (MLC), **1:**144
Marginal private cost function (MPC), **1:**229
Marginal profit, **1:**112
Marginal propensity to consume, **1:**321
Marginal propensity to consume (mpc), **1:**361
Marginal propensity to save (mps), **1:**361
Marginal revenue
    imperfectly competitive product markets, **1:**125–127
    product (MRP), **1:**118
Marginal utility, **1:**7
    diminishing, and consumer behavior, **1:**79–80
    Marshalian methodology and rise of neoclassical, **1:**27–29
Marginal willingness to pay (MWTP), **1:**229
Marginalist school of thought, **1:**6–8
Margo, Robert, **2:**570
Margolis, D., **1:**157
Margolis, J. D., **2:**792
Marinkov, M., **2:**688, **2:**689
Mark, G. P., **2:**917
Mark, M. R., **2:**752
Mark, Nelson, **1:**469, **1:**470
Market efficiency, economics of information and, **2:**734–735
Market experiments, experimental economics
        and, **2:**880–881
Market failure theory
    economics of health insurance and, **2:**719–724
    environmental economics and, **2:**632–633
    externalities and property rights, **1:**229
    regulatory economics and, **1:**266
    twentieth-century economic methodology and, **1:**35
    wildlife protection and, **2:**618–627
Market goods, valuation of, **1:**277–278
Market model, economics of crime and, **2:**750
Market production, **2:**578
Market sides, **2:**932
Markets
    competitive market and economics of strategy, **1:**185–186
    as coordinating device, **1:**4, **1:**5
    defined, **1:**69
    demand elasticities and market power, **1:**93–95
    economic aspects of cultural heritage, **2:**821–822
    market power and antitrust laws, **1:**133–134
    market power and sports economics, **2:**534
    media economics and, **2:**829–831

Markets and Hierarchies: Analysis and Antitrust Implications (Williamson), **1:**194, **1:**201, **2:**942
Markov switching (MS) modeling, **1:**292
Markowitz, Harry, **1:**207, **1:**215, **1:**216, **1:**217, **1:**219, **1:**222
Marquis, C., **2:**793
Marriage. *See* **Economic analysis of the family**
Marschak, Jacob, **1:**344
Marshall, Alfred
   aggregate demand and aggregate supply, **1:**345
   aggregate expenditures model and equilibrium output, **1:**325
   consumer behavior and, **1:**79, **1:**81
   demand elasticities and, **1:**89, **1:**98, **1:**99, **1:**99n
   economic methodology and, **1:**28, **1:**31
   HET and, **1:**7–1:8, **1:**11
   IS-LM model and, **1:**342
   Marshalian methodology, **1:**27–29
   twentieth-century economic methodology and, **1:**34, **1:**35
   urban economics and, **2:**667
Martin, G., **2:**739–740, **2:**745
Martin, J. P., **2:**593
Marx, Karl, **1:**56, **1:**58–**1:**61
   aggregate expenditures model and equilibrium output, **1:**327
   comparative economic systems and, **1:**446
   economic methodology and, **1:**27
   economics and justice, **2:**530
   economics and religion, **2:**782
   environmental economics and, **2:**638
   evolutionary economics and, **2:**924, **2:**925, **2:**928
   HET and, **1:**6
   IS-LM model and, **1:**342
   labor markets and, **1:**144
   macroeconomic models and, **1:**312
   See also **Marxian and institutional industrial relations in U.S.**
Marxian and institutional industrial relations in U.S., 1:55–66
   capitalism and labor in U.S., **1:**55–57
   class power and American employer exceptionalism, **1:**62–64
   economics and justice, **2:**529–531
   employment relations study in U.S., **1:**64–65
   evolutionary economics and, **2:**924–925
   Great Depression (1934–1947) and, **1:**61–62
   ILE/IR, **1:**60–61
   ILE/IR and New Deal, **1:**62
   industrial relations process, **1:**168–169
   institutional IR school, **1:**57–58
   Marx and capitalist employment relationship, **1:**58–60
   Marxian political economy and, **1:**61
Maslow, Abraham, **2:**621
Mason, P. L., **2:**556, **2:**557
Mass production, **1:**59
Mass transit, **2:**661
Masten, S., **2:**945, **2:**946
Masten, Scott E., **1:**45, **1:**200
Mastrict Treaty, **1:**478
Matching markets, 2:931–939
   applications, **2:**935–937
   theory, **2:**931–935
Matching Pennies (game), **1:**175 (figure)
Mathematical Psychics (Edgeworth), **1:**81
Matheson, Victor, **2:**539
Mathews, L. G., **2:**823
Mathios, Alan, **1:**270
Matsushita Electric Industrial Co. v. Zenith Radio Corp. (1986), **1:**135, **1:**137

Matthaei, Julie, **2:**768, **2:**769
Matzner, W. T., **2:**915
Maule, C., **2:**833
Maximum likelihood estimator (MLE), **1:**51, **1:**51 (figure)
May, A. M., **1:**244
Mayer, Chris, **2:**615
Mayer, K. J., **2:**946
Mayer, S., **2:**518
Mayer, W., **1:**498
Mayo, John, **1:**269, **1:**273
Mayr, Ernst, **2:**922, **2:**923
McAfee, P., **2:**937
McBride, D., **2:**767
McCabe, K., **2:**915, **2:**916
McCaffery, E. J., **2:**583
McCarthy, Anne, **2:**613
McChesney, Fred S., **2:**828
McClelland, R., **1:**304, **1:**305
McCloskey, D., **1:**37, **1:**38, **1:**39
McClure, S. M., **2:**917
McConnell, C. R., **1:**326, **1:**330
McCormack, Mark, **2:**548–549
McDonald, John F., **2:**667, **2:**668, **2:**671, **2:**672
McDonald, S., **2:**688, **2:**689
McEneaney, James, **2:**569, **2:**673
McFadden, D. L., **1:**251
McFadyen, S., **2:**830, **2:**831
McGabe, K., **2:**878–879
McGee, John, **1:**136, **1:**138, **2:**640
McGuire, Thomas, **2:**711
McIntyre, Richard, **1:**63, **1:**64, **1:**65n
McKernan, S.-M., **2:**845
McKersie, R., **1:**56
McKinnish, T., **2:**699
McManus, John, **1:**195
McManus, W. S., **2:**752
McMillan, J., **1:**227
McMillan, M., **1:**500
McMillan, Robert, **2:**519, **2:**522
McMillen, Daniel P., **2:**667, **2:**668, **2:**671, **2:**672
McNally, Dave, **2:**545
McPherson, M. S., **1:**200
McWilliams, A., **2:**786, **2:**788, **2:**792
Meade, James E., **2:**926
Mean dependent var, **1:**53
Mean square error (MSE), **1:**47
Mean-variance opportunity set, asset pricing models and, **1:**208 (figure)
Measuring and evaluating macroeconomic performance, 1:297–306
   business cycle and, **1:**302–306
   measuring pattern and robustness of economic cycle, **1:**301–302
   primary variables and data used, **1:**302–306
   theory, **1:**297–300
   through stock market cycles, **1:**300–301
Mechanism design, **1:**35–36
Mechanisms of Governance, The (Williamson), **1:**194
Medema, S., **1:**4
Media economics, 2:827–836
   athletes' salaries and, **2:**547–549
   audiences and advertising, **2:**829
   business strategies, **2:**831–832
   media as "different," **2:**826–827
   media firms, markets, competition, **2:**829–831

policy and, **2:**832–833
technological change and, **2:**834–835
Median voter model, **1:**238–240
Medicaid, **1:**260, **1:**367, **2:**710, **2:**712, **2:**717
economics of health insurance and, **2:**725, **2:**726
health economics and, **2:**710
public finance and, **1:**260
Medical Care Price Index, **2:**745
Medicare, **1:**260, **1:**359–**1:**360, **1:**367, **1:**372, **2:**710, **2:**712–713, **2:**717, **2:**722, **2:**743
economics of health insurance and, **2:**726
fiscal policy and, **1:**360
health economics and, **2:**710
Modernization Act of 2003, **2:**725
public finance and, **1:**260
Medoff, J., **1:**63, **1:**163, **1:**170, **1:**171
Meehan, M., **2:**946
Megbolugbe, I. F., **2:**673
Mehra, Rajnish, **1:**212
Meier, Stephan, **2:**899
Meiji Reforms, **1:**19
Meiji Restoration, **1:**19
Meisner, C., **2:**825
Melamed, A. D., **2:**763
Melitz, Marc, **1:**417, **1:**497
Mellewigt, T., **2:**946
Meng, Haoying, **2:**639
Meng, Xin, **2:**556
Menger, Carl, **1:**7, **1:**28, **1:**29, **1:**37, **1:**80, **1:**342
Merchandise/memorabilia, sports economics and, **2:**538
Merchandise trade balance, **1:**423
Merck, **1:**130–**1:**131
Merlo, A., **2:**750
Merrill v. Federal Open Market Committee (1981), **1:**386
Merton, Robert, **1:**209, **1:**210, **1:**211
Meru Herbs, **1:**510
Messersmith, Andy, **2:**545
Metcalf, Gilbert, **2:**642
Methodological pluralism, behavioral economics
and, **2:**864
Metrick, Andrew, **2:**625
Meyer, John, **2:**661
Michigan State University, **2:**598
Michigan Survey of Consumers, **1:**251
Microeconomics
asset pricing models, **1:**203–213
consumer behavior, **1:**79–87
costs of production: short run and long run, **1:**101–109
demand elasticities, **1:**89–100
economics of strategy, **1:**185–192
game theory, **1:**173–184
HET and, **1:**5, **1:**9
imperfectly competitive product markets, **1:**125–134
labor markets, **1:**141–151
portfolio theory and investment management, **1:**215–223
predatory pricing and strategic entry barriers, **1:**135–140
profit maximization, **1:**111–124
role of labor unions in labor markets, **1:**150, **1:**163–172
supply, demand, and equilibrium, **1:**69–78
transaction cost economics, **1:**193–202
twentieth-century economic methodology and,
1:35, **1:**36
wage determination, **1:**153–161

Microfinance, **2:**837–846
alternative practices used in, **2:**842–843
empirical evidence, **2:**842–843, **2:**845
evaluating impact and effectiveness of, **2:**843–845
microfinance institutions (MFIs), **2:**837
as response to information asymmetries, **2:**838–842
statistics about, **2:**837–838
Middle Ages, **1:**18, **2:**893
MIddle East, **1:**19
Midnight Notes Collective, **2:**647, **2:**651
Migration. *See* **Economics of migration**
Miguel, R., **2:**811–813
Mikkelson, W. H., **2:**734
Milgrom, P., **1:**137
Militancy, **1:**56
Mill, James, **1:**26, **1:**342
Mill, John Stuart, **1:**6, **1:**26–**1:**27, **1:**31, **1:**34–**1:**35, **1:**36, **1:**39, **1:**89, **1:**327, **1:**329, **1:**342, **2:**620
Millennium Poll on Corporate Social Responsibility, **2:**791
Miller, J. H., **2:**886, **2:**888, **2:**947
Miller, M., **2:**732
Miller, Marvin, **2:**544
Miller, M. H., **2:**734
Miller, T., Jr., **1:**217n, **1:**220n
Milligan, Kevin, **2:**518
Millonzi, J., **2:**833
Mills, D., **1:**137, **1:**138
Mills, Edwin S., **2:**665, **2:**666, **2:**670, **2:**671
Milwaukee Parental Choice Program, **2:**520
Milwaukee (WI) schools, **2:**520
Min, Insik, **1:**158
Mincer, Jacob, **1:**145, **1:**155, **1:**157, **2:**515–516, **2:**555
Minchin, T., **1:**62
Minhas, B., **1:**108
Minimization of conflict, **2:**757–758
Minimum wages
labor market and, **1:**149
wage determination and, **1:**159
Minnesota Timberwolves, **2:**549
Minsky, Hyman, **1:**30, **1:**315, **1:**317, **1:**345, **2:**927
Miralles, A., **2:**937, **2:**938
Mirowski, Phil, **1:**37
Mirrlees, James, **1:**259
Mises, Ludwig von, **1:**37, **1:**443–**1:**444
Mishel, L., **1:**63, **2:**701
Mishkin, Frederic S., **1:**335, **1:**385, **1:**388, **1:**406
Mitchell, T., **2:**645, **2:**646, **2:**647, **2:**648, **2:**649, **2:**650, **2:**651
Mitchell, W. C., **1:**289
Mitchell, Wesley, **1:**29
Mitra-Khan, B. H., **2:**689
"Mixed" strategies, in game theory, **1:**179
Mobil Oil, **2:**649
Mocan, H. N., **2:**751, **2:**752
Mode choice, transportation economics and, **2:**658–659
Modern consumer theory
assumptions regarding preferences, **1:**81–82
budget lines, **1:**83–84
challenges to traditional theory, **1:**86
choice when future consumption is uncertain, **1:**86
consumption bundles and, **1:**81–82, **1:**84
demand curves, **1:**84
Engel curves and cross-price demand curves, **1:**84–85
general equilibrium, **1:**86

graphical representation of indifference maps, **1:**82–83
income and substitution effects, **1:**85
intertemporal choice, **1:**85–86
labor markets, **1:**86
revealed preference, **1:**85
utility functions, **1:**83
welfare economics, **1:**86
Modern portfolio theory, **1:**216–217
Modigliani, Franco, **1:**328, **1:**344, **1:**404, **1:**486, **2:**589, **2:**732
Moffitt, R., **1:**158
Mohring, H., **2:**661
Mokyr, Joel, **1:**14, **1:**19, **2:**928
Moldovanu, B., **2:**938
Molina, Luis de, **2:**893, **2:**894
Molinero, J. M. S., **2:**800–801
Monetarism
    exchange rate and, **1:**437–438
    HET and, **1:**9
    neoclassical synthesis and Keynes, **1:**29–30
    rise of new classical economics and, **1:**310–311
Monetary approach to exchange rate determination
        (MAER), **1:**471
Monetary Conditions Index, **1:**385
Monetary equilibrium approach to business cycle theory (MEBCT),
        1:399
Monetary policy
    fiscal policy and, **1:**366–367
    2007 recession and, **1:**353–354
    See also **Monetary policy and inflation targeting**
Monetary policy and inflation targeting, 1:381–389
    effectiveness and expectations, **1:**403 (figure), **1:**404–405
    history, **1:**382–383
    inflation targeting-time of adoption and target range,
        1:386 (table)
    practice, **1:**385–388
    real output growth and inflation volatility, **1:**387 (table)
    theory, **1:**383–385
    See also Monetarism
Monetary theory of production, **1:**315
Money supply (M) theory
    debates in macroeconomic policy and, **1:**392
    macroeconomic models and, **1:**316
Money: Whence It Came, Where It Went (Galbraith), **2:**605
Moneyball: The Art of Winning an Unfair Game (Lewis),
        2:546
Moniz, A., **2:**824
Monopoly
    economics of strategy, **1:**186
    imperfectly competitive product markets, **1:**127–128
    labor input and deadweight loss, **1:**121 (figure)
    profit maximization and, **1:**119–124
    regulatory economics, **1:**267
    regulatory economics and, **1:**267–268
Monopsony, **1:**121–123
    power, **1:**143–144
    profit-maximizing labor input and deadweight loss, **1:**122 (figure)
    wage determination and, **1:**154–155
Monotonicity, **1:**82
Mont Pelerin Society, **2:**651
Montague, P. R., **2:**916
Montalvo, J. G., **2:**815, **2:**816
Montchrestien, Antoine de, **1:**4
Monteverde, K., **2:**944

Montgomery, D., **1:**59
Montgomery, R., **2:**844
Montias, J.-M., **1:**448
Montreal Protocol, **2:**635
Moore, A. T., **2:**664
Moore, B., **1:**315–**1:**316
Moore, G. H., **1:**291
Moore, J., **2:**942
Moore v. Regents of the University of California (1990), **2:**761
Moral hazards
    economics of health insurance and, **2:**722–724
    economics of information and, **2:**730
Moran, D., **2:**650
Morduch, J., **2:**840, **2:**841, **2:**845, **2:**845n
Moreno-Brid, J. C., **2:**854
Morgan, Gareth, **2:**925
Morgan, John Pierpont, **1:**392
Morgenstern, Oscar, **1:**173, **1:**183, **1:**204, **2:**873, **2:**876
Mori, Tomova, **2:**667
Morris, Cynthia Taft, **1:**15, **1:**17, **1:**19, **1:**20
Morris, Morris D., **1:**20
Morrison, Steven, **1:**272
Mortgage-backed securities (MBSs), **2:**612
Mortgage financing, **2:**612
Moulin, H., **1:**181
M3, **1:**480–484, **1:**482 (figure)
Muellbauer, J., **2:**601
Mueller, Dennis C., **1:**241, **1:**243
Mulholland, Sean E., **2:**564, **2:**565f
Mullainathan, Sendhil, **2:**569
Mullin, Joseph C., **1:**200, **1:**201
Mullin, Wallace P., **1:**200, **1:**201
Multicollinearity, **1:**50
Multiplier effect, **1:**338, **1:**361–363
Multivariate regression, **1:**46
Mumford, M., **1:**137
Mun, Thomas, **1:**419
Munch, Jakob, **2:**615
Mundell-Fleming model, **1:**9, **1:**474
Munger, Michael, **1:**243
Munn v. Illinois (1877), **1:**266
Munnell, Alicia H., **2:**569, **2:**673
Munshi, K., **2:**703
Muris, T. J., **1:**200
Murphy, Kevin M., **1:**158, **2:**538, **2:**557
Murphy, P., **2:**748
Murphy Oil Company, **1:**250
Murray, C., **1:**160
Murray, D., **1:**509
Murray, E. A., **2:**917
Murray, S., **2:**832
Musgrave, Richard, **1:**257–**1:**258, **1:**262n
Mussa, M. L., **1:**498
Mustard, D. B., **2:**750
Mutari, E., **2:**905
Muth, J. F., **1:**401
Muth, Richard, **2:**611, **2:**670, **2:**671
Mutual funds, **1:**221
Myers, C., **1:**56
Myers, S., **2:**732–733, **2:**734

Nafziger, E. W., **1:**303–**1:**304
Nagel, R., **2:**877

Nagel, Stefan, **1:**213
Nagin, D., **2:**752
Napoleonic Code, **2:**754
Napoli, P., **2:**829
Nardinelli, Clark, **2:**568
NASDAQ, **1:**217, **1:**221
Nash, John, **1:**129, **1:**131, **1:**173–**1:**174, **1:**180, **1:**188, **1:**190, **2:**876
Nash equilibrium, **1:**180, **1:**187, **1:**190
National Agricultural Statistics Service, **2:**597
National Association of Forensic Economics (NAFE), **2:**739
National Association of Manufacturers, **1:**63
National Association of Purchasing Managers, **1:**300
National Basketball Association (NBA), **2:**537, **2:**547
National Bureau of Economic Research, **1:**353
National Bureau of Economic Research (NBER), **1:**64, **1:**287, **1:**292, **1:**294, **1:**299, **1:**353, **1:**372, **2:**855
National Collegiate Athletic Association (NCAA) Division I, **2:**540
National Commission on Excellence in Education, **2:**515
National Consumers League, **2:**785
National debt/deficits, **1:**373–378. *See also* **Government budgets, debt, and deficits**
National Education Association (NEA), **1:**167
National Educational Longitudinal Survey of 1988, **2:**519
National Football League (NFL), **2:**533, **2:**538, **2:**546
National Football League Players Association, **1:**155
National Health Service (NHS), **2:**713
National Hockey League (NHL), **2:**537
National income accounting, **1:**425–426
National Income and Product Accounts (NIPA), **1:**302, **1:**319, **1:**426
National Internship Matching Program (NIMP), **2:**936
National Labor Relations Act (NLRA), **1:**57, **1:**164, **1:**168, **1:**169
    passage of, **1:**164
    role of labor unions and, **1:**168
National Labor Relations Board (NLRB), **1:**150, **1:**168
    Professional Air Traffic Controllers Organization (PATCO) and, **1:**63, **1:**150
    role of labor unions and, **1:**168
National Longitudinal Survey of Youth, **2:**569
National Occupation and Wage Estimates, **2:**742
National Oceanic and Atmospheric Administration (NOAA), **2:**822
National Park Service, **1:**232
National Recovery Act, **1:**61
National Research Council, **1:**251, **2:**702
National Residency Matching Program (NRMP), **2:**936
National Surface Transportation Infrastructure Financing Commission, **2:**662
National Surface Transportation Policy and Revenue Study Commission, **2:**662
National Survey of College Graduates, **2:**573
National Survey of Religious Identity (NSRI), **2:**781
National Union for the Total Independence of Angola (UNITA), **2:**808
Native Americans, economics of gambling and, **2:**682–683
"Natural experiments," **2:**707–708
Natural field experiments, **2:**874
Natural law, **2:**893–894
Natural Resources Canada, **2:**638
"Nature of the Firm, The" (Coase), **1:**194
Navarro, P., **2:**792

Navrud, S., **2:**823
Neal, Derek, **2:**519, **2:**522
Nechyba, T., **2:**522
Negative freedom, **2:**527–528
Negri, A., **2:**651
Neighborhood effects, race and, **2:**568–569
Neill, J., **2:**539
Nekby, Lena, **2:**559
Nelson, D., **2:**744
Nelson, E., **2:**622
Nelson, J. A., **2:**904
Nelson, Julie, **1:**145
Nelson, R., **1:**488
Nelson, R. R., **2:**927, **2:**928
Neoclassical school of thought, **1:**6–8, **1:**9
    economics and justice and, **2:**526–528
    fracturing of neoclassical hegemony, **1:**36–38
    growth model, **1:**393
    individual optimization and market equilibrium, **1:**8–9
    Keynes and monetarism, **1:**29–30
    marginal utility and Marshalian methodology, **1:**27–29
    neoclassical-Keynesian synthesis, **1:**310
    new economic growth theory and, **1:**314
    theory and, **1:**13–15
"Neoliberal" ideas, **1:**63
Nerlove, Marc, **2:**600
Nestlé, **1:**509
Net imports, **1:**319
Net national product (NNP), **1:**321
Neuberger, F., **1:**448
Neufeld, John, **1:**268
Neumark, David, **2:**556, **2:**558, **2:**574
Neuroeconomics, 2:913–920
    applications and empirical evidence, **2:**914–918
    limitations, **2:**918
    policy, **2:**918
    theory, **2:**913–914
    See also **Game theory**
Nevile, J. W., **1:**339
New classical economics, 1:399–408
    foundations of NCMI, **1:**400–402
    future of, **1:**406–407
    mark I (NCMI), **1:**399–402
    NCMII: real business cycle theory, **1:**406
    opposition to, **1:**313–314
    rise of, **1:**310–313
    theoretical foundations of NCMI, **1:**399–400
    theory, policy, empirical evidence, **1:**402–406
New Deal, **1:**61–**1:**62, **1:**63, **1:**64, **1:**164, **1:**244, **1:**266, **1:**366, **2:**646, **2:**651, **2:**927
    IR system, **1:**57, **1:**62
    National Labor Relations Act (NLRA) and, **1:**164
    regulatory economics and, **1:**266
New Economic Policy, **2:**925
New England Patriots, **2:**546
New England Program for Kidney Exchange, **2:**937
New home economics (NHE), **2:**907–908
New institutionalists (NIE), **2:**927–929
New Keynesians (NK), **1:**316–317
New Keynesians macroeconomics (NKE), **1:**313–314
New School for Social Research, **1:**4, **1:**344
New York Board of Trade (NYBOT), **1:**504
New York Mercantile Exchange (NYMEX), **2:**649

New York Stock Exchange, **1:**221, **1:**467, **2:**943

New York Times, The, **1:**386, **2:**870

New York Yankees, **2:**534, **2:**545

New Zealand, economics of aging, **2:**586 (table)

Newell, Richard G., **2:**642

Newhouse, J. P., **2:**712, **2:**716, **2:**724

Newman, A., **2:**937, **2:**938

Newman, J. L., **2:**916

Newsome, K., **1:**59

Newsome, W. T., **2:**916

Newton, Isaac, **1:**40

Ngai, Tsz Yan, **2:**639

Nichols, J. P., **2:**601

Nickell, S., **1:**479

Nickerson, Jackson A., **2:**945, **2:**946, **2:**947, **2:**948n

Niederle, Muriel, **2:**559, **2:**560, **2:**880, **2:**935, **2:**937

Niggle, C., **1:**317

Niskanen, William, **1:**243

Nison, Steve, **1:**215, **1:**218

Nissen, D., **2:**649

Nitzan, J., **2:**648, **2:**651

Nixon, Richard M., **1:**350–**1:**351, **1:**393

No Child Left Behind (NCLB) Act, **2:**521

Noam, E., **2:**833

No-fault divorce, **2:**583

Nofsinger, John, **1:**215, **1:**219

Nold, F. C., **2:**751

Nominal exchange rates, **1:**438

Nonaccelerating inflation rate of unemployment (NAIRU), **1:**298

Nonexcludability, **1:**256

Nonlinear demand curves, elasticity of demand for, **1:**91–92

Nonlinear regressions, **1:**50–51

Nonmarket goods, valuation of, **1:**278–279

Nonmarket valuation (NMV) techniques, **2:**822–823

Nonzero expected error, **1:**50

Nordhaus, William, **1:**280, **1:**364, **2:**605

Normal-form games, defined, **1:**176

Normal goods, **1:**70

Normative public choice, **1:**244–245

North, Douglass C., **1:**13, **1:**14, **1:**15, **1:**16, **1:**38, **1:**40, **1:**195, **2:**802, **2:**803, **2:**921, **2:**928

North American Association of Sports Economists, **2:**533

North American Association of State and Provincial Lotteries, **2:**679

North American Free Trade Agreement (NAFTA), **1:**417, **1:**493, **2:**851

North American Wildlife Conference, **2:**617

North Atlantic Treaty Organization (NATO), **1:**442

North Carolina State University, **2:**598

North Central Journal of Agricultural Economics, **2:**599

Northeastern Journal of Agricultural Economics, **2:**599

Norway, on value of a statistical life (VSL), **1:**279

Nossitor, T., **2:**831

Novak, James, **2:**605n

Novak, Michael, **2:**898, **2:**899

Nozick, Robert, **2:**525, **2:**528, **2:**532

Nurses, market for, **2:**710–712

Nussbaum, M., **2:**529

Nyborg, K., **2:**790

Nymoen, Ragnar, **2:**589

Nystrom, L. E., **2:**881, **2:**915

Oakland Athletics, **2:**545, **2:**546

Oakland Raiders, **2:**535

Oates, W. E., **1:**228, **1:**261, **2:**633

Oaxaca, Ronald L., **1:**158, **2:**557

Obama, Barack, **1:**65, **1:**148, **2:**870, **2:**901

O'Brien, S., **2:**770, **2:**774

Obstfeld, M., **1:**413, **1:**416, **1:**474, **1:**479, **2:**848

Ocampo, J. A., **1:**21

October Revolution of 1917, **2:**925

Odean, T., **1:**219

Odeh, Rana, **1:**347n

Odonis, Gerald, **2:**893

O'Donnell, Christopher, **2:**600

O'Driscoll, G., **1:**312

Ofcom, **2:**834

Ofer, Gur, **1:**442

Office of Farm Management, **2:**598

Office of Farm Management and Farm Economics, **2:**598

Office of Federal Contract Compliance, **1:**160

Office of Management and Budget, **1:**263n, **1:**281

Official settlements balance (OSB), **1:**421–422

Offshoring, **1:**498–499

Oguledo, V. I., **2:**699

Oikonomike, **2:**892

Oil. *See* **Political economy of oil**

Ojha, V. P., **2:**689

O'Keefe, A., **2:**827

Okun, Arthur, **1:**261, **2:**724

Old Age Survivors, **2:**743

Oligopoly

    dynamic oligopoly and economics of strategy, **1:**189–191

    economics of strategy, static oligopoly and strategic interaction, **1:**186–189

    health economics and, **2:**712

    imperfectly competitive product markets, **1:**128–133

Olivetti, Claudia, **2:**555

Olmstead, S. M., **2:**635

Olsen, P., **2:**904, **2:**909, **2:**910

Olsen, Robert, **1:**219

Olson, M., **2:**800, **2:**803

Olson, Mancur, **1:**243, **1:**270

On the Principles of Political Economy and Taxation (Ricardo), **1:**5

One-sided matching market, **2:**932, **2:**934–935

Ongena, H., **1:**479

On-the-job training, **1:**156

Open-access resources, **1:**232–233

"Open-door" policies, **1:**62

"Open" economy, **1:**324–325

Open-economy macroeconomics, **1:**474

Open enrollment policy, **2:**520–521

Openness indices (Latin America), **2:**851 (figure)

Operating budgets, government, **1:**369–370

Operations research methods, agricultural economics and, **2:**602

Opportunism, defined, **1:**194–196

Opportunity Scholarship Program, **2:**521

Optimal matching allocations, **2:**933–934

Optimization model, **1:**8

Options, **1:**434–435

Orchard View Farm v. Martin Marietta Aluminum (1980), **2:**759–760, **2:**763

Ordeshook, Peter, **1:**240–**1:**241

Ordinary least squares (OLS), **1:**46–47

Ordover, J., **1:**136, **1:**139

Organisation for Economic Co-operation and Development (OECD)

    economics and corporate social responsibility, **2:**785

economics of aging, **2:**587t
economics of civil war, **2:**813
economics of HIV/AIDS, **2:**588t, **2:**693
economics of information, **2:**736
European Monetary Union, **1:**480, **1:**481f, **1:**482f
globalization and inequality, **1:**494, **1:**496
health economics, **2:**714
international trade, **1:**416
labor markets, **1:**147
microfinance, **2:**840
monetary policy and inflation targeting, **1:**388
political economy of oil and, **2:**645–652
Organization of Petroleum Exporting Countries (OPEC),
  1:350–**1:**351, **1:**394, **1:**396, **1:**459, **1:**503, **2:**640–641, **2:**646, **2:**650
Origin of Wealth, The (Beinhocker), **1:**24
Original institutional economics (OIE), **2:**925–927
Orrenius, P. M., **2:**704
Osborn, T., **2:**622
Osborne, D. K., **2:**640
Osborne, M., **2:**790
Oscherov, Valeria, **2:**639
Osterman, P., **1:**64
Ostrom, Elinor, **1:**234, **2:**799–800
O'Sullivan, A., **2:**666, **2:**668
Oswald, Andrew, **2:**615
"Otherness," **2:**770–772
Otteson, James R., **2:**896
Ottoman Empire, **1:**19
Ottoman Middle East, **2:**648
Output, **1:**111–112
Output gap, **1:**382
Outstanding debt, **1:**370
Overbeek, H., **1:**479
Owen, B., **2:**828, **2:**830, **2:**831, **2:**832
Owens, E., **2:**750
Owens, Robert, **1:**27
Owers, J., **2:**828
Oxley, J., **2:**944, **2:**946
Ozone Transport Commission NO$_x$ Budget Program, **2:**635

Pack, H., **1:**488
Pagán, J. A., **2:**704
Page, B., **1:**373
Page, S. E., **2:**886, **2:**888
Pager, D., **2:**557
Paid work, feminist economics and, **2:**906–908
Pakenham, Thomas, **1:**21
Palacios-Huerta, I., **1:**181
Palay, Thomas, **1:**195, **1:**196, **1:**200, **2:**944
Palazzo, G., **2:**785
Paley, Mary, **2:**747
Palmer, Arnold, **2:**548–549
Palmer, Edward, **2:**594
Palmini, D., **2:**625
Panel data, **1:**51–52
Panic of 1907, **1:**392
Panksepp, J., **2:**772
Panzar, J. C., **2:**641
Papell, D. H., **1:**326
Parameters, **1:**289
Pardo, J. V., **2:**916
Pareto, Vilfredo, **1:**81, **2:**897
Pareto criterion, **1:**276

Pareto efficiency, **2:**897
Parker, R., **2:**832
Parkin, M., **1:**313
Parry, Ian W. H., **1:**248, **1:**249, **1:**251, **1:**252, **2:**659
Partch, M. M., **2:**734
Partial equilibrium approach, **1:**7, **1:**8, **1:**11
Partial-equilibrium (industry-level) analysis, of inequality and
  globalization, **1:**497
Pashigian, B. Peter, **2:**610
Passel, J. S., **2:**699, **2:**704
Pathak, P., **2:**936, **2:**938
Patinkin, D., **1:**325
Patterson, P. D., **1:**251
Patton, R., **2:**744
Paul, Satya, **2:**573
Pauly, M. V., **2:**712
Pavcnik, N., **1:**501
Payne, A. A., **2:**750
Payner, Brook, **2:**772
Payoff matrix, for firms choosing quantity of output, **1:**131 (figure)
Peacock, Alan, **2:**827, **2:**829
Peak oil, **2:**639
"Peak oil," **2:**646
Pearce, D., **2:**736
Peart, S. J., **1:**5
Pechmann, C., **2:**918
"Peculiarities" of labor market, **1:**57, **1:**58
Peebles, G., **1:**487
Peer effects, economics of education and, **2:**518–519
Peirce, Charles Saunders, **2:**925
Peltier, J., **1:**253
Peltzman, Sam, **1:**270, **1:**272
Peltzman model, **1:**270–272
Pencavel, J., **1:**155
Pence, Karen, **2:**615
Penn, J. B., **2:**603
Penner, M., **2:**692
Penner, Rudolph, **1:**360, **1:**367
Pennington, A., **2:**832
Pensieroso, L., **1:**406
Pensions, **2:**590–591, **2:**593, **2:**743
Penson, John B., Jr., **2:**599, **2:**603
Peoples, James, **2:**568
People's democracies, **1:**445
Pepsi, **1:**129
Peranson, E., **2:**936, **2:**938
Per-capita income, economics of civil war and, **2:**809–811
Perfect competition, **1:**117–119, **1:**154
Performative, **2:**771
Peri, G., **1:**479
Permit markets, **2:**634
Perotti, Roberto, **1:**367
Perry, Gregory, **2:**602, **2:**603, **2:**605
Perry, Noel, **1:**19
Perry, Reverend Arthur Latham, **2:**898
Personnel management (PM), **1:**56
Persson, S., **1:**279, **2:**811, **2:**814
Pesant de Boiguilbert, Pierre le, **2:**894
Pesenti, P., **1:**491
Peters, Edgar, **1:**219
Petersen, H. Craig, **1:**269
Peterson, J., **2:**910
Peterson, M., **2:**842

Peterson, W., **1**:298, **1**:302

Petit, Pascale, **2**:558

Petrongolo, Barbara, **2**:555

Petro-states, **2**:650–652

Petty, William, **1**:342

Pew Hispanic Center, **2**:700, **2**:702

Pharmaceuticals, market for, **2**:710–712

Phelan, P., **2**:829

Phelps, Edmund S., **1**:311, **1**:335, **1**:394, **1**:399–**1**:400, **2**:556, **2**:567, **2**:569

Phenomenology of the Social World, The (Schutz), **1**:37

Philadelphia Eagles, **2**:546

Philadelphia Phillies, **2**:544

Phillips, A. W., **1**:309, **1**:311

Phillips, C. F., Jr., **2**:641

Phillips, S., **1**:500

Phillips, W., **2**:625

Phillips curves, **1**:311, **1**:394, **1**:402–403

Phillips-Fein, K., **1**:62

Physical asset specificity, defined, **1**:196

Physicians, market for, **2**:710–712

Physiocrats, **2**:894

Picard, Robert G., **2**:828, **2**:829, **2**:831, **2**:834

Pierce, Brooks, **1**:158, **2**:557

Pierret, Charles, **2**:569

Pierson v. Post (1805), **2**:757–758

Piggott, R., **2**:602

Pigou, Arthur C., **1**:35, **1**:259, **1**:308, **1**:342, **1**:344, **2**:617, **2**:634, **2**:636

Pigouvian solution, economics of wildlife protection and, **2**:621–623

Piketty, T., **1**:494, **1**:500

Pin factory example, transaction cost economics and, **1**:199

Pindyck, Robert, **2**:639, **2**:642

Piore, Michael J., **1**:57, **2**:556

Pirouz, D., **2**:918

Pitt, M., **2**:845

Pittsburgh Steelers, **2**:546

Pizer, William, **2**:643

Placzek, D., **1**:157

Planned AE (aggregate expenditures), **1**:320

Plato, **2**:892–893

Platt, M. L., **2**:916

Plosser, C. I., **1**:302, **1**:406

Point-dependent utility functions, behavioral economics and, **2**:862–863

Point elasticity, **1**:90–91

Point-slope form, **1**:323

Poirot, C. S., **2**:922

Polachek, S. W., **2**:555, **2**:556

Polanyi, Karl, **2**:926

Polanyi, L., **2**:904

Polanyi, Michael, **1**:37, **1**:42

Polasky, S., **2**:622

Policy
aggregate demand and aggregate supply, **1**:337–338
aggregate expenditures model and equilibrium output and, **1**:324–327
agricultural economics and, **2**:603
complexity and economics, **2**:887–888
cost-benefit analysis and, **1**:275–283

demand elasticities and, **1**:98–99
economic analysis of the family, **2**:582–584
economic aspects of cultural heritage and, **2**:824
economic history and, **1**:21
economic instability and macroeconomic policy, **1**:349–355
economics and justice, **2**:530–531
economics and race, **2**:574
economics of crime and, **2**:752–753
economics of education, **2**:519–522
economics of health insurance and, **2**:720–724
economics of wildlife protection and, **2**:626
externalities and property rights, **1**:234–235
forecasting and economic policy making, **1**:293–294
international trade theory and, **1**:417–418
IS-LM model and, **1**:344–345
labor market and, **1**:147–148
media economics and, **2**:832–833
neuroeconomics and, **2**:918
new classical economics, **1**:402–406
pricing policies and demand elasticities, **1**:93–95
public finance and, **1**:261
real estate economics and, **2**:612–614
sports economics and, **2**:538–539
taxes *vs.* standards: policies for the reduction of gasoline consumption, **1**:247–254
transaction cost economics, **1**:200–201
twentieth-century economic methodology and, **1**:39
wage determination and, **1**:158–159

Polinsky, A. M., **2**:749–750

Political action committees, **1**:243

Political business cycle, public choice and, **1**:244

Political economy of oil, 2:645–653
oil as means of consumption/exploitation, **2**:646–647
oil as nonrenewable resource, **2**:645–646
oil as strategic commodity, **2**:647–650
petro-states, **2**:650–652

Political economy of violence, 2:797–805
applications and empirical evidence, **2**:802–803
future of, **2**:803–804
theory, **2**:797–802

Pollack, R., **2**:582

Pollitz, K., **2**:726

Polluter pay principle, **1**:235

Pomeranz, Kenneth, **1**:19, **1**:21

Pontusson, J., **1**:63

Poor, P. J., **2**:823

Pope, Rulon D., **2**:600

Poppen, Paul J., **2**:673, **2**:899

Popper, Karl, **1**:37

Poppo, L., **2**:945

Pork barrel legislation, **1**:240

Porter, Michael, **2**:830

Portfolio theory and investment management, 1:215–223
average annual returns and risk premiums: 1925–1996, **1**:217 (figure)
investment management, defined, **1**:219–222
portfolio theory, defined, **1**:215–219
rating of corporate bonds, **1**:220 (table)
recent changes in market behavior and, **1**:222–223

Portney, P., **1**:252

Porzecanski, R., **2**:854

Posen, Adam, **1**:385

Positive externality, **1**:228

Positive freedom, **2:**529–530

Positive law, **2:**894

Positivism, **1:**33, **1:**37

Posner, Richard A., **1:**270, **2:**749, **2:**935

"Post-Chicago" school, **1:**136–137

Post-Keynesian economics, **1:**314–317

Postlewaite, A., **2:**935

Poterba, J. M., **1:**253, **2:**588

Pothos, E. N., **2:**917

Potter, J., **1:**373

Poulsen, A., **2:**560

Pound, Louise, **2:**774n

Poverty

    civil war and, **2:**809–814

    economic history and policy, **1:**21

    inequality *vs.,* **1:**496–497

Powell, K., **2:**916

Power, M., **2:**905

Practical sciences, **2:**892–893

Pradhan, B. K., **2:**689

Prebisch, Raul, **1:**505

Predatory pricing and strategic entry barriers,
    1:135–140

    Chicago and post-Chicago schools, **1:**136–137

    current research in, **1:**138

    predation, defined, **1:**137–138

    predation and trusts, **1:**135–136

    prevalence of predatory pricing cases, **1:**139

    Wal-Mart, **1:**139

Predictably Irrational (Ariely), **1:**24, **2:**869

Preference reversals, behavioral economics and, **2:**866

Preferential trade agreements, **1:**417

Prelec, D., **2:**870, **2:**913

Prendergast, Canice, **2:**610

Prescott, Edward, **1:**10, **1:**212, **1:**384, **1:**396, **1:**399, **1:**404, **1:**405,
    1:406, **1:**407

Present value, **1:**370

Present value, forensic economics and, **2:**745

Price

    agricultural economics and, **2:**603

    Cros's Incentive Pricing Scheme, **1:**269–270

    Dow theory and, **1:**217–218

    economics of immigration and, **2:**702

    predatory pricing and strategic entry barriers,
        1:135–139

    price controls, ceilings and floors, **1:**75

    price elasticity of demand and, **1:**95

    pricing policies and demand elasticities, **1:**93–95

    real estate economics and, **2:**607–611

    of related goods, **1:**70–71

    of related goods, in production, **1:**72

    See also **Imperfectly competitive product markets; Supply,**
        demand, and equilibrium

Price ceilings, **1:**75–76

Price elasticity

    of demand and revenue, **1:**93

    factors influencing, **1:**97–98

    transportation economics and, **2:**656–657

    See also **Demand elasticities**

Price floors, **1:**75–76, **1:**509 (figure)

Price gap regulation, **1:**270

Price level targeting (PLT), **1:**382

Primary energy, **2:**638

Primitive accumulation, **1:**58

Princeton Twins Survey, **2:**516

Principles of Economics (Marshall), **1:**28, **1:**79, **1:**81, **1:**89

Principles of Economics (Menger), **1:**80

Principles of Economics (Samuelson), **1:**330

Principles of Political Economy (Mill), **1:**34

Principles of Political Economy and Taxation, The (Ricardo), **1:**25

Prisoner's Dilemma, **1:**130–132, **1:**175 (figure)

    experimental economics and, **2:**878–879

    as strategic form game, **1:**188 (table)

Private costs, **1:**106

Private "demand," economics of crime and, **2:**749

Private health insurance, **2:**709

Private market efficient equilibrium, **1:**229

Private/socially efficient market equilibria, **1:**230 (figure)

Prize, The (Yergin), **2:**638, **2:**640

Pro Mujer, **2:**840

Prob (F-statistic), **1:**53

Problem gambling, **2:**681–682

Procter & Gamble, **1:**127, **1:**509

Proctor, D. D., **2:**935

Producer price index (PPI), **1:**304

Producer surplus, **1:**113–114

Product market, **1:**119–120, **2:**791–792

Production

    of energy, **2:**647–649

    function, **1:**101–102, **2:**517–519

    information production and economics of information,
        2:736–737

    theory and agricultural economics, **2:**600–601, **2:**603

Productivity. *See* **World development in historical perspective**

Professional Air Traffic Controllers Organization (PATCO), **1:**63,
    1:150

Profit maximization, 1:111–124

    bilateral monopology, labor input, wage, and deadweight loss,
        1:123 (figure)

    competitive firm and monopoly profit-maximizing labor input,
        1:120 (figure)

    general case for, **1:**111–117

    marginal cost, average variable cost, and competitive firm's
        supply curve, **1:**117 (figure)

    marginal cost/revenue and minimum/maximum profit,
        1:113 (figure)

    market power and, **1:**119–123

    maximum profit and producer surplus, **1:**114 (figure)

    minimum and maximum profit, **1:**112 (figure)

    monopoly equilibrium and deadweight loss, **1:**121 (figure)

    monopoly labor input and deadweight loss, **1:**121 (figure)

    monopoly profit maximization with falling marginal cost,
        1:120 (figure)

    monopoly profit-maximizing output and price, **1:**120 (figure)

    monopsony profit-maximizing labor input, wage, and deadweight
        loss, **1:**122 (figure)

    in perfectly competitive economy, **1:**117–119

    profit-maximizing labor input, **1:**115 (figure)

    profit-maximizing quantity and price for a monopolist,
        1:126 (figure)

    reasons for, **1:**123–124

    shutdown point and competitive firm's demand for labor,
        1:119 (figure)

    shutdown point and competitive firm's supply curve,
        1:116 (figure)

Profit maximizing behavior, sports economics and, **2:**534–535

Progressive era, regulatory economics and, **1:**266
Progressive lending, **2:**841
Project STAR, **2:**517–518
Proletarianization, **1:**58
Propagation mechanisms, **1:**406
Property rights economics. *See* **Economics of property law**
Proportional taxes, **1:**362–363
Prospect theory, behavioral economics and, **2:**870–871
Prosperity, violence and, **2:**797–798, **2:**801–802
Prud'homme, R., **2:**660
Pryor, Frederic, **1:**448
Public choice, 1:237–246
    applied to representative democracy, **1:**240–244
    future of, **1:**245–246
    median voter model for a committee, **1:**239 (figure)
    median voter model for a representative democracy,
        1:239 (figure)
    normative, **1:**244–245
    origins of, **1:**237–238
    preference analysis, **1:**239 (table)
    rent seeking in cosmetology market, **1:**242 (figure)
    voting in direct democracy, **1:**238–240
Public enterprise, energy as, **2:**641–642
Public finance, 1:255–263
    applications and empirical research, **1:**260–261
    effects of a tax, **1:**257 (figure)
    external private benefits, **1:**258 (figure)
    future directions, **1:**262
    policy implications, **1:**261
    theory, **1:**256–259
Public Finance (Rosen, Gayer), **1:**263n
Public Finance: A Normative Theory (Tresch), **1:**262n
Public Finance and Public Policy (Gruber), **1:**263n
Public goods
    economics of cultural heritage and, **2:**820–821
    open-access resources and, **1:**232–233
Public interest theory of regulation, **1:**270
Public intervention, economics of crime and, **2:**749–750
Public ownership, government regulation and, **1:**268
Public school choice, matching markets and, **2:**936–937
Pujol, M. A., **2:**910
Puranam, P., **2:**946
Purchasing power parity (PPP), **1:**436–437, **1:**470–471
Pyle, D. H., **2:**735

Qatar, **2:**651
Qin Dynasty, **1:**19
Qualitative dependent variable, **1:**51
Quantitative techniques, agricultural economics and, **2:**602
Quantity supplied, **1:**71
Quantity theory of money (QTM), **1:**308
Queer economics, 2:767–775
    class boundaries and sexuality borders, **2:**768–770
    conventional economic thinking, **2:**767
    earnings inequality, **2:**772–774
    LBGTQ identities and, **2:**767–768
    market segmentation and sexual orientation, **2:**774
    perception of sexual orientation, **2:**772
    queer theory, **2:**770
    social rules, **2:**770–772
Quesnay, François, **2:**894
Quigley, John, **2:**611

Quindlan, A., **1:**158
Quine, Willard, **1:**37
Quirk, James, **2:**535

Rabin, M., **2:**861, **2:**862
Race. *See* **Economics and race**
Rada, P., **2:**917
Radicalism, **1:**60
Radio, media economics and, **2:**831–832
Railway Labor Act, **1:**168, **1:**169
Rainy day funds, **1:**371–373
Rajan, R. G., **2:**732, **2:**840, **2:**842
Rambaud, S. C., **1:**281
Ramirez, B., **1:**60
Ramos-Francia, M., **2:**853
Ramsey, F. P., **1:**259, **1:**280
Ramstad, Y., **2:**531
RAND Health Insurance Experiment, **2:**708, **2:**723
Randall, Alan, **2:**624
Random, defined, **1:**46
Random walk, **1:**218
Random Walk Down Wall Street, A (Malkiel), **1:**215
Rangel, A., **2:**917–918
Ransford, E., **2:**570
Ransom, M. L., **2:**557
Rao, B. Bhaskara, **1:**335, **1:**338
Raphael, S., **2:**750, **2:**752
Rapoport, H., **2:**703
Rasinski, K. A., **2:**869
Rate of return
    economics of education and, **2:**516–517
    rate-of-return regulation, **1:**269
Rates of pay, wage determination and, **1:**159
Rational behavior, **1:**8
Rational economic agent, feminist economics and, **2:**905–906
Rational expectations, **1:**311–312, **1:**394, **1:**395
    rational expectations hypothesis (REH), **1:**400–401
Rational ignorance, **1:**242
Rational voter hypothesis
    expressive voting, **1:**241
    instrumental voting, **1:**240–241
Rationality, behavioral economics and, **2:**869–870
Rationality, complexity and economics, **2:**884–886
Rattvisemarkt, **1:**507
Rausser, G. C., **2:**601
Ravallion, M., **1:**496
Ravicz, M. E., **2:**918
Rawls, John, **1:**464n, **2:**529, **2:**897
Rawls, R., **2:**626
Ray, D., **2:**815
Ray, I., **1:**178
Raynolds, L., **1:**509
Read, Leonard E., **2:**895
Ready, R. C., **2:**625, **2:**823
Reagan, Ronald, **1:**29, **1:**150, **1:**351–**1:**352, **1:**396
    labor and, **1:**63
    labor markets and, **1:**150
    "Reagan revolution," **1:**63
Real activity, **1:**382, **1:**387 (table)
Real business cycle (RBC) approach, **1:**302, **1:**406
Real business cycle (RBC) models, **1:**396–397
Real equilibrium business cycle theory (REBCT), **1:**399

Real estate economics, 2:607–616
    after 2000/future directions, **2:**614–615
    applications and empirical evidence, **2:**611–612
    development, **2:**609 (figure)
    future of, **2:**615
    policy and, **2:**612–614
    rental market, **2:**608 (figure)
    theory, **2:**607–611
    See also **Urban economics**
Real exchange rates, **1:**438
Real GDP (gross domestic product), **1:**289
Real National Income of Soviet Russia Since 1928, The (Bergson),
    1:442
Realism of assumptions, behavioral economics and, **2:**861,
    2:863–864
Rebelo, S., **1:**406
Recession
    dot-com stock market bubble, **1:**352–353
    economic measurement and forecasting, **1:**287
    economic methodology and, **1:**26
    fiscal policy and, **1:**354
    Great Recession of 2007, **1:**397–398
    Latin America's trade performance and financial crisis of 2008,
        2:855
    measuring and evaluating macroeconomic performance and,
        1:299
    monetary policy and, **1:**353–354
    real estate economics and, **2:**614
    U.S. housing boom and, **1:**352
Red Line Agreement, **2:**648, **2:**649
Redisch, M., **2:**712
Rees, A., **1:**170
Regan, Dennis T., **2:**899
Regional Clean Air Incentives Market (RECLAIM), **2:**635
Regressand, **1:**46
Regressive tax, **2:**681
Regressors, **1:**46
Regulatory economics, 1:265–273
    command-and-control (CAC) regulation, **1:**248
    demand and, **1:**71
    demand elasticities and, **1:**99
    deregulation and, **1:**272
    economics of corporate social responsibility and, **2:**793
    economics of energy markets and, **2:**640–641
    economics of gambling and, **2:**677
    HET and, **1:**4
    history of, **1:**266–268
    natural monopoly, **1:**267
    in practice, **1:**268–270
    regulatory behavior and theories of, **1:**270–272
    reregulation and, **1:**272–273
    supply and, **1:**73
    transportation economics and, **2:**661–662
Regulatory takings, economics of property law and, **2:**762–763
Reich, M., **1:**58
Reinganum, J. F., **2:**750
Reinhardt, F. L., **2:**787
Reinhart, Carmen M., **1:**433
Reisch, E., **2:**602
Reja, B., **2:**664
Relative surplus value, **1:**59
Religion. *See* **Economics and religion**

Remittances, **2:**703–704
Renner, E., **2:**842
Rent seeking, **1:**241–242
Rent theory, **2:**607–611
    economic methodology and, **1:**26
    HET and, **1:**6
Repayment, microfinance and, **2:**841
Repetition, in game theory, **1:**182
Republic, The (Plato), **2:**892
Reputation, economics of information and, **2:**735–736
Reregulation, **1:**272–273
*Researches Into the Mathematical Principles of the Theory of
    Wealth* (Cournot), **1:**6
Reserve Bank of New Zealand (RBNZ), **1:**385
Reserve clause, athletes' salaries and, **2:**544–545
Residential segregation model, **2:**888–890
Resnick, Stephen A., **1:**58, **1:**446, **1:**447, **2:**529, **2:**531, **2:**647, **2:**651
Resource depletion, prevention of, **2:**758
Retail development, real estate economics and, **2:**612
Rethinking Corporate Social Responsibility, **2:**785
Returns to scale (RTS), **1:**107
Reuer, J. J., **2:**944, **2:**945
Reunification, behavioral economics and, **2:**861
Reuter, P., **2:**748
Revealed preference, **1:**85
Revealed preference method, **1:**278
Revealed preferences, **2:**632
Revenue, changes in monopolist's total revenue resulting from price
    cut, **1:**126 (figure)
Revenue and Expenditure Control Act of 1968, **1:**363
Review of Agricultural Economics, **2:**599
Reward, neuroeconomics and, **2:**916–917
Reynal-Querol, M., **2:**811–814, **2:**815, **2:**816
Reynolds, L. G., **1:**163, **1:**333f
Rhea, Robert, **1:**217
Rhetoric of Economics, The (McCloskey), **1:**37–**1:**38
Riach, Peter A., **2:**557–558
Ricardian equivalence, **1:**366, **1:**405–406
Ricardian model of comparative advantage, international trade
    theory and, **1:**411–412
Ricardo, David
    aggregate expenditures model and equilibrium
        output, **1:**327
    agricultural economics and, **2:**600
    debates in macroeconomic policy and, **1:**391
    economic history and, **1:**14
    economic methodology and, **1:**23, **1:**25–**1:**26, **1:**27, **1:**31
    globalization and inequality, **1:**497
    HET and, **1:**5, **1:**6
    international trade and, **1:**411
    IS-LM model and, **1:**342
    macroeconomic models and, **1:**312
    new classical economics and, **1:**405
    twentieth-century economic methodology and, **1:**36
Ricardo-Viner model, **1:**413–414
Rice, T., **2:**715
Rich, Judith, **2:**557–558
Richardson, L., **2:**624
Richman, B., **2:**944
Richmond, B. J., **2:**917
Rick, S., **2:**913
Rickey, Branch, **2:**546

Ridley, Matt, **2:**637
Riedl, A., **2:**879
Riegle-Neal Act, **2:**567
Right to exclude, **2:**757–759
Right to transfer, **2:**761–763
Riker, William, **1:**240–**1:**241
Riksbank, **1:**382
Riley, J. C., **1:**15, **1:**17
Rilling, J. K., **2:**881, **2:**915
Riordan, M., **1:**135, **1:**137, **1:**138
Risk, behavioral economics and, **2:**866
Risk, neuroeconomics and, **2:**917
Risk premiums, **1:**205–207
Risk segmentation, economics of health insurance
    and, **2:**720
Rivera-Batiz, F. L., **2:**704
Robb, Alicia, **2:**573
Robbins, Lionel, **1:**37
Roberts, J., **1:**137, **2:**688, **2:**689
Robinson, J., **2:**813
Robinson, Joan, **1:**30, **1:**314, **1:**342, **1:**345
Robinson, Kenneth, **2:**603
Robinson, Marguerite, **2:**837
Robinson, Rhoda, **2:**568
Robinson-Patman Act of 1936, **1:**134, **1:**136, **1:**137
Robust estimation, **1:**52
Robust estimation procedures, **1:**52
Rocheteau, G., **2:**750
Rock, K., **2:**734
Rockwell, Llewellyn H., **2:**893, **2:**894
Rodgers, J., **2:**740, **2:**744
Rodriguez, Alex, **2:**545, **2:**549
Rodrik, D., **1:**496, **1:**501, **2:**848
Roemer, J. E., **2:**531
Roger, S., **1:**386t
Rogers, M., **2:**773
Rogers, Robert, **1:**270
Rogoff, K., **1:**138, **1:**382, **1:**474
Rogowski, Ronald, **1:**415
Rojas, C., **2:**866
Role of labor unions in labor markets, 1:150, **1:163–172**
    comparison of union/nonunion media weekly earning 2008,
        1:170 (figure)
    contemporary American unions, **1:**165–168
    earnings by occupation, 2008, **1:**171 (figure)
    history of unions, **1:**164–165
    impact of unions on labor markets, **1:**169–171
    industrial relations process, **1:**168–169
    percentage of employees that are members of unions in U.S. from
        1930 to 2000, **1:**166 (figure)
    role of unions, **1:**163–164
    union density in public/private sectors, **1:**167 (figure)
    wage determination and, **1:**155
Rolfe, J., **2:**823
Roll, Richard, **1:**209
Romalis, John, **1:**415, **1:**500
Roman Empire, **1:**16, **1:**17, **1:**18, **2:**924
Romer, Christina, **1:**367
Roncaglia, A., **2:**646, **2:**648, **2:**649, **2:**650
Roosevelt, Franklin D., **1:**61, **1:**164, **1:**244, **1:**350, **1:**366, **1:**393,
    2:646
Roosevelt, Theodore, **2:**768

Rooth, Dan-Olef, **2:**558
Rorty, Richard, **1:**37
Rosales, O., **2:**853
Rosato, P., **2:**823
Rose, C. M., **2:**758
Rose, Nancy, **2:**568
Rose-Ackerman, S., **2:**761, **2:**787
Rosen, Harvey S., **1:**263n, **1:**278, **1:**375
Rosen, Richard, **2:**614
Rosen, S., **1:**278, **2:**932
Rosenbaum, Thomas, **2:**843
Rosenberg, Alexander, **1:**37, **1:**42
Rosenberg, Richard, **2:**837–838, **2:**844
Rosenthal, Stuart S., **2:**666, **2:**667, **2:**668, **2:**669
Rosholm, Michael, **2:**615
Roson, C. Parr, **2:**603
Ross, Arthur, **1:**57
Ross, M. L., **2:**651
Ross, Michael, **2:**808
Ross, S. A., **1:**373
Ross, Stephen, **2:**535
Ross, Stephen L., **2:**673
Rosser, J. B., **1:**24
Rossi-Hansberg, E., **1:**498, **1:**499, **1:**500
Rostow, W. W., **1:**15
Rotaris, L., **2:**823
Roth, Alvin E., **2:**873, **2:**932, **2:**934, **2:**935, **2:**936, **2:**937, **2:**938
Rothschild, M., **2:**731–732
Rottenberg, Simon, **2:**534, **2:**536, **2:**544
Roubini, N., **1:**491
Rouse, Cecilia, **2:**516, **2:**520, **2:**522, **2:**558
Routledge, B. R., **2:**693
Rover, **1:**490
Roy, G., **2:**538
Roy, Tirthankar, **1:**20
Royal Dutch/Shell, **2:**648, **2:**649
R-squared, **1:**52
Rubenstein, M., **1:**216
Rubin, G., **2:**768
Rubin, Jeff, **2:**843
Rubin, Paul, **1:**243
Rubin, P. H., **2:**752
Rubinstein, A., **1:**183, **2:**884
Rubinstein, Mark, **1:**210
Rubinstein, Yona, **2:**567
Ruble, M., **2:**744
Rucker, Randal, **1:**271
Rudebusch, G. D., **1:**293
Rufolo, A. M., **2:**659, **2:**662, **2:**663
Ruggles, S., **2:**571, **2:**571f
Ruggy, John, **2:**785
Rule of Reason, **1:**134
RuPaul, **2:**770
Rupert, P., **2:**750
Rush, M., **1:**471
Russell, J. A., **2:**650
Russia
    economic history and, **1:**18
    Russian Revolution, **1:**18
Russian Research Center, **1:**441
Russo, B., **1:**373
Rustichini, A., **2:**560, **2:**913

Ruth, Babe, **2:**544
Rutherford, S., **2:**841
Rutström, E. E., **1:**279
Ryan, L., **2:**915
Ryan, Mary E., **2:**600
Rybczynski Theorem, **1:**414

Sacerdote, B., **2:**569, **2:**751
Sachs, J. D., **1:**496, **2:**651
Sachs, Jeff, **1:**40
Saez, E., **1:**494, **1:**500
Safe minimum standard (SMS), **2:**625–626
Safley, Charles, **2:**600
Sahr, Robert, **1:**374f
Saint-Simon, Claude Henri de, **1:**27
Sakellariou, C., **2:**564
Salkever, D. S., **2:**712
Sallee, J. M., **1:**251, **1:**252
Saloner, G., **1:**136, **1:**137
Sampling distributions, **1:**46–48
Sampson, R. C., **2:**945
Sam's Club, **1:**250
Samuels, W. J., **1:**4
Samuelson, Paul A.
    aggregate expenditures model and equilibrium output, **1:**319, **1:**325–**1:**326, **1:**330
    agricultural economics and, **2:**605
    consumer behavior and, **1:**81, **1:**85
    economic methodology and, **1:**30
    economics of aging and, **2:**590–591, **2:**592
    externalities and property rights, **1:**233
    globalization and inequality, **1:**497
    HET and, **1:**8, **1:**9
    international trade and, **1:**415
    IS-LM model and, **1:**346
    macroeconomic models and, **1:**309–**1:**311
    measuring and evaluating macroeconomic performance, **1:**299
    new classical economics and, **1:**399
    public finance and, **1:**256, **1:**262n
    twentieth-century economic methodology and, **1:**35, **1:**36, **1:**37, **1:**38, **1:**41, **1:**42
Sánchez-Tabernero, A., **2:**830
Sanderson, Allen, **2:**534, **2:**536, **2:**538, **2:**539
S&P/Case-Shiller Home Price Index, **1:**367, **2:**615
S&P 500, **1:**217, **1:**221, **1:**289, **1:**300
Sanfey, A. G., **2:**881, **2:**915, **2:**916
Santor, E., **1:**138, **2:**843
Sappho, **2:**769
Sara Lee, **1:**509
Sargent, Thomas J., **1:**36, **1:**293, **1:**312, **1:**371, **1:**394–**1:**395, **1:**399, **1:**403, **1:**404
Saturn Motors, **1:**64
Satyanath, S., **2:**811–813
Saunders, Lisa, **2:**568
Säve-Södeberg, Jenny, **2:**560
Savin, N. E., **2:**878
Savings and Loan banks (S&Ls), **1:**397
Savings and Loan (S&Ls) crisis, **1:**397
Savoy, R., **2:**918
Sawyer, M., **1:**316
Say, Jean Baptiste, **1:**26, **1:**36, **1:**80, **1:**307, **1:**391

Say's law, **1:**26
Scalia, Antonin, **2:**764n
"Scarcity" maintenance, **2:**647–648
Scarf, Herbert, **2:**934, **2:**935
Schannep, J., **1:**215, **1:**217, **1:**218
Schanzenbach, Diane, **2:**522
Scharfstein, D., **1:**138
Scheffman, D. T., **1:**200
Scheinkman, J. A., **2:**569
Schelling, Thomas C., **1:**38, **2:**750, **2:**888
Schelling's residential segregation model, **2:**888–890
Scheve, K. F., **1:**498
Schindler, D. L., **2:**898
Schizgal, P., **2:**916
Schmalensee, R., **1:**138, **2:**829
Schmidt, K., **2:**868
Schmidt, Martin, **2:**537, **2:**547
Schmidt-Hebbel, Klaus, **1:**388
Schmittberger, R., **2:**878
Schmitz, Andrew, **2:**624
Schmoller, Gustav von, **1:**29
Schneider, P., **2:**827
Schnitzer, M., **1:**445
Scholastics, **2:**891, **2:**892, **2:**893–894, **2:**894, **2:**899
Scholes, Myron, **1:**211
School choice, economics of education and, **2:**519–521
School of Salamanca, **2:**893, **2:**894
Schrattenholzer, Leo, **2:**643
Schultz, Theodore, **2:**515, **2:**597, **2:**604
Schultz, W., **2:**915, **2:**916
Schumpeter, Joseph, **1:**4, **1:**15, **1:**26, **1:**34, **1:**301–**1:**302, **1:**312, **1:**419, **1:**464, **2:**928
Schutz, Alfred, **1:**37
Schwager, J., **1:**217, **1:**218
Schwalberg, Barney, **1:**441
Schwartz, Anna, **1:**327
Schwartz, Shalom, **1:**448
Schwarz criterion, **1:**53
Schwarze, B., **2:**878
Scicli, Sicily, **2:**823
Scientific method, feminist economics and, **2:**904
Scott, Kirk, **2:**594
Scottish Enlightenment, **1:**33
Screening hypothesis
    economics of education and, **2:**516–517
    economics of information and, **2:**731–732
Scully, G., **2:**536
Sears, **1:**129
Seasonal Agricultural Worker (SAW), **2:**704
Seasonal unemployment, **1:**305–306
Second Empire, France, **1:**17
Second Industrial Revolution, **1:**18
Second line drugs, **2:**688
Secondary energy, **2:**638
Securities and Exchange Commission, **1:**266
Security Analysis (Graham, Dodd), **1:**215–**1:**216
Security market line (SML), **1:**209
Sefton, M., **2:**878
Seidman, Laurence, **1:**366, **1:**367, **1:**368
Seitz, Peter, **2:**545
Seki, E., **2:**863
Sela, A., **2:**938

Selén, Jan, **2:**594

Self-interested behavior
economic methodology and, **1:**23
HET and, **1:**4–5

Selten, Reinhardt, **1:**136, **1:**181, **2:**864, **2:**870

Sen, Amartya K., **1:**39, **1:**40, **1:**238, **2:**528–529, **2:**531, **2:**897

Senior, N., **1:**37

Sensitivity analysis, **1:**281

S.E. of regression, **1:**52

Sequence of individuals, **2:**935

Sequential games, **1:**132–133

Sergenti, E., **2:**811–813

Serra, Antonio, **1:**419

Seven Sisters, **2:**649, **2:**651

Seven Wonders of the World, **2:**825

Sexton, R. J., **2:**601

Shaars, M. A., **2:**598

Shaked, A., **2:**868

Shang, J., **2:**870

Shanken, Jay, **1:**213

Shapira, N. A., **2:**915, **2:**916

Shapiro, Jesse, **2:**613

Shapiro, P., **2:**662

Shapley, Lloyd S., **2:**933, **2:**934, **2:**935

Sharp, R., **2:**907, **2:**910

Sharpe, William, **1:**207

Shavell, S., **2:**749–750, **2:**764n

Shaver, D., **2:**834

Shaver, M. A., **2:**834

Shearer, B., **2:**880

Shearer, Derek, **2:**568

Shefrin, Hersh, **1:**215, **1:**218, **1:**219

Sheils, J., **2:**724

Sheiner, L. M., **2:**588

Shelanski, H. A., **1:**200, **2:**944

Shell Oil, **2:**639

Shepherd, J. M., **2:**750, **2:**752

Sherer, A. G., **2:**785

Sheridan, Niamh, **1:**388

Sherlund, Shane, **2:**615

Sherman, H. J., **1:**445, **2:**531

Sherman, Howard, **2:**921, **2:**924–925, **2:**927

Sherman, John, **1:**133

Sherman Act, **1:**133–134

Sherman Antitrust Act of 1890, **1:**133, **1:**134, **1:**137, **1:**159

Shierholz, H., **2:**701

Shiller, Robert, **1:**407, **2:**611, **2:**614, **2:**869

Shirley, C., **2:**662

Shiv, B., **2:**917

Shleifer, Andrei, **1:**40, **1:**41, **1:**448, **2:**668

Shocks, economic history and, **1:**15

Shorish, J., **2:**690

Short- and long-run output, **1:**102, **1:**469–471. *See also* **Costs of production: short run and long run**

Short-run equilibrium
in Keynesian cross diagram, **1:**325–326
under monopolistic competition, **1:**128 (figure)

Short-run output-one variable input, costs of production, **1:**103 (figure)

Short-run (specific-factors) analysis, of inequality and globalization, **1:**498

Shortle, J., **2:**624

Shoup, D. C., **2:**659

Shrestha, L., **2:**699

Shughart, William, **1:**244

Shui-bian, Chen, **1:**489

Shulman, S., **2:**701

Shumway, C. Richard, **2:**600

Shut-down
decision, **1:**104–108
profit maximization and, **1:**113 (*See also* **Profit maximization**)

Sidak, J. G., **2:**751

Siegel, D. S., **2:**786, **2:**788, **2:**791, **2:**792

Siegelman, P., **2:**557

Siegfried, John, **2:**534, **2:**536, **2:**539

Signaling, economics of information and, **2:**730–731

Silverman, B., **2:**946, **2:**947

Simmons, R., **2:**537

Simon, Curtis, **2:**568

Simon, Herbert A., **1:**8, **1:**195, **2:**790, **2:**862, **2:**864, **2:**870, **2:**884, **2:**947

Simons, H. C., **1:**163

Sims, C. A., **1:**295

Sims, E. R., **1:**252

Singapore, **2:**649

Singh, H., **2:**944

Singh, M., **1:**251

Single-payer healthcare system, **2:**715, **2:**721–722

Singleton, Kenneth, **1:**211

Sinn, Hans-Werner, **2:**593

Siphambe, H., **2:**688

Sirico, Father Robert, **2:**898, **2:**899

Sirmans, G., **2:**671

Sjaastad, L. A., **2:**697

Sjoblom, K., **2:**593

Sjögren Lindquist, Gabriella, **2:**588

Sjoquist, David, **2:**568

Skaperdas, S., **2:**807, **2:**814

Skidmore, M., **1:**253

Skill-biased technical change, **1:**498

Skinner, B. F., **2:**864

Skocpol, T., **1:**62

Skogman Thoursie, Peter, **2:**559

Skoog, G. R., **2:**740, **2:**741

Slaughter, M. J., **1:**498

Slavery
Classical School and, **1:**5–6
economic history and, **1:**21
economics and justice, **2:**530

Slesnick, F., **2:**740

Sloane, A. A., **1:**168

Slope coefficients, **1:**46

Slovic, P., **2:**866

Slutsky, E. E., **2:**861

Small, A., **2:**792

Small, Deborah, **2:**560

Small, Kenneth A., **1:**251, **2:**610, **2:**656, **2:**663, **2:**672

Small-scale randomized vouchers, **2:**520

Smetters, K. A., **1:**376

Smiley, G., **1:**327

Smith, Adam
behavioral economics and, **2:**861
costs of production and, **1:**107
debates in macroeconomic policy and, **1:**391

economic methodology and, **1:**23, **1:**24–1:25, **1:**27, **1:**31
economics of crime and, **2:**747
economics of education and, **2:**515
economics of energy markets and, **2:**637, **2:**638
economics of information and, **2:**732
economics of wildlife protection and, **2:**618
ethics and, **2:**894–897
ethics and economics, **2:**891, **2:**894, **2:**895, **2:**896–897, **2:**899
evolutionary economics and, **2:**927
expansion and, **1:**13
HET and, **1:**4–1:6, **1:**8
IS-LM model and, **1:**342
public choice and, **1:**238
public finance and, **1:**255
transaction cost economics and, **1:**199
twentieth-century economic methodology and, **1:**33, **1:**36, **1:**39
Smith, J. M., **2:**823
Smith, J. P., **2:**703, **2:**918
Smith, K., **2:**916
Smith, Mary, **2:**518
Smith, Mary Rozet, **2:**770
Smith, Rachel, **2:**605n
Smith, Robin R., **2:**673
Smith, S., **2:**741
Smith, Stefani, **2:**672
Smith, Trenton, **2:**538
Smith, Vernon, **1:**38, **1:**41, **2:**623, **2:**870, **2:**873, **2:**875, **2:**880, **2:**915
Smith College, **2:**547
Smolinski, Leon, **1:**441
"Snake," **1:**477
Snowdon, B., **1:**326, **1:**328, **1:**329, **1:**399, **1:**407
Snyder, E., **2:**946
Socal Oil, **2:**649
Social activism, **2:**792–793
Social capital
    economics of HIV/AIDS and, **2:**693–694
    queer economics and, **2:**770–772
Social change, economic methodology and, **1:**26
Social costs, **1:**106
Social good, economics and religion, **2:**778–779
Social insurance, **2:**710
Social Investment Forum, **2:**792
Social justice movement, **1:**506–507
Social Performance Task Force, **2:**844
Social preferences
    behavioral economics and, **2:**867–868
    experimental economics and, **2:**877–881
Social Security, **1:**359–1:360, **1:**367, **1:**372, **1:**375–1:376, **2:**702, **2:**710, **2:**743–744
    fiscal policy and, **1:**360
    forensic economics and, **2:**743–744
Social Security Administration, **2:**741
Social welfare, defined, **1:**276. *See also* **Regulatory economics**
Socialism, **1:**27, **1:**443–446
Socially efficient equilibrium, **1:**229
Socially responsible consumption, economics of corporate social, **2:**791–792
Sociocultural evolution, evolutionary economics and, **2:**921–923
Socioeconomic behavior, economics and religion, **2:**780–781
Söderström, Lars, **2:**586
Soft information, **2:**841

Soguel, Nils, **1:**278
Solidaridad, **1:**507
Soll, J. B., **1:**251
Solomon, B., **2:**624
Solow, Robert, **1:**13, **1:**14, **1:**108, **1:**311, **1:**314, **1:**363, **1:**393, **1:**396, **1:**397, **1:**406, **1:**487, **2:**647
Song, Shunfeng, **2:**672
Sönmez, Tayfun, **2:**936, **2:**937
Sood, N., **2:**691, **2:**726
Sorian, R., **2:**726
Sorrentino, C., **1:**166
Sotomayor, M., **2:**934
South America, economics of aging, **2:**586 (table)
Southern Cone Common Market (SCCM; MERCOSUR), **2:**851, **2:**856
Southern Journal of Agricultural Economics, **2:**599
Soviet Union, **1:**18
Soydemir, G., **2:**704
Spanish Schoolmen of Salamanca, **1:**33
Spatial patterns/structure, urban, **2:**669–670, **2:**672–674
Special interest groups
    public choice and, **1:**242–244
    regulatory economics and, **1:**271
Species preservation, economics of, **2:**625–626
Specific factors (Ricardo-Viner) model, **1:**413–414
Specification, **1:**46
Specification error, **1:**50
Spence, Michael, **2:**516, **2:**730, **2:**731–732
Spenner, Erin, **2:**539
Spielberg, F., **2:**662
Spiller, P. T., **1:**200
Spillman, W. J., **2:**600
Spirit of Democratic Capitalism, The (Novak), **2:**898
Spiritual good, economics and religion, **2:**778
Spizman, Lawrence M., **2:**739, **2:**743
Sports economics, 2:533–542
    collegiate sports, **2:**540
    competitive balance in, **2:**539
    discrimination in sports, **2:**539–540
    earnings of professional athletes and, **2:**543–551
    policy and, **2:**538–539
    theory of the sports consumer, **2:**537–538
    theory of the sports firm, **2:**534–537
    topics in, **2:**534
Spranger, J. L., **2:**560
Stabile, Mark, **2:**518
Stability, **1:**8–9
Stability and Growth Pact (SGP), **1:**477–484
Stacchetti, E., **2:**736
Stackelberg, Heinrich von, **1:**129–1:130, **1:**132, **1:**190
Stackelberg model, **1:**129–130, **1:**132, **1:**190–191
Stagflation
    debates in macroeconomic policy and, **1:**394–396
    economic instability and macroeconomic policy, **1:**351
    economic measurement and forecasting, **1:**287
    fiscal policy and, **1:**366–367
    twentieth-century economic methodology and, **1:**36
Staggers Act of 1980, **1:**272
Ståhlberg, Ann-Charlotte, **2:**593, **2:**594
Stalin, Joseph, **1:**18
Stallybrass, P., **2:**770
Stambaugh, R., **2:**792

Standard of living, **1:**462–463
Standard Oil Co. of New Jersey v. United States (1911), **1:**134,
    1:135–**1:**136, **1:**138, **2:**640
Standard Oil Trust, **2:**640, **2:**648
Standard trade model, **1:**415
Stano, M., **2:**691
Stanton, Bernard, **2:**598
"Star" system, **2:**831
Starfield, A., **2:**622
Stark, Jürgen, **1:**387
Stark, O., **2:**703
Starmer, C., **2:**869
Startz, R., **2:**569, **2:**574
State Child Health Insurance Program (SCHIP), **2:**710, **2:**717, **2:**725
State Occupational Employment and Wage Data, **2:**742
State of Working America, The, **1:**63
Stated preference method, **1:**278
Statehood, political economy of violence and, **2:**801–802
Statistical discrimination, race and, **2:**569
Statistical modeling, **1:**292
Statistical Office of the European Communities, **1:**304
Statistical Review of World Energy, **2:**645
Statman, Meir, **1:**219
Staudohar, Paul, **2:**535
Stavins, Robert N., **1:**248, **2:**642, **2:**787
Steemers, J., **2:**831
Stein, J. C., **2:**736
Step lending, **2:**841
Stern, N., **1:**280
Stern Review, **1:**280–281
Steuerle, C. Eugene, **1:**360, **1:**367
Stevenson, G., **2:**598
Stevenson, R. W., **1:**386
Stewart, Kenneth, **2:**535
Stewart, M. B., **2:**564
Stigler, George W., **1:**270, **1:**272, **2:**602, **2:**641, **2:**729,
    2:748–750
Stiglitz, Joseph E.
    aggregate expenditures model and equilibrium output, **1:**338
    economics and corporate social responsibility, **2:**788
    economics of information and, **2:**730, **2:**732, **2:**735, **2:**736
    macroeconomic models and, **1:**313, **1:**317
    microfinance and, **2:**839
    twentieth-century economic methodology and, **1:**34, **1:**40
Stilger model, **1:**270–272
St. Louis Browns, **2:**534
St. Louis Cardinals, **2:**544, **2:**546
St. Mary's City, Maryland, **2:**823
Stochastic, defined, **1:**46
Stochastic discount factors, **1:**205–207
Stock, J. H., **1:**293
Stock market
    Dow theory and, **1:**217–218
    measuring and evaluating macroeconomic performance,
        1:300–301
Stock Market Barometer, The (Hamilton), **1:**217
Stock of knowledge, **1:**14
Stockholm congestion charging policy, cost-benefit analysis
    example, **1:**281–282, 282 (table)
Stoddard, Charles, **2:**617, **2:**621
Stoics, **2:**893, **2:**894
Stoll, John, **2:**624

Stoloff, Jennifer, **2:**570
Stolper, W, **1:**497
Stolper-Samuelson Theorem, **1:**414–415, **1:**497, **1:**498, **1:**500–501
Stolypin, Pyotr, **1:**18
Stone, M., **1:**386t
St. Petersburg's paradox, **2:**873
Strahan, Philip, **2:**556
Strait of Malacca, **1:**18
Strange, William C., **2:**666, **2:**667, **2:**668, **2:**669
Strassmann, D., **2:**904
Strategic dimension of rationality, **1:**10
Strategy-proof assignment mechanism, **2:**934
Stratmann, Thomas, **1:**243
Striking, role of labor unions and, **1:**168
Stringham, E., **1:**245
Structural adjustment, **1:**505–506
Structure of Scientific Revolutions, The (Kuhn), **1:**24
Stump, R. L., **2:**944
Sturgess, B., **2:**829
Sturrock, J., **1:**373
"Subgames," **1:**181
Subsidies, media economics and, **2:**833
Substitutes, **1:**70, **1:**72
Substitution effect, **1:**79, **1:**85, **2:**680–681
Substitutions, economic history and, **1:**15
Sugden, R., **2:**861
Sugrue, L. P., **2:**916
Sullivan, Arthur, **2:**672
Sum of squared residuals (SSR), **1:**46
Summers, Lawrence H., **1:**157, **1:**313, **2:**588, **2:**721
Sumner, D. A., **2:**604
Sundén, Annika, **2:**593
Sundstrom, W. A., **1:**160
Sunstein, Cass R., **2:**863, **2:**870
Supernatural beings, economics and religion, **2:**778
Supply
    change in supply *vs.* change in quantity supplied, **1:**72 (figure)
    defined, **1:**71
    determinants of supply, **1:**71–73
    labor, **1:**142
    See also **Supply, demand, and equilibrium**
Supply, demand, and equilibrium, 1:69–78
    case studies, **1:**76–78
    change in supply *vs.* change in quantity supplied, **1:**72 (figure)
    changes in demand *vs.* changes in quantity demanded,
        1:70 (figure)
    demand, defined, **1:**69–70
    determinants of demand, **1:**70–71
    determinants of supply, **1:**71–73
    effects of a change on demand, **1:**74 (figure)
    effects of a change on supply, **1:**75 (figure)
    effects of price controls and, **1:**76
    equilibrium, **1:**73–76, **1:**73 (figure)
    supply, defined, **1:**71
    symmetry and, **1:**7
Supply shocks, **1:**337
Surowiecki, J., **2:**870
Surplus, **1:**73, **1:**113–114
Survey of Current Business, **1:**299, **1:**422, **1:**424, **1:**424t
Suzumura, K., **1:**238
Svarer, Michael, **2:**615
Svensson, Lars, **1:**383–**1:**384, **1:**388n

Swanson, T., **2:**624
Swaps, **1:**434–435
Sweden
economics of aging, **2:**586 (table), **2:**587 (table), **2:**588 (table), **2:**590 (table), **2:**594
economics of aging and, **2:**585
gender wage gap in, **2:**555 (table)
Stockholm congestion charging policy, cost-benefit analysis example, **1:**281–282, 282 (table)
Swedish National Road Administration, **1:**282
Sweezy, Paul, **1:**445
Swidler, Steve, **2:**615
System of National Accounts (SNA), **2:**906–907
Szymanski, Stefan, **2:**536

T statistic, **1:**52
Tabarrok, A., **2:**751
Tabellini, G., **1:**404
Taft, C. H., **1:**163
Taft-Hartley Act of 1947, **1:**62, **1:**167
Talani, L. S., **1:**478, **1:**480, **1:**483–**1:**484
Talbot, J., **1:**509
Tamura, Robert, **2:**564, **2:**565f
Tan, S., **2:**937
Tapert, S. F., **2:**918
Tarbell, Ida, **1:**135
Target MOTAD, **2:**602
Tariffs, **1:**417, **2:**850 (figure)
Tastes, **1:**70
Tâtonnement, **1:**7
Tauer, Loren, **2:**602
Tax Misery & Reform Index, **1:**360
Tax Policy Center, **1:**263n
Taxes
components of tax revenue, **1:**359 (figure)
economic analysis of the family and, **2:**583
economics of health insurance and, **2:**723–724
environmental economics and, **2:**634
federal tax revenue, **1:**359–360
forensic economics and, **2:**745
labor market and, **1:**148–149
public finance and effects of a tax, **1:**257 (figure)
real estate economics and, **2:**612
regressive tax and economics of gambling, **2:**681
state and local government spending and tax revenue, **1:**360
theory of taxation, **1:**257–259
tuition tax credit, **2:**520
vs. standards: policies for the reduction of gasoline consumption, **1:**247–254
Taxes *vs.* standards: policies for the reduction of gasoline consumption, 1:247–254
distributional concerns, **1:**252–253
failures in market for fuel economy, **1:**251–252
failures in market for gasoline, **1:**249–251
future research, **1:**253
justifications for/types of government intervention, **1:**248
Taylor, C., **2:**815
Taylor, C. Robert, **2:**600
Taylor, John B., **1:**313, **1:**324, **1:**326, **1:**339–**1:**340, **1:**366, **1:**383
Taylor, P., **1:**509
Tchibo, **1:**509
Technical analysis, Dow theory and, **1:**217–218

Technological change
beyond make-or-buy: advances in transaction cost economics, **2:**946–947
economic history and acceleration of, **1:**14
labor market and, **1:**149
media economics and, **2:**834–835
resource shocks, **1:**337
supply and, **1:**72
Technology standards, **1:**234–235
Teece, D., **2:**944
Television
athletes' salaries and, **2:**547–549
media economics and, **2:**831–832, **2:**834
sports economics and, **2:**538
Telser, L., **1:**136
Temporary Assistance to Needy Families (TANF), **1:**260–261
Tennessee Department of Education, **2:**517
Term Auction Facility (TAF), **1:**354
Tesfatsion, Leigh, **2:**888
Tesla Motors, **1:**250
Texaco, **2:**649
Texas Gulf Coast, **2:**649
Texas Railroad Commission, **2:**640–641, **2:**649
Texas Rangers, **2:**545
Thailand, **1:**491
Thaler, Richard H., **1:**277, **2:**545, **2:**863, **2:**866, **2:**870, **2:**917
Thatcher, Margaret, **1:**29
Thelan, K., **1:**63
Theocharis, R. D., **1:**8
Theory of Investment Value, The (Williams), **1:**216
Theory of Justice, A (Rawls), **2:**529
Theory of Moral Sentiments (Smith), **1:**4, **2:**894, **2:**896–897, **2:**899
Theory of Political Economy, The (Jevons), **1:**80
Theory of Public Finance, The (Musgrave), **1:**257
Theory of the Working Class, The (Veblen), **2:**863
Theory-oriented economics, **1:**2
Thernstrom, Abigail, **2:**574
Thernstrom, Stephan, **2:**574
Thiessen, Gordon, **1:**385
Third Republic, France, **1:**17
Third World, **1:**40
Thomas, C., **1:**139
Thomas, K., **2:**726
Thompson, E. P., **1:**17
Thompson, P., **1:**59
Thornton, D., **2:**793
Thorp, R., **1:**21
Three-Person Game (game), **1:**175 (figure)
Throsby, D., **2:**820–821, **2:**824
Thünen, Johann von, **1:**89
Thurlow, J., **2:**688
Thurman, Walter, **1:**271
Thygesen, N., **1:**478
Tiebout, Charles, **1:**259, **2:**672, **2:**697
Tiebout model, **1:**259
Tienda, M., **2:**704
Tierney, K., **2:**659
Tietenberg, T. H., **2:**632, **2:**634, **2:**635
Tiffany, S. T., **2:**914, **2:**918
Time-series data, **1:**52
Timmermann, Allan, **1:**291, **1:**294
Tintner, G., **2:**600

Tirole, J., **1:**136, **1:**248, **2:**789

Tisdell, C., **2:**624, **2:**824

Titman, Sheridan, **1:**211, **2:**732

Tobin, James, **1:**207, **1:**213n, **1:**338, **1:**401, **1:**407

Tobler, P. N., **2:**915

Todd, Petra M., **2:**516, **2:**870

Tokugawa Japan, **1:**19

Tol, Richard S. J., **2:**643

Tolley, George S., **2:**671

Tomek, William, **2:**603

Tool, M. R., **2:**528

Toossi, M., **1:**149

Tootell, Geoffrey M., **2:**569, **2:**673

Top trading cycles algorithm, **2:**935

Topel, Robert, **1:**158

Torrecillas, M. J., **1:**281

Total factor productivity (TFP), **1:**487–488

Total fixed cost (TFC), **1:**104

Total variable cost (TVC), **1:**104

Tourism, economic aspects of cultural heritage and, **2:**823–824

Toussaint-Desmoulins, N., **2:**828

Town, Robert, **2:**566

Townsend, R., **2:**843

Towse, Ruth, **2:**834–835

Toyota Prius, **1:**97

Trade
  deficit/surplus, **1:**324–325
  HET and, **1:**10–11
  liberalization process, **2:**848
  See also **Latin America's trade performance in new millenium**

Trade unions, **1:**57

Tragedy of the commons, **2:**894

Train, Kenneth E., **1:**251, **2:**642

Tranel, D., **2:**917

Transaction cost economics, 1:193–202
  applications and evidence, **1:**200–201
  policy implications, **1:**200–201
  transaction cost theory, **1:**194–200
  See also **Beyond make-or-buy: advances in transaction cost economics**

Transfair, **1:**507

Transfer payments, **1:**357

Transforming Traditional Agriculture (Schultz), **2:**604

Transition economics, **1:**446–447

Transitional Economic Systems (Douglas), **1:**446

Transitivity, **1:**82

Transportation Act of 1920, **1:**272

Transportation economics, 2:655–664
  congestion, **2:**659–661
  demand for transportation services, **2:**655–657
  issues, **2:**662–663
  mass transit, **2:**661
  mode choice, **2:**658–659
  regulation, **2:**661–662
  supply for transportation services, **2:**657–658
  See also **Urban economics**

Treasury Bills, **1:**289

Treasury Exchange Fund, **1:**425

Treatise on the Family (Becker), **2:**902

Treaty of Rome, **1:**477

Treaty on European Union, **1:**478

Tresch, Richard W., **1:**262n

Trilateral governance structure, **1:**199–200

Triple convergence, **2:**660–661

Troske, Kenneth, **2:**556

Trouard, T., **2:**915

Trudel, R., **2:**791

Trust games
  experimental economics and, **2:**878–880
  neuroeconomics and, **2:**915–916

Trusts, predation and, **1:**135–136

Tucker, R., **1:**59, **1:**60

Tuition tax credit, **2:**520

Tullock, Gordon, **1:**238, **1:**240–**1:**242, **1:**244, **1:**257

Turgot, Anne-Robert-Jacques, **2:**600

Turner, Chad S., **2:**564, **2:**565f

Turner, D., **1:**137

Turner, Margery Austin, **2:**673

Turrentine, T. S., **1:**251

Tversky, Amos, **1:**215, **1:**219, **2:**866, **2:**876, **2:**913, **2:**915, **2:**916

Twentieth-century economic methodology, 1:33–43
  absorptive capacity of formalism, **1:**38–39
  fracturing of neoclassical hegemony, **1:**36–38
  future of, **1:**39–42
  political economy and, **1:**33–36

Two-Sector Model of General Equilibrium (Johnson), **1:**263n

Two-sided matching market, **2:**932

Two theorems of welfare economics, **1:**8

Tylor, E. B., **2:**925

Uebelmesser, Silke, **2:**593

Uhl, Joseph, **2:**603

Ultimatum Game, **1:**176 (figure), **2:**868, **2:**878

Umbrella Game, **1:**177 (figure), **1:**178 (figure)

UN Convention on the Rights of the Child, **1:**507

Unbiasedness, **1:**47

Uncovered interest rate parity (UICP), **1:**436, **1:**470

Underemployment equilibrium, **1:**344

Unemployment
  differences across occupations, **1:**146–147
  economic methodology and, **1:**30
  European Monetary Union and, **1:**478–480
  full employment, defined, **1:**309
  HET and, **1:**6, **1:**9
  measuring and evaluating macroeconomic performance and, **1:**305–306

Uninsured, economics of health insurance and, **2:**725

United Kingdom, **1:**17
  economic history and, **1:**16–17, **1:**22
  economics of aging, **2:**586 (table), **2:**587 (table), **2:**588 (table), **2:**590 (table)
  gender wage gap in, **2:**555 (table)
  health economics and, **2:**713
  monetary policy and inflation targeting, **1:**386
  See also Britain

United Mine Workers, **1:**155

United Nations, **1:**465n, **2:**585, **2:**586t, **2:**588t, **2:**590, **2:**837
  Conference on Trade and Development (UNCTAD), **1:**505, **2:**850n, **2:**851f, **2:**853f, **2:**854f
  Development Fund for Women (UNIFEM), **2:**907, **2:**910n
  Development Programme (UNDP), **2:**849n, **2:**850
  Economic Commission for Latin America and the Caribbean (ECLAC), **1:**505

Millennium Development Goals, **1:**510
  UNICEF, **2:**713
United States
  economics of aging, **2:**586 (table), **2:**587 (table), **2:**588 (table)
  economics of migration and, **2:**699–700
  gasoline consumption in, **1:**247–254
  gender wage gap in, **2:**555 (table)
  globalization and inequality, **1:**500
  government of, and role of labor unions, **1:**169
  gross debt of, **1:**374–375
  health economics and reform in, **2:**713–716
  Marxian and institutional industrial relations in, **1:**55–66
  public insurance in, **2:**724–725
  recession (2007–2009) and portfolio theory/investment
      management, **1:**222–223
  regulatory economics and, **1:**265–273
  role of labor unions in, **1:**166–168 (*See also* **Role of labor
      unions in labor markets**)
  U.S. composite leading indexes, **1:**291 (table) (*See also*
      Economic measurement and forecasting)
  U.S. national debt and foreign trade debt, **1:**354–355
  See also **Government budgets, debt, and deficits;** *individual
      names of U.S. agencies*
United States Steel, **1:**62, **1:**169, **1:**201
United States v. Corn Products Refining Co. (1916), **1:**135
Universal Living Wage Campaign, **1:**149, **1:**150
University of California, Berkeley, **2:**942
University of Chicago, **1:**41, **1:**136–137, **1:**328,
      1:471, **2:**577
University of Michigan, **1:**289
University of Minnesota, **2:**598
University of Salamanca, **2:**893
Unorganized violence, **2:**797, **2:**798–799
Unpaid work, feminist economics and, **2:**906–908
Ünver, Utku, **2:**937
"Unwaged" labor, **1:**64
Uppsala University, Department of Peace and Conflict Studies,
      2:808
"Upstream" production, **2:**648
Urban economics, 2:665–675
  concept of, **2:**666
  disamenities and household bid-rent curve, **2:**671 (figure)
  spatial patterns of residents, **2:**672–674
  urban hierarchy, **2:**666–669
  urban land market, **2:**671 (figure)
  urban spatial structure, **2:**669–672
  See also **Real estate economics; Transportation economics**
Uruguay Round, **2:**694
U.S. Census Bureau, **1:**144, **1:**166f, **1:**167f, **1:**299, **1:**300, **1:**360,
      2:516, **2:**564, **2:**564f, **2:**565f, **2:**566t, **2:**567t, **2:**570f, **2:**571f,
      2:572t, **2:**573t, **2:**582, **2:**611–612, **2:**614, **2:**666, **2:**699, **2:**742,
      2:910n
U.S. Chamber of Commerce, **1:**63, **1:**167, **2:**743
U.S. Congress, **1:**250
U.S. Constitution, **1:**245, **1:**370
U.S. Department of Agriculture, **1:**99
U.S. Department of Agriculture (USDA), **1:**99, **1:**261, **1:**506, **2:**604,
      2:621
U.S. Department of Commerce, **1:**145, **1:**289
U.S. Department of Defense, **1:**261
U.S. Department of Education, **2:**521
U.S. Department of Housing and Urban Development, **2:**673

U.S. Department of Labor, **1:**145, **1:**146, **1:**300, **2:**741, **2:**742
U.S. Energy Information Administration (EIA), **2:**638
U.S. Environmental Protection Agency, **1:**266, **1:**279, **2:**635
Use rights, **2:**759–761
U.S. Fish and Wildlife Service, **2:**618
U.S. Food and Drug Administration, **2:**695, **2:**712, **2:**725
U.S. Internal Revenue Service, **2:**723
U.S. Internal Revenue Service, Statistics of Income Division, **1:**260
U.S. Justice Department, **1:**134
U.S. News & World Report, **2:**533
U.S. Peanut Program, **1:**272
U.S. Postal Service, **1:**268
USSR, comparative economic systems and, **1:**445
U.S. Statistical Abstract, **1:**145
U.S. Supreme Court, **1:**137, **1:**164, **1:**287, **1:**386, **2:**544, **2:**762
U.S. Treasury, **1:**313, **1:**364, **1:**365, **1:**373, **1:**496, **2:**615, **2:**848
Utah Pie Co. v. Continental Baking Co. (1967), **1:**137
Utility, **1:**83
  behavioral economics and, **2:**868–869
  HET and, **1:**6
  modern consumer theory, **1:**83
Utterback, J., **2:**947

Vahtrik, Lars, **2:**559
Value, of cultural heritage, **2:**821–823
Value and Capital (Hicks), **1:**81
Value chain approach, media economics and, **2:**830
Value of a statistical life (VSL), **1:**279–280, **2:**690
Value of marginal product (VMP), **1:**118
Van den Berg, H., **2:**699
Van der Wurff, R., **2:**829
Van der Zwaan, Bob C. C., **2:**643
Van Kooten, G. C., **2:**624
Vane, H. R., **1:**326, **1:**328, **1:**329, **1:**399, **1:**407
Varaiya, P., **2:**660
Vargas, J., **2:**816
Varian, H. R., **2:**786, **2:**791
Vars, Frederick, **2:**574
Vaughn, D. R., **2:**819
Veblen, Thorstein, **1:**29, **2:**863, **2:**925–926, **2:**928
Vector autoregression (VAR)–based modeling, **1:**292
Vedder, R. K., **1:**327
Vega, Marco, **1:**388
Ven Dender, Kurt, **1:**251
Venables, A. J., **2:**666
Ventura, Jesse, **2:**539
Vernon, C. J., **2:**533
Vernon, John M., **1:**272, **2:**641
Vertova, P., **2:**751
Very short-term lending facilities (VSTLFs), **1:**478
Vesterlund, Lise, **2:**559, **2:**560, **2:**880
Veterans Administration, **2:**710
Vial, J. P., **1:**181
Vicinus, M, **2:**769
Vickers, John, **2:**639
Vieira, J. C., **2:**824
Vienna Circle, **1:**33, **1:**37
Vietnam War, **1:**393
Vietor, R. H. K., **2:**787
Villeval, M.-C., **2:**560
Vincent, J. W., **2:**634
Vining, Aidan, **1:**268

Violence. *See* **Political economy of violence**

Viscusi, W. Kip, **1:**251, **1:**272, **1:**279, **2:**641, **2:**750

"Vision," **1:**34

Vitaliano, D. F., **2:**791

Vitalis, R., **2:**648, **2:**651

Vitoria, Francisco de, **2:**893

Viu, Murillo, **2:**824

Vogel, D., **2:**786

Voicu, Ioan, **2:**611

Volcker, Paul, **1:**351–**1:**352, **1:**355, **1:**396

"Volcker Recession," **1:**352, **1:**396

Volij, O., **1:**181

Voluntary transfers, economics of property law and, **2:**761

Von Allmen, Peter, **2:**535, **2:**540

Von Amsberg, J., **2:**693

Von Neumann, John, **1:**173, **1:**183, **1:**204, **2:**873, **2:**876

Von Thünen, Johann H., **2:**600, **2:**665, **2:**670

Voting

    in direct democracy, **1:**238–240

    paradox of, **1:**240–241

    See also **Public choice**

Voucher systems, health economics and, **2:**715

Vroman, S., **2:**559

Vrooman, John, **2:**536

Vukina, Tomislav, **2:**639

Wachter, S., **2:**673

Wacziarg, R., **1:**496

Wada, T., **2:**946

Wadensjö, Eskil, **2:**588

Wage determination, 1:153–161

    comparison of union/nonunion media weekly earning 2008,
        1:170 (figure)

    differences across occupations, **1:**145–146

    discrimination, **1:**158–160

    economic analysis of the family and, **2:**579–582

    economic methodology and, **1:**25

    economics of migration and, **2:**699–704

    feminist economics and paid/unpaid work, **2:**906–909

    forensic economics and, **2:**741–742

    future directions, **1:**160

    gender and, **2:**553–562

    human capital acquisition, **1:**155–158

    market structure, **1:**154–155

    queer economics and earnings inequality, **2:**772–774

    See also **Economics and race; Economics of gender; Feminist**
        economics; Labor markets

Wage fund doctrine, **1:**25, **1:**27

Wages of Wins (Berri, Schmidt, Brook), **2:**547

Wagner, R. E., **1:**238, **1:**244, **1:**246

Wagner/NLRA Act, **1:**62

Wald, L., **2:**918

Waldfogel, J., **2:**751

Walker, D. M., **2:**677, **2:**679, **2:**682

Walker, D. O., **1:**465n

Walker, G., **2:**944

Wall Street Journal, The, **1:**217, **1:**468t, **2:**870

Wallace, Neil, **1:**312, **1:**399, **1:**403

Walliser, J., **1:**376

Walls, Margaret, **1:**249, **2:**659

Wal-Mart, **1:**135, **1:**139, **1:**250

Wal-Mart Stores, Inc. v. American Drugs, Inc. (1995), **1:**139

Walras, Léon, **1:**7, **1:**28, **1:**29, **1:**80, **1:**342, **2:**689

Walsh, J., **2:**792

Walzer, M., **2:**528

Wang, H., **2:**825

Wansink, B., **2:**870

War on Poverty, **1:**393

Ward, Benjamin, **1:**441

Ward, J., **2:**740

Ward, M ., **1:**465n

Ward, R. W., **2:**601

Waring, M., **2:**907

Warner, A. M., **1:**496, **2:**651

Warner, R. S., **2:**780

Warren, George F., **2:**598

Warzala, Elaine, **2:**613

"Washington Consensus," **1:**40, **2:**848, **2:**854

Washington Mutual Savings and Loan, **1:**353

Water-diamond paradox, **1:**28

Watergate, **1:**394

Waterman, D., **2:**831

Watson, M. W., **1:**293

Watts, M., **2:**650, **2:**651

Watts, S. G., **2:**786, **2:**791

Waugh, Frederick, **2:**601

Waveform model of economic cycles, **1:**301–302

Wayland, Reverend Francis, **2:**898

Wealth and Poverty of Nations, The (Landes), **2:**637

Wealth of Nations (Smith), **1:**4, **1:**24–**1:**25, **1:**35, **1:**199, **1:**255,
        1:391, **2:**894, **2:**896–897, **2:**899

Webb, Beatrice, **1:**57, **1:**59

Webb, S., **1:**59

Weber, Bruce, **2:**767

Weber, D., **2:**944

Weber, Max, **1:**37, **1:**39, **2:**923

Webster, J., **2:**829

Webster, Timothy, **1:**145

Weeks, Jeffrey, **2:**769

Weerapana, A., **1:**339–**1:**340

Weibel, A., **2:**946

Weichselbaumer, Doris, **2:**558

Weil, David, **2:**611

Weiler, S., **2:**701

Weiler, W. C., **2:**752

Weinberg, B. A., **2:**750

Weingast, B., **2:**802

Weintraub, E. R., **1:**8, **1:**11n

Weintraub, Sidney, **1:**326, **1:**345

Weisbrod, B. A., **1:**277

Weiss, A., **2:**732, **2:**839

Weitzman, Martin, **1:**280, **2:**625

Welch, Finis, **2:**574

Welch, K. H., **1:**496

Welfare economics

    deficits and, **1:**375–377

    modern consumer theory, **1:**86

    social welfare, defined, **1:**276

    welfare capitalism, **1:**62

    welfare capitalism and aging, **2:**589–590

    welfare capitalism and comparative economic systems, **1:**445

    welfare economics of moral hazard, **2:**722 (figure)

    See also **Cost-benefit analysis; Regulatory economics**

Welfare loss, due to monopoly, **1:**127 (figure)

Welki, A. M., **2:**537
Well-defined property rights, **1:**232
Welle, P. G., **2:**634
Wenner, M., **2:**843
Werner, Pierre, **1:**477
Werner plan, **1:**477
Werner Report, **1:**477
Wessels, R., **2:**732
West, D., **1:**138
West, K. D., **1:**471
West, Kenneth D., **1:**293
West, Sarah E., **1:**248, **1:**249, **1:**251, **1:**252–**1:**253
West Texas Intermediate, **2:**649
Western Agricultural Economics Association, **2:**599
Western Climate Initiative, **2:**635
Western Economics, **2:**533
"Western imperialism," economic history and, **1:**16
Western Journal of Agricultural Economics, **2:**599
Wetlands Reserve Program, **2:**622
Wetzstein, Michael, **2:**605n
Whalen, C. J., **2:**927
Whaples, Robert, **2:**898
Wheaton, William, **2:**608, **2:**672
"Whether"/"why," corporate social responsibility and, **2:**787–790
White, A., **2:**770
Whitehouse, E., **2:**592, **2:**593
Whites. *See* **Economics and race**
Whitney, F., **1:**168
Wicksell, Knut, **1:**7, **1:**238, **1:**382
Wicksteed, Philip H., **1:**7
Wilcox, C., **2:**640
Wildlife Habitat Incentives Program, **2:**622
Wildlife protection. *See* **Economics of wildlife protection**
Wildman, S., **2:**828, **2:**829, **2:**830, **2:**831, **2:**832
Wilentz, S., **1:**63
William III (King of England), **2:**802
Williams, C., **2:**854
Williams, Eric, **1:**21
Williams, J., **2:**903, **2:**909
Williams, John Burr, **1:**215–**1:**216, **1:**217, **1:**218
Williams, J. W., **1:**304, **1:**305
Williams, R. M., **2:**904, **2:**909
Williams, Roberton C., III, **1:**249, **1:**252–**1:**253
Williams College, **2:**898
Williamson, J., **2:**848
Williamson, J. G., **1:**15, **1:**17
Williamson, Oliver E., **1:**194, **1:**195, **1:**196, **1:**197–**1:**201, **2:**928, **2:**941–943, **2:**943t, **2:**944, **2:**947
Willig, Robert D., **1:**276, **2:**641
Willingness to accept (WTA), **1:**276–277, **2:**624
Willingness to pay (WTP), **1:**80, **1:**276–277, **2:**624
Wilshire 5000, **1:**221
Wilson, Beth, **2:**611
Wilson, C., **2:**824
Wilson, P., **1:**487
Wilson, R. B., **1:**137, **1:**181
Wilson, William, **2:**569
Wilson, Woodrow, **1:**56
Windle, J., **2:**823
Windowing, **2:**832
Winegarden, C. R., **2:**581
Winkelried, Diego, **1:**388

Winkler, A. E., **2:**905
Winkler, B., **1:**479
Winkler, R. L., **1:**293
Winston, Clifford, **1:**272, **2:**656, **2:**662
Winston, G. C., **1:**200
Winter, Joachim, **2:**592
Winter, S. G., **2:**927, **2:**928
Winter-Ebmer, R., **2:**750, **2:**752
Wirth, M., **2:**829
Wisconsin Department of Agriculture, **1:**139
Wise, D. A., **2:**587, **2:**594
Witte, A. D., **2:**751
Witte, Sergei, **1:**18
Wittenberg, D. C., **1:**159
Wittman, D., **2:**579
Wohl, Martin, **2:**661
Wohlgenant, Michael, **2:**600, **2:**601
Wolf, Eric, **2:**924, **2:**925
Wolff, Richard D., **1:**58, **1:**446, **1:**447, **2:**529, **2:**531, **2:**647, **2:**651–652
Wolpin, K. I., **2:**751, **2:**752
Wolverton, A., **1:**248
Women in development (WID), **2:**909–910
Women's Policy Research, **2:**555n
Wong, R. Bin, **1:**20
Wood, Adrian, **1:**415
Woodford, Michael, **1:**383–**1:**384, **1:**399, **1:**407
Woods, Tiger, **2:**548, **2:**549
Woodward, Richard, **2:**603
Woolhandler, S., **2:**717, **2:**720
Woolridge, R., **1:**216
Workers. *See* **Labor markets; Wage determination**
Working class. *See* **Marxian and institutional industrial relations in U.S.**
World Bank, **1:**313, **1:**387t, **1:**433, **1:**464n, **1:**495, **1:**496, **1:**505, **2:**592, **2:**597, **2:**651, **2:**786, **2:**824, **2:**848, **2:**855, **2:**909
World development in historical perspective, 1:451–466
    changes in world economic and political landscape, **1:**451–454
    changing world demographics, **1:**455 (figure)
    disparities in world productivity, **1:**463 (figure)
    future of, **1:**464
    growth of world output, population, labor force (1951–2007), **1:**456 (table)
    growth of world output and trade by period, **1:**459 (figure)
    growth of world trade, **1:**458 (figure)
    long-term trend in world inflation, **1:**461 (figure)
    rise in world female labor force participation, **1:**455 (figure)
    rise in world labor productivity, **1:**460 (figure)
    rise in world life expectancy, **1:**454 (figure)
    rise in world literacy, **1:**455 (figure), **1:**460
    rise in world output and trade, **1:**458 (figure)
    rise in world per capita product, **1:**454 (figure)
    rise in world productivity, **1:**462 (figure)
    share of world output, population, labor force (1950 and 2007), **1:**456 (table)
    swings in annual world productivity growth, **1:**461 (figure)
    world economic performance in postwar era, **1:**454–463
World Energy Outlook, **2:**645
World Health Organization, **2:**695
World Heritage Sites (UNESCO), **2:**824, **2:**825
World Microfinance Forum, **2:**844

World Trade Center, **1:**288
World Trade Organization, **1:**411, **1:**464n, **1:**490, **1:**496, **1:**501, **1:**509, **2:**694, **2:**850, **2:**850n
World Values Survey, **2:**693
World War I, **1:**19, **1:**20, **1:**57, **1:**373, **1:**433, **1:**474, **2:**847
World War II, **1:**17, **1:**19, **1:**37, **1:**57, **1:**62, **1:**130, **1:**145, **1:**238, **1:**309, **1:**327, **1:**328, **1:**353, **1:**366, **1:**374, **1:**382, **1:**431, **1:**433, **1:**451–**1:**452, **1:**456, **1:**489, **2:**582, **2:**598, **2:**602, **2:**646, **2:**651, **2:**723
Worldly Philosophers, The (Heilbroner), **1:**4
Wray, L. Randall, **1:**347n, **2:**649, **2:**650
Wright, P., **2:**915, **2:**916
Wrigley, G., **1:**503
Wrongful death, forensic economics and, **2:**744
Wu, J., **2:**622
Wunder, T., **2:**926
Wydick, B., **2:**843
Wyplosz, C., **1:**479

Xie, Yu, **2:**573
Xing, X., **2:**932

Yamey, B., **1:**135
Yan, J., **2:**656, **2:**663
Yandle, T., **2:**623
Yasmeen, Wahida, **2:**573
Yasuda, Y., **2:**937
Yeager, J. C., **2:**598
Yeager, Leland B., **1:**328, **1:**464n
Yeats, A., **2:**851
Yellen, Janet L., **1:**313, **2:**729
Yeomans, M., **2:**645, **2:**646

Yergin, Daniel, **2:**638, **2:**639, **2:**640, **2:**645, **2:**647, **2:**648
Yew, Lee Kuan, **1:**489
Yezer, Anthony M., **2:**673, **2:**899
Yinger, John, **2:**673
Young, Alwyn, **1:**488
Young, Madelyn, **2:**568
Yunus, Mohamed, **2:**837, **2:**844

Zabkar, V., **2:**824
Zak, P. J., **2:**914, **2:**915
Zanatta, V., **2:**823
Zavodny, M., **2:**703
Zein-Elabdin, E., **2:**909
Zeller, M., **2:**838
Zelner, B. A., **2:**945
Zeng, Zhen, **2:**573
Zenger, Todd, **2:**945, **2:**948n
Zerbe, R. O., Jr., **1:**135, **1:**137, **1:**229
Zhou, L., **1:**178
Zhu, Yan Hong, **2:**639
Zietz, E., **2:**671
Zilberman, D., **2:**622
Zimbalist, Andrew, **1:**442, **1:**445, **2:**535, **2:**540, **2:**547
Zimmerman, David, **2:**568
Zingales, L., **2:**732, **2:**840
Zivin, J., **2:**792
Zlatoper, T. J., **2:**537
Zollo, M., **2:**944
Zoning, real estate economics and, **2:**612–613
Zusman, Pinhas, **2:**602
Zygmont, Zenon, **2:**537